C0-DKN-345

Library of
Davidson College

# Yearbook of American Universities and Colleges,
Academic Year, 1986–1987

EDITED BY
*George Thomas Kurian*

GARLAND PUBLISHING, INC.
New York & London   1988

378,73
Y391
1986-87

88-6162

© 1988 Garland Publishing, Inc.

All rights reserved

ISBN 0-8240-7942-6
ISSN — 0896-1034

Printed on acid-free, 250-year-life paper

MANUFACTURED IN THE UNITED STATES OF AMERICA

# List of Charts and Tables

## Charts

## Tables

# Table of Contents

# Introduction

## GEORGE T. KURIAN

THE YEARBOOK OF AMERICAN UNIVERSITIES AND COLLEGES is an annual report of the condition of higher education in the United States. The present first edition covers generally the academic year 1986 and 1987.

The focus of many individual universities and colleges is increasingly being turned on the future, especially the remaining years of this century and the early decades of the next. One of the principal ingredients of this effort to focus on the future is information, and often the quality of the information determines the quality of the vision as well as of the strategies required to achieve it. Universities are becoming harder to administer, as Derek Bok of Harvard confesses in a speech printed in this book, if only because the data available to university planners and decisionmakers are growing more and more complex. This *Yearbook* organizes and arranges key data under a broad range of subject headings, as well as providing interpretive studies of issues and sectors of higher education in the United States. It is designed as an information tool for university and college administrators and should also prove useful to all those involved in faculty governance as well as to other educators and to historians of education. Indeed, the *Yearbook* was designed with a second and complementary function in mind — to be a permanent historical record for higher-education watchers. As a record of a sector with over 4,000 institutions, it must to some degree be broad and general rather than narrow in on each of the constituent institutions. But it will preserve and highlight the most important data and events for the benefit of future historians as well as presenting them for the benefit of current educators.

It should be made clear that this is not a college-by-college guide to the year in higher education. At the time it was planned, the editor hoped to include a hundred or so (or perhaps more) detailed write-ups of colleges and universities where particular events of interest had taken place — expansion into non-traditional education, leadership in across-the-curriculum programs like Writing Across the Curriculum or Critical Thinking, formation or enhancement of international education programs (either singly or in consortium). But any detailed look at even a hundred campuses would have rendered the book unwieldy, and probably made it a subject of controversy when it should not be ("Why were they picked and we weren't?").

Similarly, the issues section could not be as long as we might have desired. It should be explained that the issues discussed in this volume will not all of them be discussed in next year's, and in those following, and next year's volume will presumably discuss issues not discussed here. On some, critical developments are fast-moving, on some not, and some have not yet reached the stage where they are important *as issues*. That is, the subject may be important, but there may yet be no sense of division or disagreement among those interested or on the question of whether educators should be interested.

The book is divided into sixteen sections. Of these, only the third ("Issues") is original, and that only in part. The others have all been published previously, but in widely scattered sources, some of them virtually unavailable. The point of this book is that they are here, together, conveniently, in one place.

Section II, on the Major Sectors of Higher Education in the United States, contains four chapters, by Roger L. Geiger of Penn State, on the role of the research university, by Robert Birnbaum of Columbia on the state colleges, by Allan O. Pfnister of the University of Denver on the liberal arts colleges, and by Arthur M. Cohen of UCLA on the community colleges. Section III, the "Issues" section, contains sixteen chapters, all but two of them original. Some of the concerns voiced in Section II reappear, of course, in Section III. And, as a matter of fact, the concerns voiced in Section II are not neatly separated into the concerns of the research universities, the concerns of the liberal arts colleges, and so on. Dr. Geiger, in discussing the research universities, focusses particularly on the interrelationship of undergraduate education at the research universities and the universities' research function. A considerable number of the "best and the brightest" among undergraduates are educated at these institutions — which, however, do not always see the education of undergraduates as their primary function. This finds an echo in Professor Birnbaum's discussion of the confusion in the ranks of the state universities that do not know whether to provide for the education of their undergraduates as their primary goal, or to try to expand their research capabilities, so as to attract better scholars, so as to do a better job in educating undergraduates — which will bring them straight to the research universities' current problem.

On the other hand, the community colleges, as Professor Cohen notes, have a related confusion of role. Do they exist to provide an alternative to the traditional four-year college education or to provide the first two years of the four? Are they simultaneously in competition and collaboration with the state universities? In Professor Cohen's words, "It is undoubtedly important to offer courses in the use of office equipment to people wishing to upgrade themselves within their occupations and to offer courses in painting or piano playing to people who already have college degrees, but these functions are detrimental to the perception of the college as a provider of grades 13 and 14."

If the community colleges are generally seeking to find their proper niche, some of the liberal arts colleges (the "prestigious" ones) seem to have found theirs, and the rest, Professor Pfnister argues (as the Carnegie report argued), probably have no niche to find. They are very much at risk, ground between the upper millstone of the research universities, drawing off many of the bright undergraduates, and the nether millstone of the community colleges and local state universities, providing cheaper degrees, and in many cases cheaper education as well. Small size — the vast majority are in the 750- to 1200-student range — used to be seen as an advantage as against Behemoth U. or the megaversity, but larger institutions attract better speakers, better programs, better faculty, and have more money to spend on facilities.

Still, the "prestigious" colleges have indeed found their niche and are attracting more applications than ever before. The question of the niche for another kind of liberal arts college, the Christian college, is one of the "Issues" raised in Section III, as is the question of the niche for the historically black college, both private and public. One other "niche" question, this one having to do with international education programs, is also raised in Section III.

Aside from these three chapters (chapters III.4, III.7, and III.9), Section III deals largely with issues of internal administration. In Chapter III.1, Peter Seldin discusses the question of academic culture as a form of corporate culture, "the way things are done around here" and why, and suggests that America's academic culture generally is in danger of having no stars to reach for, rather than failing to reach the star desired. This segues into Howard Altman's study of "Faculty Development in 1986" which begins with accurate — but slightly acid — portrayals of academic "types" embogged in their own Parkinsonian cultures. This is followed, as Chapter III.3, by Patrick Allen's review of the literature on faculty development.

Dean Allen also provided the discussion of the Christian liberal arts college in Chapter III.4. In Chapter III.5, he considers the relationship between funding and program performance ("Capital Infusion and Withdrawal: Program Performance at Varying Levels of Funding"), noting that although the relationship is far from monotonic and indeed may turn negative at high "quick fix" levels of funding, on the whole, advice is nice but money is better. Chapter III.6 is on growth-contracting (the process whereby a faculty member can contract with the institution for the support necessary to pursue personal and professional growth). The first growth-contracting program was developed at Gordon College (Wenham MA) in the 1970s, or else at the University of Vermont at roughly the same time, but there is no particular regional concentration of current programs.

In Chapter III.7, Reginald Wilson of the American Council on Education deals with the current status of the historically black colleges, now numbering slightly over one hundred, with eighty-seven of them four-year colleges. There are forty-one public and sixty-two private institutions, of which the prestigious ones will survive and may even strengthen, and the weakest will lose accreditation and die. The rest will survive, for a while at least, but there are not enough black students to go around, and the integrated (formerly white) research universities skim off the best.

Chapter III.8, by Dr. William Wallisch, discusses the public relations and publicity problems of colleges and universities — finding one's institution on the Top Forty Party Schools list, or under NCAA suspension or attacked on other grounds, whether legitimate or illegitimate. Bad press does not, as the author notes, mean a bad school, but it is no wonder that p.r. is an increasing concern of academic administrations, and the office that used to be off in a corner now is likely to be in a much more central location.

Chapter III.9, by John Van de Water, Director of International Education at Oregon State, discusses international programs in American colleges and universities—not only programs abroad, but programs for international students on campuses here, internationally-oriented programs taught on American campuses (as with International Business), and the "internationalization" of the curriculum. A lot is going on, but we are a long way from imparting an international perspective (including foreign languages) to the American people.

Chapter III.10, by John Bennett, Dean and Provost at Siena Heights College, is on challenges and opportunities for academic chairpersons. Dean Bennett notes the proliferation of part-timers, the need for academic entrepreneurship in raising outside funds, questions of equity and minority representation (including women), and the always-present matters of faculty evaluation and faculty development. Though managerial skills are not usually a formal requirement for academic chairpersons, the author's impression is that most of them do a pretty good job.

In Chapter III.11, Nathan Washton looks at science and technical higher education and finds that the proliferation of information, new retrieval methods (and new storage techniques), the cost of equipment, the need for subsidies in both basic and applied research, and the lack of understanding from academicians without a science or technology background, have put the colleges and universities in a squeeze. Moreover, increased political and ethical concerns over certain kinds of scientific experiments have made the task of carrying on research both more difficult and more expensive than it used to be. But Professor Washton concludes that the future looks bright for America's embryo scientists and engineers.

Chapter III.12, by Mary Deane Sorcinelli, Director of Faculty Development and Dean of the Faculties Office at Indiana (Bloomington), recounts the results of an experimental survey carried out among the faculty at Bloomington, on the personal, institutional, and societal dimensions of faculty careers. One basic concern shared by virtually all the faculty questioned—and there is no reason to think it would be different (except perhaps greater) on other campuses—was the gulf apparently existing between faculty and administration.

In Chapter III.3, Trudy Banta and Homer Fisher of the University of Tennessee at Knoxville consider the process of assessing outcomes—a consideration that ties in with the report of the Tennessee Department of Higher Education in Section X of the book. They argue for multiple and interacting techniques of assessment, and particularly for the importance of the process itself.

In Chapter III.14, Maryellen Gleason Weimer looks at techniques of instructional improvement and reports on current developments and some of their relative successes. She calls for increased general attention to the matter and echoes some of the concerns on the proper roles of the different sectors of higher education expressed in Section II.

Finally, in Chapter III.15, President Derek Bok of Harvard, in an article originally appearing in the *Harvard Magazine,* looks at higher education and high tech. President Bok's concerns are not entirely different from Professor Washton's in Chapter III.11, but his scope is wider, and he sees both greater dangers and greater opportunities, as befits that wider scope.

From the discussion of issues, the yearbook moves to providing statistical data, in Section IV. These data are divided into three sets or chapters. The first provides projections, the second current data, and the third time-series data.

Chapter IV.1 provides charts on trends in enrollment, degrees received, costs, and staff, and tables providing the data from which the charts are drawn. Chapter IV.2 provides material (in tabular form) on salaries, student attitudes, racial and ethnic makeup of student bodies, endowments, defense contracts, enrollments, student aid, state support, foreign students, public opinion, student activities, corporate gifts, ACT and SAT scores, and classification of institutions by type, size, and control. Chapter IV.3 gives time series data on enrollments, degrees, costs, funds, staff and some of the classifications of institutions provided at the end of Chapter IV.2.

Section V presents Higher Education's Man of the Year, along with a listing of new university and college presidents. In Section VI are the major speeches and documents of the year. In the speeches, Secretary of Education William Bennett appears three times, President Bok once. The documents include the Report of the National Commission on the Role and Future of State Colleges and Universities, the Congressional Economic Panel's Report on the Student-Loan Burden, two Task Force Reports (Teaching and College Quality) from the Governor's Report on Higher Education, and the Report of the Carnegie Foundation for the Advancement of Teaching, on the Undergraduate Experience in America.

Section VII presents nine lists or sets of rankings. These cover the most effective college presidents, Barron's Most Prestigious, Most Popular and Most Exciting Colleges, Great College Teachers of Our Time, the sources of university research funds, the one hundred largest institutions by enrollment, the largest by revenues and expenditures, the largest by federal obligations, the institutions enrolling the greatest number of Merit Scholars, and Edward B. Fiske's Best and Most Interesting Colleges.

Section VIII covers collective bargaining and Section IX corporate aid to higher education. These are reprinted respectively from the reports of the National Center for Collective Bargaining in Higher Education and the Professions (at Baruch College, CUNY) and of the Council for Aid to Education (formerly the Council for Financial Aid to Education), in New York.

In Section X are presented the annual reports of the federal Department of Education (in part) and of ten selected state departments of higher education. These ten were selected not so much because they represent the best state systems of higher education or even the best reports from state departments of higher education as because they recount highly interesting developments in higher education—as, for example, the University of Tennessee system's Chairs of Excellence. The ten state reports selected are those from Arkansas, Connecticut, Kentucky, Mississippi, New York, Oklahoma, Tennessee, Texas, Utah, and West Virginia.

Section XI gives interpretive summaries of major court decisions affecting higher education in such areas as faculty and staff employment and termination, and particularly contract terms, discriminatory pay or teaching loads, refusal to grant promised tenure, refusal to follow established procedures—in short, cases mostly arising from the refusal of administrators to go by the rules in dealing with faculty. Among interesting cases are those holding that provisions in faculty handbooks are part of faculty contracts, affirming the separate jurisdiction of state courts in hearing breach of contract and employment discrimination cases, and putting the burden of proof on the college or university in financial exigency cases.

Section XII is the only part of the yearbook to focus on a single institution. Because Boston University has focused its efforts in recent years on its relations with the Boston community, it seemed reasonable, in this section dealing with university-community relationships, to look at what B.U. is doing and has achieved. Next year the focus will be on other institutions or perhaps again on a single

institution with a particularly interesting record in this respect.

Section XIII covers anniversaries, including centenary anniversaries, of institutions of higher education. These are based on the reckoning of the colleges and universities involved, and while the twenty-fifth and fiftieth and sixtieth and centenary celebrations are pretty straightforward, the question of just when a college was founded in the Early Republic is more difficult to deal with. Some institutions were founded as academies before they became colleges: some of these continued to function under their original charter, while some were issued new charters. Some were founded as private institutions and became public. Some trace their ancestry and date of founding to informal log-cabin instruction years before any charter was issued. Section XIV covers name changes, institutions closing, and institutions opening in 1986.

The final section, Section XV, provides a bibliography of books and articles on higher education published in the United States (and in a few cases in Canada) in the year under review. It does not include the reports of the various state higher education departments, or Congressional hearings, or *Federal Register* items, nor does it include think-tank memos even if they have been circulated beyond the bounds of the think-tank in question. It does not include articles in newsweeklies or newspapers. In short, it is a bibliography of professional contributions to the field. The arrangement is by topic, and in the articles section (or chapter) by title rather than author within the topic areas, though by author within the topic areas in the chapter on books published. The difference is that the compiler believes the search is more likely to be by author for books and by title for articles.

Probably the most significant developments in higher education during the year covered here—besides, possibly, a certain reining-in of administrative irresponsibility in some of the legal cases—were the growth of the gulf separating the more prestigious from the less prestigious colleges and universities and the controversies over the cost of education and the assessment of outcomes—the "are we getting our money's worth?" question. Evidently, Secretary Bennett thinks not.

In future issues of the yearbook, there will be a section on grants, bequests, and gifts. Perhaps also there will be more detailed coverage of administrative personnel changes. But classification of the material into sections should remain much the same as here. While Section III, on issues, will remain, its contents will differ from year to year. Next year, for example, it is likely there will be coverage of developments and issues in programs like Critical Thinking and Writing Across the Curriculum.

The over-all picture that emerges from these reports, essays, statistics, speeches, lists and legal cases—and even from the bibliography—is, of course, of an institution, American higher education, in flux. It is entirely possible that certain currents are just beginning to flow strongly and that the next few years will see them continuing in their course until there are fundamental changes in the configuration of American universities and colleges. Some of these are alarming; some may be beneficial. Four of these currents may be noted here, to bring them particularly to the readers' attention.

First, as was already mentioned, the gap between more and less prestigious colleges is widening, and small liberal arts colleges without prestige and historically black colleges without prestige and women's colleges without prestige are in peculiarly weak positions.

Second, the size of administrative staff is growing, while faculty size is generally not. This goes along with an increasing "professionalization" of support staff (Residence Directors, Deans of Student Life, as examples), accompanied by a decreasing cross-over from faculty to staff, and in many cases an increasing sense of confrontation between faculty and administration.

Third, there is an increasing concern with teaching techniques, faculty development, and "educating" as a career rather than as a vocation. Along with this goes an emphasis on outcomes, yardstick tests, "competency" tests at the college level, and other emphasis on pedagogy. We are growing further and further away from Mark Hopkins on one end of the log and the student on the other.

Fourth, there is a tendency among institutions of all kinds—research universities, community colleges, other state universities, other private colleges—to try to be all things for all consumers. Partly this ties in with the matter of "prestige" mentioned earlier, but partly it may be seen as a kind of educational sprawl resulting from lack of planning, lack of clear role envisioning, along with a touch of the-grass-is-always-greener syndrome.

We will see what next year will bring. In the meantime, it is impossible to complete a work of this size without incurring a heavy debt of gratitude to innumerable participants in the process. Of this group, I would like to single out Peter Seldin, Professor of Management at Pace University, for his unstinting help cheerfully rendered, Jim Murray of the American Council of Education, and Gary Kuris, vice-president at Garland, who patiently shepherded the project from inception to publication.

In addition, the editor wishes to thank Dr. Jared Lobdell and Ms. Marie Ellen Larcada at Garland for their tireless labors in getting this book into print in a remarkably short period of time. Their attention and devotion to detail is evident in the pages that follow. The editor also acknowledges his gratitude to Dr. John Silber of the Boston University, and Dr. Ernest Boyer and Mr. Robert Hochstein of the Carnegie Foundation for the Advancement of Teaching. To the many others who also gave generously of their time and answered my many queries, thank you.

George Thomas Kurian

# Principal Sectors
of Higher Education

The four chapters in this section are reprinted from EDUCATION IN CONTEXT by permission of the publisher, the U.S. Department of Education.

# Research Universities:
# Their Role in Undergraduate Education

## Roger L. Geiger

The research universities form the best known portion of the American system of higher education, and yet as a group they are probably the least studied. When they are discussed, it is usually in connection with research policy rather than undergraduate education. They nevertheless occupy a strategically vital position in this area, if for no other reason than because they possess the most coveted places for college study and because they educate the country's most gifted students. Clearly their role in undergraduate education deserves attention.

The research universities are the most compartmentalized of institutions in American higher education. The undergraduate colleges of these institutions sometimes contain less than half of their enrollments, and in most cases would account for a minor portion of the budgets. Many of them operate massive, virtually autonomous hospital-medical school complexes, usually on separate campuses; the land grant research universities do extensive agricultural development work at various locations; many large university research laboratories are almost wholly supported by federal funds and quite remote from any university teaching; and almost all research universities contain various professional schools, each with its distinctive orientation. Still, in the true research university, the spirit of disinterested inquiry penetrates into the academic departments and is an active presence in the life of the institution.

The research universities are known above all else for research, naturally, and for graduate education. Behind these activities however, lie three elements that account for their character and their unity. First, they have deep and inescapable commitments to academic values (see below). This is no mere truism. As compartmentalized institutions; the research universities must harmonize commitments to many value sets, not all of which are easily compatible with the norms of academic inquiry. Nevertheless, the predominance of academic values in matters concerning faculty, graduate education, curricula, and, of course, research, is the hallmark of a research university.

Second, these institutions possess faculties that are distinguished in the eyes of their peers. Every research university obviously cannot excel in every department, but peer-rated esteem is a paramount consideration in decisions concerning the hiring, promotion, and compensation of faculty.

Third, sustaining a high volume of academic research requires a considerable resource base and resource flow. The research universities are among the wealthiest institutions of higher education—and they need to be. The annual income for research that is largely derived from external sources has to be backed up by high overhead expenditures for a distinguished faculty and a large base of research capital embedded in libraries, laboratories, and other facilities.

The Carnegie classification of American colleges and universities designates as Research I Universities the 50 institutions that receive the largest amounts of federal research funds and train the greatest number of future researchers. Using the same criteria, the next 50 institutions are dubbed Research II Universities. The National Center for Higher Education Management Systems (NCHEMS), using somewhat more restrictive criteria, counts 73 major doctoral/research universities. In either case, it should be evident that with so large a number of universities, not all will possess the three elements previously described. For our purposes, these so-called research universities might be separated into three groups—one well defined and the other two somewhat subjective.

At the peak of the research university hierarchy, there are 20 institutions which fulfill the three criteria (Geiger, in press-b). Since both total volume of research and commitment to faculty quality are important for defining research universities, the rank order lists of universities for both these criteria have been combined here. Listed below are the 16 institutions that had the largest expenditures for research and development during FY 1980 (National Science Foundation, 1981); and the 17 institutions that were rated to have the highest overall faculty quality in the recent *Assessment of Research-Doctorate Programs in the United States (1982)* (Webster, 1983):

| Rank | R&D Expenditures | Faculty Quality |
|------|------------------|-----------------|
| 1. | M.I.T. | UC Berkeley |
| 2. | Wisconsin | Stanford |
| 3. | UC San Diego | Harvard |
| 4. | Minnesota | Yale |
| 5. | Stanford | M.I.T. |
| 6. | Washington | Princeton |
| 7. | Michigan | Chicago |
| 8. | Cornell | Michigan |
| 9. | Columbia | Wisconsin |
| 10. | Harvard | UCLA |
| 11. | Penn | Columbia |
| 12. | UC Berkeley | Cornell |
| 13. | UCLA | Illinois |
| 14. | Illinois | Penn |
| 15. | Johns Hopkins | Caltech |
| 16. | Texas | Minnesota |
| 17. | ———— | Texas |

(See Appendix: tables 1 & 2)

It would be difficult to argue that any of these institutions do not belong in the top 20, although a reasonable case could be made that several others are equally deserving of the last two or three spots. Nevertheless, this list is practical and sufficient for the purpose at hand, and will consequently be used for the rest of this paper as the point of reference for the discussion of research universities (data concerning these institutions are provided in the appendices). These universities, moreover, generally act as spokesmen for research universities (Ford Foundation, 1978), and are diverse enough to represent the gamut of possibilities for this species.

A second tier of research universities that are generally smaller, less prestigious in terms of national rankings and less involved with high-dollar research can also be identified. This tier would include well-endowed, private universities like Brown, Carnegie-Mellon, Case-Western Reserve, the Claremont group, Duke, Emory, Rice, Rochester, Northwestern, Vanderbilt, and Washington University as well as such state universities as North Carolina, Virginia, and Indiana. These institutions largely share the academic values of the first group, and often have impressive levels of resources relative to their more selective commitments. Their smaller departments and graduate programs, however, do not receive sufficient recognition to place near the top in national quality rankings. These institutions might be designated as regional research universities: they are highly regarded in their respective regions and thus play an important role in research and graduate education.

A third group of research universities (but not necessarily a third or lower tier) consists of those flagship state universities, land-grant universities and large private universities that undertake substantial amounts of research, but also have major obligations for undergraduate teaching. Their intake of students tends to be less selective than that of the first two groups, and pre-professional degree programs often have larger enrollments than academic ones. Usually a considerable proportion of their research expenditures is sequestered in a medical school or devoted to agricultural stations. Academic values are generally honored in these universities, and sometimes prominently so; but they tend to be diluted by other important institutional imperatives. These multiple purposes can produce some noticeable incongruities. Texas A&M, for example, has a large and growing research and development budget and a desire to make a mark in Big Science physics research, but at the same time clings proudly to non-intellectual attitudes and patterns of behavior known as the Aggie spirit. On the whole, these institutions tend to rank more highly on measures of research volume than they do on those of faculty quality. The values and attitudes that inform research have comparatively less impact on undergraduate education.

## Unity and Diversity

Research and graduate education are the tasks that unite the research universities as a group. Indeed, these have been the principal interests of the Association of American Universities, which has represented the research universities since the beginning of this century (Geiger, in press-a). Their teaching roles, and particularly their undergraduate teaching roles, on the other hand, are the most obvious characteristics by which they differ. The 20 schools considered here, in fact, include both the largest single-campus university in the country (Minnesota) and the most selective one (Caltech). This dichotomy between research and undergraduate teaching corresponds with the distinction that Burton Clark has made between the culture of the discipline and the culture of the enterprise (Clark, 1983). Together, the two cultures account for both unity and diversity among research universities.

The competition for academic prestige is an inherent feature of the university research role. It is rooted in the processes by which scientific recognition is continuously allotted and evaluated. It is thus only natural that this preoccupation gives rise to periodic formal rankings, even though such endeavors are inherently imperfect and controversial. The rank of any university in the academic pecking order is really an abstraction; it is a somewhat artificial aggregation of the prestige of individual departments, which are in turn aggregations of the prestige of individual scholars. Nevertheless, the existence of a hierarchy is a reality that affects the behavior of individuals and institutions. The recent *Assessment of Research Doctoral Programs* is as thorough and judicious an exploration of this hierarchy as has yet been undertaken (Webster, 1983). Its findings, then, have the virtue of presenting in detail what everyone knows, or thinks they know, anyway (Table 2).

In the ranking given in Table 2, three strata are discernible among the 20 universities. At the top, 7 institutions (Berkeley, Stanford, Harvard, Yale, M.I.T., Princeton and Chicago) are distinguished by not only an abundance of very strong departments, but also by the presence of numerous excellent departments (those scoring 70 or more, two standard deviations above the mean). Caltech, as a small and specialized institution, clearly belongs in this group as well by virtue of having six departments of this caliber. The next 7 institutions constitute a second stratum /(UCLA, Michigan, Wisconsin, Columbia, Cornell, Illinois, Penn). They too have a number of strong departments, but not very many rated as excellent. Below this level the areas of academic strength become more spotty. The interesting question then becomes, how do these three levels of academic quality match up with other institutional characteristics? (See Geiger, in press-b).

Seven of the eight schools in the top stratum are private. Their most salient common characteristic is the limited size of their undergraduate colleges (Table 6). Harvard is the largest of these universities with more than 15,000 students, yet only about a third of them are undergraduates. As a result of deliberately restricting their undergraduate enrollment, they are now among the most selective of universities. Median combined SAT scores for entering freshmen in 1979-1980 exceeded 1,300 at five of the seven private institutions (Table 4). Berkeley, although an exceptional case in many regards, also fits this model by having the highest freshman SATs among public universities. Clearly, the distinguished faculty of these elite schools find teaching high-ability, well-motivated undergraduates to be a congenial accompaniment to graduate instruction and research.

The universities of the second stratum are remarkably alike. All are fairly large institutions containing numerous compartments or units. The four state universities here naturally have obligations to provide a variety of services. Service roles are present in the three private universities as well: Columbia and Penn have a special relationship to their respective metropolitan areas, which have traditionally been their sources of voluntary support; Cornell contains units of the State University of New York. The many fine academic departments found at these schools do not have the campus to themselves. The research atmosphere is consequently less rarified at these multi-purpose institutions.

Below the second stratum the effects of size tend to diverge in accordance with the differences already noted between small regional research universities and large multi-versities. The former tend to emulate the top stratum of universities to the extent that their resources permit. The latter are rather unselective in admitting undergraduates, demand heavier teaching loads, and conduct much research outside the basic academic departments. A comparison of these state universities with the others in the higher strata would seem to suggest an inverse relationship between inclusiveness and academic prestige.

## Values

It is relatively simple to specify the value system of the research universities, for it is identical to the values of the academic disciplines. In fact, the national or international disciplinary communities and the research universities are heavily dependent on one another. Through their formal and informal processes of evaluation, the disciplines ensure that contributions to the advancement of knowledge are validated, and that recognition and rewards are allocated to scholars and scientists.

Possessing the most valuable positions and facilities for conducting research, these universities have an obligation to make these opportunities available to the most capable investigators. In theory this would require exemplifying what Robert K. Merton called "the normative structure of science" (Merton, 1973). In practice it means awarding faculty positions in accordance with the reward system of science and the judgments of disciplinary peers.

Research universities bear an implicit responsibility for upholding the norms of science. Indeed, in this respect they provide moral leadership for American higher education as a whole. Other institutions may slight these values on occasion, but the research universities may not. Faculty loyalty, the flow of research funds, and much indispensable voluntary support depends upon their fealty to this code. The predominance of academic values, then, is no idle preference: it is an institutional imperative resulting from some distinctive features of higher education.

A good deal of authority in research universities is vested in academic departments. This is where the expertise necessary for exercising academic judgments resides, and this is where academic values are most strongly felt. In large measure research universities are obliged to defer to their departments in matters pertaining to personnel and subject matter if they wish to retain their most productive and prestigious faculty members. In this respect, the decentralized, competitive structure of American higher education has significant effects on the behavior of research universities. If an institution wishes to compete for academic distinction, it must honor the values set by the top research universities.

In addition to this competition for prestige, research universities are also driven by a more materialistic competition for research funds. Almost all the direct costs of separately budgeted research in American universities are paid by external grants, and a large proportion of these are awarded on the basis of peer review. Acquiring the basic resources for conducting research year after year, then, also demands that universities retain the loyalty of their grant-winning faculty.

## Resources

Howard Bowen has formulated several "laws" to describe the economic incentives and behavior of colleges and universities:

> In quest of excellence, prestige, and influence, there is virtually no limit to the amount of money an institution could spend for seemingly fruitful educational ends. [Thus,] each institution raises all the money it can [and] spends all it raises. (Bowen, 1980, 19-20)

This maxim would apply to research universities more than others. In fact, they owe their special position to their money-raising abilities.

These 20 research universities had expenditures in 1981-82 that averaged $22,580 per FTE student. By way of contrast, the other 52 institutions that NCHEMS classifies as major doctoral/research universities had per-student expenditures averaging $8,216 (NCHEMS, n.d.). One of the distinguishing features of the leading research universities is that they receive and spend relatively large amounts of money.

If direct expenditures for research are removed from the research university per-student average, $15,692 of per-student spending still remains. By way of comparison, student tuition in the private universities varied from $6,000 to $8,000, and tuition plus state appropriations in the public universities averaged over $7,500 (1981-82). If these sums are taken to represent student-derived revenues (since state appropriations depend partly upon student numbers), it becomes clear that they accounted for only about one-half of the non-research expenditures of these research universities. Where does the remainder come from?

For private research universities these extra revenues come primarily from voluntary support, and secondarily from endowment income, which itself largely represents a return on past giving (Table 3). These revenues are the most convincing single indicator of the "wealth" of these universities. Sources of voluntary support tend to vary for each institution (Geiger, in press-c), although "development", as it is euphemistically called, is so highly refined at all of these institutions that they receive substantial sums from every category of benefactor. Nevertheless, a high proportion of alumni giving correlates with a strong residential undergraduate college; universities in major cities have traditionally looked to local philanthropists; noted engineering schools have tended to encourage corporate contributions; and the large foundations have traditionally sought to bolster the private research universities generally (Council for Financial Aid to Education, 1983). It might also be noted that the medical complexes of these schools generate and consume enormous amounts of voluntary support money.

Public universities have substantially increased their development efforts in recent years. Among them, the research universities have met with considerable success. For 1982-83, 6 of the 20 leading fundraisers were public universities (Minnesota, Michigan, Illinois, Texas A&M, UCLA, and Wisconsin) not including the $100+ million efforts of the California and Texas university systems (*Chronicle of Higher Education*, May 9, 1984).

It is important to link the dynamics of voluntary support with the role of the federal government—the other principal resource base for university research. The federal role in supplying research capital was particularly prominent in the 1960s, and has declined considerably since then. The chief function of the federal government, however, has been and remains that of paying the direct costs of conducting university research (including a percentage supplement for immediate indirect costs). In the late 1960s, the percentage of university research supported by federal funds reached 75%; today it is closer to 66%. These funds naturally tend to flow to the institutions with the most competent faculties and the most complete facilities—in other words, to those with accumulated research capital. Thus, the 20 universities covered here account for about two-fifths of federally funded research and development (Geiger, in press-b).

It would be erroneous to conclude from this discussion that money is the sole resource of importance to research universities. Rather, given the values and traditions of these institutions, and their human and material capital, it is inescapable that dollars drive the system. Accordingly, financial issues are a perennial preoccupation of research universities.

## The Current Environment

The research universities do not share many of the concerns of other American colleges and universities. Their enrollments will not be affected by the shrinking of college-age cohorts. In fact, most of these schools had more applicants in 1984 than ever before. Similarly, the decline in student aptitudes has had a comparatively small impact on these selective institutions.

One common concern arises from the general financial squeeze affecting undergraduate education. The private research universities set the price ceiling in American higher education each year, and are sorely troubled that annual tuition hikes tend to restrict their potential student pool on the basis of income rather that ability. Higher tuition also raises their own costs for institutional student aid. Sustaining this very costly form of education is a risky financial juggling act.

Futhermore, the top *public* research universities happen to be found in states that have recently experienced considerable economic distress. (California, despite its tax revolt, is probably an exception here, and the University of Texas research effort has been buoyed by its oil-fueled endowment). For schools like Michigan, state indigence has prompted a reorganizational triage, as some weaker areas have been sacrificed in order to preserve academic strengths. However, the University of Washington may be the research university weakened the most, having experienced a notable faculty exodus.

Voluntary support for higher education in general has been remarkably strong in recent years, despite the turbulence of the economy. From 1975 to 1982 it actually increased on a per student, inflation-adjusted basis (*Chronicle of Higher Education*, May 9, 1984). It would appear that voluntary support to research universities has kept pace with that in other categories of colleges, a creditable achievement in light of the acceleration of development efforts across American higher education. Alumni remain the single largest source of voluntary support, followed by the category of "non-alumni individuals," which includes most major philanthropists. The most salient recent trend has been an increase in corporate giving to higher education, while the relatively static assets of foundations have provided a diminishing share of the total. The buoyancy of voluntary support has been a bright spot for higher education in general, and for the research universities in particular. In the longer term, however, one wonders how much further this pie can expand.

Ongoing federal support for university research contains an inherently political element that is hard to predict. The Reagan administration began its first term by vowing to make significant cuts in this area (Wilson, 1982), but by 1984 it was boasting of a 26% real increase in federal support for university R&D during its tenure (*Science*, April 6, 1984). This has been good news for the research universities, but it has not been sufficient to raise their downcast spirits. The consensus is that university research faces formidable problems in the years ahead.

The difficulties primarily concern the ecology of the research system and the infrastructure that supports university research. On the first point, it is now abundantly clear that the circulation of academic personnel on which the research universities have long depended has virtually ground to a halt. Academic stars are still in demand; but the normal process by which graduate students become assistant professors and ascend the academic ladder can no longer be counted upon. Academic immobility is generally bad for science, and it threatens to compound the impending crisis in graduate education. Fewer top students have been choosing graduate school in recent years; the financial backing for those that do is inadequate; and job prospects for those seeking academic careers are dismal (National Commission on Student Financial Assistance, 1983). In economic terms this may appear to be an inevitable consequence of overall stagnation in the higher education industry. However, graduate education is a vital component of the total operation of research universities.

Secondly, more than a decade of consistent pressure on research university finances has taken its toll on the infrastructure that underlies the research enterprise. The research universities themselves have taken the initiative to focus greater attention on these needs through a "Report from Fifteen University Presidents" (*Research Universities and the National Interest*, 1978) and a study commissioned by the AAU (Rosenzweig, 1982). Besides the problems besetting graduate education, both documents stressed the following areas:

1. Facilities and instrumentation — university scientists are increasingly having to work with tools that have fallen well behind the state of the art. The scientific leadership of the research universities seems to be imperiled by the scarcity of capital for these purposes.
2. University research libraries, the "laboratories of the humanities," are losing ground on two fronts: they generally lack the funds to acquire books and periodicals as comprehensively as they have in the past; and capital is needed to adapt to new informational technologies.
3. International and area studies are perhaps the outstanding examples of subjects that do not pay for them-selves in terms of student enrollments. Yet, these fields have considerable importance for broadening intellectual contacts within the university and cultivating valuable expertise for the nation. Consequently they have been developed and sustained largely through external funds. These sources are now limited, and universities are finding it difficult to sustain these efforts.

"Of the needs of the university there is, indeed, no end," lamented Harvard's Lawrence Lowell in 1920 (Geiger, in press-a). Currently, it would seem, the research universities are faced with difficult choices over which of their many needs they will be able to meet.

## Undergraduate Education

At the nation's first research university, Johns Hopkins, physicist Henry A. Rowland was once asked what he intended to do with the students in his laboratory: "Do with them? Do with them?" he replied with some annoyance, "I shall neglect them!" (Hawkins, 1960, p. 218). In the 100 years since, the stereotype has prevailed that research university faculty tend to neglect undergraduate students in favor of pursuing their own investigations. Probably any academic could cite examples to support or contradict this view; but as a generalization about research universities, it is somewhat misleading. In the late 19th century, Johns Hopkins found that it could not dispense with undergraduate education, and research universities that have faced the issue since then have reached the same conclusion (Geiger, in press-a).

There is no difficulty identifying the significance of undergraduates for public research universities. Service to their states has conventionally been defined in terms of undergraduate enrollments. And rightfully so: undergraduates constitute the clientele that is most likely to come from and remain in the state. For those private universities that receive a dominant portion of voluntary support from alumni, undergraduates are a valued and valuable resource: the loyalties that inspire this giving lie almost exclusively with classmates and the undergraduate college. Seven private research universities (Columbia, Cornell, Harvard, M.I.T., Princeton, Stanford and Yale) consistently receive more than $10 million per year from their alumni (Table 5). Also, unlike gifts from other sources, alumni contributions are largely unrestricted in nature. They are consequently a particularly vital source of revenue for this set of universities.

From an historical perspective, the leadership of the research universities in undergraduate education is readily apparent. A history of innovations might be written just from these institutions. It would have to mention the Yale Report of 1828 (defending the classical curriculum), Cornell's commitment to teach any man any subject, Harvard's elective system, high school certificates devised by Michigan, the first summer school at Chicago, selective admissions as implemented at Columbia, and the 1945 Harvard Report on general education. What Christopher Jencks and David Riesman called *The Academic Revolution* (1968) stands for the pervasive influence of these institutions on American higher education since World War II. Since Jencks and Riesman wrote, the research universities have pointed the way toward a liberalizing of academic requirements and the total abandonment of the university's *in loco parentis* role. Clearly, what happens to undergraduate education at research universities is important to higher education as a whole. Probably no set of institutions can speak more confidently about excellence in education than these 20 research universities. They measure quality by inputs (which can be measured to some extent) rather than outputs (which are far more difficult to gauge). By such criteria, the top research universities do well indeed, since they possess prestigious faculty, and because they attract a large share of the nation's brightest students. But how would they fare if it were possible to isolate and measure just their educational effects?

An initial attempt by Alexander Astin to measure the cognitive impact upon undergraduate students of just such quality inputs could discern no significant effects (Astin, 1968). In a later study, however, Astin found that selective institutions (which would include research universities) had generally positive effects on their students both during and after their academic careers. Students showed an increased sense of self-criticism and a strikingly high degree of satisfaction with their undergraduate experience. After graduation they were more likely to enroll in graduate school and, in the long term, achieve high earnings (Astin, 1977). In another study, Robert Pace found that the positive effects of research universities, compared with other types of institutions, increased significantly from 1950 to 1970 (Pace, 1974).

The selective institutions studied by Astin include both research universities and top liberal arts colleges; and it is very difficult to compare undergraduate education in these two types of institutions. David Riesman feels that the very top liberal arts colleges "are probably better than the undergraduate divisions of research universities," apparently because their faculties have a greater commitment to teaching (personal communication, 1984). Others would tip the balance toward the research universities by virtue of their generally superior faculties. Nevertheless, the superiority of the research universities in the hard sciences would be difficult to challenge. Probably most could agree that these two types embody somewhat different forms of excellence, and that one or the other might be more appropriate for certain kinds of students. Nevertheless, the superiority of the research universities in the hard sciences would remain unchallenged.

What research universities aspire to achieve with their undergraduates actually transcends the realm of quantification and standardized testing. The mental attributes that students would ideally absorb from a research environment—critical thinking, intellectual confidence, sophistication, and creativity—cannot be reduced very well to multiple choice answers. It would instead seem advisable to proceed subjectively, by first identifying the special features of undergraduate education at research universities, and then exploring the issues to which these qualities give rise.

The commitment to academic values, a distinguished faculty, and the resources to support research are the distinguishing characteristics of research universities, but their effects on undergraduate education are difficult to pin down. The value system seems to create an atmosphere that influences most undergraduates. This seems to be due in part to the intellectual example set by the faculty, and in part to the effects of intellectually active peers. Perhaps less evident is the fact that undergraduates at research universities are not the sole institutional *raison d'etre*, but rather form one component of a large and complex organism. They coexist with numerous graduate students, a faculty that is on campus most of the time, full-time researchers, and an ill-defined body of affiliated individuals. A research university is not, like some campuses, a youth ghetto; and the anti-intellectual attitudes that sometimes thrive in such an adolescent milieu accordingly have less appeal.

The existence of this complex organism, and the extensive resource base that supports it, produces an extraordinary range of opportunities for students. So great are the extracurricular offerings at most research universities that more than a modicum of intellectual curiosity could be a detriment to class work. Thus, only a fraction of these opportunities can be realized by the average undergraduate. This, however, is the nature of a research university: a movable feast where the delicacies far outstrip the appetites of the guests. Nevertheless, sampling some of these offerings, and just becoming aware of the existence of others, can in itself be an important component of a student's education. In these kinds of opportunities research universities are unequalled, but to capitalize upon them requires individual initiative. Probably the paramount factor affecting the character of undergraduate education at research universities is the mix of students. Each of these schools recruits a substantial number of very high-ability students. What varies from institution to institution is the number, aptitudes and interests of their classmates.

The research-intensive universities (Caltech, Hopkins, M.I.T.) undoubtedly have the most homogeneous student bodies because their small classes are recruited almost solely on the basis of academic abilities. The educational philosophies of these campuses encourage moving the students to the level of advanced work as quickly as possible. Interestingly, all three schools allow some or all of the freshman year to be taken on a pass-fail basis—recognition, in effect, of the preliminary nature of such work. They also make it a regular practice for undergraduates to participate in faculty research projects. The peer culture at these schools is obviously highly intellectual. For gifted and motivated students committed to scientific careers, it is difficult to imagine a better learning environment or a more effective education. However, there is no slow lane on these fast tracks.

At Harvard, Princeton, Stanford, and Yale, a somewhat different approach to undergraduate education prevails. Long ago these institutions committed themselves to choose not just the brightest students according to grades or SATs, but a diversified class from among their many qualified applicants. Exactly how each school does this is an institutional secret, although the general rules are evident. The point is that each member of these painstakingly constructed freshmen classes has the opportunity for an outstanding undergraduate education—in terms of faculty, facilities, peers, and environment. The undoubted excellence of these schools, however, is a privilege available by definition to only a few.

Public research universities have a mandate to make their resources available to a far more numerous clientele. "We will support your ambitions to be a world-class research university if you will look after our bright children," is the way Martin Trow has characterized the unwritten compact between the state of California and Berkeley (Trow, 1983). Because of the numbers involved, this clearly has a diluting effect. Thus, a world famous scholar is more likely to be encountered in the lecture room than in a seminar. The trade-off here is that more students will hear the professor, but fewer will have the opportunity for close interaction. The positive benefits of this approach should not be deprecated by comparisons with highly selective private institutions. The public research universities serve many students who are not quite up to the demanding pace of elite institutions, yet who are able and who undoubtedly learn far more than they would in a less rigorous environment. Thus, the advantages of a research university are spread more widely at the state institutions. The role of individual initiative, however, is especially significant here. On large campuses dominated by undergraduates, a student often has to exert greater effort in order to profit from the opportunities that a research university makes available.

The research university ambiance probably contributes to the effectiveness of undergraduate education most markedly at the selective public institutions like Berkeley and Michigan. However at some point, it would seem, dilution can go too far. The research university atmosphere can be overwhelmed by other elements. Specifically, the symbiotic relationship between teaching and the intellectual pursuits of the faculty begins to deteriorate when students lack sufficient preparation and motivation. Perhaps worse, the positive effects of peer culture can be lost entirely. These conditions tend to alienate research-minded faculty. Note that the state research universities in the third stratum of prestige are also those with the highest teaching burdens of lower division students (Table 6).

The character of these research universities has held stable for a generation, and is unlikely to change in the near future. Each institution responds to the logic of its own situation. Perhaps from the standpoint of the socially optimal utilization of resources, the best private research universities are too good; that is, they concentrate their abundant benefits on too few students. But they are in competition with one another for excellence, and the rarified standard to which they aspire precludes increasing their undergraduate enrollments.

State university systems, in general, might benefit from greater differentiation—in particular, from protecting the research milieu at flagship campuses. However, in most cases, higher standards of admission on these campuses would mean substituting out-of-state students for in-state ones; and diminishing size without diminishing the budget would be equally unthinkable. Thus, undergraduate education at research universities will likely continue to have two faces, each with its own special attraction.

## Caveats and Qualifications

With their many advantages compared to other colleges and universities, the research universities might produce creditable educational results for undergraduates without too great an exertion. Yet they are burdened by an extraordinary responsibility. They have the task of educating a considerable portion of the nations's most gifted youth. If for no other reason, this challenge has prevented research universities from being complacent about undergraduate education.

A perennial issue, which has been felt most acutely at the research universities, has been the tension between general education and the imperatives of specialization. "Imperatives" is not an overly strong term in light of the rapid proliferation of disciplinary knowledge, not to mention the growth of hybrid and interdisciplinary fields. Yet the desire to give to undergraduates both an acquaintance with the major areas of human knowledge and a common cultural experience remains strong (Bell, 1966). The conflict continues today, as indicated by the controversy surrounding the implementation of a Core Curriculum at Harvard. General education, nevertheless, is probably weaker today than ever. The problem is not the relentless advance of knowledge, rather, some fundamental weaknesses in the concept itself. The first of these is cultural relativity: what one generation designates as the verities of our cultural heritage and the accoutrements of all educated people is rarely accepted as such by the next generation. Second would be the current absence of consensus over what the specific content of general education out to include (Harvard took refuge here in "modes of reasoning"). Third, there seems to be no compelling evidence that institutionalized general education (as opposed to virtuoso individual performances) can actually achieve the cultural and cognitive goals that its proponents claim as justification.

Despite spasms of guilt about specialization, most disciplinary faculty have little use for general education courses. It is often alleged that this is because such courses distract them form research, or because they involve too much preparation. If one does not wholeheartedly endorse the premises of these courses, however, teaching them can be intellectually dishonest. The more closely prescribed the course, the greater the dilemma. Tellingly, the better students tend to desert general education offerings because they find greater stimulation in the disciplines (once called the "Exeter Syndrome" at Harvard). For these reasons, then, the undying impulse to ensure breadth and culture in undergraduate education has been transmuted in most research universities into distribution requirements. The permutations here are limitless, but in essence this solution harmonizes the interests of the disciplinary faculty with the consciences of the deans.

Are teaching and research complementary activities? Or, do the time demands of research and the diversion of intellectual energies inevitably occur at the expense of classroom pedagogy? These fundamental questions have been debated throughout the history of research universities, and proponents can sill be found on both sides. It nevertheless seems to this writer that active scholars at research universities are likely to be the most effective teachers for academically competent students. Actual involvement in research is still the most feasible and most natural way for a professor to keep abreast of his or her field. Furthermore, this activity is the surest means of sustaining intellectual enthusiasm towards one's subject over the duration of a teaching career. As a practical matter, research university faculty teach fewer hours per semester and fewer semesters over the years. They are consequently likely to be somewhat fresher in the classroom than faculty with unrelieved teaching burdens. Still, the synergy of teaching and research cannot be taken for granted.

Recently, two well-informed individuals independently expressed their judgments of the superior quality of undergraduate education at Yale to the author. The reasons given were the effectiveness of the Yale colleges in uniting giving and learning, and the value placed upon teaching by the Yale faculty. The first of these conditions would be impossible for most schools to duplicate (although Princeton and Penn are attempting to move in this direction); but the second would not. Yale faculty are scrupulous about meeting their classes and conscientious about their presentations. This tradition of strong teaching is recognized and encouraged institutionally; and Yale students, having been accustomed to good teaching, are a demanding audience. On research university campuses where teaching does not have this type of backing, a kind of entrepreneurial spirit can potentially distract faculty from their obligations toward students. It is not research itself that causes problems, rather excessive obligations to disseminate, market, or otherwise exploit one's work. A telling symptom of this syndrome would be courses that are perfunctorily given, with frequent cancellations, by jet-set professors.

Wayne C. Booth recently articulated a rather different concern: that the research mentality is often an outright obstacle to the obligations of teaching beginning undergraduates (Booth, 1983). This situation may be particularly acute in English Literature, where scholarship tends toward the esoteric, and where the disjunction between the goals and the reality of freshman composition can be enormous. Booth does not go so far as to endorse the position of some teaching purists who disdain scholarship entirely. Rather, he calls for scholarship that could and would be utilized by teachers. More generally, Booth essentially warns that the vitality of the conjunction can be lost when either teaching or research are overemphasized.

In light of the past leadership of research universities in undergraduate education, it would be interesting to chart the present currents of change; that is, to cite those problems that the research universities themselves have identified and acted upon.

Harvard, Princeton, Stanford, and Yale, have not only been consistently concerned about optimizing the educational experiences of their undergraduates, but these fortunate institutions possess the wherewithal to undertake significant changes when they so choose. These schools seem to be attempting, without trying to turn the clock back, to overcome some of the permissive and fissiparous developments of the late sixties and early seventies. At Harvard this has meant, above all, instituting the core curriculum—the latest and in many ways the most reasonable pendulum swing toward general education. Yale recently reinstated a foreign language requirement. Behind that step lies a consistent effort to strengthen academic standards by reducing grade and credit-hour inflation, taking a hard stand against plagiarism, and promoting writing skills. Both Princeton and Stanford have acted to enhance the educational potential of residential life in the hope of reintegrating the undergraduate college.

Do these isolated steps constitute a trend of significance for American higher education? It is noteworthy that these institutions seem to be placing greater demands upon their students in curricular coverage, in classroom performance, and as members of an academic community. They thus are running counter to the consumerism that has plagued many colleges and universities as a result of heightened competition for enrollments (Riesman, 1982). It also might be noted that academic majors are generally thriving at these schools, in contrast to the tide of vocationalism that has engulfed large sections of American higher education (Geiger, 1980a).

American higher education today is poised on the edge of a dramatic demographic reversal. For more than a decade, a large college-age cohort resulted in expanding FTEs. These fat years for colleges and universities, however, were lean ones for a large portion of their graduates, who graduated into crowded labor markets. Students instinctively responded to these conditions by discounting their educational investments, and their lack of commitment had a generally deleterious effect upon educational standards (Geiger 1980b). Continuing decreases in the college-age cohort have the potential for reversing this relationship. A healthy market for college graduates could enhance the rewards for quality in higher education. In fact, the demand for places at the best universities is already at its highest level ever. Thus, it is not entirely far-fetched to conceive of a second Academic Revolution within the coming decade. Like the last, this would be led by the major research universities; but unlike the last, the emphasis might be on fostering excellence in undergraduate education. There has been considerable realignment throughout American higher education in the past decade: it may be time for the convoluted "academic procession" that David Riesman described in the 1950s to begin marching once again (Riesman, 1956).

**TABLE 1**

# SELECTED R&D EXPENDITURES FOR
# 20 RESEARCH UNIVERSITIES
## FY 1980
(in millions of dollars)

| | Total R&D | National Rank Order | Federal R&D | Federal R&D for Medicine | B-C | Relative Rank Order | General & Educational Expenditures 1979-80 | % R&D (A/E x 100) |
|---|---|---|---|---|---|---|---|---|
| M.I.T. | 163.6 | 1 | 138.4 | 1.6 | 136.8 | 1 | 268.3 | 61.0% |
| Wisconsin | 138.2 | 2 | 89.4 | 25.1 | 64.3 | 3 | 352.9 | 39.2 |
| UC San Diego | 124.8 | 3 | 111.0 | 26.3 | 84.7 | 2 | 285.8 | 43.7 |
| Minnesota | 119.1 | 4 | 68.5 | 33.9 | 34.6 | 19 | 437.9 | 27.2 |
| Stanford | 113.1 | 5 | 102.6 | 40.7 | 61.9 | 4 | 318.4 | 35.5 |
| Washington | 111.9 | 6 | 93.1 | 36.8 | 56.3 | 6 | 329.5 | 34.0 |
| Michigan | 111.3 | 7 | 75.6 | 21.0 | 54.6 | 8 | 400.1 | 27.8 |
| Cornell | 107.6 | 8 | 70.6 | 19.1 | 51.5 | 9 | 299.7 | 35.9 |
| Columbia | 101.4 | 9 | 83.7 | 36.1 | 47.6 | 13 | 302.2 | 33.4 |
| Harvard | 100.9 | 10 | 76.4 | 20.5 | 55.9 | 7 | E426.3 | 23.7 |
| Penn | 94.2 | 11 | 70.6 | 21.4 | 49.2 | 11 | 395.2 | 23.8 |
| Berkeley | 90.4 | 12 | 64.1 | 6.3 | 57.8 | 5 | 310.5 | 29.1 |
| UCLA | 88.9 | 13 | 70.4 | 23.5 | 46.9 | 14 | 541.4 | 16.4 |
| Illinois | 88.3 | 14 | 52.8 | 2.5 | 50.3 | 10 | E318.2 | 26.2 |
| Johns Hopkins | 83.2 | 15 | 72.8 | 35.1 | 37.7 | 16 | 205.4 | 40.5 |
| Texas | 78.6 | 16 | 48.7 | neg. | 48.7 | 12 | 235.8 | 33.3 |
| Yale | 71.4 | 22 | 63.6 | 28.3 | 35.3 | 17 | 224.8 | 31.8 |
| Chicago | 58.4 | 30 | 50.1 | 15.4 | 34.7 | 18 | 291.1 | 20.1 |
| Caltech | 43.3 | 39 | 38.3 | neg. | 38.3 | 15 | 76.3 | 56.7 |
| Princeton | 27.8 | 69 | 20.9 | neg. | 20.9 | 21 | 98.1 | 28.3 |

Source: *Academic Science, FY 1980*, (NSF, 1982).

TABLE 2

# FACULTY QUALITY RATINGS

| National Rank Order | Institution | Phys. Sci., Math | Hum. | Eng. | Biol | Soc. Sci. | Progs. Rated 60 or Higher | Progs. Rated 70 or Higher | TOTAL SCORE |
|---|---|---|---|---|---|---|---|---|---|
| 1 | Berkeley | 6 | 9 | 4 | 4 | 7 | 30 | 15 | 45 |
| 2 | Stanford | 6 | 4 | 4 | 4 | 6 | 24 | 10 | 34 |
| 3 | Harvard | 5 | 5 | — | 4 | 6 | 20 | 12 | 32 |
| 4 | Yale | 6 | 7 | — | 6 | 6 | 25 | 7 | 32 |
| 5 | M.I.T. | 5 | 2 | 4 | 3 | 3 | 17 | 12 | 29 |
| 6 | Princeton | 5 | 7 | 4 | — | 5 | 21 | 7 | 28 |
| 7 | Chicago | 5 | 4 | — | 4 | 7 | 20 | 7 | 27 |
| 8 | UCLA | 5 | 5 | 2 | 6 | 6 | 24 | — | 24 |
| 8 | Michigan | 2 | 6 | 3 | 4 | 6 | 21 | 3 | 24 |
| 8 | Wisconsin | 5 | 3 | 2 | 5 | 6 | 21 | 3 | 24 |
| 11 | Columbia | 5 | 6 | — | 4 | 6 | 21 | 2 | 23 |
| 11 | Cornell | 6 | 6 | 3 | 4 | 3 | 22 | 1 | 23 |
| 13 | Illinois | 4 | 2 | 4 | 4 | 3 | 17 | 2 | 19 |
| 14 | Penn | 2 | 5 | 1 | 3 | 5 | 16 | 1 | 17 |
| 15 | Caltech | 4 | — | 4 | 1 | — | 9 | 6 | 15 |
| 16 | Minnesota | 3 | — | 2 | 2 | 4 | 11 | 2 | 13 |
| 16 | Texas | 3 | 3 | 3 | 2 | 2 | 13 | — | 13 |
| 20 | Washington | 2 | — | 1 | 5 | 2 | 10 | — | 10 |
| 21 | UC San Diego | 2 | 2 | — | 3 | 1 | 8 | — | 8 |
| 30 | Johns Hopkins | — | 1 | 1 | 1 | 2 | 5 | — | 5 |

Source: Adapted from Webster, 1983.

**TABLE 3**

## E&G REVENUES
### 1981-1982
(Raw Amounts, in $000s)

| Institution | State & Local Approp. | Tuition and Fees | Endow. Income | Government Grants & Contracts | Priv. Gifts, Grants & Contracts | Other E & G Revenue | TOTAL E & G Revenue |
|---|---|---|---|---|---|---|---|
| Caltech | $ 000 | $ 10,486 | $14,320 | $ 49,976 | $14,546 | $ 1,363 | $ 90,692 |
| Stanford | 000 | 85,671 | 37,273 | 201,434 | 50,077 | 36,470 | 410,925 |
| UC/Berkeley | 205,919 | 50,621 | 7,835 | 90,430 | 16,404 | 25,094 | 396,303 |
| UCLA | 258,998 | 66,643 | 8,900 | 122,678 | 32,835 | 79,624 | 569,679 |
| UC/San Diego | 104,650 | 21,318 | 3,174 | 121,404 | 14,970 | 31,364 | 296,879 |
| Yale | 000 | 65,714 | 32,194 | 102,357 | 28,120 | 74,324 | 302,710 |
| Chicago | 000 | 59,748 | 34,261 | 75,561 | 30,650 | 31,991 | 232,220 |
| Illinois/Urbana | 187,068 | 29,975 | 1,766 | 74,445 | 21,706 | 30,953 | 345,913 |
| Johns Hopkins | 3,646 | 39,551 | 17,060 | 104,488 | 56,338 | 45,368 | 266,452 |
| Harvard | 000 | 118,864 | 94,471 | 109,247 | 78,719 | 25,019 | 426,320 |
| M.I.T. | 000 | 71,114 | 14,835 | 168,499 | 93,313 | 996 | 340,757 |
| Princeton | 000 | 42,836 | 40,357 | 29,935 | 23,386 | 10,519 | 147,033 |
| Columbia/Main Divis. | 8,987 | 100,135 | 35,625 | 147,091 | 64,384 | 32,225 | 388,477 |
| Cornell/Endowed Colls. | 4,337 | 90,064 | 26,231 | 54,342 | 15,997 | 15,140 | 206,112 |
| Pennsylvania | 21,996 | 127,260 | 18,024 | 101,213 | 33,743 | 24,129 | 326,364 |
| Texas/Austin | 178,088 | 21,478 | 27,641 | 64,024 | 21,076 | 29,078 | 341,386 |
| Washington | 134,005 | 34,415 | 1,842 | 149,888 | 19,533 | 32,750 | 372,432 |
| Wisconsin/Madison | 187,740 | 65,701 | 3,273 | 117,887 | 23,719 | 21,357 | 419,676 |
| Minnesota, Mnpls./St. Paul | 222,361 | 64,049 | 7,997 | 102,614 | 58,461 | 66,119 | 521,600 |
| Michigan/Ann Arbor | 142,270 | 104,120 | 9,177 | 36,941 | 34,797 | 26,654 | 353,960 |
| Cornell/Statutory Coll. | 66,802 | 11,497 | 641 | 21,754 | 4,150 | 30,087 | 134,931 |

Source: National Center for Higher Education Management Systems

**TABLE 4**

# SELECTED CHARACTERISTICS,
# 20 RESEARCH UNIVERSITIES
### 1979-1980

|  | A | B | C | D |
|---|---|---|---|---|
|  | Average Salary Profess. 1981-82 | % Graduate & Professional | Undergrad. Selectivity: Verb. + Math SAT Medians | Non-Research Per Student Vol. Support* |
| Caltech | $45,700 | 52% | 1,400 | $8,836 |
| Chicago | 42,700 | 68 | 1,257 | 4,123 |
| Columbia | 42,100 | 62 | 1,285E | 3,163 |
| Cornell | 39,700 | 30 | 1,236 | 1,507 |
| Harvard | 48,500 | 58 | 1,300 + E | 6,250 |
| Johns Hopkins | 43,100 | 62 | 1,296 | 3,956 |
| M.I.T. | 43,500 | 48 | 1,355 | 4,536 |
| Pennsylvania | 42,900 | 51 | 1,290 | 1,596 |
| Princeton | 42,000 | 24 | 1,310 | 6,313 |
| Stanford | 46,000 | 44 | 1,290 | 4,605 |
| Yale | 44,800 | 46 | 1,360 | 6,023 |
| Berkeley | 42,800 | 31 | 1,240E | 360E |
| UCLA | 41,800 | 33 | 1,040E | 477E |
| UC San Diego | 40,700 | 18 | 1,090 | 612E |
| Illinois | 38,600 | 22 | 1,120 | 353 |
| Michigan | 39,800 | 37 | 1,130 | 500 |
| Minnesota | 33,400 | 23 | 980E | 630 |
| Texas | 38,700 | 22 | 1,050 | 312 |
| Washington | 37,800 | 26 | 1,070 | 350 |
| Wisconsin | 35,300 | 28 | 1,000E | 333 |

\* (Table 5: B + D − G)
      Table 4: A

Sources: *Fall Enrollments in Higher Education, 1979.* National Center for Education Statistics, 1982.
       *Academe*, 68,4 (July, 1982).

**TABLE 5**

# VOLUNTARY SUPPORT FOR 20 RESEARCH UNIVERSITIES
## 1979-1980

| | A<br>Total Voluntary Support (000,000) | B<br>Voluntary Support for Current Operations | C<br>Endowment | D<br>Endowment Contribut. to Current Opers. @5% | E<br>B&D as % of Current Operations | F<br>% Alumni Contribut. to Volunt. Support | G<br>Volunt. Support Current Research |
|---|---|---|---|---|---|---|---|
| Caltech | $15.5 | $ 8.6 | $198.4 | $ 9.9 | 20.3% | 9.0% | $ 3.7 |
| Chicago | 33.7 | 22.2 | 343.1 | 17.2 | 13.5 | 18.4 | 5.1 |
| Columbia | 38.1 | 25.6 | 533.0 | 26.7 | 17.3 | 21.5 | 8.0 |
| Cornell | 46.3 | 25.0 | 328.7 | 16.4 | 13.8 | 46.4 | 14.4 |
| Harvard | 76.2 | 33.6 | 1,491.1 | 74.6 | E25.4 | 42.7 | 10.8 |
| Johns Hopkins | 29.0 | 22.5 | 236.5 | 11.8 | 16.7 | 19.7 | 11.5 |
| M.I.T. | 38.1 | 25.7 | 550.9 | 27.5 | 19.8 | 28.6 | 14.3 |
| Pennsylvania | 49.1 | 25.1 | 224.5 | 11.2 | 9.2 | 16.5 | 8.6 |
| Princeton | 32.7 | 12.2 | 547.8 | 27.4 | 40.4 | 54.0 | 2.5 |
| Stanford | 60.1 | 31.4 | 642.6 | 32.1 | 19.9 | 26.7 | 8.5 |
| Yale | 59.6 | 36.0 | 676.4 | 33.8 | 31.0 | 57.6 | 12.3 |
| Berkeley | 11.5 | 8.7 | na | na | 2.8 | 15.6 | 2.9 |
| UCLA | 27.7 | 18.8 | na | na | 5.1 | 2.9 | 9.3 |
| UC San Diego | 8.6 | 8.0 | na | na | 2.8 | 0.7 | 3.3 |
| Illinois | 28.0 | 22.8 | 48.3 | 2.4 | E4.9 | 7.5 | 11.4 |
| Michigan | 33.9 | 26.2 | 129.1 | 6.5 | 8.2 | 20.0 | 15.9 |
| Minnesota | 40.6 | 35.5 | 106.2 | 5.3 | 9.3 | 4.7 | 10.7 |
| Texas | 23.1 | 18.2 | 57.6 | 2.9 | 8.9 | 13.9 | 8.5 |
| Washington | 24.9 | 20.6 | 70.3 | 3.5 | 7.3 | 24.0 | 13.2 |
| Wisconson | 31.1 | 23.0 | 66.8 | 3.3 | 7.5 | 22.6 | 14.6 |

Source: *Voluntary Support of Education, 1979-80 (CFAE, 1981)*

## STUDENT LEVEL AND ENROLLMENT STATUS, FALL 1982

### TABLE 6

Lower Division/Upper Division/Graduate
Part-Time and Full-Time Headcount; Raw Data Values

| Institution | Total FTE Enrollment | Lower[1] Division[2] | Upper Division[2] | Graduate[2] | Part-time Headcount | Full-time Headcount | Total Headcount |
|---|---|---|---|---|---|---|---|
| Caltech | 1,810 | 427 | 447 | 936 | 0 | 1,810 | 1,810 |
| Stanford | 12,332 | 3,260 | 3,296 | 5,469 | 2,179 | 11,605 | 13,784 |
| UC/Berkeley | 28,092 | 9,951 | 9,513 | 8,582 | 2,396 | 26,300 | 29,296 |
| UCLA | 33,259 | 11,762 | 10,110 | 9,687 | 2,682 | 31,886 | 34,568 |
| UC/San Diego | 12,687 | 6,038 | 4,038 | 2,074 | 692 | 12,410 | 13,102 |
| Yale | 10,170 | 2,611 | 2,517 | 4,960 | 398 | 9,934 | 10,332 |
| Chicago | 8,145 | 1,553 | 1,263 | 5,224 | 1,859 | 7,154 | 9,013 |
| Illinois/Urbana | 33,226 | 13,127 | 12,337 | 7,347 | 3,499 | 31,415 | 34,914 |
| Johns Hopkins | 6,599 | 1,169 | 1,134 | 3,469 | 5,033 | 4,922 | 9,955 |
| Harvard[3] | 15,866 | 1,981 | 2,077 | 8,981 | 8,143 | 13,103 | 21,252 |
| M.I.T. | 9,191 | 2,206 | 2,317 | 4,512 | 576 | 8,999 | 9,575 |
| Princeton | 6,090 | 2,239 | 2,280 | 1,512 | 94 | 6,059 | 6,153 |
| Columbia/Main Div. | 14,098 | 2,967 | 2,159 | 8,650 | 2,989 | 13,102 | 16,091 |
| Cornell/Endowed Colls. | 10,597 | 3,752 | 3,612 | 3,224 | 30 | 10,585 | 10,615 |
| Pennsylvania | 18,315 | 4,693 | 4,387 | 8,304 | 4,950 | 17,367 | 22,317 |
| Texas/Austin | 45,082 | 17,593 | 16,565 | 9,820 | 5,858 | 42,181 | 48,039 |
| Washington | 29,919 | 11,936 | 9,700 | 7,123 | 7,958 | 26,510 | 34,468 |
| Wisconsin/Madison | 37,814 | 13,017 | 14,251 | 9,486 | 6,984 | 35,246 | 42,230 |
| Minnesota, Mnpls./St. Paul | 48,697 | 22,891 | 12,277 | 11,684 | 25,050 | 39,465 | 64,515 |
| Michigan/Ann Arbor | 32,630 | 10,876 | 10,666 | 11,088 | 4,236 | 30,836 | 35,072 |
| Cornell/Statutory Coll. | 6,865 | 2,412 | 2,759 | 1,694 | 1,024 | 6,528 | 7,552 |

1. For academic years 1979-80 and earlier:
   Lower Division = 1st time freshmen + Other 1st yr + 2nd yr (FT and PT FTE)
   Upper Division = 3rd yr + 4th yr and beyond (FT and PT FTE)
   For academic years 1980-81 and later:
   Lower Division = 1st time freshmen + Other 1st yr + 2nd yr (FT only) + Total Undergrad. (PT FTE)
   Upper Division = 3rd yr + 4th yr and beyond (FT only)
2. Does not include Unclassified
3. Fall 1981; does not include Radcliffe College

Source: National Center for Higher Education Management Systems

# References

Astin, A. W. (1968). Undergraduate Achievement and Institutional Excellence. *Science*, 161, 661-68.

Astin, A. W. (1977). *Four critical years*. San Francisco: Jossey-Bass.

Bell, D. (1966). *The reforming of general education*. New York: Columbia University Press.

Booth, W. C. (1983). Arts and Scandals, 1982. *Publications of the Modern Language Associastion*, 98, 3, 312-22.

Bowen, H. R. (1980). *The costs of higher education*. San Francisco: Jossey-Bass.

Council for Financial Aid to Education (1983). *Voluntary support of education, 1981-82*. New York: CFAE. Author.

Clark, B.R. (1983). *The higher education system: Academic organization in a cross-national perspective*. Los Angeles: Univ. of Cal. Press.

Fiske, E.B. (1982). *Selective guide to colleges*. New York: Times Books.

Ford Foundation (1978). *Research universities and the national interest: a Report from fifteen university presidents*. New York. Author.

Geiger, R. L. (1980a). The college curriculum and the marketplace. *Change* (Nov.-Dec.), 17-23.

Geiger, R. L. (1980b). The changing demand for higher education in the seventies: Adaptations within three national systems. *Higher Education*, 9, 255-76.

Geiger, R. L. (in press-a). *American research universities in the 20th century, 1900-1940*. New York: Oxford University Press.

Geiger, R. L. (in press-b). Hierarchy and diversity in American research universities. In Elzinga, A. and Wittrock, B. (eds.), *The university research system: performance and policy*.

Geiger, R. L. (in press-c). *Private sectors in higher education: structure, function and change in eight countries*.

Hawkins, H. (1960). *Pioneer: a History of the Johns Hopkins University*. Ithaca: Cornell University Press.

Jencks, C. and Riesman, D. (1969). *The academic revolution*. Garden City: Anchor.

National Academy of Sciences (1982). *An assessment of research-doctoral programs in the United States*. 5 vols. Washington, D.C.: National Academy Press. Author.

National Commission on Student Financial Assistance (1983). *Signs of trouble and erosion: a Report on graduate education in America*. Washington, D.C. Author.

National Science Foundation (1980), *Academic science, FY 1980*. Washington, D.C.: NSF. Author.

Riesman, D. (1956). The academic procession. In *Constraint and variety in American higher education*. Univ. of Nebraska Press.

Riesman, D. (1981). *On higher education*. San Francisco: Jossey-Bass.

Rosenzweig, R. M. with Turlington, B. (1982). *The research universities and their patrons*. Berkeley: Univ. of California Press.

Trow, M. (1983). Organization and leadership in universities: the case of biology at Berkeley. Conference Paper, Swedish National Board of Colleges and Universities. Rosenon, Dalaro, Sweden.

Webster, D. S. (1983). America's highest ranked graduate schools, 1925-1982. *Change* (May-June), 14-24.

Wilson, J. T. (1983). *Academic science, higher education, and the federal government, 1950-1983*. Chicago: Univ. of Chicago Press.

Yale Daily News (1983). *The insider's guide to the colleges*. New York: Langdon and Weed.

# The American Liberal Arts College in The Eighties: Dinosaur or Phoenix?

## Allan O. Pfnister

### The Form and the Ideal

The American liberal arts colleges of the 1980s present a study in successful and less successful adherence to a form and to an ideal. Both the form and the ideal in question have roots in the distant past; the form is a legacy of twelfth-century Europe and the first universities in the West; the ideal derives from fifth and fourth century B.C. Greece and the citizen's education in Athens. To paraphrase George P. Schmidt's (1957) reference to the curriculum of seventeenth-century Harvard, the path from twelfth-century Paris to the American liberal arts college is devious, but recognizable, as is the path from fifth-century Athens to the ideal of liberal arts education embodied in the same American institution. It is where these two strains met and encountered the Puritan/Calvinist conviction that proof of God's favor was to be found in productive work that we find the roots of both the strength and the weakness of the American liberal arts institution of the twentieth century.

Although liberal arts institutions have been a dominant force in American higher education for nearly 300 years, in the 1980s they have come to constitute a small and decreasing proportion of the postsecondary education commonwealth. From 1640 (the year Harvard College reopened) well into the early decades of the 1900s, the independent (non-university affiliated) undergraduate liberal arts college was the most widely accepted means of higher education for most American students, and served as the door through which many passed to advanced study. At the turn of the century a French scholar (Levasseur, 1899, p. 1438) describing American higher education observed that two-thirds of the students enrolled in American post-secondary institutions were to be found in undergraduate liberal arts colleges. Well into the twentieth century these institutions continued to attract a large share of those students seeking baccalaureate degrees—even as the more complex universities, teachers colleges, agricultural colleges, and junior colleges were growing in number, size, and influence.

The years following World War II brought many changes to American society and to American education. Post-secondary education expanded in type, scope and number of institutions, and the relative position of the liberal arts college began to recede. In 1955 some 732 out of a total of 1,854 higher education institutions were identified as liberal arts colleges; these colleges registered 26% of the fall 1955 enrollment (Educational Policies Commission, 1957). By 1969 the number had decreased slightly to 721, registering less than 10% of total post-secondary enrollment; but the total number of institutions was then 2,837. By 1976 the Carnegie Council identified only 583 liberal arts colleges enrolling 5% of total post-secondary students; and by then the total number of higher education institutions had reached 3,074 (Carnegie Council, 1976).

It is little wonder that those observing the decline in position of the liberal arts institutions should begin to question the continued viability of these colleges. Mayhew (1962) characterized the liberal arts colleges as "a minority group in the presence of a majority composed of other, larger and more complex types of institutions of higher learning," and saw the attempt of these colleges to carry on the liberal tradition in the face of the increasing vocational orientation of much of American life as exceedingly difficult, perhaps impossible. Keeton and Hilberry (1969) began their report on selected liberal arts colleges with the words "The typical private liberal arts college of the mid-twentieth century is obsolete." More recently, Henry Steel Commager (1977) answered his own question—"Can the American college survive?"—by writing that the independent liberal arts college was in trouble, that it was having both an identity crisis and a financial crisis, and that he could only wonder if the college could "extricate itself from these troubles which now undermine its prosperity and imperil its existence."

Stadtman (1980) suggested that it is not so much dissolution as transformation that threatens the future of the liberal arts colleges. By taking on more of the character of comprehensive colleges they are in danger of losing their special identity; ahead is the "impending bankruptcy and failure of the liberal colleges," because "the liberal arts cannot be served in the special way this is possible when they are virtually the exclusive concern of an institution." Kerr (Keeton, 1971) is more optimistic in his introductory statement to a later Keeton volume; he writes of "a renaissance of the liberal arts college," because "they are by nature more adaptable to the new concerns of so many students, while the more massive institutions are clearly in greater trouble—some of them are turning to their own internal arts colleges to respond to students' concerns." Pfnister and Finkelstein (1984) found surprising vitality among 23 institutions in a national sample studied over a two-year period of time; these colleges not only survived the difficulties of the 1970s and the years preceding, but were entering the 1980s with a measure of strength and a determination to maintain a liberal arts emphasis.

On the other hand, Astin and Lee (1972) characterized those schools they labeled "invisible colleges" as preoccupied with survival, limited in academic resources, in financial difficulty, lacking a sense of identity, and facing severe competition from other institutions. Anderson's (1977) study of 40 single sex and/or religious colleges between the mid-1960s and mid-1970s found over half instituting significant changes in character. Anderson also noted, however, that to determine whether such changes would ultimately be successful was "not unexpectedly...complex," and that it is difficult to predict what the future would hold for these institutions.

Judgments about the viability of the American liberal arts college, often drawing on different sources of information, shaped by different research questions, or based on the examination of different samples of institutions, are obviously mixed. Although dark predictions appear to outnumber more optimistic assessments, the colleges have survived, increased in enrollment (if slowly), and experienced renewal, as institutions that closed are replaced by new ones. What then is the status of the liberal arts college in the 1980s? Are recent problems only matters of passing concern, or are they symptoms of an uncertain future?

It is the thesis of this essay that resolution of such questions is more likely to come from a reexamination of the historical development of both the *form* and the *ideal*. It is in this history that one finds the language, the rhetoric, and the traditions that undergird these institutions.

**The Form of the College.** Within 18 years of the founding of what was later to be named Harvard College, there were in the colony of the Massachusetts Bay Company approximately 100 Cambridge graduates and a third as many sons of Oxford (Rudolph, 1962). It was inevitable that any college created by these colonists would be patterned after the older foundations of England. In spite of limited resources and the lack of an established body of masters and scholars, when Henry Dunster in 1650 called for a restructuring that would identify the college as a Corporation of President and Fellows, he was placing Harvard College in the tradition of the English universities and their source, the University of Paris. In that tradition the term "college" had a special meaning.

It has been said that in the Middle Ages, "college" and "university" were terms used interchangeably. While correct in reference to the earliest efforts of Western academic institutions, it is not accurate to equate *university* with *college* when these institutions of learning assumed more formal structure (Cobban, 1975). The word *universitas* as a general term applicable to any kind of aggregate or body of persons with common purposes and independent legal status became the convenient label for the academic body only in the late fourteenth and early fifteenth centuries. An academic corporation had the right to grant degrees, and a complete academic *universitas* was one that possessed the higher faculties of theology, law, and medicine. The *collegium* came to be associated with the early hospices for the advanced students in the academic *universitas*. The first such hospice established for the University of Paris was one purchased by Jocius de Londinis in 1180 at the Hospital of the Blessed Mary of Paris, the Hotel Dieu, near the Cathedral of Notre Dame (intended to house 18 "poor clerks," it was named the College des Dix-Huit). Some 77 years later, a similar establishment by Robert de Sorbon, chaplain to Louis IX, in 1257 or 1258 provided the kind of governance structure that came to characterize later colleges of the university.

At first designed to provide maintenance and support for older students who could not otherwise afford to stay at the university, the colleges began to take on instructional responsibilities with the decision of the College d' Harcourt to admit paying scholars and for the master and/or his assistants to provide tutorial help for the scholars in the college. This instructional responsibility increased as the number of paying scholars increased. At Navarre, the master was required "diligently to hear the lessons of the scholars studying in the Faculty of Arts and faithfully to instruct them alike in life and in doctrine" (Shachner, 1938). Earlier in the development of the university, the arts students were left much to themselves, although to study in the higher faculties, one had to master the seven liberal arts which by then were the necessary prerequisite for study in the university, especially in theology. With the assumption of more instructional responsibility, the colleges admitted young students and soon became identified with preparatory studies in the arts. The limited lectures and reviews provided in colleges to supplement teaching in university schools gradually expanded, and in time colleges were able to provide full-time employment for the more qualified regent masters. By the fifteenth century the colleges were competing with the schools of the university, and the University of Paris was changing from a voluntary association of masters, each with his individual school and his own quota of pupils, to an association of colleges with full-time masters.

In England, the colleges of Oxford and Cambridge evolved out of general hospices into teaching units as in France, with one important difference: the English foundations from the beginning were independent corporations whose members owned and administered their endowments. The independence of the colleges was increased when Elizabeth I approved new statutes in 1570 which gave authority to elect the vice chancellor of Cambridge to the masters of the colleges. Oxford colleges gained similar authority in 1628.

The idea of the arts college as a residential and instructional entity designed to prepare students for admission to the advanced faculties that constituted the university proper had already experienced significant changes in France and Germany when the first American institutions were established. By the middle of the seventeenth century the ancient French universities were in decline, almost displaced by the Jesuit system of colleges, and these colleges were essentially secondary schools. By the middle of the next century the University Faculty of Arts had also taken on the character of pre-university secondary unit.

In England, in the early seventeenth century, the arts colleges were still at the height of their power as residences and teaching units. The superior, or advanced, faculties were by comparison underdeveloped, and the fellows of the colleges found themselves increasingly involved in undergraduate instruction primarily dedicated to the single aim of the "virtuous education of youth" (Curtis, 1959). As the seventeenth century wore on, the all-university lectures regained importance, and the emphasis in the undergraduate colleges shifted from general studies to specialized studies in the arts. Later the function of preparatory level arts study came to be the responsibility of the secondary grammar schools.

It was the English college of the late sixteenth and early seventeenth centuries that became the informing pattern for the North American colonial colleges, and while the English colleges continued to evolve, the colonial colleges maintained and perpetuated their adopted structure. It is not surprising that the American institutions began from the English pattern; indeed, it would have been surprising if they had not done so. Also, in retrospect, it is not surprising that the form, once adopted, underwent little change over the next 150 years. At least two factors contributed to this status: (1) American colleges were self-contained institutions, created to serve a particular constituency, and were relatively isolated from one another; and (2) they were independent foundations, responsible to local boards of control consisting of lay persons. As self-contained institutions, geographically isolated, they remained small, limited in scope, and equipped to provide little more than instruction in the arts sequence. As independent foundations, they were created by and responsive to conservative lay boards.

With the form of the residential preparatory school firmly in place, the new condition of nineteenth-century America could only lead to continuing tension between the established form and growing demands for new types of education. From the beginning, the colonies that were to become the United States also had a deep pragmatic strain. Calvinist New England found in productive work proof of God's election and bounty. The development of the nation required doers as well as thinkers.

Then, as the nation expanded westward, the colleges followed, for an important way of proving that a new settlement would soon be a great city was "to provide it as quickly as possible with all of the metropolitan hallmarks," which included not only a newspaper and a hotel, but an institution of higher learning, or at least one that aspired to be a seat of higher learning (Boorstin, 1965). Colleges or institutions aspiring to be colleges were springing up overnight, and many disappeared as quickly. It is estimated that by 1860 as many as 700 colleges had been created and had gone out of existence.

The traditional college was hard pressed to meet the new demands. Philip Lindsley turned down the presidency at Princeton to become the first president of the University of Nashville and argued in his inaugural that "the farmer, the mechanic, the manufacturer, the merchant, the sailor must be educated" (Rudolph, 1962). James Marsh, as president of the University of Vermont, was creating, or attempting to create, new programs in that institution. Jacob Abbott spearheaded reforms at Amherst, and although the reforms were short-lived, they pointed the way to broader and more inclusive curricula. In the face of such threats to tradition, the Yale Corporation in 1828 issued a report calculated to call the American colleges back to the agenda, holding that the form of the college was that of a preparatory institution, "to lay the foundation of a superior education" (Hofstadter & Smith, 1961).

**The Ideal of the College**. The American liberal arts college was heir to an ideal as well, and the report of the Yale Corporation was concerned also with the ideal. The ideal was rooted in the Athens of Aristotle, but the modifications that occurred between Athens and the New World Cambridge were profound.

In the Greece of Aristotle, education was viewed as an art. The word we translate as education is *paideia*, meaning "culture" as well as "education," and implying growth in experience as well as knowledge. Hellenistic Greek education was divided among a whole series of teachers. Elementary school masters (or *grammatistes*) taught the young person to read, write, count, and perhaps to draw. Music was under the instruction of a music master, or *mousikos*. Gymnastics was taught by professional teachers known as a *paidotribes*. Then, around the age of twelve, the young person began the study of literature, of Homer and poetry in general under a *kritikos* or *grammatikos*. At that time, study also began in advanced math under the mathematics master, *geometres*. The whole process, conducted over time, constituted the *encyclios*, a term meaning "ordinary" or "of every day occurrence" as well as "cyclic." Thus, the *encyclios paideia* was the education of the free man, the Greek citizen—as distinct from the foreigner or slave (Gwyn, 1926).

It was this *encyclios paideia* that became in Latin the "artes liberales" or "liberalis disciplina," the liberal arts. Seneca takes note that what the Greeks called *encyclioi* the Romans termed "liberales."

For the Greeks, specialization was unknown. Knowledge was not of facts but of the general principles that would later help one to a proper use of the knowledge that opens the mind to discovering the basic principles of a science. Each science, this theory holds, has its own art, or *techne*, framed by human reason and binding together the details of knowledge in a single coherent system.

Over time the contents of the *encyclios paideia* became more or less standardized, and the Greek experience modified by Roman experience was carried into western Europe through Martianus Capella (410 A.D.) in the allegory of the seven liberals arts (Stahl, Johnson, & Burge, 1977).

While Martianus Capella provided the encyclopedic description of the seven liberal arts, it was Cassiodorus (477-565 A.D.) who shifted in significant ways the nature and function of the arts. Cassiodorus, who held positions of responsibility under Theodric, retired to a monastery which he had founded and organized according to the Benedictine rule. There, he played a significant role in fostering the preservation of secular as well as ecclesiastical knowledge among the monks, giving the Benedictines the impulse to intellectual work for which they were distinguished during medieval times. It was he who found scriptural sanction for making the study of the seven liberal arts the appropriate preparation for the study of theology.

But Cassiodorus was also responsible for making more precise the distinction between the lowly arts and the liberal arts. In spite of the fact that he himself had a knack for mechanical inventions and occupied himself with developing sun dials and water clocks, he argued for making a clear division between the products of the mind in its relation to the spiritual and the works of the mind in its functional connection to the physical world. The liberal arts he praised and the mechanical arts he viewed as inferior. For Cassiodorus, the liberal arts were not preparation for the citizen and freeman but the training of the mind for the study of theology: not preparation for life, but a formal sequence that turned away from the world of work and experience and led into the professional intellectual activities.

Thus, in time, the arts cycle or sequence became the preparatory pre-university sequence in Paris, Oxford, and Cambridge, though in the latter, the advanced studies were underdeveloped. No longer the *encyclios paideia* of the Greeks, the stepwise education of the citizen, the seven liberal arts had in the medieval university become preprofessional training of the select few who would go on to study in the advanced, or superior, faculties, and the emphasis was on the grammar, rhetoric, and logic of the trivium. It was this tradition, modified by the English college experience that came to the foundations in the New World.

**Three Strains.** It was to make a statement about *form*, *ideal*, and *work* that Yale spoke out in 1828. Ticknor at Harvard, Lindsley at Nashville, Marsh at Vermont, Abbott at Amherst, and many other lesser known reformers questioned the *form* and the *ideal* of the traditional college of the early nineteenth century, and they sought to work out new accommodations with what they perceived to be the needs of the day. In this context the Yale Corporation issued its report defining the nature of liberal education, for itself and others who wished to hear.

The object of the college, Yale said, "is to *lay the foundation* of a superior education." The college is not designed to include professional subjects; its object is not to "teach that which is peculiar to any of the professions," but rather to "lay the foundation which is common to them all." This foundation education consists of two ingredients: the discipline and "the furniture of the mind." The task of the college is to expand the powers of the mind, and also to store it with knowledge that opens the way to future training. In referring to "separate schools for medicine, law, and theology, connected with the college, as well as in various parts of the country," the report used the language of the medieval university in which the higher, or superior, faculties were medicine, law, and theology. And, in emphasizing that these advanced schools were open "for the reception of all who are prepared to enter upon the appropriate studies of their several professions," Yale was describing the ancient arts faculties and the residential colleges of Paris, Oxford, and Cambridge.

Condemned and praised, faulted for its adherence to an outmoded faculty psychology and to a subject matter deemed inappropriate to the needs of an expanding nation, but also held up as a vigorous defense of humanism and the liberal arts, the Yale report nonetheless had its impact. From that point on, the American college curriculum could not be understood without reference to this first major effort to identify the philosophy and the content of the American system of higher education (Rudolph, 1977). In the years to come, any description of the liberal arts college in the American system would have to redefine the relations among a preparatory unit (whether for two or three or four years duration), the skills and knowledge presumed to be developed in this unit, and the way in which the unit is, or is not, related to the world of work.

The American college could never remain static in its treatment of *form* and *ideal*, or in its relation to the world of *work*. Indeed, most of the next 75 years of the nineteenth century were taken up by debates over the proper distribution of the elements in a responsible and responsive collegiate institution. There was the Yale pattern, followed by many, but new combinations and permutations arose with increasing frequency. Additionally, the *ideal* did not remain the possession of the independent college. As the American university took form in the later years of the century, there were those who argued for a clean break between preparatory and advanced professional and technical studies, proposing that advanced studies be reserved for the university and preparatory general studies to be the preserve of the college. Others argued against drawing such a sharp line, holding that professional studies without collegiate education were inadequate. The latter view prevailed, and the new American university became an amalgam of the older collegiate ideals and the newer advanced professional studies.

As a consequence of the university's assumption of a dual role, there seemed to be little left for the independent liberal arts college to provide. But the older collegiate institutions persisted, and made their own adaptations to the new conditions.

The first decades of the twentieth century saw the reordering of American higher education into a more systematized structure in which "the college re-emerged as a strong and secure institution within the system" (Leslie, 1976). One important adaptation was the combining of breadth and specialization. However, the new norm was not established without the surrender of some of those things which had characterized these colleges for over a century (Herbst, 1965). The debates continued, even as the transformation was being effected. An early study by the Association of American Colleges found that students tended to enroll in the more traditional subjects in spite of new and expanded opportunities (Kelley, 1921). A few years later, another survey from a broader base recorded a clear difference of opinion regarding the purpose of specialization in the undergraduate curriculum: on the one hand, intensive study was seen as an extension of general studies; on the other, it was identified clearly as having "directly or indirectly a vocational purpose" (Kelly, 1925).

## The Belief System of the Contemporary Liberal Arts College

In view of the evolution of the form and ideal of the liberal arts college sketched on the preceding pages, it is not surprising that the group of institutions labeled "liberal arts college" in the 1980s does not constitute a single homogeneous type, but contains a number of subclasses. The appropriate image to display the characteristics is less a continuum and more a cluster of overlapping circles. While sharing a substantial body of belief, the colleges in this cluster also present broad variations of theme and substance. For some, the path from Athens to the New World campus in the 1980s is recognizable: for others, the family resemblance is present, but the relationship seems more like that of distant cousins than of siblings.

In the broadest sense, this cluster of institutions is marked simply by being essentially undergraduate and independent (not affiliated with a university). In the aggregate, these independent institutions constitute the "general baccalaureate" colleges described under the new classifications employed by the National Center for Education Statistics in *The Condition of Education*. The most common subdivision of this population is that first employed by the Carnegie Commission on Higher Education, in which liberal arts colleges are labeled "Liberal Arts I" and "Liberal Arts II". The "Liberal Arts I" group consists of those colleges that scored 1,030 or more on Astin's selectivity index or were included among the 200 leading baccalaureate-granting institutions in terms of the numbers of graduates receiving Ph.D.'s at 40 leading doctorate-granting institutions from 1920 to 1966 (Carnegie Council, 1976). The remaining schools are "Liberal Arts II." Within the latter group are those institutions Astin and Lee (1972) singled out and dubbed the "invisible" colleges, an appelation not altogether welcomed by the class members.

Pfnister and Finkelstein (1984) identified five subclasses of liberal arts colleges evident in the 1950s: (1) single-purpose, traditional and elite liberal arts colleges; (2) profession-oriented, predominantly liberal arts colleges, similar to the first group but placing heavier emphasis on preparing students for further study in selected professions such as law and medicine; (3) denominational, locally oriented liberal arts colleges, institutions established to serve a religious denomination, although not necessarily limiting enrollment to members of that church; (4) general purpose community-oriented colleges, the twentieth-century version of the booster-type college described by Boorstin (1965) as the prevailing type of the early nineteenth century; and (5) teachers colleges with a liberal arts emphasis, institutions formerly dedicated to preparing teachers but now serving a broader clientele and incorporating a basic core of studies in the liberal arts.

By the end of the 1970s, the five classes could be collapsed into four on the basis of 1978 Carnegie survey data. The working labels attached to the new categories were: (1) non-professional and non-vocational colleges; (2) professionally oriented traditionals; (3) multi-purpose institutions; and (4) limited multi-purpose institutions (Pfnister & Finkelstein, 1984). The last group could be further divided into two classes, differentiated by breadth of program and relative emphasis on vocational/occupational preparation.

In the final analysis no typology proves to be wholly acceptable because each subclass of institutions examined here has much in common with other subclasses in the larger class of general baccalaureate institutions. As a consequence, there is always a certain fuzziness in the creation of such discrete subclasses. And even with the considerable variation that appears, each of these institutions ultimately identifies itself in terms of its response to *form* and *ideal* and its relation to the world of *work*. The rhetoric employed with regard to *form* and *ideal*, whatever else is mentioned, is likely to contain much of what Schmidt, (1957, pp. 241-242) refers to as the component parts of liberal education:

> A liberal education is not a thing of precise definition like an isosceles triangle, nor is it a fixed list of courses in a college catalogue taken over a given period of years. It is rather a human quality and a personal achievement, which can be attained in a variety of ways. . .

> Nevertheless, the hundreds who have written about it and the hundreds of thousands who have experienced it are convinced there is *something* there, and that something is priceless. Its component parts, if anything so vague can have component parts, might be described as follows. A liberal education means knowledge, verified and dependable, about the world of nature and its processes, and about human society both in its historic origins and its ever-changing contemporary forms. It means trained skills and abilities: to use one's own language effectively and one or more foreign languages adequately; to think critically—itself a cosmos of more specific skills to judge intelligently among alternatives; to participate helpfully in social situations. It means appreciation of people, of the moral and spiritual quality of actions; of human imagination whether displayed in painting or music, in poetry or drama, or in mathematics, astronomy, or physics. A liberal education is something like that.

A century and a half earlier, the Yale Corporation had referred to knowledge as "furniture" and asked that each student "should be instructed in those branches of knowledge, of which no one destined to the higher walks of life ought to be ignorant." The specific subjects then noted have a familiar ring, though with the passage of time our categories for describing fields of knowledge have changed. The corporation also asked that certain skills be developed—reasoning, command of one's own language, imagination, and others, constituting the "discipline of the mind." In the present-day college we would not want to be limited in library resources nor committed to heavily to the *in loco parentis* mentality of an institution serving mostly thirteen, fourteen and fifteen-year-olds; and, there are other aspects of the Yale of 1828 that just do not fit 1984. Yet, the rhetoric of the Yale report and of Schmidt are not that different.

As for liberal education and the world of *work*, as Thomas Green (1975) states, the "relation between undergraduate liberal learning and the world of work is a perennial topic." It is a perennial topic, he contends, because:

> The minimal condition of any good education system—and perhaps for the survival of any educational system—is that it facilitate some access to adult economic roles or that it provide a way of gaining economic independence. Thus, the problem of the relation between education and work is always present, and any kind of education that eschews a primary concern with this basic problem needs to give it special attention. Such is always the case with liberal studies in the undergraduate college.

Green makes the case for the American perspective— that is, that education must be related to one's economic well-being, and that liberal education especially faces a challenge in reconciling its historic separation from the world of work with present student desire to incorporate preparation for work into the educational experience. Here again is the persistent triad of *form*, *ideal*, and relation to *work* that constitutes the elements on which subclasses of liberal arts colleges build in the contemporary world.

In summary, the major points in the belief system informing these colleges in the aggregate are:

1.  A liberally educated person is both knowledgeable and skillful (in Yale's language, one has the appropriate furniture and discipline of the mind). By virtue of possessing basic knowledge and skill, one has before himself/herself the maximum range of options for the next stage of education, or for entering the world of work. By avoiding specialization, one who has a liberal education can keep options open.

2.  Although secondary schools have an important part in general acculturation of youth and in the inculcation of basic knowledge and skills, the process of acculturation cannot be completed in the secondary school years. Therefore, colleges have a continuing responsibility for completing the liberal education of those who elect further study. (There is a residual elitism in this view, because entrance into college, is outside the common schooling.)

3.  The liberal education goals of those selected for (or electing) continued education can best be met in institutions that have as their major emphasis non-specialized, non-vocational education. Moreover, whatever variations in sequencing and length of time are required or employed, the preferable form is four years of sequential experience.

Beyond these three are another collection of beliefs present in varying degrees among the colleges.

4.  The role of a liberal arts college is many-faceted. One particular task is the provision of body of common knowledge and skills. Particularly after the Committee on the objectives of a General Education in a Free Society (1955) stated that "general education" was a more appropriate term in a democracy for conveying the meaning of liberal education, general education came to be the term and concept preferred by many colleges. (The shift in terms allowed a subtle change in orientation, for now it was possible for the liberal arts college to think of itself in more general terms and as being involved in broader educational activities— as long as some component of general education was present.)

5.  The liberal arts college proper is a combination of general education and specialized education. Specialized education is an extension of the general experience of the student in the undergraduate college. (But a segment of liberal arts colleges will say that specialized study is separate from general education, that it is study calling for a high level of specialization to prepare persons for first entry into the job market.)

6.  To emphasize that liberal education is the education of the free citizen in twentieth-century America may be less relevant for the times than to emphasize that the kind of education needed is one that allows the

individual to realize more fully his or her potential. The task of higher education in contemporary America, then, is not so much to create a new body of commonly accepted knowledge but to create opportunities for exploring new possibilities and new goals. Liberal education is education for freedom; it is liberating (Gamson, 1984) education.

7. Education must be concerned with the whole person, with feelings, attitudes, and values as well as skills and intellectual ability. The unique contribution of the liberal arts colleges is (or can be) to enhance one's sense of his or her culture and its values.

There are other elements in the belief structure of the contemporary liberal arts college that parallel the general higher education belief structure, but the points above are those most frequently noted in discussion of what the liberal arts college is, or ought to be.

## The Resource Base of the Contemporary Liberal Arts College

Bowen (1980) reminds us that colleges possess both tangible and intangible assets. The tangible assets consist of land, buildings, investments, and current funds. The intangible assets include: the ability to recruit and retain qualified faculty and staff; the capacity to recruit and retain qualified students; ties to sources of appropriations, grants, and gifts; the ongoing internal organization including the division of labor, definition of roles, communication systems, rules, customs, traditions, and morale. These intangible assets together make up the "moral capital" that provides an institution with the ability to weather crises and maintain educational principles and basic mission. Of the two categories, Bowen contends the intangible are the most important, for even with the loss of tangible assets an institution can recover its position through prudent use of the intangible assets.

In assessing the resource base of the liberal arts colleges as a group in the last quarter of the twentieth century, it is difficult to identify intangible assets, because these are matters of institutional personality, history, and reputation. Tangible assets are also difficult to itemize with any precision without intensive study of individual cases. For an assessment of intangible assets, reference will be made to three recent but limited studies of institutional adaptation and recovery (Chaffee, 1984; Peck, 1983, Pfnister & Finkelstein, 1984). For insight into the condition of the physical assets, much of the data will be drawn from four sources (Leslie, Grant & Brown, 1981; Levine, 1978; Minter & Bowen, 1978; NACUBO,1981). The data bases differ among the studies, and the populations vary; yet, from the various sources it is possible to form a reasonably accurate picture of the contemporary liberal arts college.

The National Association of College and University Business Officers and the American Council of Education, under a contract with the U.S. Department of Education, analyzed data for 1975 - 1978 from the Higher Education General Information Surveys on Finance, Faculty, and Institutional Characteristics and the American Council on Education longitudinal enrollment files. Using the institutional classification codes developed by the National Center for Higher Education Management Systems, the ACE-NACUBO team developed a comprehensive picture of American higher educational institutions and their financial status, and examined the usefulness of various indicators of fiscal health. Based on data from 831 private four-year institutions, roughly the group identified in Carnegie studies as Liberal Arts I and II institutions, ACE-NACUBO provides the following profile:

|  | 1975 | 1978 | Change |
|---|---|---|---|
| Average FTE Students/Institution | 1257 | 1360 | + 8% |
| Average FTE Faculty/Institution | 70 | 66 | − 6% |
| Part-Time to Total Enrollment | 19.5 | 21.2 | + 9% |
| FTE Students to FT Faculty | 19.8 | 20.9 | + 6% |

The average size of the institutions increased from 1,257 to 1,360. The FTE faculty decreased over the four years, and the average institution had fewer FTE faculty in 1978. Proportions of part-time students increased, along with faculty-student ratios. From other analyses of the ACE-NACUBO team, 914 private four-year colleges (comprising 36% of the total sample of all types of colleges) employed 73,000 FTE faculty in 1974, or 21% of the faculty employed by all institutions of higher education in the sample. The colleges enrolled, on average, 1972 continuing education students in 1974, and increased the number of continuing education students by 1976.

Working from a narrower base of just over 700 Liberal Arts I and II colleges, Levine (1978) presents a slightly different profile:

| | L.A. I Colleges | L.A. II Colleges |
|---|---|---|
| Median number of undergraduates | 750-1000 | 750-1000 |
| Average number FTE Faculty | 76 | 64 |
| Percentage faculty with Ph.D | 57 | 38 |
| Percentage faculty with no professional publication in previous two years | 53 | 69 |
| Percentage faculty reporting more interest in teaching than research | 82 | 91 |
| Median size of department | 6-8 | 4-5 |

Leslie and others (1981) undertook a detailed study of enrollment patterns for Liberal Arts Colleges I and II over the period 1965-1977. Total enrollment for both classes of colleges increased over the 13 years studied, the LA II colleges increasing at a somewhat greater rate. Further analysis showed that on the basis of FTE enrollment, the two classes of institutions were fairly similar in the growth rate; the differences between them lay in the increasing number of part-time students in the LA II institutions and the relatively stable enrollment with limited part-time students in the LA I institutions.

Despite the differences in the compilations, the essential characteristics seem clear enough. Liberal arts colleges are small, enrolling usually less than 1,500 students. The faculty number less than 100, and departments consist of 4-7 people. Part-time enrollment is increasing, but these colleges are still predominantly peopled by full-time students. The faculty are more interested in teaching than in research and they publish infrequently. A substantial number of the faculty are teaching with less than a doctoral degree, although the proportion of the doctorates may have increased during the 1980s. There has been some reduction in the number of faculty at these institutions. How do these institutions appear in terms of fiscal transactions, income, and expenditure? The ACE-NACUBO report provides the following profile:

| | Percentage of Income, 1975 | Percentage of Income, 1978 |
|---|---|---|
| From Tuition and Fees | 50.5 | 51.2 |
| Gifts | 11.9 | 11.1 |
| Endowment Earnings | 3.6 | 3.2 |
| Appropriations | 1.5 | 1.3 |
| Government contracts | 6.1 | 7.1 |

These sources constitute an incomplete listing, accounting for only slightly over 73% of total income. The remainder is to be found in auxiliary income, with usually ranges around 22 or 23%, and the catch-all category, "other." What this table does indicate, however, is the tendency to become more tuition and government grant dependent, at a time when both are shaky sources of income. The Minter-Bowen (1978) report shows a very similar distribution.

In terms of expenditures, the profile is as follows:

| | Percentage of Expenditure, 1975 | Percentage of Expenditure, 1978 |
|---|---|---|
| Instruction | 30.8 | 29.2 |
| Research | 0.9 | 0.8 |
| Library | 3.3 | 3.2 |
| Student Services | 6.6 | 7.2 |
| Institutional Support | 15.3 | 15.6 |
| Operations and Maintenance | 9.3 | 10.0 |
| Unrestricted scholarships | 4.5 | 4.4 |

Again, the table accounts for only 70% of expenditures. With the addition of physical plant expenditures, usually 8 or 9%, and expenditures for auxiliary enterprises, the total is complete.

What does the future hold? The smaller liberal arts colleges face the most serious dangers (Dickmeyer, 1983). Those with enrollments of less than 1,000 and little or no financial reserves are the most vulnerable (Carnegie Council, 1980). For most institutions the future will be difficult, and constant monitoring of fiscal condition will be required.

In the final analysis, however, survival will depend on those intangible assets to which Bowen refers. Keller (1983), in a series of case studies, shows how even well-to-do institutions can find themselves in deep fiscal trouble, and how the combination of leadership, reputation, and "moral capital" makes the difference in recovery. Peck (1984) refers to entrepreneurial and people-oriented leadership that brought a number of liberal arts colleges from near fiscal disaster to relative fiscal health. Chaffee (1984) examines the strategic management responses of two comparable groups of liberal arts colleges facing fiscal decline in the mid-1970s. By 1980 one group had recovered and the other had not. The key to recovering appeared to be the kind of strategic management implemented with a combination of interpretive effort and responsiveness to people being the most effective approach. Pfnister and Finkelstein (1984) found that, as critical as the pattern of management and planning was, the basic array of environmental and internal attributes summed up in the term "sociological set" provided the best explanation for successful adaptation.

## Major Environmental Forces

Liberal arts colleges are subject to the same environmental forces that affect all of higher education, but some forces may have greater impact on this group of colleges. The decline in the number of students in the 18-24 age group will leave few American higher institutions untouched, but liberal arts colleges oriented toward residential students may feel the impact to a greater degree. Shifting patterns of funding will cause reassessment of financial strategy at all institutions, but tuition-dependent small liberal arts colleges may face more critical problems.

Yet the liberal arts colleges constitute clusters, not a single type, and even among these colleges the impact of environmental forces will be different. Colleges with waiting lists are not going to have the same problems as institutions which cannot adopt a final budget until after the fall enrollment is determined. Endowment and reserves vary immensely among the colleges. In a special sample of 17 institutions, Pfnister and Finkelstein (1984) found endowment capital varying from less than $400 per student to over $10,000 per student. Peat, Marwick, Mitchell and Minter (1980), in a ratio analysis report, display data for a sample of 359 private four-year institutions showing annual operating budgets ranging from less than $2 million to over $64 million.

Recognizing the variations in impact, is it still possible to say anything about the general response of this group of institutions as a whole? The final report of the Carnegie Council (1980) identifies 10 contemporary trends which in summary form are listed below:

1. The rise of the public sector; in 1950 public and private institutions enrolled almost equal shares of the total college population, but by the end of 1970s private institutions enrolled 20% and public enrolled 80% of the total.
2. A transition from a free sector to a regulated industry; federal and state regulations and regulating bodies increasingly set the directions for the activity of higher institutions, having an impact upon both public and private institutions.
3. Changing sources of financial support; since the 1930s the trend had been toward more dependence on public sources, and although there is some effort now to increase private sector giving, support for higher education will be channeled tax monies rather than private gifts.
4. An increasingly important role for large institutions; institutions of more than 10,000 students enrolled one-half of all students in American colleges and universities in 1977, and largeness rather than smallness has become the virtue.
5. Changing public confidence; skepticism over the worth of higher education has grown through the 1970s, and the public seems to hold ambivalent views about the worth of further education: wanting more education but suspecting that the additional training may not pay off in the long run.
6. Changing rates of growth; after 20 years of acceleration colleges now live with the prospect of decreases in size, or, at best, a steady state.
7. An aging faculty dominates the staffing of institutions; expansion of staff to meet the enrollment increases of the past leave institutions with a surplus, new positions are rare, and the young faculty of the 1960s are becoming the aging faculty of the 1980s and 1990s.

8. College strategies have changed from offense to defense; a feeling of harassment pervades academe, and the general reaction is to dig in, consolidate, and prepare for the worst.
9. The composition of the student body is changing in age and outlook; students are less politically active, less respectful of rules and regulations, less hopeful, more oriented to large institutions and to immediate preparation for employment.
10. The market rules supreme, and the road to survival leads through the marketplace; institutions are marketing industries, and students are consumers.

The trends that are likely to have the greatest impact on liberal arts colleges are the growth of the public sector (1) and increasing role of large institutions (4), the character of the new students (9), and the supremacy of the marketplace (10). In addition, a much longer term trend, the diversification of the educated society, will have a special meaning for the liberal arts college.

The domination by the public sector and the influence of the large institutions have a particular bearing upon the liberal arts colleges. Already noted is the fact that most liberal arts colleges fall into the 750 to 1,200 enrollment category. Whereas "bigness" was once a vice and "smallness" a virtue, the contemporary student sees in the large institution the variety of possibilities that has come to be attractive, especially since college education is more and more related to job-entry training. The smaller liberal arts college campus will continue to attract a segment of the student population, but the attractiveness of halls of ivy is considerably less in the later years of the twentieth century than it was in the early decades.

Changes in American society in the latter half of the twentieth century will also have an impact upon the way in which liberal arts colleges are viewed and supported. The liberal arts in the Greek city states, the *encyclios paideia*, implied a common culture, a homogeneity in values and outlook. In its own way, the far flung culture of the Romans also had a central focus. Americans of the latter part of the twentieth century have no such focus; the prevailing mood is of individualism, differentiation, and appreciation of the cultural pluralism that makes up the nation. America is the kaleidoscope that Alistair Cooke (1979) describes in *The Americans*, and the sole purpose of education is to promote *individual* growth, even if one is hard put to say much about *what* kind of growth is desired. Boorstin (1974) argues that the characteristic American college has become "less a place of instruction than a place of worship—worship of the growing individual." And, if subject matters are vague, options numerous, boundaries between "extracurriculum" and "curriculum" undrawn, this is to be expected, because "growth" is hard to define.

From a perspective outside American culture, Ben-David (1972) sketches the dilemma. He states that the kind of education the American colleges were intended to perpetuate assumes that "such education created a superior person. His superiority was aesthetic. . . it was also moral. . . Finally, it was an intellectual superiority, since the cultivated mind was capable of the critical reflection and intellectual autonomy of which others were not capable." It is questionable whether the principles of liberal education can ever be effective in the modern world, Ben-David suggests, but if they are, they will be limited to the few and will be found in few colleges. But, herein lies the American dilemma, for college education in the United States was not meant for a selected few, and in recent years has clearly become a system for the mass.

The more the liberal arts college adapts to the new pressures, the more it becomes similar to other institutions. By incorporating the demands of the marketplace it fades into the background of larger and more differentiated institutions that can do the job of mass education much more efficiently. The supreme challenge thus becomes that of achieving some kind of balance which retains what is valued in the original conception of the "arts" while meeting student demands.

It is not surprising that a large segment of the colleges classified as liberal arts colleges in 1970 were reclassified as comprehensive institutions in 1976, or that the Carnegie Council found it difficult to differentiate between the Liberal Arts II colleges and the comprehensive institutions (Carnegie Council, 1976).

## Undergraduate Baccalaureate Education

Given the historical antecedents, the contemporary liberal arts college comes by its bewildering variety of curricular patterns honestly. The story of the liberal arts college curriculum has been one of continuous evolution, the Carnegie Council (1976) observes; the movement has been toward increasing diversity, and in the process, "the new coexists. . . with the old, for there has been little pruning and much grafting." As a result, writes Levine (1978) there is "no such thing as *the* undergraduate curriculum in America." Each institution has a curriculum that is in some way unique.

It is in the face of threats that colleges have most vigorously asserted and or reasserted their debt to older curricular ideals. Eliot's free elective system is credited with the breakdown in the unity of the curriculum at the turn of the century (McGrath, 1966), but in his inaugural address Eliot claimed that the whole curriculum would provide a liberal education; it was only that he did not want the pattern prescribed (Thomas, 1962). Eliot's stance brought the debate to the fore again. Under Lowell, his successor, the college of Harvard University returned to a more structured form, but never to what it had been before Eliot.

The emergence of the modern American university rallied the liberal arts colleges again in the early years of the century and brought forth the Association of American Colleges, but by the 1920s the liberal arts colleges had accepted a combination of basic education and specialized education, even while debating the role of specialized education within that context. Thomas (1962) views the decade of 1920-1930, when the change gained acceptance, as "one of the most important in the history of higher education in America," because it established the form that has dominated the liberal arts college since. The liberal arts college entered the second half of the twentieth century with a conventionalized commitment to breadth and depth, but with much debate over the "proper" proportion of each. The curriculum continued to expand, and so did the number of degrees, until by the 1970s there were 650 different bachelor's degree programs for which "common abbreviations" were listed by the American Council on Education (Carnegie Foundation, 1978).

Whatever one's judgment regarding the quality or effectiveness of those elements of the curriculum labeled "general education," it is still accurate to use the tripartite division (general education, the major, and electives) to describe the variations in pattern in the contemporary liberal arts college. Based on studies of developments between 1957-1967 within a sample of 322 colleges and universities granting the baccalaureate degree, Dressel (1969) found great variation in patterns, with median requirement for basic and general education for the B.A. degree at 39%, the median for the major or concentration at 31%, and the median for electives at 29%. For the B.S. degree the median for general education was a bit lower, 30%.

The study undertaken by Blackburn, Armstrong, Conrad, Didham, and McKune (1976) was based on 271 institutions, of which 55 were liberal arts colleges. For the liberal arts sub-sample data, compiled from 1966-1967, the proportions of the total requirements for the baccalaureate distributed between the three segments were: 43 to 45% in general education; from 23-33 to 26-36% in major requirements; and from 24-34 to 29-39% in electives. (The first percentage is for private Liberal Arts I colleges, and the second for private Liberal Arts II institutions.) By 1973-1974, the proportions had shifted: 23 to 31% was in general education; from 21-34% to 25-35% was in major requirements; and from 45-56% to 44-54% was in electives. The movement was clearly to reduce the general education requirement and increase the electives, particularly in the Liberal Arts I colleges. The major or concentration remained relatively stable.

**Missions of the College Curriculum** (Carnegie Foundation, 1978) reflects the same decline in requirements in general education, but also documents the considerable difference between Liberal Arts I an II institutions in curriculum and student outlook. A high proportion (71%) of the students in Liberal Arts I institutions consider themselves intellectuals, while 66% so classed themselves in Liberal Arts II institutions. Only 19% of the Liberal Arts I students would leave college for a job, while 31% of the Liberal Arts II students would so choose. On the other hand, 70% of the Liberal Arts II students said that it was essential to get a detailed grasp of a special field while in college, compared to 53% of Liberal Arts I students.

Pfnister and Finkelstein (1984) reported that all of the colleges included in their site-visits had reviewed their general education requirements at least once during the decade of the 1970s; several had been engaged in an almost continuous review during the time and had shifted from prescribed sequences to a virtually open curriculum and back to a more structured form. In general, the more traditional liberal arts institutions (predominantly Liberal Arts I institutions) tended to decrease requirements on the supposition that the entire curriculum already emphasized the liberal arts. The institutions that had moved toward or embraced the more comprehensive structure tended to build in more specific requirements in general education.

How do we generalize for such a disparate group of institutions? We can say that the curriculum in liberal arts colleges at the beginning of the 1980s is almost evenly distributed among general education, the major, and electives, but there is great variation within this pattern. The more selective and traditional colleges tend to decrease requirements in general education and increase options with electives, while the less selective institutions tend to maintain the even division. The debates continue over proportions of the curriculum to be devoted to each aspect of the undergraduate experience, and the particular composition of courses within the general education component varies greatly.

The vagueness and almost continuous flux in the curriculum among most liberal arts colleges may be distressing to those who would like to see more order and structure, but in summarizing the mission of undergraduate education, the Carnegie Foundation (1978, p.150) states, "the curricula of modern colleges and universities can no longer be governed by the unified cultural objectives of colonial times. Instead, our heterogenous society and extraordinary increase in knowledge pose genuine dilemmas. Today, in a pluralistic society, our degree requirements are stated in terms of specific courses or areas of study and are seldom accompanied by a rationale for the selection of courses offered."

Moreover, within the liberal arts colleges, as well as within higher education generally, the curriculum as a whole has become oriented toward the student as a consumer and toward his/her concern for occupational training (Carnegie Foundation, 1978; Riesman, 1981). In the contemporary world it appears clear that most college students and their families view colleges primarily as an avenue to financial security and status.

## Matters of Vulnerability

Until the second half of the twentieth century liberal arts colleges were the model for all of higher education in relation to the oldest and, until the 1950s, the most numerous of higher institutional forms. These institutions now attract a decreasing portion of the total college enrollment and the number of liberal arts institutions appears to be decreasing (Carnegie Council, 1976). Wallis (1965) voices a popular sentiment when he contends that colleges "that confine their efforts to undergraduates will find themselves relegated, by the end of this century, to the position occupied today by the good preparatory schools. In fact they will not be in a good position."

Liberal Arts colleges have frequently confounded the forecasters and may do so again. However, that they have survived provides no guarantee that in the face of a new kind of challenge the usefulness and vigor of this distinctly American institution will continue undiminished (Bell, 1966).

**Three Thousand Futures** (Carnegie Council, 1980) concludes that the selective liberal arts colleges have a high probability of surviving, but that the less selective are among the most vulnerable of all post-secondary institutions. It is probable that the selectivity factor is less responsible for the strength of the one segment over the other than the fact that some institutions have developed the kind of attractiveness that allows them to be selective. If an institution has established a niche in its own geographical region, or in the national higher education community, then it is strengthened and reinforced with intangible resources and "moral capital," which in turn, make it more attractive and capable of surviving. Building that moral capital, however, is difficult when one is on the brink of financial disaster. The institutions that need the slack to build strength are the institutions that do not have the resources to allow slack.

Have most liberal arts college, like the dinosaur, now come to the end of their useful service, with the 123 Liberal Arts College I institutions the only remaining examples of the free-standing liberal arts college? The dinosaur was longlived, and adapted well through a long period of earth's history. A certain segment of the liberal arts colleges appears to have the strength to continue into the twenty-first century. Or, is the appropriate image the phoenix, the mythical bird that springs forth from the flames into new life? Other liberal arts colleges are adapting to the new conditions of American society by taking on new forms while maintaining or reaffirming identification with the liberal arts ideal. These are institutions that probably constitute a new class, standing between the purely comprehensive and the purely and more traditional liberal arts. Perhaps the image is not dinosaur *or* phoenix, but dinosaur and phoenix.

Even with substantial numbers of survivors, the free-standing liberal arts college as known in the past will not return to a dominant position in American higher education. But the persistence of a significant number of these institutions could continue to remind academe of the heritage of the liberal arts and could continue to have an influence on excellence in higher education quite out of proportion to their size and number.

## Notes

1. In his chapter on the classical tradition, George P. Schmidt (1957) makes the statement, "The path from the Athens of Aristotle to the new world Cambridge of Dunster and the Williamsburg of Blair is devious but recognizable" (p.43). He continues, "The Aristotelian body of knowledge and method of thinking was modified by Roman and Moslem additions, then almost lost to the Western world in the centuries of barbarism that followed the disintegration of Roman civilization. It reappeared, diluted and fragmented in the lectures of the masters of arts who were combining in the thirteenth century to establish the University of Paris." Schmidt provides more than most writers regarding the development of the ideal of the liberal arts as applied to Western Europe and later the United States, but it is my conviction that many assumptions about the Western heritage of the liberal arts as a direct legacy from Greece leads to a misunderstanding of what the American liberal arts college were about well into the nineteenth century and misunderstanding of some of the tensions affecting them in the twentieth century.

2. It is mistakenly assumed that the university grew out of the colleges during the medieval university building period. The opposite is the case; the *form* of the college arose in response to the needs of the university. The tradition of the liberal arts in the West, of course, preceded the development of both university and college, but work in the arts was required for admission to the universities. Initially the universities made little or no direct provision for young scholars to gain the requisite preparation; the students were on their own. Only later did the colleges become responsible for liberal arts instruction. Cobban (1975) contends that the college of medieval universities do not always receive the emphasis they deserve; they "were destined to occupy a commanding position in the universities of northern Europe, (and) they merit more sympathetic treatment" (p. 122).

3. For a more thorough treatment of the development see Pfnister (1980), a monograph that traces the development of the idea of the college from the College des Dix Huit to the English colleges at the time of the Elizabethan statutes of 1570 and through the subsequent modifications of the form in England and the United States.

4. Quotations from the Yale Report of 1828 are from Hofstadter and Smith (1961) volume 1, pages 275-291.

5. In addition, it should be observed that the four-year structure was the standard form of the college. There was a brief flurry of interest in turning the liberal arts curriculum into a three-year, or less, segment. The journals carry a number of proposals for such a development in the late 1800s and early 1900s. Charles W. Eliot of Harvard was an outspoken advocate of the plan.

6. With the cooperation of Verne Stadtman of the Carnegie Foundation for the Advancement of Teaching, the researchers were able to obtain the data tapes of the *1978 Carnegie Survey of Institutional Adaptations to the 1970s* for a convenient sample of 84 colleges classified as Liberal Arts I or II in 1970 by the Carnegie Commission. In this sample were 37 institutions that had remained in liberal arts category and 47 that had been reclassified by 1976. The identity of individual colleges was confidential, and only a code number appeared on the individual data.

7. Leslie's (1981) summaries of enrollments for the liberal arts colleges show that LA I institutions added few new programs, while LA II expanded rapidly in many directions. The market approach was reflected more clearly in LA II than in LA I institutions. One may ask, as did Leslie, whether this expansion of program, which secured enrollment gains, might not also have changed the nature of the colleges. Certainly, the Carnegie reclassifications in 1976 suggested that the expanded program colleges looked to be different institutions — more akin to "comprehensive colleges and universities."

8. In 1982, the Association of American Colleges launched a three-year project to attempt to "revive a consensus among the faculty, deans, presidents, and trustees on the meaning and purpose of baccalaureate degrees," according to Mark H. Curtis, president of the association. In 1982, Theodore Lockwood wrote on the first essays regarding the development of the consensus ("What should the Baccalaureate Mean?" *Change, 14* pp. 39ff.). It was obvious by that time than no consensus was forthcoming; instead, there would be several essays to describe categories of prevailing points of view.

Library of
Davidson College

# References

Anderson, R.E. (1977). *Strategic policy changes at private colleges.* New York: Teachers College Press.

Astin, A. W., & Lee, C.B.T. (1972). *The invisible colleges: A profile, of small private colleges.* New York: McGraw-Hill.

Bell, D. (1966). *The reforming of general education: The Columbia College experience in its natural setting.* New York: Columbia University Press.

Ben-David, J. (1972). *American higher education; Directions old and new.* New York: McGraw-Hill

Blackburn, R., Armstrong, E., Conrad, C., Didham, J., & McKune, T. (1976). *Changing practices in undergraduate education.* Berkeley: Carnegie Council on Policy Studies.

Boorstin, D.J. (1965). *The Americans: The national experience.* New York: Vintage Books.

Bowen, H.R. (1980). *The costs of higher education: How much do colleges spend per student and how much should they spend?* San Francisco: Jossey-Bass.

Capella, M. (1977). [The marriage of philology and Mercury.] in W. Stahl, R. Johnson, & E. Burge (Ed. and Trans.), *Marianus Capella and the seven liberal arts* (vol. 2). New York: Columbia University Press.

Carnegie Council on Policy Studies in Higher Education (1980). *Three thousand futures: The next twenty years for higher education.* San Francisco: Jossey-Bass.

Carnegie Council on Policy Studies in Higher Education (1976). *A classification of institutions of higher education.* Revised edition. Berkeley: Author.

Carnegie Foundation for the Advancement of Teaching (1978). *Missions of the college curriculum—a contemporary review with suggestions.* San Francisco: Jossey-Bass.

Chaffee, E. (1984). Successful strategic management in small private colleges. *Journal of Higher Education, 55,* 212-241.

Cobban, A. B. (1975). *The medieval universities: Their development and organization.* London: Methuen.

Commager, H.S. (1977). Can the American college survive? *Mainliner, 21,* 49-51.

Committee on the Objectives of a General Education in a Free Society (1955). *General education in a free society.* Cambridge, MA: Harvard University Press.

Cooke, A. (1980). *The Americans.* New York: Berkeley.

Curtis, M. H. (1959). *Oxford and Cambridge in transition, 1558-1642.* Oxford, England: Clarendon Press.

Dickmeyer, N. (1982). Reexamining the economics of scale and the viability of small colleges. In C. Frances (Ed.), *Successful responses to financial difficulty.* (New Directions for Higher Education No.38). San Francisco: Jossey-Bass.

Dressel, P.L., & DeLisle, F.H. (1969). *Undergraduate curriculum trends.* Washington, D.C.: American Council on Education.

Educational Policies Commission of the National Education Association. (1957). *Higher education in a decade of decision.* Washington, D.C National Educational Association.

Finkelstein, M.J., Farrar, D., & Pfnister, A. O. (1984). The adaptation of liberal arts colleges in the 1970s: An analysis of critical events. *Journal of Higher Education, 55.*

Gamson, Z.F., & Associates (1984). *Liberating education.* San Francisco: Jossey-Bass.

Green, T.F. (1975). The undergraduate college and the world of work. In D.G. Trites (Ed.), *Planning the future of the undergraduate college* (New Direction for Higher Education No. 9). San Francisco: Jossey-Bass.

Gwynn, A. (no date). *Roman education from Cicero to Quintilian.* Teachers College Press. (Original work published 1926).

Herbst, J. (1965). *The German historical school in American scholarship.* Ithaca, NY. Cornell University Press.

Hofstadter, R., & Smith, W. (Eds.). (1961). *American higher education: A documentary history* (vols. 1 & 2). Chicago: University of Chicago Press.

Keeton, M. T. (1971). *Models and mavericks: A profile of private liberal arts colleges.* New York: McGraw-Hill.

Keeton, M., & Hillberry, C. (1969). *Struggle and promise: A future for colleges.* New York: McGraw-Hill.

Keller, G. (1983). *Academic strategy: The management revolution in American higher education.* Baltimore: Johns Hopkins Univ. Press.

Kelly, F.J. (1925). *The American arts college: a limited survey.* New York: Macmillan.

Kelly, R. L. (1921). The preliminary report of the Association Commission on the organization of the college curriculum. *Association of American Colleges Bulletin, 7,* 56-60.

Leslie, L., Grant, A., & Brown, K. (1981) *Patterns of enrollments in higher education 1965 to 1977, liberal arts colleges* (topical Paper No. 19). Tucson, AZ: Center for the Study of Higher Education, University of Arizona.

Leslie, W. B. (1976). The reemergence of the American college: A multiple-case study, 1870-1920. *Liberal Education, 62,* 507-526.

Levasseur, E. (1899). Address to the American club dinner (Paris). In *Report of the commissioner of education for the year 1897-1898* (vol. 2). Washington, D.C. , Government Printing Office.

Levine, A. (1978). *Handbook on undergraduate curriculum.* San Francisco: Jossey-Bass.

McGrath, E.J. (1966). *The liberal arts college and the emergent caste system.* New York: Teachers College Press.

Mayhew, L.B. (1962). *The smaller liberal arts college.* New York: Center for Applied Research in Education.

Minter, W. J. and Bowen, H.R. (1978). *Independent higher education.* Washington, D.C: National Association of Independent Colleges and Universities.

National Association of College and University Business Officers (NACUBO) (1981). *The financial conditions of institutions of higher education.* Washington, DC: Office of Program Evaluation, U.S. Department of Education.

Peat, Marwick, & Mitchell, & Co. (1980). *Ratio analysis in higher education: A guide to assessing the institutions' financial condition.* New York, Author.

Peck, R.D. (1984). Entrepreneurship as a significant factor in successful adaptation. *Journal of Higher Education, 55.*

Pfnister, A. O. (1980). *The idea of the college in western post-secondary education: A study in adaptation from an historical and comparative perspective* (Occasional Papers in Higher Education No. 14). Denver: University of Denver School of Education.

Pfnister, A.O. (1981). *Survival and revival: The transformation of the American arts college* (Occasional Papers in Higher Education No. 15). Denver: University of Denver School of Education.

Pfnister, A.O. (1984). The role of the liberal arts college: A historical overview of the debates. *Journal of Higher Education, 55.*

Pfnister, A.O., & Finkelstein, M.J. (1984). *The morphology of change in American higher education.* Denver: University of Denver.

Riesman, D. (1981). *On higher education.* San Francisco: Jossey-Bass.

Rudolph, F. (1962). *The American college and university: A history.* New York: Knopf.

Rudolph, F. (1977). *Curriculum: A history of the American undergraduate course of study since 1636.* San Francisco: Jossey-Bass.

Schachner, N. (1938). *The medieval universities: Their development and organization.* New York: A.S. Barnes.

Schmidt, G.P. (1975). *The liberal arts college.* New Brunswick, N.J.: Rutgers University Press.

Stadtman, V. (1980). *Academic adaptations: Higher education prepares for the 1980s and 1990s.* San Francisco: Jossey-Bass.

Stahl, W. H., Johnson, R., & Burge, E.L. (1971). *Martianus Capella and the seven liberal arts (vol 1).* New York: Columbia University Press.

Thomas R. (1962). *The search for a common learning: General education 1800-1960.* New York: Columbia University Press.

Wallis, W.A. (1965). The future of the small college. In *The troubled campus* (prepared by editors of *The Atlantic*). Boston: Little, Brown.

# The Community College in the American Educational System

## Arthur M. Cohen

Educational theorists as diverse as Ivan Illich and Thomas Green have debated the configurations of the American educational system. Illich (1970) explained how the attainment of each level of schooling creates a demand for the next level and effects a form of regressive taxation, since the system's upper reaches tend to be populated by the higher income groups. He deplored the power of a system that could allocate a person's position in society by determining who was learned and thus capable of obtaining high status employment.

Green (1980) analyzed the system itself, describing it as a set of schools and colleges related by a medium of exchange comprised of the certificates, diplomas, and degrees by which the activities and outcomes of one school can be recognized as being the same as those of other schools. The system is organized in a sequence, with students prepared in one grade to continue to the next in line. It distributes educational benefits and certificates that have market value among employers. The institutions at the system's core are those whose certificates are perceived as having the greatest value, both for students going on to the next grade and among agencies outside the system. In higher education this core includes the traditional liberal arts colleges and the major research universities, along with their associated graduate and professional schools. The proprietary trade schools tend to be at the system's periphery, while corporate and professional association non-graded educational activities are outside it.

Where do American community colleges fit into the educational system? This paper discusses the educational efforts of these schools at the level of grades 13 and 14, their early attempts to gain a place near the system's core and the forces that have moved them toward the margin. And it examines the dilemma faced by community college leaders who want to maintain their institution's place in graded education but also wish to continue providing a variety of educative and quasieducative services to their constituents on an open-access basis.

## Background

Community colleges are relatively recent arrivals in the American education system, outgrowths of the junior colleges founded in the early years of the twentieth century when publicly supported higher education was beginning to move toward its current prominent position. Several forces contributed to the rise of higher education and the newly emergent two-year colleges: scientific research, the expansion of professional schools, the demand for paraprofessional and technical aides, and the drive for equality of educational opportunity for all people regardless of gender, ethnicity, or family income. The junior colleges would serve many of these people as convenient, accessible points of entry to higher levels of schooling and to the workplace.

Secondary school growth also fostered junior college development in the early decades. Between 1910 and 1940, for those students who had entered the fifth grade eight years earlier, high school graduation rates increased from 7% to 50%. Since one of the major outcomes of schooling is the demand for more schooling, the rapidly increasing number of high school graduates forced the expansion of higher education. And, since the increased percentage of the age group seeking entry to college also resulted in a demand for non-traditional curricula, collegiate institutions were forced to expand their scope as well as their size. The universities could grow and diversify only up to a point; in most states, a network of junior colleges developed to provide services the universities could not provide. This network soon became a buffer of institutions, preparing young people for university-level studies or diverting them toward other pursuits.

The first publicly supported junior colleges opened in the first decade of the twentieth century and were outnumbered by the private junior colleges until 1950. These colleges offered transferable education, enabling students to complete the first two years of baccalaureate studies; occupational programs leading to certificates of completion for curricula that might take two years or less to complete; and post-secondary terminal curricula for students who would not go on to a university but who sought an additional year or two of preparation for home and family living or for clerical and other entry level jobs in business.

Following World War II, the trend toward increased years of formal schooling moved great numbers of students into post-secondary institutions. Talk of universal higher education became common when, in 1947, the President's Commission on Higher Education recommended that post-secondary instruction be made available to all individuals who could profit from such exposure. The idea that the ultimate benefit to the state would far exceed the cost led to increased support for post-secondary institutions that would provide occupational preparation, offer instruction in citizenship and basic skills, and allow young people a place to develop during a period of prolonged adolescence. By 1950, 40% of American high school graduates were entering college. And by 1960, 75% of each age group were graduating from high school and 60% were entering college (Table 1). This increase in the rate of matriculation was enhanced by the junior colleges, which by that time were open in nearly every state and were admitting students with little regard for their prior academic preparation.

During the first 20 years after World War II, the junior colleges added functions to their transfer, occupational, and post-high school terminal programs and began calling themselves community colleges. The additional functions included community services, cultural and educational programs that typically did not lead to transfer or specific jobs, and remedial studies. Community services were added deliberately, promoted by leaders who saw a broader role for the junior college as a full-service education agency for people of all ages. Remedial studies, on the other hand, were adopted perforce as a legacy of the post-secondary terminal courses, combined with adult basic education and (starting in the 1960s) the necessity of remedying the defects in the educational experience of recent high school graduates. These additional functions, coupled with the expansion in the population and the growth in college attendance, led to substantial public community college growth. By the 1980s, nearly 1,000 community colleges were enrolling 4.5 million students, or more than one-third of all people engaged in formal post-secondary education.

Community college growth over the past four decades has resulted from a number of forces, some of which affected the growth of institutions at all levels, while others were characteristic of the two-year colleges themselves. The growth in all types of schools is attributable to society's expanding expectations of what the schools can do, the percentage of the age group participating in formal schooling, and student consumerism. Ravitch (1983) enumerates the broadened expectations assigned to the schools: "Preserve democracy, eliminate poverty, lower the crime rate, enrich the common culture, reduce unemployment, ease the assimilation of immigrants to the nation, overcome differences between ethnic groups, advance scientific and technological progress, prevent traffic accidents, raise health standards, refine moral character, and guide young people into useful occupations" (p.xii). Community colleges developed programs in each of these areas.

The community colleges fed on the student consumer movement. The traditional goals of higher education, to transmit knowledge and stimulate intellectual development, took a back seat to the presumed desires of students to find a job, protect their health, get the most for their money, and adjust to their lives. In such a climate all subjects are of equal value, and the consumer is the arbiter of what shall be studied. If most people attending school want to use their education as a tool to help gain employment and social advancement, the curriculum shifts accordingly. Therefore shift it did in the community colleges, because of their administrator-dominated leadership and commitment to serving the public. There were no vociferous alumni who would object to an expanded mission for their *alma mater*, no entrenched faculty sufficiently powerful to deflect the drive for new students and new missions. If their leaders had difficulty in modifying existing programs, they merely added new ones. Growth provides its own dynamic for change.

The colleges had been organized to provide the first two years of the baccalaureate sequence. During the 1920s and 1930s, that continued as their primary function, with the majority of students expecting to transfer to baccalaureate degree institutions. Very early in its existence, the American Association of Community and Junior Colleges adopted the definition of junior college as "an institution offering two years of instruction of strictly collegiate grade." In 1925 the association amended its definition to include the statement, "The junior college may, and is likely to, develop a different type of curriculum suited to the larger and ever-changing civic, social, religious, and vocational needs of the entire community in which the college is located. It is understood that in this case, also, the work offered shall be on a level appropriate for high-school graduates" (Bogue, 1950. p.xvii). However, the association also reiterated its original declaration that the colleges offer courses usually offered by senior institutions: "these courses must be identical, in scope and thoroughness, with corresponding courses of the standard four-year college." This early interest in transfer education survived so that by 1980 over half of junior and community college students were enrolled in courses that carried credit transferable to senior institutions.

During the 1930s and 1940s many community college leaders sought to expand occupational training as an addition to the transfer function. Pointing to the educational levels demanded by the nation's employers, they advocated the development of technological training programs. Whereas the secondary schools of the time were teaching crafts and home economics, the community colleges would prepare people to enter the work force in jobs for which craft training would not suffice. The emergent electrical, radio, aeronautical, and health technology fields all found a place in the community colleges of the time, but as late as 1960, only one-fourth of community college students were enrolled in occupational programs. With the passage of the federal Vocational Education acts in the early 1960s, occupational programs increased, so that by 1975, 35% of the students were enrolled in programs designed to lead to immediate employment. The types of degrees awarded by community colleges reflect that expansion. In 1970-71 just over 250,000 degrees were awarded with less than 43% going to occupational program graduates. In 1979-80 slightly more than 400,000 degrees were granted with more than 62% of these given to occupational program graduates (Table 2).

Programs for adult learners also became popular during this period of rapid growth. Community colleges began offering courses designed for adults who may never have attended college, or who had chosen to return for occupational upgrading or for their personal interests. The colleges particularly sought middle-aged students, providing programs specially tailored for them and offered at night and on weekends. They recruited senior citizens; and at least half offered tuition reductions, special classes, or entire programs for persons over age 65. The success of these efforts is reflected in the mean age of the community college student body, which by 1980 was 29.

The enrollment of part-time students also contributed to the growth of community colleges. In 1968 they enrolled 1.9 million degree credit students, 47% of whom were attending part-time. In 1982 enrollment climbed to 4.9 million, with 63% of these students attending part time (Table 3). Those figures do *not* include students who enrolled in non-credit courses such as hobby and recreational activities, high school completion courses, and short term occupational studies. With the exceptions of New York and North Carolina, in the 14 states with community college enrollments greater than 50,000, part-time students outnumbered the full timers. Just as the colleges made a particular effort to recruit older students, they also sought out the part timers by making attendance easy. Classes were offered at off-campus centers and in various workplaces, and students were not required to complete programs within a given span of years.

Students of lower ability swelled community college enrollments. Most American colleges have enforced some type of selectivity in admissions, but the community colleges have tended to reduce requirements. As an example, more than half of community colleges allow students to attend if they are of a minimum age (usually 18) and/or they present a high school diploma. Only one-fourth of them ask the student to present ability test scores, and few, if any, use the student's high school grade point average as a criterion for admission. This has resulted in a high proportion of students with poor prior academic records attending community colleges. Whereas 62% of the full-time students entering all post-secondary institutions in 1983 were from the top 40% of their high school classes, only 47% of that group entered community colleges (Table 4). Further, the scores of matriculants who took the American College Testing Program's battery reflect a steady decline in ability that has persisted for nearly two decades (Table 5).

The community college attracted sizable numbers of ethnic minority students and similarly high proportions of students from low income families. By 1980 nearly 40% of the ethnic minority students involved in American higher education were enrolling in the community colleges. More than half the minority population in college began in a community college. Additionally, while 54% of all first-time, full-time students entering college came from families with annual incomes of less than $35,000, 74% of the community college matriculants fell into that category (Astin, Green, Korn, & Maier, 1983).

Having a college campus within reasonable commuting distance has a marked effect on the percentage of people who attend college. Most community colleges have been built in the cities or the suburbs, locations that encourage college attendance since students may participate even while living at home or continuing full-time employment. This enchanced the attractiveness of college education for low-ability students and for those who are only casually committed to schooling.

Community colleges have also grown by acquiring educational functions previously offered by other agencies. Many of them have taken over law enforcement programs from police academies, firefighter training from fire departments, and health technology and nursing programs from hospitals. In many cities, such colleges have absorbed the adult basic education function, the literacy training that was formerly carried out by the adult division of the elementary or secondary school district. Furthermore, numerous former adult education centers and technical institutes entered the universe of community colleges when they began offering associate degrees. This has happened in several states, including Iowa, Nebraska, Wisconsin, North Carolina, South Carolina, and Georgia. And in Kentucky, Hawaii, Pennsylvania, and other states, the public universities have organized two-year branches which are included in the data on community colleges.

There is one more characteristic of community colleges which should be noted in this catalog of reasons for their growth. Compared with most four-year colleges, community colleges are more economical to operate with more modest facilities, smaller libraries, fewer laboratories, and practically no support for academic research. Data collected by the National Center for Higher Education Management Systems indicate that the public two-year colleges rank last among higher education institutions in all categories of revenue including state and local appropriations per student, tuition revenue, private gifts, and government grants and contracts. Around 70% of their revenue from state and local aid is apportioned on a per-student basis, and around 15% comes from tuition and fees. The percentage of state aid has been rising steadily over the past 40 years, while local support has diminished in commensurate fashion (Table 6). In spite of low income, however, community colleges' faculty salary scales compare favorably with those of general baccalaureate colleges and of colleges specializing in professional training. The reason is that faculty-student ratios are much higher in community colleges, standing at approximately 28 to 1 in the academic transfer courses. However, as in senior institutions, the cost savings that were supposed to accompany the introduction of instructional technology never appeared, and, coincident with the leveling in enrollment and union-negotiated class size limitations, per-student cost of instruction may soon show a rapid increase.

Access and commitment to growth have been the dominant values of community colleges. They have opened their doors to people who could not afford the expense of moving away from home and establishing full-time residence at a senior institution. Community colleges charge lower tuition fees and admit students with little regard for prior academic achievement. They organize programs for everyone, from displaced workers to illiterate adults, and programmatically accommodate people's interest in problems such as aging, substance abuse, and adjustment to divorce. They are truly the people's colleges and access for everyone is their greatest appeal.

## Faculty

Studies of community college instructors describe them as a group differing in demographic characteristics, attitudes, and values from their senior institution counterparts, and from the administrators and trustees in their own institutions. The typical community college faculty member teaching transfer credit courses holds a master's degree. This has been true since the earliest years of the community college as an institution: a 1930 study showed 59% of community college instructors with a master's, and 5% with a doctorate; by 1970 74% had master's degrees, and 15% possessed doctorates (Cohen & Brawer, 1982, p.77). Instructors of occupational subjects frequently do not have master's degrees since their certification tends to be based on experience within the trades that they teach. Members of both transfer and occupational faculty groups have relatively high teaching loads. The instructors of transfer courses teach from 13 to 16 hours per week—four or five classes with around 30 students in each. The occupational program faculty often teach longer hours since they are involved in clinics and laboratories.

Community college faculty tend not to be members of academic disciplinary associations. For example, less than 7% of those teaching history belong to the American Historical Association. The figures are similar for community college faculty membership in the American Philosophical Association, the American Sociological Association, the American Psychological Association, and so on. The reason for this is partly the fault of the associations; for example, prior to 1973 the American Sociological Association required members to have a Ph.D. Furthermore, the publications and conferences sustained by the associations tend to have little to do with the realities of teaching in community colleges. Where associations have been formed with the specific intent of involving community college instructors, their success ratio has been much higher. The Community College Humanities Association is an example. In 1983, 63% of instructors teaching history, foreign languages, political science, and other humanities disciplines claimed association membership, with most of them involved either in the CCHA or in specially designated subgroups of the major foreign language, English, and music educators' associations.

The faculty union movement has made greater inroads in community colleges than in senior institutions; more than one-third of community college instructors are working under contracts negotiated through collective bargaining. Community college faculty organization is at least partially related to a lack of disciplinary affiliation. Faculty allegiance is to local colleagues, not to a national community of scholars. The bargaining units may or may not include the part-time faculty, which is a point of some consequence since in 1980, 56% of community college instructors were part-timers (Table 7).

Are the faculty satisfied with their working conditions? Until the 1960s local secondary schools were the largest single source of community college instructors. For those who moved from a secondary school to a community college, satisfaction was high because their status had been increased and their teaching load reduced. The less satisfied instructors tended to be those hired directly from graduate school (Cohen & Brawer, 1982, p.81). General satisfaction notwithstanding, many instructors grumble about both the abilities of their students and long teaching hours. Faculty continually plead for better qualified students; several surveys of the faculty teaching humanities and the liberal arts conducted by the Center for the Study of Community Colleges have shown that around one-fourth of the faculty want stricter prerequisites for students desiring admittance to their classes. Around the same percentage of the faculty would also prefer smaller classes (Brawer, 1984).

Thus, despite the pronouncements of administrators and institutional association spokespersons who continually refer to the open access, something for everyone characteristic of their institutions, the dominant faculty ethos continues to be that of small classes with well-prepared students in attendance. In one large urban community college district, the faculty bargaining unit recently negotiated a teaching load reduction from 15 to 12 hours per week. In return, they relinquished all sabbatical leaves, instructional development grants, and travel funds. They saw lower teaching loads as more crucial to their professional well-being and satisfaction than the perquisites that faculty historically have considered essential for their professional currency.

This conflict of values, with many administrators and governing board members seeking institutional growth regardless of the characteristics of the students, and faculty desiring smaller classes, better-prepared students, and reduced teaching loads, was sidestepped throughout the period of community college expansion. The growth in occupational studies presented few problems; in most institutions separate instructional divisions were maintained. The occupational programs had their own deans, budget lines, funding sources, credentialing structures for the faculty, sets of admissions standards for the students, program goals, and student follow-up studies. But the difficulty concerning low-ability students has never been resolved. The question of how to make up for years of learning deficiencies could not easily be answered. Even though remedial programs were established, they were usually funded as a part of transfer programs and staffed by faculty with credentials similar to those held by the instructors in the transfer credit courses. Furthermore, the 1960s and 1970s saw a decline in the standards for admission to the transfer credit classes. Varying degrees of success were achieved in some colleges with small groups of functional illiterates; but poorly prepared students remained the most intransigent problem for the faculty and, indeed, the community college as an institution.

## Curriculum and Instruction

The transfer curricula in community colleges have always been marked by the types of students attending the classes and the faculty teaching them. In the early years, when most of the faculty were recruited from secondary schools, the liberal arts courses were frequently taught as modified versions of the courses presented in high schools. Centered on the textbook, there was little indication that students were expected to do independent study. In the middle years, the 1950s and 1960s, the slogan, "Our courses are just like those offered in the universities," was often heard. As more of the faculty entered community colleges directly from university graduate programs, the push to teach college-type courses increased, with new requirements for students to write papers and read beyond the assigned textbooks.

When the full extent of the decline in student abilities was felt in the community college of the 1970s, expectations in the transfer courses, and student behavior, changed notably. These modifications were traced by Richardson and others (1983) who showed how requirements for reading and writing in all courses, including general education and the liberal arts, had been reduced in one representative community college. Students were expected to read little but a textbook, and even then they were reading not for content or ideas but for the minimal amount of information needed to pass quick-score examinations. Expectations for student writing had dropped as well, so that students wrote, at most, a few pages in any course. These findings were corroborated in several studies conducted by the Center for the Study of Community Colleges which showed that nationwide, students were required to write papers in one in four humanities classes and in one out of ten science classes. Less than half the instructors in all of the liberal arts areas gave essay examinations (Cohen & Brawer, 1982, p.156). It is important to note here that this phenomenon of attenuated course requirements was not restricted to community colleges; it afflicted all of higher education. However, it was accentuated in community colleges, which have always drawn their students from among the less well-prepared. The declining abilities of high school graduates in the 1970s merely made the difficulties more pronounced.

Faculty members in most community colleges tried a variety of instructional innovations to increase the value of their courses. Audio-tutorial instruction in biology, video-taped presentations in the social sciences, computer-assisted language instruction, and taped and filmed sequences in the humanities and fine arts were all developed and used by the instructors. However, the efforts to teach the poorly prepared students, most of whom were attending part time, took its toll not only on the faculty but also on the curriculum. By 1980, 90% of the enrollment in community college liberal arts classes was in courses for which there was no prerequisite; one-third of the enrollment in mathematics classes was in courses at a lower level than algebra; and, three out of eight students taking English classes were in remedial sections.

Policies of funding and course articulation affect transfer studies in the community colleges as much as do the types of students who attend. In most states the liberal arts and occupational courses are funded on different schedules, with occupational courses receiving higher per capita reimbursements. Accreditation standards reinforce this differential funding, which affects faculty-student ratios and the equipment and assistance available to instructors in the occupational programs. State coordinating boards may also direct the community colleges to eliminate those transfer courses that are offered as junior-level options in the senior institutions. Internally, the minuscule proportion of students who complete two years at the community colleges make it difficult to maintain a full complement of specialized sophomore level courses. This has a spiraling effect: the fewer specialized courses, the fewer students stay at the colleges for their second year.

Around 50% of the community college effort is devoted to courses in the humanities, science, social science, mathematics, and fine arts. This curriculum is based on an amalgamation of the general education innovations brought into the community colleges during the 1940s and 1950s together with the liberal arts as specified in university freshman and sophomore studies. The general education/liberal arts curriculum is maintained in community colleges because it forms the core of transfer studies, hence, it is the basis of preparation for those students who wish to go on to the baccalaureate. This curriculum is also required for graduation with the associate in arts or associate in science degree; most institutions, either by state regulation or by their own internal rules, require between 18 and 30 units in general education/liberal arts. This area of the curriculum also draws some students from among those attending community colleges for their own personal interest, with up to 20% of the enrollment in those courses drawn from that group.

Liberal arts courses are influenced by the universities through formal articulation agreements and by informal arrangements between individual instructors and academic departments. Articulation agreements may be rigorous, requiring common course numbering within a state system of universities and community colleges, and senior faculty approval of syllabi and course content for those courses that carry transfer credit. On the other hand, the community colleges may be given such latitude in the construction of the transfer courses that the resemblance between a community college course and a university freshman course may stop with the course number and title. University influence is also exerted through informal associations and professional meetings where faculty from both institutions discuss textual requirements, content, ideas, and syllabi.

The academic transfer function focuses on the liberal arts because of tradition and the need to articulate those courses for the benefit of students who transfer to universities. But transfer education in community colleges has been modified through the implementation of interdisciplinary courses in the sciences, social sciences, and humanities. Instead of offering students a choice of fulfilling transfer requirements through specialized courses in history, art, music, or philosophy, those disciplines are combined into single courses with such titles as "Mirrors of the Mind" or "The Art of Being Human." And, in some community colleges, students' desire for transfer studies is being combined with their need to work through cooperative work experience-based liberal arts programs.

The community college transfer curriculum has a flat profile with a liberal arts bias. Most students enrolled in it are in introductory courses and/or courses that have no prerequisites. Add to these the remedial courses that are supposed to prepare students for the transfer credit courses, and a curriculum that is grade 13 plus remedial appears. This has opened a gap at grade 14 that makes it difficult for a student to complete two years and then transfer.

## Transfer

How many students actually transfer? The data are unreliable. In the beginning, the proportion of students completing two years at community colleges and transferring to universities probably averaged around 25%. More recently, the number of students completing two years and then transferring has remained constant, but the percentage has declined to around 5% of total enrollment. The patterns of college attendance have changed, with greater percentages of students attending part time, dropping in and out, taking courses concurrently at community colleges and universities, transferring from community colleges and back again, and transferring before obtaining 60 units or the requirements for an associate degree at the community college. Approximately one-half the students in the academic classes say that transfer is their primary goal (Center for the Study of Community Colleges, 1984), but most of the other half also take transfer credit courses to fulfill occupational program graduation requirements or for personal interest. The question becomes: who is a transfer student if nearly half the people taking courses for transfer credit are not interested in transfer?

The data on transfer students also suffer because of confounding with occupational education. A 1978 California longitudinal study showed that more than one-fourth of the students enrolled in occupational programs indicated they intended to transfer, and more than one-fourth of the students enrolled in transfer credit courses indicated they were attending college to gain job-related skills (Hunter & Sheldon, 1980). In a 1983 Los Angeles district study, 35% of the students were in the latter group (Center for the Study of Community Colleges, 1984).

Nor is the question of the number of students transferring made easier to answer when the only people counted are those who actually matriculate at senior institutions. In some states students are counted as transfers if their college of last attendance was a community college; in others they must have acquired 30 units or more at a community college before they are so counted. Few states bother to collect data on the number of their students who transfer from community colleges to senior institutions in other states. Reverse transfers— those students who leave the university, matriculate in a community college for one or two semesters, then return to university—are counted in some states and not in others (Cohen, 1979). Probably the only accurate way of determining the community colleges' contribution to baccalaureate education would be to examine the transcripts of baccalaureate-degree recipients and determine how many of their bachelors degree course requirements were acquired in community colleges. Such studies have been done in single institutions (cf. Menke, 1980) but no such data are collected systematically.

There is a paradox in the community colleges' approach to transfer studies. Most community college leaders understand the desirability of transfer education. It maintains the link with higher education that they worked to develop and fits the expectations of many of their constituents who still look to the community college as a low cost, ready-access point of entry to post-secondary study that leads to better social and career positions. On the other hand, occupational education is presumed to ameliorate social problems by providing a trained work force that will enhance the nation's economy and assist individuals by preparing them for employment at higher salaries than they could receive without specialized training. In consequence, especially since the passage of the Vocational Education acts, community college leaders have seized upon the idea of career education and upon the funds made available for it, and many of their constituents also consider career education as an equally valid function for the institution.

The paradox appears when the transfer and occupational programs are compared. Typically, students enrolled in programs leading to associate in arts degrees and/or transfer with a major in a traditional academic subject receive less guidance and are faced with fewer specific requirements. In many instances they may choose any humanities, science, or social science course from a list of options in order to fulfill a one-course or two-course graduation requirement in each of those areas. The transfer program typically has open entry; students may matriculate even when their goals are undefined. In class, they face minimal demands for reading and writing. Class size in the humanities and social sciences tends to be limited only by the size of the room or by negotiated contracts that specify maximum class size. Institutional support for the faculty in the transfer or liberal arts area may include media preparation facilities, but few faculty have access to paraprofessional assistants or readers.

In contrast, the occupational programs are much more structured. Their facilities include laboratories and workshops along with equipment and tools. Their curriculum is restrictive, with required courses to be taken in sequence. Admission to programs is selective; students may often be required to take a year or two of college-level courses before being admitted to the allied health or high technology programs. Each program typically has a lead faculty member and instructors who work together as a group.

Granted that occupational programs operate with different sets of accreditation guidelines and that state and federal money is often earmarked for them, but if they and the transfer programs were considered of equal utility the two would not be organized as differently as they are. Before the 1960s, transfer education was the more highly regarded. Facilities for occupational education were poor and the faculty in those programs were in some cases prohibited from participating in academic governance activities. More recently, career education has been on the ascent, while a concomitant reduction in the status of the traditional freshman and sophomore courses has been occurring. If both curricula were equally valued, they would be more similar in terms of teaching load, requirements for student entry, enforcement of prerequisites in curriculum, and academic support services.

Still, occupational studies are not antagonistic to transfer education. Sizeable numbers of students who complete community college programs in nursing, allied health, engineering, data processing, agriculture, forestry, and many other advanced technologies eventually transfer and complete baccalaureate studies; it may well be that more students transfer from occupational programs than from the liberal arts curricula. The genuine enemies of the transfer function are the non-sequential activities that fall within the definition of community education.

Community education is that portion of community college service that falls outside the traditional graded curriculum. It includes activities as diverse as non-credit courses in the arts and sciences, remedial and high school makeup programs in adult basic education, open forums on contemporary public issues, recreational activities, short courses in specialized occupational skills, and contract programs organized for particular industries. Figures on this area are not reliable, but the 1983 *Community, Junior, and Technical College Directory* shows 4.3 million people enrolled in community education. College leaders justify this effort with the rationale that a true community college must offer more than a graded program.

The problem with community education is that it confounds access with education, and leads to a blurring of the community college's image and function. Increasingly the college is viewed by its constituents as a place where various meritorious activities are undertaken, rather than as a place for a serious student intent on obtaining a baccalaureate degree. The problem is compounded by the varied patterns for the funding of community education, much of which is self-supporting (through fees paid by participants) but some of which is supported by funds earmarked for the graded curriculum. The latter effect is realized when the cost of the remedial courses and of the sizeable proportion of students in transfer credit courses who have no intention of transferring are recognized as costs of community education. It is undoubtedly important to offer courses in the use of office equipment to people wishing to upgrade themselves within their occupations, and to offer courses in painting or piano playing to people who already have college degrees, but these functions are detrimental to the perception of the college as a provider of grades 13 and 14.

The people served through community education efforts do not fit typical student categories. They do not enroll in programs leading to degrees; they may not even be enrolled in formally structured courses, but may be participating in events especially tailored to their interests. Therefore, any attempt to fund community education on the basis of average daily attendance, full-time equivalence, or any other category suggesting student course attendance leading to degrees or certificates is at variance with the intent of the program and the pattern of student participation.

Ideally, community education should be funded programmatically; that is, a college would be awarded a fixed sum each year to provide cultural, occupational upgrade, recreation, personal interest, community health, and semi-professional retraining programs to the people of its districts. Or, the colleges could maintain their open access policies with students taking courses that may or may not lead to degrees, and build a transfer or honors college within such a structure. Major funding would be for individuals participating in courses with reimbursement on an attendance basis, but the transfer or honors college would be operated separately with a variety of specially funded enrichment opportunities and work assistance/scholarship funds available. Another way of separating community education efforts might be to maintain transfer and occupational functions but to turn community service into an extension division, as many universities have done. This would put all community education on a self-sustaining basis (the elimination of the local tax funding of California community colleges effected in 1978 is forcing such reorganization in that state). Still another way of maintaining the traditional college with a community education component would be to place community service, remedial, and adult basic education in a separate center, with staff who might or might not have standard teaching credentials, who are teaching students 40 hours per week. Such centers have been organized under the aegis of community colleges in Chicago, Phoenix, and San Francisco.

To the extent that community education activities are merged with transfer and occupational education functions, all are weakened. Community service activities cannot flourish when they are presented by people with traditional views of instruction and when they are funded ad hoc. The transfer function is weakened when it coexists with community service activities in which people receive college transfer credit for participating in courses and events even when not working toward degrees. Those enrolled in courses that carry transfer credit who either already have associates, bachelors, or graduate degrees, or have no intention of taking courses in a sequence that leads to a degree are truly community education students. However, since they are mingled with students intending to transfer, the transfer function is diffused. Additionally, occupational programs suffer when the figures on the number of students gaining employment in the areas for which they were trained are reduced by the number of students transferring to senior institutions instead of going to work.

## The Future of Transfer Education

The prognosis for the transfer function depends in some measure on developments external to community colleges. If universities develop occupational programs better articulated with those in the community colleges, the transfer function may center on preparing students to enter junior level programs leading to bachelor's degrees in health fields, technologies, and the professions. And, if entrance to those programs continues to depend on the completion of courses in the humanities, sciences, social sciences, mathematics, and English, those areas will continue to thrive in the community colleges. Still an open question, however, is the extent to which community colleges can succeed in preparing students who lack the basic skills of reading, writing, and computation. They may be bolstered in their efforts if secondary schools tighten graduation requirements and reduce the number of functional illiterates they pass along to post-secondary education.

The transfer function will also be affected by the extent to which community college leaders seek to maintain their institutions' place in the formal education system. Many community colleges have stretched the bounds of their legitimacy within the system by community education efforts and by offering certificates that do not qualify recipients for entrance to the next level within the structure. However, a reversal of that tendency seems to be occurring, as demands for sophomore screening tests restricting entry to university upper divisions are expanding. Florida, for example, has recently instituted such a test on a state-wide basis.

The coming years will see a struggle between those who would keep the community colleges within the educational system and those who would move them closer to the system's periphery. The colleges will weaken their position whether they pass nearly all students through or pass nearly none. In the first case they will act merely as custodial institutions rewarding students with course credits that have little negotiability. Since higher education historically has been selective, the colleges that award transfer credit to students who have completed remedial or otherwise low-level courses merely jeopardize those students' chance for matriculation at the junior level. But the community college that passes very few through its transfer program similarly moves toward the periphery of the system because its educational offerings are too much at variance with those provided by the institutions at the core. Accordingly, it does a disservice to the groups it purports to serve because they are not being provided with the most important benefit of another year of schooling: a ticket allowing advancement to the next level.

The tug of war will undoubtedly continue. Community colleges are still looked upon by many as the point of entry to higher education. Although efforts to attract adults have had the effect of increasing the mean age of the student body to 29 years, the median age is 22, and modal age is 19. Most of the students entering the institutions just out of high school still expect to transfer and obtain higher degrees.

How can transfer education be strengthened? That question is being asked by many educators and agency officials. Several projects to help maintain the transfer function and traditional academic courses in community colleges have been funded by the National Endowment for the Humanities, the Ford Foundation, the Andrew W. Mellon Foundation, and other organizations and agencies whose directors realize that the community college is an important element in the nation's post-secondary education effort and that the liberal arts and transfer education are essential components of those studies.

Community colleges might enhance transfer studies by negotiating stronger articulation agreements with both receiving senior institutions and the secondary schools. Counseling can be strengthened with the addition of computerized academic and graduation information systems that keep the students apprised of their progress toward associate degrees and/or toward readying themselves for transfer to junior-level programs. Entry-level testing can be introduced as a way of directing students toward remedial or compensatory education courses within the colleges. (Prior to the 1960s most colleges had such programs, but they were allowed to lapse when testing fell into disrepute in the late 1960s and 1970s.) Liberal arts courses can be arranged in sequence and prerequisites enforced so that students in the transfer programs have some semblance of common experience. Interdisciplinary courses in the liberal arts can be required for all matriculants regardless of the degree, transfer institution, or career that they are contemplating. Academic support services, including tutorials, can be mandated so that poorly prepared students who enter transfer classes would be required to spend time in a learning laboratory working on course-related materials. Citizen advisory committees can be formed as a way of gaining lay support for the transfer program. All these efforts have been made and recent events suggest they will accelerate. The challenge lies in strengthening transfer education while maintaining access for all and continuing the broader educational efforts that have marked the community colleges in the second half of the century.

The community colleges found a niche in the educational system by offering low-cost, degree-credit, and non-credit programs in hometown settings for low-ability, part-time, minority-group, and low-income students who probably would not have otherwise participated in higher education. In so doing, they helped expand the system's boundaries by putting pressure on traditional colleges to modify their programs in order to accommodate the greater numbers of students who sought higher levels of schooling. But at what cost were these achievements accomplished? In their early years, the junior colleges were easily accessible points of entry to higher education. Their grades 13 and 14 were the culmination of high school for some students, the beginning of college for others. Now, the low percentage of students in sophomore-level courses and of students transferring (both less than 10%), coupled with the sophomore-level tests administered to students intending to transfer to the junior year in some state universities, suggest they are operating near the system's periphery. The recent calls for a renewed emphasis on excellence and quality in their programs reveal community college leaders' concern that their degrees and certificates not lose their credibility (McCabe, 1981).

The problem for community colleges now is to combine diverse educational opportunities offered for a broad clientele with a need to stay within the graded system by maintaining the value of their diplomas. In order to continue serving high-risk students, they cannot afford to exercise excessive selectivity in their graded programs. And, in order to continue offering short courses for the public through their community education activities (whether or not so designated), they cannot return to the junior college mode of grades 13 and 14 plus sequenced occupational programs.

Community colleges grew by providing access to the previously disenfranchised. Must an institution committed to access necessarily move toward the educational system's periphery? If so, the core will always be reserved for an elite group of students and schools. The efforts being made in community colleges toward tightening requirements for sequence, enforcing course prerequisites, and providing various forms of assistance for students intending to transfer, suggest that at least some college leaders recognize the need for a strong educational program within an open-access institution.

## TABLE 1

## ESTIMATED RETENTION RATES, FIFTH GRADE THROUGH COLLEGE ENTRANCE, IN PUBLIC AND NONPUBLIC SCHOOLS
### United States, 1924-32 to 1973-81

|  | Retention per 1,000 pupils who entered 5th grade | | | |
| School years pupils entered 5th grade | 9th grade | High school graduation | | 1st-time college students |
|  |  | No. | Year |  |
| 1924-25 | 612 | 302 | 1932 | 118 |
| 1934-35 | 803 | 467 | 1942 | 129 |
| 1944-45 | 872 | 553 | 1952 | 234 |
| 1954-55 | 915 | 642 | 1962 | 343 |
| 1956-57 | 930 | 676 | 1964 | 362 |
| Fall 1958 | 946 | 732 | 1966 | 384 |
| Fall 1960 | 952 | 749 | 1968 | 452 |
| Fall 1962 | 959 | 750 | 1970 | 461 |
| Fall 1964 | 975 | 748 | 1972 | 433 |
| Fall 1966 | 985 | 744 | 1974 | 448 |
| Fall 1968 | 983 | 749 | 1976 | 435 |
| Fall 1970 | 982 | 744 | 1978 | 440 |
| Fall 1971 | 985 | 743 | 1979 | 451 |
| Fall 1973 | 994 | 745 | 1981 | 469 |

Rates for 5th grade through high school graduation are based on enrollments in successive grades in successive years in public elementary and secondary schools. Rates for first-time college enrollment include full-time and part-time students enrolled in programs creditable toward a bachelor's degree.

Beginning with the class in the 5th grade in 1958, dates are based on fall enrollment and exclude upgraded pupils.

Source: U.S. Department of Education, *The Condition of Education*, 1981, and unpublished data from the National Center for Education Statistics.

**TABLE 2**

# ASSOCIATE DEGREES CONFERRED BY INSTITUTIONS OF HIGHER EDUCATION BY TYPE OF CURRICULUM
### 1970-71 to 1980-81

| Year | All Curricula | Arts and Sciences or General Programs | | Occupational Programs | |
|---|---|---|---|---|---|
| | | Number | Percentage of Total | Number | Percentage of Total |
| 1970-71 | 252,610 | 144,883 | 57.4 | 107,727 | 42.6 |
| 1971-72 | 292,119 | 158,283 | 54.2 | 133,836 | 45.8 |
| 1972-73 | 317,008 | 161,051 | 50.8 | 155,957 | 49.2 |
| 1973-74 | 343,924 | 164,659 | 47.9 | 179,265 | 52.1 |
| 1974-75 | 360,171 | 166,567 | 46.2 | 193,604 | 53.8 |
| 1975-76 | 391,454 | 175,185 | 44.8 | 216,269 | 55.2 |
| 1976-77 | 406,377 | 171,631 | 42.2 | 234,746 | 57.8 |
| 1977-78 | 412,246 | 167,036 | 40.5 | 245,210 | 59.5 |
| 1978-79 | 402,702 | 157,572 | 39.1 | 245,130 | 60.9 |
| 1979-80 | 400,910 | 154,282 | 38.5 | 246,626 | 61.5 |
| 1980-81 | 416,377 | 155,731 | 37.4 | 260,646 | 62.6 |

Sources: U.S. Department of Health, Education and Welfare, 1978, and U.S. Department of Education, *Digest of Education Statistics*, 1983-84, p. 137.

**TABLE 3**

# PART-TIME ENROLLMENT AS A
# PERCENTAGE OF TOTAL ENROLLMENTS
### 1963-1984

| Year | Opening Fall Enrollment | Part-Time Enrollment | Percentage |
|------|------------------------|----------------------|------------|
| 1963 | 914,494 | 488,976 | 53 |
| 1968 | 1,909,118 | 888,458 | 47 |
| 1969 | 2,234,669 | 1,064,187 | 48 |
| 1970 | 2,447,401 | 1,164,797 | 48 |
| 1971 | 2,678,171 | 1,290,964 | 48 |
| 1972 | 2,863,780 | 1,473,947 | 51 |
| 1973 | 3,100,951 | 1,702,886 | 55 |
| 1974 | 3,528,727 | 1,974,534 | 56 |
| 1975 | 4,069,279 | 2,222,269 | 55 |
| 1976 | 4,084,976 | 2,219,605 | 54 |
| 1977 | 4,309,984 | 2,501,789 | 58 |
| 1978 | 4,304,058 | 2,606,804 | 61 |
| 1979 | 4,487,872 | 2,788,880 | 62 |
| 1980 | 4,825,931 | 2,996,264 | 62 |
| 1981 | 4,887,675 | 3,070,087 | 63 |
| 1982 | 4,964,379 | 3,115,055 | 63 |
| 1983 | 4,947,975 | 3,113,981 | 63 |
| 1984 | 4,836,379 | 3,142,698 | 65 |

Source: American Association of Community and Junior Colleges, 1965-1984.

**TABLE 4**

## HIGH SCHOOL ACADEMIC PERFORMANCE
## OF COLLEGE FRESHMEN
### 1984

| Measure of Academic Performance | Percentage of Enrollment | |
|---|---|---|
| | All Institutions | All 2-Year Colleges |
| **Rank in high school** | | |
| top 20% | 39.7 | 24.5 |
| second 20% | 22.4 | 21.3 |
| middle 20% | 30.1 | 41.5 |
| fourth 20% | 6.7 | 11.0 |
| lowest 20% | 1.1 | 1.8 |
| **Average grade in high school** | | |
| A or A+ | 9.3 | 3.8 |
| A− | 10.7 | 6.0 |
| B+ | 18.6 | 15.4 |
| B | 25.2 | 26.4 |
| B− | 14.4 | 17.3 |
| C+ | 13.0 | 17.9 |
| C | 8.3 | 12.6 |
| D | 0.5 | 0.8 |

Source: A.W. Astin and others, *The American Freshman: National Norms for Fall 1984.*

**TABLE 5**

## MEAN ACT SCORES FOR
## TWO-YEAR COLLEGE FRESHMEN
### 1964-1979, 1982

| Year | English | Math | Social Science | Natural Science | Composite |
|---|---|---|---|---|---|
| 1964 | 17.6 | 17.4 | 18.2 | 18.5 | 18.0 |
| 1965 | 16.9 | 17.6 | 18.8 | 18.9 | 18.2 |
| 1970 | 17.2 | 17.7 | 18.0 | 19.0 | 18.1 |
| 1975 | 15.8 | 14.9 | 15.2 | 18.9 | 16.3 |
| 1977 | 15.7 | 14.2 | 14.7 | 18.5 | 15.9 |
| 1979 | 15.8 | 13.9 | 14.4 | 18.4 | 15.8 |
| 1982 | 15.7 | 13.3 | 14.5 | 18.4 | 15.6 |

Source: American College Testing Program, (1966, 1972-77, 1978-79, 1980-81, 1982-83).

**TABLE 6**

## PERCENTAGES OF INCOME FROM VARIOUS SOURCES FOR PUBLIC TWO-YEAR COLLEGES
### 1918-1981

| Source | 1918* | 1930* | 1942* | 1950* | 1959 | 1965 | 1975 | 1977 | 1980 | 1981 |
|---|---|---|---|---|---|---|---|---|---|---|
| Tuition and fees | 6 | 14 | 11 | 9 | 11 | 13 | 15 | 18 | 15 | 16 |
| Federal aid | 0 | 0 | 2 | 1 | 1 | 4 | 8 | 5 | 5 | .9 |
| State aid | 0 | 0 | 28 | 26 | 29 | 34 | 45 | 59 | 60 | 48 |
| Local aid | 94 | 85 | 57 | 49 | 44 | 33 | 24 | 15 | 11 | 17 |
| Private gifts and grants | 0 | 0 | 0 | 0 | 0 | 3 | 1 | 0 | 1 | .5 |

*Includes local junior colleges only.

Sources: Starrak and Hughes (1954); Medsker and Tillery (1971); Olivas (1979); Richardson and Leslie (1980); *Chronicle of Higher Education* (June 8, 1982).

**TABLE 7**

## NUMBERS OF FULL-TIME AND PART-TIME TWO-YEAR COLLEGE INSTRUCTORS
### 1953-1984

| Year | Total Instructors | Full-Time | | Part-Time | |
|---|---|---|---|---|---|
| | | Number | Percentage | Number | Percentage |
| 1953 | 23,762 | 12,473 | 52 | 11,289 | 48 |
| 1958 | 33,396 | 20,003 | 60 | 13,393 | 40 |
| 1963 | 44,405 | 25,438 | 57 | 18,967 | 43 |
| 1968 | 97,443 | 63,864 | 66 | 33,579 | 34 |
| 1973 | 151,947 | 89,958 | 59 | 61,989 | 41 |
| 1974 | 162,530 | 81,658 | 50 | 80,872 | 50 |
| 1975 | 181,549 | 84,851 | 47 | 96,698 | 53 |
| 1976 | 199,655 | 88,277 | 44 | 111,378 | 56 |
| 1977 | 205,528 | 89,089 | 43 | 116,439 | 57 |
| 1978 | 213,712 | 95,461 | 45 | 118,251 | 55 |
| 1979 | 212,874 | 92,881 | 44 | 119,993 | 56 |
| 1980 | 238,841 | 104,777 | 44 | 134,064 | 56 |
| 1981 | 244,228 | 104,558 | 43 | 139,670 | 57 |
| 1982 | 236,761 | 99,701 | 42 | 137,060 | 58 |
| 1983 | 251,606 | 109,436 | 43 | 142,170 | 57 |
| 1984 | 252,269 | 109,064 | 43 | 143,205 | 57 |

Source: American Association of Community and Junior Colleges, 1955-1982

## References

Astin, A.W., Green, K.C., Korn, W.S., & Maier, M.J. (1983). *The American freshman: National norms for fall 1983*. Los Angeles: UCLA Higher Education Research Institute.

Bogue, J.P. (1950). *The community college*. New York: McGraw-Hill.

Brawer, F. B. (in press). A longitudinal analysis of community college humanities faculty, 1975-1983. Community College Review.

Bushnell, D. S. (1973). *Organizing for change: New frontiers for community colleges*. New York: McGraw-Hill.

Center for the Study of the Community Colleges. (1983). *The general academic assessment in Los Angeles*. Los Angeles: Author.

Cohen, A. M. (1979). Counting the transfer students. *Junior college resource review*. Los Angeles: ERIC Clearinghouse for Junior Colleges. (ERIC Document Reproduction Service Number 172 864)

Cohen, A.M., & Brawer, F. B. (1982). *The American commmunity college*, San Francisco: Jossey-Bass.

Cross, K. P. (1981). Community colleges on the plateau. *Journal of Higher Education, 52*(2), 113-123.

Green, T. F. (1980), *Predicting the behavior of the educational system*. Syracuse, NY: Syracuse University Press.

Illich, I. (1980). *Deschooling society*. New York: Harper & Row.

McCabe, R. (1981). Now is the time to reform the American community college. *Community and Junior College Journal.* 51(8), 6-10.

Menke, D. H. (1980). *A comparison of transfer and native bachelor's degree recipients at UCLA, 1976-1978*. Unpublished doctoral dissertation, University of California at Los Angeles.

Ravitch, D. (1983). *The troubled crusade: American education, 1945-1980*. New York: Basic Books.

Richardson, R. C., Jr. (1983). *Literacy in the open-access college*. San Francisco: Jossey-Bass.

Sheldon, M. S., & Hunter, R. (1980). *Statewide longitudinal study: Report on academic wear 1978-1979. Part II—spring results*. Woodland Hills, CA: Pierce College. (ERIC Document Reproduction Service No. ED 184 636)

# State Colleges: An Unsettled Quality

## Robert Birnbaum

*The state colleges and regional universities are America's most restless institutions of higher learning. Their history spans less than 150 years, but during that time they have, typically, played four changing roles: as post-high school academies, as normal schools devoted solely to the education of teachers, as four-year liberal arts colleges with strong technical emphasis in teacher education, industrial arts, and home economics, and as comprehensive colleges giving also professional education in engineering and business administration and graduate work at the M.A. level. Some have become regional universities with research programs and Ph.D. degrees. And there still remains an unsettled quality about their functions, standards, offerings, faculties and clientele. They continue to seek a brighter place in the academic sun. (Kerr, 1969, p.vii)*

Clark Kerr's foreword to E. Alden Dunham's *Colleges of the Forgotten Americans* (1969) is as relevant today as it was fifteen years ago. Having largely completed the transformations in mission, program, enrollment, and governance foreseen by Dunham, the state colleges are still relatively invisible, understudied, and not always fully understood or appreciated by legislatures, potential students, and other internal and external constituencies. State colleges have just completed a turbulent era characterized by rapid growth, social and political unrest, significant alterations in program and structure, and insecure funding, and are now entering a period in which a demographically induced enrollment decline promises continued disruption and discontinuity. It can be expected that their "unsettled quality" will continue into the foreseeable future; in fact it may be an irresolvable consequence of the niche they occupy in the higher education system.

For the purposes of this study, the population of "state colleges" includes publicly controlled, four-year institutions other than those engaging in significant doctoral-level education, or those granting a majority of their degrees in a single program area. In 1982-1983, there were 377 state colleges representing 12% of this country's approximately 3,200 institutions of higher education. Their undergraduate enrollments in 1980-81 exceeded 2.04 million, equivalent to 22.4% of all undergraduate enrollments, and 36.6% of undergraduate enrollments in all four-year colleges. They award approximately 30% of all baccalaureate degrees. Enrollments average 2,400 in institutions offering only undergraduate degrees, and 6,700 in state colleges offering diverse masters degrees as well, making them about twice as large as comparable independent institutions in these two categories.

The state colleges are primarily comprehensive institutions placing major emphasis upon professional, rather than liberal arts, programs. In 1980-81, 69% of their degrees were awarded in professional areas such as education, business, health professions, computer science, and public affairs, with 31% given in the liberal arts. Only 36 state colleges (10%) awarded more than half of their baccalaureate degrees in non-professional subjects, while 134 (36%) gave professional degrees to at least three-quarters of their graduates.

Fifteen years ago, one out of every three degrees awarded by state colleges was in the field of education (Harcleroad, 1983); an additional but unknown number of students were also preparing for teacher certification, but received their degrees in the disciplines in which they were to teach. Although they still prepare 40% of the nation's teachers, in 1980-81 these colleges awarded more degrees in business (22.8%) than in any other field, and education degrees declined both in absolute number and as a proportion of all degrees awarded (17.2%).

While still predominantly undergraduate institutions, the state colleges are increasingly involved in graduate work at the M.A. level, and several institutions award a small number of doctoral degrees as well. Most of these graduate degrees are in the field of education, but other professional areas such as business and nursing, as well as a sprinkling of arts and science areas, are also represented. The colleges on average awarded 21% of their 1980-81 degrees at the graduate level, with 69 offering no graduate work and 47 having graduate degrees comprising one-third or more of their total degrees granted. Although 58 of the state colleges awarded doctoral degrees in 1981-82, their proportions were in almost all cases less than 1% of degrees awarded, and in no case higher than 2.8%.

## History

Identifying any large group of institutions by a single label may tend to focus attention upon their very real (but often superficial) similarities, while glossing over differences that may be less evident but more important. Reification of "state colleges" as a type can therefore lead to assuming a homogeneity among individual institutions that, in many cases, are quite dissimilar. Merely comparing the history, traditions, programs, student body, and political environment of the oldest institution now considered a state college (The College of William and Mary, founded in Virginia in 1693), with the youngest (the University of the District of Columbia, founded in 1975), lends some perspective to the wide range of characteristics of state colleges.

To underscore the diversity of state colleges, the group will be here divided into four subgroups; older colleges, multi-colleges, historically black colleges, and new colleges. These divisions are somewhat arbitrary and many state colleges could be placed into more than one of them. In briefly discussing each group, the same caveats concerning the applicability of generalizations to individual institutions should be kept in mind.

### Older Colleges

These are institutions founded prior to 1950 (about half of them before 1910) that maintain a unitary collegiate structure, restrict themselves to undergraduate programs, and focus attention upon career and professional preparation. For most, the initial purpose was the training of teachers, and they typically have moved through developmental stages as normal schools, teachers colleges with degree-granting authority in various fields of education, and more recently as state colleges with significant commitments to education but that also offer degrees in other professional areas as well as the liberal arts.

Their educational tradition and linkage to the school systems from which many drew their faculties often led to the development of college governance structures characterized by centralization, administrative dominance, and lack of faculty participation in decision making. Even though enrollment in education programs may have declined, many colleges still maintain large numbers of education faculty, often with senior rank.

These institutions tend to attract a local student body with intellectual interests and abilities reflecting a cross-section of the top two-thirds of the high school graduates in their feeder area, for whom low cost and propinquity probably prove decisive in the application process. Their parents are likely to view the institution as a safe haven preparing students for the world of work while providing an environment conducive to success and relatively free from the excesses of more cosmopolitan settings. Faculty are likely to be "locals," with strong institutional commitments and ties to the community. Of the traditional trinity of institutional purposes, the primacy of teaching is unquestioned, with service usually limited to activities in nearby communities and research eschewed almost entirely. The names of these older colleges are for the most part unfamiliar to persons outside their home state.

### Multi-Colleges

These institutions share the same historical precedents as the older colleges, but between 1955 and 1975 underwent a transformation of mission, complexity, and structure. Driven by significant enrollment increases, graduate study, liberal arts departments, and other professional schools were grafted onto an existing teacher-education base. University aspirations were developed both by state planners who encouraged them and by the well-trained new faculty who were recruited to serve in them. However, despite the common change of name from "college" to "university," authority to award the doctorate never materialized. The term "regional university" is often used to denote such institutions, although this term also can be used to refer to some non-public colleges as well.

Vestiges of their teacher-training history remain, but education programs at many of these institutions no longer play a dominant role. The rapid growth in the 1960s of arts and sciences, business, engineering, nursing, and other professional areas overwhelmed the older faculty still in place. The newer faculty brought with them fresh values born of the academic revolution, commitments to their discipline rather than to the institution, and a sense of their proper role in governance that were quite incompatible with the previous order. On some campuses, each September may have seen the faculty grow by one-third or more. Opportunities to socialize faculty into the old traditions, to develop consensus over institutional purposes and to weed out the incompetent were lost, and to a great extent the continuing unsettled quality of these institutions may be related to the consequences of this growth, as well as to the responses to external control to which the growth commonly appeared to lead.

The relatively non-selective admissions policy of most multi-colleges results in a student body of modest academic accomplishment, but the size of the institution and its more specialized offerings permit the development of islands of intellectual ferment. Low cost, convenience, and occasionally the availability of a program not available elsewhere may remain the principal reasons for attendance, but some programs may also develop a regional reputation for quality that attracts the more able, and there is often a core of faculty anxious to encourage intellectual inquiry and a group of students eager to participate. In general, however, the climate of the campus is likely to reflect a collegiate culture, and to be predominantly concerned with career preparation and with extracurricular activities.

Although teaching remains the major mission of these institutions, the expertise of a well-trained faculty and the expectations of local communities often combine to move multi-colleges towards significant programs of service, which can take such forms as collecting and analyzing regional economic data, consulting on the development of new social programs, or technically evaluating local environmental policies. Some scholarly work is done, but on many campuses the role of research remains problematic. In some cases, state-wide master plans or governing board directives specifically restrict the involvement of the state college in research, and assign that responsibility to the state university. The ambiguity created by the presence on campus of faculty who may in fact have been recruited because of their research interests, and then placed in an environment lacking institutional research support, leads to tensions which become overt when debating mission statements, promotions and tenure policy, and similar matters.

## Historically Black Colleges

Although often sharing a teacher-training background, these institutions have a different tradition and ethos justifying their identification as a unique state college sub-group. Of the 34 historically black, public, four-year institutions located in 18 states, all but one are state colleges. Almost all of them were founded in Southern and border states after the Civil War in response to the need for literacy and vocational training for black people who were denied access to existing colleges. Until the last quarter century, these institutions were the main sources of black students earning baccalaureates. Even though a majority of black students now attend predominantly white institutions, the historically black colleges still produce 30% of the degrees earned by black students in America.

Twenty-five years ago, the historically black state colleges were characterized (McGrath, 1961) as small institutions with underprepared student bodies and extensive remedial programs, emphasizing professional education in general and teacher education in particular (the only white collar positions generally available at that time to black Americans). The faculty were without terminal degrees, administration was centralized and patriarchal, and facilities were inadequate. Emphasis was placed upon teaching and service to the black community, particularly in the field of education, was considered an important part of institutional mission. Research was virtually unknown. Some dimensions of these institutions were similar to those of the older colleges, but they differed significantly, both in their lower levels of financial support and in the extent to which they existed in an often hostile political and social environment that militated against change or conspicuous self-improvement.

Since that time, the historically black institutions have developed along the same lines as other state colleges, becoming larger and more complex. Support has improved, but not to the level of comparable state institutions that have a predominantly white enrollment. The most serious problems of the historically black colleges, however, may be political rather than fiscal. Established as parallel institutions to offer "separate but equal" education in states unwilling to integrate their higher education systems, they now find their very existence threatened in 17 states by court-mandated orders to integrate the dual higher education systems that have in fact developed. The role of the federal government in this situation is unclear, with presidents of both parties pledging to preserve and support black colleges on the one hand, and the Justice Department bringing suit to integrate black and white state college systems on the other. Clearly, the integration of the systems would mean an end to the distinctive climate and opportunities offered by these institutions, and would seriously diminish the richness and diversity of the higher education system.

**New Colleges**

This category includes 88 institutions founded after 1950. Although some were developed as general-purpose institutions to meet increased enrollment demands, others were founded for three different articulated purposes.

A number of new state colleges were developed with the expressed intent of responding to the "urban crisis." In some cases this referred to explicitly professional colleges specializing in curriculum areas preparing graduates for occupations presumably in short supply in the cities. In others, it meant institutions that would serve inner-city youth, thus creating a new kind of institution—the "predominantly minority" (but not historically black) college.

A second distinctive category of new state colleges includes those developed with a special mission, in areas such as the arts, technology, or the environment. The third category includes those institutions founded to experiment with new delivery systems, and/or the provision of services to constituencies referred to as the "new learners." In some cases, these institutions may offer no instruction, but rather serve to test and certify student knowledge obtained in other settings.

While these new colleges differ significantly as individual institutions, they all share one critical, common characteristic; although they might choose to include teacher education in their curricula, they are unrestrained by the teacher education programs and traditions that so greatly influenced the development of other state colleges. Some still retain their original innovative characteristics. For most, however, the value of starting with a clean slate has been significantly eroded, if not almost completed vitiated, by internal strife, state and constituency pressures to conform to standard procedures or programs, and the difficulty of sustaining innovation with minimal resources.

## Values

The rapid enrollment growth of many of the state colleges, their evolution from a single unifying purpose to multiple and often incompatible purposes, and the increased societal expectations for higher education, have all acted to create a significant identity crisis for these institutions. As Weathersby (1983) points out, they are often easier to define by what they are not (not research institutions, not liberal arts colleges, not community colleges) than by what they are, because whatever distinctiveness they once possessed has been lost. "Such vagueness of purpose and mission has in turn led to confusion in the minds of students, employers, potential donors, and legislators about the identity, purpose, and priorities of these institutions" (p.26).

Given this problem of identity, as well as the differences in the various institutions which make up the sector, it is difficult to specify values that can be said to apply uniformly to all state colleges. There are, however, general similarities in outlook probably shared by a majority of the institutions in the sector.

First, all members of the sector are under public control, and thus are subject to a public bureaucracy that controls many administrative processes, are constantly under public scrutiny and often must discuss sensitive matters under state "sunshine" laws, and are often pressed to respond immediately to state policy initiatives without the opportunity for full campus discussion and consultation. Second, as a consequence of their public status, many of these institutions are caught in an often competitive system in which state college roles, prestige, influence, and resources are defined in relationship to those of the public research universities on one side, and community colleges on the other. Third, most state colleges belong to the American Association of State Colleges and Universities (AASCU), an organization engaged in research, development, publication, and lobbying in support of its members; and AASCU meetings and publications are influential in articulating and sharing values in the sector.

To the extent that a state college *sine qua non* exists, it would probably be the concept of "access." The colleges proudly proclaim their role in serving blue collar, first-generation, middle-American students, and defend the importance of offering education to those not served by "elite" institutions. Access is seen in perhaps its most elemental form at the historically black institutions that have traditionally admitted large numbers of underprepared students who were victimized by inadequate secondary school systems. Even at many of the older or multi-colleges, barriers to admission remain low enough to accommodate students graduating in the top two thirds or three-quarters of their high school class with special procedures set up for dealing with students not meeting even this modest criterion.

Access assumes more than just relatively non-selective admissions requirements, however, and the state colleges strongly believe that higher tuition costs are increasingly becoming a barrier to college attendance. With two other associations, AASCU was instrumental in forming the National Coalition for Lower Tuition in Higher Education, an "organized political effort to work effectively for low tuition, to make possible educational opportunity for all to fight for higher educational appropriations, which are necessary to make low tuition and quality education possible" (*Low Tuition Fact Book, 1983*).

Faced with competition from community colleges, which also support access and low tuition, state colleges are likely to point out to potential students the greater academic expertise of four-year college faculty members as measured by their relatively higher proportion of Ph.D.s, the advantage of remaining in a single institution and completing an entire program rather than suffering the discontinuities of transfer, and the higher completion rates and greater probability of achieving career goals found among students in four-year, as compared with two-year, colleges (Astin, 1977). Challenged for students by public universities in the same state, state colleges can call attention to their emphasis on teaching rather than research, and to the fact that their smaller size will lead to more personal attention. Another advantage that can be marshalled for state college support is that students at a state college will be instructed by experienced faculty, and not by graduate teaching assistants.

Although (with few exceptions) the state colleges are comprehensive institutions offering both liberal arts and professional programs, they clearly emphasize preparing students for careers. For the older institutions and multi-colleges this mission represents a continuation of the teacher-education tradition, although fields such as business currently predominate. Historically black colleges have always emphasized the role of education in preparing students to compete for employment in a discriminatory society, and the new colleges, many developed in urban areas during a period in which "relevance" was a watchword, often matched their programs to the expected vocational interests of their clientele.

The traditional arts and sciences thus play a secondary role in state colleges. They may assume greater importance in the future with renewed interest in "general education" as an essential degree component, although it is questionable whether concerns for improving competency in basic English and computational skills will eventually manifest themselves in more advanced humanities, science, and social science study. On some campuses, the liberal arts faculty have increasing difficulty in recruiting students interested in majoring in their areas; on others, liberal arts faculty see themselves as beleaguered "support departments," rather than as the college's intellectual core.

While many of these values derive from the traditions and expectations of the colleges themselves, they are reinforced by the colleges' status as agencies of the state. Driven by enrollment-related funding formulas, and with few opportunities to buffer themselves financially against short-term reversals, the colleges must offer what students want, regardless of what they may be thought to need, in order to survive. Faced with unlimited demands for service on one side, and the harsh realities of public accountability on the other, the colleges are moving away from a rhetoric of education and towards a rhetoric of administration and management. "Student credit hours per full-time equivalent faculty" becomes a term heard as often in the faculty lounge as in the president's office; fiscal exigency, layoff, and retrenchment become parts of the argot as well as the environment; and discussion of access, quality, and other core values is displaced by contingency planning, new management systems, and the need to collect data for external accountability purposes even though they may have little campus utility.

## The Environment

Because of their mission, public control, and niche in the higher education system, the state colleges will remain vulnerable to developing social, economic, and political forces. In examining the potential effects of demographic changes upon various sectors of higher education, the Carnegie Council (1980) identified the state colleges as occupying a position of average to above-average vulnerability. This means that the sector might expect an undergraduate enrollment decline by 1997 of approximately 10 to 15 percent. Decreases at any specific college could be significantly larger, and would depend upon a number of factors such as location, programs, and the existence of other institutions competing for the same applicant pool.

Institutional resources are dependent upon enrollments, and in the scramble for enrollments created by demographic trends the state colleges are not likely to fare well against either the community colleges, which are usually less expensive and more convenient, or the doctoral or system flagship universities, which are more prestigious.

The state colleges are also not likely to have the political clout of either of these other institutions and so are less likely to achieve increases in public appropriations. Local community college boards often have direct access to revenue sources or agencies. They are usually composed of men and women with important local political connections who can forcefully articulate their college's needs in the battle for community fiscal support, and who both in terms of total numbers and connections, can be an important collective force in battling for additional resources at the state level as well. The trustees of research and flagship universities are fewer in number, but in many states occupy positions considered to be of great prestige and influence. They interact with legislative and executive bodies that often include large numbers of university undergraduate or law school alumni, and in addition may have a state-wide constituency developed through their university extension and outreach activities. In the past, the power of state colleges was often magnified by their close political relationships to state-wide teachers' organizations. But the state colleges' reduced emphasis on education programs has significantly diminished the strength of this traditional coalition.

The lack of a strong political base means not only that the colleges may have greater difficulty in acquiring resources, but also that they are easier targets for retrenchment. A recent study indicated that of 4,000 faculty members (1,200 with tenure) laid off or dismissed in the past five years in four-year colleges and universities, virtually all came either from state colleges or less-well known private institutions (Scully, 1983).

In search for new clientele, state colleges are likely to try to strengthen their positions in technical education, life-long learning, and community service, thus competing head-on with community colleges. They are also likely to expand their range of graduate offerings, particularly in professional areas, thus increasing their competition with the public universities. In both cases the political constraints they will encounter, from other institutions as well as from state coordinating boards, suggest that they are not likely to fare well.

The projected demographic changes will create many critical problems for the state colleges. As interest in career-related programs increases, issues such as the nature of general education and the relationship of the college to business and industry will have to be addressed. Enrollment shifts may force consideration of the very survival of certain traditional arts and sciences departments, and raise questions concerning what the "minimum core" of the liberal arts must be. Greater interest in accepting transfer students from community colleges may create increased difficulty in articulating programs to permit two-year students to transfer their previous work into the upper division. And, the state colleges will have to continue to experiment with new delivery systems and materials to respond to part-time, older students and other "new learner" populations, thus placing greater stress on already overloaded administrative structures and further reducing the possibility of developing a sense of campus community.

## Resources

The personnel, facilities, and financial resources of individual state colleges are related to a number of variables including their history, location, and size.

State college faculty increasingly have terminal degrees in the areas in which they teach, although there are still smaller and more isolated campuses at which a faculty member with a doctorate is the exception rather than the rule. Along with other faculty, their earnings have been significantly eroded over the past decade. Average salaries in comprehensive state colleges in 1982-83 were $26,940, and in general baccalaureate state colleges $24,490 (American Association of University Professors, 1983). Their average salaries, as well as their salaries at each rank except instructor, were lower than those at public universities. The largest difference was at the full professor rank, with universities averaging $38,180, comprehensive state colleges $33,490, and baccalaureate state colleges $30,770. The average teaching load is about 12 contact hours a week (American Association of State Colleges and Universities, 1983b), higher than the 6 to 9-hour loads typically expected of university faculty. State college faculty are quick to notice these differences in teaching responsibilities and compensation—particularly in systems in which both types of institution are controlled by a single board—and to recognize that they reflect public perception of the state college's place in the academic pecking order.

Facilities run the gamut from outstanding to inadequate. In many states, community college physical plants, more recently constructed and less constrained by the regulations of state building agencies, are both more attractive and more functional than those of the four-year colleges. Libraries, science laboratories, and areas for instruction in technological subjects in particular were often constructed at state colleges for a smaller and more specialized student body, and may not have been improved to support new activities. Capital projects of any magnitude require approval at various levels of state government and often depend upon voter approval of bond issues. The state colleges are usually at a political disadvantage when they attempt to compete with public universities for these funds.

Over the past decade, due to depressed economies and projections of enrollment downturns, states have been particularly reluctant to approve new college buildings, and it is unlikely that in the near future those institutions with significant capital needs will find any relief. At the same time, renovations and other maintenance needs have been deferred to effect short-term savings. Since it is politically easier to justify the maintenance of buildings than the maintenance of faculty, some colleges may be called upon over the next few years to make budget trade-offs, and cut faculty to support the physical plant.

Equipment budgets have been particularly problematic for many state colleges. The movement into new scientific and technological arenas has not always been accompanied by appropriate equipment support. Expensive machinery or electronic components may be viewed as frills and disallowed by state budget offices, even though they are critical to the development of a sound program. Many colleges rely as much on gifts of used equipment from industry as on their own operating budget—when they can get the equipment at all. Particularly when dealing with rapidly changing biological and physical sciences, and high technology areas such as computer science, the colleges often find themselves instructing students on equipment no longer in use in the workplace.

This equipment problem has been exacerbated in recent years by restricted state budget support, and the tendency of colleges when faced with budget constraints to transfer funds from equipment and other accounts in order to maintain faculty positions. As a consequence, support for library books and equipment has become a critical issue for many campuses.

The educational and general revenues for the state colleges in fiscal 1981 came primarily from state and local appropriations (64%) and from tuition (19%), revenue sources that are highly sensitive to enrollment levels. Approximately 2% of revenues was from gifts and grants with 5% from other sources, and 10% from government grants and contracts, for a total of 17%. In contrast, public university revenues in these latter three categories were 4%, 7%, and 15% respectively, thus affording universities a larger buffer (26%) against revenue losses caused by enrollment declines or vagaries of the state.

## The Chimera of Excellence

Excellence is easy to support, but difficult to define. Over the past 40 years in higher education the one word has come to refer to a rather narrow range of beliefs, activities, and outcomes, focusing attention primarily upon cognitive performance and meritocratic values. These are the characteristics of the "university colleges," which Jencks and Riesmen (1968) identified as providing the model to which other colleges aspire, but can never really achieve.

Probably nowhere in American higher education is the discrepancy between aspiration and performance more apparent than at the state colleges. Dunham (1969) clearly identified the irony that the developing transformation of their values (sometimes internally induced, sometimes externally imposed) has the potential to change first-class teachers colleges into third-class universities. However, even modest universities can evidence aspects of "excellence" if the definition is expanded sufficiently to include a wider range of desirable values.

### The Dimensions of Excellence

Excellence is commonly thought of in terms of the academic performance of students as measured by achievement tests, of faculty qualifications as reflected in scholarly accomplishment, or of the reputation of an institution. Compared to major universities and selective independent liberal arts college, state colleges must be judged deficient on all these counts. Such a judgment, however, tends to overlook at least four important issues. First, colleges have many goals, not just ostensibly academic ones. Second, academic goals themselves are often multiple, conflicting, and inconsistent. Third, the organizational and institutional structures and processes that facilitate the effective achievement of one goal often inhibit the achievement of another. There exists no college that can optimize achievement of *all* its goals. And fourth, perceptions of excellence depend on the constituency making the judgment. Legislators and parents, foundations and community groups, administrators and alumni, cosmopolitan faculty and locals, Merit Scholars and remedial students —all are likely to have legitimate definitions that differ markedly.

The notion of excellence also tends to become confused with other ideas that appear equally desirable, if no less difficult to specify—such as "standards," "educational effectiveness," and "quality." Of these, the concepts of standards and quality appear to denote student requirements or achievements at or above a stated criterion, while excellence and effectiveness may be considered related to the impact that an institution has upon performance. Since institutions have many purposes, it may be presumed that excellence or effectiveness may be of various kinds, and in fact one scholar has developed an instrument to measure nine "dimensions" of effectiveness as seen by various campus constituencies. These include student educational satisfaction, student academic development, student career development, faculty and administrator employment satisfaction, professional development and quality of faculty, system openness and community interaction, ability to acquire resources, and organizational health (Cameron, 1982). Of these, only two (student academic development and faculty quality) appear to be related to commonly held notions of excellence.

The relatively undimensional views in rhetorical vogue today ironically ignore the pluralistic approach to values that John Gardner (1961) identified as a foundation of excellence. This does not mean that all values are of equal worth in an institution of higher education, but it does suggest that there is no definition that can be universally employed.

## The Measurement of Performance

Even if we accept a narrow definition of excellence involving only student intellectual outcomes, the problem of measuring excellence is not resolved. At least two approaches, criterion-referenced or value-added, can be taken. Using the former, we can presumably evaluate the comparative excellence of two institutions by measuring the knowledge or skills of the students they produce and comparing them to benchmarks. The institutions whose students obtain the higher test scores would by definition have the greater degree of excellence.

The value-added concept looks at the extent to which student performance has changed as a result of the college experience, rather than at the level of achievement reached. Institutions whose students evidenced the greatest amount of improvement would be judged excellent using this approach to measurement, regardless of the student's absolute performance level.

Comparisons of the quality of institutional student "outputs" indicate that they are related to the quality of student inputs so that relatively non-selective state colleges would be expected to have graduates with lower scores than the graduates of more selective institutions. However, there is no evidence to indicate that when the academic achievement of entering students is statistically controlled, the performance of students graduating from state colleges is noticeably higher or lower than that of students at other types of institutions.

It would probably be accepted as a matter of faith that, in general, state colleges have not achieved the same level of "excellence" as have selective liberal arts colleges or flagship research universities. It seems clear, though, that public perceptions of excellence depend not on educational process or on output, rather, on input. High standards of admission are considered to be evidence of excellence. To a great extent this creates a no-win situation for state colleges: low admissions requirements and extensive remedial education lead to demands for "standards;" low admission requirements and high attrition call forth attacks upon the "revolving door." But raising admissions requirements challenges the essential mission of the colleges to offer access to students of varying background and abilities.

Considering the dimensions of these issues provides new ways of looking at the concept of excellence. At some state colleges excellence will be achieved as scholarly and proficient faculty provide instruction to well-prepared and sophisticated high school graduates and hold them to universal standards of performance. At others, excellence will mean that dedicated faculty will introduce provincial students for the first time to profound ideas that will transform some and be ignored by others. Excellence may also be found at a college which accepts disadvantaged students and, in addition to providing basic skills and advanced vocational and technical training, significantly improves their self-image, feelings of competence, and dedication to community service. A state college can also find excellence in serving as a protective halfway house for potentially brilliant students who would be unable to cope immediately with a university environment, as a workshop in which students can experience racial integration for the first time and develop the understanding and tolerance necessary for helping to build a multicultural society, or as a training center from which business and industry can draw competent and stable students to fill technically demanding positions. Through various activities state colleges can also increase the aspirations of potential students, expand the cultural life of a community, assist its economy, and provide opportunities for life-long learning. In these, and many other ways, "excellence" can be manifested, even if it cannot be precisely measured.

## External Constraints on Excellence

While there may be disagreement concerning the dimensions of excellence, there are clearly a number of factors that make it difficult for some state colleges to be as effective as they might. Externally these factors include state/system coordination and control, funding provisions, and collective bargaining.

**State coordination and control.** During the past 15 years there has been an increasing tendency for decisions of campus importance to be made by groups external to the campus. In some states, individual state colleges have no independent board of trustees and are controlled instead by a single consolidated governing board responsible for a system of two or more institutions. These systems sometimes also include institutions that are not state colleges. There are 118 state colleges (31% of the total) functioning under such an arrangement. In addition, there are a large number of state colleges that have their own trustees but that remain subject to the authority of a state coordinating board that has extensive budgeting and rule-making authority. Both consolidated governing bodies and state-wide coordinating agencies can be referred to generically as "superboards." In most cases, institutions in states without superboards are subject to similar control and review by other agencies of state government, particularly in their fiscal and capital operations.

The actions of superboards tend to remove from direct campus control many critical aspects of institutional functioning, often including new program development, facilities planning, personnel policies, administrative structure, research activities, internal budget allocation, and the like. In the name of accountability such agencies can become exceptionally intrusive concerning the internal conduct of campus business. Moreover, the need to deal with a large number of disparate institutions leads to the creation of uniform regulations to bring presumed order out of apparent chaos and to offer the appearance of fairness. Many such systems were created both to provide governmental oversight and to protect the campuses from improper governmental intrusion. The ambiguity of this charge is difficult to resolve to the mutual satisfaction of both campuses and governors, and faculty and administrators at many institutions are convinced that these agencies exist primarily to carry out the will of the state, rather than to protect important institutional interests.

Superboard members are usually political appointees and, like all trustees, fulfill their responsibilities on a volunteer, part-time basis. As these systems have become more complex and difficult for lay persons to understand, effective influence has often shifted from superboards themselves to their staffs, which conduct the day-to-day business of the boards. As the locus of functional authority moves sequentially from campus trustees, then to superboards, and finally to complex state bureaucracies, colleges may begin to operate more as regulated utilities than as institutions with an identifiable character, style, and environment.

It can be debated whether the decisions made by disinterested superboards, acting from a broader perspective and assisted by extensive staff expertise, are "better" than those made by local campuses with more parochial and presumably self-serving interests in mind. Even if data were available to inform such arguments, they miss an essential point. Placing limitations on campus autonomy leads to feelings of powerlessness and anger on the part of college faculty and administration alike. Their sense of ownership of the enterprise is eroded, their professions become a job, and accountability disappears because authority is too diffused to be grasped. Faculty may find refuge in their personnel interests; administrators may find it in adherence to rules and regulations. The acknowledged reduction in morale and levels of personal commitment is evident to the state, and is used to justify further intrusions.

**Funding provisions.** State college funding arrangements have several common characteristics: they are enrollment driven or enrollment related, provide limited flexibility, offer few incentives for prudent management, and are uncertain. Each of these can severely constrain an institution's concern with excellence.

Enrollment-related formulas as a primary mechanism for determining support levels for state colleges were a major advantage during the growth era of the recent past but are now a significant handicap as colleges enter a period of stasis or decline. Although some states have moved beyond simple formulas toward more sophisticated models with time-lag provisions, and others are attempting to develop non-enrollment-related alternatives, many state colleges have little protection from environmental shifts. Issues related to student retention, grading, and transfer, for example, must thus be considered with an eye towards their impact on enrollment as well as upon educational quality. Low enrollment programs, regardless of their educational merit, are particularly vulnerable, not only from administrators under pressure to reallocate resources but also from superboard staff members anxious to identify (and then to regulate) such "obvious" examples of inefficiency and organizational slack.

**Regulations that limit flexibility.** Regulations often constrain the expenditure of funds even after they are allocated to a campus. In many institutions, budget line items developed 18 months earlier cannot be channeled to different areas which a changed environment might require without extensive negotiation with, or approval by, various state agencies. Other rules (in areas such as purchasing, for example) often prevent colleges from securing supplies and equipment not covered by master state purchase agreements, or require extended sequences of advertising and bidding with absurdly low dollar thresholds. These kinds of limits upon flexibility prevent administrators from responding to emerging needs in a timely manner, and contribute to feelings of powerlessness. They can also create tensions between administrators and faculty who, unaware of external constraints, are likely to attribute intolerable delays to inefficiency and lack of support for academic priorities on the part of campus administrators.

**Incentives for prudent management.** Management incentives are provided to a college if money saved by efficiency in one area can be applied to another, and savings generated during one time period can be used in the future. At public institutions, inflexibility in making expenditures inhibits the former; the annual budget and appropriation cycles of the state usually prevent the latter. For most colleges, funds must be spent in the year appropriated, and unexpended balances revert back to the state treasury. At many campuses, this inflexibility leads to end-of-budget-year spending orgies for equipment and supplies, whether essential or not. This apparent irrationality becomes understandable when it is realized that state budget offices may use the existence of unexpended balances (often created by their own byzantine regulations) to reduce future budgets on the grounds that they indicate a lack of need.

**Uncertainty.** In state college budget support, uncertainty is an accepted phenomenon, but one which has recently taken on new dimensions. In the past, state colleges would typically plan their budgets in cycles beginning 18 months or more before the fiscal year, even though the actual appropriations would, in some cases, not be decided upon until the fiscal year was well underway. Under such circumstances, institutions had to be extremely conservative in making expenditure decisions, and positions often remained unfilled because they were approved too late to permit adequate recruitment. Once authorized, however, institutions could generally count on expending their annual budgets, subject only to the annoyances in some states of pre-audit controls, and the regular demands in other states for savings during the current year.

Within the past few years, however, this has changed. Colleges in some states have been faced with the threat, and in some cases the actuality, of significantly altered budgets resulting from state fiscal crises during the current fiscal year itself. In some cases projected discontinuities have been great enough to lead superboards to propose changes in personnel policies that would permit colleges to circumvent existing regulations concerning periods of notice of faculty termination, or to specify criteria for a declaration of "fiscal exigency" that would presumably permit the layoff of tenured faculty in response to sudden financial shortfalls. The effects on faculty morale of such proposals, let alone their implementation, can be devastating.

**Collective bargaining.** Contracts with faculty unions exist on approximately one-third of all state college campuses, making them one of the most unionized sectors of American higher education. Although bargaining appears to be related to reduced institutional effectiveness (Cameron, 1982), it is likely that bargaining is a consequence of ineffectiveness rather than a cause. To a great extent, faculty interest in unionization is a defensive response to the feeling of powerlessness and loss of campus control created by increased intrusion of the state. Once in place, however, unionization may ironically tend to strengthen the centralization that created a desire for it. It may also accelerate tendencies towards uniformity (particularly in multicampus systems in which one contract is negotiated covering all institutions), towards loss of academic focus (particularly in those situations in which employees other than faculty belong to, or are a majority of, the bargaining unit), and toward increased intrusion by the state (particularly in states in which "management" is represented at the bargaining table by a public official unrelated to the college administration or board).

## Internal Constraints on Excellence

The status and expectations of faculty, and the background and preparation of students, are important internal considerations affecting institutional excellence.

**The status and expectations of faculty.** Probably the single most critical faculty-related influence currently affecting organizational functioning in many state colleges is high tenure density. Until recently, it was common practice to award tenure to almost all faculty members completing the probationary period. Although aggregate data (NCES, 1980) indicate that approximately 62% of full-time faculty in public four-year institutions are tenured (higher than the 54% seen in all institutional types combined), a large number of the state colleges have a tenure density of between 75% and 90%. This builds inflexibility into the system, as it becomes difficult or impossible over the short term to adjust staffing allocations in response to discontinuities in enrollment patterns. Tenure density poses a particular problem for the state colleges because they cannot increase flexibility through the use of graduate assistants as the universities do, nor do they rely on part-time instruction to the extent of community colleges.

A related phenomenon is the tension that exists on some campuses between the "old" faculty, often from education or related areas, with doctorates (if they have them) from second-tier graduate institutions, little if any scholarly productivity, and senior rank, and the "new" faculty, often of lower rank, trained in research-oriented doctoral programs of national reputation, and recruited to bring their institution into the academic mainstream. These two groups are likely to have different expectations about the proper processes and criteria for personnel actions such as promotion, differing perceptions about the appropriate role of faculty in governance, and different views of what the role and mission of the institution should be. Given the frequent lack of a clear institutional identity there are often no consistent norms or values that can help to resolve these differences, and the contending parties may fall back upon bureaucratic or political mechanisms to arrange temporary working truces. If consensus cannot be developed on the relative emphasis that should be placed on teaching (or the means of assessing it), or the importance of scholarship and publication, then seniority reigns by default. The old guard versus young Turks conflict is present in its rawest form when junior faculty see themselves held to new standards of performance that were not applied to the senior faculty who now judge them, and high tenure densities mean a lower probability of achieving tenure, even for the best and the brightest of the newcomers.

**Students.** State college students cover a wide range of abilities and aspirations that in many ways makes them typical of higher education enrollment in general. Compared to freshmen at all institutions in 1983, for example, state college freshmen closely resembled overall averages in their political orientations, high school grade distribution and rank in class, family income distribution, high school courses taken, and in the proportion planning to study for a higher degree (Astin, Green, Korn & Maier, 1983). As with other freshmen, their major reasons for going to college were (in rank order) to get a better job, to learn more about things, and to make more money.

Approximately 39% of state college freshmen report high school averages of B + or higher, making them, on average, academically stronger than students in some institutional categories (for example, public community colleges, where the figure is 27%), but weaker than students at others (for example, public universities, where the figure is 54%). Approximately 21% of state college freshmen report high school grades of C + or lower, identical to the national average but twice as high as in public universities. It is likely that at all levels of academic performance there are a number of indifferent students for whom college is a socially acceptable means of marking time. It may even be that this number is increasing.

## Conclusions about Excellence

An assessment of the present level of excellence in the state colleges depends to a great extent upon the definitions chosen and the reference groups selected. Although there are few hard data to support any clear conclusions, one would be hard-pressed to develop a strong case that the alleged "rising tide of mediocrity" has diminished the effectiveness of the state colleges as a group. Indeed, both short-term and long-term evidence suggest the contrary.

**Short-term data.** An example of short-term data includes a recent survey of higher education institutions (Watkins, 1983b) in which chief academic officers reported that new faculty hired in 1982 were more competent than those hired a year earlier. These data, disaggregated for state colleges, further indicated that faculty were seen as more concerned about their teaching and student advisement responsiblities, more willing to innovate, and more productive in terms of research and scholarship than previously. Overall, 58% of the respondents considered the quality of state college faculty performance to be increasing, while only 3% believed it to be decreasing. At the same time, it was reported that secretarial and related support for faculty was decreasing (although support for research was up), teaching loads had slightly increased, and other workload responsibilities in advising, committee work, and related non-classroom functions had become higher. In general, it appeared as if resources to support the enterprise had diminished, but quality, at least in terms of faculty performance, had increased.

A similar earlier survey (Minter & Bowen, 1980) compared the characteristics of state college faculty, students, and finances in 1979-80 with those of the previous year. Again, teaching load, advising, and committee responsibilities were all seen as increasing, while secretarial and travel support were seen as decreasing. In addition, the survey asked state college chief academic officers, student personnel officers, senior faculty, student newspaper editors, and presidents of student bodies to evaluate changes in the quality and content of educational programs during this time period. The general consensus of all groups (with the occasional disagreement of the student newspaper editor) was that there had been improvement in the overall quality of the learning environment, the quality, competence, and performance of the faculty, the rigor of academic standards, the availability of a wide range of student services, and creativity and innovation in teaching. Overall, the chief academic officers and chief student personnel officers of state colleges overwhelmingly reported an increase in the "overall quality of student learning." The presidents of these institutions reported the same patterns of increased effectiveness and decreased resources. Although almost 60% of the presidents surveyed said their institution was losing ground financially, 48% said the academic condition of the institution was improving (none said it was losing ground), and 52% noted an increase in the quality of student services.

**Long-term data.** The responses of college presidents must be viewed with a good deal of caution. Presidents tend to be optimistic, particularly when reviewing changes of quality that have taken place under their stewardship (presumably as a consequence of their educational and fiscal leadership). Faculty, on the other hand, may tend to be much more critical about their institutions. For this reason, the results of a recent study (Anderson, 1983a) of faculty perceptions of changes in institutional functioning over the 10 year period from 1970 to 1980 is instructive. Based upon responses to the Institutional Functioning Inventory (IFI), state college faculty perceived improvements in a number of areas, including development of the intellectual and aesthetic extracurriculum, concern for undergraduate learning, and concern for advancing knowledge on their campuses during this 10 year period. At the same time, they saw their colleges as becoming more diverse in terms of the backgrounds of students and faculty, and as being more concerned with meeting local needs than had previously been the case.

In addition, there appeared to be a slight increase in faculty morale during this 10 year period, even though morale at these institutions continued to be among the lowest of all institutional types included in the study. A review of state college faculty responses to specific IFI items (Anderson, 1983b) related to concern for undergraduate teaching indicates that, compared to 1970, faculty in 1980 were more concerned about how to communicate knowledge to students, more willing to talk to students about their personal concerns, more sensitive to the needs and aspirations of students, and more willing to consider teaching effectiveness in recruiting new faculty. Complementing this emphasis upon teaching, faculty also saw research and related scholarly activities receiving greater emphasis by college administrations and boards, and being reflected in an increase in faculty publications. When asked to respond to the item "The college is doing a successful job in achieving its various goals," 65% of the faculty agreed in 1980, compared to 59% in 1970.

If the quality of faculty and programs is seen as improving, there is a general consensus that the quality of state college students, as defined by traditional measures, has been deteriorating. State college student scores on the Scholastic Aptitude Test declined moderately between 1970 and 1980, paralleling the decline seen in all other higher education sectors (Anderson, 1983a). Chief academic officers at state colleges reported declines between 1978-79 and 1979-80 in the secondary school preparation of their students in reading, writing, and mathematical skills, and in preparation in the humanities, social sciences, and sciences (Minter & Bowen, 1980). More recent data collected from chief academic officers suggests that there has been little if any improvement in student preparation, even though academic standards and grading practices are reported to be more rigorous (Watkins, 1983a).

**Evaluating the level of excellence.** There is a tendency to define a problem in terms of availability of data. Pointing to test scores and relying on judgmental reports, recent criticisms of higher education have tended to obscure the fact that there is a dearth of information that might reflect educational quality more directly. The data now available do not tell us whether students are now learning more or less than in the past, whether the increase in remedial education has resulted in more or less social justice, whether graduates are more or less able to function as effective citizens and workers, or whether the state college student is more or less likely to lead a life of increased meaning and reward as consequence of having matriculated.

To some extent, present concern about the state colleges is a reflection of the continuing tension in this country between the proponents of mass and elite higher education. Critics of the level of excellence in the state colleges point to lower admissions test scores and increases in the number of remedial courses offered as indicators of serious problems requiring attention. These criticisms are often leveled without recognition of the political and social environment which led these institutions to become more flexible in offering admission to previously underrepresented groups and to take steps to ensure that the open door offered reasonable opportunities for success for these underprepared students.

It is useful to examine the condition of excellence in the state colleges and to ask how they might be improved. At the same time, considering their political and financial constraints, their heterogeneous student bodies, and the many conflicting claims on their resources and energies, an equally intriguing question is how they have managed to be as successful as they have been. Care must be taken to avoid having well-meaning proposals inadvertently disrupt those aspects of institutional functioning that have permitted the creditable performance of a most difficult task.

The major thrust of recommendations by national as well as by state-wide commissions and study groups working to improve the quality of the state colleges appears to focus attention upon raising admissions standards and on moving towards the elimination of remedial courses at the college level. These are appealing ideas to some, not only because they begin to clarify some of the differences between secondary and higher education that have become blurred over the past decade, but also because they are likely to reduce enrollments and save state funds.

The nature of the proposed solutions puts into bold relief the underlying values accompanying the concept of "excellence." The solutions appear to be based on a criterion-reference rather than a value-added approach, and to take a unidimensional rather than a multidimensional view. They apparently accept the notion that quality can be improved by inspection, rather than be built in by the application of resources to students, and also seem to think that excellence can be appropriately addressed by controlling input rather than by improving the delivery systems and strengthening the educational process.

Two diametrically opposing approaches can be taken towards of achieving excellence in the state colleges: one remedial, the other developmental. The remedial approach finds great deficiencies in the quality of the state colleges that must be corrected through bold initiatives. These include delineating the mission of the colleges with greater precision, raising admissions standards, requiring satisfactory student scores on achievement tests as a condition for moving from sophomore to junior status, further centralizing program development and curriculum evaluation processes to assure uniform application of traditional quality standards, and abolishing tenure or reducing the time required for notice of faculty termination to make allocation of personnel resources more responsive to student needs. Each of these structural changes might increase excellence as traditionally defined, but could also have significant unintended and unavoidable negative, long term consequences. For example, centralizing program criteria and review processes could stifle innovation, and abolishing tenure would almost certainly reduce faculty esprit and institutional commitment, and lead to an increase in faculty unrest. And, while erecting barriers to access will raise test scores, this is unlikely to increase social equity, or raise the level of national discourse.

The developmental approach recognizes that the condition of the state colleges is the result of many societal and educational forces over which the colleges have had relatively little control. To try to delimit the goals of these institutions is, in a real sense, an attempt to delimit the goals of the complex, multifaceted society that these colleges have been asked to serve. The developmental alternative is to maintain the present configuration of these colleges and attempt to improve them at the margins. Fiscal support for programs and activities that enrich and refresh tired faculty, support services that demonstrate societal commitment to the education of the young, enough budget slack to make life more pleasant (but not luxurious), and sufficient autonomy to encourage people of talent and conviction to consider campus administration as a career—each of these could make a real contribution to state college excellence, however, defined.

## Notes

1. Using the new classification system of the National Center for Educational Statistics (NCES), the category "State Colleges" includes 256 public colleges identified as "Comprehensive Institutions," and 121 categorized as "General Baccalaureate Institutions." The concept of "comprehensive" as used by NCES refers to the extent to which an institution offers post-baccalaureate, non-doctoral programs. In contrast, in this study the term "comprehensive" is used to refer to institutions characterized by a mix of liberal arts and professional programs such that no more that 80% of its degrees are awarded in either category.

2. Unless otherwise identified, statistics contained in this paper have been calculated by the author from data supplied by the National Center for Higher Education Management Systems (NCHEMS) from current NCES tapes.

## References

American Association of State Colleges and Universities (1983a). *Low tuition fact book*. Washington, DC: Author.

American Association of State Colleges and Universities (1983b). *Salaries, benefits, and teaching loads of member institutions*. Unpublished research report. Washington, DC: Author.

American Association of University Professors (1983). The annual report on the economic status of the profession, 1982-1983. *Academe, 69*, 2-75.

Anderson, R.E. (1983a). *Finance and effectiveness: A study of college environments*, Princeton, N.J: Educational Testing Service.

Anderson, R.E. (1983b). Unpublished data, Institute for Higher Education, Teachers College, Columbia University.

Astin, A.W. (1977). *Four critical years*. San Francisco: Jossey-Bass.

Astin, A.W. King, M., Light, J.M. & Richardson, G.T. (1973). *The American college freshman: National norms for fall 1973*. Los Angeles: Cooperative Institutional Research Program, University of California at Los Angeles.

Astin, A.W., Green, K.C., Korn, W.S., & Maier, M.J. (1983). *The American freshman: National norms for fall 1983*. Los Angeles: UCLA Higher Education Research Institute.

Cameron, K. (1982). The relationship between faculty unionism and organizational effectiveness. *Academy of Management Journal, 25*, 6-24.

Carnegie Council on Policy Studies in Higher Education (1980). *Three thousand futures: The next twenty years for higher education*. San Francisco: Jossey-Bass.

Dunham, E.A. (1969). *Colleges of the forgotten Americans*. New York: McGraw-Hill.

Gardner, J.W. (1961). *Excellence: Can we be equal and excellent too:?* New York: Harper & Bros.

Harcleroad, F.F. (1983). *The comprehensive public state colleges and universities in America: A pocket history*. Washington, D.C. American Association of State Colleges and Universities.

Jencks, C., and Riesman, D. (1968). *The academic revolution,* New York: Doubleday.

Kerr, C. (1969). Foreword. In E.A. Dunham. *Colleges of the forgotten Americans*. New York: McGraw-Hill.

Kuh, G.D. (1981). *Indices of quality in the undergraduate experience*. Washington, D.C.: American Association for Higher Education.

McGrath, E.J. (1961). *The predominantly Negro colleges and universities in transition*. New York: Teachers College, Columbia University.

Minter, W. J., & Bowen, H.R. (1980). *Preserving America's investment in human capital*. Washington, DC.: American Association of State Colleges and Universities.

National Center for Educational Statistics (1980). *The condition of education*, 1980 edition. Washington, D.C: Author.

Office for Advancement of Public Negro Colleges (1982). *A national resource: Historically public black colleges and universities*. Washington, DC: author.

Scully, M.G. (1983). 4,000 faculty members laid off in 5 years by 4-year institutions, survey shows. *Chronicle of Higher Education, 28*, 21.

Watkins, B. T. (1983a). Basic Skills of college-bound students show improvement, survey finds. *Chronicle of Higher Education, 28*, 1, 8.

Watkins, B.T. (1983b). Competence of new teachers improving, faculty quality up: survey finds. *Chronicle of Higher Education, 28*, 1, 14.

Weathersby, G.B. (1983). State colleges in transition. In J. Froomkin (Ed.). *The crisis in higher education*. New York: The Academy of Political Science.

# Issues

## III.1

# Academic Culture

## PETER SELDIN

Most, if not all, of those involved in academic pursuits would probably agree that colleges and universities — like individuals — have unique personalities. The institution's personality is known as its academic culture, and this academic culture has a lot to do with the way an institution goes about its daily business.

Academic culture is the unspoken language that tells administrators, faculty, staff, and students what is important, what is unimportant, and how they are expected to do things. In a sense, it is the ropes to know and the ropes to skip.

Loosely defined, academic culture is the amalgam of beliefs, mythology, values and tones that — even more than students and faculty — sets one institution apart from another. Most people know it as "the way we do things around here." Louis (1982) reports that these customary ways of perceiving and acting provide organizational members with clear and widely shared answers to such practical issues as (1) Who's who and who matters here, (2) How are things done around here and why, and (3) What really matters here and why?

Academic culture is a term that "describes" rather than "evaluates." It is concerned with people's general perception rather than specifically with their opinion of the college or university. For example, at one institution the department chair may wield considerable power and at another the department chair may be almost impotent. At one institution the faculty may be pressed to do extensive research and publication and at another such involvement may be at best casually regarded. One institution may encourage and support faculty, another deal with the faculty as adversaries.

Why should administrative staff, faculty, and students have a good understanding of academic culture? Deal and Kennedy (1982) offer two important reasons: (1) where a culture is clearly defined and the social information network generates widely-shared values and beliefs about the college or university — what it does and how it does it — people associated with the institution come to believe that they are part of something important and take pride in their work, and (2) one must understand and be comfortable with a culture in order to succeed in it. After several years of our exposure to a culture and its values and norms, it becomes a part of us. We become socialized by the cues, information, and behavior we see around us. Such a learning process is difficult to reverse. As a result, an administrator or faculty member attempting to move from one academic culture to another that is completely different is likely to encounter substantial difficulty in making the change.

If colleges and universities are asked to describe themselves, most will use glowing phrases similar to those used by hundreds of others. Just look at their brochures and catalogs. Virtually all institutions report that they are fervently dedicated to their students, ethical beyond a fault, fair to faculty and other employees, good neighbors, beloved by students, and admired by competitors.

# Two Examples

But this idealized self-portrait, even if arguably true (which it frequently is not), is open to challenge by those with a different perspective. And, moreover, it does not relate to the subtle and intangible aspects of the institution's academic culture. To sharpen the focus of inquiry on this topic, Seldin (1986) describes two quite different institutions. He calls them College "A" and College "B." By design they represent opposite ends of a continuum. Most colleges, of course, will fall somewhere in between.

## College "A"

Most professors at college "A" feel largely negative toward their institution. They believe that their hard work and seriousness of purpose are neither recognized nor rewarded. They complain about the absense of administrative support for faculty needs. They experience frequent conflict and back-biting between and among professors. They are angry and hurt that no one asks for their opinion about important academic issues.

The vast majority of professors share these feelings. As a result, they have become increasingly reluctant to give that extra little bit in their teaching, research, and service. In short, many of them just don't give a damn anymore.

## College "B"

This institution is the equivalent of academic nirvana. Professors at college "B" are enthusiastic and positive in their feelings about their institution. They experience an environment in which cooperation and mutual support among colleagues is commonplace. They believe that their intensive effort as teachers, researchers, and members of committees is genuinely appreciated. They know it is rewarded. They believe — with justification — that they are actively involved in academic decisions that matter.

The vast majority of professors at college "B" have these feelings. And, because they do, they willingly put in the additional time and energy necessary to excel in their work.

It would be deceptively easy to attribute the difference between the performance of professors at college "A" and college "B" to contrasting pay schedules, to the size of the institution, or to personality differences. But, in truth, when examined closely, these differences disappear as critical factors. What remains is the key ingredient that accounts for the difference in the attitudes and performance of professors at the two institutions. What remains is two vastly different academic cultures.

# The Elements of Culture

What are the definable elements of academic culture? Deal and Kennedy (1982) suggest four factors:

1. SHARED VALUES.   These are the basic concepts and beliefs of an organization. To put it another way, they are "what the institution stands for." In general, administrators, faculty and staff learn values from experience — from testing what does and what does not work in dealing with others on campus.

2. HEROES AND HEROINES.   These people personify the basic values of the institution's culture

and provide tangible role models. They have unshakable character and style. They are the ones everyone counts on when things get tough.

3. RITUALS AND CEREMONIES.   These are the formal and informal guidelines for behavior. They provide order and continuity. Rituals show people what is important, and how and where things are done. Ceremonies provide visible evidence of what a college or university stands for. For example, conducting Moving Up Day for students, or displaying a photograph of the Professor of the Year.

4. THE CULTURAL NETWORK.   This is the primary — but informal — means of communicating culture to members within the college or university community. This network spreads the lore that reinforces core values of the culture through myths and stories about its heroes and heroines.

# Diagnosing Academic Culture from the Inside

Since academic culture is so important, the obvious question is, can someone who is a member of the college or university get an accurate picture of it? The answer is yes. The key point here is that insiders, who are trying to learn about the academic culture in their institution, must disregard their biases and beliefs: instead, they must record what is seen and heard. The following list of cultural characteristics has been adapted from Schuster (1985); Robbins (1984); Likert (1967); and from experience. In order to clarify the meaning of each item, a question or two will be added.

1. INDIVIDUAL AUTONOMY.   What degree of responsibility, independence, and opportunity do individuals in the institution actually have?

2. STRUCTURE.   To what degree are rules and regulations used to control faculty, administrative staff, and students?

3. SUPPORT.   What degree of warmth and support is provided by administrators to subordinates and by faculty to students?

4. IDENTITY.   To what degree do faculty and students identify with the entire institution rather than with their own departments or disciplines.

5. QUALITY OF PERSONNEL. To what degree do administrators, faculty, staff, and students have confidence in each other's integrity and competence?

6. PERFORMANCE REWARD. To what degree is a performance reward—salary increase and promotion for faculty, test and course grade for students—based on meaningful performance criteria, standards, and evidence?

7. CONFLICT TOLERANCE. What degree of conflict exists in faculty relationships? Between faculty and administrative staff? Between faculty and students? How willing are participants to be open and honest about these conflicts?

8. COOPERATION. To what degree do people throughout the college or university work effectively together toward shared goals?

9. DECISION-MAKING PROCESS. How much genuine consultation and collaboration exists in the decision-making process, and to what extent do faculty, students, and non-instructional staff participate?

10. RISK TOLERANCE. To what degree are employees in the institution encouraged to be professionally adventuresome, innovative, and willing to take risks?

11. CONCERN FOR PEOPLE. To what degree is the college or university perceived as caring for its administrative staff? For its faculty? For its students?

12. COMMUNICATION PATTERN. To what degree does complete, accurate, and meaningful information flow upward, downward, and across the institution?

13. INTRINSIC SATISFACTION. To what extent to administrators, faculty, and staff receive from the work itself a sense of achievement, pride in a job well done, personal growth and development, feelings of competence?

14. SENSE OF COMMUNITY. To what degree do members of the college or university feel a sense of family, a sense of oneness? And to what extent do they feel a sense of genuine sharing and caring about each other?

This last characteristic of academic culture—sense of community—is unique because it is a global or summary factor. It emerges from the bottom of the funnel only after the other characteristics have gone into the top. If you want to take a quick measure of the academic culture of an institution, ask the first ten people you see on the campus this question: How would you describe the sense of community at this college or university?

Each of these fourteen areas is a continuum in which part of the culture of an academic institution can be seen. When taken together, they give insiders a reasonably good picture of the college or university.

# Diagnosing Academic Culture from the Outside

If we can learn a good deal about the academic culture of an institution from the inside, can we also learn something about culture from the outside? The answer is yes. We can learn a lot about an organization's culture from the outside by paying attention to what its people do and what they say.

First, pay attention to how the college or university greets outsiders (Gerloff, 1985). Some institutions strive to be warm and friendly to visitors, while others simply ignore visitors and pretend they are not there. The writer saw this first-hand recently when he visited colleges with his daughter, who was then a high-school senior. One factor that she used to separate institutions was what she called the "warmth factor." It was simply a count of the number of people—students, faculty or administrative staff—who made eye contact with her or smiled (even a little bit) as she took her campus tour. Surprisingly, there was considerable variation among the colleges. The numbers ranged from just two people at one institution to more than twenty at another. The warmth factor is not a scientific measure, of course, but it serves as a useful reflection of an institution's academic culture.

Second, talk to a variety of different people on and around the campus. Ask the teaching and non-instructional staff for their opinions. Consult with academic competitors. Question key members of the community. Talk to present and former students. The collective view of this array of people will be quite revealing and will provide a far deeper and more accurate picture of a college or university than is found in the flowery phrases and four-color photographs seen in campus brochures.

At Haverford College (Pennsylvania) graduating

seniors are invited to participate in "exit interviews" conducted by the college's administrators. Each interview lasts half an hour and questions range from "Did Haverford live up to your expectations?" to "What was your most memorable moment at Haverford?" The seniors are also asked to suggest any improvements they would like to see and to give a parting piece of advice to the college's president.

Third, read what the college or university writes. Despite the flowery phrases, the way a college or university presents itself to the public says a lot about how it sees itself. Deal and Kennedy (1982) suggest that annual reports, catalogs, press releases, newsletters, and magazines should be examined. What does the institution say about itself to prospective students and their parents? To its employees? To the general public? Does the institution use such communications to discuss its performance only in conventional terms—placement office statistics, degrees held by faculty, number of volumes in the library, employee sick days lost—or does it also focus on the human beings who comprise the college or university?

Fourth, analyze the physical setting of the college or university. Pay attention to its buildings. Look at their style as well as the materials used in their construction. Look at their state of repair or disrepair. Examine the landscaping. Are the trees and shrubs sparse or abundant?

Pay careful attention to the classrooms. Are the rooms well-lighted? Are the students' desks and chairs reasonably comfortable and modern? Are the administrative and faculty offices and furnishings uniformly good or are some departments quartered in luxurious surroundings while others are housed in cramped spaces with cast-off furniture? Are olive green and gray the predominant colors or are they pastel shades with brightly colored trim? Do janitors, telephone operators, receptionists, secretaries, have enough room and modern equipment to do their jobs properly or are they crammed into little cubicles and given antiquated equipment to work with?

# Summary: Inside and Outside

In summary, academic culture can be diagnosed from the inside (by those who are members of the institution) or from the outside. The key is to avoid relying on value judgments and hunches and focus instead on carefully assembling the pieces of what

you see and hear so that they fit into a cohesive whole.

The reader may say, why go through all this effort? How important really is the information that will emerge. To put the matter succinctly, it is vital. In the author's experience (as consultant/speaker at more than one hundred colleges and universities), it is of the greatest importance for administrators and faculty members to take a long and hard—and honest—look at the academic culture in their institution and at several comparable institutions. If they do—and only if they do—can they understand and improve their own institutional condition.

# Cultural Rigor Mortis

Academic culture, like an individual's personality, is stable and durable over time. Huse and Cummings (1985) say that it tends to be pervasive and taken for granted. People hold tightly to their values and beliefs: they rarely question them or consider drastic departures from what has worked in the past. Schein (1983) reports that the reason for this is that shared values, beliefs, and norms serve as crucial defense mechanisms against the anxieties of struggling for social survival within the college or university and between that institution and its larger academic environment. People are unlikely to discard those defenses and the security that they afford, even in the face of compelling contrary evidence. There is the popular story, for example, of the religious group that predicted the end of the world and, when the prophecy failed, simply put off the date of doomsday, refusing any longer to specify it.

In a college or university setting, the stability and durability of "the way things are done" is likely to result in academic stagnation, even decline. A research-oriented administration tends to remain so year after year. An autocratic college president does not appear to mellow over the years. A kind of cultural rigor mortis sets in.

The reader is urged to keep in mind that upper-echelon academic administrators set the marching pace for faculty and students. Keep in mind also that many administrators were selected for their positions precisely because their behavior and values harmonized with their superiors'. This touches on a subtle negative in the generally laudable promotion–from–within process. Filling vacant positions from the ranks is an invaluable incentive for faculty and administrative staff to work hard and efficiently. But when an individual is appointed academic vice-president after spending twenty years in the institution, it is a safe bet that the institution's academic culture will continue unchanged.

But things need not work out this way. There are some important on-going safeguards for institutions encouraging the process of revitalization. In truth, most of the time, the academic culture of a college or university does not have to be changed: it simply needs to be renewed.

# Renewing Academic Culture

The following practical advice can serve as guidelines for cultural renewal:

1. EFFECTIVE CULTURAL RENEWAL MUST START WITH A CLEAR VISION OF THE COLLEGE OR UNIVERSITY'S NEW STRATEGIC PLAN AND THE SHARED VALUES AND BELIEFS NEEDED TO MAKE IT WORK. Strategic planning must become an integral part of the academic landscape. Hard-pressed colleges and universities —contending with skyrocketing costs, a real-dollar drop in federal aid for students and research, and the first decrease in the number of high-school graduates in U.S. history—must now deal with market niches and competitive opportunities. The focus must be on the school's customers—its students. A number of institutions—including Stanford University, Carnegie-Mellon University, and the University of Miami—are already actively engaged in strategic planning.

Please note, however, that the focus here is on developing a strategic plan in order to *renew* an academic culture rather than change it completely. The latter is beyond the scope of this paper. Keller (1983, p. 153) says that "A strategic plan may bend or redirect a college's traditions and values, and it may alter its aspirations. But the strategy will never be effective if it tries to ignore powerful intangibles (such as traditions, values and hopes). They are like tides, invisable but mighty . . . The academic strategy may need to revise or update the values of the institution. But it should do so knowingly, tenderly, tactfully. Strategies work best when they are roughly consonant with . . . an institution's traditions. . . ."

2. EFFECTIVE CULTURAL RENEWAL MUST START AT THE TOP OF THE COLLEGE OR UNIVERSITY. Senior administrators, including the president, must be strongly and publicly committed to the new values and create constant pressures for change. They must also have the staying power to see the changes through.

3. SENIOR ADMINISTRATORS MUST COMMUNICATE THE RENEWED CULTURE THROUGH THEIR OWN ACTIONS. Their behavior must symbolize the kinds of values and behavior being sought. They must demonstrate an almost missionary zeal for the new values. As examples, the president of a Minnesota college demonstrated the kind of ingenuity and dedication he expected from his staff by using a snowmobile to get to work in a blizzard. The new dean of the Harvard Business School underscored his belief that his colleagues should treat their families as more important than their academic careers by refusing to work weekends and shunning the on-campus dean's house in order to live with his wife and two daughters in a restored farmhouse outside Boston where the family can keep horses.

4. COLLEGES AND UNIVERSITIES MUST HAVE AN EFFECTIVE PROGRAM FOR THE RECRUITMENT AND DEVELOPMENT OF TALENT. People are the ultimate source of renewal. A steady flow of able and highly motivated people must be brought into the institution. Equally important, there must be an effective on-going program of career development (Gardner, 1976).

5. AN HOSPITABLE ENVIRONMENT MUST BE PROVIDED FOR THE INDIVIDUAL. Colleges and universities that extinguish the spark of individuality will greatly diminish, if not eliminate, the capacity of their staff for change. Faculty and administrators who have been made to feel like cogs in the machine will behave like cogs in the machine.

6. SUPPORTING MODIFICATIONS MUST ACCOMPANY A RENEWED ACADEMIC CULTURE. Making the necessary changes in organizational structure, management style, reward system, information and control systems, interdepartmental relations, and the management of human resources will help orient people to the new behavior and values inherent in the revamped culture.

7. ACADEMIC INSTITUTIONS MUST ENCOURAGE A CLIMATE OF INTELLECTUAL FREEDOM IN WHICH HARD UNCOMFORTABLE QUESTIONS CAN BE ASKED. It must be a climate in which people are encouraged to speak their minds without risk of damaging their professional reputations or even losing their jobs.

8. COLLEGES AND UNIVERSITIES MUST FIND WAYS TO COMBAT THE VESTED INTERESTS THAT OPERATE AT EVERY LEVEL —STUDENT, FACULTY, ADMINISTRATIVE STAFF.   Every change threatens someone's privileges, someone's authority, someone's status. There can be no doubt that breaking up vested interests is difficult and time–consuming. But people must learn that the parts are subordinate to the whole, *and* that implicit in the success of the whole is the success of the parts (Gardner, 1976).

9. THOSE WHO WORK IN COLLEGES AND UNIVERSITIES MUST BELIEVE THAT IT MAKES A DIFFERENCE WHETHER THEY DO WELL OR BADLY.   Institutions run on motivation, on morale, on conviction. People have to care. They must believe—with justification—that their individual efforts mean something special to their institution.

10. NEWLY–HIRED PROFESSORS MUST BE GIVEN A CAREFULLY ORGANIZED ORIENTATION TO THE RENEWED ACADEMIC CULTURE.   Such a program's focus might be on enhancing interest in teaching and effectiveness in the classroom. Eble (1972) suggests the following items as essential in the induction of new professors: (1) communicating in tangible ways the school's interest in teaching; (2) explaining and clarifying the reward system; (3) discussing in specific terms how to gain knowledge and skill in the classroom; (4) acquainting the novitiates with their own and other departments and colleges; (5) providing relevant and factual information about the student body.

Similarly, newly–hired administrators must be given an appropriate orientation to the renewed culture because their actions can significantly promote or hinder new values and behavior. Such a program might include (1) communicating in specific terms the revised beliefs and norms and explaining the reasons for them; (2) introducing the new administrator to key members of the administrative staff, the faculty, the student body; (3) acquainting him or her with the institution's organization structure, human resources system, reward and information systems.

11. DECISION-MAKING BY CONSENSUS AND THE MOVEMENT TOWARD OPENNESS MUST CONTINUE TO GAIN FAVOR.   Group decision–making sparks new ideas, brings collective experience and expertise together, heightens an understanding of a decision in the process of making it, and clothes the decision with acceptability because a respected group made it (Seldin, 1984). Similarly, Keller (1983, p. 63) reports that an ever increasing number of administrators ". . . believe that openness about new directions is more conducive to rallying faculty, student and alumni support behind initiatives as well as productive of better academic plans because of criticisms and improvements from others. . . ." Proposed budget cuts, personnel changes, financial priorities, organizational shifts, calendar changes, and new ventures are already openly discussed by the presidents of Ohio University, Wesleyan University (Connecticut), the State University of New York at Albany, and Pace University (New York) with their faculties.

12. ALL MEMBERS OF THE ACADEMIC COMMUNITY MUST BE TREATED WITH RESPECT AND DIGNITY.   But this must be more than a slogan. It must be the real thing. It must come to life in the styles and values and beliefs of the institution. In short, it must be an integral part of its academic culture.

13. COLLEGES AND UNIVERSITIES MUST WORK HARDER AT BUILDING A STRONG BONDING AMONG MEMBERS OF THE CAMPUS COMMUNITY.   The sad truth is that at many institutions, the faculty, the administration, and the students look at each other as adversaries, engaged in a continuing struggle. Trust is often in short supply. So is institutional loyalty. Breaking down this lack of understanding and trust among various campus groups is slow painful work. It means reaching out to others. It means taking some risks. It means trying some new approaches. It means knowing that some of your efforts will fail. Creating a true campus community is admittedly difficult. But it can be done. We know the essential building blocks. They are open communication, honesty, integrity, and a shared sense of purpose.

# In Conclusion

What it comes down to is this: If administrators and faculty members want to renew the academic culture of their institution, they must take at least some of these steps. There simply is no choice.

Many academics will be skeptical. Some will say, we could never do it on our campus. Others will say, we tried some of these things before and they just did not work. Still others will say, the vested interests at our college or university are just too strong. Why should we bother to fight them?

To academics who say those things, the writer recalls the wisdom of Dr. Benjamin E. Mays, the former president of Morehouse College in Atlanta.

> It must be borne in mind that the tragedy of life doesn't lie in not reaching your goal. The tragedy lies in having no goal to reach for.
>
> It's not a disaster to be unable to capture your ideal. But it is a disaster to have no ideal to capture.
>
> It's not a disgrace not to reach the stars. But it is a disgrace to have no stars to reach for.

Each of the colleges and universities in the United States has a star to reach for. It is the shining star of a renewed culture of openness, honesty, integrity, respect, gladly learning, and gladly teaching.

# References

Deal, T. E. and Kennedy, A. A. *Corporate Cultures.* Reading, Mass.: Addison-Wesley, 1982.

Eble, K. E. *Professors As Teachers.* San Francisco: Jossey-Bass, 1972.

Gardner, J. "How to Prevent Organizational Dry Rot." In H. G. Hicks and J. D. Powell (Eds.) *Management, Organization and Human Resources.* New York: McGraw-Hill, Inc. 1976.

Gerloff, E. A. *Organizational Theory and Design.* New York: McGraw-Hill, Inc. 1985.

Keller, G. *Academic Strategy.* Baltimore: The Johns Hopkins University Press, 1983.

Likert, R. *The Human Organization.* New York: McGraw-Hill, Inc. 1967.

Louis, M. "Toward a System of Inquiry on Organizational Culture" (Paper delivered at the Western Academy of Management Meeting Colorado Springs, Colorado, April, 1982).

Huse, E. F., and Cummings, T. G. *Organizational Development and Change.* St. Paul, Minnesota, West Publishing Co. 1985.

Robbins, S. P. *Management: Concepts and Practices.* Englewood Cliffs, New Jersey: Prentice-Hall, Inc., 1984.

Schein, E. "Organizational Culture: Or, If Organizational Development Is Culture Change, Is That Possible and/or Desirable?" (Paper delivered at the Academy of Management Annual Meeting, Dallas, Texas, August, 1983).

Schuster, F. E. *Human Resource Management.* Reston, Virginia: Reston Publishing Company, Inc. 1985.

Seldin, P. "In Search of Academic Excellence: An Organizational Perspective." (Paper delivered at the Improving University Teaching International Conference, College Park, Maryland, July, 1984).

Seldin, P. "Academic Culture." (Paper delivered at the Association of American Law Schools Workshop for Senior Administrators, Washington D.C., October, 1986).

III.2

# Faculty Development in 1986:
# What Are The Issues?

## Howard B. Altman

Mary Smith is a tenured associate professor at State University, where she has been a member of the Classics Department for the past nine years. Enrollments in Classics are way down at State, students opting to pursue courses which evidently seem more "practical" to them. Mary's dean has expressed concern about the small number of Classics majors and the diminishing enrollments in lower-level Latin courses. Mary, though tenured, is the junior member of the department, and at age forty she has become increasingly nervous about her future at State.

John Jones is a full professor of History at Mercury College, a fine liberal arts institution with 1500 undergraduates and a faculty of 130. John has been at Mercury for twenty-seven years. In recent years he has developed a reputation among students for sarcasm and insensitivity to student needs and feelings. History students try to avoid his classes, as he treats them with indifference at best and contempt at worst. His last evidence of professional activity as an historian was ten years ago. John is fond of telling his junior colleagues that he "made it" back in the "good old days" when all you had to do was keep your nose clean and show up for work every day. Teaching history bores him after all these years, and he spends as little time in his office as he thinks necessary — which is less, of course, than really is needed. John is fifty-six years old. His dean sighs at the thought of having John around for at least nine more years.

Henry Roberts is a young assistant professor of Mathematics at Adams University. He is one of the most popular teachers on campus. Students flock to his classes and office hours — of which he schedules at least ten per week — because of his warm, caring, personable style and his ability to make mathematics fascinating. Henry has little interest in publishing, though he knows that Adams University expects its faculty to be professionally active. This is Henry's third year at Adams. His department chair informed him yesterday that the dean may not be willing to rehire Henry for another three-year term without some evidence of research productivity. Henry listened to this with mounting anger. What the hell did I ever become a teacher for, he asks himself.

Sandra Williams finds teaching English at Valley Community College much harder than she had ever suspected it might be. While doing a master's in English, she had never had an opportunity to teach, and this position is her first teaching assignment. She is responsible this term for two sections of freshman writing and two literature courses. She prepares her lectures in the style which she experienced as a graduate student, but they seem to fall on deaf ears. Sometimes they don't fall on any ears: absenteeism is high in her classes. Sandra wonders whether there might be more effective ways of teaching than what she has been doing, but she has no idea where to turn for help. If only her students seemed more responsive!

Mary Smith, John Jones, Henry Roberts, and Sandra Williams represent faculty types whom most readers of this essay know quite well. They probably are not the typical faculty members at our institutions, but they are not at all unknown. The mid-career faculty member with anxieties about the future, the senior professor who has lost interest in his work, the idealistic young assistant professor who loves teaching and whose future in a publish-or-perish institution seems bleak, the faculty member whose repertoire of teaching techniques needs to be extensively expanded — these are all individuals in need of institutional help. That help, broadly defined, is what is meant today by "faculty development."

# The Meaning of Faculty Development

Had Humpty Dumpty been an American professor, he might have had "faculty development" in mind when he stated in *Through the Looking Glass* that "When I use a word, it means just what I choose it to mean—neither more nor less." This is a current dilemma with "faculty development": institutions, and indeed individual faculty members, ascribe different meanings to the term. In our pluralistic system of American higher education, this is perhaps as it should be. The imprecision and multiple meanings of "faculty development," however, must not be construed as legitimate reasons for institutional do–nothing–ism in the careers and lives of faculty.

Actually, the very phrase "faculty development" —like its companion terms "faculty renewal" and "faculty revitalization"—causes problems. Probably non–existent is the faculty member who would define himself or herself as "underdeveloped, outmoded, and lacking in vitality." It is thus unfortunate that we have failed to adopt something like the term "continuing education for faculty," a term with no pejorative implications: "continuing education" has high acceptance in other professions such as medicine, dentistry, and law. But in relation to the academic profession, except as self-selected and self-directed learning, the term has never caught on. And in the absence of state licensing requirements for college and university faculty, analogous to those for physicians, dentists, and attorneys, "continuing education" for professors is next to impossible to mandate.

Historically, institutional faculty development efforts have focused on the role of the faculty member as disciplinary specialist and scholar rather than on his or her role as classroom teacher, or on any of the other institutional roles that faculty perform. Thus, Harvard University inaugurated the tradition of the "research sabbatical" in 1810, a tradition which exists a century and three quarters later on about 75 percent of American college and university campuses (Bowen and Schuster, p. 134). Likewise, funds for travel to scholarly meetings, subventions for scholarly publications, institutional research grants and released time from teaching for research are among the most treasured perquisites of faculty status on many campuses. Since these forms of faculty development are viewed by faculty—correctly —as a reward for active participation in the life of their discipline, rather than in the life of their institution, it comes as no surprise that many—if not most—faculty feel greater loyalty to their academic specialization than to the campus which pays their salary (Bowen and Schuster, p. 146).

In the early 1970s a new concept of faculty development emerged on American campuses. It was largely a positive outcome of the student unrest of the late 1960s, which had spotlighted "irrelevant courses, uninspired teaching, and impersonal faculty relationships with students" (Gaff, p. 15). With the weakening of requirements and the burgeoning of electives, professors, used to a captive audience, faced the prospect of having to compete for a clientele. Students on some campuses published evaluations of courses and instructors, and those with low marks failed to attract registrants. With the major fiscal support of both governmental and private foundations, many campuses launched extensive teaching–improvement programs. Among the better known examples were the Clinic to Improve University Teaching, at the University of Massachusetts at Amherst, and the Center for the Teaching Professions, at Northwestern University, both funded by the Kellogg Foundation. In 1972 Kenneth Eble published a book called *Professors as Teachers,* a title that should have seemed redundant but instead was viewed as precedent–setting.

The teaching improvement programs that emerged nationwide—over four hundred of them reported in a *Chronicle* survey in the late 1970s— reflected a paradox. College and university faculty, as a result of many years of formal disciplinary study, are the best educated and most inadequately trained practitioners of all professionals. The new degree recipient emerges from graduate school, steeped in the trappings of empirical or conceptual research, to face the realities of an academic appointment: classroom teaching, course preparation, test construction, student advising. (There are a few Ph.D. programs that do prepare for these—not necessarily the most prestigious.) Thoroughly imbued with the esoterica of his or her discipline, newly appointed Professor Neophyte is asked to teach three or four (or five) classes a semester—all different preparations. As Bowen and Schuster (1986) report, "Even at universities where research figures very prominently in academic reward systems, faculty on the whole spend most of their time teaching" (p. 15). If Professor Neophyte has been fortunate, he or she has had a modicum of teaching experience, probably poorly supervised, in a freshman-level course while frantically trying to keep up with the demands of graduate professors. Pierre van den Berghe's marvelously funny book, *Academic Gamesmanship: How to Make a Ph.D. Pay* (1970), encapsulates the ethos of graduate education in the author's recommendation—one hopes tongue in cheek—that the would–be successful new professor learn to consider "teaching as an annoying distraction from research . . . and students as an evil necessary to justify [one's] job in the eyes of the laymen who pay [one's] salary" (p. 78).

# Instructional Development

Given little or no training or experience in the craft of teaching, and probably (unless one majored in psychology or education) equally little knowledge about adult intellectual and social development (though psychology and education do not guarantee this), the typical newly appointed assistant professor teaches as he or she had been taught. Most new faculty know no other pedagogical approaches to their discipline than those which they had experienced themselves as students.

Institutional programs to improve teaching have as their underlying goal the improvement of student learning. Efforts to help faculty members discover new approaches to teaching that facilitate student learning, new designs for courses and curricula that embrace these approaches, and new principles for constructing valid and reliable tests to measure what students have learned—these are collectively known as *instructional development.* For some theorists such as Bergquist and Phillips (1975), instructional development is one of the components of faculty development. For others, such as Jerry Gaff (1975), instructional development and faculty development are separate, with the former focusing on students and the latter on the lives of faculty. I side with a more comprehensive view of faculty development, especially as it has evolved on American campuses during the past five years or so. Bergquist and Phillips's definition of a comprehensive faculty development program, written in 1975, still seems valid today:

> A comprehensive program of faculty development is . . . one which provides training for faculty in improved classroom performance, which assists faculty in developing a supportive environment within their academic organization, and which allows them to examine and reflect on their own personal values and attitudes as they influence their professional lives. Instructional development, organizational development, and personal development thus become the essential components of any effective program of faculty development. (p. 6)

In short, instructional development is a leading part of faculty development.

# Organizational Development

Organizational development focuses on the environment in which faculty and students work. Many faculty lead cloistered academic lives and have no sense of how their institution functions, how resources are allocated, how decisions are made, where various kinds of help may be found. A faculty member who seeks to bring about significant change in the educational process or in the operation of his or her campus is likely to encounter resistance from colleagues, obstacles from institutional regulations, and hostility from those with vested interests in the status quo—which will be almost everyone.

A program of organizational development attempts to sensitize faculty members to the environment in which they work, to its operating principles, its regulations, its pressure points. What alternative strategies exist to bring about change? What potential or real obstacles must be overcome? How can one cope with, if not obviate, resistance from colleagues? Organizational development training is especially useful for department chairpersons who, in my view, constitute the critical linchpin in any institutional effort to assist faculty. Department chairs—and deans and divisional coordinators as well—are often called upon to settle faculty conflicts, adjudicate grievances, and motivate faculty to perform in various ways. Organizational development activities that may prove valuable to faculty include the development of interdisciplinary courses, the creation of self-paced learning systems for students without regard to the conventional academic calendar, and other ways of deviating from the normative structure of the institution. Training in team–building, decision–making, and conflict management are activities strongly recommended for administrators (Bergquist and Phillips, p. 141).

# Personal Development

It is the domain of personal development for faculty—the third component in the Bergquist and Phillips design—that has received the most recent national attention. Personal development, to be of value, must be personalized. This presupposes that program administrators find out and respond to what faculty actually want and need. Colleges and universities have a poor track record nationwide in this area of faculty relations. In Howard Bowen's and Jack Schuster's important new book, *American Professors: A National Resource Imperiled* (1986), the authors stress that institutions need to exhibit greater sensitivity to individual differences among faculty and to faculty personal as well as professional needs. Too many faculty members today perceive themselves to be ignored by their institutions, or treated in an insensitive and uncaring manner. Faculty are offended by institutional decisions made without their personal involvement, by the allocation of resources without faculty input, by the placing of academic freedom or collegiality in jeopardy (p. 133). As Bowen and Schuster have written, "The faculties of America are a great national resource which has been subjected to deferred maintenance" (p. 29). McKeachie (1983) is more specific. Institutions that fail to provide faculty with a stimulating work environment, with a diversity of tasks, and with ample challenges to whet their intellectual appetites are encouraging loss of vitality and diminished productivity. "A sense of being appreciated for [the contributions they feel they are making], a feeling that the future has some bright spots, a sense of being valued by one's colleagues and administrators, these are the things that induce [faculty] performance" (p. 10).

Programs in the area of personal development are designed to meet expressed faculty interests and wishes. Workshops and short courses that allow faculty to develop new skills—in computer literacy, for example—respond to the faculty's interest in acquiring new competencies. Funds to allow faculty to take continuing education courses related to their academic area are funds well spent. Faculty exchange programs, such as the National Faculty Exchange, are another potentially valuable form of personal development. Faculty retraining programs, allowing a professor to develop the skills and knowledge to teach in a new academic area or to assume administrative responsibilities in the institution, may revitalize an otherwise demoralized faculty member who has lost interest in his or her teaching area or whose teaching area has ceased to attract sufficient numbers of students and its continuation is in question. Workshops on "how to publish your ideas" or "how to write a grant proposal" may seem quite attractive to faculty on those campuses where "publish-or-perish" is perceived as the "law of the land." Likewise, workshops on "plan-

ning for retirement" are guaranteed to attract an audience.

A recent area of attention in personal development is faculty "wellness." Aside from the obvious benefit to the institution in keeping its faculty alive—or at least *most* of its faculty alive—a wellness program can result in lower insurance costs, fewer days lost to illness, and the like. But the benefits to the participants in the program are equally impressive. Institutionally sponsored wellness activities provide an opportunity for faculty from disparate disciplines to interact and socialize, and in so doing arrive at a richer understanding of the way the institution as a whole works. Significantly, wellness activities also seem to be perceived by faculty as evidence that the institution cares about them as human beings, and not just as professors who teach, publish, and perform service of various kinds. Faculty who feel that their institution is concerned about their human welfare are more likely to reciprocate that concern in loyalty to their campus. What better pay-off could *any* faculty development program provide!

# Other Faculty Development Options

Essential to the design of any attempt at faculty development—be it instructional, organizational, or personal in nature—is that the activity respond to genuine faculty needs and wants. It makes little sense to design a workshop on some new pedagogical technique—"how to individualize instruction," for example—if no one shows up at the workshop. Most faculty members are busy people. Unless they are convinced that the commitment of their time to a faculty development activity is worthwhile, they feel free to stay away. This is especially true of tenured professors who constitute about 70 percent of the higher education faculty nationwide (Bowen and Schuster, p. 45).

There is a long and undistinguished tradition in American higher education of interpreting academic freedom to imply professorial independence in the classroom and laboratory. Professors as scholars, and even more professors as teachers, frequently work unfettered by contact with any of their colleagues. The sanctity and inviolability of the academic classroom is so well rooted—except in some enlightened community colleges—that no faculty member would deign to impugn the expertise of a colleague by suggesting to the colleague how his or her course might be better taught. Rare is the faculty member who would ask a colleague for such help. This is an especially damaging tradition in the case of new assistant professors, fresh out of graduate school, who are called upon to teach courses for the first time. To allow such new faculty to "sink or swim" is both unfair and unprofessional, and may have devastating consequences both for the new faculty member and for his or her students.

Some faculty development activities can help here. One possibility is to assign each new faculty member to a senior mentor in his or her department. It becomes the function of the mentor to work with the junior colleague, to share expertise and experience, to serve as a sounding board for ideas, to be a willing and able listener, to encourage and praise where appropriate, and to provide non–judgmental feedback. Faculty are so used to being judgmental —indeed, that is what they get paid for—that it may not be easy to find a senior colleague who can function comfortably in this role. Distinguished service as a faculty mentor is *teaching* at its best, and should be counted as teaching in faculty workloads. A campus program to train a mentor in each department to work with new and junior faculty has much to recommend it—provided the institution has competent senior faculty.

Another faculty development option, this time from organizational development, is to build faculty teams, with two or more faculty sharing teaching and other duties. Teamwork in the classroom has unfortunately never been perceived as a virtue in American education. Students learn (from kindergarten on) that, if they work with someone else, that is cheating. Education is supposed to teach us to "stand on our own two feet." But as most members of the animal kingdom can attest, four feet are frequently sturdier than two. Faculty teams working symbiotically or synergistically can accomplish far more than the same faculty members as individuals, and may do so with greater satisfaction and higher morale.

I have already suggested that, in my view, good department chairpersons are the *sine qua non* for successful faculty development programs. It is the department chair who should work most closely with the faculty in his or her unit on a regular basis. It is the department chair who can facilitate faculty development, or thwart it. The professional growth of the department faculty is as much the responsibility of the department chair, and should be at least as important to the department chair, as the state of the department's budget or the scheduling of the department's courses. Unfortunately, department chairs are usually *not* chosen because of their dedi-

cation to the professional growth of their colleagues. Those who *are* chosen may receive elaborate advice from the dean about how to evaluate department faculty for personnel actions, but probably no advice about how to help department colleagues grow and achieve their personal and professional goals as faculty. This points to the value and the importance of administrative development programs for department chairs and deans as well.

Finally, as one examines the status of faculty development practices in 1986, there is one other issue which may prove to be the most critical of all. *A faculty member's values are, and will doubtless always be, inextricably linked to the institution's reward structure.* If faculty perceive that excellence in teaching carries no greater extrinsic reward than does mediocrity, they will commit their time and efforts to those activities that do pay. Many leaders of American higher education have publicly deplored the trend, on so many campuses, of emphasizing research productivity over classroom excellence in the allocation of rewards to faculty. As Bowen and Schuster have written, "In the groves of academe, to question the importance of research approaches heresy. Still, we cannot help but wonder whether the stampede toward scholarship—or what passes for scholarship—serves the nation's needs or the long–run interests of those campuses which historically have been strongly committed to excellent teaching. We fear that the essential balance between teaching and scholarship has been lost, that the scales are tipping too far toward the latter at many institutions" (p. 150).

# In Summary

In summary, faculty development practices in 1986 reflect considerably more attention to a "whole person" approach to faculty than has been the case previously. Institutional programs have broadened their focus to include those activities that support faculty in the multiple roles they serve as teachers, as scholars, as disciplinary professionals, as experts in the community, and also as human beings with the same needs as all other human beings: support, appreciation, recognition, concern. While these new directions in faculty development make the implementation of an institutional program both more complex and, conceivably, more costly, there is every reason to expect that a broad–based approach to faculty needs and wants will have increased success in reaching the twin goals of any faculty development program: effectiveness and satisfaction.

# References

Bergquist, William H., and Phillips, Steven R. *A Handbook for Faculty Development.* Vol. I. Washington, D.C.: Council for the Advancement of Small Colleges, 1975.

Bowen, Howard R., and Schuster, Jack H. *American Professors: A National Resource Imperiled.* New York: Oxford University Press, 1986

Carnegie Foundation for the Advancement of Teaching. Change: Trendlines—"The Faculty: Deeply Troubled." *Change* 17:4 (September/October 1985), pp. 31–34.

Gaff, Jerry G. *Toward Faculty Renewal. Advances in Faculty, Instructional, and Organizational Development.* San Francisco: Jossey-Bass, 1975.

McKeachie, Wilbert J. "Older Faculty Members: Facts and Prescriptions" *AAHE Bulletin* (November 1983) pp. 8–10

Van den Berghe, Pierre. *Academic Gamesmanship: How to Make a Ph.D. Pay.* New York: Abelard-Schuman. 1970.

III.3

# Faculty Development in Higher Education
## *A Review of the Literature*

## A. PATRICK ALLEN

Faculty development is a familiar term to even a fledgling academician. There is a faculty development program, committee, center, reading room, budget, or instructional developer on almost every campus. There is general agreement that faculty development plays an important role in the vitality of colleges and universities. Yet, there is little agreement about what the term "faculty development" actually means. Webb contends that the term "faculty development" has no universal definition (1977, p. 86).

Since there is no agreement as to the meaning of the term faculty development, it is not surprising to learn that the faculty development movement has been criticized for lacking a unifying theoretical base. During the height of the faculty development boom period (1973–1978), Martin chastised the movement for not having "adequate theory, comprehensive approaches, or a deep intention" (1975, p. 3). Ten years later, this indictment is still being leveled. In a recent evaluation of a major faculty development effort sponsored by the Bush foundation, Eble concluded (1985, p. 182):

> Our conceptualizations of faculty development are not yet well developed. The studies of faculty development cited earlier have categorized faculty development activities, but as yet we know little about how these categories relate to one another, let alone their usefulness in generating hypotheses about what kind of program a particular college should develop . . .

Faculty development has been defined in many ways. Rose defines faculty development as "almost anything a faculty member does outside the classroom" (1976, p. 22). Others expand the definition to include almost everything a faculty member does in or out of the classroom. For example, faculty development has been defined as a set of activities designed to help faculty members function more

comfortably and effectively in all their roles (Munson 1975, p. 5; Wergin 1976, p. 291).

Mayhew emphasizes four rather general roles for faculty development: assisting faculty members in making their courses more attractive, creating proposals to attract external funding, developing the ability to solve significant institutional problems, and improving talents in extending professional consulting services (1979, p. 234). Obviously, Mayhew believes that the primary purpose of faculty development is to improve the faculty's ability to generate revenue. His book, intended for small college administrators, was appropriately entitled *Surviving the Eighties*.

Gaff emphasizes the idea of growth and the process of assisting professors in their instructional roles. He defines faculty development as "enhancing the talents, expanding the interests, improving the competence, and otherwise facilitating the professional and personal growth of faculty members, particularly in their roles as instructors" (1975, p. 14). Francis was one of the first to recognize that an effective faculty development program is really a form of planned change. He views faculty development as an institutional "process of change that attempts to modify the attitudes, skills and behaviors of faculty toward increased effectiveness and efficiency in meeting student, institutional, and personal objectives" (1975, p. 720).

Faculty development has also been conceptualized as a political process (Lacy 1983, p. 95), as a process of environmental modification (Ost 1976, p. 3), and visualized as a "deep-rooted, thick-trunked tree that lately has sprouted new branches" (Linquest 1981, p. 732). The "thick-trunked tree" is instructional development (rooted in the 1960s), and the new branches are organizational development and personal development. These branches began to grow in the 1970s.

Several authors argue that faculty development is a small part of a much larger process. For example,

Boyer and Crockett place faculty development inside the domain of organizational development, which they define as "a planned change strategy emphasizing more effective utilization of human resources of the organization" (1973, p. 340). For Faris, faculty development is a group process for instructional design (1970, p. 131). Whitmore, on the other hand, contends that "faculty development and curriculum redesign are interdependent aspects of the change process" (1981, p. 13).

While there is no agreement as to the precise definition of faculty development, Seldin finds three underlying assumptions of the American faculty development movement. First, teaching is the primary professional activity of most faculty. Second, instructional comportment is a combination of learned skills, attitudes, and goals. Third, faculty members can be taught how to improve their instruction (1976, p. 1). One implication of these assumptions is that the primary focus of faculty development is instructional improvement. This is particularly true of faculty development activities in the small college. However, as Gaff and Justice observe, faculty development has meant different things at different times: once it meant only the intellectual study of a field, but now it calls for a much expanded definition (1978, p. 89).

In summary, faculty development has meant different things at different times and there is no universal definition of the term. One primary emphasis is certainly instructional improvement, but a broader definition is necessary in order to encompass the immense number of activities being promoted today. With these considerations in mind, we may define faculty development as a set of institutionally sponsored activities based on the Human Resource Model, designed to enhance the total growth of faculty members — as persons, as professionals, and as members of their academic communities.

# Need for Programs

The boom period for faculty development was from 1973 to 1978. In 1973, a survey of faculty development activities revealed "more plans than programs and models" (Gerth 1973, p. 84). By 1977, the situation had changed dramatically. Centra's study found that over sixty percent of the institutions polled indicated that they had "an organized program or set of practices for faculty development and improvement of teaching" (1977, p. 47), and over two-thirds of the universities had some kind of developmental unit (1978, p. 161). Gaff cautioned, however, that

colleges still needed to institutionalize their efforts (1977, p. 514), or faculty development would become just another educational fad (1978, p. 96). Many more recent observers believe that Gaff's warnings were prophetic (Hendrickson 1982, p. 338; Toombs 1983, p. 86).

There are several theories as to why the faculty development movement did not become firmly established. Toombs argues that the programs focused more on individual needs than on the needs of the institution, thus making them expendable during times of fiscal constraint (1983, p. 86). Another suggestion is that the programs were operating under the misguided assumption that the program of the future is the program of the past: traditional sabbatical leaves, new faculty members, bigger travel budgets, and better facilities, while good things, may no longer be adequate to insure institutional quality (Miller 1972, p. 11; Preus 1979, p. 5). Others contend that the problem is a lack of financial support of faculty development activities. Ellerbe reports that less than one percent of the budget was spent on faculty development activities in his sample of community colleges (1980, 1910), and Eble contends that "faculty development has never had a prominent place in the routine budgets of American collegiate institutions" (1985, p. 8). Probably all of these factors have had an impact on faculty development's failure to take hold as a comprehensive movement.

New students, new programs, low mobility, stable enrollment patterns, harsh economic realities, external demands for quality and accountability, and the "graying of the faculty" all have demanded a new kind of faculty development program (Bergquist 1975, p. 3; Preus 1979, p. 18). Faculty mobility relieved the pressure for (and probably hid the potential of) faculty development during the 1960s and early 1970s (Group 1974, p. 16; Stordahl 1981, p. 1). Now, faculties are not only becoming less mobile, but are growing older as well. The average faculty age in 1979 was 43 years (Higher 1979, p. 5), and this average age is expected to increase to 48 years by 1990 (Gross 1977, p. 752). In fact, "if a child born today attends college at the age of eighteen, his chances of being taught by a person presently on the college faculty are 85 out of 100" (Preus 1979, p. 18). There is some evidence that faculty members develop a stronger interest in teaching — or at best a better interest in research — in the second half of their careers (Blackburn 1979, p. 568; Maehr 1984, p. 82). In addition, many authorities caution that faculty must be prepared to work with new students in new settings, and with new technologies in alternative modes of teaching and learning (Martin 1975,

p. 3; Stordahl 1981, p. 1; Levine 1981, p. 131). These conditions argue for a new type of faculty development program, inasmuch as most institutions will need to develop new responses and approaches with current personnel. Miller refers to seeking renewal from within as "intensive growth" (1974, p. 2). For intensive growth to be successful in a steady-state environment, Gallagher has maintained that faculty development opportunities must be extended to adjunct professors as well (1977, p. 3).

Hershfield points to another need for faculty development. He contends that the technology to improve educational instruction is now available, and if the faculty will not take advantage of it, someone else will (1980, p. 52). It is not clear whether that "someone" is the administration, proprietary schools, or business and industry, but the point is well taken.

A traditional, but often overlooked, problem supporting the need for faculty development programs is the general lack of preparation one receives for the teaching profession. Jacques Barzun's comments at the Conference on College Teaching thirty years ago still ring true (Dobbins 1956, p. 50):

> Just think: here is a profession in which the training does not prepare for the main task, and in the absence of that preparation does not provide apprenticeships; in which, after this double lack, there is no clear judgment of the work done, and in which the superiors of the newcomers do not care whether he succeeds or not in the task that he performs.

The President's Commission on Higher Education concluded in 1948 that college teaching is the only major learned profession that does not have a program to develop the skills essential for its practitioners (Presidents Commission 1948, p. 16). Today, these statements are still valid.

Faculty development programs are needed, according to Lowmand, because of the wide variety of duties expected of academics (1984, p. 214). Brown simply states that faculty development is needed because self-growth is a professional responsibility (1975, p. 206).

# Models for Faculty Development

The crisis in higher education during the mid-1960s began the search for new models of faculty development (Bergquist 1977, p. 3). In 1983, Sullivan, who first identified the mid-1970s as the "boom period"

for the faculty movement (1982, p. 7), warned that new models using a holistic approach and standard terminology must be adopted. "If left unattended, the faculty development movement could hang in the academic closet like the leisure suit of the 1970's" (1982, p. 13). Eble, after surveying the contemporary faculty development scene, categorizes faculty development models as being either single–focus or cafeteria (comprehensive) in their approach (1985, p. 13).

There are two basic single–focus approaches. The problem–oriented approach, used by the University of Chicago Medical School, involves a systematic search for problems and issues, and the development of strategies to deal with the areas in question (Pochyly 1977, p. 93). Many institutions fall into this category by default. That is, universities often operate by crisis–management and deal only with the most pressing issues. Unfortunately, faculty development is usually one of the things that can be kept on the back burner.

The other type of single–focus approach is the collaborative model. Many different types of collaboration are possible, but the essence of this model is that an individual faculty member chooses to pursue growth or improvement in collaboration with an instructional developer, colleague, or professional peer. Obviously, there is collaboration to some degree in all faculty development models, but in this model the collaborative relationship is at the center of the strategy and essential for its success. Wergin describes a collaborative consulting model between a faculty member and an instructional resource professional that begins with "low mutual trust and knowledge and an 'expert' consulting role, and develops into greater mutual trust and a more collaborative consulting role" (1976, p. 300). He contends that this relational shift must take place before the consulting model will be effective in creating lasting change.

The consultative model at Howard University College of Dentistry uses a three–step approach: needs assessment, inservice training, and educational research. The needs assessment includes self, student, and colleague appraisal. Then, in collaboration with an instructional specialist, an individualized program of in–service activities is designed. Faculty members are also encouraged to pursue educational research (Hutton 1977, p. 19). The centerpiece of Lhota's consultative model is a teaching center which functions as a learning resource center or "learning web" (1976, p. 35). This model resembles the instructional development program at the University of Michigan. Michigan is the university credited with the first major application of an in-structural development process in higher education, in 1963 (Gaff 1975, p. 58).

Other collaborative models include an interinstitutional model where faculty innovation – leaders teach in experimental courses and use colleagues in a similar position at a nearby college or university for support (Noonan 1973, p. 94), a psychiatric model in which "the patient must acknowledge a need for treatment if the treatment is to be effective" (Eble 1983, p. 134), a peer observation model at the University of North Carolina which encourages faculty to examine critically each other's teaching styles and effectiveness (Bell 1977, p. 17), a team model where interdisciplinary teams receive release time to pursue common goals such as course development (Armstrong 1980, p. 53), and a triad model where teachers form triads to work together for one or more terms and share "teaching goals, methods, and proposed modifications" (Sweeney 1979, p. 54). One of the assumptions of the triad model is that professors should be as comfortable sharing their knowledge about teaching as they should be about sharing their research. It should become a common professional courtesy.

In the mid-1970s, the search was on for a comprehensive model of faculty development. The single – focus models were effective, but limited in scope. In 1975, no less than five comprehensive models were introduced. These models, or their descendants, represent the major thrust of current faculty development efforts.

In his influential book, *Toward Faculty Renewal,* Gaff presented a three-part faculty development model. The major aspects of this model and their distinguishing characteristics are outlined below (1975, p. 8):

| | Faculty Development | Instructional Development | Organizational Development |
|---|---|---|---|
| Focus: | Faculty members | Courses or curriculum | Organization |
| Purpose: | Growth, skills, knowledge, and techniques | Course design, systematic instruction | Creative effective environment |
| Intellectual Base: | Social Psychology | Education & Ed. Tech | Organization Theory |
| Activities: | Seminars, workshops, evaluations | Redesign courses, writing course objectives | Action research, leadership workshops, and task forces |

Also in 1975, there was published *A Handbook for Faculty Development,* by Bergquist and Phillips.

This "how-to-do-it" manual had a great impact on the faculty development movement, particularly in the smaller colleges. The Bergquist and Phillips comprehensive model also had three major parts and was quite similar to the model proposed by Gaff. In fact, except for the substitution of the term *Personal Development* for *Faculty Development,* the two models are identical in form (Bergquist 1975, p. 5). In their second volume (1977), Bergquist and Phillips did add a fourth dimension to their model — Community Development — and argued that all three aspects of their original model must be present in a mature faculty development program (1977, p. 6). In 1978, Hipps advocated this model for nursing faculty, and warned if nursing did not get going with faculty development, nursing would be forced into it as the other areas had been (1978, p. 695). The current pressures on nursing schools suggest that Hipps was right.

Also in 1975, higher education was introduced to the concept of organizational development through planned change. This was not a new concept, but institutions of higher education are always slow at trying methods taught in their business schools. Francis offered a three stage model: consciousness raising, focal – awareness, and subsidiary awareness (1975, p. 720), and Soulier a five stage model of general awareness, supporting faculty initiatives, faculty development, department development, and maintenance (1976, pp. 4 – 7). It is important to note that in the organizational development model, faculty development is only one step in a much larger process (Richardson 1975, p. 307).

According to Birnbaum, the academic calendar can be used to promote a comprehensive program (1975, p. 227). The idea would be to reduce the teaching semester to fourteen weeks, thus leaving three weeks for corporate developmental activities. Odiorne has advanced the idea of the human resources portfolio (1984, p. 61). He suggests we view the faculty (work force) as assets in a portfolio. Some are stars, some are workhorses, some are problem employees, and others are deadwood. Each group has its own needs and should be treated differently. This model, a takeoff on the Boston Consulting Group's Product – Market Portfolio, assumes that the direction of faculty development is an administrative duty. Many faculty members resist this assumption.

Obviously, the search for the one great comprehensive theory came up empty. Instead, there are many models which may be effective, if they are used in the right place at the right time. Experts believe generally that if a single comprehensive model is to be found, it must recognize the developmental nature of faculty members. As is true of any adult, faculty members are not static in personality and attributes. They grow and pass through identifiable life stages — as a person and as a professional. A comprehensive faculty development program must recognize and allow for this process (Toombs 1975, p. 702; Ralph 1978, p. 61; Freedman 1973, p. 106; Bedsole 1978, p. 78). Adult development will be discussed further in the growth–contracting portion of the literature review.

# Faculty Development Activities

Sabbatical leaves are the oldest form of faculty support. They had their origin at Harvard in 1810, and were granted to allow professors to gain competence in a subject area (Eble 1985, p. 5). Rudolph ties the growth in sabbaticals and paid leaves in the 1890s and following years to the growing emphasis on research and scholarly publication (1968, p. 407). This is not to say, however, that sabbaticals dominated the scene in higher education. In fact, as Eble observes, little attention was paid to sabbaticals until after World War II (1985, p. 5). Now, sabbaticals and leaves of absence are quite common, and are used for such diverse activities as attending advanced courses in a field of study, preparing for conferences and seminars, retooling in another field such as computers, and pursuing special research projects (Hoem 1975, p. 32).

Faculty development activities of one kind or another can now be found around the world and in every type of institution. The first International Conference of Faculty Development convened in 1974 (Munson 1975, p. 5). Since then, activities have been reported in nursing schools, medical schools, law schools, professional schools, community colleges, liberal arts collges, major universities, urban institutions, and small and rural colleges. It is difficult to see all these activities as being usefully related to each other. Centra divides faculty development activities into four categories: traditional practices, programs conducted by experienced faculty members, instructional assistance by specialists, and assessment of teaching quality (1976, p. 47). Ellerbe's typology of faculty development practices includes workshops, seminars, and programs; analysis and assessment practices; media, technology, and course development; institution–wide programs; and miscellaneous activities (1980, p. 1910). A much simpler typology would be to classify activities by the domain of the intended improvement: instruction, professional competence, or personal growth. That is, faculty development activities are designed to assist the faculty member in becoming a better teacher, a more competent professional, or a fully functioning person.

The most widely used approaches to faculty development prior to the "boom period" (pre-1973) were to reduce student/faculty ratio, to purchase new instructional technology, and to recruit new Ph.D's from prominent universities (Bergquist 1975, p. 179). In their survey, Padgett and Thompson found the most common activities to be seminars and workshops, professional leaves, and travel (1979, p. 7). Brown and Hanger listed over 140 activities for consideration by faculty and administrators, and argued that faculty development programs must be a combination of tradition and innovation (1975, p. 202). The implication is that the incorporation of the most common activities may not produce an effective program.

What activities hold the greatest promise? The answer to this question has changed over time. For example, Goodman cites the following list of effective approaches: monthly faculty bulletins, a general professional library, faculty clubs and short and infrequent faculty meetings (1950, pp. 68–9). Miller's list of most worthwhile activities includes sabbatical leaves, private offices, financial assistance to attend professional meetings, adjustment of load for research and writing, financial assistance for further graduate study, and less than a normal load for first year teachers (1963, p. 21). Gaff and Justice, on the other hand, advocate skills training, student evaluation of teaching, technical assistance, and consultation and counseling (1978, pp. 88–9). The common wisdom holds that there are many effective activities, but they must be considered in light of the specific needs of the target group and the institution.

Faculty development activities have featured a variety of techniques to improve the instructional effectiveness of faculty members. Behavioral outcomes have been measured by ratings of videotapes, and are reported to have some impact on cognitive, behavioral, and affective outcomes (Sheets 1984, p. 747). Peer observation caused faculty to carry out critical examination of their teaching styles and effectiveness at the University of North Carolina (Bell 1977, p. 15). Understudies have been assigned to mentor–teachers in the Dallas County Community College System in order to observe instructional methods first hand (Caswell 1983, p. 2), and Carroll presents evidence that good teachers can become even better by receiving instruction in the following five step lecture method: focus, placement, definition, exemplification, and application (1981, p. 84).

Some faculty development activities recognize and focus on the developmental needs of faculty members. Freedman suggests an in-depth structured interview as a means of stimulating self-awareness that could form the basis of an effective program (1973, p. 106). Others believe that career assessment and career development activities play a key role in faculty development programming (Bedsole 1978, p. 78; Baldwin 1981, p. 83). Murphy reports that a short-term faculty exchange can be a means of promoting self-development (1980, p. 33). The recognition of the developmental nature of the teaching profession, that faculty members do seem to track through identifiable career stages, has already had a tremendous impact on the content of faculty development activities, and will probably occupy center stage in the faculty development movement's continuing efforts to develop a comprehensive philosophy.

No faculty development activity has received as much attention, affection, or criticism as has the faculty development grant. The "lack of time and money" is a traditional excuse for nonparticipation in faculty development activities, and "Dean's Grants" were supposed to address at least the second half of this problem. In his comprehensive survey of faculty development practices in 1976, Centra found that grants "to faculty members for improvement to courses or teaching were a common and highly rated practice" (1976, p. 6). Small grants also have the potential to encourage innovation as well as boost morale (Rose 1975, p. 5; Mayo 1979, p. iii; Mayhew 1979, p. 240). Rice noted that if administered properly, "challenge grants" can encourage the team approach (1979, p. 8), but Eble has cautioned that these grants will be much more successful if they are designed for the needs of specific groups of faculty—younger, mid-career, and older teachers (1972, p. 129). One additional warning: faculty grants are often used to supplement or supplant developmental budgets rather than to support faculty development. The best way to deplete the fund in a hurry is to grant money for the purchase of equipment, travel, and overload salaries (Ericksen 1984, p. 145).

In summary, faculty development activities have been around since 1810, and can now be found in all types of institutions all over the world. There is no standard typology of faculty development activities, but they can be classified by the nature of the intended impact—personal growth, professional development, or instructional improvement. There are hundreds of different activities, and each institu-tion must develop an individualized package if the program is to be effective. One key to an effective program seems to be the recognition and allowance for the developmental needs of individual faculty members. The most popular activity is the small grant or challenge grant. There is some evidence that it can boost morale and encourage innovation, but it must be carefully administered or it will be used as an auxiliary departmental budget.

# Organizational Principles

There are several underlying assumptions and operational principles which the literature in the field generally supports as essential to an effective faculty development effort. One fundamental assumption is that good teaching can be taught (Bell 1977, p. 15). If one cannot learn to be a better teacher, then the faculty development budget is merely an administrative expense. The Group for Human Development in Higher Education, credited with giving a big push to the term "Faculty Development," has contended that faculty members should give at least 10 percent of their professional time to faculty development activities (1974, p. 82). While this is a worthy objective, it is interesting to note that no one has called for a corresponding allocation of 10 percent of the instructional budget to support this goal. Also, Eble, for one, is not convinced that such a budget would actually lead to improved results in instruction since "when faculty members are given a choice about what might best further their professional development, they gravitate toward conventional support—time off and travel funds—of their own research" (1985, p. 9). In any case, it is possible to become a better teacher if one has the necessary motivation and support—to that extent, teaching can be taught.

One essential operational principle is that a program must pursue clearly defined goals within the context of institutional needs and priorities. Rose has cautioned that "the single most dangerous deficiency in professional development is this preoccupation with process. Professional developers have lost sight of the goal that gave rise to the professional development movement in the first place . . . and of the goals of their own programs" (1976, p. 22). The real goal of faculty development, according to Reilly, is program development (1983, p. 26). Individual needs and initiatives must be accommodated within the stated needs and priorities of the institution—and this has been recognized early and late in faculty development history (Kelly 1950, p. 121; Stordahl 1981, p. 1; Reilly 1983, p. 25).

During periods of financial stress, the first programs "to get the axe" are (and should be) those that do not support the institutional agenda.

Effective leadership is essential for a faculty development program, and can come from many different sources. Gaff enumerates five alternatives: administrative leadership, a faculty group or committee, an individual with a specialized appointment, a short–term project leader, or the instructional improvement center. Regardless of the alternative, there is considerable debate as to the proper role for the administration to play. One argument is that active administrative support is essential for program success (Jordan 1978, p. 18; Whitmore 1981, p. 13; Phillips 1976, p. 3). Others, however, contend that active participation by the administration will be counterproductive (Sikes 1976, p. 46; Hoyt 1977, p. 36; Warrick 1979, p. 7). Generally, the literature supports a middle-ground approach. The administration of a college or university must initially provide enthusiastic support for the program in a tangible way—then it should keep an interest in the program as it develops, but hands off.

What are the keys to a successful program? Again there is a diversity of opinion. Eble identified financial support, a sound system of development, and the lodging of responsibility with a high administrative officer as essential (1972, p. 129). Faculty development programs are most successfully operationalized, according to Brown and Hanger, if they are decentralized, faculty sponsored, centrally facilitated, visible, explicit, and traditional *and* innovative (1975, p. 202). Nelson's requirements for a successful program include flexibility, individual as well as corporate activity, and vigorous administrative leadership and support (1979, pp. 144–8). Finally, Gaff contended that the following are essential elements of a professional development program: consideration of adult psychological development, adoption of a framework, a sense of the level of institutional awareness about faculty development, and encouragement of faculty to develop professionally (1978, p. 70). Gaff's comments suggest an interesting question. If growth and development are beneficial for the individual and essential for the institution, why is there no penalty if one does not develop?

A tangible and available reward structure may be the key to program success (O'Banion 1978, p. 24; Redditt 1978, p. 39). Other important keys include the department chairperson (Plough 1979, p. 1), the separation of faculty development from faculty evaluation (North 1968, p. 15; Neff 1976, p. 427; Bell 1977, p. 17), and the recognition that faculty development is a political process, thus necessitating the need for coalition networks (Lacy 1983, p. 95).

In summary, what are the general organizational principles that can be used to establish a successful faculty development program? Obviously, inasmuch as there are a great many opinions on this subject, it would be impossible to develop a list with which all would be satisfied. However, the four general principles offered by Hynes would be supported by a strong consensus (1984, pp. 32–4). First, faculty development is a continuous process. Gaff describes faculty development programs as "evolutionary, not revolutionary" (1978, p. 50). Second, the initiative for faculty development should come primarily from faculty. Faculty development is a process of change, and faculty "ownership" and openness are essential. There is also some evidence that a strong nucleus or "critical mass" is necessary for program success (Mathis 1974, p. 26; Gaff 1978, p. 50). A critical mass is certainly easier to achieve if the program is not perceived as a threat.

Third, one must make sure seed money does not become a "money trap." The money trap occurs when means and ends are confused, and faculty members begin to pursue activities for the money rather than for the opportunities for growth and development that the money was designed to provide. And fourth and finally, it is necessary to distinguish teaching improvement from teaching effectiveness. If faculty members believe that faculty development activities are really a covert form of faculty evaluation, participation and support for these activities will be minimal, or negative.

# Participation

After studying the American faculty development scene in 1976, Seldin observed that there was not really much participation in faculty development activities. There were lots of programs, journals, committees foundation grants, and conferences, but faculty members were not turning out in large numbers (1976, p. 7). True, many glowing testimonials were coming in, reporting very positive results, but these programs almost always involved a minority of faculty members — many times the very faculty members who least needed to improve. Owens has counselled that "not all faculty will, or need to, participate in each faculty development activity: but if you provide variety, most faculty members will participate in something" (1977, p. 12). Apparently, Owens forgot to build variety into his own program, because in the same article, he reports that only 15 percent of the faculty used the Teaching Center on campus (p. 10). In a national study on the effectiveness of faculty development functions, Jordan reported that over 50 percent of the instructional centers served 30 percent or less of the faculty (1978, p. 18). These findings tend to substantiate Seldin's initial observation.

Who is this minority who participates in faculty development activities, the group that planned change strategists have referred to as the "early adapters" (Rogers and Shoemaker 1971, p. 181). They seem to be the ones who need developing the least—the competent. A study of participation in community colleges concludes that those who are already competent (as rated by students) participated most often. Therefore, faculty development helps those who need help the least (Garlock 1979, p. 10).

Ellerbe's study of technical institutes and community colleges in North Carolina supports Garlock. His findings indicate that the faculty members who were perceived as good were most active (1980 p. 1910). Gaff noted that the voluntary nature of faculty development activities would insure an atypical mix—on the average, more talented and more interested in teaching (1975, pp. 167–8). Interestingly enough, when outstanding teachers are compared with a random sample of their peers, no statistically different characteristics are found (Gaff 1971, p. 480). One explanation for the participation of competent teachers in faculty development activities is that these activities pose no threat to them. A weaker teacher could view faculty development as a form of evaluation and maybe not be interested in sharing his or her deficiencies with the instructional staff. Perhaps teachers are better than average or competent because they participate in such things as faculty development, or perhaps it works the other way around.

There are several factors that have an impact on participation. One is age. Very young faculty members are not great participators. Some are working on advanced degrees, and most are operating on the survival mode: that is, they are just trying to get through the week. Long term developmental efforts are simply not relevant. Many faculty members with over fifteen years experience feel that they are already developed, or they are involved in faculty development as a mentor, or they believe that the program really does not meet their developmental needs. That leaves the group in the middle. The most active participators seem to be those who have five to fifteen years teaching experience (Toombs 1975, p. 715).

Other factors that might influence participation are employment status, sex-role factors, attitudes, institutional size, time, and money. Gallagher reported that, provided they live close to campus, adjunct faculty are more willing to participate in faculty development activities than are regular faculty members (1977, p. 5). Sex-role characteristics and expectations also have an influence on faculty development among nursing educators (Huggins 1980, p. 29). It may be that sex-role expectations influence the perceived value of faculty development activities, thus modifying participation. If there are negative attitudes concerning faculty development, it is likely that participation will suffer. Stordahl argues that faculty may not like the idea of being "developed." He suggests that the term faculty growth or support would have a more positive reception (1981, p. 1).

Some faculty development programs pose a significant threat to faculty members (Hoyt 1977, p. 36). When faculty evaluation is coupled with development activities, many faculty members simply choose not to participate. Obviously, programs must be evaluated, but the value of using the faculty development program as the means of evaluating individual faculty members is questionable.

Institutional size can also be a factor. From his national survey of faculty development activities, Jordan concluded that the "percent of faculty served by the faculty development center (or program) is inversely related to the size of the institution" (1978, p. 17). Smaller institutions, although operating with fewer resources, may have the edge in developing effective programs.

In summary, we know that a long list of factors may influence the level of participation in faculty development activities, but we do not know why certain individuals participate and others do not, or what the participation rate should actually be for an effective program. Two things, however, are quite clear. Faculty development programs reach only a minority of faculty members, fewer than 30 percent on most campuses. The other is that the average participant is already an above–average teacher. Programs tend to help those who need it the least.

# Benefits and Impact

At the American Association of Higher Education National Conference in 1978, Gaff reviewed the then–current faculty development scene and concluded that while higher education is still learning about this phenomenon, the "evidence is beginning to accumulate that allows us to judge its worth. This evidence supports the conclusion that faculty development has yielded significant benefits to faculty members, administrators, institutions, and students'' (1978, p. 10). What exactly are these ''significant benefits''? In the same year as the conference, Gaff and Morstain reported that over 80 percent of the participants in a sixteen-institution faculty development study indicated the following benefits: contact with interesting people from other parts of the campus, increased motivation for teaching improvement, support of innovative ideas, greater awareness of one's own teaching assumptions, and personal renewal (1978, p. 77). The study concluded that faculty development activities promoted organizational development by helping faculty to become ''less insulated'' (1976, p. 79). For the small college, faculty development activities provide leaders with the opportunity to act as institutional change agents, allowed faculty members to document their value to the institution, and might even help to guide tangential interests back toward institutional needs (1978, p. 39). Since most small colleges have very limited funds with which to support faculty development activities, it is becoming increasingly necessary to give first priority to those faculty development efforts that address stated institutional needs and concerns.

Some benefits of faculty development relate directly to the instructional process. Rose suggests that a small grant fund can support innovation and stimulate faculty to try new teaching techniques (1975, p. 5). Kozma adds that classroom innovation is a function of the level of administrative and financial support at most institutions (1978, p. 442). In separate studies, Hoyt and Howard reported that students rate the teaching effectiveness of faculty who participate in faculty development significantly higher than that of those who do not participate (1977, pp. 32–5). It is not clear, however, whether participation in faculty development improves one's teaching effectiveness, or if it is simply that effective teachers participate in faculty development activities, or both.

Other benefits may include improved academic climates, better role models, and support for personal and professional development. Marker credits the small grant program at Hope College with improving the scholarly climate on campus (Nelson and Siegel 1980, p. 9). Since students learn best by example, Bailey reason, faculty development could be beneficial because growing faculty members could provide needed role models for students (1974, p. 24). Goldman provided ''empirical support that faculty development workshops promote self-actualization of its participants'' (1978, 257). This may become an increasingly important benefit

as institutions begin to deal with the developmental needs of an aging faculty (Gross 1977, p. 752).

Faculty development programs can have their down side as well. For example, faculty programs reach only a portion of those persons they are intended to reach, and the most active participators are those who need it the least, as we noted (Gaff 1975, pp. 167–8). This raises the issue of the cost-effectiveness of many programs. Some would argue that the funds could best be committed to other areas of the educational budget. Hoyt cautioned that faculty development programs may pose a real threat to many faculty members (1977, 36), the main reason being the close association of faculty development with faculty evaluation on some campuses. Growth needs to be encouraged and performance evaluation is necessary, but the assumption that these two efforts must be contained in the same program is questionable. Hodgkinson adds that some faculty find the whole idea of being developed professionally demeaning (1973, p. 119).

In summary, there are many benefits that can accrue from faculty development programs. These include benefits to students, faculty, and the institution. It is important to remember, however, that faculty development efforts can have negative effects as well, and these negatives are very real.

# Evaluation of Faculty Development Programs

Three questions can be raised with regard to evaluation of faculty development programs: why should they be evaluated, what methodology should be used, and by what criteria can the effectiveness of a program be judged? Wergin listed four shortcomings of faculty development programs: they seemed to be at the periphery of institutions, they served a number of different publics, they competed for the faculty's time, and they were plagued with a lack of data (1977, p. 70). This lack of data is troubling because programs must be evaluated in order to justify their existence and improve their effectiveness (Centra 1977, p. 47; Goldman 1978, p. 254).

In their second faculty development how-to manual, Bergquist and Phillips urge program evaluation for the following reasons: to demonstrate accountability to funding sources, to provide an evaluative summation for policy makers, to assist professional staff members in formative evaluation, to contribute information for the institutional decision-making process, and serve as a model for other campus programs (1977, p. 287). Kelly cautioned that it is important to distinguish between two similar but fundamentally different evaluation questions: (1) did the program meet its objectives? and (2) was the program any good? (Diamond 1975, p. 77). A program would not necessarily be effective simply because it meets all of its objectives, particularly if the program objectives were inappropriate or inconsequential. Durzo noted that it is also important for the administration to keep in mind that the purpose of program evaluation is to be able to reward on the basis of productivity, not to punish the people (1976, p. 4).

Obviously, then, there are many good reasons for the evaluation of faculty development programs. Perhaps the best reason is that, without evaluation, programs will have no way to document their contribution to the vitality of the institution. In these days of continual financial stress and constraint, educational programs that cannot do this will have a justifiably short future.

If faculty development programs must be evaluated, what is the best method? There is extensive agreement in the literature that the case study method utilizing data from a variety of sources is the most effective (Palola and Lehmann 1976, p. 79; Wergin 1977, p. 70; Preus 1979, p. 34). Wergin has promoted the case study because it examines the program "as a whole, including its rationale and evolution, activities, accomplishments, and difficulties" (Wergin 1977, p. 70).

What are the most common sources of evidence for case study? Nelsen lists site visits by teams of experts, questionnaires, and interviews with participants (1980, p. 136). To this list, several items can be added, including observation of the general campus milieu, and review of program documentation (Bergquist and Phillips 1977, p. 299). Cronbach pointed out that questionnaires and interviews are valuable in their ability to measure attitudes (1968, pp. 37–52). Hinricks noted that "probably the only way to really evaluate how well the job is done is to ask the people most clearly able to judge —the employees themselves" (1975, p. 481). Although Hinricks was referring to management–development activities in business and industry, there is considerable support in higher education for including student inputs as a source of evidence in the evaluation of faculty development programs (Centra 1972, p. 21; Gaff 1978, p. 59).

In any evaluation, it is essential to establish acceptable criteria for measuring performance (Bergquist and Phillips 1977, p. 290), but there are no universal measures of program performance. "Those interested in organizational effectiveness must recognize that its construct space accommo-dates a wide variety of criteria, all of which cannot be assessed in any one single study" (Cameron and Whetten 1983, p. 274). Hoyt and Howard contend that the ultimate measure of an improvement in effectiveness is the performance of students (1978, p. 26), but exactly how to get at this measure of improvement of effectiveness with any degree of validity is problematic.

A workable means of measuring program effectiveness (or success) is to identify documentable measures of program performance (Milley 1977, p. 191). While evaluating the Bush Foundation's faculty development program, Eble and McKeachie developed a comprehensive list of performance indicators (1985, p. 158):

> Among the Bush program activities, developing & revising courses, acquiring new & different teaching skills, gaining information about how students learn, improving advising procedures, observing and being observed by other teachers, acquiring knowledge of a new field, and improving scholarly competence are documentable in kind, number, and quality. That they constitute changes likely to be beneficial to instruction appears to be a sound premise.

The list of documentable indicators of program performance that Eble developed for the evaluation of the Bush program is as follows: institutional effects — changes in norms about teaching, curricular changes, communication within and among departments, organizational changes, and improved morale; and impact on faculty — motivational effects, cognitive learning, and the development of new skills in teaching (1985, 187).

Eble's work, in this writer's opinion, represents the most effective means of assessing program performance to date. Allen (1986, p. 47) utilized a list of program performance indicators (adapted from Eble) to assess the effectiveness of a faculty development program over a five-year period at different levels of financial support. This case study approach provides a wealth of data unique to each institution that can be used by program professionals, faculty committees, administrative budget panels, and external evaluation agencies in the review and analysis of faculty development programs.

# References

Armstrong, F. H. "Faculty Development Through Interdisciplinarity." *Journal of General Education* 32.1 (1980): pp. 52–63.

Bailey, S. K. "Helping Professors (and Therefore Students) to Grow." *Chronicle of Higher Education* 28 May 1974: p. 24.

Baldwin, R. G. "The Changing Development Needs of an Aging Professoriate." *New Directions in Teaching and Learning, No. 19.* Ed. C. M. N. Mehrotra. San Francisco: Jossey-Bass, 1984.

Baldwin, R. G., et al. *Expanding Faculty Options: Career Development Projects at Colleges and Universities.* Washington: American Association of Higher Education, 1981.

Bedsole, D. T., and D. C. Reddick. "An Experiment in Innovation: The Faculty Career Development Program at Austin College. *Liberal Education* 64.1 (1978): pp. 75–83.

Bell, M. E., et al. "Peer Observation as a Method of Faculty Development." *College and University Personnel Association Journal* 28.4 (1977): pp. 14–17.

Bergquist, W. H., and S. R. Phillips. *A Handbook for Faculty Development.* Washington: Council for the Advancement of Small Colleges, 1975.

⸺. *A Handbook for Faculty Development — Volume II.* Washington: Council for the Advancement of Small Colleges, 1977.

⸺. "Components of an Effective Faculty Development Program." *Journal of Higher Education* 46 Mar.–Apr. 1975: pp. 171–203.

Birnbaum, R. "Using the Calendar for Faculty Development." *Educational Record* 54.4 (1975): pp. 226–30.

Blackburn, R. T., and R. J. Havighurst. "Career Patterns of United States Male Academic Social Scientists." *Higher Education* 8 (1979): pp. 553–72.

Boyer, R. K., and C. Crockett. "Organizational Development in Higher Education: Introduction." *Journal of Higher Education* 44 Sept.–Oct. 1973: pp. 339–44.

Brown, D. G., and W. S. Hanger. "Pragmatics of Faculty Development." *Educational Record* 56.3 (1975): pp. 201–06.

Cameron, K. S., and D. A. Whetten. *Organizational Effectiveness: A Comparison of Multiple Models.* New York: Academic Press, 1983.

Carroll, M. A., and J. C. Tyson. "Good Teaching Can Become Better." *Improving College and University Teaching* 29.2 (1981): pp. 82–5.

Carroll, S. J., and H. L. Tosi. *Management by Objectives: Applications and Research.* New York: Macmillan, 1973.

Caswell, J. M. "Low Cost/High Value Staff Development Program." Annual Conference of the World Futures Society's Education Section. Dallas: February, 1983.

Centra, J. A. *Determining Faculty Effectiveness.* San Francisco: Jossey-Bass, 1979.

⸺. *Faculty Development Practices in U.S. Colleges and Universities.* Princeton: Educational Testing Service, 1976.

⸺. "Plusses and Minuses for Faculty Development." *Change* 9 (1977): pp. 47–9.

⸺. "Self-Ratings of College Teaching: A Comparison with Student Ratings." *The Utility of Student Ratings for Instructional Improvement.* Ed. J. A. Centra. Princeton: Educational Testing Service, 1972.

⸺. "Survey of Faculty Development Practices." *Faculty Development and Evaluation in Higher Education* 2.4 (1976): pp. 2–6.

⸺. "Types of Faculty Development Programs." *Journal of Higher Education* 49 Mar./Apr. 1978: pp. 151–62.

Cronbach, L. J. "Evaluation for Course Improvement." *Readings in Measurement and Evaluation.* Ed. Norman Gronlund. New York: Macmillan, 1968. Dalton, G. W., et al. "The Four Stages of Professional Careers—A New Look at Performance by Professionals." *Organizational Dynamics* Summer 1977: pp. 19–42.

Dobbins, C. G., ed. *Expanding Resources For College Teaching.* Washington: American Council on Education Studies, 1956.

Durzo, J. J. "A Summary of Implications for Implementing Instructional Development Programs." *Faculty Development and Evaluation in Higher Education* 2.2 (1976): pp. 4–8.

Eble, K. E. *The Aims of College Teaching.* San Francisco: Jossey-Bass, 1983.

⸺. *Professors as Teachers.* San Francisco: Jossey-Bass, 1972.

Eble, K. E., and W. J. McKeachie. *Improving Undergraduate Education Through Faculty Development.* San Francisco: Jossey-Bass, 1985.

Ellerbe, J. H. "Faculty Development Practices in North Carolina Technical Institutes and Community Colleges." *Dissertation Abstracts* 41 (1980): p. 1910A.

Ericksen, S. C. *The Essence of Good Teaching.* San Francisco: Jossey-Bass, 1984.

Faris, K. "Faculty Development—The Key to Instructional Development." *Viewpoints* 46.2 (1970): pp. 129–46.

Francis, J. B. "How Do We Get There From Here?" *Journal of Higher Education* 46.6 (1975): pp. 719–731.

Freedman, M. "Facilitating Faculty Development." *Facilitating Faculty Development. New Directions for Higher Education, No. 1.* Ed. M. Freedman. San Francisco: Jossey-Bass, 1973.

Gaff, J. G. "Current Issues in Faculty Development." *Liberal Education* 63.4 (1977): pp. 511–19.

⸺. "Faculty Development: What Values For Whom?" American Association of Higher Education National Conference. Chicago, 1978.

⸺. "Involving Students in Faculty Development."

*New Directions for Higher Education* 6.4 (1978): pp. 59–71.

———. "Overcoming Faculty Resistence." *New Directions for Higher Education* 6.4 (1978): pp. 43–57.

———. *Toward Faculty Renewal.* San Francisco: Jossey-Bass, 1975.

Gaff, J. G., and D. O. Justice. "Faculty Development Yesterday, Today, and Tomorrow." *Institutional Renewal Through the Improvement of Teaching* 6.4 (1978): pp. 85–98.

Gaff, J. G., and B. R. Morstain. "Evaluating the Outcomes." *Institutional Renewal Through the Improvement of Teaching* 6.4 (1978): pp. 73–84.

Gaff, J. G., and R. C. Wilson. "The Teaching Environment." *American Association of University Professors Bulletin* 57.4 (1971): pp. 475–93.

Gaff, S. S., C. Festa, and J. G. Gaff. *Professional Development: A Guide to Resources.* New Rochelle, N.Y.: Change Magazine Press, 1978.

Gallagher, J. F. "Extending Faculty Development: A Case for Adjunct Faculty." *Faculty Development and Evaluation in Higher Education* 3.2 (1977): p. 1.

Garlock, V. P. "Faculty Development at the Community College: Who Participates?" Paper. Annual Meeting of the Educational Research Association. San Francisco, 8–12 Apr. 1979.

Gerth, D. R. "Institutional Approaches to Faculty Development." *Facilitating Faculty Development. New Directions for Higher Education, No. 1.* Ed. M. Freedman. San Francisco: Jossey-Bass, 1973.

Goldman, J. A. "Effect of a Faculty Development Workshop upon Self-actualization." *Education* 98 (1978): pp. 254–8.

Goodman, J. E., ed. *Evaluation and Improvement of Instruction.* Stillwater, OK.: Oklahoma A & M College, 1950.

Gross, A. "Twilight in Academe: The Problem of the Aging Professoriate." *Phi Delta Kappan* 58.8 (1977): pp. 752–4.

———. "Faculty Growth Contracts." *Educational Horizons* 55.2 (1977): pp. 74–9.

Group for Human Development in Higher Education. *Faculty Development in a Time of Retrenchment.* New Rochelle, N.Y.: Change Magazine Press, 1974.

Heiman, J. J. "How and Why a School District Implemented MBO." *National Association of Secondary School Principals* 62 (1978): pp. 36–45.

Hendrickson, R. M. "Faculty Issues in the Eighties." *Phi Delta Kappan* 63.5 (1982): pp. 338–41.

Hershfield, A. F. "Education's Technological Revolution: An Event in Search of Leaders." *Change* 12.8 (1980): pp. 48–52.

"Higher Education Faculty: Characteristics and Opinions." *NEA Research Memo.* Washington: NEA, 1979.

Hinrichs, F. R. "A Feedback Program To Make Management Development Happen." *Personnel Journal* 54.9 (1975): pp. 478–81.

Hipps, O. S. "Faculty Development: Not Just a Bandwagon." *Nursing Outlook* 26.11 (1978): pp. 692–6.

Hodgkinson, H. L. "Adult Development Implications for Faculty and Administrators." *Educational Record* 55 (1974): pp. 263–74.

———. "Faculty Reward and Assessment Systems." *The Tenure Debate.* Ed. B. L. Smith. San Francisco: Jossey-Bass, 1973.

———. *How Much Change for a Dollar: A Look at Title III.* Washington: American Association for Higher Education, 1974.

Hoem, E. "The Professional Development Program You Can Afford." *Community and Junior College Journal* 45.8 (1975): pp. 32–4.

Hoyt, D. P., and G. S. Howard. *The Evaluation of Faculty Development Programs.* Manhattan, Kansas: Office of Educational Research, Kansas State University, 1977.

———. *The Evaluation of Faculty Development Programs.* Research Report Number 39. Manhattan, KS.: Kansas State University, 1977.

Huggins, K. *Nursing Education Research in the South.* Atlanta: Southern Regional Education Board, 1980.

Hutton, J. G. "A Professional School Faculty Development Program." *Faculty Development and Evaluation in Higher Education* 3.2 (1977): pp. 18–19.

Hynes, W. J. "Strategies for Faculty Development." *Leadership Roles of Chief Academic Officers.* Ed. D. G. Brown. New Directions for Higher Education, no. 47. San Francisco: Jossey-Bass, 1984.

Jordan, T. S. *An Examination of the Self Report Status and Effectiveness of Faculty Development Functions at Higher Education Institutions Within the United States.* Cleveland, Ohio: Cleveland State University, 1978.

Kelly, F. J., ed. *Improving College Instruction.* Washington: American Council On Education Studies, 1951.

Kozma, R. B. "Faculty Development and the Adoption and Diffusion of Classroom Innovation." *Journal of Higher Education* 49 (1978): pp. 438–49.

Lacey, P. A., ed. *New Directions for Teaching and Learning: Revitalizing Teaching Through Faculty Development, no. 15.* San Francisco: Jossey-Bass, 1983.

Levine, A. *When Dreams and Heroes Died.* San Francisco: Jossey-Bass, 1981.

Lhota, R. L. *Multidimensional Model: Adjunct Staff Development.* Council of North Central Community and Junior Colleges, 1976.

Lindquist, J. "Contract Learning Innovation Process in Higher Education." Paper. National Conference on Higher Education, Mar. 1975.

———. "Professional Development." *The Modern Amer-*

*ican College.* Ed. A. Chickering. San Francisco: Jossey-Bass, 1981.

Lowman, J. *Mastering the Techniques of Teaching.* San Francisco: Jossey-Bass, 1984.

Maehr, M. L. *The Professor of the Future: Expectations, Dilemmas, Solutions.* Ed. T. B. Massey. Proceedings of the Tenth International Conference on Improving University Teaching. College Park: University of Maryland University College, 1984.

Marsh, R. L. "Management by Objectives: A Multifaceted Faculty Evaluation Model." *Educational Technology* 19.11 (1979): pp. 44–48.

Martin, W. B. "Faculty Development and Evaluation or a Response to Student Interests and Needs." Paper. Annual Meeting of the Association of American Colleges. Washington, 1975.

Mathis, B. C. "Persuading the Institution to Experiment —Strategies for Seduction." Symposium. Improving Business Education Through Innovative Technology. Austin, Texas, March 1974.

Mayhew, L. B. *Surviving the Eighties.* San Francisco: Jossey-Bass, 1979.

Mayo, G. D. *Improving Small College Instruction Through Small Grants.* J. W. Brister Library Monograph Series 10. Memphis: Memphis State University, 1979.

Miller, R. I. *Developing Programs For Faculty Evaluation.* San Francisco: Jossey-Bass, 1974.

———. *Evaluating Faculty Performance.* San Francisco: Jossey-Bass, 1972.

Miller, W. S., and K. M. Wilson. *Faculty Development Procedures in Small Colleges.* Atlanta: Southern Regional Educational Board, 1963.

Milley, J. E. "A Case Study Approach to the Evaluation of a Faculty Development Program Which Uses Individual Development Plans." Unpublished Dissertation. Syracuse University, 1977.

Munson, P. J., et al. *So You Want To Try Faculty Development?* Richmond: Virginia Commonwealth University, 1975.

Murphy, A. F. "The Short-Term Exchange: A Means of Faculty Development." *ADFL Bulletin* 12.1 Sept. 1980, 33–35.

McCarter, W. R., and E. L. Barnes. *Organizing and Managing Small/Rural Colleges: More Bang for the Buck.* Blacksburg, Virginia: Conference on Small/Rural Colleges, Aug. 1978.

Neff, C. B. "Faculty Development Tug O'War or Up a Tree with a Tuning Fork." *Liberal Education* 62.3 (1976): pp. 427–32.

Nelsen, W. C. "Faculty Development: Prospects and Potential for the 1980's." *Liberal Education* 65 (1979): pp. 141–49.

Nelsen, W. C., and M. E. Siegel, eds. *Effective Approaches to Faculty Development.* Washington: Association of American Colleges, 1980.

Noonan, J. F. "Faculty Development Through Experimentation and Interinstitutional Cooperation." *Facilitating Faculty Development. New Directions for Higher Education, No. 1.* Ed. M. Freedman. San Francisco: Jossey-Bass, 1973.

North, J., and S. Scholl. "Revising a Faculty Evaluation System: A Workbook for Decision-Makers." Higher Education Office, 1968.

O'Banion, T. *Organizing Staff Development Programs That Work.* Washington: American Association of Community and Junior Colleges, 1978.

Odiorne, G. S., *Strategic Management of Human Resources.* San Francisco: Jossey-Bass, 1984.

Ost, D. H. "Perspective on Faculty Development." *Future* 14 (1976): pp. 2–4.

Owens, R. E. *Elevating the Importance of Teaching.* Manhattan: Kansas State University, 1977.

Padgett, S., and L. C. Thompson. "A Survey of Professional Development in Arizona Community Colleges." *Center for the Study of Higher Education.* Tucson: Arizona University, 1979.

Palola, E. G., and T. Lehmann. "Improving Student Outcomes and Institutional Decision Making With PERC." *Improving Educational Outcomes.* Ed. O. T. Lenning. San Francisco: Jossey-Bass, 1976.

Phillips, S. R. "Faculty Development: Just Another Committee?" *Faculty Development and Evaluation in Higher Education* 2.2 (1976): pp. 2–4.

Plough, T. R. "Academic Development for Department Chairpersons." Paper. Annual Forum of the Association for Institutional Research. San Diego, 13–17 May 1979.

Pochyly, D. F. "Problem-oriented Faculty Development in a Medical School." *Educational Horizons* 55.2 (1977): pp. 92–6.

President's Commission on Higher Education (Conant Commission). *Higher Education for American Democracy: A Report.* New York: Harper & Row, 1948.

Preus, P. K., and D. F. Williams. *Personalized Faculty Development: Rationale, Applications, and Evaluation.* Bear Creek, Alabama: CESCO Press, 1979.

Ralph, N. B. "Faculty Development: A Stage Conception." *Improving College and University Teaching* 26 (1978): pp. 61–8.

———. "Stages of Faculty Development." *Facilitating Faculty Development. New Directions for Higher Education, No. 1.* Ed. M. Freedman. San Francisco: Jossey-Bass, 1973.

Redditt, P. L., and W. T. William. "Teaching Improvement in a Small College." *New Directions for Higher Education.* Ed. J. Gaff. San Francisco: Jossey-Bass, 1978.

Reilly, D. H. "Faculty Development No: Program Development Yes." *Planning for Higher Education* 11.3 (1983): pp. 25–28.

Rice, R. E., and M. L. Davis. *Program Coordination of*

*Academic Planning and Professional Development.* Stockton: University of the Pacific, 1979.

Richardson, R. C. "Staff Development: A Conceptual Framework." *Journal of Higher Education* 46.1 (1975): pp. 303–12.

Rogers, E. M., and F. F. Shoemaker. *Communication of Innovation.* 2nd Edition. New York: The Free Press, 1971.

Rose, C. "Evaluation: the Misunderstood, Maligned, Misconstrued, Misused, and Missing Component of Professional Development." *Faculty Development and Evaluation in Higher Education* 2.2 (1976): pp. 22–4.

Rose, C., and G. F. Nyre. "From Retrenchment to Renewal: Faculty Development and Innovation in California State Universities and Colleges." Address. International Conference on Improving University Instruction. Heidelberg, May 1975.

Rudolph, F. *The American College and University: A History.* New York: Knopf, 1968.

Seldin, P. *Changing Practices in Faculty Evaluation.* San Francisco: Jossey-Bass, 1984.

———. *Faculty Development: The American Experience.* London: London University, 1976.

———. "Faculty Growth Contracting." *New Directions for Teaching and Learning.* Ed. K. Eble. San Francisco: Jossey-Bass, 1981.

———. "The Second International Conference on Improving University Teaching." *Faculty Development and Evaluation in Higher Education* 2.2 (1976): pp. 13–15.

Sheets, K. J., and R. C. Henry. "Assessing the Impact of Faculty Development Programs in Medical Education." *Journal of Medical Education* 59.9 (1984): pp. 746–48.

Sikes, W., and L. Barrett. *Case Studies on Faculty Development.* Washington: Council for the Advancement of Small Colleges, 1976.

Soulier, S. J. *A Description of a Conceptual Model of Institutional Renewal.* Educational Research & Improvement. Anaheim, Cal., 1976.

Stordahl, B. *Faculty Development: A Survey of the Literature of the '70's.* American Association of Higher Education—Educational Research & Improvement/Higher Education Research Currents, March 1981.

Sullivan, L. T. "Faculty Development: A Movement on the Brink." *College Board Review* 127 (1983): pp. 20–1, 29–30.

———. "Faculty Development: A Movement on the Brink—(Of What)?" *EXCEL Report.* Little Rock: Arkansas University, 1982.

Sutton, C., and G. W. Armfield. "Staff Development for Small/Rural Community Colleges: Effective Renewal with Less Resources." Paper. National Conference on Small/Rural Colleges. Blacksburg, VA., Aug. 1978.

Sweeney, J. M., and A. F. Grasha. "Improving Teaching Through Faculty Development Triads." *Educational Technology* 19.2 (1979): pp. 54–7.

Toombs, W. "A Three-dimensional View of Faculty Development." *Journal of Higher Education* 46.6 (1975): pp. 701–17.

———. "Faculty Development: The Institutional Side." *New Directions for Institutional Research, No. 40,* Dec. 1983: pp. 85–94.

Volpe, R. J. "Growth Contracting at a Small, Liberal Arts College: A Case Study of Faculty and Administrative Reactions." Unpublished dissertation. University of Pittsburgh, 1980.

Warrick, C. M. "The Academic Seven Year Itch and a Possible Home Remedy." Paper. Annual Meeting of the Western College Reading Association. Honolulu, 7–10, Apr. 1979.

Webb, J., and A. Smith. "Improving Instruction in Higher Education." *Educational Horizons* 55.2 (1977): pp. 86–91.

Webb, W. B., and C. Y. Nolan. "Student, Supervisor, and Self-Ratings of Instructional Proficiency." *The Journal of Educational Psychology* 46 (1955): pp. 42–6.

Wergin, J. J. "Evaluating Faculty Development Programs." *New Directions For Higher Education* 17.2 (1977): pp. 57–76.

———. "The Practice of Faculty Development." *Journal of Higher Education* 47.3 (1976): pp. 289–309.

Whitmore, J. R. "Lessons Learned from Dean's Grants for the Restructuring of Teacher Educaion." *Journal of Teacher Education* 32.5 (1981): pp. 7–13.

III.4

# The Small Christian College: Best Hope for the Liberal Arts?

## A. PATRICK ALLEN

As a faculty member in the College of Business, one of my favorite activities is advising new students during registration time. After looking over the course–schedule book and deflecting questions concerning the identity of the easiest professor in Writing I, I like to talk with students about their personal goals and dreams for the future. I have heard many strange and wonderful responses, but the answer that most troubles me (and the answer I hear all too often) is, "I want to be a millionaire before I am thirty–five." That is it. No dreams for a better world. No desires for a fulfilling future. No thoughts for their fellow man. They just want to make it big, and make it quick.

And this preoccupation with personal success is not exclusive to business majors. We are facing an entire generation of college students whose values are a reflection of the society in which they live. The "good life" has been glamorized to such an extent that a simple, thoughtful, purposeful life will no longer do. Now, a college education is expected to enable a student "to yank big bucks." Is it any wonder that our students are troubled when they find out that they have to take such irrelevant things as history, philosophy, and literature? They want to know what you can do with "this stuff." Are not general education courses simply a way of keeping other departments open, and something to "get out of the way" so that you can give your full attention to the major field of study? After all, is not a liberal education really a thing of the past? Who needs it in today's world?

## The Liberal Arts

It is true that the idea of a liberal education is very old. For the Greeks, *encyclios paideia* referred a lifelong learning process, an acculturation of the central values of the society in order to become an effective, participating member (Pfnister 1985,

p. 6). The Greeks knew that a liberal education was the best preparation for authentic citizenship. This type of education, however, was reserved for freemen: slaves could receive vocational training, but not a classical education. It is interesting to note that the idea that a liberal arts education should be reserved for the "ruling class" has remained with us until recent times. In the first part of this century, many state legislatures in the South were unwilling to permit liberal arts courses to be taught in black state universities. These institutions were to provide vocational training. In the 1930s, one black state college was not even allowed to teach Latin. Later, it was "smuggled into the curriculum by offering it under the title *Agricultural Latin*" (Brubacher 1976, p. 76).

In the medieval universities, the curriculum consisted of the *trivium* (grammar, logic, rhetoric) and the *quadrivium* (arithmetic, geometry, astronomy, music). You see, in the first universities, faculties had the odd notion that the proper foundation for professional life and advanced study was the ability to read, write, speak, think, and manipulate symbols. In retrospect, it was not an odd idea at all: in fact, this is still the foundation (the basic skills) necessary for a liberal education today.

But where can you get a liberal education? How is it different from vocational education? Should a university provide vocational training? Can a university provide both liberal arts instruction and vocational training? I believe the answer to the last two questions is yes: in fact, in my opinion, universities today have no choice. The problem is not to choose between liberal and vocational education, but to do both. Jose Ortega y Gassett, the great Spanish philosopher, argued that the university must prepare people to enter the professions (they have to eat), but the people must also possess the power to make their lives "a vital influence, in harmony with the height of their times. Hence it is imperative to set up once more, in the university, the teaching of the

102

culture, the system of vital ideas, which the age has attained. This is the basic function of the university. This is what the university must be, above all else" (Ortega y Gasset 1944, p. 40).

A liberal education, then, involves the transmission of culture and our cultural heritage. It prepares students to become vital participants in their world, and to shape the future. It requires the ability to read, write, speak, and think. It demands a critical mind, a historical perspective, and a sense of purpose and values. This is the business of the university.

# The Christian College

Is a Christian college a good place to get a liberal education? I believe it is, but before I defend my position, let me explain what I mean when I speak of a Christian college. It is not a college that hires only Christian professors or admits only Christian students. It is not a college whose mission is to teach biblical studies or to provide training for Christian vocations. And it is not simply an organization with religious, social, and extracurricular benefits. A Christian college is, first of all, a learning community: that is, it is a college. What makes it a Christian college is the commitment to the *integration* of faith and learning, of faith and culture. This goes beyond the mere interaction of faith and learning (you must take several religion courses). The Christian college is a learning community where the integration of faith and learning is a fundamental value (Holmes 1975, pp. 14–18).

There are at least five reasons why a Christian college is a good place to secure a liberal education. The first reason is its size. Christian colleges are generally quite small, especially when compared to most state universities. Institutions with 20,000 to 35,000 students are not uncommon among state universities. A small campus permits many opportunities for personal attention and interaction: a student can stop by after class and talk to a professor. This is hard to do when there are hundreds of students in a lecture class. A small campus also permits diversity without isolation. Larger campuses realize that smaller groups must be formed if education is to be meaningful, but the smaller groups are usually formed by discipline: all the accounting majors over here and all the chemistry majors over there. This leads to isolation and invites a mini-version of C.P. Snow's "two cultures" problem. A smaller college permits a student to know and interact with other students from a variety of disciplines.

In addition, being small permits a college the flexibility to respond quickly to the needs of the campus community. The small size permits the college to assess needs quickly and move to meet those needs without waiting for permission from different legislative bodies. Size, then, is one reason why a Christian college is a good place to receive a liberal education.

A Christian college also has the capability of building a special kind of learning climate because of the unique nature of community on a Christian campus—because it is a community of faith as well as a community of learning. Christians are comfortable with the idea of building community: it is one of our central values. We understand that being a member of a community involves a commitment to shared values and to each other. Learning, the central task of any college, is more effective in an academic *community,* and the commitment to a community of faith reinforces and affirms the learning community. As Arthur Holmes writes, "faith gives direction and meaning to learning. The goal is still educational, and membership in a Christian college community presupposes commitment to that end" (p. 97).

A third reason is a commitment to teaching: the Christian college is a teaching college. While our professors do conduct research, the primary activity is teaching. At a teaching institution, research and public service are important activities, but only to the extent that they reinforce and enrich the teaching process. With very few exceptions, the faculty is made up of teachers. I believe that the best place to receive a liberal education is from an institution where its faculty are committed to and rewarded for teaching rather than research.

A fourth reason is our concept of vocation. We understand vocation as a calling, an act of ministry. Ministry is not the exclusive domain of the clergy, and developing vocational skills is a part of the necessary preparation for a lifetime of ministry. This tends to obscure the distinction between liberal and vocational education. Rather than an "either–or" situation, this concept of vocation permits a blending of the two. I believe that the successful liberal arts institutions in the 1990s will be those who provide necessary job skills within the context of a liberal education. We can do both, and must do both to be effective.

The last reason why I believe a Christian college is a good place to receive a liberal education is that we ascribe to a set of integrative values. Universities have been criticized for falling down on the job of teaching values. The problem is that with the exception of academic honesty, the modern university cannot come to an agreement about what values to teach. So, colleges and universities "impart values under the guise of imparting none" (Billington 1984, p. 69). At a Christian college, we do share a set of core values and make no apologies for teaching them. James Bryant Conant, one of the great Harvard presidents, put it this way: "The student . . . in college and in graduate school must be concerned, in part at least, with the words 'right' and 'wrong' in both the ethical and the mathematical sense. Unless he feels the import of those general ideas and aspirations which have been a deep moving force in the lives of men, he runs the risk of partial blindness" (1945, p. viii).

# The Best Hope for the Liberal Arts?

The Christian college, as I have said, is in my opinion the best place to get a liberal education. At a time when the modern university is caught between the career interests of its students and the research interests of its faculty, the Christian college may be the best hope for sustaining a meaningful liberal arts tradition. But are we prepared and willing to do it? You see, it is far easier to say we are a liberal arts college than to be one. It is easier to copy the latest curricular trends and academic programs from a nearby state university than to carefully develop programs that are in the best interest of our students and in keeping with our fundamental mission. It is easier to say that we are just as purposeful as the next college down the road than to develop and articulate a distinctive vision for the college. We say that we provide a liberal arts education, but do we really deliver? Could we be guilty of putting designer labels on off-the-rack goods?

This is our challenge as a Christian college. We may be the best hope for the liberal arts, but we have to deliver. To do this, we must maintain a clear sense of mission and purpose. It is not enough to be "just as good as" or to be "just like" the next college. Emulation is not necessarily the way to achieve excellence. We must have a clear sense of what business we are in, and why we are in business. We must be sensitive to the needs of our constituents, but we must never become a slave to the market. The fundamental mission and core values of the institution can not be made subject to the laws of supply and demand. Some things are simply not for sale.

It is also important to articulate our values. The things that are important must be constantly repeated and reinforced. The entire academic community must understand and be committed to the

central values of the institution. This is why I believe so strongly in convocation. It is a time when the entire academic community comes together. It is the best time to build community and to articulate the values of the institution. Small colleges that no longer meet together in convocation have sacrificed one of their greatest educational opportunities.

Finally, it is important to maintain a vital general education program. General education is at the heart of a liberal arts program. Its purpose is to provide to students the knowledge, skills, and values common to all graduates without regard to the major field of study. We must be careful not to fall into the trap of copying the general education program of another college. Each institution is unique, and must develop its own curriculum and delivery system. As the recent Carnegie Report argues, "General education is not a single set of courses. It is a program with a clear objective, one that can be achieved in a variety of ways. And while there is great flexibility in the process, it is the clarity of purpose that is critical" (Boyer 1987, p. 101).

# Closing Comments

A liberal education involves the transmission of culture and the acquisition of knowledge, skills, and values which enables a student to live at the height of the times. The best place to receive a liberal education is a Christian college because of its size, an orientation toward community, a set of integrative values, a concept of vocation as ministry, and a commitment to teaching as the central activity.

The challenge for the Christian college is to deliver the product. It is easier for a college to call itself a liberal arts institution than to be one. Colleges must maintain a clear sense of mission and purpose, constantly articulate the central values of the institution, and promote an energetic and integrative general education program.

This calling will take a great deal of time and effort, but that the benefits far outweigh the costs. In my opinion, it is better to tend the flame than to guard the ashes.

# References

Billington, J. "Universities Have Fallen Down on the Job of Teaching Values." *U.S. News and World Report* October 1, 1984: 69.

Boyer, E. *College.* New York: Harper & Row, 1987.

Brubacher, J., and Rudy, W. *Higher Education in Transition.* Third Edition. New York: Harper & Row, 1976.

Hofstadter, R., and Smith W. *American Higher Education.* Volume II. Chicago: University of Chicago Press, 1961.

Holmes, A. *The Idea of a Christian College.* Grand Rapids: Eerdmans, 1975.

Ortega y Gasset, J. *Mission of the University.* New York: Norton, 1966 (org. ed. 1945).

Pfnister, A., Lisensky, R., and Sweet, S. *The New Liberal Learning.* Washington: The Council of Independent Colleges, 1985

## III.5

# Capital Infusion and Withdrawal Program Performance at Varying Levels of Funding

A. PATRICK ALLEN

Colleges and universities never have enough money. The standard faculty bromide is, "If I had more time and money, then I would be more active in faculty development activities." Actually, since time is a matter of having enough money to farm out some of one's duties or hire additional staff, the argument pretty much boils down to money. But is money the key factor in the success of faculty development activities? How does money or the lack of money affect the nature of instructional development on a college or university? In this article, some general relationships between the level of financial support and program effectiveness will be explored, followed by an examination of the dynamics of capital infusion and withdrawal (Allen 1986, p. 8).

## Financial Support

Until lately, there has been a tendency in higher education to throw money at our problems, but Hesburgh reminds us that money by itself is never enough (Hechinger 1981, p. 126):

> Higher education and every other enterprise moves forward when there is good leadership: otherwise it stagnates. We need people with vision, elan, geist, people who have standards and a certain toughness . . . Of course you need money. But if you have money and no vision, you just squander it."

Assuming we have leadership, can money have an impact on faculty development activities? Kozma reports that classroom innovation is a function of the level of support. Several instructional innovations were developed by a small faculty group when given extensive support and release time. Those given less support did improve, but to a lesser degree; while no measurable change in teaching tech-

niques were detected among the control groups (Kozma 1978, pp. 442–3). The problem is that in higher education, the "funds are divided into hundreds of small 'pots' and allocated to departments . . . Ideas (and innovations) that do not fit this 'bits and pieces' resource allocation system are excluded from consideration" (Hershfield 1980, p. 49). White adds that "the most common constraints to behavior of an individual are the constraints imposed by those allocating the resources" (1974, p. 366). Faculty development does seem to be a very "small pot" in the institutional allocation system. Two studies report that faculty development activities receive less than 1 percent of the instructional budget at most institutions (Hammons and Wallace 1976, p. 20; Ellerbe 1980, p. 1905). Does it appear likely that this funding pattern will change? Drucker is not optimistic (1980, p. 41):

> Unless challenged, every organization tends to become slack, easygoing, diffuse. It tends to allocate resources by inertia and tradition rather than by results. Above all, every organization tends to avoid unpleasantness. And nothing is less pleasant and less popular than to concentrate resources on results, because it always means saying "No."

What is the relationship between financial support and institutional size? There is some evidence that finances have a greater impact on smaller institutions (Gaff 1975, p. 168). Additional support comes from Eble. "One of our major conclusions is that in terms of cost-effectiveness, the Bush program grants had the greatest impact per dollar upon the smaller institutions" (1985, p. 216). The findings of Anderson's study, *Finance and Effectiveness: A Study of College Environments,* are less conclusive (1983, p. 119):

> There is some slight evidence that private colleges with improved finances function slightly better, the

opposite seems to hold true for public institutions . . . Overall, the results suggest that the linkage between fiscal resources and college functioning is very weak.

Several other studies were also inconclusive as to the relationship between resources and effectiveness. After a study of Title III programs, Hodgkinson concludes that there is "a general interrelationship of size of grant, size of program, and quality of institutional improvement, but the correspondences are far from absolute" (1974, p. 49). Anderson's study could not establish a positive and general relationship between finance and faculty perception of college operations (1985, p. 636). Although these studies provide mixed evidence for the relationship between financial resources and the effectiveness of faculty development activities, it is important to remember that the focus of the last two studies was on institutional effectiveness rather than specifically on faculty development or instructional improvement activities. Overall, Ericksen is probably right. "Advice about teaching is helpful, but money is better" (1984, p. 144).

# Capital Infusion and Withdrawal

Very little is known about capital infusion (an increase in the annual level of support for a faculty development program in the amount of $50,000 or more) or capital withdrawal (a decrease in the annual level of support for a faculty development program in the amount of $50,000 or more), and even less about what happens when capital infusion and withdrawal occur in the same program within a relatively short period of time—a process studied by Allen (1986).

Hynes warns that capital infusion can become a "money trap." The money trap happens when faculty members begin to pursue activities in order to get the money rather than for the improvement or development which the funds were designed to foster (Hynes 1984, p. 33). Gaff observes that regardless of the amount of capital infusion, massive organizational change is not likely (1975, p. 169). Lauderdale adds that capital infusion is more likely to support and solidify existing institutional structures than to invite a complete institutional overhaul (1971, p. 14). It appears that capital infusion can easily reach a point of diminishing returns. Too much infusion, like too much sugar, may cause its

own special problems. This is not to say that capital infusion is not helpful to an institution seeking new programs and activities. Carlberg argues that the Gordon College growth–contracting program could not have "gotten off the ground without substantial funding. It probably would have been viewed as too much work (or busy work) for too little return" (1981, p. 19). It seems, then, that capital infusion is helpful to institutions seeking new and innovative programs, but too much infusion in too short a time can quickly reach a point of diminishing returns and may even become counterproductive.

Capital withdrawal (or severe retrenchment) can obviously cause many problems as well. Mortimer cites three common results: patterns of faculty–administrative interaction undergo severe stress, there is a general decline in institutional quality, and there is a serious decline in faculty morale (1979, pp. 53–4). But what happens when capital infusion and withdrawal occur in the same program over a relatively short period of time, say three to five years? This funding pattern could occur when, after a college or university receives a large program demonstration grant, it is unable to maintain the program at anything like the original level of support (with institutional funds) after the funding period expires. Lauderdale points out that capital infusion will have little impact on dysfunctional organizational structures. If capital withdrawal follows, most changes achieved will be temporary (1971, p. 14).

Carlberg, however, is more optimistic (1981, p. 19):

> there is some evidence that now that the program is established [capital infusion], some version of it would continue should major funding run out [capital withdrawl] . . . However, it is doubtful that the current highly structured version of this program would flourish should funding become unavailable. It might again be a matter of too much work for too little return.

Milley lends support to Carlberg's optimism. In her evaluation of the Gordon College growth–contracting program, she reports that 66 percent of the participants in the 1976 program disagreed with the following statement: "If program funds were not available, I would see little value in participating in the program." Another 11 percent were uncertain, and only 23 percent agreed with the statement (Milley 1977, p. 444). It appears, then, that a growth–contracting program with substantial funding can promote participation. But will this participation have a positive cumulative impact maintaining the program's performance after capital withdrawal?

In a recent study, Allen sought to address this question (1986). He sought to answer the following question, "What is the relationship between the levels of financial support and the performance of a growth contracting program?" More specifically, this study sought to determine the impact of varying levels of funding (both aggregate program financial support and individual faculty financial support) and selected indicators of program performance (participation, participant satisfaction, impact upon the faculty, and impact upon the institution) for a small–college growth–contracting program.

The study employed an embedded single–case design. Twelve research questions were formulated to guide the investigation of Southern Nazarene University's growth–contracting program between 1979 and 1984. This was an ideal case for examination because of the program's funding pattern during the time period proposed for study. The essential organization, operation, and administration of the program did not change during the five years, but the aggregate funding levels changed dramatically (experienced capital infusion and withdrawal).

In order to provide multi–source data, three methods were used to gather data from over fifteen sources for this study: (1) review and examination of program documentation and related institutional records; (2) evaluation and assessment of all participants' growth plans and evaluation reports; and (3) in–depth interviews with sixty–three faculty participants, four nonparticipants, the Academic Dean, the chairman of the faculty development committee, and seven academic division heads.

The general analytic strategy was to develop a "descriptive framework" for organizing the case study. Within this descriptive framework, four primary modes of analysis were employed: pattern description and analysis, time–series analysis, the analysis of embedded units (organizational subunits), and explanation development.

The following general conclusions were drawn from the results of the study. There is a high positive relationship between substantial increases and decreases in the SNU growth contracting program's annual budget and each of the four dependent variables—participation, participant satisfaction, impact upon the faculty, and impact upon the institution. At higher levels of support, however, the relationship is not so direct and is influenced by other factors such as the choice of activities to pur-

sue and the degree of accomplishment of proposed activities. There is also a marked–to–high positive relationship between the amount of individual financial support and the four dependent variables. At high levels of financial support (in excess of $1000), the relationship is also influenced by the nature of activities selected by participants, the degree of project accomplishment, and the size and scope of proposed activities.

The study concluded with the following recommendations for the implementation of a growth–contracting program: (1) be sure that program priorities reflect institutional goals and needs; (2) recognize that not everyone will participate every year; (3) be sure to put enough money into the program to permit it to be successful, but do not think that money alone is enough; (4) do not spread the funds too thin; (5) be careful not to supplant institutional funds; (6) allow for the developmental needs of all faculty members; (7) be sure to seek a faculty consensus about the definition of faculty development on the campus; (8) encourage corporate activity; (9) reduce paperwork to a bare minimum; (10) maintain open communication with the faculty; (11) share program results; and (12) evaluate the program.

From this study, several points are clear. First, the capital infusion and withdrawal process is difficult for any institution to endure. Infusion brings rising expectations and anticipation of great things to come — permission to dream. But withdrawal may not only crush faculty expectations but also magnify other institutional problems as well. The study indicates that the institution might have been better off to have refused the initial grant than to have accepted the funds without the ability to maintain a reasonable level of financial support after the expiration of the grant.

Second, the study brings into question the value of "demonstration grants" — particularly to institutions who do not have the expertise or financial support to effectively maintain these programs. Perhaps the role of the federal government and private foundations needs to be more than just a source of financial support, especially if the grants may ultimately prove to be harmful.

Finally, much more needs to be learned about the capital infusion and withdrawal process. There is a dearth of good research on this subject, even though institutional experience with this process is all too familiar. It would be wasteful to spend money that ultimately does little good, and it would be stupid to utilize previous financial resources in such a manner that actually hurts the institution.

# References

Allen, A. P. "The Relationships of Growth Contracting to Levels of Financial Support: A Case Study." Unpublished dissertation. University of Oklahoma, 1987.

Anderson, R. E. "Does Money Matter?" *Journal of Higher Education* 56.6 (1985):623–639.

———. *Finance and Effectiveness: A Study of College Environments.* Princeton: Educational Testing Service, 1983.

Carlberg, R. J., ed. *Professional Development Through Growth Contracts Handbook, 1981.* Wenham, Mass.: Gordon College, 1981.

Drucker, P. F. *Managing in Turbulent Times.* New York: Harper and Row, 1980.

Eble, K. E., and W. J. McKeachie. *Improving Undergraduate Education Through Faculty Development.* San Francisco: Jossey-Bass, 1985.

Ellerbe, J. H. "Faculty Development Practices in North Carolina Technical Institutes and Community Colleges." *DAI* 41 (1980): p. 1910A.

Ericksen, S. C. *The Essence of Good Teaching.* San Francisco: Jossey-Bass, 1984.

Gaff, J. G. "Current Issues in Faculty Development." *Liberal Education* 63.4 (1977): pp 511–19.

———. *Toward Faculty Renewal.* San Francisco: Jossey-Bass, 1975.

Hammons, J. O., and T. H. S. Wallace. "Sixteen Ways to Kill a Faculty Development Program." *Educational Technology* 16.12 (1976): pp 16–20.

Hechinger, F. "Hesburgh Earned Respect the Hard Way." *New York Times,* 13 Oct., 1981.

Hershfield, A. F. "Education's Technological Revolution: An Event in Search of Leaders." *Change* 12.8 (1980): pp. 48–52.

Hodgkinson, H. L. "Adult Development Implications for Faculty and Administrators." *Educational Record* 55 (1974): pp. 263–74.

Hynes, W. J. "Strategies for Faculty Development." *Leadership Roles of Chief Academic Officers.* Ed. D. G. Brown. New Directions for Higher Education, no. 47. San Francisco: Jossey-Bass, 1984.

Kozma, R. B. "Faculty Development and the Adoption and Diffusion of Classroom Innovation." *Journal of Higher Education* 49 (1978): pp. 438–49.

Lauderdale, M., and J. Peterson. *Community Development.* Washington: Education, Training, and Research Sciences Corp., 1971.

Milley, J. E. "A Case Study Approach to the Evaluation of a Faculty Development Program Which Uses Individual Development Plans." Unpublished Dissertation. Syracuse University, 1977.

Mortimer, K. P., and M. L. Tierney. *The Three "R's" of the Eighties: Reduction, Reallocation, and Retrenchment.* Washington: American Association for Higher Education, 1979.

White, P. E. "Resources as Determinents of Organizational Behavior." *Administrative Science Quarterly* 19 (1974): pp. 366–79.

## III.6

# Growth Contracting in the Small College

## A. PATRICK ALLEN

Hard times are producing nothing less than a complete change in the character of our institutions of higher learning. Every aspect of their work is being affected. Their faculty, their students, their organization, their methods, their teaching, and their research are experiencing such alteration that we who knew them in the good old days shall shortly be unable to recognize them. Many changes are for the better. Others may wreck the whole system (Hutchins 1933, p. 714).

Although these words were written during the great depression of the 1930s, they read as though they were printed in a recent issue of the *Chronicle of Higher Education.* The 1980s will probably be characterized as the second great depression for all of higher education, but the small college has been in perennial trouble. Looking back on the relatively stable era of the 1950s, McGrath writes (1961, p. vi):

Severe financial problems related to the curriculum already exist in the independent liberal arts colleges. Indeed, their status in the structure of higher education and in the whole of American Society now rests in the balance. The outcome will be determined very largely by the willingness of faculty members to view the entire life of the college objectively, including their own special interests . . . If the crisis deepens without appropriate faculty action, the tradition of faculty control of the curriculum will necessarily be abrogated by those who have the legal and moral responsibility to preserve and advance the welfare of these colleges (1961, vi).

and ten years later, Astin cautions (1972, pp. 10–11):

If the state college and the junior college can be regarded as the second-class citizens of higher education, then the invisible college is the third-class citizen, the unassimilated, the "outsider." It faces most of the same problems as the other two but always on a more severe scale . . . Of all institutions of higher education, invisible colleges are the most likely to become extinct.

What are some of these severe problems that face the small college, and militate against faculty development efforts? Centra's comprehensive survey of faculty development activities in the United States reveals that fewer than 40 percent of smaller colleges had any type of developmental unit on campus ten years ago (1978, p. 161). This was probably due to a lack of funds rather than a lack of commitment. Sutton adds that faculty development efforts in smaller institutions tend to be focused on the curriculum, have less organization than in larger institutions, and do not meet developmental needs (1978, pp. 1–5). Another problem is that many small–college faculty members feel overwhelmed by the sheer variety of things expected of them (Lowman 1984, p. 214), and institutional expectations conflict with the predominant pattern of professional success in higher education (Miller and Wilson 1963, p. 3). When we add to all of this the fact that faculty in smaller colleges often suffer from various forms of isolation owing to such things as very small departments and rural locations (Smith 1979, pp. 3–7), it is no wonder that Akin calls faculty development in liberal arts colleges the "unfinished agenda for the 80's" (1984).

All this is not to say that being small does not have its advantages. Being small does permit the institution to change more rapidly than a large institution, and often this change process can involve an entire academic department or division with very little difficulty (Bergquist and Phillips 1975, p. 204). Smaller colleges may also benefit by having developmental activities not only run for faculty but also by the faculty (Centra 1976, p. 6), thus enhancing faculty "ownership" of the program. Parsons adds that smaller institutions can more effectively involve part–time faculty in instructional development activities (1980, p. 54). There is also evidence that small–college faculty development programs are more cost–effective (Eble 1985, p. 216), involve a higher percentage of the total faculty as participants (Jordan 1978, p. 17), and have a greater impact on the life of the institution (Gaff 1975, p. 168).

In summary, the small college is fighting for its survival and has been fighting for at least the past fifty years. An effective faculty development program will, undoubtedly, enhance the vitality of these institutions and their efforts to renew from within. However, many factors such as professional isolation, heavy teaching loads, and limited financial resources work against the best intentions. On the other hand, as we noted, there is growing evidence that faculty development programs at smaller institutions are not only cost–effective, but also have a greater impact on the institution. Therefore, while smaller colleges often face more severe versions of the same problems pressing all of higher education today, their size may in the last analysis be their biggest asset rather than the deadly liability that it is often made out to be.

# Background to Growth–Contracting Programs

Before reviewing the literature concerning growth–contracting faculty development programs, it will be helpful to provide a brief critique of two concepts which provided a springboard for the growth–contracting movement—adult development and management by objectives.

## Adult Development

One of the central themes of adult development is that, like children, adults grow and move through identifiable life stages. In his seminal work on adult development, *Childhood and Society,* Erikson discusses the following adult stages and the corresponding developmental task for each stage.

| Developmental Stage | Primary Resolution |
|---|---|
| Adolescence | Identity vs. Role Confusion |
| Young Adulthood | Intimacy vs. Isolation |
| Adulthood | Generativity vs. Stagnation |
| Old Age | Ego Integrity vs. Despair |

Erikson states that the principal task of adult life is the quest of a sense of generativity—to leave one's mark by producing something that will endure (1963, pp. 227–32). Other stage models have been

developed that build on Erikson's work, and include the concept of transition points as well as the idea of adult stages. For example, Loevinger offers a model with five adult stages and two transition levels (1976, p. 19). Levinson's model, on the other hand, features a person's "life structure" that evolves in an orderly sequence through five stages and four transition points including the now familiar "mid-life transition" (1978, p. 41). As with Erikson's model, these theories suggest that specific key issues must be resolved before one can move through a transition period and on to the next developmental stage.

Dalton applies the stage model to professional careers, and describes four unique stages of career development—apprentice, colleague, mentor, and sponsor (1976, p. 23). Ralph suggests that faculty must grow through these stages in their professional careers, and that effective faculty development programs must "reflect the fact of the growth of increasingly complex ways of thinking and acting" (1973, p. 61). Hodgkinson adds that faculty are "like other mature human beings and continue to grow psychologically" throughout their lives (1974, p. 264), and faculty development efforts must recognize the developmental nature of faculty if such programs are to be effective in meeting real needs (Bergquist and Phillips 1975, p. 181; Gross 1977, p. 752; Claxton and Murrell 1984, p. 40).

Faculty development can thus be understood as part of a specialized socialization process for teaching professionals in higher education (Brim and Wheeler 1966, p. 27). In addition to the idea that faculty development is actually a part of the process of socialization, adult–developmentalists have made several other contributions to our understanding of faculty development. First, adults are not static, but move through identifiable life stages. Second, professionals move through distinct career stages as well. Third, faculty members are professionals *and* people. Faculty development programs must recognize and allow for these growth and socialization factors if they are to be effective in promoting meaningful and lasting change.

## Management by Objectives

"Cheshire-Puss," Alice began . . . "would you tell me please, which way I ought to go from here?" "That depends on where you want to get to," said the cat. (Carroll 1971, pp. 56–7)

As the Cheshire cat reminded Alice, a road map is of little use until you know where you are and where you want to be. Management by objectives (MBO) is essentially an organizational process designed to foster agreement between the employee and a supervisor as to specific performance objectives and means of assessment. Raia defines management by objectives as (1974, p. 11)

> A philosophy of management (proactive) (participative) and a process consisting of a series of interdependent and interrelated steps: (1) the formulation of clear, concise statements of objectives; (2) the development of realistic action plans for their attainment; (3) the systematic monitoring and measuring of performance and achievement; and (4) the taking of the corrective actions necessary to achieve the planned results.

In practice, MBO works in the following way. The subordinate and superior mutually establish and agree on objectives to be accomplished. Action plans are then developed and converted into individual work plans. Periodic progress reviews and formal appraisals follow, which allow management to provide rewards based on performance (accomplishment of objectives). Before objectives and work plans can be developed, however, it is essential for the organization to establish and communicate long–range goals, strategic plans, and overall organizational objectives in order to insure that individual plans are tied to organizational needs and priorities.

Management by objectives was the most popular method used in management development programs during the 1950s (Glueck 1974, p. 385). Since then, MBO has been used in a wide variety of organizations in both the public and private sectors with an interesting array of outcomes. S. J. Carroll and H. L. Tosi review the application of MBO in sixty English firms and report that MBO helps to identify problems and improve the overall developmental climate (1973, p. 12). Management by objectives has also been reported to help clarify mission and goals, increase productivity, promote the understanding of organizational goals (Carroll and Tosi 1973, pp. 11–13), and increase job satisfaction on the part of participants (Ivancevich 1972, p. 135).

Management by objective programs have been instituted in a variety of educational settings. At the secondary level, MBO has been employed primarily wtih school boards (Moberly and Stiles 1978) and with school administrators (Heiman 1978). I. I. Dow reviews several MBO studies in secondary schools and concludes that "a modified MBO program can work in education," and will "provide the identity, commitment, and motivation necessary for creating growth in a professional organization"

(1981, pp. 379–85). In higher education, MBO programs have been implemented in many colleges and universities including the University of Tennessee, William Rainey Harper College, Brigham Young University, and the University of Utah (Temple 1973, p. 99). Heaton concludes that MBO can work in higher education and may provide an answer to the call for accountability by a wide variety of constituent groups (1975, p. 2; Fleming 1978, p. 28).

MBO has been used with administrators and faculty alike. Pearlman relates how Roosevelt University developed an "Administration by Objectives" program (1975, p. 5). At the University of Massachusetts, a similar program is called the "Management Review and Analysis Program" (Fretwell 1976, p. 4).

Winstead explains how MBO was implemented at Furman University as an aid for the institutional planning process (1977, p. 2). In spite of the fact that a workbook has been developed to assist in the step-by-step establishment of a faculty MBO program at a college or university (Deegan and Fritz 1975, p. 246), comprehensive MBO programs targeted at the faculty have not produced entirely positive results. Marsh reports that MBO can support a "multifaceted faculty evaluation model" based on mutually agreed upon criteria for evaluation between a faculty member and the department chair (1979, pp. 44–8). Wooten cautions, however, that an appraisal system employing management by objectives will be ineffective unless faculty members are allowed to participate in the administration of their areas (1980, pp. 208–10).

Cravens and Ross present a management by objectives model for faculty (based on the work of Odiorne), and cite these advantages (1976, p. 13):

> increased faculty productivity; involvement of faculty in the establishment of long and short-term goals (department and college); eliminate rivalry between faculty members; and provide deans with more specific knowledge of faculty accomplishments and constraints preventing objective accomplishment.

Their MBO model is based on three assumptions: a planning period of twelve months, department heads viewed as administrators, not coordinators; and departments and colleges *with* goals— established through faculty participation (1976, p. 14). The third assumption, established goals through faculty participation, may greatly reduce the number of colleges where this model is relevant.

Two additional studies report mixed results. Terpstra utilized "pre" and "post" questionnaires measuring perceptions of performance and satisfaction, and found that during an MBO application, faculty reported an increase in performance but a decline in satisfaction (1982, p. 353). Shetty and Carlisle, after conducting an exploratory study of faculty reactions to an application of management by objectives in a university setting concluded (1974, p. 78):

Goal setting in a university setting would increase awareness of organizational goals, improve planning, and improve evaluation: however, faculty consistently complained of (1) excessive paperwork, (2) insufficient involvement, (3) lack of departmental goals, (4) difficulty in setting goals, and (5) inadequate reviews and feedback.

Why is it that MBO programs are more successful with college and university administrators than with faculty? The key seems to be that faculty members do not always feel that they have a vital role in institutional governance. Nash points out that MBO will not work "by itself" — it must be "linked to strategy and image, based on a true spirit of participation" (1983, p. 15). Richardson criticizes MBO programs that fail to include the "means of developing a supportive governance structure, but simply focus on clearly defined organizational goals and priorities" (1975, p. 309). Reid seems to summarize the criticisms of MBO for faculty (1974, p. 286):

If we have not assured that the organizational context can support the required behavior through goal setting, sharing of objectives, developmental opportunities, self-control and recognition for achievement of predetermined goals, then we may instead be launching individuals into a period of frustration and disenchantment.

Before leaving this section on management by objectives, we will briefly trace its evolution, and examine its contribution to the development of a process that addresses at least some of the faculty concerns cited above as shortcomings of an MBO process in higher education.

Although Drucker is often credited with the invention of the term "management by objectives," he gives the credit to Alfred Sloan of General Motors. "I didn't invent the term 'management by objectives'; actually Alfred Sloan used it in the 1950's. But I put it in a central position, whereas to him it was just a side effect" (Tarrant 1976, p. 77). Drucker placed MBO in a central position by insisting that "the manager should be directed and con-

trolled by the objectives of performance rather than by his boss" (1954, p. 137). "It is the manager's specific job to make what is desirable first possible and then actual" (p. 12) . . . and "the only principle that can do this is management by objectives and self-control" (1954, p. 136).

During the 1960s, the concept of management by objectives broadened as a result of the influence of McGregor, Schleh, and Odiorne. McGregor subtitles his Theory–Y approach Management by Objectives, and promotes "management by integration" by arguing that "external control and threat of punishment are not the only means of bringing about effort toward organizational goals or objectives. Man will exercise self-direction and self-control in the service of objectives to which he is committed" (1960, pp. 47–8). Schleh introduced management by results — a slight modification of the MBO original process. He believes that a manager must focus on final results in order to integrate the work of the individual with the overall objectives of the institution (1961, p. 6). Odiorne expanded Drucker's original idea of MBO and set it in systems terms (1965). While a Dean at the University of Utah, Odiorne promoted the application of MBO in institutions of higher education.

In 1974, Raia highlighted a developmental aspect of MBO applications by citing growth planning as the last step in the MBO process (1974, p. 16). That same year, Buhl and Greenfield pointed out that growth contracting, a recently emerging form of faculty development found primarily in smaller institutions, actually represented a blending of two important concepts—adult development and management by objectives (1975, p. 115). It was not until after these two concepts gained wide understanding and support in higher education during the early 1970s that the growth–contracting movement began to flourish.

# The Growth–Contracting Process

Faculty development programs using growth contracting as their core activity go by a variety of names. Although they are typically called growth–contracting programs, they have also been referred to as growth planning programs (Sikes and Barrett 1976, p. 28), faculty support programs (Gerth 1973, p. 90), personalized faculty development activities (Preus 1979), qualitative growth development programs (Kingsley 1978), and individual activity–performance agreements (Kramer 1976, p. 2).

Whatever the program title, growth contracting is essentially a process whereby a faculty member can contract with the institution for the support necessary to pursue personal and professional growth. Volpe defines a growth contract as a "formal written, systematic outline for role definition, professional growth, and performance appraisal" (1980, p. 16). Seldin's definition is similar — "a plan written by a professor which spells out his self-development, containing his specific goals for the year, each goal accompanied by intended means of accomplishment and assessment, and a required budget" (1981, p. 90). In what follows here, growth contracting will be defined as a three-part faculty development process in which faculty members assess their own professional growth needs, develop a written growth plan, and then contract with the institution for the support necessary to accomplish the proposed plan.

Growth contracting is neither new to higher education nor exclusive to the faculty. Geller advocates the use of growth contracts as a staff development activity for student personnel professionals (1982, p. 20). There were "learning contracts" designed for out-of-class learning and growth for students even before contracting received attention as a faculty development tool (Dulley 1975, p. 53; Linquist 1976, p. 3; Feeney and Riley 1975, p. 10). Bare reports on a successful growth contracting program involving fifty-two administrators in the SUNY system (1983, p. 7). Inasmuch as administrators have more control over discretionary budgets than do individual faculty members, growth contracting may be more swiftly and successfully implemented at the administrative level than at the faculty level.

Growth contracting programs have been developed at many colleges and universities, although primarily at the smaller institutions. Twenty-one institutions were cited by Volpe as having implemented a growth contracting program, and they illustrate the diversity of its appeal: Austin College, Alvin Community College, Azusa Pacific College, College of the Mainland, Elmira College, El Paso Community College, Freed–Hardeman College, Gordon College, Hampshire College, John Brown University, Mankato State College, Ottawa University (Kansas), Spring Arbor College, St. Olaf College, University of Alabama (New College), University of Massachusetts (College of Education), University of Pennsylvania (School of Optometry), University of Texas Medical School, University of Vermont, Wharton County Junior College, and William Jewell College (Volpe 1980, pp. 19–30).

Where did the practice of growth contracting first begin? The answer to this question is not entirely clear. Although Gordon College is often credited as the first institution to develop a growth contracting program, Milley reports that the University of Vermont developed a growth contracting program called the Annual Review Process for Teaching and Learning Specialists in the Spring of 1975 — six months before Gordon College began its program (1977, p. 12). What does seem clear is that growth contracting began at about the same time in a wide variety of institutions all across the country in the mid-1970s, and that with the assistance of a large Kellogg Foundation grant, Gordon College quickly became an advocate and a model for other institutions to follow.

While not widely accepted, growth contracting has been touted as a viable substitute for tenure (O'Toole 1978, p. 27). Park suggests that a five year contract with periodic review would provide "greater flexibility both for the individual and the institution, while offering the certainty of five years of a stated and agreed upon contractual relationship" (1972, p. 36). The faculty at Dominican College in San Rafael, California, thought enough of the idea that they voluntarily gave up the tenure system to adopt a system of periodic review (Lavaroni and Savant 1977, p. 499). Dominican College, it should be noted, did not become a trend setter with this move. While the extended contract does have some appeal (especially to non-tenured faculty), supporters of the tenure system argue that it is not able to protect academic freedom in the way tenure does.

The purpose of growth contracts is to "enhance professional competences rather than specific work outcomes" (Bare 1977, p. 3). This is a subtle but important difference between growth contracting and MBO. Volpe outlines three major goals of growth contracting: to define clearly an individual's strengths and weaknesses, to outline an on-going professional development program, and to increase the reliability, validity, and objectivity of an evaluation process (1980, pp. 16–17). Gaff also argues for individual contracting as a means of increasing the objectivity of the evaluation process (1971, p. 480):

> Individual contracts not only allow faculty to work on tasks in which they excel, but also provide an explicit basis for an individualized evaluation. They can assure faculty that they will be evaluated on what they have explicitly agreed to do, a procedure which can correct the situation in some universities where some faculty are hired to teach but evaluated in terms of their research.

A vital aspect of growth contracting is self-evaluation (Bergquist and Phillips 1975, p. 45). Seldin adds that "growth contracts rest on the double assumption that instructors know their shortcomings and are also intent on overcoming them" (1984, p. 147). But are self-evaluations really accurate? Webb and Nolan report that student ratings and instructor self-ratings are highly correlated, but the supervisor's ratings are uncorrelated with any of the measures they obtained (1955, p. 46). In an Allied Health school, growth contracting participants completed the Birkman psychological instrument as a starting point for self-evaluation, but the study concludes that "self-assessments have not proved satisfactory as a means of making comparisons among individuals" (Schaffer 1980, p. 239). It would seem that self-evaluations are quite accurate and adequate for a faculty development program designed to promote faculty growth, but they are inadequate as the sole source of evidence when the intent of the program is evaluation for the purpose of promotion and tenure.

Heie, editor of the first Gordon College Handbook on growth contracts, offers eight broad principles for successful growth contracting (Hale 1979, pp. 3–8):

1. Growth contracting should be individualized to reflect the faculty member's own perceived needs for growth in light of individual strengths and weaknesses.

2. Faculty members are whole persons who need to grow in all areas of professional responsibility as well as in personal areas not directly related to their professions.

3. Within the context of common responsibilities shared by all faculty, there should be opportunities for individualizing the role of a given faculty member on the basis of particular strengths and weaknesses.

4. The success of individual efforts to achieve growth will be best realized when growth contracts are self-designed and self-imposed.

5. Successful growth contracting requires that faculty be specific in their statements of goals and in their descriptions of means of accomplishment and assessment.

6. Growth contracting should be viewed as a means for a faculty member to generate positive evidence in support of promotion and tenure consideration; but the emphasis must be on individual development, with institutional evaluation a secondary by-product.

7. Growth contracting should encourage innovation and experimentation by maximizing the potential for reward for successful attainment of goals while minimizing the penalty for failure.

8. Growth contracting should seek after the ideal of creating a sense of community wherein persons are helping other persons to grow (Heie 1979, 3–8).

Volpe notes that two other keys to success are that institutions should, "once the decision is made to adopt growth contracting, create a unique program in light of the institution's goals/objectives, needs, and character" (1980, p. 70), and they should "create a climate conducive to success: open, honest, supportive, committed, and flexible" (1980, p. 73).

Once the proper principles have been established, the following nine step procedure for implementation is offered by Heie (1979, pp. 49–51).

1. Each professor prepares an individual profile containing a self-assessment, statement of current roles, and long range plans.

2. Faculty members visit with the Dean for a "profile conference."

3. Preparation of first draft of annual individual development plan containing goals, means of accomplishment, means of assessment, and budget proposal.

4. Submission of profile and annual plan to the faculty development committee—third week in October—returned with initial comments—first Monday in November.

5. Preparation of final draft of annual plan.

6. Submission of annual plan—last Monday in November for faculty development committee action—third Monday in December.

7. Carry out annual plan.

8. Assess (according to plan)

9. Submit final report to faculty development committee prior to beginning of Fall term. Process repeats each year.

In summary, growth–contracting programs were greatly influenced by two important concepts— adult development and management by objectives. Growth contracting is a formal process in which faculty members assess their own professional growth needs, develop a written growth plan, and then contract with the institution for the support necessary to accomplish the proposed growth plan. Growth contracts have been applied in a variety of settings with faculty, staff, and administration, but are primarily used in smaller colleges and universities. Growth contracting has successfully utilized self–evaluation, but this approach may prove to be ineffective if the process is also used as an evaluation tool for faculty promotion and tenure decisions. General principles for growth contracting have been established, and a step–by–step procedure can be followed to operate the program on an annual basis.

# Evaluation of Results

While there is a good deal of support for the concept of growth contracting in higher education today, we know more about ways to establish and operate a growth–contracting program than whether growth–contracting programs are effective. In this section, three related questions will be discussed. First, what is the best way to evaluate growth–contracting programs? Second, what results have been reported concerning the performance of growth–contracting programs? Third, should performance evaluations (rank and tenure decisions) be integrated as part of the growth–contracting evaluation process?

As with faculty development programs in general, the most effective method for evaluating the performance of a growth contracting program is the case study method utilizing data for a variety of sources (Wergin 1977, p. 70; Preus 1977, p. 46; Milley 1977, p. 53; Volpe 1980, p. 34). The best supporting evidence for this approach comes from Milley. In her dissertation, her research problem was to examine various methods of evaluation and determine the most effective method for evaluating the performance of a growth–contracting program in a small college setting. Her study concluded that a case study utilizing interviews, questionnaires, and thorough analysis of program documentation was the superior method (Milley 1977, p. 33).

In a related study (and one of a very few dissertations to focus on growth contracting), Volpe supported Milley's findings with regard to the case study method (1980, p. 34). However, his study examined only the extent to which a growth–contracting program met its first–year objectives. Centra cautions that it is as important to appraise the content of the growth contracts as it is to measure the program's progress toward meeting its objectives. If this is not done, faculty members' plans "may become simple listings of conferences that they would like to attend, trips that they want to take, and the like" (Centra 1979, p. 68). The obvious implication of Centra's concern is that a program can meet its objectives and really not be a success — particularly if the objectives are inappropriate.

If it is not enough simply to find out whether the program met its objectives, then how is program performance measured? A promising approach is to use "documentable indicators of program performance." Although Milley briefly discussed the topic (1977, pp. 191–2), Eble provides the first comprehensive list of documentable performance indicators (1985, p. 158). Allen utilized a list of documentable indicators to compare a growth–contracting program's performance over five years on a year–to–year basis at varying levels of funding (1986).

What impact can growth contracting programs have on their institutions? Baldwin suggests that these programs can enhance the range of options open to mid–career faculty, and outcomes often "far exceed the modest commitment of institutional funds required to support it" (1984, p. 49). Hodgkinson noted that "the widespread adoption of something like the faculty growth contract might help convince the public that college and university teachers really do want to improve their professional competence" (1973, p. 119). Unfortunately, there is no evidence at this time to support Hodgkinson's assertion that public confidence is strengthened by faculty growth contracting.

Heie at Gordon College cites six beneficial outcomes of faculty growth contracting (1979, p. 31):

> improved communication between faculty and administration; the establishment of a reasonable and satisfying reward system; the implementation of a wide variety of self-improvement projects; assisted faculty in identifying their strengths and weaknesses; encouraged faculty to do things they would not have done otherwise; and information developed during the growth contracting period aided in personnel decisions.

In Volpe's investigation of a growth contracting program, however, the results were not so positive. He found that (1980, p. 63):

> faculty and administrators had different views of faculty development and evaluation, promotion and tenure, and the reward system; the method used to introduce growth contracting was responsible in part for its failure; growth contracting had a negative effect on a number of faculty and administrators; the objectives of the program were not accomplished; and input from the faculty in the design and development of the program was not requested.

Although Volpe did not draw any clear conclusions, the implication of his findings is that the failure of the program was a result of inept management rather than some flaw in the nature of the growth–contracting process.

There has been considerable support for the idea that growth contracts should be tied to the institutional reward system (Gross 1977, p. 76). Smith argued (1976, p. 61):

> What is needed in higher education today, if we are to have truly effective teaching, are policies and programs that combine the concepts of faculty development and evaluation into one program at the department and/or college level. Growth contracts provide the best available approach for achieving this end. A climate of trust can be developed when the growth contracting process serves both the faculty development and faculty evaluation functions of a department, college, or university.

Hodgkinson advocated growth contracts because they are "one of the few procedures where assessment techniques (built-in) were supportive of educational objectives" (1973, p. 119). Seldin notes that institutions "could use growth contracting to get away from generalities about good teaching and research, and focus in on (or tie to) instructor's daily activities as well as departmental or institutional needs (1984, p. 123). But though these writers present a strong argument for including evaluation and development in the same program, there is yet to be a single positive report concerning a growth–contracting program where it was the only institutional means of faculty evaluation for the purpose of promotion and tenure (Volpe 1980, p. 63; Carlberg 1981, p. 26). This probably reflects the fact that growth contracting works best on a voluntary basis, and faculty members provide more accurate self-evaluations in a climate of trust (Carlberg 1981, p. 26). Personnel evaluations militate against these important conditions. All this is not to say that growth contracting could not be included as part of a faculty evaluation program, but the success of the program would be enhanced if it were only one of several evaluation tools for promotion and tenure rather than the single tool used.

In summary, the best method of evaluation for a growth contracting program is the case study method using data from multiple sources. Growth contracting can have many positive outcomes for the institution, but inept management can easily cause the program to fail. Growth–contracting programs may provide important input for the faculty evaluation process concerning promotion and tenure decisions, but if it is the primary source for evaluative information, the program will probably be less than successful.

In this article, the concept of growth contracting has been presented as a viable faculty development option—particularly in the small college. Growth contracting grew in popularity in the early 1970s and was an outgrowth of two other movements—adult development and management by objectives (MBO). The history, operating principles, and evaluation of results of growth contracting are offered in the hope that other colleges might attempt to implement a program. The need for an effective faculty development program is great—precisely when the faculty development movement seems to be running out of gas.

# References

Akin, W. E., ed. *Faculty Development in Liberal Arts Colleges: An Unfinished Agenda for the 80's.* Collegeville, Pa.: Ursinus College, 1984.

Allen, A. P. "The Relationships of Growth Contracting to Levels of Financial Support: A Case Study." Unpublished dissertation. University of Oklahoma, 1986.

Astin, A. W., and C. B. T. Lee. *The Invisible Colleges.* New York: McGraw-Hill, 1972.

Astin, A. W., et al. "Faculty Development in the Time of Retrenchment." *Change* 6 (1974): pp. 43–56.

Baldwin, R. G. "The Changing Development Needs of an Aging Professoriate." *New Directions in Teaching and Learning, No. 19.* Ed. C. M. N. Mehrotra. San Francisco: Jossey-Bass, 1984.

Bare, A. C. "Individual Development Planning in Academic Settings." *College and University Personnel Association Journal* 28.4 (1977): pp. 1–7.

———. "Results of an Administrator Career Development Program." Paper. International Conference on Improving University Teaching. Dublin, Ireland, 1983.

Bergquist, W. H., and S. R. Phillips. *A Handbook for Faculty Development.* Washington: Council for the Advancement of Small Colleges 1975.

———. *A Handbook for Faculty Development—Volume II.* Washington: Council for the Advancement of Small Colleges 1977.

———. "Components of an Effective Faculty Development Program." *Journal of Higher Education* 46 Mar/Apr. 1975: pp. 171–203.

Brim, O. G. Jr., and S. Wheeler. *Socialization After Childhood: Two Essays.* New York: Wiley, 1966.

Buhl, L. C., and A. Greenfield. "Contracting for Professional Development in Academe." *Educational Record* 56.2 (1975): pp. 111–21.

Carroll, S. J., and H. L. Tosi. *Management by Objectives: Applications and Research.* New York: Macmillan, 1973.

Centra, J. A. *Determining Faculty Effectiveness.* San Francisco: Jossey-Bass, 1979.

————. *Faculty Development Practices in U.S. Colleges and Universities.* Princeton: Educational Testing Service, 1976.

————. "Plusses and Minuses for Faculty Development." *Change* 9 (1977): pp. 47–9.

————. "Self-Ratings of College Teaching: A Comparison with Student Ratings." *The Utility of Student Ratings for Instructional Improvement.* Ed. J. A. Centra. Princeton: Educational Testing Service, 1972.

————. "Survey of Faculty Development Practices." *Faculty Development and Evaluation in Higher Education* 2.4 (1976): pp. 2–6.

————. "Types of Faculty Development Programs." *Journal of Higher Education* 49 Mar./Apr. 1978: pp 151–62.

Claxton, C., and P. Murrell. "Developmental Theory as a Guide for Maintaining the Vitality of College Faculty." *Teaching and Aging. New Directions for Teaching and Learning, no. 19.* Ed. M. N. Mehrotra. San Francisco: Jossey-Bass, 1984.

Cravens, D. W., and J. B. Ross. "Management By Objectives in a University Environment." *American Assembly of Collegiate Schools of Business Bulletin* 12 (1976): pp. 12–20.

Dalton, G. W., and P. H. Thompson. "Are R&D Organizations Obsolete?" *Harvard Business Review* 54 Nov./Dec. 1976: pp. 105–116.

Deegan, A. X., and R. Fritz. *MBO Goes to College.* Boulder, Col.: Bureau of Independent Study, 1975.

Dow, I. I. "Participatory Supervision in Education: A Must For the Eighties." *Alberta Journal of Educational Research* 27.4 (1981): pp. 375–86.

Drucker, P. F. *Managing in Turbulent Times.* New York: Harper and Row, 1980.

————. *The Practice of Management.* New York: Harper and Row, 1954.

Dulley, J. "Out-of-Class Contract Learning at Justin Morrill College." *New Directions for Higher Education* 3.2 (1975): pp. 53–64.

Eble, K. E., and W. J. McKeachie. *Improving Undergraduate Education Through Faculty Development.* San Francisco: Jossey-Bass, 1985.

Erikson, E. H. *Childhood and Society.* 2nd ed. New York: Norton, 1963.

Feeney, J., and G. Riley. "Learning Contracts at New College, Sarasota." *New Directions for Higher Education.* Ed. N. Berte. San Francisco: Jossey-Bass, 1975.

Fleming, T. "Accountability: Some Considerations of a Continuing Education Dilemma." *The Journal of Educational Thought* 12.1 (1978): pp. 28–36.

Fretwell, G., et al. *A Management Review and Analysis of the University of Massachusetts.* Amherst, Mass.: University of Massachusetts, 1976.

Gaff, J. G. "Current Issues in Faculty Development." *Liberal Education* 63.4 (1977): pp. 511–19.

————. "Faculty Development: What Values For Whom?" American Association of Higher Education National Conference. Chicago, 1978.

————. "Involving Students in Faculty Development." *New Directions for Higher Education* 6.4 (1978): pp. 59–71.

————. "Overcoming Faculty Resistence." *New Directions for Higher Education* 6.4 (1978): pp. 43–57.

————. *Toward Faculty Renewal.* San Francisco: Jossey-Bass, 1975.

Gaff, J. G., and R. C. Wilson. "The Teaching Environment." *American Association of University Professors Bulletin* 57.4 (1971): pp. 475–93.

Geller, W. W. "Professional Growth Contracting." *Journal of the NAWDAC* 45.2 (1982): pp. 20–1.

Gerth, D. R. "Institutional Approaches to Faculty Development." *Facilitating Faculty Development. New Directions for Higher Education, No. 1.* Ed. M. Freedman. San Francisco: Jossey-Bass, 1973.

Glueck, W. F. *Personnel: A Diagnostic Approach.* Dallas: Business Publications, Inc., 1974.

Gross, A. "Twilight in Academe: The Problem of the Aging Professoriate." *Phi Delta Kappan* 58.8 (1977): pp. 752–4.

————. "Faculty Growth Contracts." *Educational Horizons* 55.2 (1977): pp. 74–9.

Heaton, C. P., ed. *Management by Objectives in Higher Education.* Durham, N. C.: National Laboratory for Higher Education, 1975.

Heie, H., et al. *Professional Development Through Growth Contracting Handbook.* Wenham, Mass.: Gordon College, 1979.

Heiman, J. J. "How and Why a School District Implemented MBO." *National Association of Secondary School Principals* 62 (1978): pp. 36–45.

Hodgkinson, H. L. "Adult Development Implications for Faculty and Administrators." *Educational Record* 55 (1974): pp. 263–74.

————. "Faculty Reward and Assessment Systems." *The Tenure Debate.* Ed. B. L. Smith. San Francisco: Jossey-Bass, 1973.

————. *How Much Change for a Dollar: A Look at Title III.* Washington: American Association for Higher Education, 1974.

Hutchins, R. M. "Hard Times and the Higher Learning." *Yale Review* 22 (1933): p. 714.

Ivancevich, J. M. "Longitudinal Assessment of Management By Objectives." *Administrative Science Quarterly* 17.1 (1972): pp. 126–38.

Jordan, T. S. *An Examination of the Self Report Status and Effectiveness of Faculty Development Functions at Higher Education Institutions Within the United States.* Cleveland, Ohio: Cleveland State University, 1978.

Kingsley, J. G. "Choosing Qualitative Growth: Faculty Development at William Jewell College." *The Southern Baptist Educator* 3 (1978): pp. 12–15.

Kramer, J. L. "Some Suggestions for the Management of Human Resources: Procedures at Camelot State College." *Memo to the Faculty.* Manhattan, Ks.: Kansas State University, 1976.

Lavaroni, C. W., and J. J. Savant. "Replacing Tenure with Periodic Review." *Phi Delta Kappan* 58.6 (1977): p. 499.

Levinson, D. J., et al. *The Seasons of a Man's Life.* New York: Knopf, 1978.

Lindquist, J. "Contract Learning Innovation Process in Higher Education." Paper. National Conference on Higher Education, Mar. 1975.

———. "Professional Development." *The Modern American College.* Ed. A. Chickering. San Francisco: Jossey-Bass, 1981.

Loevinger, J. *Ego Development: Conceptions and Theories.* San Francisco: Jossey-Bass, 1976.

Lowman, J. *Mastering the Techniques of Teaching.* San Francisco: Jossey-Bass, 1984.

Marsh, R. L. "Management by Objectives: A Multifaceted Faculty Evaluation Model." *Educational Technology* 19.11 (1979): pp. 44–48.

Miller, W. S., and K. M. Wilson. *Faculty Development Procedures in Small Colleges.* Atlanta: Southern Regional Educational Board, 1963.

Milley, J. E. "A Case Study Approach to the Evaluation of a Faculty Development Program Which Uses Individual Development Plans." Unpublished Dissertation. Syracuse University, 1977.

Moberly, D. L., and L. J. Stiles. "Getting a School Board to Address Its Primary Tasks." *Phi Delta Kappan* 60.3 (1978): pp. 46–53.

McGrath, E. J. *Memo to a College Faculty Member.* New York: Columbia University, 1961.

McGregor, D. *The Human Side of Enterprise.* New York: McGraw-Hill, 1960.

Nash, M. *Managing Organizational Performance.* San Francisco: Jossey-Bass, 1983.

Odiorne, G. S. *Management By Objectives: A System of Managerial Leadership.* New York: Pitman, 1965.

Odiorne, G. S. *Management Decisions by Objectives.* Englewood Cliffs, New Jersey: Prentice-Hall, 1969.

———. *Strategic Management of Human Resources.* San Francisco: Jossey-Bass, 1984.

O'Toole, J. "Tenure—A Conscientious Objection." *Change* 10.6 (1978): pp. 24–31.

Park, D. "Down With Tenure." *Change* 4.2 (1972): 32–7.

Parsons, M. H., et al. "Using Part–Time Faculty Effectively." *New Directions for Community Colleges* 8.2 (1980): pp. 28–56.

Perlman, D. H. *Management By Objectives in a University—A Progress Report.* New Orleans, Louisiana, 1975. ERIC ED 123 965.

Preus, P. K., and D. F. Williams. *Personalized Faculty Development: Rationale, Applications, and Evaluation.* Bear Creek, Alabama: CESCO Press, 1979.

Raia, A. P. *Management By Objectives.* Glenwood, Ill.: Scott, Foreman, 1974.

Ralph, N. B. "Stages of Faculty Development." *Facilitating Faculty Development. New Directions for Higher Education, No. 1.* Ed. M. Freedman. San Francisco: Jossey-Bass, 1973.

Reid, T. J. "The Context of Management Development." *Personnel Journal* 53.4 (1974): pp. 280–87.

Richardson, R. C. "Staff Development: A Conceptual Framework." *Journal of Higher Education* 46.1 (1975): pp. 303–12.

Schaffer, D. R. "A Faculty Growth Contracting Model for Allied Health Schools." *Journal of Allied Health* 9.4 (1980): pp. 239–41.

Schleh, E. C. *Management By Results.* New York: McGraw-Hill, 1961.

Seldin, P. *Changing Practices in Faculty Evaluation.* San Francisco: Jossey-Bass, 1984.

———. *Faculty Development: The American Experience.* London: London University, 1976.

———. "Faculty Growth Contracting." *New Directions for Teaching and Learning.* Ed. K. Eble. San Francisco: Jossey-Bass, 1981.

———. "The Second International Conference on Improving University Teaching." *Faculty Development and Evaluation in Higher Education* 2.2 (1976): pp. 13–15.

Shetty, Y. K., and H. M. Carlisle. "Application of Management By Objectives in a University Setting: An Exploratory Study of Faculty Reactions." *Educational Administration Quarterly* 10.2 (1974): pp. 65–81.

Sikes, W., and L. Barrett. *Case Studies on Faculty Development.* Washington: Council for the Advancement of Small Colleges, 1976.

Smith, A. B. *Faculty Development and Evaluation in Higher Education.* ERIC/Higher Education Research Report Number 8. Washington: American Association of Higher Education, 1976.

Smith, H. "Improving Educational Quality While Financial Strength Is Eroding." *New Directions for Higher Education, No. 38.* San Francisco: Jossey-Bass, 1982.

Smith, J. M. "Smaller College Sociologists Participation in Professional Organizations: Obstacles & Opportunities." Paper. Annual Meeting of the Southern Sociological Society. New Orleans, Mar. 1979.

Sutton, C., and G. W. Armfield. "Staff Development for Small/Rural Community Colleges: Effective Renewal with Less Resources." Paper. National Conference on Small/Rural Colleges. Blackburg, Va., Aug. 1978.

Tarrant, J. J. *Drucker: The Man Who Invented Corporate Society.* Boston: Cahners Books, 1976.

Temple, C. M. "Management By Objectives at the University of Tennessee." *Intellect* 102.2352 (1973): pp 98–100.

Terpstra, D. E., et al. "The Effects of MBO on Levels of Performance and Satisfaction Among University Faculty." *Group and Organization Studies* 7.3 (1982): pp. 353–66.

Volpe, R. J. "Growth Contracting at a Small, Liberal Arts College: A Case Study of Faculty and Administrative Reactions." Unpublished dissertation. University of Pittsburgh, 1980.

Webb, W. B., and C. Y. Nolan. "Student, Supervisor, and Self-Ratings of Instructional Proficiency." *The Journal of Educational Psychology* 46 (1955): pp. 42–6.

Wergin, J. J. "Evaluating Faculty Development Programs." *New Directions For Higher Education* 17.2 (1977): pp. 57–76.

———. "The Practice of Faculty Development." *Journal of Higher Education* 47.3 (1976): pp. 289–309.

Winstead, P. C. "Management By Objectives." Paper. Conference on Running Higher Education. Warrenton, VA 1–4 Feb. 1977.

Wooten, B. "Faculty Appraisal—an MBO Approach." *Journal of Business Education* 55.5 (1980): pp 208–10.

## III.7

# Historically Black Colleges

## REGINALD WILSON, PH.D.

The historically black colleges and universities have a history unique to American higher education. That history is a consequence of the presence of slavery in the American colonies, beginning with the importation of the first blacks in 1619. Slavery precluded blacks from participating in the general institutional life of the colonies even after the Declaration of Independence in 1776 declared "all men are created equal", and continuing through the establishment of the new government of the United States and its Constitution, which declared that slaves would be counted as "three-fifths of a man" in those states where slavery was permitted. Although the first college for blacks (now called Cheney University) was established in Pennsylvania in 1837, the major history of historically black universities and colleges did not begin until after the Civil War.

Before the Civil War, both slavery in the South and segregation in the North limited educational opportunity for blacks whether slave or free. There was even less opportunity for higher education for blacks then for their education generally, with some few outstanding exceptions. Oberlin College in Ohio opened its doors to black scholars before the Civil War, as did Bowdoin College in Maine. Nearly all other institutions were segregated. Nevertheless, some religious denominations and their missionaries, anticipating the end of the Civil War, recognized that the paramount need of the freedmen would be education. After President Abraham Lincoln issued the Emancipation Proclamation in January, 1863, missionaries immediately went South in those areas captured by the Union armies to establish schools and churches to educate and proselytize the newly–freed slaves.

Many of the institutions we now know as black colleges began their history as elementary schools and training institutions for the largely illiterate population. Typically, as years went by, upper grades and advanced curricula were added till these institutions achieved their present recognizable configuration. Many only became universities and accredited institutions in the 1940s and 1950s.

The historically black colleges and universities arose out of two traditions—private schools and public institutions. The private schools were the earliest established, usually by missionaries or military leaders of the Union army. The Freedmans Bureau, established to assist the economic uplift of blacks, was also instrumental in assisting the development of schools. Many of the private colleges continue to have strong church control and financial support.

Many American public colleges were established in 1862, with the passage of Justin Morrill's Land Grant act, which made provisions for each state to establish colleges to promote agriculture and education through grants from the federal government. After the passage of the "Wartime Amendments" to the Constitution—the 13th, 14th and 15th, giving full citizenship rights to blacks—it was recognized that future public colleges would also have to make equal provisions for black education. Eventually the second or 1890 Land Grant Act mandated the establishment of public colleges for black citizens in the various states of the South. These came to be known as the "1890 institutions" to distinguished them from the white colleges established under the 1862 Act. Since the Supreme Court ruled in 1896 that segregated institutions were legal (*Plessy* v. *Ferguson*), "as long as facilities were equal," these institutions were strictly separated by race, though they were never equal.

## Private Colleges

The private black colleges were the first to be established because most southern states had no provision for the development of public education for

"Negroes" and the Federal government had not yet acted to make provisions. The history of a typical institution will give some indication of how most were initiated.

After the Civil War, the black members of the Methodist Episcopal Church formed the Colored Methodist Episcopal Church, now called the Christian Methodist Epsicopal. The C.M.E. Church felt the need to establish an institution to train ministers and teachers for the "colored" schools of the South. In 1882, the church appointed three bishops as a committee to form Paine Institute, named for Bishop Robert Paine. The school held its first classes in rented quarters on Broad Street in Augusta, Georgia. The present campus site was acquired in 1886. There the school maintained farms for agriculture and animal husbandry study, as well as classrooms, a library, and residence halls.

In 1903, Paine Institute was renamed Paine College. Nevertheless, since there were no public schools for blacks in Augusta at that time, the college also offered high school courses. It was not until 1945 that the college discontinued offering secondary–school preparation. Because of the limited number of educated blacks in the early years, there were many whites on its faculty, as there continue to be today. The first black faculty member was appointed in 1888.

Paine College offers bachelor's degrees in several majors and has a Reserve Officers Training Corps Program. Religious services and emphasis are still a strong ingredient of the curriculum. Intercollegiate athletics programs are offered in seven sports.

Like Paine, the overwhelming majority of the private black colleges were established by major Protestant denominations — Baptist, Methodist, Episcopal, and Presbyterian. Missionaries from these churches or blacks educated by them were the founders of the private black colleges. They remain today under varying degrees of church control, and funds for their operation are supplied by the churches in varying degrees as well, some substantial, some with quite modest financial support. The students of these institutions today come from families where the average income is under $16,000 per year, and the present student is usually the first in his or her family to attend college. Therefore, the graduates of these schools, although giving gifts as alumni, do not give in large amounts as often is the case with private white colleges. As a result, the endowments of private black colleges are usually quite modest and the colleges are, as a consequence, more dependent on tuition to fund the majority of their operational expenses.

To offset the precariousness of their funding, the private black colleges banded together after World War II and formed the United Negro College fund (UNCF) under the leadership of Dr. Frederick Patterson, former President of Tuskeegee Institute. The UNCF each year holds a major fundraising drive that receives donations of tens of millions of dollars from corporations, wealthy individuals, and the general public. These funds are then distributed among the forty-three member institutions to supplement their operating expenses. The colleges also receive grants from several federal and foundation sources for various forms of program support. Nevertheless, the coming of desegregation in higher education and the competition for black students has made the financial situation of some colleges doubtful and, indeed, some may not survive in the next decade.

# Public Colleges

As previously indicated, most of the public black colleges came into being as a result of the 1890 Land Grant Act that mandated creating separate black colleges in those states where education was legally segregated. However, a few public black colleges were formerly private colleges, like Cheney, that were subsequently taken over by the state. Only one, Howard University, has a federal charter and receives an established portion of its budget from the U.S. Government. A look at a typical public black college will give an indication of the way these colleges developed.

In 1879 a black legislator, Pinckney B.S. Pinchback, introduced a bill in the Louisiana Legislature to create an institution "for the education of persons of color" in New Orleans. In 1880, the trustees purchased a building that was formerly the Hebrew Girls School, for the establishment of Southern University. The Federal Government granted the school Land Grant status in 1890. The Federal Government granted the school Land Grant status in 1890. In 1914 the New Orleans campus was closed and, that some year a new campus was located in Scottlandville, Louisiana. Today, the Southern University System has campuses in Baton Rouge, New Orleans, and Shreveport–Bossier City.

Southern University offers majors in dozens of disciplines at the baccalaureate level, and master's degrees in seventeen fields. It is currently developing a few selected doctoral programs. In addition, Southern University has a law school. The institution also has an ROTC program and varsity athletic sports in seven fields.

Like Southern, most of the public black colleges were established to meet the requirements of the 1890 Land Grant Act, either by establishing new institutions or by the taking over of existing private institutions. Because these were segregated schools under state control, in the early years their presidents were white men appointed by the governors of the various states. It was not until after World War II that most of these colleges had black presidents to manage them. Similarly, the faculties were always substantially white and even today the faculties of black colleges are an average of 35 percent white. After the *Brown v. Board of Education* (1954) public school desegregation decision, may of these separate colleges were made a part of their states system of higher education, but were still exclusively for blacks. It was not until the *Adams v. Califano* (1973) decision that both the white and the black public colleges and universities were required to desegregate their student bodies, their faculties, their administrative staffs, and their governing boards.

As mentioned, the black colleges already had 35 percent white faculties, and they had a few white students. Most of the white schools had no black faculty and no black students. Therefore, the court recognized and ordered that the burden of desegregation must be placed substantially on the white colleges. Nevertheless, by 1986, the black colleges had nearly 40 percent white faculties and the white colleges had only 3 percent black faculties. The black schools had 10 percent whites in the student body, the white schools had about 5 percent black students, on average. The future of the public black colleges will be discussed below.

# The Adams Case

Title VI of the 1964 Civil Rights Act directed that no public money could be used to maintain racially segregated public facilities. The Legal Defense Fund (LDF) of the National Association for the Advancement of Colored People (NAACP) noted in 1969 that the Department of Health, Education, and Welfare (HEW) had evaluated ten states, found them to be maintaining segregated colleges, and had brought no action against them to halt their receipt of Federal dollars. Therefore, the LDF went to federal court in Washington, D.C., to request an order that HEW enforce Title VI. Judge John H. Pratt

concluded that "HEW had thus knowingly failed, and continues to fail, to withhold federal funds from public colleges and universities which segregate and discriminate on the grounds of race."

On February 16, 1973, Judge Pratt ordered HEW to require the offending states to submit plans to desegregate their colleges and to terminate funds to states that did not do so. Eventually, by 1977, all seventeen states that maintained dual college systems were under the jurisdiction of the court to submit plans for segregation. HEW was to review the plans and, if it found them acceptable, was to notify the court that the state was in compliance. If HEW found them unacceptable it would then, with the court's approval, proceed to cut off federal funds from those states. Of course, if the LDF felt that HEW was accepting unsatisfactory plans, it could ask the court to reject them and demand that they file more acceptable plans. The plans had definite timetables on them, with all plans scheduled to be completed by 1986. After that, the HEW (now the Department of Education, Office of Civil Rights) was to certify to the court that the plans were implemented and that the states either were or were not in compliance.

During the years of litigation, these actions have been taking place. What most scholars of the *Adams* decision will agree on is that the federal government has been reluctant to intervene in what it perceives as state matters. Without the prodding of the LDF, little federal insistence on desegregation would have occurred. Also, it is generally agreed that states were angry at federal "interference" in their affairs and often had to be taken to court several times before moving to implement desegregation plans. Moreover, many blacks in the *Adams* states were ambivalent and fearful about the possible consequences of desegregation. They saw (1) the demise of a power base for black leaders, (2) the decline of unique institutions in the education of black people, and (3) the reluctance of white institutions to offer equal access to black students or the appointment of black faculty on their campuses.

Finally, some of the fears of both blacks and whites have been realized during the years of *Adams* litigation. The white colleges have moved to recruit some, usually the best, black high–school students. Some few black faculty and administrators are now on most white campuses. However, as indicated, no substantial black enrollment has occurred on white campuses, even in states with large black populations. On the other hand, public black campuses are well integrated at the faculty and administrative levels and have increasing numbers of white students — though generally nothing like racial balance. However, at least five historically black colleges now have a majority of white students in their student body.

# The Production of Black Leaders

The eminent black scholar, W.E.B. DuBois (1868–1963), saw the mission of the black colleges as producing a "talented tenth" who would be the leaders of the black masses. In many ways his vision was correct. The majority of the leaders in the black community have been graduates of these institutions, despite the fact that now over 80 percent of black students in the United States attend predominantly white colleges and universities. Nevertheless, in their unique role of providing pride, role models, black history, and an excellent education, these institutions continue to produce men and women who occupy prominent places in American life. For example, they have produced

Political leaders: Rev. Jesse Jackson, presidential candidate; Andrew Young, mayor of Atlanta; Congressman John Lewis; Congressman Harold Ford; Congressman Mickey Leland; Congressman George Crockett; Ernest Morial, Mayor of New Orleans; and Philadelphia Mayor, W. Wilson Goode.

Religious leaders: The Reverend Martin Luther King, Jr.; Bishop John Hurst Adams of Washington, D.C.; the Reverend Frederick Sampson of Detroit; the Reverend Joseph Lowery of the Southern Christian Leadership Conference; the Reverend Wyatt T. Walker of New York; and the Rev. Leon Sullivan of Philadelphia.

Educational leaders: Patricia Roberts Harris, late Secretary of Education; Dr. Benjamin Payton, President of Tuskegee University; Dr. John Hope Franklin, distinguished Professor at Duke University; Dr. Mary F. Berry, Distinguished Professor at Howard University; M. Carl Holman, President of the Urban Coalition; and the late Wade McCree, Professor of Law at the University of Michigan, and former Solicitor-General.

Scientific leaders; Dr. Charles Wright, physician in Detroit; Dr. Ronald McNair, the late astronaut; Dr. Sybil Mobley of Florida A & M University; Dr. Herman Branson, chemist and retired college president; and Dr. Harold Delaney, chemist on the Manhattan Project and retired college president.

These, of course, are just a small sample. There were many more in many other fields of endeavor. Moreover, graduates from these colleges in the world of sports dominate many of our professional football, basketball, and baseball teams and our Olympic amateur teams.

# The Future for Black Colleges

The future for black colleges is both easy and difficult to predict. In the case of the most prestigious institutions, their future success is as assured, as is that of other prestigious institutions with specialized audiences — women's colleges, religious colleges, and so on. They will continue to appeal to black students (and some white students) because they offer a first-rate education, a black heritage, and outstanding role models and leaders — Howard University, Hampton University, Spelman College, Morehouse College, and other outstanding schools will continue to attract outstanding students in the future.

Some of the less prestigious schools with threatened finances may very well close in the near future. The competition for good black students by other black colleges, and white colleges as well, may prove too much for their survival. Among the publics, we have already indicated that five now have mostly white students bodies. Except for their historically black blackground, these may in future be indistinguishable from other predominantly white colleges. There is also considerable pressure in various states to merge black state colleges with other state schools in the name of cost savings and efficiency. The *Adams* case is still a major factor.

As of 1984, the historically black colleges were 3 percent of all institutions of higher education in the United States. Of the 103 historically black institutions, 41 are public and 62 are private, and 87 are four-year institutions. Their total enrollment was 216,050, which is about 16 percent of all black enrollments. Between 1980 and 1984, enrollments in these schools declined by 2.7 percent.

The history of black colleges and universities has been a unique and long one of over one hundred years. They have served the black population during a period when American life was officially segregated. They have produced thousands of graduates and outstanding black leaders. Their future will be, perhaps, as unique as their past. But what it will be, we cannot be sure.

# References

Aldridge, Daniel Webster, Jr., *The Aldridge Historically Black College Guide* (Detroit: The Aldridge Group), Second Edition, 1984.

Astin, Alexander, *Minorities in American Higher Education* (San Francisco: Jossey-Bass), 1982.

Blackwell, James E., *The Black Community: Diversity and Unity* (New York: Dodd, Mead & Co), 1975.

Haynes, Leonard L., III (Ed.), *An Analysis of the Arkansas – Georgia Statewide Desegregation Plans* (Washington, D.C.: Institute for Services to Education), 1979.

Thomas, Gail E. (Ed.), *Black Students in Higher Education: Conditions and Experiences in the 1970s* (Westport: Greenwood Press), 1984.

Thompson, Daniel, *A Black Elite: A Profile of Graduates of UNCF Colleges* (Westport: Greenwood Press), 1986.

Wilson, Reginald, and Melendez, Sarah E., *Minorities in Higher Education: Fifth Annual Status Report* (Washington, D.C. American Council on Education), 1986.

# Current Developments and Issues in College and University Public Relations Covering the Year 1986

## William J. Wallisch

The September 3, 1986, issue of *The Chronicle of Higher Education* headlined its front page with the news that both Harvard and American higher education had reached the 350–year mark. Major national newspapers, magazines, and television networks gave the story good play. Harvard muttered something about its wish to keep the celebration at a small "family–affair" level, but such a modest hope could hardly have been possible. Harvard's 350th birthday was an event made in media heaven.

Other celebrations in other years were quietly observed, but not this one in 1986. The 1836 Harvard Bicentennial, for example, was probably a quiet affair, though it produced Harvard's alma mater. But the star–studded cast that showed up for the 1986 bash, one that included even Prince Charles, was a happening to be covered. And even though Harvard may have protested all the fuss, scores of others less well–known institutions looked on in lust of such exposure. Paradoxically enough, higher education is both embarrassed by and dependent upon the media spotlight it finds itself in on the occasion of its own 350th birthday. To understand that dilemma is to understand the public–relations picture of American higher education in the year 1986.

Academe has traditionally shied away from the popular media. There has always been sports coverage, graduation coverage, those nice little pieces about cultural events on campus, news about appointments, awards, and research breakthroughs. It was human interest stuff, good for the local image, fund drives, and recruitment. So, most members of the academic community grudgingly acknowledged the need for a small public–relations operation, so long as it was across campus and out of the way of serious teaching and research.

But in the several decades leading up to 1986, the issues became bigger and the stakes grew higher. Like it or not, colleges and universities added more and more to their public–relations function. Sometimes known as external affairs, or institutional advancement, the focus was growing more intense on creating the kind of public image that would shore up finances and attract students from an ever decreasing pool of college–age material. And because the media were more and more turning their attention to unfavorable news items, academic leaders were finding themselves in some very uncomfortable situations. By 1986, the American campus found itself in the public–relations business in a big way. A review of the year's issues uncovers a remarkable range of developments college and university public relations staffs had to deal with. And certainly the CEO was very much a part of everything that transpired.

Business and government executives have been involved with the press since the press has existed. As a matter of fact, there are scores of media training houses around the country that specialize in teaching executives how to handle themselves in press and television situations. As much as an academic leader might find that kind of training distasteful, it has become a matter of necessity. Academe is catching up with business: media training is taking place on campuses everywhere. The American Council on Education even offers a media–training session in its annual seminars for new college presidents. College and university presidents need only go through one bad interview or press conference to appreciate how important media skills can be. Such skills have become a very important part of the academic leadership mix.

All this suggests that schools and their leaders are emerging as personalities. Marketing is no longer a term reserved for the commercial sector. Stiff competition for students has produced a steady stream of brochures that extol the singular characteristics of colleges and universities from Maine to California. The survivors are those who have found their niche, their piece of the higher-education pie that offers students the promise of finding their own place in life after graduation.

And this marketing effort is carried out by a group of advancement professionals as good as any to be found in industry. The Council for Advancement and Support of Education, CASE, reports some 13,000 member representatives. As a prime professional association for higher education's development professionals, CASE produces a monthly publication, *Currents,* and sponsors a full schedule of advancement and public-relations workshops, seminars, and conferences. Though academe may blush at the thought of selling higher education like so much detergent or hardware, it was fully geared up to do so with the best of them in 1986. Moreover, in its 1986 Institutional Advancement Survey, CASE reported that at least one third of its members reported directly "to their institution's chief executive." (Turk 1986, p. 11). And the rest were very close to the top. Gone are the quiet days of the sleepy campus and its catalog to be had by request.

If 1986 was a year of personalities, then certainly two distinct personalities stood out as the chief spokespersons of the issues confronting academe in its 350th years. As different as night and day, Education Secretary William J. Bennett and American Council on Education President Robert H. Atwell stood their ground on what they saw as the major challenges and developments facing American higher education. Typical of what has happened in the past several decades, they did so in the middle of the media spotlight.

Of the two, Bennett has been the clear winner as headline grabber. It was difficult to pick up a newspaper or magazine and not read yet another statement from the secretary, and TV coverage was as frequent. He even took his message on an extensive tour, speaking in scores of cities all around the nation. His position as Secretary of Education enabled him to grab the limelight, taking on colleges and universities right and left for what he saw as major failings in the way they went about the business of educating America's youth. He was particularly hard on college presidents, challenging them to wage war against drugs and to see to it that college athletes take the courses they need to graduate. Speaking at the Harvard birthday celebration, he said there was "an extraordinary gap between the rhetoric and the reality of American higher education" (*Chronicle,* 10/15/86, p. 1). Zeroing in on poor teaching and curriculum, he also criticized higher education for only caring about the pursuit of federal dollars for their programs. He warned that things had to change. It made good headlines.

Far from the secretary's podium at Cambridge, Mr. Atwell addressed an audience of 1,000 senior college and university administrators at the American Council on Education's annual meeting in San Francisco. They were the accused. In answer to Bennett's charge that academe was becoming too costly, Atwell counter charged that the Reagan Administration was turning away from its social responsibilities by making a "diminished commitment to investing in the overall social good" (*Chronicle,* 10/15/86, p. 1). He did acknowledge, however, that the competition for students and funds had turned institutions against each other. He urged ACE's members to work together.

Clearly the issues of higher education in 1986 were issues that received tremendous public exposure. They were as much media events as they were real problems faced by a system of higher education besieged on all sides by financial problems and program demands. Nothing is done quietly anymore, especially when there is a media-oriented Secretary of Education speaking the hot issues from his post in Washington. This makes for a highly charged public-affairs environment that must be coped with at every level of higher education. From the campus to the associations, public relations is a big part of every consideration, every decision. And often it seems to America's academic leaders that they have little time to plan; most of the time the questions precede the strategy, forcing them into the "reactive" rather than the "proactive" mode. Without a sound plan of public-relations policy and planning, a campus is left to flounder under the weight of the issues debated by Bennett and Atwell at the top.

Reporters can come to a college president's door anytime one of the key issues gets national exposure. Let Secretary Bennett make a statement about athletics, and the media will be at most local campuses, looking for a local tie-in to the story. Let the Carnegie Foundation or a similar group release a study about higher education, and the same reporters will be knocking on local doors for the home-town angle. No matter where the issue is raised, no matter the level, campus public-relations operations will get a workout. To be in higher education in 1986 is to be in the proverbial goldfish bowl.

The issues of athletics and drugs are good examples. The unfortunate tragedy at the University of Maryland drew national attention as everyone witnessed the senseless death of well-known college athlete, Len Bias, because of a drug overdose. University officials appeared helpless in the face of it. Even beyond the tragedy of human life, the university suffered the worst kind of national exposure. The secretary's warnings about drugs on campus were being supported in living color all over America. It was a public–relations nightmare.

Even events that might seem to have no relevance can often become a serious campus public–relations concern. Though the events in far–off South Africa would certainly be appropriate for discussion within the classrooms of academe, college and university officials have found themselves in the center of controversy because many institutional portfolios contain or contained holdings in companies that do business in South Africa. The issue of divestment has raged on campuses all over America. At the Harvard birthday celebration a group of demonstrators carried a banner that said, "Derek Bok, get the word. This is not Johannesburg" (*Chronicle*, 9/10/86, p. 40). And on picturesque campuses like Colorado College and the University of North Carolina students erected native shacks, staged demonstrations, and created miles of column inches as they urged their own presidents and boards to divest themselves of any financial ties with South Africa. In this case, there was a clear moral principle involved, one that found dedicated faculty and students asking hard questions about the purity of academe: What was more important? Should higher education allow itself to be funded by parties that participated in gross social injustices, or is the financial well-being of the campus more important than such world social issues? This was, indeed, among other things, a public–relations problem of some proportion, one that still keeps presidents and boards meeting into the small hours.

And what about finances? Though Secretary Bennett chided academic leaders about their over–zealous seeking of federal funds and then further blasted them for skyrocketing tuition, the fact remains that costs soar and student pools shrink though the numbers of student may not. Even ACE's Robert Atwell rebuked his own group for its fierce infighting for the best students and the most favorable recruitment advantage. Yet the truth of the matter is that creative marketing is essential to the very survival of some — perhaps most — institutions.

Private liberal arts schools seem the hardest hit. Somehow their public-relations staffs must come up with the right recruitment strategies, or continue to face red ink and growing uncertainty.

Bad publicity can ruin a fund drive. Even something that happened on another campus can affect a school's development efforts. Everyone hangs together when public opinion is aroused against higher education. Students are demanding the kind of preparation that will guarantee jobs. Parents are overwhelmed by tuition costs. Alumni hate reading about scandals, crime, campus violence, sexual harassment cases, and a thousand and one other "difficulties" that keep public–relations people on their toes. It is far from easy to "get ahead" of any of these issues, especially when they break first in the morning papers or on the evening news. Little wonder there are so many seminars designed to help staffers cope with these issues. Have too many bad stories stacked against you and your school, you will feel it where it hurts the most: slim fund drives and falling enrollments.

College campuses today are, indeed, the crossroads of issues and emotions. Though the demonstrations of the 1960s have faded from view, that is not to say the academy has returned to being a place of peace and quiet. As 1986 came to a close, the Carnegie Foundation for the Advancement of Teaching released a report entitled *College: The Undergraduate Experience in America.* In it some very disturbing data was brought to light. For example, there seems to be confusion over the goals of the undergraduate institution, tensions abound, and there is a feeling that "the very heart of higher learning is a troubled institution" (*Chronicle,* 11/5/86, p. 1). Such institutional division against itself makes it most difficult for public–relations and development personnel to market a clear institutional picture. Yet that picture comes out loud and clear when it is picked up by educational reporters covering their beats. Media power is far reaching; reporters are believed more than a slick brochure, a tightly written catalog, or a glowing press release.

An interesting clash of ideals that got wide media coverage in 1986 was the issue surrounding the Rev. Charles Curran and his theology classes at Catholic University. In public view, open to the world, Curran was barred from his classes by no less than the Vatican itself (Evangelauf 1986, p. 44). The press gave this a lot of attention, and it received an entire edition of ABC's "Nightline" news program. For Roman Catholics it was a very emotional issue. For Catholic University it was probably something it would have preferred to keep at a much lower level of exposure. But public–relations staffs have little control over the hot developments when they are picked up at such a level of intensity. It is very difficult to conduct long-range media planning when one is travelling at the speed of light over the nation's airwaves.

Yet these issues are the stuff of academe, the very content of the curriculum. Most senior administrators often feel they are constantly reacting to yet another media event, yet another crisis that keeps them reeling, reacting, and constantly off balance.

To make matters worse, academe prides itself on being the champion of everything a free press stands for. If the First Amendment is cherished and nurtured anywhere, it is (we believe) on the American college campus, an institution that guards its own academic freedom with a vengeance. It is a place that despises cover-ups and double talk, yet, alas, it is a place that has its own media and public-relations problems as well. Like every other American institution, higher education lives in a media glare: Somehow, administrators and public-relations staff muse, things should go better.

For some schools it did go well in 1986. Many presidents do understand the realities of public relations and carry out programs that deal with a wide range of the public. In 1986 the most successful programs were those in which the top administrators played a major role. The pages of *The Chronicle of Higher Education* were filled in 1986 with stories about CEOs who got out in front and took the story of their institutions to the press. The scope of an aggressive public-relations program should include not only the press but faculty, staff, students, parents, and alumni, as well as city, state, and federal legislators. The local community is, of course, a very important target as well.

Public relations is a management function. Well-managed colleges and universities tend to organize that function around the CEO's daily routine. Likewise, when the president of an institution runs into trouble, it can turn the image of the school upside down. In 1986 there were scores of CEOs who ran afoul of either boards, legislators, or some other controlling body. Firings and forced resignations always create unfavorable headlines, and in such a case the public-relations staff finds itself carrying the load without much direction from the top. Because there is so much pressure in the top administrative ranks, the better operations have taken the time to plan for sudden traumatic changes in leadership.

But the question of institutional image goes even beyond the personality of the CEO. The Carnegie report pointed out that schools were becoming confused about their roles. And that was echoed by ACE's Robert Atwell as well. Many small undergraduate institutions came under fire for trying to give the appearance that they were assuming the role of the larger research universities. What was being said in the catalog or in marketing publications did not fit the reality of the academic program. Atwell cautioned member schools of the ACE that each should perform its own special educational mission rather than poorly imitate functions that cannot be carried out at the level at which they function—a small

liberal arts college, for example. Yet the scramble for students and new avenues of financial fortune brought on an advertising that can be witnessed in the pages of almost any newspaper. In 1986 far too many public-affairs and development campaigns created the impression that their institutions were all things to all people. In many cases actual programs did not even begin to deliver what had been promised.

Robert M. Rosenzweig, former PR chief at Stanford and now president of the Association of American Universities, wrote a thoughtful piece on the back page of the *Chronicle* (11/5/86) called, "Seeing Ourselves as Others See Us." In it he addressed one of Secretary Bennett's favorite subjects, the image presented by higher education. In this piece Dr. Rosenzweig talked about the perceptions various publics have of the American university, especially the view from Washington.

Rosenzweig's fear is that there could be a loss of America's faith in higher education. He worries that academe might not be practicing the values it preaches as it goes about the complex business of existence in the 1980s. Great investments are made in our universities, but often the perceived promise of higher education is not matched by results. Because universities are in fact complicated institutions, they often behave like the large corporations they are. Yet the university represents the world of values. If so, what about fraud and shaky financial practices? All the sins of other organizations are to be found on campus. Perhaps, he says, academe does not have an image problem but rather "a reality problem."

In fact, the best public relations has to do with providing the most accurate account of an institution in the best possible way. The image of a college or university should reflect the real things about a school that make it great (or at least good) and set it apart from others. Public affairs should always coincide with reality. Because members of the academy have traditionally distrusted the slick commercial approach, schools should be careful to give a clear picture of themselves. The truth of the matter is that education still offers our world the answers and keys to a better society for us all. Research, scholarship, and service represent the heart of academe. What happens in the classrooms and laboratories is worth reading about. What happens there has always given hope to those who believe in the university, so much so that many have sacrificed to make their children a part of it. And the view academe gives to the outside world is, therefore, something that all members of the school community should have a say in. That view should be the one found in the mission statement of a school, right in the catalog—assuming that all the members of the community have had a say in drafting that statement.

If an institution has a sense of its true self, of its directions, then whatever the media choose to highlight will in most cases be the exposure that will best advance the cause of the institution. Too often university and college public relations were carried out in 1986 as if the official public view had nothing to do with the realities of schools. The public image should beat in time with the heart of a school. And that image should never be left strictly to the public–relations staffs alone. The CEO must preside over image and it should be a cooperative venture established by all parts of the school.

Public relations is a planning venture. Professional public–relations staffs welcome partnership with the administration, faculty, and student body. Image considerations should always be incorporated into the most serious staff undertakings. After all, sooner or later most all university business becomes potentially attractive to the media. Paying attention to things before they break in the papers can mean the difference between good and bad exposure.

Yet too many presidents and chancellors avoid working closely with their public–relations staffs. Just as there is a yearly financial audit, so should there be yearly serious "image check." Everything a college or university says, publishes, and pushes in the name of image (or otherwise) should be checked by all staff agencies. Just before graduation is a good time.

The director of public relations should be chosen as carefully as the dean. And it must be someone the CEO and senior staff is comfortable with. Too often the opposite is true. One of the biggest frustrations experienced by public–relations staffs in 1986 was the isolation they felt from the rest of the campus. If deans do not report current research, news, and potential story pegs, then the public–relations function is hampered. Skim through the pages of *The Chronicle of Higher Education* and see how effective it can be when communication between the PR staff and the rest of the school is solid. Those who make the press release do the best job for an institution when they are informed. Those are the stories that make the national media. That is when superb exposure takes place. And sooner or later there must be a public release of even the most confidential planning. All the news given to the public affairs office may not be positive. Nonetheless, it must be communicated. The quicker the better.

So, like it or not, 1986 was a year of "image" for academe. From the Secretary of Education to the president of the American Council on Education, from Harvard to the small community colleges, tremendous attention was directed toward the issues of higher education. And the issues, images, and developments were packaged in video tape, magazines, brochures, newspapers, viewbooks, catalogs, slide presentations, film, radio spots, telephone campaigns, speeches to civic groups, press releases, alumni events, receptions, road shows, and every sort of mailer possible. Presidents took to the roads, airways, and airwaves. React, defend, tell the story.

All of that activity will have increased in 1987, for as 1986 drew to a close the presidential election of 1988 loomed on the horizon, and education is sure to be a major issue during that campaign. As Bennett is fueling the fire, so will the presidential aspirants take up the issues surrounding education, especially the issues of higher education. Already the plans are being unveiled. Every one of the announced candidates has a plan to fix colleges and universities, put new life into the educational process. Colorado's Senator Gary Hart was one of the first to speak up as he tried to launch a $17-million program (Palmer 1986, p. 1)—presumably now gone the way of his campaign. By the time voters go to the polls, academe will have been examined and debated coast to coast and from International Falls to Brownsville. Though few practical suggestions will be made, the candidates will have succeeded in keeping higher education squarely in the front row of public attention. And schools will have their work cut out for them as reporters follow up with their stories on campus.

Local and state politics can produce the same results. Governors and state legislatures can create headlines for higher education as dramatically as the presidential candidates. Sometimes the states focus directly on their state–supported schools, but even general concern over state budgets can end up affecting state colleges and universities. Because of a sweeping reduction in the state's budget, Utah's public supported schools were hit with a $15.4–million reduction (*Chronicle,* 12/3/86, p. 1). The headline of that story set off a chain of follow–up stories all over the nation. If Utah can do it, reporters ask, then why can't our state? That in turn causes reporters to request facts about state–university spending everywhere. It all creates more attention, more media interest. And it means more headaches for those who must provide the information. No, 1986 was not a quiet year.

And what joy to find one's institution selected by *Playboy Magazine* as one of the "Top 40 Party Colleges" in America! (*Chronicle* 3/10/86). Imagine how hectic it was for some forty public-relations offices around the country when that list came out. Fund–raising is difficult enough. Wooing alumni is hard work. Let a campus be picked for such a dubious honor and it reels from the kind of national exposure that does it little good in terms of solid image building. Parents want to see an education pay off; even students seem to judge a school by its ability to help them find a good job. No, as 1986 drew to a close, few schools wished to be recognized in the national spotlight for their party rating.

Aside from academic issues, and party ratings, sports reform continued to attract attention. This issue, however, was one that was met more or less squarely by college and university administrations. Many presidents seemed determined in 1986 to clean up their athletic departments and do the best they could to regain control of programs that had gone in separate directions for far too long. The stories that surrounded this issue very often found presidents on the offensive. For the most part they sent out a very healthy message about accountability and the office of the CEO.

The presidents seemed less sure of their own roles and that of the university in the matter of secret defense research. Many on campus do not agree with such research, saying it puts the values of academe at risk. Likewise, visits to campus by CIA and other federal recruiters can still create a flurry of backlash and subsequent press attention. Value–centered issues were faithfully covered by the media in 1986.

After reviewing the year in terms of headlines and media exposure, it might be said that the analysis finds academe in better shape than all the fuss and fury might suggest. The university has always been a focal point for issues and media concern for issues. The curriculum is meant to be a forum for free discussion. Academic freedom is the mechanism whereby the right to probe any subject is protected. And because of that freedom, society had advanced. Research and scholarship are to be protected. Learning must not be hampered by taboos, superstitions, or censorship. Such is the mission of the university, the one single place where values and truths are safe from contamination. It must be a place where honest and pure inquiry can flourish uninhibited.

A free press must then be always welcome in such a place. In spite of its business complexity, a college or university manufactures neither widgets nor (we hope) illusions. Yes, its books can be subject to audit and its leadership may fail, but its mission is still pure. Certainly the headlines of 1986 confirm the weaknesses to be found in the system. But the curriculum would also verify that and then recommend correction of the problem. Fittingly enough, a

public–relations function should speak on behalf of our system of higher education. Academe must have its own voice, a channel for information to reach the press and public as quickly and as accurately as possible. That schools have this function should be no cause to doubt their purity — the curriculum would mandate the public-relations function, though it would mandate that it be fiercely loyal to truth and candor, no matter how painful.

Ours is an information society. Academe will continue to be a major point of interest to that society. It will continue to be covered extensively by the media. In 1986 there might have been some mixed reviews. That will be for the leaders of academe to sort out in the years to come. More and more, responsibility for that will be placed on the shoulders of those who manage the public–relations process. There will be an image to maintain. Keeping in mind some of the questions raised by people like Robert Rosenzweig, those who are responsible for the image must do so with utmost integrity. Bad press does not mean a bad school. Frank and honest dealings with the media assume a partnership with the press that places equal responsibility on its members to be as careful with the reputation of higher education as those who spend their professional lives in its classrooms and board rooms.

# References

1  Judy VanSlyke Turk, "The Changing Face of CASE," *Currents,* June 1986, p. 11.

2  "Education Secretary Calls for Fundamental Changes in Colleges: ACE President Hits Guns over Butter," *Chronicle of Higher Education,* 15 Oct 1986, p. 1.

3  "Harvard's 350th Birthday Celebration Comes off Almost Without a Hitch," *Chronicle of Higher Education,* 10 Sept. 1986, p. 40.

4  "Study Finds Colleges Torn by Divisions, Confused over Roles," *Chronicle of Higher Education,* 5 Nov. 1986, p. 1.

5  Jean Evangelauf, "Catholic U. Professor, Barred from Teaching Theology," *Chronicle of Higher Education,* 3 Sept. 1986, p. 44.

6  Robert M. Rosenzweig, "Seeing Ourselves as Others See Us," *Chronicle of Higher Education,* 5 Nov. 1986, p. 104.

7  Stacy E. Palmer, "Education Already Big Issue for '88 Presidential Aspirants," *Chronicle of Higher Education,* 5 Nov. 1986, p. 1.

8  "Utah Colleges to Fire 400, Drop Scores of Programs in $15-Million Cutback," *Chronicle of Higher Education,* 3 Dec. 1986, p. 1.

9  "Some of Playboy's 'Party Colleges' Are Not Amused," *Chronicle of Higher Education,* 10 Dec. 1986, p. 2.

# III.9

# International Programs in American Universities and Colleges

## John G. Van de Water

The year 1986 was a year of transition and tension in the international dimensions of higher education in the United States. The transition reflects a fundamental shift slowly having an impact on the educational system. Educational institutions are beginning to realize that international interdependence is a present reality, not an abstract theory or a promise for the future. This realization has produced remarkably diverse responses. Colleges and universities have given increased attention to examining general education requirements, administrative structures, promotion and tenure policies, student services, and other dimensions of education, all within an increasingly international framework. The tension underlying this transition reflected two major factors. The aspirations of institutions to expand international programs and services were not matched by increased resources: expansion usually meant internal reallocation or successful outside fund–raising. The second source of tension related to the conflicts between learning to be more effective and competitive in the international marketplace and the increasing support for protection of domestic industries against foreign competition ("protectionism").

This increased activity was sustained by the rapidly changing role of the United States in the world. Our national self–sufficiency and geographic isolation are now only historical facts. We are increasingly dependent on an international or global economy. Our very survival is now linked to our ability to understand and resolve conflicts with other nuclear powers—and perhaps non–nuclear as well.

These changes are so pervasive that our universities have begun the process of responding. Across the country, the year showed these changes in numerous attempts to come to grips with the realities of international interdependence and its relationship to teaching and learning. This article examines the major developments related to this process.

The term "international education" has become common in U.S. higher education. It has gained widespread acceptance without much attention paid to defining it. The general use of the term causes considerable confusion because it is employed in a variety of conflicting or inconsistent ways. It appears, however, that a standard usage is evolving. The common use of the term is sufficiently widespread to give a definition of "international education" as follows:

> International education is the process of imparting and acquiring knowledge of the existence, diversity, and inter-relationships of the countries and cultures of the world.

This definition provides the framework for reviewing the major trends and issues in the broad array of programs and services related to the international dimensions of higher education in the United States.

In U.S. higher education there are several major areas of international activity. These include

- the teaching and research dimensions of academic disciplines, including foreign languages
- the exchange of scholars and students between and among countries
- the teaching of English as a second language
- technical assistance and international development projects

Each of these major areas has numerous components but the term "international education" is used to refer to activities involving them all. Its use is in a broad framework, referring to the international dimensions of the entire curriculum and diverse programs and services that are international in focus. Whereas comparative educators have debated for years the methodological questions related to the question whether comparative education is a discipline or a multi-disciplinary field, international educators have been concerned with policy issues, administrative structures, and the broad questions relating to the international dimensions of all disciplines and all parts of an educational institution.

# Major Trends on the Campus

There was considerable evidence throughout 1986 that international education was receiving a higher priority than in the past. New positions were established, new majors and degrees approved and implemented, and a generally higher level of interest and support was evident among students, faculty and administrators.

The major impetus for this general trend was the continuing decline in the ability of the United States to compete in the international marketplace. The year was marked by one new trade deficit after another, with each new record having an impact on the campus. A parallel series of international crises and foreign policy decisions served to strengthen the perception that the educational system needed to give more attention to understanding our allies and our adversaries.

The development of new international programs and activities raised questions at many universities regarding the coordination and administration of diverse yet interrelated programs. The expansion of activities often led to a need for developing new administrative frameworks so as to avoid duplication and to coordinate international efforts on the campus. The trend in this regard was toward the centralization of previously disparate activities.

Another major trend involved the strengthening of the curriculum, especially at the undergraduate general education level. There were two contrasting approaches to curricular reform. The dominant change involved infusing the traditional disciplinary subject matter with international content. Another approach was to develop special international courses and programs apart from the traditional curriculum. Regardless of the approach, more courses had more international content and more students were taking these courses. Professional schools shared in this trend, especially schools and colleges of business.

Foreign-language instruction continued to show increasing enrollments, with two significant trends being obvious. Efforts to link the foreign language curriculum to professional school programs contin-

ued to produce new alliances and methodologies. Also, Asian languages received a high priority and many new courses were initiated in Japanese and Chinese (and some in other Asian languages). The number of universities requiring foreign language competency to graduate increased, as did the number requiring secondary-school language preparation.

Foreign student enrollments in 1986 did not increase at the record rate of previous years but significant changes were evident. The People's Republic of China (PRC) continued to send increasing numbers of students and scholars to the United States, as did the Republic of Korea, Indonesia, and Malaysia. The number of students in the United States from Iran decreased significantly. The enrollment of foreign students in certain graduate degree programs, such as engineering, remained very high, with serious concern being expressed about the future shortage of U.S. graduates in key scientific and technical areas. Many universities responded to concerns regarding foreign graduate students teaching undergraduates by initiating special language exams and training programs for the foreign graduate teaching assistants. In some states these programs were mandated by concerned legislators.

Programs designed to provide opportunities for U.S. students to live and study abroad continued to increase in number during 1986. The number of programs in China (PRC) increased significantly, but European programs continued to dominate this area of international education. Programs providing for the direct exchange of students became more prevalent and contributed to more reciprocity in international exchange by creating opportunities for students from host universities abroad to overcome tuition obstacles in the United States. Study-abroad consortia continued to grow in popularity as the advantages of inter-institutional cooperation became more apparent. The increase in foreign language requirements also contributed to more participation in foreign study programs. The major gap in the international exchange of students remained the one between the United States and the Soviet Union. There were very few attempts to increase exchanges between the United States and developing countries, especially those in Africa. The spread of terrorist activities combined with the declining value of the dollar discouraged some applicants for study abroad.

Enrollment in programs for the teaching of English as a foreign language did not expand in 1986 as it had in preceding years. The proliferation of programs, both on and off campus, came to a halt. The major reasons for this had to do with the saturation of the market by entrepreneurial operators and a reduction in the number of students from the Middle East. Also, the improvement of English teaching in some foreign countries contributed to the reduction in demand for intensive programs in the United States, as did the decisions of some countries not to support students until they reached the minimum standards required to apply to United States universities. Also, countries such as Malaysia established in–country programs for students to spend the first two college years in a curriculum designed to facilitate transfer to a U.S. college or university.

The role of U.S. universities in technical assistance and development projects abroad remained an important aspect of international education, especially in land–grant institutions. The Agency for International Development worked closely with many U.S. universities to provide assistance to developing countries. Increased competition for AID grants and contracts came from the private sector, causing universities to question policies and procedures related to the awarding of funds to private non–university bidders. The expenditure of U.S. government funds to assist developing countries was challenged by some agriculturists who suffered through a difficult year and sought more federal support. A new development was the establishment by U.S. universities of "extension" programs for students in countries such as Malaysia. Other models for developing branch campuses of U.S. institutions were explored in China and Japan.

# Major trends at the State Level

The year of 1986 was important for the role of states in international education. New initiatives were linked to the increased recognition of the strong connection between economic development and the ability to compete in the international marketplace. In November the Report of the Southern Governors' Association Advisory Council on International Education, entitled *Cornerstone of Competition,* was published. This report was designed as a blueprint for state action to build international perspectives in the school and in the workplace. The New England states also initiated plans to strengthen international education by assigning it a higher priority than it has had at the state level. These examples are indicative of the increasingly important role assigned to international education by states seeking to improve their international trade and commerce activities.

# Major Trends at the National Government Level

At the federal level, 1986 was a year of confrontation between supporters of international education and advocates of decreased federal expenditures. The debates came to a climax on October 1st when the Senate overturned an Appropriations Committee cut of almost 25 percent in the budgets for the Fulbright program and the USIA exchange programs. In other decisions budget cuts were approved in the total funding available for international affairs programs, from maintaining U.S. embassies to USIA scholarships and AID participant training. The 99th Congress made several decisions revealing important new priorities and policies. There was a major shift in regional priorities, with Latin America in general and Central America in particular receiving a significant increase in funding for exchange and other international programs. This produced a decline in funding for programs with other world regions. Also, Congress endorsed the concept of undergraduate scholarship programs intended to reach disadvantaged but talented students from developing nations. This was a departure from previous policy that concentrated on graduate and scholar exchanges. In the process of reauthorizing higher education programs in the Department of Education, several changes were evident. The Title VI legislation included authority for new intensive summer foreign language institutes, new foreign language resource centers, and inclusion of internships overseas to build foreign language skills. The pressures to reduce federal expenditures for international education increased throughout the year and carried over to the 100th Congress.

A comprehensive immigration reform bill was passed in the closing days of the congressional session with numerous implications for foreign students and scholars in the United States. The bill that passed did not contain a controversial provision that would have required a two-year home country residency requirement for F-1 and M-1 nonimmigrant foreign students. Included in the final bill was a provision which prohibits in–country adjustment to permanent residency for nonimmigrant aliens who have fallen out of status. It also established new requirements for universities to prevent ineligible aliens from receiving federal financial aid.

International scholarship and fellowship recipients will have substantially higher tax bills as a result of the 1986 tax reform legislation. According to the new statute, degree candidates will be able to exclude from taxable income only a portion of their awards for tuition, fees, and required course expenses. Grant recipients who are not degree candidates will have to include their entire award in taxable income. In addition, Congress stipulated that withholding will be required for all awards given to F-1 and J-1 nonimmigrants. These and other changes will result in foreign scholarship recipients paying higher taxes on their awards than recipients who are U.S. citizens. Also, the new tax law is expected to decrease support for international exchange activities by decreasing tax incentives for charitable contributions.

A potentially important new legislative proposal was drafted in 1986 to create a national foundation for foreign languages and international studies. This draft served as a catalyst for extensive debates concerning government efforts in support of international education and the value of a central funding and administering body at the national level.

Professional associations continued to play important roles in various aspects of international education. The Liaison Group for International Educational Exchange emerged as an important lobbying network for its members. The Association of International Education Administrators established itself as the primary association for the increasing number of institutions that identify a principal international education administrator. The National Association for Foreign Student Affairs continued to play an important role in policy matters related to foreign students and international exchanges. The National Association of State Universities and Land Grant Colleges (NASULGC) upgraded its international activities by establishing a Division for International Programs. Participation in association meetings, professional development workshops, seminars, and other activities related to national networks in international education continued to increase throughout the year.

In summary, international education was often in the spotlight in 1986. New tensions came to the surface as more attention was directed to the international dimensions of higher education. This attention produced many changes as well as many new questions and issues that will continue to occupy the attention of international educators in the future.

# Academic Chairpersons: Challenges and Opportunities

## JOHN B. BENNETT

The stature of institutions of higher education is in good part determined by the efforts of individual department and division chairpersons or heads or coordinators. It is through their efforts at the departmental or divisional level that the fundamental business of the institution is actually coordinated. It is in the areas for which they are responsible that institutional objectives are actually met, that services are delivered, and that instruction actually occurs. For these reasons, the success of each institution is in a significant way a function of the success of the individual department chairperson.

## The Common Character

Given the importance of the chair's position, it is ironic that many institutions of higher education overlook the needs of people who continue to play such significant roles. Certainly few institutions keep in place systematic programs or procedures for providing assistance or support to current department or division chairpersons. Few have handbooks of technical information for chairpersons or provide opportunities for their continuing professional development. One is driven to conclude that most institutions hope that those selected for the responsibilities of chairperson will discover within themselves — and without the aid of the institution — ongoing resources for dealing with the complexities of the job.

Nor is the situation commonly any better at the outset of a chairperson's career. Chairpersons come to their job variously, but rarely do those assuming this position come with any substantial preparation. One might be selected because of prior publishing or scholarly honors, or because one enjoys the trust of colleagues, or because "it's one's turn", or because no one else seems to be appropriate for the position or perhaps interested in it. Some individuals will have interest in the position and will even actively seek it. More commonly, however, chairpersons back into the position and find themselves having to learn how to do things on the job.

All this is not unimportant, for the demands and the complexity of the job seem to have increased in recent years. To the already challenging workload, many institutions have added responsibilities for staffing night and weekend courses, off–campus centers, and non–credit programs. These developments have occurred as colleges and universities have struggled to adjust to the changing marketplace and equally changing societal needs. Rarely, however, have staff resources for chairpersons been strengthened. Most chairpersons find themselves having to do more with no more help than the position has ever had.

Interestingly, whether one is appointed or elected to the position seems generally to make little difference in the overall ease with which the job is accomplished. Nor, in the last analysis, does there seem to be much difference in the tasks that need to be accomplished. Faculty will need to be evaluated, curricula reviewed and perhaps revised, courses scheduled and assigned, conflicts ameliorated, budgets constructed and monitored, now as ever. But a chairperson may very well need to use quite different *strategies* on some of these issues, depending on whether he or she was elected or appointed to the position.

Most chairpersons today come to their positions through a combination of departmental consultation and administrative appointment. Some will be appointed without faculty consultation, and some will be elected without administrative involvement. The typical term is three or five years. Increasingly institutions are conducting periodic reviews of chairpersons before giving them a subsequent term.

Independent of the mode of selection, chairpersons are likely to feel considerable role ambiguity. Having special supervisory responsibilities for peers and colleagues can be awkward and can jeopardize long-standing friendships. Among themselves, faculty colleagues often have quite different understandings of the role of the chairperson. Some will regard the chairperson as chief clerk for the department, handling the minor details and protecting faculty from annoying paperwork. By contrast, others in the department will look to the chairperson to be the "white charger"—the chief advocate for the department, untiring in his or her efforts to promote it, and them, within and without the institution.

On the other hand, the dean or academic vice president is likely to look to the chairperson to reflect institution-wide perspectives and needs, rather than those closest to the hearts of department members. Certainly exhortations from the dean to increase "productivity" can be anticipated. Often chairpersons will be held responsible by both sides for matters over which they have little if any control.

One common task facing department and division chairpersons is the need to counter faculty suspicions and to deal with uneven personalities and abilities. The introduction of the new idea, or even the reintroduction of the old, is often difficult. Proposed initiatives can be met with skepticism—even, and perhaps especially, those initiatives designed to help the individuals or the department itself. The successful chairperson is often the persistent and creative one.

Sadly, some faculty members will appear to others outside the department as tired and cantankerous. Levels of energy and enthusiasm about teaching and research are often different, and occasionally some academic professionals have lost their way and seem held together primarily by a common sour disposition and apparently trapped in an unstimulating and uninteresting academic environment, which then necessarily becomes even more unstimulating and uninteresting. Knowing this all too well, the department chairperson in these circumstances is confronted with a poignant situation indeed.

Rewards for being chairperson will vary from institution to institution. Some places provide nothing by way of additional salary or released time. Most, however, recognize the additional burdens on the time, energy, and emotional health of the chair. That is, most institutions will provide a combination of released time and additional stipend, adjusted to reflect the actual circumstances under which the individual chairperson works.

Contracts are often extended beyond the traditional nine months or are supplemented by an administrative stipend ranging from $100 per term to well over $500 per month. The released time can vary from one course per term to (in extreme cases) no instructional responsibilities at all. Most arrangements involve one or two released courses per term. Where there are differential arrangements within the same institution, the relevant factors seem to be size of department and extent of such responsibilities as those for field supervision and facilities management.

Rarely, though, are monetary rewards regarded as sufficient inducements to remain in the job. Most chairpersons cite as more important the ability to direct the curriculum, to rejuvenate a tired research agenda, to reward overlooked individuals, or to apply interpersonal skills in other satisfying ways, or because they enjoy the power.

# Common Challenges

How is one to define the character of this difficult job? An effective short-hand term is that the chairperson is the "custodian of academic standards." It is to him or to her that others within the institution must turn for assurances that the department program in place is the appropriate one for the time, the temper, and the students of the institution. Changes in the discipline, in student abilities, and in faculty interests and resources usually require changes in the curriculum. Chairpersons are in the best position to recognize the need for and to implement such changes. Together, chairpersons establish and maintain the academic tone and coloring of the institution.

What from their perspective are some of the most important issues facing campuses today? A number of problems are demanding chairpersonal attention. Many of them are ongoing features of academic life. Others are more recent developments.

## Faculty Evaluation

Certainly a major task for department and division chairpersons is attending to the evaluation of faculty and non-faculty support staff within the department or division. The task is not an easy one, inasmuch as the difficulties that everyone recognizes in evaluating others are often compounded by the close collegial relations and friendships that chairpersons enjoy with colleagues and friends—these relationships and friendships sometimes being of quite long standing. Accordingly, chairpersons often will report that evaluating colleagues and dealing with inadequate performance are the two most difficult challenges of their position.

Nationally, institutions seem to be using more

sources of evidence in the evaluation of faculty members now than was the case a decade or so ago. Typically, chairpersons will now be reviewing student ratings of faculty teaching effectiveness, faculty self-reportings, and peer evaluations of scholarly competence, as well as constructing their own independent evaluation of the members in their department. Much of evaluation activity remains front-loaded—that is to say, directed overwhelmingly toward assessment of the performance of the probationary faculty member in an effort to assemble evidence for a tenure decision. Typically, far less attention has been paid to the evaluation and faculty development needs of tenured faculty members.

In fact, it is the rare institution and department that has in place any systematic procedures for the periodic and comprehensive evaluation of tenured faculty members. Many rely on a rushed and fragmentary annual evaluation that winds up serving neither the institution and its students nor the individual faculty member in question. Despite the apprehensions of some, tenure itself need not be at stake in a thorough and comprehensive evaluation. It is the ongoing performance of the individual that is under assessment, not the appropriateness of the original tenure award. In fact, periodic evaluations of senior faculty members are probably the best way to preserve the vitality of tenure and to defend it against a suspicious public.

## Faculty Development

The pronounced aging of the faculty at most institutions adds yet another dimension to this major administrative challenge for department chairpersons. Traditionally, chairpersons have viewed their major faculty development responsibilities as orienting and perhaps even mentoring the young or the new instructor. After all, it is the department chairperson who is in the best position to instruct the young person and the newcomer on relevant traditions and expectations in his or her new environment. Now, however, the older faculty member is equally in need of attention to his or her continued professional growth, and yet few department chairpersons are either prepared for, or feel comfortable in, attending to this need.

However, it would be difficult to overstate the importance of determining ways to keep the older faculty vigorous and effectively engaged in discovering and transmitting knowledge. This is preeminently the case now that federal legislation has been passed that will uncap mandatory retirement in the future. Chairpersons are the ones best positioned to help maintain morale and to combat enervating battles between cliques or age groups.

Interestingly, some institutions are already looking at the prospect of significant numbers of faculty retirements in the next few years. Most institutions will be experiencing substantial turnover by the first decade of the next century. Vacancies then will present important opportunities for redirecting the department, college, and university. Careful departmental planning will be required. In the meantime, ongoing attention must be paid to maintaining the vigor of the current professoriate.

## Entrepreneurship

Yet another development in college and university administration, fairly far advanced at some campuses, is the entrepreneurial role that many chairpersons increasingly play. This role requires that the chairperson secure funds from and establish special relationships with entities outside the normal budgetary and governance relationships of the institution. Some departments or disciplines have been pursuing such entrepreneurial activities for a good while. One thinks, for instance, of those engineering departments and business departments or schools at various institutions that have been quite successful in establishing good relationships with area and regional business enterprises, the payoffs from such relationships including increased placement opportunities for students, visiting faculty slots, enhanced donations of equipment, and even outright budget subsidies provided for faculty salaries.

A rather different form of such entrepreneurial activity relates to student recruitment. Examples here include the more humanistically-oriented disciplines that in recent times have fallen upon low student interest and as a result have had to become more aggressive in devising ways to attract and recruit students—both traditional and nontraditional. Recruiting the traditional student has involved chairpersons taking the leadership in establishing better and more effective relationships with area and regional high schools; attracting the nontraditional student has called for chairpersons to identify more creative forms of making the department's wares attractive.

Within the category of entrepreneurship, one would also want to put proposal-writing and grant-seeking. And the trend is certainly for institutions to look increasingly toward the department chairperson for leadership in such areas. Budget pressures seem inexorably to underlie and reinforce this trend. Indeed, academic administrators at all levels are finding themselves having to pay more attention now to fiscal affairs and to identify untapped possibilities of revenue. As our society, as well as the professoriate, ages, funds once available for higher education will increasingly be needed for other social services. Tight departmental budgets will become tighter.

A special development of the last ten or fifteen years has been the emergence of unusual sponsored research arrangements at various institutions. These range from rather simple agreements that, in exchange for a certain specified annual donation, a sponsoring firm will receive a certain number of reports from a university research lab or operation, all the way to very sophisticated and complicated corporate entities established as buffering units between proprietary and nonprofit partners. Some chairpersons have already found themselves playing major roles in the development and subsequent monitoring of these relationships. Potential faculty conflicts of interest will increasingly be a concern in these institutions.

## Part–Time Faculty

Another recent development in academic administration at many institutions that affects the time and energy of department and divison chairpersons is the greatly increased use of part–time or adjunct faculty members. Identifying, recruiting, and then evaluating these individuals has proven to be a major drain upon the resources of many chairpersons. There are significant departmental and collegial implications to such increased use. On the one hand, these individuals, particularly if they are professionally involved in the areas in which they instruct, can constitute a great resource in the instructional process. After all, they can speak to the application of theory as well as to experiences out of which theory itself is derived. On the other hand, removed as they are from ordinary activities and campus involvements, part–time faculty frequently serve the student less well than do full–time faculty members.

Certainly part–time faculty members are rarely involved in departmental business, curricular reflection, and joint research activities. They simply are not available. And if the odd individual is available it is usually because he or she is doing work for which there is radically inadequate compensation provided. Hence, integrating part–time faculty into the life of the department and the institution is proving to be a major challenge for many a department chairperson. Getting a handle on their teaching effectiveness, and thus attending to issues of quality control, is yet another challenge.

## Equity Concerns

An additional personnel issue that department chairpersons often confront turns on the relative proportion of women and minority individuals represented on the faculty. Within the college or university organizational structure, it is the chairperson, whether he or she knows it or not, who is at the very point where progress is most likely to occur in achieving adequate representation. We all know the difficulties of such efforts, however, and it is much easier to look for others to provide leadership than to move the department toward a more balanced representation. Similar considerations apply with regard to the curriculum and its balance in representing the contributions of women and minorities.

## Outcomes Measurements

A movement gathering considerable steam nationally and increasingly affecting department chairperson is the call to review the curriculum and the students in terms of the academic outcomes and competencies sought and those actually achieved. This movement represents a new thrust in assessment, challenging the traditional evaluation of departmental stature accomplished by reviewing faculty credentials or inputs into the program. That is, traditionally departments have reviewed themselves and been reviewed by others in terms of resources allocated (inputs) rather than outcomes accomplished (outputs). Resources, of course, are easy to quantify and measure. Outcomes are far more difficult to identify in some cases and to measure in many. But efforts must be made, as the public is increasingly disenchanted with the use of grades as an index of student accomplishment, and generally cannot evaluate inputs.

## Collective Bargaining

Another important development and issue in college and university administration from the department chairpersons' point of view is collective bargaining. On campuses that have collective bargaining or that are anticipating its arrival, chairpersons usually find themselves in unhappy situations. On the one hand, they could be part of the bargaining unit. In that case, however, their authority to

ISSUES

140

provide strong curricular and supervisory direction is frequently limited—either by clear specification of the contract or, more likely, psychologically through peer pressure. On the other hand, if the department chairperson is instead a member of management, he or she frequently feels removed from colleagues and friends of long standing and also removed from familiar sources of professional identity. In that case also authority is effectively limited, and the chairperson is constrained rather than empowered.

Thus, no matter where one places the position of department chairperson within a collective bargaining arrangement, there are disadvantages. Additionally, chairpersons are often expected to assist in implementing matters in the determination of which they had no hand. Some institutions have gone to the unusual extremes of having a special unit for their own department chairpersons. City College of the San Francisco Community College district is one example of such an arrangement.

## Evaluating the Chair

One additional matter of concern for many chairpersons is the evaluation of their own efforts and accomplishments as chairperson. Few institutions do much by way of a formal evaluation of the chair. Feedback can be erratic and incomplete. Ideally, chairpersons should be allowed and encouraged to set part of the agenda upon which they will be evaluated. Unfortunately, institutions may conspicuously fail to recognize that accomplishments of the chairperson may be purchased only at the cost of scholarly research and instructional *zing*.

# Conclusion

Chairpersons at virtually all types and sizes of institutions are plagued by role ambiguity and pushes and pulls and tugs from their different constituencies. On the one hand, they may look to the dean for leadership and guidance and be prepared to recognize his (rarely her) expectations as important in the definition of what they need to do. On the other hand, they come from the faculty, think like the faculty, and are usually regarded by faculty colleagues as one of them.

The overall challenge for the chairperson is to establish a common unity out of a collection of individuals. The academy attracts those who value their own autonomy. But the department or division must have its own unity and integrity. Often it must accommodate a diversity of personalities and value systems while also having all its members moving more or less in the same direction. And changes in the discipline, in societal needs, in student abilities, and in faculty interests dictate that its own direction will change. Often the chairperson must steer the department and make decisions with radically limited information. The challenges he or she faces are often significant and difficult. But all the evidence indicates that many departments are well served today: it can be done.

III.11

# Science and Technical Higher Education

## Nathan S. Washton

Scientific schools — medical, public health, agricultural, engineering and technical colleges and universities — must face the need for training problem solvers. It has been said that engineering students are already out of date at graduation time — too much time was spent on memorizing basic principles and not enough on solving problems.

Do medical students upon graduation feel secure in making an accurate diagnosis on their patients? Are we providing adequate support for research in making discoveries that would solve problems related to illness, disease, and poverty? Can scientific research be ordered on a platter to be completed in a given unit of time?

Professor I. Bernard Cohen of Harvard University has stated that discoveries may be intentional, accidental, or incidental. The fact that our first antibiotic, penicillin, was *accidentally* discovered did not influence the need for supporting basic scientific research. Americans are a practical people. We want results and we want them fast. Industries ask the question, "What are we getting for our investment?"

It is interesting to note for the first time, the National Institutes of Health have given grants to twenty-seven scientists to perform their research without emphasis on time. The MERIT award (*M*ethod to *E*xtend *R*esearch *In T*ime) permits scientists to continue to work for many years without applying for yearly grants for one, two, or three years. An illustration is the $2 million award recently granted to Professor Robert Bittman of Queens College to continue his research on biological membranes at the molecular level through 1996. His work is related to preventing and curing diseases through the study of cholesterol and cell membranes.

## What Price Basic Research?

The present administration in Washington deleted many funds that supported higher education in the United States. The National Science Foundation, along with other agencies, can no longer support basic scientific research projects. In many instances, non–scientific personnel were sympathetic with this approach. The feeling expressed was "Who cares if another bacterium is discovered in a can of salmon, especially if it doesn't bother us?"

We should examine the need for basic and applied research. Most individuals are receptive to financing applied research when told that the project might find a cure for cancer or another disease. Penicillin might never have been discovered by Fleming in 1939 if basic research by two British scientists Florey and Chain had not been supported ten years earlier. The purpose of the research by these three scientists had little or nothing to do with antibiotics and the control of certain infections. The accidental discovery of penicillin was the result of the encouragement and support of basic scientific research not to applied research.

It is also important to support *applied* research even when it may take many years to find a solution to the problem. In the late 1950s, billions of dollars were spent on finding a solution to the problem of launching missiles into space without their burning up prematurely. Money was appropriated for an intentional discovery. Scientists from many universities representing the disciplines of physics, engineering, mathematics, physical chemistry, meteorology, astronomy, and others, were enlisted in this call for applied research. Conventional investigations along with traditional thinking caused the scientists to look for an alloy that would not burn up in the lower atmosphere. For a long time the search continued for the right combination of metals that could withstand the tremendous temperatures. Finally, a solution was found which had nothing to do with the traditional approach of scientific investigation. The discovery was made that research in ballistics was similar to research in the evolution of launching missiles. Theoretical physicists and mathematicians found their answers.

# Funds for Technical Higher Education

Where will the financial aid come from to support the basic and applied scientific research in colleges and universities? It is anticipated that the 100th Congress will have responded more positively than the 99th to the needs of scientists who are performing vital research at their respective universities. The competition for the dollars granted by governmental agencies is very keen. Even with increases in funding by the federal government, other sources are vital to assure that necessary research is being conducted to guarantee the health, security, and prosperity of the citizens of the United States.

How much will business and industry contribute to higher education to foster either basic or applied research? Many college presidents believe that fewer contributions will be made in 1987 than in 1986 as a result of the new tax laws. There is a question as to the kind of financial support that might be forthcoming as a result of modified deductions. The other source of income would be student tuition. Students have been complaining that the continuous rise in tuition creates a genuine hardship on them as well as on their parents.

Perhaps a partial solution might be to increase the number of consortia and share the so-called "wealth" of several universities. This kind of cooperative enterprise requires faculty and administrators to place staff, equipment, supplies, space and ideas on "loan" to each other. Where there is a common problem to be investigated, a concerted effort among several universities might make the cost feasible. But to develop this type of program demands many kinds of skills in both administrative procedures and human relationships.

One of the major problems in organizing a consortium is to place the team approach above the individual. This calls for a re-assessment of faculty recognition. If three, four, or five faculty members are engaged in a common project, which one or which ones would be promoted to a higher faculty rank upon achieving their goal? Recognition in salary increases, tenure, title, and other awards could influence the success or failure of developing a consortium. The kind of educational leadership given by the administration, competitive or cooperative, is another factor. Moving students and faculty from one campus to another for courses to become cost-effective requires a positive type of motivation and cooperation.

All scientific and technical departments and institutions of higher learning have a common problem: the equipment needed for research is expensive. Engineering schools and medical and dental colleges demand versatile equipment and supplies that cost millions, and, within a group, billions of dollars. A single university, with few exceptions, could not afford to purchase the research material without outside funding. Scientific research pertaining to health, security, computer technology, and agriculture appears in hundreds of technical journals in many languages throughout the world. Faculty members read these periodicals and exchange ideas and processes. At annual meetings of numerous scientific societies, faculty members report their findings to each other with pride: it is not impossible, with this in mind, to consider the development of a new kind of scientific research consortium recognizing individual achievement through a cooperative enterprise.

Undergraduate college tuition usually helps support the financial loss of operating a graduate program, but there are limits on how often and by how much student tuition can be increased. To facilitate necessary increases, the U.S. Department of Education is recommending that more money be made available for student loans. In addition it is being suggested that students repay these loans in accordance with their ability and earning power.

On an individual university basis or a consortial basis there is an important issue that must be resolved. Who gets the percentage of the profits or royalties from research when an important commercial product is discovered — such as, for example, an antibiotic? Does the institution or faculty member receive the additional compensation? The manufacturer of computers or the pharmaceutical house operating for profit can give royalties to the institution of higher learning. This would become an important source of income to encourage further research. Some of these funds can be allocated to graduate student scholarships as well as to research equipment and research faculty.

# Mentoring — Students and Alumni

Several of our leading universities receive or have received large endowments from alumni. Most of the colleges and universities have not made alumni active participants in institutional affairs. While college presidents and development officers more than welcome the monetary contributions from alumni they also show an "inward hesitancy" for fear that the alumni might dictate some policy or request special favors.

Perhaps the real challenge for gaining loyal financial support from alumni lies in the hands of faculty. Are there special seminars and workshops for alumni when requests for financial aid are not made? Do alumni lead some of these seminars? Are there sufficient social gatherings, dances, luncheons, dinners, special occasions, where faculty invite alumni to their homes? Are placement opportunities made available as frequently as travel group activity? Mentoring is more than providing occasions for students to get together with individual faculty. Students look upon a faculty member as a mentor if he or she becomes as a role model in his or her academic credentials, in personality, and as an individual who cares. The student looks upon the mentor as a genuine friend, adviser, counselor, and someone who is readily available and accessible. The mentor also assists graduate students in the sciences to attend a number of significant professional society meetings. Such faculty members re-invite their former students to their homes or college on both informal and formal occasions. At this level alumni are asked how to obtain funds for various projects alumni who may not have the financial ability to make noteworthy contributions can volunteer their services in other ways. Faculty members, especially mentors, can become the most vital force in developing and maintaining loyal alumni.

# A Dynamic Science Curriculum

Scientific and technological subjects must be kept up to date. Thus the curriculum that is composed of the various biological and physical sciences is con-stantly changing. The dynamic curriculum is the result of new discoveries that modify existing theories. Frequently, of course, there is a lag between the class-room lecturer and the laboratory researcher. Research papers are not published in the various scientific periodicals for a period of (usually) nine months to two years from the moment the paper is received by the editor. It is a constant struggle for professors in the natural sciences and engineering to keep up with the current research and developments.

One of the major responsibilities of college and university faculty is to provide their students with the latest up-to-date and accurate information. Computer technology is undergoing very rapid changes. Retrieval information, world-wide communication within minutes or seconds on the computer, the creation of synthetic chemicals to fight disease, the development of unusually strong alloys, the application of physical chemistry in providing glass that can withstand enormous pressure and temperature changes, modified theories about the nature of the universe and space, uncovering the presence of new sub-nuclear particles represent only a part of yearly discoveries in science that affect the science curricula. Lasers are being introduced in industry in the form of compact discs and tapes. Medicine has already demonstrated the many applications of the lasers in diagnostic, preventative, and therapeutic procedures.

If it takes two years for a research paper to be published, it may take another three or four years — or more — before this information appears in textbooks. It therefore becomes imperative for instructional personnel who train scientists and engineers to attend professional technical meetings sponsored by their respective disciplines. A number of research papers have recently appeared on the scene in which emphasis is placed on ethics and human values. Genetic engineering with its implications, its applications, and the question how much this research should be brought into the curriculum raises problems with some groups. Some scientists and social scientists believe that consequences of research should be examined before undertaking specific projects. Other examples (besides those in genetic engineering) can be found in nuclear and space research.

Undergraduate courses are assessed in terms not only of up-to-dateness but also of the goals of education. Several organizations question the teaching of evolution without teaching "creationism." Moral values and character development are not listed as specific objectives in college courses in some institutions. Some faculty are bitterly opposed to the teaching of such values as the responsibility of higher education. The need for a variety of technical, private, public, denominational, and coeducational institutions is obvious.

The curriculum is heavily influenced by the meaning given general education, liberal education, specialized education, or professional education. General education may be typically defined as the common knowledge, attitudes, and skills required for intelligent living in our society. Some educators use the same definition for liberal education. A major issue is what courses or curriculum constitute the common knowledge necessary for intelligent living. Specifically, what science course or courses should be required by all undergraduates for the bachelor's degree. Should specific required courses in both the biological and physical sciences be part of the core curriculum or should a student elect one of the regular courses in biology, chemistry, geology, or physics? Some schools provide an integrated course, survey, or orientation course in the natural sciences for those students who do not consider a major in one of the basic sciences. It is almost fifty years that the pendulum swing has been going back and forth. Arguments are developed to justify each school of thought—arguments such as the importance of scientific literacy in our technical society.

What role should the laboratory play in the natural sciences and in engineering? Can an orientation or survey course provide the skills and attitudes in science necessary for better adjustment and understanding of science? Educational research in this area is extremely weak. Will a cook–book, recipe–type, laboratory manual provide skills such as problem solving and creativity? To what extent, if any, are students to be encouraged to design their own experiments under the guidance of the instructor? Are students to be permitted to identify scientific problems that are not in the textbook or laboratory manual and given the opportunity to solve them? Must all students in the sciences and engineering do the identical experiment in the laboratory at the same time? What provisions are to be made for advanced students to meet with scientists in the real world? The continuous changes in our technology demand that the scientific curricula at colleges and universities be dynamic. As faculty committees re–examine the syllabi for to bring their courses up to date, they need to plan the instructional methodology to meet the course objectives.

The strategies of teaching the basic sciences and engineering subjects go beyond the traditional lecture, demonstration, and laboratory. During the past

few years, faculty development workshops have emphasized discussion of controversial topics both in undergraduate and graduate instruction. Accepted theories and proposed hypotheses are deliberately introduced for students to do inductive and deductive reasoning. Open–ended laboratory procedures make for student creativity. Other methods of teaching such as case studies, clinical methods, research on assigned projects, reports by students (oral and written) followed by critiques in seminars, seem to motivate student learning. In making plans for the interesting strategies of teaching and learning, faculty members have found a need to consider the type of evaluation to be used. The nature of examinations will thus vary with the course objectives and with the method(s) of teaching. For example, practical quizzes in anatomy, histology, mineralogy, electronic circuitry, pathology, and so on, require more than the conventional test. K–type questions in medical schools promote a higher level of thinking and learning. The organization of a test with the correct number of questions for memory, for application, for analysis, for synthesis, for problem solving, and those based on classroom teaching will profoundly affect student grades. The balance of examination and student grades influences the students' attitude towards the instructors. Student–instructor interaction, along with the effective curriculum, can be successful as long as the instructional technology is efficient and meaningful. The evidence based on science–education research during the past few decades suggests that science–curriculum reform using activity–based approaches rather than traditional methods is more efficient than its converse in the student learning process. Miles Pickering in the September/October 1986 *Journal of College Science Teaching* writes:

> No educational improvement is without hidden costs and side effects. For a curriculum improvement, what is the cost in terms of things not learned, or in teacher and student time? Controlled studies can give us a far clearer idea of the trade-offs involved. Research offers the only change to go from a 'seat of the pants' approach to a true science, based on measured facts and controlled experiments. Our methods of teaching science should be at least as scientific as the science we teach. Controlled experiments in education can help us deliver better education.

But of course the question is not only how to teach, but what to teach.

# Curriculum Research

Each individual institution finds its own experimental ways of modifying courses and the curriculum to satisfy the changing needs of society. Liberal arts students who do not major in the natural sciences or engineering are expected to analyze and be able to interpret natural phenomena. As educated citizens, they are expected to understand science and technology that appears in newspapers such as the Science Section in the *New York Times*.

To provide greater opportunities for liberal arts students to become critical or analytical thinkers, Vassar introduced a course, "Introduction to Scientific Inquiry." A major aim of this course is to help students learn how engineers and scientists think and provide a feel for the way modern technology works. This course is taught by Psychology Professor Carol Christensen and English Professor Robert De Maria. Students evaluate statistical data, analyze controversial ideas in medical articles that appear in several periodicals, and compare those articles with the original papers published in medical and technical journals.

David Billington, Professor of Engineering at Princeton, relates aesthetics to bridges to technological principles. He writes: "Engineering is the making of things that did not previously exist, whereas science is the discovering of things that have long existed." Billington, John Truxal of the State University of New York at Stony Brook, Barrett Hazeltine of Brown University, and Leon Trilling of MIT are responsible for developing curriculum materials for liberal arts colleges where there was a lack of technological expertise. Courses such as Science, Technology and Society, have been offered for many years at MIT. Recently, Vassar College, under the leadership of Morton Travel, is offering a course in science and technology titled, "Studies in Technological Creativity: The Computer." Creativity is emphasized through the integration of artistic, scientific, and technological concepts. In another course, Holly Hummel of the Drama Department at Vassar teaches costume design and the history of costume through the computer.

Throughout the United States, one finds science and technology courses that relate social, economic, and political implications and the impact of science on contemporary society. Chemistry courses are available that stress consumer chemistry: that is, instead of determining the pH of hydrochloric acid or sodium hydroxide, students determine the degree of acidity or alkalinity of soaps, detergents, cosmetics, fruit juices, and so on. Scientific concepts and procedures are applied to every-day living where students perform real laboratory experiments away from the cook book. The History of Science, Philosophy of Science, and Science and Culture courses are also available for both the science major and social science major.

Wellesley College, with the support of the Sloan Foundation, introduced a New Liberal Arts Program in which several academic departments gave introductory courses in Technology. Interdisciplinary programs were created by the faculty. In 1986–7, the college plans to offer four additional technology courses. Although it is very important that the president and deans of the college provide leadership in curriculum experimentation, courses such as these could never mature without an enthusiastic faculty committed to this type of experimentation. The financial support from the Sloan Foundation made it possible to give faculty sufficient time and financial assistance for time off to create new courses and new programs.

Likewise, medical schools are experimenting with their curriculum. In 1985 Harvard Medical College instituted the Oliver Wendell Holmes program. The goal is to produce the best type of medical practitioner by providing outstanding learning experiences that integrate theory, research, and clinical practice. The "heart" of this program is the curriculum. The "brains" of such innovations are the faculty. Many faculty committees were organized under the supervision of the administration and educational consultants. Faculty committees were organized for courses, independent activity, student research, clinical experiences, and evaluation. About twenty-five students were excused from one fourth of required lecture time in order to do individual research or carry out clinical activity under the supervision of two professors, one clinical and one in basic science. At the very beginning of their work at the medical school, some students work with patients. The curriculum is undergoing change through research.

## *Ethical Questions*

Many educators are concerned that we do not make scientists into monsters. They believe that, by requiring a given amount of training in the social sciences, we will make scientists more sensitive to the consequences of the kind of research they perform to consequences on the general public. Ethics and morality are considered by some scientists and the lay public in determining whether support should be given to research effort that can be used for war; others consider the same effort as necessary for peace. The major issue for many institutions of higher learning is how much social science should be required for the future scientist and how much natural science for the social scientist?

## Experimentation

Experimentation in designing the curriculum should be a continuous process. Curriculum research frequently neglects at least one of the following areas: the student needs and goals, the mission of the college, the opportunities available to the graduates in employment, making good use of a talented faculty, recognition by the administration of faculty and students in developing and modifying curricula, purchasing necessary equipment and supplies to facilitate the teaching of the courses, seeking input from alumni, the quality of instruction, and, finally, an evaluation of the total program.

In the March/April 1986 issue of *Change,* Russell Edgerton writes:

> In an encounter with a string of courses, students can pick up only a tiny fragment of technological knowledge. They can learn some of the ways engineers think about things. But most crucial of all, a course can give students a toe hold of self-confidence about their ability to understand and master things technological. In a proper sequence of courses, this self-confidence can grow. Students can learn that, with effort, they can be in charge. That to me is worth fighting for.

Change in the curriculum, the faculty, the student body and the various services and equipment in the sciences is constant. American institutions of higher learning are alert to this dynamic state of learning. As a result, the future of our embryo scientists and engineers looks most encouraging.

III.12

# Faculty Careers: Personal, Institutional, and Societal Dimensions

## Mary Deane Sorcinelli

In recent years there has been an increasing interest in investigating the nature of careers in academe. At an individual level, attention has been focused on how and why faculty members decided to choose such a career, how they perceive themselves as professionals, and how needs and interests change throughout their careers (Baldwin and Blackburn, 1981; Blackburn and Havinghurst, 1979; Brown and Shukraft, 1974; Entrikin and Everett, 1981; Rice, 1984; Stumpf and Rabinowitz, 1981). At an organizational level, institutions have begun to look at the way they play their role in shaping employees' attitudes and behaviors (Kanter, 1977, 1979; Peters and Waterman, 1982). Institutions of higher education, faced with limited resources, declining enrollments, and lowered faculty mobility, are beginning to find out how their policies encourage or impede professional growth (Baldwin et al., 1981; Corcoran and Clark, 1984; Furniss, 1981; Lovett, 1984). At a societal level, of course, it is still unclear how such trends as changing student demographics and shifts in their academic interests, the questioning of the value of a liberal arts education, and the nearly irresistible forces of the market pressures outside of the university will affect the careers of faculty (Mortimer et al., 1984; Proskay, 1984).

Individual faculty members at institutions must shape their career goals and strategies not only from personal inclinations, but also in response to goals and rewards set by the institution and the economy. With these conflicting forces in mind, faculty may defer actions or even change the course of their career. The tensions among individual interests, responsibilities away from work, institutional and economic structures, cannot be avoided and should be part of any consideration of career opportunities and constraints.

The Dean of Faculties Office at a major research-oriented state university initiated a multi-focused Faculty Career Development Study in order to understand faculty careers. A primary goal of the study was to determine the interests and needs for professional development characterizing faculty members. In addition, it was hoped that the data on faculty members' understanding of their career development could point to institutional practices to encourage growth throughout the academic career.

What are the attitudes of faculty members toward their own career development? What paths provide rewards, challenges, and opportunities? What factors constrain professional growth? What is the institution doing and what could it be doing to enhance the academic careers of its faculty? These are several of the key questions that the study sought to answer.

# Methodology

To answer the questions posed above, we obtained data from a sample of 112 faculty members. Studies suggest the existence of fundamental differences among faculty in various disciplines which extend beyond subject matter into career interests and attitudes. (Blackburn et al., 1978; Fulton and Trow, 1974). The basic assumption that faculty career paths and concerns would be affected by disciplinary affiliation influenced the sampling procedure.

## The Sample

Four academic units were selected to provide a variety of academic career experiences. Faculty were randomly sampled from within one department in the humanities, one in the natural sciences, and two from professional schools. The sample was stratified by academic rank and sex. The influence of career stage (rank) on faculty opinions on career issues bears closer examination (Baldwin, 1979; Baldwin and Blackburn, 1981; Stumpf and Rabinowitz, 1981). Some 21 percent of the sample were assistant professors, 30 percent were associate professors, and 49 percent were full professors, percentages which approximate the full-time faculty population. The ranks of lecturer, instructor, and administrator were removed from consideration. Some 72 percent of the sample was male, and 28 percent female. Because of limited information on the career development of women faculty (Mathis, 1979), the sample of females was purposely larger than the 16 percent faculty population.

## Data Collection

The study employed two types of data, involving in–depth interviews followed by questionnaires. The interview guide consisted of ten open–ended questions that supplied a frame of reference for respondents, but put a minimum of restraint on their answers. The interviews provided information on career choice, strengths and weaknesses, opportunities and constraints, transitions and aspirations, and the effect of life away from work on an academic career. Questions were suggested by studies on academic careers (Baldwin, 1979; Brown and Shukraft, 1974). See Appendix A for the interview questions.

The questionnaires were completed after the interview and provided more information on interests, preferences, and incentives, as well as work and life away from work satisfactions. Questions were suggested by studies on careers (Baldwin, 1979; Blackburn and Havinghurst, 1979; Kanter, 1977; Sarason, 1977), and on work and non–work satisfaction (Gutek et al., 1983; Near, Rice, and Hunt, 1980; Near, Smith, Rice, and Hunt, 1983). While the strength of the interview was the opportunity it provided faculty members for qualitative in–depth discussion and formulation of individual perspectives, the questionnaire data provided quantitative comparisons.

The interview questions and the questionnaire were pretested, revised, and pilot–tested during December 1983 and January 1984. Interviews began in February 1984 and were completed in September 1984. Exactly 100 of the 112 questionnaires were returned, providing a response rate of 89 percent.

## A Conceptual Scheme

During the early stages of data collection and interpretation, we developed a dynamic model (see Figure 1) to assist in the analysis of interviews. The following is a brief discussion of the model's rationale, structure, and utility.

Interviews were far–reaching, lengthy, and numerous; we conducted 112, and the average time spent on each was over two hours. A basic problem was how to think about the data—that is, how to encompass and order a rich variety of information. Delineation of faculty views on career opportunities and constraints helped us appreciate the general quality of faculty academic lives, but we realized that attribution of responsibility for "the way things are" was also a critical part of interviewee responses. We needed a conceptual structure to weave issues and concerns into whole cloth.

Structurally, the model is divided into three different yet somewhat overlapping domains: the individual, the institutional, and the global. Respondents identified these three domains, both positively and negatively, as factors or agents "of responsibility" in their career development. These domains overlapped and were fluid to the degree that attribution was shared among them. It was not uncommon for a single concern, want, or state of being to have a different repercussion at each of the three levels. For example, a lack of resources for scholarship might affect productivity at an individual level, status at an institutional level (as, for example, compared to departmental colleagues), and recognition at a global level (as, for example, in ability to procure federal funding).

Each domain was further divided into categories. The individual domain emerged from issues related to academic roles and includes the categories of research, teaching, service, and personal satisfaction. The institutional domain includes the categories of rewards (both salary and recognition), resources, advancement, governance, and quality of academic life. The global domain includes the categories of economic, societal, and quality of life issues (that is, life away from work). As with the domains, the boundaries separating these clusters are permeable and there is some overlap. For example, a salary concern at the institutional level might be linked to issues of governance, advancement, and resources.

The more we worked with the model as an analytic tool, the more it began to reflect not only "what" interviewees said, but "how" they made connections between and among concerns. What finally emerged was an idea of "wheels within wheels" that could be turned to produce multiple configurations. It was then possible to demonstrate the degree to which a single issue might play out across an entire spectrum of issues. For example, an interviewee with strengths in a highly marketable research area would have quite different understandings and raise quite different concerns about resources, advancement, or marketplace pressures from those of a faculty member with a primary interest in teaching at an undergradate level. This abil-

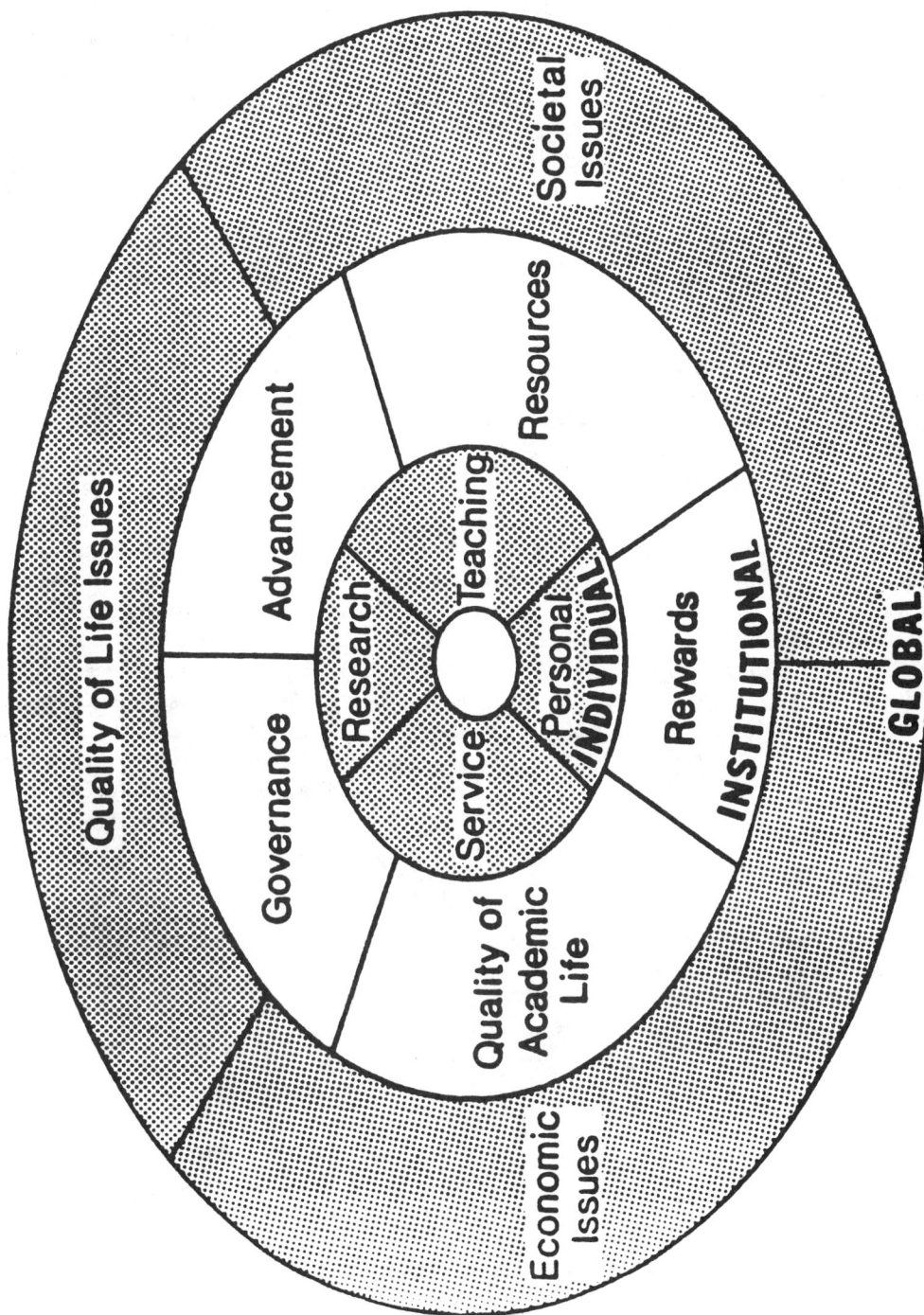

Figure I. A Model for Analysis of Career Development Issues

ity to juxtapose categories within the model respected the connections made by interviewees.

It is important to consider the model's utility in its own right. Identifying and categorizing issues and concerns certainly represents one aspect of a qualitative study. The model guided both initial classifications and the development of more detailed response categories for coding each interview. Of equal importance was the need to synthesize information across categories. The search for themes which bind discrete information into telling arguments rendered the final product more coherent by delineating the scope and depth of concerns confronting our interviewees.

Beyond the recognition of themes, the model offered a way to think about the phenomenon of career development. Once the levels and categories reflected in the data were articulated, it became a simple procedure to "turn the wheels" and build hypotheses on a host of issues. This allowed us to ask questions of the data which, without dynamic modeling, might not have been thought of. We were able to expand the study to include information as relevant where otherwise relevance might have been missed.

In summary, the use of a model to structure discrete issues and concerns helped and will help us to mine the richness of the data. It will help us to articulate the complexity of data not only among ourselves, but also to a larger audience.

## Data Analysis

The in-depth interview was selected as the major data collection instrument because of the advantages the approach offered for the exploration of contrasting perspectives and attitudes on faculty careers. Preparation for data analysis was suggested by qualitative methods of interview data analysis and interpretation (Guba and Lincoln, 1981; Wolf, 1979), and included the following activities: (1) the tape recording and taking of extensive written notes for each interview; (2) the sorting of a sample of interviews for issues, concerns and factual information; (3) the conceptualization of a model that visually represented the major career development issues, concerns, and themes that emerged from the data; (4) the designation of the appropriate coding unit as the entire interview, because of the free-flow nature of responses offered to questions (and in many cases, to unasked questions); (5) the formulation of alternative response categories for the content analysis of the interviews; (6) the testing of the interview coding instrument for intercoder agreement, with periodic revision of the instrument to ensure its applicability to later interviews; (7) the

encoding of the 112 interviews by the two interviewers; (8) the transcription on 5-×-8 cards of extensive quotations, and examples, and cases from the interview tapes in order to maintain the integrity of each interview against the threat of abstraction. Once each task was performed, we grouped results, combining thematic data with directly quoted passages and examples to underline trends and to draw conclusions concerning the attitudes of faculty members toward their careers.

Findings drawn from 112 faculty members can only estimate the range and possible dominance of certain attitudes among faculty concerning the development of their careers. The use of interviews limited the size of the sample and perhaps the generalizations drawn from the findings. However, the detailed qualitative information that this method yielded has brought and will bring an otherwise unobtainable perspective to faculty careers.

Because of the length of the interviews (one to three hours), and the breadth of responses, we have only begun to analyze this extraordinary information. This report will focus on themes suggested by preliminary analysis of the personal interviews. And while it is clear that there are career concerns peculiar to each discipline and school, rank, and sex, this paper will address the areas that concerned faculty participants across these dimensions.

This report is divided into four sections. First, it provides an overview of the study. Second, it describes the interviewees' perceptions of the opportunities for and constraints on professional growth. Third, it sets out faculty members' recommendations for career development. Finally, it presents conclusions drawn from this analysis of the interviews.

# Findings

Many respondents find personal satisfaction in their research, teaching, and service. They also appreciate the scholarly prominence of their own departments, schools, and the university. But beyond general agreement on the personal rewards of an academic career, the prestige of their departments, or the quality of academic life on the campus, faculty members expressed discontent, notably over the problems of time and salary, but also over resources, advancement, and to a lesser extent, governance.

These themes and concerns arose naturally from the ways faculty members identified their responsibilities as researchers, teachers, participants in service activities, and individuals with lives beyond these academic roles. If we consider the multiple demands on faculty members, and look at the tensions among the multiple roles they play, we can better understand their perceptions of opportunities for and constraints on career development.

## Roles

This major state university characterizes itself as an institution with a tradition of excellence in teaching based on excellence in research. Given that outlook, one would expect faculty members to view research as highly important, even essential to advancement and rewards. For many interviewees, it appeared to be the sole path to success. And because many faculty members believed in a research mission, or connected research with success, a recurring theme of the interviews was the need for more support for scholarly pursuits.

The institution sees the teaching mission as equally important and complementary to scholarship. In their own work, some interviewees found such a harmonious relationship. Nonetheless, in discussing career development, faculty members often separated their research activities from teaching. Many saw a primary investment in teaching that would take faculty down a very different path, one with limits on opportunity, reward, and recognition.

Service proved to be an unwieldy term for identifying a diverse set of activities that ranged from department, school, and university committee work or administrative roles, to service in the profession or the community at large. If investment in teaching appeared as a career path with limited opportunities for "moving up," service to the university — except for administration — was generally seen as closed off from career advancement. Service beyond the campus boundaries, while often viewed as a distraction from scholarship, did offer professional rewards and visibility.

# Opportunities

Opportunities for career development cited by faculty members were provided by the quality of the community and academic environment, institutional resources, and satisfactions from work, both personal and external to the university.

## Environment

Many of the faculty members found satisfaction in their residence in this small and attractive college town. The local environment was frequently mentioned as a source of pleasure, even an incentive to stay at the university. To use a phrase that one often heard from those with families, the town was a "nice place to bring up children." The semi-rural atmosphere and the convenience of moving from home to office to community were also cited as contributing to a pleasant career setting. Some, especially former city dwellers and single faculty, found the town parochial and provincial, and longed for the sophistication and larger social horizons of a metropolitan area. But more respondents delighted in the conveniences and security of small-town life.

The *ambience* of the university was also important. The university's School of Music, with more programs than the ordinary faculty member could possibly attend, was an obvious drawing card. Moreover, the generality of intellectual life on campus and the national prominence of individual faculty members, departments, and schools, were attractive. As one person observed, "I enjoy the feeling of being involved in a campus that has some strength of tradition behind it. There is something solid about this place that, because of my experience elsewhere, I appreciate very much."

## Resources

Approximately one third of the faculty members mentioned institutional resources that supported their development as scholars. For some, recent enlargement of classroom and research facilities better adapted to new technologies had enhanced the enhanced the physical environment. Others appreciated such resources as internal grant money and research services, and policies governing leaves and sabbaticals: "I've already benefited from grants-in-aid, summer fellowships, and the Research and Graduate Development Office seems to look for ways to help with preparing grants. My impression is that that office helps faculty."

Some faculty members also pointed to opportunities for professional development in teaching. Possibilities for interdisciplinary teaching, assignment to honors or graduate seminars, course development grants, and resources for teaching improvement provided incentives: "There are more perks for teaching. I've benefited from the Teaching Resources Center, and the Lilly Postdoctoral Fellowship. I now have a grant to develop an integrated cluster course with faculty in other departments."

## Personal Satisfaction

Despite positive remarks about the environment or the resources for scholarship, many faculty members found institutional rewards for research to be less than personal satisfaction or recognition from peers. Although nearly all participants described their efforts in research, teaching, and service, almost half of the faculty members rated research as their greatest strength and pleasures. Generating and working with knowledge provided what one respondent described as "a sense of progress of the mind." Some found the "positive atmosphere for scholarship" helpful. "There are some good people here and I think it rubs off," observed one. Others talked about how respect from colleagues and status and advancement in the department and in the university had risen with their ability to attract grants and fellowships or generate scholarly publications. One such interviewee concluded, "That's a kind of reward, how you feel your colleagues perceive you."

Success in research was also associated with the possibility of attracting professional awards, funding, or offers from outside of the university. Despite a constrained academic job market, a research record offered the promise of mobility. "I feel like I'm constantly progressing," one respondent observed. "I get invited to lots of meetings; I'm on grant panels, and I feel I could go almost anywhere and get a job that I liked. That's a very optimistic feeling, one that a lot of academics don't have." Beyond institutional rewards for research, then, faculty found personal satisfaction and disciplinary and professional recognition to be very important incentives.

About one third of the faculty members characterized their teaching as a primary strength. For most faculty members, rewards derived from teaching were largely personal. For some, the intellectual challenge of transmitting knowledge and experiences gave a sense of accomplishment. In reflecting on the teacher's potential effect on students one respondent said that, "In my field, the lifetime of a research paper is short. Turn out a student who knows how to think and you've offered society fifty years of a thinking person. What is more lasting?"

For others, establishing good relations with students, especially graduate students, was equally satisfying: "I've had a lot of excellent students who have become leaders in the discipline. It's been stimulating to interact with them and go on interacting with them in their professional careers. Here my teaching and research are so closely meshed that it's difficult to tell where graduate education leaves off and research begins."

Less than one fifth of the interviewees characterized service as their greatest strength, but it was viewed by some as personally rewarding. Whether working for the needs of minority students, a state agency, or a professional organization, a characteristic sentiment was that service provided an outlet for creativity, leadership, and action not always available in research or instruction. "I feel as if I'm in a position to make a difference," said one respondent. "My service affords avenues for impact."

More formal rewards for service within the university seemed reserved for administrators. One of several former administrators reflected, "There is no doubt I had better increments than I would have had had I continued as a professor." Others mentioned such benefits to their careers as "writing articles that stem from service activities," or "gaining professional contacts as a journal editor," or "getting additional income from consulting."

# Constraints

Given the perceived emphasis on research at this major university, perhaps the most surprising finding was the intensity with which faculty members felt the institution needed to improve the support of scholarship. There was less interest in support for teaching or service, although nearly everyone wanted to see these activities more highly rewarded. Put simply, the obstacles to career development that faculty members saw were time and money (for salary, resources, and a more nebulous category that one might describe as merit), and to a lesser degree, governance.

## *Time*

Time is a thread connecting many of the concerns of faculty in their work and their lives away from work. "Finding enough time to do my work" emerged as one of the most pressing concerns of individuals who described their semesters as fragmented by the demands of multiple responsibilities.

Part of the problem seems endemic to an academic career. Although there may be an illusion that academic life allows time for reflection, multiple responsibilities, limited time before tenure, and keeping up with the continuous advance of knowledge, all served to fragment time. Passage of time was mentioned by respondents at every rank, from the junior faculty member who viewed tenure as "a clock that's always ticking, even as we sit here talking," to a colleague nearing retirement who reflected on goals for research: "I just have so many things that I'd like to do. In fact I've got two or three books in mind. My fear is running out of time."

A central concern related to time was the incongruity between non–research assignments and the structure of rewards. While research seemed the path to career advancement, almost half of the faculty felt waylaid in their pursuit. They described not only required teaching loads but also administrative and service activities as a "tremendous drain" on time needed to maintain productivity in research. One respondent remarked, "I don't dislike teaching, but it takes a lot of time. The university requires us to spend our time teaching undergraduates and then rewards research. You can't do everything well and be very honest about it."

Other faculty members explained the tension between work roles as a rising from the very nature of research: "I love the research and I'm jealous of time taken from it. The most frustrating thing is the lack of blocks of time to concentrate. A lot of times you can't really get to the heart of something until you've thought about it or worked on it for two or three hours. Then finally you start getting involved in it and the phone rings."

Besides service or teaching responsibilities, insufficient clerical and computer support, lack of funds for released time, and fewer than necessary research assistants (or in some cases a lower quality of assistance) were cited as constraining faculty time. One respondent said, "Scholars in this place waste their time in laboratories and libraries, doing things like reading proof or monitoring equipment, when they really should have a research assistant."

Far fewer interviewees expressed a desire for more time for teaching or service than for research. Still, some indicated they might use teaching support services or better prepare for classes if there were incentives to do so. This seemed particularly true of junior faculty members, one of whom expressed the opinion of others as well: "I think my classes and evaluations would be better if I felt that was how I should spend the bulk of my time. I think I could probably figure out how to teach them or get help. But what should I spend my time doing? You've got tenure hanging over you as an issue and not doing much on teaching doesn't hurt you."

Then there was the question of time away from work, with views both favorable and unfavorable. For over three fourths of the faculty members work and life away from work were a seamless web. There were many advantages to a life in which business and pleasure were interconnected: "My avocation is my vocation. That is very unusual within society. My work—the reading, researching, thinking—is extremely satisfying to me." For most faculty members, the difficulty lay in balancing time for family responsibilities with career aspirations. One faculty member echoed the sentiments of many, "The toughest thing is to do a good job with a career that could consume all available time, pay attention

to a spouse and children, publish or perish, teach well, lead an examined life, and keep out of debt."

Others felt that the university was not conscious of the constraints imposed by dual careers, commuter marriages, and single parenthood, each of which gave rise to new demands on the time of faculty, which could affect career aspirations. A single parent attributed the deferral of a sabbatical and publications to the responsibilities of raising a child: "When my promotion didn't go through, I kind of expected someone to criticize my spending time being a parent."

Ironically, the charm of a university town, its smallness, was seen as a disadvantage for nearly half of the faculty members who cited problems with dual careers. A respondent with primary responsibility for young children in a commuter marriage reflected: "My career has taken a lot of deflections for family reasons over the last few years. If I had to take a chairmanship somewhere in order to be at a place where she could do something, well, we'd like to live together. I would not say 'no, that will interfere with my career research plans'."

Faculty members questioned the degree to which the university was aware of new pressures on academic families, and felt more flexibility in work assignments, and policies governing hiring, leaves, and sabbaticals would demonstrate sensitivity to a commitment to family as well as career.

## Money

Throughout the interviews, concerns about the environment for career development were coupled with the issue of money. A faculty member who declined to participate in the study, but discussed his rationale, explained: "I think that the study will fail to direct attention to the fundamental problem. The fundamental problem, the immediate problem, is money. And I get the impression from your survey that you won't acknowledge that." It would be impossible to ignore the connection between respondents' concerns about career opportunities and the "fundamental question" of money for salary and also for resources.

## Salary

Although faculty members were quick to acknowledge that financial reward is not the reason anyone pursues an academic career, they viewed salary as one way the institution set a value on and expressed its esteem for their contributions. In fact, one great concern was for perception of self–worth as measured by salary. Over half the faculty members interviewed felt that present salary levels as well as the process by which salaries are set inadequately rewarded achievement. Many evaluated financial rewards comparatively, primarily in terms of salaries of colleagues in other universities, those at the same rank within departments, and administrators. For some, salary was also evaluated in absolute terms against financial needs. Half the sample felt that faculty salaries generally were inadequate. Moreover, nearly half of those responding felt their own salaries were inadequate.

Faculty members were concerned about maintaining the university's reputation as a fine research institution in the face of competition with peer and lesser institutions: "I think we're going to lose younger people because our salaries are so very low. You can't get good people that way and you can't keep good people." Fear that colleagues would be lured away by higher salaries was matched by a concern about strategies used to increase salaries within the university. The procedure of "fishing for outside offers" to raise salaries was cited by nearly half the respondents as contributing to an uneven distribution of rewards within and among departments, straining collegiality and morale.

Faculty members also expressed concern about economic and societal pressures on the university. Many felt that the "notion of the university as a marketplace" had affected not only financial rewards and resources but the kind of research valued and rewarded, especially for merit pay. Some in the sample felt that their departments and the university responded to highly visible publication or marketable research. This emphasis on popular and lucrative recognition of work led "to a pursuit of laurels rather than excellence," and pitted the "popularizer" against the "specialist," the "star performer" against the "yeoman–like worker," the "basic" against the "applied" researcher, the "faddish" against more traditional lines of research.

In addition, some faculty members expressed concern over the level of administrative salaries. They described the need to take on administrative roles to supplement salary as a great distraction from scholarship. "The institution can assist in the development of my career by giving me a high enough salary so I don't have to take on an administrative position to be able to make ends meet," said one respondent. "I'd rather be doing my research and writing but only by becoming a chair will I be able to get a competitive salary."

While many faculty felt research efforts were not adequately recognized, investment in teaching was seen as further diminishing rewards. If status and value are symbolized by salary, it was clear to some

respondents that teaching was not the way to promote one's career. A concern of respondents who had strong commitments to teaching, including several who had received distinguished–teaching awards, was that they were among the "lowest paid professors in the department." While incentives for research "might be reflected in salary base" good teaching received "a plaque or one–shot cash reward."

One of the primary disadvantages of faculty committed to teaching was, of course, the absence of the "outside offer." Investment in both teaching and university service does not create the recognition necessary for offers from other institutions. As one respondent admitted, "Deep down in recent years when I've gotten really upset by my salary, if I knew how to go about getting these offers I might consider playing the game. But again, I don't know, there is something tacky about it. It's not why we, theoretically, are professors."

Finally, some faculty members expressed concern about the effect of low salaries on young families or those with college–age children. Efforts to supplement salary ranged from summer teaching to outside consulting — which, again, were viewed as necessary deterrents to career advancement. "You start thinking about what college your kids will go to, about dollars and cents, and your responsibility as a parent. You have to say, 'What does this mean to my family?'"

In summary, more than just a central concern of interviewees, salary seemed a hydra–headed creature, manifesting its influence in such diverse areas as perceptions of personal worth, research achievement, or value in the marketplace.

## Resources

Besides concerns about time and salary, nearly two thirds of the faculty members cited a third problem for researchers and that was the desirability for more scholarly resources such as graduate student fellowships, internal research support, equipment and materials. To a lesser degree, but of significance to some individuals, was the need for computer, staff, travel, or library resources.

Faculty members were concerned about funds for competing for graduate students. Respondents felt good graduates assisted faculty in their work and carried it in new directions, gave departments visibility on a national level, and had an effect on faculty recruitment. One respondent voiced the opinion of many: "We can't compete unless we have a terrific faculty and the money to offer graduate students to come here. Now what we've done over the past years is build a terrific faculty here, but unless we do the latter we're not going to succeed."

Faculty members also felt the avenues to outside funding had narrowed and wanted to see more internal funds set aside. For many, small grants were important: "There needs to be more funding available for that interim financing of research, when a person has a good idea and no other way to get it on the lab bench or out of the library books. It's surprising how far you can stretch a few dollars." Some recommended more substantial funding. As one recently tenured faculty member explained: "The funding agencies are becoming less creative and supportive. It would be nice to think that there was some way on campus to get a substantial source of funds. If it's at a critical point in your career, at least you'd have an opportunity to compete for funding independent of the granting agencies."

Teaching, too, could be improved by additional resources. Well over one third of the interviewees believed good teachers faced a number of constraints. These included large anonymous classes, heavy teaching responsibilities, and a shortage of such aids as graders, materials, and classroom facilities. "I suppose my greatest contribution is as a teacher," said one respondent. "I put a lot of effort into teaching and I try to make my courses not simply appealing to students, but rigorous. I don't give objective tests or lenient grades. But this semester I had over 600 students, which is crazy."

## Satisfactions

Personal satisfaction and respect for one's contributions was important to researchers, but seemed even more important for faculty with a strong commitment to teaching such respect. Some whose primary interests lay in teaching felt a lack of respect and recognition from colleagues for their contribution: "Sometimes the phrase 'he's a good teacher' is used as a euphemism for 'he's not a publisher, or scholar, or researcher.' That's unfortunate, but it's clearly the atmosphere in which you function."

And while nearly all of the interviewees pointed to strengths in teaching, about one fourth indicated that some of the personal rewards for teaching, particularly at the undergraduate level, were absent. Some discussed the problems in working with present–day undergraduates: "A number of the students in my courses have difficulty reading and writing. And they're mostly interested in their grades and not in the subject. I'm mostly interested in the subject and not in their grades. It doesn't tend to make for a wonderful relationship." Others faulted the structure of undergraduate education. "In grad-

uate education you develop personal relationships with your students. Undergraduates are people who pass you by. It's hard to follow up on who and what you teach because of class size or the lack of continuity from course to course."

Faculty members seemed hard–pressed for suggestions to improve undergraduate education or deal with underprepared students. Some simply stated that participation in programmatic changes to improve undergraduate teaching and learning would remove them from the structure of professional rewards. Here the complex pulls among institutional and marketplace rewards, and even life away from work were evident: "If someone said to me, 'you will be rewarded if you develop these courses just for undergraduates and work hard with these kids,' I would do it in the best of all possible worlds. But in the real world I will continue to stress research, publishing, and things that are going to do the best for me. And that's really not selfish because, like most people, I support a family. That's the hidden side of careerism. It's not as individual a pursuit as some people make it out to be."

Faculty members felt the insulation of teaching from professional and marketplace rewards might be ameliorated in several ways. One unit was experimenting with a procedure that added "merit for teaching accomplishment" (determined by chair, peer, and student assessment) to the salary base. Others advocated policies for promotion and tenure that acknowledged excellence in teaching, and perhaps even the naming of a "Distinguished Professor of Teaching" on campus.

## Dissatisfaction-Governance

Finally, and not unrelated to the environment for research and teaching was faculty members' concern for governance. On one hand, there was sympathy for administration in what everyone, critics as well as friendly observers, agreed were difficult times. The enormous problems of funding — where to find the funds to maintain the scholarly prominence of the university — were such that most faculty members personally did not want to work them out, and acknowledged the administration's efforts in this regard.

Still, about one third of the interviewees reported certain aspects of administrative attitudes toward faculty as affecting their work. Even with the practice of staffing most administrative positions with faculty who move in and out of those ranks, some faculty in the sample felt that there was an increasing distance between the faculty and the administration. This may be partly a result of the growth of the university both in size and in number of programs. In particular, the administration's difficulty in identifying with the missions and needs of departments and more generally with faculty life was cited: "One big thing they could do for career development, and this is an intangible, is to maintain and improve the quality and the intellectual vitality of the university. The administration lacks the understanding of what it means to be a professor, to pursue knowledge. They have no real understanding of scholarship or teaching."

Another area of faculty concern was an absence of leadership, of a clearly stated mission for the university. Such a statement of goals, it was suggested, might serve to harness imagination and direct efforts toward agreed upon ends. The uneasy relationship between research and teaching was evident not only in faculty members' perceptions of rewards and opportunities, but also in their views on the priorities of the university. In the absence of an agreed–upon mission, interviewees voiced divergent opinions on the responsibility of Indiana University for creating, preserving and distributing knowledge.

One faculty member who advocated a stronger administrative commitment to activities that would further the university's national reputation explained: "We don't have the right attitude. We never say, 'In the last ten years Stanford has taken the number one ranking from Harvard and in the next ten years we want to take it from Stanford.' We just don't have that push for excellence."

Another respondent reflected an equally strong sentiment about the institutional commitment to teaching, particularly the teaching of undergraduates: "We are a state university, not a Stanford or Harvard; we're not in that league. We can talk about a great research university, but our primary responsibility is to undergraduate teaching. We have not made that the issue it should be when we talk about the excellence of this university." Faculty of both opinions felt the administration should better articulate the goals and priorities of the university.

In dealing with the difficult problems facing higher education, some faculty members felt the institution must find ways to reward the diversity of roles in which faculty members find satisfaction. In their view, the current accentuation and narrowing of the "research career path" further limited development and recognition of other contributions, particularly those outside a specialized discipline: "This is a research university. Why reward someone with alternative skills? There is no forum in which that question can be debated. To argue against it is

idealistic because we all know it's that way. Whether or not it should be doesn't come up."

Yet for many who devoted considerable effort to activities other than research, the lack of rewards did not turn them away, although it clearly affected morale. Most felt an obligation to teach effectively, serve their departments and the university, and to do research as well. For some, however, continued absence of recognition had caused them to abandon teaching or service activities (undergraduate advising positions, university committees, task forces, projects in the community or state) even though they felt they had made significant contributions in these areas. These faculty members called for an academic environment that respected a variety of ways to fulfill the responsibilities of the profession: "We need a structure which rewards and encourages not only highly specialized research and teaching, but also synthesis and cooperation, innovation and risktaking. We need to send clear signals that success means something besides a Guggenheim."

## Career Directions

A final measure of the environment of career opportunities and constraints appears in the number of faculty members either considering or seeking positions in other institutions or outside of academia. Among faculty interviewed about one third were doing so. Factors influencing them included greater opportunities for advancement or new challenges, salary, and personal and family considerations (as, for example, career opportunities for spouses).

For some, the mobility of faculty was refreshing and was to be expected of a nationally ranked university: "I think we have to have a lot of this tumultuous careerism. It keeps things stirred up and it keeps the university alive." For most who were considering leaving, however, the reasons they offered for their decision touched on the constraints of the university rather than those of an academic career. Indeed, nearly three fourths of the sample indicated that if they had to do it over again, they would still pursue an academic career. One respondent summed up the attraction to an academic life: "It's like the moth to the flame. There are too many potential rewards. There is the lure of research that is an original and unique contribution. There is the lure of teaching students who keep you growing. There is the lure of growth in the directions you choose to take."

That faculty members generally are satisfied with their careers — even if concerned about possibilities for career growth — should make the enhancement of opportunities a priority. The university must maintain a climate that fosters the quality of its most important resource—the faculty.

# Recommendations

Many suggestions for enhancing the environment of opportunity emerged from the interviews with faculty members. Their recommendations spoke to the following in particular: develop incentives for research, teaching and service, and reexamine or create institutional policies.

## Incentives

Released Time: The university needs more incentives for individuals. Many suggestions concerned released time—through paid semesters-off or flexible staffing—to focus on a particular faculty role. Respondents at every rank suggested a "sabbatical summer or semester" prior to tenure for junior faculty to complete research. Mid-career faculty members needed time to acquire new skills or pursue a new area of research. Some respondents advocated a "research semester" for senior faculty members to write a seminal or synthetic piece. There was less but some interest in similar arrangements to develop teaching or service skills. Recommended was released time to get involved in administration (as, for example, with short-term assignments or internships) or in course and curriculum development. From young to long-time faculty members, there was agreement upon the need for time, which would be an incentive to their self-improvement and the improvement of the university.

Internal Support: Another form that incentives might take, according to many faculty members, would be more internal grants. Most were interested in relatively small grants requiring simple applications—for xeroxing, typing, travel, even for postage. Some saw the need for a few substantial career development grants for junior or post-tenure faculty members doing important but less market-valued research. The awarding of internal grants, and increasing incentives to seek outside funds, would give evidence that the university valued the grantees and their work.

Collegial Support: There was a desire for collegiality. By this the respondents meant really the assistance of one faculty member to another. Some faculty members suggested this might be on a volunteer basis, perhaps through reading a manuscript

or grant proposal or even visiting a classroom. Others felt the university could somehow encourage faculty members to help each other, perhaps by creating mentoring systems or "networks" across disciplines for research and teaching.

## Reexamining and Creating Policies

Evaluation of Faculty: Evaluation for reappointment, promotions, and tenure is a concern. The way out of the difficulty appears to lie in flexibility, which may mean that the present procedures are not working well. Many faculty members felt the current structure depended upon the presentation of dossiers in ways that have become almost mechanical and do not reflect or respect the difference in academic disciplines, or the extraordinary variation across schools and colleges. There was a desire for more clarity and consistency in the criteria used to evaluate performance. Several recommended more precise guidelines for dossier preparation, more systematic evaluations of teaching, and more continuous assessment of faculty members, particularly after tenure. Other faculty members wanted more generous criteria that encouraged not only traditional assessment (research advances, teaching improvement) but also expansion of career roles (research or creative activities outside an academic specialty). Beyond these, the suggestions were not always specific, but the concern was.

Leaves and Sabbaticals: For some faculty members, leave of absence and sabbatical policies have seemed inflexible. Longer institutional leaves to business, government, or other campuses, without negative consequences in terms of salary or promotion, would be attractive. Sabbaticals, especially for faculty members with working spouses or families, seemed too confined if offered within the usual term of one semester with full salary, two semesters with half. Respondents offered the alternative of "mini-sabbaticals" taken at more frequent intervals in the career. Written guidelines on how to prepare for sabbatical leave (pointers on moving, finances, and so on) also would help to maximize benefits in this critical time for career development.

Retirement Options: For many senior faculty members, the university did not seem to help the transition to retirement. One individual described his life with the university as akin to a marriage, and mentioned how his investment in the institution had been so large that it would be difficult to break the ties. A number of respondents desired to do research, teach, or somehow contribute to the university beyond the age of seventy. One suggested a central office where retired faculty members could meet. Here they might serve as research mentors to faculty or work with administrators to solve institutional problems. Others spoke for more incentives to retire early and allow young faculty "with enthusiasm, freshness, and new perspectives" to take their place. Again, flexibility seemed to be the key.

Dual Careers: Faculty members expressed a need for opportunities for spouses. The small – town, attractive for atmosphere, becomes a drawback for individuals with dual careers. If the university would perhaps show more awareness of the problems of spouses, whose skills become nearly impossible to employ within the confines of the campus, this would help. Such awareness might take the form of more flexible hiring policies for spouses, more formal counseling for dual career families, particularly new faculty, and perhaps advertising local talents to larger areas in the state.

## Rewards

In conclusion, and beyond the specific concerns of the faculty members interviewed, one must address what was often vaguely described as the need for rewards. The latter were in part salary, but this need, so often expressed, was clearly for more than that. The growth of the university during the past generation has brought many benefits, such as the growth of departments and schools with all the opportunities for collegiality. And yet there has been a loss, perhaps on the personal level. Individuals who worked hard for achievement, and attained it, often complained that they then heard nothing locally, despite state and even national recognition.

Here may be something that colleagues — especially department, school, and campus administration — could do: take notice of the achievements of faculty members and congratulate them. According to senior faculty members, when the university was smaller, and a faculty member published a book, appeared on an important scientific panel, received an award for teaching or service, a note came from the administrative offices. Faculty members who remembered the habits of old wished for a continuation of this sort of practice. Junior faculty members, some of whom felt "totally invisible" to the people making decisions about them, expressed a desire for such acknowledgement. If one were asking for changes on university and college campuses, this might be a place to begin.

# Conclusion

While a goal of the study was to determine the opportunities for and constraints on career development, it was not possible to explain faculty concerns in terms of a single issue around which others gravitated. The context of career development, as one might expect, is complex and not reducible to one prominent feature. How individuals perceived their professional strengths and weaknesses, their work, the institutional setting for that work, the community lived in, the life returned to at the end of day, and the larger economy and society — all contributed to the general view of career opportunities and constraints.

And even when a dominant concern emerged on which there seemed to be wide – spread agreement, there was still diverse opinion on who or what should be held accountable. For example, the concern about remuneration found a number of different circumstances or agents cited as responsible for the problem: a recession that ended the halcyon post – Sputnik years of state and federal funding, an administration that showed a failure of leadership and existed in a culture removed from faculty, a department or school administration that rewarded academic skills differentially, or an individual faculty member who made a pivotal career choice in youth, no regretted.

From the university, however, faculty members seemed to be asking for a more supportive institutional environment. Specifically, they sought (1) support for career growth in research, teaching, and service, and (2) an examination of institutional policies and market pressures outside the university that affect career development.

The needs for career development characterizing many of the faculty members were linked to their roles as researchers. More than any other one thing, faculty members wanted the institution to provide more time and support for research. Time was a theme that emerged again and again in the study, particularly time for scholarship. Other studies have uncovered similar faculty concern about the difficulty in balancing multiple and complex roles (Baldwin, 1979; Clark, Corcoran, and Lewis, 1984). If the institution wants to capitalize on the individual differences and strengths among faculty members, it needs to help alleviate this stress over lack of time through grants for released time, flexible staffing, leave of absences, sabbaticals, and promotion and tenure procedures.

While personal rewards provide more incentives than monetary ones (McKeachie, 1978; Newell and Spear, 1983), salaries were a critical career development concern for faculty members. Although some complained about the absolute level of their remuneration, more evaluated salaries in comparative terms and as instruments used by the administration to recognize personal worth. The linkages among salaries, research, and market place considerations were unmistakable, however. More faculty members valued research more than teaching, not only because it was an activity from which they derived considerable personal satisfaction or status in the university, but because it also was an activity that brought them greater recognition or "marketability" beyond campus boundaries. The emphasis the university places on research seems to come from the inclinations of faculty members, realities of life away from work, and a larger economy, as well as from formal rewards in the institution.

Teaching emerged as a source of satisfaction for many faculty members, and for a sizable minority it was a primary interest and pleasure. In the minds of most faculty members, however, it was an endeavor valued less than research by their colleagues, the administration, and the marketplace. While teaching held not nearly so high a priority as research for many faculty members, the interviews indicated that time and effort spend on the teaching role might change somewhat if the structure of rewards was different. The insulation of teaching from professional and marketplace rewards perhaps makes a case for sustained institutional support for instruction, particularly for high-quality undergraduate instruction.

Although most faculty members were interested in career development within their traditional disciplines, a very small number desired to develop or already had developed secondary career interests (as, for example, interdisciplinary work, creating or administrating programs and centers, consultant to a school on computers, statistics). The data indicate that there need to be ways to recognize the contributions of people who assume roles of this sort.

The connection between faculty careers and institutional policies also was unmistakable. Some interviewees felt that while a career grant might assist a few individuals, more career renewal would come from the development or rethinking of institutional policies. A consistent response to the question of how to provide support to faculty was "be more flexible." That meant more flexibility in the manner in which faculty were evaluated, in staffing, leaves, sabbatical procedures, careers for spouses, and retirement options.

This study has already initiated a dialogue between administration and faculty at Indiana, presenting the needs of faculty for the development of their careers, setting out programs to address those needs, and developing policies that acknowledge the strengths of faculty members, goals of the institution, the impact of life away from work, and larger economic and societal forces.

# Appendix A

## *Faculty Career Interviews*

1. How did you come to choose an academic career?

2. Could you briefly describe your career—the major responsibilities and interests from your first to your current position?

3. What are your major strengths as a faculty member?

4. How does the university recognize or reward your strengths? If not, how might they capitalize on and reward your skills?

5. What skills or abilities would you like to improve? If yes, are there ways the university could assist you to develop or improve the areas mentioned?

6. How can the university assist faculty in developing or enhancing their careers?

7. What are both your short and long term career goals?

8. Did you ever think of making a career change?

9. How has life outside of work made an impact on your career development?

10. If you were able to start all over again, do you think you would still choose an academic career?

# References

Baldwin, R. "Adult and Career Development: What Are the Implications for Faculty?" *Current Issues in Higher Education,* 1979, pp. 13–20.

Baldwin, R. *The Faculty Career Process—Continuity and Change: A Study of College Professors at Five Stages of the Academic Career.* Unpublished doctoral dissertation, 1979. University of Michigan, Ann Arbor.

Baldwin, R., and Blackburn, R. "The Academic Career as a Developmental Process: Implications for Higher Education." *Journal of Higher Education, 52,* 1981, pp. 598–614.

Baldwin, R., Brakeman, L. Edgerton, R., Hagberg, J., and Mahar, T. *Expanding Faculty Options: Career Development Projects at Colleges and Universities.* Washington, D.C.: American Association for Higher Education.

Blackburn, R. T., Behymer, C. E., and Hall, D. E. "Research Note: Correlates of Faculty Publications." *Sociology of Education, 51,* 1978, pp. 132–141.

Blackburn, R. and Havinghurst, R. "Career Patterns of U.S. Male Academic Social Scientists." *Higher Education,* 1979, pp. 553–572.

Clark, S. M., Corcoran, M., and Lewis, D. R. *Critical Perspectives on Faculty Career Development with Implications for Differentiated Institutional Policies.* Paper presented at American Educational Research Association, New Orleans, Louisiana, 1984.

Corcoran, M. and Clark, S. "Professional Socialization and Contemporary Career Attitudes of Three Faculty Generations." *Research in Higher Education, 20*(2), 1984, pp. 131–153.

Entrekin, L. V. and Everett, J. E. "Age and Midcareer Crisis: An Empirical Study of Academics." *Journal of Vocational Behavior, 19,* 1981, pp. 84–97.

Fulton, O., Trow, M. "Research Activity in American Higher Education." *Sociology of Education, 47,* 1974, pp. 29–73.

Furniss, T. *Reshaping Faculty Careers.* Washington, D.C.: American Council on Education, 1981.

Guba, G. E. and Lincoln, Y. S. *Effective Evaluation.* San Francisco: Jossey-Bass, 1981.

Kanter, R. M. *Men and Women of the Corporation.* New York: Basic Books, 1977.

Kanter, R. M. "Changing the Shape of Work: Reform in Academe." *Current Issues in Higher Education, 1,* 1979, pp. 3–10.

Lovett, C. M. "Vitality without Mobility: The Faculty Opportunities Audit." *Current Issues in Higher Education, 4,* 1984, pp. 1–35.

McKeachie, W. J. Financial Incentives Are Ineffective for Faculty, Mimeo, 1978.

Mortimer, K. P., Astin, A. W., Blake, J. H., Bowen, H. R., Gamson, Z. F., Hodgkinson, H. L., and Lee, B. "Involvement in Learning: Realizing the Potential of American Higher Education." *The Chronicle of Higher Education,* October 24, 1984, pp. 35–50.

Near, J., Rice, R., and Hunt, R. "The Relationship between Work and Nonwork Domains: A Review of Empirical Research," *Academy of Management Review, 5*(3), 1980, pp. 415–429.

Near, J. P., Smith, C. A., Rice, R. W., and Hunt, R. G. Job Satisfaction and Nonwork Satisfaction as Components of Life Satisfaction. *Journal of Applied Social Psychology, 13,* 1983, pp. 126–144.

Newell, L. J. and Spear, K. I. "New Dimensions for Academic Careers: Rediscovering Intrinsic Satisfactions." *Liberal Education, 69,* 1983, pp. 109–116.

Rice, E. R. "Being Professional Academically." In L. C. Buhl and L. A. Wilson, *To Improve the Academy.* Professional and Organizational Development Network in Higher Education, 3, 1984, pp. 5–11.

Sarason, S. B. *Work, Aging and Social Change: Professional and the One Life — One Career Imperative.* New York: The Free Press, 1977.

Stumpf, S. A. and Rabinowitz. "Career Stage As a Moderator of Performance Relationships with Facets of Job Satisfaction and Role Perceptions." *Journal of Vocational Behavior, 18,* 1981, pp. 202–218.

Wolf, R. L. *Strategies for Conducting Naturalistic Evaluation in Socio-Educational Settings: The Naturalistic Interview.* Occasional Paper Series. Evaluation Center, Western Michigan University, 1979.

III.13

# Assessing Outcomes:
# The Real Value Added Is in the Process

## TRUDY W. BANTA AND HOMER S. FISHER

Across the country, assessment of the outcomes of higher education is a topic of growing concern to faculty and administrators, the various publics they serve, and the agencies that influence their activities. The October 1984 National Institute of Education (NIE) report *Involvement in Learning* (item 8 in our references) contained the recommendation that each institution assess progress toward attainment of its objectives for student development. Four months later, in *Integrity in the College Curriculum,* the Association of American Colleges announced that "The colleges themselves must be held responsible for developing evaluations that the public can respect (p. 33)." An October 1985 meeting originally planned to provide a forum for discussing responses to the range of recommendations in the NIE report one year after its publication quickly became the National Conference on Assessment in Higher Education, and attracted over 700 people—nearly double the early estimates of probable attendance.

U.S. Department of Education Secretary William Bennett has announced to higher education officials that "Those who pay for education must have reliable information about the quality of the institutions they are supporting" (quoted in Knoxville *News-Sentinel,* 10/24/85). The former chairman of the National Governors' Association, Governor Lamar Alexander of Tennessee, appointed a task force on "college quality" headed by Governor John Ashcroft of Missouri, to consider ways of measuring student learning and institutional effectiveness. The Education Commission of the States is studying state strategies, including assessment, for improving undergraduate education. The six regional accrediting associations, which approve private as well as public institutions, have revised their standards to include institutional effectiveness components that require evidence of student accomplishment of educational objectives derived from assessment activities.

Considering the number of individuals, institu-

tions, agencies, and associations studying and attempting to shape outcomes assessment, it is not surprising that differing perspectives on the topic have emerged. An exchange of views at the February 1986 meeting of Governor Ashcroft's task force on college quality illustrates the lack of consensus about purposes, definitions, and methods of assessment. According to Ashcroft, "Assessment leads to quality and accountability. Standards, as measured by tests, send a strong message to young students that they will be held accountable (Jaschik, p. 14)." He went on to say that enforcing standards through testing likewise sends a message to professors and administrators that they will be held accountable for their students' performance. Ohio Governor Richard F. Celeste warned, however, that there is "a real danger of going overboard on standardized testing in higher education. The danger is imagining that some simple and uniform formula can be used to say we know how everyone stands (Jaschik, p. 14)." Instead of relying solely upon tests, Celeste urged that assessment take the form of thorough peer reviews of departments and colleges linked to competitive financing programs.

The comments of the two governors reveal the tension between those—usually outside the institution, in legislatures and state coordinating agencies—who would hold colleges and universities accountable for the quality of educational programs by imposing standards based on criteria that are easy to measure and uniform across a variety of institutions, and those—usually faculty, students, and administrators within the institution—who would prefer to use a variety of assessment activities to determine the status of programs in meeting their objectives and to suggest directions for improvement. While most within and outside academe agree that program quality in higher education should be assessed, there is little agreement about what exactly it is that should be assessed and which methods should be used.

A recent telephone survey of state academic officers conducted by the Education Commission of the States (Boyer and McGuinness, pp. 3–7) has revealed that all fifty states currently have underway initiatives for improving undergraduate education. Several of these incorporate assessment activities. In their report on the ECS survey, Boyer and McGuinness assert that "State action . . . is stimulating public colleges and universities to scrutinize their undergraduate programs (p. 7)." They also point out that some institutions "are making extensive use of outcomes data in overall institutional planning as well as in curriculum evaluation and improvement (p. 6)." However, they add (p. 6)

> Limited evidence suggests that colleges and universities can make effective use of outcomes data in their curriculum-reform efforts. Before other states act on that evidence, however, more discussion is needed on how and under what conditions the use of outcomes data can be linked to state policy without accompanying negative consequences.

Boyer and McGuinness recognize Tennessee as the first state to provide a financial incentive for public colleges and universities to define their student development objectives more clearly than they have been defined and to undertake assessment procedures to provide evidence of effectiveness in achieving those objectives. From their experience with the Tennessee performance funding initiative the authors propose to contribute to the store of evidence that prudent use of outcomes data can be linked to state policy not only "without negative consequences" but with tangible benefits for institutions.

# Performance Funding: Incentive for Assessment

Since 1979 the Tennessee Higher Education Commission (THEC) has been experimenting with a performance funding policy that provides a financial supplement to public institutions for engaging in the following instructional evaluation activities: (1) testing undergraduate students in general education; (2) conducting peer reviews and/or testing undergraduates and candidates for the master's degree in their major field; (3) surveying current students, dropouts, alumni, and/or employers to obtain their assessments of academic program quality and related student services; and (4) using the results of testing and surveys to make needed improvements in programs and services (Bogue and Brown, pp. 123–128). Until 1983, the financial sup-

plement was equivalent to 2 percent of each institution's budget for instruction; beginning in 1984 it was raised to 5 percent. Participation in instructional evaluation activities has been voluntary, but in fact the budget bonus has encouraged every state institution to undertake some or all of these assessment procedures.

The THEC performance funding policy has a number of strengths. First, it was phased in gradually over a period of three years to allow time for institutions to plan their responses to the proposed assessment program. Second, the funds provided represent a supplement to the formula–generated allocation, so that no institution has experienced undue pressure to participate or loss of anticipated funding for failure to do so. Perhaps the most important strength of this state policy is its flexibility: while there are additional rewards for high test scores, institutions also receive credit for undertaking assessment activities and demonstrating that they have been guided by the results in making program improvements. Moreover, the policy does not require institutions to use standardized tests in major fields; each program faculty is encouraged to select or develop a test that measures the achievement of its objectives for students.

Tennessee's performance funding policy thus far has avoided the overreliance on standardized tests that Ohio Governor Celeste has warned against; it has encouraged the "thorough peer reviews" he advocates; and it has stimulated colleges and universities to use outcomes data in "curriculum–reform efforts" and "overall institutional planning," as Boyer and McGuinness have suggested. The following sections provide concrete evidence of the value added to the educational process and to decision–making throughout the institution by the kind of outcomes assessment program that is suggested by the THEC performance funding policy. Most of the illustrations come from the experience of The University of Tennessee, Knoxville (UTK), the state's land–grant and research university, which has an enrollment of 25,000, including 5,500 graduate students.

# Responding to the Performance Funding Initiative

Performance funding was viewed initially as an external threat by administrators and faculty on many campuses in Tennessee. At UTK some of the negative impressions were at least neutralized in the course of a two-year study carried out with assistance from a small Kellogg Foundation grant administered by National Center for Higher Education Management Systems. Taking advantage of the time for planning offered by the THEC, three task forces —composed of students, faculty, and administrators—considered instruments available for testing students in general education and in their major and for surveying students and alumni. Then they made recommendations for integrating outcomes assessment activities in ongoing procedures vital to the life of the institution (Banta 1986).

A first principle of outcomes assessment is that there is no single set of outcomes, or approach to assessment, that is appropriate for every campus. Each institution must consider its own mission and goals, as well as goals and desired instructional outcomes for individual programs, in deciding what to assess and which of a variety of methods to use. Fortunately, the THEC performance funding guidelines provide some latitude for tailoring an assessment program to address the mission and goals of each institution.

At UTK the Kellogg project task forces enunciated three purposes for a university-wide assessment program:

(1) To establish the status of programs in meeting their objectives for student development;

(2) To provide direction for improving and strengthening curricula, methods of instruction, and related student services;

(3) To improve the quality of information used by departments, colleges and the university in making decisions about the relative priorities of certain activities and the allocation of institutional resources.

More specifically, the task forces recommended that outcomes assessment be incorporated in the well-established campus peer review process and that the enriched peer reviews be given increased importance in the institution's strategic planning and resource allocation deliberations.

The number of outcomes listed in Figure 1 as options for departments to consider in their self-study prior to peer review indicates that members of the three task forces wanted to go beyond the areas of assessment specified by the THEC. The Task Force on Measurement of Achievement in General Education asked that the ACT College Outcome Measures Project (COMP) exam be administered centrally to freshmen and seniors to permit an assessment of growth from entry to exit. COMP scores were to be provided periodically to colleges and departments. The Task Force on Measurement of Achievement in the Major recommended that the faculties of 110 academic programs select a standardized exam or construct their own to assess the status of their largest program (baccalaureate or master's-degree level) in attaining the faculty's objectives for student development in the major field. The Task Force on Measurement of Satisfaction asked two faculty specialists in survey research to design a series of related instruments to assess satisfaction of students, dropouts, alumni, and employers with the quality of university and departmental programs and services. Oversampling in departments scheduled for peer review would permit the incorporation of survey data collected centrally in departmental self-studies. Beyond the assessment information gathered by the central administration, colleges and departments were encouraged to collect and report their own data on student perceptions of growth toward objectives, placements and achievements of graduates, and external recognition received by the program.

# Benefits Resulting from Outcomes Assessment Activities

Since 1982, when a systematic outcomes assessment program was initiated at UTK, with findings incorporated in academic program reviews, strategic planning, and resource allocation procedures, benefits have begun to accrue throughout the institution.

## Academic Program Review

In 1974, UTK administrators established a peer review process that utilizes a team of two external consultants in the discipline and three internal consultants from units outside the one being reviewed. The team of five reviewers spends two and a half days gathering information from faculty, students, and administrators, to supplement that obtained from the departmental self-study prepared in advance of the visit. Prior to 1983, self-study guidelines had encouraged each department to describe its resources, including faculty credentials, abilities of incoming students, size of the library collection, levels of salaries and operating budget, and adequacy of facilities. To accommodate the focus on outcomes assessment, the guidelines were expanded to include suggestions that the department

## Figure 1

```
┌──────────────────────────────────────────────────────┐
│                      OUTCOMES                          │
│                                                        │
│  Achievement in general education (via COMP exam)      │
│                                                        │
│  Achievement in major (national or local tests)        │
│                                                        │
│  Perceptions of growth toward objectives               │
│                                                        │
│  Opinion of program quality (students, graduates,      │
│       dropouts)                                        │
│                                                        │
│  Opinion of employers concerning job-related competence│
│       of graduates                                     │
│                                                        │
│  Rate of job placement for graduates                   │
│                                                        │
│  Rate and quality of placement in graduate or profes-  │
│       sional education                                 │
│                                                        │
│  External recognition (honors, awards) achieved by     │
│       students or graduates                            │
│                                                        │
│  National program rankings                             │
└──────────────────────────────────────────────────────┘

              ┌──────────────────────────┐
              │  ACADEMIC PROGRAM REVIEW  │
              └──────────────────────────┘

    ┌──────────────────────────────────────────────┐
    │             PROGRAM IMPROVEMENT                │
    │             STRATEGIC PLANNING                 │
    │             RESOURCE ALLOCATION                │
    └──────────────────────────────────────────────┘
```

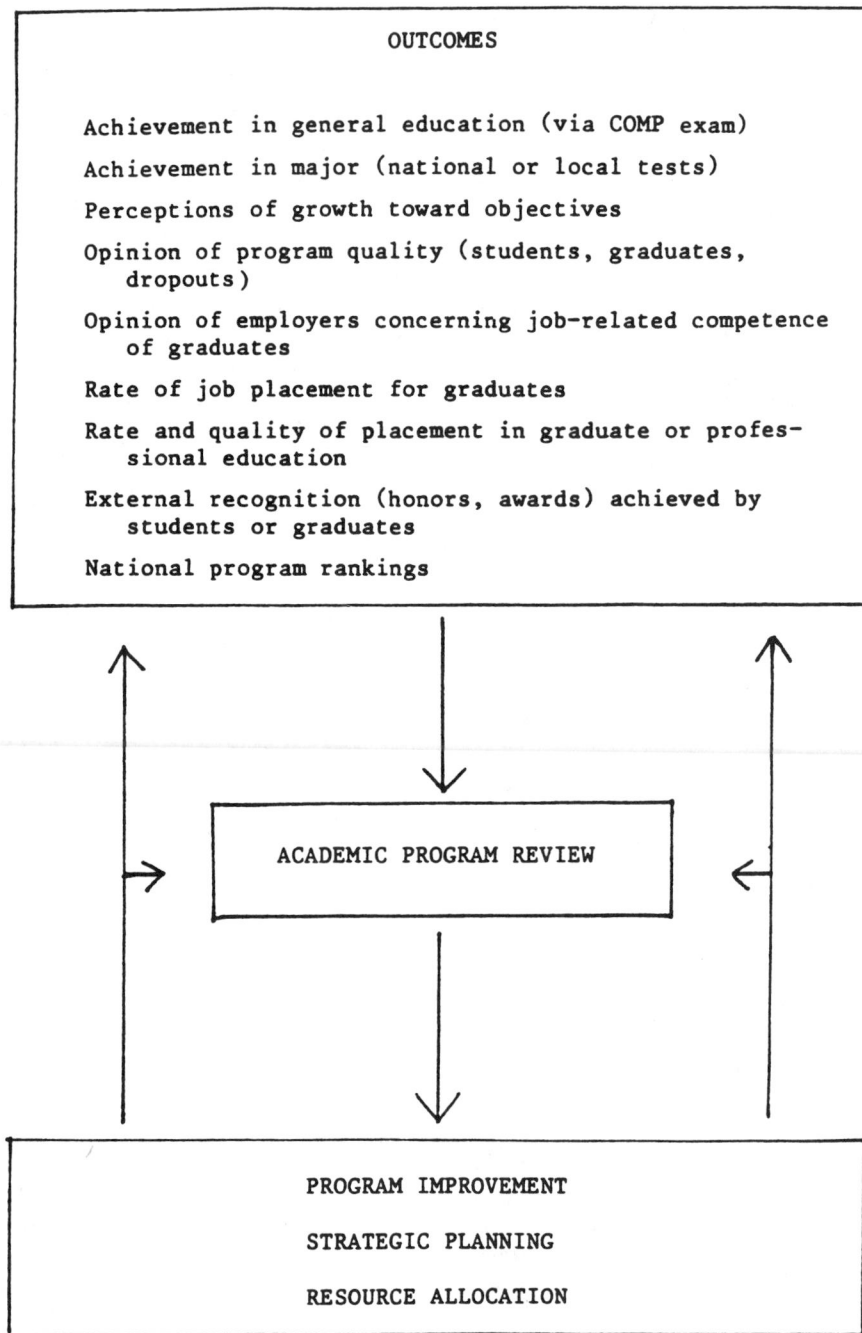

state its instructional objectives for students and then provide evidence of its effectiveness in helping students attain the objectives. The addition to the self-study of such evidence as perceptions of program quality obtained from surveys of students and alumni and students' scores on comprehensive exams in general education and the major field has enriched the content of that document. The survey responses and test scores enable the reviewers to focus their questioning of students and faculty on perceived strengths and weaknesses of the program, and many reviewers have expressed appreciation for these new tools for program evaluation.

## Strategic Planning and Resource Allocation

At UTK, a central planning group of administrators and faculty leaders seeks the best match between internal program strengths and weaknesses and external opportunities and constraints in determining strategy for the institution (Banta and Fisher, pp. 29–41). University–wide surveys of students, alumni, and dropouts have assisted the planning group in assessing both the external and the internal environment of the institution. Students' test scores and departmental survey results, along with other information from the academic program reviews, have helped the planning group determine which programs need additional support to grow or to achieve distinction, and which should be reduced in size or scope. Data from outcomes assessment also have been used to set planning goals related to enrollment and marketing, student/faculty/staff development, and improvement of equipment, physical facilities, and the library.

While academic program reviews take place only at five– to seven–year intervals, annual budget hearings permit department heads to present to the central administrative staff their goals and objectives and progress toward accomplishing these, and their associated resource needs. With the advent of outcomes assessment activities, many department heads have been able to produce new evidence of both their needs and their accomplishments. At the same time, central administrators have at their disposal improved comparative data for use in setting priorities for the allocation of funds.

Information from the various assessment activities has helped to convince central administrators at UTK that resources should be allocated for the following purposes:

(1) To strengthen the general education core as the university moves from quarters to a semester calendar.

(2) To reduce class size in selected areas.

(3) To focus attention on the need for improved strategies for student retention.

(4) To establish or expand college advising centers.

(5) To provide released time for faculty in certain units to participate in advising.

(6) To improve publications for prospective students.

Now, what has come of this determination?

## College and Departmental Decision-Making

The addition of findings from outcomes assessment activities has improved the quality of the information on which deans and department heads base decisions about academic programs and related services such as advising. Administering the ACT COMP exam to freshmen and seniors and observing patterns of growth in the six areas assessed by the instrument have provided information suggesting that the university's general education curriculum, especially in the social sciences, should be strengthened as new patterns of courses are developed for the semester system. Within individual colleges, the nature of the general education core has been shaped by the profile of specific strengths and weaknesses of students in that college, as revealed by COMP exam subscores.

The locally–developed surveys for current students, alumni, and dropouts permit colleges — and departments in the case of current students — to compare their own ratings with those of other colleges and with the university–wide average. Having access to the perceptions of those they seek to serve concerning the quality of academic programs and related services has prompted administrators and faculty in several units to

- Increase the emphasis on advising.

- Increase opportunities for faculty-student interaction.

- Initiate or expand opportunities for internships that permit students to apply their knowledge and skills in employment settings.

- Improve printed information describing the academic program.

- Initiate or expand student professional organizations.

- Increase faculty involvement in the placement of graduates.

Both deans and department heads have found that alumni, employers, advisory council members, and potential donors to their programs are favorably impressed by the seriousness with which their units have approached the collection and use of outcomes information. The ability to demonstrate high levels of student and alumni satisfaction has given a boost to development efforts across the campus.

As faculty have become involved in the development of comprehensive exams for majors, they have evolved fresh perspectives on the nature of the curriculum and the knowledge and skills students should derive from it. The test development process itself has produced a number of positive outcomes at the departmental level, including

- Increased faculty agreement concerning common learning outcomes for all students.

- Development of core objectives or competencies for students.

- Increased direction for converting courses/curricula from quarter to semester format.
- Increased consistency in the teaching of core courses.
- More clearly delineated linkage between lower-division and upper-division courses.

And following administration of the locally developed comprehensive exams and joint review of students' performance, faculties have

- Acquired baseline data on student achievement that can be used to compare the effectiveness of quarter and semester curricula.
- Identified program strengths, and weaknesses that should be corrected in the semester curriculum.
- Made curriculum changes, including stronger core curriculum within the department, and changes in requirements outside the department.

Nor are the changes limited to these.

## Faculty

As a result of looking at students' ACT COMP scores on the Communicating, Solving Problems, and Clarifying Values subscales, and reviewing students' scores on comprehensive exams in major fields, faculty members have made a number of modifications in their own instructional techniques, including increases in

- Structure for courses now that core objectives/competencies are identified.
- Number of written assignments.
- Opportunities for students to *apply* their knowledge and skills through problem-solving, term projects, field trips, internships.
- Opportunities for demonstrating complex skills on tests and in other assignments, and
- Use of scores on the local test to diagnose students' needs for remediation prior to taking the certification exam in the discipline.

Instructors increasingly are developing improved and more specific objectives for student learning and are relating course content to those objectives, then testing students to ascertain their accomplishment of the objectives. Their test development experience has placed UTK faculty in a position to be called upon to set standards and develop examinations for use at the national level by their respective professional associations. Several faculty members

involved in test development have produced papers and articles for publication in journals dealing with instruction in their discipline. Obviously these activities have enhanced the qualifications of some faculty for promotion and increases in compensation.

Participation in assessment has pointed out the need for certain types of faculty development activities on the campus. Faculty have shown increased interest in such topics as writing items for classroom tests, improving students' writing abilities, and increasing students' abilities to engage in critical thinking and problem-solving.

## Students

Students at UTK have benefited in a number of ways from the institution's instructional evaluation activities. As faculty expectations for student development have been clarified and communicated more effectively, students have been able to bring their own educational goals into sharper focus and improve the efficiency of their learning activities. Students' academic satisfaction has increased as faculty have attached added importance to good advising and interacting with students outside the classroom. Finally, most students have welcomed the additional information about their growth toward mastery of curricular objectives that has been afforded by the comprehensive exams in general education and in the major.

# Summary and Conclusions

Consensus is growing concerning the need for assessing levels of student learning and the quality of the educational process in our colleges and universities. However, there is no single set of procedures that will permit every institution to assess its student outcomes appropriately, nor does the current state of the art of measurement offer a set of procedures that will permit *any* institution to assess *all* of the intended outcomes of the education it provides. Nevertheless, there is a growing body of evidence that a given institution can select and develop procedures for outcomes assessment that support its mission and goals, and can use the results of these procedures to effect improvements in programs and services that will benefit students, faculty and administrators, departments, colleges, and the institution itself.

Assessing educational outcomes necessarily involves using tests and questionnaires that elicit relatively standardized responses and thus yield scores or ratings that are easy to interpret. Faculty and administrators can and do raise legitimate questions about the technical qualities of these "objective" instruments. However, when students' responses are not used to make decisions about individuals, but rather studied in the aggregate to gather clues about the strengths and weaknesses of programs and student services, some deviation from technical perfection may be tolerated.

Program quality must not be judged exclusively on the basis of factors that are relatively easy to quantify, such as student achievement in cognitive areas or client satisfaction. Over – reliance upon the absolute value of comprehensive test scores alone, without regard to the amount of student growth inherent in those scores, and without related information about the educational process that helped to produce the scores, will strengthen the critics of assessment — those who maintain that we should not attempt to assess *any* outcome until reliable and valid measures exist for assessing *all* outcomes of higher education.

Levels of scores by themselves can be used to establish the status of a program vis – à – vis its own goals or those of an external agency. But this is a static process. The key to an effective outcomes assessment effort is to initiate a dynamic process — using multiple sources of data to suggest program strengths and weaknesses and potential directions for improvement, then relying upon human judgment to process outcome data in combination with information about program resources in formulating recommendations for change.

More than six years of experience indicate that the current performance funding policy of the Tennessee Higher Education Commission is sufficiently flexible to permit colleges and universities to look beyond the simplistic information provided by levels of test scores to seek directions for improvements from multiple data sources. The financial carrot offered by performance funding has stimulated faculty and administrators at institutions in Tennessee (1) to formulate more specific objectives for student development, (2) to communicate these objectives to students, (3) to involve students in learning through increased faculty-student interaction and opportunities to apply knowledge and skills acquired in the classroom, (4) to assess students' progress in attaining objectives for their development, (5) to assess student satisfaction with their progress and with the process used to promote it, and (6) to make improvements indicated by the assessment data. It is in this dynamic process of using outcomes information that the real value added by higher education will be ascertained and affirmed.

# References

Association of American Colleges. "The Problem of Accountability." In *Integrity in the College Curriculum: A Report to the Academic Community.* Washington, D.C.: Association of American Colleges, 1985.

Banta, T. W. *Performance Funding in Higher Education: A Critical Analysis of Tennessee's Experience.* Boulder, CO: National Center for Higher Education Management Systems, 1986.

Banta, T. W., and Fisher, H. S. "Performance Funding: Tennessee's Experiment." In J. Folger (ed.) *Financial Incentives for Academic Quality.* New Directions for Higher Education, no 48. San Francisco: Jossey-Bass, 1984, 29–41.

Bogue, E. G., and Brown, W. "Performance Incentives for State Colleges." *Harvard Business Review,* 1982, 60 (6), 123–128.

Boyer, C. M., and McGuinness, A. C. "State Initiatives to Improve Undergraduate Education, ECS Survey Highlights." *AAHE Bulletin,* 38 (6), February 1986, 3–7.

"Colleges Must Rate Themselves, Bennett Says." *Knoxville News-Sentinel,* Thursday, October 24, 1985, A-5.

Jaschik, S. "Fear of Federal Cuts Tempers Governors' Zeal for Education." *The Chronicle of Higher Education,* 32 (1), March 5, 1986, 11, 14, 15.

Study Group on the Conditions of Excellence in American Higher Education. *Involvement in Learning: Realizing the Potential of American Higher Education.* Washington, D.C.: National Institute of Education, 1984.

# Instructional Improvement: Strategies for Implementing Changes

## Maryellen Gleason Weimer

## Background and Orientation

The instructional and faculty development literature of recent years is both abundant and rich. Research, resources, and experiences are all reported in readily available publications. These can assist instructional developers (Bergquist and Phillips 1975) assigned the tasks of creating, implementing, and operating programs designed for positive effect on instructional quality. But not all the needed answers appear in this body of literature: one very fundamental question remains unanswered—addressed, but answered tangentially, without much depth and a bit too blithely. That question is this: how do those assigned to improve instructional quality ensure that the improvements proposed are in fact implemented?

The focus of this early literature on instructional development, probably more as a matter of necessity than as a matter of design, has been on establishing programs and identifying activities that ought to occupy those engaged in instructional improvement. In addition, great effort has been expended in exploration and refinement of evaluation procedures—the measurement and description of instructional effectiveness. These focuses are appropriate and indeed they have established the foundations of the field. However, the question persists: how can implementation of proposed improvements be assured?

Most instructional development programs are service-oriented operations that propose to faculty members a variety of resources and activities aimed at increasing teaching ability. The "service" posi-

tion puts instructional developers in a place somewhat akin to that of organizations promoting weight-watching activities. Like instructional development, weight-watching is a solution only if the problem is acknowledged and steps are taken to solve it. No one—even though seriously in need—is required or forced to participate. Even the most persuasive reasons and useful resources fail if the person involved does not see fit to carry out activities that will change the situation. When everything is said and done, only one person makes the behavior changes required if weight is to be lost. Faculty members have that same ultimate prerogative about instructional improvement. They alone decide, if and when, to carry out proposed changes.

In some ways the plight of the instructional developer is less enviable than that of the weight-loss counselor. In this society there are all sorts of incentives to be thin—good health and physical attractiveness, to name two that matter to most persons. In academic communities, incentives to improve instruction are less compelling, if at all. Debate continues as to whether teaching is recognized and rewarded its due. Those who argue appear unlikely to be reconciled. But the perception that there is no reward for good teaching persists strongly in faculty minds, and it is this perception that makes the instructional developer's job a particularly challenging one.

## Myths Against Improvement

Moreover, the presence of two myths also militate against faculty members' making changes in teaching behavior. Academic communities are still peopled by faculty and administrators who believe that no one knows what makes teaching effective, that the criteria of effective instruction are unknown,

This paper was originally published in slightly different form in *Proceedings of Faculty Evaluation and Development: Lessons Learned,* Vol. 22, published by National Issues in Higher Education, Kansas State University, 1986, and is here reprinted by permission of National Issues in Higher Education and the author.

and that objective standards on which to base comparisons of faculty unavailable. The second myth—widely held even by excellent teachers—is that good teachers are born, not made. Both of these tenets of assumed instructional wisdom need to be attacked.

(1) Those who believe no one knows what makes teaching effective typically establish the claim by pointing to professor "x" in classroom "b" who tells jokes and is admired for it, and professor "y" who hollers at students in classroom "c" and is equally admired. In contrast to these anecdotal offerings are multiple empirical inquiries identifying the components of effective instruction. They have been completed regularly since the 1930s (Miller 1975, pp. 32–3). Granted, not all the lists of components identified by the empirical investigators are the same, and no universally recognized deity has deigned to bless one above all others. However, neither are the principles of literary criticism uniformly acknowledged, and this does not prevent the active practice of literary criticism, predicated upon assumptions that good writing shares recognizable components. Like literature, instruction can be improved through the use of identifiable techniques, and the absence of absolute standards of judgment does not mean that no standards may be employed. Pragmatic standards are in fact the basis of development in fields of learning generally and these pragmatic standards are designed to realize a working relationship between theory and practice. Of course, if faculty members (and administrators) believe characteristics of effective instruction are yet to be discovered, what the instructional developer recommends as the "right" or at least "better" way to teach will lack credibility. Change will be less likely to take place and instructional quality will remain unaffected.

(2) An unfortunately large number of academicians still believe good teachers are born, not made. This second myth takes the following proverbial form. At birth (for reasons yet to be revealed) a person is blessed (or conversely, cursed) with an absolute amount of teaching ability. This quantity remains constant—impervious to attempts to alter its relative proportion.

It is true that there is a certain unquantifiable and even indescribable quality—perhaps a "magic"—about truly effective instructors. Maybe the relevant distinction is the difference between being a "good" and a "great" teacher. At that point, the instructional developer may be up against the wall. Making an instructor "great" is a questionable proposition. But making an instructor "good"—that is, more effective—is a distinct possibility. The good

news from the research findings of the 1970s and the decades before is that the components of effective instruction that keep reemerging are not magical or at all mysterious. Rather, they are concrete skills that can be acquired or developed. But if the faculty member confronted by the need to make changes is constrained by beliefs about absolute amounts of teaching ability, the result is a perceived inability to do anything about what occurs in the classroom. Brilliant though the instructional developer's proposals might be, chances of implementation are slim.

# The Myths and New Strategies

The ultimate effect of these two myths is to face the instructional developer with a challenging proposition. That the issue is important seems almost too obvious to point out: the honeymoon for instructional development programs is over, and for some programs and institutions the relationship has already been severed (Gustafson and Bratton 1984). The task here is to begin to remedy that situation by proposing three strategies that instructional developers can employ to make faculty implementation of desired outcomes more likely to occur. They are being proposed with recognition of the service-oriented climate in which they must be used. They are specifically designed to work when the necessary instructional alterations cannot be forced or required. They also attack the two myths just described. The strategies are related to each other; they function synergistically; and they begin building toward a philosophical foundation on which the practices of this field might be grounded.

## Strategy 1: Behavioral Descriptive Talk about Teaching

The first strategy involves the way in which teaching ought to be described and discussed. Two recommendations: First, the talk about teaching needs to be more behavioral than it has been. Second, teaching needs to be discussed without the strongly judgmental orientation that almost always accompanies it.

Research repeatedly, for example, associates instructor interest in the subject matter with effective teaching. The admonition to teachers is "be enthusiastic!" But enthusiasm is not a tangible entity—not something to go out and secure. Rather it is an abstraction descriptive of an internal state. It is something instructors are. So, if the teaching lacks enthusiasm, the instructor is faced with changing the way he/she is. To "be" enthusiastic is not an easy assignment if you are not.

However, the presence or absence of enthusiasm is determined by the presence or absence of certain behavior associated with it. Enthusiastic instructors do things in front of students. They make gestures, speak in varying pitches, at varying rates, and at different volumes. They may move about. Their eye contact is likely to be direct and seeing. In other words, enthusiasm can be described behaviorally —in terms of what an instructor with it does. The distinction may appear small, but the significance for improving instruction is large. It becomes the difference between asking someone to change the way they *are* and to change what they *do.*

Some academicians (and administrators) are disorganized. Telling them to get organized is a lost cause; telling them to take five minutes before they start working to make a list of tasks for the day seems like a manageable proposition. Some faculty members will claim they can't be enthusiastic; few would maintain they couldn't speak louder as the importance of a point might deem it. In essence then, the first strategy makes instructional changes more likely to be implemented because the proposed alterations are specific and appear to be easy to do.

FREEDOM FROM JUDGMENT   All too frequently, teaching is thought of in bipolar extremes; good or bad, effective or ineffective. Two other characteristics typify this evaluative orientation to teaching. First, the judgments offered are likely to be comprehensive. "She's a good teacher." All the time? Every day? In every class? For every student? Second, the conclusions are often reached after only limited observation of the instructor or may even be based on the reports of students selected at random, or even with malice aforethought.

This judgmental orientation has come to permeate much of our thinking about teaching. It gains substantial reinforcement from the evaluation activities which occur almost universally at universities. Students, peers, and administrators evaluate teaching—generating data used in promotion and tenure decisions. This is all legitimate, but it adds considerably to the notion that teaching behaviors are good or bad, right or wrong, effective or ineffective in the absolute. It is possible to describe the criteria of effective instruction and rate an instructor, at a point in time, against these criteria. But this does not imply that a particular teaching technique —effective at a particular time and place with a par-

ticular group of students—is always good and right. The acts of teaching and learning are far too dynamic to be measured in such static and absolute terms.

This does not deny the necessity and for some purposes the legitimacy of the judgmental descriptions of teaching. But the contention here is that when instructional improvement is the agenda this pervasive judgmental orientation causes problems. Qualitative judgments of teaching effectiveness make faculty defensive. Rather than focusing on what they do in the classroom and might do differently, faculty members are forced to defend themselves, argue with the conclusions, and make claims to the contrary. This focus skews the procedure and makes changes less likely to occur.

The solution suggested is that discussions of teaching by instructional developers need to be descriptive and extraordinarily specific. Teaching needs to be talked about so that its overall quality is deemphasized. The conversations should aim to provide the faculty member with a clear and accurate understanding of what it is that he or she does when teaching. For example, rather than a conclusion like "You are well organized," the comment ought to be "You end each content segment with a brief summary that brings the ideas in that section together and signals students that you are about to change topics." Not "You look nervous," but "You used the same gesture repeatedly without any obvious relationship to the content. Your eyes moved quickly from student to student without seeming to focus on them." Qualitative elements remain in the examples and this is as it should be. But they are highly specific.

Observers can legitimately report how behavior affected them. "I felt that answer put me down"; not "That answer was a put down." Reports like these provide feedback rather than comprehensive and judgmental conclusions.

The effect of the descriptive approach on faculty is favorable. It diminishes the defensiveness generalized assessments frequently provoke. As personally involved as most instructors are in their teaching, their responding in ways that protect their self investment is natural. When busy defending the self, the instructor is not likely focused on accurately decoding the feedback. When interaction emphasizes descriptively what an instructor *does* as opposed to what he or she *is,* then the need to defend teaching techniques is not nearly as urgent. The observer speaks with authority *only* about the effect of the behavior on him/her. The recognition of a potentially different effect on a different person is constantly acknowledged.

Nevertheless, because this approach aids in the discovery of what one does when teaching and because behavior can be controlled and changed, the approach makes implementing change a decidedly less risky proposition. The problem is approached with a certain "tentativeness"—not in the style in which change is implemented, but in the sense of not knowing with absolute certainty whether change will be effective. Accepted from the start is the fact that the changes might work only sometimes, might be well received by some students only, or might be effective only in some courses. The point is to try them and find out. When neither success or failure are absolute, the risk of change is much more manageable.

The first strategy being suggested to help insure that instructional alterations will be implemented by faculty is to make dialogue about teaching descriptive in the sense that the components of teaching are discussed behaviorally, and descriptive in the sense that it is not judgmental.

## Strategy 2: Informed Choice About Alterations

Faculty members faced with the need to make alterations in teaching style or technique must be counseled to make informed choices based on an accurate assessment of the teaching self. This point is twofold. First, instructors must be explicitly aware of the instructional strategies they employ: a good way to test this awareness is to ask faculty members to write a description of themselves teaching that is accurate and specific enough to allow someone else to identify them teaching (without describing course content or physical characteristics like height or hair color). Second, if instructional changes are to have positive results, faculty must make appropriate choices from among a variety of potential alternative ways of behavior.

The implied contention here is that most faculty members would be unable to generate self-description of this caliber. Not only do most of them learn to teach by the seat of their pants (or skirt), they practice it pretty much the same way—without a great deal of conscious awareness of what they do, when, and with what effect. The awareness being proposed emphasizes what appears to be mundane—the nuts and bolts that hold a teaching style together. What space in the classroom is used? When are students asked questions? What students? How are points introduced? Summarized? Is there eye contact? Where? For how long? Does the tone of voice vary? Are there examples? Answers to these

questions emphasize a point that should be obvious, but frequently missed. They force an instructor to encounter the teaching self—to discover what actions combine to become the unique teaching style of the individual. Eble (1983) advocates this same personal discovery and assessment of teaching style. Carrier, Dalgaard and Simpson (1983, p. 205) assert similarly, "To teach effectively, an instructor must continually examine his teaching behavior and implicit assumptions." Until the teaching self is known, implementing change is systematic and haphazard. Precision and impact are added when the faculty member knows what is being changed and from what to what.

CHOICE OF BEHAVIOR  Behavior choice works this way. The components of effective instruction can be "packaged" in a variety of different forms. Enthusiasm is again a convenient example. As already indicated, messages of enthusiasm are communicated in a variety of different ways—gestures, movement, eye contact, tone of voice, facial expression, and so on. No magic formula exists and, in fact, the evidence is stronger that a combination is made "best" if it fits the unique rhetorical proclivities of the person involved. To put it another way, an instructor must communicate enthusiasm in ways that represent comfortable and natural communication patterns. If an instructor lectures with hands in pockets, converses out of class with hands in the same location, advising the instructor to indicate greater enthusiasm by gesturing is probably inappropriate. Gesturing for that person will seem uncomfortable and awkward—the movements will be tentative, lack conviction, and probably end up not communicating enthusiasm anyway.

To aid in the discovery of ways of teaching behavior, the query to the instructor must be, "How do you convey interest and enthusiasm outside of class?" "What do you do when you feel strongly about something?" The instructor may not know but can in that case be advised to observe. When the answer is known, the recommended ways of increasing enthusiasm in teaching ought to build on, adapt, and incorporate the strategies used elsewhere.

Obviously, the approach works only if the instructional developer counsels the faculty member to make informed choices. This makes the sort of explicit instructional awareness proposed here essential for both faculty member and instructional developer. The awareness is not difficult to develop, especially if the descriptive behavioral approach to discussions of teaching recommended earlier is adopted. The incentives in favor of the approach are strong. What the instructional developer ends up proposing to faculty members is that with guidance and adaptation, they can "do what comes naturally" in the classroom. The changes proposed and considered are adaptations of behavior used in other contexts but altered so as to fit the constraints of the classroom. The ultimate aim is to develop a teaching style that is a genuine representation of the person involved.

The approach is attractive to faculty members. To be effective, they don't have to tell jokes or jump around in the front of the room or do any other universally prescribed practice. To be effective, they must carefully and conscientiously assess their teaching styles in terms of the strategies and techniques they use generally. That assessment must be compared with specific behavioral descriptions of effective instruction and informed choices must then be made. Faculty are responsible for making the decisions and are not obligated to accept one predetermined set of remedies. It is a strategy that joins developer and faculty member in an exploration and analysis of possibilities from which a truly "individual" plan for instructional style is developed.

## Strategy 3: Implement Change Incrementally

Incorporation of instructional changes needs to be approached incrementally. This makes the instructional development plan efficient because it is developed in small manageable pieces, and as the faculty member sees it evolve, responsibility for the necessary decisions can be assumed as an almost inevitable consequence of the process.

The incremental approach has much else to commend it. Wholesale behavior changes are difficult to sustain over time. Old habits die hard. Being able to concentrate on two or three relatively minor changes, like including three internal summaries or inviting questions once in the middle of a lecture *feels* manageable, and for that reason is more likely to be managed. Moreover, with only two or three items to emphasize, chances for successful incorporation of those items increase, and the feeling of being able to orchestrate change effectively is especially desirable.

This need for success early in the instructional development process is particularly strong in cases where major repairs in a teaching performance are needed. Most faculty do not teach badly without considerable feedback to that effect. The problem is that the quality of that feedback frequently makes faculty members defensive and hostile. They feel powerless, unable to see what needs to be changed and how it might be done. Surprising though it may be, most faculty carry only a small instructional bag of tricks. Their repertoire of alternative teaching strategies is limited. Therefore, belief in the ability to make changes needs to be bolstered early on. This view rests upon the assumption that by proposing two or three manageable changes, where the chance for successful incorporation is high, faculty motivation and commitment to the whole process of improving instruction can be increased. The weight-loss metaphor is again insightful: It is easier to believe you can lose twenty pounds if you have already successfully taken off five.

Obviously then, an important ingredient of this approach is prescribing or helping the faculty member identify these first, small, sequential alterations where chance for initial success is high. For example, say the problem is massive disorganization in class presentation. Nothing in this particular class happens in any sort of obvious sequence or order. The incremental approach would start by identifying a concrete, specific problem—such as the two or three incoherent, information-dense, illegible overhead transparencies used during the lecture. Provide a model, showing how transparencies can be laid out efficiently and without a great deal of effort made readable. Encourage the instructor to make or have made a couple of new transparencies following the model. These new transparencies should be tried out in class and student response to them solicited. Doing this is easy, and the effects likely to be easily discerned. This might be followed by one which explores the question *when* transparencies can be used, followed by a series of suggestions as to *how* they can be used. All along the way, the instructor is asked questions so his or her current strategies are clearly understood in relation to a variety of possible alternatives.

The example illustrates an activity where the chance of success is good (making legible transparencies is not a particularly challenging proposition) and how the changes can be put in sequence. The objective is to motivate implementation of changes by proposing that they occur in small pieces and aiding in placing those first few pieces so that putting the rest together does not look hard. Gaff (1978, p. 205) proposes a model of "organic" change for institutional renewal and comes to the same conclusion. "The surest route to enduring change is through a series of short steps that follow each other. . . ."

Another tangential benefit of an incremental approach is that it encourages instructional developers to take a kind of "tinker" approach to teaching. Classroom performance is the object of ongoing puttering. Old parts are replaced, new ones adjusted, lubrication added for smooth running, manuals consulted for specific repair jobs. Tinkers know that with this kind of attention, most apparatus will run faithfully for years. They also know that in the act of tinkering are pleasures, satisfaction, and a sense of accomplishment. Instructors need to feel the same way about keeping the teaching learning process running smoothly.

## Conclusion

A case has been made. Instructional developers need as they continue to grow and develop to nourish their own existence by being certain that the activities and alterations they propose to improve instruction are indeed implemented. The task is challenging because the power base from which most programs of this sort operate is small and the act of implementing changes very personal. However, approaches do exist that can make the likelihood of change greater. These approaches involve descriptive behavioral discussions of teaching, development of instructional awareness as a prerequisite to identifying appropriate changes, and the in-cremental alteration of instructional practices. These build on and interact with each other in ways that begin development of a philosophy of instructional development—a task that needs to continue in the years ahead.

## References

Bergquist, W. H., and Phillips, S. R., 1975. Components of an effective faculty development program. *The Journal of Higher Education.* 46:183.

Carrier, C. A., Dalgaard, K., and Simpson, D., 1983. Theories of teaching: Foci for instructional improvement through consultation. *The Review of Higher Education* 6: 195–206.

Eble, K., 1983. *The Aims of College Teaching.* San Francisco: Jossey-Bass.

Gaff, J. G., 1978. Overcoming faculty resistance. In J. G. Gaff (Ed.), *Institutional Renewal Through the Improvement of Teaching,* 43–58. San Francisco: Jossey-Bass.

Gustafson, K., and Bratton, B., 1984. Instructional improvement centers in higher education: A status report. *Journal of Instructional Development* 7:2–7.

Miller, R., 1975. *Developing Programs for Faculty Evaluation.* San Francisco: Jossey-Bass.

III.15

# Looking into Education's High-Tech Future

## BY DEREK BOK

*Hewlett-Packard Gives Five Million Dollar Grant for Computer Equipment to Harvard Medical School*

*Digital Plans $45 Million Education Project*

*A Personal Computer for Every Freshman; Even Faculty Skeptics Are Now Enthusiasts*

In the last eighteen months, all across the country, headlines like these have signaled the sudden rush of a new technology that promises to leave a lasting imprint on the practice of education at Harvard and other universities.

Technology is already starting to affect the way in which students prepare for classes in several of our professional schools. Last fall, the Business School began requiring every entering student to purchase an IBM personal computer. Those who were unfamiliar with these machines received special instruction in their use. Software was distributed to enable students to manipulate financial data. Word processing programs were provided to assist students in preparing their reports. Because of the formidable powers of the personal computer, teachers could assign more complicated problems than before, problems that more closely resembled situations confronting corporate executives in real life.

The Law School has not yet required students to buy computers. But students and professors have formed an alliance to develop programs to help in mastering basic material such as the rules of accounting, tax, property, and evidence. Although these exercises are optional, over half the class has used them in some large courses. A more venturesome creation permits students to watch a mock trial on a screen and object at any point to the questions asked of witnesses. With each objection, a computer asks students to choose the ground for intervening

from a list of possible reasons. If the student answers correctly, the computer so states and the trial resumes. If the student gives the wrong answer — or if there is no proper ground for protest — the computer so indicates and explains why the student erred. At the end of the tape, the program automatically flashes back to every point in the testimony at which the student failed to make a valid objection.

In the Medical School, computer programs have been developed to simulate patients with a variety of diseases. With these programs, students can ask the patient questions or order medical tests and plausible answers or test results will instantly appear on the screen. By framing hypotheses and testing them in this fashion, students can eventually make a diagnosis and either have it confirmed or ask the computer where their reasoning went astray.

More conventional video technology is already in wide use to carry instruction to students at separate geographical locations. At Harvard, the Medical School is connected by closed-circuit TV to our teaching hospitals, to the Science Center in Cambridge, to MIT, and even to other, more distant institutions via satellite. Through these links, speeches and seminars at any of these institutions can be viewed by faculty and students in all the others. Elsewhere, universities have launched even more ambitious ventures. Stanford offers engineering courses by closed–circuit TV so that employees in high–tech companies throughout Silicon Valley can attend class without leaving their place of work. The University of Washington gives televised courses to supplement the education of medical students in places as distant as Alaska, Idaho, and Montana.

Networking offers a means of improving communication outside of class among people in different locations. By linking personal computers to one another, a university can permit students to send messages back and forth and ask questions of instructors or campus officials. In this way, students can seek help from many classmates simultaneously and

Assistance from Daniel A. Updegrave, vice president of EDU-COM, in obtaining this article, is gratefully acknowledged.

The article is reprinted by permission of Dr. Bok.

174

communicate with less inhibition and greater ease with their professors.

Libraries provide another fertile place for technological innovation. By next July, almost all of our new acquisitions will be registered in a computer so that librarians can instantly learn the whereabouts of a recent book or periodical, not only in our own collections but in any of a number of cooperating institutions. Medical students will soon be able to use their personal computers to search for articles in a number of journals and instantly reproduce the entire text. It is not yet possible to do the same for all books and articles in a library, since most of these materials do not exist in machine-readable form. In the not–too–distant future, however, computers may be able to conjure up on a screen the titles, tables of contents, and indexes not only of all books in a university library but of all volumes in all participating libraries across the country and abroad.

# Prospects for the New Technology

In theory, at least, the new technology has the power to transform the nature of the university. Much routine advising could shift to a network of personal computers linked to a common data base so that students could instantly have the answers to a host of factual questions about course requirements, employment interviews, campus events, and homework assignments. In time, lectures could move from classrooms to television screens so that students could listen to a professor and immediately test their comprehension of the material by working through a series of questions and problems presented by an appropriate computer program. Science concentrators could simulate many laboratory experiments on computers without leaving their residence hall. Video technology could not only transmit lectures but bring the resources of the outside world to students in living color. For example, art history majors could use a videodisc linked with a computer to explore the great museums of the world, examine the details of any painting they chose for as long as they wished, and summon up text to explain the picture and the circumstances under which it was painted.

These possibilities have fired the imagination of many apostles of the new technology. According to the president of Johns Hopkins, Steven Muller, "We are, whether fully conscious of it or not, already in an environment for higher education that represents the most drastic change since the founding of the University of Paris and Bologna . . . some

eight or nine centuries ago." [1] Because of the speed and accuracy of the computer in performing mathematical computations and processing information, "what Ph.D.s did 25 years ago will be term projects for Dartmouth students," according to Ray Neff, former director of computer services at Dartmouth. [2] "I'm not convinced that there will always be a book," says Frederick Kilgour in describing the electronic library of the future. [3] Adds Patrick Suppes, one of the pioneers in computerized instruction, "One can predict students will have access to what Philip of Macedon's son Alexander enjoyed as a royal prerogative: the personal services of a tutor as well-informed and responsive as Aristotle." [4]

Amid this general euphoria, however, one can detect quieter, more skeptical voices. According to Richard Clark, a leader in evaluating the effects of educational technology, "Five decades of research suggest that there are no learning benefits to be gained from employing different media in instruction, regardless of their obviously attractive features or advertised superiority. . . . The best current evidence is that media are mere vehicles that deliver instruction but do not influence student achievement any more than the truck that delivers our groceries causes changes in our nutrition." [5]

Experience should also make us wary of dramatic claims for the impact of new technology. Thomas Edison was clearly wrong in declaring that the phonograph would revolutionize education. Radio could not make a lasting impact on the public schools even though foundations gave generous subsidies to bring programs into the classroom. Television met a similar fate in spite of glowing predictions heralding its powers to improve learning.

In each instance, technology failed to live up to its early promise for three reasons: resistance by teachers, high cost, and the absence of demonstrable gains in student achievement. There is as yet no clear evidence that computers and videodiscs will meet a happier fate. Faculty members may be as reluctant to give way to computers as they were in the case of radios and television sets. The cost of the equipment likewise remains quite formidable. According to one professor, to provide all of the 460,000 engineering students in America with a modern computer workstation joined by a network and linked to a central data base would cost ten billion dollars. [6] True, hardware costs have been declining at a compound rate of 25 percent for a number of years. But hardware makes up only a small fraction of the total cost of computer-assisted education; the major expense lies in preparing suitable materials and maintaining the software and the machines. Thus, the overall costs of the new technology seem likely to remain high for the foreseeable future.

Finally, the educational benefits of technology also remain in dispute. There is still little proof that new devices yield lasting improvements in learning. Many studies purport to find such gains. But most of them can be explained on the grounds that students using computers were temporarily motivated by the sheer novelty of the machines or that more effort and better teaching went into the computerized courses than were devoted to the conventional classes with which they were compared. Thus, the learning improvements that early investigators reported from computer–assisted instruction shrank to virtually nothing when the same teacher taught both the experimental and the conventional classes with comparable amounts of preparation. Similarly, the gains achieved in computer experiments lasting less than four weeks dropped by more than two-thirds when the experiments continued beyond eight weeks and the novelty of the new technology began to wear off.

Undaunted by these obstacles, educators and high tech companies are spending huge sums to prove the skeptics wrong. Control Data Corporation has reputedly invested over a billion dollars in the computerized college curriculum, PLATO. With assistance from major companies, Brown, MIT, Carnegie–Mellon, and other institutions are each spending tens of millions of dollars in equipment and programming to wire their campuses. Against the backdrop of these developments, Harvard's Faculty of Arts and Sciences has launched a comprehensive review of how technology might be best put to use for research, administrative, and, not least, educational purposes. It is high time that we studied these questions, for the computer revolution is already upon us. What impact might these machines have on the nature and effectiveness of education? What kinds of innovation are feasible and not prohibitively expensive? What advantages and disadvantages could technology bring to the quality of life in the university?

# Machines That Eliminate Drudgery

Many widely used technological innovations seem principally designed to save time or eliminate drudgery and routine. Electronic bulletin boards spare students the burden of finding announcements in campus newspapers or dropping by departmental offices. On-line catalogues save a trip to the library reading room. Word processing avoids the trouble of typing new drafts, while remote-site TV can take away the need to travel from home to campus.

As these conveniences accumulate, one begins to wonder whether machines will eventually permit students to learn at home instead of going to the expense of living and attending courses on a university campus. If so, technology will not merely eliminate drudgery; it will save substantial sums by removing the need for dormitories, classrooms, and other costly facilities. The possibility is not entirely fanciful. After all, the Open University in Great Britain has enrolled 175,000 students in televised courses, and that achievement has come about without much use of microcomputers, videodiscs, and other newer devices that promise to expand the variety and challenge of instruction.

Despite the success of the Open University, the likelihood of depopulating our campuses through televised instruction seems remote. Residential universities offer compelling advantages. For many students, the opportunity for personal contact with faculty members is very important; think of the number of prominent graduates who point to a relationship or even a single encounter with a professor as a critical event in their college years. For most people, learning is also in part a group experience in which each student gains reinforcement from others. Thus, providers of televised learning, including the Open University, have found it necessary to offer tutorials, advising, periods of residency, and other devices that give more structure and human contact in order to sustain motivation. In addition, living with other young people and participating in extracurricular activities not only give pleasure; they contribute much to students' learning and to their tolerance for other points of view, their sense of responsibility, their social and emotional maturity. Apart from these benefits, the years spent living in a university afford to many people an enjoyable experience they would not willingly give up even to save a few thousand dollars a year in room and board. For all these reasons, the residential campus promises to remain a fixture despite its costs.

If the emancipating powers of technology will not do away with the residential university, will they lead to improvements in learning that go beyond mere convenience? It all depends on how students use the time technology saves them. In many cases, however, educational benefits will unquestionably occur. For example, the power of the computer has not only enabled our Business School students to avoid drudgery; it has allowed them to grapple with more complicated, realistic problems, using linear programming and other sophisticated analytic techniques that were not previously feasible for homework assignments. In the Design School, computer-generated maps and models reduce the time and skill required to complete a drawing so that students can experiment with many more ways of solving landscape planning problems. In the College, word processing in experimental sections of Expository Writing has not merely spared students the drudgery of typing over papers; teachers can now ask students to revise and rewrite until they submit a more polished piece of work than would have been possible without the new machines. In all these cases, time previously spent doing dull, repetitive tasks can now be devoted to thinking about much more challenging, important questions.

# Computer–Assisted Instruction

The new technology not only frees students from drudgery and routine, it often comes with software expressly designed to improve learning. One of the most common methods is called computer-assisted instruction (CAI). The intellectual origins of CAI go back to Thorndike's theory of stimulus-response and B. F. Skinner's development of teaching machines and programmed learning. According to Skinner, the aim of designing programmed learning was to construct a series of questions that almost every student could answer correctly. The act of giving the correct answer and the reinforcement that followed served to plant the knowledge more firmly in the student's mind.

The earliest computer-assisted instruction exemplified this method. The architects of CAI, however, soon broke with Skinner and sought to build programs that would be more challenging for the student. They stopped trying to construct only questions that would elicit correct answers and began supplying text and helpful hints that would lead erring students to recognize their mistakes and figure out the correct answer. A simple example of such a program is the following:

| | |
|---|---|
| *Computer:* | Who was the first president of the United States?<br>(1) Thomas Jefferson<br>(2) George Washington<br>(3) Abraham Lincoln |
| *Student:* | Abraham Lincoln |

| | |
|---|---|
| *Computer:* | Sorry. Abraham Lincoln was President of the United States during the Civil War from 1861–65. The first President served from 1789 to 1797 and had previously been Commander-in-Chief of the Continental Army during the American Revolution. Would you like to try again? |
| *Student:* | George Washington |
| *Computer:* | Good work. |

This basic format underlies much of the programming now in use to supplement classes in bookkeeping and accounting in the Business School and in a variety of Law School courses. In practice, of course, CAI can be much more sophisticated than the simple example given above. Some programs ask a few initial questions and, depending on the answers, branch automatically to material appropriate to the student's apparent level of ability and comprehension. Programs may also respond to wrong answers by taking the student back through the problem step-by-step to discover the source of error. Others take the form of games to motivate the student. For example, one French instructor at Harvard has used a program modeled on poker whereby teams are dealt questions and get points for giving correct answers.

Such exercises have several advantages as a supplement to regular classwork. Students have to think and cannot merely read passively to take in information. They can practice when they wish and for as long as they wish. They can proceed as rapidly or as slowly as they please, moving on to new material only when they have mastered what has gone before. Well–crafted programs give students all the help and added explanation they need and automatically move to levels of difficulty appropriate to the learner. By instantly recording whether each response is correct or not, the computer allows students to recognize areas in which they need to do further work while alerting the instructor to problems that the entire class has encountered in mastering the material. In all these ways, the machine can adapt to the special needs of each individual and offer feedback of a kind rarely available in the conventional course.

Despite these advantages, CAI has obvious limitations. The programs are highly controlled in that the student must answer the precise question posed by the machine and choose among the limited number of responses appearing on the screen. There is no room in this format for challenging students to define the problem for themselves, explore a new hypothesis of their own, or speculate about the material under study. Because of these limitations, CAI is chiefly used to help learn facts, basic routines (as in mathematical computations), or collections of rules. For universities, the principal applications have been in areas such as mastering foreign language vocabularies and grammar, or learning the rules of accounting, the elements of anatomy, and other bodies of basic information. In principle, students could do as well by conscientiously reading a printed text, supplemented by lists of questions at the end of each chapter. The hope is that computers will do the job better because they force each student to participate actively and master the material in order to complete the program.

# Developing Higher Levels of Thinking

In recent times, more and more psychologists and educators have become interested in higher levels of thinking and thus have grown impatient with the limits of conventional CAI. Cognitive psychologists have turned from the earlier theories of stimulus–response to consider more complex ways in which knowledge and reasoning interact. In particular, they are exploring how the mind seems to process information by relating it to concepts that are constantly formed and adapted to assimilate new perceptions. Researchers are also trying to find how humans combine these concepts with reasoning skills to solve problems. According to recent investigators, one's ability to think can be improved in three different ways — by enlarging the stock of relevant information; by enhancing the conceptual structures through which one extracts more meaning from new pieces of information, and by improving one's heuristics or powers of reasoning. Influenced by this work, computer experts have been looking for ways of using technology to help students develop more complex skills of problem solving by learning how to form concepts and principles from information and experience and how to apply general principles to specific cases.

An obvious way to teach these skills is by the Socratic method, long a mainstay of law school classes. The proper Socratic teacher never gives answers but only asks questions. Through an artful choice of questions, students are led to discover for themselves the inadequacies of their reasoning so that they can develop sounder generalizations and apply them to solve concrete problems. Could one program a computer to act as a Socratic teacher? After all, didn't Patrick Suppes promise us years ago that technology would soon give us the personal ser-

vices of a tutor as well informed and responsive as Aristotle?

In fact, the problem of training the computer to be a tutor has proved much more elusive than early enthusiasts assumed. One difficulty with most complicated subjects is that questions can often elicit so many answers that it is difficult to anticipate them all and provide for suitable responses in a program. Even if one could foresee all the answers, each would require a proper question in response that would in turn provoke a further profusion of answers, each requiring an appropriate question, and so on. The result is what experts call a combinatorial explosion that could exceed the capabilities of the programmer and even the computer itself.

A still more formidable problem arises from the fact that true dialogue requires each participant to interpret the responses of the other. At present, this talent lies well beyond the capacities of the machine. For one thing, the English language usually offers many ways to communicate the same idea. One can describe a home run by stating that the ball sailed over the centerfield wall or Jim blasted a round–tripper or the big first baseman muscled it out of the park. A computer would have to be programmed with more information than most machines can currently handle simply to interpret all the variations that can occur in conversing about most subjects. Worse yet, no one knows how to formulate a set of rules by which a computer can compare statements like these and recognize them as equivalents. A human being with adequate knowledge and experience perceives the similarities automatically and effortlessly. We simply do not understand how the process works.

These difficulties do not entirely rule out using computers as tutors. Some material is so structured that only a finite number of easily identifiable responses are possible. That is why a computer can be programmed to play a formidable game of checkers or even chess. Another possibility is to have the computer ask questions and require students to choose among a limited set of answers instead of allowing them to respond in any way they see fit. In this way, one can remove the problem of interpretation and reduce the combinatorial explosion to more manageable limits. Of course, resorting to multiple choices will significantly restrict the dialogue. One of the most important benefits of a Socratic exchange is forcing students to think of their own responses instead of simply choosing from a predetermined list. Even so, a computerized dialogue using multiple choice could still encourage a student to think more rigorously than is possible under a traditional CAI program. The problem is to find and encourage instructors clever and dedicated enough to work out imaginative responses to all of the answers that students can give even in this restricted form of mechanistic dialogue.

Another way of teaching higher-level reasoning comes from so-called expert systems. One of the best-known examples is MYCIN, a computer program that can rival specialists in diagnosing bacterial infections in the blood and prescribing appropriate treatments. The heart of the program consists of a few hundred rules that take the form: If X is true, then ask the following question or take the following action. These rules in turn were created after long interviews with acknowledged experts to discover how they would go about making diagnoses and prescribing treatments. Physicians can use such systems as a check on their own clinical judgments. Armed with the MYCIN program, the computer asks questions about a patient, and the doctor answers with the appropriate data. The computer will continue to seek information until it is able to arrive at a conclusion that the doctor can compare with his own judgment.

Expert systems like MYCIN can be adapted for educational use. Students can not only observe how the expert goes about solving problems but can interrupt and ask the computer to explain the steps of its reasoning and why it reached a particular conclusion or asked a particular question. In this way, the computer permits students to have greater access to an experienced mentor and to question it in more detail than would normally be possible in real life.

Like all programs, expert systems have their limitations. They are expensive to produce. They do not force students to solve problems for themselves but merely ask them to supply data and observe how the computer responds. Above all, such systems work only for a limited range of problems in which the knowledge involved is sufficiently structured, the possible relationships sufficiently finite, the inferences and conclusions sufficiently probable that programmers can deduce a series of rules with which to search for information, make and check hypotheses, and eventually reach a conclusion.

Some of these limitations can be overcome by yet another technological application. Recall the computer programs that simulate a patient and permit medical students to ask questions and order tests in an effort to diagnose the illness. With such a program, the role of the machine is entirely different. The computer does not ask questions or control the dialogue; it simply acts as a repository of information, a simulation of reality that students can explore and analyze in order to define a problem, develop and test hypotheses, and eventually arrive at a reasoned solution. If an expert system is added to the program, a student who gets stymied can ask for help at any point, and the computer will indicate what information the student should seek and why in light of what is already known. Further commands will lead the computer to summon detailed information on any aspect of the problem that arouses the student's interest.

Exercises such as the simulated patient are a powerful tool for medical education. This is particularly true in an era when doctors must learn not only to make more complicated diagnoses using a growing array of tools but also to conduct their examinations at minimal cost by avoiding unnecessary tests and procedures. Of course, simulated exercises require some simplification to reduce the countless variations of real life to a model suitable for programming. Computer programs are also incapable of capturing the wisdom and compassion of a first-rate doctor in responding to a patient's problems, questions, and anxieties. These limitations are enough to keep machines from replacing medical rounds, where students can observe doctors treating real patients on the hospital wards. Even so, as a supplement and preparation for such training, simulated patients should play a very useful role.

In making use of these devices, however, educators must remember that they are relying on a still unproven theory of how to teach problem solving. Cognitive research seems to indicate that specialists do not necessarily solve problems by the rational, step–by–step process embodied in expert systems. While they are capable of such analysis, specialists appear to function more intuitively. Instead of examining all the alternatives and methodically discarding the ones that do not fit, experts often seem to match the problem instinctively with a precept or pattern stored in their minds, adapting the pattern to the situation at hand in order to arrive at a solution. In teaching students to reason more systematically, educators assume that novices must first master this deliberate process and only then develop the expert's instincts and intuitive shortcuts as experience and knowledge accumulate. This assumption seems plausible; it underlies all instruction in problem solving whether or not the teacher makes use of technology. Nevertheless, we should not forget that the underlying assumption is still unproven.

Simulations, using videodisc or simply computers, can serve many other purposes. They can teach law students to interview witnesses, help business school students learn to diagnose a company's marketing problems and recommend solutions, or even offer a graduate student a wealth of data with which to practice constructing a research design to test hypotheses about social behavior. The strength of these programs again lies in the challenge they pose for students to think for themselves to define the problem and reason toward solutions.

Other programs can simulate environments that are either too dangerous, too expensive, or too remote and inaccessible for humans to encounter directly. For example, with the help of computer graphics, undergraduates can observe the path of the moon circling the earth and conjure up changes in the mass or velocity of the moon in order to observe the effects of gravity on the shape of its orbit. Chemistry students can conduct simulated experiments on their TV screens combining substances too dangerous for laboratory use. Biology majors can watch simulated fruit flies breed at an accelerated pace and try to deduce genetic rules from the results. Medical students can observe the workings of the circulatory system and see how the removal of blood or the cutting of the nerve regulating blood pressure affects the functioning of the entire system. In all these cases students have opportunities to visualize phenomena that would otherwise remain abstract and to manipulate variables and observe their effects in ways that may help them gain a more thorough understanding of concepts and processes that would otherwise seem remote and hard to understand.

A final use of simulated environments takes the form of elaborate computerized games in which students play different roles in competition with one another. In a business school contest, teams of students play the part of executives from different companies. In a city planning game, the teams represent political officials, planners, and business and community groups. In each case the students develop strategies and make decisions. The computer has a vast store of information based on actual experience in situations similar to those confronting the players. With this data, the computer can simulate reality by allowing participants to observe the consequences that flow from their decisions so that they can adjust their strategies accordingly and act again. Games of this sort are generally used at the end of a course, not to teach new material, but to motivate students to integrate what they have already learned by bringing their knowledge to bear on a lifelike situation with the added spur of competing against others like themselves.

All of the applications I have described are simply illustrations of what is currently feasible in a rapidly changing field. If a cheap optical scanning device became available, students and faculty could soon conjure up on their TV screens virtually any book in the university library, or indeed in any participating library. If improved authoring systems were devised, instructors could prepare better software with much less effort, and the quantity and quality of computerized material would probably rise substantially. If we could understand the art of dialogue better, teachers might program the computer to conduct more challenging discussions with students. No one knows when or even whether these developments will occur. The one thing that does seem certain is that new applications will emerge tomorrow that no one can foresee today.

# Objections to the New Technology

Now that we have looked at a sample of ingenious and arresting applications, it is time to examine these developments with a cold and skeptical eye. Despite the excitement of the new machines, what is it, exactly, that they can do to improve the process of learning? What effects will they have on the educational process?

The first point to remember is that many important tasks remain beyond the reach of the new technology. With all its powers, the computer cannot contribute much to the learning of open–ended subjects like moral philosophy, religion, historical interpretation, literary criticism, or social theory— fields of knowledge that cannot be reduced to formal rules and procedures. Since such subjects are among the most important in the curriculum, this limitation is serious indeed. Computers are also incapable of inspiring students or serving as role models. They cannot conduct a genuine dialogue because they cannot comprehend analogies or metaphors or even understand conversation beyond the five–year–old level. Finally, machines can rarely diagnose the reasons for a student's deficiencies in learning and understanding (although computers can test students and keep detailed records of their mistakes in order to help the teacher detect learning problems).

Whereas these limitations are important, they still leave ample room for applying technology to learning, especially in the major professional schools, in science departments, in engineering programs, and in many areas of social science. Other criticisms of technology, however, are more sweeping. They warn that computers may harm the entire educational process by gradually eroding some of the intangible, more humane values of university life.

A familiar concern of this kind is that computers may erect barriers that will isolate students and divide teachers from learners. If students have to spend more time with their new machines, they may become more solitary and avoid the human contact that does so much to enrich the university experience. If it really takes one hundred or two hundred hours to prepare a good program suitable for an hour's instruction, professors may withdraw to develop software leaving students to work alone at their consoles. There is also a risk of overlooking subtler benefits that come from older, less "efficient" methods of education. Lectures may be passive, but as the early devotees of self-paced instruction soon discovered, they can have an inspirational value, not replicable by machines, in showing what it means to be truly in command of an important subject. Answering student questions via computer may be more efficient, but posing a routine question to an advisor is often the way by which a shy student reaches out for help in dealing with homesickness, insecurity, and other problems to which no electronic device can possibly respond.

We also know that computers can have an unwholesome, almost addictive effect on some individuals. To borrow Joseph Weizenbaum's vivid description: "Whenever computer centers have become established . . . bright young men of dishevelled appearance, often with sunken glowing eyes, can be seen at computer consoles. . . . Their rumpled clothes, their unwashed and unshaven faces, and their uncombed hair all testify that they are oblivious to their bodies and to the world in which they live. They exist, at least when so engaged, only through and for computers. These are computer bums, compulsive programmers. They are an international phenomenon." [7]

Just what produces such behavior is not entirely clear. Sherry Turkle may come closest to the mark in describing such students as persons who do not get along easily with others and look upon the computer as a companion without emotional demands or human meanness, "a compromise between loneliness and fear of intimacy." [8] Whatever the explanation, such a fate is hardly what parents have in mind in paying many thousands of dollars a year to send their children to college.

A final concern is that computers may gradually cause faculties to place too much emphasis on problems and methods that lend themselves to programming while paying less and less attention to matters that are qualitative, speculative, and not reducible to formal rules and algorithms. Humanistic learning has suffered enough from ill-considered efforts to ape the scientists by concentrating on what is quantifiable, verifiable, and value-free. The seductive power of the new machines and their fasci-

nation for many students may only make matters worse. Do we not have a foretaste of things to come in the eagerness with which classicists fall upon computers for the analysis of ancient texts and the glee with which music instructors talk about teaching composition by machine?

Although these dangers are real, some seem exaggerated while others are avoidable given a will to do so. For example, there is no reason to conclude that computers must diminish contact between students and faculty. Virtually all of the illustrations of technology discussed in this report supplement the lecture and seminar and do not replace the instructor. Where overlap occurs, the computer replaces the least rewarding tasks of a teacher, the recitation of basic concepts and information. The contacts that students like best—the give-and-take of the seminar, the conversation of a tutorial, the Socratic discussion of a complex problem—are the very tasks the computer cannot perform effectively. At the least, therefore, the new machines should help make studying more active and rigorous. At best, technology may free instructors from routine tasks so that they can give more time to the less formal kinds of teaching and counseling students value most.

There is likewise no reason to believe that computers will necessarily isolate students and reduce their contacts with one another. As previously mentioned, most uses of technology occur outside of class and serve to enrich the process of studying, which has traditionally been a solitary activity. At worst, technology may simply perpetuate that pattern, giving students opportunities to sit alone before their computer mastering programs instead of sitting alone reading an assigned text. But it is easy to design computer exercises that will actually increase student interaction. Computer games bring students together in teams. Pairs of students can readily cooperate in working on programs in computer-assisted instruction or trying to diagnose an ailment presented on videodisc. In short, technology need not separate students and can actually be used to bring them together.

As Weizenbaum points out, one result of the new technology may be that some students become addicted and "exist only through and for computers." We must remember, however, that millions of young people arrive at college already familiar with computers. Many of them come equipped with their own models. As a result, there is little hope of preserving students from the danger of becoming obsessed with these machines whether or not universities integrate them into their teaching programs. All technology creates the possibility of abuse. One cannot reject computers on this account any more than one can give up cars because a minority will choose to drive too fast.

To many people, the greatest threat from the new technology is not the fear of isolation or addiction but the risk of undermining forms of knowledge and understanding that are not quantifiable or reducible to formal processes and rules. As one author puts it, "The issue is not whether the computer can be made to think like a human, but whether humans can and will take on the quality of digital computers." [9]

But technology need not force people to reason only in analytic or quantitative ways. For example, simulations can challenge students to speculate, to imagine new hypotheses and relationships, and to test their intuitions effortlessly. Used in this way, computers may provide one of the most effective tools yet devised to stimulate venturesome, creative thought. In fact, tenth graders have actually discovered new theorems after having a chance to experiment with geometric forms through computer manipulations.

Even with more conventional applications, machines are unlikely to do much lasting damage to intellectual discourse in fields like literature and philosophy. Ingenious applications will be made in these subjects — some useful, some ludicrous — but the limits of technology should be obvious enough not to warp the main lines of scholarly inquiry and instruction. The greater risk arises in subjects such as business management and public administration where students learn to think about problems that involve a mix of different considerations including some quantifiable elements along with other values, possibilities, and risks that are intangible and not susceptible to precise measurement. Despite protestations to the contrary, experience suggests that the seductive power of numbers, precision, and logical demonstration will lead many instructors to neglect the subtler aspects of human problems and end by caricaturing the world they seek to have their students understand.

Teachers can certainly use computers in ways that reflect these problems. For example, because ethical considerations are hard to incorporate in a program, they are simply left out of computer games that challenge business school students to act as if they were directing real corporations in a competitive environment. Because psychological and social elements are difficult to capture in programming simulated patients for medical schools, they are again omitted, thus reinforcing the tendency to ignore such factors and concentrate solely on the scientific aspects of disease.

Even so, there is little reason to believe that the clash between the humanistic and scientific approach to problems will be affected much by the uses we make of technology in education. Computers are only a recent arrival in a long series of efforts to emphasize the quantitative and verifiable in human inquiry. The struggle between what Pascal termed *l'esprit de geometrie* and *l'esprit de finesse* is an old struggle indeed. Computers may affect the debate but they are much more likely to do so through their applications to research than through their instructional uses. Modes of intellectual discourse on campus may be reinforced in the classroom but they are rarely decided there. Instead, they take their cues from norms of scholarly research derived from judgments imposed by the disciplines through peer review, refereed journals, and faculty appointments proceedings. University authorities have as much chance of affecting this process as King Canute had of stopping the waves from mounting the beach.

These concerns by no means exhaust the problems that technology will create as it continues to evolve. Few universities have had to think about what they will do if students and faculty begin to read books by computer instead of checking out volumes in the traditional way. Will they dispose of their collections? Or place them in remote storage? Most institutions have not yet decided how to distribute the royalties from educational software. Will they be treated like textbooks, where authors keep all the royalties, or like patents, where universities and their scientists share the spoils? Networking could create problems of a different sort if students begin to pepper their professors with questions they are too shy to ask in person. Although such queries may tell instructors much about the difficulties and misunderstandings experienced by their students, professors may eventually be unable to cope with all the questions that pop up on their television screens. Such problems can be multiplied may times over. On reflection, however, none of them seems more intractable than the difficulties that technological change has traditionally created for society.

# Effects on Learning

A radically different set of criticisms comes from investigators who question whether technology truly enhances learning. Remember Professor Clark's assertion that "media are mere vehicles that deliver instruction but do not influence student achievement." What Clark must mean is that technology rarely gives instruction of a kind and power that cannot be duplicated by more conventional means. Thus, the questions and answers contained in most computer–assisted instruction could also be provided, albeit in more awkward form, by a cleverly arranged workbook. The computer simulations that help develop diagnostic skills might be given by a live tutor who acted as a patient and responded to questions until students could make an accurate diagnosis. Expert systems, like MYCIN, could be duplicated by simply allowing a student to observe a real expert go about solving difficult problems. Much of what computer graphics and videodiscs provide could be approximated in only slightly more cumbersome ways by the clever use of mock–ups, videotapes, and film strips. In principle, therefore, the new technology seems unique only in allowing students to address certain kinds of problems with greater depth and sophistication through its speed and power in manipulating data.

If this were all that could be said for the new technology, one would wonder whether universities and their corporate patrons had lost their minds by spending scores of millions of dollars on such equipment. But there are other justifications to consider before we make a final reckoning.

To begin with, although in principle most advantages of technology can be duplicated by conventional methods, the truth is that few of these advantages will be achieved without the new machines. Instructors could spend two hundred hours preparing for a traditional class just as they must often do to develop an hour of computer-assisted instruction. But rarely will they actually do so. Medical schools will not provide individual tutors patient enough to allow each student to practice endlessly developing diagnostic skills. Nor will distinguished specialists be available to explain to each medical student how they reason step–by–step to arrive at a diagnosis. With student–faculty ratios of 20 or 30 to 1, a law school professor cannot work with individual students to check their progress in understanding the Socratic dialogues in which they participate vicariously in class. Nor will science majors always have an opportunity to repeat difficult experiments in the laboratory as they can by performing them in simulated form on their computer. Even the humble word processor has advantages. Without it, as Richard Marius has said, students in Expository Writing will continue to revise by merely adding a word here and changing one there; they "can seldom be made to do the so–called global revisions that involve major shifts in the argument, the elimination of some material, and the introduction of new evidence and sometimes a new point of view."[10]

The opportunities that technology makes practical have great educational value. At present, most instruction in our universities is far too passive. Professors rely excessively on the lecture. Seminars are often consumed by dull recitations of student work. Discussion groups are typically led by graduate students who lack experience in teaching, especially by the discussion method. Granted, students are challenged to think for themselves in preparing for exams and writing papers. But all too often, exam grades come back with little or no explanation, while term papers return with only a few hastily scribbled comments.

As knowledge increases and methods of analysis grow more complex, it is less and less desirable to base education so heavily on the passive experience of listening to lectures and reading texts. Habits of critical thinking, of perceiving and solving problems, of deriving useful generalizations from bodies of data all seem increasingly important and all require more active effort by the student. In the words of a recent report for the National Academy of Science, "Cognitive research confirms that knowledge learned without conceptual understanding or functional application to problems is either forgotten or remains inert when it is needed in situations that differ from ones in which the knowledge was acquired."[11] To the extent that new technology can create occasions to challenge the student with problems, opportunities for repeated practice in finding solutions, and possibilities for immediate feedback, it will provide exactly the kind of educational experiences most needed today in our universities.

Even if technology could not enhance the learning process, we can be reasonably sure that the graduates of most professional schools will need to work with computers — or at least understand their uses and limitations — in order to practice their calling in later life. With the waves of technical information that are engulfing medical practice, most physicians will have to use these machines to summon up the data they need and manipulate it to aid in reaching clinical decisions. Corporate executives already call on sophisticated computer analyses in reaching many business decisions. Even lawyers have increased recourse to computers to do their research and may look to expert systems for help in making certain kinds of professional judgments. As the use of these machines continues to expand, therefore, it is the responsibility of most professional schools to familiarize their students with the technology and make them reasonably proficient in its use. Many of the computer applications we have discussed will have precisely this effect.

Thus far, therefore, the balance of benefits and risks seems to favor the new technology. There is yet another element that tilts the scales decisively in the same direction. Over the past twenty years, computers have proved to be a major stimulus for eliciting work and thought about teaching methods and the processes by which human beings learn. By their power and versatility, the new machines have given a stimulus to the field of cognitive psychology and turned the energies of many scientists toward artificial intelligence and its applications to learning. The significance of these developments for universities is greater than one might imagine.

A striking fact about higher education is the lack of systematic effort to understand the ways in which students learn. Faculties rarely spend time thinking collectively about the educational process. When they do, they almost always discuss what students should read and study rather than how students learn and how they might be helped to learn more effectively. The reasons are not difficult to understand. Quite simply, no one is clamoring for more effective learning, while almost everyone has reasons for not caring to look too hard at the problem.

Neither alumni nor legislators try to exert much influence over the way in which faculties teach, and any effort on their part to do so would be resisted as an assault on academic freedom. Leaders in education are in a better position to make their wishes felt. Yet they continue to devote almost all their attention to arguing over what students should be taught even though very few new ideas have emerged on this subject during the past thirty years. Witness the recent flurry of well–publicized reports on the state of the liberal arts, with their stale rhetoric of crisis and their shopworn arguments in behalf of familiar positions on curricular philosophy and design.

Students are also capable of exerting influence and are not bashful about asking many things of the university. They want a reasonable chance to pick and choose what courses to take; they want lively, informed instruction; they want opportunities for extracurricular activities; they want help in finding a good job. But they are not pressing for more effective instruction. Indeed, there is some evidence suggesting that the kinds of instruction students like most tend to be least effective in helping them learn. These preferences are not deliberate or even conscious. Students simply have no way of knowing how much their intellectual skills and knowledge have grown, whether they might have developed faster at another institution, or what changes in instructional methods might help them to improve more rapidly.

The faculty has its own reasons to avoid spending much time on investigating how well their students are progressing. Professors are busy people with many interests other than teaching that compete for their attention. The last thing they need are major studies to probe the effectiveness of instruction. Either the inquiries will fail to produce convincing results and simply waste time and money or they will call for significant changes in teaching methods that will disrupt professors' lives, quite possibly in the pursuit of some seductive theory that will eventually be discredited. Fortunately for the faculty, there is a plausible reason not to mount a large institutional effort to explore how student learning might be improved. Research on this subject is extremely complicated. The goals are generally in dispute, the methodology still quite primitive, the relevant variables numerous and hard to disentangle. Because of these difficulties, the results are often intuitively suspect or simply inconclusive. Under such conditions, one can readily find reasons not to devote much time and attention to work of this kind.

In contrast to this tradition of indifference, investigators have shown a remarkable interest in experimenting with technology to try to improve the learning process. There are also good reasons to expect this interest to continue. Much of the current work has relevance for commercial products—computer hardware, videodiscs, word processors, and the like. Corporations see the possibility of burgeoning sales and are willing to invest large sums in research and development and give attractive discounts to open up university markets. Professors, in turn, are impressed by the power of the computer and often proficient in its use through their research activities. Some of them, at least, can be tempted to try the new technology in an effort to improve their courses. Students, too, are coming into the university in increasing numbers knowing how to use the computer; four million young people possessing such experience will enroll by 1987. Many of them will expect instructors to employ computers in their courses and will press them to do so, just as our own law students have asked professors to work with them to develop CAI programs to supplement courses in accounting, corporations, property, and other fields.

This growing interest may well turn out to be the greatest benefit to result from the new technology. As more people begin to use technology for educational purposes, they are bound to think more carefully about the best ways in which to help students absorb new knowledge and master new intellectual skills. One simply cannot produce good software for teaching without paying close attention to the details of how best to present the material to enhance learning and sustain student interest. This is not characteristic of traditional instruction. For most professors, lecturing requires much knowledge and a fair amount of organization but otherwise proceeds intuitively with little conscious thought about how students actually learn. The same is even true of many seminars and tutorials. The task of designing educational software, however, cannot go forward in this manner; every step of the process must proceed with a careful eye to its effect on the student or the program will not work effectively.

This is the critical difference that probably accounts for most of the gains in speed and effectiveness of learning often attributed to computer–assisted learning. It is not necessarily the machines that produce these gains. More likely, the improvements occur because of the increased time and thought that enter into creating the program. Either way, students stand to benefit from the result.

Despite these bright prospects, success is not assured and will probably not occur without the active help of those in positions of academic leadership. For all the experiments and publicity, we still have little first-rate software. Most of the programs available today are basic drill–and–practice routines that resemble expensive electronic workbooks rather than the more imaginative examples described in this report. Small wonder, since good programs often require more than two hundred hours of preparation for a single hour of instruction. To surmount this barrier university administrators will have to do much more than shower their campuses with expensive equipment. A more important step will be to persuade some of the best teachers on the faculty to take an active interest in the new technology and give them the funds and technical help they need to develop imaginative applications. As in all human enterprise, choosing the right participants will be crucial. By and large, the best teachers have thought most about how students learn and will attract the widest interest and command the greatest respect for the work they do in using technology in their courses. The greatest challenge for educators will be to find ways of persuading such teachers to develop a keen interest in lending their talents to this task.

Deans and other academic leaders will also need to take an active part in making sure that new experiments are carefully evaluated. After all, assertions about how much computers can do to improve critical thinking are assertions that rest on still unproven hypotheses. Hence, each new program deserves a careful review to try to determine whether it does in fact help students to learn more quickly, or reason better, or understand new material more thoroughly. There is also much more we need to know about the new technology. In what circumstances does it motivate students more than conventional instruction? Does CAI help some students more than others? Does the use of graphics and the chance to visualize and manipulate abstract phenomena increase comprehension? If expert systems do not reflect how an expert actually thinks, can they still help students learn to reason more effectively?

Although universities have never shown much interest in studying the learning process, they will have reasons to evaluate the new technology. Administrators will want some way of deciding whether they can justify the heavy expense of purchasing equipment and developing software. Curiosity should also lead professors to inquire into the results of their efforts to use computers. Skeptics may ask why the faculty should be any more interested than they have been up to now in trying to measure the effects of their teaching. Yet the psychological climate for conducting such evaluations should be much more promising than in the past. It is one thing to judge the effectiveness of computer–based instruction and quite another to inquire into more traditional methods of teaching. The first merely involves evaluating the effects of a machine; the second calls in question the value of the faculty members themselves. The first may simply result in canceling an order for new microcomputers; the second carries the more threatening prospect of either causing professors to feel ineffective or forcing them to consider radical changes in their methods of teaching. With ingenuity, then, and a modest use of funds, a determined administration may be able to evaluate the new technology and thus learn to use it with discrimination.

# Conclusion

In the end, therefore, with all the exaggerated claims and the media hype, we can still look upon the new technology with cautious enthusiasm. At the very least, universities should manage to use technology to engage students in a more active process of thinking and problem solving that will help them learn more effectively. At best, the new machines may also be a catalyst to hasten the development of new insights into human cognition and new ways of helping students learn.

In many ways, this last possibility is the most intriguing. It remains an embarrassing anomaly that professors, who spend so much time evaluating and criticizing other institutions, devote so little effort to finding ways to improve their own methods of instruction. The task is surely complex and results may be long in coming — but that is no more true of educational research than it is of many other fields of inquiry to which faculty members devote their energies. In view of the billions spent on higher education and its growing importance to modern society, there is an evident need to work systematically at its improvement. If technology can help in encouraging such an effort, that is reason enough to welcome its appearance.

# References

1. "The Post-Gutenberg University, Colleges Enter the Information Society," *Current Issues in Higher Education* (1983–84), p. 32.

2. *Boston Globe Magazine,* 9 December 1984, p. 33.

3. Quoted in Judith Axler Turner, "Electronic Library Planned for Researchers," *Chronicle of Higher Education.* 14 November 1984, p. 16.

4. "The Uses of Computers in Education," *Scientific American,* 215 (1966), p. 206.

5. "Reconsidering Research on Learning from Media," *Review of Educational Research,* 53 (1983), pp. 445, 450.

6. Edward A. Friedman, "The Wired University," *I. E. E. E. Spectrum,* November 1984, p. 115.

7. Quoted in Sherry Turkle, *The Second Self: Computers and the Human Spirit* (1984), pp. 205–06.

8. Op. cit., p. 307.

9. J. David Bolter, *Turing's Man* (1984), p. 150.

10. "Computers and the Winds of Words," unpublished memorandum dated 10 January 1985, on file in my office.

11. Research Briefing on Information Technology in Pre-college Education, Committee on Science, Engineering, and Public Policy of the National Academy of Sciences et al., September 1984, p. 5.

# Statistics

# Projections

Chart 1

**Trends in Bachelor's and Master's Degrees Conferred, by Sex of Recipient**

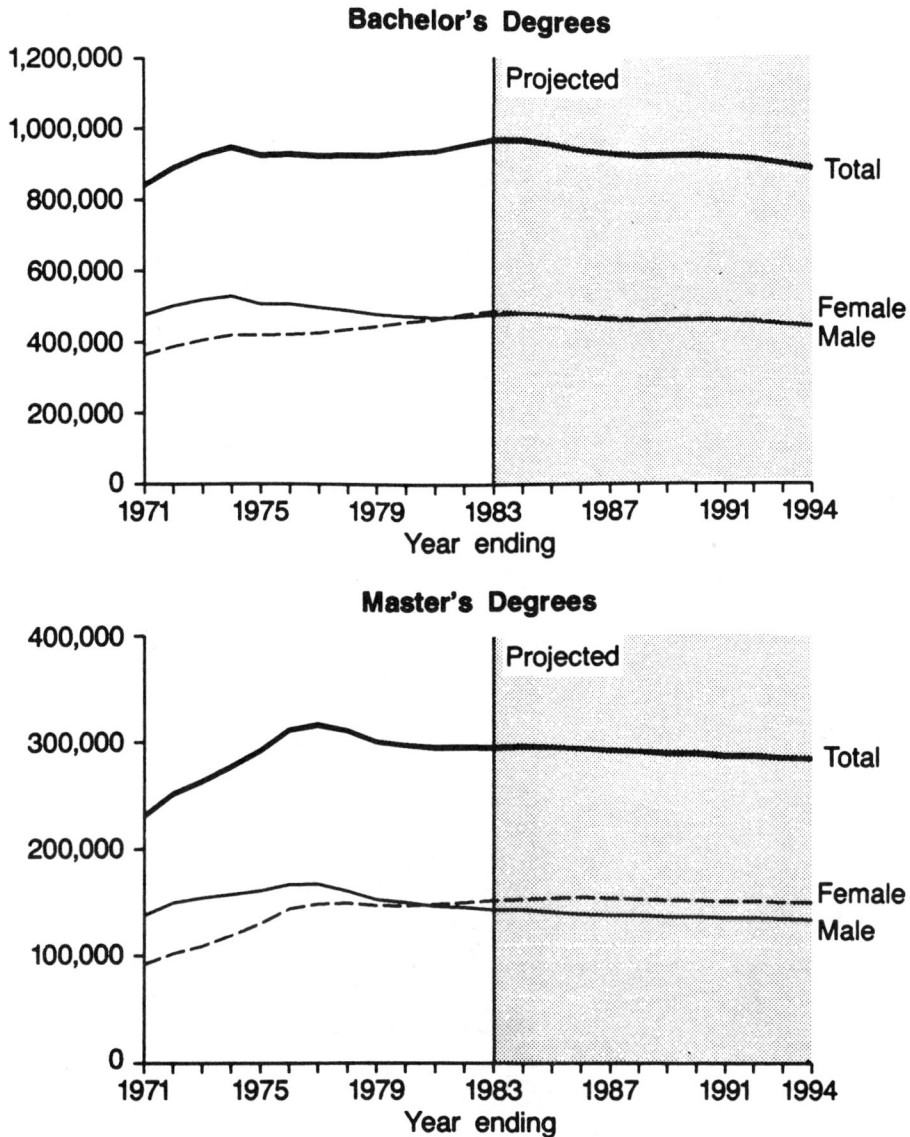

## Bachelor's Degrees

## Master's Degrees

The number of bachelor's degrees awarded annually fluctuated slightly during the 1970's and is expected to reach a high point in the first half of the 1980's. Having peaked at 317,200 in 1976-77, the number of master's degrees awarded annually has declined slightly and is expected to remain under 300,000 into the 1990's.

Source:  U.S. Dept. of Education

Chart 2

**Senior Instructional Staff in Institutions of Higher Education**

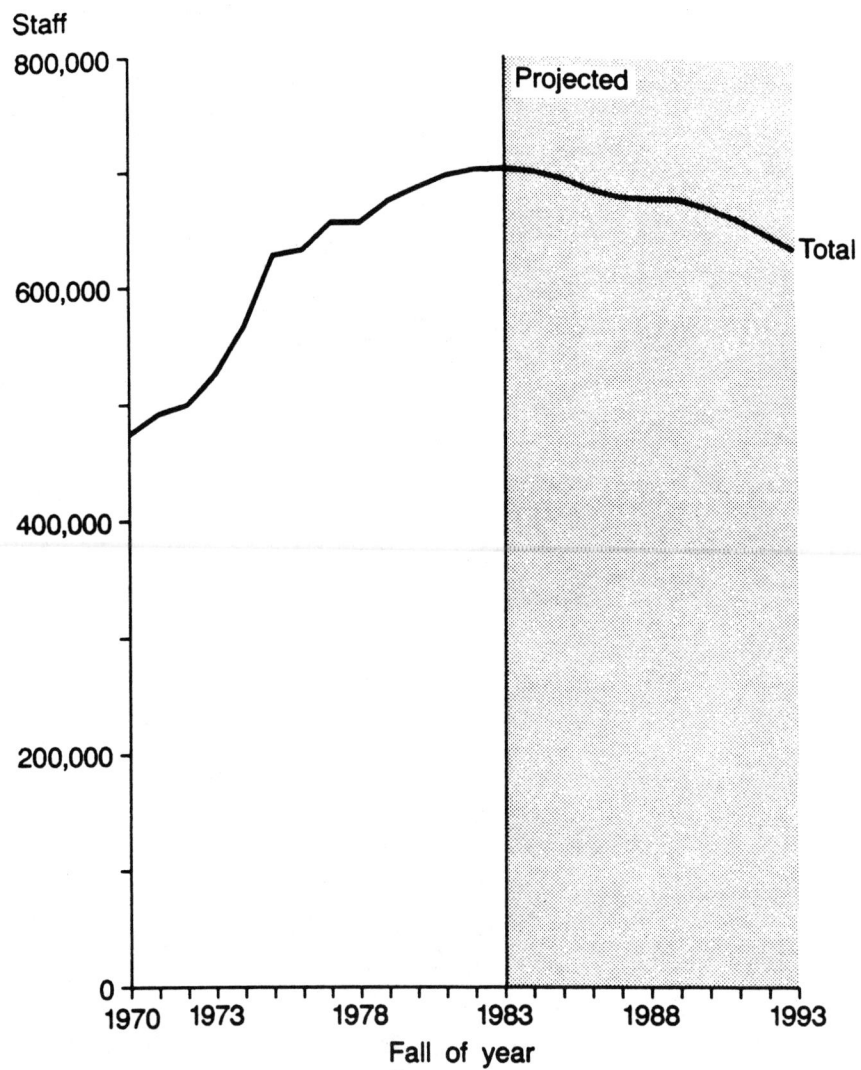

The number of instructional staff in institutions of higher education is expected to decline somewhat into the 1990's, reflecting the anticipated decrease in enrollment.

Source: U.S. Dept. of Education

Chart 3

**Full-Time-Equivalent (FTE) Enrollment Trends in Institutions of Higher Education, by Institutional Characteristics**

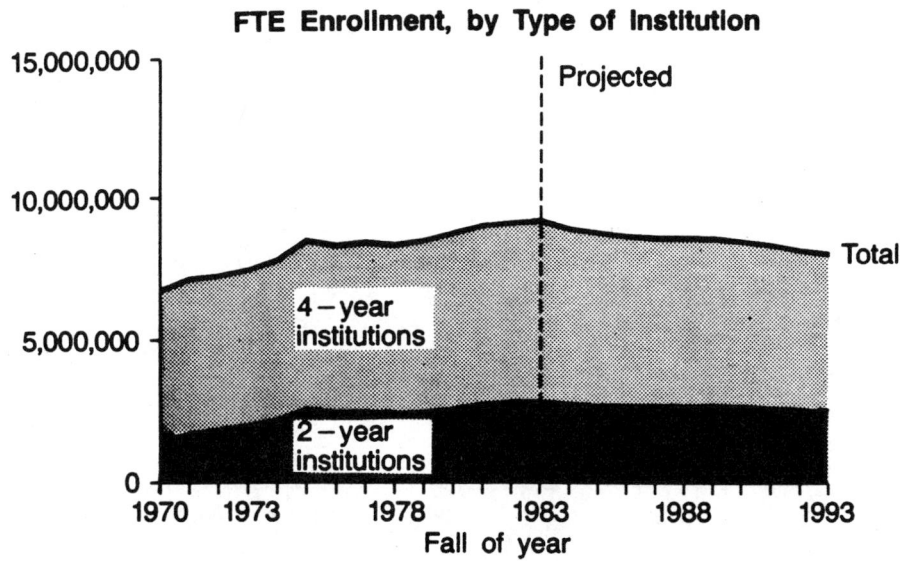

FTE Enrollment, by Type of Institution

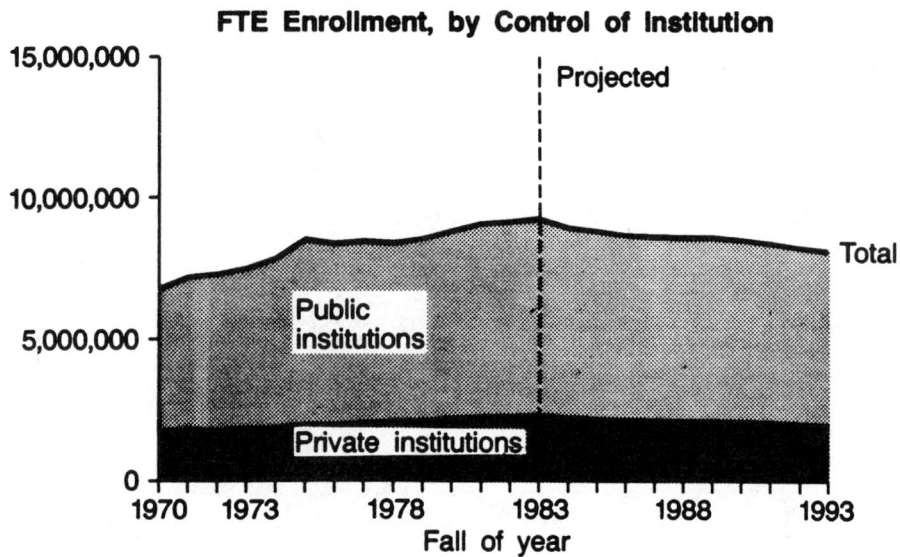

FTE Enrollment, by Control of Institution

When converted to full-time-equivalence, enrollments in both 4-year and 2-year institutions are expected to decline throughout the rest of the 1980's and into the 1990's. These declines should be felt in both public and private institutions.

Source: U.S. Dept. of Education

Chart 4

## Trends in Doctor's and First-Professional Degrees Conferred, by Sex of Recipient

### Doctor's Degrees

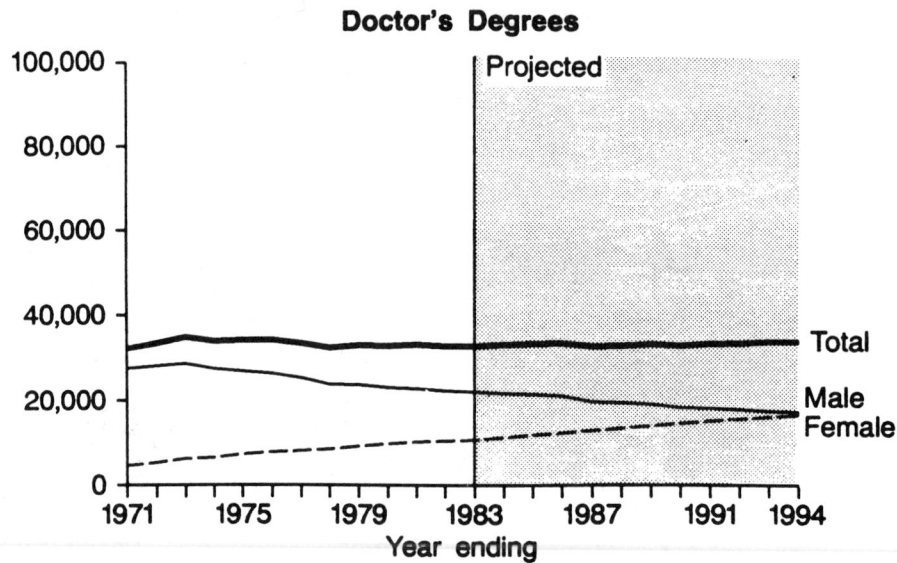

### First – Professional Degrees

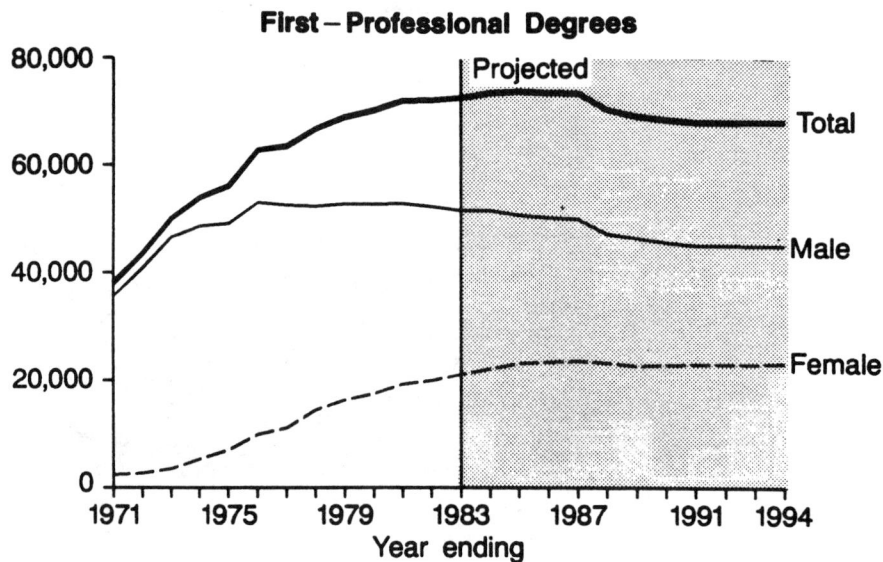

The annual number of doctor's degrees awarded in the remainder of the 1980's is expected to show little change, continuing the pattern set in the 1970's. The number of first-professional degrees awarded annually nearly doubled during the 1970's but is projected to stabilize in the mid-1980's and then decline slightly into the 1990's.

Source:  U.S. Dept. of Education

Chart 5

**National Population Trends, by Age Group**

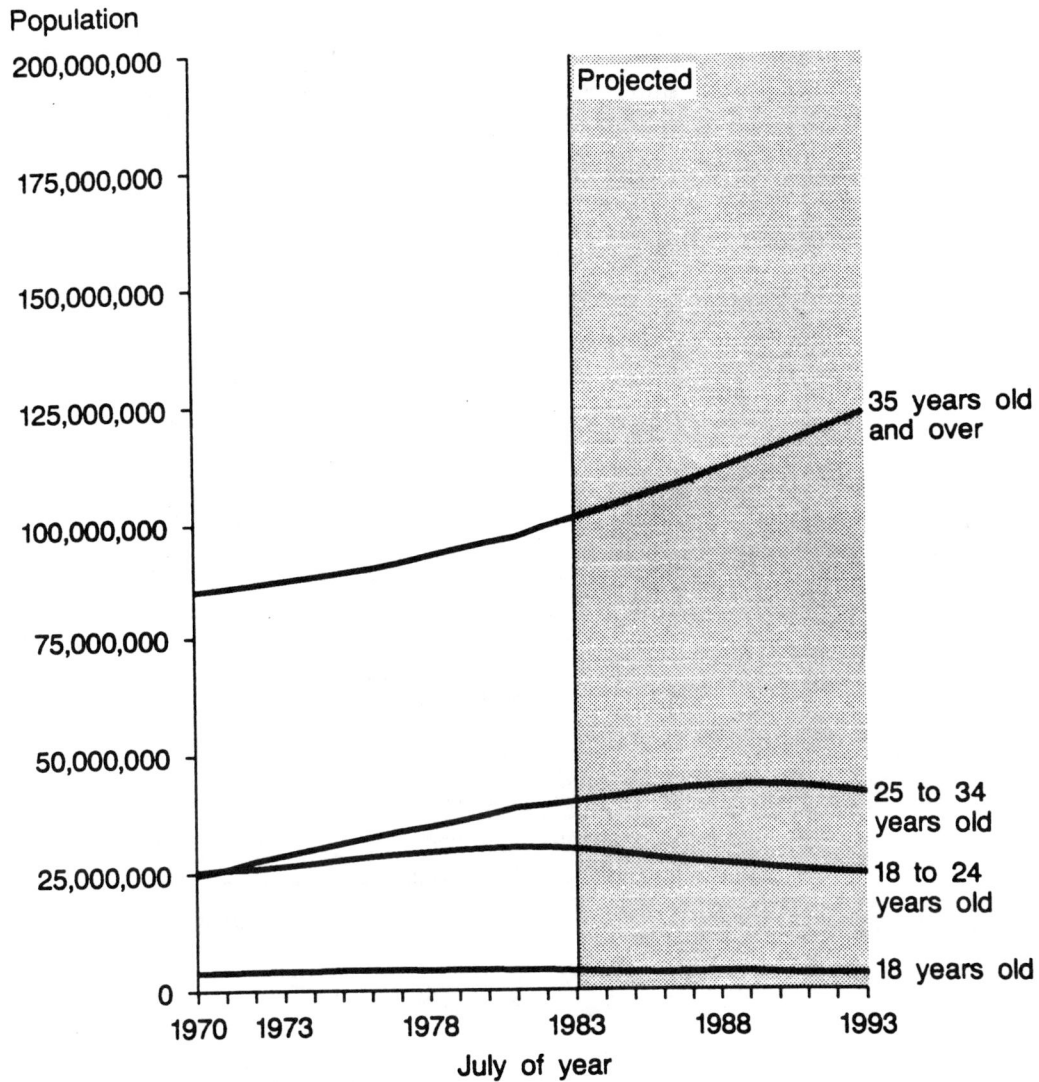

Population

200,000,000

175,000,000

150,000,000

125,000,000

100,000,000

75,000,000

50,000,000

25,000,000

0

Projected

35 years old and over

25 to 34 years old

18 to 24 years old

18 years old

1970 1973 1978 1983 1988 1993

July of year

The age composition of the national population has shifted since the 1970's. While the population in the younger adult groups is expected to decline in the 1980's and into the 1990's, the older age groups are projected to increase significantly.

Source: U.S. Dept. of Education

Chart 6

## Composition of Postsecondary Education Participants, by Type of Program

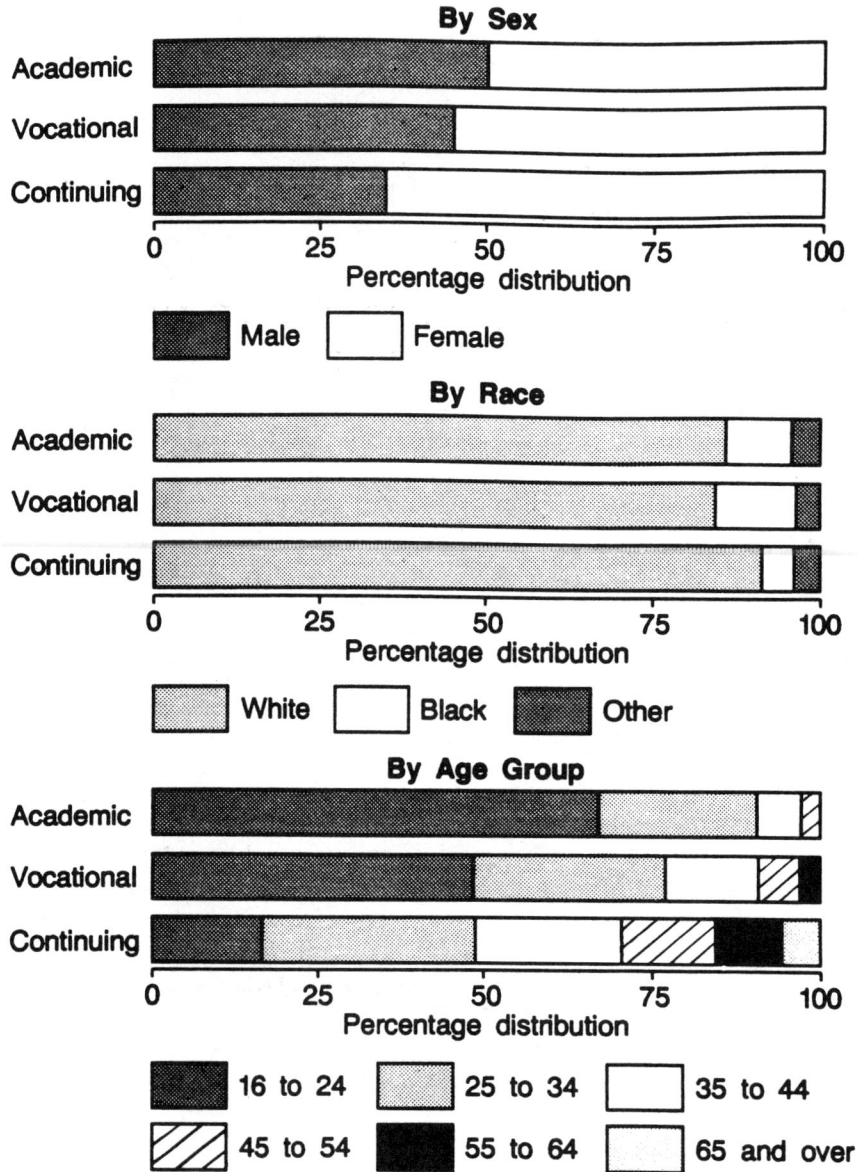

### By Sex

Academic
Vocational
Continuing

0    25    50    75    100
Percentage distribution

Male    Female

### By Race

Academic
Vocational
Continuing

0    25    50    75    100
Percentage distribution

White    Black    Other

### By Age Group

Academic
Vocational
Continuing

0    25    50    75    100
Percentage distribution

16 to 24    25 to 34    35 to 44
45 to 54    55 to 64    65 and over

While the composition of postsecondary participants in academic programs was evenly divided between the sexes, females outnumbered males in vocational and continuing education programs. Sixteen- to 24-year-olds comprised two-thirds of participants in academic programs, but they represented less than half of vocational education participants and less than a fifth of those in continuing education.

Source:  U.S. Dept. of Education

Chart 7

**Participants in Postsecondary Academic, Vocational, and Continuing Education, by Labor Force Status**

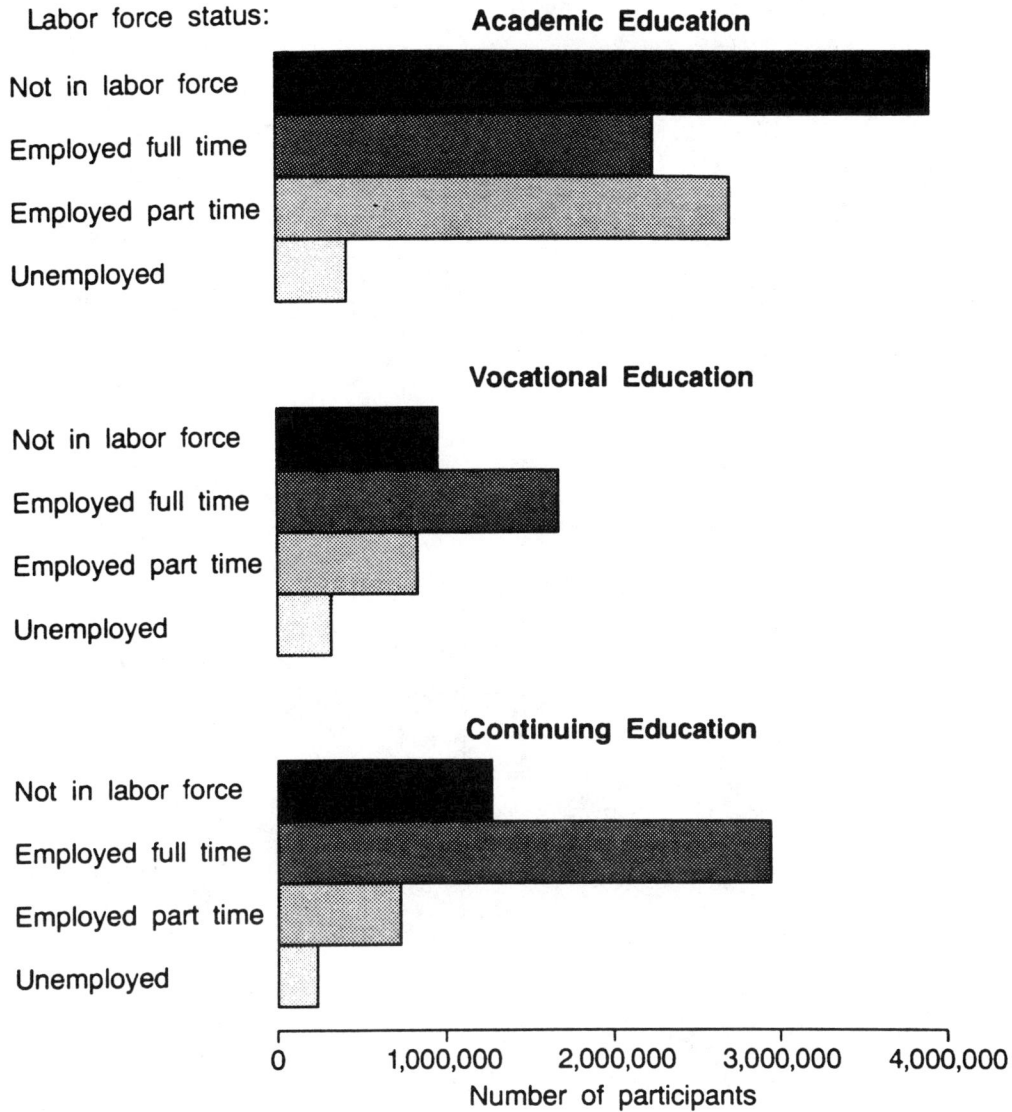

Large numbers of persons not in the labor force or employed part-time participated in academic education. The participants in vocational and continuing education were more likely to be employed full-time.

Source:  U.S. Dept. of Education

Chart 8

**Enrollment Trends in Institutions of Higher Education, by Student Characteristics**

**Enrollment, by Attendance Status**

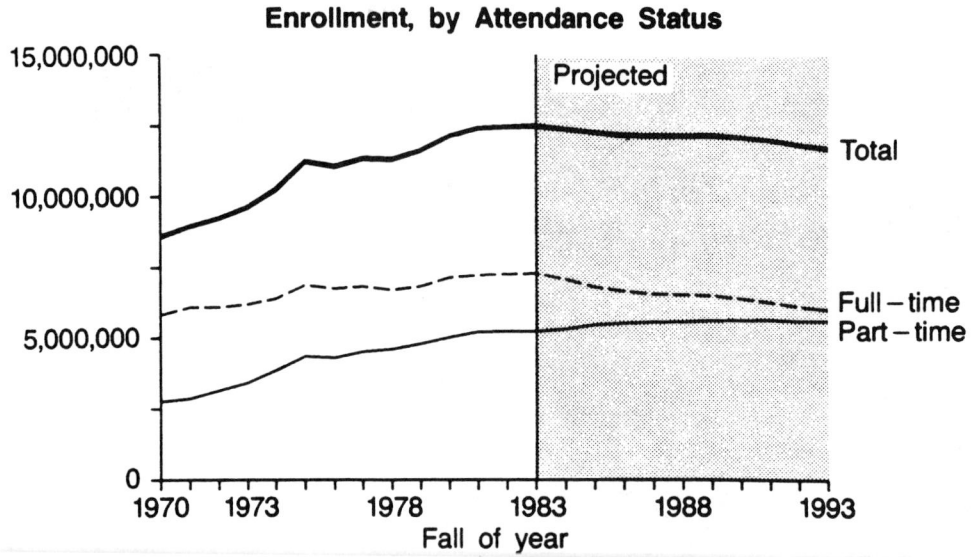

**Enrollment, by Sex**

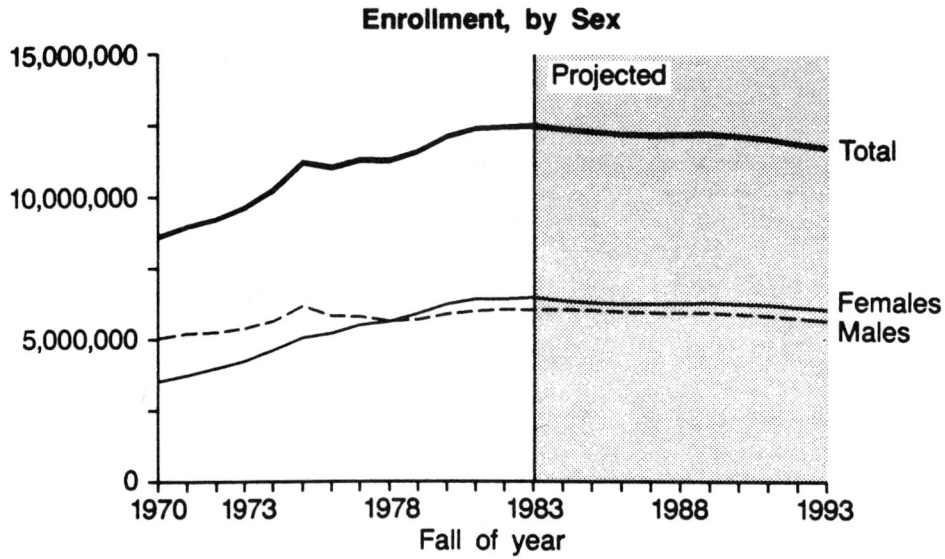

In contrast to its expansion in the 1970's, higher education enrollment is projected to decline throughout the rest of the 1980's and into the 1990's. While declines in enrollment are projected for men and full-time students, part-time enrollment is projected to increase for several more years.

Source: U.S. Dept. of Education

Chart 9

## Past and Projected Enrollment Patterns in Higher Education, by Sex and Age Group

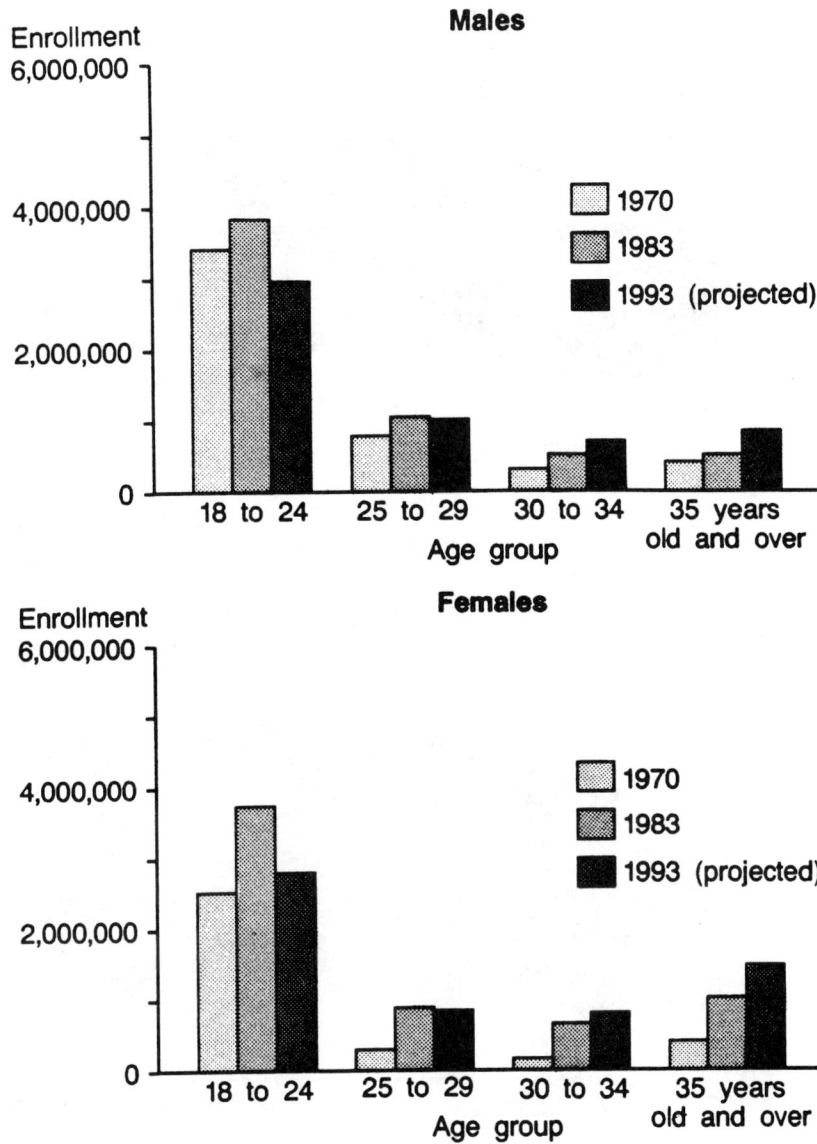

**Males**

Enrollment

Legend: 1970, 1983, 1993 (projected)

Age group: 18 to 24, 25 to 29, 30 to 34, 35 years old and over

**Females**

Enrollment

Legend: 1970, 1983, 1993 (projected)

Age group: 18 to 24, 25 to 29, 30 to 34, 35 years old and over

The number of 18- to 24-year-olds enrolled in college is projected to decline throughout the rest of the 1980's and into the 1990's, while the number of students 25 years old and over is expected to continue rising.

Source: U.S. Dept. of Education

Chart 10

**Enrollment Trends in Institutions of Higher Education, by Institutional Characteristics**

**Enrollment, by Type of Institution**

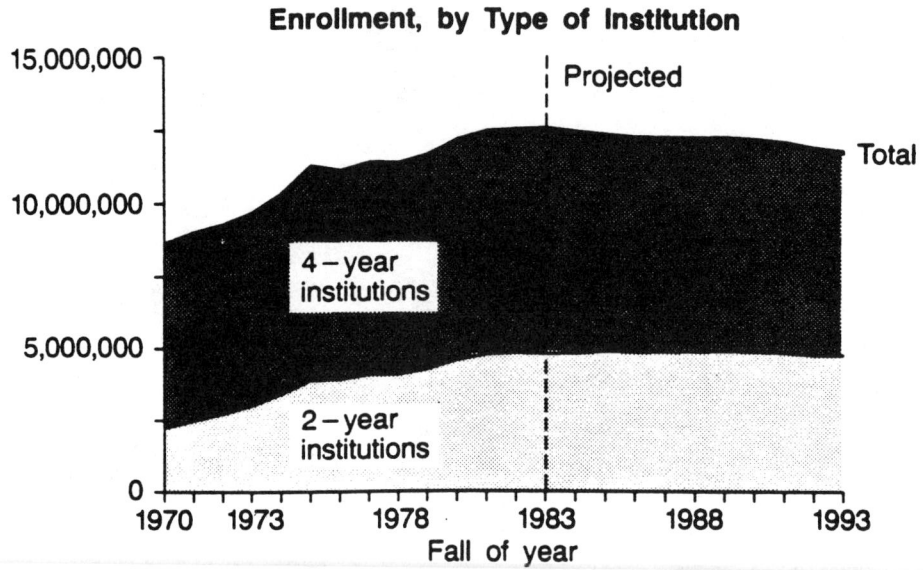

**Enrollment, by Control of Institution**

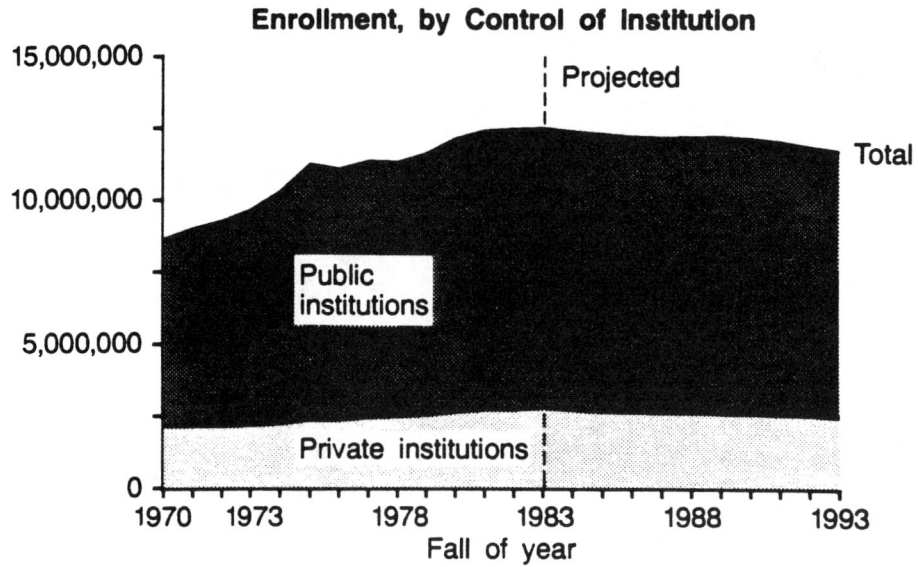

Enrollment in 4-year institutions is projected to decrease significantly during the 1980's and into the 1990's, while enrollment in 2-year institutions is projected to decline slightly in the early 1990's. Enrollments in both public and private institutions are expected to fall over the next decade.

Source: U.S. Dept. of Education

Chart 11

**- Percentage changes in public and private college costs compared to changes in the Consumer Price Index: United States, 1975–76 to 1985–86**

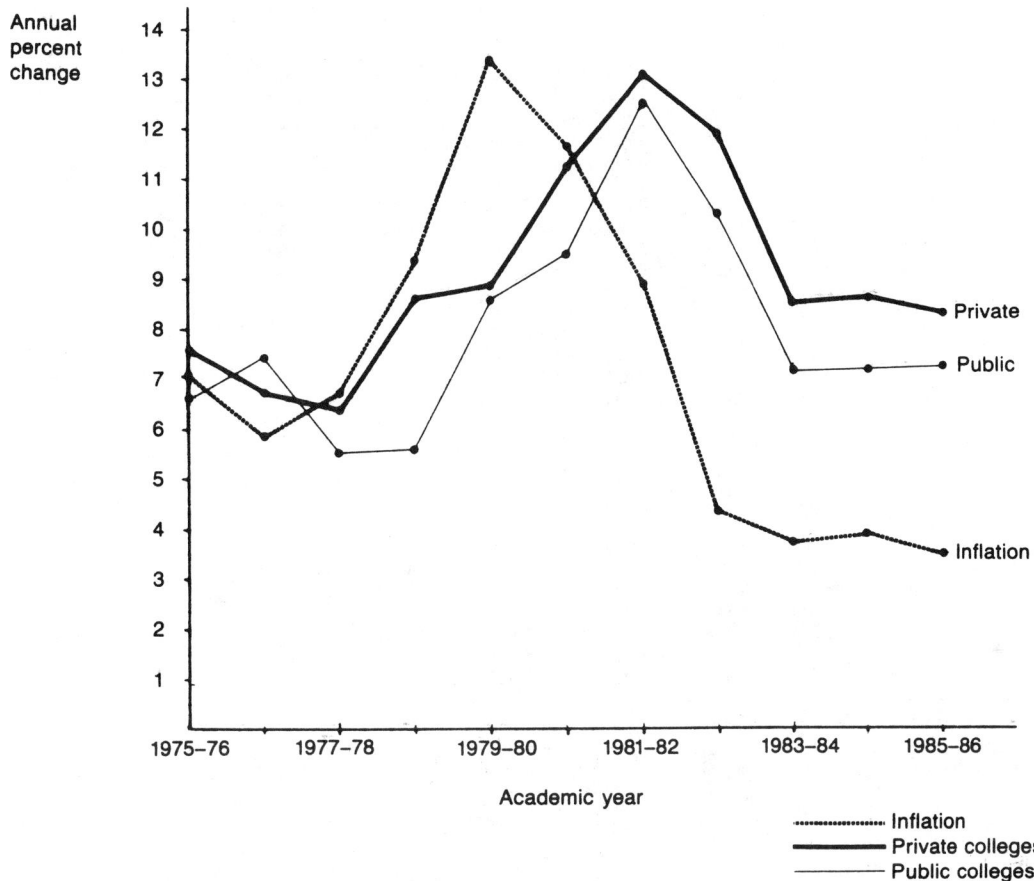

Annual
percent
change

Private

Public

Inflation

Academic year

·······················  Inflation
━━━━━━  Private colleges
─────  Public colleges

Note.—Data for 1985–86 are estimated.

SOURCE: U.S. Department of Education, Center for Statistics, survey of "Institutional Characteristics of Colleges and Universities"; and U.S. Department of Labor, Bureau of Labor Statistics.

Table 1.1

**Past and Projected Trends in Total Enrollment in Institutions of Higher Education, by Sex, Attendance Status, and Age Group: United States, Fall 1970 to Fall 1993**

| Fall of Year | Total Enrollment | Sex | | Attendance Status | | Age Group (Estimated) | |
|---|---|---|---|---|---|---|---|
| | | Male | Female | Full-Time | Part-Time | Under 25 Years Old | 25 Years Old and Over |
| 1970 | 8,581 | 5,044 | 3,537 | 5,815 | 2,766 | 6.194 | 2.386 |
| 1971 | 8,949 | 5,207 | 3,742 | 6,077 | 2,871 | 6.399 | 2.550 |
| 1972 | 9,215 | 5,239 | 3,976 | 6,072 | 3,142 | 6.401 | 2.815 |
| 1973 | 9,602 | 5,371 | 4,231 | 6,189 | 3,413 | 6.511 | 3.090 |
| 1974 | 10,224 | 5,622 | 4,601 | 6,370 | 3,853 | 6.631 | 3.593 |
| 1975 | 11,185 | 6,149 | 5,036 | 6,841 | 4,344 | 7.061 | 4.123 |
| 1976 | 11,012 | 5,811 | 5,201 | 6,717 | 4,295 | 7.066 | 3.945 |
| 1977 | 11,286 | 5,789 | 5,497 | 6,793 | 4,493 | 6.992 | 4.294 |
| 1978 | 11,259 | 5,640 | 5,619 | 6,667 | 4,592 | 7.035 | 4.225 |
| 1979 | 11,570 | 5,683 | 5,887 | 6,793 | 4,776 | 7.117 | 4.453 |
| 1980 | 12,097 | 5,874 | 6,223 | 7,098 | 4,999 | 7.560 | 4.537 |
| 1981 | 12,372 | 5,975 | 6,397 | 7,181 | 5,190 | 7.538 | 4.834 |
| 1982 | 12,426 | 6,031 | 6,394 | 7,221 | 5,205 | 7.578 | 4.848 |
| 1983 | 12,465 | 6,024 | 6,441 | 7,261 | 5,204 | 7.402 | 5.063 |
| | | | | Projected* | | | |
| 1984 | 12,345 | 6,020 | 6,325 | 7,045 | 5,300 | 7.225 | 5.120 |
| 1985 | 12,247 | 5,996 | 6,251 | 6,790 | 5,457 | 6.952 | 5.295 |
| 1986 | 12,162 | 5,944 | 6,218 | 6,645 | 5,517 | 6.734 | 5.428 |
| 1987 | 12,136 | 5,918 | 6,218 | 6,566 | 5,570 | 6.603 | 5.533 |
| 1988 | 12,141 | 5,909 | 6,232 | 6,541 | 5,600 | 6.533 | 5.608 |
| 1989 | 12,161 | 5,908 | 6,253 | 6,524 | 5,637 | 6.476 | 5.684 |
| 1990 | 12,093 | 5,867 | 6,226 | 6,430 | 5,663 | 6.351 | 5.742 |
| 1991 | 11,989 | 5,805 | 6,184 | 6,303 | 5,686 | 6.214 | 5.775 |
| 1992 | 11,810 | 5,715 | 6,095 | 6,152 | 5,658 | 6.065 | 5.745 |
| 1993 | 11,676 | 5,641 | 6,035 | 6,037 | 5,639 | 5.955 | 5.720 |

*For methodological details, see *Projections of Education Statistics to 1992-93*, 1985.

SOURCE: U.S. Department of Education, National Center for Education Statistics, Higher Education General Information Survey, *Fall Enrollment in Colleges and Universities*, various years; *Projections of Education Statistics to 1992-93*, 1985; and unpublished tabulations (December 1984).

# Table 1.2

**Past and Projected Trends in Total Enrollment in Institutions of Higher Education, by Sex, Age Group, and Percent in Full-Time Attendance Status: United States, Selected Years, Fall 1970 to Fall 1993**

| Sex and Age Group | Estimated Enrollment | | | | | | | | Projected Enrollment* | | | |
| | 1970 | | 1973 | | 1978 | | 1983 | | 1988 | | 1993 | |
| | Number (in Thousands) | Percent Full-Time | Number (in Thousands) | Percent Full-Time | Number (in Thousands) | Percent Full-Time | Number (in Thousands) | Percent Full-Time | Number (in Thousands) | Percent Full-Time | Number (in Thousands) | Percent Full-Time |
|---|---|---|---|---|---|---|---|---|---|---|---|---|
| Both sexes | 8,581 | 67.8 | 9,602 | 64.4 | 11,259 | 59.2 | 12,465 | 57.1 | 12,141 | 53.9 | 11,676 | 51.7 |
| 14 to 17 years | 258 | 93.4 | 297 | 89.6 | 263 | 91.6 | 214 | 89.2 | 213 | 89.7 | 183 | 89.6 |
| 18 and 19 years | 2,599 | 92.5 | 2,526 | 91.9 | 2,756 | 87.9 | 2,710 | 88.3 | 2,439 | 88.3 | 2,121 | 88.3 |
| 20 and 21 years | 1,880 | 87.6 | 2,109 | 85.6 | 2,213 | 82.1 | 2,392 | 82.9 | 2,023 | 82.7 | 1,888 | 82.8 |
| 22 to 24 years | 1,457 | 60.5 | 1,578 | 61.0 | 1,803 | 62.7 | 2,086 | 59.9 | 1,860 | 59.9 | 1,762 | 59.9 |
| 25 to 29 years | 1,075 | 37.9 | 1,485 | 32.6 | 1,731 | 34.7 | 2,032 | 36.4 | 2,110 | 36.4 | 1,870 | 36.4 |
| 30 to 34 years | 487 | 20.5 | 658 | 23.1 | 1,037 | 25.8 | 1,314 | 23.1 | 1,459 | 23.1 | 1,521 | 23.1 |
| 35 years and over | 824 | 16.3 | 947 | 20.5 | 1,458 | 12.9 | 1,716 | 14.8 | 2,037 | 14.9 | 2,329 | 14.9 |
| Male | 5,044 | 69.5 | 5,371 | 66.6 | 5,640 | 62.5 | 6,024 | 61.2 | 5,909 | 58.2 | 5,641 | 56.3 |
| 14 to 17 years | 129 | 96.1 | 121 | 90.9 | 105 | 90.5 | 91 | 87.0 | 92 | 87.0 | 79 | 86.1 |
| 18 and 19 years | 1,349 | 93.8 | 1,299 | 92.2 | 1,327 | 88.2 | 1,283 | 89.2 | 1,171 | 89.2 | 1,019 | 89.3 |
| 20 and 21 years | 1,095 | 90.4 | 1,149 | 86.2 | 1,157 | 84.4 | 1,205 | 84.8 | 1,033 | 84.6 | 966 | 84.7 |
| 22 to 24 years | 964 | 67.4 | 992 | 68.6 | 1,027 | 67.6 | 1,148 | 65.3 | 1,041 | 65.1 | 988 | 65.2 |
| 25 to 29 years | 783 | 41.8 | 993 | 37.0 | 985 | 38.3 | 1,087 | 40.3 | 1,150 | 40.3 | 1,022 | 40.3 |
| 30 to 34 years | 308 | 23.4 | 387 | 27.4 | 523 | 25.4 | 597 | 27.4 | 676 | 27.5 | 710 | 27.5 |
| 35 years and over | 415 | 18.1 | 428 | 28.7 | 516 | 15.7 | 613 | 14.7 | 744 | 14.8 | 855 | 14.7 |
| Female | 3,537 | 65.3 | 4,231 | 61.7 | 5,619 | 55.9 | 6,441 | 53.1 | 6,232 | 49.8 | 6,035 | 47.4 |
| 14 to 17 years | 129 | 90.7 | 175 | 89.1 | 157 | 93.0 | 123 | 91.7 | 121 | 90.9 | 104 | 91.3 |
| 18 and 19 years | 1,250 | 91.2 | 1,228 | 91.6 | 1,429 | 87.6 | 1,427 | 87.4 | 1,266 | 87.5 | 1,101 | 87.5 |
| 20 and 21 years | 785 | 83.7 | 961 | 84.8 | 1,054 | 79.7 | 1,187 | 80.9 | 989 | 80.9 | 922 | 80.8 |
| 22 to 24 years | 493 | 46.9 | 585 | 48.4 | 776 | 56.2 | 938 | 53.3 | 818 | 53.3 | 773 | 53.3 |
| 25 to 29 years | 292 | 27.4 | 492 | 23.4 | 746 | 29.8 | 945 | 31.7 | 960 | 31.7 | 849 | 31.7 |
| 30 to 34 years | 179 | 15.6 | 270 | 17.0 | 513 | 26.3 | 717 | 19.2 | 782 | 19.2 | 812 | 19.2 |
| 35 years and over | 409 | 14.4 | 518 | 13.5 | 942 | 11.4 | 1,103 | 14.9 | 1,294 | 14.9 | 1,474 | 14.9 |

*For methodological details, see *Projections of Education Statistics to 1992-93*, 1985.

NOTE: Details may not add to totals because of rounding.

SOURCE: U.S. Department of Education, National Center for Education Statistics, Higher Education General Information Survey, *Fall Enrollment in Colleges and Universities*, various years; *Projections of Education Statistics to 1992-93*, 1985, and unpublished tabulations (December 1984).

# Table 1.3

**Past and Projected Trends in Total Enrollment in Institutions of Higher Education, by Control and Type of Institution and by Level of Student: United States, Fall 1970 to Fall 1993**

| Fall of Year | Total Enrollment | Control of Institution | | Type of Institution | | Level | | |
|---|---|---|---|---|---|---|---|---|
| | | Public | Private | 4-Year | 2-Year | Undergraduate and Unclassified | Graduate and Postbaccalaureate Unclassified | First-Professional |
| 1970 | 8,581 | 6,428 | 2,153 | 6,358 | 2,223 | 7,376 | 1,031 | 175 |
| 1971 | 8,949 | 6,804 | 2,144 | 6,463 | 2,486 | 7,743 | 1,012 | 194 |
| 1972 | 9,215 | 7,071 | 2,144 | 6,459 | 2,756 | 7,941 | 1,066 | 207 |
| 1973 | 9,602 | 7,420 | 2,183 | 6,590 | 3,012 | 8,261 | 1,123 | 218 |
| 1974 | 10,224 | 7,989 | 2,235 | 6,820 | 3,404 | 8,798 | 1,190 | 236 |
| 1975 | 11,185 | 8,835 | 2,350 | 7,215 | 3,970 | 9,679 | 1,263 | 245 |
| 1976 | 11,012 | 8,653 | 2,359 | 7,129 | 3,883 | 9,429 | 1,333 | 251 |
| 1977 | 11,286 | 8,847 | 2,437 | 7,242 | 4,042 | 9,714 | 1,318 | 251 |
| 1978 | 11,259 | 8,784 | 2,475 | 7,232 | 4,028 | 9,684 | 1,319 | 257 |
| 1979 | 11,570 | 9,037 | 2,533 | 7,353 | 4,217 | 9,998 | 1,309 | 263 |
| 1980 | 12,097 | 9,457 | 2,640 | 7,571 | 4,526 | 10,475 | 1,343 | 278 |
| 1981 | 12,372 | 9,647 | 2,724 | 7,655 | 4,716 | 10,754 | 1,343 | 275 |
| 1982 | 12,426 | 9,696 | 2,730 | 7,654 | 4,772 | 10,825 | 1,323 | 278 |
| 1983 | 12,465 | 9,683 | 2,782 | 7,739 | 4,726 | 10,846 | 1,339 | 279 |
| Projected* | | | | | | | | |
| 1984 | 12,345 | 9,645 | 2,700 | 7,600 | 4,745 | 10,715 | 1,345 | 285 |
| 1985 | 12,247 | 9,591 | 2,656 | 7,437 | 4,810 | 10,551 | 1,398 | 298 |
| 1986 | 12,162 | 9,533 | 2,629 | 7,358 | 4,804 | 10,447 | 1,413 | 302 |
| 1987 | 12,136 | 9,518 | 2,618 | 7,317 | 4,819 | 10,410 | 1,424 | 302 |
| 1988 | 12,141 | 9,528 | 2,613 | 7,303 | 4,838 | 10,417 | 1,424 | 300 |
| 1989 | 12,161 | 9,548 | 2,613 | 7,306 | 4,855 | 10,439 | 1,425 | 297 |
| 1990 | 12,093 | 9,498 | 2,595 | 7,264 | 4,829 | 10,371 | 1,427 | 295 |
| 1991 | 11,989 | 9,419 | 2,570 | 7,195 | 4,794 | 10,266 | 1,430 | 293 |
| 1992 | 11,810 | 9,284 | 2,526 | 7,071 | 4,739 | 10,096 | 1,422 | 292 |
| 1993 | 11,676 | 9,185 | 2,491 | 6,968 | 4,708 | 9,968 | 1,418 | 290 |

(In Thousands)

*For methodological details, see *Projections of Education Statistics to 1992-93*, 1985.

SOURCE: U.S. Department of Education, National Center for Education Statistics, Higher Education General Information Survey, *Fall Enrollment in Colleges and Universities*, various years; *Projections of Education Statistics to 1992-93*, 1985, and unpublished tabulations (December 1984).

## Table 1.4

**Past and Projected Trends in Full-Time-Equivalent (FTE) Enrollment in Institutions of Higher Education, by Control and Type of Institution and by Level of Student: United States, Fall 1970 to Fall 1993**

| Fall of Year | Total FTE Enrollment | Control of Institution | | Type of Institution | | Level | | |
|---|---|---|---|---|---|---|---|---|
| | | Public | Private | 4-Year | 2-Year | Undergraduate and Unclassified | Graduate and Postbaccalaureate Unclassified | First-Professional |
| | | | | | | *(In Thousands)* | | |
| 1970 | 6,737 | 4,953 | 1,784 | 5,220 | 1,518 | 5.976 | 599 | 163 |
| 1971 | 7,149 | 5,344 | 1,804 | 5,430 | 1,719 | 6.351 | 613 | 185 |
| 1972 | 7,254 | 5,453 | 1,801 | 5,407 | 1,847 | 6.434 | 622 | 198 |
| 1973 | 7,453 | 5,630 | 1,824 | 5,439 | 2,014 | 6.574 | 669 | 210 |
| 1974 | 7,805 | 5,945 | 1,861 | 5,606 | 2,199 | 6.869 | 710 | 226 |
| 1975 | 8,481 | 6,523 | 1,958 | 5,899 | 2,581 | 7.493 | 758 | 229 |
| 1976 | 8,313 | 6,350 | 1,963 | 5,852 | 2,464 | 7.299 | 781 | 234 |
| 1977 | 8,415 | 6,396 | 2,018 | 5,934 | 2,480 | 7.398 | 776 | 240 |
| 1978 | 8,335 | 6,270 | 2,066 | 5,924 | 2,410 | 7.308 | 777 | 249 |
| 1979 | 8,487 | 6,393 | 2,095 | 6,017 | 2,471 | 7.460 | 778 | 250 |
| 1980 | 8,749 | 6,574 | 2,175 | 6,160 | 2,589 | 7.697 | 791 | 261 |
| 1981 | 9,012 | 6,778 | 2,234 | 6,250 | 2,764 | 7.952 | 801 | 261 |
| 1982 | 9,092 | 6,851 | 2,241 | 6,249 | 2,842 | 8.036 | 788 | 267 |
| 1983 | 9,166 | 6,881 | 2,285 | 6,324 | 2,842 | 8.095 | 806 | 266 |
| | | | | Projected* | | | | |
| 1984 | 8,866 | 6,671 | 2,195 | 6,107 | 2,759 | 7.756 | 835 | 275 |
| 1985 | 8,730 | 6,570 | 2,160 | 6,008 | 2,722 | 7.601 | 845 | 284 |
| 1986 | 8,607 | 6,480 | 2,127 | 5,908 | 2,699 | 7.467 | 852 | 288 |
| 1987 | 8,547 | 6,438 | 2,109 | 5,850 | 2,697 | 7.402 | 858 | 287 |
| 1988 | 8,533 | 6,433 | 2,100 | 5,825 | 2,708 | 7.393 | 855 | 285 |
| 1989 | 8,529 | 6,433 | 2,097 | 5,815 | 2,713 | 7.394 | 852 | 282 |
| 1990 | 8,445 | 6,371 | 2,075 | 5,761 | 2,684 | 7.316 | 849 | 280 |
| 1991 | 8,326 | 6,278 | 2,048 | 5,683 | 2,642 | 7.199 | 848 | 278 |
| 1992 | 8,165 | 6,159 | 2,007 | 5,567 | 2,598 | 7.044 | 844 | 277 |
| 1993 | 8,043 | 6,069 | 1,974 | 5,471 | 2,572 | 6.925 | 842 | 276 |

*For methodological details, see *Projections of Education Statistics to 1992-93*, 1985.

SOURCE: U.S. Department of Education, National Center for Education Statistics, Higher Education General Information Survey, *Fall Enrollment in Colleges and Universities*, various years; *Projections of Education Statistics to 1992-93*, 1985, and unpublished tabulations (December 1984).

## Table 1.5

**Estimated undergraduate tuition and fees and room and board rates in institutions of higher education, by type and control of institution: United States, 1964–65 to 1985–86**

| Year and control of institution | Total tuition, board, and room | | | | Tuition and required fees (in-State) | | | | Dormitory rooms | | | | Board (7-day basis) | | | |
|---|---|---|---|---|---|---|---|---|---|---|---|---|---|---|---|---|
| | All | University | Other 4-year | 2-year | All | University | Other 4-year | 2-year | All | University | Other 4-year | 2-year | All | University | Other 4-year | 2-year |
| 1 | 2 | 3 | 4 | 5 | 6 | 7 | 8 | 9 | 10 | 11 | 12 | 13 | 14 | 15 | 16 | 17 |
| **1964–65:** | | | | | | | | | | | | | | | | |
| Public | 950 | 1,051 | 867 | 638 | 243 | 298 | 224 | 99 | 271 | 291 | 241 | 178 | 436 | 462 | 402 | 361 |
| Private | 1,907 | 2,202 | 1,810 | 1,455 | 1,088 | 1,297 | 1,023 | 702 | 331 | 390 | 308 | 289 | 488 | 515 | 479 | 464 |
| **1965–66:[1]** | | | | | | | | | | | | | | | | |
| Public | 983 | 1,105 | 904 | 670 | 257 | 327 | 241 | 109 | 281 | 304 | 255 | 194 | 445 | 474 | 408 | 367 |
| Private | 2,005 | 2,316 | 1899 | 1,557 | 1,154 | 1,369 | 1,086 | 768 | 356 | 418 | 330 | 316 | 495 | 529 | 483 | 473 |
| **1966–67:** | | | | | | | | | | | | | | | | |
| Public | 1,026 | 1,171 | 947 | 710 | 275 | 360 | 259 | 121 | 294 | 321 | 271 | 213 | 457 | 490 | 417 | 376 |
| Private | 2,124 | 2,456 | 2,007 | 1,679 | 1,233 | 1,456 | 1,162 | 845 | 385 | 452 | 355 | 347 | 506 | 548 | 490 | 487 |
| **1967–68:** | | | | | | | | | | | | | | | | |
| Public | 1,064 | 1,199 | 997 | 789 | 283 | 366 | 268 | 144 | 313 | 337 | 292 | 243 | 468 | 496 | 437 | 402 |
| Private | 2,205 | 2,545 | 2,104 | 1,762 | 1,297 | 1,534 | 1,237 | 892 | 392 | 455 | 366 | 366 | 516 | 556 | 501 | 504 |
| **1968–69:** | | | | | | | | | | | | | | | | |
| Public | 1,117 | 1,245 | 1,063 | 883 | 295 | 377 | 281 | 170 | 337 | 359 | 318 | 278 | 485 | 509 | 464 | 435 |
| Private | 2,321 | 2,673 | 2,237 | 1,876 | 1,383 | 1,638 | 1,335 | 956 | 404 | 463 | 382 | 391 | 534 | 572 | 520 | 529 |
| **1969–70:[1]** | | | | | | | | | | | | | | | | |
| Public | 1,203 | 1,362 | 1,135 | 951 | 323 | 427 | 306 | 178 | 369 | 395 | 346 | 308 | 511 | 540 | 483 | 465 |
| Private | 2,530 | 2,820 | 2,420 | 1,993 | 1,533 | 1,809 | 1,468 | 1,034 | 436 | 503 | 409 | 413 | 561 | 608 | 543 | 546 |
| **1970–71:[1]** | | | | | | | | | | | | | | | | |
| Public | 1,287 | 1,477 | 1,206 | 998 | 351 | 478 | 332 | 187 | 401 | 431 | 375 | 338 | 535 | 568 | 499 | 473 |
| Private | 2,738 | 3,163 | 2,599 | 2,103 | 1,684 | 1,980 | 1,603 | 1,109 | 468 | 542 | 434 | 434 | 586 | 641 | 562 | 560 |
| **1971–72:** | | | | | | | | | | | | | | | | |
| Public | 1,357 | 1,579 | 1,263 | 1,073 | 376 | 526 | 354 | 192 | 430 | 463 | 400 | 366 | 551 | 590 | 509 | 515 |
| Private | 2,917 | 3,375 | 2,748 | 2,186 | 1,820 | 2,133 | 1,721 | 1,172 | 494 | 576 | 454 | 449 | 603 | 666 | 573 | 565 |
| **1972–73:** | | | | | | | | | | | | | | | | |
| Public | 1,458 | 1,668 | 1,460 | 1,197 | 407 | 566 | 455 | 233 | 476 | 500 | 455 | 398 | 575 | 602 | 550 | 566 |
| Private | 3,038 | 3,512 | 2,934 | 2,273 | 1,898 | 2,226 | 1,846 | 1,221 | 524 | 622 | 490 | 457 | 616 | 664 | 598 | 595 |
| **1973–74:** | | | | | | | | | | | | | | | | |
| Public | 1,517 | 1,707 | 1,506 | 1,274 | 438 | 581 | 463 | 274 | 480 | 505 | 464 | 409 | 599 | 621 | 579 | 591 |
| Private | 3,164 | 3,717 | 3,040 | 2,410 | 1,989 | 2,375 | 1,925 | 1,303 | 533 | 622 | 502 | 483 | 642 | 720 | 613 | 624 |
| **1974–75:** | | | | | | | | | | | | | | | | |
| Public | 1,563 | 1,760 | 1,558 | 1,339 | 432 | 599 | 448 | 277 | 506 | 527 | 497 | 424 | 625 | 634 | 613 | 638 |
| Private | 3,403 | 4,076 | 3,156 | 2,591 | 2,117 | 2,614 | 1,954 | 1,367 | 586 | 691 | 536 | 564 | 700 | 771 | 666 | 660 |
| **1975–76:** | | | | | | | | | | | | | | | | |
| Public | 1,666 | 1,935 | 1,657 | 1,386 | 433 | 642 | 469 | 245 | 544 | 573 | 533 | 442 | 689 | 720 | 655 | 699 |
| Private | 3,663 | 4,467 | 3,385 | 2,711 | 2,272 | 2,881 | 2,084 | 1,427 | 636 | 753 | 583 | 572 | 755 | 833 | 718 | 712 |

Estimated undergraduate tuition and fees and room and board rates in institutions of higher education, by type and control of institution: United States, 1964–65 to 1985–86—Continued

| Year and control of institution | Total tuition, board, and room | | | | Tuition and required fees (in-State) | | | | Dormitory rooms | | | | Board (7-day basis) | | | |
|---|---|---|---|---|---|---|---|---|---|---|---|---|---|---|---|---|
| | All | University | Other 4-year | 2-year | All | University | Other 4-year | 2-year | All | University | Other 4-year | 2-year | All | University | Other 4-year | 2-year |
| 1 | 2 | 3 | 4 | 5 | 6 | 7 | 8 | 9 | 10 | 11 | 12 | 13 | 14 | 15 | 16 | 17 |
| **1976-77:** | | | | | | | | | | | | | | | | |
| Public | 1,789 | 2,066 | 1,828 | 1,490 | 479 | 689 | 564 | 283 | 582 | 614 | 572 | 465 | 728 | 763 | 692 | 742 |
| Private | 3,907 | 4,716 | 3,714 | 2,971 | 2,467 | 3,051 | 2,351 | 1,592 | 649 | 783 | 604 | 607 | 791 | 882 | 759 | 772 |
| **1977-78:** | | | | | | | | | | | | | | | | |
| Public | 1,888 | 2,170 | 1,932 | 1,589 | 512 | 736 | 596 | 306 | 621 | 649 | 616 | 486 | 755 | 785 | 720 | 797 |
| Private | 4,158 | 5,033 | 3,968 | 3,148 | 2,624 | 3,240 | 2,520 | 1,706 | 698 | 850 | 648 | 631 | 836 | 943 | 800 | 811 |
| **1978-79:** | | | | | | | | | | | | | | | | |
| Public | 1,994 | 2,289 | 2,027 | 1,691 | 543 | 777 | 622 | 327 | 655 | 689 | 641 | 527 | 796 | 823 | 764 | 837 |
| Private | 4,514 | 5,403 | 4,326 | 3,389 | 2,867 | 3,487 | 2,771 | 1,831 | 758 | 916 | 704 | 700 | 889 | 1,000 | 851 | 858 |
| **1979-80:** | | | | | | | | | | | | | | | | |
| Public | 2,165 | 2,487 | 2,198 | 1,821 | 583 | 840 | 662 | 355 | 715 | 749 | 703 | 572 | 867 | 898 | 833 | 894 |
| Private | 4,912 | 5,888 | 4,699 | 3,755 | 3,130 | 3,811 | 3,020 | 2,062 | 827 | 999 | 768 | 769 | 955 | 1,078 | 911 | 924 |
| **1980-81:** | | | | | | | | | | | | | | | | |
| Public | 2,371 | 2,711 | 2,420 | 2,020 | 633 | 915 | 721 | 385 | 798 | 827 | 795 | 635 | 940 | 969 | 904 | 1,000 |
| Private | 5,468 | 6,566 | 5,249 | 4,290 | 3,498 | 4,275 | 3,390 | 2,413 | 917 | 1,083 | 860 | 880 | 1,053 | 1,208 | 999 | 997 |
| **1981-82:** | | | | | | | | | | | | | | | | |
| Public | 2,668 | 3,079 | 2,701 | 2,217 | 721 | 1,042 | 813 | 432 | 909 | 970 | 885 | 697 | 1,038 | 1,067 | 1,003 | 1,088 |
| Private | 6,184 | 7,439 | 5,949 | 4,840 | 3,972 | 4,887 | 3,855 | 2,697 | 1,037 | 1,226 | 970 | 1,025 | 1,175 | 1,326 | 1,124 | 1,118 |
| **1982-83:** | | | | | | | | | | | | | | | | |
| Public | 2,944 | 3,403 | 3,032 | 2,390 | 798 | 1,164 | 936 | 473 | 1,010 | 1,072 | 993 | 755 | 1,136 | 1,167 | 1,103 | 1,162 |
| Private | 6,920 | 8,537 | 6,646 | 5,364 | 4,439 | 5,583 | 4,329 | 3,008 | 1,181 | 1,453 | 1,083 | 1,177 | 1,300 | 1,501 | 1,234 | 1,179 |
| **1983-84:[3]** | | | | | | | | | | | | | | | | |
| Public | 3,156 | 3,628 | 3,285 | 2,534 | 891 | 1,284 | 1,052 | 528 | 1,087 | 1,131 | 1,092 | 801 | 1,178 | 1,213 | 1,141 | 1,205 |
| Private | 7,509 | 9,307 | 7,244 | 5,571 | 4,851 | 6,217 | 4,726 | 3,099 | 1,278 | 1,531 | 1,191 | 1,253 | 1,380 | 1,559 | 1,327 | 1,219 |
| **1984-85:[3]** | | | | | | | | | | | | | | | | |
| Public | 3,383 | 3,888 | 3,503 | 2,794 | 960 | 1,388 | 1,116 | 579 | 1,192 | 1,239 | 1,192 | 919 | 1,231 | 1,261 | 1,195 | 1,296 |
| Private | 8,156 | 10,224 | 7,831 | 5,981 | 5,281 | 6,826 | 5,126 | 3,348 | 1,430 | 1,754 | 1,320 | 1,371 | 1,445 | 1,644 | 1,385 | 1,262 |
| **1985-86:[1]** | | | | | | | | | | | | | | | | |
| Public | 3,630 | 4,160 | 3,750 | 3,000 | 1,040 | 1,510 | 1,200 | 620 | 1,300 | 1,340 | 1,310 | 1,010 | 1,290 | 1,310 | 1,240 | 1,370 |
| Private | 8,830 | 11,100 | 8,480 | 6,410 | 5,720 | 7,440 | 5,540 | 3,620 | 1,580 | 1,940 | 1,470 | 1,480 | 1,530 | 1,720 | 1,470 | 1,310 |

[1] Estimated.
[2] Data have been revised since originally published.
[3] Preliminary.

NOTE.—Data are for the entire academic year and are average charges paid by students. Tuition and fees were calculated on the basis of full-time equivalent students. Room and board were based on full-time students. The data have not been adjusted for changes in the purchasing power of the dollar.

SOURCES: U.S. Department of Education, National Center for Education Statistics, *Projections of Education Statistics*; and special tabulations from the "Institutional Characteristics of Colleges and Universities" and "Fall Enrollment in Colleges and Universities" surveys.

## Table 1.6

**Past and Projected Trends in Doctor's and First-Professional Degrees Conferred by Institutions of Higher Education, by Sex of Recipient: United States, 1970-71 to 1993-94**

| Year | Doctor's | | | | First-Professional | | | |
|------|----------|------|--------|-----------------------------|--------------------|------|--------|-----------------------------|
|      | Total    | Male | Female | Percent Awarded to Females  | Total              | Male | Female | Percent Awarded to Females  |
| 1970-71 | 32,107 | 27,530 | 4,577 | 14.3 | 37,946 | 35,544 | 2,402 | 6.3 |
| 1971-72 | 33,363 | 28,090 | 5,273 | 15.8 | 43,411 | 40,723 | 2,688 | 6.2 |
| 1972-73 | 34,777 | 28,571 | 6,206 | 17.8 | 50,018 | 46,489 | 3,529 | 7.1 |
| 1973-74 | 33,816 | 27,365 | 6,451 | 19.1 | 53,816 | 48,530 | 5,286 | 9.8 |
| 1974-75 | 34,083 | 26,817 | 7,266 | 21.3 | 55,916 | 48,956 | 6,960 | 12.4 |
| 1975-76 | 34,064 | 26,267 | 7,797 | 22.9 | 62,649 | 52,892 | 9,757 | 15.6 |
| 1976-77 | 33,232 | 25,142 | 8,090 | 24.3 | 63,359 | 52,374 | 10,985 | 17.3 |
| 1977-78 | 32,131 | 23,658 | 8,473 | 26.4 | 66,581 | 52,270 | 14,311 | 21.5 |
| 1978-79 | 32,730 | 23,541 | 9,189 | 28.1 | 68,848 | 52,652 | 16,196 | 23.5 |
| 1979-80 | 32,615 | 22,943 | 9,672 | 29.7 | 70,131 | 52,716 | 17,415 | 24.8 |
| 1980-81 | 32,958 | 22,711 | 10,247 | 31.1 | 71,956 | 52,792 | 19,164 | 26.6 |
| 1981-82 | 32,707 | 22,224 | 10,483 | 32.1 | 72,032 | 52,223 | 19,809 | 27.5 |
| 1982-83[1] | 32,700 | 22,000 | 10,700 | 32.7 | 72,500 | 51,500 | 21,000 | 29.0 |
| Projected[2] | | | | | | | | |
| 1983-84 | 33,000 | 21,700 | 11,300 | 34.2 | 73,500 | 51,500 | 22,000 | 29.9 |
| 1984-85 | 33,200 | 21,400 | 11,800 | 35.5 | 73,700 | 50,700 | 23,000 | 31.2 |
| 1985-86 | 33,400 | 21,100 | 12,300 | 36.8 | 73,500 | 50,200 | 23,300 | 31.7 |
| 1986-87 | 32,600 | 19,700 | 12,900 | 39.6 | 73,400 | 49,900 | 23,500 | 32.0 |
| 1987-88 | 32,800 | 19,400 | 13,400 | 40.9 | 70,200 | 47,100 | 23,100 | 32.9 |
| 1988-89 | 33,100 | 19,100 | 14,000 | 42.3 | 68,900 | 46,300 | 22,600 | 32.8 |
| 1989-90 | 32,800 | 18,300 | 14,500 | 44.2 | 68,300 | 45,500 | 22,800 | 33.4 |
| 1990-91 | 33,200 | 18,100 | 15,100 | 45.5 | 67,800 | 44,900 | 22,900 | 33.8 |
| 1991-92 | 33,400 | 17,800 | 15,600 | 46.7 | 67,800 | 44,900 | 22,900 | 33.8 |
| 1992-93 | 33,600 | 17,500 | 16,100 | 47.9 | 67,800 | 44,900 | 22,900 | 33.8 |
| 1993-94 | 33,700 | 17,200 | 16,500 | 49.0 | 67,800 | 44,800 | 23,000 | 33.9 |

[1]Estimated.

[2]For methodological details, see *Projections of Education Statistics to 1992-93*, 1985.

SOURCE: U.S. Department of Education, National Center for Education Statistics, Higher Education General Information Survey, *Earned Degrees Conferred by Institutions of Higher Education*, various years; *Projections of Education Statistics to 1992-93*, 1985; and unpublished tabulations (December 1984).

# Table 1.7

**Past and Projected Trends in Full-Time and Part-Time Senior Instructional Staff[1] in Institutions of Higher Education, by Control and Type of Institution: United States, Fall 1970 to Fall 1993**

| Fall of Year | Total | Employment Status | | Control | | Type | |
|---|---|---|---|---|---|---|---|
| | | Full-Time | Part-Time | Public | Private | 4-Year | 2-Year |
| | | | | | | | (In Thousands) |
| 1970............................ | **474** | 369 | 104 | 314 | 160 | 382 | 92 |
| 1971............................ | **492** | 379 | 113 | 333 | 159 | 387 | 105 |
| 1972............................ | **500** | 380 | 120 | 343 | 157 | 384 | 116 |
| 1973............................ | **527** | 389 | 138 | 365 | 162 | 401 | 126 |
| 1974............................ | **567** | 406 | 161 | 397 | 170 | 427 | 140 |
| 1975............................ | **628** | 440 | 188 | 443 | 185 | 467 | 161 |
| 1976............................ | **633** | 434 | 199 | 450 | 183 | 467 | 166 |
| 1977............................ | **°656** | 445 | 211 | 468 | 188 | 483 | 173 |
| 1978............................ | **656** | 441 | 215 | 467 | 189 | 485 | 171 |
| 1979............................ | **675** | 445 | 230 | 488 | 187 | 494 | 182 |
| 1980[2]......................... | **686** | 450 | 236 | 495 | 191 | 494 | 192 |
| 1981............................ | **696** | 452 | 245 | 500 | 196 | 498 | 198 |
| 1982[2]......................... | **701** | 455 | 246 | 506 | 195 | 499 | 202 |
| 1983[2]......................... | **702** | 457 | 245 | 507 | 195 | 500 | 202 |
| | | | Projected[3] | | | | |
| 1984............................ | **700** | 455 | 245 | 506 | 194 | 498 | 202 |
| 1985............................ | **694** | 454 | 240 | 504 | 190 | 494 | 200 |
| 1986............................ | **684** | 447 | 237 | 497 | 187 | 485 | 198 |
| 1987............................ | **678** | 443 | 235 | 493 | 185 | 480 | 198 |
| 1988............................ | **677** | 442 | 235 | 493 | 184 | 478 | 199 |
| 1989............................ | **677** | 442 | 235 | 493 | 184 | 478 | 199 |
| 1990............................ | **670** | 437 | 233 | 488 | 182 | 473 | 197 |
| 1991............................ | **661** | 431 | 230 | 481 | 180 | 467 | 194 |
| 1992............................ | **648** | 423 | 225 | 472 | 176 | 457 | 191 |
| 1993............................ | **635** | 415 | 220 | 463 | 172 | 447 | 188 |

[1]Faculty members with the title of professor, associate professor, assistant professor, instructor, lecturer, assisting professor, adjunct professor, or interim professor (or its equivalent). Excluded are graduate students with titles such as graduate or teaching fellow who assist senior staff.

[2]Estimated on the basis of enrollment.

[3]For methodological details, see *Projections of Education Statistics to 1992-93*, 1985.

NOTE: Details may not add to totals because of rounding.

SOURCE: U.S. Department of Education, National Center for Education Statistics, *Employees in Institutions of Higher Education*, various years; *Projections of Education Statistics to 1992-93*, 1985; Equal Employment Opportunity Commission, Higher Education Staff Information Report File, various years; and unpublished tabulations (December 1984).

## Table 1.8

**Past and Projected Trends in Bachelor's and Master's Degrees Conferred by Institutions of Higher Education, by Sex of Recipient: United States, 1970-71 to 1993-94**

| Year | Bachelor's | | | | Master's | | | |
|---|---|---|---|---|---|---|---|---|
| | Total | Male | Female | Percent Awarded to Females | Total | Male | Female | Percent Awarded to Females |
| 1970-71 | 839,730 | 475,594 | 364,136 | 43.4 | 230,509 | 138,146 | 92,363 | 40.1 |
| 1971-72 | 887,273 | 500,590 | 386,683 | 43.6 | 251,633 | 149,550 | 102,083 | 40.6 |
| 1972-73 | 922,362 | 518,191 | 404,171 | 43.8 | 263,371 | 154,468 | 108,903 | 41.3 |
| 1973-74 | 945,776 | 527,313 | 418,463 | 44.2 | 277,033 | 157,842 | 119,191 | 43.0 |
| 1974-75 | 922,933 | 504,841 | 418,092 | 45.3 | 292,450 | 161,570 | 130,880 | 44.8 |
| 1975-76 | 925,746 | 504,925 | 420,821 | 45.5 | 311,771 | 167,248 | 144,523 | 46.4 |
| 1976-77 | 919,549 | 495,545 | 424,004 | 46.1 | 317,164 | 167,783 | 149,381 | 47.1 |
| 1977-78 | 921,204 | 487,347 | 433,857 | 47.1 | 311,620 | 161,212 | 150,408 | 48.3 |
| 1978-79 | 921,390 | 477,344 | 444,046 | 48.2 | 301,079 | 153,370 | 147,709 | 49.1 |
| 1979-80 | 929,417 | 473,611 | 455,806 | 49.0 | 298,081 | 150,749 | 147,332 | 49.4 |
| 1980-81 | 935,140 | 469,883 | 465,257 | 49.8 | 295,739 | 147,043 | 148,696 | 50.3 |
| 1981-82 | 952,998 | 473,364 | 479,634 | 50.3 | 295,546 | 145,532 | 150,014 | 50.8 |
| 1982-83[1] | 970,000 | 480,000 | 490,000 | 50.5 | 295,000 | 143,000 | 152,000 | 51.5 |
| | | | | Projected[2] | | | | |
| 1983-84 | 970,000 | 485,000 | 485,000 | 50.0 | 296,000 | 143,000 | 153,000 | 51.7 |
| 1984-85 | 960,000 | 480,000 | 480,000 | 50.0 | 295,000 | 141,000 | 154,000 | 52.2 |
| 1985-86 | 945,000 | 470,000 | 475,000 | 50.3 | 294,000 | 139,000 | 155,000 | 52.7 |
| 1986-87 | 935,000 | 465,000 | 470,000 | 50.3 | 292,000 | 138,000 | 154,000 | 52.7 |
| 1987-88 | 927,000 | 462,000 | 465,000 | 50.2 | 291,000 | 138,000 | 153,000 | 52.6 |
| 1988-89 | 927,000 | 462,000 | 465,000 | 50.2 | 289,000 | 137,000 | 152,000 | 52.6 |
| 1989-90 | 927,000 | 462,000 | 465,000 | 50.2 | 289,000 | 137,000 | 152,000 | 52.6 |
| 1990-91 | 922,000 | 460,000 | 462,000 | 50.1 | 287,000 | 136,000 | 151,000 | 52.6 |
| 1991-92 | 915,000 | 456,000 | 459,000 | 50.2 | 287,000 | 136,000 | 151,000 | 52.6 |
| 1992-93 | 900,000 | 449,000 | 451,000 | 50.1 | 285,000 | 135,000 | 150,000 | 52.6 |
| 1993-94 | 887,000 | 442,000 | 445,000 | 50.2 | 284,000 | 134,000 | 150,000 | 52.8 |

[1]Estimated.

[2]For methodological details, see *Projections of Education Statistics to 1992-93*, 1985.

SOURCE: U.S. Department of Education, National Center for Education Statistics, Higher Education General Information Survey, *Earned Degrees Conferred by Institutions of Higher Education*, various years; *Projections of Education Statistics to 1992-93*, 1985; and unpublished tabulations (December 1984).

Table 1.9

**Past and Projected Trends in the College-Age and Adult Populations: United States, 1970 to 1993**

| Year (July 1) | (In Thousands) | | | | |
|---|---|---|---|---|---|
| | 18 Years Old and Over | 18 Years Old | 18 to 24 Years Old | 25 to 34 Years Old | 35 Years Old and Over |
| 1970 | 135,290 | 3,781 | 24,712 | 25,323 | 85,255 |
| 1971 | 137,852 | 3,878 | 25,874 | 25,958 | 86,020 |
| 1972 | 140,476 | 3,976 | 26,076 | 27,623 | 86,777 |
| 1973 | 143,145 | 4,053 | 26,635 | 28,939 | 87,571 |
| 1974 | 145,867 | 4,103 | 27,233 | 30,225 | 88,409 |
| 1975 | 148,805 | 4,256 | 28,005 | 31,471 | 89,329 |
| 1976 | 151,784 | 4,266 | 28,645 | 32,759 | 90,380 |
| 1977 | 154,776 | 4,257 | 29,174 | 33,998 | 91,604 |
| 1978 | 157,810 | 4,247 | 29,622 | 34,963 | 93,225 |
| 1979 | 160,950 | 4,316 | 30,048 | 36,203 | 94,699 |
| 1980 | 164,055 | 4,258 | 30,357 | 37,601 | 96,097 |
| 1981 | 166,809 | 4,239 | 30,486 | 39,033 | 97,290 |
| 1982 | 169,497 | 4,193 | 30,422 | 39,559 | 99,516 |
| 1983 | 171,921 | 4,022 | 30,148 | 40,334 | 101,439 |
| | | | Projected* | | |
| 1984 | 173,806 | 3,774 | 29,501 | 41,020 | 103,285 |
| 1985 | 175,792 | 3,658 | 28,739 | 41,788 | 105,265 |
| 1986 | 177,673 | 3,574 | 27,838 | 42,515 | 107,320 |
| 1987 | 179,624 | 3,667 | 27,246 | 43,098 | 109,280 |
| 1988 | 181,657 | 3,772 | 26,783 | 43,429 | 111,445 |
| 1989 | 183,673 | 3,777 | 26,375 | 43,620 | 113,678 |
| 1990 | 185,321 | 3,431 | 25,794 | 43,529 | 115,998 |
| 1991 | 186,833 | 3,317 | 25,338 | 43,159 | 118,336 |
| 1992 | 188,205 | 3,199 | 24,881 | 42,548 | 120,776 |
| 1993 | 189,633 | 3,276 | 24,583 | 41,830 | 123,220 |

*Projection data are from the middle series.

SOURCE: U.S. Department of Commerce, Bureau of the Census, *Current Population Reports*, "Population Estimates and Projections", Series P-25, No. 917, July 1982, and No. 949, May 1984.

IV.2

# Current Data

## Average Salaries for Full-Time Faculty Members at 1,700 U.S. Colleges and Universities

The following table shows average faculty salaries by rank at 1,700 colleges, universities, and multi-campus college systems in 1986-87.

The salaries, which are reported in thousands of dollars and rounded to the nearest hundred, cover all full-time members of the instructional staff except those in medical schools.

The figures are adjusted to a standard, nine-month work year.

The statistics were compiled for the American Association of University Professors by Maryse Eymonerie Associates of McLean, Va.

The designations I, IIA, IIB, III, and IV are defined in the rating table at the right, which gives the percentile distributions of salaries for each academic rank.

To maintain the confidentiality of individual salaries, a dash appears where an institution has five or fewer faculty members at that rank. A blank space indicates that the institution has no faculty members at that rank.

Average faculty salaries for institutions without academic ranks, most of which are two-year colleges, appear in a separate table.

The full salary report, which includes data on salaries by sex and fringe-benefit information, may be purchased for $25 prepaid from the American Association of University Professors, Suite 500, 1012 14th Street, N.W., Washington 20005.

### AAUP Rating Scale

*Category I: Doctoral Institutions*

| | 1+ | 1 | 2 | 3 | 4 |
|---|---|---|---|---|---|
| Professor | $62,400 | $55,900 | $50,300 | $46,700 | $42,800 |
| Associate professor | 42,800 | 39,400 | 37,000 | 35,300 | 32,500 |
| Assistant professor | 35,700 | 32,900 | 30,600 | 29,300 | 27,800 |
| Instructor | 29,300 | 25,800 | 23,800 | 22,400 | 20,500 |

*Category IIA: Comprehensive Institutions*

| | 1+ | 1 | 2 | 3 | 4 |
|---|---|---|---|---|---|
| Professor | $49,100 | $44,300 | $40,400 | $37,800 | $34,600 |
| Associate professor | 38,200 | 35,600 | 33,000 | 31,300 | 28,800 |
| Assistant professor | 31,300 | 29,500 | 27,500 | 26,100 | 24,700 |
| Instructor | 27,200 | 24,600 | 22,500 | 21,200 | 19,700 |

*Category IIB: Baccalaureate Institutions*

| | 1+ | 1 | 2 | 3 | 4 |
|---|---|---|---|---|---|
| Professor | $46,200 | $38,500 | $34,200 | $30,500 | $27,100 |
| Associate professor | 35,200 | 31,500 | 28,600 | 26,100 | 23,300 |
| Assistant professor | 28,400 | 25,900 | 24,100 | 22,400 | 20,300 |
| Instructor | 25,500 | 22,400 | 20,500 | 18,900 | 17,500 |

*Category III: 2-Year Institutions with Academic Ranks*

| | 1+ | 1 | 2 | 3 | 4 |
|---|---|---|---|---|---|
| Professor | $41,800 | $38,500 | $35,300 | $32,500 | $30,100 |
| Associate professor | 36,000 | 32,800 | 30,600 | 28,700 | 25,800 |
| Assistant professor | 30,500 | 27,900 | 26,200 | 24,400 | 21,500 |
| Instructor | 27,400 | 23,800 | 22,300 | 20,800 | 18,700 |

*Category IV: 2-Year Institutions Without Academic Ranks*

| | 1+ | 1 | 2 | 3 | 4 |
|---|---|---|---|---|---|
| All | $40,500 | $35,000 | $29,500 | $26,300 | $22,500 |

Note: Scales are based on actual distributions by average salary in 1986-87, according to data from 1,875 institutions. Percentile rankings are as follows: 1+ = 95th percentile; 1 = 80th percentile; 2 = 60th percentile; 3 = 40th percentile; 4 = 20th percentile. An average salary of $52,000 for the rank of professor in Category 1 institutions would be rated 2 because it falls between the 60th percentile ($50,300) and the 80th percentile ($55,900).

SOURCE: AMERICAN ASSOCIATION OF UNIVERSITY PROFESSORS

### ALABAMA

| | Prof | Assoc Prof | Asst Prof | Inst |
|---|---|---|---|---|
| Alabama A&M U, IIA | 32.4 | 29.1 | 24.7 | 19.4 |
| Alabama St U, IIA | 34.4 | 31.1 | 25.5 | 20.2 |
| Athens St C, IIB | 38.4 | 34.0 | 27.2 | — |
| Auburn U | | | | |
| Main campus, I | 43.8 | 34.1 | 28.7 | 19.5 |
| Montgomery, IIA | 39.2 | 33.1 | 26.5 | 21.7 |
| Birmingham-Southern C, IIB | 33.4 | 26.4 | 24.3 | — |
| Huntingdon C, IIB | 27.9 | 25.2 | 21.8 | — |
| Jacksonville St U, IIA | 35.0 | 33.8 | 28.8 | 25.7 |
| Judson C, IIB | 25.9 | — | 20.2 | — |
| Livingston U, IIB | 30.2 | 23.9 | 21.4 | 18.3 |
| SE Bible C, IIB | — | 18.6 | — | — |
| Spring Hill C, IIB | 34.2 | 28.3 | 24.6 | — |
| Stillman C, IIB | 23.9 | 20.0 | 19.8 | 16.0 |
| Troy St U | | | | |
| Main campus, IIA | 36.3 | 29.7 | 24.8 | 21.5 |
| Dothan-Ft Rucker, IIA | 35.4 | 31.5 | 28.6 | — |
| Montgomery, IIA | — | 29.2 | 26.1 | — |
| Tuskegee U, IIA | 30.5 | 24.9 | 22.5 | 18.2 |
| U of Alabama | | | | |
| Main campus, I | 45.2 | 33.9 | 28.0 | 19.7 |
| Birmingham, I | 42.1 | 32.1 | 26.0 | 20.2 |
| Huntsville, IIA | 44.5 | 32.8 | 27.2 | 21.1 |
| U of Montevallo, IIA | 34.2 | 29.4 | 25.2 | 19.4 |
| U of North Alabama, IIA | 38.7 | 31.9 | 26.8 | 13.8 |
| U of South Alabama, IIA | 37.7 | 30.7 | 27.7 | 22.2 |

### ALASKA

| | Prof | Assoc Prof | Asst Prof | Inst |
|---|---|---|---|---|
| U of Alaska | | | | |
| Anchorage, IIA | 51.8 | 42.4 | 34.0 | — |
| Co-op extension, III | | 49.1 | 44.7 | — |
| Fairbanks, IIA | 57.2 | 47.2 | 38.4 | 31.6 |
| Juneau, IIB | 56.7 | 44.4 | 36.4 | — |

### ARIZONA

| | Prof | Assoc Prof | Asst Prof | Inst |
|---|---|---|---|---|
| American Grad Sch of Internat'l Mgmt, IIB | 39.7 | 32.0 | 27.2 | — |
| Arizona St U, I | 48.8 | 37.5 | 31.1 | 23.8 |
| Grand Canyon C, IIB | 30.6 | 26.4 | 21.6 | 19.0 |
| Northern Arizona U, IIA | 44.3 | 35.1 | 28.0 | 22.1 |
| U of Arizona, I | 49.6 | 36.5 | 30.5 | 25.6 |

### ARKANSAS

| | Prof | Assoc Prof | Asst Prof | Inst |
|---|---|---|---|---|
| Arkansas C, IIB | 33.5 | 28.1 | 24.7 | — |
| Arkansas St U- | | | | |
| Main campus, IIA | 37.1 | 31.3 | 26.1 | 21.0 |
| Beebe, III | | — | 26.4 | 22.6 |
| Arkansas Tech U, IIB | 31.9 | 28.6 | 26.0 | 20.4 |
| C of the Ozarks, IIB | 23.2 | 20.9 | 19.2 | 17.3 |
| Hendrix C, IIB | 34.1 | 29.1 | 24.1 | |
| Ouachita Baptist U, IIA | 32.4 | 26.5 | 22.2 | 19.4 |
| Southern Ark U, IIB | 34.7 | 30.7 | 26.8 | 20.4 |
| U of Arkansas | | | | |
| Fayetteville, I | 42.3 | 32.9 | 27.6 | 20.7 |
| Little Rock, IIA | 41.8 | 33.0 | 27.6 | 23.2 |
| Pine Bluff, IIB | 32.0 | 28.2 | 25.8 | 21.4 |
| U of Central Ark, IIA | 37.7 | 31.5 | 25.2 | 20.1 |

### CALIFORNIA

| | Prof | Assoc Prof | Asst Prof | Inst |
|---|---|---|---|---|
| Azusa Pacific U, IIA | 29.2 | 26.0 | 23.5 | 19.9 |
| Biola U, IIA | 35.3 | 27.2 | 21.9 | 18.2 |
| California Inst of Tech, I | 65.8 | 47.8 | 38.9 | |
| Cal Lutheran C, IIA | 35.5 | 28.1 | 23.5 | 22.0 |
| California St U | | | | |
| Bakersfield, IIA | 48.8 | 37.4 | 29.9 | 26.2 |
| Chico, IIA | 48.9 | 37.4 | 30.7 | 27.3 |
| Dominguez Hills, IIA | 49.0 | 37.4 | 30.5 | — |
| Fresno, IIA | 49.4 | 37.3 | 29.9 | 27.2 |
| Fullerton, IIA | 49.2 | 38.3 | 30.3 | — |
| Hayward, IIA | 49.1 | 38.0 | 30.5 | 27.1 |
| Humboldt St U, IIA | 48.5 | 37.6 | 30.3 | — |
| Long Beach, IIA | 49.4 | 38.5 | 30.9 | 27.0 |
| Los Angeles, IIA | 48.9 | 38.2 | 31.1 | — |
| Northridge, IIA | 49.2 | 37.6 | 30.5 | 26.9 |
| Poly St U- | | | | |
| Pomona, IIA | 49.5 | 37.6 | 30.8 | — |
| San Luis Obispo, IIA | 48.5 | 38.0 | 30.5 | — |
| Sacramento, IIA | 48.9 | 37.5 | 30.1 | — |
| San Bernardino, IIA | 48.2 | 38.8 | 30.5 | — |
| San Diego St U, IIA | 49.0 | 38.3 | 31.3 | 26.5 |
| San Francisco St U, IIA | 48.5 | 37.3 | 30.4 | 26.0 |

### CALIFORNIA—Continued

| | Prof | Assoc Prof | Asst Prof | Inst |
|---|---|---|---|---|
| California St U | | | | |
| San Jose St U, IIA | 49.4 | 37.7 | 31.0 | 26.8 |
| Sonoma St U, IIA | 49.0 | 37.4 | 29.8 | — |
| Stanislaus, IIA | 49.0 | 37.7 | 30.4 | — |
| Chapman C, IIA | 36.9 | 32.1 | 28.0 | — |
| Christ C Irvine, IIB | 35.8 | 29.5 | 23.5 | — |
| Claremont McKenna C, IIB | 48.8 | 35.9 | 29.0 | — |
| C of Notre Dame, IIA | 30.0 | 23.1 | 21.0 | — |
| Fremont-Newark CC Dist, III | 40.7 | 36.9 | 33.0 | 30.6 |
| Golden Gate U, I | 48.4 | 40.1 | 33.9 | |
| Harvey Mudd C, IIB | 53.5 | 40.9 | 31.7 | — |
| Loyola Marymount U, IIA | 49.1 | 39.6 | 28.3 | 23.1 |
| Mennonite Bretheren Bible Sem, IIB | — | 27.7 | — | |
| Mills C, IIA | 44.5 | 33.8 | 28.4 | — |
| Mt Saint Mary's C, IIB | 32.5 | 28.6 | 23.6 | 20.4 |
| Naval Postgrad Sch, I | 46.9 | 36.2 | 30.4 | |
| Occidental C, IIB | 46.0 | 35.2 | 28.5 | 26.7 |
| Pacific Sch of Religion, IIA | 35.5 | — | — | |
| Pacific Union C, IIA | 26.6 | 24.8 | 23.6 | 21.7 |
| Palomar C, III | | 38.0 | | 31.0 |
| Pepperdine U, IIA | 46.2 | 37.8 | 32.2 | — |
| Pitzer C, IIB | 44.6 | — | 26.6 | |
| Point Loma Nazarene C, IIB | 35.4 | 28.4 | 22.5 | — |
| Pomona C, IIB | 52.4 | 37.6 | 29.7 | — |
| Saint Mary's C of Cal, IIA | 42.0 | 32.9 | 26.6 | |
| Santa Clara U, IIA | 58.0 | 40.5 | 32.8 | |
| Scripps C, IIB | 44.1 | 31.8 | 25.1 | — |
| Southern Cal C, IIB | 33.7 | 31.1 | 25.9 | 21.6 |
| Southwestern U, IIB | 52.3 | — | — | |
| Stanford U, I | 67.2 | 46.8 | 36.7 | |
| U of California | | | | |
| Berkeley, I | 64.0 | 42.0 | 36.2 | |
| Davis, I | 56.9 | 38.3 | 34.6 | |
| Irvine, I | 59.4 | 41.0 | 36.3 | |
| Los Angeles, I | 62.3 | 40.4 | 37.4 | |
| Riverside, I | 56.3 | 39.1 | 32.9 | |
| San Diego, I | 60.4 | 41.6 | 34.4 | |
| San Francisco, I | 68.9 | 51.9 | 42.1 | |
| Santa Barbara, I | 58.6 | 40.5 | 34.7 | |
| Santa Cruz, I | 55.7 | 38.7 | 34.2 | |
| U-Wide Services, IIA | 57.9 | 41.6 | | |
| U of La Verne, IIA | 34.3 | 24.5 | 20.8 | — |
| U of the Pacific, IIA | 39.8 | 34.2 | 29.3 | 21.4 |
| U of Redlands, IIA | 40.5 | 31.8 | 28.9 | |
| U of San Diego, IIA | 46.9 | 32.8 | 27.2 | — |
| U of Southern Cal, I | 57.7 | 41.3 | 33.3 | 29.8 |
| Westmont C, IIB | 33.7 | 28.0 | 24.5 | — |
| Whittier C, IIA | 35.1 | 30.1 | 25.1 | 25.5 |

### COLORADO

| | Prof | Assoc Prof | Asst Prof | Inst |
|---|---|---|---|---|
| Adams St C, IIA | 33.8 | 27.6 | 24.7 | 22.8 |
| Colorado C, IIB | 46.5 | 34.3 | 26.9 | — |
| Colorado Mountain C, III | 27.5 | 24.2 | — | — |
| Colorado St U, I | 41.4 | 32.8 | 28.6 | 21.2 |
| Fort Lewis C, IIB | 34.3 | 27.7 | 26.0 | — |
| Iliff Sch of Theol, IIA | 41.5 | 36.9 | — | |
| Mesa C, IIB | 33.1 | 27.9 | 23.3 | 20.5 |
| Metropolitan St C, IIB | 35.1 | 29.3 | 25.5 | 20.3 |
| Regis C, IIB | 32.6 | 27.6 | 21.7 | |
| U of Colorado | | | | |
| Boulder, I | 45.3 | 35.6 | 31.3 | 25.4 |
| Colorado Springs, IIA | 41.8 | 33.2 | 28.3 | — |
| Denver, IIA | 42.0 | 33.3 | 29.8 | 20.2 |
| U of Northern Colo, IIA | 39.5 | 29.4 | 25.0 | 23.3 |
| U of Southern Colo, IIA | 35.9 | 30.9 | 26.0 | 22.5 |
| Western St C of Colo, IIA | 33.2 | 26.0 | 22.3 | — |

### CONNECTICUT

| | Prof | Assoc Prof | Asst Prof | Inst |
|---|---|---|---|---|
| Albertus Magnus C, IIB | 29.7 | 25.5 | 22.4 | — |
| Asnuntuck CC, III | — | — | 27.1 | 22.4 |
| Central Conn St U, IIA | 45.1 | 36.9 | 31.0 | 25.8 |
| Connecticut C, IIA | 42.5 | 34.0 | 25.9 | — |
| Eastern Conn St U, IIB | 44.2 | 35.4 | 27.9 | |
| Fairfield U, IIA | 43.6 | 35.6 | 30.3 | 23.2 |
| Greater Hartford CC, III | 37.0 | 32.1 | 28.3 | 22.8 |
| Housatonic CC, III | 35.5 | 31.6 | 29.8 | — |
| Manchester CC, III | 37.4 | 32.3 | 27.9 | 22.7 |
| Mattatuck CC, III | 35.8 | 32.1 | 28.4 | 23.9 |

### CONNECTICUT—Continued

| | Prof | Assoc Prof | Asst Prof | Inst |
|---|---|---|---|---|
| Middlesex CC, III | 37.2 | 33.0 | 29.6 | 23.8 |
| Mohegan CC, III | 36.9 | 31.1 | 27.3 | 22.5 |
| NW Conn CC, III | 36.7 | 33.0 | 26.1 | — |
| Norwalk CC, III | 37.5 | 32.2 | 27.6 | 23.5 |
| Sacred Heart U, IIB | 37.0 | 29.2 | 24.3 | — |
| Saint Joseph C, IIA | 30.1 | 26.1 | 23.1 | 21.7 |
| South Central CC, III | 29.5 | 31.4 | 29.1 | 23.0 |
| Southern Conn St U, IIA | 44.3 | 36.5 | 31.1 | 24.9 |
| Trinity C, IIA | 49.0 | 36.5 | 27.8 | — |
| Tunxis CC, III | 34.9 | 31.9 | 28.7 | 22.8 |
| U of Bridgeport, IIA | 45.9 | 36.8 | 30.3 | 23.4 |
| U of Connecticut, I | 53.8 | 39.4 | 33.4 | 28.8 |
| U of Hartford, IIA | 39.8 | 32.3 | 26.6 | |
| Wesleyan U, IIA | 50.0 | 35.2 | 28.0 | — |
| Yale U, I | 63.6 | 38.3 | 30.2 | 28.1 |

### DELAWARE

| | Prof | Assoc Prof | Asst Prof | Inst |
|---|---|---|---|---|
| U of Delaware, I | 50.3 | 35.6 | 28.5 | 21.5 |

### DISTRICT OF COLUMBIA

| | Prof | Assoc Prof | Asst Prof | Inst |
|---|---|---|---|---|
| American U, I | 49.9 | 36.9 | 31.0 | 25.6 |
| Catholic U, I | 44.7 | 32.7 | 27.3 | — |
| Corcoran Sch of Art, IIB | — | 23.7 | 20.9 | |
| Gallaudet U, IIA | 44.2 | 36.1 | 28.6 | 21.5 |
| George Washington U, I | 52.6 | 37.9 | 29.9 | 21.6 |
| Georgetown U, I | 60.9 | 41.7 | 29.6 | 25.5 |
| Howard U, I | 44.2 | 33.2 | 27.5 | 23.4 |
| Mount Vernon C, IIB | — | 31.5 | 24.7 | — |
| Trinity C, IIB | 31.9 | 23.7 | 20.1 | — |

### FLORIDA

| | Prof | Assoc Prof | Asst Prof | Inst |
|---|---|---|---|---|
| Barry U, IIA | 35.3 | 29.8 | 25.2 | 20.5 |
| Bethune-Cookman C, IIB | 24.1 | 21.3 | 19.4 | 16.6 |
| Eckerd C, IIB | 36.4 | 29.3 | 24.5 | |
| Embry-Riddle Aeronautical U, IIB | 35.4 | 27.7 | 22.6 | 11.5 |
| Florida A&M U, IIA | 40.3 | 32.1 | 28.6 | 24.1 |
| Florida Atlantic U, IIA | 42.0 | 32.3 | 28.7 | 22.4 |
| Fla International U, IIA | 43.2 | 33.7 | 29.7 | 21.2 |
| Florida Southern C, IIB | 30.7 | 25.5 | 22.5 | — |
| Florida St U, I | 44.2 | 32.0 | 28.0 | 21.6 |
| Indian River CC, III | 36.5 | 32.5 | 27.9 | 26.3 |
| Jacksonville U, IIB | 29.3 | 22.6 | 20.7 | — |
| Miami-Dade CC, III | 32.4 | 27.5 | 23.0 | 18.8 |
| Rollins C, IIB | 41.4 | 31.8 | 25.6 | — |
| Stetson U, IIA | 42.8 | 31.8 | 28.4 | 18.1 |
| U of Central Florida, IIA | 41.6 | 33.4 | 28.5 | 19.9 |
| U of Florida, I | 50.8 | 38.7 | 32.9 | 23.0 |
| U of Miami, I | 48.8 | 36.0 | 29.0 | 24.3 |
| U of North Florida, IIA | 39.8 | 32.1 | 27.9 | — |
| U of South Florida, I | 44.5 | 32.7 | 28.3 | 23.4 |
| U of West Florida, IIA | 40.5 | 32.4 | 27.0 | 21.0 |

### GEORGIA

| | Prof | Assoc Prof | Asst Prof | Inst |
|---|---|---|---|---|
| Agnes Scott C, IIB | 38.5 | 31.1 | 25.2 | — |
| Albany JC, III | 31.8 | 28.4 | 26.3 | — |
| Armstrong St C, IIA | 40.0 | 31.9 | 26.6 | 20.1 |
| Atlanta Christian C, IIB | 24.5 | — | | |
| Atlanta JC, III | — | 29.2 | 26.0 | — |
| Augusta C, IIA | 40.3 | 31.3 | 26.4 | 21.2 |
| Berry C, IIB | 38.1 | 29.9 | 24.5 | — |
| Brunswick JC, III | — | 32.6 | 25.6 | 22.5 |
| Columbus C, IIA | 36.9 | 31.6 | 26.3 | 21.7 |
| Covenant C, IIB | 31.1 | 26.6 | 21.4 | |
| Emanuel County JC, III | | 29.4 | 26.6 | — |
| Floyd JC, III | 36.6 | 27.4 | 24.7 | 20.1 |
| Georgia Inst of Tech, I | 51.5 | 39.0 | 35.5 | 24.1 |
| Georgia Southern C, IIA | 39.5 | 32.9 | 25.5 | 20.7 |
| Ga Southwestern C, IIA | 38.4 | 32.6 | 27.5 | 22.7 |
| Georgia St U, I | 49.7 | 36.8 | 30.0 | 22.4 |
| Kennesaw C, IIB | 41.9 | 34.8 | 28.7 | 22.4 |
| Macon JC, III | 35.1 | 30.0 | 25.3 | 20.9 |
| Mercer U, IIA | 38.7 | 29.6 | 25.2 | 21.7 |
| North Georgia C, IIA | 37.5 | 30.0 | 28.4 | 21.7 |
| Oglethorpe U, IIB | 35.2 | 26.7 | 23.7 | |
| Paine C, IIB | 25.5 | 20.6 | 18.9 | 16.5 |
| Southern Tech Inst, IIA | 35.9 | 32.3 | 28.3 | — |
| U of Georgia, I | 50.7 | 35.3 | 28.8 | 20.8 |
| Valdosta St C, IIA | 38.9 | 32.2 | 27.7 | 21.1 |
| Waycross JC, III | — | — | 27.4 | |
| Wesleyan C, IIB | 29.3 | 25.0 | 22.2 | — |
| West Georgia C, IIA | 39.2 | 31.4 | 27.2 | 20.2 |

### HAWAII

| | Prof | Assoc Prof | Asst Prof | Inst |
|---|---|---|---|---|
| Hawaii Loa C, IIB | — | 22.4 | 20.3 | — |
| U of Hawaii | | | | |
| Hilo, IIB | 38.9 | 31.8 | 25.6 | — |
| Manoa, I | 46.8 | 35.8 | 29.2 | 22.4 |
| West Oahu, IIB | — | 29.2 | | |

### IDAHO

| | Prof | Assoc Prof | Asst Prof | Inst |
|---|---|---|---|---|
| Boise St U, IIA | 33.0 | 28.8 | 24.9 | 21.0 |
| C of Idaho, IIB | 29.0 | 27.3 | 18.4 | — |
| C of Southern Idaho, III | 26.4 | 23.0 | 21.4 | 18.9 |
| Idaho St U, IIA | 33.6 | 28.0 | 24.2 | 22.9 |
| Lewis-Clark St C, IIB | 29.3 | 25.1 | 23.0 | |
| NW Nazarene C, IIB | 27.5 | 22.4 | 20.5 | 17.9 |
| U of Idaho, I | 37.8 | 29.7 | 27.0 | — |

### ILLINOIS

| | Prof | Assoc Prof | Asst Prof | Inst |
|---|---|---|---|---|
| Augustana C, IIB | 40.4 | 32.6 | 26.0 | 22.7 |
| Aurora U, IIB | 29.4 | 27.3 | 24.5 | — |
| Barat C, IIB | 25.9 | — | 19.6 | 13.6 |
| Blackburn U, IIB | 25.6 | | | |
| Bradley U, IIA | 39.2 | 31.1 | 27.4 | 20.2 |
| Chicago St U, IIA | 33.9 | 28.3 | 24.5 | 21.5 |
| Christ Seminary-Seminex, IIB | 33.1 | — | | |
| City C's of Chicago, III | 41.7 | 38.6 | 34.4 | 28.7 |
| C of DuPage, III | 41.3 | 35.9 | 29.6 | 23.6 |
| Concordia C, IIA | 29.8 | 26.0 | 21.3 | — |
| DePaul U, IIA | 45.2 | 35.8 | 29.7 | 22.7 |
| Eastern Illinois U, IIA | 35.5 | 29.8 | 24.9 | 20.2 |
| Elmhurst C, IIB | 37.4 | 30.8 | 25.1 | 21.5 |
| Eureka C, IIB | — | 24.8 | 21.7 | — |
| Garrett-Evangelical Theol Sem, IIA | 35.8 | 32.5 | — | — |
| Greenville C, IIB | 23.6 | 20.5 | 17.6 | |

### ILLINOIS—Continued

| | Prof | Assoc Prof | Asst Prof | Inst |
|---|---|---|---|---|
| Ill Benedictine C, IIA | 34.8 | 28.5 | 25.7 | |
| Illinois Central C, III | 35.6 | 30.2 | 26.8 | 23.6 |
| Illinois C, IIB | 34.3 | 29.4 | 21.4 | — |
| Illinois Inst of Tech, I | 48.4 | 36.6 | 30.7 | 18.3 |
| Illinois St U, IIA | 40.2 | 32.4 | 27.0 | — |
| Illinois Wesleyan U, IIB | 38.0 | 29.5 | 24.8 | 24.1 |
| Judson C, IIB | 28.4 | 26.5 | 20.9 | — |
| Knox C, IIB | 36.4 | 28.8 | 22.4 | |
| Lake Forest C, IIB | 42.1 | 34.5 | 26.1 | 24.3 |
| Lewis and Clark CC, III | 33.9 | 29.4 | 26.3 | 23.4 |
| Lewis U, IIA | 30.5 | 26.3 | 22.4 | 21.7 |
| Loyola U of Chicago, I | 47.7 | 37.0 | 29.6 | 29.3 |
| Lutheran Sch of Theol Chicago, IIA | 35.6 | — | — | |
| MacCormac C, IIB | — | 20.9 | 19.0 | — |
| MacMurray C, IIB | 27.3 | 22.8 | 20.2 | — |
| McKendree C, IIB | 31.8 | 27.2 | 24.9 | 23.4 |
| Mennonite C of Nursing, IIB | | — | — | 21.7 |
| Millikin U, IIB | 38.1 | 29.0 | 24.7 | 19.5 |
| Monmouth C, IIB | 35.1 | 28.7 | 23.4 | — |
| National C of Chiropractic, IIB | 31.4 | 27.3 | 21.9 | 21.0 |
| North Central C, IIB | 37.1 | 30.4 | 25.6 | — |
| North Park C, IIB | 30.3 | 26.1 | 21.4 | 19.0 |
| Northeastern Ill U, IIA | 35.1 | 29.6 | 25.5 | — |
| Northern Illinois U, I | 43.3 | 33.9 | 27.5 | 17.5 |
| Northwestern U, I | 56.7 | 38.4 | 34.4 | |
| Olivet Nazarene C, IIB | 27.3 | 23.7 | 20.7 | 18.7 |
| Parks C of Saint Louis U, IIB | 39.7 | 30.4 | 23.3 | 25.1 |
| Principia C, IIB | 35.3 | 29.5 | 24.3 | 18.5 |
| Quincy C, IIB | 27.2 | 24.9 | 20.2 | — |
| Richland CC, III | 29.6 | 28.2 | 24.6 | — |
| Rockford C, IIB | 32.0 | 25.7 | 22.5 | — |
| Roosevelt U, IIA | 31.6 | 26.9 | 25.0 | — |
| Rosary C, IIA | — | 27.7 | 24.2 | — |
| Saint Xavier C, IIB | 33.8 | 28.6 | 23.2 | 21.6 |
| Sangamon St U, IIA | 38.6 | 33.3 | 28.2 | — |
| Sauk Valley CC, III | 31.5 | 28.3 | 23.7 | 21.3 |
| Sch of Art Inst of Chicago, IIB | 34.4 | 28.8 | 24.1 | |
| Seabury-Western Theol Sem, IIA | 22.7 | — | | — |
| Southern Illinois U | | | | |
| Carbondale, I | 43.3 | 33.3 | 28.2 | 23.4 |
| Edwardsville, IIA | 39.3 | 33.2 | 28.9 | 22.8 |
| Trinity Christian C, IIB | 31.3 | — | 25.7 | — |
| Trinity C, IIB | — | 23.4 | 21.0 | — |
| Trinity Evangelical Divinity Sch, IIA | 36.8 | 30.6 | 28.4 | — |
| U of Chicago, I | 59.4 | 39.0 | 34.0 | 24.5 |
| U of Illinois | | | | |
| Chicago, I | 50.8 | 36.2 | 31.4 | 23.5 |
| Urbana-Champaign, I | 54.0 | 38.0 | 33.1 | — |

### ILLINOIS—Continued

| | Prof | Assoc Prof | Asst Prof | Inst |
|---|---|---|---|---|
| U of Saint Mary of the Lake, IIB | 10.4 | | — | 8.7 |
| Western Illinois U, IIA | 36.4 | 31.8 | 27.8 | 17.7 |
| Wheaton C, IIA | 37.4 | 31.5 | 27.0 | |

### INDIANA

| | Prof | Assoc Prof | Asst Prof | Inst |
|---|---|---|---|---|
| Ball St U, I | 39.4 | 32.0 | 25.6 | 17.5 |
| Butler U, IIA | 36.5 | 30.7 | 24.5 | 23.5 |
| Calumet C, IIB | 22.3 | — | 16.1 | — |
| DePauw U, IIB | 41.0 | 32.5 | 25.3 | |
| Earlham C, IIB | 38.7 | 31.1 | 24.7 | |
| Fort Wayne Bible C, IIB | — | 20.8 | 18.3 | |
| Franklin C of Indiana, IIB | 26.5 | 24.2 | 21.5 | — |
| Hanover C, IIB | 39.7 | 29.0 | 24.0 | 21.8 |
| Huntington C, IIB | 29.3 | 24.5 | 20.0 | 17.2 |
| Indiana St U, I | 38.7 | 30.4 | 25.1 | 19.2 |
| Indiana U | | | | |
| Bloomington, I | 48.7 | 34.5 | 29.2 | — |
| East, III | — | 28.4 | 22.8 | |
| Indianapolis, IIA | 44.6 | 33.1 | 28.0 | — |
| Kokomo, IIB | 34.5 | 30.3 | 25.4 | |
| Northwest, IIA | 42.1 | 32.2 | 26.0 | — |
| Purdue U Ft Wayne, IIA | 38.9 | 31.2 | 24.8 | 16.6 |
| South Bend, IIA | 37.7 | 32.0 | 24.2 | — |
| Southeast, IIB | 38.0 | 29.1 | 25.0 | |
| Manchester C, IIB | 30.8 | 26.3 | 22.3 | — |
| Marion C, IIB | 26.5 | 21.9 | 18.7 | — |
| Oakland City C, IIB | 20.2 | 18.8 | 18.0 | 16.3 |
| Purdue U | | | | |
| Main campus, I | 52.0 | 36.4 | 30.6 | 20.7 |
| Calumet, IIA | 41.1 | 32.6 | 27.0 | 20.4 |
| North Central, III | 36.6 | 31.0 | 24.5 | — |
| Rose-Hulman Inst of Tech, IIA | 42.8 | 36.9 | 30.4 | |
| Saint Joseph's C, IIB | 27.6 | 24.4 | 22.5 | — |
| Saint Mary's C, IIB | 41.5 | 33.0 | 25.4 | — |
| Saint Meinrad C, IIB | — | — | 25.9 | |
| Taylor U, IIB | 28.6 | 24.8 | 21.6 | — |
| Tri-State U, IIB | 32.3 | 26.4 | 23.2 | |
| U of Evansville, IIA | 34.1 | 29.0 | 24.9 | — |
| U of Indianapolis, IIA | 34.8 | 28.3 | 23.9 | — |
| U of Notre Dame, I | 56.0 | 40.6 | 33.7 | 32.2 |
| U of Southern Ind, IIA | 36.9 | 31.1 | 26.2 | 21.0 |
| Valparaiso U, IIA | 38.4 | 30.5 | 25.9 | 19.7 |
| Vincennes U, III | 32.0 | 26.1 | 21.9 | 19.1 |
| Wabash C, IIB | 44.5 | 32.9 | 26.0 | — |

### IOWA

| | Prof | Assoc Prof | Asst Prof | Inst |
|---|---|---|---|---|
| Briar Cliff C, IIB | 29.2 | 25.9 | 22.3 | 19.5 |
| Buena Vista C, IIB | 37.2 | 29.7 | 25.0 | — |
| Central U of Iowa, IIB | 36.1 | 30.3 | 25.6 | 22.5 |
| Clarke C, IIB | 27.3 | 26.3 | 20.0 | 19.2 |
| Coe C, IIB | 35.0 | 26.9 | 21.5 | — |

*Continued on Following Page*

Table 2.1

## IOWA—Continued

| | Prof | Assoc Prof | Asst Prof | Inst |
|---|---|---|---|---|
| Cornell C, IIB | 35.7 | 28.4 | 24.0 | — |
| Dordt C, IIB | 29.5 | 26.3 | 23.0 | 22.0 |
| Graceland C, IIB | 24.7 | 21.4 | 19.5 | — |
| Grinnell C, IIB | 45.8 | 33.1 | 25.6 | 24.7 |
| Iowa St U, I | 43.9 | 33.3 | 27.9 | 19.6 |
| Iowa Wesleyan C, IIB | 20.3 | 17.3 | 15.3 | 14.9 |
| Loras C, IIA | 31.4 | 25.9 | 22.5 | 18.5 |
| Luther C, IIB | 34.4 | 28.8 | 23.2 | 20.5 |
| Morningside C, IIB | 27.8 | 23.4 | 20.7 | 18.9 |
| Mount Mercy C, IIB | 26.4 | 23.2 | 22.7 | 17.9 |
| Northwestern C, IIB | 29.2 | 25.0 | 22.4 | — |
| Palmer C of Chiropractic, IIB | 35.7 | 29.1 | 23.4 | 19.4 |
| Saint Ambrose C, IIB | 31.6 | 29.2 | 25.6 | 21.6 |
| Simpson C, IIB | 34.8 | 28.0 | 25.4 | 22.6 |
| U of Iowa, I | 46.3 | 35.3 | 29.4 | 29.0 |
| U of Northern Iowa, IIA | 37.4 | 30.7 | 26.2 | 21.5 |
| Upper Iowa U, IIB | — | 22.8 | 18.7 | 17.0 |
| Waldorf C, III | 26.4 | 23.4 | 20.4 | — |
| Wartburg C, IIB | 32.5 | 27.3 | 22.6 | 17.1 |
| Westmar C, IIB | — | — | 18.8 | 18.9 |

## KANSAS

| | Prof | Assoc Prof | Asst Prof | Inst |
|---|---|---|---|---|
| Baker U, IIB | 26.5 | 22.2 | 19.6 | |
| Benedictine C, IIB | 27.1 | 23.6 | 20.0 | 17.1 |
| Bethany C, IIB | 29.2 | 25.1 | 21.3 | — |
| Bethel C, IIB | 25.2 | 23.4 | 20.4 | — |
| Emporia St U, IIA | 34.2 | 29.2 | 25.9 | — |
| Fort Hays St U, IIA | 33.5 | 27.8 | 24.3 | 20.4 |
| Friends U, IIB | 24.6 | 21.3 | 20.0 | — |
| Kansas St U, I | 40.3 | 30.6 | 27.1 | 21.2 |
| Kansas Tech Inst, III | 30.4 | 28.9 | 25.8 | — |
| Kansas Wesleyan U, IIB | 22.0 | 18.1 | 16.6 | — |
| Marymount C of Kan, IIB | — | 20.2 | 18.5 | — |
| Ottawa U, IIB | 25.1 | 22.8 | 19.5 | — |
| Pittsburg St U, IIA | 33.7 | 30.2 | 25.0 | 20.2 |
| Saint Mary C, IIB | 25.9 | 23.3 | 18.6 | 16.2 |
| Tabor C, IIB | 26.0 | 21.9 | 19.3 | — |
| U of Kansas, I | 42.8 | 31.5 | 28.6 | 19.1 |
| Wichita St U, IIA | 41.3 | 31.5 | 26.1 | 19.9 |

## KENTUCKY

| | Prof | Assoc Prof | Asst Prof | Inst |
|---|---|---|---|---|
| Asbury C, IIB | 26.8 | 22.5 | 19.0 | 16.5 |
| Asbury Theol Sem, IIA | 31.0 | 27.8 | — | — |
| Bellarmine C, IIB | 36.1 | 28.9 | 23.9 | — |
| Berea C, IIB | 35.0 | 28.4 | 23.6 | 19.0 |
| Centre C of Ky, IIB | 36.4 | 28.9 | 24.3 | — |
| Eastern Kentucky U, IIA | 34.1 | 29.3 | 25.3 | 20.0 |
| Georgetown C, IIB | 29.5 | 25.5 | 21.5 | 17.6 |
| Ky Christian C, IIB | 23.6 | — | — | |
| Kentucky St U, IIA | 32.2 | 27.8 | 24.4 | 21.3 |
| Lees C, III | 20.6 | — | 18.0 | |
| Morehead St U, IIA | 34.8 | 28.5 | 25.1 | 20.0 |
| Murray St U, IIA | 35.0 | 30.1 | 25.7 | 21.3 |
| Northern Kentucky U, IIA | 37.0 | 30.8 | 23.9 | 22.4 |
| Pikeville C, IIB | — | 22.5 | 20.4 | 17.0 |
| Spalding U, IIB | 27.8 | 22.5 | 22.3 | 18.4 |
| Thomas More C, IIB | 28.6 | 23.1 | 19.9 | — |
| Transylvania U, IIB | 32.7 | 27.8 | 25.9 | — |
| U of Kentucky, I | 45.4 | 33.7 | 28.7 | 28.9 |
| U of Kentucky CC, III | 30.5 | 25.1 | 20.9 | 19.8 |
| U of Louisville, IIA | 43.3 | 32.5 | 26.9 | 21.3 |
| Western Kentucky U, IIA | 35.3 | 29.3 | 25.6 | 20.1 |

## LOUISIANA

| | Prof | Assoc Prof | Asst Prof | Inst |
|---|---|---|---|---|
| Centenary C of La, IIB | 33.5 | 29.0 | 23.8 | 19.0 |
| Grambling St U, IIA | 30.7 | 29.3 | 25.2 | 20.0 |
| Louisiana C, IIB | 28.5 | 24.7 | 23.2 | — |
| Louisiana St U | | | | |
| A&M C, I | 44.9 | 34.0 | 29.0 | 20.3 |
| Alexandria, III | 30.8 | 26.1 | 22.0 | 18.9 |
| Eunice, III | — | 27.1 | 24.2 | 20.9 |
| Shreveport, IIA | 34.5 | 30.9 | 26.0 | 22.5 |
| Louisiana Tech U, IIA | 35.1 | 29.1 | 25.7 | 21.7 |
| Loyola U, IIA | 43.4 | 35.5 | 29.1 | 22.6 |
| McNeese St U, IIA | 33.2 | 30.1 | 25.7 | 22.0 |
| Nicholls St U, IIA | 33.1 | 28.8 | 24.9 | 21.0 |
| Northeast La U, IIA | 36.7 | 30.8 | 26.0 | 19.6 |
| Our Lady of Holy Cross C, IIB | — | 21.9 | 19.9 | 23.5 |
| Southeastern La U, IIA | 33.2 | 30.0 | 25.4 | 20.1 |
| Southern U A&M C, IIA | 33.1 | 28.2 | 23.9 | 19.4 |
| Tulane U, I | 48.3 | 36.2 | 29.7 | 20.4 |
| U of New Orleans, IIA | 38.9 | 30.8 | 25.2 | 19.2 |
| U of SW Louisiana, IIA | 38.2 | 31.3 | 27.0 | 21.7 |
| Xavier U of La, IIB | 26.0 | 23.1 | 20.3 | 18.2 |

## MAINE

| | Prof | Assoc Prof | Asst Prof | Inst |
|---|---|---|---|---|
| Bates C, IIB | 46.5 | 35.4 | 25.4 | 25.5 |
| Bowdoin C, IIB | 50.0 | 35.9 | 27.8 | — |
| Colby C, IIB | 49.7 | 35.6 | 26.8 | 25.6 |
| Husson C, IIB | 30.8 | 27.7 | 25.4 | — |
| Saint Joseph's C, IIB | — | — | 19.0 | — |
| U of Maine | | | | |
| Augusta, III | 31.6 | 24.3 | 20.0 | — |
| Farmington, IIB | 34.6 | 27.4 | 22.7 | 20.0 |
| Fort Kent, IIB | — | 27.1 | 23.0 | — |
| Machias, IIB | 31.4 | 28.9 | 20.8 | |
| Orono, IIA | 40.0 | 30.6 | 25.2 | 13.6 |
| Presque Isle, IIB | 34.3 | 28.0 | 21.8 | |
| U of Southern Maine, IIA | 39.2 | 31.4 | 25.0 | 18.5 |

## MARYLAND

| | Prof | Assoc Prof | Asst Prof | Inst |
|---|---|---|---|---|
| Allegany CC, III | 31.8 | 25.9 | 22.0 | 20.4 |
| Anne Arundel CC, III | 41.1 | 35.0 | 28.2 | 24.6 |
| Bowie St C, IIB | 41.6 | 35.3 | 28.3 | 20.6 |
| Capitol Inst of Tech, IIB | — | 26.4 | 21.6 | |
| Catonsville CC, III | 42.5 | 35.4 | 29.7 | 23.4 |
| Cecil CC, III | 33.4 | — | 25.5 | 19.1 |
| Charles County CC, III | 35.9 | 32.7 | 24.7 | — |
| Chesapeake C, III | — | 28.2 | 23.0 | — |
| C of Notre Dame of Maryland, IIB | 31.1 | 26.0 | 24.2 | — |
| Columbia Union C, IIB | 23.7 | 22.8 | 21.1 | 18.3 |
| CC of Baltimore, III | 35.2 | 29.2 | 25.6 | 21.4 |
| Coppin St C, IIB | 40.9 | 32.4 | 27.2 | 23.0 |
| Dundalk CC, III | 38.5 | 29.4 | 30.3 | — |
| Essex CC, III | 43.4 | 33.9 | 28.9 | 22.2 |
| Frederick CC, III | 39.4 | 29.5 | 23.7 | — |
| Frostburg St C, IIA | 39.1 | 31.5 | 27.5 | 23.7 |
| Garrett CC, III | — | — | 20.9 | — |
| Goucher C, IIB | 37.0 | 28.0 | 23.6 | 19.8 |
| Hagerstown JC, III | 32.5 | 28.9 | 22.5 | — |
| Harford CC, III | 39.0 | 34.9 | 31.1 | 22.1 |
| Hood C, IIA | 38.2 | 30.4 | 25.1 | 20.6 |
| Howard CC, III | 39.2 | 33.6 | 26.5 | 20.6 |
| Johns Hopkins U, I | 59.8 | 40.5 | 33.5 | 26.8 |
| Peabody Inst, IIB | 30.2 | | | |
| Loyola C, IIA | 42.5 | 36.1 | 28.9 | — |
| Montgomery C, III | 39.7 | 31.2 | 26.9 | 23.3 |
| Morgan St U, IIA | 45.6 | 35.9 | 30.7 | 24.6 |
| Mount Saint Mary's C, IIB | 37.2 | 29.5 | 23.1 | — |
| Prince George's CC, III | 38.9 | 33.6 | 26.5 | — |

## MARYLAND—Continued

| | Prof | Assoc Prof | Asst Prof | Inst |
|---|---|---|---|---|
| Saint Mary's C of Md, IIB | 41.4 | 32.6 | 25.0 | 22.1 |
| Salisbury St C, IIA | 39.8 | 31.5 | 25.8 | 21.5 |
| Towson St U, IIA | 41.9 | 35.4 | 28.3 | 22.2 |
| U of Baltimore, IIA | 47.4 | 39.4 | 31.4 | — |
| U of Maryland | | | | |
| Baltimore City, I | 55.3 | 43.9 | 32.6 | 24.2 |
| Baltimore County, IIA | 51.5 | 36.6 | 30.6 | 22.2 |
| College Park, I | 52.8 | 38.0 | 31.2 | 23.2 |
| Eastern Shore, IIA | — | 35.4 | 33.2 | 27.7 |
| Washington Bible C, IIB | — | 20.9 | — | |
| Washington C, IIB | 36.0 | 30.3 | 23.2 | |
| Western Maryland C, IIA | 36.9 | 30.6 | 26.6 | — |
| Wor-Wic Tech CC, III | — | 30.0 | 26.2 | 22.6 |

## MASSACHUSETTS

| | Prof | Assoc Prof | Asst Prof | Inst |
|---|---|---|---|---|
| Amherst C, IIB | 52.2 | 37.3 | 29.8 | |
| Andover Newton Theol Sch, IIA | 32.5 | — | — | |
| Anna Maria C, IIB | — | 27.9 | 23.9 | — |
| Assumption C, IIB | 38.0 | 31.2 | 26.6 | — |
| Babson C, IIB | 57.1 | 44.5 | 36.6 | — |
| Berklee C of Music, IIB | 33.6 | 27.8 | 22.9 | 18.7 |
| Boston C, I | 51.9 | 38.6 | 31.5 | 27.6 |
| Brandeis U, I | 52.4 | 37.8 | 29.5 | — |
| Bridgewater St C, IIA | 39.0 | 34.6 | 30.2 | 23.7 |
| Bristol CC, III | 35.0 | 29.6 | 26.3 | 22.3 |
| Bunker Hill CC, III | 34.1 | 29.6 | 25.8 | 21.9 |
| Cape Cod CC, III | 35.9 | 30.2 | 27.5 | 24.7 |
| Chamberlayne JC, III | — | — | 21.5 | — |
| Clark U, IIA | 48.5 | 36.2 | 29.3 | — |
| C of Our Lady of the Elms, IIB | — | 25.7 | 23.4 | — |
| C of the Holy Cross, IIB | 46.2 | 34.8 | 27.1 | 22.8 |
| Dean JC, III | 30.9 | 30.1 | 21.5 | 18.2 |
| Emerson C, IIA | 48.6 | 38.0 | 30.0 | — |
| Emmanuel C, IIB | 34.5 | 28.2 | 24.2 | 20.3 |
| Episcopal Divinity Sch, IIB | 22.5 | | — | |
| Fitchburg St C, IIB | 38.5 | 33.7 | 29.1 | 24.2 |
| Gordon C, IIB | 32.4 | 27.7 | 23.1 | — |
| Gordon-Conwell Theol Sem, IIA | 35.9 | 31.3 | 24.0 | |
| Hampshire C, IIB | 40.5 | 32.2 | 26.5 | |
| Harvard U, I | 69.7 | 36.9 | 34.0 | 19.8 |
| Mass Inst of Tech, I | 62.4 | 43.9 | 35.7 | 25.9 |
| Merrimack C, IIB | 39.0 | 32.6 | 26.1 | |
| Mount Holyoke C, IIB | 45.9 | 34.0 | 26.7 | 21.6 |
| North Shore CC, III | 36.6 | 29.5 | 25.2 | 21.7 |
| Northeastern U, I | 49.5 | 37.9 | 31.8 | 22.2 |
| Regis C, IIB | 35.3 | 29.4 | 25.2 | — |
| Roxbury CC, III | 34.8 | 30.6 | 24.8 | 20.4 |
| Simmons C, IIA | 46.7 | 36.0 | 29.8 | 26.4 |
| Smith C, IIA | 50.6 | 36.6 | 28.6 | 21.3 |
| Southeastern Mass U, IIA | 42.0 | 34.6 | 30.4 | — |
| Springfield C, IIA | 36.8 | 29.2 | 23.3 | 17.3 |
| Springfield Tech CC, III | 35.6 | 30.5 | 27.0 | 23.5 |
| Stonehill C, IIB | 35.8 | 29.4 | 25.2 | |
| Suffolk U, IIA | 48.4 | 38.5 | 29.7 | 25.8 |
| Tufts U, I | 51.2 | 38.1 | 32.1 | |
| U of Massachusetts | | | | |
| Amherst, I | 52.6 | 41.3 | 32.4 | 29.3 |
| Boston, IIA | 51.0 | 42.0 | 34.5 | — |
| Wellesley C, IIB | 54.9 | 37.8 | 31.7 | 25.9 |
| W New England C, IIA | 45.9 | 35.1 | 30.0 | 23.7 |
| Wheaton C, IIB | 44.4 | 33.6 | 26.4 | — |
| Wheelock C, IIB | 37.2 | 28.8 | 22.8 | 22.0 |
| Williams C, IIB | 52.2 | 36.3 | 29.3 | |
| Worcester Poly Inst, IIA | 48.7 | 38.6 | 34.3 | |

## MICHIGAN

| | Prof | Assoc Prof | Asst Prof | Inst |
|---|---|---|---|---|
| Adrian C, IIB | 31.4 | 24.8 | 20.8 | — |
| Albion C, IIB | 39.8 | 31.8 | 25.5 | 20.2 |
| Alma C, IIB | 36.5 | 29.9 | 24.0 | — |
| Aquinas C, IIB | 32.4 | 29.6 | 22.8 | — |
| Calvin C, IIB | 34.8 | 30.2 | 25.8 | 21.8 |
| Central Michigan U, IIA | 41.4 | 34.8 | 28.9 | 22.8 |
| Concordia C, IIB | 28.4 | 24.7 | 21.7 | — |
| Eastern Michigan U, IIA | 39.1 | 33.9 | 28.5 | 25.1 |
| Ferris St C, IIB | 37.1 | 31.8 | 28.2 | 25.0 |
| Grand Rapids Baptist C, IIB | 25.8 | 22.8 | 19.1 | |
| Grand Valley St C, IIA | 39.4 | 33.2 | 25.9 | — |
| Hope C, IIB | 35.2 | 30.9 | 24.1 | 20.9 |
| Jordan C, IIB | — | | 18.8 | 15.1 |
| Kalamazoo C, IIB | 38.1 | 28.9 | 25.7 | — |
| Lake Superior St C, IIB | 35.3 | 31.2 | 26.7 | 22.5 |
| Madonna C, IIB | 34.3 | 27.1 | 23.1 | 21.4 |
| Marygrove C, IIA | 28.0 | 23.4 | 18.9 | 16.5 |
| Mercy C of Detroit, IIB | 31.5 | 25.4 | 21.0 | 18.6 |
| Michigan St U, I | 46.1 | 34.8 | 29.7 | 22.8 |
| Michigan Tech U, IIA | 49.2 | 36.4 | 30.5 | 22.8 |
| Nazareth C, IIB | — | 26.3 | 21.6 | 19.7 |
| Northern Michigan U, IIA | 39.5 | 33.0 | 25.2 | 21.4 |
| Northwestern Mich C, III | 36.8 | 30.3 | 26.1 | 21.9 |
| Oakland U, IIA | 43.9 | 34.4 | 29.7 | 27.2 |
| Olivet C, IIB | 27.6 | 23.6 | 18.4 | — |
| Siena Heights C, IIB | | 24.7 | 23.4 | — |
| Spring Arbor C, IIB | 25.8 | 23.2 | 20.4 | — |
| U of Detroit, I | 37.4 | 33.2 | 27.2 | 19.6 |
| U of Michigan | | | | |
| Ann Arbor, I | 55.9 | 41.8 | 34.7 | 23.6 |
| Dearborn, IIA | 40.7 | 30.9 | 27.9 | |
| Flint, IIA | 41.5 | 34.1 | 27.2 | — |
| Wayne St U, I | 42.2 | 36.7 | 31.3 | 23.1 |
| Western Michigan U, I | 41.1 | 33.4 | 28.0 | 20.7 |

## MINNESOTA

| | Prof | Assoc Prof | Asst Prof | Inst |
|---|---|---|---|---|
| Augsburg C, IIB | 29.1 | 24.4 | 21.5 | 17.7 |
| Bemidji St U, IIA | 39.7 | 31.5 | 24.6 | 18.9 |
| Bethel C, IIB | 32.2 | 26.8 | 22.9 | 20.6 |
| Carleton C, IIB | 45.7 | 36.6 | 27.7 | 23.6 |
| C of Saint Benedict, IIB | 36.1 | 28.7 | 24.4 | 20.9 |
| C of Saint Catherine, IIB | 35.1 | 29.3 | 24.5 | 21.1 |
| C of Saint Scholastica, IIB | — | 27.1 | 24.1 | 22.5 |
| C of Saint Thomas, IIA | 42.9 | 34.2 | 28.3 | 22.5 |
| Concordia C Moorhead, IIB | 36.6 | 30.3 | 24.3 | 18.9 |
| Gustavus Adolphus C, IIB | 37.7 | 31.0 | 25.2 | 21.4 |
| Hamline U, IIB | 32.3 | 25.6 | 22.6 | |
| Macalester C, IIB | 44.6 | 32.6 | 25.9 | 22.7 |
| Metropolitan St U, IIB | 40.5 | 34.7 | 28.1 | |
| Minneapolis C of Art & Design, IIB | 32.2 | 26.8 | 21.9 | 17.2 |
| Minnesota Bible C, IIB | 29.8 | | | |
| Moorhead St U, IIA | 42.1 | 33.8 | 27.3 | 20.7 |
| Northwestern C, IIB | 30.7 | 25.4 | 22.7 | — |
| Saint Cloud St U, IIA | 42.2 | 32.5 | 27.6 | 19.7 |
| Saint John's U, IIB | 40.1 | 33.4 | 26.7 | 21.8 |
| Saint Mary's C, IIA | 34.8 | 27.5 | 23.2 | — |
| Saint Olaf C, IIB | 40.7 | 32.2 | 25.3 | 22.2 |
| Saint Paul Bible C, IIB | — | 25.0 | 21.9 | 18.7 |
| Southwest St U, IIB | 42.6 | 33.9 | 27.7 | — |

## MINNESOTA—Continued

| | Prof | Assoc Prof | Asst Prof | Inst |
|---|---|---|---|---|
| U of Minnesota | | | | |
| Duluth, IIA | 44.4 | 34.9 | 28.3 | 23.5 |
| Morris, IIB | 42.3 | 32.1 | 26.6 | 22.8 |
| Twin Cities, I | 50.2 | 36.4 | 31.3 | 24.8 |
| Tech C Crookston, III | — | 32.6 | 28.4 | 23.3 |
| Tech C Waseca, III | — | 30.9 | 27.9 | — |

## MISSISSIPPI

| | Prof | Assoc Prof | Asst Prof | Inst |
|---|---|---|---|---|
| Alcorn St U, IIB | 29.6 | 25.2 | 20.5 | 16.2 |
| Delta St U, IIA | 32.5 | 27.5 | 23.1 | 19.2 |
| Millsaps C, IIB | 35.2 | 28.5 | 24.2 | — |
| Mississippi St U, I | 39.5 | 31.2 | 26.3 | 19.8 |
| Miss U for Women, IIA | 30.5 | 24.3 | 23.0 | 19.8 |
| Miss Valley St U, IIB | 28.4 | 24.9 | 21.2 | 17.3 |
| Reformed Theol Sem, IIB | 34.1 | — | — | |
| U of Mississippi, I | 38.6 | 30.6 | 25.0 | 18.7 |
| U of Southern Miss, I | 40.4 | 31.6 | 26.7 | 19.9 |

## MISSOURI

| | Prof | Assoc Prof | Asst Prof | Inst |
|---|---|---|---|---|
| Avila C, IIB | 29.1 | 26.7 | 21.0 | 21.2 |
| Central Bible C, IIB | — | 23.6 | 19.6 | 16.0 |
| Central Methodist C, IIB | 27.2 | 25.1 | 22.4 | 18.5 |
| Central Missouri State U, IIA | 36.4 | 31.5 | 26.4 | 20.4 |
| Columbia C, IIB | 23.5 | 22.9 | 19.6 | 17.6 |
| Concordia Sem, IIA | 29.2 | 26.1 | 21.5 | |
| Culver-Stockton C, IIB | 32.0 | 23.8 | 20.1 | — |
| Drury C, IIB | 33.3 | 30.9 | 22.9 | 19.8 |
| Evangel C, IIB | 27.7 | 25.5 | 20.8 | 16.0 |
| Fontbonne C, IIB | 19.0 | 18.3 | 14.8 | — |
| Hannibal-LaGrange C, III | — | — | 20.0 | 17.6 |
| Harris-Stowe St C, IIB | 31.3 | 25.3 | 26.0 | — |
| Kansas City Art Inst, IIB | 31.7 | 25.6 | — | |
| Lincoln U, IIA | 30.9 | 26.9 | 22.8 | 19.5 |
| Lindenwood C, IIA | 28.7 | 23.7 | 21.1 | — |
| Maryville C, IIB | 30.2 | 24.1 | 19.0 | — |
| Missouri Baptist C, IIB | — | — | 16.2 | — |
| Mo Southern St C, IIB | 37.8 | 32.0 | 27.1 | 22.9 |
| Mo Western St C, IIB | 35.6 | 31.3 | 26.1 | 21.0 |
| Northeast Mo St U, IIA | 39.1 | 32.8 | 27.3 | 22.9 |
| Northwest Mo St U, IIA | 38.3 | 32.4 | 25.8 | 22.0 |
| Park C, IIB | 25.7 | 20.2 | 16.5 | |
| Rockhurst C, IIB | 36.4 | 28.8 | 25.3 | 21.8 |
| St Louis CC | | | | |
| Florissant Valley, III | 39.5 | 32.7 | 26.4 | — |
| Forest Park, III | 38.7 | 33.1 | 26.0 | 22.4 |
| Meramec, III | 37.9 | 32.4 | 25.8 | 22.2 |
| Saint Louis U, I | 45.1 | 32.7 | 27.4 | 23.3 |
| Sch of the Ozarks, IIB | 28.7 | 24.0 | 21.3 | |
| Southeast Mo St U, IIA | 37.8 | 32.1 | 27.3 | 23.0 |
| Southwest Baptist U, IIB | 28.2 | 21.2 | 20.3 | 20.1 |
| Southwest Mo St U, IIA | 39.7 | 33.5 | 28.0 | 21.4 |
| Tarkio C, IIB | — | 22.1 | 21.0 | 17.5 |
| U of Missouri | | | | |
| Columbia, I | 41.6 | 32.0 | 28.6 | 20.9 |
| Kansas City, I | 40.9 | 32.2 | 27.6 | 18.8 |
| Rolla, IIA | 44.3 | 35.2 | 31.3 | — |
| St Louis, IIA | 42.1 | 32.6 | 27.5 | 29.6 |
| Washington U, I | 51.2 | 37.1 | 29.7 | 21.2 |
| Westminster C, IIB | 32.9 | 27.0 | 23.1 | — |
| William Jewell C, IIB | 31.3 | 26.5 | 22.5 | 19.8 |

## MONTANA

| | Prof | Assoc Prof | Asst Prof | Inst |
|---|---|---|---|---|
| Carroll C, IIB | 30.9 | 25.9 | 21.6 | |
| C of Great Falls, IIB | 24.8 | 20.9 | 19.4 | — |
| Eastern Montana C, IIA | 31.3 | 27.4 | 23.3 | 20.0 |
| Montana C of Mineral Science & Tech, IIB | 39.3 | 31.3 | 25.8 | 21.4 |
| Montana St U, IIA | 38.5 | 30.9 | 26.1 | 20.4 |
| Northern Montana C, IIA | 31.5 | 27.7 | 24.9 | 20.3 |
| Rocky Mountain C, IIB | 28.8 | 23.9 | 20.0 | — |
| U of Montana, I | 33.7 | 27.5 | 24.3 | 20.2 |
| Western Montana C, IIA | 32.6 | 26.1 | 21.8 | |

## NEBRASKA

| | Prof | Assoc Prof | Asst Prof | Inst |
|---|---|---|---|---|
| Bellevue C, IIB | — | 23.1 | 20.4 | |
| Chadron St C, IIA | 34.6 | 27.1 | 22.8 | 18.9 |
| C of Saint Mary, IIB | — | 24.2 | 22.5 | 20.2 |
| Concordia Teachers C, IIA | 24.5 | 22.3 | 17.6 | — |
| Creighton U, IIA | 44.3 | 33.1 | 26.2 | 20.8 |
| Dana C, IIB | 23.9 | 21.2 | 19.6 | — |
| Doane C, IIB | 29.9 | 25.5 | 21.5 | — |
| Hastings C, IIB | 29.7 | 25.7 | 22.2 | 17.9 |
| Kearney St C, IIA | 34.6 | 28.5 | 23.6 | 19.0 |
| Midland Lutheran C, IIB | 27.5 | 24.1 | 22.5 | 20.1 |
| Neb Wesleyan U, IIB | 33.0 | 27.3 | 24.1 | — |
| Peru St C, IIB | 32.3 | 25.7 | 23.2 | 19.7 |
| Union C, IIB | 22.2 | 22.9 | 21.7 | 22.0 |
| U of Nebraska | | | | |
| Lincoln, I | 40.1 | 30.3 | 26.6 | 17.9 |
| Omaha, IIA | 34.4 | 27.6 | 24.1 | 22.6 |
| Wayne St C, IIA | 34.9 | 28.0 | 23.4 | 19.6 |
| York C, III | — | 23.5 | — | — |

## NEVADA

| | Prof | Assoc Prof | Asst Prof | Inst |
|---|---|---|---|---|
| U of Nevada | | | | |
| Reno, I | 44.6 | 35.7 | 29.5 | — |
| Las Vegas, IIA | 45.0 | 36.7 | 30.9 | 27.3 |

## NEW HAMPSHIRE

| | Prof | Assoc Prof | Asst Prof | Inst |
|---|---|---|---|---|
| Colby-Sawyer C, IIB | 27.7 | 22.0 | 20.3 | — |
| Dartmouth C, IIA | 52.7 | 37.5 | 30.5 | 22.5 |
| Franklin Pierce C, IIB | 30.8 | 27.7 | 22.1 | — |
| Franklin Pierce Law Center, IIB | 51.3 | | — | |
| NH Voc Tech C | | | | |
| Claremont, III | 25.6 | 20.9 | 19.0 | — |
| Laconia, III | 26.5 | 22.0 | — | |
| Manchester, III | 25.4 | 21.6 | — | |
| Stratham, III | 24.7 | 21.0 | — | |
| Plymouth St C, IIA | 36.7 | 29.6 | 25.4 | — |
| U of New Hampshire, I | 43.4 | 33.3 | 27.8 | — |

## NEW JERSEY

| | Prof | Assoc Prof | Asst Prof | Inst |
|---|---|---|---|---|
| Atlantic CC, III | 38.8 | 34.0 | 28.3 | — |
| Caldwell C, III | 28.5 | 23.9 | 16.8 | — |
| Centenary C, IIB | — | 22.8 | 19.7 | — |
| C of Saint Elizabeth, IIB | 30.4 | 26.5 | 21.5 | 18.5 |
| County C of Morris, III | 42.0 | 35.1 | 28.4 | 24.6 |
| Cumberland County C, III | — | 34.4 | 32.5 | 27.4 |
| Drew U, I | 43.7 | 32.9 | 26.2 | 22.8 |
| Fairleigh Dickinson U, IIA | 42.2 | 34.4 | 28.9 | 22.9 |
| Felician C, IIB | 23.9 | 20.8 | 19.7 | 17.7 |
| Georgian Court C, IIB | 30.7 | 31.2 | 25.9 | 20.7 |
| Hudson County CC, III | — | 26.2 | 22.3 | 18.0 |
| Kean C of NJ, IIA | 47.5 | 35.4 | 29.6 | 22.2 |
| Monmouth C, IIA | 41.9 | 34.8 | 28.3 | — |

## NEW JERSEY—Continued

| | Prof | Assoc Prof | Asst Prof | Inst |
|---|---|---|---|---|
| Montclair St C, IIA | 47.8 | 38.7 | 31.3 | 24.5 |
| Princeton Theol Sem, I | 52.5 | 45.7 | 33.1 | — |
| Princeton U, I | 63.4 | 40.1 | 31.0 | 26.2 |
| Rider C, IIA | 45.8 | 37.9 | 31.7 | — |
| Rutgers U | | | | |
| Camden, IIB | 63.5 | 42.9 | 32.6 | 26.7 |
| New Brunswick, I | 59.4 | 42.2 | 32.6 | 24.0 |
| Newark, IIA | 62.3 | 44.6 | 35.8 | 26.1 |
| Saint Peter's C, IIB | 34.2 | 28.1 | 23.3 | 21.6 |
| Union County C, III | 43.7 | 32.6 | 27.0 | 22.0 |
| Upsala C, IIB | 33.2 | 27.5 | 21.9 | 18.8 |
| Westminster Choir C, IIA | 36.5 | 27.8 | 19.9 | 16.4 |
| William Paterson C, IIA | 48.1 | 38.5 | 30.8 | 23.5 |

## NEW MEXICO

| | Prof | Assoc Prof | Asst Prof | Inst |
|---|---|---|---|---|
| C of Santa Fe, IIB | 23.0 | 22.5 | 19.1 | |
| Eastern NM U, IIA | 36.4 | 30.7 | 25.7 | 21.8 |
| Roswell, III | | | — | 24.4 |
| NM Highlands U, IIA | 32.9 | 26.9 | 23.4 | — |
| New Mexico Inst of Mining & Tech, I | 38.6 | 28.6 | 28.2 | — |
| NM Military Inst, III | — | 29.0 | 24.6 | 23.7 |
| New Mexico St U | | | | |
| Main campus, I | 40.1 | 31.6 | 26.3 | 19.7 |
| Alamogordo, III | — | 29.7 | 23.1 | 22.6 |
| Carlsbad, III | — | — | 25.7 | — |
| Dona Ana, III | | | 20.4 | 19.8 |
| Grants, III | | — | — | 19.2 |
| San Juan C, III | — | — | 27.7 | 25.7 |
| U of New Mexico, I | 41.7 | 30.7 | 26.3 | 20.3 |
| Western NM U, IIA | 34.2 | 29.3 | 23.4 | — |

## NEW YORK

| | Prof | Assoc Prof | Asst Prof | Inst |
|---|---|---|---|---|
| Albany C of Pharmacy, IIB | 40.5 | 32.2 | — | — |
| Alfred U, IIA | 39.7 | 32.7 | 27.9 | — |
| Bard C, IIB | 39.3 | 32.1 | 24.7 | |
| Barnard C, IIB | 51.9 | 35.0 | 28.9 | 21.6 |
| Canisius C, IIB | 37.9 | 32.0 | 26.8 | — |
| Cazenovia C, III | 28.1 | — | 20.4 | 16.3 |
| Clarkson U, IIA | 54.9 | 40.9 | 34.8 | 32.8 |
| Colgate U, IIB | 50.9 | 38.6 | 29.5 | 24.5 |
| C of Aeronautics, III | 27.1 | 27.3 | 24.4 | 19.9 |
| C of Mt St Vincent, IIB | 34.1 | 26.9 | 23.7 | — |
| C of New Rochelle, IIA | 39.8 | 32.7 | 26.5 | 22.3 |
| Columbia U, I | 61.5 | 43.7 | 33.3 | — |
| Teachers C, I | 50.5 | 38.0 | 28.7 | 20.5 |
| Concordia C, IIB | 27.9 | 23.3 | 19.2 | — |
| Cornell U | | | | |
| Endowed C's, I | 56.6 | 40.7 | 32.4 | — |
| D'Youville C, IIB | 31.0 | 23.5 | 19.8 | 18.0 |
| Dominican C of Blauvelt, IIB | — | 29.2 | 25.1 | 21.3 |
| Elmira C, IIA | 34.1 | 24.9 | 22.6 | 19.3 |
| Fordham U, I | 52.6 | 39.4 | 29.9 | 26.8 |
| Hamilton C, IIB | 46.8 | 35.1 | 27.2 | — |
| Hartwick C, IIB | 37.4 | 32.1 | 24.3 | — |
| Hilbert C, III | — | — | 19.2 | 16.5 |
| Hobart-William Smith C's, IIB | 43.3 | 33.5 | 26.3 | 22.0 |
| Hofstra U, I | 49.1 | 38.2 | 31.6 | 28.8 |
| Houghton C, IIB | 28.3 | 24.4 | 21.3 | — |
| Iona C, IIA | 45.0 | 37.0 | 29.8 | 26.0 |
| Ithaca C, IIB | 41.4 | 33.1 | 25.9 | 19.1 |
| JC of Albany, III | 28.0 | 24.1 | 18.8 | 17.9 |
| Le Moyne C, IIB | 39.7 | 32.4 | 25.8 | 24.1 |
| Long Island U, IIA | 42.5 | 33.9 | 27.6 | 22.6 |
| Manhattan C, IIA | 44.7 | 37.6 | 29.8 | 22.0 |
| Manhattanville C, IIA | 39.2 | 35.1 | 25.7 | — |
| Marist C, IIB | 42.2 | 33.5 | 26.3 | 20.0 |
| Marymount C, IIB | 36.0 | 29.7 | 23.8 | — |
| Marymount Manhattan C, IIB | — | 29.1 | 24.9 | — |
| Molloy C, IIB | 32.9 | 25.1 | 21.8 | 16.5 |
| Mount Saint Mary C, IIB | 34.8 | 28.9 | 23.6 | 19.5 |
| Nazareth C of Rochester, IIB | 37.4 | 31.0 | 24.9 | — |
| NY Inst of Tech, IIA | 43.3 | 36.1 | 28.2 | 24.8 |
| New York U, I | 59.1 | 40.4 | 34.5 | 25.2 |
| Niagara U, IIA | 35.6 | 29.7 | 25.1 | — |
| Pace U, IIA | 49.0 | 38.2 | 31.5 | 28.1 |
| Pratt Inst, IIA | 39.4 | 32.8 | 27.1 | |
| Rensselaer Poly Inst, I | 55.8 | 40.3 | 34.6 | |
| Rockefeller U, I | 74.4 | 42.8 | 28.9 | 25.3 |
| Russell Sage C, IIA | 37.9 | 28.8 | 24.7 | 19.9 |
| Saint Bonaventure U, IIA | 36.0 | 30.2 | 26.7 | 24.2 |
| Saint Francis C, IIB | 42.1 | 33.6 | 24.6 | 23.6 |
| Saint Lawrence U, IIB | 47.2 | 34.4 | 27.4 | — |
| Saint Thomas Aquinas C, IIB | 36.1 | 29.6 | 24.5 | — |
| Siena C, IIB | 37.4 | 28.4 | 23.9 | |
| Skidmore C, IIB | 45.8 | 33.5 | 27.1 | 21.2 |
| St U of New York | | | | |
| Albany, I | 57.1 | 41.6 | 31.5 | |
| Binghamton, I | 55.4 | 39.7 | 30.0 | |
| Buffalo, I | 57.5 | 41.5 | 33.1 | — |
| Stony Brook, I | 58.1 | 40.6 | 30.8 | — |
| Empire St C, IIB | 41.2 | 35.2 | 27.7 | 25.9 |
| C at Brockport, IIA | 46.4 | 37.8 | 31.5 | 22.1 |
| C at Buffalo, IIA | 43.5 | 34.0 | 26.9 | 24.4 |
| C at Cortland, IIA | 43.2 | 33.3 | 26.9 | 21.5 |
| C at Fredonia, IIA | 44.9 | 34.9 | 28.2 | 21.8 |
| C at Geneseo, IIA | 45.0 | 35.2 | 25.7 | 23.1 |
| C at New Paltz, IIA | 43.8 | 36.5 | 29.5 | — |
| C at Old Westbury, IIB | 47.6 | 37.4 | 28.2 | — |
| C at Oneonta, IIA | 43.5 | 34.8 | 28.2 | — |
| C at Oswego, IIA | 43.5 | 33.6 | 26.3 | 24.4 |
| C at Plattsburgh, IIA | 43.3 | 35.9 | 28.1 | 22.4 |
| C at Potsdam, IIA | 42.8 | 32.8 | 28.2 | 20.5 |
| C at Purchase, IIB | 43.2 | 33.6 | 26.2 | |
| St C of Optometry, IIA | 51.7 | 42.4 | 31.4 | — |
| A&T C | | | | |
| Alfred, III | 40.1 | 35.0 | 27.8 | 22.2 |
| Canton, III | 38.3 | 30.9 | 26.7 | 23.9 |
| Cobleskill, III | 39.7 | 31.4 | 26.9 | 22.9 |
| Delhi, III | 38.9 | 31.8 | 26.9 | 19.5 |
| Farmingdale, III | 42.5 | 32.8 | 26.6 | 23.3 |
| Morrisville, III | 40.4 | 32.8 | 25.9 | 22.2 |
| C of Environmental Sci & Forestry, IIA | 45.2 | 36.6 | 28.0 | — |
| Maritime C, IIB | 44.5 | 32.9 | 28.2 | 21.8 |
| C of Tech, IIA | — | 35.1 | 29.5 | — |
| Fashion Inst of Tech, III | 59.9 | 49.5 | 38.1 | 30.2 |
| Cornell U | | | | |
| Statutory C's, I | 50.1 | 38.7 | 31.8 | 25.8 |
| C of Ceramics at Alfred U, IIA | 47.5 | 37.5 | 32.2 | 28.7 |
| Adirondack CC, III | 34.9 | 28.5 | 23.3 | 21.0 |
| Cayuga County CC, III | 33.3 | 25.9 | 21.7 | — |
| Clinton CC, III | 31.6 | 26.9 | 24.3 | — |
| Columbia-Greene CC, III | 34.6 | 29.4 | 23.2 | 20.4 |
| CC of Finger Lake, III | 31.3 | 26.6 | 22.5 | 18.8 |
| Corning CC, III | 36.9 | 27.5 | 21.3 | — |
| Dutchess CC, III | 43.5 | 37.1 | 29.6 | 23.1 |

## NEW YORK—Continued

| | Prof | Assoc Prof | Asst Prof | Inst |
|---|---|---|---|---|
| St U of New York | | | | |
| Erie CC | | | | |
| City, III | 36.6 | — | 26.9 | 21.5 |
| South, III | 36.8 | 32.4 | 26.7 | 23.5 |
| North, III | 38.0 | 32.2 | 27.4 | 22.4 |
| Fulton-Montgomery CC, III | 35.9 | 31.6 | 26.2 | 20.2 |
| Genesee CC, III | 30.8 | 25.3 | 21.2 | — |
| Hudson Valley CC, III | 34.0 | 30.4 | 24.8 | 20.0 |
| Jamestown CC, III | 35.1 | 29.1 | 23.0 | 19.4 |
| Jefferson CC, III | 39.9 | 32.8 | 25.0 | 16.8 |
| Monroe CC, III | 39.4 | 33.8 | 28.0 | 23.5 |
| Nassau CC, III | 52.4 | 42.1 | 33.9 | 28.6 |
| Niagara County CC, III | 38.0 | 31.7 | 25.5 | 21.5 |
| Onondaga CC, III | 36.2 | 29.9 | 26.5 | 21.7 |
| Rockland CC, III | 36.7 | 33.3 | 25.3 | 18.9 |
| Schenectady Co CC, III | 33.8 | 27.1 | 21.5 | — |
| Sullivan County CC, III | 35.7 | 31.0 | 25.5 | — |
| Tompkins-Cortland CC, III | 33.0 | 26.2 | 23.0 | 18.8 |
| Ulster County CC, III | 37.0 | 30.7 | 26.7 | 22.4 |
| Westchester CC, III | 55.0 | 48.4 | 42.0 | — |
| Syracuse U, I | 46.8 | 33.8 | 28.2 | 24.8 |
| Utica C, IIB | 32.5 | 26.9 | 21.6 | — |
| Trocaire C, III | — | — | 19.6 | 17.5 |
| Union C, IIA | 45.8 | 35.3 | 26.5 | 24.8 |
| U of Rochester, I | 54.3 | 39.3 | 31.7 | 23.8 |
| Vassar C, IIB | 48.9 | 34.8 | 27.3 | 22.9 |
| Wells C, IIB | 30.9 | 25.8 | 21.1 | — |

## NORTH CAROLINA

| | Prof | Assoc Prof | Asst Prof | Inst |
|---|---|---|---|---|
| Appalachian St U, IIA | 38.3 | 32.4 | 29.1 | 22.5 |
| Atlantic Christian C, IIB | 26.7 | 21.7 | 18.9 | 19.6 |
| Belmont Abbey C, IIB | 26.4 | 24.0 | 20.8 | — |
| Catawba C, IIB | 29.0 | 24.3 | 20.2 | 17.8 |
| Davidson C, IIB | 42.1 | 35.1 | 25.7 | — |
| Duke U, I | 57.4 | 40.2 | 32.0 | 31.7 |
| East Carolina U, IIA | 42.4 | 34.2 | 28.2 | 24.3 |
| Elizabeth City St U, IIB | 36.2 | 31.3 | 28.1 | — |
| Elon C, IIB | 30.6 | 25.3 | 22.5 | 18.4 |
| Fayetteville St U, IIB | 41.4 | 33.9 | 28.7 | 25.6 |
| Greensboro C, IIB | 27.7 | 22.8 | — | — |
| High Point C, IIB | 31.9 | 26.7 | 22.4 | — |
| Johnson C Smith U, IIB | 30.9 | 25.6 | 21.2 | 18.2 |
| Lenoir-Rhyne C, IIB | 29.5 | 26.4 | 23.1 | — |
| Mars Hill C, IIB | 27.2 | 24.1 | 21.5 | 17.6 |
| Methodist C, IIB | 26.6 | 21.8 | 20.4 | 19.5 |
| NC A&T St U, IIA | 41.0 | 35.4 | 29.4 | 25.0 |
| NC Central U, IIA | 42.7 | 33.8 | 29.4 | 27.1 |
| NC Sch of the Arts, IIB | | | | 31.0 |
| North Carolina St U, I | 52.8 | 38.2 | 33.1 | 26.6 |
| Pembroke St U, IIB | 40.8 | 33.8 | 26.5 | — |
| Pfeiffer C, IIB | 23.6 | 23.7 | 19.0 | — |
| Piedmont Bible C, IIB | 15.2 | | | |
| Saint Andrews Presbyterian C, IIB | 33.0 | 27.6 | 21.8 | — |
| Salem C, IIB | 31.7 | 26.8 | 23.9 | — |
| Southeastern Baptist Theol Sem, IIA | 28.9 | — | — | |
| U of North Carolina | | | | |
| Asheville, IIB | 42.2 | 33.1 | 28.3 | — |
| Chapel Hill, I | 53.2 | 38.5 | 31.4 | 28.1 |
| Charlotte, IIA | 42.1 | 35.0 | 29.3 | |
| Greensboro, I | 48.4 | 35.4 | 29.3 | 23.7 |
| Wilmington, IIB | 41.8 | 34.3 | 28.6 | |
| Wake Forest U, IIA | 45.4 | 35.1 | 27.3 | 20.9 |
| Western Carolina U, IIA | 40.3 | 34.4 | 28.2 | 23.5 |
| Winston-Salem St U, IIB | 37.9 | 30.3 | 27.6 | 22.2 |

## NORTH DAKOTA

| | Prof | Assoc Prof | Asst Prof | Inst |
|---|---|---|---|---|
| Dickinson St C, IIB | 30.5 | 28.5 | 25.7 | 22.7 |
| Jamestown C, IIB | 27.5 | 25.7 | 20.3 | 18.2 |
| Mayville St C, IIB | 33.4 | 29.0 | 23.7 | — |
| Minot St C, IIB | 35.2 | 30.6 | 25.9 | 23.4 |
| North Dakota St U, IIA | 38.9 | 31.6 | 27.0 | 18.9 |
| U of North Dakota, I | 37.9 | 30.8 | 26.5 | 23.0 |
| Valley City St C, IIB | 32.9 | 30.5 | 25.2 | 24.1 |

## OHIO

| | Prof | Assoc Prof | Asst Prof | Inst |
|---|---|---|---|---|
| Air Force Inst of Tech, IIA | 44.0 | 36.3 | 33.7 | — |
| Antioch U, IIA | 28.9 | 23.6 | 22.1 | |
| Baldwin-Wallace C, IIB | 33.0 | 27.8 | 23.0 | — |
| Bluffton C, IIB | 24.6 | 21.2 | 19.5 | — |
| Bowling Green St U, I | 46.6 | 36.4 | 29.3 | 21.1 |
| Firelands, III | — | 36.0 | 28.0 | 23.8 |
| Capital U, IIB | 33.0 | 25.4 | 22.3 | 20.3 |
| Case Western Reserve U, I | 51.2 | 36.6 | 31.1 | 22.5 |
| Cedarville C, IIB | 30.4 | 25.4 | 22.4 | — |
| Clark Tech C, III | — | 28.8 | 25.6 | 20.6 |
| Cleveland St U, IIA | 48.8 | 36.8 | 30.3 | 24.6 |
| C of Mt Saint Joseph, IIB | 28.3 | 24.8 | 21.4 | 19.7 |
| C of Wooster, IIB | 37.8 | 29.0 | 24.2 | 23.1 |
| Denison U, IIB | 40.7 | 32.5 | 25.4 | 21.7 |
| Findlay C, IIB | 30.3 | 26.7 | 21.1 | 19.6 |
| Hebrew Union C, IIA | 58.6 | 39.1 | — | — |
| Heidelberg C, IIB | 30.2 | 25.2 | 21.3 | 17.6 |
| Hiram C, IIB | 32.6 | 26.1 | 22.1 | 19.1 |
| Jefferson Tech C, III | | 31.0 | 26.6 | 24.1 |
| John Carroll U, IIA | 38.2 | 31.8 | 26.8 | 24.4 |
| Kent St U | | | | |
| Main campus, I | 45.1 | 35.0 | 29.0 | 22.7 |
| Ashtabula, III | — | 33.2 | 28.5 | — |
| Liverpool, III | | — | 25.6 | — |
| Salem, III | — | — | 25.9 | — |
| Stark, III | — | 34.5 | 29.2 | — |
| Trumbull, III | — | 33.4 | 25.4 | — |
| Tuscarawas, III | — | 34.6 | 28.6 | — |
| Kenyon C, IIB | 47.5 | 34.9 | 25.7 | 21.4 |
| Lakeland CC, III | 36.7 | 35.1 | 34.3 | 30.0 |
| Lorain County CC, III | — | 35.4 | 28.9 | 23.1 |
| Lourdes C, IIB | | — | — | 19.5 |
| Marietta C, IIB | 32.4 | 28.3 | 25.8 | — |
| Miami U | | | | |
| Hamilton, III | — | 35.4 | 27.6 | 24.7 |
| Middletown, III | — | 34.5 | 28.4 | 30.7 |
| Oxford, I | 47.0 | 36.0 | 29.1 | 25.1 |
| Mount Union C, IIB | 33.7 | 26.9 | 23.5 | 21.0 |
| Mount Vernon Nazarene C, IIB | 27.2 | 24.0 | 20.7 | — |
| Muskingum Area Tech C, III | — | 26.6 | 24.0 | 21.6 |
| Muskingum C, IIB | 34.1 | 28.5 | 22.7 | — |
| Notre Dame C, IIB | — | — | 20.7 | — |
| Oberlin C, IIB | 45.1 | 33.3 | 26.8 | 24.2 |
| Ohio C of Podiatric Med, IIB | — | 43.4 | 35.4 | |
| Ohio Dominican C, IIB | 31.0 | 24.9 | 21.7 | — |
| Ohio Northern U, IIB | 36.0 | 29.0 | 25.7 | 21.5 |
| Ohio St U | | | | |
| Main campus, I | 54.0 | 39.6 | 33.1 | 23.7 |
| Ag Tech Inst, IIB | | 30.2 | 26.8 | — |
| Lima, IIB | | 35.2 | 28.9 | — |
| Mansfield, IIB | — | 33.8 | 27.9 | — |

## OHIO—Continued

| | Prof | Assoc Prof | Asst Prof | Inst |
|---|---|---|---|---|
| Ohio St U | | | | |
| Marion, IIB | — | 35.0 | 25.9 | — |
| Newark, IIB | — | 33.8 | 31.2 | — |
| Ohio U | | | | |
| Athens, I | 46.0 | 36.0 | 29.7 | 23.7 |
| Belmont, III | | — | 30.5 | |
| Chillicothe, III | | 30.7 | 27.2 | — |
| Lancaster, III | | 33.4 | 25.8 | |
| Zanesville, III | — | 32.6 | 26.7 | — |
| Ohio Wesleyan U, IIB | 34.0 | 26.3 | 23.0 | |
| Otterbein C, IIB | 32.7 | 25.9 | 22.5 | 18.5 |
| Rio Grande C, IIB | 24.5 | 26.8 | 24.1 | 17.5 |
| Trinity Lutheran | | | | |
| Seminary, IIA | 29.6 | 28.0 | — | — |
| United Theol Sem, IIB | 27.7 | 26.3 | | |
| U of Akron | | | | |
| Main campus, I | 46.8 | 36.0 | 30.7 | 25.6 |
| Wayne General & | | | | |
| Tech C, III | — | 27.8 | 22.8 | — |
| U of Cincinnati | | | | |
| Main campus, I | 50.7 | 38.1 | 29.5 | 22.4 |
| Claremont General & | | | | |
| Tech C, III | — | 34.5 | 27.2 | — |
| Raymond Walters | | | | |
| General & Tech C, III | 40.3 | 33.8 | 26.2 | 19.3 |
| U of Dayton, IIA | 39.8 | 34.0 | 26.8 | 17.3 |
| U of Toledo, I | 47.0 | 36.8 | 30.1 | 23.4 |
| Ursuline C, IIB | — | — | 21.7 | 19.8 |
| Walsh C, IIB | 29.7 | 25.1 | 22.5 | — |
| Wilberforce U, IIB | — | 20.5 | 16.8 | 14.3 |
| Wilmington C, IIB | 30.1 | 26.2 | 21.5 | — |
| Wittenberg U, IIB | 40.8 | 32.0 | 24.8 | 20.9 |
| Wright St U | | | | |
| Main campus, IIA | 49.0 | 37.0 | 30.7 | 22.5 |
| Lake, III | — | — | 28.0 | — |
| Xavier U, IIA | 38.4 | 31.4 | 27.2 | 21.7 |
| Youngstown St U, IIA | 43.9 | 36.3 | 27.5 | 23.0 |

## OKLAHOMA

| | Prof | Assoc Prof | Asst Prof | Inst |
|---|---|---|---|---|
| Bacone C, III | | — | 17.1 | 15.1 |
| Cameron U, IIB | 33.9 | 29.9 | 25.6 | 18.6 |
| Central St U, IIA | 37.9 | 34.6 | 31.7 | 26.8 |
| East Central U, IIB | 35.8 | 32.9 | 28.5 | 22.8 |
| Langston U, IIB | 33.2 | 26.1 | 24.8 | 24.3 |
| Oklahoma Baptist U, IIB | 29.5 | 24.9 | 21.9 | 19.3 |
| Okla Christian C, IIB | 32.6 | 29.0 | 23.1 | 19.6 |
| Oklahoma St U, I | 40.0 | 31.8 | 27.7 | 22.2 |
| Phillips U, IIB | 27.3 | 23.5 | 20.4 | — |
| SE Oklahoma St U, IIA | 33.5 | 30.7 | 26.6 | 22.5 |
| U of Oklahoma, I | 41.4 | 31.4 | 27.0 | 17.5 |
| U of Tulsa, IIA | 47.8 | 34.7 | 27.7 | 19.8 |

## OREGON

| | Prof | Assoc Prof | Asst Prof | Inst |
|---|---|---|---|---|
| Eastern Oregon St C, IIB | 34.1 | 27.7 | 23.6 | — |
| George Fox C, IIB | 25.5 | 21.7 | 17.9 | — |
| Lewis and Clark C, IIA | 44.5 | 30.8 | 22.6 | — |
| Linfield C, IIB | 30.2 | 26.1 | 21.6 | — |
| Oregon Inst of Tech, IIB | 36.8 | 31.6 | 27.1 | 23.1 |
| Oregon St U, I | 41.6 | 33.5 | 28.0 | 20.2 |
| Portland St U, IIA | 38.0 | 30.5 | 27.8 | 22.2 |
| Reed C, IIA | 41.1 | 31.5 | 25.9 | |
| Southern Ore St C, IIA | 35.1 | 28.2 | 23.0 | — |
| U of Oregon, I | 41.1 | 32.0 | 26.7 | 20.5 |
| U of Portland, IIA | 36.9 | 29.6 | 25.1 | |
| Warner Pacific C, IIB | — | 23.5 | 21.1 | |
| Western Baptist C, IIB | 20.3 | — | | — |
| Western Ore St C, IIA | 32.5 | 28.1 | 23.7 | — |
| W St Chiropractic C, IIA | — | — | 22.2 | |
| Willamette U, IIA | 39.4 | 29.6 | 25.5 | — |

## PENNSYLVANIA

| | Prof | Assoc Prof | Asst Prof | Inst |
|---|---|---|---|---|
| Academy of the | | | | |
| New Church, IIB | — | — | 33.0 | 26.8 |
| Albright C, IIB | 39.0 | 31.2 | 26.8 | 24.8 |
| Allegheny C, IIA | 41.1 | 31.7 | 25.3 | 21.1 |
| Allentown C | | | | |
| of Saint Francis, IIB | 34.7 | 30.0 | 24.5 | 18.9 |
| Alvernia C, IIB | — | 20.5 | 18.4 | 16.1 |
| Beaver C, IIB | 37.3 | 27.3 | 23.5 | 16.3 |
| Bryn Mawr C, I | 44.1 | 35.4 | 26.6 | — |
| Bucknell U, IIA | 47.6 | 36.7 | 28.9 | — |
| Carlow C, IIB | 34.2 | 24.9 | 19.6 | 17.2 |
| Carnegie Mellon U, I | 60.1 | 40.8 | 36.1 | 35.7 |
| CC of Allegheny County | | | | |
| Allegheny, III | 33.9 | 31.0 | 27.7 | — |
| Boyce, III | 35.3 | 30.7 | 27.3 | — |
| North, III | 28.4 | 26.1 | 22.8 | — |
| South, III | 34.1 | 29.5 | 23.1 | — |
| Cedar Crest C, IIB | 30.2 | 24.5 | 21.1 | — |
| Chatham C, IIB | 35.1 | 29.1 | 23.0 | 20.4 |
| Chestnut Hill C, IIB | — | 25.8 | 18.4 | — |
| Clarion U, IIA | 41.2 | 33.4 | 27.1 | 21.0 |
| C Misericordia, IIB | — | 26.0 | 21.7 | — |
| Dickinson C, IIB | 42.4 | 32.6 | 25.7 | 22.7 |
| Drexel U, I | 50.6 | 36.1 | 31.9 | 25.4 |
| Duquesne U, IIA | 37.2 | 28.9 | 24.7 | 19.0 |
| Eastern Baptist | | | | |
| Theol Sem, IIB | 29.6 | — | — | |
| Eastern C, IIB | 31.1 | 27.2 | 23.7 | 22.2 |
| Edinboro U, IIA | 40.7 | 33.7 | 27.4 | — |
| Franklin | | | | |
| and Marshall C, IIB | 48.1 | 36.4 | 25.3 | 23.7 |
| Gannon U, IIA | 35.8 | 31.9 | 27.6 | 21.8 |
| Geneva C, IIB | 28.6 | 25.2 | 21.1 | — |
| Gettysburg C, IIB | 46.0 | 34.7 | 26.0 | 27.8 |
| Harrisburg Area CC, III | 36.0 | 30.1 | 23.2 | 20.8 |
| Haverford C, IIB | 49.0 | 36.9 | 29.1 | — |
| Immaculata C, IIB | 33.1 | 29.8 | — | — |
| Indiana U, IIA | 41.1 | 33.4 | 26.4 | 19.4 |
| Juniata C, IIB | 36.8 | 28.4 | 24.4 | — |
| Keystone JC, III | 27.9 | 22.9 | 19.7 | 17.0 |
| King's C, IIB | 34.6 | 30.0 | 25.1 | — |
| La Salle U, IIB | 42.1 | 34.4 | 27.8 | 23.0 |
| Lackawanna JC, III | — | — | 16.9 | 13.4 |
| Lafayette C, IIB | 51.3 | 37.8 | 28.4 | 26.8 |
| Lancaster Bible C, IIB | — | — | 17.5 | — |
| Lebanon Valley C, IIB | 29.0 | 27.6 | 22.4 | — |
| Lehigh U, I | 50.8 | 37.3 | 30.8 | 33.1 |
| Lock Haven U, IIB | 42.1 | 34.5 | 25.6 | 21.8 |
| Lutheran Theol Sem, IIA | 25.5 | — | — | — |
| Lycoming C, IIB | 35.4 | 29.1 | 23.8 | 22.0 |
| Marywood C, IIA | 31.7 | 27.7 | 23.3 | 19.9 |
| Mercyhurst C, IIB | 31.2 | 26.5 | 22.0 | 20.3 |
| Millersville U, IIA | 40.7 | 33.3 | 26.6 | 21.7 |
| Montgomery Co CC, III | 37.9 | 32.6 | 27.0 | — |
| Moravian C, IIB | 36.7 | 29.1 | 24.5 | — |
| Muhlenberg C, IIB | 40.8 | 31.7 | 25.5 | — |
| Neumann C, IIB | — | 23.5 | 21.9 | 20.5 |
| Northampton County | | | | |
| Area CC, III | 31.8 | 29.5 | 25.5 | — |
| Peirce JC, III | 29.5 | 25.9 | 22.0 | 18.6 |
| Pennsylvania St U | | | | |
| Main campus, I | 50.4 | 36.8 | 30.5 | 19.6 |
| IIA campuses | 42.9 | 36.9 | 30.1 | 25.5 |
| III campuses | 40.6 | 31.8 | 26.1 | 21.4 |

# *Regional Differences in This Year's Average Faculty Salaries*

| | West | | North Central | | Northeast | | South | | | |
|---|---|---|---|---|---|---|---|---|---|---|
| | Pacific | Mountain | West North Central | East North Central | Middle Atlantic | New England | West South Central | East South Central | South Atlantic | All |
| **Doctoral institutions** | | | | | | | | | | |
| Professor | $56,610 | $44,020 | $44,380 | $49,580 | $55,680 | $55,700 | $46,120 | $44,500 | $50,540 | $50,500 |
| Associate professor | 38,030 | 33,650 | 33,030 | 36,500 | 39,400 | 38,210 | 33,770 | 33,340 | 36,740 | 36,210 |
| Assistant professor | 32,990 | 28,630 | 28,420 | 30,580 | 31,880 | 31,750 | 28,790 | 27,950 | 30,670 | 30,360 |
| Instructor | 22,090 | 22,610 | 20,830 | 21,860 | 23,570 | 25,420 | 21,110 | 20,620 | 23,220 | 22,130 |
| Lecturer | 31,820 | 24,060 | 19,900 | 23,790 | 25,730 | 29,370 | 22,160 | 20,750 | 24,800 | 26,090 |
| All ranks | 45,520 | 36,490 | 36,340 | 39,580 | 43,390 | 43,950 | 35,810 | 35,160 | 39,080 | 39,800 |
| **Comprehensive institutions** | | | | | | | | | | |
| Professor | $47,380 | $37,810 | $38,190 | $39,730 | $43,290 | $44,420 | $37,410 | $37,410 | $41,150 | $42,160 |
| Associate professor | 36,130 | 31,360 | 31,190 | 32,790 | 34,540 | 34,030 | 31,150 | 30,810 | 33,530 | 33,200 |
| Assistant professor | 29,440 | 26,390 | 26,190 | 27,480 | 28,220 | 27,920 | 26,810 | 28,850 | 28,230 | 27,310 |
| Instructor | 25,040 | 22,130 | 21,050 | 22,030 | 22,500 | 21,980 | 21,040 | 21,070 | 21,870 | 21,220 |
| Lecturer | 25,600 | 24,960 | 19,440 | 22,120 | 25,340 | 28,320 | 19,340 | 18,500 | 23,610 | 22,790 |
| All ranks | 41,050 | 31,160 | 30,610 | 32,690 | 34,960 | 35,410 | 30,030 | 30,260 | 32,890 | 33,750 |
| **Baccalaureate institutions** | | | | | | | | | | |
| Professor | $40,020 | $35,000 | $33,890 | $34,770 | $40,140 | $43,790 | $32,830 | $31,820 | $34,150 | $36,170 |
| Associate professor | 30,590 | 28,210 | 27,600 | 28,700 | 31,230 | 32,280 | 28,220 | 26,080 | 28,520 | 29,210 |
| Assistant professor | 25,120 | 23,760 | 23,170 | 23,720 | 25,200 | 26,550 | 24,720 | 22,400 | 23,920 | 24,070 |
| Instructor | 21,720 | 19,630 | 20,270 | 19,740 | 20,990 | 22,130 | 20,970 | 17,980 | 20,290 | 19,840 |
| Lecturer | 19,430 | — | 22,060 | 20,000 | 23,520 | 30,030 | 21,470 | 20,200 | 23,360 | 23,240 |
| All ranks | 31,290 | 29,080 | 26,850 | 28,070 | 30,560 | 33,030 | 27,220 | 25,730 | 27,660 | 28,480 |
| **2-year institutions with academic ranks** | | | | | | | | | | |
| Professor | $40,690 | $28,940 | $37,640 | $38,170 | $39,500 | $33,200 | $36,500 | $30,780 | $36,670 | $37,170 |
| Associate professor | 37,800 | 26,730 | 31,720 | 33,360 | 32,480 | 28,080 | 30,280 | 26,390 | 30,300 | 31,330 |
| Assistant professor | 33,000 | 24,160 | 26,110 | 28,820 | 27,200 | 24,260 | 26,500 | 22,710 | 25,840 | 26,590 |
| Instructor | 30,800 | 22,860 | 23,470 | 25,180 | 22,390 | 21,710 | 23,650 | 20,460 | 21,300 | 22,270 |
| Lecturer | — | — | — | 20,600 | 18,930 | 16,870 | — | — | 19,720 | 19,540 |
| All ranks | 37,230 | 25,090 | 31,020 | 31,610 | 32,210 | 28,260 | 28,650 | 24,860 | 29,920 | 30,100 |
| **2-year institutions without academic ranks** | | | | | | | | | | |
| All | $31,790 | $27,530 | $26,510 | $31,470 | $17,040 | $23,570 | $26,220 | $21,930 | $23,590 | $31,240 |
| **All institutions except 2-year institutions without academic rank** | | | | | | | | | | |
| Professor | $51,050 | $41,520 | $40,470 | $44,820 | $48,080 | $49,660 | $42,340 | $39,620 | $44,860 | $45,530 |
| Associate professor | 36,580 | 32,220 | 31,130 | 34,050 | 35,370 | 35,190 | 32,350 | 30,790 | 33,990 | 33,820 |
| Assistant professor | 30,770 | 27,210 | 26,040 | 28,440 | 28,590 | 28,900 | 27,350 | 25,820 | 28,210 | 27,920 |
| Instructor | 23,850 | 22,200 | 29,810 | 21,890 | 22,360 | 22,690 | 21,210 | 20,410 | 21,800 | 21,330 |
| Lecturer | 31,250 | 24,200 | 20,010 | 22,830 | 25,260 | 29,140 | 21,660 | 19,660 | 24,080 | 24,930 |
| All ranks | 42,370 | 33,820 | 31,990 | 35,470 | 37,030 | 38,490 | 32,880 | 31,140 | 34,690 | 35,470 |

— No data reported.

Note: Salary figures are based on 1,875 institutions.
Pacific: Alaska, Cal., Hawaii, Ore., Wash; Mountain: Ariz., Colo., Idaho, Mont., Nev., N.M., Utah, Wyo.; West North Central: Iowa, Kan., Minn., Mo., Neb., N.D., S.D.; East North Central: Ill., Ind., Mich., Ohio, Wis.; Middle Atlantic: N.J., N.Y., Pa., New England: Conn., Me., Mass., N.H., R.I., Vt.; West South Central: Ark., La., Okla., Tex.; East South Central: Ala., Ky., Miss., Tenn.; South Atlantic: Del., D.C., Fla., Ga., Md., N.C., S.C., Va., W.Va.

SOURCE: AMERICAN ASSOCIATION OF UNIVERSITY PROFESSORS

## PENNSYLVANIA—Continued

| | Prof | Assoc Prof | Asst Prof | Inst |
|---|---|---|---|---|
| Philadelphia C | | | | |
| of Pharmacy & Sci, IIA | 43.4 | 32.7 | 25.7 | 21.5 |
| Philadelphia C | | | | |
| of Textiles & Sci, IIA | 38.7 | 32.6 | 27.9 | — |
| Point Park C, IIB | 30.4 | 26.2 | 20.9 | 18.8 |
| Rosemont C, IIB | 31.7 | 29.2 | 19.3 | — |
| Saint Joseph's U, IIB | 42.5 | 33.0 | 28.3 | 22.5 |
| Seton Hill C, IIB | 30.2 | 24.4 | 19.4 | 16.0 |
| Shippensburg U, IIA | 41.1 | 33.3 | 27.1 | — |
| Susquehanna U, IIB | 37.7 | 29.7 | 24.2 | — |
| Swarthmore C, IIB | 50.5 | 34.2 | 27.5 | — |
| Temple U, I | 46.3 | 36.2 | 30.0 | 22.6 |
| Thiel C, IIB | 30.2 | 25.0 | 21.4 | — |
| U of Pennsylvania, I | 59.6 | 43.3 | 35.8 | — |
| U of Pittsburgh | | | | |
| Main campus, I | 51.5 | 36.4 | 29.4 | 19.6 |
| Bradford, IIB | — | 29.6 | 26.0 | 19.2 |
| Greensburg, III | 32.9 | 27.0 | 23.9 | 17.2 |
| Johnstown, IIB | 39.2 | 32.4 | 25.8 | 21.0 |
| Titusville, III | | 29.4 | — | — |
| U of Scranton, IIA | 37.6 | 30.9 | 26.9 | 22.8 |
| Ursinus C, IIB | 37.9 | 31.5 | 25.7 | — |
| Villa Maria C, IIB | — | 21.9 | 18.7 | 17.8 |
| Villanova U, IIA | 47.2 | 36.8 | 30.4 | 21.5 |
| Washington | | | | |
| and Jefferson C, IIB | 34.8 | 30.9 | 25.6 | 19.6 |
| Westminster C, IIB | 33.0 | 27.5 | 22.4 | — |
| Westmoreland Co CC, III | — | 28.3 | 24.7 | 22.8 |
| Widener U, IIA | 43.3 | 36.8 | 28.7 | 25.5 |
| Wilkes C, IIA | 34.5 | 26.8 | 23.6 | 19.3 |
| Williamsport Area CC, III | 30.5 | 29.5 | 28.0 | 25.2 |
| York C of Pa, IIB | 43.3 | 36.8 | 28.5 | 23.8 |

## RHODE ISLAND

| | Prof | Assoc Prof | Asst Prof | Inst |
|---|---|---|---|---|
| Brown U, I | 53.3 | 36.7 | 30.4 | — |
| Bryant C, IIA | 43.7 | 40.4 | 31.5 | 27.1 |
| CC of Rhode Island, III | 32.5 | 27.7 | 22.7 | — |
| Providence C, IIA | 41.4 | 36.8 | 27.4 | 27.5 |
| Rhode Island C, IIA | 37.5 | 31.6 | 26.6 | 21.7 |
| RI Sch of Design, IIB | 40.1 | 32.0 | 25.6 | — |
| Salve Regina- | | | | |
| Newport C, IIA | 34.7 | 28.7 | 24.4 | 19.8 |
| U of Rhode Island, I | 43.5 | 34.2 | 29.9 | 22.2 |

## SOUTH CAROLINA

| | Prof | Assoc Prof | Asst Prof | Inst |
|---|---|---|---|---|
| Baptist C | | | | |
| of Charleston, IIB | 23.4 | 20.5 | 18.8 | — |
| Central Wesleyan C, IIB | 20.9 | 17.8 | 14.6 | — |
| Citadel, IIA | 39.7 | 31.8 | 28.5 | — |
| Clemson U, I | 46.3 | 34.4 | 29.6 | 20.7 |
| Coker C, IIB | 26.7 | 23.8 | 21.3 | — |
| C of Charleston, IIA | 38.6 | 33.8 | 26.5 | 19.5 |
| Columbia C, IIB | 29.4 | 24.3 | 22.9 | 19.8 |
| Converse C, IIB | 31.6 | 27.8 | 23.9 | 22.3 |
| Erskine C, IIB | 26.3 | 21.4 | 18.3 | — |
| Francis Marion C, IIB | 37.1 | 29.4 | 24.9 | 18.3 |
| Furman U, IIB | 39.2 | 29.5 | 24.7 | 21.2 |
| Lander C, IIB | 35.9 | 31.0 | 26.2 | 20.2 |
| Limestone C, IIB | 21.9 | 21.0 | 21.6 | — |

## SOUTH CAROLINA—Continued

| | Prof | Assoc Prof | Asst Prof | Inst |
|---|---|---|---|---|
| Morris C, IIB | 23.1 | 21.9 | 18.2 | 16.1 |
| Newberry C, IIB | 25.1 | 22.7 | 19.7 | — |
| North Greenville C, III | — | — | 17.9 | 15.7 |
| Presbyterian C, IIB | 34.6 | 27.2 | 23.3 | 20.1 |
| South Carolina St C, IIB | 38.8 | 31.8 | 26.4 | 21.4 |
| U of South Carolina | | | | |
| Main campus, I | 46.1 | 33.2 | 28.9 | 21.2 |
| Aiken, IIB | 34.6 | 28.0 | 23.6 | 18.7 |
| Beaufort, III | — | 26.3 | — | — |
| Coastal, IIB | 34.3 | 28.5 | 26.1 | 22.5 |
| Lancaster, III | — | 27.3 | 24.6 | — |
| Salkehatchie, III | — | — | 22.8 | — |
| Spartanburg, IIB | 33.9 | 29.4 | 24.1 | 21.4 |
| Sumter, III | — | 28.7 | 25.3 | — |
| Union, III | — | — | — | 20.8 |
| Voorhees C, IIB | 22.8 | — | 18.4 | 15.8 |
| Winthrop C, IIA | 39.9 | 32.5 | 26.5 | 19.7 |
| Wofford C, IIB | 38.2 | 29.8 | 25.4 | — |

## SOUTH DAKOTA

| | Prof | Assoc Prof | Asst Prof | Inst |
|---|---|---|---|---|
| Black Hills St C, IIB | 31.8 | 27.3 | 23.9 | 19.2 |
| Mount Marty C, IIB | 25.9 | 20.7 | 17.9 | — |
| Northern St C, IIA | 34.6 | 28.0 | 24.2 | 21.1 |
| Sioux Falls C, IIB | 24.9 | 22.4 | 20.7 | — |
| SD Sch of Mines | | | | |
| & Tech, IIA | 36.8 | 29.9 | 26.2 | 21.1 |
| South Dakota St U, IIA | 34.2 | 28.3 | 24.1 | 21.4 |
| U of South Dakota, I | 37.7 | 29.0 | 24.8 | 18.8 |

## TENNESSEE

| | Prof | Assoc Prof | Asst Prof | Inst |
|---|---|---|---|---|
| Austin Peay St U, IIA | 35.0 | 27.4 | 23.0 | 18.0 |
| Belmont C, IIB | 31.6 | 25.7 | 23.2 | 22.2 |
| Bethel C, IIB | — | 20.3 | 19.4 | — |
| Bryan C, IIB | — | 21.1 | 19.0 | — |
| Carson-Newman C, IIB | 30.2 | 24.8 | 23.0 | — |
| Chattanooga St | | | | |
| Tech CC, III | 34.8 | 31.0 | 28.8 | 22.4 |
| Christian Brothers C, IIB | 34.0 | 25.9 | 24.4 | |
| Cleveland St CC, III | 30.2 | 26.5 | 23.6 | |
| Columbia St CC, III | — | 30.7 | 27.6 | 22.0 |
| David Lipscomb C, IIB | 32.0 | 26.9 | 23.1 | 19.5 |
| Dyersburg St CC, III | 28.8 | 26.1 | 22.6 | 20.6 |
| East Tennessee St U, IIA | 38.8 | 32.6 | 26.9 | 21.1 |
| Freed-Hardeman C, IIB | 31.8 | 27.3 | 23.1 | 17.0 |
| Hiwassee C, III | 19.0 | 18.2 | 16.6 | 15.6 |
| Jackson St CC, III | 30.1 | 27.2 | 24.0 | 20.0 |
| Lambuth C, IIB | 24.9 | 23.7 | 21.2 | |
| Lane C, IIB | 21.2 | 18.8 | 17.9 | 16.1 |
| Lee C, IIB | 27.8 | 23.3 | 20.4 | 17.9 |
| Maryville C, IIB | 27.0 | 22.6 | 20.8 | 16.9 |
| Middle Tenn St U, IIA | 41.5 | 34.5 | 27.4 | 21.5 |
| Rhodes C, IIB | 40.0 | 31.3 | 23.9 | — |
| Roane St CC, III | 32.6 | 27.2 | 22.8 | 18.2 |
| St Tech Inst Memphis, III | 32.2 | 26.8 | 23.4 | 20.8 |
| Tennessee Tech U, IIA | 40.8 | 33.0 | 27.5 | 20.8 |
| Tusculum C, IIB | 21.1 | — | 18.3 | — |
| Union U, IIB | 28.8 | 24.6 | 21.7 | 18.9 |
| U of Tennessee | | | | |
| Chattanooga, IIA | 38.6 | 31.8 | 27.3 | 20.2 |

## TENNESSEE—Continued

| | Prof | Assoc Prof | Asst Prof | Inst |
|---|---|---|---|---|
| U of Tennessee | | | | |
| Inst of Ag, IIA | 43.5 | 36.3 | 30.7 | 20.8 |
| Knoxville, I | 45.6 | 33.3 | 29.1 | 21.2 |
| Martin, IIB | 35.7 | 30.6 | 26.6 | 21.5 |
| U of the South, IIA | 40.4 | 30.1 | 25.5 | — |
| Vanderbilt U, I | 54.7 | 37.7 | 29.9 | 29.4 |
| Volunteer St CC, III | 31.4 | 26.7 | 22.9 | 19.4 |

## TEXAS

| | Prof | Assoc Prof | Asst Prof | Inst |
|---|---|---|---|---|
| Abilene Christian U, IIA | 32.9 | 28.3 | 24.4 | 19.0 |
| Angelo St U, IIA | 36.2 | 32.7 | 26.9 | 21.2 |
| Austin C, IIB | 38.1 | 29.6 | 25.6 | — |
| Baylor U, I | 46.0 | 36.3 | 29.9 | 23.5 |
| Bishop C, IIB | 24.2 | 24.6 | 24.0 | — |
| Corpus Christi St U, IIA | 36.5 | 28.8 | 23.5 | — |
| Del Mar C, III | 37.9 | 32.3 | 29.1 | 24.7 |
| East Texas St U, IIA | 37.1 | 29.4 | 25.9 | 22.5 |
| Texarkana, IIB | 37.4 | 32.8 | — | — |
| Hardin-Simmons U, IIA | 33.2 | 26.9 | 24.1 | 20.6 |
| Houston Baptist U, IIA | 30.1 | 28.9 | 24.4 | 22.1 |
| Incarnate Word C, IIB | 29.3 | 26.0 | 20.6 | |
| Jarvis Christian C, IIB | 29.7 | 23.9 | 19.8 | 16.7 |
| Lamar U Orange Ctr, III | | — | 23.3 | 18.3 |
| Lubbock Christian C, IIB | 23.1 | 20.3 | 16.3 | — |
| McMurry C, IIB | 28.1 | 24.6 | 24.0 | 20.8 |
| Midwestern St U, IIA | 38.0 | 30.8 | 24.2 | 19.5 |
| North Texas St U, I | 39.9 | 32.2 | 28.1 | 21.9 |
| Odessa C, III | 37.6 | 30.8 | 27.9 | 26.9 |
| Our Lady | | | | |
| of the Lake U, IIA | 33.0 | 27.5 | 23.8 | 19.5 |
| Pan American U, IIA | 39.4 | 31.5 | 26.1 | 20.8 |
| Prairie View A&M U, IIA | 37.7 | 32.2 | 27.1 | 24.0 |
| Rice U, I | 55.9 | 39.3 | 31.8 | 22.9 |
| S F Austin St U, IIA | 37.3 | 31.1 | 25.5 | 19.9 |
| Saint Mary's U, IIA | 41.3 | 30.0 | 26.6 | — |
| Sam Houston St U, IIA | 37.5 | 31.9 | 26.4 | 22.8 |
| San Antonio C, III | 34.6 | 31.3 | 27.8 | 24.3 |
| Schreiner C, III | 29.0 | — | 21.1 | 17.9 |
| Southern Methodist U, I | 54.8 | 37.2 | 31.3 | 21.3 |
| Southwest Tex St U, IIA | 37.6 | 31.2 | 24.6 | 19.1 |
| SW Assemblies | | | | |
| of God C, IIB | — | — | 19.7 | — |
| Southwestern U, IIB | 45.0 | 34.3 | 27.4 | 25.8 |
| Sul Ross St U, IIA | 34.1 | 29.1 | 23.3 | 19.2 |
| Tarleton St U, IIA | 34.1 | 29.6 | 25.5 | 20.7 |
| Texas A&I U, IIA | 34.0 | 28.5 | 25.6 | 17.9 |
| Texas A&M U | | | | |
| Main campus, I | 46.7 | 35.3 | 29.0 | 19.3 |
| Galveston, IIB | — | 28.1 | 24.5 | |
| Texas Christian U, I | 47.3 | 35.6 | 30.1 | 26.4 |
| Texas Lutheran C, IIB | 32.6 | 28.8 | 24.9 | — |
| Texas Southern U, I | 35.1 | 31.0 | 20.3 | 16.7 |
| Texas Tech U, I | 43.2 | 32.5 | 27.0 | 19.3 |
| Texas Wesleyan C, IIB | 29.7 | 26.2 | 24.5 | — |
| Texas Woman's U, I | 38.9 | 30.9 | 25.3 | 22.3 |
| Trinity U, IIA | 48.7 | 35.7 | 28.2 | — |
| U of Dallas, IIA | 33.1 | 30.2 | 27.6 | — |
| U of Houston | | | | |
| Clear Lake, IIA | 40.6 | 33.9 | 30.3 | 24.2 |
| Downtown, IIB | 40.2 | 32.2 | 26.2 | — |

## TEXAS—Continued

| | Prof | Assoc Prof | Asst Prof | Inst |
|---|---|---|---|---|
| U of Houston U Park, I | 47.8 | 34.0 | 29.2 | 24.9 |
| U of Saint Thomas, IIA | 27.7 | 25.3 | 22.7 | — |
| U of Texas | | | | |
| Arlington, I | 42.5 | 32.0 | 27.4 | — |
| Austin, I | 49.7 | 34.0 | 29.9 | 22.6 |
| Dallas, I | 48.1 | 34.0 | 30.3 | — |
| Permian Basin, IIA | 35.2 | 28.6 | 25.3 | — |
| San Antonio, IIA | 38.9 | 31.4 | 26.3 | — |
| Tyler, IIA | 39.0 | 32.1 | 25.7 | 22.4 |
| West Texas St U, IIA | 35.7 | 29.1 | 24.7 | 20.8 |

## UTAH

| | Prof | Assoc Prof | Asst Prof | Inst |
|---|---|---|---|---|
| Dixie C, III | — | 28.8 | 28.1 | 18.9 |
| Snow C, III | 31.4 | 27.9 | 24.4 | 21.5 |
| Southern Utah St C, IIB | 33.3 | 26.8 | 23.5 | 20.2 |
| U of Utah, I | 44.5 | 31.6 | 28.0 | 22.6 |
| Utah St U, I | 40.4 | 31.7 | 26.0 | 22.5 |
| Utah Tech C | | | | |
| at Salt Lake, III | 29.0 | 25.4 | 23.1 | 22.0 |
| Weber St C, IIA | 35.5 | 29.4 | 25.7 | 20.9 |

## VERMONT

| | Prof | Assoc Prof | Asst Prof | Inst |
|---|---|---|---|---|
| Champlain C, III | 30.5 | 25.8 | 24.9 | 18.6 |
| Green Mountain C, IIB | 26.3 | 24.0 | 21.6 | — |
| Lyndon St C, IIB | 32.5 | 28.3 | 25.0 | — |
| Middlebury C, IIB | 50.3 | 35.4 | 28.8 | 27.3 |
| Norwich U, IIA | 33.3 | 26.8 | 24.2 | 18.5 |
| Saint Michael's C, IIB | 36.3 | 29.6 | 23.1 | — |
| U of Vermont, I | 46.1 | 34.3 | 28.1 | 22.7 |

## VIRGINIA

| | Prof | Assoc Prof | Asst Prof | Inst |
|---|---|---|---|---|
| Averett C, IIB | 26.9 | 24.1 | 21.3 | — |
| Blue Ridge CC, III | — | 30.5 | 26.9 | 22.5 |
| Bridgewater C, IIB | 29.9 | 24.7 | 21.8 | — |
| Central Virginia CC, III | 35.6 | 31.8 | 27.9 | — |
| Christendom C, IIB | | — | 25.0 | |
| Christopher | | | | |
| Newport C, IIB | 35.5 | 31.3 | 28.4 | 23.6 |
| C of William and Mary, I | 47.0 | 38.8 | 30.2 | 24.3 |
| Richard Bland C, III | — | 29.0 | — | — |
| Dabney Lancaster CC, III | — | 34.9 | 26.9 | 23.5 |
| Danville CC, III | 31.4 | 30.1 | 25.8 | — |
| E Mennonite C, IIB | 23.9 | 21.6 | 18.9 | — |
| Emory and Henry C, IIB | 30.8 | 26.1 | 23.4 | — |
| Ferrum C, IIB | 26.9 | 22.8 | 20.0 | — |
| George Mason U, IIA | 47.8 | 36.3 | 31.0 | 25.5 |
| Germanna CC, III | — | 31.7 | 25.5 | 21.1 |
| Hampden-Sydney C, IIB | 36.9 | 30.1 | 25.0 | |
| Hollins C, IIB | 40.1 | 32.6 | 23.7 | — |
| J Sargeant | | | | |
| Reynolds CC, III | 33.6 | 31.5 | 26.6 | 23.8 |
| James Madison U, IIA | 39.4 | 33.8 | 29.3 | 21.6 |
| John Tyler CC, III | 33.1 | 30.3 | 25.3 | 23.2 |
| Longwood C, IIB | 38.9 | 33.1 | 25.9 | 23.0 |
| Lord Fairfax CC, III | — | 27.0 | 25.4 | — |
| Lynchburg C, IIA | 34.5 | 28.2 | 23.3 | — |
| Mary Baldwin C, IIB | 31.6 | 24.1 | 23.2 | 22.0 |

*Continued on Following Page*

### VIRGINIA—Continued

| | Prof | Assoc Prof | Asst Prof | Inst |
|---|---|---|---|---|
| Mary Washington C, IIA | 37.8 | 33.4 | 26.2 | 23.1 |
| Marymount U, IIB | 37.5 | 27.9 | 23.6 | 18.3 |
| Mountain Empire CC, III | — | 29.9 | 25.6 | 22.5 |
| New River CC, III | 35.9 | 31.5 | 26.2 | 21.1 |
| Norfolk St U, IIA | 40.4 | 35.4 | 29.4 | 22.1 |
| Northern Virginia CC, III | 35.9 | 32.7 | 28.2 | 24.4 |
| Old Dominion U, IIA | 48.0 | 35.7 | 30.8 | 23.8 |
| Patrick Henry CC, III | — | 30.4 | 26.0 | — |
| Paul D Camp CC, III | — | 29.4 | 24.8 | — |
| Piedmont Virginia CC, III | 33.8 | 28.9 | 25.3 | — |
| Presbyterian Sch of Christian Ed, IIB | 30.3 | — | — | — |
| Radford U, IIA | 39.6 | 33.0 | 27.3 | 21.7 |
| Randolph-Macon C, IIB | 36.6 | 29.6 | 24.8 | — |
| Randolph-Macon Woman's C, IIB | 37.7 | 28.1 | 23.3 | — |
| Rappahannock CC, III | — | 31.6 | 25.0 | — |
| Roanoke C, IIB | 37.7 | 29.2 | 24.5 | — |
| Shenandoah C & Conserv of Music, IIB | 26.3 | 24.0 | 19.1 | — |
| Southside Va CC, III | — | 28.1 | 25.3 | — |
| Southwest Va CC, III | 33.7 | 30.6 | 27.2 | 23.7 |
| Sweet Briar C, IIB | 38.3 | 30.3 | 23.9 | — |
| Thomas Nelson CC, III | 34.6 | 29.9 | 26.5 | 22.6 |
| Tidewater CC, III | 31.8 | 28.9 | 25.6 | 22.6 |
| U of Richmond, IIA | 45.5 | 35.0 | 27.8 | 19.7 |
| U of Virginia, I | 59.0 | 39.9 | 32.0 | 23.1 |

### VIRGINIA—Continued

| | Prof | Assoc Prof | Asst Prof | Inst |
|---|---|---|---|---|
| U of Virginia Clinch Valley C, IIB | 36.8 | 29.8 | 24.8 | — |
| Va Commonwealth U, I | 45.5 | 37.4 | 31.7 | 23.8 |
| Va Highlands CC, III | — | 30.3 | 26.2 | — |
| Virginia Military Inst, IIB | 42.0 | 36.8 | 29.4 | — |
| Va Poly Inst & St U, I | 54.0 | 38.3 | 33.1 | 22.7 |
| Virginia St U, IIA | 37.5 | 32.7 | 29.5 | 24.4 |
| Virginia Wesleyan C, IIB | 34.3 | 29.8 | 22.9 | 22.5 |
| Virginia Western CC, III | 35.7 | 31.2 | 26.5 | 22.3 |
| Washington & Lee U, IIB | 44.4 | 33.1 | 26.6 | 21.1 |
| Wytheville CC, III | 33.3 | 30.0 | 25.7 | 23.7 |

### WASHINGTON

| | Prof | Assoc Prof | Asst Prof | Inst |
|---|---|---|---|---|
| Central Wash U, IIA | 36.5 | 30.8 | 25.1 | — |
| Pacific Lutheran U, IIA | 36.2 | 29.4 | 24.4 | — |
| Saint Martin's C, IIB | — | 23.7 | 20.9 | — |
| Seattle Pacific U, IIB | 33.1 | 27.7 | 24.1 | 19.9 |
| Seattle U, IIA | 36.6 | 29.4 | 25.9 | 22.9 |
| U of Puget Sound, IIA | 39.9 | 31.6 | 25.7 | 21.9 |
| U of Washington, I | 47.9 | 33.7 | 30.7 | — |
| Washington St U, I | 42.2 | 32.1 | 28.5 | 22.5 |
| Western Wash U, IIA | 38.2 | 31.7 | 26.9 | — |
| Whitman C, IIB | 39.0 | 32.6 | 25.7 | 22.3 |
| Whitworth C, IIB | 34.2 | 27.9 | 23.0 | 17.4 |

### WEST VIRGINIA

| | Prof | Assoc Prof | Asst Prof | Inst |
|---|---|---|---|---|
| Alderson Broaddus C, IIB | 27.1 | 22.9 | 19.0 | 17.3 |
| Bethany C, IIB | 28.1 | 22.3 | 21.5 | — |
| Bluefield St C, IIB | 29.7 | 25.2 | 20.6 | 19.2 |
| Concord C, IIB | 31.3 | 26.6 | 21.9 | 18.5 |
| Davis & Elkins C, IIB | 27.6 | 23.4 | 20.6 | 17.5 |
| Fairmont St C, IIB | 31.1 | 27.2 | 22.9 | 23.1 |
| Glenville St C, IIB | 29.9 | 25.5 | 21.8 | 19.7 |
| Marshall U, IIA | 34.0 | 28.8 | 23.3 | 17.7 |
| Shepherd C, IIB | 32.2 | 27.2 | 24.3 | 20.6 |
| West Liberty St C, IIB | 31.3 | 25.8 | 21.0 | 18.7 |
| West Virginia C of Grad Studies, IIA | 37.0 | 32.5 | — | |
| West Va Inst of Tech, IIB | 26.8 | 27.8 | 23.8 | 20.1 |
| West Va Northern CC, III | 29.1 | 23.8 | 20.3 | 16.3 |
| West Virginia U, I | 39.8 | 32.0 | 26.0 | 19.4 |
| Potomac St C, III | 32.7 | 25.8 | 21.5 | 17.8 |
| West Va Wesleyan C, IIB | 28.2 | 24.4 | 22.0 | — |

### WISCONSIN

| | Prof | Assoc Prof | Asst Prof | Inst |
|---|---|---|---|---|
| Alverno C, IIB | 29.9 | 25.9 | 21.3 | 18.4 |
| Beloit C, IIB | 35.3 | 29.4 | 24.2 | — |
| Carroll C, IIB | 35.9 | 30.3 | 26.7 | |
| Carthage C, IIB | 30.0 | 23.6 | 22.7 | 17.3 |
| Concordia C of Wis, IIB | — | 21.3 | 19.6 | — |
| Edgewood C, IIB | 29.8 | 22.7 | 20.2 | — |

### WISCONSIN—Continued

| | Prof | Assoc Prof | Asst Prof | Inst |
|---|---|---|---|---|
| Inst of Paper Chemistry, IIA | 52.9 | 40.0 | 33.0 | — |
| Lakeland C, IIB | 26.5 | 21.7 | 20.8 | — |
| Lawrence U, IIB | 42.2 | 33.1 | 24.9 | |
| Marquette U, I | 49.3 | 36.9 | 30.8 | |
| Milwaukee Sch of Engineering, IIB | 34.8 | 26.7 | 25.8 | 23.8 |
| Mount Mary C, IIA | — | 25.4 | 20.4 | — |
| Mount Senario C, IIB | — | 18.4 | 16.4 | 14.5 |
| Northland C, IIB | 23.2 | — | 19.4 | — |
| Ripon C, IIB | 38.7 | 29.8 | 25.0 | — |
| Saint Norbert C, IIB | 38.8 | 31.8 | 24.9 | — |
| U of Wisconsin Centers, III | 35.8 | 30.1 | 24.6 | 21.5 |
| Eau Claire, IIA | 39.0 | 31.1 | 27.2 | 23.4 |
| Green Bay, IIA | 40.3 | 32.1 | 27.3 | — |
| La Crosse, IIA | 39.0 | 34.4 | 29.1 | 27.2 |
| Madison, I | 49.3 | 36.1 | 32.8 | 26.4 |
| Milwaukee, I | 46.8 | 34.7 | 30.2 | 27.7 |
| Oshkosh, IIA | 40.4 | 34.0 | 29.5 | 24.0 |
| Parkside, IIA | 42.3 | 32.3 | 28.2 | |
| Platteville, IIA | 38.5 | 33.1 | 29.1 | — |
| River Falls, IIA | 37.4 | 29.7 | 26.8 | — |
| Stevens Point, IIA | 38.8 | 31.4 | 27.3 | 22.8 |
| Stout, IIA | 37.9 | 31.5 | 26.7 | 24.5 |
| Superior, IIA | 40.6 | 31.1 | 26.7 | — |
| Whitewater, IIA | 39.5 | 32.9 | 28.8 | 25.1 |

### WISCONSIN—Continued

| | Prof | Assoc Prof | Asst Prof | Inst |
|---|---|---|---|---|
| Viterbo C, IIB | — | 25.9 | 21.1 | 19.7 |

### WYOMING

| | Prof | Assoc Prof | Asst Prof | Inst |
|---|---|---|---|---|
| Central Wyoming C, III | 31.6 | — | 26.3 | 23.8 |
| Northwest CC, III | — | 31.7 | 25.6 | 22.3 |
| U of Wyoming, I | 43.4 | 32.4 | 28.1 | — |
| Western Wyo CC, III | 37.6 | 34.5 | 30.6 | 25.3 |

### PUERTO RICO

| | Prof | Assoc Prof | Asst Prof | Inst |
|---|---|---|---|---|
| Antillian C, IIB | — | — | 15.6 | 14.0 |
| Arecibo Tech U C, III | 26.2 | 22.8 | 18.9 | 16.5 |
| Catholic U of PR, IIB | 19.4 | 15.5 | 13.5 | 11.7 |
| Inter American U of Puerto Rico, IIA | 20.3 | 17.6 | 15.2 | 13.2 |
| Mendez Ed Fdn Sys Puerto Rico JC, III | | — | 14.9 | 12.5 |
| U of Turabo, IIB | 22.3 | 17.7 | 15.5 | 11.5 |
| U Metropolitan, IIB | — | — | 15.4 | 9.8 |
| U of Puerto Rico Cayey U C, IIB | 30.0 | 23.1 | 18.9 | 16.3 |
| Humacao U C, IIB | 28.4 | 23.5 | 19.5 | 16.2 |
| Ponce Tech U C, III | — | 17.9 | 15.7 | 13.0 |
| Rio Piedras, IIA | 29.4 | 23.8 | 19.8 | 16.3 |
| U of Sacred Heart, IIB | 23.6 | 19.4 | 16.4 | 13.6 |

### GUAM

| | Prof | Assoc Prof | Asst Prof | Inst |
|---|---|---|---|---|
| U of Guam, IIA | 40.8 | 34.8 | 26.4 | 21.3 |

## *2-Year and 4-Year Institutions Without Academic Ranks*

### ALABAMA

| | |
|---|---|
| Alabama Aviation & Tech C, IV | 27.7 |
| Alabama Tech C, IV | 26.8 |
| Alexander City St JC, IV | 29.0 |
| Atmore St Tech Inst, IV | 24.5 |
| Ayers St Tech C, IV | 31.2 |
| Bessemer St Tech C, IV | 30.3 |
| Bishop St JC, IV | 25.9 |
| Brewer St JC, IV | 27.8 |
| Calhoun St CC, IV | 27.5 |
| Carver St Tech C, IV | 29.2 |
| Chattahoochee Valley St CC, IV | 28.1 |
| Drake St Tech C, IV | 29.1 |
| Enterprise St JC, IV | 27.7 |
| Faulkner St JC, IV | 29.0 |
| Freed St Tech C, IV | 31.3 |
| Gadsden St JC, IV | 27.1 |
| G C Wallace St CC, IV | 26.6 |
| Dothan, IV | 29.1 |
| Selma, IV | 28.7 |
| Hobson St Tech C, IV | 30.5 |
| Ingram St Tech Inst, IV | 30.5 |
| Jefferson Davis St JC, IV | 26.9 |
| Jefferson St JC, IV | 29.3 |
| Lawson St CC, IV | 28.5 |
| L B Wallace St JC, IV | 26.5 |
| MacArthur St Tech C, IV | 28.3 |
| Muscle Shoals St Tech C, IV | 29.2 |
| Nunnelley St Tech C, IV | 27.3 |
| Northeast Alabama St JC, IV | 27.4 |
| Northwest Alabama St JC, IV | 26.3 |
| Northwest Ala St Tech C, IV | 30.8 |
| Opelika St Tech C, IV | 29.5 |
| Patterson St Tech C, IV | 30.3 |
| Patrick Henry St JC, IV | 28.0 |
| Reid St Tech C, IV | 27.9 |
| Shelton St CC, IV | 29.4 |
| Snead St JC, IV | 28.3 |
| Southern Union St JC, IV | 27.7 |
| Southwest St Tech C, IV | 31.8 |
| Sparks St Tech C, IV | 30.8 |
| Trenholm St Tech C, IV | 30.3 |
| Walker C, IV | 25.2 |
| Walker St Tech C, IV | 27.9 |

### ALASKA

| | |
|---|---|
| U of Alaska | |
| Anchorage CC, IV | 45.0 |
| Islands CC, IV | 40.8 |
| Kenai Peninsula CC, IV | 43.7 |
| Ketchikan CC, IV | 39.9 |
| Kuskokwim CC, IV | 55.7 |
| Matanuska-Susitna CC, IV | 40.8 |
| Northwest CC, IV | 55.2 |
| Prince William Sound CC, IV | 39.9 |
| Tanana Valley CC, IV | 43.7 |

### ARIZONA

| | |
|---|---|
| Arizona Western C, IV | 29.8 |
| Cochise C, IV | 27.7 |
| Eastern Arizona C, IV | 31.0 |
| Mohave CC, IV | 26.4 |
| Northland Pioneer C, IV | 27.6 |
| Pima CC, IV | 28.4 |
| Yavapai C, IV | 31.6 |

### ARKANSAS

| | |
|---|---|
| S Ark U Tech Branch, IV | 23.1 |
| Southern Baptist C, IV | 16.3 |

### CALIFORNIA

| | |
|---|---|
| Allan Hancock C, IV | 34.5 |
| Antelope Valley C, IV | 36.1 |
| Barstow C, IV | 35.1 |
| Butte C, IV | 36.7 |
| Cabrillo C, IV | 29.0 |
| California Inst of the Arts, IIA | 28.7 |
| Cerritos C, IV | 41.7 |
| Chabot C, IV | 38.3 |
| Chaffey C, IV | 35.7 |
| Citrus C, IV | 40.4 |
| City C of San Francisco, IV | 37.3 |
| Coast CC Dist, IV | 39.7 |
| C of the Canyons, IV | 37.4 |
| C of the Desert, IV | 35.3 |
| C of the Redwoods, IV | 38.0 |
| C of the Sequoias, IV | 38.6 |
| Compton CC, IV | 30.9 |
| Contra Costa CC Dist, IV | 44.1 |
| Cuesta C, IV | 38.0 |
| El Camino C, IV | 40.2 |
| Foothill-De Anza CC Dist, IV | 44.5 |
| Fresno Pacific C, IIB | 23.3 |
| Gavilan C, IV | 36.8 |

### CALIFORNIA—Continued

| | |
|---|---|
| Glendale CC Dist, IV | 38.1 |
| Grossmont C, IV | 36.1 |
| Hartnell C, IV | 35.8 |
| Imperial Valley C, IV | 32.2 |
| Kern CC Dist, IV | 35.2 |
| Lake Tahoe CC, IV | 35.2 |
| Lassen C, IV | 32.5 |
| Long Beach City C, IV | 42.3 |
| Los Angeles CC Dist, IV | 38.3 |
| Los Rios CC Dist, IV | 35.8 |
| Marin CC Dist, IV | 38.4 |
| Mendocino-Lake CC Dist, IV | 35.0 |
| Menlo C, IIB | 32.8 |
| Merced C, IV | 35.4 |
| Mira Costa C, IV | 39.0 |
| Monterey Peninsula C, IV | 34.5 |
| Mount San Antonio C, IV | 40.5 |
| Mount San Jacinto C, IV | 35.0 |
| Napa Valley C, IV | 34.1 |
| North Orange Co CC Dist, IV | 40.0 |
| Pacific Oaks C, IIA | 22.3 |
| Palo Verde C, IV | 35.3 |
| Pasadena Area CC Dist, IV | 38.5 |
| Peralta CC's Dist, IV | 37.0 |
| Rancho Santiago C, IV | 39.9 |
| Rio Hondo C, IV | 40.7 |
| Riverside City C, IV | 37.1 |
| Saddleback CC Dist, IV | 41.8 |
| San Diego CC Dist, IV | 31.1 |
| San Joaquin Delta C, IV | 43.9 |
| San Jose CC Dist, IV | 38.9 |
| San Mateo CC Dist, IV | 39.3 |
| Santa Barbara City C, IV | 34.5 |
| Santa Monica C, IV | 41.2 |
| Santa Rosa JC, IV | 39.8 |
| Shasta C, IV | 38.2 |
| Sierra C, IV | 37.0 |
| Siskiyou Joint CC Dist, IV | 35.1 |
| Solano CC, IV | 38.7 |
| Southwestern C, IV | 36.6 |
| State Center CC Dist, IV | 38.1 |
| Taft C, IV | 40.7 |
| Ventura County CC Dist, IV | 36.8 |
| Victor Valley CC Dist, IV | 34.1 |
| West Hills CC Dist, IV | 36.5 |
| West Valley Joint CC Dist, IV | 39.2 |
| Woodbury U, IIA | 30.0 |
| Yosemite CC Dist, IV | 37.3 |
| Yuba C, IV | 37.0 |

### COLORADO

| | |
|---|---|
| Arapahoe CC, IV | 24.9 |
| Colorado Northwestern CC, IV | 29.5 |
| CC of Aurora, IV | 24.0 |
| CC of Denver, IV | 25.6 |
| Northeastern JC, IV | 25.5 |
| Otero JC, IV | 24.9 |
| Pikes Peak CC, IV | 24.7 |
| Red Rocks CC, IV | 33.7 |

### CONNECTICUT

| | |
|---|---|
| Hartford Sem, IIB | 38.3 |

### DELAWARE

| | |
|---|---|
| Delaware Tech and CC | |
| Southern, IV | 30.8 |
| Stanton-Wilmington, IV | 28.8 |
| Terry, IV | 28.1 |

### FLORIDA

| | |
|---|---|
| Broward CC, IV | 28.8 |
| Lake City CC, IV | 23.4 |
| Lake-Sumter CC, IV | 25.6 |
| Polk CC, IV | 21.8 |
| Valencia CC, IV | 29.9 |

### GEORGIA

| | |
|---|---|
| Truett McConnell C, IV | 19.7 |

### HAWAII

| | |
|---|---|
| U of Hawaii | |
| Honolulu CC, IV | 29.6 |
| Kapiolani CC, IV | 30.9 |
| Kauai CC, IV | 28.6 |
| Leeward CC, IV | 30.9 |
| Maui CC, IV | 29.5 |
| Windward CC, IV | 28.7 |

### IDAHO

| | |
|---|---|
| North Idaho C, IV | 27.0 |

### ILLINOIS

| | |
|---|---|
| Belleville Area C, IV | 34.6 |
| Carl Sandburg C, IV | 20.4 |
| Chicago C of Commerce, IV | 18.5 |
| C of Lake County, IV | 35.0 |
| Danville Area CC, IV | 26.6 |
| Elgin CC, IV | 31.1 |
| Governors St U, IIA | 33.0 |
| Harrington Inst of Interior Design, IV | 27.3 |
| Highland CC, IV | 28.3 |
| Illinois Eastern CC's, IV | 23.3 |
| John A Logan C, IV | 29.4 |
| Kankakee CC, IV | 25.8 |
| Kaskaskia C, IV | 25.9 |
| Lake Land CC, IV | 26.3 |
| Lincoln C, IV | 20.6 |
| McHenry County C, IV | 30.0 |
| Moraine Valley CC, IV | 29.8 |
| Morton C, IV | 33.0 |
| NAES C, IIB | 19.1 |
| National C of Ed, IIA | 26.5 |
| Parkland C, IV | 33.4 |
| Ray C of Design, IIB | 22.8 |
| Rock Valley C, IV | 30.3 |
| Springfield C in Illinois, IV | 19.4 |
| State CC, IV | 24.6 |
| Triton C, IV | 35.0 |

### IOWA

| | |
|---|---|
| Des Moines Area CC, IV | 24.9 |
| Indian Hills CC, IV | 22.1 |
| Iowa Lakes CC, IV | 22.5 |
| North Iowa Area CC, IV | 29.4 |
| Western Iowa Tech CC, IV | 22.8 |

### KANSAS

| | |
|---|---|
| Allen County CC, IV | 25.5 |
| Barton County CC, IV | 24.4 |
| Butler County CC, IV | 24.2 |
| Central C, IV | 16.1 |
| Coffeyville CC, IV | 22.7 |
| Colby CC, IV | 23.1 |
| Cowley County CC, IV | 25.8 |
| Hesston C, IV | 17.6 |
| Hutchinson CC, IV | 27.4 |
| Johnson County CC, IV | 32.3 |
| Kansas City Kansas CC, IV | 28.7 |
| Neosho County CC, IV | 24.2 |
| Seward County CC, IV | 25.6 |

### KENTUCKY

| | |
|---|---|
| Midway C, IV | 18.7 |
| Saint Catharine C, IV | 16.6 |

### MARYLAND

| | |
|---|---|
| Maryland Inst C of Art, IIB | 27.3 |
| Saint John's C, IIB | 31.0 |

### MICHIGAN

| | |
|---|---|
| Detroit C of Business, IIB | 26.3 |
| Grand Rapids JC, IV | 34.9 |
| Mid Michigan CC, IV | 25.4 |
| Montcalm CC, IV | 29.4 |
| Schoolcraft C, IV | 35.8 |
| Suomi C, IV | 25.7 |
| West Shore CC, IV | 28.4 |

### MINNESOTA

| | |
|---|---|
| Anoka-Ramsey CC, IV | 31.5 |
| Austin CC, IV | 33.7 |
| Bethany Lutheran C, IV | 18.5 |
| Brainerd CC, IV | 30.3 |
| Fergus Falls CC, IV | 31.9 |
| Hibbing CC, IV | 26.7 |
| Inver Hills CC, IV | 31.3 |
| Itasca CC, IV | 30.6 |
| Lakewood CC, IV | 32.4 |
| Mesabi CC, IV | 31.1 |
| Minneapolis CC, IV | 31.6 |
| Normandale CC, IV | 31.4 |
| North Hennepin CC, IV | 32.0 |
| Northland CC, IV | 31.4 |
| Rainy River CC, IV | 27.1 |
| Rochester CC, IV | 31.0 |
| Vermillion CC, IV | 31.0 |
| Willmar CC, IV | 30.7 |
| Worthington CC, IV | 31.2 |

### MISSISSIPPI

| | |
|---|---|
| Coahoma JC, IV | 17.8 |
| Copiah-Lincoln JC, IV | 19.4 |

### MISSISSIPPI—Continued

| | |
|---|---|
| East Central JC, IV | 18.8 |
| East Mississippi JC, IV | 18.8 |
| Hinds JC, IV | 21.2 |
| Holmes JC, IV | 19.4 |
| Itawamba JC, IV | 21.1 |
| Jones County JC, IV | 24.2 |
| Meridian JC, IV | 21.9 |
| Mississippi Delta JC, IV | 21.7 |
| Mississippi Gulf Coast JC, IV | 22.7 |
| Northeast Mississippi JC, IV | 21.9 |
| Northwest Mississippi JC, IV | 21.9 |
| Pearl River JC, IV | 19.8 |
| Southwest Mississippi JC, IV | 20.6 |
| Wood JC, IV | 15.7 |

### MISSOURI

| | |
|---|---|
| Stephens C, IIB | 22.0 |
| Three Rivers CC, IV | 20.2 |
| Trenton JC, IV | 20.7 |

### MONTANA

| | |
|---|---|
| Flathead Valley CC, IV | 28.7 |
| Miles CC, IV | 25.3 |

### NEBRASKA

| | |
|---|---|
| Grace C of the Bible, IIB | 17.7 |
| McCook CC, IV | 22.2 |
| Metropolitan Tech CC, IV | 22.8 |
| Mid-Plains Tech CC Area, IV | 24.9 |
| Northeast Tech CC, IV | 21.9 |
| Southeast CC Area, IV | 21.4 |
| Western Tech CC Area, IV | 23.1 |

### NEVADA

| | |
|---|---|
| Western Nevada CC, IV | 31.4 |

### NEW MEXICO

| | |
|---|---|
| Northern New Mexico CC, IV | 20.4 |
| Saint John's C, IIB | 30.1 |

### NEW YORK

| | |
|---|---|
| Friends World C, IIB | 20.6 |
| Sarah Lawrence C, IIA | 34.5 |

### NORTH CAROLINA

| | |
|---|---|
| Bladen Tech C, IV | 19.4 |
| Blue Ridge Tech C, IV | 23.3 |
| Brunswick Tech C, IV | 20.9 |
| Carteret Tech C, IV | 20.8 |
| Fayetteville Tech Inst, IV | 24.0 |
| Halifax CC, IV | 20.5 |
| Haywood Tech C, IV | 21.9 |
| Isothermal CC, IV | 21.9 |
| Johnston Tech C, IV | 19.7 |
| Lees-McRae C, IV | 19.6 |
| Mayland Tech C, IV | 20.6 |
| McDowell Tech C, IV | 20.0 |
| Mitchell CC, IV | 21.2 |
| Montreat-Anderson C, IV | 21.5 |
| Nash Tech C, IV | 23.2 |
| Piedmont Tech C, IV | 19.3 |
| Richmond Tech C, IV | 24.0 |
| Southeastern CC, IV | 19.9 |
| Tri-County CC, IV | 18.7 |
| Vance-Granville CC, IV | 22.7 |
| Wayne CC, IV | 23.0 |

### NORTH DAKOTA

| | |
|---|---|
| Bismarck JC, IV | 29.4 |
| Lake Region CC, IV | 22.5 |
| ND St Sch of Science, IV | 27.8 |
| ND St U Bottineau, IV | 26.1 |
| U of ND Williston Ctr, IV | 26.8 |

### OHIO

| | |
|---|---|
| Art Acad of Cincinnati, IIB | 18.2 |
| Cincinnati Tech C, IV | 26.6 |
| Columbus Tech Inst, IV | 25.1 |
| Cuyahoga CC Dist, IV | 36.8 |
| Marion Tech C, IV | 25.1 |

### OKLAHOMA

| | |
|---|---|
| Bartlesville Wesleyan C, IIB | 18.4 |
| Connors St C, IV | 24.8 |
| Eastern Oklahoma St C, IV | 27.0 |

### OKLAHOMA—Continued

| | |
|---|---|
| Rose St C, IV | 25.3 |
| Saint Gregory's C, IV | 21.4 |
| Sayre JC, IV | 24.3 |
| Seminole JC, IV | 24.8 |

### OREGON

| | |
|---|---|
| Clackamas CC, IV | 28.4 |
| Pacific Northwest C of Art, IIB | 18.0 |

### RHODE ISLAND

| | |
|---|---|
| Roger Williams C, IIB | 33.0 |

### SOUTH CAROLINA

| | |
|---|---|
| Aiken Tech C, IV | 24.1 |
| Anderson C, IV | 23.2 |
| Beaufort Tech C, IV | 21.4 |
| Chesterfield-Marlboro Tech C, IV | 25.8 |
| Clinton JC, IV | 6.8 |
| Denmark Tech C, IV | 20.2 |
| Florence-Darlington Tech C, IV | 23.9 |
| Greenville Tech C, IV | 23.1 |
| Horry-Georgetown Tech C, IV | 22.5 |
| Midlands Tech C, IV | 24.4 |
| Orangeburg Calhoun Tech C, IV | 22.2 |
| Piedmont Tech C, IV | 22.0 |
| Spartanburg Methodist C, IV | 22.7 |
| Spartanburg Tech C, IV | 22.6 |
| Sumter Area Tech C, IV | 21.7 |
| Tri-County Tech C, IV | 22.6 |
| Trident Tech C, IV | 30.4 |
| York Tech C, IV | 23.0 |

### TENNESSEE

| | |
|---|---|
| Tomlinson C, IV | 19.7 |

### TEXAS

| | |
|---|---|
| Austin CC, IV | 26.0 |
| El Paso County CC Dist, IV | 25.9 |
| Galveston C, IV | 27.8 |
| Hill JC, IV | 23.4 |
| Howard County JC Dist, IV | 25.7 |
| Midland C, IV | 38.7 |
| North Harris County C Dist, IV | 31.2 |
| Paris JC, IV | 22.6 |
| San Jacinto C, IV | 29.8 |
| Texas Southmost C, IV | 27.1 |
| Texas St Tech Inst | |
| Sweetwater, IV | 26.3 |
| Waco, IV | 22.7 |
| Trinity Valley CC, IV | 26.9 |

### UTAH

| | |
|---|---|
| C of Eastern Utah, IV | 25.7 |
| Utah Tech C at Provo, IV | 26.6 |

### VIRGINIA

| | |
|---|---|
| Southern Sem JC, IV | 19.0 |
| Virginia Intermont C, IIB | 18.0 |

### WASHINGTON

| | |
|---|---|
| Centralia C, IV | 27.2 |
| Columbia Basin C, IV | 28.3 |
| Cornish Inst, IIB | 16.0 |
| Evergreen St C, IIB | 32.7 |
| Grays Harbor C, IV | 28.3 |
| Lower Columbia C, IV | 25.5 |
| Peninsula C, IV | 29.8 |
| Pierce C, IV | 26.7 |
| Seattle CC Dist, IV | 28.6 |
| Skagit Valley C, IV | 26.3 |
| South Puget Sound CC, IV | 26.0 |
| Tacoma CC, IV | 32.0 |
| Washington St CC Dist, IV | 26.8 |
| Wenatchee Valley C, IV | 27.2 |

### WISCONSIN

| | |
|---|---|
| District One Tech Inst, IV | 30.9 |
| Mid-State Tech Inst, IV | 29.6 |
| Milwaukee Area Tech C, IV | 35.6 |
| Milwaukee Inst of Art & Design, IIB | 20.9 |
| Waukesha Co Tech Inst, IV | 33.6 |

### WYOMING

| | |
|---|---|
| Casper C, IV | 27.5 |

### TRUST TERRITORY

| | |
|---|---|
| CC of Micronesia, IV | 11.8 |

# Median Salaries of Administrators, 1986-87

| | All institutions | 1-year change | Public institutions | Private institutions | All universities | 4-year colleges | 2-year colleges |
|---|---|---|---|---|---|---|---|
| Chief executive of a system | $84,959 | + 4.7% | $84,959 | $82,236 | $98,800 | $70,000 | $75,000 |
| Chief executive of a single institution | 70,000 | + 6.2% | 69,875 | 71,000 | 85,680 | 68,865 | 62,441 |
| Executive vice-president | 58,916 | + 4.5% | 60,000 | 55,000 | 72,100 | 53,593 | 53,000 |
| Chief academic officer | 54,796 | + 6.4% | 58,266 | 50,000 | 70,044 | 51,500 | 48,695 |
| Chief budget officer | 44,527 | + 5.4% | 44,979 | 41,650 | 48,000 | 38,964 | 41,379 |
| Chief business officer | 52,000 | + 6.3% | 53,800 | 49,202 | 66,675 | 49,488 | 46,721 |
| Chief development officer | 47,092 | + 5.8% | 48,072 | 45,600 | 58,435 | 44,000 | 39,630 |
| Chief development and public-relations officer | 54,000 | + 9.3% | 55,000 | 53,141 | 66,500 | 51,000 | 37,022 |
| Chief health-professions officer | 67,392 | +11.3% | 64,400 | 82,500 | 104,816 | 37,800 | 42,350 |
| Chief personnel and human-resources officer | 40,000 | + 6.8% | 42,996 | 34,570 | 45,600 | 32,500 | 39,450 |
| Chief physical-plant officer | 38,000 | + 4.5% | 40,158 | 34,000 | 47,797 | 33,300 | 33,208 |
| Chief planning officer | 49,000 | + 4.3% | 50,500 | 44,750 | 56,500 | 41,750 | 44,405 |
| Chief planning and budget officer | 52,998 | + 5.7% | 58,538 | 46,000 | 60,000 | 45,900 | 47,161 |
| Chief public-relations officer | 35,424 | + 6.7% | 38,773 | 31,000 | 46,867 | 30,000 | 31,500 |
| Chief student-affairs officer | 45,773 | + 6.1% | 50,110 | 38,430 | 57,000 | 39,000 | 44,691 |
| Administrator, grants and contracts | 38,892 | + 2.7% | 41,112 | 35,000 | 45,000 | 28,510 | 34,120 |
| Administrator, hospital medical center | 94,700 | +12.7% | 92,940 | 100,006 | 100,000 | — | — |
| Bursar | 29,940 | + 9.2% | 31,260 | 27,269 | 34,971 | 24,837 | 27,941 |
| Chaplain | 26,200 | + 2.1% | 28,113 | 26,100 | 31,009 | 24,700 | 23,600 |
| Comptroller | 40,000 | + 4.9% | 42,974 | 36,040 | 47,961 | 34,255 | 37,333 |
| General counsel | 56,442 | + 6.5% | 55,650 | 62,993 | 58,300 | 51,100 | 47,515 |
| Registrar | 32,952 | + 6.3% | 37,510 | 28,100 | 40,308 | 28,938 | 32,386 |
| Director, accounting | 32,330 | + 7.0% | 35,000 | 28,090 | 38,500 | 26,650 | 30,800 |
| Director, admissions | 35,020 | + 4.7% | 36,000 | 33,800 | 42,400 | 33,406 | 31,836 |
|    Admissions and financial aid | 40,000 | + 6.7% | 40,132 | 39,541 | 44,870 | 39,541 | 35,144 |
|    Admissions and registrar | 39,853 | + 3.1% | 41,128 | 30,788 | 46,103 | 33,072 | 37,914 |
| Director, affirmative action & equal employment | 39,828 | + 7.6% | 39,669 | 39,000 | 40,250 | 33,800 | 39,317 |
| Director, alumni affairs | 28,680 | +10.3% | 32,159 | 25,116 | 34,250 | 24,464 | 22,500 |
| Director, athletics | 40,000 | + 3.6% | 44,000 | 34,655 | 49,992 | 34,000 | 35,904 |
|    Men's | — | — | — | — | 43,783 | 28,500 | 36,000 |
|    Women's | — | — | — | — | 37,000 | 24,960 | 27,600 |
| Director, auxiliary services | 40,044 | + 9.0% | 41,000 | 35,600 | 44,628 | 33,935 | 32,315 |
| Director, bookstore | 23,256 | + 5.7% | 26,365 | 19,915 | 31,350 | 19,750 | 21,672 |
| Director, campus recreation and intramurals | 26,724 | + 1.0% | 29,364 | 22,550 | 30,500 | 22,500 | 21,477 |
| Director, campus security | 28,940 | + 5.2% | 31,658 | 25,099 | 34,475 | 25,000 | 26,303 |
| Director, church relations | 26,130 | — | 32,820 | 25,600 | — | 25,000 | — |
| Director, community services | 35,000 | + 6.9% | 36,277 | 28,220 | 37,689 | 27,906 | 34,879 |
| Director, computer center | 40,720 | + 5.4% | 44,165 | 34,775 | 51,000 | 34,729 | 38,173 |
|    Academic operations | 37,685 | + 2.9% | 40,000 | 35,000 | 45,096 | 31,185 | 33,079 |
|    Administrative operations | 38,500 | + 6.4% | 41,468 | 35,700 | 46,675 | 33,254 | 34,350 |
| Director, development and alumni affairs | 38,713 | + 9.7% | 39,650 | 37,400 | 50,000 | 35,352 | 33,667 |
| Director, educational-media services | 31,164 | + 4.8% | 34,871 | 23,880 | 35,880 | 24,136 | 32,892 |
| Director, food services | 31,028 | + 3.1% | 32,113 | 30,500 | 39,068 | 26,000 | 25,502 |
| Director, foreign students | 28,434 | + 4.2% | 29,715 | 24,872 | 29,112 | 23,812 | 23,345 |
| Director, housing and food services | — | — | 46,656 | 42,400 | — | 34,920 | — |
| Director, information office | 30,000 | + 5.3% | 32,376 | 27,250 | 36,300 | 25,603 | 27,354 |
| Director, information systems | 44,736 | + 3.4% | 45,337 | 42,200 | 50,325 | 37,656 | 43,000 |
| Director, institutional research | 38,280 | + 5.6% | 40,000 | 33,000 | 43,680 | 32,136 | 36,267 |
| Director, internal audit | 38,447 | + 5.9% | 38,304 | 39,000 | 40,000 | 31,698 | 34,215 |
| Director, international studies | — | — | — | — | 42,500 | 31,298 | 38,851 |
| Director, learning-resources center | 34,130 | + 5.1% | 37,169 | 25,000 | 37,442 | 25,908 | 36,876 |
| Director, library services | 37,500 | + 5.6% | 42,400 | 32,000 | 50,000 | 32,000 | 33,753 |
| Director, news bureau | 27,690 | + 3.2% | 29,400 | 24,000 | 30,000 | 23,023 | 25,215 |
| Director, personnel and affirmative action | 33,600 | + 5.7% | 34,329 | — | 38,727 | 28,875 | 33,600 |
| Director, publications | 29,500 | + 8.1% | 32,643 | 26,028 | 34,500 | 24,995 | 25,596 |
| Director, purchasing | 31,497 | + 5.8% | 32,550 | 28,000 | 35,915 | 26,500 | 29,562 |
| Director, risk management and insurance | 41,500 | + 9.1% | 42,100 | 41,500 | 42,800 | 31,000 | 33,102 |
| Director, special and deferred gifts | 36,000 | + 8.1% | 41,000 | 34,388 | 41,617 | 32,400 | 30,000 |
| Director, student activities | 27,214 | + 4.5% | 30,992 | 21,962 | 31,936 | 21,480 | 29,900 |
| Director, student counseling | 34,081 | + 2.5% | 37,095 | 28,090 | 39,003 | 28,000 | 35,391 |
| Director, student financial aid | 30,899 | + 4.3% | 33,463 | 27,300 | 37,200 | 27,300 | 30,009 |
| Director, student health services | | | | | | | |
|    Physician | 61,509 | + 5.0% | 63,900 | 48,495 | 66,600 | 40,000 | 23,210 |
|    Nurse | 22,300 | + 1.9% | 25,793 | 20,000 | 25,662 | 19,500 | 23,507 |
| Director, student housing | 27,900 | + 8.9% | 32,832 | 23,665 | 34,430 | 23,300 | 23,130 |
| Director, student placement | 29,264 | + 4.0% | 32,096 | 25,000 | 34,980 | 24,570 | 28,106 |
| Director, student union | 32,639 | + 4.9% | 36,088 | 27,288 | 36,187 | 26,787 | 33,495 |
| Dean, architecture | 64,500 | + 2.8% | — | 61,300 | 65,749 | 45,213 | — |
| Dean, agriculture | 69,756 | +10.0% | 89,756 | — | 71,000 | — | 43,560 |
| Dean, arts and letters | 48,936 | + 2.0% | 48,936 | 42,800 | 60,980 | 44,748 | 40,656 |
| Dean, arts and sciences | 57,681 | + 7.5% | 57,681 | 57,024 | 63,816 | 51,188 | 43,470 |
| Dean, business | 55,790 | + 7.3% | 55,698 | 55,790 | 66,300 | 46,700 | 42,050 |
| Dean, communications | — | — | — | 56,500 | 65,500 | 32,400 | 43,302 |
| Dean, continuing education | 44,616 | + 9.4% | 45,102 | 42,000 | 53,510 | 39,300 | 41,425 |
| Dean, dentistry | 94,329 | + 7.9% | 89,338 | 96,500 | 95,748 | — | — |
| Dean, education | 55,259 | + 6.3% | 58,000 | 42,200 | 60,000 | 41,893 | 39,181 |
| Dean, engineering | 68,496 | + 5.1% | 68,900 | 68,000 | 76,464 | 52,000 | 44,325 |
| Dean, extension | 54,430 | + 8.9% | 54,430 | — | 65,500 | 30,000 | 41,359 |
| Dean, fine arts | 51,151 | + 4.3% | 54,564 | 40,000 | 60,000 | 35,250 | 41,328 |
| Dean, graduate programs | 57,680 | + 3.0% | 59,600 | 50,891 | 60,284 | 44,944 | — |
| Dean, health-related professions | 50,003 | + 3.2% | 50,003 | 55,450 | 63,000 | 54,000 | 40,613 |
| Dean, home economics | — | — | — | 33,600 | 64,500 | — | 41,228 |
| Dean, humanities | 43,500 | + 3.1% | 45,874 | 33,150 | 57,000 | 34,731 | 41,792 |
| Dean, instruction | — | — | — | — | — | — | 46,295 |
| Dean, law | 89,000 | + 7.2% | 86,820 | 90,000 | 90,000 | 41,420 | — |
| Dean, library and information sciences | — | — | — | — | 57,043 | 42,744 | 44,859 |
| Dean, mathematics | 40,750 | − 2.9% | 41,853 | 32,000 | — | 33,075 | 41,319 |
| Dean, medicine | 120,000 | +14.3% | 109,920 | 145,000 | 125,000 | — | — |
| Dean, music | 55,640 | + 6.0% | 62,250 | 47,500 | 64,000 | 44,056 | 46,446 |
| Dean, nursing | 50,000 | + 5.5% | 53,457 | 43,990 | 60,000 | 39,400 | 38,167 |
| Dean, pharmacy | 70,826 | + 3.4% | 76,309 | 66,000 | 71,506 | — | — |
| Dean, sciences | 48,168 | + 4.0% | 49,658 | 35,435 | 62,974 | 37,440 | 41,738 |
| Dean, social sciences | 42,400 | − 1.2% | 44,750 | 31,183 | 57,700 | 31,900 | 42,540 |
| Dean, social work | 63,305 | + 0.8% | 66,096 | 55,000 | 66,800 | 41,600 | — |
| Dean, special programs | — | — | — | 35,738 | — | 36,800 | 37,840 |
| Dean, undergraduate programs | — | — | — | — | 56,500 | 48,400 | 46,300 |
| Dean, vocational education | 45,000 | + 5.9% | 45,000 | — | 56,604 | 46,650 | 43,480 |

— No data

Note: The results are based on a national sample of 3,190 colleges and universities. The rate of response to the survey was 51 per cent. The figures are intended only to give a broad overview of salaries.

SOURCE: COLLEGE AND UNIVERSITY PERSONNEL ASSOCIATION

Table 2.2

# Shifts in Students' Attitudes

**By ELIZABETH GREENE**

Dramatic shifts in the attitudes, aspirations, and abilities of college freshmen over the last two decades pose significant threats to the future of liberal-arts education, according to a report that analyzes 20 years of surveys of a total of nearly six million first-year students.

Concerned with being financially well-off, more freshmen than ever before have said in recent years that they plan to choose majors and careers in big-money fields, the authors of the report say.

The study, *The American Freshman: Twenty Year Trends, 1966-1985*, also says that students have become more worried about their ability to finance their education.

## Career-Specific Majors

Using data from 20 years of freshman surveys conducted by the Cooperative Institutional Research Program (CIRP), now based at the University of California at Los Angeles, the authors—Alexander W. Astin and Kenneth C. Green—outline and analyze the changes that have occurred in students' academic interests, educational achievements, life goals, and values—many of them, they say, attributable to the women's movement.

"Increased student interest in career-specific majors such as business has been accompanied by rising materialistic and power values, while decreased student interest in education, social science, the arts, humanities, nursing, social work, allied health, and the clergy are reflected in declining altruism and social concern," says Mr. Astin, the director of the program.

"The traditional liberal-arts fields are clearly in serious trouble, and some of the fields are virtually moribund," say the authors. Shifts in student demands have forced institutions to reduce the size of their faculties in some liberal-arts areas and eliminate some of their course offerings, they add.

Many liberal-arts disciplines, they say, have "witnessed what can only be described as a bear market." Especially sharp declines have taken place in the humanities, the fine and performing arts, and the social sciences. In 1966, more than half the freshmen said they intended to major in those areas. In 1985, fewer than one-fourth planned to do so.

Between 1966 and 1985 the percentage of entering freshmen planning to major in education dropped 35 per cent—although, with the current wave of educational reform, a small renewal of interest has been evident in the past three years. Among the various career-goal groups, today's aspiring teachers are the least well-prepared, the authors say.

"We do not think that it is overstating the case to say that our schools are approaching a state of crisis," they add.

In addition, interest in the physical sciences has declined by one-half in the last 20 years, and mathematics and statistics have lost more than 80 per cent of their students. The authors warn of increasing shortages in the nation's pool of highly trained professionals.

They also make suggestions for increasing student interest in the liberal arts and for rebuilding that curriculum.

"One very practical question," they say, "is whether the higher education community should adapt passively to these 'market' trends in student expectations, or whether the inherent dangers in such trends should be recognized and curricula revised accordingly."

The annual freshman survey was begun in 1966 by Mr. Astin at the American Council on Education and moved with him to U.C.L.A. seven years later. The survey, which still has the council's sponsorship, has become a much-used gauge of student trends, providing the most comprehensive data of its kind.

Each year, roughly 280,000 college freshmen at about 550 two-and four-year colleges and universities nationwide participate in the annual survey. The retrospective study includes data from nearly six million students at more than 1,250 institutions.

Many of the study's findings can be attributed to the difficult economic upheavals of the last decade, which have had a serious impact on the families of today's students, Mr. Green says. A college degree is no longer perceived to be a sure ticket to a good job and a sound tomorrow, he observes.

Students, he adds, have become preoccupied with insuring that their futures will be secure.

"A lot of what we see is portfolio-building," Mr. Green says. Students are thinking, " 'I don't want this kind of risk in my future. I want to be sure that everything is going to be O.K.' "

The authors point out that the percentage of freshmen who cited "being very well-off financially" as "essential or very important" increased from 44 per cent in 1967 to 71 per cent in 1985. The percentage citing "developing a meaningful philosophy of life" dropped from 83 per cent in 1967 to 43 per cent in 1985.

## Advanced Training Unpopular

Some of the most dramatic changes have occurred in the students' preferences for majors and careers, with shifts toward business and away from the humanities and social sciences.

In recent years, students have expressed the greatest interest in career areas that do not require education beyond the bachelor's degree and are relatively high-paying; interest has been declining in areas that require advanced training or are relatively low-paying.

Those choices reflect increased opportunities for women as well as changing social values, perceptions about the labor market for college graduates, and the impact of television, according to the authors.

In addition, the authors say, the students' choices reflect a decline in academic skills. In 1985, two in every five freshmen indicated that an "important" or "very important" reason for deciding to go to college was "to improve my reading and study skills," nearly doubling the 1971 figure. The number of freshmen reporting they would need tutoring also nearly doubled.

Business has emerged as the No. 1 major and career choice for college freshmen. Intended majors in business rose from 14 per cent in 1966 to 25 per cent in 1985, and interest in business careers more than doubled. Computer science and engineering have also become more popular, though interest has been declining since their peak in 1982, as labor-market conditions in those areas has worsened.

The study shows a shift in federal aid from grants to loans, and an attempt on the part of colleges to compensate for the loss of federal grant funds by providing more assistance themselves.

It also reveals an increasing concern on the part of students about their ability to pay for their education. Almost 9 per cent expressed such concern in 1967; almost 14 per cent did so in 1985. Since 1978, more students have been taking on part-time work.

Significant changes have taken place in the makeup of the student body, especially in the demographics of blacks and women.

## Minority Presence Doubled

Between the mid-1960's and mid-1970's, the representation of minorities in entering freshman classes nearly doubled. The increase was largest for blacks, whose representation rose from 5 per cent in 1966 to 9 per cent in 1985. The authors attribute the changes to improving high-school completion rates.

While traditionally more men than women pursued postsecondary education, today women make up the majority of today's freshmen. Between 1969, when the women's movement was gaining momentum, and 1985 the percentage of female freshmen increased from 43 to 52.

The changing role of women in American society is reflected in less sex-biased student attitudes. The number of freshmen believing "the activities of married women are best confined to the home and family" has decreased dramatically since 1967, from 57 per cent to 22 per cent in 1985.

Women's choices of majors and careers have changed considerably, away from the traditionally "feminine" fields of schoolteaching, nursing, social work, and homemaking, toward business, law, medicine, science, and engineering, coupled with greater interest in advanced degrees.

Copyright: 1986. *The Chronicle of Higher Education.* Reprinted with Permission.

# Views and Characteristics of this Year's Freshmen

A national profile based on responses of 204,000 students who entered college in the fall of 1986

## Characteristics

| Age by December 31, 1986: | |
|---|---|
| 16 or younger | 0.1% |
| 17 | 2.8% |
| 18 | 72.1% |
| 19 | 19.0% |
| 20 | 1.9% |
| 21-24 | 1.9% |
| 25-29 | 0.9% |
| 30-39 | 0.9% |
| 40-54 | 0.3% |
| 55 or older | 0.0% |

| Racial/ethnic background: | |
|---|---|
| White | 85.8% |
| Black | 8.5% |
| American Indian | 0.9% |
| Asian-American | 2.5% |
| Mexican-American | 1.2% |
| Puerto Rican-American | 0.9% |
| Other | 2.0% |

| Average grade in high school: | |
|---|---|
| A or A+ | 10.7% |
| A− | 11.8% |
| B+ | 18.3% |
| B | 24.8% |
| B− | 14.1% |
| C+ | 12.5% |
| C | 7.3% |
| D | 0.4% |

| Academic rank in high school: | |
|---|---|
| Top 20% | 41.7% |
| Second 20% | 22.3% |
| Middle 20% | 28.8% |
| Fourth 20% | 6.1% |
| Lowest 20% | 1.1% |

| Year of high-school graduation: | |
|---|---|
| 1986 | 92.2% |
| 1985 | 2.8% |
| 1984 | 0.9% |
| 1983 or earlier | 2.4% |
| H. S. equivalency (G. E. D. test) | 1.4% |
| Never completed high school | 0.3% |

| Have met or exceeded recommended years of study, as proposed by the National Commission on Excellence in Education, in: | |
|---|---|
| English (4 years) | 93.6% |
| Mathematics (3 years) | 88.1% |
| Foreign language (2 years) | 71.1% |
| Physical science (2 years) | 53.6% |
| Biological science (2 years) | 35.5% |
| History, American government (1 year) | 98.9% |
| Computer science (.5 years) | 59.1% |
| Art or music (1 year) | 63.0% |

| Marital status: | |
|---|---|
| Not married | 98.0% |
| Married, living with spouse | 1.6% |
| Married, not living with spouse | 0.4% |

| Disabilities: | |
|---|---|
| Health-related | 0.8% |
| Hearing | 0.6% |
| Learning | 0.8% |
| Orthopedic | 0.7% |
| Speech | 0.2% |
| Visual | 1.7% |
| Other | 0.9% |

| Current religious preference: | |
|---|---|
| Jewish | 3.2% |
| Protestant | 29.5% |
| Roman Catholic | 36.0% |
| None | 10.0% |
| Other | 21.2% |

| Residence planned during fall term: | |
|---|---|
| With parents or relatives | 29.8% |
| Other private home or apartment | 8.0% |
| College dormitory | 58.4% |
| Fraternity or sorority house | 0.6% |
| Other campus housing | 2.2% |
| Other | 1.0% |

| Residence preferred during fall term: | |
|---|---|
| With parents or relatives | 16.4% |
| Other private home or apartment | 29.2% |
| College dormitory | 39.7% |
| Fraternity or sorority house | 6.8% |
| Other campus housing | 5.4% |
| Other | 2.5% |

| Father's occupation: | |
|---|---|
| Artist (incl. performer) | 0.8% |
| Businessman | 30.2% |
| Member of clergy or religious worker | 1.0% |
| Engineer | 8.4% |
| Farmer or forester | 3.1% |
| Lawyer | 1.7% |
| Military career officer | 1.7% |
| Physician or dentist | 2.3% |
| Other health professional | 1.4% |
| Research scientist | 0.6% |
| Teacher or administrator, college | 1.0% |
| Teacher or administrator, elementary school | 0.7% |
| Teacher or administrator, secondary school | 3.6% |
| Worker, skilled | 10.4% |
| Worker, semi-skilled | 4.5% |
| Worker, unskilled | 3.1% |
| Other occupation | 23.0% |
| Unemployed | 2.6% |

| Father's education: | |
|---|---|
| Grammar school or less | 4.1% |
| Some high school | 8.7% |
| High-school diploma | 27.4% |
| Postsecondary other than college | 5.0% |
| Some college | 14.1% |
| College degree | 20.3% |
| Some graduate school | 2.7% |
| Graduate degree | 17.8% |

| Mother's occupation: | |
|---|---|
| Artist (incl. performer) | 1.6% |
| Businesswoman | 13.4% |
| Member of clergy or religious worker | 0.1% |
| Clerical worker | 11.3% |
| Engineer | 0.2% |
| Farmer or forester | 0.3% |
| Homemaker (full-time) | 20.6% |
| Lawyer | 0.2% |
| Nurse | 7.5% |
| Physician or dentist | 0.3% |
| Other health professional | 1.8% |
| Research scientist | 0.1% |
| Social, welfare, or recreation worker | 1.2% |
| Teacher or administrator, college | 0.4% |
| Teacher or administrator, elementary school | 5.9% |
| Teacher or administrator, secondary school | 3.6% |
| Worker, skilled | 2.1% |
| Worker, semi-skilled | 3.0% |
| Worker, unskilled | 2.1% |
| Other occupation | 17.6% |
| Unemployed | 6.7% |

| Mother's education: | |
|---|---|
| Grammar school or less | 3.0% |
| Some high school | 6.8% |
| High-school diploma | 36.3% |
| Postsecondary other than college | 7.8% |
| Some college | 16.4% |
| College degree | 18.1% |
| Some graduate school | 2.9% |
| Graduate degree | 8.7% |

| Students estimate chances are very good that they will: | |
|---|---|
| Change major field | 13.1% |
| Change career choice | 12.1% |
| Fail one or more courses | 1.4% |
| Graduate with honors | 11.3% |
| Be elected to student office | 3.2% |
| Get a job to pay college expenses | 36.7% |
| Work full-time while attending college | 3.6% |
| Join a social fraternity or sorority | 17.2% |
| Study abroad while enrolled | 10.4% |
| Play varsity athletics | 14.2% |
| Be elected to an honor society | 6.6% |
| Make at least a B average | 39.8% |
| Need extra time to complete degree | 6.5% |
| Need tutoring in some courses | 11.0% |
| Work at outside job | 20.3% |
| Seek vocational counseling | 5.4% |
| Seek personal counseling | 3.5% |
| Get a bachelor's degree | 67.6% |
| Participate in student protests | 4.7% |
| Drop out temporarily | 1.2% |
| Drop out permanently | 0.8% |
| Transfer to another college | 10.0% |

| Students estimate chances are very good that they will: (Continued) | |
|---|---|
| Be satisfied with college | 52.5% |
| Find employment in preferred field | 69.6% |
| Marry while in college | 4.4% |
| Marry within a year after college | 15.3% |

| Number of other colleges applied to for admission this year: | |
|---|---|
| None | 35.3% |
| One | 17.2% |
| Two | 16.0% |
| Three | 14.0% |
| Four | 7.7% |
| Five | 4.7% |
| Six or more | 5.1% |

| Number of other college acceptances this year: | |
|---|---|
| None | 18.2% |
| One | 28.7% |
| Two | 23.4% |
| Three | 15.8% |
| Four | 7.5% |
| Five | 3.3% |
| Six or more | 3.0% |

| College attended is student's: | |
|---|---|
| First choice | 71.4% |
| Second choice | 21.3% |
| Third choice | 4.8% |
| Other | 2.5% |

| Distance from home to college: | |
|---|---|
| 5 miles or less | 8.2% |
| 6-10 miles | 9.3% |
| 11-50 miles | 27.7% |
| 51-100 miles | 16.6% |
| 101-500 miles | 28.0% |
| More than 500 miles | 10.1% |

| Reasons noted as very important in deciding to go to college: | |
|---|---|
| Parents' wishes | 16.9% |
| Could not find job | 3.9% |
| To get away from home | 9.4% |
| To be able to get a better job | 83.1% |
| To gain general education | 61.6% |
| To improve reading and study skills | 40.3% |
| Nothing better to do | 2.5% |
| To become a more cultured person | 32.2% |
| To be able to make more money | 70.6% |
| To learn more about things | 74.1% |
| To prepare for graduate school | 47.1% |

| Reasons noted as very important in selecting college attended: | |
|---|---|
| Relatives' wishes | 7.7% |
| Teachers' advice | 4.4% |
| Good academic reputation | 59.2% |
| Good social reputation | 27.2% |
| Offered financial assistance | 21.5% |
| Offers special education programs | 23.5% |
| Low tuition | 22.4% |
| Advice of guidance counselor | 8.4% |
| Wanted to live near home | 18.8% |
| Friend's suggestion | 8.4% |
| Recruited by college | 3.7% |
| Recruited by athletic department | 4.6% |
| Graduates go to top graduate schools | 25.8% |
| Graduates get good jobs | 46.8% |
| Not offered aid by first choice | 4.7% |

| Highest degree planned at college attended: | |
|---|---|
| None | 3.3% |
| Vocational certificate | 1.6% |
| Associate (or equivalent) | 21.6% |
| Bachelor's | 56.5% |
| Master's | 12.0% |
| Ph.D. or Ed.D. | 1.6% |
| M.D., D.O., D.D.S., or D.V.M. | 1.2% |
| LL.B. or J.D. | 0.6% |
| B.D. or M.Div. | 0.2% |
| Other | 1.2% |

| Highest degree planned anywhere: | |
|---|---|
| None | 2.0% |
| Vocational certificate | 1.2% |
| Associate (or equivalent) | 6.3% |
| Bachelor's | 36.8% |
| Master's | 33.0% |
| Ph.D. or Ed.D. | 9.7% |
| M.D., D.O., D.D.S., or D.V.M. | 5.6% |

| Highest degree planned anywhere: (Continued) | |
|---|---|
| LL.B. or J.D. | 3.7% |
| B.D. or M.Div. | 0.3% |
| Other | 1.6% |

| Probable major field of study: | |
|---|---|
| **Arts and Humanities** | |
| Art, fine and applied | 2.1% |
| English | 1.2% |
| History | 0.7% |
| Journalism | 1.6% |
| Foreign language | 0.6% |
| Music | 1.1% |
| Philosophy | 0.1% |
| Speech | 0.1% |
| Theater or drama | 0.6% |
| Theology or religion | 0.2% |
| Other | 0.7% |
| **Biological Science** | |
| Biology (general) | 1.9% |
| Biochemistry or biophysics | 0.5% |
| Botany | 0.1% |
| Marine science | 0.4% |
| Microbiology or bacteriology | 0.2% |
| Zoology | 0.3% |
| Other | 0.5% |
| **Business** | |
| Accounting | 6.2% |
| Business administration (general) | 7.6% |
| Finance | 1.8% |
| Marketing | 2.7% |
| Management | 5.4% |
| Secretarial studies | 1.5% |
| Other | 1.7% |
| **Education** | |
| Business education | 0.3% |
| Elementary education | 3.9% |
| Music or art education | 0.3% |
| Physical education or recreation | 1.3% |
| Secondary education | 1.3% |
| Special education | 0.7% |
| Other | 0.3% |
| **Engineering** | |
| Aeronautical engineering | 1.6% |
| Civil engineering | 0.9% |
| Chemical engineering | 0.7% |
| Electrical or electronic engineering | 3.8% |
| Industrial engineering | 0.4% |
| Mechanical engineering | 2.0% |
| Other | 1.5% |
| **Physical Science** | |
| Astronomy | 0.1% |
| Atmospheric science | 0.1% |
| Chemistry | 0.7% |
| Earth science | 0.2% |
| Marine science | 0.1% |
| Mathematics | 0.7% |
| Physics | 0.4% |
| Statistics | 0.0% |
| Other | 0.1% |
| **Professional** | |
| Architecture, urban planning | 1.0% |
| Home economics | 0.4% |
| Health technology | 1.1% |
| Library science | 0.0% |
| Nursing | 2.7% |
| Pharmacy | 0.6% |
| Pre-dental, pre-medical, pre-veterinary | 2.9% |
| Therapy (physical, occupational, etc.) | 1.8% |
| Other | 1.2% |
| **Social Science** | |
| Anthropology | 0.1% |
| Economics | 0.5% |
| Ethnic studies | 0.0% |
| Geography | 0.0% |
| Political science | 2.5% |
| Psychology | 3.4% |
| Social work | 1.0% |
| Sociology | 0.3% |
| Women's studies | 0.0% |
| Other | 0.2% |
| **Technical** | |
| Building trades | 0.3% |
| Data processing, computer programming | 1.6% |
| Drafting or design | 0.6% |
| Electronics | 0.5% |
| Mechanics | 0.5% |
| Other | 0.5% |
| **Other Fields** | |
| Agriculture | 1.2% |
| Communications | 2.5% |
| Computer science | 1.9% |
| Forestry | 0.6% |
| Law enforcement | 1.4% |

| Probable major field of study: Other Fields (Continued) | |
|---|---|
| Military science | 0.1% |
| Other | 1.4% |
| Undecided | 6.5% |

| Probable career occupation: | |
|---|---|
| Accountant or actuary | 5.9% |
| Actor or entertainer | 1.0% |
| Architect or urban planner | 1.5% |
| Artist | 1.6% |
| Business (clerical) | 1.4% |
| Business executive | 12.9% |
| Business proprietor | 3.7% |
| Business salesperson or buyer | 1.6% |
| Clergy (minister or priest) | 0.2% |
| Clergy (other) | 0.1% |
| Clinical psychologist | 1.4% |
| Computer programmer or analyst | 3.5% |
| Conservationist or forester | 0.8% |
| Dentist | 0.6% |
| Dietitian or home economist | 0.2% |
| Educator (college) | 0.3% |
| Educator (elementary) | 4.4% |
| Educator (secondary) | 2.9% |
| Engineer | 9.7% |
| Farmer or rancher | 0.6% |
| Foreign-service worker | 1.0% |
| Homemaker (full-time) | 0.1% |
| Interior decorator | 0.6% |
| Interpreter | 0.2% |
| Journalist or writer | 2.3% |
| Lab technician or hygienist | 0.7% |
| Law-enforcement officer | 1.1% |
| Lawyer or judge | 4.0% |
| Military person | 1.3% |
| Musician | 1.1% |
| Nurse | 2.7% |
| Optometrist | 0.2% |
| Pharmacist | 0.7% |
| Physician | 3.7% |
| Research scientist | 1.4% |
| School counselor | 0.3% |
| School principal | 0.0% |
| Social, welfare, or recreation worker | 1.4% |
| Statistician | 0.1% |
| Therapist | 2.1% |
| Veterinarian | 0.9% |
| Skilled trades | 1.4% |
| Other occupation | 6.8% |
| Undecided | 11.6% |

| Estimated parental income: | |
|---|---|
| Less than $6,000 | 3.9% |
| $6,000-$9,999 | 3.7% |
| $10,000-$14,499 | 6.4% |
| $15,000-$19,999 | 6.5% |
| $20,000-$24,999 | 7.9% |
| $25,000-$29,999 | 8.2% |
| $30,000-$34,999 | 10.4% |
| $35,000-$39,999 | 9.7% |
| $40,000-$49,999 | 12.4% |
| $50,000-$59,999 | 10.2% |
| $60,000-$74,999 | 8.3% |
| $75,000-$99,999 | 5.3% |
| $100,000-$149,999 | 3.6% |
| $150,000 or more | 3.6% |

| Number of parents' dependents: | |
|---|---|
| One | 7.5% |
| Two | 14.5% |
| Three | 22.3% |
| Four | 28.2% |
| Five | 17.1% |
| Six or more | 10.4% |

| Number of other dependents currently attending college: | |
|---|---|
| None | 69.2% |
| One | 23.3% |
| Two | 5.5% |
| Three or more | 2.0% |

| Concern about financing college: | |
|---|---|
| None | 36.3% |
| Some | 49.6% |
| Major | 14.1% |

| Support from parental aid: | |
|---|---|
| None | 26.6% |
| $1-$499 | 10.9% |
| $500-$999 | 8.3% |
| $1,000-$1,499 | 7.8% |
| $1,500-$1,999 | 5.3% |
| $2,000-$3,000 | 9.2% |
| Over $3,000 | 31.9% |

| Other savings: | |
|---|---|
| None | 74.0% |
| $1-$499 | 13.4% |
| $500-$999 | 5.2% |

*Continued on Following Page*

Note: Because of multiple responses, sections may not add to 100 per cent.

Table 2.3

**Other savings: (Continued)**
- $1,000-$1,499 ........ 3.1%
- $1,500-$1,999 ........ 1.2%
- $2,000-$3,000 ........ 1.2%
- Over $3,000 ........ 1.9%

**Support from Pell Grant:**
- None ........ 83.1%
- $1-$499 ........ 4.4%
- $500-$999 ........ 4.9%
- $1,000-$1,499 ........ 3.6%
- $1,500-$1,999 ........ 2.5%
- $2,000-$3,000 ........ 1.5%

**Support from Supplemental Educational Opportunity Grant:**
- None ........ 94.7%
- $1-$499 ........ 1.9%
- $500-$999 ........ 1.6%
- $1,000-$1,499 ........ 1.0%
- $1,500-$1,999 ........ 0.5%
- $2,000-$3,000 ........ 0.3%

**Support from state scholarship or grant:**
- None ........ 86.5%
- $1-$499 ........ 5.1%
- $500-$999 ........ 3.7%
- $1,000-$1,499 ........ 2.6%
- $1,500-$1,999 ........ 1.2%
- $2,000-$3,000 ........ 0.9%

**Support from college grant:**
- None ........ 82.2%
- $1-$499 ........ 3.9%
- $500-$999 ........ 4.1%
- $1,000-$1,499 ........ 3.1%
- $1,500-$1,999 ........ 1.4%
- $2,000-$3,000 ........ 2.0%
- Over $3,000 ........ 3.3%

**Support from private grant:**
- None ........ 93.1%
- $1-$499 ........ 2.7%
- $500-$999 ........ 1.9%
- $1,000-$1,499 ........ 1.1%
- $1,500-$1,999 ........ 0.4%
- $2,000-$3,000 ........ 0.5%
- Over $3,000 ........ 0.4%

**Support from College Work-Study grant:**
- None ........ 89.6%
- $1-$499 ........ 3.5%
- $500-$999 ........ 3.9%
- $1,000-$1,499 ........ 2.2%
- $1,500-$1,999 ........ 0.6%
- $2,000-$3,000 ........ 0.2%

**Support from part-time employment:**
- None ........ 66.7%
- $1-$499 ........ 20.0%
- $500-$999 ........ 8.4%
- $1,000-$1,499 ........ 3.2%
- $1,500-$1,999 ........ 0.8%
- $2,000-$3,000 ........ 0.4%
- Over $3,000 ........ 0.3%

**Support from summer employment:**
- None ........ 49.9%
- $1-$499 ........ 23.9%
- $500-$999 ........ 14.0%
- $1,000-$1,499 ........ 7.5%
- $1,500-$1,999 ........ 2.4%
- $2,000-$3,000 ........ 1.6%
- Over $3,000 ........ 0.7%

**Support from federal Guaranteed Student Loan:**
- None ........ 74.6%
- $1-$499 ........ 1.5%
- $500-$999 ........ 3.1%
- $1,000-$1,499 ........ 5.0%
- $1,500-$1,999 ........ 9.0%
- $2,000-$3,000 ........ 6.6%

**Support from college loan:**
- None ........ 96.0%
- $1-$499 ........ 0.7%
- $500-$999 ........ 0.9%
- $1,000-$1,499 ........ 0.8%
- $1,500-$1,999 ........ 0.5%
- $2,000-$3,000 ........ 0.7%
- Over $3,000 ........ 0.5%

**Support from National Direct Student Loan:**
- None ........ 93.8%
- $1-$499 ........ 1.1%
- $500-$999 ........ 1.8%
- $1,000-$1,499 ........ 1.5%
- $1,500-$1,999 ........ 1.1%
- $2,000-$3,000 ........ 0.6%

## Attitudes and Activities

| | All institutions | | | 2-year colleges | | 4-year colleges | | | | Universities | | Predominantly black colleges | |
|---|---|---|---|---|---|---|---|---|---|---|---|---|---|
| | Men | Women | Total | Public | Private | Public | Pvt., non-sectarian | Protestant | Catholic | Public | Private | Public | Private |
| **Activities in the past year:** | | | | | | | | | | | | | |
| Used a personal computer* | 26.9% | 21.8% | 24.2% | 19.9% | 19.8% | 26.4% | 25.1% | 23.9% | 24.0% | 27.8% | 30.6% | 23.6% | 27.2% |
| Played a musical instrument | 39.1% | 44.9% | 42.2% | 35.9% | 39.9% | 41.8% | 47.1% | 51.2% | 42.0% | 46.1% | 50.9% | 41.7% | 45.5% |
| Attended a religious service | 80.0% | 86.1% | 83.2% | 78.0% | 88.2% | 86.0% | 84.1% | 90.3% | 92.1% | 83.2% | 85.3% | 89.2% | 93.9% |
| Participated in a speech or debate | 23.2% | 23.6% | 23.4% | 16.8% | 21.4% | 25.2% | 28.7% | 27.2% | 25.7% | 26.7% | 31.2% | 28.4% | 37.0% |
| Was president of one or more student organizations | 24.8% | 27.7% | 26.3% | 19.3% | 27.4% | 27.5% | 30.6% | 31.7% | 29.6% | 29.0% | 37.8% | 34.0% | 41.9% |
| Was bored in class | 90.5% | 91.2% | 90.9% | 84.5% | 90.5% | 92.9% | 93.9% | 94.5% | 94.4% | 95.2% | 94.8% | 86.0% | 90.0% |
| Had a major part in a play | 17.4% | 17.5% | 17.5% | 13.8% | 19.0% | 18.5% | 22.6% | 23.4% | 18.3% | 17.3% | 20.3% | 25.6% | 28.1% |
| Won a varsity letter in sports | 54.4% | 38.5% | 46.1% | 37.1% | 46.6% | 50.9% | 49.2% | 52.7% | 52.3% | 49.8% | 50.2% | 46.5% | 43.9% |
| Didn't complete homework on time | 72.9% | 65.0% | 68.8% | 64.0% | 74.5% | 70.8% | 72.3% | 72.6% | 70.9% | 70.8% | 66.7% | 67.5% | 72.4% |
| Won an award in an art contest | 16.7% | 15.9% | 16.3% | 14.4% | 20.2% | 15.9% | 21.0% | 17.0% | 16.7% | 16.5% | 17.0% | 18.5% | 19.1% |
| Edited the school paper, yearbook, or magazine | 13.1% | 22.4% | 18.0% | 13.6% | 17.0% | 18.5% | 22.9% | 19.9% | 21.0% | 19.3% | 26.2% | 15.2% | 19.7% |
| Tutored another student | 40.0% | 43.1% | 41.6% | 30.0% | 29.4% | 43.0% | 48.1% | 44.1% | 48.0% | 51.4% | 62.4% | 38.1% | 53.4% |
| Wrote a computer program | 52.8% | 39.0% | 45.6% | 41.3% | 36.4% | 48.6% | 45.1% | 45.3% | 47.5% | 49.9% | 49.5% | 40.8% | 47.6% |
| Participated in a science contest | 18.3% | 12.0% | 15.0% | 10.5% | 15.4% | 16.1% | 16.8% | 17.0% | 15.3% | 18.3% | 20.6% | 21.7% | 27.1% |
| Did extra course work or reading* | 9.6% | 13.7% | 11.8% | 8.5% | 11.7% | 12.4% | 14.8% | 12.8% | 12.8% | 13.3% | 17.3% | 16.3% | 21.9% |
| Was a guest in a teacher's home | 32.8% | 32.9% | 32.9% | 26.2% | 35.6% | 34.9% | 38.8% | 43.0% | 34.0% | 34.0% | 37.2% | 42.2% | 39.5% |
| Studied with other students | 84.8% | 89.3% | 87.2% | 80.2% | 86.2% | 89.4% | 90.2% | 90.7% | 92.1% | 91.7% | 92.3% | 89.8% | 92.5% |
| Overslept and missed class or an appointment | 31.7% | 29.8% | 30.7% | 29.4% | 33.8% | 29.7% | 33.5% | 31.3% | 32.2% | 31.5% | 31.7% | 31.3% | 30.9% |
| Smoked cigarettes* | 7.9% | 11.5% | 9.8% | 15.1% | 13.5% | 7.6% | 8.2% | 6.1% | 8.5% | 6.0% | 5.2% | 3.8% | 2.7% |
| Performed volunteer work | 67.4% | 71.1% | 69.4% | 63.3% | 70.8% | 70.4% | 73.5% | 74.6% | 77.4% | 70.7% | 79.1% | 68.7% | 74.7% |
| Missed school because of illness* | 2.9% | 5.8% | 4.4% | 3.6% | 7.0% | 4.7% | 5.4% | 5.2% | 5.2% | 4.1% | 4.3% | 7.6% | 5.3% |
| Attended a recital or concert | 72.7% | 79.0% | 76.0% | 67.7% | 76.2% | 78.0% | 81.7% | 81.6% | 80.7% | 80.3% | 83.7% | 74.8% | 81.5% |
| Drank beer | 72.8% | 60.7% | 66.5% | 67.7% | 63.0% | 66.2% | 60.1% | 56.3% | 74.5% | 71.1% | 62.8% | 37.2% | 35.1% |
| Stayed up all night | 77.4% | 75.7% | 76.5% | 74.4% | 77.4% | 77.0% | 77.1% | 76.8% | 79.0% | 78.8% | 75.8% | 71.4% | 76.3% |
| Felt overwhelmed* | 12.9% | 21.6% | 17.5% | 13.0% | 18.9% | 18.3% | 19.9% | 22.0% | 21.1% | 19.8% | 20.2% | 16.8% | 17.8% |
| Felt depressed* | 6.4% | 10.3% | 8.4% | 7.6% | 11.2% | 9.0% | 9.0% | 10.4% | 8.8% | 7.9% | 7.7% | 11.1% | 11.2% |
| **Political views:** | | | | | | | | | | | | | |
| Far left | 2.5% | 1.5% | 2.0% | 2.2% | 2.4% | 1.9% | 2.2% | 2.0% | 1.6% | 1.7% | 1.7% | 3.7% | 3.5% |
| Liberal | 21.2% | 22.7% | 22.0% | 19.2% | 21.0% | 21.9% | 26.6% | 21.8% | 22.4% | 23.7% | 25.5% | 26.2% | 34.6% |
| Middle of the road | 51.9% | 59.8% | 56.0% | 62.0% | 59.0% | 56.6% | 48.4% | 50.7% | 54.6% | 53.4% | 44.7% | 50.1% | 44.5% |
| Conservative | 22.4% | 15.4% | 18.7% | 15.2% | 16.3% | 18.3% | 21.3% | 24.0% | 20.3% | 20.1% | 26.8% | 17.5% | 16.4% |
| Far right | 2.0% | 0.7% | 1.3% | 1.4% | 1.3% | 1.3% | 1.4% | 1.5% | 1.0% | 1.2% | 1.3% | 2.5% | 1.1% |
| **Agree strongly or somewhat that:** | | | | | | | | | | | | | |
| Government isn't protecting the consumer | 58.5% | 66.7% | 62.8% | 66.6% | 66.4% | 63.7% | 62.3% | 62.2% | 61.8% | 58.0% | 53.8% | 74.4% | 73.9% |
| Government isn't promoting disarmament | 58.6% | 72.8% | 66.0% | 65.0% | 62.0% | 65.6% | 69.6% | 66.6% | 70.4% | 65.7% | 68.4% | 74.6% | 78.4% |
| Government isn't controlling pollution | 76.3% | 79.6% | 78.0% | 77.4% | 76.3% | 78.0% | 80.5% | 78.2% | 78.2% | 77.7% | 79.1% | 76.9% | 80.4% |
| Government should discourage the use of energy | 67.0% | 72.2% | 69.7% | 68.4% | 67.1% | 70.9% | 71.6% | 69.2% | 69.9% | 70.2% | 70.1% | 69.2% | 70.9% |
| Taxes should be raised to reduce the federal deficit | 27.4% | 19.4% | 23.2% | 19.6% | 20.5% | 23.4% | 25.4% | 25.0% | 22.8% | 26.7% | 28.5% | 23.1% | 18.1% |
| Military spending should be increased | 34.8% | 19.7% | 26.9% | 27.9% | 29.8% | 29.3% | 23.9% | 26.2% | 22.0% | 25.7% | 22.4% | 31.2% | 20.9% |
| Nuclear disarmament is attainable | 52.7% | 56.4% | 54.6% | 54.4% | 53.7% | 55.3% | 55.8% | 54.5% | 57.2% | 54.0% | 52.9% | 52.4% | 55.2% |
| The death penalty should be abolished | 21.4% | 29.1% | 25.4% | 24.2% | 26.9% | 25.8% | 29.2% | 26.9% | 31.8% | 22.8% | 28.3% | 45.4% | 41.1% |
| We need a national health-care plan | 58.8% | 65.2% | 62.1% | 67.0% | 67.4% | 62.5% | 62.6% | 58.9% | 62.1% | 55.8% | 53.8% | 75.8% | 74.2% |
| Abortion should be legalized | 58.3% | 59.0% | 58.6% | 55.9% | 52.9% | 60.4% | 60.1% | 52.8% | 46.4% | 65.8% | 57.9% | 56.3% | 66.0% |
| High-school grading was too easy | 49.7% | 47.9% | 48.7% | 46.2% | 42.0% | 47.0% | 50.8% | 51.3% | 49.5% | 52.2% | 56.9% | 35.5% | 37.8% |
| Women's activities should be confined to the home | 27.0% | 14.3% | 20.3% | 22.3% | 23.2% | 20.7% | 19.6% | 20.6% | 19.7% | 17.2% | 17.7% | 33.1% | 22.6% |
| Couples should live together before marriage | 56.0% | 46.8% | 51.1% | 55.3% | 47.3% | 50.4% | 49.0% | 39.7% | 43.7% | 52.9% | 46.7% | 52.4% | 49.8% |
| Women should have job equality | 87.3% | 96.3% | 92.0% | 90.4% | 90.8% | 92.3% | 92.6% | 92.4% | 92.6% | 93.6% | 94.0% | 89.0% | 93.3% |
| The wealthy should pay a larger share of taxes | 72.8% | 71.5% | 72.1% | 74.5% | 68.4% | 74.3% | 69.5% | 70.5% | 69.1% | 70.3% | 66.3% | 73.1% | 75.9% |
| Marijuana should be legalized | 25.0% | 18.0% | 21.3% | 22.4% | 21.2% | 20.7% | 21.8% | 16.6% | 18.9% | 22.7% | 19.2% | 22.5% | 18.3% |
| Busing to achieve racial balance in schools is all right | 53.6% | 58.4% | 56.1% | 59.2% | 60.8% | 55.9% | 57.7% | 55.6% | 56.1% | 51.4% | 50.5% | 69.7% | 71.3% |
| Homosexual relations should be prohibited | 62.5% | 42.8% | 52.2% | 58.1% | 60.6% | 52.4% | 47.8% | 55.0% | 47.9% | 45.6% | 40.5% | 60.0% | 56.2% |
| Colleges have the right to regulate off-campus behavior | 13.7% | 11.2% | 12.4% | 13.1% | 14.6% | 12.9% | 13.8% | 13.6% | 10.9% | 9.4% | 11.9% | 27.1% | 19.6% |
| Students should help evaluate faculty members | 70.4% | 70.2% | 70.3% | 66.4% | 63.8% | 69.9% | 72.6% | 71.1% | 71.6% | 75.1% | 76.9% | 63.9% | 67.9% |
| Colleges have the right to ban a speaker | 28.0% | 23.4% | 25.6% | 28.1% | 30.4% | 25.5% | 24.5% | 25.5% | 24.9% | 22.3% | 22.1% | 33.0% | 27.1% |
| Colleges should divest of South African investments | 50.7% | 43.3% | 46.9% | 42.9% | 38.6% | 46.5% | 52.9% | 46.5% | 47.5% | 50.2% | 56.3% | 47.3% | 59.5% |
| Chief benefit of college is to increase earnings | 74.3% | 67.5% | 70.7% | 77.7% | 72.5% | 71.9% | 62.1% | 64.7% | 66.4% | 68.3% | 56.0% | 80.1% | 77.6% |
| **Objectives considered essential or very important:** | | | | | | | | | | | | | |
| Achieving in a performing art | 9.7% | 11.3% | 10.5% | 7.3% | 12.2% | 11.1% | 15.7% | 12.8% | 10.7% | 10.6% | 14.3% | 14.7% | 12.8% |
| Becoming an authority in his or her field | 72.4% | 71.3% | 71.8% | 68.1% | 70.9% | 73.9% | 72.2% | 71.1% | 72.5% | 74.9% | 74.4% | 77.7% | 83.9% |
| Obtaining recognition from colleagues | 55.1% | 54.3% | 54.7% | 50.3% | 54.4% | 57.1% | 55.6% | 52.3% | 56.3% | 58.4% | 57.5% | 60.9% | 68.4% |
| Influencing the political structure | 17.1% | 12.3% | 14.5% | 10.9% | 13.6% | 15.4% | 18.0% | 16.0% | 17.7% | 15.7% | 19.8% | 24.7% | 28.0% |
| Influencing social values | 29.3% | 35.3% | 32.5% | 28.3% | 36.1% | 33.6% | 38.3% | 38.0% | 37.1% | 31.4% | 35.0% | 43.9% | 47.4% |
| Raising a family | 66.3% | 67.7% | 67.0% | 64.3% | 67.9% | 67.3% | 68.0% | 70.7% | 70.8% | 67.4% | 72.5% | 56.5% | 62.9% |
| Having administrative responsibility | 45.2% | 43.4% | 44.2% | 43.0% | 43.9% | 46.6% | 41.5% | 41.1% | 47.0% | 45.8% | 42.7% | 51.7% | 53.8% |
| Being very well-off financially | 76.9% | 69.8% | 73.2% | 75.6% | 73.4% | 73.9% | 68.1% | 65.3% | 71.0% | 74.5% | 68.5% | 84.9% | 87.1% |
| Helping others who are in difficulty | 48.0% | 65.5% | 57.2% | 52.6% | 62.4% | 59.4% | 62.3% | 63.0% | 61.6% | 55.5% | 60.2% | 69.2% | 75.5% |
| Making a contribution to scientific theory | 16.0% | 9.5% | 12.6% | 10.7% | 9.1% | 12.3% | 13.5% | 10.4% | 10.9% | 16.2% | 16.9% | 15.7% | 20.6% |
| Writing original works | 11.0% | 11.5% | 11.3% | 7.9% | 10.0% | 11.9% | 16.2% | 12.6% | 12.0% | 12.3% | 16.1% | 13.9% | 14.1% |
| Creating artistic works | 10.0% | 11.8% | 10.9% | 8.7% | 14.3% | 10.5% | 17.0% | 10.6% | 10.8% | 11.7% | 11.9% | 12.6% | 10.5% |
| Being successful in his or her own business | 53.5% | 44.9% | 49.0% | 49.2% | 56.5% | 47.8% | 49.7% | 46.7% | 51.1% | 49.4% | 45.4% | 63.5% | 67.9% |
| Helping clean up the environment | 18.7% | 13.5% | 15.9% | 16.0% | 18.2% | 16.0% | 17.9% | 15.5% | 14.5% | 15.2% | 14.4% | 24.9% | 25.9% |
| Developing a philosophy of life | 40.7% | 40.6% | 40.6% | 33.6% | 42.0% | 41.3% | 48.6% | 45.2% | 42.9% | 42.8% | 50.8% | 53.1% | 62.6% |
| Participating in community action | 16.3% | 20.4% | 18.5% | 14.3% | 20.8% | 19.8% | 22.5% | 22.2% | 21.7% | 19.0% | 21.6% | 31.4% | 39.9% |
| Promoting racial understanding | 25.3% | 29.0% | 27.2% | 21.3% | 28.3% | 29.5% | 35.7% | 31.1% | 30.3% | 26.8% | 33.9% | 58.7% | 70.8% |
| Being an expert on finance and commerce | 30.1% | 20.8% | 25.2% | 22.8% | 24.0% | 27.3% | 24.4% | 23.9% | 29.0% | 26.7% | 26.6% | 41.6% | 41.1% |

* Frequently only; all other activities frequently or occasionally

SOURCE: "THE AMERICAN FRESHMAN: NATIONAL NORMS FOR FALL 1986," BY ALEXANDER W. ASTIN, PUBLISHED BY AMERICAN COUNCIL ON EDUCATION AND UNIVERSITY OF CALIFORNIA AT LOS ANGELES

# Racial and Ethnic Makeup of College and University Enrollments

The following tables show colleges' and universities' enrollments of American Indian, Asian, black, Hispanic, and white students, as well as foreign students, in fall 1984 and earlier years.

The figures were collected by the U.S. Department of Education, which gathers such data every two years for its Office for Civil Rights.

The full definitions of the racial and ethnic categories are as follows: American Indian or Alaskan native; Asian or Pacific islander; black, non-Hispanic; Hispanic; and white, non-Hispanic. The figures in those categories cover U.S. citizens and resident aliens. Foreign students include all non-resident aliens, regardless of their racial or ethnic background.

The national figures include students in the 50 states and the District of Columbia, and exclude those in Puerto Rico and other outlying areas.

The national totals are based on enrollment at about 3,300 colleges and universities. Because of underreporting and non-reporting of some data, total enrollments are slightly lower than figures appearing in other government statistical reports.

In the table of enrollment by institution, which omits about 200 colleges for which the government estimated data, the total enrollment is given in the first column and is followed by the percentages of students in each of the six categories. Because of rounding, the figures may not equal 100 per cent.

## Minority Enrollment by State in 1984

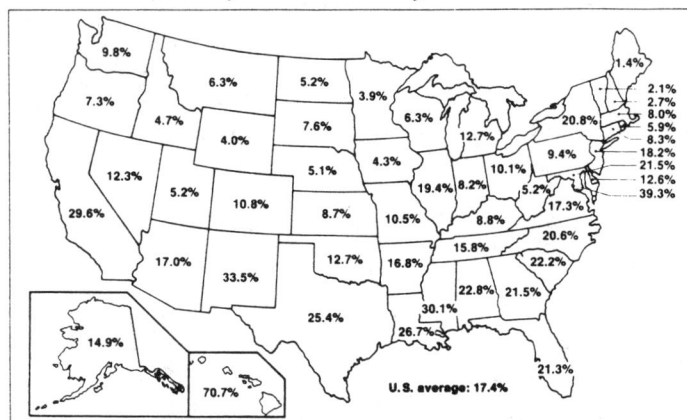

CHRONICLE MAP BY PETER H. STAFFORD                 SOURCE: DEPARTMENT OF EDUCATION

The map shows the proportion of enrollments in each state that comprises American Indian, Asian, black, and Hispanic students. The percentages are based on total enrollment minus foreign students.

### Enrollment since 1976 and 2-year changes

|  | 1976 | 1978 | 1980 | 1982 | 1984 |
|---|---|---|---|---|---|
| American Indian | 76,000 | 78,000 +2.6% | 84,000 +7.7% | 88,000 +4.8% | 83,000 -5.7% |
| Asian | 198,000 | 235,000 +18.7% | 286,000 +21.7% | 351,000 +22.7% | 382,000 +8.8% |
| Black | 1,033,000 | 1,054,000 +2.0% | 1,107,000 +5.0% | 1,101,000 -0.5% | 1,070,000 -2.8% |
| Hispanic | 384,000 | 417,000 +8.6% | 472,000 +13.2% | 519,000 +10.0% | 529,000 +1.9% |
| White | 9,076,000 | 9,194,000 +1.3% | 9,833,000 +7.0% | 9,997,000 +1.7% | 9,767,000 -2.3% |
| Foreign | 219,000 | 253,000 +15.5% | 305,000 +20.6% | 331,000 +8.5% | 332,000 +0.3% |
| All students | 10,986,000 | 11,231,000 +2.2% | 12,087,000 +7.6% | 12,386,000 +2.5% | 12,162,000 -1.8% |

### 1984 enrollment by ethnic and racial groups

|  | American Indian | Asian | Black | Hispanic | White | Foreign |
|---|---|---|---|---|---|---|
| Public | 71,642 | 317,454 | 841,336 | 452,514 | 7,524,802 | 217,163 |
| Men | 32,262 | 169,568 | 340,030 | 213,705 | 3,542,374 | 150,563 |
| Women | 39,380 | 147,886 | 501,306 | 238,809 | 3,982,428 | 66,600 |
| Private | 11,030 | 64,292 | 228,549 | 76,272 | 2,242,043 | 114,681 |
| Men | 4,794 | 35,974 | 94,485 | 37,325 | 1,125,232 | 78,076 |
| Women | 6,236 | 28,318 | 134,064 | 38,947 | 1,116,811 | 36,605 |
| Undergraduate | 68,815 | 301,187 | 897,185 | 436,614 | 7,549,607 | 197,678 |
| Men | 30,842 | 160,564 | 368,089 | 206,337 | 3,620,973 | 131,840 |
| Women | 37,973 | 140,603 | 529,096 | 230,277 | 3,928,634 | 65,838 |
| Graduate | 3,634 | 28,543 | 52,834 | 24,402 | 882,253 | 108,687 |
| Men | 1,706 | 17,865 | 19,961 | 11,676 | 436,893 | 81,368 |
| Women | 1,928 | 10,678 | 32,873 | 12,726 | 445,360 | 27,319 |
| Professional | 980 | 9,240 | 13,243 | 7,913 | 241,597 | 3,391 |
| Men | 616 | 5,786 | 7,017 | 5,152 | 162,537 | 2,518 |
| Women | 364 | 3,454 | 6,226 | 2,761 | 79,060 | 873 |
| Unclassified | 9,243 | 42,796 | 106,623 | 59,857 | 1,093,388 | 22,088 |
| Men | 3,892 | 21,327 | 39,448 | 27,865 | 447,203 | 12,913 |
| Women | 5,351 | 21,469 | 67,175 | 31,992 | 646,185 | 9,175 |
| Total | 82,672 | 381,746 | 1,069,885 | 528,786 | 9,766,845 | 331,844 |
| Men | 37,056 | 205,542 | 434,515 | 251,030 | 4,667,606 | 228,639 |
| Women | 45,616 | 176,204 | 635,370 | 277,756 | 5,099,239 | 103,205 |

### 1984 enrollment by type of institution

|  | Total | American Indian | Asian | Black | Hispanic | White | Foreign |
|---|---|---|---|---|---|---|---|
| **Public** |  |  |  |  |  |  |  |
| Universities | 17.5% | 12.7% | 17.1% | 9.3% | 9.2% | 18.6% | 28.5% |
| Other 4-year | 24.9% | 23.0% | 23.5% | 30.4% | 23.9% | 24.5% | 22.2% |
| 2-year | 35.1% | 50.9% | 42.5% | 39.0% | 52.5% | 34.0% | 14.7% |
| **Private** |  |  |  |  |  |  |  |
| Universities | 6.0% | 2.4% | 7.3% | 4.0% | 4.1% | 6.0% | 14.0% |
| Other 4-year | 14.5% | 7.2% | 8.9% | 13.6% | 8.5% | 15.0% | 19.6% |
| 2-year | 2.0% | 3.8% | 0.7% | 3.7% | 1.8% | 1.9% | 1.0% |
| Total | 100.0% | 100.0% | 100.0% | 100.0% | 100.0% | 100.0% | 100.0% |

Note: This table shows, for example, that while 17.5 per cent of all students were enrolled at public universities in 1984, only 12.7 per cent of American Indian students attended such institutions.

### 1984 enrollment by level

|  | Total | American Indian | Asian | Black | Hispanic | White | Foreign |
|---|---|---|---|---|---|---|---|
| Undergraduate | 100.0% | 0.7% | 3.2% | 9.5% | 4.6% | 79.9% | 2.1% |
| Graduate | 100.0% | 0.3% | 2.6% | 4.8% | 2.2% | 80.2% | 9.9% |
| Professional | 100.0% | 0.4% | 3.3% | 4.8% | 2.9% | 87.4% | 1.2% |
| Unclassified | 100.0% | 0.7% | 3.2% | 8.0% | 4.5% | 82.0% | 1.6% |

Note: This table shows, for example, that American Indian students accounted for 0.7 per cent of all undergraduates nationwide, but only 0.3 per cent of all graduate students.

|  | Total | American Indian | Asian | Black | Hispanic | White | Foreign |
|---|---|---|---|---|---|---|---|
| Alabama | 171,632 | 282 | 912 | 36,487 | 637 | 129,610 | 3,704 |
| Alaska | 26,958 | 1,929 | 534 | 999 | 425 | 22,280 | 791 |
| Arizona | 209,122 | 7,014 | 3,672 | 5,952 | 18,028 | 169,499 | 4,957 |
| Arkansas | 78,777 | 317 | 589 | 11,731 | 290 | 64,086 | 1,764 |
| California | 1,627,719 | 20,565 | 166,837 | 108,772 | 169,308 | 1,106,522 | 55,715 |
| Colorado | 164,387 | 1,367 | 3,006 | 4,103 | 8,786 | 142,262 | 4,863 |
| Connecticut | 161,578 | 468 | 2,347 | 7,174 | 3,150 | 144,418 | 4,021 |
| Delaware | 31,873 | 41 | 366 | 3,256 | 300 | 27,391 | 519 |
| District of Columbia | 79,750 | 112 | 1,914 | 23,418 | 1,785 | 42,112 | 10,409 |
| Florida | 443,778 | 955 | 5,570 | 40,400 | 44,491 | 337,396 | 14,966 |
| Georgia | 196,318 | 333 | 2,058 | 36,852 | 1,804 | 150,269 | 5,002 |
| Hawaii | 49,979 | 143 | 31,574 | 1,065 | 825 | 13,939 | 2,433 |
| Idaho | 43,302 | 447 | 622 | 282 | 630 | 40,609 | 712 |
| Illinois | 647,154 | 2,003 | 18,918 | 82,138 | 20,126 | 512,029 | 11,940 |
| Indiana | 249,953 | 576 | 2,565 | 13,659 | 3,225 | 223,002 | 6,926 |
| Iowa | 153,041 | 476 | 1,574 | 3,229 | 1,109 | 141,370 | 5,283 |
| Kansas | 141,915 | 1,789 | 1,442 | 6,458 | 2,267 | 125,658 | 4,301 |
| Kentucky | 141,935 | 310 | 720 | 10,693 | 540 | 127,839 | 1,833 |
| Louisiana | 179,989 | 411 | 1,701 | 40,500 | 3,059 | 125,698 | 8,620 |
| Maine | 52,712 | 190 | 168 | 281 | 120 | 51,741 | 212 |
| Maryland | 234,305 | 623 | 7,360 | 38,120 | 3,251 | 179,979 | 4,972 |
| Massachusetts | 418,371 | 922 | 8,701 | 14,778 | 7,597 | 370,456 | 15,917 |
| Michigan | 503,605 | 2,729 | 6,178 | 47,541 | 6,120 | 429,064 | 11,973 |
| Minnesota | 214,743 | 1,287 | 3,059 | 2,681 | 1,137 | 201,800 | 4,779 |
| Mississippi | 104,325 | 219 | 571 | 29,902 | 340 | 71,958 | 1,335 |
| Missouri | 240,573 | 677 | 2,803 | 19,143 | 2,212 | 210,610 | 5,128 |
| Montana | 37,056 | 1,795 | 152 | 161 | 191 | 33,987 | 770 |
| Nebraska | 97,422 | 637 | 698 | 2,593 | 936 | 90,566 | 1,992 |
| Nevada | 43,007 | 1,152 | 1,057 | 1,691 | 1,301 | 37,248 | 558 |
| New Hampshire | 53,050 | 135 | 237 | 649 | 378 | 50,807 | 844 |
| New Jersey | 305,323 | 884 | 8,005 | 28,473 | 16,773 | 243,768 | 7,420 |
| New Mexico | 66,447 | 3,144 | 632 | 1,466 | 16,502 | 43,199 | 1,504 |
| New York | 992,919 | 4,708 | 28,779 | 109,477 | 58,574 | 765,758 | 25,623 |
| North Carolina | 309,227 | 2,288 | 2,950 | 55,597 | 1,745 | 241,456 | 5,191 |
| North Dakota | 37,589 | 1,395 | 144 | 257 | 98 | 34,820 | 875 |
| Ohio | 518,107 | 1,297 | 4,979 | 41,183 | 3,841 | 454,988 | 11,819 |
| Oklahoma | 167,891 | 5,809 | 2,436 | 10,178 | 1,905 | 140,315 | 7,248 |
| Oregon | 141,809 | 1,169 | 5,200 | 1,848 | 1,766 | 127,639 | 4,187 |
| Pennsylvania | 528,638 | 855 | 7,615 | 35,852 | 4,628 | 470,102 | 9,586 |
| Rhode Island | 69,144 | 138 | 911 | 2,006 | 974 | 63,845 | 1,270 |
| South Carolina | 126,873 | 184 | 746 | 26,027 | 718 | 97,125 | 2,073 |
| South Dakota | 32,478 | 1,623 | 130 | 338 | 317 | 29,341 | 729 |
| Tennessee | 200,476 | 346 | 1,194 | 28,439 | 930 | 165,107 | 4,460 |
| Texas | 795,345 | 2,586 | 16,812 | 70,706 | 104,114 | 571,878 | 29,249 |
| Utah | 101,860 | 885 | 2,070 | 608 | 1,469 | 92,067 | 4,761 |
| Vermont | 30,787 | 53 | 160 | 247 | 163 | 29,711 | 453 |
| Virginia | 282,765 | 590 | 5,874 | 38,903 | 2,713 | 229,861 | 4,824 |
| Washington | 230,661 | 2,816 | 10,648 | 5,389 | 3,225 | 202,888 | 5,695 |
| West Virginia | 79,008 | 111 | 565 | 3,128 | 265 | 73,754 | 1,185 |
| Wisconsin | 270,862 | 1,625 | 3,318 | 9,056 | 2,659 | 248,874 | 5,330 |
| Wyoming | 23,424 | 190 | 116 | 205 | 387 | 21,770 | 756 |
| U.S. service schools | 51,816 | 72 | 557 | 5,794 | 652 | 44,374 | 367 |
| Total U.S. | 12,161,778 | 82,672 | 381,746 | 1,069,885 | 528,786 | 9,766,845 | 331,844 |

*Continued on Following Pages*

Table 2.4

# Racial and Ethnic Makeup of 1984 Enrollments at Over 3,100 Colleges

| | Total | American Indian | Asian | Black | Hispanic | White | Foreign |
|---|---|---|---|---|---|---|---|
| **ALABAMA** | | | | | | | |
| Alabama A & M U | 4,109 | 0.0% | 0.0% | 75.2% | 0.0% | 6.1% | 18.7% |
| Alabama Aviation and Tech C | 374 | 0.0 | 0.3 | 17.4 | 1.6 | 78.6 | 2.1 |
| Alabama Christian C | 1,645 | 0.0 | 0.2 | 52.0 | 0.4 | 45.2 | 2.2 |
| Alabama St U | 3,787 | 0.0 | 0.1 | 97.6 | 0.1 | 0.4 | 1.8 |
| Alabama Tech C | 586 | 0.0 | 0.0 | 9.9 | 0.7 | 89.4 | 0.0 |
| Alexander City St JC | 1,098 | 0.5 | 0.4 | 21.2 | 0.1 | 77.4 | 0.5 |
| Athens St C | 1,220 | 0.2 | 0.2 | 6.7 | 0.2 | 92.0 | 0.7 |
| Auburn U | | | | | | | |
| Main campus | 18,888 | 0.1 | 0.6 | 3.1 | 0.3 | 94.3 | 1.6 |
| Montgomery | 5,084 | 0.2 | 0.7 | 15.8 | 0.4 | 83.0 | 0.0 |
| Birmingham Southern C | 1,542 | 0.2 | 1.0 | 10.5 | 0.2 | 87.9 | 0.3 |
| Booker T Washington Business C | 308 | 0.0 | 0.0 | 100.0 | 0.0 | 0.0 | 0.0 |
| Brewer St JC | 676 | 0.0 | 0.0 | 10.9 | 0.0 | 89.1 | 0.0 |
| Chattahoochee Valley CC | 1,395 | 0.2 | 0.3 | 30.7 | 0.2 | 66.7 | 1.9 |
| Concordia C | 326 | 0.0 | 0.0 | 100.0 | 0.0 | 0.0 | 0.0 |
| Douglas MacArthur St Tech C | 472 | 0.0 | 0.2 | 15.7 | 0.0 | 84.1 | 0.0 |
| Enterprise St JC | 2,073 | 0.4 | 2.6 | 12.3 | 2.0 | 82.7 | 0.0 |
| Faulkner St JC | 1,710 | 0.6 | 0.9 | 15.2 | 0.2 | 83.0 | 0.1 |
| Gadsden St JC | 2,990 | 0.3 | 0.3 | 12.7 | 0.5 | 78.9 | 7.2 |
| Geo Wallace St CC | | | | | | | |
| Dothan | 2,885 | 0.2 | 0.6 | 14.3 | 0.3 | 84.4 | 0.2 |
| Hanceville | 2,543 | 0.0 | 0.0 | 1.9 | 0.0 | 97.9 | 0.2 |
| Selma | 1,368 | 0.0 | 0.1 | 34.9 | 0.0 | 65.1 | 0.0 |
| Hobson St Tech C | 500 | 0.2 | 0.0 | 45.0 | 0.0 | 54.8 | 0.0 |
| Huntingdon C | 752 | 0.0 | 0.0 | 8.2 | 0.5 | 90.6 | 0.7 |
| Jacksonville St U | 6,564 | 0.4 | 0.3 | 16.3 | 0.8 | 79.7 | 2.4 |
| Jefferson Davis St JC | 819 | 0.5 | 0.0 | 24.7 | 0.0 | 74.8 | 0.0 |
| Jefferson St JC | 6,030 | 0.2 | 0.5 | 12.7 | 0.2 | 85.5 | 0.9 |
| John C Calhoun St CC | 5,486 | 0.2 | 0.4 | 9.4 | 0.4 | 89.0 | 0.6 |
| Judson C | 386 | 0.0 | 0.0 | 4.7 | 0.5 | 93.3 | 1.6 |
| Lawson St CC | 1,552 | 0.0 | 0.0 | 99.0 | 0.0 | 1.0 | 0.0 |
| Livingston U | 1,500 | 0.0 | 0.6 | 34.9 | 0.0 | 64.5 | 0.0 |
| Lurleen B Wallace St JC | 774 | 0.0 | 0.0 | 15.8 | 0.0 | 83.5 | 0.8 |
| Marion Military Inst | 343 | 0.0 | 0.6 | 6.4 | 0.6 | 92.1 | 0.3 |
| Miles C | 582 | 0.0 | 0.0 | 97.6 | 0.0 | 0.2 | 2.2 |
| Mobile C | 891 | 0.0 | 0.6 | 13.4 | 0.1 | 85.5 | 0.4 |
| N F Nunnelly St Tech C | 609 | 0.0 | 0.3 | 19.2 | 0.2 | 80.3 | 0.0 |
| Northeast Alabama St JC | 1,003 | 0.2 | 0.1 | 1.5 | 0.0 | 98.2 | 0.0 |
| Northwest Alabama St JC | 1,066 | 0.0 | 0.0 | 6.2 | 0.0 | 93.7 | 0.1 |
| Oakwood C | 1,330 | 0.0 | 0.0 | 85.4 | 0.1 | 0.0 | 14.5 |
| Patrick Henry St JC | 683 | 0.1 | 0.0 | 20.1 | 0.0 | 79.8 | 0.0 |
| RETS Electronic Inst | 809 | 0.0 | 0.0 | 29.9 | 0.1 | 70.0 | 0.0 |
| S D Bishop St JC | 1,587 | 0.2 | 0.0 | 77.6 | 0.0 | 21.2 | 0.9 |
| Samford U | 4,007 | 0.2 | 0.5 | 5.3 | 0.2 | 92.5 | 1.4 |
| Selma U | 351 | 0.0 | 0.0 | 99.1 | 0.0 | 0.9 | 0.0 |
| Snead St JC | 1,109 | 0.0 | 0.0 | 2.2 | 0.0 | 97.8 | 0.0 |
| Southeastern Bible C | 157 | 0.0 | 0.6 | 1.9 | 0.0 | 94.9 | 2.5 |
| Southern JC of Business | 1,783 | 0.0 | 0.0 | 58.7 | 0.0 | 40.4 | 0.8 |
| Southern Union St JC | 1,794 | 0.1 | 0.2 | 16.9 | 0.1 | 82.1 | 0.6 |
| Southwest St Tech C | 894 | 0.0 | 0.3 | 31.2 | 0.7 | 67.8 | 0.0 |
| Spring Hill C | 1,125 | 0.1 | 0.6 | 5.1 | 1.9 | 90.9 | 1.4 |
| Stillman C | 731 | 0.0 | 0.0 | 94.1 | 0.0 | 0.1 | 5.7 |
| Talladega C | 503 | 0.2 | 0.0 | 93.6 | 1.6 | 4.0 | 0.6 |
| Troy St U | | | | | | | |
| Main campus | 5,309 | 0.2 | 0.5 | 22.0 | 1.0 | 75.4 | 1.0 |
| Dothan-Ft Rucker | 1,568 | 0.4 | 0.4 | 8.4 | 0.6 | 89.9 | 0.3 |
| Montgomery | 2,096 | 0.5 | 1.5 | 24.0 | 1.0 | 72.3 | 0.7 |
| Tuskegee U | 3,275 | 0.0 | 0.2 | 87.3 | 0.4 | 3.0 | 9.1 |
| U S Sports Acad | 89 | 0.0 | 0.0 | 0.0 | 0.0 | 94.4 | 5.6 |
| U of Alabama | | | | | | | |
| Main campus | 15,626 | 0.2 | 0.7 | 8.9 | 0.4 | 87.3 | 2.4 |
| Birmingham | 13,517 | 0.1 | 1.0 | 17.9 | 0.3 | 79.6 | 1.1 |
| Huntsville | 5,863 | 0.1 | 2.2 | 5.4 | 0.8 | 89.8 | 1.7 |
| U of Montevallo | 2,782 | 0.1 | 0.1 | 9.2 | 0.2 | 87.9 | 2.4 |
| U of North Alabama | 5,197 | 0.1 | 0.3 | 8.3 | 0.3 | 90.7 | 0.3 |
| U of South Alabama | 9,342 | 0.4 | 0.4 | 10.5 | 0.5 | 82.8 | 5.4 |
| Walker C | 714 | 0.0 | 0.1 | 8.1 | 0.0 | 91.7 | 0.0 |
| Walker St Tech C | 744 | 0.0 | 0.0 | 15.1 | 0.0 | 84.9 | 0.0 |
| **ALASKA** | | | | | | | |
| Alaska Bible C | 62 | 8.1% | 0.0% | 8.1% | 0.0% | 79.0% | 4.8% |
| Alaska Pacific U | 688 | 8.6 | 1.7 | 6.7 | 2.0 | 78.8 | 2.2 |
| Sheldon Jackson C | 236 | 56.9 | 0.4 | 0.8 | 0.4 | 41.9 | 0.4 |
| U of Alaska | | | | | | | |
| Anchorage | 4,074 | 4.0 | 1.8 | 4.4 | 1.3 | 83.6 | 5.1 |
| Anchorage CC | 8,649 | 4.4 | 3.3 | 5.9 | 2.3 | 82.7 | 1.4 |
| Fairbanks | 5,536 | 10.3 | 1.5 | 2.2 | 1.4 | 79.2 | 5.4 |
| Islands CC | 425 | 14.1 | 0.2 | 0.9 | 1.6 | 81.2 | 1.9 |
| Juneau | 1,650 | 6.9 | 1.0 | 0.4 | 1.1 | 88.4 | 2.2 |
| Kenai Peninsula CC | 1,155 | 3.9 | 0.8 | 0.5 | 0.9 | 92.3 | 1.6 |
| Ketchikan CC | 528 | 11.9 | 1.1 | 0.8 | 0.4 | 84.8 | 1.1 |
| Kodiak CC | 747 | 7.1 | 1.9 | 0.8 | 1.9 | 86.6 | 1.7 |
| Kuskokwim CC | 247 | 50.2 | 2.4 | 0.4 | 0.4 | 45.7 | 0.8 |
| Matanuska-Susitna CC | 1,050 | 3.3 | 0.4 | 0.7 | 0.7 | 94.4 | 0.6 |
| Northwest CC | 141 | 51.1 | 0.0 | 0.7 | 0.0 | 45.4 | 2.8 |
| Tanana Valley CC | 1,803 | 4.8 | 1.3 | 5.7 | 1.3 | 83.9 | 3.0 |
| **ARIZONA** | | | | | | | |
| Amer Grad Sch of Mgmt | 1,082 | 0.0% | 0.1% | 0.1% | 0.0% | 75.2% | 24.6% |
| American Indian Bible C | 75 | 89.3 | 0.0 | 0.0 | 4.0 | 6.7 | 0.0 |
| Arizona Automotive Inst | 1,111 | 2.7 | 3.8 | 4.8 | 16.7 | 71.6 | 0.4 |
| Arizona C of the Bible | 161 | 1.2 | 0.0 | 2.5 | 3.1 | 92.5 | 0.6 |
| Arizona St U | 40,538 | 1.2 | 2.1 | 2.0 | 4.6 | 86.5 | 3.7 |
| Arizona Western C | 3,718 | 2.4 | 0.8 | 3.7 | 28.5 | 64.5 | 0.1 |
| Central Arizona C | 3,477 | 8.7 | 0.5 | 3.0 | 17.9 | 69.8 | 0.0 |
| Cochise C | 3,961 | 1.3 | 3.4 | 6.5 | 19.4 | 67.1 | 2.2 |
| C of Ganado | 268 | 92.5 | 0.4 | 0.0 | 0.7 | 6.3 | 0.0 |
| DeVry Inst of Tech | 4,007 | 1.0 | 5.1 | 3.5 | 8.2 | 81.0 | 1.2 |
| Eastern Arizona C | 3,403 | 5.5 | 1.9 | 2.8 | 16.1 | 73.6 | 0.0 |
| Grand Canyon C | 1,379 | 2.5 | 1.0 | 5.9 | 4.2 | 85.4 | 1.0 |
| Maricopa Co CC District | | | | | | | |
| Glendale CC | 13,002 | 0.8 | 2.0 | 2.5 | 8.4 | 86.2 | 0.2 |
| Maricopa Tech CC | 2,877 | 4.3 | 1.8 | 12.4 | 13.4 | 68.0 | 0.1 |
| Mesa CC | 14,907 | 1.6 | 1.7 | 2.6 | 8.4 | 85.1 | 0.6 |
| Phoenix C | 11,836 | 3.1 | 2.4 | 5.1 | 10.7 | 78.3 | 0.5 |
| Rio Salado CC | 12,497 | 1.5 | 0.6 | 2.8 | 7.6 | 87.5 | 0.0 |
| Scottsdale CC | 7,313 | 2.1 | 0.6 | 1.4 | 2.0 | 93.5 | 0.3 |
| South Mountain CC | 1,154 | 1.9 | 0.3 | 39.2 | 36.5 | 21.9 | 0.3 |
| Mohave CC | 3,121 | 2.0 | 0.7 | 0.2 | 2.9 | 94.2 | 0.0 |
| Navajo CC | 1,962 | 80.0 | 0.1 | 1.1 | 1.8 | 17.0 | 0.0 |
| Northern Arizona U | 11,824 | 5.5 | 0.6 | 1.4 | 5.6 | 82.9 | 3.9 |
| Northland Pioneer C | 4,536 | 22.4 | 0.6 | 0.6 | 4.8 | 71.5 | 0.0 |
| Pima CC | 20,882 | 2.1 | 2.3 | 3.7 | 17.3 | 72.5 | 2.1 |
| Prescott C | 187 | 0.5 | 0.0 | 0.5 | 2.1 | 94.7 | 2.1 |
| Southwestern Conservative Baptist Bible C | 147 | 2.7 | 0.7 | 0.0 | 6.1 | 89.1 | 1.4 |
| U of Arizona | 30,307 | 0.8 | 1.8 | 1.3 | 6.4 | 83.3 | 6.3 |
| U of Phoenix | 3,864 | 1.0 | 4.0 | 7.0 | 8.5 | 79.5 | 0.0 |
| Western International U | 311 | 0.0 | 0.0 | 0.0 | 0.0 | 85.2 | 14.8 |
| Yavapai C | 5,203 | 5.2 | 0.2 | 0.3 | 3.0 | 91.2 | 0.0 |
| **ARKANSAS** | | | | | | | |
| American C | 1,689 | 0.2% | 0.2% | 70.6% | 1.2% | 27.7% | 0.0% |
| Arkansas Baptist C | 150 | 0.0 | 0.0 | 99.3 | 0.0 | 0.7 | 0.0 |
| Arkansas C | 664 | 0.0 | 0.2 | 2.0 | 0.0 | 97.7 | 0.2 |
| Arkansas St U | | | | | | | |
| Main campus | 8,319 | 0.5 | 0.4 | 9.6 | 0.2 | 85.8 | 3.4 |
| Beebe | 753 | 0.9 | 0.3 | 4.4 | 0.4 | 94.0 | 0.0 |
| Arkansas Tech U | 3,575 | 0.3 | 0.4 | 3.7 | 0.3 | 94.9 | 0.4 |
| Capital City JC | 584 | 0.0 | 0.3 | 57.2 | 0.0 | 42.0 | 0.5 |
| **ARKANSAS—Continued** | | | | | | | |
| Central Baptist C | 238 | 0.0% | 0.0% | 1.7% | 0.0% | 98.3% | 0.0% |
| C of the Ozarks | 660 | 0.8 | 0.0 | 4.5 | 0.0 | 84.2 | 10.5 |
| Crowley's Ridge C | 111 | 0.0 | 0.0 | 3.6 | 0.0 | 96.4 | 0.0 |
| East Arkansas CC | 1,183 | 0.0 | 0.6 | 31.6 | 0.1 | 67.8 | 0.0 |
| Garland County CC | 1,536 | 0.3 | 0.3 | 6.3 | 0.6 | 92.2 | 0.3 |
| Harding U Main campus | 2,828 | 0.1 | 0.2 | 2.0 | 0.2 | 95.5 | 2.0 |
| Harding Grad Sch Religion | 207 | 0.0 | 0.0 | 4.8 | 0.0 | 91.3 | 3.9 |
| Henderson St U | 2,944 | 0.3 | 0.2 | 16.9 | 0.3 | 81.4 | 0.8 |
| Hendrix C | 965 | 0.0 | 2.0 | 6.0 | 0.6 | 91.0 | 0.4 |
| John Brown U | 831 | 0.0 | 0.4 | 1.1 | 0.1 | 94.5 | 4.0 |
| Mississippi County CC | 1,214 | 0.0 | 1.5 | 17.3 | 0.7 | 80.5 | 0.0 |
| National Education Center Arkansas C of Tech | 594 | 0.0 | 0.0 | 27.1 | 0.0 | 71.9 | 1.0 |
| North Arkansas CC | 1,002 | 0.3 | 0.0 | 0.2 | 0.3 | 99.0 | 0.2 |
| Ouachita Baptist U | 1,400 | 0.0 | 0.2 | 9.1 | 0.4 | 88.6 | 1.7 |
| Philander Smith C | 549 | 0.2 | 0.0 | 59.2 | 0.0 | 0.2 | 40.4 |
| Phillips County CC | 1,476 | 0.8 | 0.2 | 45.7 | 0.6 | 52.7 | 0.0 |
| Rich Mountain CC | 329 | 0.0 | 0.3 | 0.0 | 0.0 | 99.7 | 0.0 |
| Shorter C | 78 | 0.0 | 0.0 | 65.4 | 0.0 | 0.0 | 34.6 |
| Southern Arkansas U | | | | | | | |
| Main campus | 2,127 | 0.2 | 0.2 | 21.5 | 0.2 | 77.4 | 0.5 |
| El Dorado | 640 | 0.2 | 0.3 | 18.1 | 0.8 | 80.6 | 0.0 |
| Tech | 677 | 0.0 | 0.3 | 15.2 | 0.3 | 84.2 | 0.0 |
| Southern Baptist C | 476 | 0.2 | 0.0 | 4.8 | 0.2 | 94.5 | 0.2 |
| U of Arkansas | | | | | | | |
| Main campus | 14,882 | 0.8 | 1.0 | 5.5 | 0.5 | 88.1 | 4.1 |
| Little Rock | 10,242 | 0.2 | 1.9 | 12.4 | 0.7 | 83.1 | 1.7 |
| Med Sciences | 1,365 | 0.1 | 1.0 | 6.5 | 0.2 | 91.6 | 0.6 |
| Monticello | 1,915 | 0.3 | 0.3 | 23.1 | 0.3 | 75.8 | 0.2 |
| Pine Bluff | 2,640 | 0.2 | 0.2 | 80.5 | 0.0 | 18.3 | 0.8 |
| U of Central Arkansas | 6,245 | 0.0 | 0.0 | 13.3 | 0.0 | 85.3 | 1.4 |
| Westark CC | 3,709 | 1.4 | 2.2 | 3.3 | 0.6 | 90.9 | 1.6 |
| **CALIFORNIA** | | | | | | | |
| Allan Hancock C | 6,672 | 2.1% | 4.4% | 4.5% | 12.3% | 75.4% | 1.3% |
| American Acad of Dramatic Arts-West | 209 | 1.4 | 1.0 | 2.9 | 4.3 | 80.4 | 10.0 |
| American Baptist Sem of the West | 128 | 0.8 | 7.0 | 18.8 | 21.1 | 48.4 | 3.9 |
| American Film Inst Ctr Advanced Film Studies | 143 | 0.0 | 5.6 | 5.6 | 1.4 | 74.1 | 13.3 |
| Antelope Valley C | 6,430 | 1.3 | 3.4 | 5.4 | 7.4 | 82.2 | 0.4 |
| Art Center C of Design | 1,179 | 0.3 | 9.8 | 1.0 | 3.8 | 73.7 | 11.3 |
| Azusa Pacific U | 2,578 | 0.2 | 3.1 | 3.9 | 4.0 | 75.9 | 12.9 |
| Bakersfield C | 10,242 | 1.9 | 3.3 | 5.3 | 15.0 | 73.4 | 1.2 |
| Barstow C | 1,381 | 1.9 | 2.8 | 8.3 | 16.0 | 67.9 | 3.1 |
| Bethany Bible C | 539 | 0.9 | 1.9 | 0.6 | 6.1 | 89.4 | 1.1 |
| Biola U | 3,027 | 0.6 | 6.6 | 3.8 | 2.9 | 82.9 | 3.2 |
| Brooks Inst | 662 | 0.0 | 5.9 | 0.8 | 3.2 | 79.5 | 10.7 |
| Butte C | 6,697 | 3.5 | 1.2 | 1.2 | 4.7 | 88.2 | 1.2 |
| Cabrillo C | 9,391 | 1.0 | 3.0 | 0.9 | 7.6 | 85.8 | 1.7 |
| California Baptist C | 597 | 0.3 | 3.4 | 6.7 | 3.7 | 79.2 | 6.7 |
| Cal C of Arts and Crafts | 1,035 | 1.4 | 8.7 | 3.3 | 3.3 | 70.6 | 12.8 |
| Cal C of Podiatric Med | 407 | 1.0 | 11.3 | 2.7 | 2.0 | 81.6 | 1.5 |
| California Inst of the Arts | 842 | 0.2 | 3.3 | 6.5 | 4.2 | 78.5 | 7.2 |
| Cal Inst of Integral Studies | 133 | 1.5 | 3.0 | 4.5 | 2.3 | 85.0 | 3.8 |
| California Inst of Tech | 1,816 | 0.3 | 11.3 | 0.8 | 1.8 | 63.5 | 22.3 |
| California Inst of Transpersonal Psychology | 136 | 0.0 | 2.9 | 0.0 | 0.7 | 95.6 | 0.7 |
| California Lutheran C | 2,282 | 0.4 | 3.2 | 3.3 | 6.0 | 83.7 | 3.4 |
| California Maritime Acad | 456 | 0.7 | 3.1 | 2.9 | 3.1 | 86.2 | 4.2 |
| Cal Sch of Prof Psychology | | | | | | | |
| Berkeley | 348 | 0.3 | 2.6 | 2.9 | 3.4 | 90.2 | 0.6 |
| Fresno | 159 | 0.0 | 1.3 | 3.8 | 1.3 | 92.5 | 1.3 |
| Los Angeles | 403 | 0.0 | 4.2 | 5.0 | 6.9 | 83.1 | 0.7 |
| San Diego | 389 | 0.3 | 1.0 | 1.3 | 5.7 | 87.9 | 3.9 |
| California St U System | | | | | | | |
| Bakersfield | 3,397 | 1.6 | 3.3 | 6.6 | 11.5 | 74.1 | 2.9 |
| Chico | 13,352 | 0.9 | 3.1 | 1.6 | 4.4 | 87.1 | 2.9 |
| Dominguez Hills | 7,403 | 1.1 | 11.7 | 34.1 | 10.3 | 39.1 | 3.7 |
| Fresno | 15,447 | 1.1 | 5.8 | 3.3 | 13.1 | 69.6 | 7.1 |
| Fullerton | 21,588 | 1.4 | 12.2 | 2.5 | 8.9 | 73.7 | 1.4 |
| Hayward | 11,562 | 1.6 | 15.3 | 9.8 | 6.3 | 64.1 | 2.8 |
| Humboldt St U | 5,487 | 2.8 | 2.0 | 0.9 | 3.7 | 89.3 | 1.3 |
| Long Beach | 29,521 | 0.9 | 16.7 | 6.3 | 8.7 | 64.1 | 3.3 |
| Los Angeles | 16,590 | 0.7 | 26.1 | 11.6 | 24.8 | 31.7 | 5.0 |
| Northridge | 25,796 | 0.7 | 10.1 | 5.7 | 8.8 | 72.9 | 1.7 |
| Poly St U at San Luis Obispo | 15,131 | 0.8 | 7.2 | 1.3 | 5.3 | 84.5 | 0.9 |
| Sacramento | 20,226 | 1.3 | 9.3 | 5.4 | 6.4 | 75.6 | 2.1 |
| San Bernardino | 5,497 | 1.2 | 3.3 | 7.6 | 12.2 | 74.5 | 1.3 |
| San Diego St U | 32,235 | 1.0 | 7.5 | 3.5 | 8.0 | 77.7 | 2.3 |
| San Francisco St U | 20,589 | 0.9 | 22.2 | 7.9 | 6.4 | 57.7 | 4.8 |
| San Jose St U | 22,264 | 3.5 | 17.5 | 5.0 | 7.6 | 62.9 | 3.3 |
| Sonoma St U | 4,945 | 0.9 | 2.9 | 3.7 | 4.6 | 83.7 | 4.2 |
| Stanislaus | 3,807 | 1.2 | 3.6 | 3.3 | 9.2 | 77.2 | 5.6 |
| St Poly U at Pomona | 15,742 | 0.9 | 14.5 | 3.7 | 12.7 | 66.2 | 2.1 |
| Cal Western Sch of Law | 505 | 1.0 | 2.8 | 1.8 | 1.4 | 90.3 | 2.8 |
| Cañada C | 7,082 | 0.5 | 5.8 | 4.3 | 9.7 | 79.2 | 0.4 |
| Center for Early Education | 48 | 0.0 | 0.0 | 8.3 | 2.1 | 87.5 | 2.1 |
| Cerritos C | 18,308 | 1.6 | 4.0 | 4.8 | 34.8 | 39.9 | 14.9 |
| Chabot C | 17,778 | 2.2 | 11.7 | 7.7 | 10.3 | 66.8 | 1.4 |
| Chaffey CC | 10,200 | 1.4 | 18.2 | 5.5 | 0.5 | 73.1 | 1.2 |
| Chapman C | 6,200 | 0.2 | 1.1 | 1.2 | 1.6 | 92.0 | 3.9 |
| Christ C Irvine | 394 | 0.5 | 1.8 | 3.3 | 3.0 | 88.1 | 3.3 |
| Christian Heritage C | 434 | 0.9 | 3.0 | 2.3 | 2.8 | 88.9 | 2.1 |
| Church Divinity Sch of the Pacific | 95 | 0.0 | 0.0 | 1.1 | 1.1 | 93.7 | 4.2 |
| Citrus C | 7,563 | 0.8 | 5.2 | 5.4 | 16.0 | 68.9 | 3.7 |
| Claremont Graduate Sch | 1,742 | 0.3 | 2.1 | 3.7 | 2.2 | 76.5 | 15.2 |
| Claremont McKenna C | 843 | 0.4 | 8.1 | 3.7 | 5.6 | 78.3 | 4.0 |
| Cleveland Chiropractic C | 404 | 1.0 | 10.4 | 1.2 | 5.2 | 79.5 | 2.7 |
| Coast CC District | | | | | | | |
| Coastline CC | 12,286 | 0.9 | 5.4 | 0.8 | 4.4 | 88.3 | 0.3 |
| Golden West C | 15,654 | 1.3 | 11.5 | 1.0 | 6.4 | 77.4 | 2.3 |
| Orange Coast C | 21,581 | 1.3 | 9.2 | 1.2 | 6.2 | 79.0 | 3.0 |
| Cogswell C | 292 | 0.7 | 16.1 | 4.1 | 9.9 | 34.6 | 34.6 |
| Coleman C | 771 | 1.0 | 4.9 | 1.8 | 7.1 | 85.1 | 0.0 |
| C of the Canyons | 3,527 | 0.3 | 3.5 | 1.2 | 6.4 | 87.8 | 0.7 |
| C of the Desert | 5,110 | 0.9 | 1.9 | 2.9 | 16.4 | 77.5 | 0.4 |
| C of Law U of San Fernando Valley | 183 | 0.0 | 1.1 | 2.7 | 3.8 | 92.3 | 0.0 |
| C of Notre Dame | 1,128 | 0.9 | 4.0 | 2.8 | 3.5 | 72.8 | 16.0 |
| C of Oceaneering | 92 | 0.0 | 1.1 | 1.1 | 8.7 | 67.4 | 21.7 |
| C of Osteopathic Med of the Pacific | 361 | 1.7 | 5.3 | 1.1 | 3.3 | 86.4 | 2.2 |
| C of the Siskiyous | 2,184 | 2.4 | 1.5 | 3.4 | 2.7 | 89.7 | 0.5 |
| Columbia C-Columbia | 2,619 | 0.7 | 0.8 | 0.6 | 2.7 | 95.2 | 0.0 |
| Columbia C-Hollywood | 311 | 0.0 | 2.3 | 6.4 | 6.1 | 47.3 | 37.9 |
| Compton CC | 3,543 | 2.7 | 78.9 | 0.8 | 4.3 | 11.1 | 2.2 |
| Contra Costa CC District | | | | | | | |
| Contra Costa C | 6,217 | 0.8 | 14.3 | 25.3 | 8.7 | 49.9 | 0.9 |
| Diablo Valley C | 16,668 | 0.8 | 5.5 | 2.4 | 4.5 | 86.4 | 0.5 |
| Los Medanos C | 4,493 | 1.6 | 4.8 | 7.1 | 11.8 | 74.4 | 0.3 |
| Cuesta C | 5,440 | 1.4 | 2.9 | 1.4 | 4.9 | 88.2 | 1.1 |
| Cuyamaca C | 2,299 | 1.7 | 5.8 | 1.9 | 7.8 | 81.9 | 0.9 |
| Cypress C | 12,880 | 1.8 | 10.5 | 2.2 | 8.2 | 76.8 | 0.3 |
| D-Q U | 206 | 77.7 | 1.5 | 0.5 | 8.3 | 12.1 | 0.0 |
| Dominican C of San Rafael | 725 | 0.3 | 4.6 | 3.0 | 4.3 | 79.9 | 8.0 |
| Dominican Sch of Philosophy and Theol | 100 | 0.0 | 13.0 | 0.0 | 10.0 | 74.0 | 3.0 |
| Don Bosco Tech Inst | 282 | 0.4 | 11.3 | 0.4 | 56.4 | 31.6 | 0.0 |
| El Camino C | 24,476 | 1.0 | 13.4 | 20.7 | 11.7 | 52.2 | 1.0 |
| **CALIFORNIA—Continued** | | | | | | | |
| Fielding Inst | 535 | 0.0% | 0.9% | 2.4% | 0.9% | 95.7% | 0.0% |
| Foothill-De Anza CC District | | | | | | | |
| De Anza C | 26,256 | 0.9 | 15.6 | 3.6 | 7.7 | 71.5 | 0.7 |
| Foothill C | 12,893 | 1.3 | 10.6 | 4.4 | 6.8 | 74.8 | 2.1 |
| Franciscan Sch of Theol | 126 | 0.0 | 3.2 | 1.6 | 7.9 | 75.4 | 11.9 |
| Fresno Pacific C | 1,032 | 0.7 | 0.9 | 1.7 | 11.3 | 79.1 | 6.3 |
| Fuller Theol Sem | 2,938 | 1.8 | 3.9 | 3.2 | 3.0 | 82.8 | 5.4 |
| Fullerton C | 17,220 | 1.3 | 9.2 | 2.0 | 10.9 | 76.5 | 0.2 |
| Gavilan C | 2,155 | 1.7 | 3.2 | 0.8 | 22.9 | 69.7 | 1.7 |
| Glendale CC | 10,145 | 1.7 | 12.3 | 2.0 | 18.5 | 59.3 | 6.3 |
| Golden Gate U | 10,441 | 0.4 | 8.5 | 6.4 | 2.4 | 74.2 | 8.1 |
| Graduate Theol Union | 372 | 0.3 | 2.4 | 1.3 | 3.0 | 83.9 | 9.1 |
| Grossmont C | 13,472 | 1.7 | 4.3 | 2.3 | 7.1 | 83.6 | 1.0 |
| Hartnell C | 6,210 | 1.4 | 9.9 | 3.7 | 24.2 | 59.8 | 1.1 |
| Harvey Mudd C | 556 | 0.0 | 15.8 | 0.7 | 3.1 | 77.0 | 3.4 |
| Heald C-San Jose | 960 | 0.0 | 6.9 | 4.4 | 9.4 | 78.3 | 1.0 |
| Holy Family C | 56 | 0.0 | 0.0 | 0.0 | 8.9 | 91.1 | 0.0 |
| Holy Names C | 645 | 0.8 | 6.8 | 9.0 | 4.7 | 56.1 | 22.6 |
| Humphreys C | 316 | 1.9 | 4.7 | 3.5 | 9.2 | 79.4 | 1.3 |
| Imperial Valley C | 3,370 | 1.6 | 1.7 | 4.0 | 59.9 | 30.6 | 2.2 |
| International Sch of Theol | 131 | 0.8 | 0.8 | 2.3 | 2.3 | 83.2 | 10.7 |
| Jesuit Sch of Theol | 193 | 0.0 | 1.6 | 0.0 | 2.6 | 80.8 | 15.0 |
| John F Kennedy U | 1,791 | 0.3 | 2.2 | 3.7 | 2.6 | 88.8 | 2.3 |
| LIFE Bible C | 453 | 0.4 | 3.5 | 4.9 | 10.4 | 76.8 | 4.0 |
| Life Chiropractic C West | 417 | 0.2 | 3.8 | 1.7 | 3.1 | 89.2 | 1.9 |
| Loma Linda U | 4,610 | 0.2 | 14.8 | 7.6 | 7.0 | 60.4 | 9.9 |
| Los Angeles Baptist C | 304 | 0.7 | 3.0 | 3.6 | 1.0 | 91.1 | 0.7 |
| LA C of Chiropractic | 775 | 0.1 | 5.7 | 1.7 | 5.2 | 82.3 | 5.0 |
| Los Angeles CC District | | | | | | | |
| East Los Angeles C | 12,364 | 0.5 | 19.1 | 4.1 | 63.7 | 10.5 | 2.2 |
| Los Angeles City C | 15,184 | 0.5 | 24.9 | 24.3 | 25.8 | 20.9 | 3.6 |
| Los Angeles Harbor C | 7,988 | 0.8 | 14.6 | 14.6 | 19.0 | 50.0 | 1.1 |
| Los Angeles Mission C | 3,082 | 0.7 | 4.8 | 8.5 | 36.7 | 47.7 | 1.5 |
| Los Angeles Pierce C | 18,906 | 0.6 | 8.8 | 3.5 | 9.7 | 75.3 | 2.0 |
| Los Angeles Southwest C | 4,153 | 0.3 | 0.5 | 94.6 | 2.4 | 1.1 | 1.1 |
| LA Trade-Tech C | 11,888 | 0.6 | 12.0 | 38.8 | 31.5 | 14.5 | 2.6 |
| Los Angeles Valley C | 17,701 | 0.9 | 8.6 | 6.0 | 14.9 | 67.9 | 1.7 |
| West Los Angeles C | 6,908 | 0.4 | 7.3 | 51.9 | 7.7 | 31.7 | 0.9 |
| Los Rios CC District | | | | | | | |
| American River C | 20,452 | 2.0 | 4.7 | 5.7 | 5.1 | 82.0 | 0.5 |
| Cosumnes River C | 5,298 | 1.8 | 8.6 | 14.2 | 8.9 | 66.5 | 0.1 |
| Sacramento City C | 13,186 | 1.6 | 15.5 | 13.8 | 11.1 | 55.2 | 2.8 |
| Loyola Marymount U | 6,410 | 0.4 | 5.9 | 4.3 | 11.5 | 71.2 | 6.7 |
| Marymount Palos Verdes C | 756 | 0.7 | 8.2 | 7.3 | 8.7 | 59.7 | 15.4 |
| Mendocino C | 3,037 | 3.3 | 1.2 | 0.7 | 4.1 | 90.3 | 0.6 |
| Menlo C | 646 | 0.3 | 1.6 | 0.5 | 1.7 | 76.3 | 19.7 |
| Mennonite Brethren Biblical Sem | 131 | 0.0 | 0.0 | 0.0 | 2.3 | 66.4 | 31.3 |
| Merced C | 5,736 | 1.1 | 7.8 | 6.6 | 13.2 | 66.4 | 4.9 |
| Mills C | 935 | 0.2 | 7.1 | 8.0 | 3.1 | 73.4 | 8.2 |
| Mira Costa C | 5,274 | 0.8 | 4.3 | 5.8 | 9.1 | 79.2 | 0.7 |
| Modesto JC | 8,952 | 1.3 | 5.9 | 1.3 | 10.3 | 80.6 | 0.6 |
| Monterey Inst of International Studies | 436 | 0.2 | 3.0 | 0.9 | 4.8 | 73.8 | 17.2 |
| Mount Saint Mary's C | 1,222 | 0.5 | 9.2 | 11.5 | 19.3 | 57.4 | 2.1 |
| Mount San Antonio C | 20,693 | 1.1 | 6.2 | 7.7 | 22.0 | 62.9 | 0.2 |
| Mount San Jacinto C | 2,715 | 1.4 | 1.3 | 2.8 | 9.1 | 85.1 | 0.4 |
| National Tech Sch | 700 | 0.0 | 17.4 | 25.1 | 22.1 | 33.0 | 2.3 |
| National U | 8,735 | 0.5 | 5.3 | 10.1 | 7.2 | 71.7 | 5.1 |
| New C of California | 735 | 1.9 | 3.0 | 13.7 | 14.7 | 63.3 | 3.4 |
| Occidental C | 1,578 | 0.4 | 12.0 | 2.8 | 6.3 | 75.2 | 3.4 |
| Ohlone C | 7,214 | 1.5 | 12.4 | 3.6 | 9.7 | 70.9 | 2.0 |
| Otis Art Inst of Parsons Sch of Design | 709 | 0.1 | 8.3 | 4.5 | 8.2 | 67.4 | 11.4 |
| Pacific Christian C | 465 | 1.5 | 3.7 | 1.9 | 3.7 | 86.7 | 2.6 |
| Pacific Coast Baptist Bible C | 277 | 0.4 | 5.1 | 1.4 | 4.7 | 85.9 | 2.5 |
| Pacific Grad Sch of Psych | 172 | 0.6 | 0.6 | 0.6 | 1.2 | 95.9 | 1.2 |
| Pacific Lutheran Theol Sem | 167 | 0.0 | 1.2 | 1.2 | 0.6 | 94.0 | 3.0 |
| Pacific Sch of Religion | 243 | 0.4 | 3.7 | 3.3 | 0.8 | 81.9 | 9.9 |
| Pacific Union C | 1,403 | 0.6 | 10.1 | 3.6 | 4.8 | 68.9 | 12.1 |
| Palo Verde C | 586 | 0.9 | 0.7 | 10.1 | 26.7 | 61.0 | 0.7 |
| Pasadena City C | 17,666 | 0.7 | 11.7 | 9.8 | 15.9 | 51.8 | 10.0 |
| Patten C | 191 | 0.0 | 7.3 | 44.0 | 7.9 | 40.8 | 0.0 |
| Pepperdine U | 6,836 | 0.8 | 4.3 | 4.3 | 3.9 | 77.0 | 9.6 |
| Peralta CC District | | | | | | | |
| C of Alameda | 5,001 | 0.8 | 15.9 | 36.9 | 6.6 | 38.1 | 2.6 |
| Feather River C | 1,124 | 2.6 | 1.6 | 1.3 | 2.9 | 90.7 | 0.8 |
| Laney C | 9,651 | 0.8 | 19.0 | 33.0 | 5.8 | 37.5 | 3.9 |
| Merritt C | 6,700 | 1.0 | 12.0 | 31.6 | 4.9 | 49.2 | 1.4 |
| Vista C | 4,720 | 0.5 | 8.8 | 16.1 | 6.7 | 67.2 | 0.7 |
| Pitzer C | 761 | 0.3 | 4.6 | 6.0 | 11.2 | 71.0 | 7.0 |
| Point Loma Nazarene C | 1,917 | 0.9 | 2.3 | 1.9 | 3.8 | 87.6 | 3.4 |
| Pomona C | 1,360 | 0.0 | 10.1 | 3.0 | 6.3 | 78.4 | 2.1 |
| Porterville C | 1,887 | 2.5 | 2.8 | 2.0 | 14.3 | 73.7 | 4.7 |
| Queen of Holy Rosary C | 232 | 0.0 | 2.6 | 1.3 | 9.9 | 86.2 | 0.0 |
| Rand Graduate Inst of Policy Studies | 57 | 0.0 | 3.5 | 1.8 | 1.8 | 70.2 | 22.8 |
| Rio Hondo C | 10,517 | 1.6 | 6.2 | 3.0 | 45.8 | 39.9 | 3.5 |
| Riverside City C | 13,647 | 2.7 | 3.2 | 10.3 | 12.0 | 70.8 | 1.0 |
| Saddleback C | 21,493 | 1.4 | 4.6 | 1.3 | 4.6 | 87.4 | 0.7 |
| Saint John's C | 126 | 0.0 | 8.7 | 1.6 | 29.4 | 60.3 | 0.0 |
| Saint Joseph's C | 112 | 0.0 | 26.8 | 0.0 | 13.4 | 50.0 | 9.8 |
| Saint Mary's C of California | 3,590 | 0.5 | 2.7 | 4.5 | 5.0 | 83.9 | 3.3 |
| Saint Patrick's Sem | 104 | 0.0 | 9.6 | 1.0 | 3.8 | 77.9 | 7.7 |
| San Bernardino Valley C | 10,742 | 2.3 | 4.1 | 12.2 | 20.0 | 59.8 | 1.6 |
| San Diego CC District | | | | | | | |
| San Diego City C | 11,034 | 1.5 | 9.1 | 18.9 | 13.8 | 50.1 | 6.5 |
| San Diego Mesa C | 17,137 | 1.3 | 8.0 | 4.1 | 7.5 | 76.1 | 2.9 |
| San Diego Miramar C | 3,707 | 2.8 | 10.8 | 5.8 | 6.1 | 73.4 | 1.1 |
| San Francisco Art Inst | 644 | 0.3 | 4.8 | 2.6 | 4.7 | 74.8 | 12.7 |
| San Francisco CC District | 21,344 | 0.6 | 40.7 | 11.2 | 9.9 | 34.8 | 2.8 |
| San Francisco C of Mortuary Science | 41 | 0.0 | 2.4 | 19.5 | 12.2 | 65.9 | 0.0 |
| San Francisco Conservatory of Music | 219 | 0.9 | 12.8 | 2.7 | 1.8 | 66.7 | 15.1 |
| San Francisco Theol Sem | 1,050 | 0.1 | 5.0 | 3.4 | 0.8 | 75.0 | 15.8 |
| San Joaquin Delta C | 14,520 | 1.8 | 11.3 | 5.1 | 12.3 | 67.8 | 1.7 |
| San Jose Bible C | 175 | 1.1 | 6.3 | 5.1 | 1.7 | 85.7 | 0.0 |
| San Jose CC District | | | | | | | |
| Evergreen Valley C | 6,668 | 7.6 | 16.5 | 5.3 | 11.8 | 57.0 | 1.8 |
| San Jose City C | 11,061 | 7.0 | 11.7 | 3.3 | 9.9 | 67.5 | 0.7 |
| Santa Ana C | 20,255 | 1.2 | 14.0 | 3.2 | 15.3 | 62.3 | 3.9 |
| Santa Barbara City C | 9,760 | 0.8 | 3.7 | 2.5 | 12.2 | 78.8 | 2.1 |
| Santa Monica C | 18,827 | 1.0 | 9.5 | 10.3 | 10.2 | 64.4 | 4.6 |
| Sch of Theol at Claremont | 233 | 0.4 | 12.9 | 6.0 | 3.0 | 70.0 | 7.7 |
| Scripps C | 604 | 0.5 | 6.5 | 3.8 | 5.1 | 80.6 | 3.5 |
| Shasta C | 8,622 | 3.3 | 0.6 | 0.8 | 2.8 | 92.4 | 0.1 |
| Sierra C | 8,667 | 1.8 | 1.1 | 0.6 | 3.7 | 90.9 | 1.9 |
| Simpson C | 321 | 0.0 | 7.2 | 6.9 | 4.4 | 78.2 | 3.4 |
| Southern California C | 917 | 1.4 | 2.8 | 2.0 | 9.7 | 80.5 | 3.6 |
| Southern California C of Optometry | 398 | 0.0 | 23.1 | 1.3 | 4.0 | 71.1 | 0.5 |
| Southwestern C | 10,146 | 0.7 | 15.7 | 5.8 | 30.3 | 45.8 | 1.7 |
| Southwestern U Sch of Law | 1,015 | 0.2 | 3.9 | 1.8 | 3.5 | 89.4 | 1.2 |
| Stanford U | 13,947 | 0.5 | 6.2 | 4.9 | 6.0 | 68.1 | 14.4 |
| Starr King Sch for the Ministry | 51 | 0.0 | 0.0 | 0.0 | ,0.0 | 96.1 | 3.9 |
| St Center CC District | | | | | | | |
| Fresno City C | 12,736 | 1.4 | 7.1 | 9.2 | 20.9 | 60.4 | 0.9 |
| Kings River CC | 3,123 | 1.5 | 4.8 | 1.9 | 30.3 | 61.0 | 0.5 |
| Sysorex Inst | 8 | 0.0 | 0.0 | 0.0 | 0.0 | 0.0 | 100.0 |

| | Total | American Indian | Asian | Black | Hispanic | White | Foreign |
|---|---|---|---|---|---|---|---|
| **CALIFORNIA—Continued** | | | | | | | |
| Taft C | 979 | 1.9% | 2.1% | 8.4% | 3.1% | 82.6% | 1.8% |
| US International U | 2,539 | 0.3 | 3.2 | 4.8 | 4.6 | 60.4 | 26.7 |
| U of California | | | | | | | |
| Berkeley | 29,939 | 0.5 | 19.3 | 4.3 | 5.7 | 63.6 | 6.6 |
| Davis | 18,147 | 0.6 | 14.3 | 3.1 | 4.7 | 72.9 | 4.5 |
| Hastings C of Law | 1,490 | 0.7 | 8.5 | 4.0 | 5.8 | 80.7 | 0.3 |
| Irvine | 11,706 | 0.5 | 22.8 | 3.0 | 7.5 | 61.9 | 4.2 |
| Los Angeles | 32,171 | 0.6 | 18.3 | 5.6 | 8.1 | 61.6 | 5.9 |
| Riverside | 4,486 | 0.7 | 11.9 | 5.6 | 9.5 | 66.7 | 5.6 |
| San Diego | 13,069 | 0.5 | 13.6 | 2.8 | 6.4 | 72.3 | 4.4 |
| San Francisco | 3,629 | 0.4 | 17.4 | 4.0 | 6.9 | 68.3 | 3.1 |
| Santa Barbara | 15,917 | 0.6 | 6.5 | 2.4 | 6.4 | 80.8 | 3.3 |
| Santa Cruz | 6,488 | 0.5 | 9.0 | 2.8 | 6.3 | 78.9 | 2.5 |
| U of Judaism | 160 | 0.0 | 0.6 | 0.0 | 0.0 | 96.2 | 3.1 |
| U of La Verne | 5,073 | 0.1 | 3.7 | 10.5 | 11.8 | 68.2 | 5.7 |
| U of the Pacific | 5,806 | 0.3 | 11.7 | 2.9 | 4.3 | 74.6 | 6.2 |
| U of the Redlands | 2,643 | 0.5 | 3.5 | 5.1 | 4.3 | 83.4 | 3.3 |
| U of San Diego | 5,264 | 0.3 | 3.1 | 1.3 | 5.5 | 87.1 | 2.7 |
| U of San Francisco | 5,752 | 0.3 | 10.6 | 3.8 | 4.6 | 55.6 | 25.1 |
| U of Santa Clara | 7,453 | 0.4 | 14.2 | 1.2 | 4.9 | 73.3 | 6.0 |
| U of Southern California | 30,373 | 0.3 | 12.6 | 5.6 | 5.6 | 62.6 | 13.2 |
| U of West Los Angeles | 685 | 0.6 | 4.7 | 25.5 | 6.1 | 62.5 | 0.6 |
| Ventura County CC District | | | | | | | |
| Moorpark C | 8,955 | 1.3 | 3.6 | 1.2 | 6.9 | 86.2 | 0.8 |
| Oxnard C | 4,546 | 1.4 | 12.9 | 6.5 | 28.3 | 50.4 | 0.5 |
| Ventura C | 10,725 | 1.4 | 4.5 | 2.4 | 16.4 | 74.5 | 0.8 |
| Victor Valley C | 4,149 | 1.5 | 1.4 | 6.5 | 7.2 | 79.8 | 3.6 |
| West Coast Christian C | 199 | 2.5 | 10.6 | 4.0 | 20.6 | 41.7 | 20.6 |
| West Coast U | 641 | 0.0 | 7.8 | 3.9 | 3.9 | 56.0 | 28.4 |
| West Hills C | 1,965 | 2.6 | 4.2 | 5.5 | 18.8 | 68.4 | 0.5 |
| Western St U C of Law Orange County | 1,561 | 1.0 | 3.2 | 2.8 | 5.7 | 87.3 | 0.0 |
| Western St U C of Law of San Diego | 624 | 0.5 | 2.1 | 3.7 | 5.4 | 88.3 | 0.0 |
| Westminster Theol Sem | 99 | 0.0 | 12.1 | 1.0 | 2.0 | 78.8 | 6.1 |
| Westmont C | 1,208 | 0.3 | 1.4 | 0.9 | 1.8 | 94.5 | 1.0 |
| Whittier C | 1,608 | 0.4 | 4.2 | 3.4 | 13.0 | 69.8 | 9.2 |
| Woodbury U | 950 | 0.3 | 7.6 | 12.9 | 12.6 | 30.9 | 35.6 |
| World C West | 82 | 0.0 | 2.4 | 4.9 | 8.5 | 79.3 | 4.9 |
| Wright Inst | 188 | 1.1 | 2.7 | 10.1 | 4.8 | 79.3 | 2.1 |
| Yeshiva Ohr Elchonon Chabad / West Coast Talmudical Sem | 48 | 0.0 | 0.0 | 0.0 | 0.0 | 100.0 | 0.0 |
| Yuba C | 7,501 | 2.0 | 1.9 | 3.7 | 8.9 | 83.3 | 0.2 |
| **COLORADO** | | | | | | | |
| Adams St C | 2,050 | 0.7% | 0.7% | 2.1% | 23.1% | 72.8% | 0.5% |
| Aims CC | 4,253 | 1.1 | 0.7 | 0.3 | 7.3 | 80.8 | 9.8 |
| Arapahoe CC | 5,687 | 1.1 | 1.6 | 1.1 | 3.0 | 90.0 | 3.2 |
| Bel-Rea Inst of Animal Tech | 146 | 0.0 | 0.0 | 0.7 | 0.0 | 99.3 | 0.0 |
| Colorado C | 1,923 | 0.7 | 2.0 | 2.0 | 3.1 | 91.0 | 1.3 |
| Colorado Inst of Art | 1,130 | 1.9 | 1.8 | 4.6 | 6.6 | 84.5 | 0.5 |
| Colorado Mountain C | 8,155 | 0.7 | 0.3 | 0.2 | 2.1 | 96.6 | 0.0 |
| Colorado Northwestern CC | 1,202 | 0.6 | 0.5 | 1.7 | 3.5 | 93.3 | 0.4 |
| Colorado Sch of Mines | 2,882 | 0.2 | 1.5 | 0.3 | 2.3 | 85.6 | 10.0 |
| Colorado St U | 18,094 | 0.4 | 1.6 | 1.1 | 2.7 | 91.3 | 2.9 |
| Colorado Tech C | 599 | 0.7 | 0.0 | 6.0 | 5.0 | 75.3 | 13.0 |
| CC of Aurora | 1,883 | 0.8 | 3.1 | 10.6 | 4.8 | 80.5 | 0.2 |
| Denver Auraria CC | 2,995 | 1.8 | 3.3 | 11.0 | 11.4 | 57.0 | 15.5 |
| Denver Conservative Baptist Sem | 544 | 0.0 | 1.8 | 1.5 | 1.3 | 92.8 | 2.6 |
| Denver Tech C | 288 | 0.3 | 1.7 | 18.8 | 11.8 | 66.7 | 0.7 |
| Fort Lewis C | 3,769 | 8.1 | 0.5 | 0.5 | 3.0 | 86.7 | 1.3 |
| Front Range CC | 5,148 | 1.3 | 1.2 | 1.4 | 7.4 | 84.7 | 4.1 |
| Iliff Sch of Theol | 274 | 0.4 | 0.7 | 2.6 | 1.1 | 93.1 | 2.2 |
| Lamar CC | 297 | 2.0 | 0.0 | 4.7 | 10.1 | 81.8 | 1.3 |
| Loretto Heights C | 717 | 0.6 | 1.7 | 2.8 | 6.1 | 85.8 | 3.1 |
| Mesa C | 3,552 | 0.4 | 0.5 | 0.8 | 3.6 | 94.5 | 0.3 |
| Metropolitan St C | 13,997 | 0.4 | 3.1 | 5.0 | 7.6 | 82.6 | 1.4 |
| Morgan CC | 559 | 0.2 | 0.2 | 0.2 | 3.2 | 95.2 | 1.1 |
| Naropa Inst | 211 | 0.9 | 1.4 | 0.5 | 1.9 | 86.3 | 9.0 |
| Nazarene Bible C | 433 | 0.5 | 0.5 | 3.2 | 3.5 | 91.9 | 0.5 |
| Northeastern JC | 1,635 | 0.5 | 0.1 | 0.9 | 3.6 | 94.7 | 0.1 |
| Otero JC | 651 | 0.2 | 0.0 | 2.0 | 24.7 | 72.8 | 0.3 |
| Parks C | 785 | 1.9 | 1.0 | 9.7 | 13.2 | 73.4 | 0.8 |
| Pikes Peak CC | 5,545 | 1.5 | 1.9 | 7.4 | 6.5 | 80.6 | 2.1 |
| Pueblo CC | 1,331 | 0.8 | 0.5 | 2.9 | 35.3 | 60.1 | 0.4 |
| Red Rocks CC | 3,781 | 1.4 | 0.8 | 1.2 | 4.3 | 88.7 | 3.6 |
| Regis C | 3,196 | 0.3 | 1.0 | 4.1 | 4.0 | 90.2 | 0.5 |
| Rockmont C | 175 | 0.0 | 1.7 | 4.0 | 1.7 | 89.1 | 3.4 |
| Saint Thomas Sem | 112 | 0.9 | 0.9 | 0.0 | 8.9 | 87.5 | 1.8 |
| Trinidad St JC | 832 | 1.9 | 0.2 | 2.8 | 25.8 | 65.4 | 3.8 |
| U of Colorado | | | | | | | |
| Boulder | 22,299 | 0.6 | 3.0 | 1.3 | 3.0 | 89.2 | 2.9 |
| Colorado Springs | 5,446 | 0.3 | 1.7 | 2.3 | 3.9 | 91.4 | 0.4 |
| Denver | 10,790 | 0.5 | 4.5 | 2.9 | 3.8 | 85.9 | 2.5 |
| Health Sciences Center | 1,455 | 0.8 | 2.7 | 1.0 | 3.6 | 90.9 | 1.0 |
| U of Denver | 7,879 | 0.5 | 1.2 | 1.9 | 2.3 | 86.0 | 8.0 |
| U of Northern Colorado | 9,287 | 0.4 | 0.9 | 1.6 | 4.2 | 91.5 | 1.3 |
| U of Southern Colorado | 4,802 | 0.5 | 1.0 | 4.4 | 19.7 | 69.3 | 5.1 |
| Western Bible C | 164 | 0.0 | 2.4 | 1.2 | 0.6 | 94.5 | 1.2 |
| Western St C of Colorado | 2,508 | 0.2 | 0.6 | 0.8 | 1.8 | 95.3 | 1.2 |
| Yeshiva Toras Chaim Talmudical Sem | 33 | 0.0 | 0.0 | 0.0 | 0.0 | 78.8 | 21.2 |
| **CONNECTICUT** | | | | | | | |
| Albertus Magnus C | 440 | 0.0% | 1.8% | 7.3% | 1.1% | 86.6% | 3.2% |
| Asnuntuck CC | 1,970 | 0.1 | 0.2 | 4.9 | 0.4 | 93.2 | 1.2 |
| Bais Binyomin Acad | 33 | 0.0 | 0.0 | 0.0 | 0.0 | 100.0 | 0.0 |
| Briarwood C | 487 | 0.0 | 0.0 | 3.3 | 1.6 | 95.1 | 0.0 |
| Bridgeport Engr Inst | 869 | 0.0 | 2.3 | 4.5 | 2.6 | 89.0 | 1.6 |
| Connecticut C | 1,911 | 0.1 | 0.6 | 0.9 | 0.4 | 95.1 | 2.9 |
| Connecticut St U System | | | | | | | |
| Central Conn St U | 13,333 | 0.2 | 1.2 | 2.7 | 1.5 | 93.5 | 1.0 |
| Eastern Connecticut St U | 3,873 | 1.1 | 0.5 | 2.8 | 1.7 | 93.5 | 0.4 |
| Southern Conn St U | 10,733 | 0.0 | 0.2 | 4.7 | 0.8 | 92.8 | 1.6 |
| Western Conn St U | 5,778 | 2.0 | 1.1 | 2.0 | 1.2 | 92.8 | 1.0 |
| Fairfield U | 5,104 | 0.0 | 0.1 | 0.9 | 0.7 | 97.3 | 0.9 |
| Greater Hartford CC | 3,430 | 0.4 | 1.4 | 27.3 | 7.9 | 59.5 | 3.5 |
| Greater New Haven Tech C | 1,125 | 0.3 | 2.0 | 6.4 | 1.5 | 89.7 | 0.1 |
| Hartford C for Women | 197 | 0.0 | 2.5 | 14.2 | 6.1 | 72.6 | 4.6 |
| Hartford Graduate Ctr | 2,239 | 0.4 | 1.6 | 0.7 | 0.6 | 94.1 | 2.6 |
| Hartford Sem | 110 | 0.0 | 2.7 | 10.0 | 0.9 | 86.4 | 0.0 |
| Hartford St Tech C | 1,858 | 0.2 | 3.3 | 5.5 | 2.4 | 88.6 | 0.0 |
| Holy Apostles C | 171 | 0.0 | 1.2 | 0.6 | 1.8 | 96.5 | 0.0 |
| Housatonic Regional CC | 2,386 | 0.2 | 1.0 | 13.7 | 7.6 | 73.2 | 4.2 |
| Manchester CC | 6,231 | 0.9 | 1.1 | 4.3 | 1.6 | 92.0 | 0.1 |
| Mattatuck CC | 3,584 | 0.1 | 0.4 | 3.5 | 1.8 | 93.4 | 0.9 |
| Middlesex CC | 2,690 | 0.1 | 0.1 | 3.6 | 1.7 | 92.9 | 1.6 |
| Mitchell C | 921 | 0.1 | 0.7 | 5.3 | 1.7 | 88.7 | 3.5 |
| Mohegan CC | 2,099 | 0.1 | 0.8 | 2.2 | 1.0 | 95.7 | 0.1 |
| Northwestern Conn CC | 2,343 | 0.2 | 0.8 | 0.3 | 0.2 | 98.2 | 0.4 |
| Norwalk CC | 3,357 | 0.3 | 1.2 | 15.4 | 6.5 | 74.1 | 2.6 |
| Norwalk St Tech C | 1,707 | 0.4 | 4.0 | 9.2 | 6.0 | 79.3 | 1.1 |
| Paier C of Art Inc | 385 | 0.0 | 0.5 | 0.5 | 1.3 | 97.1 | 0.5 |
| Post C | 1,507 | 0.1 | 0.3 | 4.8 | 1.5 | 93.3 | 0.0 |
| Quinebaug Valley CC | 1,131 | 0.4 | 0.3 | 0.2 | 2.8 | 96.3 | 0.0 |
| Quinnipiac C | 3,139 | 0.0 | 0.3 | 1.1 | 0.4 | 98.0 | 0.1 |
| Sacred Heart U | 4,972 | 0.1 | 0.9 | 3.7 | 3.3 | 91.0 | 1.1 |
| Saint Alphonsus C | 43 | 0.0 | 4.7 | 2.3 | 14.0 | 79.1 | 0.0 |
| Saint Basil's C | 18 | 0.0 | 0.0 | 0.0 | 0.0 | 100.0 | 0.0 |
| Saint Joseph C | 1,223 | 0.2 | 0.7 | 2.3 | 1.4 | 95.0 | 0.4 |
| South Central CC | 2,245 | 0.2 | 0.8 | 22.1 | 6.0 | 68.6 | 2.3 |
| Thames Valley St Tech C | 1,402 | 0.4 | 0.6 | 1.4 | 1.0 | 96.5 | 0.1 |
| Trinity C | 2,108 | 0.1 | 2.3 | 2.4 | 2.3 | 91.7 | 1.2 |
| Tunxis CC | 3,043 | 0.1 | 0.5 | 1.3 | 1.2 | 94.2 | 2.7 |
| U of Bridgeport | 6,337 | 0.1 | 2.4 | 2.6 | 0.9 | 86.2 | 7.8 |

| | Total | American Indian | Asian | Black | Hispanic | White | Foreign |
|---|---|---|---|---|---|---|---|
| **CONNECTICUT—Continued** | | | | | | | |
| U of Connecticut | | | | | | | |
| Main campus | 22,976 | 0.2% | 1.9% | 3.0% | 1.8% | 91.5% | 1.6% |
| Health Center | 506 | 0.0 | 4.2 | 3.8 | 2.4 | 89.1 | 0.6 |
| U of Hartford | 7,611 | 0.9 | 2.0 | 3.4 | 1.5 | 87.8 | 4.4 |
| U of New Haven | 7,044 | 0.0 | 0.5 | 2.6 | 1.1 | 87.5 | 8.1 |
| Waterbury St Tech C | 1,801 | 0.3 | 0.8 | 1.6 | 0.9 | 96.2 | 0.1 |
| Wesleyan U | 3,204 | 0.0 | 3.7 | 6.6 | 2.0 | 85.5 | 2.2 |
| Yale U | 10,749 | 0.2 | 4.6 | 5.0 | 2.4 | 79.4 | 8.5 |
| **DELAWARE** | | | | | | | |
| Delaware St C | 2,209 | 0.0% | 0.2% | 58.9% | 0.7% | 38.2% | 1.9% |
| Delaware Tech & CC | | | | | | | |
| Southern | 1,808 | 0.4 | 0.4 | 12.5 | 1.1 | 85.1 | 0.5 |
| Stanton-Wilmington | 4,025 | 0.2 | 1.7 | 12.1 | 1.4 | 83.6 | 1.1 |
| Terry | 1,297 | 0.3 | 1.1 | 13.0 | 1.5 | 83.4 | 0.6 |
| Goldey Beacom C | 1,918 | 0.3 | 1.0 | 8.5 | 1.3 | 87.9 | 1.0 |
| U of Delaware | 18,083 | 0.1 | 1.3 | 3.4 | 0.7 | 92.5 | 2.1 |
| Wesley C | 1,472 | 0.0 | 0.9 | 11.3 | 1.8 | 85.3 | 0.7 |
| Wilmington C | 1,080 | 0.0 | 0.8 | 12.6 | 1.1 | 84.5 | 0.9 |
| **DISTRICT OF COLUMBIA** | | | | | | | |
| American U | 10,489 | 0.2% | 2.3% | 8.4% | 3.4% | 71.9% | 13.7% |
| Beacon C | 12 | 0.0 | 0.0 | 0.0 | 0.0 | 75.0 | 25.0 |
| Benjamin Franklin U | 303 | 0.7 | 4.0 | 31.7 | 5.0 | 45.9 | 12.9 |
| Catholic U | 6,780 | 0.1 | 2.6 | 4.7 | 2.7 | 81.7 | 8.3 |
| Corcoran Sch of Art | 418 | 0.2 | 1.9 | 8.9 | 2.9 | 78.5 | 7.7 |
| De Sales Sch of Theol | 26 | 0.0 | 0.0 | 3.8 | 11.5 | 84.6 | 0.0 |
| Defense Intelligence C | 618 | 0.3 | 0.6 | 8.1 | 1.1 | 86.7 | 3.1 |
| Dominican House of Studies | 38 | 0.0 | 0.0 | 0.0 | 0.0 | 94.7 | 5.3 |
| Gallaudet C | 1,458 | 0.3 | 1.5 | 6.3 | 2.1 | 72.2 | 17.6 |
| George Washington U | 19,322 | 0.2 | 4.0 | 6.3 | 2.2 | 75.8 | 11.5 |
| Georgetown U | 11,986 | 0.1 | 2.6 | 5.7 | 3.3 | 80.2 | 8.0 |
| Howard U | 11,454 | 0.1 | 0.9 | 79.7 | 0.4 | 1.6 | 17.3 |
| Mount Vernon C | 454 | 0.2 | 1.8 | 7.3 | 3.3 | 78.4 | 9.0 |
| Oblate C | 42 | 0.0 | 0.0 | 4.8 | 14.3 | 81.0 | 0.0 |
| Southeastern U | 960 | 0.0 | 0.0 | 28.0 | 1.9 | 5.1 | 65.0 |
| Strayer C | 1,321 | 0.0 | 3.6 | 42.3 | 1.4 | 32.9 | 19.9 |
| Trinity C | 838 | 0.1 | 0.1 | 22.1 | 3.5 | 70.2 | 4.1 |
| U of the District of Columbia | 12,832 | 0.1 | 1.6 | 76.5 | 1.8 | 5.3 | 14.9 |
| Wesley Theol Sem | 399 | 0.0 | 0.8 | 9.8 | 0.8 | 84.7 | 4.0 |
| **FLORIDA** | | | | | | | |
| Art Inst of Ft Lauderdale | 1,167 | 0.3% | 0.8% | 8.1% | 8.6% | 77.3% | 5.1% |
| Baptist Bible Inst | 358 | 0.6 | 0.3 | 0.3 | 0.0 | 98.3 | 0.6 |
| Barry U | 3,931 | 0.2 | 1.1 | 7.6 | 15.1 | 70.8 | 5.2 |
| Bethune Cookman C | 1,708 | 0.0 | 0.1 | 92.2 | 0.8 | 0.8 | 6.2 |
| Brevard CC | 10,709 | 0.4 | 1.3 | 5.5 | 2.0 | 87.8 | 3.0 |
| Broward CC | 19,500 | 0.4 | 1.4 | 6.6 | 5.8 | 83.6 | 2.2 |
| Central Florida CC | 2,522 | 0.6 | 1.0 | 8.8 | 2.8 | 86.1 | 0.7 |
| Chipola JC | 1,291 | 0.5 | 0.3 | 13.9 | 1.1 | 84.2 | 0.0 |
| Clearwater Christian C | 199 | 0.5 | 0.5 | 1.0 | 2.5 | 90.5 | 5.0 |
| C of Boca Raton | 823 | 0.0 | 1.5 | 2.9 | 5.3 | 81.7 | 8.6 |
| Daytona Beach CC | 7,271 | 0.0 | 1.0 | 6.6 | 1.6 | 89.8 | 1.0 |
| Eckerd C | 1,073 | 0.1 | 0.9 | 3.4 | 2.0 | 83.6 | 10.1 |
| Edison CC | 6,022 | 0.2 | 0.5 | 3.0 | 2.3 | 93.5 | 0.6 |
| Edward Waters C | 748 | 0.0 | 0.0 | 93.3 | 0.0 | 1.7 | 4.9 |
| Embry-Riddle Aeronautical U | 9,593 | 0.2 | 1.2 | 5.4 | 4.8 | 83.2 | 5.2 |
| Florida Bible C | 140 | 0.0 | 1.4 | 0.7 | 11.4 | 80.0 | 6.4 |
| Florida C | 395 | 0.0 | 0.0 | 4.3 | 1.0 | 93.9 | 0.8 |
| Florida Inst of Tech | 6,997 | 0.2 | 0.4 | 1.3 | 2.0 | 82.3 | 13.8 |
| Florida JC at Jacksonville | 13,959 | 0.3 | 2.1 | 15.6 | 1.7 | 80.0 | 0.3 |
| Florida Keys CC | 1,562 | 0.2 | 1.5 | 3.7 | 5.8 | 88.7 | 0.2 |
| Florida Memorial C | 1,760 | 0.0 | 0.3 | 60.9 | 31.4 | 2.6 | 4.8 |
| Florida Southern C | 3,096 | 0.1 | 0.3 | 2.3 | 1.1 | 93.7 | 2.4 |
| Gulf Coast CC | 3,976 | 0.3 | 1.5 | 8.4 | 0.9 | 88.3 | 0.6 |
| Hillsborough CC | 12,198 | 0.3 | 1.7 | 9.4 | 10.0 | 77.5 | 1.2 |
| Indian River CC | 6,104 | 0.3 | 1.0 | 6.7 | 0.7 | 88.7 | 2.6 |
| Jacksonville U | 2,099 | 0.3 | 2.0 | 6.1 | 5.3 | 81.6 | 4.7 |
| Jones C Jacksonville | 1,572 | 0.6 | 0.4 | 36.4 | 2.3 | 58.8 | 1.5 |
| Lake City CC | 1,946 | 0.4 | 0.6 | 13.4 | 1.1 | 83.5 | 1.0 |
| Lake-Sumter CC | 1,722 | 0.2 | 0.6 | 7.1 | 0.8 | 91.0 | 0.3 |
| Manatee JC | 6,025 | 0.2 | 0.6 | 4.1 | 1.1 | 92.6 | 1.4 |
| Miami Christian C | 353 | 0.3 | 0.8 | 8.8 | 11.3 | 77.1 | 1.7 |
| Miami-Dade CC | 37,675 | 0.2 | 1.2 | 13.6 | 49.7 | 30.1 | 5.3 |
| Morris JC of Business | 278 | 0.0 | 1.4 | 9.7 | 3.6 | 82.4 | 2.9 |
| National Ed Ctr Bauder C | 825 | 0.0 | 1.1 | 16.1 | 8.1 | 74.7 | 0.0 |
| National Education Center Tampa Tech Inst | 1,958 | 0.1 | 0.8 | 15.7 | 8.8 | 73.2 | 1.3 |
| New England Inst of Tech-Palm Beach | 333 | 0.0 | 1.2 | 28.8 | 6.9 | 62.8 | 0.3 |
| North Florida JC | 840 | 0.1 | 0.6 | 14.8 | 0.1 | 84.4 | 0.0 |
| Nova U | 6,641 | 0.2 | 0.9 | 11.8 | 4.7 | 78.9 | 3.5 |
| Okaloosa-Walton JC | 3,592 | 0.2 | 1.5 | 5.7 | 1.4 | 91.1 | 0.1 |
| Orlando C | 906 | 0.0 | 0.9 | 15.9 | 4.4 | 76.0 | 2.8 |
| Palm Beach Atlantic C | 977 | 0.3 | 0.6 | 6.3 | 3.5 | 83.1 | 6.1 |
| Palm Beach JC | 11,637 | 0.1 | 0.8 | 6.0 | 4.2 | 87.3 | 1.6 |
| Pasco-Hernando CC | 2,879 | 0.6 | 0.5 | 2.8 | 1.4 | 94.7 | 0.0 |
| Pensacola JC | 7,653 | 0.7 | 2.5 | 10.5 | 1.2 | 84.8 | 0.3 |
| Polk CC | 4,488 | 0.2 | 0.8 | 9.8 | 1.5 | 87.3 | 0.4 |
| Ringling Sch of Art and Design | 399 | 0.0 | 0.0 | 1.8 | 2.3 | 91.5 | 4.5 |
| Rollins C | 3,648 | 0.4 | 0.8 | 3.9 | 2.2 | 90.0 | 2.7 |
| Saint John Vianney C Sem | 66 | 0.0 | 0.0 | 1.5 | 33.3 | 50.0 | 15.2 |
| Saint Johns River CC | 1,463 | 0.2 | 0.5 | 4.9 | 1.5 | 92.5 | 0.3 |
| Saint Leo C | 7,012 | 0.0 | 0.2 | 16.6 | 2.8 | 79.1 | 1.3 |
| Saint Petersburg JC | 15,865 | 0.4 | 1.1 | 4.5 | 1.6 | 91.6 | 0.8 |
| Saint Thomas U | 3,595 | 0.0 | 1.8 | 7.8 | 52.4 | 35.5 | 2.4 |
| Saint Vincent De Paul Regional Sem | 119 | 0.0 | 0.0 | 4.2 | 33.6 | 58.0 | 4.2 |
| Seminole CC | 5,092 | 0.4 | 1.4 | 5.2 | 3.4 | 88.5 | 1.2 |
| Santa Fe CC | 7,296 | 0.1 | 0.9 | 8.8 | 4.2 | 81.7 | 4.2 |
| Southeastern C of the Assemblies of God | 1,021 | 0.3 | 0.2 | 3.1 | 4.1 | 91.5 | 0.8 |
| SE C of Osteopathic Med | 273 | 0.7 | 1.5 | 1.5 | 3.3 | 92.7 | 0.4 |
| St U System of Florida | | | | | | | |
| Florida A&M U | 5,269 | 0.1 | 0.5 | 81.1 | 1.3 | 12.5 | 4.6 |
| Florida Atlantic U | 10,239 | 0.1 | 2.1 | 4.5 | 5.1 | 83.4 | 4.9 |
| Florida International U | 16,116 | 0.1 | 2.1 | 8.1 | 37.0 | 45.8 | 6.8 |
| Florida St U | 20,984 | 0.2 | 0.6 | 7.1 | 2.6 | 86.8 | 2.7 |
| U of Central Florida | 15,822 | 0.2 | 2.0 | 4.3 | 3.7 | 87.8 | 2.1 |
| U of Florida | 35,496 | 0.1 | 1.6 | 5.5 | 5.2 | 83.3 | 4.3 |
| U of North Florida | 6,032 | 0.2 | 1.4 | 8.6 | 1.2 | 87.1 | 1.5 |
| U of South Florida | 27,690 | 0.1 | 1.1 | 3.5 | 4.6 | 88.5 | 2.2 |
| U of West Florida | 6,057 | 0.3 | 1.3 | 5.2 | 1.6 | 89.9 | 1.6 |
| Stetson U | 2,739 | 0.2 | 0.4 | 1.9 | 2.1 | 93.1 | 2.2 |
| Tallahassee CC | 4,885 | 0.3 | 0.9 | 15.5 | 4.1 | 79.1 | 0.0 |
| Tampa C | 1,583 | 0.3 | 1.5 | 11.5 | 6.4 | 70.4 | 9.9 |
| United Electronics Inst of Florida | 1,029 | 0.0 | 0.6 | 7.2 | 6.5 | 69.7 | 16.0 |
| U of Miami | 13,708 | 0.1 | 1.5 | 4.0 | 20.0 | 61.4 | 12.9 |
| U of Tampa | 2,047 | 0.3 | 0.9 | 4.0 | 3.6 | 85.0 | 6.3 |
| Valencia CC | 11,432 | 0.4 | 1.9 | 7.5 | 5.3 | 83.1 | 1.9 |
| Warner Southern C | 335 | 0.6 | 0.0 | 5.1 | 0.0 | 88.4 | 6.0 |
| Webber C | 353 | 0.6 | 0.6 | 11.3 | 4.2 | 75.4 | 7.9 |
| **GEORGIA** | | | | | | | |
| Abraham Baldwin Agricultural C | 1,979 | 0.1% | 0.2% | 11.2% | 0.2% | 86.3% | 2.1% |
| Agnes Scott C | 539 | 0.0 | 1.1 | 6.3 | 2.0 | 89.2 | 1.3 |
| Albany JC | 1,770 | 0.6 | 0.6 | 20.8 | 0.5 | 77.5 | 0.1 |
| Albany St C | 1,893 | 0.3 | 0.4 | 82.6 | 0.4 | 16.3 | 0.0 |
| Andrew C | 319 | 0.0 | 0.0 | 16.3 | 0.9 | 69.9 | 12.9 |
| Armstrong St C | 2,680 | 0.1 | 0.8 | 13.2 | 0.4 | 85.0 | 0.4 |
| Art Inst of Atlanta | 1,051 | 0.0 | 1.7 | 28.4 | 1.1 | 68.7 | 0.0 |

| | Total | American Indian | Asian | Black | Hispanic | White | Foreign |
|---|---|---|---|---|---|---|---|
| **GEORGIA—Continued** | | | | | | | |
| Atlanta Christian C | 149 | 0.0% | 3.4% | 14.8% | 0.0% | 81.9% | 0.0% |
| Atlanta C of Art | 247 | 0.0 | 2.8 | 12.1 | 2.0 | 81.8 | 1.2 |
| Atlanta JC | 1,453 | 0.3 | 0.3 | 88.6 | 0.7 | 1.5 | 8.5 |
| Atlanta U | 1,023 | 0.0 | 24.9 | 72.2 | 0.5 | 2.3 | 0.0 |
| Augusta C | 4,091 | 0.3 | 1.6 | 14.9 | 1.1 | 82.0 | 0.1 |
| Bainbridge JC | 575 | 0.0 | 0.9 | 20.5 | 0.0 | 78.4 | 0.2 |
| Bauder Fashion C | 610 | 0.5 | 0.0 | 23.9 | 1.5 | 73.8 | 0.3 |
| Berry C | 1,396 | 0.0 | 0.1 | 3.4 | 0.5 | 94.8 | 1.2 |
| Brewton-Parker C | 1,277 | 0.0 | 0.0 | 22.2 | 0.0 | 75.6 | 2.3 |
| Brunswick JC | 1,243 | 0.3 | 1.0 | 20.4 | 1.3 | 76.8 | 0.1 |
| Clark C | 1,879 | 0.0 | 0.0 | 95.2 | 0.0 | 0.0 | 4.8 |
| Clayton JC | 3,358 | 0.4 | 0.7 | 8.1 | 1.1 | 89.4 | 0.4 |
| Columbia Theol Sem | 483 | 0.0 | 2.9 | 3.9 | 0.4 | 88.4 | 4.3 |
| Columbus C | 3,985 | 0.4 | 1.5 | 18.7 | 1.2 | 76.6 | 1.6 |
| Covenant C | 511 | 0.0 | 1.4 | 2.0 | 1.6 | 92.4 | 2.7 |
| Crandall JC | 547 | 0.0 | 0.0 | 47.3 | 0.0 | 52.7 | 0.0 |
| Dalton JC | 1,622 | 0.1 | 0.1 | 2.0 | 0.2 | 97.4 | 0.1 |
| Dekalb CC | 14,877 | 0.4 | 1.4 | 19.8 | 1.1 | 74.9 | 2.4 |
| DeVry Inst of Tech | 2,783 | 0.3 | 2.3 | 38.0 | 1.7 | 55.6 | 2.1 |
| Draughon's JC | 701 | 0.0 | 1.0 | 60.6 | 0.1 | 38.2 | 0.0 |
| Emanuel County JC | 416 | 0.0 | 0.0 | 19.2 | 0.0 | 80.8 | 0.0 |
| Emmanuel C | 352 | 0.0 | 0.0 | 7.4 | 0.0 | 92.6 | 0.0 |
| Emmanuel Sch of Ministries | 35 | 0.0 | 0.0 | 2.9 | 0.0 | 94.3 | 2.9 |
| Emory U | 8,533 | 0.1 | 1.5 | 5.3 | 1.7 | 86.2 | 5.2 |
| Floyd JC | 1,278 | 0.2 | 0.2 | 7.7 | 0.2 | 91.5 | 0.2 |
| Fort Valley St C | 1,837 | 0.1 | 0.1 | 90.1 | 0.1 | 6.9 | 2.7 |
| Gainesville JC | 1,744 | 0.1 | 0.2 | 4.0 | 0.5 | 94.0 | 1.2 |
| Georgia C | 3,795 | 0.1 | 0.4 | 17.4 | 0.4 | 80.5 | 1.1 |
| Georgia Inst of Tech Main campus | 10,958 | 0.1 | 3.5 | 5.7 | 2.2 | 81.7 | 6.6 |
| Georgia Military C | 1,403 | 0.5 | 0.7 | 37.5 | 8.1 | 53.0 | 0.2 |
| Georgia Southern C | 6,526 | 0.1 | 0.3 | 11.7 | 0.6 | 86.3 | 1.1 |
| Georgia Southwestern C | 2,259 | 0.3 | 0.3 | 19.7 | 0.2 | 78.9 | 0.5 |
| Georgia St U | 21,386 | 0.1 | 1.2 | 16.4 | 1.3 | 77.8 | 3.1 |
| Gordon JC | 1,365 | 0.2 | 0.3 | 13.4 | 0.2 | 83.4 | 2.4 |
| Gupton Jones C of Funeral Service | 163 | 0.0 | 0.0 | 33.7 | 0.0 | 66.3 | 0.0 |
| Interdenominational Theol Center | 311 | 0.0 | 0.0 | 90.7 | 0.0 | 2.9 | 6.4 |
| Kennesaw C | 5,821 | 0.2 | 0.8 | 2.4 | 0.9 | 94.4 | 1.3 |
| La Grange C | 947 | 0.1 | 0.3 | 8.3 | 0.1 | 87.0 | 4.1 |
| Life Chiropractic C | 1,596 | 0.1 | 0.8 | 2.3 | 1.8 | 93.7 | 1.3 |
| Macon JC | 2,828 | 0.2 | 0.5 | 16.6 | 0.4 | 82.4 | 0.0 |
| Med C of Georgia | 2,320 | 0.1 | 1.5 | 6.5 | 1.2 | 88.3 | 2.3 |
| Mercer U | | | | | | | |
| Main campus | 2,771 | 0.2 | 0.6 | 12.2 | 1.0 | 85.1 | 0.9 |
| Atlanta | 1,975 | 0.2 | 0.3 | 11.4 | 0.8 | 77.0 | 10.3 |
| S Sch of Pharmacy | 351 | 0.0 | 1.7 | 16.2 | 3.1 | 71.2 | 7.7 |
| Middle Georgia C | 1,293 | 0.0 | 0.4 | 10.8 | 0.4 | 87.2 | 1.2 |
| Morehouse C | 2,056 | 0.0 | 0.0 | 96.1 | 0.0 | 0.0 | 3.9 |
| Morehouse Sch of Med | 127 | 1.6 | 5.5 | 78.0 | 0.0 | 13.4 | 1.6 |
| Morris Brown C | 1,086 | 0.0 | 1.8 | 98.1 | 0.1 | 0.0 | 0.0 |
| North Georgia C | 1,979 | 0.2 | 0.2 | 2.8 | 0.2 | 96.4 | 0.2 |
| Oglethorpe U | 1,017 | 0.0 | 1.5 | 8.0 | 2.7 | 87.9 | 0.0 |
| Phillips C | 522 | 0.2 | 1.5 | 42.0 | 1.0 | 55.0 | 0.4 |
| Piedmont C | 387 | 0.0 | 1.3 | 14.0 | 0.5 | 82.2 | 2.1 |
| Reinhardt C | 514 | 0.0 | 0.0 | 4.1 | 0.0 | 94.6 | 1.4 |
| Savannah C of Art & Design | 438 | 0.0 | 0.9 | 8.7 | 0.5 | 89.0 | 0.9 |
| Savannah St C | 2,011 | 0.1 | 0.1 | 81.1 | 0.9 | 14.1 | 3.6 |
| Shorter C | 726 | 0.0 | 0.3 | 4.7 | 0.0 | 92.4 | 2.6 |
| South Georgia C | 1,059 | 0.0 | 0.5 | 16.1 | 0.3 | 78.1 | 5.0 |
| Southern Tech Inst | 3,610 | 0.2 | 0.7 | 8.9 | 0.6 | 87.0 | 2.5 |
| Spelman C | 1,604 | 0.0 | 0.0 | 97.8 | 0.0 | 0.0 | 2.2 |
| Thomas County CC | 391 | 0.3 | 0.0 | 22.0 | 0.3 | 76.0 | 1.5 |
| Tift C | 488 | 0.2 | 0.8 | 19.3 | 0.2 | 79.5 | 0.0 |
| Toccoa Falls C | 642 | 0.0 | 0.2 | 0.9 | 1.1 | 93.5 | 4.4 |
| Truett McConnell C | 902 | 0.0 | 0.0 | 12.9 | 0.0 | 87.1 | 0.0 |
| U of Georgia | 25,230 | 0.1 | 0.4 | 5.3 | 0.6 | 89.4 | 4.1 |
| Valdosta St C | 6,095 | 0.1 | 0.3 | 14.7 | 0.6 | 83.5 | 0.8 |
| Waycross JC | 469 | 0.4 | 0.4 | 13.9 | 0.2 | 84.9 | 0.2 |
| Wesleyan C | 368 | 0.0 | 0.5 | 10.3 | 2.2 | 83.7 | 3.3 |
| West Georgia C | 6,250 | 0.1 | 0.3 | 12.8 | 0.2 | 86.1 | 0.4 |
| Young Harris C | 382 | 0.0 | 0.0 | 0.8 | 0.0 | 99.2 | 0.0 |
| **HAWAII** | | | | | | | |
| Chaminade U of Honolulu | 2,366 | 0.2% | 29.6% | 5.1% | 1.4% | 59.2% | 4.6% |
| Hawaii Loa C | 426 | 1.6 | 23.0 | 2.6 | 3.1 | 45.5 | 24.2 |
| Hawaii Pacific C | 3,383 | 0.8 | 21.9 | 12.1 | 6.0 | 39.8 | 19.3 |
| U of Hawaii | | | | | | | |
| Manoa | 19,964 | 0.2 | 66.7 | 0.9 | 0.8 | 26.2 | 5.3 |
| Hilo | 3,234 | 0.7 | 62.6 | 1.0 | 1.9 | 29.9 | 4.0 |
| West Oahu C | 435 | 0.0 | 55.6 | 3.7 | 1.8 | 38.6 | 0.2 |
| Honolulu CC | 4,549 | 0.2 | 77.3 | 2.0 | 1.5 | 14.7 | 4.4 |
| Kapiolani CC | 5,264 | 0.2 | 76.8 | 1.0 | 1.5 | 18.9 | 1.6 |
| Kauai CC | 1,159 | 0.2 | 67.0 | 0.3 | 1.6 | 30.3 | 0.8 |
| Leeward CC | 5,751 | 0.2 | 73.2 | 2.3 | 2.3 | 21.5 | 0.5 |
| Maui CC | 2,087 | 0.2 | 59.8 | 0.4 | 1.1 | 36.4 | 2.0 |
| Windward CC | 1,363 | 0.5 | 49.3 | 1.5 | 1.9 | 45.2 | 1.6 |
| **IDAHO** | | | | | | | |
| Boise Bible C | 80 | 1.2% | 0.0% | 0.0% | 1.2% | 97.5% | 0.0% |
| Boise St U | 11,584 | 0.8 | 1.5 | 0.8 | 2.3 | 93.9 | 0.8 |
| C of Idaho | 975 | 0.3 | 1.0 | 0.7 | 1.6 | 95.6 | 0.7 |
| C of Southern Idaho | 3,014 | 1.2 | 0.7 | 0.6 | 2.7 | 93.4 | 1.3 |
| Idaho St U | 7,043 | 1.4 | 3.7 | 1.0 | 1.6 | 92.2 | 0.1 |
| Lewis-Clark St C | 2,033 | 2.7 | 0.2 | 0.2 | 0.7 | 94.1 | 2.0 |
| North Idaho C | 2,274 | 1.8 | 0.3 | 0.5 | 0.9 | 95.5 | 1.0 |
| Northwest Nazarene C | 1,012 | 2.0 | 1.4 | 0.5 | 1.1 | 93.9 | 1.2 |
| Ricks C | 6,318 | 0.6 | 0.3 | 0.2 | 0.7 | 94.1 | 4.1 |
| U of Idaho | 8,970 | 0.7 | 1.2 | 0.7 | 0.7 | 94.0 | 2.7 |
| **ILLINOIS** | | | | | | | |
| Alfred Adler Inst of Chicago | 94 | 0.0% | 0.0% | 3.2% | 0.0% | 95.7% | 1.1% |
| American Conserv Music | 222 | 0.0 | 5.9 | 17.6 | 8.1 | 61.3 | 7.2 |
| Augustana C | 2,193 | 0.4 | 0.3 | 6.7 | 1.0 | 90.0 | 1.7 |
| Aurora C | 1,566 | 0.0 | 0.7 | 8.0 | 3.6 | 87.3 | 0.4 |
| Barat C | 547 | 0.0 | 0.4 | 4.6 | 0.2 | 86.5 | 8.4 |
| Belleville Area C | 12,480 | 0.6 | 1.4 | 8.1 | 0.9 | 88.2 | 0.8 |
| Bethany Theol Sem | 138 | 0.0 | 1.4 | 0.7 | 0.7 | 92.8 | 4.3 |
| Black Hawk C | | | | | | | |
| East | 811 | 0.1 | 0.0 | 1.6 | 0.9 | 97.4 | 0.0 |
| Quad Cities | 4,983 | 0.3 | 1.2 | 5.2 | 3.6 | 89.7 | 0.0 |
| Blackburn C | 465 | 0.0 | 1.9 | 6.5 | 2.2 | 87.3 | 2.2 |
| Bradley U | 5,286 | 0.0 | 1.5 | 6.6 | 1.4 | 89.0 | 1.4 |
| Brisk Rabbinical C | 26 | 0.0 | 0.0 | 0.0 | 0.0 | 100.0 | 0.0 |
| Carl Sandburg C | 2,144 | 0.4 | 0.8 | 3.9 | 1.3 | 93.1 | 0.5 |
| Catholic Theol Union-Chicago | 351 | 0.0 | 0.9 | 2.6 | 3.7 | 79.8 | 13.1 |
| Chicago C of Osteo Med | 395 | 0.0 | 3.3 | 1.3 | 0.8 | 94.4 | 0.3 |
| Chicago Sch of Professional Psychology | 131 | 0.0 | 0.0 | 2.3 | 0.0 | 97.7 | 0.0 |
| Chicago St U | 7,404 | 0.2 | 0.6 | 82.7 | 1.9 | 12.9 | 1.6 |
| Chicago Theol Sem | 166 | 0.0 | 4.8 | 22.3 | 0.0 | 72.9 | 0.0 |
| Christ Seminary-Seminex | 88 | 0.0 | 0.0 | 1.1 | 1.1 | 97.7 | 0.0 |
| City C's of Chicago | | | | | | | |
| City-Wide C | 7,024 | 0.5 | 3.8 | 37.6 | 6.8 | 51.3 | 0.0 |
| Kennedy-King C | 8,067 | 1.1 | 0.6 | 96.3 | 0.7 | 1.3 | 0.0 |
| Loop C | 8,433 | 1.2 | 10.5 | 61.3 | 8.2 | 18.5 | 0.3 |
| Malcolm X C | 6,424 | 0.9 | 2.1 | 88.9 | 4.5 | 3.5 | 0.0 |
| Olive Harvey C | 7,799 | 1.0 | 0.3 | 92.4 | 3.1 | 3.1 | 0.0 |
| Daley C | 10,320 | 0.5 | 1.4 | 20.1 | 8.1 | 69.7 | 0.0 |
| Truman C | 10,926 | 1.1 | 15.6 | 16.2 | 12.2 | 55.0 | 0.0 |
| Wright C | 8,960 | 0.4 | 7.6 | 11.1 | 11.6 | 69.2 | 0.1 |
| C of DuPage | 18,648 | 0.1 | 4.4 | 1.7 | 1.9 | 91.9 | 0.1 |

*Continued on Following Page*

| | Total | American Indian | Asian | Black | Hispanic | White | Foreign |
|---|---|---|---|---|---|---|---|
| **ILLINOIS—Continued** | | | | | | | |
| C of Lake County | 10,931 | 0.3% | 2.3% | 6.7% | 3.4% | 87.3% | 0.0% |
| C of Saint Francis | 3,850 | 0.1 | 0.8 | 2.7 | 0.8 | 95.6 | 0.0 |
| Columbia C | 4,907 | 1.2 | 1.4 | 33.4 | 5.6 | 57.5 | 0.9 |
| Concordia C | 1,290 | 0.0 | 0.5 | 3.6 | 0.5 | 93.6 | 1.8 |
| Danville Area CC | 2,574 | 0.8 | 0.6 | 13.2 | 0.7 | 84.5 | 0.1 |
| DeLourdes C | 194 | 0.0 | 8.2 | 4.1 | 4.1 | 83.5 | 0.0 |
| DePaul U | 12,326 | 0.2 | 3.8 | 10.0 | 3.7 | 81.3 | 0.9 |
| DeVry Inst of Tech | 7,049 | 0.3 | 6.2 | 17.3 | 6.8 | 68.7 | 0.7 |
| Dr William Scholl C of Podiatric Med | 510 | 0.6 | 2.0 | 5.7 | 2.2 | 89.0 | 0.6 |
| Eastern Illinois U | 10,419 | 0.0 | 0.8 | 4.0 | 0.5 | 94.0 | 0.7 |
| East-West U | 396 | 0.0 | 9.6 | 88.4 | 1.0 | 1.0 | 0.0 |
| Elgin CC | 5,533 | 0.3 | 3.0 | 2.6 | 2.7 | 91.3 | 0.1 |
| Elmhurst C | 3,438 | 0.2 | 1.1 | 1.5 | 1.1 | 95.5 | 0.5 |
| Eureka C | 522 | 0.0 | 0.0 | 9.8 | 0.0 | 88.9 | 1.3 |
| Felician C | 325 | 0.3 | 7.4 | 4.9 | 10.8 | 73.5 | 3.1 |
| Forest Inst of Professional Psychology | 146 | 0.0 | 1.4 | 1.4 | 0.7 | 95.9 | 0.7 |
| Garrett-Evangelical Theol Sem | 353 | 0.0 | 2.3 | 11.9 | 0.0 | 83.0 | 2.8 |
| Gem City C | 190 | 0.0 | 0.0 | 1.6 | 0.0 | 98.4 | 0.0 |
| George Williams C | 1,158 | 0.1 | 1.5 | 8.3 | 2.2 | 85.5 | 2.5 |
| Governors St U | 4,921 | 0.2 | 1.1 | 16.7 | 1.7 | 78.9 | 1.4 |
| Greenville C | 650 | 0.0 | 0.6 | 4.6 | 1.2 | 91.4 | 2.2 |
| Harrington Inst of Interior Design | 395 | 0.0 | 3.3 | 3.0 | 0.8 | 91.4 | 1.5 |
| Hebrew Theol C | 83 | 0.0 | 0.0 | 0.0 | 0.0 | 96.4 | 3.6 |
| Highland CC | 2,665 | 0.2 | 0.5 | 2.1 | 0.1 | 97.1 | 0.0 |
| Illinois Benedictine C | 2,162 | 0.0 | 2.7 | 2.4 | 1.4 | 93.4 | 0.0 |
| Illinois Central C | 5,793 | 0.5 | 1.1 | 2.6 | 0.7 | 95.1 | 0.1 |
| Illinois C | 746 | 0.0 | 0.3 | 0.7 | 0.1 | 98.7 | 0.3 |
| Illinois C of Optometry | 531 | 0.0 | 5.5 | 2.1 | 2.4 | 88.5 | 1.5 |
| Illinois Eastern CC System | | | | | | | |
| Frontier CC | 3,844 | 0.1 | 0.3 | 0.2 | 0.1 | 99.3 | 0.0 |
| Lincoln Trail C | 975 | 0.1 | 0.9 | 0.7 | 0.3 | 97.7 | 0.2 |
| Olney Central C | 2,046 | 0.0 | 0.1 | 0.3 | 0.8 | 98.5 | 0.2 |
| Wabash Valley C | 1,749 | 0.2 | 0.5 | 1.8 | 0.2 | 97.1 | 0.3 |
| Illinois Inst of Tech | 6,432 | 0.1 | 7.9 | 8.4 | 2.9 | 72.1 | 8.6 |
| Illinois Sch of Professional Psychology | 347 | 0.3 | 1.2 | 2.0 | 0.6 | 94.5 | 1.4 |
| Illinois St U | 20,903 | 0.1 | 0.9 | 6.0 | 0.9 | 90.6 | 1.5 |
| Illinois Tech C | 342 | 0.9 | 5.3 | 65.2 | 7.6 | 21.1 | 0.0 |
| Illinois Valley CC | 3,983 | 0.0 | 0.7 | 1.3 | 0.9 | 97.1 | 0.1 |
| Illinois Wesleyan U | 1,641 | 0.0 | 1.4 | 5.1 | 0.7 | 92.4 | 0.4 |
| John A Logan C | 3,479 | 0.2 | 0.7 | 4.3 | 0.5 | 94.1 | 0.2 |
| John Marshall Law Sch | 1,509 | 0.1 | 0.6 | 2.5 | 1.4 | 95.4 | 0.1 |
| John Wood CC | 3,664 | 0.2 | 0.9 | 1.6 | 0.2 | 96.9 | 0.2 |
| Joliet JC | 9,845 | 0.2 | 0.8 | 9.8 | 3.5 | 85.5 | 0.1 |
| Judson C | 410 | 0.0 | 0.5 | 4.6 | 4.4 | 89.0 | 1.5 |
| Kankakee CC | 3,881 | 0.1 | 0.8 | 12.7 | 0.5 | 85.8 | 0.1 |
| Kaskaskia C | 2,644 | 0.5 | 0.6 | 5.8 | 1.0 | 91.8 | 0.2 |
| Keller Grad Sch of Mgmt | 1,013 | 0.0 | 2.0 | 7.6 | 0.9 | 89.5 | 0.0 |
| Kendall C | 278 | 0.0 | 0.7 | 32.0 | 2.2 | 61.2 | 4.0 |
| Kishwaukee C | 3,315 | 0.4 | 2.1 | 4.1 | 1.8 | 91.0 | 0.6 |
| Knox C | 903 | 0.1 | 2.8 | 5.8 | 1.1 | 79.6 | 10.6 |
| Lake Forest C | 1,151 | 0.2 | 1.8 | 4.1 | 1.3 | 91.2 | 1.4 |
| Lake Land C | 3,386 | 0.4 | 0.7 | 3.5 | 0.5 | 94.8 | 0.1 |
| Lewis and Clark CC | 4,747 | 0.2 | 0.3 | 6.6 | 0.3 | 92.5 | 0.1 |
| Lewis U | 2,826 | 0.0 | 1.0 | 12.0 | 2.4 | 83.7 | 0.8 |
| Lincoln Christian C | 472 | 0.0 | 0.2 | 0.6 | 0.2 | 97.5 | 1.5 |
| Lincoln C | 1,280 | 0.5 | 0.9 | 31.3 | 2.8 | 64.5 | 0.0 |
| Lincoln Land CC | 6,610 | 0.2 | 0.7 | 5.4 | 0.5 | 93.0 | 0.1 |
| Loyola U of Chicago | 14,174 | 0.2 | 4.5 | 8.7 | 5.2 | 80.9 | 0.5 |
| Lutheran Sch of Theol at Chicago | 280 | 0.0 | 0.4 | 3.9 | 1.4 | 80.7 | 13.6 |
| MacCormac C | 715 | 0.0 | 1.1 | 5.6 | 50.3 | 42.4 | 0.6 |
| Mallinckrodt C | 287 | 0.3 | 4.2 | 2.4 | 3.8 | 81.5 | 7.7 |
| McCormick Theol Sem | 548 | 0.0 | 5.3 | 6.0 | 7.1 | 80.5 | 1.1 |
| McHenry County C | 3,497 | 0.0 | 0.3 | 0.1 | 0.5 | 99.0 | 0.0 |
| McKendree C | 973 | 0.5 | 0.7 | 10.3 | 1.3 | 87.1 | 0.1 |
| Meadville / Lombard Theol Sch | 35 | 0.0 | 0.0 | 5.7 | 0.0 | 91.4 | 2.9 |
| Mennonite C of Nursing | 91 | 0.0 | 0.0 | 6.6 | 0.0 | 93.4 | 0.0 |
| Metropolitan Business C | 47 | 8.5 | 8.5 | 10.6 | 6.4 | 66.0 | 0.0 |
| Midstate C | 446 | 0.0 | 0.4 | 9.9 | 0.4 | 88.6 | 0.7 |
| Midwest C of Engineering | 264 | 0.0 | 10.2 | 3.0 | 1.5 | 81.4 | 3.8 |
| Millikin U | 1,601 | 0.1 | 0.4 | 4.1 | 0.7 | 94.3 | 0.4 |
| Monmouth C | 608 | 0.0 | 0.0 | 2.3 | 0.0 | 94.7 | 3.0 |
| Moody Bible Inst | 1,358 | 0.1 | 1.3 | 1.3 | 0.6 | 91.7 | 5.0 |
| Moraine Valley CC | 13,990 | 0.2 | 1.1 | 4.5 | 2.2 | 91.5 | 0.6 |
| Morrison Inst of Tech | 202 | 0.5 | 1.0 | 12.4 | 1.0 | 85.1 | 0.0 |
| Morton C | 3,413 | 0.2 | 1.3 | 0.1 | 5.6 | 92.5 | 0.3 |
| Mundelein C | 1,171 | 0.3 | 2.1 | 15.8 | 7.0 | 74.0 | 0.9 |
| NAES C | 68 | 82.4 | 0.0 | 0.0 | 0.0 | 17.6 | 0.0 |
| National C of Chiropractic | 908 | 0.2 | 0.7 | 0.8 | 1.7 | 94.4 | 2.3 |
| National C of Education | 3,313 | 0.2 | 4.3 | 10.4 | 4.8 | 80.1 | 0.1 |
| North Central C | 1,644 | 0.2 | 2.1 | 3.0 | 1.9 | 92.5 | 0.2 |
| North Park C & Theol Sem | 1,491 | 0.2 | 3.4 | 8.6 | 11.9 | 74.6 | 1.3 |
| Northeastern Illinois U | 10,075 | 0.3 | 7.1 | 11.9 | 10.3 | 69.3 | 1.2 |
| Northern Baptist Theol Sem | 230 | 0.0 | 1.7 | 10.4 | 8.3 | 71.7 | 7.8 |
| Northern Illinois U | 23,689 | 0.3 | 1.9 | 4.6 | 1.4 | 89.2 | 2.6 |
| Northwestern U | 15,829 | 0.4 | 5.4 | 6.2 | 1.5 | 80.7 | 5.7 |
| Oakton CC | 10,742 | 0.1 | 4.6 | 2.0 | 1.4 | 91.8 | 0.0 |
| Olivet Nazarene C | 1,740 | 0.0 | 0.6 | 3.7 | 0.9 | 93.9 | 0.9 |
| Parkland C | 7,712 | 0.5 | 1.9 | 6.6 | 1.1 | 88.8 | 1.1 |
| Prairie St C | 5,234 | 0.2 | 0.9 | 13.5 | 2.8 | 82.7 | 0.0 |
| Quincy C | 860 | 0.0 | 1.4 | 2.0 | 1.0 | 92.8 | 2.8 |
| Rend Lake C | 2,960 | 0.4 | 0.0 | 2.0 | 0.2 | 97.3 | 0.1 |
| Richland CC | 3,117 | 0.2 | 0.6 | 13.7 | 0.2 | 85.4 | 0.0 |
| Robert Morris C | 2,102 | 0.1 | 1.0 | 33.2 | 14.7 | 50.9 | 0.0 |
| Rock Valley C | 8,363 | 0.3 | 0.7 | 4.5 | 1.2 | 92.6 | 0.7 |
| Rockford C | 1,421 | 0.4 | 0.6 | 1.5 | 0.2 | 94.9 | 2.4 |
| Roosevelt U | 6,400 | 0.4 | 3.7 | 25.9 | 3.2 | 57.7 | 9.1 |
| Rosary C | 1,567 | 0.1 | 2.0 | 5.6 | 2.9 | 89.3 | 0.1 |
| Saint Augustine CC | 774 | 0.0 | 0.0 | 0.0 | 99.9 | 0.1 | 0.0 |
| Saint Mary of the Lake Sem | 198 | 0.0 | 0.5 | 3.5 | 2.5 | 93.4 | 0.0 |
| Saint Xavier C | 2,369 | 0.0 | 1.3 | 11.9 | 1.1 | 85.1 | 0.5 |
| Sangamon St U | 3,027 | 0.1 | 1.2 | 5.4 | 0.6 | 90.5 | 2.3 |
| Sauk Valley C | 2,685 | 0.3 | 0.9 | 0.8 | 2.7 | 95.3 | 0.0 |
| Sch of Art Inst of Chicago | 1,691 | 0.3 | 4.5 | 7.9 | 2.8 | 81.0 | 3.5 |
| Seabury-Western Theol Sem | 82 | 1.2 | 0.0 | 3.7 | 0.0 | 95.1 | 0.0 |
| Shawnee C | 1,914 | 0.2 | 0.5 | 16.7 | 0.0 | 82.6 | 0.0 |
| Sherwood Conserv Music | 38 | 0.0 | 10.5 | 13.2 | 2.6 | 65.8 | 7.9 |
| Shimer C | 77 | 0.0 | 0.0 | 19.5 | 2.6 | 76.6 | 1.3 |
| Southeastern Illinois C | 2,252 | 0.6 | 0.8 | 11.8 | 1.3 | 84.9 | 0.6 |
| Southern Illinois U | | | | | | | |
| Carbondale | 22,776 | 0.2 | 1.5 | 9.5 | 1.4 | 78.5 | 8.9 |
| Edwardsville | 10,820 | 0.2 | 1.1 | 12.9 | 0.8 | 82.9 | 2.2 |
| Spertus C of Judaica | 167 | 0.0 | 0.0 | 7.8 | 1.8 | 87.4 | 3.0 |
| Spoon River C | 1,612 | 0.1 | 0.6 | 2.2 | 0.5 | 96.5 | 0.1 |
| Springfield C in Illinois | 507 | 0.4 | 0.8 | 5.3 | 0.4 | 93.1 | 0.0 |
| State CC at East St Louis | 1,375 | 0.0 | 0.1 | 97.2 | 0.0 | 1.7 | 1.0 |
| Thornton CC | 7,378 | 0.1 | 0.8 | 19.4 | 2.6 | 76.8 | 0.2 |
| Trinity Christian C | 532 | 0.0 | 1.1 | 7.9 | 1.5 | 88.7 | 0.8 |
| Trinity C | 592 | 0.5 | 2.2 | 5.9 | 3.7 | 85.1 | 2.5 |
| Trinity Evangelical Divinity Sch | 971 | 0.0 | 3.7 | 3.8 | 0.6 | 86.2 | 5.7 |
| Triton C | 22,046 | 0.3 | 2.3 | 9.9 | 4.9 | 82.3 | 0.3 |
| U of Chicago | 9,287 | 0.2 | 5.4 | 2.9 | 1.8 | 82.3 | 7.4 |
| U of Health Sciences Chicago Med Sch | 826 | 0.1 | 5.2 | 1.2 | 1.2 | 90.8 | 1.5 |
| U of Illinois | | | | | | | |
| Chicago | 24,067 | 0.4 | 9.3 | 10.1 | 7.3 | 68.3 | 4.5 |
| Urbana-Champaign | 34,760 | 0.2 | 4.6 | 3.3 | 1.6 | 85.3 | 4.9 |
| Vandercook C of Music | 162 | 0.0 | 0.0 | 22.2 | 1.9 | 74.1 | 1.9 |
| Waubonsee CC | 5,280 | 0.4 | 0.6 | 4.4 | 4.4 | 89.0 | 1.2 |

| | Total | American Indian | Asian | Black | Hispanic | White | Foreign |
|---|---|---|---|---|---|---|---|
| **ILLINOIS—Continued** | | | | | | | |
| West Suburban C of Nursing | 72 | 0.0% | 2.8% | 4.2% | 1.4% | 91.7% | 0.0% |
| Western Illinois U | 11,732 | 0.2 | 0.7 | 8.7 | 1.2 | 85.8 | 3.5 |
| Wheaton C | 2,572 | 0.1 | 3.0 | 0.6 | 0.5 | 93.2 | 2.6 |
| William Rainey Harper C | 13,724 | 0.2 | 2.2 | 1.3 | 1.9 | 92.4 | 1.9 |
| **INDIANA** | | | | | | | |
| Ancilla Domini C | 473 | 0.0% | 0.4% | 0.6% | 0.4% | 98.5% | 0.0% |
| Anderson C | 2,022 | 2.3 | 0.3 | 4.2 | 0.2 | 91.0 | 2.0 |
| Ball St U | 17,370 | 0.3 | 0.5 | 3.2 | 0.6 | 94.4 | 1.0 |
| Bethel C | 550 | 0.0 | 0.4 | 1.3 | 0.2 | 96.4 | 1.8 |
| Calumet C | 1,130 | 0.0 | 0.3 | 11.5 | 13.6 | 74.5 | 0.1 |
| Christian Theol Sem | 312 | 0.0 | 1.0 | 4.2 | 0.0 | 94.2 | 0.6 |
| Clark C | 537 | 0.0 | 0.7 | 55.7 | 0.9 | 40.2 | 2.4 |
| Concordia Theol Sem | 517 | 0.0 | 0.0 | 2.5 | 0.6 | 96.9 | 0.0 |
| DePauw U | 2,336 | 0.0 | 1.1 | 1.5 | 0.6 | 96.6 | 0.3 |
| Earlham C | 1,049 | 0.0 | 1.1 | 4.9 | 0.3 | 91.2 | 2.5 |
| Fort Wayne Bible C | 400 | 0.2 | 1.7 | 5.2 | 0.7 | 90.2 | 1.7 |
| Franklin C of Indiana | 705 | 0.1 | 0.1 | 2.1 | 0.4 | 95.7 | 1.4 |
| Goshen Biblical Sem | 113 | 0.0 | 0.0 | 0.0 | 1.8 | 87.6 | 10.6 |
| Goshen C | 1,045 | 0.1 | 1.1 | 2.7 | 3.0 | 86.4 | 6.8 |
| Grace C | 845 | 0.5 | 0.4 | 0.9 | 0.9 | 95.7 | 1.5 |
| Grace Schs Inc | 407 | 0.0 | 1.5 | 1.7 | 0.5 | 92.6 | 3.7 |
| Hanover C | 1,015 | 0.1 | 0.1 | 0.5 | 0.4 | 96.7 | 2.2 |
| Holy Cross JC | 364 | 0.0 | 0.0 | 3.3 | 0.3 | 96.4 | 0.0 |
| Huntington C | 366 | 0.0 | 0.0 | 1.4 | 0.5 | 96.7 | 1.4 |
| Indiana Central U | 2,999 | 1.0 | 0.6 | 5.3 | 0.6 | 92.2 | 0.3 |
| Indiana St U | | | | | | | |
| Main campus | 11,618 | 0.2 | 2.2 | 7.8 | 0.4 | 79.1 | 10.4 |
| Evansville | 3,848 | 0.1 | 0.3 | 2.7 | 0.2 | 95.9 | 0.8 |
| Indiana U | | | | | | | |
| Bloomington | 32,715 | 0.2 | 1.3 | 4.3 | 1.1 | 87.1 | 6.0 |
| East | 1,326 | 0.2 | 0.4 | 4.0 | 0.9 | 94.3 | 0.3 |
| Kokomo | 2,499 | 0.4 | 0.4 | 1.8 | 0.9 | 96.4 | 0.2 |
| Northwest | 4,686 | 0.1 | 0.7 | 23.0 | 6.8 | 69.0 | 0.4 |
| Purdue U Fort Wayne | 10,171 | 0.1 | 0.6 | 3.5 | 0.6 | 94.9 | 0.4 |
| Purdue U Indianapolis | 23,366 | 0.2 | 2.0 | 7.6 | 0.8 | 88.4 | 1.0 |
| South Bend | 5,442 | 0.1 | 0.6 | 3.9 | 0.6 | 94.5 | 0.3 |
| Southeast | 4,399 | 0.2 | 0.3 | 1.8 | 0.2 | 97.4 | 0.2 |
| Indiana Voc-Tech CC | | | | | | | |
| Central Indiana | 4,427 | 0.4 | 0.5 | 21.5 | 0.8 | 76.8 | 0.0 |
| Columbus | 1,840 | 0.2 | 0.3 | 1.0 | 0.9 | 97.7 | 0.0 |
| Eastcentral | 1,824 | 0.4 | 0.2 | 7.7 | 0.1 | 91.7 | 0.0 |
| Kokomo | 1,388 | 0.4 | 0.4 | 4.6 | 0.7 | 93.9 | 0.0 |
| Lafayette | 1,291 | 0.4 | 0.6 | 0.5 | 0.0 | 98.5 | 0.0 |
| Northcentral | 2,352 | 1.1 | 0.3 | 6.3 | 0.7 | 91.6 | 0.0 |
| Northeast | 3,318 | 0.1 | 0.5 | 6.5 | 0.5 | 92.4 | 0.0 |
| Northwest | 3,314 | 0.5 | 0.4 | 32.5 | 8.5 | 58.2 | 0.0 |
| Southcentral | 1,370 | 0.5 | 0.5 | 3.1 | 0.1 | 95.8 | 0.0 |
| Southeast | 711 | 0.4 | 0.1 | 0.6 | 0.4 | 98.5 | 0.0 |
| Southwest | 2,069 | 0.3 | 0.3 | 2.4 | 0.2 | 96.8 | 0.0 |
| Wabash Valley | 1,667 | 0.5 | 0.4 | 3.6 | 0.6 | 95.0 | 0.0 |
| Whitewater | 1,005 | 0.4 | 0.2 | 3.7 | 0.2 | 95.5 | 0.0 |
| ITT Tech Inst-Fort Wayne | 1,252 | 0.0 | 0.2 | 6.3 | 0.3 | 93.1 | 0.0 |
| Manchester C | 1,028 | 0.2 | 0.4 | 1.9 | 0.5 | 95.5 | 1.5 |
| Marian C | 1,044 | 0.0 | 0.7 | 9.4 | 0.5 | 87.8 | 1.6 |
| Marion C | 1,038 | 0.2 | 0.3 | 4.4 | 0.4 | 93.3 | 1.4 |
| Martin Center C | 140 | 0.0 | 0.0 | 92.1 | 0.0 | 7.9 | 0.0 |
| Mennonite Biblical Sem | 81 | 0.0 | 0.0 | 0.0 | 0.0 | 56.8 | 43.2 |
| Mid-America C of Funeral Service | 97 | 0.0 | 0.0 | 8.2 | 0.0 | 91.8 | 0.0 |
| Oakland City C | 736 | 0.0 | 0.5 | 2.4 | 0.0 | 96.9 | 0.1 |
| Purdue U | | | | | | | |
| Main campus | 31,852 | 0.2 | 1.7 | 3.0 | 1.2 | 89.1 | 4.7 |
| Calumet | 7,446 | 0.2 | 0.8 | 7.5 | 6.5 | 84.9 | 0.1 |
| North Central | 2,616 | 0.2 | 0.6 | 2.4 | 1.0 | 95.9 | 0.0 |
| Rose Hulman Inst of Tech | 1,346 | 0.0 | 1.0 | 0.7 | 0.1 | 96.4 | 1.7 |
| Saint Francis C | 1,296 | 0.2 | 1.0 | 2.1 | 0.5 | 95.5 | 0.6 |
| Saint Joseph's C | 933 | 0.0 | 1.0 | 2.6 | 1.3 | 94.7 | 0.4 |
| Saint Mary-of-the-Woods C | 670 | 0.9 | 0.3 | 2.8 | 1.0 | 92.2 | 2.7 |
| Saint Mary's C | 1,726 | 0.0 | 0.8 | 0.2 | 0.9 | 96.9 | 1.2 |
| Saint Meinrad C | 168 | 0.0 | 0.0 | 1.2 | 4.2 | 93.5 | 1.2 |
| Saint Meinrad Sch of Theol | 147 | 0.0 | 2.0 | 2.0 | 5.4 | 89.8 | 0.7 |
| Taylor U | 1,445 | 0.1 | 0.4 | 1.1 | 0.4 | 96.5 | 1.5 |
| Tri-State U | 965 | 0.0 | 1.9 | 2.3 | 0.1 | 79.6 | 16.2 |
| U of Evansville | 4,208 | 0.1 | 0.4 | 2.8 | 0.2 | 90.9 | 5.6 |
| U of Notre Dame | 9,461 | 0.3 | 1.5 | 2.2 | 3.1 | 89.1 | 3.7 |
| Valparaiso U | 3,958 | 0.4 | 0.6 | 1.4 | 0.6 | 94.8 | 2.3 |
| Vincennes U | 6,688 | 0.0 | 0.2 | 5.5 | 0.2 | 91.9 | 2.1 |
| Wabash C | 786 | 0.0 | 2.5 | 4.3 | 1.9 | 90.3 | 0.9 |
| **IOWA** | | | | | | | |
| American Inst of Business | 1,063 | 0.0% | 0.5% | 1.1% | 0.2% | 98.2% | 0.0% |
| Briar Cliff C | 1,293 | 0.3 | 0.5 | 0.8 | 0.6 | 97.4 | 0.4 |
| Buena Vista C | 1,683 | 0.0 | 0.5 | 0.6 | 0.1 | 98.8 | 0.0 |
| Central U of Iowa | 1,537 | 0.1 | 0.6 | 2.0 | 0.3 | 94.0 | 3.0 |
| Clarke C | 922 | 0.0 | 0.4 | 0.9 | 0.2 | 96.9 | 1.6 |
| Coe C | 1,302 | 0.0 | 0.7 | 2.7 | 1.1 | 87.6 | 8.0 |
| Cornell C | 1,073 | 0.6 | 1.3 | 2.8 | 1.1 | 88.9 | 5.3 |
| Des Moines Area CC | 8,056 | 0.2 | 2.2 | 2.8 | 1.3 | 92.9 | 0.6 |
| Divine Word C | 89 | 0.0 | 29.2 | 3.4 | 4.5 | 56.2 | 6.7 |
| Dordt C | 1,103 | 0.2 | 0.3 | 0.1 | 0.0 | 84.8 | 14.7 |
| Eastern Iowa CC District | 4,548 | 0.6 | 0.7 | 3.5 | 1.8 | 92.9 | 0.5 |
| Ellsworth CC | 925 | 0.1 | 0.2 | 4.0 | 0.0 | 95.4 | 0.3 |
| Faith Baptist Bible C | 357 | 0.0 | 0.6 | 0.3 | 0.0 | 98.9 | 0.3 |
| Graceland C | 993 | 0.6 | 0.8 | 2.0 | 1.6 | 90.8 | 4.1 |
| Grand View C | 1,323 | 0.1 | 3.8 | 4.2 | 0.7 | 87.9 | 3.3 |
| Grinnell C | 1,220 | 0.0 | 2.6 | 4.3 | 0.6 | 87.4 | 5.2 |
| Hamilton Tech C | 447 | 1.1 | 0.9 | 1.6 | 3.1 | 93.3 | 0.0 |
| Hawkeye Inst of Tech | 1,809 | 0.1 | 0.3 | 3.6 | 0.3 | 95.6 | 0.1 |
| Indian Hills CC | 2,196 | 0.0 | 0.7 | 0.4 | 0.1 | 98.6 | 0.1 |
| Iowa Central CC | 2,867 | 0.0 | 1.1 | 0.8 | 0.0 | 98.1 | 0.0 |
| Iowa Lakes CC | 1,436 | 0.2 | 0.3 | 0.9 | 0.1 | 98.5 | 0.1 |
| Iowa St U | 26,994 | 0.1 | 1.1 | 2.2 | 0.7 | 88.5 | 7.4 |
| Iowa Wesleyan C | 652 | 0.0 | 0.5 | 5.2 | 0.3 | 93.9 | 0.2 |
| Iowa Western CC | 2,866 | 0.2 | 0.2 | 0.8 | 0.4 | 97.6 | 0.9 |
| Kirkwood CC | 6,340 | 1.2 | 0.9 | 0.9 | 0.5 | 95.2 | 1.3 |
| Loras C | 1,995 | 0.0 | 0.8 | 0.6 | 0.0 | 98.6 | 0.1 |
| Luther C | 2,090 | 0.1 | 2.4 | 1.1 | 0.1 | 93.9 | 2.4 |
| Maharishi International U | 1,114 | 1.0 | 1.5 | 1.1 | 0.9 | 69.9 | 25.6 |
| Marshalltown CC | 1,383 | 1.1 | 2.7 | 0.5 | 0.2 | 94.4 | 1.2 |
| Marycrest C | 1,453 | 0.1 | 0.1 | 2.8 | 0.6 | 94.6 | 1.9 |
| Morningside C | 1,205 | 2.9 | 0.7 | 2.5 | 0.2 | 91.1 | 2.7 |
| Mount Mercy C | 1,287 | 0.0 | 0.7 | 1.9 | 0.2 | 97.0 | 0.2 |
| Mount Saint Clare C | 348 | 0.0 | 0.3 | 0.0 | 0.0 | 99.1 | 0.6 |
| National Ed Center-National Inst of Tech | 280 | 0.0 | 3.6 | 3.9 | 0.0 | 92.5 | 0.0 |
| North Iowa Area CC | 2,096 | 0.1 | 0.6 | 1.7 | 0.6 | 96.9 | 0.0 |
| Northeast Iowa Tech Inst | 1,021 | 0.8 | 0.0 | 0.0 | 0.8 | 98.4 | 0.0 |
| Northwest Iowa Tech C | 470 | 0.4 | 0.9 | 0.2 | 0.9 | 97.7 | 0.0 |
| Northwestern C | 900 | 0.3 | 0.1 | 0.7 | 0.0 | 96.7 | 2.2 |
| Open Bible C | 80 | 0.0 | 0.0 | 1.2 | 1.2 | 96.2 | 1.2 |
| Palmer C of Chiropractic | 1,812 | 0.4 | 0.2 | 0.7 | 0.7 | 91.2 | 6.8 |
| Saint Ambrose C | 2,236 | 0.1 | 0.9 | 3.5 | 1.2 | 93.9 | 0.4 |
| Simpson C | 1,224 | 0.2 | 0.3 | 2.0 | 0.3 | 96.7 | 0.5 |
| Sioux Empire C | 151 | 6.6 | 0.0 | 10.6 | 0.7 | 81.5 | 0.7 |
| Southeastern CC | 1,938 | 0.0 | 0.7 | 3.0 | 0.5 | 95.7 | 0.1 |
| Southwestern CC | 673 | 0.0 | 0.0 | 0.4 | 0.0 | 99.6 | 0.0 |
| U of Dubuque | 1,157 | 1.2 | 0.0 | 1.3 | 0.1 | 91.8 | 5.6 |
| U of Iowa | 30,798 | 0.4 | 1.3 | 2.0 | 1.1 | 90.3 | 5.0 |
| U of Northern Iowa | 12,090 | 0.1 | 0.4 | 1.8 | 0.4 | 96.5 | 0.8 |
| U of Osteopathic Med and Health Sciences | 897 | 0.2 | 2.0 | 1.7 | 1.1 | 94.2 | 0.8 |
| Upper Iowa U | 970 | 0.1 | 1.8 | 12.4 | 0.7 | 82.3 | 2.8 |
| Vennard C | 201 | 1.5 | 1.0 | 0.5 | 1.0 | 91.0 | 5.0 |
| Waldorf C | 423 | 0.0 | 0.2 | 1.2 | 0.0 | 98.6 | 0.0 |
| Wartburg C | 1,155 | 0.1 | 0.3 | 2.2 | 0.0 | 93.9 | 3.5 |

| | Total | American Indian | Asian | Black | Hispanic | White | Foreign |
|---|---|---|---|---|---|---|---|
| **IOWA—Continued** | | | | | | | |
| Wartburg Theol Sem | 247 | 0.0% | 0.0% | 0.0% | 2.0% | 92.7% | 5.3% |
| Western Iowa Tech CC | 1,294 | 2.2 | 0.8 | 0.8 | 0.9 | 95.0 | 0.5 |
| Westmar C | 507 | 0.0 | 0.6 | 1.8 | 0.2 | 91.5 | 5.9 |
| William Penn C | 472 | 0.2 | 0.2 | 9.5 | 1.7 | 82.4 | 5.9 |
| **KANSAS** | | | | | | | |
| Allen County CC | 2,012 | 0.0% | 0.0% | 1.2% | 1.0% | 97.4% | 0.3% |
| Baker U | 829 | 0.0 | 0.1 | 6.9 | 0.5 | 90.0 | 2.5 |
| Barton County CC | 2,356 | 0.4 | 0.5 | 2.5 | 0.8 | 95.8 | 0.0 |
| Benedictine C | 891 | 0.0 | 0.4 | 3.5 | 3.6 | 89.7 | 2.8 |
| Bethany C | 810 | 0.1 | 0.5 | 3.7 | 1.6 | 91.9 | 2.2 |
| Bethel C | 667 | 0.1 | 0.9 | 6.6 | 0.4 | 88.5 | 3.4 |
| Butler County CC | 3,402 | 1.2 | 1.1 | 8.2 | 2.4 | 86.2 | 0.9 |
| Central Baptist Theol Sem | 157 | 0.0 | 0.6 | 22.3 | 1.3 | 73.9 | 1.9 |
| Central C | 293 | 1.4 | 1.0 | 5.5 | 1.0 | 90.1 | 1.0 |
| Cloud County CC | 1,986 | 0.0 | 0.0 | 1.0 | 0.0 | 98.9 | 0.1 |
| Coffeyville CC | 1,420 | 2.9 | 0.1 | 15.7 | 1.8 | 78.7 | 0.8 |
| Colby CC | 1,663 | 0.0 | 0.0 | 1.6 | 0.1 | 98.3 | 0.0 |
| Cowley County CC | 1,679 | 1.6 | 0.8 | 4.0 | 1.9 | 91.5 | 0.2 |
| Dodge City CC | 1,379 | 0.9 | 0.1 | 2.6 | 3.2 | 93.0 | 0.1 |
| Donnelly C | 813 | 0.4 | 3.3 | 60.9 | 4.6 | 14.5 | 16.4 |
| Emporia St U | 5,498 | 0.3 | 0.1 | 2.7 | 0.9 | 93.3 | 2.7 |
| Fort Hays St U | 5,412 | 0.4 | 0.5 | 1.0 | 0.9 | 95.7 | 1.5 |
| Friends Bible C | 116 | 0.0 | 0.0 | 0.0 | 4.3 | 94.0 | 1.7 |
| Friends U | 887 | 0.5 | 1.0 | 3.8 | 0.8 | 89.2 | 4.7 |
| Garden City CC | 1,259 | 0.5 | 1.9 | 3.9 | 9.5 | 84.0 | 0.2 |
| Haskell Indian JC | 774 | 100.0 | 0.0 | 0.0 | 0.0 | 0.0 | 0.0 |
| Hesston C | 501 | 1.2 | 1.4 | 4.2 | 2.8 | 86.8 | 3.6 |
| Highland CC | 1,265 | 1.7 | 0.7 | 6.0 | 1.8 | 89.8 | 0.0 |
| Hutchinson CC | 3,439 | 0.4 | 0.3 | 3.5 | 1.6 | 93.4 | 0.8 |
| Independence CC | 907 | 0.0 | 0.2 | 6.5 | 1.2 | 92.0 | 0.1 |
| Johnson County CC | 8,103 | 0.2 | 0.8 | 1.5 | 0.8 | 96.7 | 0.0 |
| Kansas City Kansas CC | 3,569 | 0.4 | 1.0 | 19.0 | 3.0 | 76.4 | 0.1 |
| Kansas Newman C | 891 | 0.7 | 1.1 | 7.2 | 3.9 | 84.7 | 2.4 |
| Kansas St U | 18,089 | 0.3 | 0.7 | 2.8 | 1.6 | 89.6 | 5.0 |
| Kansas Tech Inst | 629 | 0.2 | 0.8 | 0.5 | 1.4 | 97.1 | 0.0 |
| Kansas Wesleyan | 528 | 0.0 | 0.6 | 9.1 | 3.2 | 84.3 | 2.8 |
| Labette CC | 2,413 | 1.0 | 0.5 | 3.6 | 1.3 | 93.0 | 0.6 |
| Manhattan Christian C | 192 | 0.0 | 1.0 | 3.6 | 0.5 | 91.7 | 3.1 |
| Marymount C of Kansas | 625 | 0.0 | 1.1 | 4.5 | 1.1 | 93.3 | 0.0 |
| McPherson C | 484 | 0.4 | 0.4 | 5.6 | 0.0 | 90.3 | 3.3 |
| Mid-America Nazarene C | 1,053 | 0.4 | 0.4 | 0.9 | 0.5 | 95.3 | 2.5 |
| Neosho County CC | 1,001 | 0.8 | 0.1 | 3.3 | 1.2 | 94.6 | 0.0 |
| Ottawa U | 1,704 | 0.6 | 0.5 | 5.6 | 1.3 | 89.4 | 2.6 |
| Pittsburg St U | 4,927 | 0.7 | 0.3 | 1.4 | 0.7 | 94.9 | 2.0 |
| Pratt CC | 1,611 | 0.1 | 0.0 | 4.1 | 1.6 | 94.0 | 0.1 |
| Saint John's C | 258 | 0.0 | 1.2 | 3.9 | 1.6 | 91.5 | 1.9 |
| Saint Mary C | 1,009 | 0.4 | 2.3 | 19.4 | 5.5 | 70.3 | 2.2 |
| Saint Mary of the Plains C | 705 | 0.1 | 0.0 | 3.0 | 4.5 | 92.2 | 0.1 |
| Seward County CC | 1,203 | 0.6 | 1.7 | 2.7 | 2.3 | 92.8 | 0.0 |
| Southwestern C | 551 | 1.6 | 1.5 | 12.9 | 0.4 | 81.9 | 1.8 |
| Sterling C | 343 | 0.0 | 0.9 | 11.1 | 0.3 | 86.6 | 1.2 |
| Tabor C | 398 | 0.3 | 0.0 | 4.8 | 0.3 | 91.7 | 3.0 |
| U of Kansas | | | | | | | |
| Main campus | 23,901 | 0.5 | 1.2 | 3.3 | 1.1 | 87.3 | 6.7 |
| Med Center | 2,308 | 0.4 | 2.8 | 1.2 | 1.0 | 93.1 | 1.5 |
| Washburn U of Topeka | 7,094 | 0.7 | 0.6 | 5.4 | 3.1 | 89.7 | 0.5 |
| Wichita St U | 16,623 | 2.5 | 2.9 | 5.9 | 2.1 | 82.1 | 4.4 |
| **KENTUCKY** | | | | | | | |
| Alice Lloyd C | 543 | 0.0% | 0.0% | 0.2% | 0.0% | 99.8% | 0.0% |
| Asbury C | 1,067 | 0.2 | 0.5 | 0.3 | 0.3 | 96.3 | 2.4 |
| Asbury Theol Sem | 746 | 0.0 | 0.3 | 0.7 | 0.4 | 92.6 | 6.0 |
| Bellarmine C | 2,709 | 0.0 | 0.4 | 2.3 | 0.3 | 96.6 | 0.3 |
| Berea C | 1,586 | 0.0 | 0.4 | 6.1 | 0.1 | 88.6 | 4.9 |
| Bowling Green JC of Business | 525 | 0.0 | 0.0 | 31.8 | 0.0 | 68.2 | 0.0 |
| Brescia C | 815 | 0.0 | 0.0 | 1.3 | 0.0 | 94.1 | 4.5 |
| Campbellsville C | 637 | 0.0 | 0.0 | 3.0 | 0.0 | 93.4 | 3.6 |
| Centre C | 747 | 0.1 | 0.4 | 1.2 | 0.3 | 97.3 | 0.7 |
| Cumberland C | 2,106 | 0.2 | 0.0 | 4.1 | 0.5 | 92.3 | 2.9 |
| Draughon's JC of Business | 425 | 0.0 | 0.0 | 24.9 | 0.0 | 75.1 | 0.0 |
| Eastern Kentucky U | 12,357 | 0.1 | 0.2 | 6.2 | 0.2 | 92.6 | 0.8 |
| Georgetown C | 1,290 | 0.4 | 0.2 | 3.1 | 0.5 | 95.5 | 0.3 |
| Inst of Electronic Tech | 185 | 0.5 | 0.0 | 3.8 | 0.5 | 95.1 | 0.0 |
| Kentucky Christian C | 572 | 0.0 | 0.0 | 0.2 | 0.0 | 99.5 | 0.3 |
| Kentucky C of Business | 418 | 0.0 | 0.0 | 16.3 | 0.0 | 81.8 | 1.9 |
| Kentucky St U | 2,066 | 0.0 | 0.3 | 42.9 | 0.1 | 55.1 | 1.5 |
| Kentucky Wesleyan C | 821 | 0.0 | 0.2 | 4.4 | 0.0 | 93.5 | 1.8 |
| Lees JC | 329 | 0.0 | 1.8 | 4.9 | 0.0 | 93.3 | 0.0 |
| Lexington Theol Sem | 134 | 0.0 | 1.5 | 8.2 | 0.0 | 89.6 | 0.7 |
| Lindsey Wilson C | 547 | 0.0 | 0.0 | 7.9 | 0.0 | 91.8 | 0.4 |
| Louisville Presbyterian Theol Sem | 190 | 0.0 | 0.5 | 1.1 | 0.0 | 96.8 | 1.6 |
| Louisville Tech Inst | 335 | 0.0 | 0.0 | 3.6 | 0.0 | 96.4 | 0.0 |
| Midway C | 352 | 0.0 | 0.0 | 1.7 | 0.0 | 96.9 | 1.4 |
| Morehead St U | 6,174 | 0.1 | 0.1 | 2.9 | 0.3 | 94.7 | 1.9 |
| Murray St U | 7,335 | 0.1 | 0.4 | 5.1 | 0.4 | 92.7 | 1.3 |
| National Education Center-Ky C of Tech | 655 | 0.2 | 0.8 | 13.3 | 0.3 | 85.5 | 0.0 |
| Northern Kentucky U | 8,873 | 0.0 | 0.2 | 1.4 | 0.0 | 97.9 | 0.4 |
| Owensboro JC of Business | 265 | 0.0 | 0.0 | 2.3 | 0.0 | 97.7 | 0.0 |
| Pikeville C | 453 | 0.0 | 0.0 | 1.8 | 0.0 | 98.2 | 0.0 |
| RETS Electronic Inst | 878 | 0.1 | 0.0 | 7.9 | 0.5 | 91.6 | 0.0 |
| Saint Catharine C | 178 | 0.0 | 0.0 | 7.9 | 0.0 | 86.5 | 5.6 |
| S Baptist Theol Sem | 2,335 | 0.0 | 0.2 | 2.3 | 0.6 | 93.7 | 3.3 |
| Spalding U | 1,126 | 0.1 | 0.2 | 7.0 | 0.6 | 91.2 | 0.9 |
| Sue Bennett C | 310 | 0.0 | 0.0 | 5.2 | 0.3 | 93.5 | 1.0 |
| Thomas More C | 1,319 | 0.2 | 0.8 | 0.5 | 0.4 | 97.7 | 0.5 |
| Transylvania U | 787 | 0.0 | 0.6 | 2.4 | 0.6 | 95.7 | 0.6 |
| Union C | 879 | 0.0 | 0.5 | 4.1 | 0.0 | 95.1 | 0.3 |
| U of Kentucky | 20,637 | 0.3 | 0.8 | 3.1 | 0.6 | 92.8 | 2.4 |
| U of Kentucky CC System | 23,742 | 0.5 | 0.6 | 8.2 | 0.3 | 90.2 | 0.2 |
| U of Louisville | 19,747 | 0.3 | 1.2 | 8.4 | 0.6 | 87.9 | 1.6 |
| Watterson C | 2,972 | 0.0 | 0.0 | 70.7 | 1.6 | 27.5 | 0.1 |
| Western Kentucky U | 11,771 | 0.1 | 0.3 | 6.9 | 0.2 | 91.0 | 1.5 |
| **LOUISIANA** | | | | | | | |
| Centenary C of Louisiana | 1,254 | 0.2% | 0.2% | 17.1% | 0.6% | 80.4% | 1.5% |
| Delgado CC | 8,006 | 0.3 | 3.5 | 33.3 | 4.8 | 53.7 | 4.4 |
| Dillard U | 1,214 | 0.0 | 0.0 | 98.9 | 0.0 | 0.0 | 1.1 |
| Grambling St U | 4,767 | 0.0 | 0.1 | 95.8 | 0.1 | 1.6 | 2.3 |
| Louisiana C | 1,062 | 0.7 | 1.5 | 7.5 | 0.9 | 88.2 | 1.1 |
| Louisiana St U | | | | | | | |
| Baton Rouge | 30,186 | 0.2 | 0.5 | 6.8 | 1.4 | 82.4 | 8.7 |
| Alexandria | 1,985 | 0.1 | 0.8 | 16.1 | 0.6 | 82.4 | 0.0 |
| Eunice | 1,644 | 0.1 | 0.0 | 14.5 | 0.4 | 85.0 | 0.0 |
| Med Center | 2,552 | 0.0 | 1.6 | 7.6 | 1.4 | 88.9 | 0.4 |
| Shreveport | 4,690 | 0.3 | 1.5 | 7.5 | 0.6 | 89.8 | 0.2 |
| U of New Orleans | 16,356 | 0.2 | 2.6 | 16.6 | 4.1 | 74.2 | 2.4 |
| Louisiana Tech U | 10,825 | 0.2 | 0.8 | 11.5 | 0.7 | 82.9 | 4.0 |
| Loyola U in New Orleans | 4,859 | 0.5 | 0.7 | 13.4 | 5.1 | 76.6 | 3.7 |
| McNeese St U | 7,910 | 0.3 | 0.5 | 16.6 | 0.6 | 81.1 | 1.0 |
| New Orleans Baptist Theol Sem | 1,850 | 0.0 | 0.4 | 2.9 | 0.8 | 95.9 | 0.1 |
| Nicholls St U | 7,387 | 0.4 | 0.1 | 12.4 | 1.6 | 84.3 | 1.3 |
| Northeast Louisiana U | 11,558 | 0.5 | 0.4 | 19.2 | 0.3 | 75.4 | 4.2 |
| Northwestern St U of La | 6,206 | 0.6 | 1.0 | 17.4 | 2.1 | 77.6 | 1.2 |
| Notre Dame Sem Graduate Sch of Theol | 117 | 0.0 | 0.0 | 6.0 | 2.6 | 90.6 | 0.9 |
| Our Lady of Holy Cross C | 622 | 0.5 | 2.6 | 15.3 | 3.9 | 77.7 | 0.2 |
| Phillips C of Greater Orleans | 1,706 | 0.0 | 1.3 | 36.1 | 10.4 | 51.2 | 1.0 |
| Saint Bernard Parish CC | 620 | 1.0 | 1.6 | 2.1 | 3.5 | 91.6 | 0.2 |
| Saint Joseph Sem C | 155 | 0.0 | 10.3 | 6.5 | 1.3 | 81.9 | 0.0 |
| Southeastern Louisiana U | 8,992 | 0.4 | 0.8 | 9.4 | 0.5 | 87.0 | 1.9 |

| Institution | Total | American Indian | Asian | Black | Hispanic | White | Foreign |
|---|---|---|---|---|---|---|---|
| **LOUISIANA—Continued** | | | | | | | |
| Southern U and A&M C | | | | | | | |
| Main campus | 9,784 | 0.0% | 0.1% | 88.1% | 0.5% | 3.6% | 7.6% |
| New Orleans | 2,870 | 0.0 | 0.6 | 91.4 | 0.6 | 2.6 | 4.8 |
| Shreveport-Bossier | 621 | 0.0 | 0.0 | 98.1 | 0.0 | 1.9 | 0.0 |
| Tulane U | 10,232 | 0.2 | 1.6 | 4.8 | 3.1 | 84.8 | 5.5 |
| U of Southwestern La | 16,316 | 0.1 | 0.5 | 14.9 | 0.7 | 71.1 | 12.7 |
| Xavier U of Louisiana | 2,071 | 0.0 | 0.4 | 93.5 | 0.2 | 4.5 | 1.4 |
| **MAINE** | | | | | | | |
| Andover C | 441 | 0.0% | 0.0% | 0.9% | 0.5% | 98.6% | 0.0% |
| Bangor Theol Sem | 130 | 0.0 | 0.8 | 0.8 | 0.0 | 96.9 | 1.5 |
| Bates C | 1,519 | 0.0 | 1.6 | 2.0 | 0.5 | 95.4 | 0.5 |
| Beal C | 456 | 0.0 | 0.0 | 0.0 | 0.0 | 100.0 | 0.0 |
| Bowdoin C | 1,399 | 0.1 | 1.8 | 2.3 | 0.5 | 94.9 | 0.5 |
| Casco Bay C | 245 | 0.0 | 0.0 | 0.4 | 0.0 | 99.6 | 0.0 |
| Central Maine Med Center Sch of Nursing | 79 | 0.0 | 0.0 | 0.0 | 0.0 | 100.0 | 0.0 |
| Central Maine Voc-Tech Inst | 422 | 0.2 | 0.0 | 0.0 | 0.0 | 99.8 | 0.0 |
| Colby C | 1,718 | 0.0 | 0.8 | 1.5 | 0.8 | 94.9 | 2.0 |
| C of the Atlantic | 117 | 0.0 | 0.0 | 0.0 | 0.0 | 98.3 | 1.7 |
| Eastern Me Voc-Tech Inst | 858 | 0.2 | 0.1 | 0.0 | 0.0 | 99.7 | 0.0 |
| Husson C | 1,493 | 0.9 | 1.0 | 1.5 | 0.9 | 94.6 | 1.2 |
| Kennebec Valley Voc-Tech Inst | 681 | 0.0 | 0.1 | 0.0 | 0.0 | 99.9 | 0.0 |
| Maine Maritime Acad | 621 | 0.2 | 0.5 | 0.5 | 0.2 | 97.3 | 1.4 |
| Northern Maine Voc-Tech Inst | 1,229 | 0.7 | 0.3 | 1.1 | 0.7 | 97.2 | 0.0 |
| Portland Sch of Art | 250 | 0.0 | 0.4 | 0.0 | 0.4 | 99.2 | 0.0 |
| Saint Joseph's C | 8,264 | 0.4 | 0.0 | 1.1 | 0.0 | 98.5 | 0.0 |
| S Me Voc-Tech Inst | 1,466 | 0.0 | 0.1 | 0.0 | 0.1 | 95.7 | 4.1 |
| Thomas C | 832 | 0.0 | 0.0 | 0.2 | 0.6 | 98.0 | 1.2 |
| Unity C | 274 | 0.0 | 0.0 | 0.0 | 0.4 | 99.3 | 0.4 |
| U of Maine | | | | | | | |
| Augusta | 3,368 | 0.1 | 0.2 | 0.0 | 0.1 | 99.6 | 0.0 |
| Farmington | 2,140 | 0.0 | 0.0 | 0.1 | 0.1 | 99.6 | 0.0 |
| Fort Kent | 661 | 0.0 | 0.0 | 0.0 | 0.0 | 99.8 | 0.2 |
| Machias | 834 | 3.0 | 0.0 | 0.4 | 0.1 | 96.2 | 0.4 |
| Orono | 11,177 | 0.7 | 0.4 | 0.3 | 0.2 | 98.2 | 0.2 |
| Presque Isle | 1,210 | 0.7 | 0.6 | 0.9 | 1.3 | 95.6 | 0.8 |
| U of Southern Maine | 8,769 | 0.2 | 0.1 | 0.1 | 0.1 | 99.5 | 0.1 |
| U of New England | 923 | 0.2 | 0.1 | 0.2 | 0.7 | 98.2 | 0.7 |
| Westbrook C | 1,138 | 0.1 | 0.8 | 0.0 | 0.0 | 98.2 | 0.9 |
| **MARYLAND** | | | | | | | |
| Allegany CC | 2,134 | 0.0% | 0.0% | 1.8% | 0.0% | 98.1% | 0.0% |
| Anne Arundel CC | 8,894 | 0.4 | 1.5 | 6.7 | 1.0 | 89.9 | 0.4 |
| Baltimore Hebrew C | 231 | 0.0 | 0.0 | 0.4 | 0.0 | 99.6 | 0.0 |
| Bowie St C | 2,361 | 0.3 | 1.3 | 65.8 | 0.6 | 25.8 | 6.2 |
| Capitol Inst of Tech | 1,045 | 0.2 | 12.7 | 17.2 | 1.4 | 64.6 | 3.8 |
| Catonsville CC | 11,209 | 0.2 | 1.5 | 14.7 | 0.6 | 82.9 | 0.2 |
| Cecil CC | 1,423 | 0.8 | 0.5 | 3.0 | 0.2 | 95.3 | 0.2 |
| Charles County CC | 4,463 | 0.3 | 1.2 | 10.4 | 0.7 | 87.2 | 0.2 |
| Chesapeake C | 1,811 | 0.1 | 0.6 | 8.4 | 0.5 | 90.4 | 0.1 |
| C of Notre Dame of Md | 1,756 | 0.5 | 1.1 | 10.4 | 2.1 | 84.7 | 1.3 |
| Columbia Union C | 886 | 0.3 | 4.3 | 25.2 | 3.3 | 60.6 | 6.3 |
| CC of Baltimore | 7,516 | 0.0 | 0.8 | 78.0 | 0.5 | 20.7 | 0.0 |
| Coppin St C | 2,434 | 0.4 | 2.6 | 89.4 | 0.2 | 3.2 | 4.2 |
| Dundalk CC | 3,203 | 0.3 | 0.4 | 8.2 | 0.4 | 90.5 | 0.0 |
| Eastern Christian C | 56 | 0.0 | 1.8 | 1.8 | 0.0 | 96.4 | 0.0 |
| Essex CC | 9,861 | 0.6 | 1.3 | 5.4 | 0.7 | 91.9 | 0.0 |
| Frederick CC | 3,200 | 0.3 | 0.5 | 4.1 | 0.9 | 93.9 | 0.3 |
| Frostburg St C | 3,546 | 0.2 | 0.4 | 7.4 | 0.8 | 90.9 | 0.3 |
| Garrett CC | 569 | 0.0 | 0.2 | 3.2 | 0.2 | 96.5 | 0.0 |
| Goucher C | 984 | 0.3 | 3.6 | 5.8 | 2.6 | 85.0 | 2.7 |
| Hagerstown Business C | 259 | 0.0 | 0.8 | 6.2 | 0.0 | 92.3 | 0.8 |
| Hagerstown JC | 2,497 | 0.1 | 0.4 | 5.3 | 0.6 | 93.6 | 0.0 |
| Harford CC | 4,285 | 0.2 | 1.2 | 7.3 | 0.7 | 90.5 | 0.0 |
| Hood C | 1,736 | 0.1 | 1.0 | 3.2 | 2.4 | 91.9 | 1.3 |
| Howard CC | 3,420 | 0.2 | 2.6 | 11.7 | 1.0 | 84.1 | 0.4 |
| Johns Hopkins U | 10,586 | 0.2 | 4.8 | 5.2 | 1.2 | 82.7 | 5.8 |
| Loyola C | 5,171 | 0.1 | 1.5 | 3.8 | 0.8 | 91.5 | 2.3 |
| Md C of Art and Design | 83 | 0.0 | 2.4 | 25.3 | 1.2 | 69.9 | 1.2 |
| Maryland Inst C of Art | 1,244 | 0.2 | 2.6 | 7.1 | 1.8 | 85.3 | 3.1 |
| Montgomery C | | | | | | | |
| Germantown | 2,564 | 0.3 | 2.5 | 3.3 | 1.3 | 92.1 | 0.4 |
| Rockville | 12,682 | 0.2 | 6.2 | 5.8 | 3.5 | 81.2 | 3.1 |
| Takoma Park | 4,650 | 0.2 | 7.9 | 24.0 | 4.8 | 58.0 | 5.1 |
| Morgan St U | 4,206 | 0.2 | 0.4 | 87.3 | 0.2 | 4.3 | 7.5 |
| Mount Saint Mary's C | 1,708 | 0.1 | 0.6 | 2.5 | 0.8 | 95.9 | 0.0 |
| Ner Israel Rabbinical C | 325 | 0.0 | 0.0 | 0.0 | 0.0 | 100.0 | 0.0 |
| Peabody Inst of Johns Hopkins U | 429 | 0.2 | 4.2 | 4.2 | 1.2 | 76.7 | 13.5 |
| Prince Georges CC | 14,083 | 0.3 | 3.6 | 37.8 | 1.6 | 55.4 | 1.4 |
| Saint John's C | | | | | | | |
| Main campus | 384 | 0.0 | 1.6 | 0.5 | 1.6 | 94.5 | 1.8 |
| Santa Fe | 353 | 0.3 | 0.6 | 0.0 | 1.4 | 95.5 | 2.3 |
| Saint Mary's C of Maryland | 1,299 | 0.5 | 0.5 | 5.1 | 0.5 | 92.9 | 0.5 |
| Saint Mary's Sem and U | 336 | 0.0 | 0.0 | 0.0 | 0.0 | 100.0 | 0.0 |
| Salisbury St C | 4,487 | 0.2 | 0.5 | 6.7 | 0.5 | 91.8 | 0.3 |
| Sojourner-Douglass C | 387 | 0.0 | 0.3 | 99.2 | 0.0 | 0.5 | 0.0 |
| Towson St U | 15,106 | 0.1 | 1.4 | 10.3 | 0.8 | 86.7 | 0.6 |
| U of Baltimore | 5,178 | 0.3 | 1.9 | 16.1 | 0.7 | 78.1 | 3.0 |
| U of Maryland | | | | | | | |
| College Park | 38,307 | 0.4 | 5.8 | 7.9 | 2.2 | 79.0 | 4.7 |
| Baltimore County | 8,153 | 0.2 | 5.0 | 11.9 | 1.3 | 80.1 | 1.6 |
| Baltimore Prof Schs | 4,633 | 0.1 | 4.4 | 10.8 | 1.2 | 81.8 | 1.6 |
| U C | 11,640 | 0.4 | 5.2 | 16.8 | 1.9 | 75.2 | 0.4 |
| Eastern Shore | 1,230 | 0.2 | 1.5 | 68.0 | 0.7 | 23.0 | 6.7 |
| Villa Julie C | 1,328 | 0.0 | 0.5 | 13.6 | 0.6 | 85.3 | 0.1 |
| Washington Bible C | 524 | 0.4 | 7.1 | 19.3 | 0.4 | 67.2 | 5.7 |
| Washington C | 865 | 0.1 | 0.2 | 0.7 | 0.7 | 95.8 | 2.4 |
| Washington Theol Union | 167 | 0.0 | 1.2 | 1.8 | 1.8 | 95.2 | 0.0 |
| Western Maryland C | 1,585 | 0.0 | 0.4 | 3.0 | 0.5 | 96.1 | 0.1 |
| Wor-Wic Tech CC | 856 | 0.1 | 0.1 | 22.4 | 0.6 | 76.8 | 0.0 |
| **MASSACHUSETTS** | | | | | | | |
| American International C | 1,859 | 0.0% | 0.0% | 11.2% | 1.0% | 83.8% | 3.9% |
| Amherst C | 1,543 | 0.1 | 3.8 | 6.4 | 2.1 | 85.4 | 2.2 |
| Andover Newton Theol Sch | 458 | 0.4 | 0.0 | 4.6 | 1.5 | 91.3 | 2.2 |
| Anna Maria C | 1,749 | 0.1 | 1.0 | 2.8 | 1.0 | 94.1 | 1.1 |
| Aquinas JC at Milton | 389 | 0.0 | 0.0 | 0.3 | 0.0 | 99.7 | 0.0 |
| Arthur D Little Management Ed Inst | 67 | 0.0 | 1.5 | 3.0 | 1.5 | 4.5 | 89.6 |
| Assumption C | 2,474 | 0.0 | 0.1 | 0.6 | 1.9 | 97.2 | 0.2 |
| Atlantic Union C | 600 | 0.2 | 0.7 | 21.8 | 9.2 | 55.3 | 12.8 |
| Babson C | 3,187 | 0.0 | 0.9 | 1.4 | 0.8 | 91.1 | 5.7 |
| Bay Path JC | 686 | 0.1 | 0.1 | 2.3 | 0.4 | 95.9 | 1.0 |
| Bay St JC of Business | 541 | 0.0 | 0.7 | 13.5 | 9.1 | 73.8 | 3.0 |
| Becker JC | | | | | | | |
| Leicester | 547 | 0.0 | 0.2 | 0.9 | 0.2 | 98.4 | 0.4 |
| Worcester | 911 | 0.0 | 0.0 | 0.9 | 0.2 | 98.8 | 0.1 |
| Bentley C | 8,085 | 0.1 | 0.9 | 0.7 | 1.1 | 96.0 | 1.3 |
| Berklee C of Music | 2,425 | 0.3 | 1.0 | 8.3 | 2.0 | 66.0 | 22.4 |
| Berkshire Christian C | 126 | 0.0 | 0.0 | 6.3 | 0.8 | 88.1 | 4.8 |
| Blue Hills Regional Tech Inst | 465 | 0.2 | 0.2 | 1.5 | 1.3 | 96.8 | 0.0 |
| Boston Architecture Ctr | 642 | 0.0 | 2.3 | 2.0 | 3.7 | 91.9 | 0.0 |
| Boston C | 14,209 | 0.2 | 2.8 | 2.0 | 2.9 | 89.6 | 2.6 |
| Boston Conservatory | 420 | 0.2 | 1.2 | 6.0 | 2.9 | 83.8 | 6.0 |
| Boston U | 27,630 | 0.2 | 3.1 | 3.1 | 2.0 | 83.5 | 8.2 |
| Bradford C | 404 | 0.0 | 0.7 | 3.5 | 3.7 | 82.4 | 9.7 |
| Brandeis U | 3,536 | 0.1 | 2.5 | 2.5 | 2.3 | 85.2 | 7.2 |
| Cambridge C | 439 | 0.9 | 3.6 | 23.2 | 3.9 | 65.6 | 2.7 |
| Catherine Laboure C | 661 | 0.3 | 0.4 | 10.7 | 1.2 | 86.8 | 0.6 |
| Central New England C of Tech | 556 | 0.0 | 1.3 | 0.9 | 0.9 | 93.2 | 3.8 |
| **MASSACHUSETTS—Continued** | | | | | | | |
| Chamberlayne JC | 806 | 0.5% | 1.7% | 7.6% | 1.6% | 78.5% | 10.0% |
| Clark U | 3,185 | 0.0 | 0.9 | 1.8 | 1.9 | 89.1 | 6.2 |
| C of the Holy Cross | 2,590 | 0.0 | 0.3 | 1.7 | 1.0 | 96.7 | 0.4 |
| C of Our Lady of the Elms | 900 | 0.1 | 0.1 | 2.8 | 0.6 | 95.9 | 0.6 |
| Curry C | 1,244 | 0.1 | 0.6 | 3.4 | 0.3 | 94.5 | 1.2 |
| Dean JC | 2,354 | 0.0 | 0.1 | 1.3 | 0.2 | 98.0 | 0.4 |
| Emerson C | 2,287 | 0.1 | 0.3 | 4.1 | 1.7 | 90.4 | 3.3 |
| Emmanuel C | 979 | 0.1 | 0.4 | 3.5 | 4.1 | 89.5 | 2.5 |
| Endicott C | 669 | 0.0 | 1.6 | 1.3 | 2.8 | 93.6 | 0.6 |
| Episcopal Divinity Sch | 117 | 0.0 | 0.0 | 3.4 | 0.9 | 92.3 | 3.4 |
| Fisher JC | 4,384 | 0.4 | 0.6 | 4.9 | 1.4 | 91.9 | 0.7 |
| Forsyth Sch of Dental Hygienists | 137 | 0.7 | 0.7 | 0.7 | 1.5 | 91.2 | 5.1 |
| Franklin Inst of Boston | 449 | 0.2 | 5.1 | 8.2 | 0.4 | 79.1 | 6.9 |
| Gordon C | 1,073 | 0.0 | 1.5 | 2.3 | 0.7 | 94.3 | 1.1 |
| Gordon-Conwell Theol Sem | 861 | 0.0 | 1.5 | 10.9 | 6.5 | 78.9 | 2.2 |
| Hampshire C | 1,049 | 0.2 | 1.3 | 2.0 | 1.8 | 89.2 | 5.4 |
| Harvard U | 19,977 | 0.3 | 4.4 | 4.2 | 3.1 | 78.8 | 9.2 |
| Hebrew C | 160 | 0.0 | 0.0 | 0.0 | 0.0 | 80.0 | 20.0 |
| Hellenic C-Holy Cross Greek Orthodox Sch of Theol | 219 | 0.0 | 0.9 | 5.9 | 0.0 | 78.1 | 15.1 |
| Lasell JC | 492 | 0.0 | 0.4 | 2.6 | 0.8 | 91.1 | 5.1 |
| Lesley C | 2,980 | 0.2 | 0.8 | 1.9 | 0.8 | 94.6 | 1.7 |
| Marian Court JC of Business | 250 | 0.4 | 0.0 | 0.4 | 0.8 | 98.4 | 0.0 |
| Mass Bd of Regents Sys | | | | | | | |
| Southeastern Mass U | 7,125 | 0.2 | 0.7 | 1.7 | 0.5 | 95.8 | 1.1 |
| U of Lowell | 15,800 | 0.3 | 2.5 | 0.8 | 0.9 | 91.9 | 3.6 |
| U of Massachusetts | | | | | | | |
| Amherst | 27,162 | 0.2 | 1.4 | 2.2 | 1.7 | 90.1 | 4.3 |
| Boston | 11,711 | 0.5 | 3.7 | 9.8 | 3.6 | 79.9 | 2.6 |
| Med Sch at Worcester | 457 | 0.0 | 3.3 | 2.2 | 2.0 | 92.6 | 0.0 |
| Bridgewater St C | 8,313 | 0.1 | 0.4 | 0.9 | 0.3 | 98.0 | 0.3 |
| Fitchburg St C | 6,693 | 0.1 | 0.3 | 2.4 | 0.7 | 96.3 | 0.2 |
| Framingham St C | 5,653 | 0.2 | 0.4 | 0.3 | 0.3 | 98.5 | 0.4 |
| Massachusetts C of Art | 1,730 | 0.3 | 3.0 | 3.1 | 2.0 | 90.8 | 0.9 |
| Mass Maritime Acad | 803 | 0.1 | 0.6 | 0.4 | 0.6 | 97.1 | 1.1 |
| North Adams St C | 2,729 | 0.0 | 0.2 | 1.4 | 0.4 | 97.4 | 0.5 |
| Salem St C | 8,654 | 0.3 | 0.8 | 2.4 | 0.8 | 95.0 | 0.7 |
| Westfield St C | 4,607 | 0.0 | 0.1 | 2.5 | 0.7 | 96.3 | 0.4 |
| Worcester St C | 7,062 | 0.1 | 0.1 | 0.8 | 0.5 | 97.8 | 0.8 |
| Berkshire CC | 3,017 | 0.0 | 0.4 | 1.5 | 0.5 | 97.6 | 0.0 |
| Bristol CC | 4,718 | 0.2 | 0.9 | 1.6 | 1.0 | 95.5 | 0.8 |
| Bunker Hill CC | 6,977 | 0.3 | 10.8 | 10.1 | 4.7 | 72.0 | 2.0 |
| Cape Cod CC | 4,251 | 0.2 | 0.4 | 2.4 | 0.8 | 96.1 | 0.1 |
| Greenfield CC | 2,396 | 0.1 | 0.3 | 0.4 | 0.5 | 98.1 | 0.6 |
| Holyoke CC | 4,704 | 0.4 | 0.5 | 1.5 | 1.7 | 95.6 | 0.3 |
| Massachusetts Bay CC | 4,236 | 0.0 | 0.8 | 1.0 | 0.8 | 96.9 | 0.5 |
| Massasoit CC | 6,113 | 0.2 | 0.6 | 4.5 | 1.4 | 93.3 | 0.0 |
| Middlesex CC | 6,772 | 0.2 | 1.4 | 1.6 | 1.1 | 95.7 | 0.0 |
| Mount Wachusett CC | 2,900 | 0.4 | 1.0 | 3.4 | 1.7 | 93.0 | 0.5 |
| Northern Essex CC | 6,110 | 0.5 | 0.8 | 0.4 | 1.8 | 96.0 | 0.4 |
| North Shore CC | 5,993 | 0.1 | 0.5 | 1.7 | 1.6 | 95.8 | 0.4 |
| Quinsigamond CC | 4,782 | 0.2 | 0.9 | 2.0 | 2.7 | 94.0 | 0.3 |
| Roxbury CC | 1,444 | 0.2 | 1.9 | 45.8 | 17.2 | 24.7 | 10.2 |
| Springfield Tech CC | 6,762 | 0.3 | 0.3 | 6.9 | 4.5 | 87.2 | 0.8 |
| Mass C of Pharmacy & Allied Health Sciences | 1,194 | 0.1 | 0.8 | 5.6 | 1.8 | 81.7 | 10.0 |
| Massachusetts Inst of Tech | 9,606 | 0.2 | 6.8 | 3.3 | 2.1 | 65.3 | 22.3 |
| Massachusetts Sch of Professional Psychology | 179 | 0.0 | 0.6 | 1.7 | 1.7 | 95.0 | 1.1 |
| Merrimack C | 3,643 | 0.0 | 0.2 | 0.6 | 0.9 | 97.6 | 0.7 |
| MGH Inst of Health Professions | 154 | 0.0 | 1.3 | 1.3 | 1.3 | 94.2 | 1.9 |
| Mount Holyoke C | 1,966 | 0.1 | 4.4 | 5.1 | 1.6 | 84.1 | 4.7 |
| New England C of Optometry | 357 | 0.0 | 3.9 | 1.1 | 1.4 | 91.6 | 2.0 |
| New England Conservatory of Music | 738 | 0.0 | 2.3 | 1.6 | 1.1 | 77.4 | 17.6 |
| New England Inst of Applied Arts and Sciences | 135 | 0.0 | 0.0 | 5.2 | 0.0 | 93.3 | 1.5 |
| New England Sch of Law | 967 | 0.1 | 1.0 | 2.5 | 1.1 | 95.2 | 0.0 |
| Newbury C | 3,848 | 0.1 | 2.4 | 19.2 | 10.7 | 64.5 | 3.1 |
| Nichols C | 1,092 | 0.0 | 0.1 | 0.3 | 0.4 | 98.7 | 0.5 |
| Northeastern U | 36,219 | 0.6 | 2.8 | 5.5 | 1.2 | 85.9 | 4.0 |
| Pine Manor C | 568 | 0.5 | 1.1 | 1.9 | 1.2 | 80.3 | 15.0 |
| Quincy JC | 2,945 | 0.0 | 0.3 | 0.6 | 1.4 | 97.2 | 0.5 |
| Radcliffe C | 2,691 | 0.4 | 9.1 | 7.9 | 4.9 | 72.4 | 5.4 |
| Regis C | 1,180 | 0.0 | 0.8 | 0.6 | 5.1 | 90.3 | 3.2 |
| Saint Hyacinth C-Sem | 39 | 0.0 | 0.0 | 0.0 | 5.1 | 87.2 | 7.7 |
| Saint John's Sem | 218 | 0.0 | 0.0 | 0.9 | 3.2 | 95.4 | 0.5 |
| Sch of the Museum of Fine Arts-Boston | 1,021 | 0.2 | 0.6 | 0.9 | 1.5 | 90.8 | 6.1 |
| Simmons C | 3,138 | 0.1 | 1.1 | 3.3 | 1.5 | 91.3 | 2.7 |
| Simon's Rock of Bard C | 324 | 0.0 | 1.9 | 2.8 | 0.6 | 92.3 | 2.5 |
| Smith C | 2,752 | 0.1 | 6.3 | 3.7 | 2.0 | 82.9 | 5.1 |
| Springfield C | 2,353 | 0.0 | 0.5 | 6.0 | 1.6 | 89.4 | 2.4 |
| Stonehill C | 2,786 | 0.1 | 0.2 | 0.7 | 0.3 | 98.3 | 0.3 |
| Suffolk U | 6,124 | 0.2 | 0.5 | 2.0 | 1.0 | 93.8 | 2.6 |
| Swain Sch of Design | 149 | 0.0 | 0.7 | 6.0 | 0.0 | 89.9 | 3.4 |
| Tufts U | 7,507 | 0.1 | 3.8 | 3.3 | 1.7 | 85.3 | 5.8 |
| Wang Inst of Graduate Studies | 55 | 0.0 | 3.6 | 1.8 | 0.0 | 89.1 | 5.5 |
| Wellesley C | 2,297 | 0.2 | 9.4 | 5.4 | 3.0 | 76.8 | 5.2 |
| Wentworth Inst of Tech | 4,034 | 0.3 | 2.7 | 5.5 | 2.0 | 81.7 | 7.8 |
| Western New England C | 5,140 | 0.3 | 0.8 | 2.3 | 1.0 | 94.3 | 1.4 |
| Weston Sch of Theol | 212 | 0.0 | 0.0 | 0.0 | 1.4 | 92.0 | 6.6 |
| Wheaton C | 1,105 | 0.0 | 1.9 | 2.8 | 0.4 | 92.4 | 2.5 |
| Wheelock C | 671 | 0.1 | 0.1 | 1.2 | 1.2 | 95.7 | 1.6 |
| Williams C | 2,012 | 0.1 | 4.2 | 5.0 | 1.2 | 85.5 | 3.9 |
| Worcester JC | 1,480 | 0.5 | 1.6 | 1.1 | 1.2 | 93.8 | 1.8 |
| Worcester Polytechnic Inst | 3,812 | 0.1 | 1.7 | 0.3 | 0.4 | 91.7 | 5.8 |
| **MICHIGAN** | | | | | | | |
| Adrian C | 1,220 | 0.0% | 0.0% | 4.2% | 1.8% | 92.8% | 1.2% |
| Albion C | 1,586 | 0.0 | 1.2 | 2.1 | 0.4 | 95.0 | 1.3 |
| Alma C | 1,016 | 0.0 | 0.5 | 1.4 | 0.6 | 97.0 | 0.5 |
| Alpena CC | 1,878 | 0.1 | 0.4 | 2.4 | 0.7 | 96.3 | 0.1 |
| Andrews U | 3,028 | 0.3 | 3.9 | 15.4 | 8.0 | 50.7 | 21.7 |
| Aquinas C | 2,831 | 0.2 | 0.5 | 2.6 | 1.2 | 94.9 | 0.6 |
| Baker JC of Business | 2,424 | 0.3 | 1.6 | 10.4 | 1.3 | 86.3 | 0.0 |
| Bay De Noc CC | 1,801 | 2.2 | 0.2 | 0.0 | 0.3 | 97.2 | 0.1 |
| Calvin C | 3,972 | 0.1 | 0.4 | 0.5 | 0.1 | 89.6 | 9.4 |
| Calvin Theol Sem | 238 | 0.0 | 2.9 | 1.7 | 0.8 | 70.2 | 24.4 |
| Center for Creative Studies C of Art and Design | 1,141 | 0.0 | 0.4 | 6.7 | 0.9 | 90.3 | 1.7 |
| Center for Humanistic Studies | 66 | 0.0 | 0.0 | 6.1 | 0.0 | 90.9 | 3.0 |
| Central Michigan U | 16,788 | 0.4 | 0.3 | 1.9 | 0.7 | 95.3 | 1.3 |
| Charles S Mott CC | 11,158 | 1.1 | 0.6 | 14.1 | 1.5 | 82.6 | 0.1 |
| Cleary C | 989 | 0.0 | 0.1 | 11.8 | 0.4 | 86.9 | 0.8 |
| Concordia C | 487 | 0.6 | 0.2 | 2.7 | 0.0 | 93.2 | 3.3 |
| Cranbrook Acad of Art | 147 | 0.0 | 3.4 | 1.4 | 0.7 | 78.9 | 15.6 |
| Devenport C | 4,219 | 0.5 | 0.3 | 6.6 | 1.1 | 91.3 | 0.1 |
| Delta C | 10,243 | 0.4 | 0.4 | 8.1 | 2.9 | 88.1 | 0.1 |
| Detroit C of Business | 3,318 | 0.8 | 0.5 | 37.5 | 1.8 | 59.2 | 0.2 |
| Detroit C of Law | 809 | 0.2 | 1.4 | 6.7 | 0.6 | 91.0 | 0.1 |
| Eastern Michigan U | 17,093 | 0.3 | 1.2 | 9.0 | 1.2 | 83.6 | 4.7 |
| Ferris St C | 10,546 | 0.2 | 0.3 | 4.0 | 0.5 | 94.1 | 0.9 |
| Glen Oaks CC | 1,213 | 0.2 | 0.5 | 1.6 | 0.5 | 95.7 | 1.4 |
| GMI Engr and Mgmt Inst | 2,998 | 0.4 | 3.8 | 5.1 | 1.4 | 81.9 | 7.3 |
| Gogebic CC | 1,600 | 0.8 | 0.2 | 21.6 | 0.7 | 76.7 | 0.0 |
| Grace Bible C | 141 | 0.7 | 0.0 | 2.1 | 1.4 | 95.7 | 0.0 |
| Grand Rapids Bible C and Sem | 951 | 0.2 | 0.2 | 1.7 | 0.5 | 95.6 | 1.8 |
| Grand Rapids JC | 8,913 | 0.5 | 1.4 | 6.6 | 1.7 | 89.3 | 0.5 |
| **MICHIGAN—Continued** | | | | | | | |
| Grand Valley St C | 7,153 | 0.4% | 0.4% | 3.7% | 1.1% | 93.1% | 1.3% |
| Great Lakes Bible C | 141 | 0.0 | 0.0 | 2.8 | 1.4 | 95.7 | 0.0 |
| Highland Park CC | 2,416 | 0.0 | 0.1 | 96.2 | 0.1 | 2.2 | 1.3 |
| Hillsdale C | 1,033 | 0.0 | 0.0 | 1.3 | 0.0 | 96.8 | 1.9 |
| Hope C | 2,550 | 0.1 | 0.9 | 0.6 | 0.8 | 95.5 | 2.0 |
| Jackson CC | 6,074 | 0.6 | 1.7 | 10.1 | 0.7 | 86.7 | 0.1 |
| Jordan C | 1,711 | 0.4 | 0.4 | 44.0 | 1.9 | 52.9 | 0.6 |
| Kalamazoo C | 1,218 | 0.1 | 3.4 | 1.5 | 0.7 | 91.5 | 2.9 |
| Kalamazoo Valley CC | 8,281 | 0.4 | 0.8 | 8.4 | 0.9 | 87.6 | 1.8 |
| Kellogg CC | 4,553 | 0.5 | 0.7 | 8.6 | 0.9 | 88.7 | 0.6 |
| Kendall Sch of Design | 687 | 0.6 | 0.6 | 0.9 | 1.2 | 96.4 | 0.4 |
| Kirtland CC | 1,333 | 0.5 | 0.0 | 1.5 | 0.6 | 97.4 | 0.1 |
| Lake Michigan C | 3,199 | 0.2 | 1.2 | 12.2 | 1.3 | 84.0 | 1.1 |
| Lake Superior St C | 2,783 | 2.9 | 0.3 | 1.1 | 0.3 | 74.7 | 20.7 |
| Lansing CC | 19,157 | 0.7 | 1.4 | 5.6 | 1.8 | 89.4 | 1.1 |
| Lawrence Inst of Tech | 6,121 | 0.6 | 1.5 | 7.7 | 1.1 | 87.2 | 2.0 |
| Lewis C of Business | 377 | 0.0 | 0.0 | 100.0 | 0.0 | 0.0 | 0.0 |
| Macomb CC | 30,892 | 0.5 | 0.9 | 1.9 | 0.6 | 96.0 | 0.2 |
| Madonna C | 3,878 | 0.2 | 0.6 | 7.3 | 1.0 | 88.8 | 2.2 |
| Marygrove C | 1,182 | 0.3 | 0.1 | 68.3 | 0.8 | 30.2 | 0.3 |
| Mercy C of Detroit | 2,445 | 0.1 | 0.9 | 31.9 | 0.7 | 65.8 | 0.4 |
| Michigan Christian C | 360 | 0.0 | 0.6 | 23.3 | 1.4 | 73.6 | 1.1 |
| Michigan St U | 42,193 | 0.3 | 1.2 | 5.8 | 1.1 | 87.1 | 4.5 |
| Michigan Tech U | 6,935 | 0.3 | 0.9 | 0.3 | 0.5 | 94.8 | 3.1 |
| Mid Michigan CC | 1,761 | 0.6 | 0.1 | 0.4 | 0.2 | 97.8 | 0.9 |
| Monroe County CC | 2,880 | 0.2 | 0.3 | 0.7 | 0.6 | 98.2 | 0.0 |
| Montcalm CC | 1,398 | 0.3 | 0.4 | 10.9 | 0.6 | 87.8 | 0.0 |
| Muskegon Business C | 1,464 | 0.2 | 0.3 | 6.6 | 2.0 | 90.9 | 0.0 |
| Muskegon CC | 4,623 | 1.8 | 0.6 | 6.6 | 1.1 | 89.9 | 0.0 |
| Nazareth C | 820 | 0.2 | 0.4 | 7.1 | 1.6 | 90.7 | 0.0 |
| North Central Michigan C | 1,692 | 2.3 | 0.3 | 0.1 | 0.5 | 96.6 | 0.2 |
| Northern Michigan U | 7,824 | 1.5 | 0.5 | 2.8 | 0.4 | 94.1 | 0.8 |
| Northwestern Michigan C | 3,222 | 0.8 | 0.2 | 0.1 | 0.3 | 98.0 | 0.6 |
| Northwood Inst | 2,079 | 0.0 | 0.3 | 7.0 | 0.8 | 87.0 | 4.9 |
| Oakland CC | 26,605 | 0.4 | 0.7 | 6.6 | 1.4 | 90.2 | 0.6 |
| Oakland U | 11,935 | 0.3 | 1.1 | 5.0 | 0.8 | 92.3 | 0.5 |
| Olivet C | 679 | 0.4 | 0.4 | 13.4 | 1.3 | 84.4 | 0.0 |
| Reformed Bible C | 219 | 0.0 | 5.0 | 3.7 | 3.2 | 62.1 | 26.0 |
| Sacred Heart Sem C | 203 | 0.0 | 2.5 | 4.4 | 0.5 | 92.6 | 0.0 |
| Saginaw Valley St C | 4,833 | 0.5 | 0.7 | 6.4 | 2.8 | 89.1 | 0.5 |
| Saint Clair County CC | 3,885 | 0.2 | 0.2 | 1.2 | 0.4 | 97.8 | 0.3 |
| Saint John's Provincial Sem | 200 | 0.0 | 0.5 | 0.5 | 1.5 | 97.5 | 0.0 |
| Saint Mary's C | 241 | 0.0 | 0.0 | 5.0 | 0.0 | 90.9 | 4.1 |
| Schoolcraft C | 8,512 | 0.3 | 0.9 | 1.6 | 0.2 | 97.0 | 0.0 |
| Siena Heights C | 1,480 | 0.1 | 0.3 | 7.6 | 2.4 | 86.5 | 3.1 |
| Southwestern Michigan C | 2,365 | 1.1 | 0.4 | 7.0 | 0.8 | 90.3 | 0.5 |
| Spring Arbor C | 1,046 | 0.0 | 0.4 | 14.4 | 1.0 | 82.0 | 2.2 |
| Thomas M Cooley Law Sch | 1,128 | 0.3 | 0.4 | 1.2 | 0.7 | 97.4 | 0.0 |
| U of Detroit | 5,820 | 0.3 | 1.6 | 16.8 | 1.3 | 73.6 | 6.4 |
| U of Michigan | | | | | | | |
| Ann Arbor | 34,467 | 0.4 | 3.7 | 4.7 | 1.6 | 82.8 | 6.9 |
| Dearborn | 6,321 | 0.6 | 1.8 | 6.6 | 1.8 | 89.1 | 0.2 |
| Flint | 5,596 | 1.1 | 0.9 | 9.3 | 1.7 | 86.8 | 0.2 |
| Walsh C of Accountancy and Business Admin | 2,025 | 0.6 | 1.0 | 2.6 | 0.6 | 95.0 | 0.1 |
| Washtenaw CC | 7,858 | 0.8 | 2.2 | 12.5 | 0.6 | 83.4 | 0.4 |
| Wayne County CC | 12,505 | 0.9 | 0.9 | 61.2 | 1.3 | 32.7 | 3.1 |
| Wayne St U | 29,070 | 0.8 | 3.3 | 21.9 | 1.8 | 69.7 | 2.5 |
| West Shore CC | 1,083 | 0.5 | 0.4 | 0.7 | 0.5 | 98.0 | 0.0 |
| Western Michigan U | 20,233 | 0.2 | 0.4 | 5.5 | 0.5 | 88.4 | 5.0 |
| Western Theol Sem | 177 | 0.0 | 1.1 | 0.6 | 0.0 | 94.9 | 3.4 |
| William Tyndale C | 302 | 0.0 | 1.3 | 21.5 | 1.3 | 74.2 | 1.7 |
| **MINNESOTA** | | | | | | | |
| Alexandria Area Tech Inst | 1,560 | 0.8% | 0.3% | 0.2% | 0.2% | 98.5% | 0.0% |
| Augsburg C | 1,617 | 1.8 | 0.7 | 2.8 | 0.4 | 90.8 | 3.5 |
| Bethany Lutheran C | 246 | 0.4 | 0.0 | 1.2 | 0.4 | 97.2 | 0.8 |
| Bethel C | 1,861 | 0.0 | 0.3 | 0.2 | 0.0 | 98.9 | 0.6 |
| Bethel Theol Sem | 466 | 0.0 | 1.1 | 2.6 | 0.9 | 90.8 | 4.7 |
| Carleton C | 1,855 | 0.3 | 4.2 | 4.0 | 2.3 | 88.4 | 0.7 |
| C of Saint Benedict | 2,173 | 0.1 | 0.7 | 0.3 | 0.2 | 88.9 | 9.8 |
| C of Saint Catherine | 2,395 | 0.1 | 0.9 | 0.8 | 0.9 | 95.2 | 2.1 |
| C of Saint Scholastica | 1,434 | 1.3 | 0.3 | 0.7 | 0.2 | 96.8 | 0.7 |
| C of Saint Teresa | 474 | 0.4 | 0.4 | 1.1 | 1.7 | 94.5 | 1.9 |
| C of Saint Thomas | 6,435 | 0.4 | 0.8 | 0.9 | 0.8 | 96.5 | 0.7 |
| Concordia C at Moorhead | 2,467 | 0.6 | 0.4 | 0.4 | 0.2 | 96.1 | 2.3 |
| Concordia C-Saint Paul | 741 | 0.1 | 4.6 | 4.3 | 0.0 | 85.6 | 5.4 |
| Crosier Sem | 26 | 0.0 | 11.5 | 0.0 | 0.0 | 88.5 | 0.0 |
| Dr Martin Luther C | 559 | 0.4 | 0.2 | 0.4 | 0.0 | 98.7 | 0.4 |
| Golden Valley Lutheran C | 429 | 0.9 | 2.3 | 7.2 | 0.2 | 87.4 | 1.9 |
| Gustavus Adolphus C | 2,214 | 0.0 | 0.8 | 1.0 | 0.0 | 97.3 | 0.8 |
| Luther NW Theol Sem | 837 | 0.2 | 0.1 | 0.6 | 0.4 | 97.3 | 1.4 |
| Macalester C | 1,696 | 0.8 | 1.4 | 4.1 | 2.7 | 77.4 | 13.7 |
| Mayo Grad Sch of Med | 987 | 0.3 | 3.2 | 0.8 | 0.8 | 92.4 | 2.4 |
| Mayo Med Sch | 157 | 1.9 | 1.3 | 4.5 | 2.5 | 89.8 | 0.0 |
| Med Inst of Minnesota | 226 | 1.3 | 1.3 | 2.7 | 0.0 | 94.7 | 0.0 |
| Minneapolis C of Art Design | 604 | 0.3 | 1.7 | 1.3 | 0.3 | 93.7 | 2.6 |
| Minneapolis Bible C | 86 | 0.0 | 2.3 | 0.0 | 0.0 | 94.2 | 3.5 |
| Minnesota CC's System | | | | | | | |
| Anoka-Ramsey CC | 4,229 | 0.3 | 0.6 | 0.3 | 0.4 | 98.2 | 0.2 |
| Arrowhead CC Hibbing | 4,099 | 1.6 | 0.1 | 0.2 | 0.0 | 96.2 | 1.9 |
| Austin CC | 988 | 0.0 | 0.2 | 0.5 | 0.2 | 96.1 | 3.0 |
| Brainerd CC | 653 | 0.8 | 0.0 | 0.8 | 0.0 | 98.3 | 0.2 |
| Fergus Falls CC | 583 | 0.2 | 0.0 | 1.0 | 0.0 | 96.9 | 1.9 |
| Inver Hills CC | 3,624 | 0.4 | 0.7 | 1.3 | 0.7 | 96.6 | 0.4 |
| Lakewood CC | 3,948 | 0.0 | 0.0 | 0.0 | 0.0 | 100.0 | 0.0 |
| Minneapolis CC | 2,729 | 3.3 | 3.1 | 9.6 | 0.6 | 80.7 | 2.7 |
| Normandale CC | 6,349 | 0.2 | 1.6 | 0.6 | 0.2 | 97.0 | 0.5 |
| North Hennepin CC | 4,555 | 0.0 | 0.0 | 0.0 | 0.0 | 100.0 | 0.0 |
| Northland CC | 703 | 1.3 | 0.1 | 2.0 | 0.1 | 96.4 | 0.0 |
| Rochester CC | 3,158 | 0.3 | 1.4 | 0.5 | 0.2 | 97.2 | 0.5 |
| Willmar CC | 898 | 0.8 | 1.0 | 0.1 | 0.7 | 97.2 | 0.2 |
| Worthington CC | 639 | 0.0 | 0.2 | 0.2 | 0.0 | 99.5 | 0.2 |
| National Ed Ctr-Brown Inst | 1,329 | 0.5 | 3.2 | 2.9 | 0.6 | 92.7 | 0.2 |
| North Central Bible C | 1,130 | 0.5 | 1.7 | 3.1 | 1.3 | 92.0 | 1.3 |
| Northwest Tech Inst | 57 | 0.0 | 0.0 | 0.0 | 0.0 | 100.0 | 0.0 |
| Northwestern C | 994 | 0.6 | 0.2 | 0.8 | 0.0 | 97.2 | 1.2 |
| NW C of Chiropractic | 533 | 0.2 | 0.8 | 0.8 | 0.2 | 97.0 | 1.1 |
| NW Electronics Inst | 1,090 | 0.6 | 8.0 | 1.7 | 0.2 | 89.0 | 0.6 |
| Pillsbury Baptist Bible C | 383 | 0.0 | 0.0 | 0.5 | 0.0 | 95.8 | 3.7 |
| Saint John's U | 2,024 | 0.0 | 0.4 | 0.1 | 0.6 | 97.3 | 1.5 |
| Saint Mary's C | 1,480 | 0.5 | 0.3 | 1.0 | 0.5 | 97.5 | 0.3 |
| Saint Mary's JC | 825 | 1.2 | 0.8 | 2.7 | 1.1 | 93.9 | 0.2 |
| Saint Olaf C | 3,010 | 0.1 | 1.0 | 0.9 | 0.1 | 96.2 | 1.7 |
| Saint Paul Bible C | 636 | 0.6 | 3.0 | 0.8 | 0.5 | 94.2 | 0.9 |
| Saint Paul Tech-Voc Inst | 1,952 | 1.2 | 12.2 | 5.2 | 3.7 | 77.7 | 0.0 |
| Sch of the Associated Arts | 100 | 0.0 | 2.0 | 1.0 | 1.0 | 96.0 | 0.0 |
| St U System of Minnesota | | | | | | | |
| Bemidji St U | 4,262 | 3.6 | 0.2 | 0.3 | 0.2 | 94.6 | 1.0 |
| Mankato St U | 13,845 | 0.2 | 0.5 | 0.6 | 0.3 | 95.9 | 2.5 |
| Metropolitan St U | 3,687 | 1.3 | 1.1 | 3.6 | 0.5 | 93.5 | 0.0 |
| Moorhead St U | 6,918 | 0.5 | 0.4 | 0.2 | 0.4 | 96.7 | 1.7 |
| Saint Cloud St U | 12,363 | 0.3 | 0.6 | 0.6 | 0.2 | 96.8 | 1.5 |
| Southwest St U | 2,089 | 0.2 | 0.7 | 0.5 | 0.1 | 96.6 | 1.9 |
| Winona St U | 5,265 | 0.1 | 0.3 | 0.2 | 0.2 | 97.0 | 2.2 |
| United Theol Sem | 216 | 2.3 | 0.5 | 0.9 | 0.9 | 94.0 | 1.4 |
| U of Minnesota | | | | | | | |
| Duluth | 11,562 | 1.9 | 0.5 | 0.5 | 0.2 | 95.1 | 1.7 |
| Minneapolis-St Paul | 62,266 | 0.4 | 2.5 | 1.6 | 0.8 | 90.9 | 3.8 |
| Morris | 1,849 | 1.5 | 1.4 | 5.2 | 1.1 | 90.1 | 0.8 |
| Tech C at Crookston | 1,147 | 0.5 | 0.1 | 0.6 | 2.2 | 95.9 | 0.7 |
| Tech C at Waseca | 1,120 | 0.1 | 0.0 | 0.2 | 0.0 | 99.7 | 0.0 |
| **MISSISSIPPI** | | | | | | | |
| Alcorn St U | 2,395 | 0.0% | 0.4% | 96.5% | 0.0% | 3.1% | 0.0% |

*Continued on Following Page*

| | Total | American Indian | Asian | Black | Hispanic | White | Foreign |
|---|---|---|---|---|---|---|---|
| **MISSISSIPPI—Continued** | | | | | | | |
| Belhaven C | 730 | 0.0% | 0.3% | 4.5% | 0.1% | 91.9% | 3.2% |
| Blue Mountain C | 318 | 0.0 | 0.0 | 3.5 | 0.0 | 96.2 | 0.3 |
| Coahoma JC | 1,457 | 0.0 | 0.1 | 97.2 | 0.0 | 2.7 | 0.0 |
| Copiah-Lincoln JC | 1,722 | 0.0 | 0.1 | 29.0 | 0.0 | 71.0 | 0.0 |
| Delta St U | 3,475 | 0.0 | 0.7 | 18.4 | 0.1 | 80.7 | 0.1 |
| East Central JC | 842 | 8.9 | 0.0 | 27.1 | 0.0 | 64.0 | 0.0 |
| East Mississippi JC | 1,088 | 0.1 | 1.1 | 34.8 | 0.3 | 63.7 | 0.0 |
| Hinds JC | 7,358 | 0.1 | 0.4 | 29.2 | 0.1 | 70.1 | 0.0 |
| Holmes JC | 869 | 0.0 | 0.3 | 31.6 | 0.0 | 67.8 | 0.2 |
| Itawamba JC | 2,560 | 0.0 | 0.0 | 15.0 | 0.1 | 84.8 | 0.0 |
| Jackson St U | 6,088 | 0.0 | 0.2 | 92.5 | 0.2 | 4.4 | 2.8 |
| Jones County JC | 2,442 | 0.2 | 0.0 | 21.6 | 0.0 | 78.0 | 0.2 |
| Mary Holmes C | 704 | 0.0 | 0.3 | 99.1 | 0.0 | 0.3 | 0.3 |
| Meridian JC | 2,541 | 1.1 | 0.4 | 21.3 | 0.8 | 76.0 | 0.4 |
| Millsaps C | 1,301 | 0.0 | 1.2 | 5.2 | 0.4 | 92.9 | 0.4 |
| Mississippi C | 2,837 | 0.0 | 0.2 | 9.4 | 0.2 | 90.0 | 0.2 |
| Mississippi Delta JC | 1,627 | 0.0 | 0.2 | 41.6 | 0.1 | 58.1 | 0.0 |
| Mississippi Gulf Coast JC | 6,967 | 0.6 | 1.1 | 13.7 | 1.0 | 83.2 | 0.4 |
| Mississippi St U | 12,775 | 0.1 | 0.0 | 10.9 | 0.0 | 84.8 | 4.1 |
| Mississippi U for Women | 2,197 | 0.0 | 0.5 | 16.4 | 0.2 | 82.7 | 0.1 |
| Mississippi Valley St U | 2,396 | 0.0 | 0.1 | 99.3 | 0.0 | 0.4 | 0.2 |
| Northeast Mississippi JC | 2,277 | 0.0 | 0.1 | 10.5 | 0.0 | 89.4 | 0.0 |
| Northwest Mississippi JC | 4,136 | 0.0 | 0.0 | 35.0 | 0.5 | 64.5 | 0.0 |
| Pearl River JC | 1,615 | 0.0 | 0.0 | 17.6 | 0.0 | 82.4 | 0.0 |
| Prentiss Normal and Industrial Inst | 90 | 0.0 | 0.0 | 100.0 | 0.0 | 0.0 | 0.0 |
| Reformed Theol Sem | 232 | 0.0 | 0.0 | 4.7 | 0.4 | 81.9 | 12.9 |
| Rust C | 870 | 0.0 | 0.0 | 94.7 | 0.0 | 0.5 | 4.8 |
| Southeastern Baptist C | 72 | 0.0 | 0.0 | 20.8 | 0.0 | 76.4 | 2.8 |
| Southwest Mississippi JC | 1,475 | 0.0 | 0.0 | 27.1 | 0.0 | 72.9 | 0.0 |
| U of Mississippi | | | | | | | |
| Main campus | 8,712 | 0.1 | 0.5 | 6.2 | 0.2 | 88.6 | 4.5 |
| Med Center | 1,737 | 0.1 | 2.0 | 9.2 | 0.5 | 86.6 | 1.7 |
| U of Southern Mississippi | 13,250 | 0.3 | 1.9 | 12.3 | 1.1 | 84.4 | 0.0 |
| Utica JC | 640 | 0.2 | 0.2 | 98.7 | 0.0 | 0.8 | 0.2 |
| Wesley C | 81 | 0.0 | 0.0 | 2.5 | 0.0 | 97.5 | 0.0 |
| William Carey C | 1,746 | 0.0 | 0.2 | 22.2 | 0.3 | 74.6 | 2.6 |
| Wood JC | 380 | 0.0 | 0.0 | 8.5 | 0.0 | 88.7 | 2.8 |
| **MISSOURI** | | | | | | | |
| Aquinas Inst | 89 | 0.0% | 0.0% | 3.4% | 0.0% | 87.6% | 9.0% |
| Assemblies of God Graduate Sch | 223 | 0.9 | 0.9 | 0.4 | 2.2 | 86.5 | 9.0 |
| Avila C | 1,662 | 0.5 | 0.8 | 6.9 | 1.4 | 90.4 | 0.0 |
| Bailey Tech Sch | 38 | 0.0 | 0.0 | 15.8 | 7.9 | 76.3 | 0.0 |
| Baptist Bible C | 1,227 | 0.5 | 0.4 | 1.3 | 0.6 | 97.2 | 0.0 |
| Basic Inst of Tech | 188 | 0.5 | 0.5 | 23.4 | 0.0 | 75.5 | 0.0 |
| Calvary Bible C | 429 | 0.2 | 0.9 | 2.1 | 0.7 | 94.9 | 1.2 |
| Cardinal Glennon C | 80 | 0.0 | 0.0 | 2.5 | 0.0 | 97.5 | 0.0 |
| Central Bible C | 1,038 | 1.0 | 0.3 | 0.5 | 1.5 | 92.3 | 4.4 |
| Central Christian C of the Bible | 132 | 0.0 | 0.0 | 1.5 | 0.0 | 97.7 | 0.8 |
| Central Methodist C | 611 | 0.2 | 0.3 | 6.5 | 0.2 | 91.5 | 1.3 |
| Central Missouri St U | 8,979 | 0.0 | 0.4 | 6.7 | 0.5 | 89.3 | 3.1 |
| Cleveland Chiropractic C | 369 | 0.3 | 0.0 | 1.4 | 0.5 | 93.2 | 4.6 |
| Columbia C | 2,745 | 1.5 | 1.4 | 14.7 | 2.8 | 78.5 | 1.0 |
| Conception Sem C | 105 | 1.0 | 2.9 | 1.0 | 3.8 | 91.4 | 0.0 |
| Concordia Sem | 616 | 0.0 | 1.0 | 1.6 | 0.2 | 95.0 | 2.3 |
| Cottey C | 348 | 1.1 | 0.9 | 0.6 | 2.3 | 89.1 | 6.0 |
| Covenant Theol Sem | 144 | 0.0 | 0.7 | 1.4 | 0.0 | 87.5 | 10.4 |
| Crowder C | 1,179 | 0.0 | 0.1 | 0.7 | 0.2 | 99.0 | 0.1 |
| Culver-Stockton C | 646 | 0.0 | 0.2 | 8.0 | 0.2 | 91.6 | 0.0 |
| DeVry Inst of Tech | 2,081 | 0.1 | 1.8 | 7.8 | 1.0 | 88.4 | 1.0 |
| Drury C | 2,400 | 0.4 | 0.4 | 3.5 | 0.7 | 94.1 | 0.9 |
| East Central C | 2,355 | 0.2 | 0.1 | 0.3 | 0.3 | 99.2 | 0.0 |
| Eden Theol Sem | 186 | 0.0 | 0.0 | 2.2 | 0.0 | 97.3 | 0.5 |
| Evangel C | 1,777 | 0.3 | 0.3 | 2.2 | 2.1 | 94.5 | 0.5 |
| Fontbonne C | 952 | 0.4 | 2.3 | 11.1 | 0.9 | 80.9 | 4.3 |
| Hannibal-LaGrange C | 638 | 0.0 | 0.3 | 3.6 | 0.0 | 95.9 | 0.2 |
| Harris-Stowe St C | 1,175 | 0.1 | 0.3 | 73.8 | 0.3 | 20.7 | 4.9 |
| International Graduate Sch | 112 | 0.0 | 4.5 | 22.3 | 1.8 | 71.4 | 0.0 |
| Jefferson C | 3,023 | 0.2 | 0.2 | 0.9 | 0.4 | 98.4 | 0.1 |
| Kansas City Art Inst | 475 | 0.8 | 1.9 | 2.5 | 1.5 | 90.9 | 2.3 |
| Kemper Military Sch and C | 81 | 0.0 | 0.0 | 18.5 | 7.4 | 64.2 | 9.9 |
| Kenrick Sem | 86 | 0.0 | 0.0 | 1.2 | 1.2 | 97.7 | 0.0 |
| Kirksville C of Osteo Med | 536 | 0.4 | 2.1 | 1.1 | 1.3 | 94.8 | 0.4 |
| Lincoln U | 2,951 | 0.3 | 0.7 | 35.8 | 0.4 | 57.2 | 5.6 |
| Lindenwood C | 1,755 | 0.0 | 0.1 | 8.0 | 0.3 | 88.8 | 2.8 |
| Logan C of Chiropractic | 633 | 0.2 | 0.8 | 0.8 | 1.3 | 94.9 | 2.1 |
| Maryville C | 2,247 | 0.0 | 0.5 | 4.2 | 0.5 | 91.4 | 3.4 |
| Metropolitan CC's System | | | | | | | |
| Longview CC | 5,703 | 0.2 | 0.6 | 4.2 | 0.8 | 94.0 | 0.2 |
| Maple Woods CC | 2,704 | 0.2 | 0.8 | 0.4 | 0.8 | 97.7 | 0.1 |
| Penn Valley CC | 5,247 | 0.6 | 2.9 | 37.1 | 3.5 | 51.0 | 4.9 |
| Pioneer CC | 319 | 0.3 | 2.5 | 72.1 | 1.6 | 23.5 | 0.0 |
| Mineral Area CC | 1,609 | 0.1 | 0.1 | 0.3 | 0.1 | 99.3 | 0.1 |
| Missouri Baptist C | 478 | 0.0 | 0.8 | 17.4 | 0.2 | 80.5 | 1.0 |
| Missouri Southern St C | 4,323 | 1.0 | 0.4 | 0.5 | 0.4 | 97.4 | 0.2 |
| Missouri Valley C | 462 | 0.6 | 1.1 | 16.2 | 1.1 | 81.0 | 0.0 |
| Missouri Western St C | 4,069 | 0.4 | 0.3 | 3.0 | 0.9 | 95.2 | 0.1 |
| Moberly Area JC | 1,050 | 0.3 | 0.4 | 10.1 | 0.6 | 87.9 | 0.8 |
| Nazarene Theol Sem | 463 | 0.0 | 0.4 | 0.9 | 0.9 | 92.4 | 5.4 |
| Northeast Missouri St U | 7,349 | 0.1 | 0.2 | 2.3 | 0.2 | 93.1 | 4.0 |
| Northwest Missouri St U | 4,974 | 0.0 | 0.1 | 2.4 | 0.2 | 94.9 | 2.4 |
| Park C | 3,272 | 0.6 | 0.4 | 5.0 | 4.0 | 89.0 | 1.0 |
| Platt C | 174 | 0.0 | 1.1 | 1.7 | 0.0 | 97.1 | 0.0 |
| Research C of Nursing | 145 | 0.0 | 2.1 | 7.6 | 0.0 | 90.3 | 0.0 |
| Rockhurst C | 2,869 | 0.1 | 0.9 | 6.4 | 2.2 | 89.7 | 0.6 |
| Saint Louis Christian C | 153 | 0.0 | 0.0 | 3.9 | 0.0 | 96.1 | 0.0 |
| Saint Louis C of Pharmacy | 685 | 0.0 | 2.6 | 3.4 | 0.9 | 93.1 | 0.0 |
| Saint Louis CC | | | | | | | |
| Florissant Valley | 11,628 | 0.3 | 0.7 | 18.6 | 0.8 | 79.7 | 0.2 |
| Forest Park | 7,351 | 0.2 | 1.0 | 41.8 | 0.6 | 55.2 | 1.2 |
| Meramec | 12,649 | 0.2 | 0.7 | 2.4 | 0.4 | 96.0 | 0.3 |
| Saint Louis Consv Music | 111 | 0.0 | 1.8 | 2.7 | 0.9 | 79.3 | 15.3 |
| Saint Louis U | | | | | | | |
| Main campus | 8,567 | 0.2 | 3.1 | 8.7 | 2.5 | 83.6 | 1.9 |
| Parks C | 1,112 | 0.1 | 2.3 | 4.4 | 3.1 | 80.5 | 9.5 |
| Saint Mary's C of O'Fallon | 651 | 0.0 | 0.2 | 1.5 | 0.0 | 97.7 | 0.6 |
| Saint Mary's Sem C | 34 | 0.0 | 5.9 | 2.9 | 5.9 | 79.4 | 5.9 |
| Saint Paul Sch of Theol | 133 | 0.8 | 1.5 | 2.3 | 0.0 | 95.5 | 0.0 |
| Saint Paul's C | 104 | 0.0 | 0.0 | 5.8 | 0.0 | 94.2 | 0.0 |
| Sch of the Ozarks | 1,222 | 0.0 | 0.0 | 0.7 | 0.0 | 96.4 | 2.9 |
| Southeast Missouri St U | 9,186 | 0.1 | 0.3 | 6.1 | 0.2 | 90.3 | 3.0 |
| Southwest Baptist U | 1,792 | 0.0 | 1.7 | 0.5 | 0.1 | 97.6 | 0.1 |
| Southwest Missouri St U | 15,121 | 0.2 | 0.8 | 0.8 | 0.2 | 97.6 | 0.4 |
| State Fair CC | 1,615 | 1.9 | 0.2 | 3.5 | 0.5 | 93.5 | 0.3 |
| Stephens C | 1,094 | 0.5 | 0.4 | 5.9 | 0.5 | 91.2 | 1.6 |
| Tarkio C | 620 | 0.0 | 0.2 | 17.9 | 3.2 | 77.6 | 1.1 |
| Three Rivers CC | 1,313 | 0.0 | 0.0 | 2.8 | 0.0 | 97.2 | 0.0 |
| Trenton JC | 608 | 0.0 | 0.0 | 2.3 | 0.0 | 97.7 | 0.0 |
| U of Missouri | | | | | | | |
| Columbia | 23,585 | 0.3 | 1.1 | 3.6 | 0.7 | 89.4 | 4.9 |
| Kansas City | 11,464 | 0.5 | 2.4 | 7.7 | 1.7 | 86.2 | 1.6 |
| Rolla | 6,967 | 0.2 | 3.1 | 2.5 | 1.1 | 88.2 | 4.9 |
| St Louis | 11,596 | 0.3 | 1.1 | 9.6 | 0.6 | 88.0 | 0.4 |
| Washington U | 10,610 | 0.2 | 4.9 | 5.0 | 1.9 | 82.9 | 5.0 |
| Webster U | 5,358 | 0.1 | 0.7 | 11.1 | 1.0 | 82.7 | 4.4 |
| Wentworth Military Acad | 236 | 0.0 | 0.8 | 7.6 | 2.1 | 86.9 | 2.5 |
| Westminster C | 615 | 0.0 | 0.8 | 2.3 | 0.2 | 95.3 | 1.5 |
| William Jewell C | 1,991 | 0.3 | 0.4 | 2.6 | 0.4 | 95.7 | 0.7 |
| William Woods C | 781 | 0.3 | 0.0 | 2.7 | 0.0 | 96.9 | 0.1 |
| **MONTANA** | | | | | | | |
| Blackfeet CC | 239 | 90.0% | 0.0% | 0.0% | 0.0% | 10.0% | 0.0% |
| Carroll C | 1,528 | 0.5 | 0.3 | 0.2 | 0.3 | 97.6 | 1.1 |
| **MONTANA—Continued** | | | | | | | |
| C of Great Falls | 1,360 | 3.8% | 1.8% | 2.8% | 1.8% | 89.3% | 0.4% |
| Dawson CC | 753 | 22.7 | 0.7 | 0.4 | 0.0 | 75.7 | 0.5 |
| Dull Knife Memorial C | 237 | 93.2 | 0.0 | 1.7 | 0.0 | 5.1 | 0.0 |
| Miles CC | 813 | 3.1 | 0.4 | 0.0 | 0.6 | 95.7 | 0.2 |
| Montana U System | | | | | | | |
| Eastern Montana C | 4,208 | 4.4 | 0.5 | 0.3 | 1.0 | 93.5 | 0.2 |
| Montana C of Mineral Science and Tech | 2,124 | 0.4 | 0.1 | 0.3 | 0.7 | 92.1 | 6.4 |
| Montana St U | 11,026 | 1.5 | 0.4 | 0.3 | 0.2 | 95.0 | 2.7 |
| Northern Montana C | 1,811 | 8.7 | 0.6 | 0.6 | 0.8 | 88.9 | 0.4 |
| U of Montana | 9,213 | 2.6 | 0.3 | 0.5 | 0.6 | 93.1 | 2.9 |
| Western Montana C | 894 | 1.2 | 0.1 | 0.0 | 0.2 | 98.4 | 0.0 |
| Rocky Mountain C | 503 | 2.6 | 0.4 | 1.8 | 0.4 | 90.1 | 4.8 |
| Salish Kootenai CC | 478 | 67.2 | 0.0 | 0.0 | 0.0 | 32.8 | 0.0 |
| **NEBRASKA** | | | | | | | |
| Bellevue C | 2,605 | 0.2% | 0.6% | 6.2% | 2.1% | 89.1% | 1.8% |
| Bishop Clarkson C of Nursing | 517 | 0.0 | 0.2 | 2.5 | 0.6 | 96.7 | 0.0 |
| Central CC | 8,209 | 0.5 | 0.3 | 0.2 | 0.5 | 98.4 | 0.0 |
| Chadron St C | 2,105 | 0.3 | 0.9 | 0.7 | 0.7 | 97.5 | 0.0 |
| C of Saint Mary | 1,055 | 0.7 | 0.4 | 6.3 | 0.9 | 91.0 | 0.8 |
| Concordia Teachers C | 968 | 0.7 | 0.2 | 3.0 | 0.3 | 94.6 | 1.1 |
| Creighton U | 5,913 | 0.3 | 4.0 | 3.3 | 2.1 | 87.6 | 2.7 |
| Dana C | 461 | 0.2 | 0.0 | 3.7 | 0.0 | 95.9 | 0.2 |
| Doane C | 736 | 0.1 | 0.3 | 3.4 | 0.5 | 89.9 | 5.7 |
| Grace C of the Bible | 272 | 0.0 | 0.0 | 1.1 | 0.4 | 95.2 | 3.3 |
| Hastings C | 811 | 0.1 | 0.4 | 1.0 | 0.4 | 97.4 | 0.7 |
| Kearney St C | 8,035 | 0.0 | 0.4 | 0.1 | 0.3 | 98.8 | 0.3 |
| Metropolitan Tech CC Area | 6,018 | 2.0 | 1.0 | 11.0 | 1.0 | 85.0 | 0.0 |
| Mid-Plains CC Area | 2,497 | 0.0 | 0.3 | 0.3 | 1.3 | 98.0 | 0.0 |
| Midland Lutheran C | 848 | 0.0 | 0.1 | 6.0 | 0.2 | 92.1 | 1.5 |
| Nebraska Christian C | 140 | 0.0 | 0.0 | 1.4 | 2.1 | 95.0 | 1.4 |
| Nebraska Indian CC | 289 | 90.3 | 0.0 | 1.0 | 0.3 | 8.3 | 0.0 |
| Nebraska Wesleyan U | 1,320 | 0.2 | 0.5 | 0.9 | 0.2 | 94.2 | 4.0 |
| Northeast Tech CC Area | 2,298 | 0.4 | 0.0 | 0.0 | 0.0 | 99.4 | 0.1 |
| Peru St C | 1,249 | 0.4 | 0.1 | 4.5 | 0.4 | 94.4 | 0.2 |
| Southeast Tech CC Area | 5,228 | 0.2 | 0.7 | 1.1 | 0.5 | 96.8 | 0.8 |
| Union C | 871 | 1.6 | 0.6 | 4.7 | 2.2 | 81.3 | 9.6 |
| U of Nebraska | | | | | | | |
| Lincoln | 24,228 | 0.2 | 0.5 | 1.6 | 0.9 | 91.9 | 4.8 |
| Med Center | 2,495 | 0.2 | 1.9 | 2.2 | 1.2 | 93.3 | 1.3 |
| Omaha | 13,832 | 0.3 | 0.4 | 4.7 | 1.2 | 91.6 | 1.9 |
| Wayne St C | 2,547 | 0.4 | 0.2 | 1.3 | 0.2 | 97.3 | 0.6 |
| Western Tech CC Area | 1,480 | 1.2 | 0.1 | 0.6 | 4.6 | 93.3 | 0.1 |
| York C | 395 | 0.3 | 0.3 | 5.1 | 1.3 | 92.7 | 0.5 |
| **NEVADA** | | | | | | | |
| Old C | 155 | 0.0% | 1.9% | 1.3% | 2.6% | 90.3% | 3.9% |
| Sierra Nevada C | 152 | 0.0 | 2.0 | 0.0 | 3.9 | 92.8 | 1.3 |
| U of Nevada System | | | | | | | |
| Las Vegas | 10,989 | 0.4 | 3.2 | 5.6 | 4.2 | 85.6 | 1.0 |
| Reno | 9,681 | 0.8 | 1.8 | 1.4 | 1.8 | 90.4 | 3.7 |
| Clark County CC | 9,824 | 6.8 | 2.6 | 8.1 | 3.5 | 78.6 | 0.4 |
| Northern Nevada CC | 1,520 | 4.5 | 0.6 | 0.1 | 3.3 | 91.4 | 0.0 |
| Truckee Meadows CC | 7,430 | 2.1 | 2.9 | 1.7 | 2.8 | 90.0 | 0.5 |
| Western Nevada CC | 3,256 | 4.1 | 1.3 | 0.6 | 1.7 | 92.3 | 0.0 |
| **NEW HAMPSHIRE** | | | | | | | |
| Castle JC | 149 | 0.0% | 0.0% | 0.0% | 2.0% | 98.0% | 0.0% |
| Colby-Sawyer C | 449 | 0.0 | 0.2 | 0.2 | 0.0 | 98.7 | 0.9 |
| Daniel Webster C | 1,156 | 0.0 | 0.6 | 1.7 | 0.7 | 96.7 | 0.3 |
| Dartmouth C | 4,622 | 1.0 | 1.8 | 4.9 | 0.8 | 87.4 | 4.1 |
| Franklin Pierce C | 2,293 | 0.3 | 0.4 | 2.5 | 0.9 | 94.9 | 0.9 |
| Franklin Pierce Law Center | 325 | 0.0 | 0.3 | 1.2 | 0.3 | 98.2 | 0.0 |
| Hawthorne C | 628 | 0.0 | 0.0 | 1.6 | 0.0 | 94.6 | 3.8 |
| Hesser C | 1,983 | 0.0 | 0.4 | 1.1 | 0.2 | 98.2 | 0.2 |
| Magdalen C | 70 | 0.0 | 1.4 | 0.0 | 2.9 | 90.0 | 5.7 |
| McIntosh C | 547 | 0.0 | 0.0 | 2.7 | 0.9 | 96.3 | 0.0 |
| New England C | 1,241 | 0.0 | 0.0 | 0.4 | 0.2 | 84.2 | 15.2 |
| New Hampshire C | 7,262 | 0.0 | 0.4 | 2.5 | 3.0 | 90.7 | 3.3 |
| New Hampshire Tech Inst | 1,989 | 0.1 | 0.0 | 0.1 | 0.0 | 99.8 | 0.0 |
| NH Voc-Tech C's | | | | | | | |
| Berlin | 275 | 0.0 | 0.0 | 0.0 | 0.0 | 100.0 | 0.0 |
| Claremont | 375 | 0.0 | 0.3 | 0.5 | 0.3 | 98.7 | 0.3 |
| Laconia | 214 | 0.0 | 0.5 | 0.0 | 0.0 | 99.5 | 0.0 |
| Manchester | 1,534 | 0.0 | 0.5 | 0.4 | 0.0 | 99.2 | 0.0 |
| Stratham | 673 | 0.0 | 0.1 | 0.1 | 0.0 | 99.7 | 0.0 |
| Notre Dame C | 764 | 1.3 | 0.5 | 0.5 | 0.5 | 97.0 | 0.1 |
| Rivier C | 2,257 | 0.1 | 0.4 | 0.1 | 0.5 | 98.4 | 0.3 |
| Saint Anselm C | 1,917 | 0.1 | 0.2 | 0.2 | 0.3 | 98.9 | 0.4 |
| U Sys of New Hampshire | | | | | | | |
| Keene St C | 3,512 | 0.2 | 0.1 | 0.2 | 0.1 | 99.1 | 0.3 |
| Plymouth St C | 3,577 | 0.2 | 0.3 | 0.5 | 0.3 | 98.4 | 0.3 |
| Sch of Lifelong Learning | 1,416 | 0.4 | 0.6 | 0.8 | 0.2 | 97.9 | 0.0 |
| U of New Hampshire | 12,314 | 0.3 | 0.3 | 0.4 | 0.3 | 97.7 | 1.0 |
| U of NH Manchester | 365 | 0.0 | 0.3 | 0.5 | 0.0 | 99.2 | 0.0 |
| White Pines C | 63 | 0.0 | 0.0 | 1.6 | 1.6 | 92.1 | 4.8 |
| **NEW JERSEY** | | | | | | | |
| Assumption C for Sisters | 18 | 0.0% | 16.7% | 0.0% | 0.0% | 83.3% | 0.0% |
| Atlantic CC | 4,019 | 0.9 | 1.1 | 10.5 | 2.8 | 83.3 | 1.3 |
| Bergen CC | 11,247 | 0.5 | 2.4 | 4.5 | 5.1 | 85.5 | 1.9 |
| Berkeley Sch | 715 | 0.0 | 0.0 | 6.6 | 7.7 | 85.5 | 0.3 |
| Beth Medrash Govoha | 965 | 0.0 | 0.0 | 0.0 | 0.8 | 91.5 | 7.6 |
| Bloomfield C | 1,631 | 0.2 | 1.7 | 37.5 | 5.3 | 54.5 | 0.7 |
| Brookdale CC | 11,089 | 0.2 | 2.4 | 5.4 | 1.7 | 90.3 | 0.0 |
| Burlington County C | 5,835 | 0.5 | 2.2 | 12.9 | 2.3 | 81.6 | 0.4 |
| Caldwell C | 704 | 0.1 | 1.3 | 8.5 | 4.4 | 84.2 | 1.4 |
| Camden County C | 8,148 | 0.1 | 1.4 | 9.9 | 1.7 | 86.9 | 0.0 |
| Centenary C | 1,160 | 0.5 | 0.3 | 6.0 | 0.2 | 91.9 | 1.0 |
| C of Saint Elizabeth | 919 | 0.0 | 0.8 | 6.9 | 2.9 | 87.6 | 1.8 |
| County C of Morris | 11,000 | 0.1 | 1.8 | 1.4 | 2.1 | 93.6 | 1.0 |
| Cumberland County C | 2,336 | 2.4 | 0.0 | 13.1 | 6.9 | 77.0 | 0.4 |
| Don Bosco C | 66 | 0.0 | 7.6 | 1.5 | 9.1 | 66.7 | 15.2 |
| Drew U | 2,380 | 0.0 | 1.8 | 4.5 | 1.3 | 88.7 | 3.7 |
| Essex County C | 5,806 | 0.1 | 4.9 | 62.4 | 16.1 | 8.0 | 8.5 |
| Fairleigh Dickinson U | | | | | | | |
| Edward Williams C | 1,061 | 0.1 | 3.1 | 19.5 | 7.6 | 67.6 | 2.1 |
| Florham Park-Madison | 4,275 | 0.2 | 1.5 | 2.5 | 1.1 | 94.1 | 0.6 |
| Rutherford | 3,090 | 0.2 | 1.8 | 6.1 | 5.0 | 83.3 | 3.7 |
| Teaneck | 7,011 | 0.3 | 2.9 | 6.2 | 4.3 | 79.1 | 7.2 |
| Felician C | 627 | 0.0 | 3.0 | 6.5 | 3.3 | 86.4 | 0.6 |
| Georgian Court C | 1,572 | 0.1 | 0.2 | 4.1 | 2.7 | 92.6 | 0.3 |
| Glassboro St C | 8,714 | 0.6 | 1.5 | 10.1 | 4.3 | 83.3 | 0.3 |
| Gloucester County C | 3,565 | 0.6 | 0.0 | 7.5 | 0.5 | 77.1 | 14.2 |
| Hudson County CC | 3,477 | 0.0 | 5.6 | 17.1 | 54.1 | 21.1 | 2.2 |
| Immaculate Conception Sem | 151 | 0.0 | 1.3 | 2.0 | 4.0 | 92.7 | 0.0 |
| Jersey City St C | 8,449 | 0.4 | 5.3 | 16.8 | 15.8 | 58.3 | 3.4 |
| Kean C of New Jersey | 12,758 | 0.2 | 1.7 | 10.5 | 9.0 | 75.9 | 2.7 |
| Mercer County CC | 9,171 | 0.3 | 2.0 | 13.3 | 2.6 | 81.2 | 0.6 |
| Middlesex County C | 11,197 | 0.3 | 4.2 | 5.9 | 5.9 | 82.9 | 0.8 |
| Monmouth C | 4,224 | 0.1 | 1.6 | 3.6 | 1.5 | 91.4 | 1.8 |
| Montclair St C | 14,241 | 1.3 | 0.9 | 6.4 | 6.6 | 83.4 | 1.4 |
| New Brunswick Theol Sem | 120 | 0.0 | 6.7 | 31.7 | 10.8 | 50.8 | 0.0 |
| New Jersey Inst of Tech | 7,540 | 0.1 | 8.4 | 7.1 | 6.4 | 70.2 | 7.8 |
| Northeastern Bible C | 263 | 0.8 | 2.7 | 12.2 | 5.3 | 77.2 | 1.9 |
| Ocean County C | 5,612 | 0.5 | 0.4 | 1.3 | 0.8 | 97.0 | 0.1 |
| Passaic County CC | 2,987 | 0.5 | 5.5 | 27.5 | 37.4 | 29.2 | 0.0 |
| Princeton Theol Sem | 859 | 0.1 | 3.0 | 3.3 | 1.0 | 84.6 | 7.9 |
| Princeton U | 6,277 | 0.2 | 4.4 | 5.1 | 3.5 | 72.7 | 14.1 |
| Rabbinical C of America | 230 | 0.0 | 0.0 | 0.0 | 0.0 | 64.8 | 35.2 |
| Ramapo C of New Jersey | 4,611 | -0.2 | 0.3 | 4.9 | 2.6 | 90.5 | 1.5 |
| Rider C | 5,062 | 0.2 | 0.3 | 1.9 | 0.9 | 95.5 | 1.1 |
| **NEW JERSEY—Continued** | | | | | | | |
| Rutgers U | | | | | | | |
| Camden | 4,732 | 0.2% | 2.1% | 9.0% | 2.7% | 85.8% | 0.3% |
| Newark | 9,381 | 0.1 | 3.7 | 20.4 | 7.7 | 66.3 | 1.8 |
| New Brunswick | 33,728 | 0.1 | 5.0 | 7.2 | 3.7 | 81.3 | 2.7 |
| Saint Peter's C | 4,022 | 0.4 | 3.7 | 8.8 | 14.9 | 71.2 | 0.9 |
| Salem CC | 1,177 | 0.3 | 0.7 | 14.5 | 1.0 | 83.2 | 0.3 |
| Seton Hall U | 8,965 | 0.1 | 0.9 | 6.2 | 3.6 | 88.1 | 1.1 |
| Somerset County C | 4,626 | 0.1 | 2.0 | 2.4 | 1.1 | 94.6 | 0.0 |
| Stevens Inst of Tech | 3,323 | 0.0 | 8.6 | 2.5 | 4.5 | 69.5 | 15.0 |
| Stockton St C | 4,750 | 0.3 | 0.8 | 9.0 | 1.6 | 88.0 | 0.3 |
| Talmudical Acad of NJ | 44 | 0.0 | 0.0 | 0.0 | 0.0 | 100.0 | 0.0 |
| Thomas A Edison C | 4,231 | 0.0 | 0.0 | 7.3 | 2.5 | 83.5 | 6.8 |
| Trenton St C | 8,826 | 0.3 | 0.7 | 7.3 | 1.7 | 89.0 | 0.9 |
| Union County C | 8,006 | 0.0 | 1.9 | 13.3 | 6.5 | 78.3 | 0.0 |
| U of Med and Dentistry of New Jersey | 2,095 | 0.0 | 4.9 | 8.3 | 6.5 | 79.2 | 1.1 |
| Upsala C | 1,822 | 0.2 | 1.4 | 21.7 | 4.2 | 71.7 | 0.8 |
| Westminster Choir C | 396 | 0.0 | 0.8 | 8.8 | 1.5 | 80.8 | 8.1 |
| William Paterson C | 10,033 | 0.2 | 1.1 | 5.6 | 3.6 | 89.5 | 0.0 |
| **NEW MEXICO** | | | | | | | |
| C of Sante Fe | 854 | 7.6% | 1.3% | 3.7% | 39.2% | 44.8% | 3.3% |
| C of the Southwest | 211 | 0.0 | 0.0 | 3.3 | 9.0 | 87.2 | 0.5 |
| Eastern New Mexico U | | | | | | | |
| Main campus | 5,571 | 1.6 | 0.8 | 5.6 | 15.0 | 74.6 | 2.3 |
| Roswell | 1,285 | 1.4 | 0.5 | 2.6 | 24.2 | 71.1 | 0.3 |
| New Mexico Highlands U | 2,105 | 3.0 | 0.4 | 3.1 | 71.7 | 20.5 | 1.2 |
| NM Inst of Mining & Tech | 1,244 | 1.8 | 1.9 | 0.6 | 6.9 | 80.1 | 8.6 |
| New Mexico JC | 2,594 | 0.7 | 0.5 | 3.6 | 10.7 | 84.3 | 0.2 |
| New Mexico Military Inst | 424 | 0.7 | 5.2 | 9.7 | 15.8 | 63.9 | 4.7 |
| New Mexico St U | | | | | | | |
| Main campus | 13,540 | 1.9 | 0.5 | 1.3 | 24.8 | 68.0 | 3.4 |
| Alamogordo | 1,396 | 1.6 | 0.9 | 4.0 | 14.1 | 79.4 | 0.0 |
| Carlsbad | 921 | 0.8 | 0.2 | 0.9 | 18.8 | 79.4 | 0.0 |
| Grants | 507 | 11.8 | 0.2 | 0.4 | 31.2 | 56.4 | 0.0 |
| Northern New Mexico CC | 1,047 | 6.5 | 0.1 | 0.4 | 73.8 | 19.0 | 0.2 |
| San Juan C | 2,218 | 24.5 | 0.3 | 0.3 | 8.8 | 65.6 | 0.5 |
| Santa Fe CC | 1,821 | 2.5 | 0.1 | 0.2 | 53.4 | 43.8 | 0.0 |
| U of Albuquerque | 1,181 | 8.3 | 1.1 | 4.6 | 30.0 | 52.8 | 3.2 |
| U of New Mexico | | | | | | | |
| Main campus | 26,079 | 3.1 | 1.4 | 1.9 | 22.8 | 68.3 | 2.5 |
| Gallup | 1,491 | 53.1 | 0.7 | 0.7 | 11.2 | 34.3 | 0.0 |
| Western New Mexico U | 1,840 | 2.3 | 0.7 | 3.0 | 41.1 | 51.6 | 1.2 |
| **NEW YORK** | | | | | | | |
| Acad of Aeronautics | 1,485 | 0.0% | 6.1% | 19.9% | 26.0% | 45.9% | 2.0% |
| Adelphi U | 10,717 | 0.1 | 1.5 | 10.3 | 3.4 | 84.7 | 0.0 |
| Albany C of Pharmacy | 633 | 0.2 | 1.3 | 1.4 | 0.3 | 95.6 | 1.3 |
| Albany Law Sch | 696 | 0.1 | 1.0 | 2.7 | 1.9 | 94.0 | 0.3 |
| Albany Med C | 593 | 0.0 | 7.1 | 1.5 | 1.7 | 89.5 | 0.2 |
| Alfred U | 1,645 | 0.1 | 0.1 | 2.2 | 0.6 | 96.5 | 0.4 |
| American Acad of Dramatic Arts | 249 | 0.0 | 1.2 | 7.6 | 2.0 | 78.3 | 10.8 |
| American Acad McAllister Inst of Funeral Service | 154 | 0.0 | 0.6 | 30.5 | 3.9 | 63.6 | 1.3 |
| Bank Street C of Ed | 443 | 0.2 | 1.8 | 10.8 | 12.4 | 74.7 | 0.0 |
| Bard C | 707 | 0.0 | 0.7 | 3.5 | 3.0 | 88.4 | 4.4 |
| Berkeley Sch | 723 | 0.0 | 0.1 | 10.9 | 3.0 | 85.1 | 0.8 |
| Berkeley Sch-Hicksville | 352 | 0.0 | 0.6 | 10.8 | 3.4 | 85.2 | 0.0 |
| Berkeley Sch of New York | 735 | 0.0 | 0.3 | 18.8 | 28.0 | 52.1 | 0.8 |
| Beth Israel Sch Nursing | 184 | 0.0 | 4.3 | 13.0 | 7.1 | 73.9 | 1.6 |
| Boricua C | 951 | 0.0 | 0.0 | 0.3 | 99.5 | 0.2 | 0.0 |
| Bramson ORT Tech Inst | 151 | 2.0 | 11.3 | 19.9 | 8.6 | 58.3 | 0.0 |
| Briarcliffe Secretarial Sch | 622 | 0.0 | 0.2 | 8.0 | 5.1 | 86.0 | 0.6 |
| Brooklyn Law Sch | 1,183 | 0.1 | 2.1 | 5.8 | 5.0 | 87.0 | 0.0 |
| Bryant & Stratton Bus Inst | 1,282 | 1.1 | 0.9 | 32.9 | 4.5 | 60.6 | 0.0 |
| Bryant & Stratton Bus Inst | 5,704 | 0.6 | 0.5 | 16.2 | 0.9 | 81.8 | 0.0 |
| Bryant & Stratton Bus Inst | 1,561 | 0.8 | 0.1 | 15.8 | 0.1 | 83.2 | 0.0 |
| Canisius C | 4,383 | 0.1 | 0.5 | 6.9 | 0.8 | 91.6 | 0.0 |
| Cathedral C of the Immaculate Conception | 91 | 0.0 | 2.2 | 8.8 | 11.0 | 78.0 | 0.0 |
| Cazenovia C | 801 | 0.4 | 0.1 | 6.5 | 0.9 | 91.9 | 0.2 |
| Central City Business Inst | 1,057 | 2.6 | 0.0 | 12.7 | 0.9 | 83.8 | 0.0 |
| Central Yeshiva Tomchei Tmimim Lubavitz | 383 | 0.0 | 0.0 | 0.0 | 0.0 | 60.3 | 39.7 |
| Christ The King Sem | 140 | 0.0 | 0.0 | 2.9 | 0.0 | 97.1 | 0.0 |
| City U of New York | | | | | | | |
| Bernard Baruch C | 15,581 | 1.1 | 7.8 | 19.4 | 13.1 | 56.4 | 2.2 |
| Mount Sinai Sch of Med | 469 | 0.0 | 7.0 | 3.8 | 7.9 | 81.2 | 0.0 |
| Clarkson U | 4,183 | 0.3 | 0.5 | 0.1 | 0.2 | 94.5 | 4.4 |
| Cochran Sch of Nursing | 85 | 0.0 | 0.0 | 17.6 | 2.4 | 77.6 | 2.4 |
| Colgate Rochester Divinity Sch Bexley Hall-Crozer Theol Sem | 273 | 0.7 | 1.1 | 15.4 | 0.0 | 82.4 | 0.4 |
| Colgate U | 2,615 | 0.2 | 3.7 | 3.6 | 2.1 | 88.5 | 2.0 |
| C for Human Service | 287 | 1.0 | 0.3 | 76.0 | 12.9 | 9.8 | 0.0 |
| C of Insurance | 1,093 | 0.0 | 5.9 | 11.1 | 11.3 | 67.9 | 3.9 |
| C of Mt Saint Vincent | 1,079 | 0.1 | 0.7 | 6.9 | 8.2 | 83.2 | 0.8 |
| C of New Rochelle | 4,826 | 0.0 | 0.5 | 50.0 | 8.5 | 40.6 | 0.4 |
| C of Saint Rose | 2,840 | 0.1 | 0.1 | 1.6 | 0.6 | 96.4 | 1.1 |
| Columbia U | | | | | | | |
| Main division | 17,017 | 0.2 | 8.3 | 4.2 | 3.4 | 82.4 | 1.5 |
| Barnard C | 2,187 | 0.0 | 12.4 | 4.8 | 3.7 | 74.7 | 4.3 |
| Teachers C | 3,538 | 0.0 | 2.5 | 10.0 | 5.8 | 73.0 | 8.8 |
| Concordia C | 560 | 0.0 | 1.8 | 9.5 | 3.2 | 75.0 | 10.5 |
| Cooper Union | 1,065 | 0.1 | 14.5 | 2.5 | 3.8 | 73.0 | 6.2 |
| Cornell U | | | | | | | |
| Endowed C's | 10,462 | 0.3 | 7.7 | 4.6 | 3.9 | 73.4 | 10.2 |
| Med Center | 526 | 0.0 | 3.8 | 7.8 | 5.3 | 80.0 | 3.0 |
| Statutory C's | 7,958 | 0.3 | 3.7 | 5.7 | 3.0 | 86.7 | 0.7 |
| Culinary Inst of America | 1,841 | 0.1 | 0.7 | 1.8 | 0.5 | 94.7 | 2.2 |
| Daeman C | 1,603 | 0.4 | 0.4 | 15.8 | 2.9 | 79.6 | 0.8 |
| Darkei No'am Rabbinical C | 55 | 0.0 | 0.0 | 0.0 | 0.0 | 100.0 | 0.0 |
| Dominican C of Blauvelt | 1,643 | 0.0 | 2.7 | 3.6 | 3.4 | 89.8 | 0.5 |
| Dowling C | 1,836 | 0.0 | 0.7 | 4.5 | 2.1 | 92.2 | 0.6 |
| D'Youville C | 1,272 | 1.1 | 0.5 | 13.4 | 5.3 | 79.2 | 0.5 |
| Elizabeth Seton C | 1,291 | 0.0 | 3.0 | 35.1 | 11.0 | 50.0 | 0.9 |
| Elmira C | 2,090 | 0.4 | 0.8 | 1.8 | 0.6 | 94.8 | 1.6 |
| Five Towns C | 358 | 0.3 | 0.6 | 9.5 | 2.2 | 86.6 | 0.8 |
| Fordham U | 12,340 | 0.2 | 1.4 | 6.8 | 7.1 | 83.0 | 1.4 |
| Friends World C | 238 | 0.4 | 0.4 | 5.0 | 2.1 | 82.8 | 9.2 |
| General Theol Sem | 162 | 0.6 | 0.0 | 4.3 | 0.6 | 91.4 | 3.1 |
| Hadar Hatorah Rabbinical Sem | 275 | 0.0 | 0.0 | 0.0 | 0.0 | 100.0 | 0.0 |
| Hamilton C | 1,626 | 0.1 | 1.4 | 2.9 | 1.2 | 92.2 | 2.3 |
| Hartwick C | 1,441 | 0.1 | 0.3 | 0.4 | 0.3 | 96.8 | 1.9 |
| Hilbert C | 709 | 0.6 | 0.0 | 3.4 | 1.1 | 94.8 | 0.1 |
| Hobart and Smith C's | 1,829 | 0.0 | 0.4 | 5.1 | 0.7 | 92.4 | 1.3 |
| Hofstra U | 6,794 | 0.3 | 1.3 | 5.3 | 2.9 | 88.9 | 1.4 |
| Houghton C | 1,262 | 0.3 | 1.0 | 3.4 | 1.0 | 91.0 | 3.2 |
| Inst for Advanced Studies in Humanities | 289 | 0.0 | 0.0 | 0.0 | 0.0 | 90.7 | 9.3 |
| Inst of Design and Construction | 197 | 0.0 | 2.5 | 23.9 | 13.7 | 57.4 | 2.5 |
| Interboro Inst | 854 | 0.0 | 0.4 | 78.1 | 16.7 | 4.4 | 0.4 |
| Iona C | 6,140 | 0.2 | 0.8 | 5.5 | 3.5 | 89.3 | 0.7 |
| Ithaca C | 5,488 | 0.3 | 0.6 | 2.0 | 0.9 | 94.6 | 1.6 |
| Jamestown Business C | 312 | 0.3 | 0.0 | 0.0 | 0.0 | 99.7 | 0.0 |
| Jewish Theol Sem America | 382 | 0.0 | 0.0 | 0.0 | 0.0 | 91.4 | 8.6 |
| Juilliard Sch | 1,153 | 0.1 | 7.5 | 1.7 | 2.0 | 69.9 | 18.8 |
| Katharine Gibbs Sch | 273 | 0.0 | 0.0 | 2.9 | 0.7 | 96.0 | 0.4 |
| Katharine Gibbs Sch | 443 | 0.2 | 0.7 | 7.2 | 8.1 | 83.7 | 0.0 |
| Keuka C | 420 | 1.0 | 0.7 | 3.8 | 1.4 | 93.1 | 0.0 |
| King's C | 708 | 0.3 | 1.8 | 6.2 | 3.4 | 87.3 | 1.0 |

| NEW YORK—Continued | Total | American Indian | Asian | Black | Hispanic | White | Foreign |
|---|---|---|---|---|---|---|---|
| Lab Inst of Merchandising | 259 | 0.0% | 0.0% | 11.2% | 5.8% | 82.6% | 0.4% |
| Le Moyne C | 2,213 | 0.0 | 0.5 | 1.4 | 0.7 | 97.2 | 0.1 |
| Long Island C Hospital Sch of Nursing | 151 | 0.7 | 1.3 | 31.8 | 7.9 | 58.3 | 0.0 |
| Long Island U | | | | | | | |
| Brooklyn | 4,690 | 0.4 | 5.9 | 38.3 | 11.2 | 38.6 | 5.7 |
| C W Post | 9,285 | 0.2 | 1.0 | 8.5 | 2.2 | 86.8 | 1.3 |
| Southampton | 590 | 0.0 | 0.2 | 9.5 | 3.7 | 84.9 | 1.7 |
| Machzikei Hadath Rabbinical C | 76 | 0.0 | 0.0 | 0.0 | 0.0 | 100.0 | 0.0 |
| Manhattan C | 4,737 | 0.0 | 1.7 | 2.8 | 6.8 | 85.0 | 3.7 |
| Manhattan Sch of Music | 801 | 0.5 | 7.7 | 3.7 | 2.9 | 70.4 | 14.7 |
| Manhattanville C | 1,275 | 0.0 | 1.6 | 6.9 | 4.5 | 80.8 | 6.3 |
| Mannes C of Music | 418 | 0.0 | 6.0 | 2.2 | 3.3 | 83.7 | 4.8 |
| Maria C of Albany | 957 | 0.0 | 0.2 | 2.9 | 1.1 | 95.7 | 0.0 |
| Maria Regina C | 518 | 0.2 | 0.2 | 3.5 | 1.0 | 94.8 | 0.4 |
| Marist C | 4,219 | 0.1 | 0.4 | 8.5 | 4.1 | 85.8 | 1.1 |
| Maryknoll Sch of Theol | 114 | 0.0 | 0.0 | 0.9 | 0.0 | 89.5 | 9.6 |
| Marymount C | 1,202 | 0.0 | 1.3 | 10.7 | 5.2 | 82.8 | 0.0 |
| Marymount Manhattan C | 1,895 | 0.0 | 2.2 | 18.3 | 10.8 | 65.9 | 2.9 |
| Mater Dei C | 550 | 12.7 | 0.5 | 2.2 | 1.5 | 82.9 | 0.2 |
| Medaille C | 787 | 0.6 | 0.1 | 45.7 | 1.0 | 52.1 | 0.4 |
| Mercy C | 8,137 | 2.0 | 0.6 | 18.1 | 9.4 | 55.2 | 14.8 |
| Mesivta Eastern Parkway Rabbinical Sem | 45 | 0.0 | 0.0 | 0.0 | 0.0 | 95.6 | 4.4 |
| Molloy C | 1,656 | 0.1 | 0.8 | 6.9 | 1.6 | 90.3 | 0.3 |
| Monroe Business Inst | 2,251 | 0.0 | 1.1 | 47.8 | 42.0 | 8.9 | 0.1 |
| Mt Saint Alphonsus Sem | 30 | 0.0 | 0.0 | 10.0 | 6.7 | 83.3 | 0.0 |
| Mount Saint Mary C | 1,131 | 0.0 | 0.4 | 10.9 | 3.3 | 85.5 | 0.0 |
| Nazareth C of Rochester | 2,532 | 0.2 | 0.7 | 3.0 | 0.9 | 95.2 | 0.1 |
| New Sch for Social Research | 6,371 | 0.4 | 4.3 | 7.8 | 4.8 | 78.6 | 4.1 |
| New York Chiropractic C | 846 | 0.0 | 0.7 | 0.2 | 1.5 | 95.5 | 2.0 |
| NY C Podiatric Med | 552 | 0.0 | 2.5 | 10.3 | 3.3 | 83.9 | 0.0 |
| New York Inst of Tech | | | | | | | |
| Main campus | 9,473 | 0.0 | 0.9 | 3.5 | 1.6 | 84.5 | 9.5 |
| New York | 3,605 | 0.1 | 1.5 | 6.4 | 3.1 | 62.1 | 26.8 |
| New York Law Sch | 1,216 | 0.2 | 3.0 | 5.9 | 6.4 | 84.0 | 0.4 |
| New York Med C | 1,268 | 0.1 | 5.0 | 5.0 | 3.6 | 84.8 | 1.6 |
| New York Sch of Interior Design | 23 | 0.0 | 0.0 | 0.0 | 0.0 | 0.0 | 100.0 |
| New York Theol Sem | 235 | 0.4 | 5.5 | 48.1 | 8.9 | 37.0 | 0.0 |
| New York U | 33,014 | 0.2 | 7.1 | 5.2 | 5.0 | 78.1 | 4.4 |
| Niagara U | 3,347 | 0.6 | 0.9 | 5.6 | 1.0 | 79.6 | 12.4 |
| Nyack C | 874 | 0.0 | 4.9 | 5.0 | 4.8 | 83.1 | 2.2 |
| Ohr Hameir Theol Sem | 31 | 0.0 | 0.0 | 0.0 | 0.0 | 100.0 | 0.0 |
| Olean Business Inst | 156 | 0.6 | 0.0 | 0.0 | 0.0 | 99.4 | 0.0 |
| Pace U | | | | | | | |
| New York | 12,771 | 0.6 | 6.8 | 19.5 | 10.3 | 60.5 | 2.3 |
| Pleasantville-Briarcliff | 4,552 | 0.9 | 1.2 | 3.3 | 2.6 | 91.2 | 0.8 |
| White Plains | 4,968 | 0.8 | 1.9 | 4.7 | 2.2 | 89.1 | 1.3 |
| Paul Smith's C of Arts and Sciences | 891 | 0.0 | 0.0 | 0.4 | 0.3 | 97.8 | 1.5 |
| Plaza Business Inst | 387 | 0.0 | 1.0 | 38.5 | 38.5 | 21.2 | 0.8 |
| Polytechnic Inst of NY | 5,105 | 0.0 | 22.9 | 5.6 | 4.7 | 57.9 | 8.9 |
| Pratt Inst | 3,603 | 0.0 | 6.6 | 14.9 | 6.2 | 59.6 | 12.7 |
| Rabbi Isaac Elchanen Theol Sem | 236 | 0.0 | 0.0 | 0.0 | 0.0 | 97.0 | 3.0 |
| Rabbinical Sem M'kor Chaim | 85 | 0.0 | 0.0 | 0.0 | 0.0 | 100.0 | 0.0 |
| Rensselaer Poly Inst | 6,811 | 0.1 | 4.9 | 2.0 | 2.6 | 80.9 | 9.5 |
| Rika Breuer Teachers Sem | 103 | 0.0 | 0.0 | 0.0 | 0.0 | 100.0 | 0.0 |
| Roberts Wesleyan C | 631 | 1.3 | 1.7 | 3.6 | 1.7 | 86.7 | 4.9 |
| Rochester Business Inst | 363 | 0.0 | 0.0 | 23.1 | 1.4 | 74.9 | 0.6 |
| Rochester Inst of Tech | 14,326 | 0.3 | 1.8 | 2.9 | 1.1 | 92.4 | 1.6 |
| Rockefeller U | 107 | 0.0 | 4.7 | 0.0 | 0.9 | 72.9 | 21.5 |
| Russell Sage C | | | | | | | |
| Main campus | 3,426 | 0.2 | 0.6 | 2.2 | 0.4 | 95.9 | 0.7 |
| JC of Albany | 1,126 | 0.0 | 1.0 | 21.1 | 3.0 | 72.6 | 2.3 |
| Saint Anthony on Hudson Sem | 39 | 0.0 | 0.0 | 0.0 | 0.0 | 92.3 | 7.7 |
| Saint Bernard's Inst | 84 | 0.0 | 0.0 | 0.0 | 1.2 | 98.8 | 0.0 |
| Saint Bonaventure U | 2,675 | 0.2 | 0.3 | 0.6 | 0.3 | 97.8 | 0.8 |
| Saint Francis C | 2,422 | 0.4 | 2.5 | 23.0 | 9.4 | 62.5 | 2.2 |
| Saint John Fisher C | 2,259 | 0.3 | 0.4 | 3.2 | 0.8 | 95.0 | 0.3 |
| Saint John's U | 19,123 | 0.1 | 2.2 | 4.5 | 3.3 | 87.3 | 2.7 |
| Saint Joseph's C | | | | | | | |
| New York | 928 | 0.0 | 12.2 | 40.1 | 7.2 | 38.7 | 1.8 |
| Branch campus | 1,440 | 0.0 | 0.3 | 3.3 | 8.3 | 88.1 | 0.0 |
| Saint Joseph's Sem & C | 208 | 0.0 | 0.0 | 1.4 | 4.3 | 93.8 | 0.5 |
| Saint Lawrence U | 2,338 | 1.1 | 0.4 | 1.5 | 0.3 | 94.0 | 2.7 |
| Saint Thomas Aquinas C | 1,984 | 0.0 | 0.6 | 4.2 | 3.5 | 91.7 | 0.0 |
| Saint Vladimir's Orthodox Theol Sem | 89 | 0.0 | 0.0 | 0.0 | 0.0 | 86.5 | 13.5 |
| Sara Schenirer Teachers Sem | 123 | 0.0 | 0.0 | 0.0 | 0.0 | 99.2 | 0.8 |
| Sarah Lawrence C | 1,063 | 0.3 | 2.0 | 3.0 | 2.3 | 90.3 | 2.2 |
| Sch of Visual Arts | 5,082 | 0.0 | 3.8 | 7.3 | 4.8 | 82.5 | 1.6 |
| Sem of the Immaculate Conception | 180 | 0.0 | 0.0 | 1.7 | 3.9 | 92.8 | 1.7 |
| Siena C | 3,318 | 0.0 | 0.7 | 1.4 | 0.8 | 97.0 | 0.1 |
| Skidmore C | 2,537 | 0.0 | 1.3 | 4.1 | 1.3 | 92.0 | 1.3 |
| St U of New York | | | | | | | |
| Albany | 15,938 | 0.2 | 1.9 | 4.4 | 2.3 | 87.6 | 3.5 |
| Binghamton | 11,984 | 0.1 | 2.3 | 3.3 | 1.9 | 90.2 | 2.2 |
| Buffalo | | | | | | | |
| Main campus | 22,953 | 0.5 | 3.5 | 5.7 | 1.7 | 82.3 | 6.3 |
| Health Sciences Center | 3,207 | 0.6 | 3.0 | 3.8 | 1.0 | 87.2 | 4.3 |
| Stony Brook | | | | | | | |
| Main campus | 14,676 | 0.2 | 8.7 | 5.9 | 4.2 | 74.4 | 6.7 |
| Health Sciences Center | 1,572 | 0.1 | 2.9 | 4.8 | 3.6 | 86.9 | 1.7 |
| Empire St C | 5,661 | 0.2 | 1.1 | 11.2 | 4.0 | 82.9 | 0.5 |
| C at Brockport | 7,162 | 0.3 | 0.7 | 7.2 | 1.5 | 88.9 | 1.3 |
| C at Buffalo | 11,548 | 0.5 | 0.5 | 8.7 | 1.3 | 87.4 | 1.5 |
| C at Cortland | 6,430 | 0.3 | 0.8 | 1.6 | 1.1 | 95.4 | 0.7 |
| C at Fredonia | 4,985 | 0.2 | 0.4 | 2.1 | 0.7 | 96.2 | 0.4 |
| C at Genesso | 5,282 | 0.2 | 0.2 | 0.8 | 0.5 | 98.3 | 0.0 |
| C at New Paltz | 7,344 | 1.1 | 1.4 | 10.9 | 4.0 | 79.7 | 2.9 |
| C at Old Westbury | 3,743 | 4.5 | 2.3 | 33.0 | 10.9 | 46.3 | 3.0 |
| C at Oneonta | 5,884 | 0.1 | 0.4 | 1.5 | 0.8 | 96.0 | 1.2 |
| C at Oswego | 7,694 | 0.2 | 0.5 | 1.9 | 1.1 | 95.8 | 0.4 |
| C at Plattsburgh | 6,044 | 0.2 | 0.3 | 2.4 | 0.9 | 94.1 | 2.1 |
| C at Potsdam | 4,416 | 0.2 | 0.4 | 0.3 | 0.5 | 98.2 | 0.3 |
| C at Purchase | 3,865 | 0.1 | 0.3 | 3.5 | 2.4 | 91.9 | 1.9 |
| Downstate Med Center | 1,320 | 0.0 | 2.7 | 14.2 | 3.9 | 77.2 | 2.0 |
| Upstate Med Center | 931 | 1.1 | 2.3 | 2.7 | 1.9 | 91.2 | 0.9 |
| C of Optometry | 248 | 0.0 | 3.6 | 3.6 | 1.6 | 90.3 | 0.8 |
| A&T at Alfred | 3,837 | 1.0 | 0.5 | 1.2 | 0.5 | 96.7 | 0.1 |
| A&T at Canton | 2,326 | 0.1 | 0.1 | 0.0 | 0.0 | 99.7 | 0.0 |
| A&T at Cobleskill | 2,734 | 0.0 | 0.3 | 1.2 | 1.0 | 97.1 | 0.3 |
| A&T at Delhi | 2,389 | 0.2 | 0.2 | 2.6 | 1.0 | 95.9 | 0.1 |
| A&T at Farmingdale | 12,987 | 0.1 | 0.8 | 4.6 | 2.2 | 92.2 | 0.1 |
| A&T at Morrisville | 3,054 | 0.2 | 0.5 | 4.9 | 0.9 | 93.3 | 0.2 |
| C of Environmental Science & Forestry | 1,496 | 0.0 | 0.6 | 0.8 | 0.2 | 91.2 | 7.2 |
| Maritime C | 1,029 | 0.4 | 1.7 | 1.7 | 1.5 | 84.5 | 10.2 |
| C of Tech at Utica-Rome | 2,189 | 0.2 | 0.9 | 2.5 | 0.8 | 94.2 | 1.4 |
| Fashion Inst of Tech | 10,732 | 0.0 | 11.0 | 14.9 | 10.0 | 61.9 | 2.2 |
| C of Ceramics Alfred U | 778 | 0.0 | 0.9 | 0.6 | 0.4 | 91.6 | 6.4 |
| Adirondack CC | 2,878 | 0.2 | 0.1 | 0.9 | 0.5 | 98.0 | 0.2 |
| Broome CC | 6,475 | 0.2 | 1.0 | 2.0 | 0.4 | 94.9 | 1.3 |
| Cayuga County CC | 3,053 | 0.1 | 0.3 | 2.5 | 1.0 | 96.1 | 0.0 |
| Clinton CC | 1,586 | 0.3 | 0.6 | 9.6 | 4.1 | 85.4 | 0.0 |
| Columbia-Greene CC | 1,356 | 0.4 | 0.1 | 3.6 | 0.6 | 93.6 | 1.6 |
| CC of the Finger Lakes | 2,952 | 0.2 | 0.2 | 1.5 | 0.2 | 97.9 | 0.1 |
| Corning CC | 3,136 | 0.2 | 0.4 | 1.8 | 0.2 | 97.4 | 0.1 |
| Dutchess CC | 7,084 | 0.2 | 1.7 | 6.7 | 1.8 | 89.0 | 0.6 |

| NEW YORK—Continued | Total | American Indian | Asian | Black | Hispanic | White | Foreign |
|---|---|---|---|---|---|---|---|
| St U of New York—Continued | | | | | | | |
| Erie CC | | | | | | | |
| North | 5,549 | 0.3% | 0.5% | 11.0% | 1.9% | 85.8% | 0.5% |
| City | 2,273 | 0.0 | 0.2 | 9.3 | 0.6 | 89.5 | 0.4 |
| South | 3,233 | 0.5 | 0.6 | 12.3 | 2.9 | 83.0 | 0.6 |
| Fulton-Montgomery CC | 1,824 | 0.8 | 0.4 | 1.9 | 1.5 | 90.6 | 4.7 |
| Genesee CC | 2,636 | 0.4 | 0.1 | 1.3 | 0.1 | 98.1 | 0.1 |
| Herkimer County CC | 2,011 | 0.0 | 0.0 | 1.3 | 0.0 | 98.5 | 0.1 |
| Hudson Valley CC | 8,040 | 0.7 | 0.7 | 2.3 | 0.4 | 94.9 | 1.0 |
| Jamestown CC | 3,947 | 1.1 | 0.3 | 1.5 | 0.9 | 96.3 | 0.0 |
| Jefferson CC | 1,750 | 0.2 | 0.3 | 1.3 | 0.2 | 97.9 | 0.1 |
| Mohawk Valley CC | 6,359 | 0.3 | 0.3 | 6.7 | 0.8 | 91.6 | 0.3 |
| Monroe CC | 11,479 | 0.4 | 2.0 | 7.8 | 1.9 | 88.0 | 0.0 |
| Nassau CC | 21,132 | 0.4 | 1.1 | 8.2 | 3.1 | 87.0 | 0.2 |
| Niagara County CC | 4,518 | 1.3 | 0.0 | 5.3 | 0.7 | 91.7 | 1.0 |
| North Country CC | 1,687 | 1.2 | 0.4 | 1.0 | 0.4 | 97.0 | 0.0 |
| Onondaga CC | 7,262 | 0.4 | 0.5 | 2.6 | 0.4 | 96.1 | 0.0 |
| Orange County CC | 5,245 | 0.2 | 0.6 | 4.1 | 3.3 | 91.4 | 0.5 |
| Rockland CC | 8,949 | 0.9 | 2.9 | 10.4 | 4.5 | 80.6 | 0.8 |
| Schenectady County CC | 3,216 | 0.5 | 0.9 | 5.8 | 0.8 | 92.0 | 0.1 |
| Suffolk County CC | | | | | | | |
| Selden | 12,542 | 0.2 | 0.6 | 3.0 | 2.1 | 94.1 | 0.0 |
| Eastern | 1,964 | 0.1 | 0.2 | 2.5 | 2.4 | 94.9 | 0.0 |
| Western | 5,109 | 0.1 | 0.3 | 2.5 | 2.1 | 94.9 | 0.0 |
| Sullivan County CC | 1,656 | 0.0 | 0.3 | 12.9 | 1.8 | 85.0 | 0.0 |
| Tompkins-Cortland CC | 2,803 | 0.2 | 0.9 | 1.7 | 0.5 | 95.8 | 0.9 |
| Ulster County CC | 3,197 | 0.1 | 0.6 | 1.7 | 4.9 | 92.6 | 0.2 |
| Westchester CC | 7,759 | 0.3 | 2.1 | 12.8 | 5.1 | 79.0 | 0.7 |
| Syracuse U | | | | | | | |
| Main campus | 21,044 | 0.2 | 1.4 | 5.4 | 1.6 | 85.5 | 5.9 |
| Utica C | 2,352 | 0.0 | 0.7 | 4.8 | 0.8 | 93.2 | 0.5 |
| Taylor Business Inst | 1,372 | 0.0 | 1.7 | 58.1 | 36.9 | 2.4 | 0.9 |
| Tech Career Inst | 2,455 | 0.0 | 2.5 | 43.3 | 9.5 | 41.1 | 3.5 |
| Tobe-Coburn Sch of Fashion Careers | 521 | 0.0 | 3.1 | 12.7 | 6.1 | 76.6 | 1.5 |
| Torah Temimah Talmudical Sem | 101 | 0.0 | 0.0 | 0.0 | 0.0 | 100.0 | 0.0 |
| Touro C | 3,433 | 0.6 | 0.9 | 36.5 | 4.6 | 45.8 | 11.7 |
| Trocaire C | 993 | 0.6 | 0.0 | 3.8 | 0.7 | 94.7 | 0.2 |
| Union C | 3,288 | 0.0 | 2.4 | 1.6 | 0.7 | 94.3 | 0.9 |
| U of Rochester | 8,559 | 0.2 | 3.7 | 3.1 | 1.2 | 85.2 | 6.7 |
| Utica Sch of Commerce | 331 | 0.0 | 0.0 | 10.0 | 1.2 | 88.8 | 0.0 |
| Vassar C | 2,258 | 0.1 | 3.7 | 4.6 | 1.6 | 87.9 | 2.1 |
| Villa Maria C of Buffalo | 686 | 0.0 | 0.3 | 15.0 | 0.1 | 84.5 | 0.0 |
| Wadhams Hall Sem-C | 65 | 0.0 | 0.0 | 1.5 | 0.0 | 76.9 | 21.5 |
| Wagner C | 2,235 | 0.1 | 0.5 | 6.0 | 1.2 | 72.7 | 19.6 |
| Webb Inst of Naval Architecture | 87 | 0.0 | 1.1 | 0.0 | 1.1 | 97.7 | 0.0 |
| Wells C | 475 | 0.2 | 0.8 | 2.7 | 0.6 | 93.3 | 2.3 |
| Wendell Castle Workshop | 26 | 0.0 | 0.0 | 3.8 | 0.0 | 92.3 | 3.8 |
| Westchester Business Inst | 797 | 0.0 | 1.3 | 35.9 | 12.7 | 49.2 | 1.0 |
| Wood Sch | 451 | 0.0 | 0.7 | 16.6 | 26.8 | 55.9 | 0.0 |
| Yeshiva Karlin Stolin Inst | 84 | 0.0 | 0.0 | 0.0 | 0.0 | 89.3 | 10.7 |
| Yeshiva U | 4,146 | 0.0 | 2.2 | 1.7 | 2.1 | 90.4 | 3.5 |
| **NORTH CAROLINA** | | | | | | | |
| Anson Tech C | 572 | 0.2% | 0.0% | 29.9% | 0.2% | 69.8% | 0.0% |
| Asheville Buncombe Tech C | 2,406 | 0.9 | 0.0 | 4.9 | 0.0 | 93.8 | 0.4 |
| Atlantic Christian C | 1,348 | 0.5 | 0.5 | 11.1 | 0.2 | 86.6 | 1.1 |
| Barber-Scotia C | 389 | 0.0 | 0.5 | 99.5 | 0.0 | 0.0 | 0.0 |
| Beaufort County CC | 1,086 | 0.1 | 0.6 | 22.4 | 0.1 | 76.7 | 0.1 |
| Belmont Abbey C | 890 | 0.6 | 0.7 | 3.5 | 1.5 | 90.2 | 3.6 |
| Bennett C | 575 | 0.0 | 0.0 | 99.8 | 0.0 | 0.2 | 0.0 |
| Bladen Tech Inst | 380 | 2.4 | 0.0 | 35.3 | 0.0 | 62.4 | 0.0 |
| Blue Ridge Tech C | 1,138 | 0.1 | 0.5 | 2.8 | 0.5 | 95.8 | 0.3 |
| Brevard C | 658 | 2.0 | 0.0 | 5.3 | 1.2 | 88.3 | 3.2 |
| Brookstone C of Business | 44 | 0.0 | 0.0 | 52.3 | 0.0 | 47.7 | 0.0 |
| Brunswick Tech C | 463 | 0.0 | 0.2 | 19.7 | 0.0 | 80.1 | 0.0 |
| Caldwell CC and Tech Inst | 2,175 | 0.1 | 0.3 | 5.1 | 0.2 | 93.9 | 0.4 |
| Campbell U | 3,338 | 0.5 | 1.7 | 8.0 | 1.6 | 85.7 | 2.6 |
| Cape Fear Tech Inst | 1,813 | 0.3 | 0.5 | 17.9 | 0.4 | 80.6 | 0.2 |
| Carteret Tech C | 1,057 | 0.4 | 0.7 | 6.5 | 0.9 | 91.5 | 0.1 |
| Catawba C | 910 | 0.1 | 0.5 | 11.8 | 0.3 | 86.9 | 0.3 |
| Catawba Valley Tech C | 2,315 | 0.2 | 0.5 | 5.7 | 0.3 | 93.3 | 0.1 |
| Cecils JC | 192 | 0.5 | 1.0 | 9.4 | 0.5 | 88.5 | 0.0 |
| Central Carolina Tech C | 1,936 | 0.3 | 0.2 | 18.4 | 0.5 | 80.0 | 0.6 |
| Central Piedmont CC | 26,235 | 0.5 | 2.3 | 16.0 | 0.5 | 77.9 | 2.8 |
| Chowan C | 911 | 0.3 | 2.0 | 27.2 | 0.7 | 66.4 | 3.4 |
| Cleveland Tech C | 1,193 | 0.3 | 0.7 | 19.8 | 0.2 | 79.0 | 0.1 |
| Coastal Carolina CC | 3,073 | 0.3 | 1.5 | 16.7 | 3.0 | 78.6 | 0.0 |
| C of the Albemarle | 1,487 | 0.1 | 0.5 | 14.6 | 0.4 | 84.4 | 0.0 |
| Craven CC | 1,963 | 0.1 | 1.1 | 16.3 | 2.5 | 79.8 | 0.3 |
| Davidson C | 1,373 | 0.0 | 1.2 | 3.9 | 0.4 | 94.2 | 0.1 |
| Davidson County CC | 2,169 | 0.3 | 0.2 | 7.0 | 0.2 | 92.3 | 0.0 |
| Duke U | 10,025 | 0.1 | 2.6 | 4.0 | 1.3 | 87.2 | 4.9 |
| Durham Tech Inst | 3,811 | 0.6 | 2.5 | 40.0 | 0.7 | 56.2 | 0.0 |
| East Coast Bible C | 279 | 0.0 | 1.1 | 9.0 | 0.4 | 89.6 | 0.0 |
| Edgecombe Tech C | 981 | 0.5 | 0.1 | 44.6 | 0.0 | 54.7 | 0.0 |
| Elon C | 2,803 | 0.1 | 0.2 | 8.1 | 0.1 | 91.0 | 0.4 |
| Fayetteville Tech Inst | 5,473 | 1.3 | 1.6 | 29.9 | 2.4 | 64.7 | 0.1 |
| Forsyth Tech Inst | 3,086 | 0.3 | 0.6 | 21.4 | 0.3 | 77.5 | 0.0 |
| Gardner-Webb C | 1,885 | 0.2 | 0.5 | 8.4 | 0.3 | 90.6 | 0.1 |
| Gaston C | 2,986 | 0.2 | 1.1 | 9.1 | 0.4 | 87.8 | 1.4 |
| Greensboro C | 524 | 1.0 | 0.0 | 14.7 | 0.8 | 82.1 | 1.5 |
| Guilford C | 1,636 | 0.6 | 0.0 | 4.8 | 1.0 | 89.1 | 4.5 |
| Guilford Tech CC | 4,745 | 0.3 | 0.8 | 19.3 | 0.4 | 78.6 | 0.7 |
| Halifax CC | 1,006 | 1.3 | 0.1 | 39.8 | 0.0 | 58.8 | 0.0 |
| Hardbarger JC of Business | 710 | 0.8 | 0.4 | 33.8 | 0.4 | 64.5 | 0.0 |
| Haywood Tech C | 957 | 0.1 | 0.3 | 0.9 | 0.3 | 98.0 | 0.3 |
| High Point C | 1,333 | 0.0 | 0.6 | 6.8 | 1.4 | 89.6 | 1.6 |
| Isothermal CC | 2,390 | 0.2 | 0.1 | 8.3 | 0.1 | 91.3 | 0.0 |
| James Sprunt Tech C | 743 | 0.1 | 0.1 | 37.3 | 0.3 | 62.2 | 0.0 |
| John Wesley C | 77 | 1.3 | 0.0 | 1.3 | 0.0 | 97.4 | 0.0 |
| Johnson C Smith U | 1,277 | 0.0 | 0.0 | 97.7 | 0.0 | 0.2 | 2.1 |
| Johnston Tech C | 1,654 | 0.8 | 0.2 | 20.3 | 0.1 | 78.6 | 0.0 |
| Lees-McRae C | 670 | 0.0 | 0.0 | 9.4 | 0.0 | 90.0 | 0.6 |
| Lenoir CC | 1,980 | 0.1 | 0.3 | 32.5 | 0.4 | 66.8 | 0.0 |
| Lenoir-Rhyne C | 1,475 | 0.2 | 0.3 | 4.9 | 1.1 | 92.7 | 0.7 |
| Livingstone C | 741 | 0.1 | 0.0 | 84.8 | 0.0 | 15.1 | 0.0 |
| Louisburg C | 725 | 0.0 | 0.1 | 11.7 | 0.4 | 87.4 | 0.3 |
| Mars Hill C | 1,357 | 0.7 | 0.0 | 4.1 | 0.1 | 94.7 | 0.5 |
| Martin CC | 776 | 0.0 | 0.9 | 35.1 | 0.3 | 63.8 | 0.0 |
| Mayland Tech C | 549 | 0.2 | 0.4 | 4.2 | 0.2 | 95.1 | 0.0 |
| McDowell Tech C | 599 | 0.0 | 0.2 | 6.7 | 0.3 | 92.8 | 0.0 |
| Meredith C | 1,761 | 0.1 | 0.5 | 2.6 | 0.3 | 95.7 | 0.8 |
| Methodist C | 953 | 0.7 | 1.2 | 18.8 | 2.8 | 74.1 | 2.4 |
| Mitchell CC | 1,332 | 0.2 | 0.5 | 12.9 | 0.0 | 86.4 | 0.0 |
| Montgomery Tech C | 506 | 1.4 | 0.0 | 28.1 | 0.2 | 70.4 | 0.0 |
| Montreat-Anderson C | 386 | 0.3 | 0.0 | 5.2 | 0.8 | 89.3 | 4.4 |
| Mount Olive C | 665 | 0.2 | 1.7 | 16.7 | 0.5 | 81.1 | 0.0 |
| Nash Tech Inst | 1,410 | 2.4 | 0.1 | 26.2 | 0.0 | 71.2 | 0.0 |
| North Carolina Wesleyan C | 1,143 | 0.4 | 0.1 | 17.1 | 0.6 | 80.7 | 1.1 |
| Pamlico Tech C | 134 | 0.0 | 0.0 | 32.1 | 0.0 | 67.9 | 0.0 |
| Peace C | 513 | 0.2 | 0.4 | 0.8 | 0.2 | 98.4 | 0.0 |
| Pfeiffer C | 811 | 0.1 | 0.6 | 8.1 | 0.4 | 90.4 | 0.4 |
| Piedmont Bible C | 322 | 0.0 | 0.3 | 0.9 | 0.3 | 96.6 | 1.9 |
| Piedmont Tech C | 415 | 0.5 | 0.0 | 35.2 | 0.7 | 63.6 | 0.0 |
| Pitt CC | 2,710 | 0.1 | 0.3 | 24.1 | 0.0 | 73.7 | 1.6 |
| Queens C | 1,230 | 0.2 | 0.9 | 7.0 | 0.3 | 90.9 | 0.7 |
| Randolph Tech C | 1,144 | 0.2 | 0.4 | 4.5 | 0.1 | 94.7 | 0.1 |
| Richmond Tech C | 983 | 4.8 | 0.1 | 28.3 | 0.3 | 66.4 | 0.1 |
| Roanoke Bible C | 142 | 0.0 | 0.0 | 0.7 | 0.0 | 99.3 | 0.0 |
| Roanoke-Chowan Tech C | 710 | 0.0 | 0.0 | 46.6 | 0.0 | 53.2 | 0.1 |
| Robeson Tech C | 1,101 | 30.3 | 0.4 | 20.5 | 0.4 | 48.4 | 0.0 |
| Rockingham CC | 1,529 | 0.0 | 0.1 | 17.3 | 0.0 | 82.7 | 0.0 |
| Rowan Tech C | 1,996 | 0.2 | 0.2 | 13.0 | 0.0 | 86.6 | 0.1 |

| NORTH CAROLINA—Continued | Total | American Indian | Asian | Black | Hispanic | White | Foreign |
|---|---|---|---|---|---|---|---|
| Rutledge C | | | | | | | |
| Greensboro | 276 | 0.0% | 0.0% | 79.7% | 0.0% | 20.3% | 0.0% |
| Raleigh | 246 | 0.0 | 0.0 | 89.8 | 0.4 | 8.9 | 0.8 |
| Winston-Salem | 325 | 0.3 | 0.9 | 77.2 | 0.6 | 20.6 | 0.3 |
| Sacred Heart C | 379 | 0.0 | 2.1 | 5.0 | 0.5 | 57.8 | 34.6 |
| Saint Andrew's Presbyterian C | 736 | 1.0 | 0.1 | 12.2 | 0.8 | 84.5 | 1.4 |
| Saint Augustine's C | 1,716 | 0.0 | 0.0 | 100.0 | 0.0 | 0.0 | 0.0 |
| Saint Mary's C | 273 | 0.0 | 0.0 | 1.1 | 0.0 | 96.0 | 2.9 |
| Salem C | 707 | 0.6 | 0.1 | 1.4 | 0.3 | 96.3 | 1.3 |
| Sampson Tech Inst | 836 | 2.3 | 0.0 | 29.4 | 0.6 | 67.7 | 0.0 |
| Sandhills CC | 1,718 | 1.7 | 0.2 | 15.2 | 0.3 | 82.7 | 0.0 |
| Shaw U | 1,772 | 0.1 | 0.0 | 78.3 | 0.0 | 1.0 | 20.7 |
| Southeastern CC | 1,714 | 3.0 | 0.6 | 22.4 | 0.0 | 74.0 | 0.0 |
| Southwestern Tech C | 1,215 | 11.4 | 0.3 | 1.5 | 0.1 | 86.7 | 0.0 |
| Stanly Tech C | 1,072 | 0.1 | 0.3 | 9.5 | 0.2 | 88.9 | 1.0 |
| Surry CC | 2,759 | 0.1 | 0.1 | 3.8 | 0.1 | 95.9 | 0.0 |
| Tech C of Alamance | 2,253 | 0.4 | 0.3 | 16.2 | 0.2 | 82.9 | 0.0 |
| Tri-County CC | 724 | 1.2 | 0.0 | 0.6 | 0.1 | 98.1 | 0.0 |
| U of North Carolina Sys | | | | | | | |
| Appalachian St U | 10,029 | 0.3 | 0.2 | 4.6 | 0.5 | 94.0 | 0.5 |
| East Carolina U | 15,140 | 0.6 | 0.6 | 11.2 | 0.6 | 86.0 | 1.0 |
| Elizabeth City St U | 1,557 | 0.3 | 0.2 | 82.7 | 0.2 | 15.9 | 0.8 |
| Fayetteville St U | 2,679 | 0.7 | 0.4 | 74.4 | 1.3 | 22.4 | 0.9 |
| North Carolina A&T St U | 5,426 | 0.2 | 0.4 | 82.4 | 0.1 | 10.7 | 6.2 |
| North Carolina Central U | 4,552 | 0.1 | 0.5 | 82.9 | 0.3 | 14.7 | 1.5 |
| NC Sch of the Arts | 505 | 0.0 | 0.8 | 12.3 | 0.8 | 84.2 | 2.0 |
| NC St U Raleigh | 23,733 | 0.3 | 2.0 | 8.1 | 0.7 | 85.3 | 3.5 |
| Pembroke St U | 2,197 | 24.6 | 0.5 | 14.3 | 0.5 | 59.4 | 0.7 |
| U of North Carolina | | | | | | | |
| Asheville | 2,651 | 0.1 | 0.6 | 4.8 | 0.6 | 92.9 | 0.8 |
| Chapel Hill | 21,652 | 0.6 | 1.1 | 8.3 | 0.7 | 87.4 | 1.9 |
| Charlotte | 10,830 | 0.3 | 1.7 | 8.6 | 0.7 | 84.9 | 3.8 |
| Greensboro | 10,293 | 0.3 | 0.7 | 9.9 | 0.4 | 87.1 | 1.5 |
| Wilmington | 5,857 | 0.2 | 0.6 | 7.0 | 0.5 | 91.4 | 0.4 |
| Western Carolina U | 6,385 | 1.4 | 0.4 | 5.4 | 0.4 | 91.0 | 1.3 |
| Winston-Salem St U | 2,443 | 0.1 | 0.4 | 85.3 | 0.2 | 14.0 | 0.1 |
| Vance-Granville CC | 1,373 | 0.3 | 0.4 | 37.9 | 0.6 | 60.7 | 0.0 |
| Wake Forest U | 4,961 | 0.1 | 0.7 | 3.3 | 0.5 | 94.4 | 0.9 |
| Wake Tech C | 4,332 | 0.3 | 1.1 | 16.5 | 0.3 | 80.8 | 1.0 |
| Warren Wilson C | 463 | 0.2 | 1.5 | 2.6 | 0.2 | 86.2 | 9.3 |
| Wayne CC | 2,003 | 0.1 | 0.3 | 24.4 | 0.2 | 74.8 | 0.1 |
| Western Piedmont CC | 2,055 | 0.1 | 0.9 | 6.4 | 0.0 | 92.5 | 0.0 |
| Wilkes CC | 2,935 | 0.2 | 0.2 | 4.1 | 0.1 | 95.3 | 0.2 |
| Wilson County Tech Inst | 1,370 | 0.2 | 0.1 | 31.2 | 0.2 | 68.2 | 0.1 |
| Wingate C | 1,562 | 0.2 | 0.2 | 5.1 | 0.1 | 93.4 | 1.0 |
| **NORTH DAKOTA** | | | | | | | |
| Jamestown C | 571 | 0.5% | 0.0% | 2.6% | 0.4% | 96.0% | 0.5% |
| Little Hoop CC | 109 | 87.2 | 0.0 | 0.0 | 0.0 | 12.8 | 0.0 |
| Mary C | 1,207 | 6.2 | 0.2 | 0.2 | 0.0 | 92.6 | 0.8 |
| ND St Bd of Higher Ed Sys | | | | | | | |
| Bismarck JC | 2,406 | 1.5 | 0.2 | 0.1 | 0.2 | 97.5 | 0.4 |
| Dickinson St C | 1,248 | 1.3 | 0.0 | 0.3 | 0.2 | 97.4 | 0.8 |
| Lake Region CC | 810 | 5.7 | 1.6 | 2.7 | 1.1 | 88.6 | 0.2 |
| Mayville St C | 728 | 0.7 | 0.0 | 0.7 | 0.1 | 96.4 | 2.1 |
| Minot St C | 3,047 | 1.6 | 0.5 | 3.3 | 0.7 | 90.0 | 4.0 |
| ND St Sch of Science | 2,932 | 1.7 | 0.5 | 0.4 | 0.1 | 96.3 | 0.9 |
| North Dakota State U | | | | | | | |
| Main campus | 9,998 | 0.5 | 0.4 | 0.2 | 0.1 | 95.7 | 3.1 |
| Bottineau | 501 | 3.2 | 0.0 | 0.8 | 0.0 | 90.2 | 5.8 |
| U of North Dakota | | | | | | | |
| Main campus | 11,060 | 2.4 | 0.5 | 0.4 | 0.4 | 93.3 | 3.0 |
| Williston | 667 | 4.2 | 0.3 | 0.0 | 0.6 | 94.8 | 0.1 |
| Valley City St C | 1,044 | 0.8 | 0.0 | 0.3 | 0.0 | 98.8 | 0.2 |
| Northwest Bible C | 151 | 0.0 | 0.0 | 6.6 | 0.0 | 93.4 | 0.0 |
| Standing Rock CC | 261 | 95.4 | 0.0 | 0.0 | 0.0 | 4.6 | 0.0 |
| Trinity Bible C | 420 | 1.9 | 0.5 | 1.2 | 1.2 | 94.0 | 1.2 |
| Turtle Mountain CC | 339 | 92.3 | 0.0 | 0.3 | 0.0 | 7.4 | 0.0 |
| **OHIO** | | | | | | | |
| ATES Tech Inst | 540 | 0.0% | 0.0% | 6.3% | 5.0% | 88.7% | 0.0% |
| Antioch U | 3,426 | 0.5 | 0.9 | 20.5 | 2.3 | 73.6 | 2.2 |
| Antonelli Inst of Art and Photography | 164 | 0.0 | 0.0 | 8.5 | 0.0 | 91.5 | 0.0 |
| Art Acad of Cincinnati | 235 | 0.0 | 0.4 | 4.3 | 0.4 | 94.0 | 0.9 |
| Ashland C | 3,211 | 0.1 | 0.0 | 7.8 | 0.1 | 88.6 | 3.3 |
| Athenaeum of Ohio | 179 | 0.0 | 0.0 | 2.8 | 0.0 | 97.2 | 0.0 |
| Baldwin-Wallace C | 3,705 | 0.0 | 3.2 | 9.2 | 3.7 | 82.8 | 1.1 |
| Belmont Tech C | 2,056 | 0.0 | 0.0 | 1.8 | 0.0 | 98.2 | 0.0 |
| Bluffton C | 573 | 0.0 | 0.0 | 1.7 | 0.0 | 95.3 | 3.0 |
| Borromeo C of Ohio | 122 | 0.0 | 0.0 | 4.9 | 2.5 | 91.0 | 1.6 |
| Bowling Green St U | | | | | | | |
| Main campus | 17,104 | 0.1 | 0.6 | 3.5 | 0.6 | 93.7 | 1.5 |
| Firelands | 1,074 | 0.1 | 0.0 | 0.7 | 0.3 | 98.9 | 0.1 |
| Capital U | 2,645 | 0.1 | 0.3 | 6.4 | 0.5 | 91.9 | 0.8 |
| Case Western Reserve U | 8,352 | 0.2 | 4.0 | 3.6 | 0.8 | 80.6 | 10.8 |
| Cedarville C | 1,815 | 0.1 | 0.3 | 0.8 | 0.4 | 98.4 | 0.0 |
| Central Ohio Tech C | 1,327 | 0.3 | 0.4 | 2.3 | 0.4 | 96.6 | 0.0 |
| Chatfield C | 124 | 0.0 | 0.0 | 0.8 | 0.0 | 99.2 | 0.0 |
| Cincinnati Bible Sem | 892 | 0.0 | 0.6 | 1.7 | 0.3 | 95.7 | 1.7 |
| Cincinnati C of Mortuary Science | 110 | 0.0 | 0.0 | 10.9 | 0.0 | 89.1 | 0.0 |
| Cincinnati Tech | 3,902 | 0.2 | 0.5 | 13.7 | 0.4 | 84.9 | 0.4 |
| Circleville Bible C | 186 | 0.5 | 0.5 | 1.1 | 0.0 | 96.8 | 1.1 |
| Clark Tech C | 2,399 | 0.2 | 0.3 | 7.7 | 0.2 | 91.4 | 0.3 |
| Cleveland Inst of Art | 542 | 0.2 | 1.1 | 6.6 | 0.6 | 90.6 | 0.9 |
| Cleveland Inst of Electronics | 23,373 | 0.0 | 0.0 | 0.0 | 0.0 | 100.0 | 0.0 |
| Cleveland Inst of Music | 270 | 0.0 | 4.1 | 3.3 | 2.6 | 80.0 | 10.0 |
| Cleveland St U | 18,032 | 0.5 | 0.7 | 10.8 | 0.5 | 86.0 | 1.5 |
| C of Mount Saint Joseph-On-The-Ohio | 1,942 | 0.0 | 0.7 | 4.4 | 0.1 | 94.6 | 0.2 |
| C of Wooster | 1,792 | 0.2 | 1.4 | 4.1 | 0.3 | 86.8 | 7.3 |
| Columbus C of Art and Design | 1,285 | 0.2 | 1.0 | 7.2 | 0.6 | 88.9 | 2.0 |
| Columbus Tech Inst | 8,484 | 1.4 | 0.3 | 15.4 | 0.7 | 81.7 | 0.4 |
| Cuyahoga CC District | 24,972 | 0.7 | 1.3 | 25.9 | 1.3 | 69.3 | 1.5 |
| Davis JC | 539 | 0.2 | 0.0 | 7.4 | 1.5 | 90.9 | 0.0 |
| Defiance C | 904 | 0.0 | 0.0 | 5.6 | 2.2 | 87.2 | 5.0 |
| Denison U | 2,121 | 0.1 | 0.8 | 4.9 | 0.5 | 92.7 | 1.0 |
| DeVry Inst of Tech | 3,630 | 0.1 | 0.9 | 12.3 | 0.6 | 85.0 | 1.1 |
| Dyke C | 1,313 | 0.2 | 0.4 | 56.7 | 1.3 | 41.1 | 0.4 |
| Edison St CC | 2,373 | 0.4 | 0.5 | 0.8 | 0.2 | 97.9 | 0.2 |
| Electronic Tech Inst | 1,240 | 0.0 | 0.5 | 13.1 | 1.6 | 84.8 | 0.0 |
| Findlay C | 1,415 | 0.1 | 0.4 | 6.1 | 1.5 | 85.7 | 6.3 |
| Franklin U | 4,618 | 0.1 | 0.8 | 12.8 | 0.5 | 84.1 | 1.7 |
| Hebrew Union C Jewish Inst of Religion | 140 | 0.0 | 0.0 | 0.0 | 0.0 | 91.4 | 8.6 |
| California branch | 78 | 0.0 | 0.0 | 0.0 | 0.0 | 94.9 | 5.1 |
| Heidelberg C | 968 | 0.2 | 0.3 | 4.0 | 1.1 | 88.3 | 6.0 |
| Hiram C | 1,108 | 0.0 | 0.5 | 3.8 | 0.3 | 95.4 | 0.0 |
| Hocking Tech C | 3,665 | 0.0 | 0.0 | 0.8 | 0.1 | 97.2 | 1.9 |
| ITT Tech Inst | 556 | 0.0 | 0.7 | 4.1 | 0.0 | 95.1 | 0.0 |
| Jefferson Tech C | 1,449 | 0.0 | 0.1 | 4.3 | 0.1 | 95.4 | 0.1 |
| John Carroll U | 3,666 | 0.0 | 0.8 | 3.4 | 1.0 | 94.3 | 0.5 |
| Kent St U | | | | | | | |
| Main campus | 20,324 | 0.1 | 0.6 | 5.6 | 0.5 | 89.9 | 3.3 |
| Ashtabula | 850 | 0.2 | 0.4 | 1.5 | 0.5 | 97.1 | 0.4 |
| East Liverpool | 629 | 0.3 | 0.2 | 6.0 | 0.0 | 93.3 | 0.2 |
| Salem | 568 | 0.0 | 0.0 | 1.2 | 0.4 | 98.4 | 0.0 |
| Stark County | 1,647 | 0.1 | 0.4 | 5.2 | 0.2 | 93.8 | 0.2 |
| Trumbull | 1,585 | 0.3 | 0.2 | 7.4 | 0.1 | 92.0 | 0.0 |
| Tuscarawas | 955 | 0.1 | 0.1 | 0.9 | 0.3 | 98.2 | 0.3 |
| Kenyon C | 1,458 | 0.0 | 0.9 | 1.0 | 0.5 | 96.3 | 1.4 |
| Kettering C of Med Arts | 463 | 0.2 | 1.3 | 5.6 | 1.9 | 90.5 | 0.4 |
| Lakeland CC | 9,209 | 0.1 | 0.5 | 1.7 | 0.3 | 97.4 | 0.0 |
| Lima Tech C | 1,885 | 0.3 | 0.5 | 4.5 | 0.7 | 93.8 | 0.1 |

*Continued on Following Page*

| | Total | American Indian | Asian | Black | Hispanic | White | Foreign |
|---|---|---|---|---|---|---|---|
| **OHIO—Continued** | | | | | | | |
| Lorain County CC | 6,495 | 0.1% | 0.1% | 5.4% | 2.9% | 91.3% | 0.2% |
| Lourdes C | 719 | 0.1 | 0.4 | 3.3 | 0.4 | 95.3 | 0.4 |
| Malone C | 917 | 0.0 | 0.5 | 3.3 | 0.1 | 94.4 | 1.6 |
| Marietta C | 1,307 | 0.0 | 0.2 | 0.3 | 0.2 | 97.9 | 1.4 |
| Marion Tech C | 1,366 | 0.5 | 0.7 | 7.5 | 0.4 | 90.4 | 0.5 |
| Med C of Ohio at Toledo | 730 | 0.0 | 4.5 | 3.7 | 0.4 | 89.5 | 1.9 |
| Methodist Theol Sch of Ohio | 251 | 0.0 | 1.2 | 7.2 | 0.8 | 89.2 | 1.6 |
| Miami-Jacobs JC of Business | 569 | 0.0 | 0.0 | 27.8 | 0.2 | 72.1 | 0.0 |
| Miami U | | | | | | | |
| Hamilton | 1,772 | 0.1 | 0.7 | 3.0 | 0.2 | 96.0 | 0.0 |
| Middletown | 1,334 | 0.1 | 0.7 | 2.5 | 0.3 | 96.3 | 0.0 |
| Oxford | 15,430 | 0.1 | 1.2 | 2.4 | 0.3 | 96.0 | 0.0 |
| Mount Union C | 922 | 0.2 | 0.9 | 6.2 | 1.4 | 91.2 | 0.1 |
| Mount Vernon Nazarene C | 1,065 | 0.0 | 0.1 | 0.9 | 0.8 | 98.0 | 0.2 |
| Muskingum Area Tech C | 1,447 | 0.1 | 0.0 | 2.3 | 0.1 | 97.5 | 0.0 |
| Muskingum C | 1,036 | 0.4 | 0.7 | 1.9 | 0.4 | 95.0 | 1.6 |
| North Central Tech C | 1,872 | 0.0 | 0.2 | 2.3 | 0.2 | 97.3 | 0.0 |
| Northeastern Ohio U's C of Med | 398 | 0.5 | 9.5 | 1.5 | 0.8 | 87.7 | 0.0 |
| Northwest Tech C | 897 | 0.4 | 0.0 | 0.2 | 2.3 | 97.0 | 0.0 |
| Northwestern Business C Tech Center | 918 | 0.0 | 0.0 | 6.9 | 0.3 | 92.8 | 0.0 |
| Notre Dame C | 673 | 0.0 | 0.4 | 22.4 | 0.9 | 74.6 | 1.6 |
| Oberlin C | 2,751 | 0.1 | 4.3 | 6.7 | 1.4 | 86.1 | 1.4 |
| Ohio C of Podiatric Med | 551 | 0.2 | 2.0 | 12.0 | 2.5 | 81.5 | 1.8 |
| Ohio Dominican C | 1,053 | 0.0 | 0.5 | 12.0 | 4.1 | 68.6 | 14.9 |
| Ohio Northern U | 2,439 | 0.1 | 0.7 | 1.8 | 0.4 | 94.6 | 2.4 |
| Ohio St U | | | | | | | |
| Main campus | 53,446 | 0.1 | 1.6 | 4.5 | 0.8 | 88.1 | 4.9 |
| A&T Inst | 564 | 0.0 | 0.0 | 0.9 | 0.7 | 98.2 | 0.2 |
| Lima | 939 | 0.2 | 0.4 | 2.0 | 0.6 | 96.7 | 0.0 |
| Mansfield | 1,089 | 0.0 | 0.6 | 2.2 | 0.5 | 96.8 | 0.0 |
| Marion | 795 | 0.4 | 0.5 | 2.8 | 0.4 | 96.0 | 0.0 |
| Newark | 935 | 0.2 | 0.3 | 1.0 | 0.4 | 98.0 | 0.1 |
| Ohio U | | | | | | | |
| Main campus | 14,684 | 0.3 | 0.4 | 5.3 | 0.4 | 84.1 | 9.5 |
| Belmont | 1,077 | 0.0 | 0.0 | 0.3 | 0.0 | 99.6 | 0.1 |
| Chillicothe | 1,186 | 0.4 | 0.1 | 2.4 | 0.2 | 96.9 | 0.1 |
| Lancaster | 1,529 | 0.4 | 0.2 | 0.6 | 0.2 | 98.4 | 0.2 |
| Zanesville | 1,036 | 0.0 | 0.0 | 1.3 | 0.3 | 98.3 | 0.2 |
| Ohio Wesleyan U | 1,563 | 0.1 | 1.1 | 5.1 | 0.7 | 84.5 | 8.6 |
| Otterbein C | 1,592 | 0.1 | 0.9 | 1.6 | 0.3 | 93.2 | 3.8 |
| Owens Tech C | 4,779 | 0.3 | 0.3 | 6.6 | 1.8 | 89.5 | 1.5 |
| Pontifical C Josephinum | 220 | 0.0 | 3.6 | 0.5 | 11.4 | 84.5 | 0.0 |
| Rio Grande C | 1,622 | 0.1 | 0.2 | 1.7 | 0.2 | 95.9 | 1.9 |
| Saint Mary Sem | 89 | 0.0 | 0.0 | 0.0 | 0.0 | 100.0 | 0.0 |
| Shawnee St CC | 2,314 | 0.3 | 0.1 | 3.4 | 0.2 | 95.8 | 0.1 |
| Sinclair CC | 16,247 | 0.3 | 1.1 | 14.9 | 0.6 | 82.8 | 0.4 |
| Southern Ohio C | 5,390 | 0.1 | 0.2 | 33.6 | 0.4 | 65.5 | 0.2 |
| Southern St CC | 1,277 | 0.5 | 0.0 | 2.0 | 0.0 | 97.5 | 0.1 |
| Stark Tech C | 3,400 | 0.4 | 0.4 | 4.6 | 0.3 | 94.2 | 0.1 |
| Terra Tech C | 2,312 | 0.1 | 0.1 | 1.1 | 2.2 | 96.3 | 0.1 |
| Tiffin U | 556 | 0.0 | 0.2 | 5.0 | 0.9 | 92.1 | 1.8 |
| Trinity Lutheran Sem | 321 | 0.0 | 0.0 | 6.5 | 0.0 | 91.0 | 2.5 |
| United Theol Sem | 291 | 0.0 | 0.3 | 8.2 | 0.3 | 89.7 | 1.4 |
| U of Akron | | | | | | | |
| Main campus | 26,644 | 0.4 | 0.7 | 6.6 | 0.3 | 89.5 | 2.4 |
| Wayne Gen & Tech C | 983 | 1.0 | 0.3 | 0.4 | 0.4 | 97.8 | 0.1 |
| U of Cincinnati | | | | | | | |
| Main campus | 30,830 | 0.3 | 2.4 | 10.5 | 0.8 | 84.4 | 1.5 |
| Clermont Gen & Tech C | 1,206 | 0.7 | 0.2 | 1.1 | 0.4 | 97.3 | 0.2 |
| Raymond Walters General and Tech C | 3,213 | 0.6 | 1.4 | 6.5 | 1.2 | 90.0 | 0.3 |
| U of Dayton | 10,693 | 0.1 | 1.0 | 5.2 | 1.2 | 91.3 | 1.3 |
| U of Steubenville | 878 | 0.2 | 0.7 | 1.1 | 1.9 | 92.8 | 3.2 |
| U of Toledo | 21,039 | 0.5 | 1.1 | 6.4 | 1.2 | 84.7 | 6.1 |
| Urbana C | 573 | 0.0 | 0.0 | 22.7 | 0.2 | 68.8 | 8.4 |
| Ursuline C | 1,559 | 0.3 | 0.8 | 7.3 | 0.5 | 90.3 | 0.8 |
| Virginia Marti C of Fashion and Art | 167 | 0.0 | 2.4 | 40.1 | 6.0 | 50.9 | 0.6 |
| Walsh C | 1,225 | 0.0 | 0.2 | 7.1 | 2.5 | 84.2 | 5.9 |
| Washington Tech C | 872 | 0.3 | 0.6 | 0.6 | 0.1 | 98.4 | 0.0 |
| West Side Inst of Tech | 535 | 0.6 | 1.5 | 10.3 | 1.3 | 86.4 | 0.0 |
| Wilberforce U | 915 | 0.1 | 0.0 | 98.4 | 0.0 | 0.2 | 1.3 |
| Wilmington C | 1,332 | 0.0 | 0.1 | 14.9 | 0.1 | 82.0 | 2.9 |
| Wittenberg U | 2,183 | 0.0 | 0.6 | 3.8 | 0.8 | 93.8 | 1.0 |
| Wright St U | | | | | | | |
| Main campus | 14,580 | 0.2 | 1.4 | 6.2 | 0.7 | 90.1 | 1.5 |
| Western Ohio | 868 | 0.1 | 0.1 | 0.1 | 0.2 | 99.3 | 0.1 |
| Xavier U | 6,785 | 0.2 | 0.8 | 6.0 | 1.5 | 89.8 | 1.6 |
| Youngstown C of Business and Professional Drafting | 697 | 0.0 | 0.0 | 32.6 | 0.4 | 67.0 | 0.0 |
| Youngstown St U | 15,252 | 0.1 | 0.2 | 6.8 | 0.7 | 90.3 | 1.8 |
| **OKLAHOMA** | | | | | | | |
| Bacone C | 398 | 48.0% | 0.5% | 12.3% | 0.5% | 38.7% | 0.0% |
| Bartlesville Wesleyan C | 634 | 3.0 | 0.6 | 3.8 | 0.8 | 90.7 | 1.1 |
| Bethany Nazarene C | 1,275 | 1.6 | 1.0 | 1.6 | 1.7 | 89.1 | 5.0 |
| Cameron U | 5,496 | 4.8 | 2.3 | 14.5 | 3.7 | 74.1 | 0.6 |
| Carl Albert JC | 1,972 | 6.5 | 0.1 | 4.2 | 0.5 | 88.5 | 0.4 |
| Central State U | 13,264 | 1.6 | 1.6 | 8.9 | 0.9 | 80.9 | 6.1 |
| Connors St C | 1,246 | 4.0 | 1.4 | 10.0 | 0.4 | 84.3 | 0.0 |
| East Central Okla St U | 4,046 | 6.2 | 0.6 | 4.5 | 0.7 | 87.7 | 0.3 |
| Eastern Oklahoma St C | 1,675 | 5.9 | 0.2 | 5.4 | 0.5 | 87.4 | 0.5 |
| El Reno JC | 1,595 | ·1.7 | 0.3 | 4.1 | 3.1 | 88.0 | 2.8 |
| Flaming Rainbow U | 221 | 66.5 | 0.0 | 0.0 | 1.4 | 32.1 | 0.0 |
| Hillsdale Free Will Baptist C | 156 | 2.6 | 1.3 | 7.1 | 2.6 | 84.6 | 1.9 |
| Langston U | 1,802 | 1.5 | 1.4 | 51.0 | 0.6 | 33.4 | 12.1 |
| Murray St C | 1,389 | 4.9 | 0.1 | 4.1 | 0.3 | 90.4 | 0.3 |
| Northeastern Okla A&M C | 2,536 | 6.4 | 0.2 | 6.3 | 0.4 | 82.5 | 4.2 |
| Northeastern Okla St U | 7,266 | 15.0 | 0.3 | 6.1 | 0.7 | 76.9 | 1.0 |
| Northern Oklahoma C | 1,843 | 3.0 | 0.6 | 1.7 | 0.4 | 93.1 | 1.1 |
| Northwestern Okla St U | 1,663 | 1.1 | 0.2 | 2.6 | 0.7 | 93.6 | 1.9 |
| Oklahoma Baptist U | 1,532 | 3.0 | 0.8 | 1.6 | 1.9 | 91.4 | 1.3 |
| Oklahoma Christian C | 1,465 | 1.0 | 0.5 | 4.6 | 0.5 | 93.1 | 0.3 |
| Oklahoma City CC | 7,806 | 2.0 | 4.4 | 4.2 | 1.4 | 86.3 | 1.8 |
| Oklahoma City U | 2,687 | 2.1 | 0.8 | 4.5 | 1.0 | 79.8 | 11.8 |
| Oklahoma C of Business and Tech | 774 | 8.4 | 1.4 | 24.3 | 1.4 | 63.6 | 0.9 |
| Oklahoma C of Osteopathic Med and Surgery | 325 | 5.5 | 2.5 | 3.4 | 1.2 | 87.4 | 0.0 |
| Oklahoma Panhandle St U | 1,173 | 1.0 | 0.5 | 5.3 | 3.5 | 89.2 | 0.5 |
| Oklahoma St U | | | | | | | |
| Main campus | 22,237 | 1.9 | 1.1 | 2.7 | 0.7 | 85.2 | 8.4 |
| Tech Inst | 2,877 | 2.2 | 2.8 | 5.6 | 1.5 | 87.0 | 0.8 |
| Rogers St C | 2,583 | 8.2 | 2.5 | 1.9 | 0.4 | 70.5 | 16.4 |
| Rose St C | 9,876 | 2.5 | 2.2 | 13.2 | 1.6 | 78.4 | 2.1 |
| Saint Gregory's C | 290 | 4.1 | 3.8 | 6.2 | 4.5 | 76.6 | 4.8 |
| Sayre JC | 485 | 1.2 | 0.6 | 0.2 | 1.6 | 96.3 | 0.0 |
| Seminole JC | 1,481 | 8.2 | 0.2 | 4.5 | 0.5 | 85.7 | 0.9 |
| Southeastern Okla St U | 3,826 | 6.1 | 3.6 | 3.5 | 0.8 | 80.9 | 5.1 |
| Southwestern C of Christian Ministries | 82 | 0.0 | 3.7 | 2.4 | 1.2 | 92.7 | 0.0 |
| Southwestern Okla St U | 4,657 | 2.1 | 0.8 | 2.7 | 0.9 | 91.8 | 1.8 |
| Tulsa JC | 15,332 | 2.3 | 1.1 | 6.3 | 0.9 | 89.4 | 0.0 |
| U of Oklahoma | | | | | | | |
| Health Sciences Center | 2,555 | 3.2 | 2.2 | 4.7 | 1.3 | 85.2 | 3.4 |
| Norman | 21,365 | 2.3 | 1.7 | 4.2 | 1.0 | 84.9 | 5.9 |
| U of Science and Arts of Oklahoma | 1,296 | 8.6 | 0.7 | 4.7 | 0.9 | 79.2 | 5.9 |
| U of Tulsa | 5,326 | 1.9 | 0.8 | 2.7 | 0.7 | 84.0 | 10.0 |
| Western Oklahoma St C | 2,155 | 1.2 | 1.2 | 6.5 | 4.5 | 86.6 | 0.0 |
| **OREGON** | | | | | | | |
| Bassist C | 234 | 0.9% | 4.3% | 3.4% | 3.4% | 88.0% | 0.0% |
| Blue Mountain CC | 2,511 | 1.4 | 0.5 | 0.0 | 1.0 | 97.0 | 0.0 |
| Central Oregon CC | 1,769 | 1.9 | 0.3 | 0.1 | 1.1 | 96.3 | 0.3 |
| Chemeketa CC | 6,676 | 0.5 | 1.5 | 0.5 | 1.2 | 96.1 | 0.2 |
| Clackamas CC | 4,203 | 0.2 | 2.5 | 0.4 | 0.5 | 96.1 | 0.4 |
| Clatsop CC | 1,722 | 0.3 | 2.1 | 0.9 | 1.4 | 95.2 | 0.1 |
| Columbia Christian C | 240 | 0.8 | 0.8 | 6.3 | 0.0 | 91.7 | 0.4 |
| Concordia C | 447 | 0.7 | 1.1 | 3.4 | 0.4 | 62.9 | 31.5 |
| Eugene Bible C | 162 | 1.2 | 0.6 | 0.0 | 1.9 | 90.1 | 6.2 |
| George Fox C | 669 | 0.1 | 0.6 | 1.0 | 0.3 | 97.0 | 0.9 |
| ITT Tech Inst | 840 | 0.5 | 1.4 | 1.4 | 3.8 | 92.3 | 0.6 |
| Judson Baptist C | 98 | 0.0 | 0.0 | 2.0 | 2.0 | 93.9 | 2.0 |
| Lane CC | 6,944 | 2.0 | 1.3 | 1.0 | 1.4 | 93.1 | 1.3 |
| Lewis and Clark C | 3,012 | 0.6 | 2.8 | 0.7 | 0.7 | 89.0 | 6.1 |
| Linfield C | 1,966 | 0.3 | 2.3 | 0.7 | 0.9 | 92.5 | 3.3 |
| Linn-Benton CC | 5,428 | 0.5 | 1.1 | 0.4 | 0.3 | 97.1 | 0.6 |
| Marylhurst C for Lifelong Learning | 679 | 0.3 | 1.8 | 1.0 | 0.1 | 95.1 | 1.6 |
| Mount Angel Sem | 116 | 0.0 | 7.8 | 0.0 | 14.7 | 70.7 | 6.9 |
| Mount Hood CC | 6,524 | 0.8 | 2.4 | 1.5 | 0.9 | 94.1 | 0.3 |
| Multnomah Sch of the Bible | 765 | 0.7 | 1.0 | 0.7 | 1.0 | 92.8 | 3.8 |
| Northwest Christian C | 236 | 0.0 | 0.0 | 0.4 | 0.4 | 93.2 | 5.9 |
| Oregon Graduate Center | 105 | 0.0 | 1.0 | 0.0 | 0.0 | 73.3 | 25.7 |
| Oregon Grad Sch of Professional Psychology | 62 | 0.0 | 0.0 | 0.0 | 0.0 | 100.0 | 0.0 |
| Oregon Polytechnic Inst | 178 | 0.0 | 7.9 | 4.5 | 1.1 | 85.4 | 1.1 |
| Oregon St Sys of Higher Ed | | | | | | | |
| Eastern Oregon St C | 1,602 | 1.1 | 1.4 | 1.1 | 1.7 | 90.1 | 4.5 |
| Oregon Health Sciences U | 1,185 | 0.3 | 5.6 | 0.1 | 0.6 | 92.8 | 0.6 |
| Oregon Inst of Tech | 2,700 | 2.2 | 2.2 | 1.0 | 1.0 | 92.3 | 1.4 |
| Oregon St U | 15,624 | 1.5 | 4.5 | 1.0 | 1.3 | 87.3 | 4.3 |
| Portland St U | 14,390 | 0.7 | 6.4 | 2.0 | 1.1 | 86.4 | 3.4 |
| Southern Oregon St C | 4,432 | 1.0 | 0.7 | 0.8 | 1.4 | 94.9 | 1.2 |
| U of Oregon | 15,840 | 0.6 | 3.7 | 1.1 | 1.2 | 85.4 | 8.0 |
| Western Oregon St C | 2,820 | 0.4 | 0.7 | 0.2 | 0.5 | 94.4 | 3.8 |
| Pacific Northwest C of Art | 199 | 0.0 | 2.0 | 1.5 | 0.0 | 95.0 | 1.5 |
| Pacific U | 1,061 | 0.8 | 14.6 | 1.0 | 2.0 | 80.1 | 1.5 |
| Portland CC | 20,877 | 0.5 | 7.2 | 3.1 | 1.8 | 86.2 | 1.3 |
| Rogue CC | 2,646 | 1.2 | 0.3 | 0.1 | 1.1 | 97.0 | 0.3 |
| Southwestern Oregon CC | 2,550 | 1.3 | 1.3 | 0.2 | 1.2 | 95.8 | 0.2 |
| Treasure Valley CC | 1,394 | 0.1 | 2.0 | 0.4 | 5.4 | 92.0 | 0.1 |
| Umpqua CC | 1,394 | 0.6 | 0.9 | 0.1 | 0.9 | 97.4 | 0.0 |
| U of Portland | 2,861 | 0.6 | 4.7 | 1.6 | 0.9 | 80.6 | 11.6 |
| Warner Pacific C | 395 | 1.5 | 0.8 | 3.8 | 0.0 | 81.0 | 12.9 |
| Western Baptist C | 282 | 1.1 | 1.1 | 1.1 | 0.7 | 96.1 | 0.0 |
| Western Conservative Baptist Sem | 462 | 0.2 | 3.9 | 1.3 | 0.9 | 93.1 | 0.6 |
| Western Evangelical Sem | 129 | 0.0 | 1.6 | 2.3 | 0.0 | 84.5 | 11.6 |
| Western Sts Chiropractic C | 428 | 0.5 | 1.6 | 0.5 | 0.9 | 94.6 | 1.9 |
| Willamette U | 1,866 | 0.3 | 2.9 | 1.3 | 1.4 | 92.2 | 1.8 |
| **PENNSYLVANIA** | | | | | | | |
| Acad of the New Church | 156 | 0.0% | 0.0% | 0.0% | 0.0% | 83.3% | 16.7% |
| Albright C | 2,049 | 0.1 | 1.4 | 0.5 | 0.5 | 96.6 | 0.8 |
| Allegheny C | 1,955 | 0.0 | 1.3 | 2.5 | 0.7 | 93.2 | 2.2 |
| Allentown C of Saint Francis De Sales | 1,298 | 0.2 | 0.8 | 0.4 | 0.9 | 97.5 | 0.2 |
| Alliance C | 282 | 0.0 | 0.0 | 2.8 | 0.0 | 95.4 | 1.8 |
| Alvernia C | 729 | 0.1 | 0.3 | 2.5 | 1.1 | 94.8 | 1.2 |
| American C | 1,875 | 0.0 | 0.0 | 0.0 | 0.0 | 100.0 | 0.0 |
| Antonelli Inst of Art & Photography | 346 | 0.0 | 0.3 | 9.5 | 2.9 | 86.1 | 1.2 |
| Art Inst of Philadelphia | 1,339 | 0.1 | 2.0 | 18.5 | 2.2 | 76.4 | 0.8 |
| Art Inst of Pittsburgh | 1,961 | 0.2 | 0.7 | 11.4 | 0.8 | 86.9 | 0.0 |
| Baptist Bible C of Pa | 756 | 0.0 | 0.5 | 0.8 | 0.4 | 97.5 | 0.8 |
| Beaver C | 2,146 | 0.0 | 1.4 | 9.3 | 0.8 | 86.9 | 1.6 |
| Berean Inst | 172 | 0.0 | 0.0 | 88.4 | 6.4 | 1.2 | 4.1 |
| Bryn Mawr C | 1,782 | 0.3 | 7.0 | 3.6 | 2.0 | 80.6 | 6.5 |
| Bucknell U | 3,339 | 0.1 | 1.5 | 1.7 | 1.1 | 93.4 | 2.1 |
| Bucks County CC | 9,642 | 0.2 | 1.0 | 1.1 | 0.5 | 97.1 | 0.0 |
| Butler County CC | 2,109 | 0.0 | 0.1 | 0.7 | 0.0 | 99.2 | 0.0 |
| Cabrini C | 935 | 0.0 | 0.7 | 4.8 | 1.0 | 93.3 | 0.2 |
| Carlow C | 1,246 | 0.4 | 0.2 | 11.4 | 0.6 | 86.8 | 0.6 |
| Carnegie Mellon U | 6,251 | 0.1 | 3.5 | 1.6 | 0.5 | 90.4 | 3.8 |
| Cedar Crest C | 1,051 | 0.2 | 0.7 | 1.0 | 0.8 | 97.0 | 0.4 |
| Central Pennsylvania Business Sch | 722 | 0.3 | 0.1 | 2.8 | 0.4 | 95.8 | 0.6 |
| Chatham C | 536 | 0.0 | 0.6 | 12.1 | 0.6 | 85.1 | 1.7 |
| Chestnut Hill C | 1,184 | 0.0 | 0.0 | 7.0 | 6.0 | 86.0 | 1.0 |
| C Misericordia | 1,292 | 0.0 | 0.0 | 0.5 | 0.0 | 99.2 | 0.2 |
| Combs C of Music | 76 | 0.0 | 9.2 | 26.3 | 0.0 | 64.5 | 0.0 |
| CC of Allegheny County | | | | | | | |
| Allegheny | 7,474 | 0.5 | 1.1 | 22.5 | 0.5 | 74.4 | 1.0 |
| Boyce | 4,736 | 0.3 | 0.8 | 6.7 | 0.1 | 92.0 | 0.2 |
| North | 3,303 | 0.6 | 0.3 | 2.6 | 0.2 | 96.2 | 0.0 |
| South | 5,197 | 0.4 | 0.3 | 3.9 | 0.3 | 95.1 | 0.1 |
| CC of Beaver County | 2,377 | 0.0 | 0.2 | 5.8 | 0.0 | 94.0 | 0.0 |
| CC of Philadelphia | 14,965 | 0.5 | 5.0 | 52.4 | 4.1 | 38.0 | 0.0 |
| Curtis Inst of Music | 166 | 0.0 | 2.4 | 4.2 | 1.2 | 65.7 | 26.5 |
| Dean Inst of Tech | 162 | 0.0 | 0.0 | 8.6 | 0.0 | 91.4 | 0.0 |
| Delaware County CC | 7,254 | 0.1 | 0.8 | 4.7 | 0.3 | 94.1 | 0.0 |
| Delaware Valley C of Science and Ag | 1,534 | 0.0 | 0.0 | 4.0 | 0.0 | 96.0 | 0.0 |
| Dickinson C | 1,888 | 0.0 | 0.8 | 0.7 | 0.3 | 96.3 | 1.8 |
| Dickinson Sch of Law | 520 | 0.4 | 0.2 | 1.9 | 0.8 | 96.0 | 0.8 |
| Drexel U | 12,566 | 0.0 | 5.2 | 5.3 | 1.1 | 82.9 | 5.4 |
| Dropsie C | 50 | 0.0 | 6.0 | 2.0 | 0.0 | 90.0 | 2.0 |
| Duquesne U | 6,598 | 0.2 | 0.2 | 3.2 | 0.6 | 93.5 | 2.2 |
| Eastern Baptist Theol Sem | 391 | 0.0 | 2.6 | 14.6 | 6.1 | 71.9 | 4.9 |
| Eastern C | 937 | 0.2 | 2.0 | 7.0 | 1.3 | 86.7 | 2.8 |
| Electronic Inst-Harrisburg | 306 | 0.0 | 4.6 | 0.7 | 0.3 | 94.4 | 0.0 |
| Electronic Inst-Pittsburgh | 356 | 0.0 | 0.0 | 3.9 | 0.0 | 96.1 | 0.0 |
| Elizabethtown C | 1,788 | 0.1 | 1.0 | 1.2 | 0.1 | 96.9 | 0.7 |
| Erie Business Center | 321 | 0.0 | 0.0 | 5.3 | 0.0 | 94.7 | 0.0 |
| Evangelical Sch of Theol | 53 | 0.0 | 0.0 | 0.0 | 0.0 | 100.0 | 0.0 |
| Faith Theol Sem | 47 | 0.0 | 0.0 | 0.0 | 0.0 | 8.5 | 91.5 |
| Franklin and Marshall C | 2,793 | 0.0 | 1.9 | 2.1 | 0.8 | 93.7 | 1.5 |
| Gannon U | 4,185 | 0.4 | 0.4 | 2.3 | 0.5 | 94.0 | 2.5 |
| Geneva C | 1,225 | 0.2 | 1.0 | 3.6 | 0.2 | 93.3 | 1.7 |
| Gettysburg C | 1,951 | 0.1 | 0.4 | 0.5 | 0.6 | 97.2 | 1.2 |
| Gratz C | 309 | 0.0 | 0.0 | 2.9 | 0.0 | 94.8 | 2.3 |
| Grove City C | 2,184 | 0.1 | 0.2 | 0.1 | 0.1 | 98.4 | 1.0 |
| Gwynedd-Mercy C | 2,107 | 0.0 | 1.3 | 2.8 | 1.2 | 94.6 | 0.0 |
| Hahnemann U | 2,089 | 0.1 | 2.8 | 13.3 | 6.5 | 76.7 | 0.6 |
| Harcum JC | 983 | 0.3 | 0.8 | 11.5 | 0.8 | 85.7 | 0.9 |
| Harrisburg Area CC | 6,866 | 0.1 | 2.4 | 5.1 | 0.9 | 91.4 | 0.2 |
| Haverford C | 1,085 | 0.0 | 3.6 | 3.5 | 4.0 | 87.8 | 1.1 |
| Holy Family C | 1,528 | 0.0 | 0.7 | 2.2 | 1.2 | 95.9 | 0.1 |
| Hussian Sch of Art | 155 | 0.0 | 0.0 | 8.4 | 0.6 | 91.0 | 0.0 |
| Immaculata C | 1,836 | 0.0 | 0.5 | 1.1 | 1.1 | 94.8 | 2.4 |
| Juniata C | 1,185 | 0.0 | 1.1 | 0.3 | 0.1 | 97.0 | 1.4 |
| Keystone JC | 1,092 | 0.0 | 0.3 | 2.2 | 0.5 | 95.5 | 1.6 |
| King's C | 2,271 | 0.0 | 0.4 | 0.3 | 0.7 | 98.4 | 0.2 |
| Lackawanna JC | 1,060 | 0.2 | 0.2 | 1.3 | 0.5 | 97.8 | 0.0 |
| Lafayette C | 2,332 | 0.0 | 1.0 | 2.5 | 0.7 | 93.7 | 2.0 |
| Lancaster Bible C | 359 | 0.0 | 0.0 | 0.6 | 0.6 | 98.9 | 0.0 |
| Lancaster Theol Sem | 244 | 0.0 | 0.8 | 4.5 | 0.0 | 93.9 | 0.8 |
| LaRoche C | 1,780 | 0.0 | 0.3 | 2.8 | 0.4 | 96.4 | 0.1 |
| LaSalle U | 6,333 | 0.0 | 0.4 | 5.7 | 0.6 | 93.3 | 0.0 |
| Lebanon Valley C | 1,287 | 0.0 | 0.9 | 0.6 | 0.0 | 97.8 | 0.7 |
| Lehigh County CC | 3,306 | 0.2 | 1.6 | 1.1 | 1.7 | 95.1 | 0.4 |
| Lehigh U | 6,280 | 0.0 | 5.3 | 1.4 | 1.1 | 90.9 | 1.3 |
| Lincoln Tech Inst | 932 | 0.0 | 0.8 | 1.1 | 0.6 | 97.4 | 0.1 |
| Lincoln U | 1,167 | 0.0 | 0.2 | 90.0 | 0.8 | 5.1 | 4.0 |
| Lutheran Theol Sem | 247 | 0.4 | 0.0 | 1.2 | 0.0 | 97.6 | 0.8 |
| Lutheran Theol Sem-Philadelphia | 259 | 0.8 | 0.0 | 17.0 | 0.8 | 80.3 | 1.2 |
| Luzerne County CC | 4,259 | 0.1 | 0.3 | 1.0 | 0.2 | 98.5 | 0.0 |
| **PENNSYLVANIA—Continued** | | | | | | | |
| Lycoming C | 1,258 | 0.1% | 0.3% | 0.6% | 0.2% | 98.6% | 0.2% |
| Lyons Tech Inst | 98 | 0.0 | 0.0 | 51.0 | 5.1 | 43.9 | 0.0 |
| Manor JC | 450 | 0.0 | 0.4 | 6.0 | 0.7 | 92.2 | 0.7 |
| Mary Immaculate Sem | 48 | 0.0 | 0.0 | 0.0 | 0.0 | 97.9 | 2.1 |
| Marywood C | 3,207 | 0.0 | 0.1 | 0.4 | 0.2 | 98.3 | 1.1 |
| McCarrie Schs of Health Sciences and Tech | 251 | 0.0 | 2.4 | 50.6 | 1.2 | 45.8 | 0.0 |
| Median Sch of Allied Health Careers | 90 | 0.0 | 0.0 | 0.0 | 0.0 | 100.0 | 0.0 |
| Med C of Pennsylvania | 544 | 0.4 | 3.1 | 5.9 | 1.7 | 88.2 | 0.7 |
| Mercyhurst C | 1,643 | 0.1 | 0.3 | 4.1 | 0.2 | 94.3 | 1.0 |
| Messiah C | 1,761 | 0.0 | 0.6 | 1.6 | 0.9 | 94.9 | 1.9 |
| Montgomery County CC | 7,239 | 0.3 | 2.2 | 4.0 | 0.7 | 92.4 | 0.4 |
| Moore C of Art | 541 | 0.7 | 1.3 | 7.4 | 2.4 | 86.0 | 2.2 |
| Moravian C | 1,729 | 0.0 | 1.6 | 0.4 | 0.8 | 97.2 | 0.0 |
| Mount Aloysius JC | 551 | 0.0 | 0.2 | 4.4 | 0.2 | 95.3 | 0.0 |
| Muhlenberg C | 2,185 | 0.0 | 0.6 | 0.2 | 0.4 | 98.2 | 0.5 |
| National Education Center-Vale Tech Inst | 350 | 0.0 | 0.3 | 2.3 | 3.1 | 94.3 | 0.0 |
| Neumann C | 982 | 0.0 | 0.8 | 3.0 | 0.7 | 95.5 | 0.0 |
| New Sch of Music | 54 | 0.0 | 1.9 | 1.9 | 0.0 | 81.5 | 14.8 |
| Northampton County Area CC | 4,168 | 0.1 | 0.9 | 1.5 | 2.1 | 95.0 | 0.4 |
| Northeastern Christian JC | 207 | 0.0 | 0.0 | 38.6 | 1.0 | 58.0 | 2.4 |
| O S Johnson Sch of Tech | 537 | 0.0 | 0.6 | 0.2 | 0.0 | 99.3 | 0.0 |
| Peirce JC | 1,642 | 0.1 | 0.5 | 38.4 | 2.0 | 57.1 | 1.9 |
| Penn Tech Inst | 496 | 0.0 | 0.0 | 3.6 | 0.0 | 96.4 | 0.0 |
| Pennco Tech | 700 | 0.0 | 0.7 | 16.6 | 2.4 | 80.3 | 0.0 |
| Pa C of Optometry | 590 | 0.3 | 2.9 | 4.2 | 1.7 | 89.8 | 1.0 |
| Pa C of Podiatric Med | 458 | 0.4 | 1.1 | 4.1 | 0.4 | 93.0 | 0.9 |
| Pennsylvania Inst of Tech | 399 | 0.0 | 1.0 | 16.5 | 1.3 | 80.7 | 0.5 |
| Pennsylvania St U | | | | | | | |
| Main campus | 34,401 | 0.2 | 1.4 | 3.4 | 0.8 | 91.0 | 3.3 |
| Allentown | 482 | 0.2 | 2.9 | 0.4 | 0.8 | 95.6 | 0.0 |
| Altoona | 2,081 | 0.2 | 0.4 | 2.9 | 0.2 | 96.2 | 0.0 |
| Beaver | 1,142 | 0.3 | 0.5 | 4.6 | 0.4 | 94.2 | 0.1 |
| Behrend | 1,989 | 0.2 | 0.6 | 3.7 | 0.4 | 95.1 | 0.1 |
| Berks | 1,092 | 0.0 | 1.8 | 0.6 | 0.7 | 96.8 | 0.0 |
| Capitol | 2,595 | 0.0 | 1.9 | 2.7 | 0.4 | 94.7 | 0.2 |
| Delaware | 1,504 | 0.3 | 1.0 | 6.8 | 0.5 | 91.4 | 0.1 |
| DuBois | 868 | 0.2 | 0.2 | 0.3 | 0.2 | 99.0 | 0.0 |
| Fayette | 835 | 0.1 | 0.0 | 2.6 | 0.1 | 97.1 | 0.0 |
| Hazleton | 1,105 | 0.1 | 1.1 | 0.7 | 0.3 | 97.6 | 0.2 |
| King of Prussia Graduate Center | 533 | 0.4 | 4.5 | 4.9 | 0.8 | 89.5 | 0.0 |
| McKeesport | 1,449 | 0.0 | 0.8 | 5.2 | 0.6 | 93.4 | 0.0 |
| Hershey Med Center | 757 | 0.1 | 1.6 | 1.6 | 1.8 | 93.9 | 0.9 |
| Mont Alto | 797 | 0.3 | 2.8 | 1.5 | 0.5 | 95.0 | 0.0 |
| New Kensington | 1,270 | 0.2 | 0.5 | 0.9 | 0.2 | 98.2 | 0.0 |
| Ogontz | 3,492 | 0.0 | 1.8 | 6.5 | 0.6 | 91.0 | 0.0 |
| Schuylkill | 951 | 0.2 | 0.8 | 1.1 | 0.8 | 97.1 | 0.0 |
| Shenango Valley | 1,067 | 0.1 | 0.2 | 3.2 | 0.1 | 96.4 | 0.0 |
| Wilkes-Barre | 686 | 0.0 | 0.1 | 0.1 | 0.0 | 99.7 | 0.0 |
| Worthington Scranton | 1,202 | 0.1 | 0.7 | 0.4 | 0.2 | 98.7 | 0.0 |
| York | 1,111 | 0.2 | 2.8 | 1.8 | 0.2 | 95.0 | 0.1 |
| Philadelphia C of Art | 1,527 | 0.1 | 3.1 | 8.3 | 2.4 | 84.2 | 1.8 |
| Philadelphia C of the Bible | 541 | 0.0 | 1.5 | 5.4 | 0.9 | 90.6 | 1.7 |
| Philadelphia C of Osteopathic Med | 833 | 0.1 | 0.8 | 2.2 | 0.4 | 96.4 | 0.1 |
| Philadelphia C of the Performing Arts | 414 | 0.0 | 0.7 | 21.0 | 2.9 | 70.3 | 5.1 |
| Philadelphia C of Pharmacy and Science | 1,111 | 0.1 | 3.5 | 2.3 | 0.7 | 90.8 | 2.6 |
| Philadelphia C of Textiles and Science | 2,746 | 0.0 | 0.6 | 11.2 | 0.8 | 81.3 | 6.1 |
| Pittsburgh Inst of Aeronautics | 440 | 0.0 | 0.0 | 1.4 | 0.9 | 97.7 | 0.0 |
| Pittsburgh Tech Inst | 254 | 0.0 | 0.0 | 6.3 | 0.0 | 93.3 | 0.4 |
| Pittsburgh Theol Sem | 399 | 0.0 | 0.8 | 5.0 | 0.0 | 93.0 | 1.3 |
| Point Park C | 2,594 | 0.0 | 0.0 | 6.9 | 0.0 | 84.9 | 8.2 |
| Reading Area CC | 1,384 | 1.2 | 2.0 | 4.7 | 4.2 | 87.9 | 0.0 |
| Robert Morris C | 5,714 | 0.2 | 0.1 | 4.9 | 0.1 | 93.6 | 1.0 |
| Rosemont C | 559 | 0.7 | 0.9 | 2.1 | 3.2 | 93.0 | 0.0 |
| Saint Charles Borromeo Sem | 495 | 0.0 | 0.6 | 0.6 | 1.2 | 97.6 | 0.0 |
| Saint Francis C | 1,615 | 0.0 | 0.2 | 1.2 | 0.2 | 98.0 | 0.4 |
| Saint Joseph's U | 5,760 | 0.0 | 1.2 | 6.1 | 1.5 | 88.1 | 3.0 |
| Saint Vincent C and Sem | 1,226 | 0.0 | 0.0 | 1.1 | 0.9 | 96.8 | 1.2 |
| Seton Hill C | 870 | 0.1 | 1.1 | 2.9 | 4.9 | 89.9 | 1.0 |
| Spring Garden C | 1,255 | 0.2 | 1.4 | 5.8 | 0.8 | 88.4 | 3.5 |
| St System of Higher Ed | | | | | | | |
| Bloomsburg U | 6,189 | 0.1 | 0.3 | 2.4 | 0.3 | 96.7 | 0.1 |
| California U | 5,085 | 0.2 | 0.4 | 5.8 | 0.3 | 93.1 | 0.2 |
| Cheney U | 1,795 | 0.7 | 3.5 | 90.8 | 0.1 | 1.4 | 3.6 |
| Clarion U | | | | | | | |
| Main campus | 5,297 | 0.1 | 0.1 | 2.6 | 0.2 | 94.2 | 2.8 |
| Venango | 591 | 0.0 | 0.3 | 0.3 | 0.0 | 99.2 | 0.2 |
| East Stroudsburg U | 4,235 | 0.1 | 0.5 | 2.5 | 0.9 | 94.8 | 1.2 |
| Edinboro U | 6,053 | 0.3 | 0.4 | 4.0 | 0.3 | 93.8 | 1.2 |
| Indiana U | 12,806 | 0.0 | 0.3 | 4.6 | 0.3 | 93.4 | 1.3 |
| Kutztown U | 6,001 | 0.1 | 0.7 | 2.3 | 0.6 | 95.8 | 0.5 |
| Lock Haven U | 2,624 | 0.0 | 0.3 | 2.5 | 0.4 | 94.7 | 2.1 |
| Mansfield U | 2,939 | 0.0 | 0.1 | 3.0 | 0.1 | 95.5 | 1.3 |
| Millersville U | 6,770 | 0.1 | 1.8 | 3.4 | 0.8 | 93.1 | 0.8 |
| Shippensburg U | 6,121 | 0.2 | 0.5 | 3.5 | 0.5 | 94.7 | 0.5 |
| Slippery Rock U | 6,479 | 0.1 | 0.2 | 2.7 | 0.3 | 95.7 | 1.0 |
| West Chester U | 9,528 | 0.1 | 0.9 | 6.3 | 0.4 | 91.4 | 0.9 |
| Susquehanna U | 1,789 | 0.1 | 0.2 | 0.7 | 0.2 | 98.4 | 0.3 |
| Swarthmore C | 1,326 | 0.1 | 4.2 | 6.9 | 1.4 | 82.1 | 5.3 |
| Temple U | 28,772 | 0.3 | 2.6 | 15.1 | 1.8 | 78.6 | 1.5 |
| Thaddeus Stevens St Sch of Tech | 264 | 0.0 | 3.0 | 2.7 | 1.9 | 92.4 | 0.0 |
| Thiel C | 875 | 0.0 | 0.7 | 3.8 | 0.5 | 93.8 | 1.3 |
| Thomas Jefferson U | 2,015 | 0.3 | 3.2 | 4.9 | 1.3 | 89.5 | 0.7 |
| Tracey-Warner Sch | 94 | 0.0 | 3.2 | 57.4 | 4.3 | 34.0 | 1.1 |
| Triangle Inst of Tech | 249 | 0.0 | 0.0 | 25.3 | 0.0 | 73.9 | 0.8 |
| Triangle Inst of Tech-Erie | 210 | 0.0 | 1.4 | 9.0 | 1.0 | 88.6 | 0.0 |
| Triangle Inst of Tech-Greensburg | 171 | 0.0 | 0.0 | 0.0 | 0.0 | 99.4 | 0.6 |
| Trinity Episcopal Sch for the Ministry | 103 | 0.0 | 0.0 | 0.0 | 1.0 | 94.2 | 4.9 |
| United Wesleyan C | 223 | 0.4 | 0.4 | 1.3 | 4.5 | 92.4 | 0.9 |
| U of Pennsylvania | 22,065 | 0.3 | 3.4 | 5.0 | 1.7 | 80.5 | 9.1 |
| U of Pittsburgh | | | | | | | |
| Main campus | 29,197 | 0.1 | 1.6 | 8.1 | 0.5 | 85.0 | 4.7 |
| Bradford | 974 | 0.2 | 0.4 | 3.8 | 0.1 | 95.2 | 0.3 |
| Greensburg | 1,471 | 0.0 | 0.3 | 0.8 | 0.1 | 98.8 | 0.0 |
| Johnstown | 3,223 | 0.0 | 0.4 | 1.0 | 0.2 | 98.4 | 0.0 |
| Titusville | 323 | 0.0 | 0.3 | 0.9 | 0.0 | 98.8 | [illegible] |
| U of Scranton | 4,684 | 0.0 | 0.1 | 0.2 | 0.0 | 97.4 | [illegible] |
| Ursinus C | 2,136 | 0.0 | 1.2 | 0.2 | 0.2 | 98.0 | 0.4 |
| Valley Forge Christian C | 601 | 0.0 | 0.0 | 3.8 | 1.5 | 88.9 | 5.8 |
| Valley Forge Military JC | 151 | 0.0 | 2.0 | 9.3 | 1.3 | [illegible] | 10.6 |
| Villa Maria C | 668 | 0.0 | 0.3 | 1.9 | 0.3 | [illegible] | 0.0 |
| Villanova U | 11,665 | 0.3 | 1.1 | 1.3 | 0.7 | [illegible] | 0.0 |
| Washington and Jefferson C | 1,227 | 0.0 | 0.6 | 1.4 | [illegible] | 97.1 | 0.7 |
| Waynesburg C | 821 | 0.0 | 0.9 | 5.8 | [illegible] | 89.8 | 3.5 |
| Westminster C | 1,344 | 0.1 | 0.0 | 0.7 | 0.2 | 98.7 | 0.4 |
| Westminster Theol Sem | 476 | 0.0 | 11.8 | 3.2 | 0.8 | 71.6 | 12.6 |
| Westmoreland County CC | 3,496 | 0.3 | 0.1 | 1.1 | 0.1 | 98.4 | 0.0 |
| Widener U | | | | | | | |
| Pennsylvania campus | 5,665 | 0.2 | 0.1 | 7.5 | 0.2 | 91.3 | 0.7 |
| Brandywine C | 737 | 0.0 | 0.0 | 6.0 | 0.0 | 93.8 | 0.3 |
| Delaware Law Sch | 885 | 0.2 | 0.1 | 2.5 | 0.7 | 96.5 | 0.0 |
| Wilkes C | 2,731 | 0.0 | 0.8 | 0.7 | 0.2 | 97.7 | 0.6 |

| | Total | American Indian | Asian | Black | Hispanic | White | Foreign |
|---|---|---|---|---|---|---|---|
| **PENNSYLVANIA—Continued** | | | | | | | |
| Williamson Free Sch | 104 | 0.0% | 0.0% | 2.9% | 0.0% | 97.1% | 0.0% |
| Williamsport Area CC | 4,084 | 0.1 | 0.3 | 0.9 | 0.1 | 98.6 | 0.0 |
| Wilson C | 310 | 0.0 | 1.0 | 4.2 | 2.9 | 84.2 | 7.7 |
| York C of Pennsylvania | 4,570 | 0.0 | 0.0 | 2.1 | 0.4 | 97.2 | 0.4 |
| **RHODE ISLAND** | | | | | | | |
| Barrington C | 442 | 0.5% | 0.9% | 4.8% | 1.8% | 91.2% | 0.9% |
| Brown U | 7,099 | 0.1 | 5.3 | 6.0 | 2.8 | 80.6 | 5.2 |
| Bryant C | 6,505 | 0.0 | 0.3 | 0.3 | 0.2 | 98.4 | 0.7 |
| CC of Rhode Island | 12,317 | 0.3 | 1.2 | 4.0 | 1.4 | 93.2 | 0.0 |
| Johnson and Wales C | 5,786 | 0.3 | 0.8 | 6.6 | 3.4 | 88.5 | 0.4 |
| New England Inst of Tech | 1,505 | 0.0 | 0.6 | 2.5 | 0.8 | 96.1 | 0.0 |
| Providence C | 5,679 | 0.1 | 0.0 | 1.0 | 0.3 | 98.1 | 0.6 |
| Rhode Island C | 8,574 | 0.4 | 0.9 | 3.0 | 1.7 | 93.7 | 0.3 |
| Rhode Island Sch of Design | 1,792 | 0.2 | 2.1 | 1.1 | 1.3 | 84.3 | 11.0 |
| Roger Williams C | | | | | | | |
| Main campus | 2,531 | 0.0 | 0.7 | 1.5 | 1.7 | 90.1 | 6.0 |
| Providence | 1,232 | 0.0 | 0.4 | 1.9 | 2.0 | 95.0 | 0.7 |
| Salve Regina-the Newport C | 2,087 | 0.0 | 0.5 | 0.6 | 0.7 | 97.2 | 1.0 |
| U of Rhode Island | 13,616 | 0.2 | 1.2 | 1.6 | 0.8 | 93.3 | 2.9 |
| **SOUTH CAROLINA** | | | | | | | |
| Aiken Tech C | 1,032 | 0.3% | 0.5% | 25.8% | 0.4% | 73.1% | 0.0% |
| Anderson C | 1,165 | 0.0 | 0.3 | 7.0 | 0.5 | 91.0 | 1.1 |
| Baptist C at Charleston | 1,649 | 0.1 | 0.8 | 20.9 | 0.8 | 74.2 | 3.2 |
| Beaufort Tech C | 1,187 | 0.5 | 0.5 | 42.4 | 0.7 | 54.3 | 1.6 |
| Benedict C | 1,495 | 0.1 | 0.0 | 96.9 | 0.0 | 0.0 | 3.1 |
| Central Wesleyan C | 397 | 0.0 | 0.0 | 10.8 | 0.0 | 87.4 | 1.8 |
| Chesterfield-Marlboro Tech C | 602 | 1.2 | 0.0 | 28.7 | 0.0 | 69.8 | 0.3 |
| Citadel Military C of SC | 3,048 | 0.1 | 0.5 | 6.7 | 0.4 | 91.1 | 1.1 |
| Claflin C | 653 | 0.0 | 0.0 | 98.8 | 0.0 | 0.9 | 0.3 |
| Clemson U | 12,926 | 0.1 | 0.2 | 4.7 | 0.3 | 91.4 | 3.3 |
| Clinton JC | 95 | 0.0 | 0.0 | 100.0 | 0.0 | 0.0 | 0.0 |
| Coker C | 320 | 0.0 | 0.6 | 14.1 | 0.3 | 84.1 | 0.9 |
| C of Charleston | 5,395 | 0.1 | 0.9 | 7.1 | 0.4 | 89.9 | 1.6 |
| Columbia Bible C | 885 | 0.1 | 0.3 | 1.5 | 0.7 | 91.1 | 6.3 |
| Columbia C | 1,186 | 0.1 | 0.8 | 20.5 | 0.3 | 77.3 | 0.9 |
| Columbia JC of Business | 515 | 0.0 | 0.0 | 75.7 | 0.2 | 24.1 | 0.0 |
| Converse C | 1,050 | 0.4 | 0.2 | 6.3 | 0.1 | 92.8 | 0.3 |
| Denmark Tech C | 657 | 0.0 | 0.0 | 97.4 | 0.3 | 2.3 | 0.0 |
| Erskine C and Sem | 636 | 0.2 | 0.2 | 7.1 | 0.6 | 90.4 | 1.6 |
| Florence Darlington Tech C | 1,986 | 0.2 | 0.3 | 27.2 | 0.3 | 72.1 | 0.1 |
| Francis Marion C | 3,232 | 0.1 | 0.2 | 13.5 | 0.2 | 85.9 | 0.1 |
| Furman U | 2,969 | 0.0 | 0.3 | 3.2 | 0.5 | 95.9 | 0.0 |
| Greenville Tech C | 6,007 | 0.0 | 0.4 | 14.1 | 0.4 | 84.5 | 0.6 |
| Horry-Georgetown Tech C | 1,304 | 0.1 | 1.6 | 20.8 | 0.2 | 76.7 | 0.7 |
| Lander C | 2,281 | 0.4 | 0.2 | 15.7 | 0.4 | 83.0 | 0.4 |
| Limestone C | 1,151 | 0.0 | 0.5 | 17.9 | 0.1 | 81.1 | 0.4 |
| Lutheran Theol S Sem | 168 | 0.0 | 0.0 | 13.1 | 0.0 | 86.9 | 0.0 |
| Med U of SC | 2,033 | 0.0 | 1.6 | 4.5 | 0.3 | 91.9 | 1.5 |
| Midlands Tech C | 4,980 | 0.1 | 1.3 | 27.2 | 3.5 | 67.7 | 0.1 |
| Morris C | 600 | 0.0 | 0.0 | 99.8 | 0.0 | 0.2 | 0.0 |
| Newberry C | 625 | 0.0 | 0.2 | 15.8 | 0.2 | 83.7 | 0.2 |
| Nielsen Electronics Inst | 291 | 0.0 | 6.2 | 67.0 | 0.0 | 26.8 | 0.0 |
| North Greenville C | 501 | 0.0 | 0.0 | 11.6 | 0.0 | 88.4 | 0.0 |
| Orangeburg Calhoun Tech C | 1,307 | 0.7 | 0.1 | 45.4 | 0.0 | 53.9 | 0.0 |
| Piedmont Tech C | 1,580 | 0.3 | 0.4 | 28.4 | 0.4 | 70.5 | 0.0 |
| Presbyterian C | 897 | 0.2 | 0.2 | 4.1 | 0.2 | 94.4 | 0.8 |
| Rutledge C-Columbia | 504 | 0.0 | 0.2 | 85.1 | 0.2 | 14.5 | 0.0 |
| Rutledge C-Greenville | 347 | 0.0 | 0.0 | 55.0 | 0.0 | 45.0 | 0.0 |
| Rutledge C-Spartanburg | 383 | 0.0 | 0.0 | 50.1 | 0.3 | 48.6 | 1.0 |
| Sherman C of Straight Chiropractic | 346 | 0.6 | 0.9 | 1.2 | 1.2 | 87.6 | 8.7 |
| South Carolina St C | 4,226 | 0.0 | 0.0 | 92.7 | 0.0 | 6.5 | 0.8 |
| Spartanburg Methodist C | 1,006 | 0.0 | 0.0 | 19.2 | 0.4 | 80.1 | 0.3 |
| Spartanburg Tech C | 1,653 | 0.2 | 0.5 | 13.6 | 0.4 | 85.0 | 0.4 |
| Sumter Area Tech C | 1,620 | 0.5 | 0.5 | 41.0 | 1.7 | 56.2 | 0.0 |
| Tri-County Tech C | 2,162 | 0.5 | 0.6 | 11.5 | 0.6 | 86.0 | 0.7 |
| Trident Tech C | 4,685 | 0.3 | 1.4 | 21.1 | 1.0 | 75.7 | 0.5 |
| U of South Carolina | | | | | | | |
| Aiken | 1,936 | 0.2 | 0.5 | 14.5 | 0.4 | 84.0 | 0.5 |
| Beaufort | 753 | 0.3 | 0.4 | 16.3 | 2.8 | 80.1 | 0.1 |
| Coastal Carolina | 2,627 | 0.2 | 0.6 | 7.5 | 0.5 | 90.3 | 0.9 |
| Columbia | 23,301 | 0.1 | 0.8 | 13.0 | 0.6 | 81.3 | 4.1 |
| Lancaster | 847 | 0.2 | 0.0 | 15.0 | 0.1 | 84.7 | 0.0 |
| Salkehatchie | 446 | 0.0 | 0.4 | 21.5 | 0.4 | 77.6 | 0.0 |
| Spartanburg | 2,606 | 0.2 | 0.9 | 10.7 | 0.7 | 87.3 | 0.2 |
| Sumter | 1,160 | 0.1 | 1.0 | 17.8 | 0.7 | 79.8 | 0.5 |
| Union | 324 | 0.0 | 0.0 | 17.9 | 0.0 | 82.1 | 0.0 |
| Vorhees C | 560 | 0.0 | 0.0 | 98.7 | 0.0 | 0.4 | 0.9 |
| Williamsburg Tech C | 357 | 0.0 | 0.0 | 46.5 | 0.0 | 53.5 | 0.0 |
| Winthrop C | 5,055 | 0.2 | 0.5 | 14.0 | 0.6 | 83.9 | 0.9 |
| Wofford C | 1,046 | 0.2 | 0.8 | 8.0 | 0.3 | 89.9 | 0.9 |
| York Tech C | 1,898 | 0.4 | 0.4 | 19.2 | 0.0 | 80.0 | 0.1 |
| **SOUTH DAKOTA** | | | | | | | |
| Augustana C | 1,914 | 0.6% | 0.4% | 0.6% | 0.1% | 96.0% | 2.3% |
| Black Hill St C | 1,825 | 5.0 | 0.4 | 0.4 | 0.9 | 92.5 | 0.7 |
| North Central U CC Center | 298 | 0.0 | 0.0 | 0.0 | 0.0 | 100.0 | 0.0 |
| Dakota St C | 977 | 0.4 | 0.4 | 1.1 | 0.3 | 96.4 | 1.3 |
| Dakota Wesleyan U | 571 | 8.6 | 1.2 | 2.3 | 0.4 | 85.8 | 1.8 |
| Freeman JC | 54 | 1.9 | 0.0 | 1.9 | 0.0 | 90.7 | 5.6 |
| Huron C | 369 | 6.5 | 0.5 | 12.5 | 1.4 | 78.3 | 0.8 |
| Mount Marty C | 722 | 0.4 | 0.4 | 1.5 | 0.1 | 97.5 | 0.0 |
| National C | 2,712 | 4.6 | 1.5 | 6.5 | 9.2 | 76.9 | 1.3 |
| N American Baptist Sem | 138 | 0.0 | 0.7 | 0.7 | 0.0 | 86.2 | 12.3 |
| Northern St C | 2,718 | 1.6 | 0.1 | 0.1 | 0.2 | 97.5 | 0.4 |
| Oglala Lakota C | 752 | 90.2 | 0.0 | 0.0 | 0.0 | 9.8 | 0.0 |
| Presentation C | 356 | 11.8 | 0.8 | 0.6 | 0.8 | 84.3 | 1.7 |
| Sinte Gleska C | 444 | 72.7 | 0.0 | 0.0 | 0.0 | 27.3 | 0.0 |
| Sioux Falls C | 872 | 0.5 | 0.1 | 0.9 | 0.2 | 96.8 | 1.5 |
| SD Sch of Mines and Tech | 2,583 | 1.0 | 1.2 | 0.5 | 0.4 | 90.1 | 6.7 |
| South Dakota St U | 8,117 | 0.5 | 0.1 | 0.0 | 0.1 | 94.6 | 4.6 |
| U of South Dakota | 7,051 | 2.1 | 0.2 | 0.4 | 0.1 | 97.0 | 0.2 |
| **TENNESSEE** | | | | | | | |
| American Baptist Theol Sem | 126 | 0.0% | 0.0% | 87.3% | 0.0% | 0.0% | 12.7% |
| Aquinas JC | 361 | 0.0 | 0.0 | 8.3 | 0.0 | 90.6 | 1.1 |
| Belmont C | 2,125 | 0.1 | 0.0 | 3.4 | 0.6 | 91.0 | 4.8 |
| Bethel C | 520 | 0.0 | 0.0 | 9.4 | 0.0 | 86.7 | 3.8 |
| Bristol C | 588 | 0.0 | 0.2 | 2.6 | 0.0 | 97.3 | 0.0 |
| Bryan C | 506 | 0.2 | 0.6 | 1.6 | 0.0 | 95.3 | 2.4 |
| Carson-Newman C | 1,716 | 0.0 | 0.4 | 6.6 | 0.1 | 92.8 | 0.0 |
| Christian Brothers C | 1,540 | 0.1 | 1.1 | 20.5 | 0.6 | 72.3 | 5.5 |
| Church of God Sch of Theol | 184 | 0.0 | 0.0 | 3.8 | 4.9 | 80.4 | 10.9 |
| Cooper Inst | 168 | 0.0 | 0.0 | 41.1 | 0.0 | 58.9 | 0.0 |
| David Lipscomb C | 2,311 | 0.1 | 0.3 | 2.7 | 0.3 | 95.8 | 0.9 |
| Draughon's JC | 783 | 0.0 | 0.0 | 78.2 | 0.0 | 21.6 | 0.3 |
| Draughon's JC-Knoxville | 1,741 | 0.0 | 0.0 | 13.9 | 1.4 | 84.2 | 0.5 |
| Draughon's JC of Business | 545 | 0.0 | 0.0 | 36.3 | 0.6 | 59.1 | 4.0 |
| Emmanuel Sch of Religion | 132 | 0.0 | 0.0 | 0.0 | 0.0 | 91.7 | 8.3 |
| Free Will Baptist Bible C | 421 | 0.2 | 0.0 | 0.7 | 0.2 | 98.1 | 0.7 |
| Freed-Hardeman C | 1,071 | 0.1 | 0.0 | 5.8 | 0.1 | 92.4 | 1.6 |
| Hiwassee C | 956 | 0.0 | 0.0 | 3.6 | 0.0 | 94.2 | 2.2 |
| John A Gupton C | 34 | 0.0 | 0.0 | 23.5 | 0.0 | 76.5 | 0.0 |
| Johnson Bible C | 376 | 0.0 | 0.0 | 1.3 | 0.3 | 97.1 | 1.3 |
| King C | 547 | 0.0 | 1.3 | 0.2 | 0.4 | 88.1 | 10.1 |
| Knoxville Business C | 270 | 0.0 | 3.0 | 34.4 | 1.9 | 60.7 | 0.0 |
| Knoxville C | 560 | 0.0 | 0.0 | 93.9 | 0.2 | 1.8 | 4.1 |
| Lambuth C | 625 | 0.0 | 0.6 | 14.6 | 0.3 | 81.4 | 3.0 |
| Lane C | 690 | 0.0 | 0.0 | 98.3 | 0.0 | 0.1 | 1.6 |
| **TENNESSEE—Continued** | | | | | | | |
| LeMoyne-Owen C | 844 | 0.0% | 0.0% | 98.0% | 0.0% | 0.0% | 2.0% |
| Lee C | 1,154 | 1.0 | 0.0 | 5.4 | 4.7 | 85.2 | 3.7 |
| Lincoln Memorial U | 1,425 | 0.1 | 0.0 | 2.0 | 0.1 | 89.6 | 8.2 |
| Martin C | 290 | 0.0 | 0.0 | 15.2 | 0.0 | 78.3 | 6.6 |
| Maryville C | 594 | 0.0 | 0.2 | 5.7 | 0.5 | 88.0 | 5.6 |
| McKenzie C | 376 | 0.0 | 0.3 | 23.9 | 0.3 | 74.5 | 1.1 |
| Meharry Med C | 715 | 0.7 | 2.8 | 79.7 | 2.4 | 6.0 | 8.4 |
| Memphis Acad of Arts | 244 | 0.0 | 0.0 | 20.1 | 0.8 | 73.4 | 5.7 |
| Memphis Theol Sem | 164 | 0.0 | 0.0 | 29.3 | 0.0 | 69.5 | 1.2 |
| Mid-America Baptist Theol Sem | 466 | 0.0 | 0.0 | 1.3 | 0.0 | 98.3 | 0.4 |
| Mid-South Bible C | 162 | 0.6 | 0.0 | 29.6 | 0.0 | 68.5 | 1.2 |
| Milligan C | 610 | 0.0 | 0.3 | 1.1 | 0.2 | 96.9 | 1.5 |
| Morristown C | 178 | 0.0 | 0.0 | 92.7 | 0.0 | 0.0 | 7.3 |
| O'More C of Design | 130 | 0.0 | 0.0 | 0.8 | 1.5 | 97.7 | 0.0 |
| Rhodes C | 1,046 | 0.0 | 1.2 | 3.5 | 0.4 | 93.9 | 1.0 |
| Scarritt C | 96 | 0.0 | 1.0 | 6.3 | 3.1 | 85.4 | 4.2 |
| Southern C of Optometry | 422 | 0.7 | 1.7 | 1.9 | 2.8 | 92.2 | 0.7 |
| Southern C of Seventh-Day Adventists | 1,622 | 0.4 | 2.2 | 8.3 | 5.2 | 81.3 | 2.7 |
| St U & CC Sys of Tennessee | | | | | | | |
| Austin Peay St U | 5,282 | 0.3 | 1.1 | 15.9 | 2.1 | 78.9 | 1.6 |
| East Tennessee St U | 9,869 | 0.3 | 0.6 | 2.7 | 0.3 | 95.2 | 1.0 |
| Memphis St U | 21,296 | 0.1 | 0.4 | 18.6 | 0.2 | 77.8 | 2.9 |
| Middle Tennessee St U | 11,236 | 0.2 | 0.2 | 7.3 | 0.3 | 88.9 | 3.1 |
| Tennessee St U | 7,646 | 0.2 | 1.1 | 65.1 | 0.2 | 31.0 | 2.4 |
| Tennessee Tech U | 7,494 | 0.1 | 0.7 | 1.9 | 0.1 | 93.1 | 4.0 |
| Chattanooga St Tech CC | 4,728 | 0.4 | 0.4 | 11.3 | 0.3 | 87.5 | 0.1 |
| Cleveland St CC | 3,102 | 0.3 | 0.8 | 3.3 | 0.5 | 95.1 | 0.0 |
| Columbia St CC | 2,556 | 0.1 | 0.1 | 5.9 | 0.2 | 93.6 | 0.2 |
| Dyersburg St CC | 1,618 | 0.0 | 0.2 | 12.2 | 0.1 | 87.5 | 0.1 |
| Jackson St CC | 2,776 | 0.0 | 0.0 | 12.4 | 0.0 | 87.6 | 0.0 |
| Motlow St CC | 2,451 | 0.2 | 0.2 | 5.1 | 0.2 | 94.3 | 0.0 |
| Nashville St Tech Inst | 4,946 | 0.2 | 1.3 | 13.7 | 0.6 | 84.1 | 0.1 |
| Roane St CC | 3,521 | 0.2 | 0.8 | 3.0 | 0.2 | 95.8 | 0.0 |
| St Tech Inst Memphis | 6,780 | 0.4 | 0.7 | 31.7 | 0.7 | 66.4 | 0.1 |
| Shelby St CC | 4,674 | 0.1 | 0.3 | 57.6 | 0.3 | 41.7 | 0.0 |
| Tri-Cities St Tech Inst | 1,733 | 0.0 | 0.0 | 2.2 | 0.0 | 97.8 | 0.0 |
| Volunteer St CC | 3,323 | 0.2 | 0.4 | 3.1 | 0.6 | 95.6 | 0.0 |
| Walters St CC | 4,023 | 0.0 | 0.2 | 3.1 | 0.2 | 96.1 | 0.3 |
| Tenn Inst of Electronics | 216 | 0.0 | 0.0 | 0.9 | 0.5 | 98.6 | 0.0 |
| Tennessee Temple U | 2,496 | 0.1 | 0.0 | 2.1 | 1.1 | 95.9 | 0.7 |
| Tennessee Wesleyan C | 432 | 1.2 | 0.0 | 4.4 | 0.5 | 90.0 | 3.9 |
| Tomlinson C | 246 | 0.4 | 1.6 | 7.7 | 1.2 | 82.1 | 6.9 |
| Tusculum C | 382 | 0.0 | 0.0 | 11.0 | 0.0 | 86.9 | 2.1 |
| Union U | 1,458 | 0.0 | 0.0 | 4.4 | 0.0 | 95.4 | 0.2 |
| U of the South | 1,158 | 0.0 | 0.2 | 2.5 | 0.4 | 95.6 | 1.3 |
| U of Tennessee | | | | | | | |
| Ctr for Health Sciences | 1,883 | 0.1 | 2.8 | 3.0 | 0.5 | 93.1 | 0.5 |
| Chattanooga | 7,464 | 0.3 | 0.7 | 11.3 | 0.5 | 84.9 | 2.3 |
| Knoxville | 26,158 | 0.2 | 0.8 | 4.4 | 0.3 | 90.9 | 3.4 |
| Martin | 5,366 | 0.2 | 0.5 | 13.6 | 0.2 | 80.9 | 4.6 |
| Vanderbilt U | 9,046 | 0.1 | 1.0 | 3.4 | 0.5 | 89.9 | 5.1 |
| **TEXAS** | | | | | | | |
| Abilene Christian U | 4,617 | 0.2% | 0.7% | 3.2% | 0.9% | 91.0% | 4.0% |
| Alvin CC | 4,070 | 0.4 | 0.6 | 11.6 | 9.8 | 76.8 | 0.9 |
| Amarillo C | 6,151 | 0.9 | 3.2 | 3.4 | 7.0 | 84.3 | 1.2 |
| Amber U | 864 | 1.6 | 0.7 | 13.3 | 2.4 | 74.8 | 7.2 |
| American Tech U | 492 | 1.2 | 2.2 | 18.3 | 8.1 | 69.1 | 1.0 |
| Angelina C | 2,391 | 0.2 | 0.3 | 16.3 | 1.8 | 81.5 | 0.0 |
| Angelo St U | 6,162 | 0.2 | 0.6 | 3.9 | 10.2 | 83.3 | 1.7 |
| Austin C | 1,173 | 0.3 | 2.2 | 2.7 | 4.6 | 89.0 | 1.1 |
| Austin CC | 17,807 | 0.4 | 2.8 | 6.9 | 12.8 | 74.7 | 2.3 |
| Austin Presbyterian Theol Sem | 177 | 0.0 | 1.7 | 3.4 | 2.3 | 91.5 | 1.1 |
| Bauder Fashion C | 476 | 0.6 | 1.3 | 11.3 | 6.1 | 80.5 | 0.2 |
| Baylor C of Dentistry | 607 | 0.5 | 3.0 | 1.2 | 4.4 | 90.4 | 0.5 |
| Baylor C of Med | 899 | 0.3 | 6.2 | 2.4 | 7.0 | 80.0 | 4.0 |
| Baylor U | 10,943 | 0.4 | 1.4 | 1.8 | 2.1 | 92.6 | 1.6 |
| Bee County C | 2,240 | 0.5 | 0.4 | 3.0 | 44.0 | 51.6 | 0.4 |
| Bishop C | 1,107 | 0.0 | 0.0 | 66.6 | 0.0 | 0.0 | 33.4 |
| Blinn C | 3,499 | 0.4 | 0.7 | 6.9 | 6.1 | 82.3 | 3.7 |
| Brazosport C | 3,576 | 0.2 | 0.9 | 7.0 | 9.8 | 81.2 | 1.0 |
| Central Texas C | 5,777 | 0.4 | 2.2 | 19.7 | 9.0 | 67.9 | 0.7 |
| Cisco JC | 1,774 | 1.1 | 0.3 | 6.6 | 6.3 | 85.6 | 0.1 |
| Clarendon C | 723 | 0.1 | 0.4 | 4.0 | 1.0 | 94.5 | 0.0 |
| C of the Mainland | 2,901 | 0.7 | 2.1 | 14.2 | 9.0 | 72.5 | 1.5 |
| Concordia Lutheran C | 463 | 0.9 | 0.2 | 3.9 | 7.3 | 84.2 | 3.5 |
| Cooke County C | 1,687 | 0.6 | 0.8 | 2.8 | 2.0 | 93.4 | 0.4 |
| Criswell Center for Biblical Studies | 358 | 0.0 | 0.6 | 0.3 | 0.6 | 98.6 | 0.0 |
| Dallas Baptist C | 1,563 | 0.7 | 2.0 | 17.2 | 4.4 | 71.2 | 4.5 |
| Dallas Bible C | 217 | 0.0 | 1.4 | 15.2 | 1.4 | 79.3 | 2.8 |
| Dallas Christian C | 121 | 0.0 | 0.8 | 4.1 | 5.8 | 87.6 | 1.7 |
| Dallas County CC System | | | | | | | |
| Brookhaven C | 6,952 | 0.4 | 3.6 | 4.1 | 4.6 | 86.4 | 0.9 |
| Cedar Valley C | 2,205 | 0.3 | 0.5 | 45.4 | 3.4 | 50.2 | 0.1 |
| Eastfield C | 8,514 | 0.5 | 3.2 | 8.0 | 6.3 | 81.6 | 0.4 |
| El Centro C | 5,506 | 0.6 | 2.1 | 48.0 | 9.3 | 38.4 | 1.5 |
| Mountain View C | 5,288 | 0.9 | 3.8 | 22.7 | 11.3 | 60.8 | 0.5 |
| North Lake C | 5,667 | 0.4 | 2.4 | 5.1 | 4.7 | 86.6 | 0.8 |
| Richland C | 13,672 | 0.3 | 3.9 | 5.5 | 3.7 | 85.8 | 0.8 |
| Dallas Theol Sem | 1,228 | 0.2 | 2.4 | 2.9 | 1.1 | 84.9 | 8.4 |
| Del Mar C | 9,639 | 0.3 | 0.6 | 3.4 | 45.7 | 49.7 | 0.2 |
| DeVry Inst of Tech | 2,200 | 0.5 | 6.8 | 16.4 | 11.0 | 62.3 | 3.0 |
| East Texas Baptist C | 714 | 0.6 | 0.0 | 7.7 | 1.4 | 88.8 | 1.5 |
| East Texas St U | 7,100 | 0.7 | 0.5 | 9.6 | 2.6 | 79.6 | 6.9 |
| East Texas St U Texarkana | 1,272 | 1.1 | 0.3 | 11.6 | 0.7 | 84.4 | 1.9 |
| El Paso CC | 14,062 | 0.5 | 1.1 | 6.9 | 64.5 | 25.8 | 1.2 |
| Episcopal Theol Sem of The Southwest | 74 | 0.0 | 1.4 | 1.4 | 4.1 | 86.5 | 6.8 |
| Fashion & Art Inst of Dallas | 480 | 0.2 | 0.4 | 10.6 | 5.0 | 83.7 | 0.0 |
| Frank Phillips C | 959 | 3.5 | 0.3 | 2.9 | 0.8 | 92.4 | 0.0 |
| Galveston C | 2,014 | 0.1 | 2.3 | 20.1 | 15.2 | 61.9 | 0.3 |
| Grayson County JC | 5,142 | 0.3 | 0.8 | 3.7 | 1.6 | 93.4 | 0.1 |
| Hardin-Simmons U | 1,834 | 0.1 | 0.5 | 3.1 | 4.7 | 90.6 | 1.0 |
| Henderson County JC | 3,795 | 0.3 | 0.4 | 18.1 | 3.7 | 75.2 | 2.3 |
| Hill JC | 1,159 | 0.1 | 0.5 | 5.2 | 3.6 | 90.5 | 0.1 |
| Houston Baptist U | 2,624 | 0.3 | 5.8 | 7.6 | 6.4 | 75.2 | 4.8 |
| Houston CC | 25,118 | 0.2 | 7.2 | 22.0 | 10.1 | 60.0 | 0.5 |
| Howard County JC Dist | 1,167 | 0.9 | 0.7 | 4.7 | 13.3 | 79.3 | 1.0 |
| Howard Payne U | 817 | 0.1 | 0.2 | 6.5 | 5.1 | 87.5 | 0.5 |
| Huston-Tillotson C | 587 | 0.0 | 0.5 | 57.8 | 1.5 | 0.7 | 39.5 |
| Incarnate Word C | 1,350 | 0.4 | 1.0 | 9.6 | 31.6 | 53.2 | 4.1 |
| Jacksonville C | 240 | 0.8 | 2.1 | 8.7 | 0.8 | 75.8 | 11.7 |
| Jarvis Christian C | 533 | 0.0 | 0.0 | 99.6 | 0.2 | 0.2 | 0.0 |
| Kilgore C | 4,469 | 0.3 | 0.5 | 11.1 | 0.8 | 87.2 | 0.2 |
| Lamar U | 15,835 | 0.4 | 0.3 | 19.7 | 3.6 | 71.1 | 4.9 |
| Laredo JC | 4,038 | 0.0 | 0.1 | 0.3 | 87.8 | 6.4 | 5.4 |
| Lee C | 4,879 | 0.4 | 1.1 | 15.6 | 9.2 | 72.9 | 0.8 |
| LeTourneau C | 898 | 0.6 | 0.7 | 0.7 | 0.2 | 91.6 | 6.2 |
| Lon Morris C | 300 | 0.3 | 0.7 | 15.0 | 2.7 | 74.7 | 6.7 |
| Lubbock Christian C | 1,038 | 0.9 | 0.7 | 6.6 | 5.2 | 81.9 | 4.8 |
| McLennan CC | 4,732 | 0.1 | 0.7 | 14.3 | 5.4 | 78.9 | 0.5 |
| McMurry C | 1,482 | 0.4 | 0.9 | 8.5 | 7.8 | 81.7 | 0.6 |
| Midland C | 3,417 | 0.1 | 1.3 | 4.6 | 10.9 | 82.2 | 0.9 |
| Midwestern St U | 4,857 | 0.4 | 2.0 | 4.3 | 3.5 | 87.6 | 2.2 |
| Miss Wades Fashion C | 172 | 0.0 | 0.0 | 33.1 | 9.3 | 54.7 | 2.9 |
| Navarro C | 2,816 | 0.1 | 1.0 | 13.2 | 2.3 | 83.1 | 0.3 |
| North Harris County C | 10,949 | 0.3 | 3.3 | 4.6 | 7.0 | 84.0 | 0.7 |
| North Texas St U | 21,414 | 0.2 | 0.4 | 6.2 | 2.9 | 79.2 | 11.1 |
| Oblate Sch of Theol | 127 | 0.0 | 0.0 | 0.0 | 17.3 | 73.2 | 9.4 |
| Odessa C | 4,916 | 0.2 | 1.6 | 4.3 | 16.2 | 77.1 | 0.6 |
| Our Lady of the Lake U | 1,685 | 0.4 | 0.5 | 8.2 | 49.0 | 39.4 | 2.4 |
| Pan American U | 10,042 | 0.2 | 0.6 | 0.8 | 77.9 | 19.6 | 0.9 |
| Panola JC | 1,370 | 0.1 | 0.3 | 17.0 | 0.5 | 82.0 | 0.1 |
| **TEXAS—Continued** | | | | | | | |
| Paris JC | 2,142 | 0.7% | 0.5% | 9.4% | 1.1% | 86.5% | 1.9% |
| Paul Quinn C | 355 | 0.0 | 0.3 | 97.7 | 0.0 | 1.1 | 0.8 |
| Ranger JC | 698 | 0.7 | 0.4 | 25.1 | 9.2 | 62.0 | 2.6 |
| Rice U | 4,040 | 0.2 | 4.2 | 3.8 | 2.8 | 80.9 | 8.1 |
| Saint Edward's U | 2,356 | 0.4 | 0.8 | 4.8 | 20.1 | 58.7 | 15.2 |
| Saint Mary's U of San Antonio | 3,306 | 0.2 | 0.8 | 4.4 | 34.6 | 54.9 | 5.0 |
| Sam Houston St U | 10,472 | 0.3 | 0.4 | 6.4 | 3.8 | 85.6 | 3.5 |
| Saint Philip's C | 6,313 | 0.5 | 1.4 | 24.3 | 40.8 | 31.9 | 1.1 |
| San Antonio C | 22,274 | 0.4 | 1.3 | 6.5 | 42.7 | 45.9 | 3.1 |
| San Jacinto C | | | | | | | |
| Central | 13,155 | 0.3 | 1.6 | 3.5 | 8.7 | 79.6 | 6.4 |
| North | 3,577 | 0.3 | 2.5 | 13.6 | 11.0 | 70.4 | 2.2 |
| Schreiner C | 489 | 0.0 | 0.2 | 4.5 | 9.6 | 82.4 | 3.3 |
| South Plains C | 3,671 | 0.3 | 0.9 | 7.9 | 16.5 | 73.2 | 1.3 |
| South Texas C of Law | 1,186 | 0.3 | 1.3 | 2.6 | 4.5 | 91.1 | 0.3 |
| Southern Methodist U | 9,261 | 0.3 | 1.8 | 3.0 | 3.3 | 88.5 | 3.1 |
| Southwest Texas JC | 2,483 | 0.2 | 0.3 | 1.1 | 55.9 | 42.0 | 0.5 |
| Southwest Texas St U | 19,222 | 0.2 | 0.5 | 4.1 | 10.4 | 82.7 | 2.1 |
| Southwestern Adventist C | 683 | 0.4 | 1.3 | 5.6 | 14.8 | 70.1 | 7.8 |
| Southwestern Assemblies of God C | 579 | 0.9 | 0.5 | 2.1 | 9.3 | 87.0 | 0.2 |
| Southwestern Christian C | 272 | 0.0 | 0.0 | 86.8 | 0.0 | 0.4 | 12.9 |
| Southwestern U | 1,001 | 0.0 | 1.2 | 2.0 | 4.6 | 89.2 | 3.0 |
| Stephen F Austin St U | 12,549 | 0.1 | 0.2 | 4.3 | 1.8 | 92.8 | 0.7 |
| Sul Ross St U | 2,241 | 0.3 | 0.4 | 3.9 | 34.1 | 58.5 | 2.9 |
| Tarrant County JC | 25,990 | 0.4 | 2.0 | 9.8 | 5.5 | 81.8 | 0.6 |
| Temple JC | 2,334 | 0.2 | 0.8 | 9.6 | 7.8 | 81.4 | 0.3 |
| Texarkana C | 3,585 | 0.3 | 0.2 | 12.7 | 0.6 | 86.0 | 0.3 |
| Texas A&M U | | | | | | | |
| Main campus | 36,827 | 0.1 | 1.7 | 1.6 | 4.6 | 87.6 | 4.3 |
| Galveston | 608 | 0.2 | 1.0 | 0.8 | 3.0 | 92.6 | 2.5 |
| Prairie View A&M U | 4,437 | 0.1 | 1.2 | 89.5 | 0.9 | 7.8 | 0.5 |
| Tarleton St U | 4,624 | 0.1 | 0.6 | 2.2 | 1.6 | 92.6 | 2.9 |
| Texas Chiropractic C | 449 | 0.0 | 0.4 | 1.3 | 1.3 | 94.9 | 2.0 |
| Texas Christian U | 6,747 | 0.3 | 0.4 | 4.4 | 2.8 | 92.0 | 0.0 |
| Texas C | 573 | 0.0 | 0.0 | 67.2 | 0.0 | 0.2 | 32.6 |
| Texas C of Osteo Med | 395 | 1.5 | 3.0 | 1.8 | 6.8 | 86.8 | 0.0 |
| Texas Lutheran C | 1,377 | 0.1 | 1.1 | 6.8 | 9.2 | 81.9 | 0.9 |
| Texas Southern U | 8,910 | 0.1 | 0.9 | 66.8 | 2.5 | 2.3 | 27.3 |
| Texas Southmost C | 4,886 | 0.3 | 0.4 | 0.2 | 80.1 | 16.4 | 2.7 |
| Texas St Tech Inst | | | | | | | |
| Amarillo | 1,118 | 1.2 | 2.1 | 3.7 | 13.4 | 77.8 | 1.8 |
| Rio Grande | 2,359 | 0.1 | 0.2 | 0.3 | 82.9 | 15.7 | 0.9 |
| Sweetwater | 502 | 0.0 | 0.6 | 4.2 | 13.9 | 81.3 | 0.0 |
| Waco | 4,609 | 0.4 | 1.1 | 10.2 | 7.8 | 79.5 | 1.0 |
| Texas Tech U | 23,406 | 0.2 | 1.0 | 2.3 | 5.0 | 86.5 | 4.9 |
| Texas Tech U Health Sciences Center | 709 | 0.1 | 4.4 | 1.8 | 7.9 | 85.5 | 0.3 |
| Texas Woman's U | 8,259 | 0.3 | 1.6 | 12.4 | 5.5 | 74.5 | 5.7 |
| Trinity U | 2,850 | 0.4 | 1.6 | 0.8 | 7.3 | 87.7 | 2.1 |
| Tyler JC | 6,889 | 0.3 | 0.2 | 15.3 | 1.2 | 82.0 | 1.0 |
| U of Dallas | 2,466 | 0.4 | 2.7 | 1.7 | 3.8 | 82.4 | 9.0 |
| U of Houston | | | | | | | |
| Clear Lake | 6,392 | 0.4 | 3.3 | 4.6 | 4.6 | 85.6 | 1.5 |
| Downtown | 6,391 | 0.2 | 9.8 | 26.5 | 16.3 | 36.7 | 10.6 |
| U Park | 31,095 | 0.4 | 6.4 | 8.8 | 6.1 | 71.3 | 7.0 |
| Victoria | 926 | 0.3 | 0.4 | 2.9 | 7.1 | 89.1 | 0.1 |
| U of Mary Hardin-Baylor | 1,181 | 0.0 | 0.3 | 7.5 | 8.2 | 76.2 | 7.8 |
| U of Saint Thomas | 1,983 | 0.3 | 2.6 | 6.0 | 12.0 | 74.0 | 5.1 |
| U System of South Texas | | | | | | | |
| Corpus Christi St U | 3,589 | 0.3 | 1.1 | 2.4 | 26.4 | 69.0 | 0.8 |
| Laredo St U | 928 | 0.0 | 0.3 | 1.3 | 76.7 | 11.6 | 10.0 |
| Texas A&I U | 5,509 | 0.4 | 1.9 | 4.4 | 49.1 | 39.8 | 4.4 |
| U of Texas | | | | | | | |
| Austin | 47,973 | 0.2 | 3.0 | 3.3 | 8.7 | 78.0 | 6.8 |
| Arlington | 23,397 | 0.4 | 5.1 | 6.4 | 3.9 | 78.1 | 6.1 |
| Dallas | 7,442 | 0.4 | 4.3 | 3.7 | 2.8 | 81.3 | 7.6 |
| El Paso | 15,322 | 0.3 | 0.7 | 2.2 | 47.3 | 41.1 | 8.5 |
| Health Science Centers | | | | | | | |
| Dallas | 1,398 | 0.4 | 3.1 | 3.4 | 5.9 | 84.0 | 3.1 |
| Houston | 2,800 | 0.2 | 5.7 | 6.1 | 6.6 | 77.5 | 3.9 |
| San Antonio | 2,332 | 0.6 | 3.2 | 2.7 | 12.6 | 80.2 | 0.7 |
| Med Branch at Galveston | 2,505 | 0.4 | 5.5 | 4.6 | 6.4 | 83.1 | 0.1 |
| Permian Basin | 2,003 | 0.4 | 1.4 | 2.2 | 6.6 | 88.4 | 0.9 |
| San Antonio | 12,612 | 0.1 | 2.2 | 3.0 | 22.0 | 72.6 | 0.0 |
| Tyler | 3,546 | 0.4 | 0.4 | 7.4 | 0.9 | 89.8 | 1.2 |
| Vernon Regional JC | 1,849 | 0.7 | 1.3 | 10.8 | 6.8 | 80.2 | 0.2 |
| Victoria C | 2,889 | 0.1 | 0.6 | 3.6 | 17.0 | 78.2 | 0.6 |
| Wayland Baptist U | 1,707 | 0.3 | 0.9 | 5.9 | 8.1 | 83.4 | 1.5 |
| Weatherford C | 1,532 | 3.3 | 0.2 | 4.0 | 1.3 | 83.2 | 8.0 |
| West Texas St U | 6,474 | 0.2 | 1.4 | 3.1 | 6.0 | 87.0 | 2.2 |
| Western Texas C | 1,319 | 0.2 | 0.0 | 4.6 | 9.2 | 85.5 | 0.5 |
| Wharton County JC | 2,527 | 0.0 | 0.8 | 12.0 | 14.7 | 72.4 | 0.1 |
| Wiley C | 546 | 0.0 | 0.0 | 93.8 | 0.0 | 0.2 | 6.0 |
| **UTAH** | | | | | | | |
| Brigham Young U | | | | | | | |
| Main campus | 29,571 | 0.9% | 0.6% | 0.1% | 0.4% | 93.3% | 4.8% |
| Hawaii | 1,936 | 0.0 | 31.0 | 0.4 | 0.0 | 33.6 | 35.1 |
| Stevens Henager C | 759 | 0.7 | 2.0 | 7.8 | 4.3 | 85.1 | 0.1 |
| Utah Higher Education Sys | | | | | | | |
| U of Utah | 24,568 | 0.6 | 2.2 | 0.5 | 1.8 | 90.9 | 4.0 |
| Utah St U | 11,544 | 0.3 | 1.2 | 0.5 | 0.6 | 90.0 | 7.5 |
| Southern Utah St C | 2,529 | 3.8 | 0.6 | 0.7 | 0.9 | 92.9 | 1.2 |
| Weber St C | 10,130 | 0.9 | 1.4 | 1.4 | 2.3 | 91.2 | 2.8 |
| C of Eastern Utah | 1,113 | 0.4 | 0.6 | 3.7 | 6.7 | 88.4 | 0.1 |
| Dixie C | 1,904 | 1.6 | 0.6 | 1.4 | 0.3 | 94.7 | 1.3 |
| Snow C | 1,317 | 1.4 | 1.0 | 0.9 | 0.8 | 90.2 | 5.7 |
| Utah Tech C | | | | | | | |
| Provo | 5,821 | 1.6 | 2.1 | 0.2 | 2.0 | 91.5 | 2.5 |
| Salt Lake | 8,289 | 1.2 | 3.3 | 0.6 | 3.6 | 90.7 | 0.6 |
| Westminster C of Salt Lake City | 1,234 | 0.7 | 1.4 | 1.8 | 3.3 | 87.0 | 5.8 |
| **VERMONT** | | | | | | | |
| Bennington C | 584 | 0.0% | 1.2% | 1.9% | 1.9% | 87.7% | 7.4% |
| Burlington C | 167 | 1.2 | 0.0 | 2.4 | 1.2 | 95.2 | 0.0 |
| Champlain C | 1,801 | 0.0 | 0.0 | 0.2 | 0.0 | 99.6 | 0.2 |
| C of Saint Joseph the Provider | 387 | 0.5 | 0.3 | 1.3 | 0.3 | 97.4 | 0.3 |
| Green Mountain C | 385 | 0.0 | 0.0 | 0.8 | 0.0 | 96.9 | 2.3 |
| Marlboro C | 190 | 0.0 | 0.0 | 1.1 | 1.6 | 95.3 | 2.1 |
| Middlebury C | 2,012 | 0.8 | 0.0 | 1.0 | 0.8 | 97.0 | 0.3 |
| Norwich U | 1,586 | 0.6 | 0.6 | 2.0 | 1.5 | 93.9 | 1.4 |
| Vermont C | 942 | 0.1 | 0.3 | 5.1 | 2.1 | 90.1 | 2.2 |
| Saint Michael's C | 2,009 | 0.0 | 0.1 | 0.1 | 0.1 | 94.9 | 4.8 |
| Sch for Int'l Training | 438 | 0.2 | 0.5 | 1.4 | 0.0 | 72.4 | 25.6 |
| Southern Vermont C | 482 | 0.0 | 0.0 | 1.9 | 1.0 | 95.0 | 2.1 |
| Sterling C | 70 | 0.0 | 0.0 | 0.0 | 0.0 | 98.6 | 1.4 |
| Trinity C | 945 | 0.0 | 0.0 | 0.1 | 0.0 | 99.9 | 0.0 |
| U of Vermont | 10,908 | 0.0 | 1.1 | 0.5 | 0.5 | 97.2 | 0.7 |
| Vermont St C's System | | | | | | | |
| Castleton St C | 2,043 | 0.2 | 0.1 | 0.6 | 0.3 | 98.7 | 0.1 |
| CC of Vermont | 2,344 | 0.5 | 0.3 | 0.1 | 0.3 | 98.8 | 0.0 |
| Johnson St C | 1,128 | 0.0 | 0.3 | 0.4 | 0.4 | 96.5 | 2.5 |
| Lyndon St C | 1,014 | 0.0 | 0.2 | 0.4 | 0.6 | 98.5 | 0.3 |
| Vermont Tech C | 755 | 0.0 | 0.7 | 0.0 | 0.1 | 98.9 | 0.3 |
| **VIRGINIA** | | | | | | | |
| Averett C | 952 | 0.0% | 0.2% | 8.4% | 0.4% | 88.8% | 2.2% |
| Bluefield C | 326 | 0.0 | 0.9 | 4.3 | 0.0 | 92.9 | 1.8 |
| Bridgewater C | 791 | 0.1 | 0.0 | 1.5 | 0.0 | 97.2 | 1.1 |
| Christopher Newport C | 4,268 | 0.3 | 1.1 | 10.6 | 0.4 | 87.0 | 0.5 |
| C of William and Mary | 6,640 | 0.2 | 1.3 | 4.1 | 0.9 | 91.0 | 2.5 |
| Richard Bland C | 934 | 0.2 | 1.5 | 15.8 | 0.9 | 81.6 | 0.0 |
| Eastern Mennonite C | 919 | 0.0 | 0.2 | 1.4 | 1.4 | 93.7 | 3.3 |

*Continued on Following Page*

| | Total | American Indian | Asian | Black | Hispanic | White | Foreign |
|---|---|---|---|---|---|---|---|
| **VIRGINIA—Continued** | | | | | | | |
| Eastern Va Med Sch | 359 | 0.0% | 5.3% | 7.2% | 2.2% | 85.0% | 0.3% |
| Emory and Henry C | 768 | 0.0 | 0.1 | 2.0 | 0.5 | 97.3 | 0.1 |
| Ferrum C | 1,580 | 0.3 | 0.2 | 7.4 | 0.6 | 91.1 | 0.4 |
| George Mason U | 15,534 | 0.3 | 4.5 | 3.7 | 2.0 | 86.1 | 3.4 |
| Hampden-Sydney C | 752 | 0.0 | 0.0 | 1.2 | 0.3 | 98.4 | 0.1 |
| Hampton U | 4,260 | 0.0 | 0.2 | 90.8 | 0.3 | 5.8 | 2.8 |
| Hollins C | 982 | 0.0 | 0.2 | 2.4 | 0.3 | 95.6 | 1.4 |
| James Madison U | 10,016 | 0.1 | 0.5 | 5.9 | 0.5 | 92.9 | 0.1 |
| Longwood C | 2,713 | 0.1 | 0.7 | 7.9 | 0.1 | 91.0 | 0.1 |
| Lynchburg C | 2,150 | 0.0 | 0.3 | 2.1 | 0.4 | 95.1 | 2.1 |
| Mary Baldwin C | 908 | 0.1 | 1.1 | 3.3 | 1.1 | 94.1 | 0.3 |
| Mary Washington C | 3,049 | 0.2 | 1.0 | 4.1 | 1.1 | 93.2 | 0.4 |
| Marymount C of Va | 2,088 | 0.2 | 2.7 | 6.8 | 2.8 | 81.3 | 6.1 |
| National Business C | 1,196 | 0.1 | 0.2 | 35.4 | 2.2 | 61.8 | 0.4 |
| Norfolk St U | 7,233 | 0.1 | 0.2 | 85.7 | 0.2 | 9.5 | 4.3 |
| Old Dominion U | 15,626 | 0.5 | 2.0 | 9.4 | 1.3 | 84.3 | 2.5 |
| Protestant Episcopal Theol Sem in Va | 212 | 0.0 | 0.0 | 2.8 | 0.0 | 92.0 | 5.2 |
| Radford U | 6,802 | 0.2 | 0.8 | 2.7 | 0.6 | 95.3 | 0.3 |
| Randolph-Macon C | 965 | 0.4 | 0.6 | 2.0 | 0.5 | 95.9 | 0.6 |
| Randolph-Macon Woman's C | 742 | 0.0 | 0.9 | 1.3 | 0.8 | 94.9 | 2.0 |
| Roanoke C | 1,455 | 0.1 | 0.3 | 1.3 | 0.1 | 98.2 | 0.0 |
| Saint Paul's C | 697 | 0.0 | 0.0 | 97.4 | 0.0 | 1.6 | 1.0 |
| Shenandoah C and Conservatory of Music | 932 | 0.0 | 0.9 | 6.3 | 0.0 | 92.8 | 0.0 |
| Southern Sem JC | 246 | 0.0 | 0.0 | 3.7 | 0.0 | 95.5 | 0.8 |
| Sweet Briar C | 725 | 0.0 | 0.0 | 3.2 | 0.0 | 93.7 | 3.2 |
| Union Theol Sem in Va | 257 | 0.0 | 0.4 | 1.2 | 0.0 | 94.9 | 3.5 |
| U of Richmond | 4,578 | 0.2 | 0.5 | 3.3 | 0.4 | 95.1 | 0.5 |
| U of Virginia | | | | | | | |
| Main campus | 17,143 | 0.1 | 2.2 | 6.8 | 0.4 | 88.4 | 2.1 |
| Clinch Valley C | 891 | 0.1 | 1.6 | 2.5 | 0.3 | 95.5 | 0.0 |
| Virginia Commonwealth U | 19,773 | 0.3 | 2.0 | 14.6 | 0.9 | 81.4 | 0.8 |
| Virginia CC System | | | | | | | |
| Blue Ridge | 2,016 | 0.1 | 0.5 | 2.3 | 0.2 | 96.7 | 0.0 |
| Central Virginia | 3,565 | 0.2 | 0.6 | 11.7 | 0.1 | 87.3 | 0.1 |
| Dabney S Lancaster | 1,213 | 0.2 | 0.1 | 6.3 | 0.1 | 93.2 | 0.0 |
| Danville | 2,012 | 0.1 | 0.3 | 18.4 | 0.2 | 80.9 | 0.0 |
| Eastern Shore | 378 | 0.0 | 0.0 | 19.3 | 0.0 | 80.4 | 0.3 |
| Germanna | 1,758 | 0.1 | 0.5 | 8.6 | 0.6 | 90.0 | 0.1 |
| J Sargeant Reynolds | 9,190 | 0.2 | 1.4 | 25.5 | 0.4 | 72.1 | 0.3 |
| John Tyler | 3,904 | 0.4 | 1.2 | 21.8 | 0.5 | 76.1 | 0.1 |
| Lord Fairfax | 1,679 | 0.0 | 0.1 | 2.1 | 0.2 | 97.6 | 0.1 |
| Mountain Empire | 2,501 | 0.0 | 0.2 | 1.7 | 0.1 | 97.9 | 0.0 |
| New River | 2,737 | 0.0 | 0.2 | 3.8 | 0.4 | 95.1 | 0.4 |
| Northern Virginia | 32,053 | 0.3 | 6.8 | 7.6 | 3.0 | 80.2 | 2.0 |
| Patrick Henry | 1,598 | 0.0 | 0.2 | 11.1 | 0.4 | 88.2 | 0.0 |
| Paul D Camp | 1,154 | 0.2 | 0.3 | 37.2 | 0.1 | 62.2 | 0.0 |
| Piedmont Virginia | 3,644 | 0.2 | 1.3 | 8.2 | 0.6 | 89.3 | 0.4 |
| Rappahannock | 1,318 | 0.5 | 0.2 | 18.8 | 0.2 | 80.2 | 0.0 |
| Southside Virginia | 1,465 | 0.1 | 0.2 | 30.6 | 0.1 | 68.9 | 0.1 |
| Southwest Virginia | 3,520 | 0.0 | 0.3 | 0.9 | 0.1 | 98.6 | 0.1 |
| Thomas Nelson | 6,151 | 0.4 | 1.7 | 24.5 | 0.9 | 72.2 | 0.3 |
| Tidewater | 14,976 | 0.4 | 3.5 | 14.1 | 0.9 | 80.7 | 0.4 |
| Virginia Highlands | 1,595 | 0.1 | 0.3 | 1.6 | 0.2 | 97.9 | 0.1 |
| Virginia Western | 5,722 | 0.1 | 0.5 | 7.3 | 0.1 | 91.6 | 0.3 |
| Wytheville | 1,584 | 0.1 | 0.2 | 2.0 | 0.1 | 97.6 | 0.0 |
| Virginia Intermont C | 517 | 0.4 | 0.4 | 5.6 | 2.7 | 85.1 | 5.8 |
| Virginia Military Inst | 1,338 | 0.1 | 2.0 | 5.7 | 1.4 | 89.2 | 1.6 |
| Va Polytech Inst & St U | 23,303 | 0.1 | 1.4 | 4.2 | 0.6 | 88.4 | 5.2 |
| Virginia St U | 4,108 | 0.1 | 0.4 | 85.9 | 0.2 | 10.7 | 2.8 |
| Virginia Union U | 1,298 | 0.0 | 0.0 | 99.9 | 0.0 | 0.1 | 0.0 |
| Virginia Wesleyan C | 976 | 0.2 | 1.8 | 8.1 | 0.8 | 87.4 | 1.6 |
| Washington and Lee U | 1,705 | 0.1 | 0.1 | 2.0 | 0.6 | 95.9 | 1.3 |
| **WASHINGTON** | | | | | | | |
| Art Inst of Seattle | 602 | 0.3% | 1.3% | 2.2% | 2.3% | 93.0% | 0.8% |
| Bellevue CC | 7,779 | 0.4 | 4.5 | 1.4 | 1.1 | 91.7 | 0.9 |
| Big Bend CC | 1,578 | 1.6 | 0.4 | 0.9 | 3.6 | 91.1 | 2.3 |
| Central Washington U | 7,375 | 1.4 | 1.8 | 1.6 | 2.1 | 92.0 | 1.1 |
| Centralia C | 2,776 | 0.9 | 0.7 | 0.1 | 0.3 | 97.6 | 0.3 |
| Clark C | 6,217 | 0.8 | 1.7 | 0.4 | 0.4 | 96.2 | 0.6 |
| Columbia Basin CC | 4,967 | 0.3 | 1.5 | 0.4 | 1.5 | 96.2 | 0.1 |
| Cornish Inst | 555 | 1.1 | 1.6 | 4.5 | 1.4 | 89.0 | 2.3 |
| Eastern Washington U | 8,527 | 1.2 | 1.0 | 1.3 | 1.6 | 92.0 | 2.9 |
| Edmonds CC | 5,775 | 1.3 | 2.6 | 1.8 | 1.0 | 91.3 | 2.0 |
| Everett CC | 5,248 | 1.8 | 2.8 | 0.4 | 0.8 | 94.2 | 0.1 |
| Evergreen St C | 2,826 | 2.2 | 2.5 | 3.7 | 1.6 | 89.3 | 0.8 |
| Fort Steilacoom CC | 6,865 | 1.7 | 5.4 | 8.7 | 3.0 | 80.1 | 1.2 |
| Gonzaga U | 3,210 | 0.8 | 2.6 | 0.7 | 1.9 | 82.3 | 11.7 |
| Grays Harbor C | 2,114 | 3.5 | 1.3 | 0.3 | 0.4 | 94.4 | 0.1 |
| Green River CC | 4,685 | 1.2 | 2.8 | 1.0 | 1.2 | 93.5 | 0.2 |
| Griffin C | 1,472 | 1.9 | 16.4 | 13.2 | 1.7 | 65.8 | 0.9 |
| Heritage C | 339 | 15.3 | 2.9 | 0.3 | 19.2 | 39.5 | 22.7 |
| Highline CC | 6,887 | 1.3 | 6.1 | 2.3 | 1.6 | 88.6 | 0.1 |
| John Bastyr C of Naturopathic Med | 152 | 0.7 | 2.6 | 2.6 | 0.7 | 86.2 | 7.2 |
| Lower Columbia C | 2,866 | 1.1 | 0.9 | 0.2 | 0.5 | 97.1 | 0.1 |
| Lutheran Bible Inst of Seattle | 207 | 1.0 | 2.4 | 1.4 | 0.0 | 90.3 | 4.8 |
| Northwest C of the Assemblies of God | 690 | 2.0 | 2.3 | 0.4 | 1.2 | 91.6 | 2.5 |
| Olympic C | 5,692 | 1.5 | 5.2 | 3.4 | 2.0 | 87.9 | 0.1 |
| Pacific Lutheran U | 3,694 | 0.5 | 3.0 | 1.8 | 0.7 | 88.4 | 5.5 |
| Peninsula C | 2,441 | 2.5 | 0.9 | 0.1 | 1.3 | 95.0 | 0.3 |
| Puget Sound Christian C | 122 | 0.8 | 1.6 | 1.6 | 0.8 | 93.4 | 1.6 |
| Saint Martin's C | 508 | 3.7 | 3.0 | 1.6 | 1.2 | 71.1 | 19.5 |
| Seattle CC District | | | | | | | |
| Central | 5,382 | 1.5 | 10.6 | 11.2 | 1.9 | 73.4 | 1.3 |
| North | 5,467 | 1.0 | 10.5 | 2.4 | 1.3 | 84.8 | 0.1 |
| South | 3,736 | 1.6 | 9.5 | 4.6 | 1.8 | 80.7 | 1.9 |
| **WASHINGTON—Continued** | | | | | | | |
| Seattle Pacific U | 2,935 | 0.8% | 3.4% | 1.5% | 0.3% | 89.1% | 4.8% |
| Seattle U | 4,626 | 0.7 | 5.8 | 2.6 | 0.9 | 81.1 | 8.9 |
| Shoreline CC | 5,604 | 0.7 | 4.9 | 1.4 | 1.0 | 88.1 | 3.9 |
| Skagit Valley C | 3,894 | 1.7 | 1.5 | 0.7 | 2.0 | 93.2 | 0.9 |
| South Puget Sound CC | 2,959 | 1.0 | 3.0 | 0.6 | 1.0 | 94.2 | 0.1 |
| Tacoma CC | 4,010 | 1.4 | 5.6 | 6.8 | 1.6 | 82.0 | 2.6 |
| U of Puget Sound | 3,924 | 0.6 | 4.0 | 1.7 | 0.6 | 92.2 | 0.8 |
| U of Washington | 34,450 | 0.9 | 11.1 | 2.9 | 1.4 | 79.2 | 4.5 |
| Walla Walla C | 1,635 | 0.3 | 1.8 | 1.5 | 1.5 | 81.8 | 13.1 |
| Walla Walla CC | 3,357 | 1.1 | 0.7 | 3.6 | 2.6 | 90.6 | 1.4 |
| Washington St CC District | | | | | | | |
| Spokane | 6,065 | 0.9 | 1.5 | 0.5 | 0.7 | 96.3 | 0.1 |
| Spokane Falls | 8,239 | 1.3 | 1.7 | 1.1 | 1.0 | 94.7 | 0.2 |
| Washington St U | 16,484 | 0.7 | 3.0 | 2.1 | 0.9 | 88.6 | 4.7 |
| Wenatchee Valley C | 2,059 | 4.3 | 1.3 | 0.3 | 1.4 | 92.2 | 0.5 |
| Western Washington U | 9,144 | 0.9 | 2.0 | 0.6 | 0.7 | 94.0 | 1.8 |
| Whatcom CC | 1,963 | 4.9 | 1.5 | 0.4 | 0.8 | 91.8 | 0.6 |
| Whitman C | 1,185 | 0.3 | 5.0 | 1.0 | 1.0 | 90.7 | 2.0 |
| Whitworth C | 1,764 | 0.7 | 2.0 | 1.4 | 0.6 | 92.7 | 2.6 |
| Yakima Valley CC | 3,426 | 4.8 | 1.2 | 1.0 | 6.2 | 85.5 | 1.3 |
| **WEST VIRGINIA** | | | | | | | |
| Alderson Broaddus C | 781 | 0.3% | 0.8% | 2.6% | 0.6% | 93.5% | 2.3% |
| Appalachian Bible C | 188 | 0.0 | 0.0 | 1.6 | 1.6 | 96.8 | 0.0 |
| Beckley C | 1,669 | 0.0 | 0.7 | 5.8 | 0.0 | 93.6 | 0.0 |
| Bluefield St C | 2,597 | 0.1 | 0.3 | 10.2 | 0.1 | 87.9 | 1.4 |
| Concord C | 2,217 | 0.1 | 0.5 | 6.0 | 0.3 | 92.9 | 0.2 |
| Fairmont St C | 5,004 | 0.2 | 0.3 | 2.8 | 0.2 | 96.3 | 0.2 |
| Glenville St C | 1,914 | 0.1 | 0.7 | 1.6 | 0.1 | 97.5 | 0.0 |
| Huntington JC | 426 | 0.0 | 0.0 | 9.9 | 0.0 | 90.1 | 0.0 |
| Marshall U | 11,318 | 0.1 | 0.6 | 3.4 | 0.2 | 94.4 | 1.2 |
| National Education Center National Inst Tech | 387 | 0.0 | 0.0 | 5.2 | 0.3 | 94.6 | 0.0 |
| Ohio Valley C | 290 | 0.0 | 0.0 | 1.7 | 0.3 | 97.2 | 0.7 |
| Parkersburg County C | 2,977 | 0.1 | 0.4 | 0.7 | 0.4 | 98.4 | 0.0 |
| Potomac St C | 875 | 0.2 | 0.2 | 7.0 | 0.1 | 92.3 | 0.1 |
| Salem C | | | | | | | |
| Main campus | 833 | 0.1 | 1.6 | 13.2 | 0.7 | 83.4 | 1.0 |
| Clarksburg | 337 | 0.0 | 0.0 | 0.3 | 0.0 | 99.7 | 0.0 |
| Shepherd C | 3,534 | 0.2 | 0.4 | 3.1 | 0.1 | 96.2 | 0.0 |
| Southern W Va CC | 2,359 | 0.7 | 0.6 | 2.0 | 0.1 | 96.6 | 0.0 |
| West Liberty St C | 2,524 | 0.1 | 0.3 | 1.7 | 0.2 | 97.6 | 0.1 |
| West Va C of Grad Studies | 2,715 | 0.2 | 1.0 | 4.6 | 0.3 | 93.8 | 0.1 |
| West Virginia Inst of Tech | 3,210 | 0.2 | 3.0 | 6.9 | 0.4 | 88.6 | 1.0 |
| West Virginia Northern CC | 3,540 | 0.2 | 0.6 | 2.8 | 0.2 | 96.1 | 0.0 |
| West Va Sch of Osteo Med | 235 | 0.9 | 1.7 | 2.1 | 0.4 | 94.9 | 0.0 |
| West Virginia St C | 4,295 | 0.2 | 0.7 | 13.4 | 0.2 | 85.0 | 0.5 |
| West Virginia U | 19,070 | 0.1 | 0.9 | 2.2 | 0.5 | 92.1 | 4.2 |
| West Virginia Wesleyan C | 1,539 | 0.1 | 0.6 | 3.0 | 0.5 | 93.2 | 2.6 |
| Wheeling C | 1,088 | 0.2 | 1.3 | 1.4 | 0.6 | 94.6 | 1.9 |
| **WISCONSIN** | | | | | | | |
| Alverno C | 1,512 | 1.0% | 0.5% | 10.9% | 2.2% | 84.8% | 0.5% |
| Beloit C | 976 | 0.1 | 2.3 | 2.5 | 1.3 | 88.9 | 4.9 |
| Blackhawk Tech Inst | 2,300 | 0.5 | 0.5 | 6.0 | 0.4 | 92.6 | 0.0 |
| Cardinal Stritch C | 1,982 | 0.1 | 0.4 | 8.1 | 0.6 | 90.3 | 0.5 |
| Carroll C | 1,568 | 0.3 | 0.6 | 3.2 | 1.5 | 93.8 | 0.7 |
| Carthage C | 1,502 | 0.0 | 0.4 | 4.7 | 0.9 | 93.5 | 0.5 |
| Concordia C | 811 | 0.4 | 1.1 | 7.2 | 0.1 | 88.8 | 2.5 |
| District One Tech Inst | 3,037 | 0.6 | 1.2 | 0.2 | 0.3 | 97.7 | 0.0 |
| Edgewood C | 681 | 0.3 | 0.0 | 2.6 | 0.7 | 92.4 | 4.0 |
| Fox Valley Tech Inst | 3,601 | 0.4 | 0.5 | 0.1 | 0.3 | 98.6 | 0.1 |
| Holy Redeemer C | 49 | 0.0 | 0.0 | 2.0 | 4.1 | 87.8 | 6.1 |
| Inst of Paper Chemistry | 104 | 0.0 | 1.0 | 0.0 | 0.0 | 95.2 | 3.8 |
| Lakeland C | 955 | 0.4 | 0.8 | 6.7 | 0.6 | 91.2 | 0.2 |
| Lawrence U | 1,062 | 0.4 | 0.8 | 1.7 | 0.2 | 94.4 | 2.5 |
| Madison Area Tech C | 5,930 | 0.6 | 2.5 | 1.7 | 0.8 | 94.3 | 0.1 |
| Madison Business C | 419 | 0.5 | 0.0 | 1.7 | 0.0 | 96.2 | 1.7 |
| Marian C of Fond Du Lac | 456 | 0.0 | 1.3 | 0.9 | 1.3 | 96.1 | 0.4 |
| Marquette U | 11,630 | 0.2 | 3.9 | 3.5 | 2.4 | 87.4 | 2.6 |
| Med C of Wisconsin | 856 | 0.1 | 5.0 | 3.7 | 5.4 | 84.1 | 1.6 |
| Mid-State Tech Inst | 1,819 | 1.1 | 0.4 | 0.1 | 0.2 | 98.2 | 0.0 |
| Milwaukee Area Tech C | 20,783 | 1.1 | 1.7 | 15.9 | 2.0 | 78.9 | 0.2 |
| Milwaukee Inst of Art & Design | 363 | 1.1 | 0.6 | 1.9 | 1.4 | 94.2 | 0.8 |
| Milwaukee Sch of Engr | 2,553 | 0.0 | 2.6 | 4.0 | 0.3 | 91.8 | 1.3 |
| Moraine Park Voc-Tech & Adult Ed | 4,846 | 0.3 | 0.7 | 0.3 | 0.8 | 97.9 | 0.0 |
| Mount Mary C | 1,291 | 0.5 | 0.8 | 4.0 | 0.7 | 92.7 | 1.3 |
| Mount Senario C | 751 | 12.1 | 2.3 | 3.7 | 2.4 | 77.2 | 2.3 |
| Nashotah House | 74 | 0.0 | 1.4 | 0.0 | 0.0 | 98.6 | 0.0 |
| Nicolet C & Tech Inst | 1,168 | 5.0 | 0.3 | 0.3 | 0.4 | 94.0 | 0.0 |
| North Central Tech Inst | 3,646 | 1.0 | 1.0 | 0.1 | 0.1 | 97.8 | 0.0 |
| Northeast Wis Tech Inst | 4,380 | 2.7 | 0.8 | 0.2 | 0.4 | 95.7 | 0.2 |
| Northland C | 586 | 8.2 | 0.0 | 1.4 | 1.7 | 86.9 | 1.9 |
| Northwestern C | 241 | 0.0 | 0.0 | 0.4 | 0.0 | 98.8 | 0.8 |
| Ripon C | 860 | 0.3 | 1.0 | 0.8 | 0.7 | 95.6 | 1.5 |
| Sacred Heart Sch of Theol | 100 | 0.0 | 1.0 | 0.0 | 2.0 | 91.0 | 6.0 |
| Saint Norbert C | 1,741 | 0.2 | 0.2 | 0.1 | 0.1 | 99.4 | 0.1 |
| Silver Lake C | 393 | 0.0 | 0.5 | 0.0 | 0.3 | 98.5 | 0.8 |
| SW Wis Voc-Tech Inst | 1,080 | 0.0 | 0.0 | 0.2 | 0.0 | 99.8 | 0.0 |
| Stratton C | 572 | 0.9 | 0.7 | 37.9 | 2.3 | 57.2 | 1.0 |
| U of Wisconsin | | | | | | | |
| Eau Claire | 10,767 | 0.3 | 0.3 | 0.3 | 0.3 | 97.2 | 1.7 |
| Green Bay | 4,876 | 1.5 | 0.5 | 1.1 | 0.3 | 93.5 | 3.1 |
| La Crosse | 9,109 | 0.4 | 0.4 | 0.7 | 0.4 | 97.5 | 0.7 |
| Madison | 44,218 | 0.2 | 1.8 | 1.8 | 1.2 | 89.0 | 6.1 |
| Milwaukee | 26,464 | 0.6 | 1.3 | 6.3 | 1.8 | 87.5 | 2.5 |
| Oshkosh | 11,103 | 0.5 | 0.6 | 1.2 | 0.5 | 96.6 | 0.8 |
| Parkside | 5,544 | 0.3 | 1.1 | 3.6 | 1.8 | 92.8 | 0.3 |
| Platteville | 5,293 | 0.2 | 0.3 | 0.7 | 0.2 | 97.1 | 1.4 |
| River Falls | 5,287 | 0.4 | 0.4 | 0.7 | 0.2 | 96.8 | 1.6 |
| Stevens Point | 9,008 | 1.1 | 0.4 | 0.5 | 0.4 | 95.7 | 1.9 |
| **WISCONSIN—Continued** | | | | | | | |
| U of Wisconsin—Continued | | | | | | | |
| Stout | 7,383 | 0.7% | 0.4% | 1.0% | 0.3% | 94.4% | 3.3% |
| Superior | 2,095 | 1.1 | 0.7 | 1.3 | 0.1 | 93.9 | 2.9 |
| Whitewater | 10,737 | 0.2 | 0.4 | 1.7 | 0.7 | 95.8 | 1.2 |
| Centers | 10,042 | 0.4 | 0.9 | 1.4 | 0.5 | 96.6 | 0.2 |
| Viterbo C | 1,074 | 0.2 | 0.7 | 0.6 | 0.6 | 97.5 | 0.6 |
| Waukesha Co Tech Inst | 4,813 | 0.3 | 0.3 | 0.1 | 0.5 | 98.8 | 0.0 |
| Western Wis Tech Inst | 4,432 | 0.4 | 6.5 | 0.4 | 0.3 | 92.4 | 0.0 |
| Wisconsin Consv of Music | 54 | 0.0 | 0.0 | 29.6 | 1.9 | 57.4 | 11.1 |
| Wisconsin Indianhead Voc-Tech & Adult Ed | 1,899 | 3.3 | 0.4 | 0.4 | 0.1 | 95.7 | 0.0 |
| Wisconsin Lutheran C | 107 | 0.0 | 0.0 | 5.6 | 0.0 | 94.4 | 0.0 |
| Wis Sch of Electronics | 421 | 0.2 | 0.0 | 1.7 | 0.7 | 97.1 | 0.2 |
| Wisconsin Sch of Professional Psychology | 37 | 0.0 | 0.0 | 0.0 | 0.0 | 100.0 | 0.0 |
| **WYOMING** | | | | | | | |
| Casper C | 3,248 | 0.7% | 0.3% | 0.2% | 1.1% | 97.1% | 0.6% |
| Central Wyoming C | 865 | 9.5 | 0.1 | 1.2 | 0.7 | 88.1 | 0.5 |
| Eastern Wyoming C | 1,125 | 0.2 | 0.0 | 0.4 | 2.3 | 97.1 | 0.0 |
| Laramie County CC | 3,125 | 0.4 | 0.7 | 2.9 | 2.8 | 81.8 | 11.4 |
| Northwest CC | 1,719 | 0.2 | 0.0 | 0.1 | 3.4 | 95.8 | 0.5 |
| Sheridan C | 1,601 | 0.6 | 0.0 | 0.4 | 0.0 | 98.4 | 0.6 |
| U of Wyoming | 10,087 | 0.5 | 0.7 | 0.8 | 1.4 | 93.1 | 3.6 |
| Western Wyoming CC | 1,654 | 0.4 | 0.6 | 0.5 | 2.0 | 96.6 | 0.0 |
| **U.S. SERVICE SCHOOLS** | | | | | | | |
| Uniformed Services U of the Health Sciences | 729 | 0.3% | 6.7% | 2.5% | 2.2% | 87.9% | 0.4% |
| US Air Force Acad | 4,414 | 0.5 | 3.3 | 6.8 | 4.6 | 84.8 | 0.0 |
| US Coast Guard Acad | 785 | 0.5 | 4.1 | 1.4 | 1.8 | 89.9 | 2.3 |
| US Merchant Marine Acad | 1,079 | 0.2 | 1.9 | 1.9 | 1.8 | 92.0 | 2.2 |
| US Military Acad | 4,608 | 0.4 | 2.6 | 8.1 | 3.9 | 84.7 | 0.2 |
| US Naval Acad | 4,571 | 0.4 | 3.7 | 4.6 | 4.4 | 86.4 | 0.5 |
| **AMERICAN SAMOA** | | | | | | | |
| American Samoa CC | 871 | 1.7% | 80.5% | 0.0% | 0.0% | 0.0% | 17.8% |
| **GUAM** | | | | | | | |
| Guam CC | 1,740 | 0.2% | 77.5% | 1.0% | 0.7% | 8.7% | 11.8% |
| U of Guam | 2,692 | 0.3 | 69.6 | 0.8 | 1.4 | 10.0 | 17.9 |
| **NORTHERN MARIANAS** | | | | | | | |
| Northern Marianas C | 431 | 0.0% | 95.1% | 0.0% | 0.2% | 4.6% | 0.0% |
| **PUERTO RICO** | | | | | | | |
| American C of PR | 3,827 | 0.0% | 0.0% | 0.0% | 100% | 0.0% | 0.0% |
| Antillian C | 918 | 0.0 | 0.0 | 1.1 | 93.8 | 0.5 | 4.6 |
| Bayamon Central U | 2,841 | 0.0 | 0.0 | 0.0 | 99.9 | 0.0 | 0.1 |
| Caguas City C | 912 | 0.0 | 0.0 | 0.0 | 100.0 | 0.0 | 0.0 |
| Caribbean Center for Advanced Studies | 347 | 0.0 | 0.0 | 0.0 | 96.8 | 2.0 | 1.2 |
| Caribbean U C | 3,594 | 0.0 | 0.0 | 0.0 | 100.0 | 0.0 | 0.0 |
| Catholic U of PR | 13,308 | 0.0 | 0.0 | 0.0 | 99.8 | 0.0 | 0.2 |
| Ctr for Advanced Studies on PR and the Caribbean | 260 | 0.0 | 0.0 | 0.0 | 100.0 | 0.0 | 0.0 |
| Conserv of Music of PR | 259 | 0.0 | 0.0 | 0.0 | 100.0 | 0.0 | 0.0 |
| Electronic Data Processing C of Puerto Rico | 2,522 | 0.0 | 0.0 | 0.0 | 100.0 | 0.0 | 0.0 |
| Fundacion Ed Ana Mendez | | | | | | | |
| Colegio U Metropolitan | 5,017 | 0.0 | 0.0 | 0.0 | 100.0 | 0.0 | 0.0 |
| Puerto Rico JC | 4,853 | 0.0 | 0.0 | 0.0 | 100.0 | 0.0 | 0.0 |
| U Del Turabo | 7,435 | 0.0 | 0.0 | 0.0 | 100.0 | 0.0 | 0.0 |
| Huertas JC | 1,008 | 0.0 | 0.0 | 0.0 | 100.0 | 0.0 | 0.0 |
| Inst Comercial de PR JC | 1,653 | 0.0 | 0.0 | 0.0 | 100.0 | 0.0 | 0.0 |
| Inst Tech Comercial JC | 443 | 0.0 | 0.0 | 0.0 | 100.0 | 0.0 | 0.0 |
| Inter-American U | | | | | | | |
| Aguadilla | 2,760 | 0.0 | 0.0 | 0.0 | 100.0 | 0.0 | 0.0 |
| Arecibo | 3,531 | 0.0 | 0.0 | 0.0 | 100.0 | 0.0 | 0.0 |
| Barranquitas | 1,458 | 0.0 | 0.0 | 0.0 | 100.0 | 0.0 | 0.0 |
| Fajardo | 1,861 | 0.0 | 0.0 | 0.0 | 100.0 | 0.0 | 0.0 |
| Guayama | 1,374 | 0.0 | 0.0 | 0.0 | 100.0 | 0.0 | 0.0 |
| Metropolitan | 13,249 | 0.0 | 0.0 | 0.0 | 100.0 | 0.0 | 0.0 |
| Ponce | 2,788 | 0.0 | 0.0 | 0.0 | 100.0 | 0.0 | 0.0 |
| San German | 6,727 | 0.0 | 0.0 | 0.0 | 100.0 | 0.0 | 0.0 |
| Ponce Sch of Med | 184 | 0.0 | 2.2 | 0.0 | 88.0 | 8.7 | 1.1 |
| Ramirez C of Business and Tech | 851 | 0.0 | 0.0 | 0.0 | 100.0 | 0.0 | 0.0 |
| Tech C of the Municipality of San Juan | 1,070 | 0.0 | 0.0 | 0.0 | 100.0 | 0.0 | 0.0 |
| U Central Del Caribe Med Sch Cayey | 321 | 0.0 | 0.3 | 0.3 | 89.4 | 10.0 | 0.0 |
| U Politecnica of PR | 1,257 | 0.0 | 0.0 | 0.0 | 100.0 | 0.0 | 0.0 |
| U of Puerto Rico | | | | | | | |
| Cayey U C | 3,420 | 0.0 | 0.0 | 0.0 | 100.0 | 0.0 | 0.0 |
| Humacao U C | 3,447 | 0.0 | 0.0 | 0.0 | 100.0 | 0.0 | 0.0 |
| Mayaguez | 9,831 | 0.0 | 0.0 | 0.0 | 100.0 | 0.0 | 0.0 |
| Med Sciences | 3,151 | 0.0 | 0.0 | 0.0 | 99.7 | 0.0 | 0.3 |
| Rio Piedras | 21,523 | 0.0 | 0.0 | 0.0 | 100.0 | 0.0 | 0.0 |
| Aguadilla Regional C | 1,518 | 0.0 | 0.0 | 0.0 | 100.0 | 0.0 | 0.0 |
| Arecibo Tech U C | 3,589 | 0.0 | 0.0 | 0.0 | 100.0 | 0.0 | 0.0 |
| Bayamon Tech U C | 4,090 | 0.0 | 0.0 | 0.0 | 100.0 | 0.0 | 0.0 |
| La Montana Regional C | 558 | 0.0 | 0.0 | 0.0 | 98.2 | 1.8 | 0.0 |
| Carolina Regional C | 1,436 | 0.0 | 0.0 | 0.0 | 98.1 | 1.9 | 0.0 |
| Ponce Tech U C | 1,892 | 0.0 | 0.0 | 0.0 | 100.0 | 0.0 | 0.0 |
| U of the Sacred Heart | 8,019 | 0.0 | 0.0 | 0.0 | 100.0 | 0.0 | 0.0 |
| **TRUST TERRITORY** | | | | | | | |
| CC of Micronesia | 334 | 0.0% | 100% | 0.0% | 0.0% | 0.0% | 0.0% |
| Micronesian Occupational C | 462 | 0.0 | 100.0 | 0.0 | 0.0 | 0.0 | 0.0 |
| **VIRGIN ISLANDS** | | | | | | | |
| C of the Virgin Islands | 2,820 | 0.1% | 0.9% | 77.5% | 34.0% | 9.8% | 8.3% |

# University Endowments

College and university endowments gained an average of 25.51 per cent in fiscal 1985, the National Association of College and University Business Officers reported last week.

The figure includes changes in the market value of the investments as well as interest and dividends.

The gain, which is based on the performance of 277 investment pools at 284 institutions participating in the association's annual survey of endowments, was slightly lower than expected. A composite index based on the same asset mix as the average investment pool gained 28.01 per cent.

Last year the average endowment was invested as follows:

stocks, 51.7 per cent; bonds, 30.9 per cent; cash, 13.3 per cent; real estate, 2.1 per cent; other assets, 2.0 per cent.

The market value of the 277 investment pools on June 30, 1985, was $32.3-billion, an amount that represented about three-quarters of all endowments held by colleges and universities.

A summary of the 1985 survey appears in *Business Officer*, NACUBO's monthly magazine. The full report, *Results of the 1985 NACUBO Comparative Performance Study and Endowment Questionnaire*, may be purchased from NACUBO at P.O. Box 35024, Washington 20013. The price, prepaid, is $30 for association members and $50 for others.

## Gains in Fiscal 1985

|  | 1 year | 3 years | 5 years | 10 years |
|---|---|---|---|---|
| **All endowments** | +25.51% | +19.84% | +14.26% | +11.21% |
| Funds over $100-million | +25.92% | +20.94% | +15.00% | +12.01% |
| $25-million to $100-million | +26.21% | +20.48% | +14.44% | +11.20% |
| Under $25-million | +24.79% | +18.74% | +13.69% | +10.68% |
| **Comparative measurements** | | | | |
| **Equities** | | | | |
| Dow Jones Industrial Average | +23.81% | +24.02% | +15.00% | + 9.87% |
| Standard & Poor's 500 Index | +30.86% | +25.12% | +16.45% | +12.49% |
| **Bonds** | | | | |
| Salomon Brothers Bond Index | +41.45% | +23.24% | +11.55% | + 8.30% |
| Shearson Lehman Bond Index | +34.33% | +22.57% | +13.06% | + 9.60% |
| Consumer Price Index | + 3.70% | + 3.50% | + 5.39% | + 7.21% |
| Higher Education Price Index [†] | + 6.72% | + 6.14% | + 7.80% | + 7.64% |

Note: Data are based on 277 investment pools of 284 colleges and universities. Gains are changes in market value, plus dividends and interest, for periods ending June 30, 1985.

[†] An index of changes in prices paid by colleges and universities for goods and services, developed by D. Kent Halstead, National Institute for Education.

SOURCE: NATIONAL ASSOCIATION OF COLLEGE AND UNIVERSITY BUSINESS OFFICERS

## Value of 100 Endowments on June 30, 1985

| 1985 rank | Institution | Market value June 30, 1984 | Market value June 30, 1985 |
|---|---|---|---|
| 1. | University of Texas System [1] | $2,273,302,000 | $2,927,200,000 |
| 2. | Harvard University | 2,486,300,000 | 2,694,800,000 |
| 3. | Princeton University | 1,287,900,000 | 1,519,240,000 |
| 4. | Yale University | 1,060,670,000 | 1,308,690,000 |
| 5. | Stanford University [1] | 943,986,000 | 1,083,890,000 |
| 6. | Columbia University | 855,221,000 | 978,640,000 |
| 7. | Massachusetts Inst. of Technology | 645,575,000 | 770,167,000 |
| 8. | University of California | 559,411,000 | 716,809,000 |
| 9. | University of Chicago | 517,100,000 | 640,800,000 |
| 10. | Washington University (Mo.) | 474,684,000 | 622,076,000 |
| 11. | Rice University | 462,156,000 | 570,678,000 |
| 12. | University of Rochester | 588,276,000 | 567,696,000 |
| 13. | Northwestern University [1] | 449,784,000 | 552,201,000 |
| 14. | Emory University [1] | 457,830,000 | 535,825,000 |
| 15. | Cornell University | 417,671,000 | 518,956,000 |
| 16. | New York University [1] | 384,000,000 | 450,708,000 |
| 17. | University of Pennsylvania | 329,436,000 | 437,064,000 |
| 18. | Johns Hopkins University | 304,029,000 | 393,129,000 |
| 19. | Rockefeller University | 328,621,000 | 391,284,000 |
| 20. | Dartmouth College | 318,879,000 | 386,021,000 |
| 21. | Vanderbilt University | 261,864,000 | 318,322,000 |
| 22. | University of Notre Dame | 254,680,000 | 306,930,000 |
| 23. | California Institute of Technology [2] | 233,700,000 | 284,300,000 |
| 24. | University of Southern California | 233,829,000 | 267,602,000 |
| 25. | University of Virginia | 211,667,000 | 256,477,000 |
| 26. | Duke University | 195,676,000 | 252,071,000 |
| 27. | Case Western Reserve University | 189,201,000 | 244,126,000 |
| 28. | Southern Methodist University [3] | 174,225,000 | 233,659,000 |
| 29. | Smith College | 171,108,000 | 222,378,000 |
| 30. | Brown University | 175,200,000 | 222,300,000 |
| 31. | University of Delaware | 176,868,000 | 212,660,000 |
| 32. | Wellesley College | 158,223,000 | 205,000,000 |
| 33. | University of Michigan | 165,635,000 | 203,675,000 |
| 34. | Williams College | 164,133,000 | 199,996,000 |
| 35. | Carnegie Mellon University | 162,508,000 | 193,458,000 |
| 36. | Wesleyan University | 156,847,000 | 188,675,000 |
| 37. | University of Minnesota | not reported | 181,288,000 |
| 38. | Baylor University [3] | 158,772,000 | 175,611,000 |
| 39. | Grinnell College | 126,958,000 | 175,053,000 |
| 40. | Swarthmore College | 143,548,000 | 174,429,000 |
| 41. | University of Cincinnati | 145,010,000 | 169,387,000 |
| 42. | George Washington University | 134,795,000 | 169,194,000 |
| 43. | Loyola University of Chicago | 108,074,000 | 169,009,000 |
| 44. | Amherst College | 132,309,000 | 168,134,000 |
| 45. | Ohio State University | 121,444,000 | 167,281,000 |
| 46. | University of Richmond | 127,734,000 | 162,748,000 |
| 47. | University of Pittsburgh | 130,445,000 | 160,463,000 |
| 48. | Vassar College | 128,048,000 | 156,100,000 |
| 49. | Baylor College of Medicine | 106,844,000 | 153,341,000 |
| 50. | Berea College | 119,832,000 | 150,261,000 |
| 51. | Wake Forest University | $122,805,000 | $145,633,000 |
| 52. | Pomona College | 111,771,000 | 143,551,000 |
| 53. | Rensselaer Polytechnic Institute | 119,513,000 | 141,372,000 |
| 54. | Tulane University | 119,419,000 | 140,121,000 |
| 55. | Georgetown University | 95,076,000 | 139,072,000 |
| 56. | Lehigh University | 99,955,000 | 128,138,000 |
| 57. | Middlebury College | 100,524,000 | 125,791,000 |
| 58. | Lafayette College | 88,272,000 | 113,073,000 |
| 59. | University of Nebraska | 100,749,000 | 112,075,000 |
| 60. | Thomas Jefferson University | 85,269,000 | 108,738,000 |
| 61. | Brandeis University | not reported | 107,160,000 |
| 62. | Boston University | 85,896,000 | 104,316,000 |
| 63. | University of Florida | not reported | 104,188,000 |
| 64. | Tufts University | 58,616,000 | 97,675,000 |
| 65. | Washington State University | not reported | 97,158,000 |
| 66. | Carleton College | 75,056,000 | 96,988,000 |
| 67. | Mount Holyoke College | 76,397,000 | 96,757,000 |
| 68. | Kansas U. Endowment Association | 73,990,000 | 95,134,000 |
| 69. | Saint Louis University | 73,491,000 | 94,921,000 |
| 70. | State University of New York [3] | 72,448,000 | 92,620,000 |
| 71. | Rochester Institute of Technology | 75,547,000 | 91,160,000 |
| 72. | Bowdoin College | not reported | 89,697,000 |
| 73. | Syracuse University | 72,502,000 | 89,636,000 |
| 74. | Academy of the New Church | 65,492,000 | 89,198,000 |
| 75. | University of Miami [3] | 64,196,000 | 80,564,000 |
| 76. | Rutgers University | 67,496,000 | 80,515,000 |
| 77. | University of North Carolina-Chapel Hill | 59,859,000 | 79,902,000 |
| 78. | Earlham College | 60,127,000 | 75,816,000 |
| 79. | Mount Sinai School of Medicine | not reported | 74,770,000 |
| 80. | Trinity College (Conn.) | 59,899,000 | 74,107,000 |
| 81. | Occidental College | 69,474,000 | 73,262,000 |
| 82. | Hamilton College (N.Y.) | 60,813,000 | 73,261,000 |
| 83. | University of Washington | 58,602,000 | 72,909,000 |
| 84. | University of Wisconsin System | 60,070,000 | 70,937,000 |
| 85. | Colgate University [3] | 54,277,000 | 69,786,000 |
| 86. | University of Illinois Foundation | 49,532,000 | 68,151,000 |
| 87. | Union College (N.Y.) | not reported | 68,043,000 |
| 88. | Southwestern University | 52,008,000 | 67,314,000 |
| 89. | Butler University [3] | 61,781,000 | 64,585,000 |
| 90. | Worcester Polytechnic Institute | 55,148,000 | 64,456,000 |
| 91. | Colorado College | 51,901,000 | 63,914,000 |
| 92. | Whitman College | 53,306,000 | 63,603,000 |
| 93. | Radcliffe College | 39,923,000 | 62,516,000 |
| 94. | Bucknell University | 52,194,000 | 62,214,000 |
| 95. | University of the South | 48,884,000 | 60,654,000 |
| 96. | Hampton University | 40,129,000 | 58,785,000 |
| 97. | Pepperdine University [4] | 53,749,000 | 55,965,000 |
| 98. | Santa Clara University | 45,326,000 | 55,873,000 |
| 99. | Claremont McKenna College | 44,887,000 | 55,241,000 |
| 100. | Haverford College | not reported | 54,927,000 |

[1] As of August 31, 1985
[2] As of September 30, 1985
[3] As of May 31, 1985
[4] As of July 31, 1985

Note: Table includes the top 100 institutions participating in the comparative-performance study by the National Association of College and University Business Officers.

Table 2.5

# Defense Contracts for Non-Profit Organizations

Colleges, universities, and other non-profit organizations received $2.48-billion in Department of Defense contract funds in fiscal 1985. That represents an increase of 17 per cent over the 1984 total of $2.12-billion.

The contracts covered research, development, testing, and evaluation for military projects and also included federal civil water-resource projects. The figures include contracts over $25,000 and exclude funds for training.

Some 320 educational and nonprofit organizations were among the 2,330 contractors in fiscal 1985. The table below shows those that had contracts of $500,000 or more.

Contracts to colleges, universities, and other non-profit organizations accounted for 13 per cent of the $18.94-billion the Pentagon spent on research last year. In 1984, such organizations received 12 per cent of the total funds.

The Massachusetts Institute of Technology, the top higher-education contractor, was the 14th leading contractor overall, with contracts of $360-million. The Johns Hopkins University, with $304-million, ranked 18th among all contractors.

| | Amount | | | Amount |
|---|---|---|---|---|
| 1. Massachusetts Inst. of Technology | $360,104,000 | | 76. Northeastern University | $2,476,000 |
| 2. Charles S. Draper Laboratory | 305,238,000 | | 77. Arizona State University | 2,461,000 |
| 3. Johns Hopkins University | 304,310,000 | | 78. Oklahoma State University | 2,443,000 |
| 4. Aerospace Corporation | 291,520,000 | | 79. Emmanuel College | 2,436,000 |
| 5. Mitre Corporation | 260,995,000 | | 80. Polytechnic Institute of New York | 2,413,000 |
| 6. University of California System | 58,453,000 | | 81. University of Hawaii | 2,329,000 |
| 7. SRI International | 55,727,000 | | 82. Northwestern University | 2,268,000 |
| 8. IIT Research Institute | 45,701,000 | | 83. Mayo Foundation | 2,128,000 |
| 9. Institute for Defense Analyses | 42,838,000 | | 84. Michigan State University | 2,075,000 |
| 10. University of Texas System | 39,871,000 | | 85. University of North Carolina | 1,999,000 |
| 11. Georgia Tech Research Corporation | 35,952,000 | | 86. Auburn University | 1,972,000 |
| 12. Stanford University | 32,716,000 | | 87. Lehigh University | 1,962,000 |
| 13. Carnegie Mellon University | 29,511,000 | | 88. Duke University | 1,929,000 |
| 14. Rand Corporation | 27,252,000 | | 89. Syracuse University | 1,922,000 |
| 15. University of Southern California | 25,891,000 | | 90. La Jolla Institute | 1,880,000 |
| 16. Battelle Memorial Institute | 25,631,000 | | 91. University of Alabama | 1,715,000 |
| 17. Pennsylvania State University | 24,848,000 | | 92. Florida State University | 1,562,000 |
| 18. Hudson Institute | 23,498,000 | | 93. Rutgers University | 1,467,000 |
| 19. University of Dayton | 18,743,000 | | 94. American Society for Engineering Education | 1,361,000 |
| 20. University of Washington | 17,739,000 | | 95. University of Connecticut Foundation | 1,346,000 |
| 21. Analytic Services, Inc. | 17,000,000 | | 96. Drexel University | 1,329,000 |
| 22. New Mexico State University | 15,630,000 | | 96. Wright State University | 1,329,000 |
| 23. University of New Mexico | 14,887,000 | | 98. George Washington University | 1,328,000 |
| 24. Southwest Research Institute | 14,342,000 | | 99. University of Kansas | 1,309,000 |
| 25. Utah State University | 13,378,000 | | 100. Palisades Institute for Research Services | 1,289,000 |
| 26. University of Illinois | 11,942,000 | | 101. Michigan Technological University | 1,239,000 |
| 27. Woods Hole Oceanographic Institution | 11,548,000 | | 102. University of Denver | 1,237,000 |
| 28. University of Maryland | 11,307,000 | | 103. Colorado State University | 1,223,000 |
| 29. Trustees of Columbia University | 10,874,000 | | 104. Dartmouth College | 1,152,000 |
| 30. Environmental Research Institute of Michigan | 9,844,000 | | 105. Stevens Institute of Technology | 1,142,000 |
| 31. Logistics Management Institute | 8,996,000 | | 106. Louisiana State University System | 1,136,000 |
| 32. University of Wisconsin System | 8,633,000 | | 107. University of Missouri | 1,054,000 |
| 33. National Academy of Sciences | 8,560,000 | | 108. Trustees of Boston College | 1,048,000 |
| 34. Cornell University | 7,195,000 | | 109. University of Tennessee | 1,046,000 |
| 35. University of Pennsylvania | 6,290,000 | | 110. Armour Pharmaceutical Company | 1,045,000 |
| 36. University of Massachusetts | 6,141,000 | | 111. City University of New York | 1,034,000 |
| 37. University of Michigan | 5,994,000 | | 111. Howard University | 1,034,000 |
| 38. California Institute of Technology | 5,951,000 | | 113. University of Virginia | 1,028,000 |
| 39. Human Resources Research Organization | 5,678,000 | | 114. Clemson University | 1,025,000 |
| 40. Southeastern Center for Electrical Engineering Education | 5,576,000 | | 115. Clarkson University | 987,000 |
| 41. University of Florida | 5,550,000 | | 116. University of Houston System | 981,000 |
| 42. Yale University | 5,507,000 | | 117. University of Delaware | 962,000 |
| 43. Salk Institute | 5,463,000 | | 118. University of Georgia | 955,000 |
| 44. Southern Research Institute | 5,323,000 | | 119. Washington State University | 935,000 |
| 45. University of Utah | 5,197,000 | | 120. Wayne State University | 913,000 |
| 46. Harvard University | 4,637,000 | | 121. Iowa State University | 891,000 |
| 47. Princeton University | 4,556,000 | | 122. University of Cincinnati | 847,000 |
| 48. Battelle-Columbus Laboratories | 4,374,000 | | 122. Colorado School of Mines | 847,000 |
| 49. Texas A&M University System | 4,366,000 | | 124. San Diego State University Foundation | 837,000 |
| 50. Riverside Research Institute | 4,213,000 | | 125. Virginia Commonwealth University | 789,000 |
| 51. Virginia Polytechnic Institute and State University | 4,197,000 | | 126. Brigham Young University | 785,000 |
| 52. Georgia Institute of Technology | 4,088,000 | | 126. University of Oklahoma | 785,000 |
| 53. Rensselaer Polytechnic Institute | 4,051,000 | | 128. North Texas State University | 781,000 |
| 54. Syracuse Research Corporation | 3,967,000 | | 129. University of Nebraska | 779,000 |
| 55. Purdue University | 3,935,000 | | 130. Catholic University of America | 770,000 |
| 56. University of Arizona | 3,811,000 | | 131. Mississippi State University | 747,000 |
| 57. State University of New York and SUNY Research Foundation | 3,793,000 | | 132. Indiana University Foundation | 733,000 |
| 58. Ohio State University | 3,790,000 | | 133. Vanderbilt University | 732,000 |
| 59. University of Rochester | 3,738,000 | | 134. Midwest Research Institute | 720,000 |
| 60. Trustees of Boston University | 3,691,000 | | 135. Illinois Institute of Technology | 718,000 |
| 61. Research Triangle Institute | 3,665,000 | | 136. University of Notre Dame | 697,000 |
| 62. University of Minnesota | 3,601,000 | | 137. University of Oregon | 694,000 |
| 63. Brown University | 3,530,000 | | 138. University of Chicago | 678,000 |
| 64. New York University | 3,417,000 | | 139. Agouron Institute | 670,000 |
| 65. University of Rhode Island | 3,413,000 | | 140. Applied Research Laboratories Inc. | 663,000 |
| 66. University of Miami | 3,204,000 | | 141. University of Lowell | 650,000 |
| 67. Wentworth Institute of Technology | 3,199,000 | | 142. Rice University | 619,000 |
| 68. University of Colorado | 3,164,000 | | 143. University of Mississippi | 603,000 |
| 69. North Carolina State University | 3,162,000 | | 144. Consortium of Universities (D.C.) | 580,000 |
| 70. University of Pittsburgh | 3,143,000 | | 145. Research Institute of Colorado | 576,000 |
| 71. Oregon State University | 2,808,000 | | 146. Texas Tech University | 572,000 |
| 72. New Mexico Institute of Mining and Technology | 2,716,000 | | 147. University of Denver | 561,000 |
| 73. University of Iowa | 2,676,000 | | 148. Kansas State University | 560,000 |
| 74. Georgetown University | 2,545,000 | | 149. Oakland University | 548,000 |
| 75. Case Western Reserve University | 2,542,000 | | 150. George Mason University | 544,000 |
| | | | 151. Washington University (Mo.) | 537,000 |
| | | | 152. Atlanta University | 500,000 |

Table 2.6

SOURCE: U.S. DEPARTMENT OF DEFENSE

# 1985 Enrollment and Degrees at 343 Graduate Schools

| | Public institutions | | Private institutions | | All institutions | |
|---|---|---|---|---|---|---|
| | Fall 1985 | 1-year change | Fall 1985 | 1-year change | Fall 1985 | 1-year change |
| **Total graduate-school enrollment** | | | | | | |
| Ph.D.-granting institutions ........... | 506,883 | +1.8% | 210,845 | −0.4% | 717,728 | +1.2% |
| Master's-degree-only institutions ..... | 115,013 | +4.4% | 25,087 | +2.9% | 140,100 | +4.1% |
| All institutions ...................... | 621,896 | +2.3% | 235,932 | 0.0% | 857,828 | +1.6% |
| **Full-time graduate-school enrollment** | | | | | | |
| Ph.D.-granting institutions ........... | 216,581 | +1.1% | 92,756 | +1.3% | 309,337 | +1.2% |
| Master's-degree-only institutions ..... | 21,692 | −2.7% | 7,047 | +15.3% | 28,739 | +1.2% |
| All institutions ...................... | 238,273 | +0.7% | 99,803 | +2.2% | 338,076 | +1.2% |
| **Part-time graduate-school enrollment** | | | | | | |
| Ph.D.-granting institutions ........... | 262,849 | +2.9% | 114,427 | −1.6% | 377,276 | +1.5% |
| Master's-degree-only institutions ..... | 90,305 | +6.2% | 18,040 | −1.3% | 108,345 | +4.9% |
| All institutions ...................... | 353,154 | +3.8% | 132,467 | −1.6% | 485,621 | +2.2% |
| **First-time graduate students** | | | | | | |
| Ph.D.-granting institutions ........... | 120,613 | +1.8% | 50,399 | +0.6% | 171,012 | +1.4% |
| Master's-degree-only institutions ..... | 27,035 | +5.8% | 7,705 | +1.9% | 34,740 | +4.9% |
| All institutions ...................... | 147,648 | +2.5% | 58,104 | +0.7% | 205,752 | +2.0% |
| **Applications received** | | | | | | |
| Ph.D.-granting institutions ........... | 414,892 | +4.2% | 179,036 | +2.0% | 593,928 | +3.5% |
| Master's-degree-only institutions ..... | 44,814 | +5.8% | 12,938 | +1.5% | 57,752 | +4.8% |
| All institutions ...................... | 459,706 | +4.4% | 191,974 | +1.9% | 651,680 | +3.7% |
| **Graduate assistants** | | | | | | |
| Ph.D.-granting institutions ........... | 121,807 | +6.6% | 30,308 | +5.1% | 152,115 | +6.3% |
| Master's-degree-only institutions ..... | 5,824 | +1.8% | 609 | −0.5% | 6,433 | +1.6% |
| All institutions ...................... | 127,631 | +6.4% | 30,917 | +5.0% | 158,548 | +6.1% |
| **Graduate fellows** | | | | | | |
| Ph.D.-granting institutions ........... | 21,000 | +3.7% | 15,054 | +4.7% | 36,054 | +4.1% |
| Master's-degree-only institutions ..... | 344 | +20.3% | 78 | +25.8% | 422 | +21.3% |
| All institutions ...................... | 21,344 | +3.9% | 15,132 | +4.8% | 36,476 | +4.3% |
| **Degrees awarded in 1984-85** | | | | | | |
| Ph.D. ............................. | 20,027 | +0.7% | 8,523 | −3.8% | 28,550 | −0.7% |
| Master's ........................... | 126,747 | −0.3% | 56,659 | +10.3% | 183,406 | +2.7% |

Note: The figures are based on the reports of 343 of the 385 institutions that are members of the Council of Graduate Schools.

SOURCE: COUNCIL OF GRADUATE SCHOOLS IN THE UNITED STATES AND GRADUATE EXAMINATIONS BOARD

Table 2.7

# Fall 1985 Enrollment

## By type and control of institution

| | All students | | | Full-time students | | | Part-time students | | |
|---|---|---|---|---|---|---|---|---|---|
| **Public institutions** | Total | Men | Women | Total | Men | Women | Total | Men | Women |
| Doctoral | 2,400,817 | 1,241,164 | 1,159,653 | 1,813,810 | 968,114 | 845,696 | 587,007 | 273,050 | 313,957 |
| Comprehensive | 2,206,206 | 1,017,892 | 1,188,314 | 1,427,475 | 691,703 | 735,772 | 778,731 | 326,189 | 452,542 |
| General baccalaureate | 396,413 | 183,479 | 212,934 | 237,966 | 115,669 | 122,297 | 158,447 | 67,810 | 90,637 |
| Specialized | 197,979 | 129,561 | 68,418 | 160,108 | 111,677 | 48,431 | 37,871 | 17,884 | 19,987 |
| 2-year | 4,249,048 | 1,850,456 | 2,398,592 | 1,465,320 | 710,375 | 754,945 | 2,783,728 | 1,140,081 | 1,634,647 |
| New* | 28,810 | 14,936 | 13,874 | 15,567 | 8,824 | 6,743 | 13,243 | 6,112 | 7,131 |
| All | 9,479,273 | 4,437,488 | 5,041,785 | 5,120,246 | 2,606,362 | 2,513,884 | 4,359,027 | 1,831,126 | 2,527,901 |
| **Private institutions** | | | | | | | | | |
| Doctoral | 632,565 | 346,318 | 286,247 | 467,309 | 264,650 | 202,659 | 165,256 | 81,668 | 83,588 |
| Comprehensive | 657,004 | 325,569 | 331,435 | 419,516 | 211,342 | 208,174 | 237,488 | 114,227 | 123,261 |
| General baccalaureate | 759,927 | 330,271 | 429,656 | 570,472 | 258,513 | 311,959 | 189,455 | 71,758 | 117,697 |
| Specialized | 387,101 | 218,409 | 168,692 | 251,426 | 152,782 | 98,644 | 135,675 | 65,627 | 70,048 |
| 2-year | 260,293 | 111,814 | 148,479 | 204,314 | 90,174 | 114,140 | 55,979 | 21,640 | 34,339 |
| New* | 70,892 | 48,581 | 22,311 | 41,938 | 23,897 | 18,041 | 28,954 | 24,684 | 4,270 |
| All | 2,767,782 | 1,380,962 | 1,386,820 | 1,954,975 | 1,001,358 | 953,617 | 812,807 | 379,604 | 433,203 |
| **All institutions** | | | | | | | | | |
| Doctoral | 3,033,382 | 1,587,482 | 1,445,900 | 2,281,119 | 1,232,764 | 1,048,355 | 752,263 | 354,718 | 397,545 |
| Comprehensive | 2,863,210 | 1,343,461 | 1,519,749 | 1,846,991 | 903,045 | 943,946 | 1,016,219 | 440,416 | 575,803 |
| General baccalaureate | 1,156,340 | 513,750 | 642,590 | 808,438 | 374,182 | 434,256 | 347,902 | 139,568 | 208,334 |
| Specialized | 585,080 | 347,970 | 237,110 | 411,534 | 264,459 | 147,075 | 173,546 | 83,511 | 90,035 |
| 2-year | 4,509,341 | 1,962,270 | 2,547,071 | 1,669,634 | 800,549 | 869,085 | 2,839,707 | 1,161,721 | 1,677,986 |
| New* | 99,702 | 63,517 | 36,185 | 57,505 | 32,721 | 24,784 | 42,197 | 30,796 | 11,401 |
| All | 12,247,055 | 5,818,450 | 6,428,605 | 7,075,221 | 3,607,720 | 3,467,501 | 5,171,834 | 2,210,730 | 2,961,104 |

## By student level

| | Total | Men | Women | Total | Men | Women | Total | Men | Women |
|---|---|---|---|---|---|---|---|---|---|
| **Undergraduates** | | | | | | | | | |
| Doctoral institutions | 2,094,738 | 1,087,728 | 1,007,010 | 1,799,134 | 946,153 | 852,981 | 295,604 | 141,575 | 154,029 |
| Comprehensive | 2,175,200 | 1,039,286 | 1,135,914 | 1,684,363 | 818,253 | 866,110 | 490,837 | 221,033 | 269,804 |
| General baccalaureate | 993,686 | 445,539 | 548,147 | 781,248 | 359,611 | 421,637 | 212,438 | 85,928 | 126,510 |
| Specialized | 342,778 | 205,052 | 137,726 | 276,008 | 173,101 | 102,907 | 66,770 | 31,951 | 34,819 |
| 2-year | 3,722,106 | 1,636,456 | 2,085,652 | 1,571,521 | 751,684 | 819,837 | 2,150,587 | 884,722 | 1,265,815 |
| New* | 85,564 | 56,013 | 29,551 | 50,117 | 27,918 | 22,199 | 35,447 | 28,095 | 7,352 |
| All | 9,414,074 | 4,470,074 | 4,944,000 | 6,162,391 | 3,076,720 | 3,085,671 | 3,251,683 | 1,393,354 | 1,858,329 |
| **First-time freshmen** | | | | | | | | | |
| All | 2,292,222 | 1,075,736 | 1,216,486 | 1,602,038 | 774,858 | 827,180 | 690,184 | 300,878 | 389,306 |
| **Graduate students** | | | | | | | | | |
| Doctoral institutions | 600,228 | 325,960 | 274,268 | 327,090 | 192,084 | 135,006 | 273,138 | 133,876 | 139,262 |
| Comprehensive | 381,945 | 170,448 | 211,497 | 86,932 | 43,496 | 43,436 | 295,013 | 126,952 | 168,061 |
| General baccalaureate | 37,809 | 16,284 | 21,525 | 7,197 | 3,911 | 3,286 | 30,612 | 12,373 | 18,239 |
| Specialized | 101,662 | 59,895 | 41,767 | 46,672 | 28,795 | 17,877 | 54,990 | 31,100 | 23,890 |
| 2-year | 3,677 | 2,630 | 1,047 | 534 | 245 | 289 | 3,143 | 2,385 | 758 |
| New* | 4,217 | 2,007 | 2,210 | 2,542 | 1,288 | 1,254 | 1,675 | 719 | 956 |
| All | 1,129,538 | 577,224 | 552,314 | 470,967 | 269,819 | 201,148 | 658,571 | 307,405 | 351,166 |
| **First professional** | | | | | | | | | |
| Doctoral institutions | 129,508 | 81,100 | 48,408 | 121,962 | 76,771 | 45,191 | 7,546 | 4,329 | 3,217 |
| Comprehensive | 40,438 | 25,162 | 15,276 | 33,670 | 21,029 | 12,641 | 6,768 | 4,133 | 2,635 |
| General baccalaureate | 7,709 | 5,320 | 2,389 | 6,314 | 4,317 | 1,997 | 1,395 | 1,003 | 392 |
| Specialized | 93,088 | 65,788 | 27,300 | 81,783 | 58,199 | 23,584 | 11,305 | 7,589 | 3,716 |
| New* | 3,457 | 2,422 | 1,035 | 2,890 | 2,052 | 838 | 567 | 370 | 197 |
| All | 274,200 | 179,792 | 94,408 | 246,619 | 162,638 | 84,251 | 27,581 | 17,424 | 10,157 |
| **Unclassified** | | | | | | | | | |
| All | 1,429,243 | 591,360 | 837,883 | 195,244 | 98,813 | 96,431 | 1,233,999 | 492,547 | 741,452 |

## By state

| | Public institutions | Private institutions | Total | | Public institutions | Private institutions | Total |
|---|---|---|---|---|---|---|---|
| Alabama | 158,688 | 20,655 | 179,343 | New Jersey | 237,297 | 60,361 | 297,658 |
| Alaska | 26,510 | 969 | 27,479 | New Mexico | 66,059 | 2,236 | 68,295 |
| Arizona | 202,036 | 14,818 | 216,854 | New York | 563,251 | 436,847 | 1,000,098 |
| Arkansas | 66,123 | 11,835 | 77,958 | North Carolina | 267,044 | 60,244 | 327,288 |
| California | 1,444,207 | 206,232 | 1,650,439 | North Dakota | 34,802 | 3,137 | 37,939 |
| Colorado | 142,031 | 19,283 | 161,314 | Ohio | 379,164 | 135,581 | 514,745 |
| Connecticut | 98,616 | 60,732 | 159,348 | Oklahoma | 146,827 | 22,346 | 169,173 |
| Delaware | 27,933 | 3,950 | 31,883 | Oregon | 119,612 | 18,355 | 137,967 |
| District of Columbia | 12,747 | 66,121 | 78,868 | Pennsylvania | 300,523 | 232,675 | 533,198 |
| Florida | 362,241 | 89,151 | 451,392 | Rhode Island | 35,389 | 34,538 | 69,927 |
| Georgia | 148,956 | 47,870 | 196,826 | South Carolina | 105,854 | 26,048 | 131,902 |
| Hawaii | 43,246 | 6,691 | 49,937 | South Dakota | 23,339 | 9,433 | 32,772 |
| Idaho | 33,666 | 9,002 | 42,668 | Tennessee | 147,951 | 46,894 | 194,845 |
| Illinois | 520,224 | 158,465 | 678,689 | Texas | 677,192 | 92,500 | 769,692 |
| Indiana | 193,833 | 56,734 | 250,567 | Utah | 69,426 | 34,568 | 103,994 |
| Iowa | 109,765 | 43,132 | 152,897 | Vermont | 18,844 | 12,572 | 31,416 |
| Kansas | 127,220 | 14,139 | 141,359 | Virginia | 250,754 | 41,662 | 292,416 |
| Kentucky | 110,836 | 30,888 | 141,724 | Washington | 201,532 | 30,021 | 231,553 |
| Louisiana | 153,173 | 24,003 | 177,176 | West Virginia | 66,531 | 10,128 | 76,659 |
| Maine | 33,188 | 19,013 | 52,201 | Wisconsin | 238,735 | 36,334 | 275,069 |
| Maryland | 198,992 | 32,657 | 231,649 | Wyoming | 24,204 | 0 | 24,204 |
| Massachusetts | 185,602 | 235,573 | 421,175 | U.S. Service Schools | 54,052 | 0 | 54,052 |
| Michigan | 434,270 | 73,023 | 507,293 | Total | 9,479,273 | 2,767,782 | 12,247,055 |
| Minnesota | 173,984 | 47,178 | 221,162 | American Samoa | 758 | 0 | 758 |
| Mississippi | 90,704 | 10,476 | 101,180 | Guam | 4,601 | 0 | 4,601 |
| Missouri | 168,829 | 72,317 | 241,146 | North Marianas | 318 | 0 | 318 |
| Montana | 32,032 | 3,926 | 35,958 | Puerto Rico | 56,438 | 99,479 | 155,917 |
| Nebraska | 81,202 | 16,567 | 97,769 | Trust Territories, Pacific Islands | 724 | 0 | 724 |
| Nevada | 43,368 | 288 | 43,656 | Virgin Islands | 2,572 | 0 | 2,572 |
| New Hampshire | 26,669 | 25,614 | 52,283 | | | | |

Table 2.8

* New institutions not yet classified.

SOURCE: U.S. DEPARTMENT OF EDUCATION, CENTER FOR STATISTICS

# Trends in Student Aid, 1980-81 to 1985-86

## Total amounts, in millions of dollars, not adjusted for inflation

| Federally supported programs | Academic Years | | | | Estimated 1984-85 | Estimated 1985-86 | Percent change 1980-81 to 1985-86 |
| | 1980-81 | 1981-82 | 1982-83 | 1983-84 | | | |
|---|---|---|---|---|---|---|---|
| **Generally available aid** | | | | | | | |
| Pell Grants | $2,387 | $2,299 | $2,417 | $2,796 | $3,042 | $3,749 | + 57.1% |
| Supplemental Educational Opportunity Grants | 366 | 361 | 343 | 361 | 360 | 396 | + 8.2% |
| State Student Incentive Grants | 76 | 77 | 73 | 60 | 76 | 76 | 0.0 |
| College Work Study | 658 | 624 | 615 | 683 | 649 | 693 | + 5.3% |
| National Direct Student Loans | 695 | 580 | 598 | 682 | 763 | 841 | + 21.0% |
| Guaranteed Student Loans and Parent Loans for Undergraduate Students | 6,201 | 7,226 | 6,694 | 7,578 | 8,604 | 9,411 | + 51.8% |
| Subtotal | 10,384 | 11,168 | 10,741 | 12,160 | 13,494 | 15,166 | + 46.1% |
| **Specially directed aid** | | | | | | | |
| Social Security | 1,883 | 1,996 | 733 | 220 | 35 | 0 | −100.0% |
| Veterans | 1,714 | 1,351 | 1,356 | 1,033 | 904 | 746 | − 56.5% |
| Other grants | 119 | 102 | 81 | 59 | 55 | 48 | − 59.7% |
| Other loans | 61 | 88 | 157 | 219 | 244 | 248 | +306.6% |
| Subtotal | 3,777 | 3,536 | 2,327 | 1,531 | 1,238 | 1,042 | − 72.4% |
| **Total federal aid** | 14,161 | 14,704 | 13,067 | 13,690 | 14,732 | 16,208 | + 14.5% |
| State grant programs | 801 | 921 | 1,006 | 1,106 | 1,222 | 1,374 | + 71.5% |
| Institutionally awarded aid | 2,138 | 2,323 | 2,517 | 2,883 | 3,173 | 3,426 | + 60.2% |
| **Total federal, state, and institutional aid** | $17,101 | $17,947 | $16,590 | $17,679 | $19,128 | $21,008 | + 22.9% |

## Total amounts, in millions of constant 1982 dollars

| Federally supported programs | Academic Years | | | | Estimated 1984-85 | Estimated 1985-86 | Percent change 1980-81 to 1985-86 |
| | 1980-81 | 1981-82 | 1982-83 | 1983-84 | | | |
|---|---|---|---|---|---|---|---|
| **Generally available aid** | | | | | | | |
| Pell Grants | $2,660 | $2,358 | $2,376 | $2,651 | $2,753 | $3,298 | + 24.0% |
| Supplemental Educational Opportunity Grants | 408 | 371 | 337 | 342 | 326 | 348 | − 14.7% |
| State Student Incentive Grants | 85 | 79 | 72 | 57 | 69 | 67 | − 21.2% |
| College Work Study | 734 | 640 | 605 | 648 | 587 | 610 | − 16.9% |
| National Direct Student Loans | 774 | 595 | 588 | 647 | 690 | 740 | − 4.4% |
| Guaranteed Student Loans and Parent Loans for Undergraduate Students | 6,911 | 7,411 | 6,580 | 7,185 | 7,785 | 8,280 | + 19.8% |
| Subtotal | 11,573 | 11,453 | 10,558 | 11,529 | 12,210 | 13,343 | + 15.3% |
| **Specially directed aid** | | | | | | | |
| Social Security | 2,099 | 2,047 | 721 | 209 | 32 | 0 | −100.0% |
| Veterans | 1,911 | 1,385 | 1,333 | 979 | 818 | 656 | − 65.7% |
| Other grants | 132 | 105 | 80 | 56 | 50 | 42 | − 68.2% |
| Other loans | 68 | 90 | 155 | 208 | 221 | 218 | +220.6% |
| Subtotal | 4,209 | 3,626 | 2,287 | 1,451 | 1,120 | 917 | − 78.2% |
| **Total federal aid** | 15,782 | 15,079 | 12,845 | 12,981 | 13,331 | 14,260 | − 9.6% |
| State grant programs | 893 | 944 | 989 | 1,048 | 1,106 | 1,209 | + 35.4% |
| Institutionally awarded aid | 2,383 | 2,382 | 2,474 | 2,734 | 2,871 | 3,014 | + 26.5% |
| **Total federal, state, and institutional aid** | $19,059 | $18,406 | $16,308 | $16,763 | $17,307 | $18,483 | − 3.0% |

## Number of student-aid recipients and amount of aid per recipient

| | Academic Years | | | | Estimated 1984-85 | Estimated 1985-86 | Percent change 1980-81 to 1985-86 |
| | 1980-81 | 1981-82 | 1982-83 | 1983-84 | | | |
|---|---|---|---|---|---|---|---|
| **Pell Grants** | | | | | | | |
| Recipients | 2,806,000 | 2,744,000 | 2,539,000 | 2,802,000 | 2,919,000 | 2,954,000 | + 5.3% |
| Aid per recipient—current dollars | $851 | $838 | $952 | $998 | $1,042 | $1,269 | + 49.1% |
| Aid per recipient—constant dollars | $948 | $859 | $936 | $946 | $943 | $1,116 | + 17.7% |
| **Supplemental Educational Opportunity Grants** | | | | | | | |
| Recipients | 717,000 | 659,000 | 641,000 | 649,000 | 655,000 | 720,000 | + 0.4% |
| Aid per recipient—current dollars | $513 | $549 | $535 | $557 | $550 | $550 | + 7.2% |
| Aid per recipient—constant dollars | $572 | $563 | $526 | $528 | $498 | $484 | − 15.4% |
| **College Work Study** | | | | | | | |
| Recipients | 819,000 | 739,000 | 720,000 | 772,000 | 737,000 | 788,000 | − 3.8% |
| Aid per recipient—current dollars | $806 | $844 | $854 | $886 | $880 | $879 | + 9.1% |
| Aid per recipient—constant dollars | $898 | $866 | $839 | $840 | $796 | $773 | − 13.9% |
| **National Direct Student Loans** | | | | | | | |
| Recipients | 813,000 | 684,000 | 675,000 | 719,000 | 867,000 | 956,000 | + 17.6% |
| Aid per recipient—current dollars | $853 | $848 | $886 | $949 | $880 | $880 | + 3.2% |
| Aid per recipient—constant dollars | $951 | $870 | $871 | $900 | $796 | $774 | − 18.6% |
| **Guaranteed Student Loans** | | | | | | | |
| Recipients | 2,899,000 | 3,138,000 | 2,947,000 | 3,145,000 | 3,504,000 | 3,798,000 | + 31.0% |
| Aid per recipient—current dollars | $2,134 | $2,281 | $2,209 | $2,307 | $2,326 | $2,323 | + 8.9% |
| Aid per recipient—constant dollars | $2,379 | $2,340 | $2,172 | $2,188 | $2,104 | $2,044 | − 14.1% |
| **Parent Loans for Undergraduate Students** | | | | | | | |
| Recipients | 6,000 | 26,000 | 75,000 | 123,000 | 171,000 | 216,000 | +3,500.0% |
| Aid per recipient—current dollars | $2,333 | $2,577 | $2,440 | $2,610 | $2,655 | $2,727 | + 16.9% |
| Aid per recipient—constant dollars | $2,600 | $2,643 | $2,399 | $2,475 | $2,402 | $2,399 | − 7.7% |
| **State Grants and State Student Incentive Grants** | | | | | | | |
| Recipients | 1,140,000 | 1,448,000 | 1,493,000 | 1,528,000 | 1,580,000 | 1,585,000 | + 39.0% |
| Aid per recipient—current dollars | $736 | $690 | $723 | $763 | $821 | $914 | + 24.2% |
| Aid per recipient—constant dollars | $820 | $708 | $711 | $723 | $743 | $804 | − 2.0% |

**Note:** Several of the "federally supported" aid programs include small amounts of money from sources other than the federal government. For example, College Work Study includes some contributions by institutions, although most of the funds in the program are federal. National Direct Student Loans are financed from federal and capital contributions and collections from borrowers.

Federal State Student Incentive Grant expenditures are reported under "federally supported" aid and excluded from state awards.

Guaranteed Student Loan and Parent Loans for Undergraduate Students funds come mostly from private sources. The federal government subsidizes interest payments and repays defaults. Amounts reported represent loan commitments rather than amounts loaned, but there is not much difference between the two. The estimated 1985-86 figure assumes no decrease in loan volume as a result of changes effected by the Gramm-Rudman-Hollings deficit-reduction law beginning March 1, 1986.

Veterans' benefits are payments for postsecondary education and training to veterans and their dependents.

SOURCE: THE COLLEGE BOARD

Table 2.9

# State Appropriations for Higher Education . . . . . .

The following figures were compiled by Edward R. Hines of Illinois State University. The table omits footnotes qualifying some of the figures.

## *Annual Appropriations*

| | Appropriations 1986-87 (add 000) | 2-year change |
|---|---|---|
| **ALABAMA** | | |
| U of Alabama | $ 182,529 | +12% |
| Auburn U | 104,318 | +14% |
| U of South Alabama | 35,889 | +14% |
| Jacksonville St U | 15,840 | +12% |
| Troy St U | 14,809 | +20% |
| Alabama A&M U | 15,148 | +36% |
| Alabama St U | 14,958 | +37% |
| U of North Alabama | 12,030 | +12% |
| U of Montevallo | 8,752 | +10% |
| Livingston U | 5,316 | +11% |
| Athens St C | 2,715 | + 9% |
| Junior colleges | 58,550 | +11% |
| Aid to private institutions | 2,601 | − 3% |
| Student aid | 1,224 | + 2% |
| Other appropriations | 82,215 | n/c |
| **Total** | **$ 556,894** | **+11%** |
| **ALASKA** | | |
| U of Alaska | $ 98,213 | −16% |
| Community colleges | 45,318 | −11% |
| Student aid | 60,000 | − 2% |
| Other appropriations | 3,555 | n/c |
| **Total** | **$ 207,086** | **−11%** |
| **ARIZONA** | | |
| U of Arizona | $ 208,574 | +26% |
| Arizona St U | 154,797 | +30% |
| Northern Arizona U | 52,745 | +26% |
| Community colleges | 59,905 | +25% |
| Other appropriations | 4,055 | n/c |
| **Total** | **$ 480,076** | **+27%** |
| **ARKANSAS** | | |
| U of Arkansas | $ 163,940 | + 7% |
| Arkansas St U | 26,942 | +13% |
| U of Central Arkansas | 19,402 | + 6% |
| Southern Arkansas U | 11,750 | +11% |
| Arkansas Tech U | 10,846 | +10% |
| Henderson St U | 8,649 | + 5% |
| Community colleges | 20,790 | +11% |
| Student aid | 7,747 | +32% |
| Other appropriations | 3,116 | n/c |
| **Total** | **$ 273,182** | **+10%** |
| **CALIFORNIA** | | |
| U of California | | |
| Los Angeles | $ 403,919 | +22% |
| Berkeley | 322,196 | +24% |
| Davis | 290,267 | +37% |
| San Diego | 181,059 | +28% |
| San Francisco | 142,221 | +23% |
| Irvine | 140,185 | +27% |
| Santa Barbara | 123,557 | +25% |
| Riverside | 97,852 | +37% |
| Santa Cruz | 66,631 | +21% |
| Administration | 35,278 | n/c |
| California St U | | |
| San Diego | 113,088 | +11% |
| Long Beach | 94,956 | + 9% |
| San Jose | 87,909 | + 9% |
| Northridge | 86,121 | +11% |
| San Luis Obispo | 81,859 | +12% |
| San Francisco | 80,920 | +11% |
| Sacramento | 80,607 | +13% |
| Fresno | 77,235 | +17% |
| Los Angeles | 74,808 | + 5% |
| Pomona | 71,704 | +12% |
| Fullerton | 70,128 | + 9% |
| Chico | 66,865 | +11% |
| Hayward | 50,765 | + 7% |
| Humboldt | 40,065 | + 1% |
| Dominguez Hills | 30,702 | + 2% |
| San Bernardino | 29,034 | +22% |
| Sonoma | 28,501 | + 5% |
| Bakersfield | 21,452 | +14% |
| Stanislaus | 21,187 | + 5% |
| Other appropriations | 212,041 | n/c |
| Community colleges | 1,199,057 | + 8% |
| Hastings C of Law | 11,365 | +32% |
| California Maritime Academy | 6,068 | +28% |
| Student aid commission | 118,590 | +46% |
| Other appropriations | 4,459 | n/c |
| **Total** | **$4,562,651** | **+18%** |

Note: Some totals may be inconsistent with itemized figures because of rounding.
n/c Not comparable
* Estimated
† Total is preliminary, and figures for campuses are not available.

| | Appropriations 1986-87 (add 000) | 2-year change |
|---|---|---|
| **COLORADO** | | |
| U of Colorado | $ 155,773 | +10% |
| St Board of Agriculture (for Colorado St U, U of Southern Colo, and Ft. Lewis C) | 82,812 | +14% |
| U of Northern Colorado | 23,221 | + 6% |
| Colorado Sch of Mines | 10,019 | +14% |
| State colleges (Mesa, Metropolitan, Western, and Adams St) | 39,427 | + 5% |
| Community colleges | 55,564 | + 7% |
| Occupational education | 24,018 | + 9% |
| Student aid | 24,328 | + 5% |
| Other appropriations | 7,970 | n/c |
| **Total** | **$ 423,132** | **+10%** |
| **CONNECTICUT** | | |
| U of Connecticut | $ 162,159 | +18% |
| St U System | | |
| Central Connecticut | 25,063 | +19% |
| Southern Connecticut | 24,898 | +18% |
| Western Connecticut | 11,912 | +22% |
| Eastern Connecticut | 9,778 | 25% |
| Central office | 1,761 | +46% |
| Regional community colleges | 45,492 | +23% |
| State tech colleges | 14,984 | +30% |
| Other appropriations | 72,600 | n/c |
| **Total** | **$ 368,648** | **+22%** |
| **DELAWARE** | | |
| U of Delaware | $ 57,661 | +14% |
| Delaware St C | 14,564 | +14% |
| Tech & community colleges | 21,472 | +14% |
| Other appropriations | 3,100 | n/c |
| **Total** | **$ 96,797** | **+14%** |
| **FLORIDA** | | |
| U of Florida | $ 302,218 | +22% |
| U of South Florida | 144,866 | +31% |
| Florida St U | 117,801 | +19% |
| Florida International U | 56,393 | +29% |
| U of Central Florida | 52,470 | +27% |
| Florida Atlantic U | 39,867 | +27% |
| Florida A&M U | 38,385 | +44% |
| U of West Florida | 26,758 | +22% |
| U of North Florida | 20,649 | +25% |
| Contracts to private insts | 13,499 | +25% |
| Community colleges | 392,662 | +17% |
| Student aid | 20,705 | +24% |
| Aid to private college students | 15,989 | +34% |
| Other appropriations | 35,442 | n/c |
| **Total** | **$1,277,704** | **+24%** |
| **GEORGIA** | | |
| U of Georgia | $ 212,756 | +15% |
| Medical C of Georgia | 91,296 | +11% |
| Georgia St U | 76,295 | +14% |
| Georgia Inst of Tech | 72,972 | +19% |
| Georgia Southern C | 20,393 | +12% |
| West Georgia C | 16,335 | +10% |
| Valdosta St C | 15,198 | +20% |
| Kennesaw C | 13,240 | +53% |
| Columbus C | 12,461 | + 9% |
| Southern Tech Inst | 10,867 | +43% |
| Fort Valley St C | 10,182 | +11% |
| Georgia St C | 9,900 | +19% |
| Savannah St C | 9,850 | +12% |
| Albany St C | 9,617 | + 9% |
| Augusta C | 9,141 | +11% |
| Armstrong St C | 8,036 | + 7% |
| Georgia Southwestern C | 7,813 | +10% |
| North Georgia C | 6,351 | +12% |
| Clayton St C | 5,984 | +16% |
| Junior colleges | 65,663 | +27% |
| Student aid | 1,912 | +44% |
| Other appropriations | 27,742 | n/c |
| **Total** | **$ 714,004** | **+17%** |
| **HAWAII** | | |
| U of Hawaii | $ 197,580 | +18% |
| Other appropriations | 45,965 | n/c |
| Less tuition and other revenue | −22,700 | n/c |
| **Total** | **$ 220,845** | **+18%** |
| **IDAHO** | | |
| U of Idaho | $ 52,177 | +13% |
| Boise St U | 25,957 | + 9% |
| Idaho St U | 23,160 | +16% |
| Lewis-Clark St C | 3,988 | +16% |
| Community colleges | 5,815 | +11% |
| Vocational education | 13,546 | + 9% |
| Student aid | 267 | 0% |
| Other appropriations | 1,120 | n/c |
| **Total** | **$ 126,030** | **+12%** |
| **ILLINOIS** | | |
| U of Illinois | $ 485,459 | +16% |
| Southern Illinois U | 165,218 | +17% |
| Northern Illinois U | 79,301 | +19% |
| Illinois St U | 59,784 | +15% |
| Western Illinois U | 41,995 | +16% |
| Eastern Illinois U | 31,943 | +18% |
| Northeastern Illinois U | 28,224 | +30% |
| Chicago St U | 22,347 | +18% |
| Governors St U | 16,166 | +10% |
| Sangamon St U | 15,693 | +13% |

| | Appropriations 1986-87 (add 000) | 2-year change |
|---|---|---|
| **ILLINOIS—Continued** | | |
| Community colleges | 203,240 | +19% |
| Student aid | 141,395 | +22% |
| Other appropriations | 99,849 | n/c |
| **Total** | **$1,390,614** | **+18%** |
| **INDIANA** | | |
| Indiana U | $ 256,337 | +17% |
| Purdue U | 181,046 | +20% |
| Ball St U | 74,112 | +21% |
| Indiana St U | 51,165 | +14% |
| U of Southern Indiana | 7,878 | +23% |
| Indiana Voc-Tech C | 39,005 | +49% |
| Vincennes U | 15,747 | +25% |
| Student aid | 31,956 | +32% |
| Other appropriations | 3,286 | n/c |
| **Total** | **$ 660,532** | **+20%** |
| **IOWA** | | |
| U of Iowa | $ 141,999 | + 3% |
| Iowa St U | 129,249 | + 4% |
| U of Northern Iowa | 41,016 | + 4% |
| Board of Regents | 461 | − 1% |
| Aid to area colleges | 68,053 | + 2% |
| Student aid | 23,832 | − 2% |
| **Total** | **$ 404,610** | **+ 3%** |
| **KANSAS** | | |
| U of Kansas | $ 133,804 | − 2% |
| Kansas St U | 86,009 | + 8% |
| Wichita St U | 36,525 | + 6% |
| Pittsburg St U | 16,308 | + 3% |
| Emporia St U | 16,103 | − 1% |
| Fort Hays St U | 15,730 | + 4% |
| Kansas Tech Inst | 3,136 | + 7% |
| Washburn U of Topeka | 4,446 | + 8% |
| Community colleges | 27,056 | + 6% |
| Student aid | 5,293 | +11% |
| Other appropriations* | 6,325 | n/c |
| **Total** | **$ 350,735** | **+ 4%** |
| **KENTUCKY** | | |
| U of Kentucky | $ 192,377 | +14% |
| U of Louisville | 94,817 | +12% |
| Eastern Kentucky U | 38,895 | +10% |
| Western Kentucky U | 38,218 | +12% |
| Murray St U | 28,892 | +10% |
| Morehead St U | 23,506 | +11% |
| Northern Kentucky U | 19,832 | +11% |
| Kentucky St U | 13,050 | +17% |
| Kentucky Higher Education Assistance Authority | 8,575 | n/c |
| Other appropriations | 10,793 | n/c |
| **Total** | **$ 468,955** | **+15%** |
| **LOUISIANA** | | |
| Louisiana St U | $ 309,637 | − 3% |
| Southern U | 44,592 | + 4% |
| U of Southwestern La | 34,824 | − 4% |
| Louisiana Tech U | 25,562 | − 1% |
| Northeast Louisiana U | 24,627 | − 3% |
| Southeastern La U | 17,800 | − 2% |
| Northwestern St U of La | 16,248 | − 4% |
| Nicholls St U | 16,077 | − 4% |
| McNeese St U | 17,652 | − 1% |
| Grambling St U | 16,412 | +11% |
| Delgado CC | 12,438 | + 3% |
| Student aid | 1,388 | n/c |
| Other appropriations | 4,465 | n/c |
| **Total** | **$ 541,722** | **− 3%** |
| **MAINE** | | |
| U of Maine | $ 101,026 | +39% |
| Maine Maritime Academy | 4,028 | +19% |
| Vocational education | 16,302 | +29% |
| Student aid | 3,860 | +61% |
| **Total** | **$ 125,216** | **+37%** |
| **MARYLAND** | | |
| U of Maryland | $ 312,681 | +22% |
| State colleges | | |
| Towson | 33,095 | +13% |
| Morgan | 24,361 | +22% |
| Frostburg | 14,387 | +13% |
| Salisbury | 12,027 | +14% |
| U of Baltimore | 11,745 | +19% |
| Bowie | 10,421 | +18% |
| Coppin | 9,631 | +14% |
| St Mary's C of Maryland | 6,270 | +17% |
| Trustees | 5,963 | −13% |
| Community colleges | 98,143 | + 6% |
| Aid to private colleges | 16,675 | +26% |
| Student aid | 8,940 | n/c |
| Other appropriations | 5,636 | n/c |
| **Total** | **$ 569,975** | **+17%** |
| **MASSACHUSETTS** | | |
| U of Massachusetts | $ 251,154 | +19% |
| U of Lowell | 54,801 | +36% |
| Southeastern Mass U | 32,115 | +26% |
| Salem St C | 20,545 | +17% |
| Bridgewater St C | 19,513 | +15% |
| Fitchburg St C | 16,542 | +17% |
| Worcester St C | 13,177 | +18% |
| Westfield St C | 13,123 | +14% |
| Framingham St C | 13,012 | +15% |
| Mass Maritime Academy | 9,184 | +18% |
| North Adams St C | 8,925 | +16% |

| | Appropriations 1986-87 (add 000) | 2-year change |
|---|---|---|
| **MASSACHUSETTS—Continued** | | |
| Mass C of Art | $ 8,590 | +11% |
| Community colleges | 130,530 | +20% |
| Student aid | 75,300 | +51% |
| Other appropriations | 149,868 | n/c |
| **Total** | **$ 816,379** | **+27%** |
| **MICHIGAN** | | |
| U of Michigan | $ 252,224 | +23% |
| Michigan St U | 222,464 | +22% |
| Wayne St U | 152,553 | +22% |
| Western Michigan U | 69,276 | +20% |
| Eastern Michigan U | 52,307 | +21% |
| Central Michigan U | 45,175 | +21% |
| Ferris St C | 33,339 | +20% |
| Michigan Tech U | 33,124 | +24% |
| Northern Michigan U | 32,020 | +19% |
| Oakland U | 29,900 | +20% |
| Grand Valley St C | 20,346 | +21% |
| Saginaw Valley St C | 12,242 | +40% |
| Lake Superior St C | 8,643 | +19% |
| Community colleges | 186,722 | +17% |
| Student aid | 77,717 | n/c |
| Other appropriations | 507 | n/c |
| **Total** | **$1,228,559** | **+22%** |
| **MINNESOTA** | | |
| U of Minnesota | $ 364,522 | +18% |
| State universities | 118,180 | +11% |
| Area voc-tech insts | 135,140 | +16% |
| Community colleges | 58,599 | +10% |
| Mayo Medical School | 916 | −24% |
| Student aid | 62,729 | +11% |
| Other appropriations | 7,101 | n/c |
| **Total** | **$ 747,187** | **+15%** |
| **MISSISSIPPI** | | |
| U of Mississippi | $ 81,790 | + 2% |
| Mississippi St U | 68,834 | − 1% |
| U of Southern Mississippi | 36,130 | + 1% |
| Jackson St U | 14,765 | −17% |
| Delta St U | 9,156 | −14% |
| Alcorn St U | 6,579 | −26% |
| Mississippi Valley State U | 5,533 | −26% |
| Mississippi U for Women | 5,878 | −31% |
| Vocational education | 38,659 | + 1% |
| Community colleges | 50,000 | − 1% |
| Student aid | 792 | n/c |
| Other appropriations | 9,237 | n/c |
| **Total** | **$ 327,353** | **− 5%** |
| **MISSOURI** | | |
| U of Missouri | $ 255,608 | +28% |
| Southwest Missouri St U | 37,770 | +36% |
| Central Missouri St U | 26,162 | +23% |
| Southeast Missouri St U | 25,196 | +32% |
| Northeast Missouri St U | 20,626 | +37% |
| Northwest Missouri St U | 14,934 | +28% |
| Missouri Western St C | 9,864 | +21% |
| Missouri Southern St C | 10,111 | +32% |
| Lincoln U | 8,338 | +15% |
| Harris-Stowe C | 4,213 | +29% |
| Aid to public CC's | 51,845 | +20% |
| Student aid | 8,644 | +13% |
| Other appropriations | 3,109 | n/c |
| **Total** | **$ 476,420** | **+19%** |
| **MONTANA** | | |
| U of Montana | $ 26,728 | − 2% |
| Montana St U | 40,511 | − 4% |
| Eastern Montana C | 10,441 | − 3% |
| Northern Montana C | 6,051 | − 4% |
| Western Montana C | 3,139 | + 6% |
| C of Mineral Science & Tech | 7,984 | −14% |
| Community colleges | 3,102 | − 4% |
| Student aid | 4,418 | 0% |
| Other appropriations | 793 | n/c |
| **Total** | **$ 103,167** | **− 4%** |
| **NEBRASKA** | | |
| U of Nebraska | $ 167,735 | + 2% |
| State colleges | | |
| Kearney | 11,585 | + 6% |
| Wayne | 6,165 | + 1% |
| Chadron | 5,874 | + 3% |
| Peru | 3,231 | − 1% |
| System office | 228 | + 6% |
| Aid to tech CC's | 22,447 | − 3% |
| Coordinating commission | 90 | n/c |
| **Total** | **$ 217,355** | **+ 2%** |
| **NEVADA** | | |
| U of Nevada | $ 75,306 | +33% |
| Community colleges | 18,924 | +36% |
| Other appropriations | 8,189 | n/c |
| **Total** | **$ 102,419** | **+30%** |
| **NEW HAMPSHIRE** | | |
| U of New Hampshire | $ 31,694 | +25% |
| Plymouth St C | 6,073 | +35% |
| Keene St C | 5,680 | +30% |
| Sch for Lifelong Learning | 553 | +92% |
| NH Tech Inst | 2,947 | +56% |
| Voc-tech insts | 7,009 | +39% |
| Other appropriations | 2,005 | n/c |
| **Total** | **$ 55,961** | **+31%** |

Table 2.10

# for 1986-87, with Changes over 2 Years

| | Appropriations 1986-87 (add 000) | 2-year change |
|---|---|---|
| **NEW JERSEY** | | |
| Rutgers U | $ 207,100 | +20% |
| U of Medicine & Dentistry of NJ | 125,431 | +22% |
| NJ Inst of Tech | 32,030 | +42% |
| Montclair St C | 29,341 | +17% |
| William Paterson C | 27,621 | +18% |
| Trenton St C | 26,161 | +16% |
| Kean C of NJ | 24,584 | +15% |
| Glassboro St C | 24,485 | +20% |
| Jersey City St C | 21,839 | +14% |
| Stockton St C | 13,716 | +15% |
| Ramapo C of NJ | 12,637 | +17% |
| Thomas A Edison St C | 2,356 | +26% |
| Aid to county colleges | 83,765 | +21% |
| Aid to private colleges | 18,127 | +42% |
| Student aid | 71,356 | +10% |
| Other appropriations* | 178,028 | n/c |
| **Total** | **$ 898,577** | **+19%** |
| **NEW MEXICO** | | |
| U of New Mexico | $ 106,223 | + 5% |
| New Mexico St U | 66,599 | − 3% |
| Eastern New Mexico U | 19,753 | − 4% |
| NM Inst of Mining & Tech | 11,758 | − 3% |
| NM Highlands U | 9,629 | − 2% |
| Western New Mexico U | 6,767 | +18% |
| Community colleges | 6,362 | + 3% |
| Student aid | 5,616 | +32% |
| Other appropriations | 845 | n/c |
| **Total** | **$ 233,552** | **+ 2%** |
| **NEW YORK** | | |
| State U of NY centers | | |
| Stony Brook | $ 234,470 | +19% |
| Buffalo | 157,803 | + 7% |
| Albany | 71,424 | + 4% |
| Binghamton | 50,814 | + 8% |
| St U of NY med centers | | |
| Downstate | 122,802 | +11% |
| Upstate | 98,385 | + 9% |
| State U of NY colleges | | |
| Buffalo | 37,435 | + 3% |
| Brockport | 28,167 | − 7% |
| Oswego | 27,781 | 0% |
| New Paltz | 25,000 | + 2% |
| Oneonta | 22,714 | + 1% |
| Cortland | 22,346 | + 2% |
| Plattsburgh | 21,819 | + 1% |
| Geneseo | 20,169 | − 1% |
| Potsdam | 19,485 | − 2% |
| Fredonia | 20,185 | + 1% |
| Purchase | 17,809 | 0% |
| Old Westbury | 14,309 | + 2% |
| Statutory colleges | | |
| Cornell U | 87,869 | + 6% |
| Ceramics at Alfred U | 5,596 | +11% |
| Specialized colleges | | |
| Environmental Science & Forestry | 16,662 | + 8% |
| Empire State | 12,998 | +12% |
| Technology | 10,644 | +17% |
| Optometry | 10,271 | +18% |
| Maritime | 7,865 | + 8% |
| Ag & tech colleges | | |
| Farmingdale | 26,684 | + 7% |
| Alfred | 15,907 | 0% |
| Cobleskill | 11,242 | + 2% |
| Morrisville | 11,059 | + 3% |
| Delhi | 10,747 | + 6% |
| Canton | 9,160 | + 2% |
| University-wide programs | 111,356 | n/c |
| Aid to City U of NY | 449,557 | + 7% |
| Aid to community colleges | 275,530 | +21% |
| Aid to private colleges | 154,430 | +17% |
| Student aid | 451,183 | n/c |
| Other appropriations | 361,889 | n/c |
| Less student fees and other income | −331,641 | −21% |
| **Total** | **$2,720,779** | **+15%** |
| **NORTH CAROLINA** | | |
| U of North Carolina | | |
| Chapel Hill | $ 215,513 | +21% |
| North Carolina St U | 189,984 | +23% |
| East Carolina U | 92,606 | +20% |
| Greensboro | 42,361 | +24% |
| Appalachian St U | 39,679 | +24% |
| Charlotte | 39,542 | +30% |
| NC A&T St U | 28,718 | +28% |
| Western Carolina U | 28,339 | +33% |
| NC Central U | 22,970 | +20% |
| Wilmington | 23,011 | +32% |
| Winston-Salem St U | 13,002 | +27% |
| Fayetteville St U | 13,517 | +40% |
| Asheville | 11,067 | +33% |
| Pembroke St U | 10,696 | +38% |
| Elizabeth City St U | 9,397 | +27% |
| NC Sch of the Arts | 7,111 | +33% |
| NC Memorial Hospital | 24,937 | + 7% |
| Student aid | 34,423 | +19% |
| Other appropriations | 17,706 | +35% |
| CC's and tech insts | 304,873 | +19% |
| Veterans' aid | 2,668 | − 7% |
| **Total** | **$1,172,120** | **+22%** |
| **OHIO** | | |
| Ohio St U | $ 265,727 | +21% |
| U of Cincinnati | 119,168 | +18% |
| U of Akron | 61,496 | +20% |
| Ohio U | 56,655 | +28% |
| Kent St U | 55,461 | +16% |
| U of Toledo | 51,865 | +21% |
| Wright St U | 51,647 | +33% |
| Bowling Green St U | 50,723 | +18% |
| Cleveland St U | 46,482 | +21% |
| Miami U | 43,840 | +24% |
| Youngstown St U | 36,038 | +20% |
| Northeastern Ohio U's C of Medicine | 22,138 | +16% |
| Central St U | 12,052 | +38% |
| Northeastern Med C | 11,320 | +16% |
| Case Western Reserve U Medical and Dental Schs | 6,319 | 0% |
| Community colleges | 78,243 | +31% |
| Technical colleges | 72,620 | +35% |
| University branches | 40,463 | +24% |
| **OHIO—Continued** | | |
| Student aid | 50,528 | n/c |
| Other appropriations | 75,425 | n/c |
| **Total** | **$1,208,210** | **+25%** |
| **OKLAHOMA** | | |
| U of Oklahoma | $ 107,677 | + 4% |
| Oklahoma St U | 100,561 | + 4% |
| Central St U | 20,985 | + 3% |
| Northeastern Okla St U | 13,842 | + 6% |
| Southwestern Okla St U | 11,262 | + 3% |
| Cameron U | 9,503 | + 2% |
| Southeastern Okla St U | 8,699 | + 3% |
| East Central U | 8,632 | + 6% |
| Okla C of Osteo Medicine | 6,193 | + 3% |
| Langston U | 4,648 | + 6% |
| Northwestern Okla St U | 3,892 | + 1% |
| Okla Panhandle St U | 3,624 | + 3% |
| U of Science & Arts | 3,488 | + 2% |
| Community colleges | 64,823 | + 3% |
| Other appropriations | 17,723 | n/c |
| **Total** | **$ 385,552** | **+ 5%** |

## How the States Rank

| | 1986-87 appropriations (a) | | 2-year change | | | 10-year change | | |
|---|---|---|---|---|---|---|---|---|
| | Amount | Rank | not adjusted for inflation(b) | adjusted for inflation(c) | Rank | not adjusted for inflation(d) | adjusted for inflation(e) | Rank |
| Alabama | $ 556,894,000 | 20 | +11% | + 5% | 33 | +122% | + 15% | 31 |
| Alaska | 207,086,000 | 39 | −11% | −16% | 50 | +219% | + 66% | 3 |
| Arizona | 480,076,000 | 23 | +27% | +21% | 4 | +160% | + 35% | 12 |
| Arkansas | 273,182,000 | 33 | +10% | + 4% | 35 | +138% | + 23% | 23 |
| California | 4,562,651,000 | 1 | +18% | +11% | 19 | +150% | + 29% | 18 |
| Colorado | 423,132,000 | 26 | +10% | + 4% | 34 | +105% | + 6% | 38 |
| Connecticut | 368,648,000 | 29 | +22% | +15% | 12 | +153% | + 31% | 15 |
| Delaware | 96,797,000 | 47 | +14% | + 8% | 27 | +123% | + 16% | 30 |
| Florida | 1,277,704,000 | 5 | +24% | +18% | 8 | +194% | + 52% | 6 |
| Georgia | 714,004,000 | 14 | +17% | +11% | 22 | +169% | + 39% | 11 |
| Hawaii | 220,845,000 | 37 | +18% | +12% | 18 | +126% | + 17% | 29 |
| Idaho | 126,030,000 | 40 | +12% | + 6% | 28 | + 82% | − 6% | 48 |
| Illinois | 1,390,614,000 | 4 | +18% | +11% | 20 | +100% | + 3% | 41 |
| Indiana | 660,532,000 | 16 | +20% | +14% | 13 | +109% | + 8% | 35 |
| Iowa | 404,610,000 | 27 | + 3% | − 2% | 43 | + 92% | 0% | 44 |
| Kansas | 350,735,000 | 30 | + 4% | − 1% | 42 | +102% | + 5% | 39 |
| Kentucky | 468,955,000 | 25 | +15% | + 9% | 26 | +128% | + 18% | 28 |
| Louisiana | 541,722,000 | 21 | − 3% | − 8% | 46 | +151% | + 30% | 17 |
| Maine | 125,216,000 | 41 | +37% | +30% | 1 | +194% | + 53% | 4 |
| Maryland | 569,975,000 | 19 | +17% | +11% | 21 | +133% | + 21% | 25 |
| Massachusetts | 816,379,000 | 12 | +27% | +21% | 5 | +248% | + 81% | 1 |
| Michigan | 1,228,559,000 | 6 | +22% | +16% | 10 | +107% | + 7% | 37 |
| Minnesota | 747,187,000 | 13 | +15% | + 9% | 25 | +130% | + 19% | 27 |
| Mississippi | 327,353,000 | 32 | − 5% | −10% | 48 | +113% | + 10% | 34 |
| Missouri | 476,420,000 | 24 | +19% | +13% | 16 | +101% | + 4% | 40 |
| Montana | 103,167,000 | 45 | − 4% | − 9% | 47 | +116% | + 12% | 33 |
| Nebraska | 217,355,000 | 38 | + 2% | − 3% | 45 | + 78% | − 8% | 49 |
| Nevada | 102,419,000 | 46 | +30% | +23% | 3 | +142% | + 25% | 22 |
| New Hampshire | 55,961,000 | 49 | +31% | +24% | 2 | +145% | + 27% | 21 |
| New Jersey | 898,577,000 | 11 | +19% | +13% | 15 | +227% | + 70% | 2 |
| New Mexico | 233,552,000 | 36 | + 2% | − 3% | 44 | +185% | + 48% | 8 |
| New York | 2,720,779,000 | 2 | +15% | + 9% | 23 | +117% | + 13% | 32 |
| North Carolina | 1,172,120,000 | 8 | +22% | +16% | 11 | +187% | + 49% | 7 |
| North Dakota | 124,430,000 | 42 | +11% | + 5% | 32 | +155% | + 32% | 13 |
| Ohio | 1,208,210,000 | 7 | +25% | +19% | 7 | +145% | + 27% | 20 |
| Oklahoma | 385,552,000 | 28 | + 5% | − 1% | 41 | +153% | + 31% | 14 |
| Oregon | 335,998,000 | 31 | +19% | +13% | 14 | + 90% | − 1% | 45 |
| Pennsylvania | 1,108,982,000 | 9 | +12% | + 6% | 30 | + 68% | − 13% | 50 |
| Rhode Island | 117,149,000 | 43 | +12% | + 6% | 29 | +108% | + 8% | 36 |
| South Carolina | 520,248,000 | 22 | +15% | + 9% | 24 | +147% | + 28% | 19 |
| South Dakota | 73,223,000 | 48 | +19% | +13% | 17 | + 86% | − 4% | 46 |
| Tennessee | 608,083,000 | 18 | +23% | +16% | 9 | +169% | + 40% | 10 |
| Texas | 2,141,392,000 | 3 | − 9% | −14% | 49 | +133% | + 21% | 24 |
| Utah | 257,249,000 | 34 | + 9% | + 3% | 37 | +152% | + 31% | 16 |
| Vermont | 46,778,000 | 50 | +12% | + 6% | 31 | +132% | + 21% | 26 |
| Virginia | 901,452,000 | 10 | +26% | +20% | 6 | +185% | + 48% | 9 |
| Washington | 609,937,000 | 17 | + 9% | + 3% | 38 | + 97% | + 2% | 42 |
| West Virginia | 241,087,000 | 35 | +10% | + 4% | 36 | + 93% | 0% | 43 |
| Wisconsin | 666,525,000 | 15 | + 8% | + 2% | 39 | + 83% | − 5% | 47 |
| Wyoming | 111,583,000 | 44 | + 7% | + 2% | 40 | +194% | + 53% | 5 |
| **Total U. S.** | **$ 32,377,114,000** | | **+14%** | **+ 8%** | | **+134%** | **+ 21%** | |

Note: Percentages shown are rounded. Rankings are based on unrounded figures.

(a) Reported by Edward R. Hines of Illinois State University as state tax funds appropriated for operating expenses for higher education, for student aid, and for governing and coordinating boards. Amount of appropriations may be changed in some states because of increases or decreases in revenue. Not included are appropriations for capital outlays and money from sources other than state taxes, such as student fees. Included are appropriations for annual operating expenses even if appropriated to some other state agency for ultimate allocation to colleges and universities.

(b) Increase in appropriations for 1986-87 over 1984-85, as reported by Edward R. Hines.

(c) Two-year increase in appropriations adjusted for inflation of 5.5 per cent, as indicated by the Labor Department's Consumer Price Indexes for June, 1986, and June, 1984.

(d) Increase in appropriations for 1986-87 over 1976-77, as reported by Edward R. Hines.

(e) Ten-year increase in appropriations adjusted for inflation of 92.8 per cent, as indicated by the Labor Department's Consumer Price Indexes for June, 1986, and June, 1976.

| | Appropriations 1986-87 (add 000) | 2-year change |
|---|---|---|
| **OREGON** | | |
| Oregon St U | $ 83,099 | +24% |
| U of Oregon | 48,158 | +22% |
| Oregon Health Sci U | 55,913 | +18% |
| Portland St U | 33,395 | +23% |
| Southern Oregon St C | 11,125 | +24% |
| Oregon Inst of Tech | 9,647 | +26% |
| Western Oregon St C | 8,771 | +15% |
| Eastern Oregon St C | 6,465 | +19% |
| Community colleges | 59,571 | +10% |
| Student aid | 11,013 | +16% |
| Other appropriations | 8,841 | n/c |
| **Total** | **$ 335,998** | **+19%** |
| **PENNSYLVANIA** | | |
| Pennsylvania St U | $ 181,924 | +12% |
| Temple U | 110,283 | +12% |
| U of Pittsburgh | 100,324 | +12% |
| Lincoln U | 7,563 | +13% |
| Indiana U of Pa | 39,753 | +13% |
| West Chester U of Pa | 28,419 | +13% |
| Bloomsburg U of Pa | 21,275 | +11% |
| Millersville U of Pa | 21,178 | +12% |
| Edinboro U of Pa | 20,687 | +16% |
| Slippery Rock U of Pa | 20,175 | +13% |
| Shippensburg U of Pa | 19,324 | +11% |
| Clarion U of Pa | 19,286 | +11% |
| Kutztown U of Pa | 18,793 | +12% |
| California U of Pa | 17,153 | + 8% |
| East Stroudsburg U of Pa | 15,820 | +11% |
| Cheyney U of Pa | 12,162 | + 8% |
| Mansfield U of Pa | 12,002 | +10% |
| Lock Haven U of Pa | 11,709 | +11% |
| Thaddeus Stevens St Sch of Tech | 3,049 | + 3% |
| Private, state-aided insts | 61,627 | +18% |
| Community colleges* | 77,500 | +12% |
| Other appropriations | 288,976 | n/c |
| **Total** | **$1,108,982** | **+12%** |
| **RHODE ISLAND** | | |
| U of Rhode Island | $ 58,294 | +13% |
| Rhode Island C | 26,472 | +11% |
| CC of Rhode Island | 21,046 | +13% |
| Student aid | 8,528 | + 9% |
| Other appropriations | 2,809 | n/c |
| **Total** | **$ 117,149** | **+12%** |
| **SOUTH CAROLINA** | | |
| U of South Carolina | $ 143,877 | +18% |
| Clemson U | 96,125 | +14% |
| Medical U of SC | 94,267 | +10% |
| South Carolina St C | 17,388 | − 1% |
| Winthrop C | 16,443 | + 8% |
| C of Charleston | 17,089 | +10% |
| Citadel Military C of SC | 12,306 | + 7% |
| Francis Marion C | 9,497 | +17% |
| Lander C | 7,109 | +17% |
| Commission on Higher Ed | 3,252 | n/c |
| Aid to private college students | 15,815 | +20% |
| Technical and comprehensive colleges | 87,080 | +24% |
| **Total** | **$ 520,248** | **+15%** |
| **SOUTH DAKOTA** | | |
| U of South Dakota | $ 24,770 | +12% |
| South Dakota St U | 30,307 | +14% |
| SD Sch of Mines & Tech | 7,721 | + 6% |
| Northern St C | 6,648 | +12% |
| Black Hills St C | 5,221 | +13% |
| Dakota St C | 4,125 | + 7% |
| Vocational education | 5,826 | +49% |
| Student aid | 430 | +20% |
| Other appropriations | 5,615 | n/c |
| Less estimated tuition | −17,440 | n/c |
| **Total** | **$ 73,223** | **+19%** |
| **TENNESSEE** | | |
| U of Tennessee | $ 245,071 | +20% |
| St U System | | |
| Memphis | 64,657 | +23% |
| East Tennessee | 42,684 | +19% |
| Middle Tennessee | 35,234 | +22% |
| Tennessee Tech U | 28,803 | +23% |
| Tennessee | 22,696 | +10% |
| Austin Peay | 15,012 | +22% |
| Administration | 2,024 | +24% |
| Community colleges | 58,567 | +14% |
| State tech insts | 27,278 | +19% |
| Area voc-tech schools | 23,242 | +19% |
| Student aid | 11,253 | +53% |
| Other appropriations | 31,562 | n/c |
| **Total** | **$ 608,083** | **+23%** |
| **TEXAS** | | |
| **Total †** | **$2,141,392** | **− 9%** |
| **UTAH** | | |
| U of Utah | $ 113,797 | + 9% |
| Utah St U | 60,509 | +13% |
| Weber St C | 30,490 | + 8% |
| Utah Tech C Provo | 11,331 | +13% |
| Utah Tech C Salt Lake | 13,146 | +15% |
| Southern Utah St C | 9,239 | +11% |
| Snow C | 5,251 | + 8% |
| Dixie C | 5,465 | +20% |

*Continued on Following Page*

# 1986-87 State Appropriations for Higher Education

| | Appropriations 1986-87 (add 000) | 2-year change |
|---|---|---|
| **UTAH—Continued** | | |
| C of Eastern Utah | 4,687 | +19% |
| Other appropriations | 3,334 | n/c |
| Total | $ 257,249 | + 9% |
| **VERMONT** | | |
| U of Vermont | $ 24,731 | +10% |
| State colleges | 12,352 | +14% |
| Student aid | 9,600 | +14% |
| Other appropriations | 95 | n/c |
| Total | $ 46,778 | +12% |
| **VIRGINIA** | | |
| Virginia Polytech Inst and St U | $ 144,838 | +23% |
| Va Commonwealth U | 150,840 | +31% |
| U of Virginia | 132,989 | +22% |
| Old Dominion U | 40,446 | +19% |
| C of William and Mary | 34,966 | +22% |
| George Mason U | 40,271 | +29% |
| James Madison U | 26,348 | +31% |
| Norfolk St U | 22,441 | +25% |
| Radford U | 18,200 | +34% |
| Virginia St U | 13,598 | + 2% |
| Longwood C | 8,897 | +27% |
| Mary Washington C | 8,174 | +17% |
| Virginia Military Inst | 8,470 | +35% |
| Christopher Newport C | 7,566 | +21% |
| Community colleges | 148,403 | +16% |
| Student aid | 37,712 | +24% |

| | Appropriations 1986-87 (add 000) | 2-year change |
|---|---|---|
| **VIRGINIA—Continued** | | |
| Other appropriations | 57,293 | n/c |
| Total | $ 901,452 | +26% |
| **WASHINGTON** | | |
| U of Washington | $ 179,841 | + 8% |
| Washington St U | 107,259 | + 8% |
| Western Washington U | 30,667 | + 9% |
| Eastern Washington U | 29,546 | + 7% |
| Central Washington U | 25,295 | + 6% |
| Evergreen St C | 13,789 | + 7% |
| Community colleges | 205,560 | + 9% |
| Student aid | 15,977 | +29% |
| Other appropriations | 2,023 | n/c |
| Total | $ 609,937 | + 9% |
| **WEST VIRGINIA** | | |
| West Virginia U | $ 107,661 | + 9% |
| Marshall U | 30,393 | +12% |
| Fairmont St C | 9,147 | +12% |
| W Va Inst of Tech | 8,043 | +11% |
| West Virginia St C | 7,737 | +10% |
| West Liberty St C | 6,626 | + 7% |
| Shepherd C | 6,140 | +15% |
| Concord C | 5,322 | + 8% |
| W Va C of Graduate Studies | 4,643 | +10% |
| Glenville St C | 4,518 | + 8% |
| West Virginia Sch of Osteopathic Medicine | 4,412 | + 7% |

| | Appropriations 1986-87 (add 000) | 2-year change |
|---|---|---|
| **WEST VIRGINIA—Continued** | | |
| Bluefield St C | 4,330 | +11% |
| Community colleges | 10,388 | + 8% |
| Student aid | 4,310 | + 2% |
| Other appropriations | 27,417 | n/c |
| Total | $ 241,067 | +10% |
| **WISCONSIN** | | |
| U of Wisconsin System | | |
| Madison | $ 216,142 | + 6% |
| Milwaukee | 68,037 | +10% |
| Oshkosh | 26,072 | + 5% |
| Eau Claire | 25,133 | + 4% |
| Stevens Point | 21,306 | + 3% |
| Whitewater | 21,259 | + 7% |
| La Crosse | 19,850 | + 5% |
| Stout | 18,894 | + 6% |
| River Falls | 14,796 | + 6% |
| Platteville | 14,159 | + 6% |
| Parkside | 14,044 | +14% |
| Green Bay | 12,482 | + 7% |
| Superior | 8,714 | +11% |
| Two-year centers | 18,010 | + 6% |
| Extension | 33,963 | + 8% |
| Systemwide programs | 16,651 | + 7% |
| Medical C of Wisconsin | 5,501 | −15% |
| Voc-tech adult education | 80,842 | +13% |
| Higher education aids board | 30,670 | +20% |
| Total | $ 666,525 | + 8% |

## Biennial Appropriations

| | Appropriations 1985-87 (add 000) | 2-year change |
|---|---|---|
| **NORTH DAKOTA** | | |
| North Dakota St U | $ 91,112 | +12% |
| U of North Dakota | 90,076 | +15% |
| ND St Sch of Science | 18,504 | + 2% |
| Minot St C | 13,016 | +11% |
| Dickinson St C | 9,368 | +10% |
| Valley City St C | 7,415 | + 9% |
| Mayville St C | 6,389 | + 9% |
| Community colleges | 9,497 | +51% |
| Student aid | 1,310 | +15% |
| Other appropriations | 2,173 | n/c |
| Total | $ 248,860 | +11% |
| **WYOMING** | | |
| U of Wyoming | $ 150,387 | + 5% |
| Community colleges | 65,958 | +14% |
| Other appropriations | 6,821 | n/c |
| Total | $ 223,166 | + 7% |

Note:  Some totals may be inconsistent with itemized figures because of rounding.
n/c  Not comparable
*  Estimated
†  Total is preliminary, and figures for campuses are not available.

# Foreign Students in U.S. Institutions, 1985-86

## Institutions with largest enrollments

| Rank | Institution | Number of foreign students | Proportion of total enrollment |
|---|---|---|---|
| 1. | Miami-Dade Community College | 4,730 | 11.5% |
| 2. | University of Southern California | 3,741 | 12.3% |
| 3. | University of Texas, Austin | 3,132 | 6.8% |
| 4. | University of Wisconsin, Madison | 2,873 | 6.8% |
| 5. | Ohio State University, main campus | 2,690 | 5.3% |
| 6. | Columbia University and Teachers College, and Barnard College | 2,679 | 10.8% |
| 7. | Boston University | 2,493 | 11.1% |
| 8. | University of California, Los Angeles | 2,488 | 7.2% |
| 9. | University of Minnesota, Minneapolis-St. Paul | 2,473 | 6.3% |
| 10. | University of Houston, University Park | 2,434 | 8.2% |
| 11. | University of Michigan, Ann Arbor | 2,413 | 6.8% |
| 12. | North Texas State University | 2,398 | 11.3% |
| 13. | Southern Illinois University, Carbondale | 2,299 | 10.1% |
| 14. | University of Arizona | 2,290 | 7.5% |
| 15. | University of Southwestern Louisiana | 2,246 | 13.8% |
| 16. | Iowa State University | 2,178 | 8.2% |
| 17. | New York University | 2,098 | 4.7% |
| 18. | George Washington University | 2,077 | 12.8% |
| 19. | Indiana University, Bloomington | 2,048 | 6.4% |
| 20. | Harvard University | 2,042 | 12.5% |
| 21. | University of Maryland, College Park | 2,023 | 5.2% |
| 22. | University of Pennsylvania | 2,012 | 11.8% |
| 23. | Howard University | 1,997 | 19.8% |
| 24. | University of California, Berkeley | 1,967 | 6.3% |
| 25. | Michigan State University | 1,985 | 4.8% |
| 26. | California State University, Los Angeles | 1,979 | 9.2% |
| 27. | Oklahoma State University, main campus | 1,969 | 9.3% |
| 28. | University of Illinois, Urbana-Champaign | 1,959 | 5.4% |
| 29. | University of Miami | 1,916 | 14.3% |
| 30. | Northeastern University | 1,888 | 8.6% |
| 31. | Massachusetts Institute of Technology | 1,886 | 19.4% |
| 32. | Louisiana State University, Baton Rouge | 1,864 | 6.4% |
| 33. | State University of New York, Buffalo | 1,855 | 7.1% |
| 34. | California State University, Long Beach | 1,802 | 5.5% |
| 35. | Stanford University | 1,780 | 14.7% |
| 36. | Northern Virginia Community College | 1,774 | 5.4% |
| 37. | Cornell University | 1,718 | 10.0% |
| 38. | University of Florida | 1,712 | 4.8% |
| 39. | University of Kansas | 1,660 | 6.7% |
| 40. | University of Washington | 1,652 | 5.4% |
| 41. | Arizona State University | 1,645 | 4.1% |
| 42. | Purdue University | 1,633 | 5.1% |
| 43. | University of Iowa | 1,623 | 5.5% |
| 44. | Texas A&M University, main campus | 1,596 | 4.5% |
| 45. | City University of New York, City College | 1,560 | 13.5% |
| 46. | Pennsylvania State University, main campus | 1,531 | 2.5% |
| 47. | University of Oregon, main campus | 1,519 | 9.3% |
| 48. | Oregon State University | 1,503 | 9.9% |
| 49. | Southern University and A&M College, main campus | 1,500 | 15.7% |
| 50. | University of Toledo | 1,482 | 6.1% |
| 51. | American University | 1,437 | 15.5% |
| 52. | University of Texas, Arlington | 1,428 | 6.2% |
| 53. | University of Missouri, Columbia | 1,405 | 6.1% |
| 54. | University of Hawaii, Manoa | 1,399 | 7.1% |
| 55. | University of Massachusetts, Amherst | 1,393 | 5.4% |
| 56. | University of Pittsburgh, main campus | 1,349 | 4.7% |
| 57. | Brigham Young University | 1,335 | 4.8% |
| 58. | Ohio University, main campus | 1,327 | 8.8% |
| 59. | Syracuse University, main campus | 1,285 | 6.1% |
| 60. | University of Illinois, Chicago | 1,254 | 5.0% |
| 61. | Temple University | 1,237 | 4.4% |
| 62. | University of the District of Columbia | 1,231 | 9.7% |
| 63. | Texas Southern University | 1,217 | 14.3% |
| 64. | State University of New York, Stony Brook | 1,174 | 8.2% |
| 64. | University of Texas, El Paso | 1,174 | 8.3% |
| 66. | Rutgers University, New Brunswick | 1,173 | 3.1% |
| 67. | University of Oklahoma, Norman | 1,169 | 5.8% |
| 68. | Georgetown University | 1,147 | 9.6% |
| 69. | University of San Francisco | 1,135 | 25.1% |
| 70. | Wayne State University | 1,117 | 3.9% |
| 71. | University of Georgia | 1,104 | 4.3% |
| 72. | California State University, Fresno | 1,088 | 6.4% |
| 73. | Florida International University | 1,083 | 7.0% |
| 74. | Indiana State University | 1,081 | 9.4% |
| 75. | Western Michigan University | 1,035 | 4.9% |
| 76. | Texas Tech University | 1,023 | 4.5% |
| 77. | University of Nebraska, Lincoln | 1,018 | 4.3% |
| 78. | Central State University | 1,004 | 7.6% |

## Distribution by field of study

| Field of study | 1984-1985 Number of foreign students | 1984-1985 Proportion of foreign students | 1985-1986 Number of foreign students | 1985-1986 Proportion of foreign students |
|---|---|---|---|---|
| Agriculture | 7,540 | 2.2% | 7,400 | 2.1% |
| Allied health | 3,060 | 0.9% | 3,200 | 0.9% |
| Architecture & environmental design | 6,340 | 1.9% | 6,540 | 1.9% |
| Area & ethnic studies | 1,020 | 0.3% | 830 | 0.2% |
| Business & management | 64,930 | 19.0% | 64,970 | 18.9% |
| Communications | 4,060 | 1.2% | 4,310 | 1.3% |
| Communications technologies | 390 | 0.1% | 590 | 0.2% |
| Computer & information sciences | 27,520 | 8.0% | 27,910 | 8.1% |
| Education | 12,140 | 3.6% | 11,680 | 3.4% |
| Engineering | 75,370 | 22.0% | 74,580 | 21.7% |
| English language | 11,010 | 3.2% | 12,870 | 3.7% |
| Foreign languages | 2,850 | 0.8% | 2,790 | 0.8% |
| Health sciences | 10,350 | 3.0% | 10,680 | 3.1% |
| Home economics | 1,870 | 0.5% | 1,980 | 0.6% |
| Industrial arts | 860 | 0.3% | 890 | 0.3% |
| Law | 1,720 | 0.5% | 1,650 | 0.5% |
| Letters | 6,250 | 1.8% | 5,190 | 1.6% |
| Liberal & general studies | 9,440 | 2.8% | 10,470 | 3.0% |
| Library & archival sciences | 610 | 0.2% | 690 | 0.2% |
| Life sciences | 9,950 | 2.9% | 10,040 | 2.9% |
| Mathematics | 8,110 | 2.4% | 8,000 | 2.3% |
| Military sciences | 130 | — | 130 | — |
| Military technologies | 90 | — | — | — |
| Multi/interdisciplinary studies | 2,400 | 0.7% | 2,090 | 0.6% |
| Parks & recreation | 200 | — | 230 | 0.1% |
| Personal & social development | 1,320 | 0.4% | 1,360 | 0.4% |
| Philosophy & religion | 1,300 | 0.4% | 1,390 | 0.4% |
| Physical sciences | 15,020 | 4.4% | 15,630 | 4.6% |
| Protective services | 570 | 0.2% | 470 | 0.1% |
| Psychology | 3,240 | 0.9% | 3,260 | 1.0% |
| Public affairs | 2,600 | 0.8% | 2,700 | 0.8% |
| Science technologies | 990 | 0.3% | 1,160 | 0.3% |
| Social sciences | 17,370 | 5.1% | 17,220 | 5.0% |
| Theology | 2,630 | 0.8% | 2,540 | 0.7% |
| Visual & performing arts | 8,700 | 2.5% | 7,970 | 2.3% |
| Vocational home economics | 220 | 0.1% | 270 | 0.1% |
| Undeclared | 19,940 | 5.8% | 20,100 | 5.9% |
| Total | 342,110 | 100.0% | 343,780 | 100.0% |

## Where they come from

| Rank | Country or territory | Students | Rank | Country or territory | Students |
|---|---|---|---|---|---|
| 1. | Taiwan | 23,770 | 33. | Cyprus | 2,140 |
| 2. | Malaysia | 23,020 | 33. | Syria | 2,140 |
| 3. | Republic of Korea | 18,660 | 35. | Jamaica | 2,110 |
| 4. | India | 16,070 | 36. | Peru | 2,050 |
| 5. | Canada | 15,410 | 37. | Ethiopia | 1,940 |
| 6. | Iran | 14,210 | 38. | Bangladesh | 1,930 |
| 7. | China | 13,980 | 39. | Italy | 1,890 |
| 8. | Nigeria | 13,710 | 40. | Norway | 1,820 |
| 9. | Japan | 13,360 | 41. | Nicaragua | 1,800 |
| 10. | Hong Kong | 10,710 | 41. | Sri Lanka | 1,800 |
| 11. | Indonesia | 8,210 | 43. | South Africa | 1,790 |
| 12. | Lebanon | 7,090 | 44. | Spain | 1,740 |
| 13. | Venezuela | 7,040 | 45. | Kenya | 1,720 |
| 14. | Thailand | 6,940 | 46. | Bahamas | 1,610 |
| 15. | Saudi Arabia | 6,900 | 47. | Panama | 1,590 |
| 16. | Jordan | 6,590 | 48. | Australia | 1,530 |
| 17. | United Kingdom | 5,940 | 49. | Pacific Is. Trust Terr. | 1,520 |
| 18. | Mexico | 5,460 | 50. | Cuba | 1,420 |
| 19. | Pakistan | 5,440 | 51. | Netherlands | 1,410 |
| 20. | West Germany | 4,730 | 52. | Sweden | 1,400 |
| 21. | Greece | 4,440 | 53. | Haiti | 1,340 |
| 22. | Colombia | 4,010 | 53. | Iraq | 1,340 |
| 23. | Singapore | 3,930 | 55. | Argentina | 1,320 |
| 24. | Philippines | 3,920 | 56. | Ghana | 1,230 |
| 25. | Kuwait | 3,810 | 57. | Chile | 1,160 |
| 26. | France | 3,680 | 58. | United Arab Emirates | 1,150 |
| 27. | Vietnam | 3,270 | 59. | El Salvador | 1,140 |
| 28. | Brazil | 2,840 | 60. | Cameroon | 1,130 |
| 29. | Israel | 2,600 | 61. | Honduras | 1,090 |
| 30. | Turkey | 2,460 | 62. | Ecuador | 1,080 |
| 31. | Egypt | 2,270 | 63. | Ireland | 1,030 |
| 32. | Trinidad & Tobago | 2,250 | 64. | Liberia | 1,020 |
| | | | 65. | Bolivia | 1,000 |

## Number of foreign students by state

| Rank | State | Students | Rank | State | Students | Rank | State | Students | Rank | State | Students |
|---|---|---|---|---|---|---|---|---|---|---|---|
| 1. | California | 47,586 | 14. | New Jersey | 7,045 | 27. | Tennessee | 4,155 | 40. | West Virginia | 1,249 |
| 2. | New York | 31,360 | 15. | Maryland | 6,276 | 28. | Colorado | 4,099 | 41. | North Dakota | 936 |
| 3. | Texas | 26,875 | 16. | Iowa | 5,858 | 29. | Connecticut | 3,906 | 42. | New Hampshire | 934 |
| 4. | Florida | 17,948 | 17. | Missouri | 5,805 | 30. | Utah | 3,837 | 43. | Idaho | 883 |
| 5. | Massachusetts | 17,652 | 18. | Washington | 5,789 | 31. | Alabama | 3,817 | 44. | Delaware | 791 |
| 6. | Illinois | 13,319 | 19. | Virginia | 5,780 | 32. | Hawaii | 3,261 | 45. | South Dakota | 770 |
| 7. | Ohio | 12,357 | 20. | Georgia | 5,755 | 33. | Nebraska | 2,018 | 46. | Montana | 738 |
| 8. | Michigan | 12,094 | 21. | Wisconsin | 5,676 | 34. | South Carolina | 2,005 | 47. | Vermont | 614 |
| 9. | Pennsylvania | 11,496 | 22. | Arizona | 5,631 | 35. | Arkansas | 1,912 | 48. | Nevada | 512 |
| 10. | District of Columbia | 9,832 | 23. | North Carolina | 5,525 | 36. | Kentucky | 1,719 | 49. | Wyoming | 421 |
| 11. | Louisiana | 8,923 | 24. | Oregon | 5,314 | 37. | Mississippi | 1,690 | 50. | Maine | 377 |
| 12. | Oklahoma | 7,519 | 25. | Minnesota | 5,124 | 38. | New Mexico | 1,553 | 51. | Alaska | 234 |
| 13. | Indiana | 7,133 | 26. | Kansas | 4,587 | 39. | Rhode Island | 1,468 | | | |

SOURCE: INSTITUTE OF INTERNATIONAL EDUCATION

Table 2.11

# How the Public Views Higher Education

| Support for federal aid | 1983 | 1984 | 1985 | 1986 |
|---|---|---|---|---|
| Grants to low-income students | | | | |
| Strongly favor | 50% | 53% | 46% | 55% |
| Somewhat favor | 35% | 35% | 38% | 32% |
| Somewhat oppose | 10% | 7% | 8% | 7% |
| Strongly oppose | 4% | 4% | 6% | 3% |
| Low-interest loans to middle-income students | | | | |
| Strongly favor | 51% | 46% | 40% | 54% |
| Somewhat favor | 39% | 39% | 41% | 35% |
| Somewhat oppose | 6% | 7% | 12% | 6% |
| Strongly oppose | 3% | 4% | 6% | 3% |
| Aid to colleges with a large percentage of low-income students | | | | |
| Strongly favor | 50% | 46% | 37% | 46% |
| Somewhat favor | 34% | 39% | 45% | 36% |
| Somewhat oppose | 10% | 7% | 10% | 8% |
| Strongly oppose | 4% | 4% | 6% | 5% |
| **College costs** | | | | |
| College costs are rising at a rate that will put college out of reach of most people | | | | |
| Agree | 80% | 80% | 77% | 82% |
| Disagree | 17% | 17% | 22% | 16% |
| Most people can afford to pay for a college education | | | | |
| Agree | 33% | 36% | 39% | 32% |
| Disagree | 64% | 61% | 60% | 65% |
| I would be able to afford college at this time only with low-interest loans or grants | | | | |
| Agree | 68% | 75% | 70% | 70% |
| Disagree | 27% | 21% | 28% | 27% |
| I am better able to afford college today than I would have been five years ago | | | | |
| Agree | 48% | 50% | 48% | 52% |
| Disagree | 47% | 47% | 50% | 44% |
| **Quality of a college education** | | | | |
| The quality of a college education is | | | | |
| Generally improving | 36% | 44% | 44% | 36% |
| Staying about the same | 37% | 33% | 37% | 35% |
| Generally declining | 17% | 13% | 16% | 21% |

Note: "Don't know" and "No opinion" responses are omitted. The telephone survey of 1,010 adults was conducted in December 1986. The statistical margin of error at the 95-per-cent confidence level is plus or minus 3 percentage points.

SOURCE: OPINION RESEARCH CORPORATION

Table 2. 12

# Revenues and Expenditures of Colleges and Universities, 1984-85

| | Public institutions | | Private institutions | | All institutions | |
|---|---|---|---|---|---|---|
| | 1984-85 | Per cent of total | 1984-85 | Per cent of total | 1984-85 | Per cent of total |
| **Revenues** | | | | | | |
| Tuition and fees ........................... | $8,647,637,000 | 14.5% | $12,635,691,000 | 38.7% | $21,283,329,000 | 23.0% |
| Appropriations | | | | | | |
| Federal .............................. | 1,349,183,000 | 2.3% | 221,407,000 | 0.7% | 1,570,590,000 | 1.7% |
| State ................................. | 26,065,494,000 | 43.6% | 307,666,000 | 0.9% | 26,373,160,000 | 28.5% |
| Local ................................. | 1,970,829,000 | 3.3% | 2,455,000 | — | 1,973,284,000 | 2.1% |
| Government grants and contracts | | | | | | |
| Federal .............................. | 4,960,635,000 | 8.3% | 4,977,900,000 | 15.2% | 9,938,535,000 | 10.7% |
| State ................................. | 899,923,000 | 1.5% | 309,928,000 | 1.0% | 1,209,851,000 | 1.3% |
| Local ................................. | 207,932,000 | 0.4% | 205,996,000 | 0.6% | 413,927,000 | 0.5% |
| Private gifts, grants, and contracts......... | 1,845,606,000 | 3.1% | 3,050,719,000 | 9.3% | 4,896,325,000 | 5.3% |
| Endowment income ....................... | 342,833,000 | 0.6% | 1,753,465,000 | 5.4% | 2,096,298,000 | 2.3% |
| Sales and services ....................... | 11,967,500,000 | 20.0% | 7,734,412,000 | 23.7% | 19,701,912,000 | 21.3% |
| Other.................................... | 1,536,586,000 | 2.6% | 1,478,897,000 | 4.5% | 3,015,483,000 | 3.3% |
| Total current-fund revenues ............... | $59,794,159,000 | 100.0% | $32,678,536,000 | 100.0% | $92,472,694,000 | 100.0% |
| **Expenditures** | | | | | | |
| Instruction ................................ | $20,287,410,000 | 34.8% | $ 8,489,773,000 | 26.8% | $28,777,183,000 | 32.0% |
| Research ................................. | 5,119,191,000 | 8.8% | 2,432,701,000 | 7.7% | 7,551,892,000 | 8.4% |
| Public service............................. | 2,316,270,000 | 4.0% | 544,825,000 | 1.7% | 2,861,095,000 | 3.2% |
| Libraries.................................. | 1,557,489,000 | 2.7% | 804,304,000 | 2.5% | 2,361,793,000 | 2.6% |
| Other academic support................... | 2,710,209,000 | 4.6% | 1,002,251,000 | 3.2% | 3,712,460,000 | 4.2% |
| Student services ......................... | 2,684,343,000 | 4.6% | 1,493,893,000 | 4.7% | 4,178,236,000 | 4.6% |
| Institutional support...................... | 5,191,693,000 | 8.9% | 3,395,523,000 | 10.7% | 8,587,216,000 | 9.5% |
| Plant operation and maintenance ......... | 5,040,869,000 | 8.6% | 2,304,612,000 | 7.3% | 7,345,482,000 | 8.2% |
| Scholarships and fellowships .............. | 1,374,803,000 | 2.4% | 2,295,551,000 | 7.3% | 3,670,355,000 | 4.1% |
| Mandatory transfers...................... | 591,269,000 | 1.0% | 424,344,000 | 1.3% | 1,015,613,000 | 1.1% |
| Auxiliary enterprises ..................... | 6,431,577,000 | 11.0% | 3,580,671,000 | 11.3% | 10,012,248,000 | 11.1% |
| Hospitals ................................. | 4,914,560,000 | 8.4% | 3,095,581,000 | 9.8% | 8,010,141,000 | 8.9% |
| Other.................................... | 94,867,000 | 0.2% | 1,772,683,000 | 5.6% | 1,867,550,000 | 2.1% |
| Total current-fund expenditures and mandatory transfers ................ | $58,314,550,000 | 100.0% | $31,636,713,000 | 100.0% | $89,951,263,000 | 100.0% |

Note: Because of rounding, details may not add up to totals.

SOURCE: CENTER FOR STATISTICS, U.S. DEPARTMENT OF EDUCATION

Table 2.13

# Average Faculty Salaries for 1986-87

| | Public | | Private | | Church-related | | All | |
|---|---|---|---|---|---|---|---|---|
| | Salary | 1-year increase | Salary | 1-year increase | Salary | 1-year increase | Salary | 1-year increase |
| **Doctoral institutions** | | | | | | | | |
| Professor | $48,740 | 6.3% | $56,900 | 5.9% | $51,120 | 6.1% | $50,500 | 6.2% |
| Associate professor | 35,590 | 5.8% | 38,820 | 5.8% | 37,440 | 6.5% | 36,210 | 5.8% |
| Assistant professor | 29,930 | 5.9% | 32,040 | 6.2% | 30,490 | 5.1% | 30,360 | 5.9% |
| Instructor | 21,440 | 4.9% | 24,890 | 4.2% | 26,260 | 6.1% | 22,130 | 4.8% |
| Lecturer | 26,060 | — | 26,650 | — | 24,310 | — | 26,090 | — |
| All ranks | 38,670 | 6.1% | 44,620 | 5.9% | 39,030 | 5.7% | 39,800 | 6.0% |
| **Comprehensive institutions** | | | | | | | | |
| Professor | $42,290 | 6.5% | $42,680 | 6.2% | $39,800 | 3.9% | $42,160 | 6.3% |
| Associate professor | 33,340 | 6.0% | 33,140 | 6.0% | 32,130 | 5.1% | 33,200 | 5.9% |
| Assistant professor | 27,520 | 5.6% | 26,650 | 6.1% | 26,670 | 4.6% | 27,310 | 5.5% |
| Instructor | 21,640 | 4.0% | 19,070 | 4.0% | 21,180 | 3.6% | 21,220 | 4.0% |
| Lecturer | 22,470 | — | 24,210 | — | 26,530 | — | 22,790 | — |
| All ranks | 34,050 | 6.1% | 33,010 | 6.0% | 32,140 | 4.5% | 33,750 | 5.9% |
| **Baccalaureate institutions** | | | | | | | | |
| Professor | $36,870 | 3.2% | $40,460 | 5.5% | $32,480 | 5.2% | $36,170 | 4.9% |
| Associate professor | 31,210 | 4.2% | 30,650 | 5.5% | 26,910 | 5.4% | 29,210 | 5.1% |
| Assistant professor | 25,940 | 4.3% | 24,990 | 5.9% | 22,500 | 4.8% | 24,070 | 5.0% |
| Instructor | 21,590 | 4.8% | 19,520 | 4.7% | 18,990 | 6.2% | 19,840 | 5.4% |
| Lecturer | 22,810 | — | 26,250 | — | 19,130 | — | 23,240 | — |
| All ranks | 29,660 | 4.0% | 30,780 | 5.5% | 26,170 | 5.2% | 28,480 | 5.0% |
| **2-year institutions with academic ranks** | | | | | | | | |
| Professor | $37,460 | 6.3% | $27,210 | 5.6% | $23,890 | 8.3% | $37,170 | 6.3% |
| Associate professor | 31,560 | 6.7% | 24,720 | 6.5% | 21,330 | 6.9% | 31,330 | 6.7% |
| Assistant professor | 26,940 | 6.8% | 20,030 | 4.9% | 19,200 | 7.0% | 26,590 | 6.7% |
| Instructor | 22,750 | 7.0% | 16,190 | 4.1% | 16,570 | 6.7% | 22,270 | 6.9% |
| Lecturer | 19,540 | — | — | — | — | — | 19,540 | — |
| All ranks | 30,490 | 6.6% | 21,120 | 5.3% | 20,310 | 7.3% | 30,100 | 6.6% |
| **2-year institutions without academic ranks** | | | | | | | | |
| All | $31,430 | 3.9% | $20,280 | 9.1% | $19,830 | 4.7% | $31,240 | 3.9% |
| **All institutions except 2-year institutions without academic ranks** | | | | | | | | |
| Professor | $45,280 | 6.3% | $50,270 | 5.9% | $37,620 | 5.1% | $45,530 | 6.1% |
| Associate professor | 34,170 | 5.9% | 34,910 | 5.8% | 30,090 | 5.3% | 33,820 | 5.8% |
| Assistant professor | 28,470 | 5.8% | 28,310 | 6.1% | 24,600 | 4.8% | 27,920 | 5.7% |
| Instructor | 21,180 | 4.9% | 20,440 | 4.3% | 19,900 | 5.6% | 21,330 | 4.9% |
| Lecturer | 24,730 | — | 26,410 | — | 24,080 | — | 24,930 | — |
| All ranks | 35,790 | 6.0% | 37,760 | 5.8% | 29,670 | 5.1% | 35,470 | 5.9% |

— No data reported.
Note: Salary figures are based on 1,875 institutions; percentage increases are based on 1,766 institutions.

SOURCE: AMERICAN ASSOCIATION OF UNIVERSITY PROFESSORS

Table 2.14

# Net Migration of Students by State, 1984

| | Number of first-time students | Percentage from out of state | Number of state residents who left | Number of students from out of state | Net migration |
|---|---|---|---|---|---|
| Alabama ...... | 54,722 | 16% | 4,775 | 8,569 | + 3,794 |
| Alaska ........ | 4,986 | 9% | 2,660 | 424 | − 2,236 |
| Arizona ....... | 78,792 | 16% | 4,674 | 12,625 | + 7,951 |
| Arkansas ..... | 25,501 | 13% | 4,244 | 3,391 | − 853 |
| California ..... | 319,119 | 6% | 24,384 | 20,326 | − 4,058 |
| Colorado ..... | 51,912 | 17% | 8,210 | 8,842 | + 632 |
| Connecticut ... | 52,390 | 15% | 18,016 | 8,054 | − 9,962 |
| Delaware ..... | 10,581 | 40% | 3,050 | 4,214 | + 1,164 |
| D. C. ......... | 22,502 | 71% | 3,301 | 15,934 | +12,633 |
| Florida ....... | 134,295 | 13% | 16,647 | 16,963 | + 316 |
| Georgia ....... | 59,562 | 20% | 8,614 | 11,772 | + 3,158 |
| Hawaii ........ | 15,611 | 12% | 2,867 | 1,833 | − 1,034 |
| Idaho ........ | 13,185 | 28% | 3,007 | 3,633 | + 626 |
| Illinois ........ | 170,594 | 7% | 29,233 | 12,243 | −16,990 |
| Indiana ....... | 71,558 | 18% | 8,248 | 13,178 | + 4,930 |
| Iowa ......... | 49,397 | 18% | 6,871 | 8,929 | + 2,058 |
| Kansas ....... | 46,836 | 15% | 4,670 | 6,976 | + 2,306 |
| Kentucky ..... | 43,246 | 16% | 5,304 | 7,005 | + 1,701 |
| Louisiana ..... | 52,081 | 13% | 4,486 | 6,585 | + 2,099 |
| Maine ........ | 16,223 | 17% | 3,630 | 2,697 | − 933 |
| Maryland ..... | 76,484 | 14% | 16,998 | 10,842 | − 6,156 |
| Massachusetts | 135,906 | 22% | 18,589 | 30,125 | +11,536 |
| Michigan ..... | 135,015 | 7% | 12,857 | 8,897 | − 3,960 |
| Minnesota .... | 42,251 | 19% | 11,591 | 8,003 | − 3,588 |
| Mississippi .... | 40,603 | 10% | 3,499 | 4,123 | + 624 |
| Missouri ...... | 68,647 | 18% | 9,246 | 12,186 | + 2,940 |
| Montana ...... | 11,613 | 13% | 2,326 | 1,493 | − 833 |
| Nebraska ..... | 29,150 | 13% | 3,690 | 3,786 | + 96 |
| Nevada ....... | 15,749 | 6% | 2,257 | 914 | − 1,343 |
| New Hampshire | 13,371 | 39% | 4,932 | 5,183 | + 251 |
| New Jersey ... | 79,318 | 6% | 42,336 | 4,398 | − 37,938 |
| New Mexico .. | 17,662 | 20% | 3,896 | 3,529 | − 367 |
| New York ..... | 309,688 | 10% | 42,574 | 32,416 | − 10,158 |
| North Carolina | 113,631 | 14% | 5,986 | 16,293 | +10,307 |
| North Dakota . | 9,514 | 31% | 2,110 | 2,912 | + 802 |
| Ohio ......... | 130,008 | 11% | 16,690 | 14,262 | − 2,428 |
| Oklahoma .... | 53,855 | 9% | 4,430 | 4,715 | + 285 |
| Oregon ....... | 47,734 | 13% | 5,219 | 6,126 | + 907 |
| Pennsylvania .. | 168,753 | 17% | 24,055 | 28,383 | + 4,328 |
| Rhode Island . | 26,500 | 34% | 4,082 | 9,084 | + 5,002 |
| South Carolina | 46,788 | 13% | 4,430 | 5,923 | + 1,493 |
| South Dakota . | 10,067 | 26% | 2,244 | 2,571 | + 327 |
| Tennessee .... | 61,345 | 18% | 6,560 | 10,781 | + 4,221 |
| Texas ......... | 205,129 | 9% | 10,976 | 18,566 | + 7,590 |
| Utah ......... | 32,110 | 20% | 2,315 | 6,456 | + 4,141 |
| Vermont ...... | 11,016 | 40% | 2,286 | 4,358 | + 2,072 |
| Virginia ....... | 91,209 | 18% | 14,452 | 15,999 | + 1,547 |
| Washington ... | 67,429 | 8% | 7,791 | 5,683 | − 2,108 |
| West Virginia . | 21,943 | 21% | 3,009 | 4,506 | + 1,497 |
| Wisconsin .... | 95,535 | 11% | 8,155 | 10,118 | + 1,963 |
| Wyoming ..... | 7,994 | 15% | 1,551 | 1,199 | − 352 |
| **Total** ......... | **3,469,110** | **13%** | **468,023** | **468,023** | **0** |

SOURCE: U.S.DEPARTMENT OF EDUCATION

Table 2.15

# Number of Colleges and Universities by Enrollment in Fall, 1985

| | Universities | Other 4-year | 2-year | Total |
|---|---|---|---|---|
| **Private institutions** | 62 | 1,383 | 363 | 1,808 |
| Under 200 | 0 | 256 | 71 | 327 |
| 200 to 499 | 0 | 226 | 135 | 361 |
| 500 to 999 | 0 | 319 | 97 | 416 |
| 1,000 to 2,499 | 0 | 396 | 48 | 444 |
| 2,500 to 4,999 | 5 | 134 | 8 | 147 |
| 5,000 to 9,999 | 25 | 44 | 3 | 72 |
| 10,000 to 19,999 | 24 | 8 | 0 | 32 |
| 20,000 to 29,999 | 5 | 0 | 1 | 6 |
| 30,000 or more | 3 | 0 | 0 | 3 |
| **Public institutions** | 94 | 470 | 929 | 1,493 |
| Under 200 | 0 | 0 | 3 | 3 |
| 200 to 499 | 0 | 9 | 26 | 35 |
| 500 to 999 | 0 | 29 | 96 | 125 |
| 1,000 to 2,499 | 0 | 93 | 311 | 404 |
| 2,500 to 4,999 | 1 | 107 | 221 | 329 |
| 5,000 to 9,999 | 7 | 125 | 161 | 293 |
| 10,000 to 19,999 | 33 | 90 | 88 | 211 |
| 20,000 to 29,999 | 31 | 15 | 20 | 66 |
| 30,000 or more | 22 | 2 | 3 | 27 |
| **Public and private** | 156 | 1,853 | 1,292 | 3,301 |
| Under 200 | 0 | 256 | 74 | 330 |
| 200 to 499 | 0 | 235 | 161 | 396 |
| 500 to 999 | 0 | 348 | 193 | 541 |
| 1,000 to 2,499 | 0 | 489 | 359 | 848 |
| 2,500 to 4,999 | 6 | 241 | 229 | 476 |
| 5,000 to 9,999 | 32 | 169 | 164 | 365 |
| 10,000 to 19,999 | 57 | 98 | 88 | 243 |
| 20,000 to 29,999 | 36 | 15 | 21 | 72 |
| 30,000 or more | 25 | 2 | 3 | 30 |

Note: The university data are for institutions with a significant level of activity in doctoral-level education as measured by the number of doctoral recipients and the diversity in doctoral-level program offerings.

SOURCE: U.S. DEPARTMENT OF EDUCATION

Table 2.16

# Hours Students Spent Each Week on Various Activities

| Studying or doing homework: | | Talking with teacher outside of class: | | Using a personal computer: | | Religious services or meetings: | |
|---|---|---|---|---|---|---|---|
| None | 2.3% | None | 19.3% | None | 51.7% | None | 33.3% |
| 1-2 | 16.5% | 1-2 | 54.2% | 1-2 | 25.4% | 1-2 | 47.9% |
| 3-5 | 31.7% | 3-5 | 18.6% | 3-5 | 13.6% | 3-5 | 13.5% |
| 6-10 | 28.3% | 6-10 | 5.1% | 6-10 | 5.9% | 6-10 | 3.7% |
| 11-15 | 12.6% | 11-15 | 1.6% | 11-15 | 1.7% | 11-15 | 0.8% |
| 16-20 | 5.4% | 16-20 | 0.6% | 16-20 | 0.8% | 16-20 | 0.3% |
| 21-30 | 2.3% | 21-30 | 0.3% | 21-30 | 0.3% | 21-30 | 0.2% |
| Over 30 | 0.9% | Over 30 | 0.2% | Over 30 | 0.5% | Over 30 | 0.3% |

| Exercising or sports: | | Partying: | | Working for pay: | | Student clubs or groups: | |
|---|---|---|---|---|---|---|---|
| None | 7.5% | None | 18.0% | None | 27.6% | None | 35.2% |
| 1-2 | 17.4% | 1-2 | 20.0% | 1-2 | 3.9% | 1-2 | 27.3% |
| 3-5 | 21.2% | 3-5 | 24.3% | 3-5 | 6.4% | 3-5 | 21.4% |
| 6-10 | 20.0% | 6-10 | 18.3% | 6-10 | 10.0% | 6-10 | 9.6% |
| 11-15 | 15.6% | 11-15 | 8.8% | 11-15 | 12.7% | 11-15 | 3.6% |
| 16-20 | 9.4% | 16-20 | 4.8% | 16-20 | 18.4% | 16-20 | 1.6% |
| 21-30 | 4.4% | 21-30 | 2.3% | 21-30 | 13.6% | 21-30 | 0.6% |
| Over 30 | 4.6% | Over 30 | 3.4% | Over 30 | 7.4% | Over 30 | 0.7% |

| Socializing with friends: | | Watching television: | | Volunteer work: | | Hobbies: | |
|---|---|---|---|---|---|---|---|
| None | 0.5% | None | 6.4% | None | 55.6% | None | 10.2% |
| 1-2 | 4.4% | 1-2 | 23.8% | 1-2 | 26.8% | 1-2 | 28.0% |
| 3-5 | 13.6% | 3-5 | 30.9% | 3-5 | 11.0% | 3-5 | 31.6% |
| 6-10 | 23.6% | 6-10 | 22.0% | 6-10 | 3.9% | 6-10 | 16.8% |
| 11-15 | 20.7% | 11-15 | 9.2% | 11-15 | 1.3% | 11-15 | 6.9% |
| 16-20 | 16.5% | 16-20 | 4.1% | 16-20 | 0.6% | 16-20 | 3.2% |
| 21-30 | 9.5% | 21-30 | 1.8% | 21-30 | 0.3% | 21-30 | 1.3% |
| Over 30 | 11.3% | Over 30 | 2.0% | Over 30 | 0.5% | Over 30 | 2.0% |

Table 2.17

# Corporate Gifts to Education

| | Corporate contributions to education | 1-year change | As per cent of pretax net income | As per cent of all giving by corporations |
|---|---|---|---|---|
| 1970 . . . . . . . . | $ 320,000,000 | − 14.7% | 0.42% | 40.2% |
| 1971 . . . . . . . . | 345,000,000 | + 7.8% | 0.40% | 39.9% |
| 1972 . . . . . . . . | 365,000,000 | + 5.8% | 0.36% | 36.2% |
| 1973 . . . . . . . . | 410,000,000 | + 12.3% | 0.33% | 34.9% |
| 1974 . . . . . . . . | 445,000,000 | + 8.5% | 0.33% | 37.1% |
| 1975 . . . . . . . . | 450,000,000 | + 1.1% | 0.34% | 37.4% |
| 1976 . . . . . . . . | 560,000,000 | + 24.4% | 0.34% | 37.7% |
| 1977* . . . . . . . | 665,000,000 | + 18.8% | 0.33% | 37.1% |
| 1978* . . . . . . . | 780,000,000 | + 17.3% | 0.33% | 37.4% |
| 1979* . . . . . . . | 880,000,000 | + 12.8% | 0.34% | 38.5% |
| 1980* . . . . . . . | 980,000,000 | + 11.4% | 0.41% | 41.5% |
| 1981* . . . . . . . | 1,090,000,000 | + 11.2% | 0.48% | 43.4% |
| 1982* . . . . . . . | 1,250,000,000 | + 14.7% | 0.74% | 43.0% |
| 1983* . . . . . . . | 1,525,000,000 | + 22.0% | 0.73% | 42.0% |
| 1984* . . . . . . . | 1,700,000,000 | + 11.5% | 0.72% | 42.5% |
| 1985 . . . . . . . . | 1,875,000,000 | + 10.3% | 0.84% | 42.6% |

*Revised from earlier estimate          SOURCE: COUNCIL FOR FINANCIAL AID TO EDUCATION

Table 2.18

# College Admissions Test Scores by State, 1986

| | Test | Average score | 1-year change | Per cent tested | | Test | Average score | 1-year change | Per cent tested |
|---|---|---|---|---|---|---|---|---|---|
| Alabama . . . . . . . . . . | ACT | 18.2 | + 0.6 | 49.6% | Missouri . . . . . . . . . . | ACT | 19.2 | + 0.4 | 47.9% |
| Alaska . . . . . . . . . . . | ACT | 18.1 | + 0.5 | 37.6% | Montana . . . . . . . . . . | ACT | 19.8 | + 0.3 | 51.5% |
| Arizona . . . . . . . . . . | ACT | 19.3 | + 0.6 | 36.8% | Nebraska . . . . . . . . . | ACT | 20.0 | + 0.3 | 61.8% |
| Arkansas . . . . . . . . | ACT | 18.1 | + 0.7 | 52.3% | Nevada . . . . . . . . . . | ACT | 19.0 | + 0.5 | 40.1% |
| California . . . . . . . . . | SAT | 904 | 0 | 43.3% | New Hampshire . . . . . | SAT | 935 | − 4 | 61.0% |
| Colorado . . . . . . . . . | ACT | 19.9 | + 0.2 | 59.9% | New Jersey . . . . . . . . | SAT | 889 | 0 | 66.0% |
| Connecticut . . . . . . . . | SAT | 914 | − 1 | 69.5% | New Mexico . . . . . . . . | ACT | 17.9 | + 0.4 | 52.3% |
| Delaware . . . . . . . . . | SAT | 917 | − 1 | 59.6% | New York . . . . . . . . . | SAT | 898 | − 2 | 64.8% |
| D.C. . . . . . . . . . . . . | SAT | 852 | + 8 | 53.5% | North Carolina . . . . . . | SAT | 835 | + 2 | 51.3% |
| Florida . . . . . . . . . . | SAT | 895 | + 11 | 44.4% | North Dakota . . . . . . . | ACT | 18.5 | + 0.4 | 61.2% |
| Georgia . . . . . . . . . . | SAT | 842 | + 5 | 55.4% | Ohio . . . . . . . . . . . . | ACT | 19.3 | + 0.1 | 46.4% |
| Hawaii . . . . . . . . . . . | SAT | 880 | + 3 | 51.3% | Oklahoma . . . . . . . . . | ACT | 17.8 | + 0.3 | 48.1% |
| Idaho . . . . . . . . . . . | ACT | 19.2 | + 0.4 | 52.4% | Oregon . . . . . . . . . . | SAT | 930 | + 2 | 46.0% |
| Illinois . . . . . . . . . . . | ACT | 19.1 | + 0.2 | 60.2% | Pennsylvania . . . . . . . | SAT | 894 | + 1 | 54.4% |
| Indiana . . . . . . . . . . | SAT | 874 | − 1 | 49.5% | Rhode Island . . . . . . . | SAT | 898 | + 3 | 58.7% |
| Iowa . . . . . . . . . . . . | ACT | 20.6 | + 0.3 | 56.3% | South Carolina . . . . . . | SAT | 826 | + 11 | 50.0% |
| Kansas . . . . . . . . . . | ACT | 19.2 | + 0.1 | 60.6% | South Dakota . . . . . . . | ACT | 19.9 | + 0.7 | 61.9% |
| Kentucky . . . . . . . . . | ACT | 18.1 | ±0.2 | 50.9% | Tennessee . . . . . . . . | ACT | 18.0 | + 0.4 | 56.6% |
| Louisiana . . . . . . . . . | ACT | 16.9 | + 0.4 | 57.5% | Texas . . . . . . . . . . . | SAT | 877 | − 1 | 39.3% |
| Maine . . . . . . . . . . . | SAT | 900 | + 2 | 51.8% | Utah . . . . . . . . . . . . | ACT | 19.1 | + 0.2 | 61.7% |
| Maryland . . . . . . . . . | SAT | 911 | + 1 | 53.8% | Vermont . . . . . . . . . . | SAT | 916 | − 3 | 61.8% |
| Massachusetts . . . . . . | SAT | 909 | + 3 | 66.5% | Virginia . . . . . . . . . . | SAT | 908 | 0 | 58.9% |
| Michigan . . . . . . . . . | ACT | 18.9 | 0 | 51.2% | Washington* . . . . . . . | — | — | — | — |
| Minnesota . . . . . . . . | ACT | 20.3 | + 0.1 | 30.5% | West Virginia . . . . . . . | ACT | 17.7 | + 0.3 | 47.5% |
| Mississippi . . . . . . . . | ACT | 16.3 | + 0.8 | 60.3% | Wisconsin . . . . . . . . . | ACT | 20.5 | + 0.2 | 38.8% |
| | | | | | Wyoming . . . . . . . . . | ACT | 19.7 | + 0.3 | 55.6% |
| | | | | | U.S. average . . . . . . . | ACT | 18.8 | + 0.2 | |
| | | | | | | SAT | 906 | 0 | |

Note: The ACT (American College Testing Program's ACT Assessment) is scored on a scale from 1 to 36. The SAT (the College Board's Scholastic Aptitude Test) is scored on a scale from 400 to 1,600. For each state one score is given, depending on which test was taken by more students. The table shows the percentage of high-school graduates who took the test.

*Omitted because fewer than 35 per cent of the students took either test.

SOURCE: U.S. DEPARTMENT OF EDUCATION

Table 2.19

# Median Salaries of Administrators in 'Secondary' Positions, 1986-87

by Richard C. Creal and Jan P. Miller of the College and University Personnel Association, along with John M. Toller, personnel director at the University of Connecticut.

The figures, based on reports from 1,637 colleges and universities, are intended to give only a broad overview of administrative salaries. Comparative analyses between positions or among institutions are available in the full report, or through special studies purchased from the personnel association.

Copies of the report, *1986-87 Administrative Compensation Survey,* are available from the order desk, CUPA, 11 Dupont Circle, Suite 120, Washington 20036; (202) 462-1038.

The price is $50 per copy for members, $125 for non-members who participated in the survey, and $200 for others.

| | All universities | All 4-year colleges | Public 2-year colleges | All institutions |
|---|---|---|---|---|
| **Assistant to president:** | | | | |
| Institution | $44,500 | $31,800 | $32,100 | $36,700 |
| System | 57,900 | — | 39,068 | 46,073 |
| **Director:** | | | | |
| Annual giving | 32,750 | 26,730 | — | 28,938 |
| Conferences | 31,800 | 23,000 | — | 28,801 |
| Corporate and foundation relations | 38,435 | 30,282 | — | 34,007 |
| Estate planning | 42,000 | 31,619 | — | 39,000 |
| Governmental and legislative relations | 51,700 | — | — | 49,995 |
| Health and safety | 35,192 | — | — | 33,924 |
| Medical-center | | | | |
| Public relations | 41,855 | — | — | 44,040 |
| Personnel | 40,500 | — | — | 40,500 |
| Sports information | 25,402 | 18,825 | — | 23,145 |
| Telecommunications | 37,300 | 23,784 | 31,150 | 34,176 |
| **Manager:** | | | | |
| Benefits | 28,000 | 23,200 | 22,457 | 26,795 |
| Building maintenance trades | 30,680 | 26,041 | 26,784 | 28,466 |
| Custodial services | 27,540 | 21,000 | 22,980 | 24,492 |
| Employee relations | 33,000 | — | — | 32,682 |
| Employment | 29,001 | 23,650 | 26,000 | 28,000 |
| Landscape and grounds | 27,935 | 22,480 | 24,337 | 25,335 |
| Payroll | 27,800 | 19,740 | 23,462 | 24,710 |
| Personnel information | 31,039 | — | — | 29,550 |
| Power plant | 32,859 | 29,486 | — | 31,687 |
| Technical trades | 32,700 | 26,700 | 26,281 | 30,500 |
| Training and development | 30,420 | — | — | 30,420 |
| Wage and salary | 31,200 | — | 25,028 | 30,000 |
| **Associate director:** | | | | |
| Admissions | 31,251 | 23,550 | 24,003 | 27,400 |
| Affirmative action and equal employment | 31,263 | — | — | 30,935 |
| Bookstore | 25,152 | 15,300 | 20,538 | 21,736 |
| Budget | 38,500 | 31,860 | 28,169 | 36,750 |
| Computer center | 43,000 | 27,527 | 37,764 | 37,100 |
| Academic | 41,300 | 28,800 | — | 35,300 |
| Administrative | 44,000 | 27,700 | — | 38,220 |
| Food services | 32,221 | 22,486 | — | 28,345 |
| Institutional research | 35,000 | — | 34,710 | 32,616 |
| Personnel | 33,991 | 27,000 | 31,237 | 32,500 |
| Physical plant and facilities management | 38,004 | 26,677 | 31,657 | 33,882 |
| Publications | 26,031 | 18,500 | — | 23,000 |
| Purchasing | 30,702 | 22,200 | 24,980 | 28,300 |
| Student counseling | 33,617 | 20,667 | — | 28,560 |
| Student financial aid | 28,176 | 19,939 | 25,625 | 24,200 |
| Student housing | 30,924 | 18,500 | — | 25,692 |
| Student union | 28,425 | 21,000 | — | 26,155 |
| **Associate:** | | | | |
| Bursar | 27,600 | 16,821 | — | 26,600 |
| General counsel | 46,461 | — | — | 45,000 |
| Registrar | 31,851 | 21,300 | 26,805 | 27,500 |
| Assistant director, admissions | 23,742 | 19,000 | 24,434 | 21,300 |
| Assistant registrar | 24,521 | 18,800 | 22,943 | 22,000 |
| **Librarian:** | | | | |
| Acquisitions | 29,238 | 23,300 | 28,221 | 26,832 |
| Circulation | 25,053 | 20,441 | 28,556 | 23,130 |
| Public services | 34,053 | 24,357 | 26,203 | 29,018 |
| Reference | 28,518 | 22,475 | 27,063 | 25,517 |
| Technical services | 32,868 | 23,485 | 27,915 | 27,252 |
| **Coordinator,** resource development | 26,222 | 22,600 | — | 25,080 |
| Data base administrator | 37,592 | 28,000 | 35,315 | 35,316 |
| Student union, business manager | 27,196 | — | — | 26,829 |
| **Programmer:** | | | | |
| Analyst I* | 27,768 | 24,500 | 27,477 | 27,137 |
| Analyst II** | 22,050 | 19,775 | 22,660 | 22,000 |
| **Systems:** | | | | |
| Analyst I* | 33,340 | 28,800 | 31,131 | 32,096 |
| Analyst II** | 28,044 | 22,660 | 26,616 | 26,921 |
| **Housing officer:** | | | | |
| Administrative operations | 27,500 | — | — | 25,643 |
| Family housing | 27,500 | — | — | 27,500 |
| Residence life | 25,122 | 17,183 | — | 22,980 |

—  No data or insufficient number of responses.
*  Highest level
**  Lowest level

Table 2.20

SOURCE: COLLEGE AND UNIVERSITY PERSONNEL ASSOCIATION

# Average Faculty Salaries by Rank in Selected Fields, 1986-87

| Field | 261 Public Institutions | | | | | | 478 Private Institutions | | | | | |
|---|---|---|---|---|---|---|---|---|---|---|---|---|
| | Professor | Associate professor | Assistant professor* | New assistant professor | Instructor | All ranks | Professor | Associate professor | Assistant professor* | New assistant professor | Instructor | All ranks |
| Accounting | $46,023 | $38,378 | $32,969 | $34,295 | $23,606 | $36,223 | $44,913 | $37,134 | $29,408 | $31,072 | $22,234 | $33,879 |
| Agribusiness and agricultural production | 36,738 | 30,178 | 26,964 | — | 20,781 | 31,144 | — | — | — | — | — | — |
| Anthropology | 41,471 | 32,592 | 26,071 | — | — | 35,217 | 43,406 | 32,274 | 25,477 | 24,022 | — | 33,981 |
| Architecture and environmental design | 38,676 | 33,004 | 26,800 | — | — | 32,488 | 43,619 | 33,969 | 27,732 | 25,668 | 21,434 | 35,982 |
| Area and ethnic studies | 43,717 | 35,781 | 28,776 | — | — | 34,559 | 46,746 | 36,393 | 27,973 | — | — | 37,199 |
| Audiology and speech pathology | 42,055 | 33,182 | 28,473 | 22,980 | 21,916 | 32,867 | 43,070 | 31,749 | 24,507 | 22,907 | 22,322 | 30,162 |
| Business administration and management | 43,937 | 36,570 | 31,560 | 32,524 | 22,250 | 35,245 | 45,659 | 35,563 | 28,797 | 32,912 | 23,820 | 33,825 |
| Business and management | 45,372 | 37,724 | 31,460 | 32,280 | 23,831 | 35,846 | 49,523 | 37,412 | 31,278 | 28,547 | 22,855 | 37,253 |
| Business economics | 42,549 | 34,503 | 29,601 | 28,807 | 23,748 | 34,875 | 44,215 | 33,543 | 28,143 | 23,828 | 21,177 | 33,478 |
| Chemistry | 40,367 | 32,346 | 25,931 | 24,615 | 20,278 | 35,029 | 41,821 | 30,402 | 24,897 | — | 18,003 | 34,609 |
| Communications | 39,845 | 31,608 | 25,818 | 25,322 | 20,838 | 29,917 | 37,444 | 31,195 | 24,723 | 24,971 | 20,078 | 28,726 |
| Communications technologies | 39,247 | 32,244 | 25,824 | — | 22,885 | 31,876 | 35,439 | 31,309 | 25,367 | 25,377 | 21,465 | 27,587 |
| Computer and information science | 44,885 | 37,104 | 31,615 | 32,326 | 23,425 | 34,384 | 44,627 | 34,602 | 28,518 | 28,467 | 22,017 | 32,154 |
| Curriculum and instruction | 39,263 | 32,480 | 26,878 | 23,843 | 21,655 | 33,046 | 43,976 | 35,162 | 25,298 | — | — | 34,336 |
| Dramatic arts | 41,077 | 31,646 | 24,649 | 22,459 | 20,680 | 31,078 | 38,166 | 29,409 | 24,004 | 21,997 | 19,914 | 28,517 |
| Education | 40,183 | 32,821 | 26,480 | 25,055 | 21,405 | 33,615 | 37,142 | 29,829 | 24,073 | 22,817 | 20,503 | 29,786 |
| Education administration | 40,297 | 32,948 | 27,086 | 25,915 | 20,965 | 36,301 | 41,350 | 28,728 | 25,361 | — | — | 31,468 |
| Engineering | 45,866 | 37,548 | 32,467 | 32,155 | 23,829 | 38,273 | 51,835 | 38,637 | 32,963 | 33,399 | 25,614 | 42,934 |
| Fine arts | 38,516 | 30,995 | 25,244 | 23,489 | 21,358 | 31,910 | 37,054 | 28,737 | 23,491 | 22,602 | 20,144 | 29,124 |
| Foreign languages | 40,284 | 31,743 | 25,280 | 23,028 | 21,037 | 31,754 | 38,353 | 29,563 | 23,901 | 22,794 | 18,623 | 29,128 |
| Geography | 40,499 | 31,419 | 26,183 | 25,055 | 21,166 | 33,778 | 40,234 | 32,277 | 24,881 | — | — | 33,446 |
| Geological sciences | 41,155 | 32,972 | 27,219 | 22,876 | 20,965 | 35,231 | 45,631 | 33,520 | 27,272 | 26,520 | — | 37,776 |
| History | 39,728 | 32,047 | 25,517 | 24,701 | 21,096 | 35,205 | 39,330 | 30,284 | 23,798 | 21,981 | 18,500 | 32,671 |
| Home economics | 39,224 | 32,386 | 26,283 | 22,805 | 21,012 | 29,414 | 34,885 | 26,617 | 23,057 | 24,571 | 18,105 | 24,744 |
| Letters | 39,224 | 31,369 | 25,151 | 22,805 | 19,358 | 31,055 | 37,888 | 29,243 | 23,166 | 22,081 | 17,830 | 29,653 |
| Library and archival sciences | 39,410 | 31,458 | 25,448 | 23,389 | 20,441 | 28,030 | 36,936 | 27,876 | 23,503 | 24,817 | 19,165 | 26,026 |
| Life sciences | 39,704 | 31,860 | 26,233 | 25,045 | 19,932 | 34,104 | 39,701 | 30,312 | 24,653 | 25,014 | 17,515 | 32,240 |
| Mathematics | 41,298 | 32,986 | 27,322 | 26,513 | 20,070 | 32,486 | 42,705 | 31,341 | 25,263 | 21,292 | 19,732 | 31,894 |
| Multi-interdisciplinary studies | 39,134 | 32,561 | 25,716 | 23,848 | 21,777 | 30,971 | 35,721 | 26,575 | 21,843 | 22,998 | 18,003 | 26,154 |
| Music | 38,831 | 30,892 | 25,172 | 23,418 | 21,152 | 31,047 | 35,768 | 27,736 | 22,889 | — | 19,858 | 28,136 |
| Nursing | 41,421 | 32,264 | 26,587 | 27,174 | 22,081 | 27,862 | 37,489 | 29,328 | 23,428 | 24,462 | 20,081 | 24,894 |
| Philosophy and religion | 40,228 | 31,829 | 25,315 | 22,766 | 19,840 | 33,877 | 36,741 | 29,273 | 23,575 | 22,002 | 19,190 | 30,687 |
| Physical education | 39,367 | 32,374 | 27,030 | 24,369 | 22,546 | 30,421 | 35,835 | 29,525 | 24,100 | 21,676 | 20,064 | 26,533 |
| Physical science | 40,272 | 32,196 | 26,376 | 24,623 | 20,594 | 33,587 | 40,474 | 29,361 | 25,977 | — | 17,220 | 32,485 |
| Physics | 41,556 | 33,481 | 27,202 | 25,677 | 21,724 | 36,081 | 46,523 | 33,415 | 26,781 | 25,344 | 19,388 | 38,701 |
| Political science | 40,749 | 32,185 | 25,473 | 23,098 | 21,491 | 33,906 | 42,246 | 31,368 | 24,327 | 23,206 | 19,663 | 33,119 |
| Psychology | 40,841 | 32,771 | 25,997 | 24,150 | 20,719 | 34,479 | 39,838 | 29,839 | 24,064 | 23,474 | 18,872 | 31,444 |
| Reading education | 37,336 | 30,098 | 26,055 | — | 21,282 | 31,422 | 43,955 | 31,097 | 21,625 | — | — | 28,772 |
| Secretarial and related programs | 37,574 | 31,927 | 25,342 | — | 20,409 | 29,020 | — | 24,241 | 19,427 | — | 15,699 | 20,464 |
| Social sciences | 39,245 | 30,884 | 25,796 | 25,445 | 21,252 | 31,544 | 42,078 | 31,332 | 24,919 | 25,344 | 20,555 | 32,528 |
| Sociology | 40,245 | 32,482 | 25,934 | 22,984 | 21,076 | 33,092 | 38,563 | 28,966 | 24,111 | 22,228 | 19,054 | 29,914 |
| Special education | 38,684 | 31,335 | 25,707 | 24,391 | 20,438 | 31,354 | 39,305 | 28,640 | 22,551 | 22,033 | 16,753 | 27,770 |
| Student counseling and personnel services | 40,283 | 33,075 | 25,875 | 24,006 | 23,305 | 34,520 | 39,675 | 30,688 | 23,743 | — | — | 32,448 |
| Teacher education, general programs | 38,562 | 31,498 | 26,043 | 24,355 | 20,479 | 32,483 | 33,499 | 27,865 | 22,518 | 21,464 | 17,434 | 26,875 |
| Theology | — | — | — | — | — | — | 35,320 | 29,252 | 24,051 | 24,336 | 20,243 | 30,132 |
| Visual and performing arts | 37,919 | 30,260 | 24,705 | 23,130 | 20,966 | 30,271 | 38,126 | 30,601 | 24,339 | 22,571 | 20,451 | 30,056 |
| Vocational and technical education | 39,420 | 31,647 | 27,030 | 28,248 | 21,407 | 30,877 | — | — | — | — | — | — |
| **All major fields** | **$40,606** | **$32,560** | **$27,168** | **$26,220** | **$21,523** | **$32,960** | **$41,175** | **$31,301** | **$25,440** | **$25,276** | **$20,049** | **$31,849** |

Note: Data are based on reports from 261 public institutions that are members of the American Association of State Colleges and Universities and from 478 private colleges and universities. The data are included in the averages for all ranks and for all fields.
* Includes data for new assistant professors.
— Indicates fewer than 10 positions in a rank or fewer than 50 of all ranks.

SOURCE: COLLEGE AND UNIVERSITY PERSONNEL ASSOCIATION

Table 2.21

**—Total enrollment in institutions of higher education, by control of institution, sex, level of enrollment, and attendance status: United States, fall 1985**

| Level of enrollment and attendance status | All institutions | | | Public institutions | | | Private institutions | | |
|---|---|---|---|---|---|---|---|---|---|
| | Total | Men | Women | Total | Men | Women | Total | Men | Women |
| 1 | 2 | 3 | 4 | 5 | 6 | 7 | 8 | 9 | 10 |
| **All students** ............... | **12,247,055** | **5,818,450** | **6,428,605** | **9,479,273** | **4,437,488** | **5,041,785** | **2,767,782** | **1,380,962** | **1,386,820** |
| Full-time .................. | 7,075,221 | 3,607,720 | 3,467,501 | 5,120,246 | 2,606,362 | 2,513,884 | 1,954,975 | 1,001,358 | 953,617 |
| Part-time ................. | 5,171,834 | 2,210,730 | 2,961,104 | 4,359,027 | 1,831,126 | 2,527,901 | 812,807 | 379,604 | 433,203 |
| Total undergraduate students[1] ...... | 10,596,674 | 4,962,080 | 5,634,594 | 8,477,125 | 3,952,548 | 4,524,577 | 2,119,549 | 1,009,532 | 1,110,017 |
| Undergraduate students ........ | 9,414,074 | 4,470,074 | 4,944,000 | 7,443,611 | 3,516,141 | 3,927,470 | 1,970,463 | 953,933 | 1,016,530 |
| Full-time ................. | 6,162,391 | 3,076,720 | 3,085,671 | 4,549,901 | 2,286,260 | 2,263,641 | 1,612,490 | 790,460 | 822,030 |
| Part-time ................. | 3,251,683 | 1,393,354 | 1,858,329 | 2,893,710 | 1,229,881 | 1,663,829 | 357,973 | 163,473 | 194,500 |
| Unclassified students below the baccalaureate ........... | 1,182,600 | 492,006 | 690,594 | 1,033,514 | 436,407 | 597,107 | 149,086 | 55,599 | 93,487 |
| Full-time ................. | 157,201 | 79,726 | 77,475 | 137,875 | 70,157 | 67,718 | 19,326 | 9,569 | 9,757 |
| Part-time ................. | 1,025,399 | 412,280 | 613,119 | 895,639 | 366,250 | 529,389 | 129,760 | 46,030 | 83,730 |
| Total postbaccalaureate students ................... | 1,650,381 | 856,370 | 794,011 | 1,002,148 | 484,940 | 517,208 | 648,233 | 371,430 | 276,803 |
| First-professional students ....... | 274,200 | 179,792 | 94,408 | 111,808 | 71,373 | 40,435 | 162,392 | 108,419 | 53,973 |
| Full-time ................. | 246,619 | 162,368 | 84,251 | 106,693 | 68,392 | 38,301 | 139,926 | 93,976 | 45,950 |
| Part-time ................. | 27,581 | 17,424 | 10,157 | 5,115 | 2,981 | 2,134 | 22,466 | 14,443 | 8,023 |
| Graduate students ............. | 1,129,538 | 577,224 | 552,314 | 703,076 | 341,863 | 361,213 | 426,462 | 235,361 | 191,101 |
| Full-time ................. | 470,967 | 269,819 | 201,148 | 297,023 | 167,860 | 129,163 | 173,944 | 101,959 | 71,985 |
| Part-time ................. | 658,571 | 307,405 | 351,166 | 406,053 | 174,003 | 232,050 | 252,518 | 133,402 | 119,116 |
| Unclassified postbaccalaureate students ................... | 246,643 | 99,354 | 147,289 | 187,264 | 71,704 | 115,560 | 59,379 | 27,650 | 31,729 |
| Full-time ................. | 38,043 | 19,087 | 18,956 | 28,754 | 13,693 | 15,061 | 9,289 | 5,394 | 3,895 |
| Part-time ................. | 208,600 | 80,267 | 128,333 | 158,510 | 58,011 | 100,499 | 50,090 | 22,256 | 27,834 |

[1]Includes students enrolled for an undergraduate degree and also unclassified students below the baccalaureate level.

SOURCE: U.S. Department of Education, Center for Education Statistics, "Fall Enrollment in Colleges and Universities, 1985" survey. (This table was prepared July 1986.)

Table 2.22

CURRENT DATA

### —Total enrollment in institutions of higher education, by level of enrollment and State: Fall 1985

| State or other area | Total enrollment | Level of enrollment | | | | |
|---|---|---|---|---|---|---|
| | | Undergraduate | First-professional | Graduate | Unclassified | |
| | | | | | Below the baccalaureate | Post-baccalaureate |
| 1 | 2 | 3 | 4 | 5 | 6 | 7 |
| United States | 12,247,055 | 9,414,074 | 274,200 | 1,129,538 | 1,182,600 | 246,643 |
| Alabama | 179,343 | 155,096 | 3,019 | 14,218 | 5,389 | 1,621 |
| Alaska | 27,479 | 11,765 | ... | 1,190 | 13,894 | 630 |
| Arizona | 216,854 | 179,075 | 1,390 | 16,557 | 13,730 | 6,102 |
| Arkansas | 77,958 | 65,551 | 1,422 | 6,503 | 3,591 | 891 |
| California | 1,650,439 | 1,258,019 | 31,153 | 119,415 | 206,144 | 35,708 |
| Colorado | 161,314 | 119,737 | 3,112 | 14,804 | 19,244 | 4,417 |
| Connecticut | 159,348 | 117,289 | 3,326 | 25,524 | 9,628 | 3,581 |
| Delaware | 31,883 | 25,459 | ... | 2,347 | 3,959 | 118 |
| District of Columbia | 78,868 | 44,022 | 8,859 | 19,340 | 3,105 | 3,542 |
| Florida | 451,392 | 349,090 | 6,991 | 33,467 | 52,403 | 9,441 |
| Georgia | 196,826 | 154,971 | 7,694 | 21,439 | 9,809 | 2,913 |
| Hawaii | 49,937 | 39,450 | 496 | 4,011 | 4,601 | 1,379 |
| Idaho | 42,668 | 35,623 | 249 | 4,145 | 1,777 | 874 |
| Illinois | 678,689 | 482,201 | 17,362 | 62,612 | 104,986 | 11,528 |
| Indiana | 250,567 | 205,926 | 5,735 | 24,933 | 9,417 | 4,556 |
| Iowa | 152,897 | 126,044 | 5,753 | 15,369 | 5,195 | 536 |
| Kansas | 141,359 | 107,363 | 2,348 | 13,946 | 11,841 | 5,861 |
| Kentucky | 141,724 | 109,576 | 4,596 | 11,655 | 11,900 | 3,997 |
| Louisiana | 177,176 | 140,909 | 4,974 | 17,427 | 9,305 | 4,561 |
| Maine | 52,201 | 34,172 | 569 | 2,094 | 15,230 | 136 |
| Maryland | 231,649 | 184,719 | 3,322 | 24,508 | 15,273 | 3,827 |
| Massachusetts | 421,175 | 282,368 | 13,245 | 55,552 | 59,069 | 10,941 |
| Michigan | 507,293 | 424,890 | 10,093 | 41,789 | 22,544 | 7,977 |
| Minnesota | 221,162 | 181,734 | 6,099 | 16,598 | 12,536 | 4,195 |
| Mississippi | 101,180 | 88,785 | 1,771 | 7,262 | 1,795 | 1,567 |
| Missouri | 241,146 | 176,687 | 9,077 | 25,633 | 26,531 | 3,218 |
| Montana | 35,958 | 30,662 | 217 | 2,054 | 1,358 | 1,667 |
| Nebraska | 97,769 | 75,381 | 2,740 | 9,604 | 9,347 | 697 |
| Nevada | 43,656 | 36,526 | 259 | 1,646 | 4,324 | 901 |
| New Hampshire | 52,283 | 39,603 | 638 | 4,737 | 6,088 | 1,217 |
| New Jersey | 297,658 | 222,512 | 5,764 | 31,008 | 30,831 | 7,543 |
| New Mexico | 68,295 | 46,319 | 618 | 7,109 | 13,697 | 552 |
| New York | 1,000,098 | 714,337 | 24,832 | 120,507 | 111,967 | 28,455 |
| North Carolina | 327,288 | 244,968 | 5,934 | 20,970 | 51,211 | 4,205 |
| North Dakota | 37,939 | 32,242 | 441 | 2,061 | 1,983 | 1,212 |
| Ohio | 514,745 | 421,390 | 13,144 | 49,398 | 24,798 | 6,015 |
| Oklahoma | 169,173 | 125,833 | 4,139 | 16,461 | 18,267 | 4,473 |
| Oregon | 137,967 | 107,371 | 3,240 | 9,987 | 14,043 | 3,326 |
| Pennsylvania | 533,198 | 413,986 | 15,049 | 59,704 | 38,891 | 5,568 |
| Rhode Island | 69,927 | 50,522 | 448 | 5,842 | 11,223 | 1,892 |
| South Carolina | 131,902 | 107,063 | 2,615 | 10,872 | 8,087 | 3,265 |
| South Dakota | 32,772 | 26,183 | 464 | 2,634 | 2,873 | 618 |
| Tennessee | 194,845 | 154,508 | 5,525 | 14,220 | 15,382 | 5,210 |
| Texas | 769,692 | 617,234 | 18,598 | 77,515 | 42,038 | 14,307 |
| Utah | 103,994 | 93,156 | 1,203 | 7,360 | 796 | 1,479 |
| Vermont | 31,416 | 23,226 | 731 | 2,113 | 4,977 | 369 |
| Virginia | 292,416 | 197,884 | 5,911 | 23,913 | 57,575 | 7,133 |
| Washington | 231,553 | 191,266 | 3,248 | 14,625 | 17,649 | 4,765 |
| West Virginia | 76,659 | 61,336 | 1,256 | 8,259 | 4,847 | 961 |
| Wisconsin | 275,069 | 210,982 | 3,694 | 20,639 | 33,585 | 6,169 |
| Wyoming | 24,204 | 18,314 | 201 | 1,295 | 3,867 | 527 |
| U.S. Service Schools | 54,052 | 50,749 | 636 | 2,667 | ... | ... |
| Outlying areas | 164,890 | 146,529 | 3,131 | 8,527 | 6,549 | 154 |
| American Samoa | 758 | 758 | ... | ... | ... | ... |
| Guam | 4,601 | 3,247 | ... | 330 | 1,024 | ... |
| Northern Marianas | 318 | 215 | ... | ... | 103 | ... |
| Puerto Rico | 155,917 | 140,936 | 3,131 | 8,016 | 3,680 | 154 |
| Trust Territory of the Pacific | 724 | 697 | ... | ... | 27 | ... |
| Virgin Islands | 2,572 | 676 | ... | 181 | 1,715 | ... |

--- Data not reported or not applicable.

SOURCE: U.S. Department of Education, Center for Education Statistics, "Fall Enrollment in Colleges and Universities, 1985" survey. (This table was prepared July 1986.)

Table 2.23

**—Total enrollment in private institutions of higher education, by attendance status, sex, and State: Fall 1984 and fall 1985**

| State or other area | Fall 1984 | | | | | Fall 1985 | | | | |
|---|---|---|---|---|---|---|---|---|---|---|
| | Total | Full-time | | Part-time | | Total | Full-time | | Part-time | |
| | | Men | Women | Men | Women | | Men | Women | Men | Women |
| 1 | 2 | 3 | 4 | 5 | 6 | 7 | 8 | 9 | 10 | 11 |
| United States .... | 2,764,570 | 1,005,319 | 945,463 | 383,743 | 430,045 | 2,767,782 | 1,001,358 | 953,617 | 379,604 | 433,203 |
| Alabama .......... | 22,052 | 8,972 | 9,743 | 1,146 | 2,191 | 20,655 | 8,672 | 8,806 | 1,122 | 2,055 |
| Alaska ........... | 986 | 186 | 307 | 132 | 361 | 969 | 214 | 303 | 126 | 326 |
| Arizona .......... | 13,492 | 9,008 | 3,492 | 535 | 457 | 14,818 | 9,812 | 3,806 | 708 | 492 |
| Arkansas ......... | 12,024 | 4,808 | 5,815 | 609 | 792 | 11,835 | 4,544 | 5,795 | 562 | 934 |
| California ........ | 205,576 | 77,225 | 62,778 | 37,617 | 27,956 | 206,232 | 77,623 | 64,453 | 36,437 | 27,719 |
| Colorado ......... | 19,509 | 6,959 | 7,003 | 2,656 | 2,891 | 19,283 | 7,181 | 7,139 | 2,350 | 2,613 |
| Connecticut ....... | 60,822 | 19,001 | 18,021 | 11,627 | 12,173 | 60,732 | 18,828 | 17,912 | 11,459 | 12,533 |
| Delaware ......... | 4,450 | 609 | 1,147 | 1,115 | 1,579 | 3,950 | 607 | 1,112 | 839 | 1,392 |
| District of Columbia ... | 66,300 | 21,338 | 21,470 | 11,868 | 11,624 | 66,121 | 21,119 | 21,738 | 11,490 | 11,774 |
| Florida ........... | 89,906 | 35,328 | 26,916 | 16,573 | 11,089 | 89,151 | 36,678 | 27,525 | 14,318 | 10,630 |
| Georgia .......... | 46,834 | 19,398 | 19,194 | 4,097 | 4,145 | 47,870 | 19,131 | 19,704 | 4,506 | 4,529 |
| Hawaii ........... | 6,175 | 2,060 | 1,432 | 1,679 | 1,004 | 6,691 | 2,207 | 1,512 | 1,806 | 1,166 |
| Idaho ............ | 8,385 | 3,057 | 3,768 | 714 | 846 | 9,002 | 3,254 | 4,093 | 728 | 927 |
| Illinois .......... | 156,565 | 55,776 | 48,199 | 24,219 | 28,371 | 158,465 | 55,368 | 48,571 | 25,145 | 29,381 |
| Indiana .......... | 57,339 | 25,925 | 20,425 | 3,844 | 7,145 | 56,734 | 25,258 | 20,472 | 3,779 | 7,225 |
| Iowa ............ | 43,269 | 17,514 | 16,064 | 3,977 | 5,714 | 43,132 | 16,965 | 16,151 | 4,062 | 5,954 |
| Kansas .......... | 14,705 | 5,177 | 5,512 | 1,341 | 2,675 | 14,139 | 4,999 | 5,210 | 1,321 | 2,609 |
| Kentucky ......... | 30,853 | 11,280 | 12,713 | 2,284 | 4,576 | 30,888 | 11,270 | 12,752 | 2,277 | 4,589 |
| Louisiana ......... | 25,142 | 9,893 | 9,805 | 2,350 | 3,094 | 24,003 | 9,268 | 9,621 | 2,306 | 2,808 |
| Maine ........... | 19,278 | 3,952 | 4,838 | 885 | 9,603 | 19,013 | 3,977 | 4,970 | 872 | 9,194 |
| Maryland ......... | 32,408 | 8,817 | 10,038 | 6,100 | 7,453 | 32,657 | 9,042 | 9,797 | 6,259 | 7,559 |
| Massachusetts ...... | 235,882 | 80,724 | 80,891 | 33,743 | 40,524 | 235,573 | 80,861 | 81,565 | 32,978 | 40,169 |
| Michigan ......... | 72,200 | 23,346 | 25,172 | 10,036 | 13,646 | 73,023 | 22,915 | 25,731 | 10,065 | 14,312 |
| Minnesota ......... | 46,840 | 19,145 | 19,414 | 3,329 | 4,952 | 47,178 | 18,581 | 19,547 | 3,794 | 5,256 |
| Mississippi ........ | 11,698 | 3,813 | 4,564 | 1,068 | 2,253 | 10,476 | 3,340 | 3,959 | 1,175 | 2,002 |
| Missouri .......... | 70,828 | 27,092 | 21,310 | 10,590 | 11,836 | 72,317 | 25,990 | 20,553 | 12,433 | 13,341 |
| Montana .......... | 4,345 | 1,005 | 1,462 | 782 | 1,096 | 3,926 | 969 | 1,360 | 686 | 911 |
| Nebraska ......... | 17,201 | 5,954 | 6,322 | 2,002 | 2,923 | 16,567 | 5,714 | 5,980 | 1,875 | 2,998 |
| Nevada .......... | 307 | 105 | 68 | 69 | 65 | 288 | 107 | 66 | 53 | 62 |
| New Hampshire ..... | 25,726 | 9,208 | 8,919 | 3,197 | 4,402 | 25,614 | 9,059 | 8,893 | 3,376 | 4,286 |
| New Jersey ....... | 61,942 | 19,996 | 17,438 | 11,478 | 13,030 | 60,361 | 19,364 | 16,928 | 11,065 | 13,004 |
| New Mexico ....... | 2,246 | 458 | 673 | 406 | 709 | 2,236 | 422 | 632 | 417 | 765 |
| New York ......... | 440,619 | 150,666 | 147,618 | 61,288 | 81,047 | 436,847 | 149,883 | 149,037 | 58,584 | 79,343 |
| North Carolina ..... | 59,832 | 25,149 | 26,092 | 3,631 | 4,960 | 60,244 | 25,109 | 26,434 | 3,611 | 5,090 |
| North Dakota ...... | 3,144 | 956 | 1,377 | 257 | 554 | 3,137 | 977 | 1,367 | 238 | 555 |
| Ohio ............ | 136,825 | 45,021 | 39,685 | 34,636 | 17,483 | 135,581 | 44,348 | 39,479 | 34,133 | 17,621 |
| Oklahoma ......... | 22,212 | 9,232 | 7,446 | 2,939 | 2,595 | 22,346 | 9,298 | 7,665 | 2,947 | 2,436 |
| Oregon .......... | 18,579 | 8,059 | 6,663 | 1,871 | 1,986 | 18,355 | 8,193 | 6,618 | 1,680 | 1,864 |
| Pennsylvania ....... | 227,497 | 83,870 | 77,058 | 30,180 | 36,389 | 232,675 | 85,635 | 79,522 | 30,572 | 36,946 |
| Rhode Island ....... | 34,638 | 13,183 | 11,947 | 4,714 | 4,794 | 34,538 | 13,425 | 12,210 | 4,381 | 4,522 |
| South Carolina ..... | 26,266 | 10,479 | 12,277 | 1,481 | 2,029 | 26,048 | 10,172 | 12,467 | 1,405 | 2,004 |
| South Dakota ...... | 8,450 | 2,555 | 3,578 | 791 | 1,526 | 9,433 | 2,687 | 4,134 | 836 | 1,776 |
| Tennessee ........ | 48,140 | 20,054 | 21,417 | 2,586 | 4,083 | 46,894 | 19,541 | 20,707 | 2,457 | 4,189 |
| Texas ........... | 91,620 | 37,475 | 32,467 | 11,656 | 10,022 | 92,500 | 37,628 | 33,167 | 11,526 | 10,179 |
| Utah ............ | 34,648 | 14,668 | 11,643 | 4,239 | 4,098 | 34,568 | 13,811 | 11,646 | 4,450 | 4,661 |
| Vermont .......... | 12,594 | 5,212 | 5,203 | 760 | 1,419 | 12,572 | 5,120 | 5,253 | 710 | 1,489 |
| Virginia .......... | 38,005 | 13,620 | 16,709 | 2,929 | 4,747 | 41,662 | 14,902 | 18,712 | 3,255 | 4,793 |
| Washington ....... | 29,810 | 10,762 | 11,880 | 3,182 | 3,986 | 30,021 | 10,643 | 11,545 | 3,552 | 4,281 |
| West Virginia ...... | 10,625 | 3,513 | 4,140 | 1,032 | 1,940 | 10,128 | 3,281 | 3,802 | 1,103 | 1,942 |
| Wisconsin ......... | 35,781 | 13,716 | 13,350 | 3,503 | 5,212 | 36,334 | 13,366 | 13,196 | 3,775 | 5,997 |
| Wyoming ......... | --- | --- | --- | --- | --- | --- | --- | --- | --- | --- |
| Outlying areas ..... | 93,318 | 29,211 | 44,696 | 7,770 | 11,641 | 99,479 | 31,242 | 48,561 | 7,717 | 11,959 |
| American Samoa ... | --- | --- | --- | --- | --- | --- | --- | --- | --- | --- |
| Guam ............ | --- | --- | --- | --- | --- | --- | --- | --- | --- | --- |
| Northern Marianas ... | --- | --- | --- | --- | --- | --- | --- | --- | --- | --- |
| Puerto Rico ........ | 93,318 | 29,211 | 44,696 | 7,770 | 11,641 | 99,479 | 31,242 | 48,561 | 7,717 | 11,959 |
| Trust Territory of the Pacific ......... | --- | --- | --- | --- | --- | --- | --- | --- | --- | --- |
| Virgin Islands ....... | --- | --- | --- | --- | --- | --- | --- | --- | --- | --- |

---Data not reported or not applicable.

SOURCE: U.S. Department of Education, Center for Education Statistics, "Fall Enrollment in Colleges and Universities" surveys. (This table was prepared July 1986.)

Table 2.24

### —Total enrollment in public institutions of higher education, by attendance status, sex, and State: Fall 1984 and fall 1985

| State or other area | Fall 1984 | | | | | Fall 1985 | | | | |
|---|---|---|---|---|---|---|---|---|---|---|
| | Total | Full-time Men | Full-time Women | Part-time Men | Part-time Women | Total | Full-time Men | Full-time Women | Part-time Men | Part-time Women |
| 1 | 2 | 3 | 4 | 5 | 6 | 7 | 8 | 9 | 10 | 11 |
| United States .... | 9,477,370 | 2,642,190 | 2,505,416 | 1,832,322 | 2,497,442 | 9,479,273 | 2,606,362 | 2,513,884 | 1,831,126 | 2,527,901 |
| Alabama .......... | 149,579 | 50,113 | 52,660 | 22,287 | 24,519 | 158,688 | 51,678 | 54,423 | 25,492 | 27,095 |
| Alaska ........... | 26,005 | 3,976 | 4,027 | 7,156 | 10,846 | 26,510 | 4,182 | 4,387 | 7,172 | 10,769 |
| Arizona .......... | 196,537 | 42,400 | 39,062 | 50,329 | 64,746 | 202,036 | 42,429 | 39,595 | 51,790 | 68,222 |
| Arkansas ......... | 66,753 | 22,403 | 22,763 | 7,765 | 13,822 | 66,123 | 21,706 | 23,014 | 7,736 | 13,667 |
| California ........ | 1,459,579 | 308,010 | 297,755 | 372,186 | 481,628 | 1,444,207 | 303,200 | 295,849 | 367,170 | 477,988 |
| Colorado ......... | 144,885 | 47,511 | 41,635 | 23,925 | 31,814 | 142,031 | 46,498 | 41,489 | 22,875 | 31,169 |
| Connecticut ....... | 100,754 | 23,126 | 24,756 | 20,855 | 32,017 | 98,616 | 22,375 | 24,132 | 19,745 | 32,364 |
| Delaware ......... | 27,422 | 8,385 | 10,048 | 3,951 | 5,038 | 27,933 | 8,365 | 10,297 | 4,135 | 5,136 |
| District of Columbia .. | 13,450 | 2,431 | 2,420 | 3,822 | 4,777 | 12,747 | 2,388 | 2,204 | 3,573 | 4,582 |
| Florida ........... | 354,156 | 78,858 | 80,225 | 79,846 | 115,227 | 362,241 | 79,082 | 81,565 | 82,645 | 118,949 |
| Georgia .......... | 150,035 | 47,643 | 46,838 | 24,162 | 31,392 | 148,956 | 46,927 | 46,941 | 23,452 | 31,636 |
| Hawaii ........... | 43,806 | 12,484 | 13,326 | 8,396 | 9,600 | 43,246 | 12,069 | 12,906 | 8,264 | 10,007 |
| Idaho ............ | 34,918 | 12,201 | 9,630 | 5,400 | 7,687 | 33,666 | 11,574 | 9,511 | 5,258 | 7,323 |
| Illinois .......... | 504,549 | 115,008 | 108,444 | 111,674 | 169,423 | 520,224 | 118,065 | 113,364 | 115,958 | 172,837 |
| Indiana .......... | 192,618 | 62,180 | 57,210 | 33,426 | 39,802 | 193,833 | 60,998 | 57,444 | 33,949 | 41,442 |
| Iowa ............ | 109,800 | 44,148 | 36,392 | 12,257 | 17,003 | 109,765 | 43,854 | 36,922 | 12,201 | 16,788 |
| Kansas .......... | 127,211 | 38,076 | 33,044 | 22,286 | 33,805 | 127,220 | 37,777 | 33,199 | 21,902 | 34,342 |
| Kentucky ......... | 112,702 | 36,036 | 36,930 | 15,063 | 24,673 | 110,836 | 34,357 | 36,049 | 15,347 | 25,083 |
| Louisiana ........ | 154,846 | 53,885 | 51,408 | 19,554 | 29,999 | 153,173 | 55,654 | 54,342 | 17,078 | 26,099 |
| Maine ........... | 33,436 | 10,769 | 9,515 | 5,455 | 7,697 | 33,188 | 10,582 | 9,472 | 5,315 | 7,819 |
| Maryland ......... | 201,894 | 44,470 | 47,077 | 44,884 | 65,463 | 198,992 | 44,020 | 46,094 | 43,905 | 64,973 |
| Massachusetts ..... | 183,084 | 48,171 | 52,051 | 34,671 | 48,191 | 185,602 | 47,078 | 52,071 | 35,047 | 51,406 |
| Michigan ......... | 433,134 | 113,699 | 109,782 | 92,097 | 117,556 | 434,270 | 109,865 | 108,366 | 95,011 | 121,028 |
| Minnesota ........ | 168,726 | 53,682 | 49,276 | 26,630 | 39,138 | 173,984 | 53,459 | 49,975 | 28,375 | 42,175 |
| Mississippi ....... | 92,641 | 34,188 | 36,053 | 8,763 | 13,637 | 90,704 | 33,437 | 35,887 | 8,508 | 12,872 |
| Missouri.......... | 170,092 | 51,412 | 48,091 | 29,030 | 41,559 | 168,829 | 49,094 | 47,629 | 29,337 | 42,769 |
| Montana .......... | 32,716 | 13,251 | 10,962 | 3,428 | 5,075 | 32,032 | 12,859 | 11,124 | 3,172 | 4,877 |
| Nebraska ......... | 80,221 | 24,412 | 20,877 | 15,063 | 19,869 | 81,202 | 23,842 | 21,076 | 15,196 | 21,088 |
| Nevada .......... | 42,700 | 7,136 | 5,955 | 14,386 | 15,223 | 43,368 | 6,739 | 6,244 | 12,629 | 17,756 |
| New Hampshire .... | 27,323 | 8,831 | 9,174 | 4,170 | 5,148 | 26,669 | 8,669 | 9,157 | 3,592 | 5,251 |
| New Jersey ....... | 243,388 | 57,377 | 60,485 | 51,232 | 74,294 | 237,297 | 55,792 | 58,188 | 50,458 | 72,859 |
| New Mexico ....... | 64,261 | 19,008 | 17,001 | 11,022 | 17,230 | 66,059 | 19,039 | 17,149 | 11,819 | 18,052 |
| New York ........ | 567,151 | 159,738 | 175,968 | 94,023 | 137,422 | 563,251 | 154,637 | 174,911 | 93,308 | 140,395 |
| North Carolina ..... | 249,417 | 67,671 | 73,813 | 45,877 | 62,056 | 267,044 | 69,162 | 77,456 | 50,438 | 69,988 |
| North Dakota ...... | 34,441 | 15,546 | 12,059 | 2,976 | 3,860 | 34,802 | 15,328 | 12,117 | 3,142 | 4,215 |
| Ohio ............ | 381,610 | 116,862 | 110,899 | 67,793 | 86,056 | 379,164 | 114,674 | 111,496 | 65,768 | 87,226 |
| Oklahoma ......... | 145,822 | 43,038 | 36,566 | 27,162 | 39,056 | 146,827 | 42,292 | 36,942 | 27,499 | 40,094 |
| Oregon .......... | 123,231 | 37,904 | 32,780 | 23,112 | 29,435 | 119,612 | 37,083 | 32,907 | 21,545 | 28,077 |
| Pennsylvania ...... | 301,172 | 100,221 | 91,357 | 46,174 | 63,420 | 300,523 | 99,454 | 92,196 | 45,645 | 63,228 |
| Rhode Island ...... | 34,507 | 8,020 | 9,300 | 6,564 | 10,623 | 35,389 | 8,482 | 9,672 | 6,455 | 10,780 |
| South Carolina ..... | 105,213 | 34,497 | 35,448 | 14,865 | 20,403 | 105,854 | 34,372 | 36,037 | 14,677 | 20,768 |
| South Dakota ...... | 24,023 | 9,626 | 8,239 | 2,585 | 3,573 | 23,339 | 9,090 | 7,977 | 2,578 | 3,694 |
| Tennessee ....... | 152,797 | 46,784 | 45,449 | 25,656 | 34,908 | 147,951 | 44,447 | 43,852 | 24,954 | 34,698 |
| Texas ........... | 703,717 | 191,055 | 170,737 | 151,208 | 190,717 | 677,192 | 184,976 | 168,331 | 142,547 | 181,338 |
| Utah ............ | 67,215 | 25,238 | 17,596 | 13,639 | 10,742 | 69,426 | 24,801 | 17,942 | 14,298 | 12,385 |
| Vermont .......... | 18,192 | 5,900 | 6,314 | 2,087 | 3,891 | 18,844 | 5,923 | 6,242 | 2,328 | 4,351 |
| Virginia .......... | 245,104 | 63,706 | 66,977 | 47,014 | 67,407 | 250,754 | 64,044 | 67,005 | 49,299 | 70,406 |
| Washington ....... | 200,857 | 64,843 | 59,393 | 28,832 | 47,789 | 201,532 | 64,164 | 60,142 | 29,290 | 47,936 |
| West Virginia ...... | 68,384 | 22,449 | 20,365 | 9,142 | 16,428 | 66,531 | 21,398 | 20,495 | 8,588 | 16,050 |
| Wisconsin ........ | 235,084 | 79,200 | 75,243 | 34,798 | 45,843 | 238,735 | 79,085 | 75,791 | 36,649 | 47,210 |
| Wyoming ......... | 23,424 | 7,482 | 6,519 | 3,515 | 5,908 | 24,204 | 7,232 | 6,446 | 3,892 | 6,634 |
| U.S. Service Schools ... | 52,788 | 47,130 | 5,522 | 129 | 7 | 54,052 | 48,065 | 5,862 | 120 | 5 |
| Outlying areas ..... | 65,134 | 20,801 | 28,622 | 6,093 | 9,618 | 65,411 | 20,819 | 28,956 | 6,184 | 9,452 |
| American Samoa .... | 871 | 200 | 209 | 182 | 280 | 758 | 191 | 178 | 185 | 204 |
| Guam ............ | 4,432 | 1,092 | 1,082 | 1,064 | 1,194 | 4,601 | 1,153 | 1,119 | 1,165 | 1,164 |
| Northern Marianas ... | 431 | 22 | 22 | 189 | 198 | 318 | 45 | 58 | 82 | 133 |
| Puerto Rico ........ | 55,784 | 18,823 | 26,566 | 3,965 | 6,430 | 56,438 | 18,821 | 26,867 | 4,180 | 6,570 |
| Trust Territory of the Pacific .......... | 796 | 450 | 192 | 81 | 73 | 724 | 458 | 199 | 27 | 40 |
| Virgin Islands ....... | 2,820 | 214 | 551 | 612 | 1,443 | 2,572 | 151 | 535 | 545 | 1,341 |

SOURCE: U.S. Department of Education, Center for Education Statistics, "Fall Enrollment in Colleges and Universitites" surveys. (This table was prepared July 1986.)

Table 2.25

## —Total enrollment in all institutions of higher education, by attendance status, sex, and State: Fall 1984 and fall 1985

| State or other area | Fall 1984 | | | | | Fall 1985 | | | | |
|---|---|---|---|---|---|---|---|---|---|---|
| | Total | Full-time | | Part-time | | Total | Full-time | | Part-time | |
| | | Men | Women | Men | Women | | Men | Women | Men | Women |
| 1 | 2 | 3 | 4 | 5 | 6 | 7 | 8 | 9 | 10 | 11 |
| United States .... | 12,241,940 | 3,647,509 | 3,450,879 | 2,216,065 | 2,927,487 | 12,247,055 | 3,607,720 | 3,467,501 | 2,210,730 | 2,961,104 |
| Alabama .......... | 171,631 | 59,085 | 62,403 | 23,433 | 26,710 | 179,343 | 60,350 | 63,229 | 26,614 | 29,150 |
| Alaska ............ | 26,991 | 4,162 | 4,334 | 7,288 | 11,207 | 27,479 | 4,396 | 4,690 | 7,298 | 11,095 |
| Arizona .......... | 210,029 | 51,408 | 42,554 | 50,864 | 65,203 | 216,854 | 52,241 | 43,401 | 52,498 | 68,714 |
| Arkansas ........ | 78,777 | 27,211 | 28,578 | 8,374 | 14,614 | 77,958 | 26,250 | 28,809 | 8,298 | 14,601 |
| California ........ | 1,665,155 | 385,235 | 360,533 | 409,803 | 509,584 | 1,650,439 | 380,823 | 360,302 | 403,607 | 505,707 |
| Colorado .......... | 164,394 | 54,470 | 48,638 | 26,581 | 34,705 | 161,314 | 53,679 | 48,628 | 25,225 | 33,782 |
| Connecticut ........ | 161,576 | 42,127 | 42,777 | 32,482 | 44,190 | 159,348 | 41,203 | 42,044 | 31,204 | 44,897 |
| Delaware .......... | 31,872 | 8,994 | 11,195 | 5,066 | 6,617 | 31,883 | 8,972 | 11,409 | 4,974 | 6,528 |
| District of Columbia .. | 79,750 | 23,769 | 23,890 | 15,690 | 16,401 | 78,868 | 23,507 | 23,942 | 15,063 | 16,356 |
| Florida ............ | 444,062 | 114,186 | 107,141 | 96,419 | 126,316 | 451,392 | 115,760 | 109,090 | 96,963 | 129,579 |
| Georgia .......... | 196,869 | 67,041 | 66,032 | 28,259 | 35,537 | 196,826 | 66,058 | 66,645 | 27,958 | 36,165 |
| Hawaii .......... | 49,981 | 14,544 | 14,758 | 10,075 | 10,604 | 49,937 | 14,276 | 14,418 | 10,070 | 11,173 |
| Idaho ............ | 43,303 | 15,258 | 13,398 | 6,114 | 8,533 | 42,668 | 14,828 | 13,604 | 5,986 | 8,250 |
| Illinois ............ | 661,114 | 170,784 | 156,643 | 135,893 | 197,794 | 678,689 | 173,433 | 161,935 | 141,103 | 202,218 |
| Indiana ............ | 249,957 | 88,105 | 77,635 | 37,270 | 46,947 | 250,567 | 86,256 | 77,916 | 37,728 | 48,667 |
| Iowa ............ | 153,069 | 61,662 | 52,456 | 16,234 | 22,717 | 152,897 | 60,819 | 53,073 | 16,263 | 22,742 |
| Kansas .......... | 141,916 | 43,253 | 38,556 | 23,627 | 36,480 | 141,359 | 42,776 | 38,409 | 23,223 | 36,951 |
| Kentucky .......... | 143,555 | 47,316 | 49,643 | 17,347 | 29,249 | 141,724 | 45,627 | 48,801 | 17,624 | 29,672 |
| Louisiana .......... | 179,988 | 63,778 | 61,213 | 21,904 | 33,093 | 177,176 | 64,922 | 63,963 | 19,384 | 28,907 |
| Maine ............ | 52,714 | 14,721 | 14,353 | 6,340 | 17,300 | 52,201 | 14,559 | 14,442 | 6,187 | 17,013 |
| Maryland .......... | 234,302 | 53,287 | 57,115 | 50,984 | 72,916 | 231,649 | 53,062 | 55,891 | 50,164 | 72,532 |
| Massachusetts ...... | 418,966 | 128,895 | 132,942 | 68,414 | 88,715 | 421,175 | 127,939 | 133,636 | 68,025 | 91,575 |
| Michigan .......... | 505,334 | 137,045 | 134,954 | 102,133 | 131,202 | 507,293 | 132,780 | 134,097 | 105,076 | 135,340 |
| Minnesota .......... | 215,566 | 72,827 | 68,690 | 29,959 | 44,090 | 221,162 | 72,040 | 69,522 | 32,169 | 47,431 |
| Mississippi .......... | 104,339 | 38,001 | 40,617 | 9,831 | 15,890 | 101,180 | 36,777 | 39,846 | 9,683 | 14,874 |
| Missouri .......... | 240,920 | 78,504 | 69,401 | 39,620 | 53,395 | 241,146 | 75,084 | 68,182 | 41,770 | 56,110 |
| Montana .......... | 37,061 | 14,256 | 12,424 | 4,210 | 6,171 | 35,958 | 13,828 | 12,484 | 3,858 | 5,788 |
| Nebraska .......... | 97,422 | 30,366 | 27,199 | 17,065 | 22,792 | 97,769 | 29,556 | 27,056 | 17,071 | 24,086 |
| Nevada ............ | 43,007 | 7,241 | 6,023 | 14,455 | 15,288 | 43,656 | 6,846 | 6,310 | 12,682 | 17,818 |
| New Hampshire ..... | 53,049 | 18,039 | 18,093 | 7,367 | 9,550 | 52,283 | 17,728 | 18,050 | 6,968 | 9,537 |
| New Jersey ....... | 305,330 | 77,373 | 77,923 | 62,710 | 87,324 | 297,658 | 75,156 | 75,116 | 61,523 | 85,863 |
| New Mexico ........ | 66,507 | 19,466 | 17,674 | 11,428 | 17,939 | 68,295 | 19,461 | 17,781 | 12,236 | 18,817 |
| New York .......... | 1,007,770 | 310,404 | 323,586 | 155,311 | 218,469 | 1,000,098 | 304,520 | 323,948 | 151,892 | 219,738 |
| North Carolina ..... | 309,249 | 92,820 | 99,905 | 49,508 | 67,016 | 327,288 | 94,271 | 103,890 | 54,049 | 75,078 |
| North Dakota ...... | 37,585 | 16,502 | 13,436 | 3,233 | 4,414 | 37,939 | 16,305 | 13,484 | 3,380 | 4,770 |
| Ohio ............ | 518,435 | 161,883 | 150,584 | 102,429 | 103,539 | 514,745 | 159,022 | 150,975 | 99,901 | 104,847 |
| Oklahoma .......... | 168,034 | 52,270 | 44,012 | 30,101 | 41,651 | 169,173 | 51,590 | 44,607 | 30,446 | 42,530 |
| Oregon ............ | 141,810 | 45,963 | 39,443 | 24,983 | 31,421 | 137,967 | 45,276 | 39,525 | 23,225 | 29,941 |
| Pennsylvania ........ | 528,669 | 184,091 | 168,415 | 76,354 | 99,809 | 533,198 | 185,089 | 171,718 | 76,217 | 100,174 |
| Rhode Island ........ | 69,145 | 21,203 | 21,247 | 11,278 | 15,417 | 69,927 | 21,907 | 21,882 | 10,836 | 15,302 |
| South Carolina ...... | 131,479 | 44,976 | 47,725 | 16,346 | 22,432 | 131,902 | 44,544 | 48,504 | 16,082 | 22,772 |
| South Dakota ........ | 32,473 | 12,181 | 11,817 | 3,376 | 5,099 | 32,772 | 11,777 | 12,111 | 3,414 | 5,470 |
| Tennessee ........ | 200,937 | 66,838 | 66,866 | 28,242 | 38,991 | 194,845 | 63,988 | 64,559 | 27,411 | 38,887 |
| Texas ............ | 795,337 | 228,530 | 203,204 | 162,864 | 200,739 | 769,692 | 222,604 | 201,498 | 154,073 | 191,517 |
| Utah ............ | 101,863 | 39,906 | 29,239 | 17,878 | 14,840 | 103,994 | 38,612 | 29,588 | 18,748 | 17,046 |
| Vermont .......... | 30,786 | 11,112 | 11,517 | 2,847 | 5,310 | 31,416 | 11,043 | 11,495 | 3,038 | 5,840 |
| Virginia ............ | 283,109 | 77,326 | 83,686 | 49,943 | 72,154 | 292,416 | 78,946 | 85,717 | 52,554 | 75,199 |
| Washington ........ | 230,667 | 75,605 | 71,273 | 32,014 | 51,775 | 231,553 | 74,807 | 71,687 | 32,842 | 52,217 |
| West Virginia ........ | 79,009 | 25,962 | 24,505 | 10,174 | 18,368 | 76,659 | 24,679 | 24,297 | 9,691 | 17,992 |
| Wisconsin .......... | 270,865 | 92,916 | 88,593 | 38,301 | 51,055 | 275,069 | 92,451 | 88,987 | 40,424 | 53,207 |
| Wyoming .......... | 23,424 | 7,482 | 6,519 | 3,515 | 5,908 | 24,204 | 7,232 | 6,446 | 3,892 | 6,634 |
| U.S. Service Schools .. | 52,788 | 47,130 | 5,522 | 129 | 7 | 54,052 | 48,065 | 5,862 | 120 | 5 |
| Outlying areas ..... | 158,452 | 50,012 | 73,318 | 13,863 | 21,259 | 164,890 | 52,061 | 77,517 | 13,901 | 21,411 |
| American Samoa .... | 871 | 200 | 209 | 182 | 280 | 758 | 191 | 178 | 185 | 204 |
| Guam ............ | 4,432 | 1,092 | 1,082 | 1,064 | 1,194 | 4,601 | 1,153 | 1,119 | 1,165 | 1,164 |
| Northern Marianas ... | 431 | 22 | 22 | 189 | 198 | 318 | 45 | 58 | 82 | 133 |
| Puerto Rico ........ | 149,102 | 48,034 | 71,262 | 11,735 | 18,071 | 155,917 | 50,063 | 75,428 | 11,897 | 18,529 |
| Trust Territory of the Pacific ............ | 796 | 450 | 192 | 81 | 73 | 724 | 458 | 199 | 27 | 40 |
| Virgin Islands ....... | 2,820 | 214 | 551 | 612 | 1,443 | 2,572 | 151 | 535 | 545 | 1,341 |

SOURCE: U.S. Department of Education, Center for Education Statistics, "Fall Enrollment in Colleges and Universities" surveys. (This table was prepared July 1986.)

Table 2.26

### —Selected statistics on traditionally black institutions of higher education:[1] United States, 1983-84 and fall 1985

| Item | Total | Public 4-year | Public 2-year | Private 4-year | Private 2-year |
|---|---|---|---|---|---|
| 1 | 2 | 3 | 4 | 5 | 6 |
| Number of institutions, fall 1985 | 99 | 38 | 5 | 49 | 7 |
| **Total enrollment, fall 1985** | 213,776 | 146,111 | 6,050 | 60,292 | 1,323 |
| Men | 94,998 | 65,617 | 2,370 | 26,387 | 624 |
| Women | 118,778 | 80,494 | 3,680 | 33,905 | 699 |
| Full-time enrollment | 165,670 | 105,485 | 4,662 | 54,270 | 1,253 |
| Men | 75,429 | 49,440 | 1,714 | 23,676 | 599 |
| Women | 90,241 | 56,045 | 2,948 | 30,594 | 654 |
| Part-time enrollment | 48,106 | 40,626 | 1,388 | 6.022 | 70 |
| Men | 19,569 | 16,177 | 656 | 2,711 | 25 |
| Women | 28,537 | 24,449 | 732 | 2,211 | 45 |
| **Earned degrees conferred, 1983-84[2]** | | | | | |
| Associate | 1,849 | 1,101 | 399 | 120 | 229 |
| Men | 630 | 410 | 100 | 29 | 91 |
| Women | 1,219 | 691 | 299 | 91 | 138 |
| Bachelor's | 21,229 | 13,789 | --- | 7,433 | 7 |
| Men | 9,344 | 6,283 | --- | 3,054 | 7 |
| Women | 11,885 | 7,506 | --- | 4,379 | --- |
| Master's | 4,090 | 3,194 | --- | 896 | --- |
| Men | 1,780 | 1,400 | --- | 380 | --- |
| Women | 2,310 | 1,794 | --- | 516 | --- |
| Doctor's | 118 | 22 | --- | 96 | --- |
| Men | 74 | 11 | --- | 63 | --- |
| Women | 44 | 11 | --- | 33 | --- |
| First-professional | 913 | 239 | --- | 674 | --- |
| Men | 565 | 166 | --- | 399 | --- |
| Women | 348 | 73 | --- | 275 | --- |
| **Financial statistics, fiscal year 1984, in thousands of dollars[2]** | | | | | |
| Current-fund revenues | $1,757,100 | $937,526 | $25,305 | $781,676 | $12,594 |
| Tuition and fees | 317,856 | 124,218 | 3,216 | 187,641 | 2,780 |
| Federal Government[3] | 398,736 | 133,759 | 5,144 | 256,299 | 3,534 |
| State governments[3] | 477,976 | 453,830 | 12,597 | 11,467 | 83 |
| Local governments[3] | 64,146 | 62,495 | 1,381 | 271 | --- |
| Private gifts, grants, and contracts | 90,764 | 8,081 | 664 | 78,794 | 3,225 |
| Endowment income | 20,648 | 1,259 | 0 | 19,201 | 187 |
| Sales and services | 343,838 | 135,287 | 1,914 | 204,125 | 2,512 |
| Other sources | 43,136 | 18,596 | 390 | 23,878 | 272 |
| Current-fund expenditures | 1,723,305 | 915,461 | 27,082 | 769,218 | 11,544 |
| Educational and general expenditures | 1,382,512 | 793,021 | 25,558 | 554,524 | 9,410 |
| Auxiliary enterprises | 206,056 | 122,440 | 1,524 | 79,957 | 2,135 |
| Hospitals | 134,736 | --- | --- | 134,736 | --- |
| Endowment, market value | 278,507 | 14,886 | --- | 263,387 | 235 |
| Buildings, replacement value | 4,183,929 | 2,748,302 | 66,197 | 1,343,500 | 25,931 |

[1]Includes institutions which were established prior to 1954 for the education of black students mainly in the southern and border States.

[2]Tabulation includes degree and finance data for Lomax-Hannon Junior College, but excludes enrollment data.

[3]Includes appropriations, grants, and contracts.

---Data not reported or not applicable.

NOTE.—Because of rounding, details may not add to totals.

SOURCE: U.S. Department of Education, Center for Education Statistics, "Fall Enrollment in Higher Education, 1985," "Degrees and Formal Awards Conferred, 1983-84," and "Financial Statistics of Institutions of Higher Education, Fiscal Year 1984" surveys. (This table was prepared September 1986.)

Table 2.27

### —Average salary of full-time instructional faculty on 9-month contracts in institutions of higher education, by type and control of institution and by State: 1985-86

| State or other area | Average, all institutions | Public institutions | | | Private institutions | | |
|---|---|---|---|---|---|---|---|
| | | Total | 4-year | 2-year | Total | 4-year | 2-year |
| 1 | 2 | 3 | 4 | 5 | 6 | 7 | 8 |
| **United States** | $32,392 | $32,750 | $34,033 | $29,590 | $31,402 | $31,732 | $19,436 |
| Alabama | 29,108 | 30,132 | 30,932 | 27,510 | 22,499 | 22,562 | 21,165 |
| Alaska | 42,696 | 43,463 | 42,637 | 45,114 | 22,446 | 22,446 | ... |
| Arizona | 34,118 | 34,450 | 35,864 | 31,765 | 25,541 | 26,141 | 17,528 |
| Arkansas | 27,427 | 28,088 | 29,064 | 22,479 | 21,455 | 21,557 | 13,100 |
| California | 39,002 | 39,636 | 42,085 | 36,119 | 32,603 | 32,760 | 20,559 |
| Colorado | 31,003 | 31,220 | 32,845 | 24,338 | 29,481 | 29,664 | 20,134 |
| Connecticut | 36,464 | 36,470 | 38,638 | 30,021 | 36,456 | 36,621 | 22,434 |
| Delaware | 32,134 | 32,718 | 33,824 | 26,493 | 21,309 | 21,309 | ... |
| District of Columbia | 35,014 | 33,662 | 33,662 | ... | 35,302 | 35,302 | ... |
| Florida | 29,334 | 29,526 | 33,062 | 24,802 | 28,603 | 28,769 | 18,190 |
| Georgia | 30,378 | 31,356 | 32,323 | 26,272 | 27,175 | 27,690 | 18,769 |
| Hawaii | 30,444 | 31,027 | 32,376 | 28,001 | 20,430 | 20,430 | ... |
| Idaho | 28,266 | 28,588 | 29,223 | 24,992 | 22,267 | 22,267 | ... |
| Illinois | 32,789 | 32,488 | 33,545 | 30,839 | 33,427 | 33,575 | 18,957 |
| Indiana | 30,279 | 30,319 | 31,883 | 20,438 | 30,181 | 30,250 | 18,727 |
| Iowa | 27,959 | 29,442 | 31,512 | 22,411 | 25,451 | 25,523 | 21,383 |
| Kansas | 28,274 | 29,766 | 31,272 | 25,459 | 20,048 | 20,452 | 16,304 |
| Kentucky | 27,324 | 28,359 | 29,488 | 22,238 | 23,248 | 23,787 | 17,181 |
| Louisiana | 28,202 | 27,709 | 27,960 | 24,383 | 30,795 | 30,795 | ... |
| Maine | 27,444 | 27,363 | 28,354 | 22,347 | 27,684 | 27,684 | ... |
| Maryland | 32,797 | 32,667 | 33,852 | 30,590 | 33,307 | 33,362 | 20,269 |
| Massachusetts | 36,582 | 35,452 | 37,715 | 29,833 | 37,309 | 37,967 | 20,985 |
| Michigan | 33,039 | 34,268 | 34,828 | 32,693 | 26,334 | 26,460 | 24,600 |
| Minnesota | 32,373 | 34,404 | 35,852 | 30,403 | 28,209 | 28,349 | 20,778 |
| Mississippi | 24,273 | 24,562 | 27,804 | 19,206 | 20,804 | 21,818 | 14,586 |
| Missouri | 29,033 | 29,508 | 29,938 | 27,842 | 27,886 | 28,356 | 16,015 |
| Montana | 27,730 | 28,451 | 28,604 | 26,170 | 22,006 | 22,242 | 20,893 |
| Nebraska | 27,693 | 28,263 | 29,405 | 22,248 | 25,732 | 25,925 | 19,731 |
| Nevada | 32,394 | 32,404 | 33,752 | 27,381 | 24,000 | 24,000 | ... |
| New Hampshire | 30,237 | 29,161 | 30,851 | 22,203 | 31,639 | 32,112 | 15,557 |
| New Jersey | 35,313 | 35,057 | 36,860 | 30,603 | 35,942 | 36,028 | 25,638 |
| New Mexico | 29,485 | 29,715 | 30,340 | 26,903 | 20,557 | 20,557 | ... |
| New York | 35,845 | 36,879 | 38,813 | 33,586 | 34,634 | 35,058 | 18,108 |
| North Carolina | 29,585 | 31,444 | 33,114 | 20,311 | 24,150 | 24,564 | 20,273 |
| North Dakota | 27,618 | 28,241 | 28,939 | 26,125 | 18,801 | 18,820 | 18,756 |
| Ohio | 32,212 | 33,748 | 35,664 | 26,898 | 28,259 | 28,278 | 13,602 |
| Oklahoma | 29,479 | 29,972 | 31,127 | 26,371 | 27,414 | 27,763 | 18,754 |
| Oregon | 28,629 | 28,838 | 29,921 | 27,707 | 27,773 | 27,773 | ... |
| Pennsylvania | 31,956 | 31,657 | 32,928 | 27,886 | 32,305 | 32,715 | 19,436 |
| Rhode Island | 33,519 | 31,394 | 32,769 | 26,967 | 36,014 | 36,014 | ... |
| South Carolina | 27,895 | 29,251 | 31,319 | 21,606 | 22,738 | 23,229 | 18,839 |
| South Dakota | 25,234 | 26,784 | 26,784 | ... | 21,027 | 21,402 | 16,071 |
| Tennessee | 29,389 | 30,127 | 31,498 | 24,099 | 27,644 | 27,927 | 17,942 |
| Texas | 31,311 | 31,311 | 32,432 | 28,930 | 31,309 | 31,493 | 17,983 |
| Utah | 31,475 | 31,664 | 33,452 | 25,597 | 22,002 | 22,002 | ... |
| Vermont | 28,843 | 30,956 | 31,438 | 25,539 | 26,439 | 26,724 | 23,351 |
| Virginia | 30,769 | 31,638 | 33,673 | 25,746 | 26,935 | 27,049 | 18,048 |
| Washington | 30,376 | 30,924 | 33,837 | 27,521 | 27,980 | 27,980 | ... |
| West Virginia | 26,225 | 27,105 | 27,667 | 21,809 | 21,555 | 21,805 | 17,362 |
| Wisconsin | 31,233 | 31,736 | 33,177 | 29,259 | 28,344 | 28,344 | ... |
| Wyoming | 32,065 | 32,065 | 36,198 | 27,551 | ... | ... | ... |
| U.S. Service Schools | 38,205 | 38,205 | 38,205 | ... | ... | ... | ... |
| Outlying areas | 23,580 | 23,645 | 23,611 | 24,177 | 10,227 | 10,227 | ... |
| American Samoa | ... | ... | ... | ... | ... | ... | ... |
| Guam | 27,575 | 27,575 | 29,242 | 24,729 | ... | ... | ... |
| Northern Marianas | ... | ... | ... | ... | ... | ... | ... |
| Puerto Rico | 23,180 | 23,250 | 23,221 | 24,064 | 10,227 | 10,227 | ... |
| Trust Territory of the Pacific | 13,406 | 13,406 | ... | 13,406 | ... | ... | ... |
| Virgin Islands | 25,804 | 25,804 | 25,804 | ... | ... | ... | ... |

---Data not reported or not applicable.

SOURCE: U.S. Department of Education, Center for Education Statistics, "Salaries, Tenure, and Fringe Benefits of Full-Time Instructional Faculty, 1985-86" survey. (This table was prepared September 1986.)

Table 2.28

## —Institutions of higher education and branches, by control of institution, highest level of offering, and sex of student body: United States, 1985-86

| Highest level of offering and sex of student body | Total | Public | | | | | Private | | | | |
| | | Federal[1] | State | Local (city, county, or district) | State and local | State-related | Independent nonprofit | Organized as profit-making | Religious group | | |
| | | | | | | | | | Protestant | Catholic | Other[2] |
| 1 | 2 | 3 | 4 | 5 | 6 | 7 | 8 | 9 | 10 | 11 | 12 |
| **All institutions** | 3,340 | 13 | 883 | 173 | 398 | 31 | 828 | 220 | 524 | 235 | 35 |
| Coeducational | 3,126 | 13 | 881 | 173 | 398 | 31 | 726 | 218 | 505 | 168 | 13 |
| Men only | 99 | 0 | 1 | 0 | 0 | 0 | 47 | 0 | 3 | 30 | 18 |
| Women only | 102 | 0 | 1 | 0 | 0 | 0 | 48 | 2 | 14 | 34 | 3 |
| Coordinate[3] | 13 | 0 | 0 | 0 | 0 | 0 | 7 | 0 | 2 | 3 | 1 |
| Less than 4 years beyond high school | 1,309 | 3 | 356 | 170 | 383 | 20 | 121 | 190 | 43 | 20 | 3 |
| Coeducational | 1,282 | 3 | 356 | 170 | 383 | 20 | 107 | 188 | 40 | 13 | 2 |
| Men only | 6 | 0 | 0 | 0 | 0 | 0 | 4 | 0 | 0 | 2 | 0 |
| Women only | 20 | 0 | 0 | 0 | 0 | 0 | 9 | 2 | 3 | 5 | 1 |
| Coordinate[3] | 1 | 0 | 0 | 0 | 0 | 0 | 1 | 0 | 0 | 0 | 0 |
| 4- or 5-year baccalaureate degree | 707 | 5 | 73 | 1 | 5 | 2 | 242 | 19 | 286 | 70 | 4 |
| Coeducational | 627 | 5 | 72 | 1 | 5 | 2 | 209 | 19 | 275 | 37 | 2 |
| Men only | 31 | 0 | 1 | 0 | 0 | 0 | 10 | 0 | 2 | 16 | 2 |
| Women only | 46 | 0 | 0 | 0 | 0 | 0 | 22 | 0 | 8 | 16 | 0 |
| Coordinate[3] | 3 | 0 | 0 | 0 | 0 | 0 | 1 | 0 | 1 | 1 | 0 |
| First-professional degree | 93 | 0 | 9 | 0 | 0 | 0 | 67 | 2 | 11 | 2 | 2 |
| Coeducational | 80 | 0 | 9 | 0 | 0 | 0 | 58 | 2 | 10 | 1 | 0 |
| Men only | 12 | 0 | 0 | 0 | 0 | 0 | 9 | 0 | 0 | 1 | 2 |
| Women only | 1 | 0 | 0 | 0 | 0 | 0 | 0 | 0 | 1 | 0 | 0 |
| Coordinate[3] | 0 | 0 | 0 | 0 | 0 | 0 | 0 | 0 | 0 | 0 | 0 |
| Master's degree | 566 | 2 | 148 | 1 | 0 | 3 | 196 | 5 | 103 | 105 | 3 |
| Coeducational | 525 | 2 | 148 | 1 | 0 | 3 | 181 | 5 | 100 | 82 | 3 |
| Men only | 12 | 0 | 0 | 0 | 0 | 0 | 4 | 0 | 0 | 8 | 0 |
| Women only | 24 | 0 | 0 | 0 | 0 | 0 | 9 | 0 | 2 | 13 | 0 |
| Coordinate[3] | 5 | 0 | 0 | 0 | 0 | 0 | 2 | 0 | 1 | 2 | 0 |
| Beyond master's but less than doctorate | 153 | 0 | 100 | 0 | 4 | 0 | 25 | 0 | 13 | 9 | 2 |
| Coeducational | 146 | 0 | 100 | 0 | 4 | 0 | 22 | 0 | 13 | 7 | 0 |
| Men only | 5 | 0 | 0 | 0 | 0 | 0 | 1 | 0 | 0 | 2 | 2 |
| Women only | 2 | 0 | 0 | 0 | 0 | 0 | 2 | 0 | 0 | 0 | 0 |
| Coordinate[3] | 0 | 0 | 0 | 0 | 0 | 0 | 0 | 0 | 0 | 0 | 0 |
| Doctorate | 473 | 3 | 197 | 1 | 6 | 6 | 153 | 1 | 68 | 29 | 9 |
| Coeducational | 462 | 3 | 196 | 1 | 6 | 6 | 148 | 1 | 67 | 28 | 6 |
| Men only | 4 | 0 | 0 | 0 | 0 | 0 | 0 | 0 | 1 | 1 | 2 |
| Women only | 3 | 0 | 1 | 0 | 0 | 0 | 2 | 0 | 0 | 0 | 0 |
| Coordinate[3] | 4 | 0 | 0 | 0 | 0 | 0 | 3 | 0 | 0 | 0 | 1 |
| Undergraduate nondegree-granting | 15 | 0 | 0 | 0 | 0 | 0 | 11 | 1 | 0 | 0 | 3 |
| Coeducational | 2 | 0 | 0 | 0 | 0 | 0 | 1 | 1 | 0 | 0 | 0 |
| Men only | 7 | 0 | 0 | 0 | 0 | 0 | 6 | 0 | 0 | 0 | 1 |
| Women only | 6 | 0 | 0 | 0 | 0 | 0 | 4 | 0 | 0 | 0 | 2 |
| Coordinate[3] | 0 | 0 | 0 | 0 | 0 | 0 | 0 | 0 | 0 | 0 | 0 |
| Graduate nondegree-granting | 22 | 0 | 0 | 0 | 0 | 0 | 13 | 0 | 0 | 0 | 9 |
| Coeducational | 0 | 0 | 0 | 0 | 0 | 0 | 0 | 0 | 0 | 0 | 0 |
| Men only | 22 | 0 | 0 | 0 | 0 | 0 | 13 | 0 | 0 | 0 | 9 |
| Women only | 0 | 0 | 0 | 0 | 0 | 0 | 0 | 0 | 0 | 0 | 0 |
| Coordinate[3] | 0 | 0 | 0 | 0 | 0 | 0 | 0 | 0 | 0 | 0 | 0 |

[1]Includes ten U.S. Service Schools, Haskell Indian Junior College, Institute of American Indian Arts, and Oglala Sioux Community College.
[2]Includes Jewish, Latter-Day Saints, Greek Orthodox, Russian Orthodox, and Unitarian.
[3]Institutions with separate colleges for men and women.

SOURCE: U.S. Department of Education, Center for Education Statistics, "Institutional Characteristics of Colleges and Universities, 1985-86" survey. (This table was prepared September 1986.)

Table 2.29

## —Institutions of higher education and branches,[1] by type, control, and size of enrollment: United States, fall 1985

| Control of institution and size of enrollment | All institutions | | Universities | | All other 4-year institutions | | 2-year institutions | |
|---|---|---|---|---|---|---|---|---|
| | Number | Enrollment | Number | Enrollment | Number | Enrollment | Number | Enrollment |
| 1 | 2 | 3 | 4 | 5 | 6 | 7 | 8 | 9 |
| **Public and private institutions** .............. | **3,301** | **12,247,055** | **156** | **2,870,692** | **1,853** | **4,845,286** | **1,292** | **4,531,077** |
| Under 200 ................. | 330 | 37,212 | 0 | 0 | 256 | 28,336 | 74 | 8,876 |
| 200 to 499 ................ | 396 | 138,014 | 0 | 0 | 235 | 81,845 | 161 | 56,169 |
| 500 to 999 ................ | 541 | 394,540 | 0 | 0 | 348 | 255,648 | 193 | 138,892 |
| 1,000 to 2,499 ........... | 848 | 1,362,623 | 0 | 0 | 489 | 774,196 | 359 | 588,427 |
| 2,500 to 4,999 ........... | 476 | 1,689,457 | 6 | 24,870 | 241 | 851,981 | 229 | 812,606 |
| 5,000 to 9,999 ........... | 365 | 2,536,917 | 32 | 243,128 | 169 | 1,144,771 | 164 | 1,149,018 |
| 10,000 to 19,999 .......... | 243 | 3,276,747 | 57 | 802,504 | 98 | 1,291,203 | 88 | 1,183,040 |
| 20,000 to 29,999 .......... | 72 | 1,715,055 | 36 | 873,298 | 15 | 352,284 | 21 | 489,473 |
| 30,000 or more ........... | 30 | 1,096,490 | 25 | 926,892 | 2 | 65,022 | 3 | 104,576 |
| **Public institutions** ........ | **1,493** | **9,479,273** | **94** | **2,141,112** | **470** | **3,068,428** | **929** | **4,269,733** |
| Under 200 ................. | 3 | 517 | 0 | 0 | 0 | 0 | 3 | 517 |
| 200 to 499 ................ | 35 | 13,479 | 0 | 0 | 9 | 3,435 | 26 | 10,044 |
| 500 to 999 ................ | 125 | 94,418 | 0 | 0 | 29 | 22,571 | 96 | 71,847 |
| 1,000 to 2,499 ........... | 404 | 683,808 | 0 | 0 | 93 | 165,520 | 311 | 518,288 |
| 2,500 to 4,999 ........... | 329 | 1,183,190 | 1 | 4,529 | 107 | 394,563 | 221 | 784,098 |
| 5,000 to 9,999 ........... | 293 | 2,055,572 | 7 | 58,818 | 125 | 865,531 | 161 | 1,131,223 |
| 10,000 to 19,999 .......... | 211 | 2,878,569 | 33 | 496,027 | 90 | 1,199,502 | 88 | 1,183,040 |
| 20,000 to 29,999 .......... | 66 | 1,571,140 | 31 | 752,756 | 15 | 352,284 | 20 | 466,100 |
| 30,000 or more ........... | 27 | 998,580 | 22 | 828,982 | 2 | 65,022 | 3 | 104,576 |
| **Private institutions** ........ | **1,808** | **2,767,782** | **62** | **729,580** | **1,383** | **1,776,858** | **363** | **261,344** |
| Under 200 ................. | 327 | 36,695 | 0 | 0 | 256 | 28,336 | 71 | 8,359 |
| 200 to 499 ................ | 361 | 124,535 | 0 | 0 | 226 | 78,410 | 135 | 46,125 |
| 500 to 999 ................ | 416 | 300,122 | 0 | 0 | 319 | 233,077 | 97 | 67,045 |
| 1,000 to 2,499 ........... | 444 | 678,815 | 0 | 0 | 396 | 608,676 | 48 | 70,139 |
| 2,500 to 4,999 ........... | 147 | 506,267 | 5 | 20,341 | 134 | 457,418 | 8 | 28,508 |
| 5,000 to 9,999 ........... | 72 | 481,345 | 25 | 184,310 | 44 | 279,240 | 3 | 17,795 |
| 10,000 to 19,999 .......... | 32 | 398,178 | 24 | 306,477 | 8 | 91,701 | 0 | 0 |
| 20,000 to 29,999 .......... | 6 | 143,915 | 5 | 120,542 | 0 | 0 | 1 | 23,373 |
| 30,000 or more ........... | 3 | 97,910 | 3 | 97,910 | 0 | 0 | 0 | 0 |

[1]Data represent those institutions and enrollments reported in the "Fall Enrollment in Colleges and Universities" survey.

SOURCE: U.S. Department of Education, Center for Education Statistics, "Fall Enrollment in Colleges and Universities, 1985" survey. (This table was prepared July 1986.)

Table 2.30

## —Institutions of higher education and branches, by type, control of institution, and State: 1985-86

| State or other area | Total | All institutions | | Universities | | All other 4-year institutions | | 2-year institutions | |
|---|---|---|---|---|---|---|---|---|---|
| | | Public | Private | Public | Private | Public | Private | Public | Private |
| 1 | 2 | 3 | 4 | 5 | 6 | 7 | 8 | 9 | 10 |
| **United States** | **3,340** | **1,498** | **1,842** | **94** | **62** | **472** | **1,401** | **932** | **379** |
| Alabama | 78 | 53 | 25 | 2 | 0 | 14 | 17 | 37 | 8 |
| Alaska | 15 | 12 | 3 | 1 | 0 | 2 | 3 | 9 | 0 |
| Arizona | 31 | 19 | 12 | 2 | 0 | 1 | 9 | 16 | 3 |
| Arkansas | 36 | 20 | 16 | 1 | 0 | 9 | 11 | 10 | 5 |
| California | 290 | 137 | 153 | 2 | 4 | 29 | 124 | 106 | 25 |
| Colorado | 48 | 28 | 20 | 2 | 1 | 11 | 11 | 15 | 8 |
| Connecticut | 48 | 24 | 24 | 1 | 1 | 6 | 20 | 17 | 3 |
| Delaware | 8 | 5 | 3 | 1 | 0 | 1 | 3 | 3 | 0 |
| District of Columbia | 19 | 2 | 17 | 0 | 5 | 2 | 12 | 0 | 0 |
| Florida | 87 | 37 | 50 | 2 | 1 | 7 | 37 | 28 | 12 |
| Georgia | 80 | 34 | 46 | 1 | 1 | 17 | 30 | 16 | 15 |
| Hawaii | 12 | 9 | 3 | 1 | 0 | 2 | 3 | 6 | 0 |
| Idaho | 10 | 6 | 4 | 1 | 0 | 3 | 3 | 2 | 1 |
| Illinois | 162 | 59 | 103 | 3 | 4 | 9 | 83 | 47 | 16 |
| Indiana | 75 | 28 | 47 | 4 | 1 | 9 | 36 | 15 | 10 |
| Iowa | 59 | 19 | 40 | 2 | 1 | 1 | 33 | 16 | 6 |
| Kansas | 52 | 29 | 23 | 3 | 0 | 5 | 20 | 21 | 3 |
| Kentucky | 45 | 9 | 36 | 2 | 0 | 6 | 21 | 1 | 15 |
| Louisiana | 31 | 20 | 11 | 1 | 2 | 13 | 8 | 6 | 1 |
| Maine | 30 | 13 | 17 | 1 | 0 | 7 | 12 | 5 | 5 |
| Maryland | 56 | 32 | 24 | 1 | 1 | 12 | 21 | 19 | 2 |
| Massachusetts | 121 | 31 | 90 | 1 | 7 | 13 | 64 | 17 | 19 |
| Michigan | 92 | 44 | 48 | 3 | 1 | 12 | 41 | 29 | 6 |
| Minnesota | 69 | 29 | 40 | 1 | 0 | 9 | 32 | 19 | 8 |
| Mississippi | 42 | 25 | 17 | 2 | 0 | 7 | 12 | 16 | 5 |
| Missouri | 92 | 28 | 64 | 1 | 2 | 12 | 52 | 15 | 10 |
| Montana | 16 | 9 | 7 | 2 | 0 | 4 | 3 | 3 | 4 |
| Nebraska | 28 | 13 | 15 | 1 | 1 | 6 | 12 | 6 | 2 |
| Nevada | 8 | 6 | 2 | 1 | 0 | 1 | 2 | 4 | 0 |
| New Hampshire | 28 | 12 | 16 | 1 | 0 | 3 | 12 | 8 | 4 |
| New Jersey | 60 | 31 | 29 | 1 | 2 | 13 | 24 | 17 | 3 |
| New Mexico | 20 | 17 | 3 | 2 | 0 | 4 | 3 | 11 | 0 |
| New York | 301 | 86 | 215 | 2 | 12 | 39 | 158 | 45 | 45 |
| North Carolina | 128 | 74 | 54 | 2 | 2 | 14 | 34 | 58 | 18 |
| North Dakota | 19 | 11 | 8 | 2 | 0 | 4 | 4 | 5 | 4 |
| Ohio | 142 | 59 | 83 | 8 | 1 | 14 | 63 | 37 | 19 |
| Oklahoma | 47 | 29 | 18 | 2 | 1 | 12 | 13 | 15 | 4 |
| Oregon | 46 | 21 | 25 | 2 | 0 | 6 | 24 | 13 | 1 |
| Pennsylvania | 206 | 62 | 144 | 3 | 4 | 22 | 103 | 37 | 37 |
| Rhode Island | 13 | 3 | 10 | 1 | 0 | 1 | 10 | 1 | 0 |
| South Carolina | 63 | 33 | 30 | 2 | 0 | 10 | 20 | 21 | 10 |
| South Dakota | 18 | 7 | 11 | 2 | 0 | 5 | 8 | 0 | 3 |
| Tennessee | 80 | 24 | 56 | 1 | 1 | 9 | 40 | 14 | 15 |
| Texas | 158 | 98 | 60 | 6 | 4 | 33 | 49 | 59 | 7 |
| Utah | 14 | 9 | 5 | 2 | 1 | 2 | 2 | 5 | 2 |
| Vermont | 22 | 6 | 16 | 1 | 0 | 3 | 14 | 2 | 2 |
| Virginia | 72 | 39 | 33 | 3 | 0 | 12 | 30 | 24 | 3 |
| Washington | 53 | 33 | 20 | 2 | 0 | 4 | 18 | 27 | 2 |
| West Virginia | 29 | 16 | 13 | 1 | 0 | 11 | 9 | 4 | 4 |
| Wisconsin | 63 | 30 | 33 | 1 | 1 | 12 | 28 | 17 | 4 |
| Wyoming | 8 | 8 | 0 | 1 | 0 | 0 | 0 | 7 | 0 |
| U.S. Service Schools | 10 | 10 | 0 | 0 | 0 | 9 | 0 | 1 | 0 |
| **Outlying areas** | **48** | **20** | **28** | **1** | **0** | **10** | **18** | **9** | **10** |
| American Samoa | 1 | 1 | 0 | 0 | 0 | 0 | 0 | 1 | 0 |
| Guam | 2 | 2 | 0 | 0 | 0 | 1 | 0 | 1 | 0 |
| Northern Marianas | 1 | 1 | 0 | 0 | 0 | 0 | 0 | 1 | 0 |
| Puerto Rico | 41 | 13 | 28 | 1 | 0 | 8 | 18 | 4 | 10 |
| Trust Territory of the Pacific | 2 | 2 | 0 | 0 | 0 | 0 | 0 | 2 | 0 |
| Virgin Islands | 1 | 1 | 0 | 0 | 0 | 1 | 0 | 0 | 0 |

SOURCE: U.S. Department of Education, Center for Education Statistics, "Institutional Characteristics of Colleges and Universities, 1985-86" survey. (This table was prepared March 1986.)

Table 2.31

## —Institutions of higher education and branches, by level, control of institution, and State: 1985-86

| State or other area | Total | Doctoral[1] | | Comprehensive[2] | | General baccalaureate[3] | | Specialized[4] | | 2-year[5] | | New[6] | |
|---|---|---|---|---|---|---|---|---|---|---|---|---|---|
| | | Public | Private | Public | Private | Public | Private | Public | Private | Public | Private | Public | Private |
| 1 | 2 | 3 | 4 | 5 | 6 | 7 | 8 | 9 | 10 | 11 | 12 | 13 | 14 |
| United States | 3,340 | 109 | 62 | 254 | 164 | 118 | 588 | 67 | 515 | 917 | 347 | 33 | 166 |
| Alabama | 78 | 3 | 0 | 12 | 2 | 1 | 9 | 0 | 1 | 21 | 7 | 16 | 6 |
| Alaska | 15 | 0 | 0 | 2 | 0 | 1 | 0 | 0 | 2 | 9 | 1 | 0 | 0 |
| Arizona | 31 | 2 | 0 | 1 | 0 | 0 | 2 | 0 | 6 | 16 | 1 | 0 | 3 |
| Arkansas | 36 | 1 | 0 | 4 | 1 | 4 | 7 | 1 | 2 | 9 | 6 | 1 | 0 |
| California | 290 | 8 | 8 | 19 | 22 | 0 | 17 | 3 | 65 | 105 | 14 | 2 | 27 |
| Colorado | 48 | 3 | 1 | 4 | 0 | 4 | 5 | 2 | 6 | 14 | 2 | 1 | 6 |
| Connecticut | 48 | 1 | 1 | 4 | 7 | 1 | 4 | 1 | 6 | 17 | 4 | 0 | 2 |
| Delaware | 8 | 1 | 0 | 0 | 0 | 1 | 1 | 0 | 1 | 3 | 1 | 0 | 0 |
| District of Columbia | 19 | 0 | 5 | 1 | 1 | 0 | 3 | 0 | 8 | 0 | 0 | 1 | 0 |
| Florida | 87 | 3 | 1 | 6 | 6 | 0 | 12 | 0 | 11 | 28 | 10 | 0 | 10 |
| Georgia | 80 | 2 | 1 | 9 | 2 | 4 | 16 | 3 | 9 | 16 | 15 | 0 | 3 |
| Hawaii | 12 | 1 | 0 | 0 | 0 | 2 | 2 | 0 | 1 | 6 | 0 | 0 | 0 |
| Idaho | 10 | 1 | 0 | 2 | 0 | 1 | 2 | 0 | 0 | 2 | 1 | 0 | 1 |
| Illinois | 162 | 5 | 4 | 7 | 7 | 0 | 31 | 0 | 38 | 47 | 11 | 0 | 12 |
| Indiana | 75 | 3 | 1 | 6 | 6 | 3 | 20 | 0 | 9 | 16 | 10 | 0 | 1 |
| Iowa | 59 | 2 | 0 | 1 | 1 | 0 | 26 | 0 | 6 | 16 | 6 | 0 | 1 |
| Kansas | 52 | 2 | 0 | 4 | 0 | 1 | 16 | 1 | 3 | 21 | 4 | 0 | 0 |
| Kentucky | 45 | 2 | 0 | 4 | 1 | 2 | 12 | 0 | 6 | 1 | 15 | 0 | 2 |
| Louisiana | 31 | 1 | 1 | 9 | 1 | 3 | 6 | 1 | 2 | 6 | 1 | 0 | 0 |
| Maine | 30 | 0 | 0 | 2 | 0 | 3 | 6 | 2 | 5 | 5 | 4 | 1 | 2 |
| Maryland | 56 | 1 | 1 | 7 | 3 | 4 | 7 | 1 | 9 | 19 | 3 | 0 | 1 |
| Massachusetts | 121 | 1 | 7 | 8 | 10 | 2 | 20 | 3 | 23 | 17 | 22 | 0 | 8 |
| Michigan | 92 | 4 | 1 | 7 | 2 | 3 | 17 | 1 | 17 | 29 | 9 | 0 | 2 |
| Minnesota | 69 | 1 | 0 | 6 | 2 | 3 | 15 | 0 | 13 | 16 | 9 | 3 | 1 |
| Mississippi | 42 | 3 | 0 | 3 | 2 | 2 | 6 | 1 | 3 | 16 | 6 | 0 | 0 |
| Missouri | 92 | 2 | 2 | 7 | 2 | 2 | 18 | 2 | 27 | 15 | 7 | 0 | 8 |
| Montana | 16 | 0 | 0 | 2 | 0 | 2 | 3 | 2 | 0 | 3 | 3 | 0 | 1 |
| Nebraska | 28 | 1 | 0 | 3 | 1 | 2 | 6 | 1 | 5 | 6 | 1 | 0 | 2 |
| Nevada | 8 | 1 | 0 | 1 | 0 | 0 | 1 | 0 | 0 | 4 | 0 | 0 | 1 |
| New Hampshire | 28 | 1 | 1 | 0 | 1 | 2 | 5 | 0 | 4 | 7 | 4 | 2 | 1 |
| New Jersey | 60 | 1 | 2 | 6 | 4 | 5 | 6 | 2 | 13 | 17 | 4 | 0 | 0 |
| New Mexico | 20 | 2 | 0 | 4 | 0 | 0 | 3 | 0 | 0 | 10 | 0 | 1 | 0 |
| New York | 301 | 6 | 12 | 19 | 25 | 7 | 39 | 7 | 80 | 47 | 41 | 0 | 18 |
| North Carolina | 128 | 3 | 1 | 6 | 2 | 6 | 27 | 1 | 4 | 57 | 19 | 1 | 1 |
| North Dakota | 19 | 1 | 0 | 1 | 0 | 4 | 2 | 0 | 2 | 5 | 1 | 0 | 3 |
| Ohio | 142 | 8 | 2 | 3 | 5 | 1 | 32 | 2 | 22 | 45 | 13 | 0 | 9 |
| Oklahoma | 47 | 2 | 0 | 4 | 4 | 5 | 5 | 3 | 4 | 15 | 4 | 0 | 1 |
| Oregon | 46 | 2 | 0 | 2 | 2 | 1 | 10 | 3 | 8 | 13 | 2 | 0 | 3 |
| Pennsylvania | 206 | 3 | 4 | 14 | 10 | 5 | 49 | 2 | 39 | 37 | 33 | 1 | 9 |
| Rhode Island | 13 | 1 | 1 | 1 | 2 | 0 | 3 | 0 | 2 | 1 | 2 | 0 | 0 |
| South Carolina | 63 | 2 | 0 | 3 | 2 | 6 | 14 | 1 | 4 | 21 | 8 | 0 | 2 |
| South Dakota | 18 | 1 | 0 | 1 | 0 | 3 | 5 | 1 | 3 | 1 | 3 | 0 | 0 |
| Tennessee | 80 | 2 | 1 | 7 | 0 | 0 | 25 | 1 | 12 | 13 | 15 | 1 | 3 |
| Texas | 158 | 7 | 2 | 21 | 13 | 2 | 19 | 7 | 13 | 59 | 8 | 2 | 5 |
| Utah | 14 | 2 | 1 | 0 | 0 | 2 | 2 | 0 | 0 | 5 | 2 | 0 | 0 |
| Vermont | 22 | 1 | 0 | 0 | 4 | 3 | 6 | 0 | 2 | 2 | 3 | 0 | 1 |
| Virginia | 72 | 3 | 0 | 7 | 4 | 5 | 19 | 0 | 4 | 24 | 3 | 0 | 3 |
| Washington | 53 | 2 | 0 | 3 | 7 | 1 | 3 | 0 | 5 | 27 | 1 | 0 | 4 |
| West Virginia | 29 | 1 | 0 | 1 | 0 | 8 | 7 | 2 | 1 | 4 | 4 | 0 | 1 |
| Wisconsin | 63 | 2 | 1 | 10 | 0 | 1 | 17 | 0 | 9 | 17 | 4 | 0 | 2 |
| Wyoming | 8 | 1 | 0 | 0 | 0 | 0 | 0 | 0 | 0 | 7 | 0 | 0 | 0 |
| U.S. Service Schools | 10 | 0 | 0 | 0 | 0 | 0 | 0 | 10 | 0 | 0 | 0 | 0 | 0 |
| Outlying areas | 48 | 0 | 0 | 3 | 3 | 3 | 5 | 2 | 4 | 3 | 12 | 9 | 4 |
| American Samoa | 1 | 0 | 0 | 0 | 0 | 0 | 0 | 0 | 0 | 1 | 0 | 0 | 0 |
| Guam | 2 | 0 | 0 | 1 | 0 | 0 | 0 | 0 | 0 | 0 | 0 | 1 | 0 |
| Northern Marianas | 1 | 0 | 0 | 0 | 0 | 0 | 0 | 0 | 0 | 0 | 0 | 1 | 0 |
| Puerto Rico | 41 | 0 | 0 | 2 | 3 | 2 | 5 | 2 | 4 | 1 | 12 | 6 | 4 |
| Trust Territory of the Pacific | 2 | 0 | 0 | 0 | 0 | 0 | 0 | 0 | 0 | 1 | 0 | 1 | 0 |
| Virgin Islands | 1 | 0 | 0 | 0 | 0 | 1 | 0 | 0 | 0 | 0 | 0 | 0 | 0 |

[1]These institutions have a significant level of activity in doctoral-level education as measured by the number of doctoral recipients and the diversity in doctoral-level program offerings.

[2]These institutions have diverse postbaccalaureate programs, but do not engage in significant doctoral-level education.

[3]These institutions primarily emphasize general undergraduate education.

[4]These baccalaureate or postbaccalaureate institutions are characterized by an emphasis in one field of study, such as business or engineering.

[5]These institutions confer at least 75 percent of their degrees and awards below the bachelor's degree level.

[6]These institutions are new additions to the Higher Education General Information Survey universe (not necessarily newly organized). When degree and award data become available, they will be reclassified.

SOURCE: U.S. Department of Education, Center for Education Statistics, "Institutional Characteristics of Colleges and Universities, 1985-86" survey. (This table was prepared March 1986.)

Table 2.32

## —Institutions of higher education and branches, by control of institution and State: 1985-86

| State or other area | Total | Public | | | | | Private | | | | |
|---|---|---|---|---|---|---|---|---|---|---|---|
| | | Federal[1] | State | Local (city, county, or district) | State and local | State-related | Independent nonprofit | Organized as profit-making | Religious group | | |
| | | | | | | | | | Protestant | Catholic | Other[2] |
| 1 | 2 | 3 | 4 | 5 | 6 | 7 | 8 | 9 | 10 | 11 | 12 |
| United States | 3,340 | 13 | 883 | 173 | 398 | 31 | 828 | 220 | 524 | 235 | 35 |
| Alabama | 78 | 0 | 53 | 0 | 0 | 0 | 9 | 4 | 11 | 1 | 0 |
| Alaska | 15 | 0 | 12 | 0 | 0 | 0 | 1 | 0 | 2 | 0 | 0 |
| Arizona | 31 | 0 | 3 | 4 | 12 | 0 | 5 | 4 | 3 | 0 | 0 |
| Arkansas | 36 | 0 | 13 | 1 | 6 | 0 | 1 | 3 | 12 | 0 | 0 |
| California | 290 | 0 | 32 | 2 | 103 | 0 | 96 | 15 | 23 | 18 | 1 |
| Colorado | 48 | 0 | 24 | 3 | 1 | 0 | 7 | 8 | 3 | 2 | 0 |
| Connecticut | 48 | 0 | 24 | 0 | 0 | 0 | 18 | 2 | 0 | 4 | 0 |
| Delaware | 8 | 0 | 4 | 0 | 0 | 1 | 2 | 0 | 1 | 0 | 0 |
| District of Columbia | 19 | 1 | 0 | 1 | 0 | 0 | 8 | 1 | 2 | 6 | 0 |
| Florida | 87 | 0 | 14 | 18 | 5 | 0 | 23 | 11 | 11 | 5 | 0 |
| Georgia | 80 | 0 | 33 | 1 | 0 | 0 | 16 | 8 | 22 | 0 | 0 |
| Hawaii | 12 | 0 | 9 | 0 | 0 | 0 | 2 | 0 | 1 | 0 | 0 |
| Idaho | 10 | 0 | 4 | 2 | 0 | 0 | 2 | 0 | 1 | 0 | 1 |
| Illinois | 162 | 0 | 14 | 10 | 35 | 0 | 51 | 11 | 27 | 12 | 2 |
| Indiana | 75 | 0 | 28 | 0 | 0 | 0 | 9 | 7 | 20 | 11 | 0 |
| Iowa | 59 | 0 | 4 | 3 | 12 | 0 | 11 | 3 | 17 | 8 | 1 |
| Kansas | 52 | 1 | 8 | 11 | 9 | 0 | 2 | 0 | 15 | 6 | 0 |
| Kentucky | 45 | 0 | 9 | 0 | 0 | 0 | 7 | 10 | 14 | 5 | 0 |
| Louisiana | 31 | 0 | 17 | 0 | 3 | 0 | 1 | 1 | 4 | 5 | 0 |
| Maine | 30 | 0 | 13 | 0 | 0 | 0 | 11 | 4 | 1 | 1 | 0 |
| Maryland | 56 | 0 | 13 | 12 | 7 | 0 | 15 | 1 | 2 | 5 | 1 |
| Massachusetts | 121 | 0 | 29 | 2 | 0 | 0 | 67 | 2 | 5 | 15 | 1 |
| Michigan | 92 | 0 | 15 | 25 | 4 | 0 | 26 | 0 | 13 | 9 | 0 |
| Minnesota | 69 | 0 | 26 | 1 | 2 | 0 | 11 | 3 | 16 | 10 | 0 |
| Mississippi | 42 | 0 | 12 | 7 | 6 | 0 | 2 | 2 | 13 | 0 | 0 |
| Missouri | 92 | 0 | 13 | 11 | 4 | 0 | 25 | 6 | 22 | 10 | 1 |
| Montana | 16 | 0 | 6 | 1 | 2 | 0 | 3 | 1 | 1 | 2 | 0 |
| Nebraska | 28 | 0 | 7 | 4 | 2 | 0 | 5 | 0 | 8 | 2 | 0 |
| Nevada | 8 | 0 | 6 | 0 | 0 | 0 | 2 | 0 | 0 | 0 | 0 |
| New Hampshire | 28 | 0 | 12 | 0 | 0 | 0 | 10 | 2 | 0 | 4 | 0 |
| New Jersey | 60 | 0 | 12 | 0 | 19 | 0 | 12 | 1 | 5 | 9 | 2 |
| New Mexico | 20 | 1 | 13 | 1 | 2 | 0 | 3 | 0 | 0 | 0 | 0 |
| New York | 301 | 0 | 34 | 0 | 52 | 0 | 152 | 27 | 7 | 11 | 18 |
| North Carolina | 128 | 0 | 33 | 0 | 40 | 1 | 2 | 11 | 39 | 2 | 0 |
| North Dakota | 19 | 0 | 10 | 0 | 1 | 0 | 4 | 0 | 3 | 1 | 0 |
| Ohio | 142 | 0 | 53 | 0 | 6 | 0 | 25 | 15 | 25 | 14 | 4 |
| Oklahoma | 47 | 0 | 24 | 0 | 5 | 0 | 5 | 2 | 10 | 1 | 0 |
| Oregon | 46 | 0 | 8 | 10 | 3 | 0 | 14 | 2 | 7 | 2 | 0 |
| Pennsylvania | 206 | 0 | 16 | 10 | 7 | 29 | 70 | 22 | 28 | 24 | 0 |
| Rhode Island | 13 | 0 | 3 | 0 | 0 | 0 | 8 | 0 | 0 | 2 | 0 |
| South Carolina | 63 | 0 | 27 | 0 | 6 | 0 | 7 | 6 | 17 | 0 | 0 |
| South Dakota | 18 | 0 | 6 | 1 | 0 | 0 | 2 | 1 | 6 | 2 | 0 |
| Tennessee | 80 | 0 | 24 | 0 | 0 | 0 | 14 | 9 | 31 | 2 | 0 |
| Texas | 158 | 0 | 46 | 25 | 27 | 0 | 12 | 5 | 36 | 7 | 0 |
| Utah | 14 | 0 | 9 | 0 | 0 | 0 | 1 | 1 | 0 | 0 | 3 |
| Vermont | 22 | 0 | 6 | 0 | 0 | 0 | 14 | 0 | 0 | 2 | 0 |
| Virginia | 72 | 0 | 39 | 0 | 0 | 0 | 10 | 1 | 21 | 1 | 0 |
| Washington | 53 | 0 | 31 | 0 | 2 | 0 | 7 | 3 | 7 | 3 | 0 |
| West Virginia | 29 | 0 | 16 | 0 | 0 | 0 | 5 | 2 | 5 | 1 | 0 |
| Wisconsin | 63 | 0 | 15 | 3 | 12 | 0 | 13 | 3 | 7 | 10 | 0 |
| Wyoming | 8 | 0 | 1 | 4 | 3 | 0 | 0 | 0 | 0 | 0 | 0 |
| U.S. Service Schools | 10 | 10 | 0 | 0 | 0 | 0 | 0 | 0 | 0 | 0 | 0 |
| Outlying areas | 48 | 1 | 16 | 1 | 2 | 0 | 19 | 5 | 1 | 3 | 0 |
| American Samoa | 1 | 0 | 1 | 0 | 0 | 0 | 0 | 0 | 0 | 0 | 0 |
| Guam | 2 | 0 | 1 | 0 | 1 | 0 | 0 | 0 | 0 | 0 | 0 |
| Northern Marianas | 1 | 0 | 0 | 0 | 1 | 0 | 0 | 0 | 0 | 0 | 0 |
| Puerto Rico | 41 | 0 | 12 | 1 | 0 | 0 | 19 | 5 | 1 | 3 | 0 |
| Trust Territory of the Pacific | 2 | 1 | 1 | 0 | 0 | 0 | 0 | 0 | 0 | 0 | 0 |
| Virgin Islands | 1 | 0 | 1 | 0 | 0 | 0 | 0 | 0 | 0 | 0 | 0 |

[1]Includes ten U.S. Service Schools, Defense Intelligence College (District of Columbia), Haskell Indian Junior College (Kansas), Institute of American Indian Arts (New Mexico), and Micronesian Occupational College (Trust Territory of the Pacific).

[2]Includes Jewish, Latter-Day Saints, Greek Orthodox, Russian Orthodox, and Unitarian.

SOURCE: U.S. Department of Education, Center for Education Statistics, "Institutional Characteristics of Colleges and Universities, 1985-86" survey. (This table was prepared September 1986.)

Table 2.33

# Time Series Data

**—Foreign students enrolled in institutions of higher education in the United States and outlying areas, by continent, region, and selected countries of origin: 1980-81 to 1985-86**

| Continent, region, and country | 1980-81 | | 1982-83 | | 1983-84 | | 1984-85 | | 1985-86 | |
|---|---|---|---|---|---|---|---|---|---|---|
| | Number | Percent | Number | Percent | Number | Percent | Number | Percent | Number | Percent |
| 1 | 2 | 3 | 4 | 5 | 6 | 7 | 8 | 9 | 10 | 11 |
| Total | 311,880 | 100.0 | 336,990 | 100.0 | 338,890 | 100.0 | 342,110 | 100.0 | 343,780 | 100.0 |
| Africa | 38,180 | 12.2 | 42,690 | 12.7 | 41,690 | 12.3 | 39,520 | 11.6 | 34,190 | 9.9 |
| Eastern Africa | 6,260 | 2.0 | 6,770 | 2.0 | 7,050 | 2.1 | 7,080 | 2.1 | 6,730 | 2.0 |
| Central Africa | 1,130 | 0.4 | 1,330 | 0.4 | 1,330 | 0.4 | 1,350 | 0.4 | 1,540 | 0.4 |
| North Africa | 7,310 | 2.3 | 7,070 | 2.1 | 6,840 | 2.0 | 6,490 | 1.9 | 5,980 | 1.7 |
| Southern Africa | 1,480 | 0.5 | 1,970 | 0.6 | 2,110 | 0.6 | 2,160 | 0.6 | 2,360 | 0.7 |
| West Africa | 22,000 | 7.1 | 25,550 | 7.6 | 24,360 | 7.2 | 22,440 | 6.6 | 17,580 | 5.1 |
| Nigeria | 17,350 | 5.6 | 20,710 | 6.1 | 20,080 | 5.9 | 18,370 | 5.4 | 13,710 | 4.0 |
| Europe | 25,330 | 8.1 | 31,570 | 9.4 | 31,860 | 9.4 | 33,350 | 9.7 | 34,310 | 10.0 |
| Eastern Europe | 1,670 | 0.5 | 2,000 | 0.6 | 1,810 | 0.5 | 1,690 | 0.5 | 1,770 | 0.5 |
| Western Europe | 23,660 | 7.6 | 29,570 | 8.8 | 30,050 | 8.9 | 31,660 | 9.3 | 32,540 | 9.5 |
| Federal Republic of Germany | 3,310 | 1.1 | --- | --- | 3,790 | 1.1 | 4,190 | 1.2 | 4,730 | 1.4 |
| Greece | 3,750 | 1.2 | --- | --- | 5,030 | 1.5 | 4,870 | 1.4 | 4,440 | 1.3 |
| United Kingdom | 4,440 | 1.4 | --- | --- | 5,860 | 1.7 | 6,030 | 1.8 | 5,940 | 1.7 |
| Latin America | 49,810 | 16.0 | 56,810 | 16.9 | 52,350 | 15.4 | 48,560 | 14.2 | 45,480 | 13.2 |
| Caribbean | 10,650 | 3.4 | 10,710 | 3.2 | 11,170 | 3.3 | 11,010 | 3.2 | 11,100 | 3.2 |
| Central America | 12,970 | 4.2 | 14,420 | 4.3 | 12,400 | 3.7 | 12,550 | 3.7 | 12,740 | 3.7 |
| Mexico | 6,730 | 2.2 | --- | --- | 5,600 | 1.7 | 5,750 | 1.7 | 5,460 | 1.6 |
| South America | 26,190 | 8.4 | 31,680 | 9.4 | 28,780 | 8.5 | 25,000 | 7.3 | 21,640 | 6.3 |
| Venezuela | 11,750 | 3.8 | 15,490 | 4.6 | 13,440 | 4.0 | 10,290 | 3.0 | 7,040 | 2.0 |
| Middle East | 84,710 | 27.2 | 67,280 | 20.0 | 60,660 | 17.9 | 56,580 | 16.5 | 52,720 | 15.3 |
| Iran | 47,550 | 15.2 | 26,760 | 7.9 | 20,360 | 6.0 | 16,640 | 4.9 | 14,210 | 4.1 |
| Jordan | 6,140 | 2.0 | 6,820 | 2.0 | 6,890 | 2.0 | 6,750 | 2.0 | 6,590 | 1.9 |
| Lebanon | 6,770 | 2.2 | 7,110 | 2.1 | 6,680 | 2.0 | 6,940 | 2.0 | 7,090 | 2.1 |
| Saudia Arabia | 10,440 | 3.3 | 9,250 | 2.7 | 8,630 | 2.5 | 7,760 | 2.3 | 6,900 | 2.0 |
| North America[1] | 14,790 | 4.7 | 14,570 | 4.3 | 15,670 | 4.6 | 15,960 | 4.7 | 16,030 | 4.7 |
| Canada | 14,320 | 4.6 | 14,020 | 4.2 | 15,150 | 4.5 | 15,370 | 4.5 | 15,410 | 4.5 |
| Oceania | 4,180 | 1.3 | 4,040 | 1.2 | 4,090 | 1.2 | 4,190 | 1.2 | 4,030 | 1.2 |
| South and East Asia | 94,640 | 30.3 | 119,650 | 35.5 | 132,270 | 39.0 | 143,680 | 42.0 | 156,830 | 45.6 |
| East Asia | 51,650 | 16.6 | 60,710 | 18.0 | 66,520 | 19.6 | 72,630 | 21.2 | 80,720 | 23.5 |
| China | 2,770 | 0.9 | --- | --- | 8,140 | 2.4 | 10,100 | 3.0 | 13,980 | 4.1 |
| Hong Kong | 9,660 | 3.1 | 8,610 | 2.6 | 9,420 | 2.8 | 10,130 | 3.0 | 10,710 | 3.1 |
| Japan | 13,500 | 4.3 | 13,610 | 4.0 | 13,010 | 3.8 | 13,160 | 3.8 | 13,360 | 3.9 |
| Korea, Republic of | 6,150 | 2.0 | 11,360 | 3.4 | 13,860 | 4.1 | 16,430 | 4.8 | 18,660 | 5.4 |
| Taiwan | 19,460 | 6.2 | 20,770 | 6.2 | 21,960 | 6.5 | 22,590 | 6.6 | 23,770 | 6.9 |
| South Central Asia | 14,540 | 4.7 | 20,710 | 6.1 | 21,930 | 6.5 | 23,340 | 6.8 | 25,800 | 7.5 |
| India | 9,250 | 3.0 | 12,890 | 3.8 | 13,730 | 4.1 | 14,610 | 4.3 | 16,070 | 4.7 |
| Pakistan | 2,990 | 1.0 | --- | --- | 4,280 | 1.3 | 4,750 | 1.4 | 5,440 | 1.6 |
| South East Asia | 28,450 | 9.1 | 38,230 | 11.3 | 43,820 | 12.9 | 47,710 | 13.9 | 50,310 | 14.6 |
| Indonesia | 3,250 | 1.0 | --- | --- | 6,110 | 1.8 | 7,190 | 2.1 | 8,210 | 2.4 |
| Malaysia | 6,010 | 1.9 | 14,020 | 4.2 | 18,150 | 5.4 | 21,720 | 6.3 | 23,020 | 6.7 |
| Thailand | 6,550 | 2.1 | 6,800 | 2.0 | 6,940 | 2.0 | 7,220 | 2.1 | 6,940 | 2.0 |
| Stateless | 240 | 0.1 | 380 | 0.1 | 300 | 0.1 | 270 | 0.1 | 190 | 0.1 |

[1]Excludes Mexico and Central America, which are included with Latin America.

---Data not available.

NOTE.—Data are for "nonimmigrants," i.e., students who have not migrated to this country. The distribution by continent and region includes estimates for students whose country of origin is unknown. Because of rounding, details may not add to totals.

SOURCE: Institute of International Education, *Open Doors: 1980-81; Open Doors: 1982-83;* and *Open Doors: 1983-84;* and unpublished data (latest edition copyright ©1985 by the Institute of International Education. All rights reserved.) (This table was prepared October 1986.)

Table 3.1

### —Total enrollment in institutions of higher education, by type and control of institution and attendance status: United States, fall 1979 to fall 1985

| Type and control of institution and attendance status | 1979 | 1980 | 1981 | 1982 | 1983 | 1984 | 1985 | Percent change, 1979 to 1985 |
|---|---|---|---|---|---|---|---|---|
| 1 | 2 | 3 | 4 | 5 | 6 | 7 | 8 | 9 |
| **All institutions** | **11,569,899** | **12,096,895** | **12,371,672** | **12,425,780** | **12,464,661** | **12,241,940** | **12,247,055** | **5.9** |
| Doctoral[1] | 2,962,756 | 3,028,868 | 3,046,363 | 3,028,176 | 3,043,612 | 3,029,832 | 3,033,382 | 2.4 |
| Full-time | 2,221,216 | 2,278,610 | 2,291,489 | 2,282,777 | 2,283,434 | 2,277,707 | 2,281,119 | 2.7 |
| Part-time | 741,540 | 750,258 | 754,874 | 745,399 | 760,178 | 752,125 | 752,263 | 1.4 |
| Comprehensive[2] | 2,746,604 | 2,813,735 | 2,839,524 | 2,837,745 | 2,877,348 | 2,864,555 | 2,863,210 | 4.2 |
| Full-time | 1,775,281 | 1,816,746 | 1,825,327 | 1,835,152 | 1,873,566 | 1,852,459 | 1,846,991 | 4.0 |
| Part-time | 971,323 | 996,989 | 1,014,197 | 1,002,593 | 1,003,782 | 1,012,096 | 1,016,219 | 4.6 |
| General baccalaureate[3] | 1,121,749 | 1,172,667 | 1,185,922 | 1,181,015 | 1,149,861 | 1,146,430 | 1,156,340 | 3.1 |
| Full-time | 827,802 | 849,697 | 855,352 | 839,067 | 817,180 | 808,259 | 808,438 | -2.3 |
| Part-time | 293,947 | 322,970 | 330,570 | 341,948 | 332,681 | 338,171 | 347,902 | 18.4 |
| Specialized[4] | 492,164 | 543,277 | 559,458 | 575,443 | 599,106 | 590,093 | 585,080 | 18.9 |
| Full-time | 357,960 | 401,337 | 406,852 | 417,354 | 424,655 | 417,233 | 411,534 | 15.0 |
| Full-time | 134,204 | 141,940 | 152,606 | 158,089 | 174,451 | 172,860 | 173,546 | 29.3 |
| Two-year[5] | 4,246,232 | 4,472,085 | 4,630,108 | 4,665,939 | 4,725,379 | 4,526,735 | 4,509,341 | 6.2 |
| Full-time | 1,611,414 | 1,710,344 | 1,748,292 | 1,774,508 | 1,829,228 | 1,697,093 | 1,669,634 | 3.6 |
| Part-time | 2,634,818 | 2,761,741 | 2,881,816 | 2,891,431 | 2,896,151 | 2,829,642 | 2,839,707 | 7.8 |
| New[6] | 394 | 66,263 | 110,297 | 137,462 | 69,355 | 84,295 | 99,702 | --- |
| Full-time | 366 | 41,224 | 53,938 | 71,760 | 32,987 | 45,637 | 57,505 | --- |
| Part-time | 28 | 25,039 | 56,359 | 65,702 | 36,368 | 38,658 | 42,197 | --- |
| **Public institutions** | **9,036,822** | **9,457,394** | **9,647,032** | **9,696,087** | **9,682,734** | **9,477,370** | **9,479,273** | **4.9** |
| Doctoral[1] | 2,304,514 | 2,363,946 | 2,367,447 | 2,366,260 | 2,410,724 | 2,395,847 | 2,400,817 | 4.2 |
| Full-time | 1,753,559 | 1,803,777 | 1,808,147 | 1,803,007 | 1,822,398 | 1,812,016 | 1,813,810 | 3.4 |
| Part-time | 550,955 | 560,169 | 559,300 | 563,253 | 588,326 | 583,831 | 587,007 | 6.5 |
| Comprehensive[2] | 2,147,468 | 2,207,559 | 2,227,725 | 2,224,856 | 2,208,259 | 2,201,428 | 2,206,206 | 2.7 |
| Full-time | 1,387,090 | 1,424,569 | 1,435,979 | 1,442,663 | 1,450,817 | 1,431,413 | 1,427,475 | 2.9 |
| Part-time | 760,378 | 782,990 | 791,746 | 782,193 | 757,442 | 770,015 | 778,731 | 2.4 |
| General baccalaureate[3] | 375,396 | 395,330 | 401,857 | 410,084 | 397,002 | 392,294 | 396,413 | 5.6 |
| Full-time | 234,718 | 240,418 | 244,161 | 247,599 | 242,802 | 238,551 | 237,966 | 1.4 |
| Part-time | 140,678 | 154,912 | 157,696 | 162,485 | 154,200 | 153,743 | 158,447 | 12.6 |
| Specialized[4] | 143,817 | 180,029 | 185,948 | 193,443 | 198,834 | 198,275 | 197,979 | 37.7 |
| Full-time | 114,917 | 149,458 | 154,287 | 161,748 | 162,400 | 161,685 | 160,108 | 39.3 |
| Part-time | 28,900 | 30,571 | 31,661 | 31,695 | 36,434 | 36,590 | 37,871 | 31.0 |
| Two-year[5] | 4,065,627 | 4,283,678 | 4,432,157 | 4,463,945 | 4,456,073 | 4,267,379 | 4,249,048 | 4.5 |
| Full-time | 1,470,863 | 1,562,975 | 1,595,799 | 1,616,857 | 1,614,670 | 1,492,300 | 1,465,320 | -0.4 |
| Part-time | 2,594,764 | 2,720,703 | 2,836,358 | 2,847,088 | 2,841,403 | 2,775,079 | 2,783,728 | 7.3 |
| New[6] | 0 | 26,852 | 31,898 | 37,499 | 11,842 | 22,147 | 28,810 | --- |
| Full-time | 0 | 6,489 | 8,132 | 12,218 | 6,028 | 11,641 | 15,567 | --- |
| Part-time | 0 | 20,363 | 23,766 | 25,281 | 5,814 | 10,506 | 13,243 | --- |
| **Private institutions** | **2,533,077** | **2,639,501** | **2,724,640** | **2,729,693** | **2,781,927** | **2,764,570** | **2,767,782** | **9.3** |
| Doctoral[1] | 658,242 | 664,922 | 678,916 | 661,916 | 632,888 | 633,985 | 632,565 | -3.9 |
| Full-time | 467,657 | 474,833 | 483,342 | 479,770 | 461,036 | 465,691 | 467,309 | -0.1 |
| Part-time | 190,585 | 190,089 | 195,574 | 182,146 | 171,852 | 168,294 | 165,256 | -13.3 |
| Comprehensive[2] | 599,136 | 606,176 | 611,799 | 612,889 | 669,089 | 663,127 | 657,004 | 9.7 |
| Full-time | 388,191 | 392,177 | 389,348 | 392,489 | 422,749 | 421,046 | 419,516 | 8.1 |
| Part-time | 210,945 | 213,999 | 222,451 | 220,400 | 246,340 | 242,081 | 237,488 | 12.6 |
| General baccalaureate[3] | 746,353 | 777,337 | 784,065 | 770,931 | 752,859 | 754,136 | 759,927 | 1.8 |
| Full-time | 593,084 | 609,279 | 611,191 | 591,468 | 574,378 | 569,708 | 570,472 | -3.8 |
| Part-time | 153,269 | 168,058 | 172,874 | 179,463 | 178,481 | 184,428 | 189,455 | 23.6 |
| Specialized[4] | 348,347 | 363,248 | 373,510 | 382,000 | 400,272 | 391,818 | 387,101 | 11.1 |
| Full-time | 243,043 | 251,879 | 252,565 | 255,606 | 262,255 | 255,548 | 251,426 | 3.4 |
| Part-time | 105,304 | 111,369 | 120,945 | 126,394 | 138,017 | 136,270 | 135,675 | 28.8 |
| Two-year[5] | 180,605 | 188,407 | 197,951 | 201,994 | 269,306 | 259,356 | 260,293 | [7] 44.1 |
| Full-time | 140,551 | 147,369 | 152,493 | 157,651 | 214,558 | 204,793 | 204,314 | [7] 45.4 |
| Part-time | 40,054 | 41,038 | 45,458 | 44,343 | 54,748 | 54,563 | 55,979 | [7] 39.8 |
| New[6] | 394 | 39,411 | 78,399 | 99,963 | 57,513 | 62,148 | 70,892 | --- |
| Full-time | 366 | 34,735 | 45,806 | 59,542 | 26,959 | 33,996 | 41,938 | --- |
| Part-time | 28 | 4,676 | 32,593 | 40,421 | 30,554 | 28,152 | 28,954 | --- |

[1] These institutions have a significant level of activity in doctoral-level education as measured by the number of doctoral recipients and the diversity in doctoral-level program offerings.

[2] These institutions have diverse postbaccalaureate programs but do not engage in significant doctoral-level education.

[3] These institutions primarily emphasize general undergraduate education.

[4] These baccalaureate or postbaccalaureate institutions are characterized by an emphasis in one field of study, such as business or engineering.

[5] These institutions confer at least 75 percent of their degrees and awards below the bachelor's degree level.

[6] These institutions are new additions to the Higher Education General Information Survey universe (not necessarily newly organized). When degree and award data become available, they will be reclassified.

[7] Large percentage increase is due primarily to the addition of colleges accredited by the National Association of Trade and Technical Schools in 1980 and 1981.

---Data not available.

SOURCE: U.S. Department of Education, Center for Education Statistics, "Fall Enrollment in Colleges and Universities" surveys. (This table was prepared July 1986.)

Table 3.2

Table 3.3 — Enrollment and number of institutions of higher education, by affiliation[1] of institution: United States, fall 1980 to fall 1985

| Affiliation | Total, fall 1980 | Total, fall 1983 | Total, fall 1984 | Enrollment Fall 1985 — Total | Full-time Men | Full-time Women | Part-time Men | Part-time Women | No. of inst.[2] Fall 1980 | No. of inst.[2] Fall 1985 |
|---|---|---|---|---|---|---|---|---|---|---|
| (col) 1 | 2 | 3 | 4 | 5 | 6 | 7 | 8 | 9 | 10 | 11 |
| All institutions | 12,096,895 | 12,464,661 | 12,241,940 | 12,247,055 | 3,607,347 | 3,467,238 | 2,210,679 | 2,961,091 | 3,226 | 3,301 |
| Public institutions | 9,457,394 | 9,682,734 | 9,477,370 | 9,479,273 | 2,606,362 | 2,513,884 | 1,831,126 | 2,527,901 | 1,493 | 1,493 |
| Federal | 50,989 | 54,800 | 54,358 | 55,787 | 48,741 | 6,331 | 539 | 176 | 12 | 12 |
| State | 5,879,057 | 5,964,595 | 5,883,571 | 5,924,118 | 1,963,955 | 1,884,583 | 887,272 | 1,188,308 | 881 | 881 |
| State and local | 2,360,972 | 2,538,044 | 2,465,058 | 2,439,409 | 389,989 | 421,901 | 668,889 | 958,630 | 379 | 397 |
| State related | 154,964 | 149,385 | 145,992 | 148,094 | 58,644 | 47,325 | 19,852 | 22,273 | 31 | 31 |
| Local | 1,011,412 | 975,910 | 928,391 | 911,865 | 145,033 | 153,744 | 254,574 | 358,514 | 190 | 172 |
| Private institutions | 2,639,501 | 2,781,927 | 2,764,570 | 2,767,782 | 1,000,985 | 953,354 | 379,553 | 433,190 | 1,733 | 1,808 |
| Independent nonprofit | 1,521,614 | 1,554,187 | 1,528,571 | 1,529,779 | 562,590 | 497,668 | 226,639 | 242,882 | 795 | 811 |
| Organized as profit making | 111,714 | 192,740 | 190,151 | 195,991 | 76,400 | 74,321 | 32,650 | 12,620 | 164 | 211 |
| Religiously affiliated | 1,006,173 | 1,035,000 | 1,045,848 | 1,042,012 | 361,995 | 381,365 | 120,264 | 177,688 | 774 | 786 |
| Advent Christian Church | 143 | 142 | 126 | 103 | 48 | 46 | 6 | 3 | 1 | ... |
| African Methodist Episcopal Zion Church | 1,091 | 939 | 836 | 702 | 416 | 278 | 5 | 3 | 3 | 2 |
| African Methodist Episcopal | 4,541 | 3,715 | 3,404 | 3,473 | 1,401 | 1,837 | 96 | 139 | 6 | 6 |
| American Baptist | 6,131 | 7,477 | 8,554 | 8,307 | 2,506 | 2,815 | 1,133 | 1,853 | 11 | 12 |
| American Lutheran and Lutheran Church in America | 3,092 | 2,999 | 2,770 | 2,730 | 913 | 798 | 406 | 613 | 3 | 3 |
| American Lutheran | 21,608 | 20,746 | 21,100 | 21,258 | 7,974 | 9,740 | 1,555 | 1,989 | 13 | 12 |
| Assemblies of God Church | 7,814 | 7,745 | 7,972 | 7,899 | 3,685 | 3,154 | 587 | 473 | 10 | 11 |
| Baptist | 38,231 | 39,559 | 39,152 | 41,163 | 16,958 | 16,316 | 4,020 | 3,869 | 33 | 36 |
| Brethren Church | 3,925 | 4,391 | 4,463 | 4,664 | 1,795 | 1,186 | 898 | 785 | 3 | 3 |
| Brethren in Christ Church | 1,301 | 1,612 | 1,761 | 1,846 | 650 | 1,117 | 27 | 52 | 1 | 1 |
| Christian and Missionary Alliance Church | 1,705 | 1,854 | 1,831 | 1,740 | 765 | 691 | 167 | 117 | 3 | 3 |
| Christian Church (Disciples of Christ) | 14,913 | 15,413 | 15,132 | 15,311 | 4,847 | 5,458 | 2,536 | 2,470 | 12 | 11 |
| Christian Churches and Churches of Christ | 1,342 | 1,457 | 1,591 | 1,543 | 757 | 521 | 150 | 115 | 7 | 10 |
| Christian Methodist Episcopal | 2,486 | 1,972 | 1,845 | 1,661 | 813 | 705 | 60 | 83 | 4 | 3 |
| Christian Reformed Church | 5,408 | 5,291 | 5,313 | 5,268 | 2,461 | 2,447 | 192 | 168 | 3 | 3 |
| Church of Christ (Scientist) | 2,773 | ... | ... | ... | ... | ... | ... | ... | 6 | ... |
| Church of God of Prophecy | ... | 270 | 246 | 245 | 96 | 119 | 20 | 10 | ... | 1 |
| Church of God | 6,082 | 6,091 | 6,187 | 5,990 | 2,407 | 2,463 | 598 | 522 | 9 | 9 |
| Church of New Jerusalem | 170 | 164 | 156 | 155 | 72 | 64 | 5 | 14 | 1 | 1 |
| Church of the Brethren | 8,482 | 8,699 | 9,302 | 8,684 | 2,590 | 2,880 | 1,471 | 1,743 | 6 | 6 |
| Church of the Nazarene | 11,716 | 11,140 | 10,834 | 10,757 | 4,258 | 4,609 | 843 | 1,047 | 10 | 10 |
| Churches of Christ | 9,343 | 11,775 | 11,486 | 10,945 | 4,674 | 4,617 | 895 | 759 | 9 | 13 |
| Cumberland Presbyterian | 594 | 659 | 684 | 636 | 277 | 221 | 65 | 73 | 2 | 2 |
| Evangelical Congregational Church | 80 | 60 | 53 | 71 | 13 | 0 | 48 | 10 | 1 | 1 |
| Evangelical Convent Church of America | 1,401 | 1,545 | 1,491 | 1,539 | 542 | 698 | 104 | 195 | 1 | 1 |
| Evangelical Free Church of America | 833 | 935 | 1,563 | 1,613 | 758 | 270 | 429 | 156 | 1 | 2 |
| Evangelical Lutheran Church | 743 | 724 | 575 | 589 | 339 | 136 | 107 | 7 | 3 | 3 |
| Free Methodist | 5,543 | 5,552 | 5,602 | 5,643 | 1,865 | 2,419 | 543 | 816 | 5 | 5 |
| Free Will Baptist Church | 1,132 | 1,198 | 1,242 | 1,191 | 436 | 442 | 183 | 130 | 4 | 3 |
| Friends United Meeting | 1,109 | 1,443 | ... | ... | ... | ... | ... | ... | 1 | ... |

—Enrollment and number of institutions of higher education, by affiliation[1] of institution: United States, fall 1980 to fall 1985—Continued

| | | | | Enrollment | | | | | Number of institutions[2] | |
| | | | | | Fall 1985 | | | | | |
| | | | | | Full-time | | Part-time | | | |
| Affiliation | Total, fall 1980 | Total, fall 1983 | Total, fall 1984 | Total | Men | Women | Men | Women | Fall 1980 | Fall 1985 |
| 1 | 2 | 3 | 4 | 5 | 6 | 7 | 8 | 9 | 10 | 11 |
| Friends | 5,157 | 4,889 | 6,962 | 7,077 | 3,323 | 2,701 | 443 | 610 | 5 | 7 |
| General Conference Mennonite Church | 820 | 1,369 | 1,321 | 1,303 | 567 | 541 | 73 | 122 | 2 | 3 |
| Greek Orthodox | 204 | 303 | 219 | 161 | 126 | 22 | 11 | 2 | 1 | 1 |
| Interdenominational | 1,254 | 1,565 | 1,598 | 1,438 | 662 | 426 | 178 | 172 | 4 | 6 |
| Jewish | 5,738 | 5,191 | 5,444 | 5,472 | 4,226 | 735 | 278 | 233 | 24 | 22 |
| Latter Day Saints | 39,172 | 39,277 | 38,973 | 39,406 | 15,900 | 14,324 | 4,551 | 4,631 | 4 | 4 |
| Lutheran Church—Missouri Synod | 11,727 | 12,209 | 11,940 | 11,507 | 5,029 | 4,983 | 468 | 1,027 | 15 | 15 |
| Lutheran Church in America | 23,877 | 22,977 | 23,108 | 22,659 | 9,158 | 9,640 | 1,368 | 2,493 | 20 | 20 |
| Mennonite Brethren Church | 1,344 | 1,510 | 1,561 | 1,548 | 450 | 432 | 224 | 442 | 3 | 3 |
| Mennonite Church | 4,008 | 2,794 | 2,632 | 2,490 | 993 | 1,234 | 108 | 155 | 6 | 5 |
| Missionary Church Inc. | 487 | 543 | 550 | 573 | 142 | 164 | 38 | 229 | 1 | 1 |
| Moravian Church | 2,434 | 2,545 | 2,436 | 2,352 | 655 | 1,086 | 238 | 373 | 2 | 2 |
| Multiple Protestant Denominations | 5,526 | 4,982 | 5,083 | 4,964 | 1,616 | 2,679 | 273 | 396 | 8 | 7 |
| North American Baptist | 155 | 147 | 138 | 133 | 62 | 19 | 35 | 17 | 1 | 1 |
| Pentecostal Holiness Church | 767 | 402 | 469 | 470 | 214 | 217 | 17 | 22 | 3 | 3 |
| Presbyterian U.S. and United Presbyterian | 1,580 | 14,709 | 50,679 | 52,290 | 20,499 | 20,960 | 4,642 | 6,189 | 3 | 58 |
| Presbyterian, U.S. | 16,914 | 14,499 | --- | --- | --- | --- | --- | --- | 24 | --- |
| Protestant Episcopal | 5,396 | 5,258 | 5,323 | 5,344 | 2,344 | 2,626 | 151 | 223 | 12 | 13 |
| Protestant, other | 4,072 | 3,564 | 2,765 | 2,390 | 1,151 | 797 | 229 | 213 | 11 | 8 |
| Reformed Church in America | 2,713 | 5,149 | 5,284 | 5,238 | 2,142 | 2,572 | 264 | 260 | 4 | 5 |
| Reformed Episcopal Church | 67 | --- | --- | --- | --- | --- | --- | --- | 1 | --- |
| Reformed Presbyterian Church | 2,014 | 1,292 | 1,225 | 1,191 | 608 | 388 | 112 | 83 | 4 | 1 |
| Reorganized Latter-Day Saints Church | 4,274 | 4,237 | 4,265 | 4,517 | 1,923 | 1,251 | 879 | 464 | 2 | 2 |
| Roman Catholic | 422,842 | 445,030 | 456,936 | 452,992 | 132,519 | 151,173 | 61,954 | 107,346 | 229 | 234 |
| Russian Orthodox | 47 | 43 | 47 | 36 | 34 | 0 | 2 | 0 | 1 | 1 |
| Seventh-Day Adventists | 19,168 | 17,525 | 17,131 | 15,993 | 6,380 | 6,314 | 1,341 | 1,958 | 11 | 11 |
| Southern Baptist | 85,281 | 88,556 | 88,837 | 88,869 | 33,956 | 32,760 | 10,250 | 11,903 | 54 | 56 |
| Unitarian Universalist | 87 | 91 | 86 | 88 | 40 | 36 | 8 | 4 | 2 | 2 |
| United Brethren Church | 545 | 448 | 366 | 447 | 204 | 181 | 39 | 23 | 1 | 1 |
| United Church of Christ | 14,169 | 13,911 | 12,180 | 12,568 | 4,295 | 4,455 | 1,547 | 2,271 | 16 | 14 |
| United Methodist | 127,099 | 127,064 | 127,281 | 127,238 | 46,787 | 50,606 | 12,823 | 17,022 | 91 | 94 |
| United Presbyterian, U.S.A. | 28,650 | 22,275 | --- | --- | --- | --- | --- | --- | 30 | --- |
| Wesleyan Church | 3,583 | 2,584 | 2,516 | 2,394 | 918 | 1,067 | 174 | 235 | 5 | 4 |
| Wisconsin Evangelical Lutheran Synod | 808 | 629 | 559 | 520 | 173 | 344 | 2 | 1 | 1 | 1 |
| Other religiously affiliated | 462 | 1,866 | 2,663 | 2,618 | 583 | 585 | 395 | 355 | 7 | 7 |

[1]Affiliation as reported by institutions of higher education.
[2]Includes only institutions which reported enrollment.
--- Data not applicable or not reported

SOURCE: U.S. Department of Education, Center for Education Statistics, "Fall Enrollment in Colleges and Universities" surveys (This table was prepared August 1986).

## —Total first-time-freshman enrollment in institutions of higher education, by sex of student, attendance status, and type and control of institution: United States, fall 1955 to fall 1985

[In thousands]

| Year | Total enrollment | Men | | | Women | | | Type of institution, by control | | | |
|---|---|---|---|---|---|---|---|---|---|---|---|
| | | | | | | | | 4-year | | 2-year | |
| | | Total | Full-time | Part-time | Total | Full-time | Part-time | Public | Private | Public | Private |
| 1 | 2 | 3 | 4 | 5 | 6 | 7 | 8 | 9 | 10 | 11 | 12 |
| 1955[1] | 670 | 416 | --- | --- | 254 | --- | --- | [2]283 | [2]247 | [2]117 | [2]23 |
| 1956[1] | 718 | 443 | --- | --- | 275 | --- | --- | [2]293 | [2]262 | [2]137 | [2]25 |
| 1957[1] | 724 | 442 | --- | --- | 282 | --- | --- | [2]294 | [2]263 | [2]141 | [2]27 |
| 1958[1] | 775 | 465 | --- | --- | 310 | --- | --- | [2]328 | [2]272 | [2]146 | [2]29 |
| 1959[1] | 822 | 488 | --- | --- | 334 | --- | --- | [2]348 | [2]292 | [2]153 | [2]28 |
| 1960[1] | 923 | 540 | --- | --- | 384 | --- | --- | [2]396 | [2]313 | [2]182 | [2]32 |
| 1961[1] | 1,018 | 592 | --- | --- | 426 | --- | --- | [2]438 | [2]336 | [2]210 | [2]34 |
| 1962[1] | 1,031 | 598 | --- | --- | 432 | --- | --- | [2]445 | [2]325 | [2]225 | [2]36 |
| 1963[1] | 1,046 | 604 | --- | --- | 442 | --- | --- | --- | --- | --- | --- |
| 1964[1] | 1,225 | 702 | --- | --- | 523 | --- | --- | [2]539 | [2]363 | [2]275 | [2]47 |
| 1965[1] | 1,442 | 829 | --- | --- | 613 | --- | --- | [2]642 | [2]399 | [2]348 | [2]53 |
| 1966 | 1,554 | 890 | --- | --- | 665 | --- | --- | [2]626 | [2]383 | [2]478 | [2]67 |
| 1967 | 1,641 | 931 | 761 | 170 | 710 | 574 | 136 | [2]645 | [2]368 | [2]561 | [2]67 |
| 1968 | 1,893 | 1,082 | 847 | 235 | 810 | 624 | 187 | [2]725 | [2]378 | [2]718 | [2]72 |
| 1969 | 1,967 | 1,118 | 876 | 242 | 849 | 649 | 200 | [2]737 | [2]393 | [2]776 | [2]61 |
| 1970 | 2,063 | 1,152 | 896 | 256 | 911 | 691 | 221 | [2]754 | [2]397 | [2]854 | [2]58 |
| 1971 | 2,119 | 1,171 | 896 | 275 | 949 | 710 | 238 | [2]738 | [2]386 | [2]937 | [2]58 |
| 1972 | 2,153 | 1,158 | 858 | 299 | 995 | 716 | 279 | 680 | 381 | 1,037 | 55 |
| 1973 | 2,226 | 1,182 | 867 | 315 | 1,044 | 740 | 304 | 699 | 379 | 1,089 | 59 |
| 1974 | 2,366 | 1,244 | 896 | 348 | 1,122 | 777 | 345 | 746 | 386 | 1,176 | 58 |
| 1975 | 2,515 | 1,328 | 942 | 386 | 1,187 | 821 | 366 | 772 | 395 | 1,284 | 64 |
| 1976 | 2,347 | 1,170 | 855 | 316 | 1,177 | 808 | 369 | 717 | 414 | 1,153 | 63 |
| 1977 | 2,394 | 1,156 | 840 | 316 | 1,239 | 841 | 398 | 737 | 405 | 1,186 | 67 |
| 1978 | 2,390 | 1,142 | 817 | 324 | 1,248 | 834 | 414 | 737 | 407 | 1,174 | 73 |
| 1979 | 2,503 | 1,180 | 840 | 340 | 1,323 | 866 | 457 | 760 | 415 | 1,254 | 74 |
| 1980 | 2,588 | 1,219 | 862 | 357 | 1,369 | 887 | 481 | 765 | 418 | 1,314 | 91 |
| 1981 | 2,595 | 1,218 | 852 | 366 | 1,378 | 886 | 492 | 754 | 419 | 1,318 | 104 |
| 1982 | 2,505 | 1,199 | 837 | 362 | 1,306 | 851 | 455 | 731 | 404 | 1,254 | 116 |
| 1983 | 2,444 | 1,159 | 825 | 334 | 1,285 | 853 | 431 | 728 | 404 | 1,190 | 122 |
| 1984 | 2,357 | 1,112 | 786 | 326 | 1,245 | 827 | 418 | 714 | 403 | 1,130 | 110 |
| 1985 | 2,292 | 1,076 | 775 | 301 | 1,216 | 827 | 389 | 717 | 399 | 1,060 | 116 |

[1]Excludes first-time freshmen in occupational programs not creditable towards a bachelor's degree.

[2]Data for 2-year branches of 4-year college systems are aggregated with the 4-year institutions.

---Data not available.

NOTE.—Alaska and Hawaii are included in all years. Because of rounding, details may not add to totals.

SOURCE: U.S. Department of Education, National Center for Education Statistics, *Fall Enrollment in Higher Education,* various years; and Center for Education Statistics, "Fall Enrollment in Colleges and Universities" surveys. (This table was prepared September 1986.)

Source: U.S. Dept. of Education

Table 3.4

**—Full-time-equivalent enrollment in institutions of higher education, by type and control of institution: United States, fall 1970 to fall 1985**

| Year | All institutions | | | Public institutions | | | Private institutions | | |
|---|---|---|---|---|---|---|---|---|---|
| | Total | 4-year | 2-year | Total | 4-year | 2-year | Total | 4-year | 2-year |
| 1 | 2 | 3 | 4 | 5 | 6 | 7 | 8 | 9 | 10 |
| 1970[1] | 6,737,819 | 5,219,855 | 1,517,964 | 4,953,144 | 3,540,559 | 1,412,585 | 1,784,675 | 1,679,296 | 105,379 |
| 1971[1] | 7,148,575 | 5,429,703 | 1,718,872 | 5,344,356 | 3,731,009 | 1,613,347 | 1,804,219 | 1,698,694 | 105,525 |
| 1972 | 7,253,739 | 5,406,821 | 1,846,918 | 5,452,848 | 3,706,239 | 1,746,609 | 1,800,891 | 1,700,582 | 100,309 |
| 1973 | 7,453,448 | 5,439,218 | 2,014,230 | 5,629,555 | 3,721,031 | 1,908,524 | 1,823,893 | 1,718,187 | 105,706 |
| 1974 | 7,805,453 | 5,606,249 | 2,199,204 | 5,944,804 | 3,847,550 | 2,097,254 | 1,860,649 | 1,758,699 | 101,950 |
| 1975 | 8,479,685 | 5,900,401 | 2,579,284 | 6,522,310 | 4,056,500 | 2,465,810 | 1,957,375 | 1,843,901 | 113,474 |
| 1976 | 8,312,502 | 5,848,001 | 2,464,501 | 6,349,903 | 3,998,450 | 2,351,453 | 1,962,599 | 1,849,551 | 113,048 |
| 1977 | 8,415,339 | 5,935,076 | 2,480,263 | 6,396,476 | 4,039,071 | 2,357,405 | 2,018,863 | 1,896,005 | 122,858 |
| 1978 | 8,348,482 | 5,932,573 | 2,415,909 | 6,279,199 | 3,996,126 | 2,283,073 | 2,069,283 | 1,936,447 | 132,836 |
| 1979 | 8,487,317 | 6,016,072 | 2,471,245 | 6,392,617 | 4,059,304 | 2,333,313 | 2,094,700 | 1,956,768 | 137,932 |
| 1980 | 8,819,013 | 6,161,372 | 2,657,641 | 6,642,294 | 4,158,267 | 2,484,027 | 2,176,719 | 2,003,105 | [2]173,614 |
| 1981 | 9,014,521 | 6,249,847 | 2,764,674 | 6,781,300 | 4,208,506 | 2,572,794 | 2,233,221 | 2,041,341 | [2]191,880 |
| 1982 | 9,091,648 | 6,248,923 | 2,842,725 | 6,850,589 | 4,220,648 | 2,629,941 | 2,241,059 | 2,028,275 | 212,784 |
| 1983 | 9,166,399 | 6,325,223 | 2,841,176 | 6,881,480 | 4,265,808 | 2,615,672 | 2,284,919 | 2,059,415 | 225,504 |
| 1984 | 8,951,695 | 6,292,711 | 2,658,984 | 6,684,664 | 4,237,895 | 2,446,769 | 2,267,031 | 2,054,816 | 212,215 |
| 1985 | 8,943,433 | 6,294,339 | 2,649,094 | 6,667,781 | 4,239,622 | 2,428,159 | 2,275,652 | 2,054,717 | 220,935 |

[1]Data for 2-year branch campuses of 4-year systems are included with the 4-year institutions.

[2]Large increases are due to the addition of schools accredited by the National Association of Trade and Technical Schools in 1980 and 1981.

SOURCE: U.S. Department of Education, Center for Education Statistics, "Fall Enrollment in Colleges and Universities" surveys. (This table was prepared July 1986.)

Table 3.5

## —Total enrollment in institutions of higher education, by State: Fall 1970 to fall 1985

| State or other area | Fall 1970 | Fall 1975 | Fall 1980 | Fall 1981 | Fall 1982 | Fall 1983 | Fall 1984 | Fall 1985 |
|---|---|---|---|---|---|---|---|---|
| 1 | 2 | 3 | 4 | 5 | 6 | 7 | 8 | 9 |
| United States | 8,580,887 | 11,184,859 | 12,096,895 | 12,371,672 | 12,425,780 | 12,464,661 | 12,241,940 | 12,247,055 |
| Alabama | 103,936 | 164,700 | 164,306 | 166,375 | 167,753 | 171,381 | 171,631 | 179,343 |
| Alaska | 9,471 | 13,998 | 21,296 | 24,754 | 24,556 | 26,045 | 26,991 | 27,479 |
| Arizona | 109,619 | 173,542 | 202,716 | 205,169 | 210,683 | 213,437 | 210,029 | 216,854 |
| Arkansas | 52,039 | 65,547 | 77,607 | 76,032 | 76,972 | 76,702 | 78,777 | 77,958 |
| California | 1,257,245 | 1,787,932 | 1,790,993 | 1,885,757 | 1,842,963 | 1,730,847 | 1,665,155 | 1,650,439 |
| Colorado | 123,395 | 149,814 | 162,916 | 167,977 | 171,821 | 172,650 | 164,394 | 161,314 |
| Connecticut | 124,700 | 148,491 | 159,632 | 162,367 | 162,194 | 164,344 | 161,576 | 159,348 |
| Delaware | 25,260 | 32,389 | 32,939 | 32,061 | 32,454 | 31,945 | 31,872 | 31,883 |
| District of Columbia | 77,158 | 84,190 | 86,675 | 88,553 | 82,793 | 80,367 | 79,750 | 78,868 |
| Florida | 235,525 | 344,267 | 411,891 | 426,570 | 436,606 | 443,436 | 444,062 | 451,392 |
| Georgia | 126,511 | 173,585 | 184,159 | 191,384 | 198,367 | 201,453 | 196,869 | 196,826 |
| Hawaii | 36,562 | 46,671 | 47,181 | 48,121 | 51,788 | 52,065 | 49,981 | 49,937 |
| Idaho | 34,567 | 39,075 | 43,018 | 42,758 | 42,975 | 42,911 | 43,303 | 42,668 |
| Illinois | 452,146 | 584,089 | 644,245 | 659,623 | 683,969 | 673,084 | 661,114 | 678,689 |
| Indiana | 192,668 | 213,820 | 247,253 | 251,826 | 253,529 | 256,470 | 249,957 | 250,567 |
| Iowa | 108,902 | 121,678 | 140,449 | 143,105 | 147,862 | 152,968 | 153,069 | 152,897 |
| Kansas | 102,485 | 120,833 | 136,605 | 138,453 | 141,661 | 141,709 | 141,916 | 141,359 |
| Kentucky | 98,591 | 125,253 | 143,066 | 144,154 | 144,159 | 146,503 | 143,555 | 141,724 |
| Louisiana | 120,728 | 153,213 | 160,058 | 174,656 | 176,505 | 179,647 | 179,988 | 177,176 |
| Maine | 34,134 | 40,443 | 43,264 | 44,012 | 47,719 | 53,347 | 52,714 | 52,201 |
| Maryland | 149,607 | 205,570 | 225,526 | 229,936 | 234,585 | 239,232 | 234,302 | 231,649 |
| Massachusetts | 303,809 | 384,485 | 418,415 | 417,830 | 407,557 | 423,348 | 418,966 | 421,175 |
| Michigan | 392,726 | 496,405 | 520,131 | 513,033 | 508,240 | 515,760 | 505,334 | 507,293 |
| Minnesota | 160,788 | 184,756 | 206,691 | 210,713 | 214,133 | 214,219 | 215,566 | 221,162 |
| Mississippi | 73,967 | 99,962 | 102,364 | 105,974 | 105,932 | 109,728 | 104,339 | 101,180 |
| Missouri | 183,930 | 223,115 | 234,421 | 243,672 | 244,238 | 248,329 | 240,920 | 241,146 |
| Montana | 30,062 | 30,843 | 35,177 | 35,959 | 36,811 | 37,877 | 37,061 | 35,958 |
| Nebraska | 66,915 | 74,705 | 89,488 | 93,507 | 94,390 | 95,162 | 97,422 | 97,769 |
| Nevada | 13,669 | 30,187 | 40,455 | 39,936 | 42,212 | 43,768 | 43,007 | 43,656 |
| New Hampshire | 29,400 | 41,030 | 46,794 | 48,524 | 52,208 | 53,143 | 53,049 | 52,283 |
| New Jersey | 216,121 | 297,114 | 321,610 | 322,797 | 322,284 | 314,468 | 305,330 | 297,658 |
| New Mexico | 44,461 | 51,944 | 58,283 | 60,413 | 63,483 | 66,094 | 66,507 | 68,295 |
| New York | 806,479 | 1,005,063 | 992,237 | 1,014,863 | 1,012,421 | 1,022,521 | 1,007,770 | 1,000,098 |
| North Carolina | 171,925 | 251,786 | 287,537 | 295,771 | 300,910 | 301,675 | 309,249 | 327,288 |
| North Dakota | 31,495 | 29,743 | 34,069 | 35,446 | 36,224 | 37,591 | 37,585 | 37,939 |
| Ohio | 376,267 | 436,052 | 489,145 | 521,396 | 532,361 | 535,592 | 518,435 | 514,745 |
| Oklahoma | 110,155 | 146,613 | 160,295 | 162,825 | 168,186 | 174,171 | 168,034 | 169,173 |
| Oregon | 122,177 | 145,281 | 157,458 | 149,924 | 141,312 | 141,172 | 141,810 | 137,967 |
| Pennsylvania | 411,044 | 470,536 | 507,716 | 517,879 | 529,341 | 545,112 | 528,669 | 533,198 |
| Rhode Island | 45,898 | 64,479 | 66,869 | 68,339 | 68,351 | 70,811 | 69,145 | 69,927 |
| South Carolina | 69,518 | 133,023 | 132,476 | 132,394 | 136,727 | 134,532 | 131,479 | 131,902 |
| South Dakota | 30,639 | 30,260 | 32,761 | 35,015 | 35,074 | 34,879 | 32,473 | 32,772 |
| Tennessee | 135,103 | 181,435 | 204,581 | 200,183 | 201,806 | 207,777 | 200,937 | 194,845 |
| Texas | 442,225 | 624,390 | 701,391 | 716,297 | 758,839 | 795,741 | 795,337 | 769,692 |
| Utah | 81,687 | 87,323 | 93,987 | 97,048 | 99,431 | 103,324 | 101,863 | 103,994 |
| Vermont | 22,209 | 29,095 | 30,628 | 30,573 | 30,648 | 31,306 | 30,786 | 31,416 |
| Virginia | 151,915 | 244,671 | 280,504 | 286,015 | 281,026 | 288,588 | 283,109 | 292,416 |
| Washington | 183,544 | 227,168 | 303,603 | 278,680 | 227,812 | 229,639 | 230,667 | 231,553 |
| West Virginia | 63,153 | 78,619 | 81,973 | 82,375 | 82,891 | 83,202 | 79,009 | 76,659 |
| Wisconsin | 202,058 | 240,701 | 269,086 | 275,325 | 276,176 | 277,751 | 270,865 | 275,069 |
| Wyoming | 15,220 | 18,078 | 21,147 | 21,235 | 22,713 | 23,844 | 23,424 | 24,204 |
| U.S. Service Schools | 17,079 | 36,897 | 49,808 | 54,088 | 60,129 | 52,994 | 52,788 | 54,052 |
| Outlying areas | 67,237 | 104,270 | 137,749 | 146,081 | 162,740 | 169,269 | 158,452 | 164,890 |
| American Samoa | --- | 689 | 976 | 987 | 1,007 | 845 | 871 | 758 |
| Guam | 2,719 | 3,800 | 3,217 | 5,127 | 5,041 | 3,436 | 4,432 | 4,601 |
| Northern Marianas | --- | --- | --- | --- | --- | 173 | 431 | 318 |
| Puerto Rico | 63,073 | 97,517 | 131,184 | 137,171 | 153,350 | 161,215 | 149,102 | 155,917 |
| Trust Territory of the Pacific | --- | 185 | 224 | 188 | 598 | 736 | 796 | 724 |
| Virgin Islands | 1,445 | 2,079 | 2,148 | 2,608 | 2,744 | 2,864 | 2,820 | 2,572 |

---Data not reported or not applicable.

SOURCE: U.S. Department of Education, Center for Education Statistics, "Fall Enrollment in Colleges and Universities" surveys. (This table was prepared July 1986.)

Table 3.6

## —Total enrollment in institutions of higher education, by type, control of institution, and State: Fall 1984 and fall 1985

| State or other area | Fall 1984 | | | | Fall 1985 | | | |
|---|---|---|---|---|---|---|---|---|
| | Public 4-year | Public 2-year | Private 4-year | Private 2-year | Public 4-year | Public 2-year | Private 4-year | Private 2-year |
| 1 | 2 | 3 | 4 | 5 | 6 | 7 | 8 | 9 |
| United States | 5,198,273 | 4,279,097 | 2,512,894 | 251,676 | 5,209,540 | 4,269,733 | 2,506,438 | 261,344 |
| Alabama | 102,452 | 47,127 | 17,521 | 4,531 | 104,676 | 54,012 | 16,806 | 3,849 |
| Alaska | 11,260 | 14,745 | 986 | --- | 10,523 | 15,987 | 969 | --- |
| Arizona | 82,669 | 113,868 | 11,213 | 2,279 | 84,119 | 117,917 | 13,459 | 1,359 |
| Arkansas | 54,254 | 12,499 | 8,968 | 3,056 | 53,933 | 12,190 | 8,861 | 2,974 |
| California | 463,747 | 995,832 | 196,114 | 9,462 | 463,726 | 980,481 | 194,990 | 11,242 |
| Colorado | 100,931 | 43,954 | 15,827 | 3,682 | 100,538 | 41,493 | 15,253 | 4,030 |
| Connecticut | 58,352 | 42,402 | 59,217 | 1,605 | 57,870 | 40,746 | 59,007 | 1,725 |
| Delaware | 20,292 | 7,130 | 4,450 | --- | 20,452 | 7,481 | 3,950 | --- |
| District of Columbia | 13,450 | --- | 66,300 | --- | 12,747 | --- | 66,121 | --- |
| Florida | 143,705 | 210,451 | 82,058 | 7,848 | 146,336 | 215,905 | 82,103 | 7,048 |
| Georgia | 112,706 | 37,329 | 38,099 | 8,735 | 114,619 | 34,337 | 38,737 | 9,133 |
| Hawaii | 23,633 | 20,173 | 6,175 | --- | 23,243 | 20,003 | 6,691 | --- |
| Idaho | 29,630 | 5,288 | 2,067 | 6,318 | 28,545 | 5,121 | 2,122 | 6,880 |
| Illinois | 184,593 | 319,956 | 148,432 | 8,133 | 187,244 | 332,980 | 146,343 | 12,122 |
| Indiana | 158,028 | 34,590 | 51,602 | 5,737 | 159,304 | 34,529 | 50,781 | 5,953 |
| Iowa | 69,882 | 39,918 | 40,905 | 2,364 | 69,943 | 39,822 | 40,608 | 2,524 |
| Kansas | 83,852 | 43,359 | 13,098 | 1,607 | 83,947 | 43,273 | 12,702 | 1,437 |
| Kentucky | 88,960 | 23,742 | 20,862 | 9,991 | 87,069 | 23,767 | 20,778 | 10,110 |
| Louisiana | 140,399 | 14,447 | 23,436 | 1,706 | 138,235 | 14,938 | 22,297 | 1,706 |
| Maine | 28,780 | 4,656 | 18,057 | 1,221 | 28,685 | 4,503 | 17,770 | 1,243 |
| Maryland | 102,584 | 99,310 | 32,066 | 342 | 104,065 | 94,927 | 32,292 | 365 |
| Massachusetts | 108,499 | 74,585 | 216,170 | 19,712 | 110,562 | 75,040 | 216,178 | 19,395 |
| Michigan | 225,479 | 207,655 | 63,118 | 9,082 | 229,020 | 205,250 | 62,958 | 10,065 |
| Minnesota | 124,106 | 44,620 | 42,612 | 4,228 | 127,303 | 46,681 | 42,737 | 4,441 |
| Mississippi | 53,025 | 39,616 | 9,715 | 1,983 | 52,558 | 38,146 | 8,982 | 1,494 |
| Missouri | 111,739 | 58,353 | 68,412 | 2,416 | 110,979 | 57,850 | 69,467 | 2,850 |
| Montana | 29,276 | 3,440 | 3,391 | 954 | 28,503 | 3,529 | 3,007 | 919 |
| Nebraska | 54,491 | 25,730 | 16,517 | 684 | 55,077 | 26,125 | 15,936 | 631 |
| Nevada | 20,670 | 22,030 | 307 | --- | 21,292 | 22,076 | 288 | --- |
| New Hampshire | 20,819 | 6,504 | 22,984 | 2,742 | 20,574 | 6,095 | 22,973 | 2,641 |
| New Jersey | 134,089 | 109,299 | 60,148 | 1,794 | 130,925 | 106,372 | 58,432 | 1,929 |
| New Mexico | 50,379 | 13,882 | 2,246 | --- | 51,252 | 14,807 | 2,236 | --- |
| New York | 321,448 | 245,703 | 402,869 | 37,750 | 320,520 | 242,731 | 400,671 | 36,176 |
| North Carolina | 125,929 | 123,488 | 52,646 | 7,186 | 128,731 | 138,313 | 53,424 | 6,820 |
| North Dakota | 27,125 | 7,316 | 2,349 | 795 | 27,535 | 7,267 | 2,306 | 831 |
| Ohio | 259,363 | 122,247 | 100,964 | 35,861 | 260,542 | 118,622 | 99,039 | 36,542 |
| Oklahoma | 90,971 | 54,851 | 19,075 | 3,137 | 91,995 | 54,832 | 18,874 | 3,472 |
| Oregon | 58,593 | 64,638 | 18,401 | 178 | 59,647 | 59,965 | 18,035 | 320 |
| Pennsylvania | 186,121 | 115,051 | 208,627 | 18,870 | 189,369 | 111,154 | 208,898 | 23,777 |
| Rhode Island | 22,190 | 12,317 | 34,638 | --- | 22,772 | 12,617 | 34,538 | --- |
| South Carolina | 68,666 | 36,547 | 21,142 | 5,124 | 69,098 | 36,756 | 20,899 | 5,149 |
| South Dakota | 24,023 | --- | 7,742 | 708 | 23,339 | --- | 8,569 | 864 |
| Tennessee | 103,694 | 49,103 | 40,385 | 7,755 | 101,430 | 46,521 | 40,673 | 6,221 |
| Texas | 381,975 | 321,742 | 89,680 | 1,940 | 371,035 | 306,157 | 89,648 | 2,852 |
| Utah | 48,771 | 18,444 | 32,741 | 1,907 | 50,281 | 19,145 | 33,087 | 1,481 |
| Vermont | 15,093 | 3,099 | 10,723 | 1,871 | 15,210 | 3,634 | 10,701 | 1,871 |
| Virginia | 138,437 | 106,667 | 36,563 | 1,442 | 141,380 | 109,374 | 40,067 | 1,595 |
| Washington | 78,806 | 122,051 | 29,208 | 602 | 77,923 | 123,609 | 28,855 | 1,166 |
| West Virginia | 58,633 | 9,751 | 7,806 | 2,819 | 57,404 | 9,127 | 7,640 | 2,488 |
| Wisconsin | 151,884 | 83,200 | 34,262 | 1,519 | 154,502 | 84,233 | 34,680 | 1,654 |
| Wyoming | 10,087 | 13,337 | --- | --- | 10,123 | 14,081 | --- | --- |
| U.S. Service Schools | 19,733 | 33,055 | --- | --- | 18,840 | 35,212 | --- | --- |
| Outlying areas | 56,714 | 8,420 | 74,269 | 19,049 | 57,106 | 8,305 | 79,569 | 19,910 |
| American Samoa | --- | 871 | --- | --- | --- | 758 | --- | --- |
| Guam | 2,692 | 1,740 | --- | --- | 2,769 | 1,832 | --- | --- |
| Northern Marianas | --- | 431 | --- | --- | --- | 318 | --- | --- |
| Puerto Rico | 51,202 | 4,582 | 74,269 | 19,049 | 51,765 | 4,673 | 79,569 | 19,910 |
| Trust Territory of the Pacific | --- | 796 | --- | --- | --- | 724 | --- | --- |
| Virgin Islands | 2,820 | --- | --- | --- | 2,572 | --- | --- | --- |

---Data not available or not applicable.

SOURCE: U.S. Department of Education, Center for Education Statistics, "Fall Enrollment in Colleges and Universities" surveys. (This table was prepared July 1986.)

Table 3.7

**—Full-time-equivalent enrollment in institutions of higher education, by type, control of institution, and State: Fall 1984 and fall 1985**

| State or other area | Fall 1984 | | | | | Fall 1985 | | | | |
|---|---|---|---|---|---|---|---|---|---|---|
| | Total | Public 4-year | Public 2-year | Private 4-year | Private 2-year | Total | Public 4-year | Public 2-year | Private 4-year | Private 2-year |
| 1 | 2 | 3 | 4 | 5 | 6 | 7 | 8 | 9 | 10 | 11 |
| United States | 8,951,695 | 4,237,895 | 2,446,769 | 2,054,816 | 212,215 | 8,943,433 | 4,239,622 | 2,428,159 | 2,054,717 | 220,935 |
| Alabama | 145,293 | 87,931 | 37,290 | 15,824 | 4,248 | 149,895 | 89,514 | 41,507 | 15,343 | 3,531 |
| Alaska | 13,548 | 7,108 | 5,823 | 617 | --- | 14,098 | 7,083 | 6,370 | 645 | --- |
| Arizona | 131,451 | 67,683 | 50,996 | 10,586 | 2,186 | 134,954 | 67,081 | 53,743 | 12,883 | 1,247 |
| Arkansas | 64,006 | 44,932 | 7,982 | 8,111 | 2,981 | 63,230 | 44,749 | 7,686 | 7,888 | 2,907 |
| California | 1,059,937 | 393,099 | 497,432 | 160,662 | 8,744 | 1,062,439 | 393,084 | 497,941 | 160,899 | 10,515 |
| Colorado | 122,762 | 84,167 | 22,180 | 12,910 | 3,505 | 121,804 | 84,188 | 21,238 | 12,500 | 3,878 |
| Connecticut | 110,098 | 43,372 | 21,727 | 43,762 | 1,237 | 107,803 | 42,847 | 20,360 | 43,341 | 1,255 |
| Delaware | 25,276 | 17,048 | 5,361 | 2,867 | --- | 25,750 | 17,547 | 5,427 | 2,776 | --- |
| District of Columbia | 59,844 | 7,648 | --- | 52,196 | | 59,198 | 7,239 | --- | 51,959 | |
| Florida | 304,409 | 109,556 | 121,485 | 65,658 | 7,710 | 308,315 | 111,069 | 123,660 | 66,673 | 6,913 |
| Georgia | 161,101 | 92,979 | 25,758 | 34,294 | 8,070 | 161,952 | 95,218 | 23,474 | 34,774 | 8,486 |
| Hawaii | 37,359 | 19,645 | 13,173 | 4,541 | --- | 36,986 | 19,132 | 12,917 | 4,937 | --- |
| Idaho | 32,724 | 22,181 | 3,202 | 1,747 | 5,594 | 32,649 | 21,556 | 3,193 | 1,808 | 6,092 |
| Illinois | 436,287 | 156,543 | 155,808 | 116,790 | 7,146 | 450,504 | 157,749 | 167,767 | 114,254 | 10,734 |
| Indiana | 196,418 | 123,382 | 22,525 | 45,100 | 5,411 | 195,630 | 123,873 | 21,895 | 44,187 | 5,675 |
| Iowa | 128,646 | 60,209 | 31,072 | 35,218 | 2,147 | 128,492 | 60,867 | 30,658 | 34,678 | 2,289 |
| Kansas | 101,023 | 66,569 | 22,509 | 10,508 | 1,437 | 100,807 | 66,514 | 22,860 | 10,143 | 1,290 |
| Kentucky | 112,855 | 71,068 | 14,869 | 17,606 | 9,312 | 110,539 | 68,826 | 14,731 | 17,431 | 9,551 |
| Louisiana | 149,386 | 117,337 | 10,427 | 19,916 | 1,706 | 148,983 | 118,327 | 9,879 | 19,071 | 1,706 |
| Maine | 38,174 | 21,211 | 3,285 | 12,587 | 1,091 | 37,993 | 20,965 | 3,393 | 12,533 | 1,102 |
| Maryland | 151,636 | 77,367 | 50,923 | 23,024 | 322 | 148,091 | 78,817 | 45,347 | 23,595 | 332 |
| Massachusetts | 319,574 | 83,826 | 43,312 | 177,989 | 14,447 | 321,022 | 84,360 | 43,933 | 178,559 | 14,170 |
| Michigan | 359,563 | 186,486 | 114,574 | 50,895 | 7,608 | 354,690 | 187,165 | 108,164 | 51,003 | 8,358 |
| Minnesota | 168,550 | 94,831 | 31,428 | 38,432 | 3,859 | 170,958 | 96,691 | 31,984 | 38,378 | 3,905 |
| Mississippi | 88,942 | 46,835 | 32,380 | 7,890 | 1,837 | 86,846 | 46,752 | 31,442 | 7,290 | 1,362 |
| Missouri | 179,529 | 91,040 | 31,999 | 54,330 | 2,160 | 178,090 | 90,392 | 31,296 | 53,876 | 2,526 |
| Montana | 29,967 | 25,344 | 1,817 | 2,162 | 644 | 29,992 | 25,149 | 1,879 | 2,340 | 624 |
| Nebraska | 71,475 | 44,064 | 12,776 | 14,154 | 481 | 70,778 | 44,140 | 12,713 | 13,401 | 524 |
| Nevada | 22,260 | 14,644 | 7,381 | 235 | --- | 23,093 | 14,874 | 7,990 | 229 | --- |
| New Hampshire | 41,869 | 17,259 | 3,948 | 18,253 | 2,409 | 41,733 | 17,092 | 3,780 | 18,624 | 2,237 |
| New Jersey | 204,712 | 95,872 | 63,303 | 44,073 | 1,464 | 201,270 | 95,010 | 61,496 | 43,273 | 1,491 |
| New Mexico | 46,167 | 37,380 | 7,334 | 1,453 | --- | 47,169 | 37,986 | 7,637 | 1,546 | --- |
| New York | 771,255 | 245,416 | 175,446 | 316,488 | 33,905 | 763,596 | 242,716 | 170,136 | 318,464 | 32,280 |
| North Carolina | 241,126 | 109,765 | 76,384 | 48,069 | 6,908 | 249,901 | 111,903 | 82,909 | 48,555 | 6,534 |
| North Dakota | 32,496 | 23,869 | 6,071 | 1,961 | 595 | 32,456 | 23,966 | 5,881 | 1,938 | 671 |
| Ohio | 386,631 | 209,418 | 72,835 | 84,474 | 19,904 | 383,898 | 210,436 | 69,921 | 83,042 | 20,499 |
| Oklahoma | 125,823 | 75,509 | 31,056 | 16,414 | 2,844 | 126,691 | 76,077 | 31,118 | 16,323 | 3,173 |
| Oregon | 103,945 | 49,396 | 38,436 | 15,935 | 178 | 102,247 | 50,533 | 35,627 | 15,767 | 320 |
| Pennsylvania | 419,839 | 157,856 | 77,118 | 167,421 | 17,444 | 422,349 | 160,010 | 73,097 | 167,269 | 21,973 |
| Rhode Island | 51,941 | 16,799 | 6,691 | 28,451 | --- | 53,016 | 17,135 | 6,892 | 28,989 | --- |
| South Carolina | 107,894 | 56,518 | 27,221 | 19,373 | 4,782 | 109,303 | 58,074 | 27,249 | 19,109 | 4,871 |
| South Dakota | 26,797 | 19,720 | --- | 6,559 | 518 | 26,988 | 18,998 | --- | 7,376 | 614 |
| Tennessee | 158,171 | 84,624 | 29,398 | 37,229 | 6,920 | 152,967 | 82,798 | 27,260 | 37,042 | 5,867 |
| Texas | 587,686 | 317,851 | 190,956 | 77,038 | 1,841 | 566,736 | 306,823 | 180,051 | 77,107 | 2,755 |
| Utah | 83,719 | 39,908 | 13,554 | 28,746 | 1,511 | 84,095 | 40,038 | 14,263 | 28,561 | 1,233 |
| Vermont | 25,530 | 12,592 | 1,677 | 9,662 | 1,599 | 25,649 | 12,632 | 1,847 | 9,618 | 1,552 |
| Virginia | 200,324 | 114,734 | 52,677 | 31,576 | 1,337 | 204,928 | 116,789 | 51,645 | 35,059 | 1,435 |
| Washington | 171,478 | 71,007 | 74,910 | 24,963 | 598 | 171,668 | 70,599 | 75,760 | 24,177 | 1,132 |
| West Virginia | 60,348 | 45,691 | 5,520 | 7,010 | 2,127 | 58,438 | 44,663 | 5,416 | 6,570 | 1,789 |
| Wisconsin | 212,441 | 129,846 | 52,090 | 29,057 | 1,448 | 211,749 | 131,817 | 49,481 | 28,914 | 1,537 |
| Wyoming | 16,713 | 9,118 | 7,595 | --- | --- | 17,037 | 9,003 | 8,034 | --- | --- |
| U.S. Service Schools | 52,697 | 19,642 | 33,055 | --- | --- | 53,968 | 18,756 | 35,212 | --- | --- |
| Outlying areas | 139,888 | 50,105 | 6,739 | 65,459 | 17,585 | 145,530 | 50,013 | 6,696 | 70,382 | 18,439 |
| American Samoa | 720 | --- | 720 | --- | --- | 497 | --- | 497 | --- | --- |
| Guam | 2,921 | 2,086 | 835 | --- | --- | 3,049 | 2,133 | 916 | --- | --- |
| Northern Marianas | 158 | --- | 158 | --- | --- | 183 | --- | 183 | --- | --- |
| Puerto Rico | 133,730 | 46,354 | 4,332 | 65,459 | 17,585 | 139,627 | 46,386 | 4,420 | 70,382 | 18,439 |
| Trust Territory of the Pacific | 694 | --- | 694 | --- | --- | 680 | --- | 680 | --- | --- |
| Virgin Islands | 1,665 | 1,665 | --- | --- | --- | 1,494 | 1,494 | --- | --- | --- |

---Indicates data not available or not applicable.
SOURCE: U.S. Department of Education, Center for Education Statistics, "Fall Enrollment in Colleges and Universities" surveys. (This table was prepared July 1986.)

Table 3.8

**—Enrollment of persons 14 to 34 years of age[1] in institutions of higher education, by race/ethnicity, sex, and year of college: United States, October 1965 to October 1985**

| Characteristic | 1965 | 1970 | 1975 | 1976 | 1977 | 1978 | 1979 | 1980 | 1981[2] | 1982 | 1983 | 1984 | 1985 |
|---|---|---|---|---|---|---|---|---|---|---|---|---|---|
| 1 | 2 | 3 | 4 | 5 | 6 | 7 | 8 | 9 | 10 | 11 | 12 | 13 | 14 |
| | Numbers in thousands | | | | | | | | | | | | |
| **All students** | **5,675** | **7,413** | **9,697** | **9,950** | **10,217** | **9,838** | **9,978** | **10,180** | **10,734** | **10,919** | **10,825** | **10,859** | **10,863** |
| **White** | | | | | | | | | | | | | |
| Total | 5,317 | 6,759 | 8,514 | 8,644 | 8,812 | 8,514 | 8,709 | 8,875 | 9,162 | 9,328 | 9,242 | 9,269 | 9,334 |
| Men | 3,326 | 4,066 | 4,771 | 4,658 | 4,717 | 4,508 | 4,400 | 4,438 | 4,620 | 4,650 | 4,718 | 4,709 | 4,633 |
| Women | 1,991 | 2,693 | 3,743 | 3,986 | 4,095 | 4,006 | 4,309 | 4,437 | 4,543 | 4,679 | 4,524 | 4,559 | 4,701 |
| **Black** | | | | | | | | | | | | | |
| Total | 274 | 522 | 948 | 1,062 | 1,103 | 1,022 | 1,002 | 1,007 | 1,133 | 1,127 | 1,102 | 1,138 | 1,049 |
| Men | 126 | 253 | 442 | 489 | 490 | 452 | 434 | 437 | 505 | 482 | 497 | 544 | 458 |
| Women | 148 | 269 | 506 | 573 | 614 | 569 | 568 | 570 | 628 | 645 | 605 | 594 | 591 |
| **Hispanic origin[3]** | | | | | | | | | | | | | |
| Total | --- | --- | 411 | 427 | 418 | 377 | 440 | 443 | 510 | 493 | 523 | 524 | 579 |
| Men | --- | --- | 219 | 223 | 223 | 196 | 226 | 222 | 258 | 216 | 253 | 232 | 280 |
| Women | --- | --- | 192 | 204 | 194 | 181 | 214 | 221 | 252 | 278 | 270 | 292 | 299 |
| **Year of college** | | | | | | | | | | | | | |
| First | 1,861 | 2,212 | 2,886 | 2,632 | 2,936 | 2,766 | 2,885 | 2,957 | 3,096 | 2,990 | 2,987 | 3,024 | 2,956 |
| Second | 1,256 | 1,739 | 2,376 | 2,535 | 2,364 | 2,286 | 2,291 | 2,411 | 2,560 | 2,617 | 2,624 | 2,454 | 2,585 |
| Third | 896 | 1,248 | 1,492 | 1,748 | 1,681 | 1,658 | 1,653 | 1,716 | 1,799 | 1,815 | 1,805 | 1,981 | 1,931 |
| Fourth | 803 | 1,074 | 1,354 | 1,356 | 1,427 | 1,445 | 1,458 | 1,403 | 1,598 | 1,688 | 1,595 | 1,599 | 1,642 |
| Fifth or higher | 859 | 1,140 | 1,589 | 1,680 | 1,810 | 1,681 | 1,691 | 1,692 | 1,682 | 1,810 | 1,814 | 1,802 | 1,749 |
| | Percentage distribution | | | | | | | | | | | | |
| All students | 100.0 | 100.0 | 100.0 | 100.0 | 100.0 | 100.0 | 100.0 | 100.0 | 100.0 | 100.0 | 100.0 | 100.0 | 100.0 |
| **White** | | | | | | | | | | | | | |
| Total | 93.7 | 91.2 | 87.8 | 86.9 | 86.2 | 86.5 | 87.3 | 87.2 | 85.4 | 85.4 | 85.4 | 85.4 | 85.9 |
| Men | 58.6 | 54.8 | 49.2 | 46.8 | 46.2 | 45.8 | 44.1 | 43.6 | 43.0 | 42.6 | 43.6 | 43.4 | 42.6 |
| Women | 35.1 | 36.3 | 38.6 | 40.1 | 40.1 | 40.7 | 43.2 | 43.6 | 42.3 | 42.9 | 41.8 | 42.0 | 43.3 |
| **Black** | | | | | | | | | | | | | |
| Total | 4.8 | 7.0 | 9.8 | 10.7 | 10.8 | 10.4 | 10.0 | 9.9 | 10.6 | 10.3 | 10.2 | 10.5 | 9.7 |
| Men | 2.2 | 3.4 | 4.6 | 4.9 | 4.8 | 4.6 | 4.3 | 4.3 | 4.7 | 4.4 | 4.6 | 5.0 | 4.2 |
| Women | 2.6 | 3.6 | 5.2 | 5.8 | 6.0 | 5.8 | 5.7 | 5.6 | 5.9 | 5.9 | 5.6 | 5.5 | 5.4 |
| **Hispanic origin[3]** | | | | | | | | | | | | | |
| Total | --- | --- | 4.2 | 4.3 | 4.1 | 3.8 | 4.4 | 4.4 | 4.8 | 4.5 | 4.8 | 4.8 | 5.3 |
| Men | --- | --- | 2.3 | 2.2 | 2.2 | 2.0 | 2.3 | 2.2 | 2.4 | 2.0 | 2.3 | 2.1 | 2.6 |
| Women | --- | --- | 2.0 | 2.1 | 1.9 | 1.8 | 2.1 | 2.2 | 2.3 | 2.5 | 2.5 | 2.7 | 2.8 |
| **Year of college** | | | | | | | | | | | | | |
| First | 32.8 | 29.8 | 29.8 | 26.5 | 28.7 | 28.1 | 28.9 | 29.0 | 28.8 | 27.4 | 27.6 | 27.8 | 27.2 |
| Second | 22.1 | 23.5 | 24.5 | 25.5 | 23.1 | 23.2 | 23.0 | 23.7 | 23.8 | 24.0 | 24.2 | 22.6 | 23.8 |
| Third | 15.8 | 16.8 | 15.4 | 17.6 | 16.5 | 16.9 | 16.6 | 16.9 | 16.8 | 16.6 | 16.7 | 18.2 | 17.8 |
| Fourth | 14.1 | 14.5 | 14.0 | 13.6 | 14.0 | 14.7 | 14.6 | 13.8 | 14.9 | 15.5 | 14.7 | 14.7 | 15.1 |
| Fifth or higher | 15.1 | 15.4 | 16.4 | 16.9 | 17.7 | 17.1 | 16.9 | 16.6 | 15.7 | 16.6 | 16.8 | 16.6 | 16.1 |

[1]Totals differ from those shown in other tables. This table presents data collected in sample surveys of households rather than surveys of institutions.

[2]Controlled to 1980 census base.

[3]Persons of Hispanic origin may be of any race.

---Data not available.

NOTE.—Data are based on samples of civilian noninstitutional population. Because of rounding, details may not add to totals.

SOURCE: U.S. Department of Commerce, Bureau of the Census, *Current Population Reports*, Series P-20, No. 409. (This table was prepared October 1986.)

Table 3.9

**—Average salary of full-time instructional faculty on 9-month contracts in institutions of higher education, by academic rank and type and control of institution: United States, 1980-81, 1982-83, 1984-85, and 1985-86**

| Academic year, control and type of institution | Average salary, all faculty | Average salary, by rank | | | | | | Average salary, by sex | |
|---|---|---|---|---|---|---|---|---|---|
| | | Professor | Associate professor | Assistant professor | Instructor | Lecturer | No academic rank | Men | Women |
| 1 | 2 | 3 | 4 | 5 | 6 | 7 | 8 | 9 | 10 |
| **1980-81** | | | | | | | | | |
| All institutions | $23,302 | $30,753 | $23,214 | $18,901 | $15,178 | $17,301 | $22,334 | $24,499 | $19,996 |
| 4-year | 23,693 | 31,016 | 23,265 | 18,867 | 15,056 | 17,375 | 17,380 | 24,909 | 19,809 |
| University | 25,949 | 33,622 | 24,392 | 19,684 | 15,530 | 17,327 | 17,856 | 27,206 | 20,736 |
| Other 4-year | 22,230 | 28,798 | 22,558 | 18,398 | 14,887 | 17,425 | 17,334 | 23,271 | 19,372 |
| 2-year | 21,898 | 26,528 | 22,750 | 19,166 | 15,621 | 16,222 | 22,615 | 22,736 | 20,434 |
| Public institutions | 23,745 | 31,077 | 23,772 | 19,431 | 15,613 | 17,620 | 22,820 | 24,873 | 20,673 |
| 4-year | 24,373 | 31,442 | 23,898 | 19,442 | 15,486 | 17,712 | 19,240 | 25,509 | 20,608 |
| University | 25,571 | 32,945 | 24,268 | 19,637 | 15,305 | 17,426 | 17,358 | 26,788 | 20,564 |
| Other 4-year | 23,500 | 30,097 | 23,639 | 19,315 | 15,567 | 17,997 | 19,798 | 24,499 | 20,633 |
| 2-year | 22,177 | 26,880 | 22,947 | 19,370 | 15,928 | 16,458 | 22,875 | 22,965 | 20,778 |
| Private institutions | 22,093 | 29,994 | 21,833 | 17,767 | 14,192 | 15,899 | 15,946 | 23,493 | 18,073 |
| 4-year | 22,325 | 30,089 | 21,887 | 17,816 | 14,316 | 15,971 | 16,706 | 23,669 | 18,326 |
| University | 26,897 | 35,227 | 24,730 | 19,792 | 16,197 | 16,956 | 18,933 | 28,251 | 21,176 |
| Other 4-year | 19,996 | 26,173 | 20,502 | 16,939 | 13,905 | 14,741 | 16,617 | 21,040 | 17,342 |
| 2-year | 15,065 | 18,645 | 17,685 | 14,663 | 12,155 | 12,441 | 14,993 | 16,075 | 13,892 |
| **1982-83** | | | | | | | | | |
| All institutions | 27,196 | 35,540 | 26,921 | 22,056 | 17,601 | 20,072 | 25,557 | 28,664 | 23,261 |
| 4-year | 27,758 | 35,889 | 27,013 | 22,055 | 17,440 | 20,116 | 19,624 | 29,240 | 23,139 |
| University | 30,710 | 39,373 | 28,502 | 23,398 | 17,956 | 20,170 | 19,850 | 32,269 | 24,396 |
| Other 4-year | 25,921 | 33,121 | 26,113 | 21,315 | 17,275 | 20,064 | 19,594 | 27,167 | 22,568 |
| 2-year | 25,252 | 30,680 | 26,131 | 22,058 | 18,128 | 19,383 | 25,900 | 26,268 | 23,536 |
| Public institutions | 27,488 | 35,473 | 27,346 | 22,538 | 18,003 | 20,048 | 26,113 | 28,851 | 23,892 |
| 4-year | 28,293 | 35,918 | 27,511 | 22,588 | 17,789 | 20,087 | 21,189 | 29,661 | 23,876 |
| University | 29,893 | 38,041 | 28,086 | 23,112 | 17,430 | 19,869 | 19,160 | 31,390 | 23,908 |
| Other 4-year | 27,152 | 34,124 | 27,112 | 22,245 | 17,940 | 20,277 | 22,333 | 28,323 | 23,858 |
| 2-year | 25,567 | 31,058 | 26,349 | 22,290 | 18,484 | 19,547 | 26,189 | 26,524 | 23,917 |
| Private institutions | 26,393 | 35,701 | 25,876 | 21,054 | 16,675 | 20,176 | 17,786 | 28,159 | 21,451 |
| 4-year | 26,691 | 35,828 | 25,949 | 21,118 | 16,849 | 20,232 | 19,072 | 28,380 | 21,785 |
| University | 32,842 | 42,658 | 29,692 | 24,095 | 19,678 | 21,088 | 22,740 | 34,540 | 25,721 |
| Other 4-year | 23,819 | 31,095 | 24,294 | 19,929 | 16,336 | 18,960 | 18,957 | 25,128 | 20,545 |
| 2-year | 16,595 | 20,829 | 19,689 | 17,164 | 14,055 | 13,438 | 15,811 | 17,346 | 15,845 |
| **1984-85** | | | | | | | | | |
| All institutions | 30,447 | 39,743 | 29,945 | 24,668 | 20,230 | 22,334 | 27,683 | 32,182 | 25,941 |
| 4-year | 31,255 | 40,249 | 30,091 | 24,731 | 19,312 | 22,414 | 22,048 | 32,994 | 26,015 |
| University | 34,543 | 44,119 | 31,704 | 26,365 | 19,784 | 22,433 | 22,404 | 36,370 | 27,389 |
| Other 4-year | 29,189 | 37,209 | 29,096 | 23,828 | 19,158 | 22,397 | 21,998 | 30,654 | 25,383 |
| 2-year | 27,530 | 33,498 | 28,700 | 24,176 | 22,136 | 21,125 | 28,085 | 28,620 | 25,767 |
| Public institutions | 30,646 | 39,521 | 30,355 | 25,155 | 20,887 | 22,497 | 28,269 | 32,240 | 26,566 |
| 4-year | 31,764 | 40,176 | 30,595 | 25,287 | 19,711 | 22,511 | 23,283 | 33,344 | 26,813 |
| University | 33,388 | 42,282 | 31,064 | 25,905 | 19,190 | 22,066 | 21,820 | 35,132 | 26,680 |
| Other 4-year | 30,598 | 38,416 | 30,262 | 24,883 | 19,936 | 22,871 | 24,023 | 31,954 | 26,887 |
| 2-year | 27,864 | 33,805 | 28,937 | 24,473 | 22,544 | 22,311 | 28,378 | 28,891 | 26,172 |
| Private institutions | 29,910 | 40,280 | 28,963 | 23,666 | 18,401 | 21,641 | 20,337 | 32,028 | 24,186 |
| 4-year | 30,247 | 40,409 | 29,049 | 23,757 | 18,612 | 22,018 | 21,528 | 32,278 | 24,560 |
| University | 37,515 | 48,606 | 33,470 | 27,474 | 21,887 | 23,512 | 24,933 | 39,515 | 29,310 |
| Other 4-year | 26,789 | 34,787 | 27,047 | 22,258 | 18,034 | 19,544 | 21,412 | 28,351 | 23,060 |
| 2-year | 18,510 | 23,580 | 21,377 | 18,440 | 15,758 | 11,267 | 18,278 | 19,460 | 17,575 |
| **1985-86** | | | | | | | | | |
| All institutions | 32,392 | 42,268 | 31,787 | 26,277 | 20,918 | 23,770 | 29,088 | 34,294 | 27,576 |
| 4-year | 33,270 | 42,803 | 31,940 | 26,335 | 20,383 | 23,805 | 24,055 | 35,174 | 27,696 |
| University | 36,837 | 46,994 | 33,704 | 28,242 | 20,784 | 23,807 | 24,139 | 38,841 | 29,243 |
| Other 4-year | 31,078 | 39,610 | 30,864 | 25,314 | 20,253 | 23,802 | 24,043 | 32,688 | 26,994 |
| 2-year | 29,259 | 36,076 | 30,483 | 25,823 | 22,434 | 23,154 | 29,420 | 30,490 | 27,294 |
| Public institutions | 32,750 | 42,328 | 32,367 | 26,951 | 21,553 | 23,839 | 29,597 | 34,528 | 28,299 |
| 4-year | 34,033 | 43,044 | 32,642 | 27,100 | 20,895 | 23,862 | 25,142 | 35,786 | 28,680 |
| University | 35,835 | 45,322 | 33,133 | 27,887 | 20,226 | 23,557 | 23,706 | 37,771 | 28,567 |
| Other 4-year | 32,757 | 41,170 | 32,296 | 26,597 | 21,180 | 24,101 | 25,705 | 34,260 | 28,742 |
| 2-year | 29,590 | 36,418 | 30,733 | 26,162 | 22,818 | 23,500 | 29,712 | 30,758 | 27,693 |
| Private institutions | 31,402 | 42,118 | 30,400 | 24,891 | 19,314 | 23,477 | 21,577 | 33,656 | 25,523 |
| 4-year | 31,732 | 42,260 | 30,486 | 24,987 | 19,483 | 23,574 | 23,394 | 33,900 | 25,889 |
| University | 39,519 | 51,355 | 35,307 | 29,125 | 22,743 | 24,540 | 26,603 | 41,680 | 31,106 |
| Other 4-year | 28,198 | 36,455 | 28,365 | 23,412 | 18,910 | 22,093 | 23,295 | 29,882 | 24,280 |
| 2-year | 19,436 | 24,519 | 22,291 | 19,297 | 16,419 | 9,231 | 18,783 | 20,412 | 18,504 |

SOURCE: U.S. Department of Education, National Center for Education Statistics, *Faculty Salaries, Tenure, and Benefits, 1980-81;* and Center for Education Statistics, "Salaries, Tenure, and Fringe Benefits of Full-Time Instructional Faculty" surveys. (This table was prepared September 1986.)

Table 3.10

### —Full-time instructional faculty with tenure for institutions reporting tenure status, by academic rank and sex and by type and control of institution: United States, 1980-81, 1982-83, 1984-85, and 1985-86

| Academic year, type, and control of institution | All ranks | Percent with tenure, by rank | | | | | | Percent with tenure, by sex | |
|---|---|---|---|---|---|---|---|---|---|
| | | Professor | Associate professor | Assistant professor | Instructor | Lecturer | No academic rank | Men | Women |
| 1 | 2 | 3 | 4 | 5 | 6 | 7 | 8 | 9 | 10 |
| **1980-81** | | | | | | | | | |
| All institutions | 64.8 | 95.8 | 82.9 | 27.9 | 9.2 | 11.9 | 77.4 | 70.0 | 49.7 |
| 4-year | 62.7 | 95.8 | 82.2 | 24.1 | 6.6 | 10.7 | 24.7 | 68.3 | 44.0 |
| University | 64.5 | 96.7 | 83.7 | 15.3 | 5.4 | 4.3 | 3.5 | 70.0 | 41.0 |
| Other 4-year | 61.3 | 94.9 | 81.2 | 29.7 | 7.1 | 17.8 | 32.4 | 67.0 | 45.5 |
| 2-year | 74.5 | 95.6 | 89.2 | 58.9 | 19.8 | 34.8 | 81.1 | 78.8 | 66.6 |
| Public institutions | 68.0 | 96.6 | 85.9 | 32.5 | 11.8 | 14.3 | 79.4 | 72.8 | 54.0 |
| 4-year | 65.7 | 96.6 | 85.3 | 27.6 | 8.7 | 12.8 | 12.2 | 71.1 | 47.5 |
| University | 66.0 | 96.9 | 86.5 | 16.8 | 6.1 | 4.9 | 4.5 | 71.3 | 42.8 |
| Other 4-year | 65.5 | 96.3 | 84.4 | 35.5 | 10.0 | 21.4 | 17.2 | 70.9 | 50.2 |
| 2-year | 75.2 | 95.9 | 89.5 | 59.5 | 20.3 | 35.8 | 81.8 | 79.3 | 67.5 |
| Private institutions | 55.9 | 93.8 | 75.2 | 17.5 | 3.0 | 1.5 | 43.4 | 62.2 | 37.2 |
| 4-year | 56.0 | 93.8 | 75.2 | 17.4 | 2.8 | 1.5 | 37.5 | 62.2 | 37.2 |
| University | 60.4 | 96.3 | 75.8 | 11.5 | 3.5 | 1.8 | 0.6 | 66.3 | 36.5 |
| Other 4-year | 53.6 | 92.0 | 74.9 | 20.2 | 2.6 | 1.2 | 43.4 | 59.8 | 37.4 |
| 2-year | 49.5 | 84.7 | 77.3 | 35.2 | 8.8 | 0.0 | 52.2 | 57.3 | 39.5 |
| **1982-83** | | | | | | | | | |
| All institutions | 65.4 | 95.6 | 82.1 | 26.8 | 9.0 | 11.0 | 77.2 | 70.4 | 51.0 |
| 4-year | 63.2 | 95.6 | 81.4 | 23.1 | 6.2 | 9.8 | 23.6 | 68.9 | 45.2 |
| University | 65.5 | 96.8 | 83.8 | 14.6 | 4.9 | 3.6 | 0.7 | 70.9 | 42.9 |
| Other 4-year | 61.6 | 94.4 | 79.8 | 28.4 | 6.7 | 16.3 | 32.7 | 67.3 | 46.4 |
| 2-year | 75.0 | 95.3 | 88.9 | 58.4 | 19.9 | 32.3 | 81.2 | 78.9 | 68.2 |
| Public institutions | 68.9 | 96.4 | 85.5 | 31.8 | 11.3 | 13.3 | 79.2 | 73.6 | 55.7 |
| 4-year | 66.7 | 96.5 | 84.9 | 27.0 | 7.9 | 11.9 | 11.1 | 72.0 | 49.0 |
| University | 67.5 | 97.2 | 87.0 | 16.5 | 5.5 | 4.3 | 0.9 | 72.7 | 45.0 |
| Other 4-year | 66.1 | 95.7 | 83.3 | 34.6 | 9.0 | 19.1 | 19.4 | 71.4 | 51.4 |
| 2-year | 75.7 | 95.7 | 89.1 | 59.0 | 20.3 | 32.6 | 81.7 | 79.4 | 69.0 |
| Private institutions | 55.9 | 93.4 | 73.8 | 16.3 | 3.6 | 1.2 | 43.3 | 62.0 | 38.1 |
| 4-year | 56.0 | 93.5 | 73.8 | 16.1 | 3.2 | 1.2 | 35.8 | 62.1 | 38.0 |
| University | 60.3 | 95.8 | 74.9 | 10.3 | 3.2 | 1.4 | 0.0 | 66.0 | 37.8 |
| Other 4-year | 53.7 | 91.9 | 73.2 | 18.8 | 3.2 | 0.9 | 40.9 | 59.8 | 38.1 |
| 2-year | 49.9 | 78.9 | 77.2 | 35.6 | 13.7 | 0.0 | 56.7 | 55.8 | 42.2 |
| **1984-85** | | | | | | | | | |
| All institutions | 66.0 | 95.8 | 82.3 | 25.6 | 14.9 | 10.7 | 76.4 | 71.1 | 51.8 |
| 4-year | 64.0 | 95.8 | 81.6 | 22.0 | 5.7 | 8.9 | 20.7 | 69.7 | 46.3 |
| University | 66.6 | 97.0 | 84.7 | 13.5 | 5.2 | 2.9 | 0.4 | 72.0 | 44.6 |
| Other 4-year | 62.2 | 94.7 | 79.5 | 27.3 | 5.9 | 14.7 | 28.5 | 67.9 | 47.2 |
| 2-year | 75.2 | 95.2 | 88.7 | 56.7 | 38.2 | 40.3 | 81.6 | 78.9 | 68.9 |
| Public institutions | 69.0 | 96.5 | 85.4 | 30.0 | 18.6 | 12.9 | 78.9 | 73.8 | 56.1 |
| 4-year | 67.0 | 96.6 | 84.9 | 25.3 | 7.4 | 10.7 | 11.1 | 72.4 | 49.7 |
| University | 67.9 | 97.1 | 87.4 | 14.7 | 5.8 | 3.6 | 0.5 | 73.3 | 46.0 |
| Other 4-year | 66.2 | 96.1 | 82.9 | 32.9 | 8.2 | 16.9 | 19.7 | 71.5 | 51.9 |
| 2-year | 75.8 | 95.3 | 89.0 | 57.4 | 38.6 | 43.7 | 82.1 | 79.4 | 69.8 |
| Private institutions | 57.4 | 93.8 | 74.4 | 16.0 | 3.5 | 1.2 | 37.7 | 63.7 | 39.7 |
| 4-year | 57.5 | 93.8 | 74.4 | 15.8 | 2.2 | 1.1 | 30.1 | 63.8 | 39.6 |
| University | 62.7 | 96.8 | 76.5 | 10.3 | 3.0 | 1.0 | 0.0 | 68.4 | 40.6 |
| Other 4-year | 54.9 | 91.8 | 73.4 | 18.2 | 2.1 | 1.3 | 33.8 | 61.1 | 39.3 |
| 2-year | 51.2 | 91.8 | 72.5 | 33.6 | 28.9 | 5.6 | 56.4 | 58.2 | 41.7 |
| **1985-86** | | | | | | | | | |
| All institutions | 66.0 | 95.8 | 82.2 | 25.1 | 10.7 | 9.3 | 75.3 | 71.3 | 51.7 |
| 4-year | 64.1 | 95.8 | 81.5 | 21.5 | 5.7 | 8.3 | 20.0 | 69.9 | 46.4 |
| University | 66.8 | 97.0 | 85.0 | 13.0 | 5.0 | 3.2 | 0.3 | 72.3 | 45.4 |
| Other 4-year | 62.2 | 94.8 | 79.2 | 26.6 | 6.0 | 13.0 | 27.0 | 68.1 | 46.8 |
| 2-year | 75.1 | 95.1 | 88.5 | 56.4 | 27.3 | 28.6 | 80.4 | 79.1 | 68.5 |
| Public institutions | 68.9 | 96.5 | 85.4 | 29.1 | 13.4 | 10.9 | 77.2 | 73.9 | 55.6 |
| 4-year | 66.9 | 96.6 | 84.9 | 24.4 | 7.3 | 9.7 | 11.1 | 72.5 | 49.3 |
| University | 68.1 | 97.1 | 87.8 | 14.0 | 5.8 | 3.4 | 0.3 | 73.5 | 46.4 |
| Other 4-year | 66.0 | 96.2 | 82.7 | 31.8 | 8.0 | 15.0 | 18.3 | 71.6 | 51.1 |
| 2-year | 75.7 | 95.2 | 89.0 | 57.4 | 28.0 | 28.7 | 80.8 | 79.5 | 69.2 |
| Private institutions | 57.6 | 93.8 | 73.8 | 16.0 | 2.7 | 2.1 | 40.3 | 63.9 | 40.3 |
| 4-year | 57.7 | 93.9 | 73.9 | 15.9 | 2.5 | 2.1 | 32.1 | 64.0 | 40.3 |
| University | 63.0 | 96.7 | 76.6 | 10.1 | 2.2 | 2.8 | 0.0 | 68.4 | 42.7 |
| Other 4-year | 55.1 | 92.0 | 72.6 | 18.3 | 2.5 | 1.0 | 34.6 | 61.6 | 39.5 |
| 2-year | 48.4 | 89.9 | 63.6 | 24.9 | 9.3 | 0.0 | 57.5 | 56.1 | 39.3 |

SOURCE: U.S. Department of Education, National Center for Education Statistics, *Faculty Salaries, Tenure, and Benefits, 1980-81*; and unpublished data; and Center for Education Statistics, "Salaries, Tenure, and Fringe Benefits of Full-Time Instructional Faculty" surveys. (This table was prepared September 1986.)

Table 3.11

## —Institutions of higher education, by control and type of institution: United States, 1949-50 to 1985-86

| Year | All institutions | | | Publicly controlled | | | Privately controlled | | |
|---|---|---|---|---|---|---|---|---|---|
| | Total | 4-year | 2-year | Total | 4-year | 2-year | Total | 4-year | 2-year |
| 1 | 2 | 3 | 4 | 5 | 6 | 7 | 8 | 9 | 10 |
| **Excluding branch campuses** | | | | | | | | | |
| 1949-50 | 1,851 | 1,327 | 524 | 641 | 344 | 297 | 1,210 | 983 | 227 |
| 1950-51 | 1,852 | 1,312 | 540 | 636 | 341 | 295 | 1,216 | 971 | 245 |
| 1951-52 | 1,832 | 1,326 | 506 | 641 | 350 | 291 | 1,191 | 976 | 215 |
| 1952-53 | 1,882 | 1,355 | 527 | 639 | 349 | 290 | 1,243 | 1,006 | 237 |
| 1953-54 | 1,863 | 1,345 | 518 | 662 | 369 | 293 | 1,201 | 976 | 225 |
| 1954-55 | 1,849 | 1,333 | 516 | 648 | 353 | 295 | 1,201 | 980 | 221 |
| 1955-56 | 1,850 | 1,347 | 503 | 650 | 360 | 290 | 1,200 | 987 | 213 |
| 1956-57 | 1,878 | 1,355 | 523 | 656 | 359 | 297 | 1,222 | 996 | 226 |
| 1957-58 | 1,930 | 1,390 | 540 | 666 | 366 | 300 | 1,264 | 1,024 | 240 |
| 1958-59 | 1,947 | 1,394 | 553 | 673 | 366 | 307 | 1,274 | 1,028 | 246 |
| 1959-60 | 2,004 | 1,422 | 582 | 695 | 367 | 328 | 1,309 | 1,055 | 254 |
| 1960-61 | 2,021 | 1,431 | 590 | 700 | 368 | 332 | 1,321 | 1,063 | 258 |
| 1961-62 | 2,033 | 1,443 | 590 | 718 | 374 | 344 | 1,315 | 1,069 | 246 |
| 1962-63 | 2,093 | 1,468 | 625 | 740 | 376 | 364 | 1,353 | 1,092 | 261 |
| 1963-64 | 2,132 | 1,499 | 633 | 760 | 386 | 374 | 1,372 | 1,113 | 259 |
| 1964-65 | 2,175 | 1,521 | 654 | 799 | 393 | 406 | 1,376 | 1,128 | 248 |
| 1965-66 | 2,230 | 1,551 | 679 | 821 | 401 | 420 | 1,409 | 1,150 | 259 |
| 1966-67 | 2,329 | 1,577 | 752 | 880 | 403 | 477 | 1,449 | 1,174 | 275 |
| 1967-68 | 2,374 | 1,588 | 786 | 934 | 414 | 520 | 1,440 | 1,174 | 266 |
| 1968-69 | 2,483 | 1,619 | 864 | 1,011 | 417 | 594 | 1,472 | 1,202 | 270 |
| 1969-70 | 2,525 | 1,639 | 886 | 1,060 | 426 | 634 | 1,465 | 1,213 | 252 |
| 1970-71 | 2,556 | 1,665 | 891 | 1,089 | 435 | 654 | 1,467 | 1,230 | 237 |
| 1971-72 | 2,606 | 1,675 | 931 | 1,137 | 440 | 697 | 1,469 | 1,235 | 234 |
| 1972-73 | 2,665 | 1,701 | 964 | 1,182 | 449 | 733 | 1,483 | 1,252 | 231 |
| 1973-74 | 2,720 | 1,717 | 1,003 | 1,200 | 440 | 760 | 1,520 | 1,277 | 243 |
| 1974-75 | 2,747 | 1,744 | 1,003 | 1,214 | 447 | 767 | 1,533 | 1,297 | 236 |
| 1975-76 | 2,765 | 1,767 | 998 | 1,219 | 447 | 772 | 1,546 | 1,320 | 226 |
| 1976-77 | 2,785 | 1,783 | 1,002 | 1,231 | 452 | 779 | 1,554 | 1,331 | 223 |
| 1977-78 | 2,826 | 1,808 | 1,018 | 1,241 | 454 | 787 | 1,585 | 1,354 | 231 |
| 1978-79 | 2,954 | 1,843 | 1,111 | 1,308 | 463 | 845 | 1,646 | 1,380 | 266 |
| 1979-80 | 2,975 | 1,863 | 1,112 | 1,310 | 464 | 846 | 1,665 | 1,399 | 266 |
| 1980-81 | 3,056 | 1,861 | 1,195 | 1,334 | 465 | 869 | 1,722 | 1,396 | 326 |
| 1981-82 | 3,083 | 1,883 | 1,200 | 1,340 | 471 | 869 | 1,743 | 1,412 | 331 |
| 1982-83 | 3,111 | 1,887 | 1,224 | 1,336 | 472 | 864 | 1,775 | 1,415 | 360 |
| 1983-84 | 3,117 | 1,914 | 1,203 | 1,325 | 474 | 851 | 1,792 | 1,440 | 352 |
| 1984-85 | 3,146 | 1,911 | 1,235 | 1,329 | 461 | 868 | 1,817 | 1,450 | 367 |
| 1985-86 | 3,155 | 1,915 | 1,240 | 1,326 | 461 | 865 | 1,829 | 1,454 | 375 |
| **Including branch campuses** | | | | | | | | | |
| 1974-75 | 3,004 | 1,866 | 1,138 | 1,433 | 537 | 896 | 1,571 | 1,329 | 242 |
| 1975-76 | 3,026 | 1,898 | 1,128 | 1,442 | 545 | 897 | 1,584 | 1,353 | 231 |
| 1976-77 | 3,046 | 1,913 | 1,133 | 1,455 | 550 | 905 | 1,591 | 1,363 | 228 |
| 1977-78 | 3,095 | 1,938 | 1,157 | 1,473 | 552 | 921 | 1,622 | 1,386 | 236 |
| 1978-79 | 3,134 | 1,941 | 1,193 | 1,474 | 550 | 924 | 1,660 | 1,391 | 269 |
| 1979-80 | 3,152 | 1,957 | 1,195 | 1,475 | 549 | 926 | 1,677 | 1,408 | 269 |
| 1980-81 | 3,231 | 1,957 | 1,274 | 1,497 | 552 | 945 | 1,734 | 1,405 | 329 |
| 1981-82 | 3,253 | 1,979 | 1,274 | 1,498 | 558 | 940 | 1,755 | 1,421 | 334 |
| 1982-83 | 3,280 | 1,984 | 1,296 | 1,493 | 560 | 933 | 1,787 | 1,424 | 363 |
| 1983-84 | 3,284 | 2,013 | 1,271 | 1,481 | 565 | 916 | 1,803 | 1,448 | 355 |
| 1984-85 | 3,331 | 2,025 | 1,306 | 1,501 | 566 | 935 | 1,830 | 1,459 | 371 |
| 1985-86 | 3,340 | 2,029 | 1,311 | 1,498 | 566 | 932 | 1,842 | 1,463 | 379 |

SOURCE: U.S. Department of Education, Center for Education Statistics, *Education Directory, Colleges and Universities* and "Fall Enrollment in Higher Education" and "Institutional Characteristics of Colleges and Universities" surveys. (This table was prepared March 1986.)

Table 3.12

## Table 3.13 — Average undergraduate tuition and fees and room and board rates in institutions of higher education, by type and control of institution: United States, 1964-65 to 1986-87

| Year and control of institution | Total tuition, room, and board | | | | Tuition and required fees (in State) | | | | Dormitory rooms | | | | Board (7-day basis) | | | |
|---|---|---|---|---|---|---|---|---|---|---|---|---|---|---|---|---|
| | All | University | Other 4-year | 2-year | All | University | Other 4-year | 2-year | All | University | Other 4-year | 2-year | All | University | Other 4-year | 2-year |
| 1 | 2 | 3 | 4 | 5 | 6 | 7 | 8 | 9 | 10 | 11 | 12 | 13 | 14 | 15 | 16 | 17 |
| 1964-65 | | | | | | | | | | | | | | | | |
| Public | $950 | $1,051 | $867 | $638 | $243 | $298 | $224 | $99 | $271 | $291 | $241 | $178 | $436 | $462 | $402 | $361 |
| Private | 1,907 | 2,202 | 1,810 | 1,455 | 1,088 | 1,297 | 1,023 | 702 | 331 | 390 | 308 | 289 | 488 | 515 | 479 | 464 |
| 1965-66 [1] | | | | | | | | | | | | | | | | |
| Public | 983 | 1,105 | 904 | 670 | 257 | 327 | 241 | 109 | 281 | 304 | 255 | 194 | 445 | 474 | 408 | 367 |
| Private | 2,005 | 2,316 | 1,899 | 1,557 | 1,154 | 1,369 | 1,086 | 768 | 356 | 418 | 330 | 316 | 495 | 529 | 483 | 473 |
| 1966-67 | | | | | | | | | | | | | | | | |
| Public | 1,026 | 1,171 | 947 | 710 | 275 | 360 | 259 | 121 | 294 | 321 | 271 | 213 | 457 | 490 | 417 | 376 |
| Private | 2,124 | 2,456 | 2,007 | 1,679 | 1,233 | 1,456 | 1,162 | 845 | 385 | 452 | 355 | 347 | 506 | 548 | 490 | 487 |
| 1967-68 [1] | | | | | | | | | | | | | | | | |
| Public | 1,064 | 1,199 | 997 | 789 | 283 | 366 | 268 | 144 | 313 | 337 | 292 | 243 | 468 | 496 | 437 | 402 |
| Private | 2,205 | 2,545 | 2,104 | 1,762 | 1,297 | 1,534 | 1,237 | 892 | 392 | 455 | 366 | 366 | 516 | 556 | 501 | 504 |
| 1968-69 | | | | | | | | | | | | | | | | |
| Public | 1,117 | 1,245 | 1,063 | 883 | 295 | 377 | 281 | 170 | 337 | 359 | 318 | 278 | 485 | 509 | 464 | 435 |
| Private | 2,321 | 2,673 | 2,237 | 1,876 | 1,383 | 1,638 | 1,335 | 956 | 404 | 463 | 382 | 391 | 534 | 572 | 520 | 529 |
| 1969-70 [1] | | | | | | | | | | | | | | | | |
| Public | 1,203 | 1,362 | 1,135 | 951 | 323 | 427 | 306 | 178 | 369 | 395 | 346 | 308 | 511 | 540 | 483 | 465 |
| Private | 2,530 | 2,920 | 2,420 | 1,993 | 1,533 | 1,809 | 1,468 | 1,034 | 436 | 503 | 409 | 413 | 561 | 608 | 543 | 546 |
| 1970-71 [1] | | | | | | | | | | | | | | | | |
| Public | 1,287 | 1,477 | 1,206 | 998 | 351 | 478 | 332 | 187 | 401 | 431 | 375 | 338 | 535 | 568 | 499 | 473 |
| Private | 2,738 | 3,163 | 2,599 | 2,103 | 1,684 | 1,980 | 1,603 | 1,109 | 468 | 542 | 434 | 434 | 586 | 641 | 562 | 560 |
| 1971-72 | | | | | | | | | | | | | | | | |
| Public | 1,357 | 1,579 | 1,263 | 1,073 | 376 | 526 | 354 | 192 | 430 | 463 | 400 | 366 | 551 | 590 | 509 | 515 |
| Private | 2,917 | 3,375 | 2,748 | 2,186 | 1,820 | 2,133 | 1,721 | 1,172 | 494 | 576 | 454 | 449 | 603 | 666 | 573 | 565 |
| 1972-73 | | | | | | | | | | | | | | | | |
| Public | 1,458 | 1,668 | 1,460 | 1,197 | 407 | 566 | 455 | 233 | 476 | 500 | 455 | 398 | 575 | 602 | 550 | 566 |
| Private | 3,038 | 3,512 | 2,934 | 2,273 | 1,898 | 2,226 | 1,846 | 1,221 | 524 | 622 | 490 | 457 | 616 | 664 | 598 | 595 |
| 1973-74 | | | | | | | | | | | | | | | | |
| Public | 1,517 | 1,707 | 1,506 | 1,274 | 438 | 581 | 463 | 274 | 480 | 505 | 464 | 409 | 599 | 621 | 579 | 591 |
| Private | 3,164 | 3,717 | 3,040 | 2,410 | 1,989 | 2,375 | 1,925 | 1,303 | 533 | 622 | 502 | 483 | 642 | 720 | 613 | 624 |
| 1974-75 | | | | | | | | | | | | | | | | |
| Public | 1,563 | 1,760 | 1,558 | 1,339 | 432 | 599 | 448 | 277 | 506 | 527 | 497 | 424 | 625 | 634 | 613 | 638 |
| Private | 3,403 | 4,076 | 3,156 | 2,591 | 2,117 | 2,614 | 1,954 | 1,367 | 586 | 691 | 536 | 564 | 700 | 771 | 666 | 660 |
| 1975-76 | | | | | | | | | | | | | | | | |
| Public | 1,666 | 1,935 | 1,657 | 1,386 | 433 | 642 | 469 | 245 | 544 | 573 | 533 | 442 | 689 | 720 | 655 | 699 |
| Private | 3,663 | 4,467 | 3,385 | 2,711 | 2,272 | 2,881 | 2,084 | 1,427 | 636 | 753 | 583 | 572 | 755 | 833 | 718 | 712 |
| 1976-77 | | | | | | | | | | | | | | | | |
| Public | 1,789 | 2,066 | 1,828 | 1,490 | 479 | 689 | 564 | 283 | 582 | 614 | 572 | 465 | 728 | 763 | 692 | 742 |
| Private | 3,907 | 4,716 | 3,714 | 2,971 | 2,467 | 3,051 | 2,351 | 1,592 | 649 | 783 | 604 | 607 | 791 | 882 | 759 | 772 |
| 1977-78 | | | | | | | | | | | | | | | | |
| Public | 1,888 | 2,170 | 1,932 | 1,589 | 512 | 736 | 596 | 306 | 621 | 649 | 616 | 486 | 755 | 785 | 720 | 797 |
| Private | 4,158 | 5,033 | 3,968 | 3,148 | 2,624 | 3,240 | 2,520 | 1,706 | 698 | 850 | 648 | 631 | 836 | 943 | 800 | 811 |

—Average undergraduate tuition and fees and room and board rates in institutions of higher education, by type and control of institution: United States, 1964-65 to 1986-87—Continued

| Year and control of institution | Total tuition, room, and board | | | | Tuition and required fees (in State) | | | | Dormitory rooms | | | | Board (7-day basis) | | | |
|---|---|---|---|---|---|---|---|---|---|---|---|---|---|---|---|---|
| | All | University | Other 4-year | 2-year | All | University | Other 4-year | 2-year | All | University | Other 4-year | 2-year | All | University | Other 4-year | 2-year |
| 1 | 2 | 3 | 4 | 5 | 6 | 7 | 8 | 9 | 10 | 11 | 12 | 13 | 14 | 15 | 16 | 17 |
| **1978-79** | | | | | | | | | | | | | | | | |
| Public | 1,994 | 2,289 | 2,027 | 1,691 | 543 | 777 | 622 | 327 | 655 | 689 | 641 | 527 | 796 | 823 | 764 | 837 |
| Private | 4,514 | 5,403 | 4,326 | 3,389 | 2,867 | 3,487 | 2,771 | 1,831 | 758 | 916 | 704 | 700 | 889 | 1,000 | 851 | 858 |
| **1979-80** | | | | | | | | | | | | | | | | |
| Public | 2,165 | 2,487 | 2,198 | 1,821 | 583 | 840 | 662 | 355 | 715 | 749 | 703 | 572 | 867 | 898 | 833 | 894 |
| Private | 4,912 | 5,888 | 4,699 | 3,755 | 3,130 | 3,811 | 3,020 | 2,062 | 827 | 999 | 768 | 769 | 955 | 1,078 | 911 | 924 |
| **1980-81** | | | | | | | | | | | | | | | | |
| Public | 2,371 | 2,711 | 2,420 | 2,020 | 633 | 915 | 721 | 385 | 798 | 827 | 795 | 635 | 940 | 969 | 904 | 1,000 |
| Private | 5,468 | 6,566 | 5,249 | 4,290 | 3,498 | 4,275 | 3,390 | 2,413 | 917 | 1,083 | 860 | 880 | 1,053 | 1,208 | 999 | 997 |
| **1981-82** | | | | | | | | | | | | | | | | |
| Public | 2,668 | 3,079 | 2,701 | 2,217 | 721 | 1,042 | 813 | 432 | 909 | 970 | 885 | 697 | 1,038 | 1,067 | 1,003 | 1,088 |
| Private | 6,184 | 7,439 | 5,949 | 4,840 | 3,972 | 4,887 | 3,855 | 2,697 | 1,037 | 1,226 | 970 | 1,025 | 1,175 | 1,326 | 1,124 | 1,118 |
| **1982-83** | | | | | | | | | | | | | | | | |
| Public | 2,944 | 3,403 | 3,032 | 2,390 | 798 | 1,164 | 936 | 473 | 1,010 | 1,072 | 993 | 755 | 1,136 | 1,167 | 1,103 | 1,162 |
| Private | 6,920 | 8,537 | 6,646 | 5,364 | 4,439 | 5,583 | 4,329 | 3,008 | 1,181 | 1,453 | 1,083 | 1,177 | 1,300 | 1,501 | 1,234 | 1,179 |
| **1983-84** | | | | | | | | | | | | | | | | |
| Public | 3,156 | 3,628 | 3,285 | 2,534 | 891 | 1,284 | 1,052 | 528 | 1,087 | 1,131 | 1,092 | 801 | 1,178 | 1,213 | 1,141 | 1,205 |
| Private | 7,509 | 9,307 | 7,244 | 5,571 | 4,851 | 6,217 | 4,726 | 3,099 | 1,278 | 1,531 | 1,191 | 1,253 | 1,380 | 1,559 | 1,327 | 1,219 |
| **1984-85 [2]** | | | | | | | | | | | | | | | | |
| Public | 3,408 | 3,899 | 3,518 | 2,807 | 971 | 1,386 | 1,117 | 584 | 1,196 | 1,237 | 1,200 | 921 | 1,241 | 1,276 | 1,201 | 1,302 |
| Private | 8,202 | 10,243 | 7,849 | 6,203 | 5,314 | 6,843 | 5,135 | 3,485 | 1,426 | 1,753 | 1,309 | 1,424 | 1,462 | 1,647 | 1,405 | 1,294 |
| **1985-86 [1]** | | | | | | | | | | | | | | | | |
| Public | 3,640 | 4,170 | 3,750 | 3,010 | 1,040 | 1,510 | 1,200 | 620 | 1,300 | 1,340 | 1,310 | 1,010 | 1,300 | 1,320 | 1,240 | 1,380 |
| Private | 8,870 | 11,110 | 8,500 | 6,630 | 5,750 | 7,450 | 5,550 | 3,760 | 1,580 | 1,940 | 1,460 | 1,530 | 1,540 | 1,720 | 1,490 | 1,340 |
| **1986-87 [1]** | | | | | | | | | | | | | | | | |
| Public | 3,820 | 4,370 | 3,940 | 3,160 | 1,100 | 1,590 | 1,270 | 650 | 1,360 | 1,400 | 1,370 | 1,060 | 1,360 | 1,380 | 1,300 | 1,450 |
| Private | 9,470 | 11,870 | 9,070 | 7,060 | 6,230 | 8,060 | 6,000 | 4,060 | 1,640 | 2,020 | 1,520 | 1,600 | 1,600 | 1,790 | 1,550 | 1,400 |

[1] Estimated.

[2] Data have been revised since originally published.

NOTE.—Data are for the entire academic year and are average charges paid by students. Tuition and fees were calculated on the basis of full-time-equivalent students but are not adjusted to reflect student residency. Room and board were based on full-time students. The data have not been adjusted for changes in purchasing power of the dollar.

SOURCES: U.S. Department of Education, Center for Education Statistics, *Projections of Education Statistics;* and "Institutional Characteristics of Colleges and Universities" and "Fall Enrollment in Colleges and Universities" surveys. (This table was prepared September 1986.)

**—Physical plant value and endowment funds per student in institutions of higher education, by type and control of institution: United States, 1975-76 to 1984-85**

| Control and level of institution | Institutions | | Plant value (end of year) | | Market value of endowment funds (end of year) | |
|---|---|---|---|---|---|---|
| | Number[1] | Enrollment,[2] in thousands | Total, in thousands of dollars | Per full-time-equivalent student | Total, in thousands of dollars | Per full-time-equivalent student |
| 1 | 2 | 3 | 4 | 5 | 6 | 7 |
| **1975-76** | | | | | | |
| All institutions | 3,026 | 8,480 | $66,348,304 | $7,824 | $15,488,266 | $1,827 |
| 4-year institutions | 1,898 | 5,900 | 57,333,509 | 9,717 | 15,337,285 | 2,599 |
| 2-year institutions | 1,128 | 2,579 | 9,014,795 | 3,495 | 150,981 | 59 |
| Publicly controlled institutions | 1,442 | 6,522 | 44,795,168 | 6,868 | 2,932,737 | 450 |
| 4-year institutions | 545 | 4,057 | 36,440,349 | 8,983 | 2,886,157 | 711 |
| 2-year institutions | 897 | 2,466 | 8,354,819 | 3,388 | 46,580 | 19 |
| Privately controlled institutions | 1,584 | 1,957 | 21,553,136 | 11,011 | 12,555,529 | 6,414 |
| 4-year institutions | 1,353 | 1,844 | 20,893,160 | 11,331 | 12,451,128 | 6,753 |
| 2-year institutions | 231 | 113 | 659,976 | 5,816 | 104,401 | 920 |
| **1979-80** | | | | | | |
| All institutions | 3,152 | 8,487 | 83,733,387 | 9,866 | 20,743,045 | 2,444 |
| 4-year institutions | 1,957 | 6,016 | 71,524,828 | 11,889 | 20,541,897 | 3,415 |
| 2-year institutions | 1,195 | 2,471 | 12,208,559 | 4,940 | 201,148 | 81 |
| Publicly controlled institutions | 1,475 | 6,393 | 56,970,126 | 8,912 | 3,708,329 | 580 |
| 4-year institutions | 549 | 4,059 | 45,523,288 | 11,215 | 3,628,794 | 894 |
| 2-year institutions | 926 | 2,333 | 11,446,838 | 4,906 | 79,535 | 34 |
| Privately controlled institutions | 1,677 | 2,095 | 26,763,261 | 12,777 | 17,034,716 | 8,132 |
| 4-year institutions | 1,408 | 1,957 | 26,001,540 | 13,288 | 16,913,103 | 8,643 |
| 2-year institutions | 269 | 138 | 761,721 | 5,522 | 121,613 | 882 |
| **1982-83** | | | | | | |
| All institutions | 3,280 | 9,092 | --- | --- | 32,691,133 | 3,596 |
| 4-year institutions | 1,984 | 6,249 | --- | --- | 32,388,498 | 5,183 |
| 2-year institutions | 1,296 | 2,843 | --- | --- | 302,636 | 106 |
| Publicly controlled institutions | 1,493 | 6,851 | --- | --- | 5,825,940 | 850 |
| 4-year institutions | 560 | 4,221 | --- | --- | 5,696,596 | 1,350 |
| 2-year institutions | 933 | 2,630 | --- | --- | 129,345 | 49 |
| Privately controlled institutions | 1,787 | 2,241 | --- | --- | 26,865,193 | 11,988 |
| 4-year institutions | 1,424 | 2,028 | --- | --- | 26,691,902 | 13,160 |
| 2-year institutions | 363 | 213 | --- | --- | 173,291 | 814 |
| **1983-84** | | | | | | |
| All institutions | 3,284 | 9,166 | 99,986,781 | 10,908 | 32,975,610 | 3,597 |
| 4-year institutions | 2,013 | 6,324 | 85,784,845 | 13,564 | 32,644,125 | 5,162 |
| 2-year institutions | 1,271 | 2,842 | 14,201,936 | 4,997 | 331,486 | 117 |
| Publicly controlled institutions | 1,481 | 6,881 | 70,837,004 | 10,294 | 6,038,051 | 877 |
| 4-year institutions | 565 | 4,266 | 57,375,678 | 13,451 | 5,887,180 | 1,380 |
| 2-year institutions | 916 | 2,616 | 13,461,326 | 5,146 | 150,871 | 58 |
| Privately controlled institutions | 1,803 | 2,285 | 29,149,777 | 12,757 | 26,937,560 | 11,789 |
| 4-year institutions | 1,448 | 2,059 | 28,409,167 | 13,799 | 26,756,944 | 12,997 |
| 2-year institutions | 355 | 226 | 740,610 | 3,275 | 180,615 | 799 |
| **1984-85** | | | | | | |
| All institutions | 3,331 | 8,952 | 114,763,986 | 12,820 | 39,916,361 | 4,459 |
| 4-year institutions | 2,025 | 6,293 | 98,417,404 | 15,640 | 39,524,453 | 6,281 |
| 2-year institutions | 1,306 | 2,659 | 16,346,582 | 6,148 | 391,908 | 147 |
| Publicly controlled institutions | 1,501 | 6,685 | 77,314,401 | 11,566 | 7,344,312 | 1,099 |
| 4-year institutions | 566 | 4,238 | 61,924,903 | 14,612 | 7,172,486 | 1,692 |
| 2-year institutions | 935 | 2,447 | 15,389,498 | 6,290 | 171,826 | 70 |
| Privately controlled institutions | 1,830 | 2,267 | 37,449,585 | 16,519 | 32,572,049 | 14,368 |
| 4-year institutions | 1,459 | 2,055 | 36,492,501 | 17,759 | 32,351,967 | 15,744 |
| 2-year institutions | 371 | 212 | 957,084 | 4,510 | 220,082 | 1,037 |

[1]Includes main and branch campuses.
[2]Total resident and extension enrollment, fall 1975 through fall 1984, expressed in terms of full-time-equivalent students.
---Data not available.

NOTE.—Because of rounding, details may not add to totals.

SOURCE: U.S. Department of Education, Center for Education Statistics, "Financial Statistics of Institutions of Higher Education" and "Fall Enrollment in Colleges and Universities" surveys. (This table was prepared November 1986.)

Table 3.14

## —Earned degrees conferred by institutions of higher education, by level of degree and sex of student: United States, 1869-70 to 1986-87

| Year | Bachelor's degrees | | | Master's degrees | | | First-professional degrees | | | Doctor's degrees | | |
|------|-------|-----|-------|-------|-----|-------|-------|-----|-------|-------|-----|-------|
| | Total | Men | Women | Total | Men | Women | Total | Men | Women | Total | Men | Women |
| 1 | 2 | 3 | 4 | 5 | 6 | 7 | 8 | 9 | 10 | 11 | 12 | 13 |
| 1869-70 | [1]9,371 | [1]7,993 | [1]1,378 | 0 | 0 | 0 | [2] | [2] | [2] | 1 | 1 | 0 |
| 1879-80 | [1]12,896 | [1]10,411 | [1]2,485 | 879 | 868 | 11 | [2] | [2] | [2] | 54 | 51 | 3 |
| 1889-90 | [1]15,539 | [1]12,857 | [1]2,682 | 1,015 | 821 | 194 | [2] | [2] | [2] | 149 | 147 | 2 |
| 1899-1900 | [1]27,410 | [1]22,173 | [1]5,237 | 1,583 | 1,280 | 303 | [2] | [2] | [2] | 382 | 359 | 23 |
| 1909-10 | [1]37,199 | [1]28,762 | [1]8,437 | 2,113 | 1,555 | 558 | [2] | [2] | [2] | 443 | 399 | 44 |
| 1919-20 | [1]48,622 | [1]31,980 | [1]16,642 | 4,279 | 2,985 | 1,294 | [2] | [2] | [2] | 615 | 522 | 93 |
| 1929-30 | [1]122,484 | [1]73,615 | [1]48,869 | 14,969 | 8,925 | 6,044 | [2] | [2] | [2] | 2,299 | 1,946 | 353 |
| 1939-40 | [1]186,500 | [1]109,546 | [1]76,954 | 26,731 | 16,508 | 10,223 | [2] | [2] | [2] | 3,290 | 2,861 | 429 |
| 1949-50 | [1]432,058 | [1]328,841 | [1]103,217 | 58,183 | 41,220 | 16,963 | [2] | [2] | [2] | 6,420 | 5,804 | 616 |
| 1959-60 | [1]392,440 | [1]254,063 | [1]138,377 | 74,435 | 50,898 | 23,537 | [2] | [2] | [2] | 9,829 | 8,801 | 1,028 |
| 1960-61 | 369,995 | 228,500 | 141,495 | 81,690 | 55,267 | 26,423 | 25,253 | 24,577 | 676 | 10,575 | 9,463 | 1,112 |
| 1961-62 | 388,680 | 234,671 | 154,009 | 88,414 | 59,710 | 28,704 | 25,607 | 24,836 | 771 | 11,622 | 10,377 | 1,245 |
| 1962-63 | 416,928 | 246,129 | 170,799 | 95,470 | 64,198 | 31,272 | 26,590 | 25,753 | 837 | 12,822 | 11,448 | 1,374 |
| 1963-64 | 466,944 | 270,319 | 196,625 | 105,551 | 70,339 | 35,212 | 27,209 | 26,357 | 852 | 14,490 | 12,955 | 1,535 |
| 1964-65 | 501,713 | 289,003 | 212,710 | 117,152 | 77,544 | 39,608 | 28,290 | 27,283 | 1,007 | 16,467 | 14,692 | 1,775 |
| 1965-66 | 520,923 | 299,871 | 221,052 | 140,548 | 93,063 | 47,485 | 30,124 | 28,982 | 1,142 | 18,237 | 16,121 | 2,116 |
| 1966-67 | 558,852 | 322,948 | 235,904 | 157,707 | 103,092 | 54,615 | 31,695 | 30,401 | 1,294 | 20,617 | 18,163 | 2,454 |
| 1967-68 | 632,758 | 358,105 | 274,653 | 176,749 | 113,519 | 63,230 | 33,939 | 32,402 | 1,537 | 23,089 | 20,183 | 2,906 |
| 1968-69 | 729,071 | 410,785 | 318,286 | 193,756 | 121,531 | 72,225 | 35,114 | 33,595 | 1,519 | 26,188 | 22,752 | 3,436 |
| 1969-70 | 792,656 | 451,380 | 341,276 | 208,291 | 125,624 | 82,667 | 34,578 | 32,794 | 1,784 | 29,866 | 25,890 | 3,976 |
| 1970-71 | 839,730 | 475,594 | 364,136 | 230,509 | 138,146 | 92,363 | 37,946 | 35,544 | 2,402 | 32,107 | 27,530 | 4,577 |
| 1971-72 | 887,273 | 500,590 | 386,683 | 251,633 | 149,550 | 102,083 | 43,411 | 40,723 | 2,688 | 33,363 | 28,090 | 5,273 |
| 1972-73 | 922,362 | 518,191 | 404,171 | 263,371 | 154,468 | 108,903 | 50,018 | 46,489 | 3,529 | 34,777 | 28,571 | 6,206 |
| 1973-74 | 945,776 | 527,313 | 418,463 | 277,033 | 157,842 | 119,191 | 53,816 | 48,530 | 5,286 | 33,816 | 27,365 | 6,451 |
| 1974-75 | 922,933 | 504,841 | 418,092 | 292,450 | 161,570 | 130,880 | 55,916 | 48,956 | 6,960 | 34,083 | 26,817 | 7,266 |
| 1975-76 | 925,746 | 504,925 | 420,821 | 311,771 | 167,248 | 144,523 | 62,649 | 52,892 | 9,757 | 34,064 | 26,267 | 7,797 |
| 1976-77 | 919,549 | 495,545 | 424,004 | 317,164 | 167,783 | 149,381 | 64,359 | 52,374 | 11,985 | 33,232 | 25,142 | 8,090 |
| 1977-78 | 921,204 | 487,347 | 433,857 | 311,620 | 161,212 | 150,408 | 66,581 | 52,270 | 14,311 | 32,131 | 23,658 | 8,473 |
| 1978-79 | 921,390 | 477,344 | 444,046 | 301,079 | 153,370 | 147,709 | 68,848 | 52,652 | 16,196 | 32,730 | 23,541 | 9,189 |
| 1979-80 | 929,417 | 473,611 | 455,806 | 298,081 | 150,749 | 147,332 | 70,131 | 52,716 | 17,415 | 32,615 | 22,943 | 9,672 |
| 1980-81 | 935,140 | 469,883 | 465,257 | 295,739 | 147,043 | 148,696 | 71,956 | 52,792 | 19,164 | 32,958 | 22,711 | 10,247 |
| 1981-82 | 952,998 | 473,364 | 479,634 | 295,546 | 145,532 | 150,014 | 72,032 | 52,223 | 19,809 | 32,707 | 22,224 | 10,483 |
| 1982-83 | 969,510 | 479,140 | 490,370 | 289,921 | 144,697 | 145,224 | 73,136 | 51,310 | 21,826 | 32,775 | 21,902 | 10,873 |
| 1983-84 | 974,309 | 482,319 | 491,990 | 284,263 | 143,595 | 140,668 | 74,407 | 51,334 | 23,073 | 33,209 | 22,064 | 11,145 |
| 1984-85 | 979,477 | 482,528 | 496,949 | 286,251 | 143,390 | 142,861 | 75,063 | 50,455 | 24,608 | 32,943 | 21,700 | 11,243 |
| 1985-86[3] | 979,000 | 483,000 | 496,000 | 285,000 | 142,000 | 143,000 | 75,400 | 50,400 | 25,000 | 32,800 | 21,200 | 11,600 |
| 1986-87[3] | 978,000 | 480,000 | 498,000 | 286,000 | 142,000 | 144,000 | 75,600 | 50,300 | 25,300 | 32,700 | 20,800 | 11,900 |

[1]Includes first-professional degrees.
[2]First-professional degrees are included with bachelor's degrees.
[3]Projected.

SOURCE: U.S. Department of Education, National Center for Education Statistics, *Earned Degrees Conferred*; and Center for Education Statistics, ''Degrees and Other Formal Awards Conferred'' surveys. (This table was prepared November 1986.)

Table 3.15

**—Full-time and part-time senior instructional staff[1] in institutions of higher education, by employment status and control and type of institution: United States, fall 1970 to fall 1986**

[In thousands]

| Year | Total | Employment status | | Control | | Type | |
|---|---|---|---|---|---|---|---|
| | | Full-time | Part-time | Public | Private | 4-year | 2-year |
| 1 | 2 | 3 | 4 | 5 | 6 | 7 | 8 |
| 1970 .......... | 474 | 369 | 104 | 314 | 160 | 382 | 92 |
| 1971[2] .......... | 492 | 379 | 113 | 333 | 159 | 387 | 105 |
| 1972 .......... | 500 | 380 | 120 | 343 | 157 | 384 | 116 |
| 1973[2] .......... | 527 | 389 | 138 | 365 | 162 | 401 | 126 |
| 1974[2] .......... | 567 | 406 | 161 | 397 | 170 | 427 | 140 |
| 1975[2] .......... | 628 | 440 | 188 | 443 | 185 | 467 | 161 |
| 1976 .......... | 633 | 434 | 199 | 450 | 183 | 467 | 166 |
| 1977 .......... | 678 | 448 | 230 | 492 | 186 | 485 | 193 |
| 1979[2] .......... | 675 | 445 | 230 | 488 | 187 | 494 | 182 |
| 1980[2] .......... | 686 | 450 | 236 | 495 | 191 | 494 | 192 |
| 1981 .......... | 705 | 461 | 244 | 509 | 196 | 493 | 212 |
| 1983 .......... | 723 | 469 | 254 | 511 | 212 | 503 | 220 |
| 1985[2] .......... | 710 | 456 | 254 | 499 | 211 | 500 | 210 |
| 1986[3] .......... | 701 | 440 | 260 | 493 | 208 | 492 | 209 |

[1]Includes faculty members with the title of professor, assistant professor, instructor, lecturer, assisting professor, adjunct professor, or interim professor (or the equivalent). Excluded are graduate students with titles such as graduate or teaching fellow who assist senior staff.

[2]Estimated on the basis of enrollment.

[3]Projected.

NOTE.—Because of rounding, details may not add to totals. Some data have been revised from previously published figures. For methodological details on estimates and projections, see *Projections of Education Statistics to 1992-93.*

SOURCE: U.S. Department of Education, National Center for Education Statistics, *Employees in Institutions of Higher Education,* various years; *Projections of Education Statistics to 1992-93,* 1985; Center for Education Statistics, unpublished projections; and U.S. Equal Employment Opportunity Commission, Higher Education Staff Information Report File, 1977, 1981, and 1983. (This table was prepared October 1986.)

Table 3.16

## —Average salary of full-time instructional faculty in institutions of higher education, by academic rank and sex: United States, 1972-73 to 1985-86

| Academic year and sex | Constant (1985-86) dollars[1] All ranks | Current dollars | | | | | | |
|---|---|---|---|---|---|---|---|---|
| | | All ranks | Professor | Associate professor | Assistant professor | Instructor | Lecturer | Undesignated or no academic rank |
| 1 | 2 | 3 | 4 | 5 | 6 | 7 | 8 | 9 |
| **1972-73** | | | | | | | | |
| Total ............... | $35,205 | $13,850 | $19,182 | $14,572 | $12,029 | $10,737 | $11,637 | $12,676 |
| Male .................. | 36,641 | 14,415 | 19,405 | 14,714 | 12,190 | 11,147 | 12,105 | 13,047 |
| Female ................ | 30,312 | 11,925 | 17,122 | 13,827 | 11,510 | 10,099 | 10,775 | 11,913 |
| **1975-76** | | | | | | | | |
| Total ............... | 32,631 | 16,634 | 22,611 | 17,026 | 13,966 | 13,682 | 12,887 | 15,201 |
| Male .................. | 34,111 | 17,388 | 22,866 | 17,167 | 14,154 | 14,440 | 13,577 | 15,764 |
| Female ................ | 28,037 | 14,292 | 20,257 | 16,336 | 13,506 | 12,580 | 11,870 | 14,098 |
| **1979-80** | | | | | | | | |
| Total ............... | 29,951 | 21,367 | 28,371 | 21,431 | 17,459 | 14,021 | 16,151 | 20,479 |
| Male .................. | 31,431 | 22,423 | 28,653 | 21,627 | 17,712 | 14,321 | 16,987 | 21,247 |
| Female ................ | 25,785 | 18,395 | 25,910 | 20,642 | 16,971 | 13,749 | 15,142 | 19,069 |
| **1980-81** | | | | | | | | |
| Total ............... | 29,278 | 23,302 | 30,753 | 23,214 | 18,901 | 15,178 | 17,301 | 22,334 |
| Male .................. | 30,782 | 24,499 | 31,082 | 23,451 | 19,227 | 15,545 | 18,281 | 23,170 |
| Female ................ | 25,124 | 19,996 | 27,959 | 22,295 | 18,302 | 14,854 | 16,168 | 20,843 |
| **1981-82** | | | | | | | | |
| Total ............... | 29,424 | 25,449 | 33,437 | 25,278 | 20,608 | 16,450 | 18,756 | 24,331 |
| Male .................. | 30,981 | 26,796 | 33,799 | 25,553 | 21,025 | 16,906 | 19,721 | 25,276 |
| Female ................ | 25,207 | 21,802 | 30,438 | 24,271 | 19,866 | 16,054 | 17,676 | 22,672 |
| **1982-83** | | | | | | | | |
| Total ............... | 30,147 | 27,196 | 35,540 | 26,921 | 22,056 | 17,601 | 20,072 | 25,557 |
| Male .................. | 31,774 | 28,664 | 35,956 | 27,262 | 22,586 | 18,160 | 21,225 | 26,541 |
| Female ................ | 25,785 | 23,261 | 32,221 | 25,738 | 21,130 | 17,102 | 18,830 | 23,855 |
| **1984-85** | | | | | | | | |
| Total ............... | 31,331 | 30,447 | 39,743 | 29,945 | 24,668 | 20,230 | 22,334 | 27,683 |
| Male .................. | 33,117 | 32,182 | 40,269 | 30,392 | 25,330 | 21,159 | 23,557 | 28,670 |
| Female ................ | 26,694 | 25,941 | 35,824 | 28,517 | 23,575 | 19,362 | 21,004 | 26,050 |
| **1985-86** | | | | | | | | |
| Total ............... | 32,392 | 32,392 | 42,268 | 31,787 | 26,277 | 20,918 | 23,770 | 29,088 |
| Male .................. | 34,294 | 34,294 | 42,833 | 32,273 | 27,094 | 21,693 | 25,238 | 30,267 |
| Female ................ | 27,576 | 27,576 | 38,252 | 30,300 | 24,966 | 20,237 | 22,273 | 27,171 |

[1]Data adjusted, using the consumer price index prepared by the Bureau of Labor Statistics, averaged on an academic year time frame.

NOTE.—Data for 1972-73 and 1975-76 are for faculty on 9- to 10-month contracts; data for 1979-80 to 1985-86 are for faculty on 9-month contracts.

SOURCE: U.S. Department of Education, National Center for Education Statistics, "Salaries, Tenure, and Fringe Benefits of Full-Time Instructional Faculty" surveys; and Center for Education Statistics, "Salaries, Tenure, and Fringe Benefits of Full-Time Instructional Faculty" surveys. (This table was prepared September 1986.)

Table 3.17

**—Total enrollment in 4-year and 2-year institutions of higher education, by control of institution: United States, fall 1963 to fall 1985**

| Year | All institutions | | | Public institutions | | | Private institutions | | |
|---|---|---|---|---|---|---|---|---|---|
| | Total | 4-year | 2-year | Total | 4-year | 2-year | Total | 4-year | 2-year |
| 1 | 2 | 3 | 4 | 5 | 6 | 7 | 8 | 9 | 10 |
| 1963[1] | 4,765,867 | 3,921,355 | 844,512 | 3,065,848 | 2,330,819 | 735,029 | 1,700,019 | 1,590,536 | 109,483 |
| 1964[1] | 5,280,020 | 4,291,094 | 988,926 | 3,467,708 | 2,592,929 | 874,779 | 1,812,312 | 1,698,165 | 114,147 |
| 1965[1] | 5,920,864 | 4,747,912 | 1,172,952 | 3,969,596 | 2,928,332 | 1,041,264 | 1,951,268 | 1,819,580 | 131,688 |
| 1966[1] | 6,389,872 | 5,063,902 | 1,325,970 | 4,348,917 | 3,159,748 | 1,189,169 | 2,040,955 | 1,904,154 | 136,801 |
| 1967[1] | 6,911,748 | 5,398,986 | 1,512,762 | 4,816,028 | 3,443,975 | 1,372,053 | 2,095,720 | 1,955,011 | 140,709 |
| 1968[1] | 7,513,091 | 5,720,795 | 1,792,296 | 5,430,652 | 3,784,178 | 1,646,474 | 2,082,439 | 1,936,617 | 145,822 |
| 1969[1] | 8,004,660 | 6,028,002 | 1,976,658 | 5,896,868 | 4,050,144 | 1,846,724 | 2,107,792 | 1,977,858 | 129,934 |
| 1970[1] | 8,580,887 | 6,357,679 | 2,223,208 | 6,428,134 | 4,326,162 | 2,101,972 | 2,152,753 | 2,031,517 | 121,236 |
| 1971[1] | 8,948,644 | 6,462,733 | 2,485,911 | 6,804,309 | 4,438,442 | 2,365,867 | 2,144,335 | 2,024,291 | 120,044 |
| 1972 | 9,214,860 | 6,458,674 | 2,756,186 | 7,070,635 | 4,429,696 | 2,640,939 | 2,144,225 | 2,028,978 | 115,247 |
| 1973 | 9,602,123 | 6,592,074 | 3,010,049 | 7,419,516 | 4,529,895 | 2,889,621 | 2,182,607 | 2,062,179 | 120,428 |
| 1974 | 10,223,729 | 6,819,735 | 3,403,994 | 7,988,500 | 4,703,018 | 3,285,482 | 2,235,229 | 2,116,717 | 118,512 |
| 1975 | 11,184,859 | 7,214,740 | 3,970,119 | 8,834,508 | 4,998,142 | 3,836,366 | 2,350,351 | 2,216,598 | 133,753 |
| 1976 | 11,012,137 | 7,128,816 | 3,883,321 | 8,653,477 | 4,901,691 | 3,751,786 | 2,358,660 | 2,227,125 | 131,535 |
| 1977 | 11,285,787 | 7,242,845 | 4,042,942 | 8,846,993 | 4,945,224 | 3,901,769 | 2,438,794 | 2,297,621 | 141,173 |
| 1978 | 11,260,092 | 7,231,951 | 4,028,141 | 8,785,893 | 4,912,203 | 3,873,690 | 2,474,199 | 2,319,748 | 154,451 |
| 1979 | 11,569,899 | 7,353,233 | 4,216,666 | 9,036,822 | 4,980,012 | 4,056,810 | 2,533,077 | 2,373,221 | 159,856 |
| 1980 | 12,096,895 | 7,570,608 | 4,526,287 | 9,457,394 | 5,128,612 | 4,328,782 | 2,639,501 | 2,441,996 | [2]197,505 |
| 1981 | 12,371,672 | 7,655,461 | 4,716,211 | 9,647,032 | 5,166,324 | 4,480,708 | 2,724,640 | 2,489,137 | [2]235,503 |
| 1982 | 12,425,780 | 7,654,074 | 4,771,706 | 9,696,087 | 5,176,434 | 4,519,653 | 2,729,693 | 2,477,640 | 252,053 |
| 1983 | 12,464,661 | 7,741,195 | 4,723,466 | 9,682,734 | 5,223,404 | 4,459,330 | 2,781,927 | 2,517,791 | 264,136 |
| 1984 | 12,241,940 | 7,711,167 | 4,530,773 | 9,477,370 | 5,198,273 | 4,279,097 | 2,764,570 | 2,512,894 | 251,676 |
| 1985 | 12,247,055 | 7,715,978 | 4,531,077 | 9,479,273 | 5,209,540 | 4,269,733 | 2,767,782 | 2,506,438 | 261,344 |

[1]Data for 2-year branch campuses of 4-year institutions are included with the 4-year institutions.

[2]Large increases are due to the addition of schools accredited by the National Association of Trade and Technical Schools in 1980 and 1981.

SOURCE: U.S. Department of Education, Center for Education Statistics, "Fall Enrollment in Colleges and Universities" surveys. (This table was prepared September 1986.)

## Table 3.18

**—Total enrollment in institutions of higher education, by attendance status, sex, and age: United States, fall 1970, 1975, 1980, and 1985**

| Characteristic | 1970 | | | 1975 | | | 1980 | | | 1985 | | |
|---|---|---|---|---|---|---|---|---|---|---|---|---|
| | Total | Full-time | Part-time | Total | Full-time | Part-time | Total | Full-time | Part-time | Total | Full-time | Part-time |
| 1 | 2 | 3 | 4 | 5 | 6 | 7 | 8 | 9 | 10 | 11 | 12 | 13 |
| **Men and women, total** | **8,581** | **5,815** | **2,766** | **11,185** | **6,841** | **4,344** | **12,097** | **7,098** | **4,999** | **12,247** | **7,075** | **5,172** |
| 14 to 17 years old | 259 | 242 | 17 | 278 | 242 | 36 | 247 | 216 | 31 | 235 | 203 | 32 |
| 18 and 19 years old | 2,600 | 2,406 | 194 | 2,786 | 2,510 | 276 | 2,901 | 2,580 | 320 | 2,600 | 2,322 | 278 |
| 20 and 21 years old | 1,880 | 1,647 | 233 | 2,243 | 1,854 | 390 | 2,423 | 2,060 | 364 | 2,383 | 1,975 | 408 |
| 22 to 24 years old | 1,457 | 881 | 576 | 1,754 | 1,008 | 746 | 1,989 | 1,174 | 815 | 1,933 | 1,227 | 705 |
| 25 to 29 years old | 1,074 | 407 | 668 | 1,774 | 692 | 1,082 | 1,871 | 610 | 1,261 | 1,953 | 695 | 1,258 |
| 30 to 34 years old | 487 | 100 | 388 | 967 | 279 | 687 | 1,243 | 264 | 979 | 1,261 | 310 | 951 |
| 35 years old and over | 823 | 134 | 689 | 1,383 | 256 | 1,127 | 1,422 | 193 | 1,229 | 1,885 | 345 | 1,540 |
| **Men, total** | **5,044** | **3,505** | **1,540** | **6,149** | **3,926** | **2,222** | **5,874** | **3,689** | **2,185** | **5,818** | **3,608** | **2,211** |
| 14 to 17 years old | 130 | 124 | 5 | 126 | 109 | 17 | 99 | 84 | 15 | 121 | 102 | 19 |
| 18 and 19 years old | 1,349 | 1,265 | 84 | 1,397 | 1,269 | 128 | 1,375 | 1,229 | 146 | 1,230 | 1,108 | 122 |
| 20 and 21 years old | 1,095 | 990 | 105 | 1,245 | 1,053 | 192 | 1,259 | 1,104 | 154 | 1,216 | 1,027 | 189 |
| 22 to 24 years old | 964 | 650 | 314 | 1,047 | 686 | 362 | 1,064 | 687 | 377 | 1,048 | 730 | 318 |
| 25 to 29 years old | 783 | 327 | 456 | 1,122 | 474 | 649 | 993 | 379 | 615 | 991 | 395 | 596 |
| 30 to 34 years old | 308 | 72 | 236 | 557 | 184 | 373 | 576 | 129 | 447 | 574 | 149 | 424 |
| 35 years old and over | 415 | 75 | 340 | 654 | 152 | 502 | 507 | 77 | 430 | 639 | 97 | 542 |
| **Women, total** | **3,537** | **2,311** | **1,225** | **5,036** | **2,915** | **2,120** | **6,223** | **3,409** | **2,814** | **6,429** | **3,468** | **2,961** |
| 14 to 17 years old | 129 | 117 | 12 | 152 | 133 | 19 | 148 | 132 | 17 | 113 | 101 | 12 |
| 18 and 19 years old | 1,250 | 1,140 | 110 | 1,389 | 1,241 | 147 | 1,526 | 1,352 | 174 | 1,370 | 1,214 | 156 |
| 20 and 21 years old | 786 | 657 | 128 | 998 | 800 | 198 | 1,165 | 955 | 209 | 1,166 | 948 | 218 |
| 22 to 24 years old | 493 | 231 | 262 | 706 | 322 | 384 | 925 | 487 | 438 | 885 | 497 | 388 |
| 25 to 29 years old | 291 | 80 | 212 | 652 | 218 | 433 | 878 | 232 | 646 | 962 | 299 | 662 |
| 30 to 34 years old | 179 | 28 | 151 | 410 | 95 | 315 | 667 | 135 | 531 | 687 | 161 | 527 |
| 35 years old and over | 409 | 59 | 349 | 729 | 105 | 625 | 914 | 115 | 799 | 1,246 | 248 | 998 |

NOTE.—Distribution by age is based on samples of civilian noninstitutional population. Because of rounding, details may not add to totals.

SOURCE: U.S. Department of Education, Center for Education Statistics, "Fall Enrollment in Colleges and Universities" surveys; and U.S. Department of Commerce, Bureau of the Census, *Current Population Reports*, "Social and Economic Characteristics of Students," various years. (This table was prepared October 1986.)

## Table 3.19

**—Total enrollment in institutions of higher education, by type and control of institution:
United States, fall 1979 to fall 1985**

| Type and control of institution | 1979 | 1980 | 1981 | 1982 | 1983 | 1984 | 1985 | Percent change, 1979 to 1985 |
|---|---|---|---|---|---|---|---|---|
| 1 | 2 | 3 | 4 | 5 | 6 | 7 | 8 | 9 |
| **All institutions** ............. | **11,569,899** | **12,096,895** | **12,371,672** | **12,425,780** | **12,464,661** | **12,241,940** | **12,247,055** | **5.85** |
| Universities ................. | 2,839,582 | 2,902,014 | 2,901,344 | 2,883,735 | 2,888,813 | 2,870,329 | 2,870,692 | 1.10 |
| Other 4-year institutions ........ | 4,513,651 | 4,668,594 | 4,754,117 | 4,770,339 | 4,852,382 | 4,840,838 | 4,845,286 | 7.35 |
| 2-year institutions ............ | 4,216,666 | 4,526,287 | 4,716,211 | 4,771,706 | 4,723,466 | 4,530,773 | 4,531,077 | 7.46 |
| Public institutions ........... | 9,036,822 | 9,457,394 | 9,647,032 | 9,696,087 | 9,682,734 | 9,477,370 | 9,479,273 | 4.90 |
| Universities ................. | 2,099,525 | 2,154,283 | 2,152,474 | 2,152,547 | 2,154,790 | 2,138,621 | 2,141,112 | 1.98 |
| Other 4-year institutions ........ | 2,880,487 | 2,974,329 | 3,013,850 | 3,023,887 | 3,068,614 | 3,059,652 | 3,068,428 | 6.52 |
| 2-year institutions ............ | 4,056,810 | 4,328,782 | 4,480,708 | 4,519,653 | 4,459,330 | 4,279,097 | 4,269,733 | 5.25 |
| Private institutions ........... | 2,533,077 | 2,639,501 | 2,724,640 | 2,729,693 | 2,781,927 | 2,764,570 | 2,767,782 | 9.27 |
| Universities ................. | 740,057 | 747,731 | 748,870 | 731,188 | 734,023 | 731,708 | 729,580 | -1.42 |
| Other 4-year institutions ........ | 1,633,164 | 1,694,265 | 1,740,267 | 1,746,452 | 1,783,768 | 1,781,186 | 1,776,858 | 8.80 |
| 2-year institutions ............ | 159,856 | 197,505 | 235,503 | 252,053 | 264,136 | 251,676 | 261,344 | [1]63.49 |

[1]Large percentage increase is due primarily to the addition of colleges accredited by the National Association of Trade and Technical Schools in 1980 and 1981.

SOURCE: U.S. Department of Education, Center for Education Statistics, "Fall Enrollment in Colleges and Universities" surveys. (This table was prepared July 1986.)

Table 3.20

# People

## V.1

# Higher Education's Man of the Year: Ernest L. Boyer

Dr. Ernest L. Boyer is President of the Carnegie Foundation for the Advancement of Teaching, Princeton, New Jersey, and Senior Fellow of the Woodrow Wilson School, Princeton University.

Before joining the Carnegie Foundation in 1980, Dr. Boyer served as the twenty–third United States Commissioner of Education, administering a $12 billion federal budget.

For seven years (1970–1977) Dr. Boyer was Chancellor of the State University of New York (SUNY).

- As head of the largest university in the United States, he directed a system of sixty-four institutions with over 350,000 students

Ernest LeRoy Boyer was born in Dayton, Ohio, where he attended public schools. He earned his Ph.D. degree at the University of Southern California (Language Disorders, Psychology).

- In 1959 Dr. Boyer was Post–Doctoral Fellow at the University of Iowa Hospital (Medical Audiology)
- In 1976 Dr. Boyer was a Visiting Fellow at Cambridge University
- And in 1984 he was named a Distinguished Fulbright Professor — traveling to India

In 1983 Dr. Boyer, in a national survey, was selected by his peers as the leading educator in the nation.

- For five consecutive years he has been listed by *U.S. News and World Report* as one of the top educators in the nation

Dr. Boyer holds honorary degrees from more than eighty United States colleges and universities.

- And in 1971 he was awarded the President's Medal from Tel Aviv University

Ernest L. Boyer's most recent book is *College: The Undergraduate Experience in America,* published by Harper & Row. A policy study on education in children's early years is underway.

Dr. Boyer taught at Loyola University (Los Angeles). In 1956 he became Academic Dean at Upland College (California). There he introduced an experimental mid-year term — the nation's first so-called 4–1–4 calendar — subsequently adopted by many other colleges.

In 1960 Dr. Boyer became Director of the Commission to Improve the Education of Teachers at the Western College Association.

In 1962 he went to the University of California, Santa Barbara as Director of the Center for Coordinated Education.

In 1965 Dr. Boyer joined the State University of New York as Executive Dean; in 1968 he was named Executive Vice Chancellor and on September 1, 1970, was appointed Chancellor. As Chancellor he

- initiated a five-year review of college presidents
- developed an experimental three-year A.B. degree program
- launched a new non-campus institution called Empire State College
- established a new rank for Distinguished Teaching Professor
- and negotiated the first undergraduate exchange program with the Soviet Union

While serving as U.S. Commissioner of Education, he emphasized excellence in education and the centrality of language.

Dr. Boyer has been named by three Presidents of the United States to National Commissions:

- The National Commission on the Financing of Postsecondary Education
- The President's Advisory Council on Women's Educational Programs

- The President's Commission on Foreign Language and International Education

Dr. Boyer served as President of the National Association of State Universities and Land–Grant Colleges from 1974 to 1975.

Dr. Boyer was also a Fellow at the Aspen Institute. He has been a member of both the Saratoga Performing Arts Center, and the Kennedy Center for the Performing Arts. Dr. Boyer currently is a member of the Council on Foreign Relations, The National Council for American Overseas Schools for the Department of State and a Trustee of several colleges including Haverford College in Pennsylvania.

Dr. Boyer is a Quaker. He is married to the former Kathryn Garis Tyson, a certified nurse-midwife. They have four children: Ernest, Jr., Beverly, Craig, and Stephen.

# Ernest Boyer: The Establishment in High Gear

The official résumé of Ernest Boyer, the 57-year-old president of the Carnegie Foundation for the Advancement of Teaching, bulges with awards, trusteeships, and honorary degrees—more than 60 of the latter by mid-1985. What it omits are such entries as his oft-repeated observations that "a rising tide of reports on educational reform is threatening to engulf us" or that "reports on reforming education won't reform education." Like many of Boyer's semi-jesting throwaway lines, these remarks provide nourishment for serious thought. So does nearly everything within Ernest Boyer's ever-expanding field of vision.

With income-producing assets worth more than $35 million (including a superb bond portfolio and substantial holdings of blue-chip common stocks), the Foundation Boyer heads is no presumptuous intruder in education's executive suites. To the degree that such characterizations count, the 80-year-old Carnegie Foundation for the Advancement of Teaching emblemizes the Establishment in American education. Consequently, whether he communicates officially or muses casually, its president almost automatically legitimizes a subject merely by addressing it. With the license to deploy the Foundation's prestige and resources nearly as he pleases, Boyer holds one of the most powerful wild cards in education's deck. He uses it wisely and effectively, whether the topic is college athletics, art as language, or the perils of top-down education reform.

Boyer has spent a generation in the public eye, and he does not inspire indifference. Former associates follow his professional odyssey with fascination—and, some will admit, naked envy. What began as a routine passage through academe as an expert on learning disorders and audiology—Boyer's doctorate from the University of Southern California in 1955 was in these areas—quickly

Source: "Shining Lights in High Places: Education's Top Four Leaders and Their Heirs," by George Kaplan. Copyright September 1985, Phi Delta Kappan Inc. Reprinted by permission.

evolved into a career in administration and educational policy. By the mid-1960s Boyer had become vice chancellor of the rapidly expanding State University of New York (SUNY) system, and in 1970 he assumed full command of the 64-institution, 350,000-student system. The precipitate expansion of SUNY finally peaked a few years later, as operating budgets began to level off or dip. After 12 years in the system, it was time for Boyer to move on. The SUNY network today is one of the nation's best, albeit grossly underappreciated, state systems of higher education.

Boyer's service as U.S. Commissioner of Education (1977–79) in the Carter Administration thrust him between a rock and a hard place. His boss, Joseph Califano, Jr., the hard-driving, turf-guarding Secretary of Health, Education, and Welfare, seldom encouraged the independence of his subordinates—a role to which Boyer was not accustomed in any case—and the capital's interest in education had come to focus almost exclusively on the wrenching but digressive debate over the creation of a Cabinet-level Department of Education.

But Boyer did not squander his time in Washington. Although he did not ingratiate himself with the permanent staff of the U.S. Office of Education, he competently administered the largest federal education budget to that point in history. More significantly, perhaps, his ceaseless push for a blend of equity, access, and quality anticipated today's well-advertised search for excellence—no small achievement in an Administration that sometimes seemed to consider "quality" a reactionary cuss word. For the first time, too, everything he said, wrote, or did bore the label, "Made in Washington." In the pre-Reagan era, this carried some weight.

Free from the billion-dollar budgetary headaches and fragile legislative egos that trouble the sleep of public office-holders, Boyer has, since 1983, directed his formidable talents of analysis and persuasion to the Great School Debate. A key substantive

ERNEST L. BOYER

contributor to that debate through *High School*— one of the stronger entries in "the rising tide of reform reports"—he is an awesomely articulate, if constantly questioning, advocate of the main premises of the reform movement. He remains critical of its lack of focus on issues of equity and laments the continuing absence of a shared agenda for schools and colleges—a long-time concern of his organization. Whether the drive for excellence will succeed will depend, Boyer contends, on the readiness of educators to step forward to provide the necessary post-legislative momentum to extend renewal beyond regulation into the transitional phase that began a year or so ago. But he is not certain that our "institutional junkies," a self-explanatory Boyer-coined phrase, possess the compassion and flexibility to carry it off.

Boyer continually tries to explain the immense complexity of the links between the schools and society. A legendary brain-picker and quick reader whose work week customarily extends to 80 or 90 hours, he seldom dwells on the classics or on intellectual history. This could have been perceived as a shortcoming, but it may ultimately be a virtue, for it liberates Boyer from uncritical dependence on overworked disciplines that may have passed their prime as the sole guiding principles of schooling in a democracy.

Though he has a reputation as a scrapper, Boyer is cautious, both by Quaker preference and as the custodian of the Carnegie legacy in education. Only rarely does he lead the crowd into an issue. When he moves, a half step behind some of his peers, it is in measured paces rather than flying leaps. He sees no particular virtue in perching indefinitely on the cutting edge of any topic. But when public interest in a theme develops, no one in U.S. education deals more masterfully with the communications media or imparts a more human brand of legitimacy to the "new" topic. Ernest Boyer's sense of an issue's ripeness is rare in education.

As the quest for quality proceeds from the legislative halls to the classrooms, Boyer urges reformers to heed the signals of the new age in which we are already living. Such shifting social patterns as single-parent families, two wage-earning parents, and the need for child care in the workplace are altering school/family relations. Evidence is also accumulating that some degree of intervention in the early years may be important to the education of at least some children. Like it or not, these forces, along with those stemming from research on brain theory and the definition of intelligence, may subtly transform the schools.

At the same time, educators must reckon with the images of the world that television conveys to children of all ages. Boyer senses that children are "becoming too smart too young." Schools must also come to terms with a culture of self-learning in which instruction by teachers lacking formal credentials may combine, perhaps awkwardly, with classroom learning to educate our children. At the other end of the chronological learning spectrum, Boyer is convinced that adult and lifelong learning will become major social and cultural features of American education and that we shortchange global interdependence at our peril.

These trends will dictate the development of new combinations of specialized and interdisciplinary learning. Indeed, notes Boyer, it may even be time to move beyond the historic "Carnegie unit" toward new measures of interdisciplinary achievement. This is a courageous stand for the keeper of the Carnegie flame, but no more so than his crusade against the public address system, "this Orwellian interruption," in our schools.

V.3

# New College and University Presidents

## 1986–87

| | | | |
|---|---|---|---|
| UNIVERSITY OF ALABAMA AT BIRMINGHAM | Charles A. McCallum | BOROUGH OF MANHATTAN COMMUNITY COLLEGE | Augusta Souza Kappner |
| UNIVERSITY OF ALASKA AT JUNEAU | Marshall L. Lind (Chancellor) | BRIARCLIFF COLLEGE | Sr. Margaret Wick |
| AMARILLO COLLEGE | George Miller | UNIVERSITY OF BRIDGEPORT | Janet D. Greenwood |
| ANTELOPE VALLEY COLLEGE | Allan W. Kurki | BRIDGEWATER STATE COLLEGE | Gerard T. Indelicato |
| AQUINAS JUNIOR COLLEGE | Dorothy Mulcahy Oppenheim | BROWARD COMMUNITY COLLEGE | Willis N. Holcombe |
| ARTHUR D. LITTLE MANAGEMENT EDUCATION INSTITUTE | Frank G. Feeley | BURLINGTON COUNTY COLLEGE | Robert Messina |
| ASPEN INSTITUTE FOR HUMANISTIC STUDIES | Colin W. Williams | UNIVERSITY OF CALIFORNIA AT DAVIS | Theodore L. Hullar (Chancellor) |
| AUGUSTA COLLEGE (GEORGIA) | Richard S. Wallace | UNIVERSITY OF CALIFORNIA AT RIVERSIDE | Rosemary S. J. Schraer |
| AUGUSTANA COLLEGE | Lloyd Svendsbye | | |
| BANGOR THEOLOGICAL SEMINARY | Malcolm L. Warford | UNIVERSITY OF CALIFORNIA AT SANTA BARBARA | Barbara S. Uehling |
| BELMONT TECHNICAL COLLEGE (OHIO) | Steve Maradian | UNIVERSITY OF CALIFORNIA AT SANTA CRUZ | Robert B. Stevens |
| BENNETT COLLEGE (NORTH CAROLINA) | Gloria Dean Randle Scott | CAMDEN COMMUNITY COLLEGE | Robert W. Ramsey |
| BENNINGTON COLLEGE | Elizabeth Coleman | | |
| BLOOMFIELD COLLEGE | John F. Noonan | CAMPION COLLEGE | Rev. Joseph Schner |
| | | CARLETON COLLEGE | Stephen R. Lewis |

| | | | |
|---|---|---|---|
| CASE WESTERN RESERVE UNIVERSITY | Agnar Pytte | DARTMOUTH COLLEGE | James O. Freedman |
| | | DEANE COLLEGE | Fred Brown |
| CANUGA COUNTY COMMUNITY COLLEGE | Lawrence H. Poole | UNIVERSITY OF DELAWARE | Russel C. Jones |
| CENTRAL ARIZONA COLLEGE | Kathleen F. Arns | DELAWARE VALLEY COLLEGE | William H. Rorer III |
| CENTRAL CONNECTICUT STATE UNIVERSITY | John W. Shumaker | DeVRY INSTITUTE OF TECHNOLOGY | E. Arthur Stunard |
| CENTRAL PIEDMONT COMMUNITY COLLEGE | Ruth G. Shaw | DIVINE WORD COLLEGE | Rev. Joseph Simon |
| | | DIXIE COLLEGE | Douglas Alder |
| CHADRON STATE COLLEGE | Samuel H. Rankin, Jr. | DYERSBURG STATE COMMUNITY COLLEGE | Karen Bowyer |
| CHRISTIAN THEOLOGICAL SEMINARY (INDIANA) | Richard D. N. Dickinson | EAST CAROLINA UNIVERSITY | Ralph Eakin |
| | | EASTERN MENNONITE COLLEGE | Joseph L. Lapp |
| CHRISTOPHER NEWPORT COLLEGE | Anthony Santoro | EASTERN WASHINGTON UNIVERSITY | Alexander F. Schilt |
| CLARK TECHNICAL COLLEGE | Albert A. Salerno | EASTFIELD COLLEGE | Dan Sundermann |
| CLEARWATER CHRISTIAN COLLEGE | George Youstra | EAST TEXAS STATE UNIVERSITY | Jerry Morris |
| COLORADO COMMUNITY COLLEGE | Jerome F. Wartgow | EL CENTRO COLLEGE | Wright L. Lassiter |
| | | ELMIRA COLLEGE | Thomas K. Meier |
| UNIVERSITY OF COLORADO AT BOULDER | James Corbridge (Chancellor) | UNIVERSITY OF EVANSVILLE | Wallace B. Graves (Chancellor) |
| | | FELICIAN COLLEGE | Sr. M. Charlene Endecavage |
| COLUMBIA THEOLOGICAL COLLEGE (GEORGIA) | Douglas W. Oldenburg | FERRUM COLLEGE | Jerry M. Boone |
| | | FLORIDA INSTITUTE OF TECHNOLOGY | Donald D. Glower |
| CORNISH COLLEGE OF THE ARTS | Robert N. Funk | FLORIDA INTERNATIONAL UNIVERSITY | Modesto Maidique |
| DALLAS THEOLOGICAL SEMINARY | Donald K. Campbell | | |
| | | FORT WAYNE BIBLE COLLEGE | Donald D. Gerig |
| DANVILLE COMMUNITY COLLEGE | Arnold R. Oliver | FRANKLIN UNIVERSITY (OHIO) | Paul J. Otte |

| | | | |
|---|---|---|---|
| FRESNO CITY COLLEGE | Ernest R. Leach | LAKE ERIE COLLEGE | Clodius R. Smith |
| GANNON UNIVERSITY | Joseph R. Scottino | LEE COLLEGE (TEXAS) | Vivian Bowling Blevins |
| GARRETT COMMUNITY COLLEGE | Stephen Herman | LEE COLLEGE | Charles P. Conn |
| UNIVERSITY OF GEORGIA | Charles B. Knapp | UNIVERSITY OF LETHBRIDGE | Howard Tennant |
| GLENDALE COMMUNITY COLLEGE | John A. Davitt | LEXINGTON THEOLOGICAL SEMINARY | Daniel Cobb |
| GOLDEN GATE BAPTIST THEOLOGICAL SEMINARY | Rev. William O. Crews | LINCOLN UNIVERSITY (PENNSYLVANIA) | Niara Sudarkasa |
| GREATER NEW HAVEN STATE TECHNICAL COLLEGE | George D. Harris | LONG ISLAND CAMPUS OF BERKELEY SCHOOLS | Thomas L. Heaton |
| | | LORAIN COUNTY COMMUNITY COLLEGE | Roy A. Church |
| HAHNEMANN UNIVERSITY | Iqbal F. Paroc | LOUISIANA TECHNICAL UNIVERSITY | Don Reneau |
| HAMPDEN SYDNEY COLLEGE | James R. Leutze | MACMURRAY COLLEGE (ILLINOIS) | Edward J. Mitchell |
| HANOVER COLLEGE | Russell L. Nichols | | |
| BERKIMER COMMUNITY COLLEGE | Ronald F. Williams | UNIVERSITY OF MAINE AT FORT KENT | Barbara Leondar |
| HOPE COLLEGE | John H. Jacobson, Jr. | UNIVERSITY OF MAINE | Robert L. Woodbury (Chancellor) |
| UNIVERSITY OF HOUSTON SYSTEM | Wilbur L. Meier, Jr. | MANHATTAN CAMPUS OF BERKELEY SCHOOLS | John E. Clow |
| UNIVERSITY OF HOUSTON AT VICTORIA | Glenn A. Goerke | MANHATTAN COLLEGE | Br. Thomas J. Scanlan |
| COLLEGE OF IDAHO | Robert L. Hendren, Jr. | MARIAN COLLEGE | Edward L. Henry |
| INDIANA UNIVERSITY | Thomas Ehrlich | MARYCREST COLLEGE | Wanda Durrett Bigharm |
| KENNEDY-KING COLLEGE OF THE CITY COLLEGES OF CHICAGO | Harold Pates | MARY HOLMES COLLEGE | Alvin F. Anderson |
| UNIVERSITY OF KING'S COLLEGE | Marion Fry | MARYLAND TECHNICAL COLLEGE | Virginia Foxx |
| COLLEGE OF LAKE COUNTY | Daniel J. Lavista | MARYVILLE COLLEGE | Richard I. Ferrin |

| | |
|---|---|
| MASSACHUSETTS COLLEGE OF PHARMACY | Louis P. Jeffrey |
| MCNEESE STATE UNIVERSITY | Robert D. Hebert |
| MIDDLESEX COUNTY COMMUNITY COLLEGE | Flora Mancuso Edwards |
| MINNESOTA STATE UNIVERSITY SYSTEM | Robert Carothers (Chancellor) |
| UNIVERSITY OF MONTANA | James V. Koch |
| MOODY BIBLE INSTITUTE | Joseph Stowell |
| MORAVIAN COLLEGE | Roger Harry Martin |
| MOREHEAD STATE UNIVERSITY (KENTUCKY) | C. Nelson Grote |
| MOTLOW STATE COMMUNITY COLLEGE | A. Frank Glass |
| MOUNT ALLISON UNIVERSITY | Don Wells |
| MOUNT ST. CLARE COLLEGE | Rev. Charles E. Lang |
| COLLEGE OF MOUNT ST. JOSEPH | Sr. Frances M. Thrallkill |
| UNIVERSITY OF NEVADA SYSTEM | Mark H. Dawson (Chancellor) |
| NORTHEAST IOWA TECHNICAL INSTITUTE | Ron Hutkin |
| NORTHEASTERN ILLINOIS UNIVERSITY | Gordon H. Lamb |
| NORTHERN ILLINOIS UNIVERSITY | John E. LaTourette |
| NORTH IDAHO COLLEGE | Carl R. Bennett |
| NORTH PARK COLLEGE & THEOLOGICAL SEMINARY | David G. Horner |
| NORTHWESTERN MICHIGAN COLLEGE | Phillip E. Runkel |
| NORTHWESTERN STATE UNIVERSITY (LOUISIANA) | Robert A. Alost |
| NORWALK STATE TECHNICAL COLLEGE | John K. Fisher |
| UNIVERSITY OF NOTRE DAME | Edward A. Malloy |
| NOTRE DAME SEMINARY | Rev. Gregory M. Aymond |
| ORANGE COUNTY COMMUNITY COLLEGE | William F. Messner |
| UNIVERSITY OF THE PACIFIC | Bill L. Atchley |
| PORTLAND STATE UNIVERSITY | Natale A. Sicuro |
| POST COLLEGE (CONNECTICUT) | N. Patrick Yarborough |
| PRATT COMMUNITY COLLEGE | Thomas C. Henry |
| QUINNIPINC COLLEGE | John L. Lahey |
| RANDOLPH-MACON WOMEN'S COLLEGE | Linda Koch Lorimer |
| RED ROCKS COMMUNITY COLLEGE | Thomas K. Thomas |
| REFORMED BIBLE COLLEGE | Edwin D. Roels |
| UNIVERSITY OF RICHMOND | Samuel A. Banks |
| ROCKY MOUNT COLLEGE | Arthur H. DeRosser |
| ROCKY MOUNTAIN COLLEGE | James J. R. Ritterskamp, Jr. |
| SACRED HEART UNIVERSITY | Robert A. Preston |
| COLLEGE OF ST. BENEDICT | Sr. Colman D. Connell |

| | | | |
|---|---|---|---|
| ST. CHARLES COUNTY COMMUNITY COLLEGE | Donald D. Shook | STATE UNIVERSITY OF NEW YORK AGRICULTURAL AND TECHNICAL COLLEGE AT ALFRED | John O. Hunter |
| ST. LAWRENCE UNIVERSITY | Patti McGill Peterson | STATE UNIVERSITY OF NEW YORK AT WESTBURY | Eudora Pettigrew |
| ST. LOUIS UNIVERSITY | Rev. Lawrence Biondi | | |
| ST. LEO COLLEGE | Rev. Monsignor Frank M. Mouch | SUMTER AREA TECHNICAL COLLEGE | Herbert C. Robbins |
| ST. MARY'S COLLEGE (MISSOURI) | Patricia C. Hahn | TENNESSEE STATE UNIVERSITY | Otis Floyd |
| ST. MARY'S COLLEGE (NORTH CAROLINA) | Clauston L. Jenkins | TENNESSEE TECHNICAL UNIVERSITY | Angelo A. Volpe |
| ST. PAUL'S COLLEGE (VIRGINIA) | Marvin B. Scott | UNIVERSITY OF TENNESSEE AT MARTIN | Margaret N. Perry |
| ST. THOMAS UNIVERSITY (FLORIDA) | Rev. Patrick H. O'Neill | TEXAS A&M UNIVERSITY | Perry L. Adkisson (Chancellor) |
| SAN BARNARDINO VALLEY COLLEGE | Manuel G. Rivera | UNIVERSITY OF TEXAS HEALTH SCIENCES CENTER AT DALLAS | Kern Wildenthal |
| SAUK VALLEY COMMUNITY COLLEGE | Richard L. Behrendt | | |
| SETON HALL COLLEGE | JoAnn Boyle | TEXAS WOMEN'S UNIVERSITY | Shirley Sears Chater |
| SKIDMORE COLLEGE | David H. Porter | THAMES VALLEY STATE TECHNICAL COLLEGE | Eileen Baccus Mitchell |
| SKYLINE COLLEGE | Linda Graef Salter | | |
| SOUTH CENTRAL COMMUNITY COLLEGE (CONNECTICUT) | Antonio Perez | THOMAS COLLEGE (MAINE) | Cyril M. Joly, Jr. |
| | | THOMAS MORE COLLEGE | Charles J. Bensman |
| SOUTHEASTERN LOUISIANA UNIVERSITY | G. Warren Smith | THOMAS NELSON COMMUNITY COLLEGE | Robert G. Templin, Jr. |
| SOUTHERN OREGON STATE COLLEGE | Joseph Cox | TOMPKINS CORTLAND COMMUNITY COLLEGE | Eduardo J. Marti |
| SOUTHWEST STATE UNIVERSITY (MINNESOTA) | Douglas M. Treadway | | |
| STATE COLLEGES AND UNIVERSITIES OF LOUISIANA | J. Larry Crain | TRENT UNIVERSITY | John Stubbs |
| | | TRENTON JUNIOR COLLEGE | Donald Gatzke |

| | |
|---|---|
| TROY STATE UNIVERSITY AT DOTHAN | Thomas E. Harrison |
| TRUCKEE MEADOWS COMMUNITY COLLEGE | John W. Gwaltney |
| U.S. NAVAL ACADEMY | Ronald F. Marryott (Superintendent) |
| UNITED THEOLOGICAL SEMINARY OF THE TWIN CITIES | Rev. Benjamin Griffin |
| UPSALA COLLEGE | David E. Schramm |
| URSULINE COLLEGE | Sr. Anne M. Diederich |
| WARREN WILSON COLLEGE | John J. Carey |
| WENATCHEE VALLEY COLLEGE | Arnie Heuchert |
| WESTERN NEW MEXICO UNIVERSITY | Rudolph Gomez |
| WESTFIELD STATE COLLEGE | Irving H. Buchen |
| WESTMINSTER COLLEGE (PENNSYLVANIA) | Oscar E. Remick |
| WESTMORELAND COUNTY COMMUNITY COLLEGE | Daniel C. Krezenski |
| WEST OAHU COLLEGE OF THE UNIVERSITY OF HAWAII | Edward J. Kormondy |
| WEST VIRGINIA BOARD OF REGENTS | Thomas W. Cole, Jr. (Chancellor) |
| WEST VIRGINIA INSTITUTE OF TECHNOLOGY | Robert C. Gillespie |
| WEST VIRGINIA WESLEYAN COLLEGE | Thomas B. Courtice |
| WILEY COLLEGE | Earl W. Rand |
| WILLMAR COMMUNITY COLLEGE | Harold G. Conradi |
| UNIVERSITY OF WISCONSIN SYSTEM | Stephen R. Portch (Chancellor) |
| UNIVERSITY OF WISCONSIN AT GREEN BAY | David I. Outcalt |
| WOOD JUNIOR COLLEGE | Sale D. Randle |
| WRIGHT COLLEGE OF THE CITY COLLEGES OF CHICAGO | Raymond F. LeFevour |
| UNIVERSITY OF WYOMING | Terry P. Roar |

# Speeches and Documents

# Address by William J. Bennett, United States Secretary of Education

## *at Harvard University, Cambridge, Massachusetts, on October 10, 1986*

During the Roman Saturnalia even slaves could speak freely. On the occasion of Harvard College's 350th anniversary, let me invoke ancient custom and ask that, I, a public servant, be permitted to speak freely. And so I shall speak about the condition, as I see it, of American higher education today. I am not confident that this condition is an entirely healthy one.

It gives me no pleasure to say this. I spent the majority of my adult years on college and university campuses, and my memories of those years are fine ones. Even now it is a special pleasure to get back onto college campuses, and talk to students and professors, and browse in the bookstores, and remind myself of all the reasons these institutions should be worthy of allegiance and esteem. And so I'm glad to be here, at Harvard, today, to help the college celebrate its 350th birthday.

I'm glad not simply because Harvard is a representative institution of American higher education. I'm personally glad to be back. I spent three very interesting years here, and it's good to return. I say this not out of excessive sentimentality about Harvard. In fact, I received some publicity for a comment I made soon after becoming Secretary of Education, that it is possible to live a fulfilled life without a Harvard degree. Well, it is. But it's also possible to live a fulfilled life with one. In any case, a fulfilled life depends on many things; an education is only one of them.

I want to discuss today the question of the extent to which our colleges and universities in general contribute seriously to the fulfillment, to the betterment, of the lives of their students, of the young men and women given over to their charge. I have been concerned with this question since I myself was an undergraduate and then a graduate student; but perhaps not so intensely until I arrived at Harvard in 1968. I came as a law student, and became also a proctor in Matthews, and a tutor in Social Studies. I had a good time, and learned some things and treasure some memories.

Let me mention one set of memories in particular. My job as a freshman proctor was far and away the best part of my years here. I had a good time doing it, I made some fast friends, I learned a great deal, and I think I was able to be of some actual help to those whose well–being was my direct and ongoing responsibility. Every year, from the photographs and records that were available, I memorized my freshmen before they arrived, so that I could greet them by name and be somewhat familiar with their interests and talents. I made it a point not to conform to the pretentious practice of keeping proctor's office hours — mere graduate or law students acting like full professors; my freshmen were always welcome in my room, and they made use of this welcome. We spent a lot of time together, at parties, at our own softball and football games, and in serious and considerably less than serious discussion. To some of them, I'm proud to say, I occasionally gave a hard time; I was tough on drugs, and I would not sign course–change cards if I thought a student was going after gut courses or otherwise undercutting his academic opportunities.

Proctoring was the highlight of my experience at Harvard, though I enjoyed the tutoring as well, and law school was at least interesting. But out of these various Harvard experiences, and especially from the intense experience and illuminating vantage point of a proctor, I formed some notions both about this university and about American higher education in general. My subsequent experiences at other colleges and universities have served to strengthen these notions into convictions.

One of my fundamental convictions is this: There is an extraordinary gap between the rhetoric and the reality of American higher education. The gap is so wide, in fact, that we face the real possibility — not today, perhaps not tomorrow, but someday — of an erosion of public support for the enterprise.

The rhetoric of contemporary American higher education, the terms in which its practitioners and advocates speak of it, is often exceedingly pious, self–congratulatory, and suffused with the aura of moral superiority. The spokesmen for higher education tend to invoke the mission of the university as if they were reciting the Nicene Creed: one, holy, universal, and apostolic church. To be sure, being modern and sophisticated, they also know the rhetorical uses of a little well–placed deprecation, and they can speak winningly of the need for constant self–inspection and self–improvement. But try, as I have tried, to criticize American higher education by the one yardstick that matters—namely, the relative success or failure of our colleges and universities at discharging the educational responsibilities that they bear. From the reaction, you would think I had hurled a rock through the stained–glass window of a cathedral. The response to my criticism was not "Prove it," or "You're wrong for the following reasons"; it was more like "How dare you"—"Who do you think you are?" Well, I know who I am, having been a student at three colleges and universities, and a teacher at six. I know who I am, but does the university know what it is? The university claims to educate, to improve the minds—even the hearts—of young men and women. Sometimes it does this, to be sure—but not as often, and not as wholeheartedly and as purposefully and as successfully as it should.

Let's take Harvard as an example. Considering the vast sums that parents pay for the privilege of sending their children to a college like Harvard, it may seem gauche and impertinent to ask whether the sacrifice is matched by the value of the education received in exchange. But the question is nevertheless worth asking, for the fact is that neither those fees themselves, nor a $3.1 billion endowment, nor a library system staggering in its holdings, nor research laboratories and scientific facilities that are the envy of the world, nor well–furnished centers for the study of domestic and international affairs, nor first–class museums and theaters, nor a faculty justly renowned for its scholarship and intellectual brilliance, nor even, for that matter, a brainy and resourceful student body—the fact is that none of these things is evidence that Harvard or any similarly situated university is really fulfilling its obligation *to its own students* of seeing to it that when they leave after four years, they leave as educated men and women.

That Harvard is a place where one *can* get a good education, no one can doubt. The reason has largely to do with the presence here on one campus of all those resources I've just enumerated, and especially the final two items on the list: the bright young men and women whom the college attracts as students, and the gifted scholars with whom they are placed

in proximity. From such a combination of active elements, exciting things will occur. It's a good bet. But it does not occur in other cases—and I would fault Harvard and other universities for this: there's not that much effort to see to it, systematically and devotedly, that real education occurs. Under the justification of deferring to individual decisions and choices, much is left to chance. Sometimes a proctor, a professor, a dean, steps in and takes a real interest in a student's education—but that's often the luck of the draw.

Our students deserve better. They deserve a university's real and sustained attention to their intellectual and their moral well–being. And they deserve a good general education—at a minimum, a systematic familiarization with our own Western tradition of learning, with the classical and Jewish–Christian heritage, the facts of American and European history, the political organization of Western societies, the great works of Western art and literature, the major achievements of the scientific disciplines—in short, the basic body of knowledge which universities once took it upon themselves as their obligation to transmit, under the name of a liberal education, from ages past to ages present and future.

As the distinguished historian James H. Billington has remarked, American universities have as a rule given up on this once central task—with the result that not only do students now tend to lack a knowledge of their own tradition, they often have no standpoint from which to appreciate any other tradition, or even to *have* a sense of tradition. Billington characterizes the typical undergraduate curriculum of today as a "smorgasbord." If this Scandinavian metaphor betrays too Western a bias, I would propose instead the metaphor of an old–style Chinese menu, the kind that used to adorn the Hong Kong restaurant on Mass Ave, where a customer could pick at leisure from Column A and Column B. Whatever may be said of this as a meal, it is not a model for a college curriculum.

But, one might respond, here at Harvard, we have the Core Curriculum. Well, I could respond in turn, do you? You have a symbolic nod, a head feint, in the direction of a core curriculum. I have studied the Harvard catalog, and I agree that under the heading of the Core Curriculum we find an agglomeration of courses, many of them obviously meaty and important, taught by eminent scholars, on a wide variety of subjects. But it seems to me that many of them could more appropriately find their place among the individual offerings of the various departments of instruction, from where, indeed, they give every appearance of having been plucked, only to be regrouped in new combinations. In what sense, however, do these courses constitute a *core*—i.e., the central, foundational part of a liberal education? Some of the courses are real core courses—and my sense is that in fact students, to their credit, often flock to such classes. But they do not constitute a true curriculum. I think students would benefit from a real core curriculum—i.e., a *set* of fundamental courses, ordered, purposive, coherent. I cannot discern such a core curriculum here.

Now despite this, many Harvard students get an education—or at least they learn a lot. And of course there is a limit to what any curriculum can accomplish. But if Harvard were more intentional about it, more committed to ensuring that its undergraduates received an education commensurate with the promise held out by the Core Curriculum, it would be doing even better by its students, and it would set a clearer example for all the institutions that look to it. There are too many intellectual and educational casualties among the student body of Harvard. Of course there would be some under any plan; but there are more than there have to be, and that's because luck, serendipity, chance, peer pressure, and a kind of institutional negligence—often a very high-minded negligence—are not the best guarantors of a general education. Some people don't get educated here—too many for the greatest university in the country. If we say to parents and taxpayers and donors when we take their money—often large amounts of it—that we'll educate their sons and daughters—let's do so. Let's do what we promise.

After all, American colleges and universities are quick to proclaim their duty to address all sorts of things that are wrong in the world, to speak truth to power, to discourse on the most complex social and moral issues beyond their walls, and to instruct political and business and religious leaders on the proper path to follow. But they have a prior duty, which is to see to the education of the young people in their charge. They ought to be expected to take a proctor's interest in that education—this is, after all, what they are paid for. Some do—perhaps especially the smaller, less famous, institutions. But too often our institutions—especially our most prestigious institutions—fail in the discharge of their educational responsibilities. And they ought to be held to account for this—not just by parents and trustees and donors and taxpayers, but above all by students.

I was interested to read in *The Chronicle of Higher Education* of a recent comprehensive survey of undergraduates that found the following: two fifths reported that *no* professor at their institution took a "special personal interest" in their academic prog-

ress; and fewer than one fifth rated their institution's academic advisory programs "highly adequate," while nearly three of five rated them merely "adequate" or worse. Students should not accept this state of affairs as inevitable, or pre-ordained; I think that demanding greater guidance, a more serious assumption of responsibility by their institutions, is a worthy cause for student activism. Commencement exercises at Harvard College used to conclude—perhaps they still do—with the president's welcoming the new graduates into the company of educated men and women. If students feel that their years at Harvard are failing to prepare them adequately for membership in that privileged company, they should let Harvard know.

Let me add that Harvard would, I think, be prepared to listen. One approach that may help foster quality and focus and purpose in undergraduate education goes by the name of assessment—that is, assessing what students actually learn. I suggest, near the beginning of my tenure as Secretary of Education, that more attention to this issue might be desirable. At the time many in higher education refused even to consider it. But I do want to pay tribute to your President, my former crackerjack labor law teacher, Mr. Bok. He thinks the question of quality and assessing quality is important, as he said in his last annual report, and he's beginning to do something about it, with a faculty seminar, among other things, here at Harvard. Good for him. That's leadership. I hope others will follow—and we in the Department of Education stand ready to help.

Students should make other demands of colleges and universities as well. William James said the purpose of a college education is to help you to know a good man when you see him. (We can add "and a good woman.") He said a college education's best claim is that it helps you to value what deserves to be valued: "The only rational ground for pre-eminent admiration of any single college," James said, speaking of Harvard, "would be its pre-eminent spiritual tone." And James warned that all too often, "to be a college man, even a Harvard man, affords no sure guarantee for anything but a more educated cleverness in the service of popular idols and vulgar ends."

Notice that James is talking about both intellectual and moral discernment. What of moral discernment in particular? Most of our colleges would not dream of claiming to offer a moral education to their students, to their charges. Most do not seek to improve the individual moral sense of their students—much less their faculty. But there is no shortage of moralizing and moral posturing—especially the kind that does not cost anything of the individual, that does not take time or self–denial or effort. Chekhov wrote, "You can't become a saint through other people's sins," but many seem to think that's just how you do it. I remember some teachers and tutors in the 1970s who were at a fever pitch over international justice and the welfare of others in general, but in particular they did not want to give much time to those on their own campus whom they were charged to help. The advantage of a concern for justice in general, for justice somewhere else, is that it takes less time than pursuing justice in particular, and it has the added benefit of not interfering with meals, socializing, and other engagements.

Now where are many of our colleges and universities on the issues of their responsibility to protect their students and their obligation to foster moral discernment in their students? With the exception of a relatively few places — mostly religious or military institutions, I gather — higher education is silent. Many colleges freely dispense guidance to those beyond their walls, and such guidance is to be welcomed in a free society; but colleges that aim, as they might put it, to "lead" society's conscience on various social problems should not, when faced by a real problem within their competence to deal with, duck or throw up their hands. When it comes to drugs on campus, too many college presidents say, well, that's a society–wide problem — there's little we can do about it. This unaccustomed modesty from higher education is puzzling. I think moral responsibility begins at home. To be interested — intensely interested — in broader issues is fine, but to neglect one's basic responsibilities is not. It is true that dealing with the drug problem requires a more sustained effort than signing a petition or mounting a demonstration; it requires individual and institutional time and long–term commitment. These have not been very forthcoming on very many of our campuses.

Earlier on, I compared the modern university with the old church. Although I am known, generally and correctly, as a friend of religion, let me say this: the self–righteousness that has given so many religious institutions and spokesmen a bad name has found an even more secure and hospitable home in the modern university. Even more, because in the old churches most divines did not forget that the first injunction was, heal thyself; they knew they had to attend to their own souls, and then those of their parishioners, before preaching to the outside world. The residents of the modern university all too often take it upon themselves to preach, without even a cursory acknowledgment that they should first attend to healing themselves.

There is another analogy that can be drawn be-tween the contemporary university and the old church. The old church fell into some disrepute because its exhortations to poverty and holiness were too often belied by the worldliness and sumptuousness of its clerics. Similarly, American higher education simply refuses to acknowledge the obvious fact that, in general, it is rich. Whether this refusal is due to calculation or self–deception, I do not know, but in all the debates over student aid and federal tax policy, somehow this basic fact has been neglected. Now reasonable people can differ over student aid or tax policies — but these differences should be based on facts. And the fact is that the American people have been very generous to higher education in this country.

From higher education's publicity you would think that hosts of institutions are on the brink of collapse, others near the abyss, but this is not so. The number of institutions of higher education in the United States has increased from 1,852 in 1950 to 2,230 in 1965 to 3,231 in 1980 to 3,331 today. The number of public institutions continues to increase; the number of private institutions continues to increase. This is fine — but let's not pretend this is a shrinking enterprise, in a perilous state.

And let's not pretend the wealth of this increasing number of institutions is shrinking, either. Gross national spending on higher education in this nation has gone, in constant 1985–1986 dollars from $12 billion in 1950 to $53 billion in 1965 to over $100 billion today. The wealth — the endowments — of our institutions of higher education have also continued to increase — especially in the past few years. In fact, the Reagan–era stock market may be the best thing to have happened in a long while to American higher education.

But to say this is to adopt a false criterion of well–being for our institutions of higher education, a criterion their spokesmen too often adopt. It is to mistake a means for an end. Now I work in Washington, and I see higher education much of the time through its representatives there. Of those representatives I would say this: I have never seen a greater interest in *money* — money, cash, bucks — among anybody. The higher education lobbyists put Harvard Square hawkers to shame. They are, admittedly, very good at getting their funds from a Congress seemingly enraptured by the pieties, pontifications, and poor-mouthings of American higher education. But very few words can be heard from any of these representatives about other aspects of higher education — issues like purpose, quality, curriculum, the moral authority and responsibilities of universities; most of the time, all we hear from them are pleas for money, for more money.

For example, just the other week, the American Council on Education appointed a thirty–three–member national "Commission on National Challenges in Higher Education"; the purpose was to provide "a new, exciting agenda" for American higher education. But this agenda is limited in an interesting way: the commission will *not* deal with such issues as what should be taught or what students are learning. Rather, the president of the ACE said, "We will be looking at such questions as 'What does higher education mean . . . to the people who fund us?' and 'What are their responsibilities?'" (Press Release) Notice: *their* responsibilities. And the purpose of the exercise, it is reported, is that "it is hoped that, by highlighting the importance of education to the nation, the Commission can coax additional funds from Congress." Is it likely that this report will be an examination of the real national challenges in higher education? Even supporters of increased government spending in higher education are coming to find the spectacle in Washington a bit much. Thus the *Washington Post* recently took issue with colleges' objections to the new tax bill under the headline, "Crying Towel for Colleges." And there is some danger that higher education's tendency to cry "Wolf" so insistently and so tiresomely will lead even Congress, one of these days, to balk.

Money is a means. It can be used for good and ill. In some cases money has aided good things, but in others money has aided in a kind of corruption. Money has meant growth and expansion, which in some places has meant a diffusion and loss of focus, a loss of central purpose. And more money has given many in our universities the opportunity to avoid doing one thing above all — actually teaching large numbers of students; or, in some cases, any students. Bennett's axiom: After a certain point, the more money you have, the fewer distinguished professors you will have in the classroom. This is an oddity of academic life. X dollars buys the students one professor, 2x dollars buys them two, but 3x and 4x and 5x dollars gradually remove the professor from the student, and 6x dollars may replace all the classroom professors with graduate students. So money is not an unambiguous good. In any case, it's often not that hard to get money — but to bring quality and focus and purpose to a place, now that's harder.

My final topic is tolerance: the university as a home for the free exchange of ideas. We are all too familiar with recent incidents of denial of free speech on college campuses. There was even an incident here at Harvard, last spring, though I was glad to see Harvard invited the victimized speakers

back. Still, as Wayne State University President David Adamany said earlier this year, "The whole nation knows that faculty members, students, academic administrators, and some governing boards have in recent years silenced unpopular speakers — especially speakers on the right. . . . The shame for those of us who are active liberals is that we do not join in a chorus of condemnation of our colleagues when right–leaning speakers are kept off of our campuses by threat or are silenced by disorder." Perhaps such a chorus of condemnation may now — finally — begin to emerge, as in the recent speech by Yale President Benno Schmidt; such a chorus had better emerge, and triumph — or else the game really will be up.

And we should also be careful not to allow a more subtle and pervasive kind of conformism and intolerance to permeate our institutions of higher education. Let me put it simply. Prestigious, selective, leading universities — whatever modifier you wish — have a tendency in our time to show a liberal bias. This is partly because most of the people in the humanities and social sciences departments in these universities stand to the left of center. A 1984 Carnegie Foundation survey of the professoriate found that, among philosophy faculty at four–year institutions, 21.7 percent designated themselves as "left," *none* as "strongly conservative"; for the sociologists, the percentages were 37 percent versus .9 percent; for historians, 12.9 percent versus 3.0 percent. As the values–forming teachers of the young, these professors may tend to tilt students in the direction of their own beliefs. (Also many students coming to such universities think that a general liberal bias is expected of them.) So certain views are in a minority, and indeed are unpopular.

This need not be a great problem, as long as we are very careful that a generally shared political viewpoint does not lead to the explicit or implicit censorship of unpopular ideas. Unpopular views — views unpopular in the academy, that is — should not merely be grudgingly tolerated there; they should be respected and fostered. Harvard professor James Q. Wilson wrote over a decade ago that of the five institutions of which he had been a part — the Catholic Church, the University of Redlands, the U.S. Navy, the University of Chicago, and Harvard — it was Harvard that was perhaps the least open to free and uninhibited discussion. Combatting this sort of intolerance, if it is present, requires more than allowing an occasional dissenting outside speaker to appear on campus. It requires self-criticism and self–examination; it requires a conscious striving by the academy against the tendency to become home to a "herd of independent minds." For if you cannot hold or express or argue for an unorthodox view at a university without risk of penalty, either explicit penalty or social disdain, the university will collapse like a deck of cards, falling of its own weight. If we cannot protect the basic principle of academic freedom, then we cannot even begin to hope that our colleges and universities will evolve into a recognizable imitation of what they claim to be.

Let me conclude: Universities deserve the kind of scrutiny they like to give to others. Universities cost a lot, and they puff and boast a lot. From time to time, it's not a bad idea to look at what's really going on, and to ask some hard questions. I've tried to do a bit of that today, and I've tried to do it for the sake of our students. I hope that some in American higher education will take seriously the questions I've raised, and ask *themselves* how our colleges and universities today can do better by their students — who are after all the purpose of the enterprise. If we are not doing as well as we might by them, we should begin to see to it that we do better.

VI.2

# ADDRESS BY WILLIAM J. BENNETT, UNITED STATES SECRETARY OF EDUCATION: The Future of Federal Student Financial Aid

*Sponsored by the Institute for Educational Affairs, Catholic University, Washington, D.C., November 19, 1986.*

Last month, in Cambridge, I spoke to the students, faculty, and administration of Harvard University about the condition of higher education in America. My talk was principally about the *quality* of America's colleges and universities: I said that too many students, at Harvard and elsewhere, are not getting the education, moral or intellectual, that they have been promised and that they deserve.

In the weeks since, the concerns I expressed at Harvard have been seconded by some very distinguished members of the university community. Two weeks ago, in the most comprehensive examination of American higher education in recent memory, Ernest Boyer issued a call for, among other things, more coherent curricula, more emphasis on teaching, and more attention to students' moral well–being. And in a speech delivered at Harvard University a week ago, Cornell University President Frank Rhodes stated that American higher education has lost the sense of moral and intellectual purpose so essential to the integrity of the university, and to the education of her students.

These contributions to the debate are good signs. They are signs of the beginning of a candid, constructive conversation on the purpose and quality of American higher education. I hope this conversation will continue. I hope that we may see it lead eventually to a real, profound, and much–needed reform of the American academy.

With this discussion underway, I would like to turn my attention today to the other side of the higher education coin: whereas at Harvard I spoke primarily of quality, today I would like to address the side of the coin that is finances. I think, in the end, we will find the issues of cost and quality closely related; I think we would do well to consider these two issues together.

The difficulties of families in meeting college costs are the stuff of contemporary lore, and they are the subjects of countless articles, proposals, and conferences such as this one. Between 1975 and 1986, average college costs rose 150 percent: from $1,972 to $4,917. That's 36 percent faster than inflation. In the last five years, college costs have risen 85 percent faster than the rate of inflation. Between 1975 and 1985, college costs rose 25 percent faster than median family income. And for families in which only one parent works, costs increased almost 50 percent faster than income.

There are growing signs of frustration and exasperation with the difficulties of meeting these costs. A recent poll found that over 75 percent of Americans believe that college costs are climbing at such a rate that soon a college education will be out of reach of the average American. In his new report on higher education, Ernest Boyer lists college costs as the chief concern of prospective college students and their parents. The second greatest concern, not surprisingly, is obtaining financial aid. Over two thirds of college–bound students, Mr. Boyer reports, consider college costs "outrageous."

In the past few years, we have seen the emergence of numerous plans to help families meet these increasingly difficult college costs. Representatives of several of these plans are speaking here today. These programs are encouraging. They are signs of genuine concern and effort among some state and college officials. I believe they will help make college costs more manageable for many American students and their families. Today I would like to emphasize, however, that in the long run dealing with the issue of college costs will require more than creative financing. It will require reforms on the part of colleges and reforms on the part of the federal government.

First, we need to see where we stand. There are some colleges and universities that are in serious financial circumstances, but the basic fact—often obscured, sometimes denied—is that in general our colleges and universities are in very good financial shape. The Reagan years have been good to our colleges and universities. Not only have a growing economy—and increased student aid—allowed colleges dramatically to raise their prices; our institutions of higher education have also raised increasing sums by other means. In each of the last ten years, revenues from donations have increased over the year before. In 1985, a record year like the nine previous, colleges received $6.32 billion from corporations, alumni, and other sources, an increase of about 13 percent over 1984. Funds received from corporations alone increased by nearly 25 percent. Furthermore, the Reagan–era stock market has done wonders for many universities' endowments. Endowment income in 1985 was $2.1 billion, an increase of 60 percent from 1981.

Nonetheless, our universities tend to complain about their financial condition; they do, in fact, protest too much. Recently, the Association of American Universities has circulated a note around Capitol Hill with the request that Federal officials view our universities as "rich but needy . . . , able to pursue institutional self—interest but in a spirit of altruism . . . , economically successful but incorruptible." The conflicting testimony of ledger and lobbyist has indeed become untenable. And as we hear talk of the danger of universities going under, the number of both public and private institutions of higher learning continues to increase: from 1,852 in 1950 to 2,230 in 1965, to 3,231 in 1980, and to 3,331 today. Higher education remains a growth industry.

Given, then, that colleges have been doing well financially, why is it that college costs have risen so much? The prevailing wisdom is that the increases of the 1980s are to make up for losses to inflation in the 1970s. It is said that they are needed to return faculty salaries to where they were in the early 1970s and to address long–deferred maintenance needs in the physical plant.

A look at where the money is actually going, however, suggests otherwise. Between 1975 and 1984 (the last year for which figures are available) the share of college expenditures on plant operation and maintenance increased only slightly; at public universities from 10.2 to 10.8 percent of the budget, at private institutions from 10.0 to 10.2. Faculty salaries over the same period did increase by over 80 percent. Yet the share of spending on instruction, which consists mainly of faculty salaries, stayed even—no increase at all. Many colleges found they could offset higher salaries by offering them to fewer people; promotion and tenure were offered less often, and low–paid part–time faculty—so–called gypsy faculty—were hired to teach more and more courses. It is not clear that this is the best result from the point of view of the students. As Mr. Boyer notes in his report, these instructors often "do not have deep institutional commitments and their connections with . . . students are tenuous at best."

In any case, it is clear that instructional costs and expenses for operation and maintenance cannot account for the enormous increases we have seen in college costs. How then to explain them? Well, I think what is required, first of all, is an understanding of our universities' nature as financial institutions. Even so good a spokesman for higher education as Robert Rosenzweig, President of the Association of American Universities, has acknowledged that, in certain respects, higher education is an industry. Our universities have become preoccupied with raising money; they have become very adept at the task. We see this in increasing donations and increasing endowments. And we see this in the cost increases as well. Some of our colleges and universities charge what the market will bear. And lately, they have found that it will bear quite a lot indeed. The heart of the matter is that colleges raise costs *because they can*. And a very important factor in that ability to raise costs has been the availability of federal student aid.

As Larry Gladieux, director of the Washington office of the College Board, has put it, "In the college market there seems to be a bidding up of costs and quality, and the people seem willing to pay for it. . . . [T]he availability of student aid has at least facilitated things." The calculation is apparent in a *New York Times* article on college costs published last spring: asked what their costs would be for the following year, officials at one Ivy League school told the reporter that tuition would not be determined until more information was available on levels of federal aid for that year.

Colleges are more or less assured that where students cannot meet their costs, the federal government will help out. And when the federal government is expected to help meet a large share of the difference between a student's wherewithal and the college's charges, colleges can more easily afford to let costs rise. The wealthiest students can always pay, and those who can't are, by definition, needy.

For this reason, controlling college costs inevitably will require some adjustment, some reform, of federal student aid itself. In our discussion of easing college costs, we must always remain mindful of this fact. Trying to control college costs merely by increasing aid is like the dog chasing his tail around the tree; the faster he runs, the faster the tail runs away.

To date, federal policy essentially has been to increase the dog's speed. The dog, of course, has gotten no closer to his tail; he has only become exhausted: he's burning more energy, using more fuel. The fact is that the federal government can no more afford to bear the skyrocketing cost of college than can the American student or the American family. Since 1965, federal student aid (including capital leveraged from the private market) has ballooned from $200 million to $14.5 billion — over 7000 percent. The federal government now has over $40 billion in outstanding loan insurance commitments. This year alone, the Guaranteed Student Loan program will cost the government $3 billion. And despite the expected collection of at least $184 million in delinquent loans through a joint effort with the IRS, it is projected that loan defaults this year will cost the taxpayers over $1.1 billion. That's up from $254 million in 1980, and $117 million in 1975.

This year's reauthorization of the Higher Education Act did not address this fundamental need for reform. Indeed, the new act will allow federal student aid costs to increase by over 20 percent a year compared with where we were last year.

This cannot go on. The system must change; our approach to rising college costs must change. It must change because, as we've seen, the federal aid budget is already running out of control. And it must change because, as we've seen, in the end more loan money does not make it easier for families to meet college costs. Rather, in the end, more loan money makes it easier for colleges to raise college costs. Thus the spiral continues: colleges raise costs, there is pressure on the federal government to meet those costs, student aid increases to meet them, and up costs go all over again. Rather than addressing the true problem, the central problem, the problem of soaring college costs, loan increases will only encourage the problem — extend it, deepen it. They will do so at the expense of heavily burdened family and federal budgets, and they will do so to the benefit of college budgets already profiting from other sources.

As *The Chronicle of Higher Education* has reported, among experts on student aid programs there is fairly broad agreement that federal aid policy must be reformed. Increasing recognition of the nature of this problem may also account for the changing public mood: a survey by the Opinion Research Corporation reveals that in the last two years support for student aid increases has dropped ten percentage points.

Right now, in preparing the 1988 budget, we are considering how federal aid programs might be reformed so as to help halt this spiral. Among other things, in the needs analysis system governing grants and loans, we are considering excluding any increase in tuition and costs greater than the inflation rate plus 1 percent. We believe that for colleges to increase costs beyond inflation, and for the government to subsidize those increases, contributes unnecessarily and irresponsibly to rising college costs. The federal government should not subsidize such increases. Refusing to do so may prove one way of reining costs in.

What other changes might be made to ease the crunch of college costs? Allow me, for a moment, to offer my own broader view of what student aid should look like in the future. Here is my blueprint.

At the heart of federal programs should be grants for the neediest students. Need-based grants contribute admirably to the democratic purposes of our educational system, and we would want to continue to operate grant programs much as we do now.

What will be necessary, though, is a considerable change in our loan programs. Effective reform would require overcoming two particularly vexing aspects of the current system: the unmanageable debt placed on students, and the government's subsidization of that debt.

The problem of student debt recently has received a good deal of media attention. Under the present system, students agree to pay the bulk of their loans in the years immediately after graduation. As we all know, financially these are a graduate's least rewarding years. The result is that, already in a somewhat precarious financial situation, the borrower must now struggle to meet his loan payments. Some students feel compelled to reject jobs in low-income professions in favor of high paying jobs that enable them to meet their payments. There is, of course, a third alternative, illegal but all too frequent: default.

For the government, the most burdensome aspect in the design of current loan programs is that, in addition to guaranteeing the loan, the government subsidizes the cost of the loan. Guaranteed Student Loans are subsidized at the 91-day Treasury Bill rate plus 3.25 percent. It is this subsidy, not the loan itself, that has come to constitute a major liability for the government and for our loan programs. In fiscal year 1986, aggregate GSL costs for interest and special allowances ran to $2.1 billion. A one-point rise in the T-Bill rate would cost the government nearly $500 million a year in additional subsidies. In periods of high inflation, this becomes for the government a potentially disastrous liability: in the late 1970s, the cost of subsidizing a loan sometimes approached the size of the loan itself.

For the borrower, then, we would want a loan program that offered sizeable sums, but on a more manageable repayment schedule: smaller payments spread over a longer term. The best imaginable schedule would be one that allowed the borrower — now the recent graduate — to pay what he is able as he makes his way in the working world. Let him pay according to his means. Rather than fitting his career to his payments, let him fit his payments to his career.

For the federal government, the ideal program would eliminate loan subsidies. The subsidy is a generous extra from the federal government, but it is not essential to the loan itself. And it can be inimical to a sound and stable program.

What I have outlined is a plan that answers the most pressing needs of both student and government. And it is a plan that in fact exists, if only on a small scale. It can be found in the Higher Education Reauthorization Act, as the Administration's new Income Contingent Loan pilot program, or ICLs.

ICLs will, like the plan I have outlined, offer the borrower substantial sums on appreciably more manageable terms. Payments would begin nine months after graduation. For the first two years they would be at a fixed rate between $20 and $50, depending on the size of the loan. At the end of this two year period, the payments would become contingent on the borrower's Adjusted Gross Income for the prior year. There would be no minimum payment, and yearly payments would never exceed 15 percent of the beneficiary's income. Special deferments would still be available.

For the government, ICLs would transfer payment of the interest on the loan from the government to the recipient. Recipients would repay their loans at the Treasury Bill rate plus 3 percent — still a better rate than any bank will offer for an unsecured loan. Note that it is switching the interest burden from the government to the recipient that would make it possible to offer large loans with longer repayment periods.

Today, I am sending letters to the presidents of all 3331 of the nation's colleges and universities, inviting them to apply for participation in the five-year pilot ICL program. Ten of the applicants will be chosen to participate in the first year of the program,

involving $5 million a year for the years 1987 to 1991. We're hoping to expand the program in future years.

I will also again be asking Congress to allow institutions partaking in the $900 million cash flow from NDSL revolving funds to consider administering these funds along terms similar to the ICL. I am making this request in the interest of helping to ease the current loan burden on government and students. And I am asking them to do it as a contribution to shaping the student loan programs of the future.

ICLs are not a new idea. Nor are they a particularly Republican or conservative idea: they have been proposed by parties as diverse as Milton Friedman, Michael McPherson of Williams College, and the Carnegie Commission on Higher Education, chaired by Clark Kerr. The Reverend William Byron of Catholic University has been a leading advocate.

Support for ICLs is broad, I believe, because they point clearly to the direction that federal student aid programs must take. They recognize, first of all, the federal interest in helping needy students obtain an education. By extending the repayment period and diminishing early payments, ICLs recognize that the financial rewards of a college education are seldom immediate. And by shifting the cost of the loan from the government — that is, the taxpayer — to the recipient, ICLs recognize that as much as education benefits the nation, the fullest, most direct, and most tangible benefits of that college education come to the individual receiving the education. The college graduate will earn $640,000 more than the high school graduate over his lifetime, an income gain of almost 53 percent. It is only sensible — and only fair — that that beneficiary pay the cost rather than taxpayers, the majority of whom do not themselves enjoy the financial rewards of a college education.

Finally, I believe that by exposing the true, full cost of a college education to the student borrower, ICLs may help engender a much broader reform of higher education. No longer will the costs of college be hidden by federal subsidies. Rather than spending someone else's money, students will find themselves making decisions about their own. This cannot help but make students more conscious of how much they pay their college, and of the quality of the education they receive in return. After all, they'll be paying for it.

This returns me, in a sense, to where I began: the question of quality, as well as cost, in higher education in America. I believe that there could be no change more auspicious for American higher education — for the quality, as well as the cost —

than the consumer considering these two fundamental matters together. Students and parents must begin to ask whether they're getting their money's worth. We must have a demystification of American higher education.

Higher education today operates in a sort of black box; it is very hard to know what is actually going on inside. We have very little means of assessing what is being achieved. The few data we do have on college performance are not encouraging. We know, for instance, that between 1964 and 1982 student performance declined on eleven of the fifteen major Subject Area Tests of the Graduate Record Examinations. We know that, whereas in 1945 Jacques Barzun reported that most college professors taught fifteen hours a week, today that number is down to five hours at our major universities, less than seven overall. (Ed. note: This statement aroused controversy.)

What is needed is a little more consumer information; a little truth in advertising. Let's have our universities open that black box. Let's have them show their performance, their worth, their influence. Let's publish drop-out rates, and scores on entrance and exit exams; let's see the value added.

This summer, in their report on education, *Time for Results*, the nation's governors indicated their intention more closely to examine the performance of their state universities. Make no mistake: in the future we are going to see more assessment, more attention to the relative cost and quality of our institutions of higher learning. The appearance of new cost–conscious college guides are evidence that prospective students and their parents are also becoming mindful of educational value. It would be nice for our colleges themselves to take the lead. When they do, some universities will indeed prove worth their tuitions; I suspect that some will not.

At the beginning of this decade, Americans were particularly alarmed by the meteoric rise of costs in two important areas of our national life: higher education, and medicine. As the decade has progressed, we have grown accustomed to thinking about hospital cost containment. And today, hospital costs, which once seemed uncontrollable, are now stabilizing, even declining. It's time that we demand the same of our colleges. In addition to hospital cost containment, let us speak of college cost containment. I for one am confident that a more thorough, more responsible look at college costs and college performance will in the long run only serve to increase Americans' confidence in our colleges and universities, and will improve a system of higher education that is, in many respects, the wonder and envy of the world.

# Testimony of William J. Bennett, United States Secretary of Education

*Presented Before The Committee on Labor and Human Resources Subcommittee on Education, Arts, and the Humanities, United States Senate January 28, 1986*

Mr. Chairman and members of the committee, I am pleased to have this opportunity to testify before your Subcommittee on the accreditation of postsecondary institutions. In order properly to consider this topic, however, it should be placed within the context of broader issues concerning the quality of postsecondary education. So I will discuss both the particular issue of accreditation and the broader issue of quality in my remarks today.

## The Achievement of American Postsecondary Education

Let me say at the outset that our nation has created the world's finest system of postsecondary education. At its best, it combines the finest research and teaching with the greatest variety of educational programs available anywhere. It offers more choices, more second chances, and more intellectual freedom to students and their teachers than any other system of education in all of history. It is a system composed of universities, colleges, junior colleges, trade schools, and professional and technical schools of almost every description. Together they provide our citizens with multiple opportunities to tailor an educational program to their changing goals and circumstances throughout life.

Today 62 percent of American high school graduates go on to enroll in postsecondary institutions, with total enrollments at almost 18 million. Expenditures by postsecondary institutions have nearly doubled since 1966; they totalled $90 billion in 1984. Funding from federal, state, and local governments accounted for almost half this total — $44 billion in 1984, up from $26 billion in 1966 when adjusted for inflation. The private sector has also provided substantial and steadily increasing support for postsecondary education. Last year private giving to higher education totaled $5.6 billion, including $1.25 billion from American corporations and $1 billion from foundations.

It is clear that the American people have been generous to our institutions of postsecondary education. This generosity derives from the knowledge that these institutions are an indispensable foundation of our economic progress and national well–being, and from the firm belief that they offer a gateway to the American dream. But, given the importance and the growing cost of postsecondary education, it is only reasonable that students, parents, government officials, and others should look for — and should expect to find — evidence that they are getting their money's worth. This is a particularly important matter for students from less financially fortunate homes, students for whom postsecondary education may be a crucial avenue to success.

This morning, I would like to discuss signs of inadequate quality in postsecondary education; evidence of practices that ill serve students and taxpayers; some indicators that the postsecondary education community is beginning to work on behalf of quality improvement; and what I believe may be the largest single challenge facing our postsecondary education system, namely the development of very substantially improved mechanisms for determining whether its institutions are in fact achieving the results to which they aspire.

Then I will talk about where responsibility for quality improvement lies, emphasizing that the primary burden should be borne by the institutions themselves, by voluntary mechanisms of the postsecondary education community such as accreditation, and by the states. Finally, I will review some ways in which the federal government may be able to help in these matters, paying particular attention to the complex system by which we rely on private accreditation as a major indicator of eligibility for federal financial assistance of many kinds.

# Challenges to the Quality of Postsecondary Education

As I said at the beginning of my remarks, many students receive an excellent education from our post-secondary institutions. But the health and vitality of these institutions depend upon the creation and maintenance of rigorous standards of achievement for students, faculty members, and institutions themselves. From a growing number of sources, both inside and outside the walls of the academy, concern has recently been expressed that many of our institutions of postsecondary education are not establishing or applying suitable standards of quality.

1. AREAS OF CONCERN IN VOCATIONAL AND PROFESSIONAL EDUCATION  Among the diverse parts of our postsecondary education system different problems have been identified. A 1984 General Accounting Office study of proprietary schools found that many do not establish or enforce meaningful "ability to benefit" standards. The Higher Education Act requires that students admitted to postsecondary institutions have either a high school diploma, its equivalent, or — in lieu of these — the "ability to benefit" from the training offered. But when 61 percent of Pell grant recipients admitted under the "ability to benefit" clause do not complete their educational programs, one can wonder how vigorously this standard is being applied. The GAO study also found situations where federal aid recipients who had never graduated from high school enrolled on the "ability to benefit" basis — but then had in fact no chance to benefit from the training, because state licensing standards for employment in their field required a high school diploma.

Audit reports and program reviews, as well as other indicators, suggest that some institutions have been admitting students without adequately assessing their ability. The program reviews conducted by the Department of Education show that many institutions do not give admissions tests or conduct other assessments of ability. Even in instances where admission tests are given, they are sometimes geared to third- and fourth-grade-level questions. Often there is no relationship between the test and the educational subject matter the institution is offering; often passing scores have never been defined.

In an effort to address this problem, the Department submitted legislation with its Fiscal Year 1986 Budget Proposal to allow only students with high school diplomas to qualify for financial aid, thus eliminating the "ability to benefit" exception provided in the law. This has yet to be enacted.

A related problem is the fact that some proprietary schools, accredited by the state or by accrediting agencies, are graduating large numbers of students who fail the relevant state licensing examination. Without their professional license, these graduates cannot find employment.

Indeed, this problem, whether due to lax admissions standards or inadequate instruction, is not limited to vocational or proprietary institutions. Some colleges and universities also graduate large numbers of students from such professional programs as accounting and pharmacy who are unable to pass certification examinations. Also, the advent of state teacher testing has produced shocking evidence of poor performance by some institutions. In some states, as many as 70 percent of the graduates of certain accredited teacher training colleges fail the National Teacher Examination.

Institutions are defrauding students, and in many cases they are ripping off the American public, when they admit individuals who are manifestly unprepared for the work that will be required of them, or when they graduate students who cannot satisfy minimum standards in their field of study.

2. THE DECLINE IN QUALITY OF UNDERGRADUATE EDUCATION  There is also widening agreement that the quality of undergraduate liberal arts education at many institutions is not what it should be.

We have all heard reports that many of our graduates do not possess the knowledge, skills, or, in some cases the civic virtues of a highly educated person. Some evidence is fragmentary, anecdotal, or impressionistic; other evidence is more tangible: student performance declined in eleven of fifteen major Subject Area Tests of the Graduate Record Examinations between 1964 and 1982.

We have seen five major reports in just over one year that have been critical of various aspects of undergraduate education. These reports contain some troubling findings. For example, a 1984–85 survey by the American Council on Education indicates that a student can obtain a bachelor's degree from 72 percent of all American colleges and universities without having studied American literature and history; from 75 percent without having studied European history; and from 86 percent without having studied the civilizations of classical Greece and Rome. The Modern Language Association reports that, in 1966, 89 percent of all institutions required foreign language study for the bachelor's degree;

this dropped to 53 percent in 1975, and to 47 percent in 1983.

As the recent Association of American Colleges report *(Integrity in the College Curriculum)* states, higher education has gone through a period in which there seemed to be more confidence "about the length of college education than its content and purpose." The simple accumulation of credit hours — what is sometimes called "seat time" — became the primary yardstick. The neglect of the real purposes and goals of education strikes at the very integrity of higher education.

I am encouraged by the signs that our colleges and universities are now recognizing the need to improve the quality of undergraduate education. For, while construed by some as an indictment of higher education, these reports are, in fact, a promising sign. They have recognized the danger of declining quality and provided guidance on how the problems can be overcome. These reports are, for the most part, products of the academy. They are by its members to its members, and it is the members of the academy who must take the lead to solve these problems.

# The Importance of Assessment

I therefore believe that the quality of postsecondary education must be improved, but also that the primary force for that improvement must come from the institutions themselves. These institutions, and particularly our traditional colleges and universities, must do a better job of providing a coherent and rigorous curriculum for students. They must do a more conscientious job of stating their goals, of gauging their own success in relation to those goals, and of making their results available to everyone — students, prospective students, parents, citizens, and taxpayers. As a recent report by the Association of American Colleges stated:

> As difficult as it may be to develop the most searching and appropriate methods of evaluation and assessment, an institution that lacks refined instruments of program evaluation and rigorous instruments of student assessment is contributing to the debasement of baccalaureate education.

Apart from the essential skills and fundamental knowledge that we expect all colleges and universities to impart, there are individual institutional goals that vary enormously from school to school. It is only sensible that each school appraise its own progress toward those goals. This is the surest way to turn the lofty statements of college catalogues into actual classroom practice. If we are to keep our promises to students, we must be willing to honestly assess our strengths — and our shortcomings. Such acknowledgment is the surest way to maintain institutional integrity; it is also the best way to maintain institutional sovereignty and self-government.

Some institutions of higher education are in fact beginning to assess student outcomes as a means of assessing learning. While their methods vary, colleges and universities are beginning to set competency levels in certain content areas that must be met before a student can be promoted. For example, the University of Arizona requires all students to pass a writing proficiency examination near the mid–point of their undergraduate career, and the University of Massachusetts at Boston requires undergraduates to pass a writing proficiency examination before they can take upper–division courses.

Assessments can use many different methods — standardized tests, interviews, questionnaires, reviews of students' written work over four years, reviews of extracurricular activity, studies of alumni and dropouts, surveys of students' use of time, and surveys of graduates' use of time. Some results could be expressed in numerical terms; many obviously could not. In large, complex universities, assessment might be conducted separately by schools, colleges, or departments.

But no matter what the form, judgments need to be made so that institutions can assure the public and themselves that they are doing what they say they are doing. Such assessment should also hold a central place in the accreditation of all postsecondary institutions. Today that is not the case.

# State Government Responsibilities

Because they are responsible for licensing or otherwise recognizing the educational institutions that operate within their borders, state governments also play an essential role in any effort to improve the accountability of postsecondary education. A number of states have recently begun to take action to assure that their institutions meet tougher standards of educational quality. On the national level, the National Governors Association (NGA) has identified raising standards in higher education as one of its initiatives for the next five years. Governor John Ashcroft of Missouri, who chairs NGA's College Quality task force, has resolved to investigate what states can do to improve consumer information about higher education, the assessment of undergraduate performance, and institutional management. NGA hearings next month will focus on postsecondary assessment. Governor Thomas Kean of New Jersey has said that the Education Commission of the States should "think deeply about how to inspire effective State action to improve undergraduate education."

One of the strategies some states are adopting for strengthening higher education is mandating requirements for evaluating student performance. "Value–added" testing, or testing at entry and graduation, is beginning to gain acceptance in a number of States. State coordinating boards in South Dakota and Tennessee already require this form of outcome assessment. Colorado, New Jersey, Maryland, and Virginia are considering value–added proposals.

In 1982, Florida adopted a "rising junior" examination policy. This policy requires that all students from community colleges or in State colleges or universities pass the Florida College Level Academic Skills Test before being given junior class status. The requirement has been expanded to private college students who receive financial aid from state sources.

State governments are also beginning to take important steps to promote excellence by awarding a portion of their financial support to colleges and universities on the basis of reliable measures of institutional quality. Tennessee is currently employing a performance funding program that uses assessment as a way of making decisions about a portion of higher education funding. It rewards institutions for performance on established criteria. This effort emphasizes student learning in general education, student learning in a major field, and other criteria.

# Reviewing Accreditation Standards

Although the Department of Education is prohibited by law—and properly so—from prescribing the curriculum of any school, college, or university, the department is required by law to determine the eligibility of institutions to receive federal funds. Rather than evaluate thousands of separate schools, the federal government relies upon the private and voluntary accrediting bodies through which the postsecondary community determines its own institutional membership.

The 1952 Korean War GI bill required the Commissioner of Education to establish a list of accrediting agencies that he determined "to be (a) reliable authority as to the quality of training offered by an educational institution." Although this list was not exclusive, the 1952 law established the principle that accreditation by a recognized private agency

was sufficient to make an institution eligible for federal funds.

The 1958 National Defense Education Act provided that one way for an institution to participate in NDEA programs was for it to be "accredited by a nationally recognized accrediting agency or association." Although it left the responsibility of "recognizing" accrediting bodies to the Commissioner of Education, NDEA again indicated Congress' intention to accept "accreditation" as established by nongovernmental agencies as a sufficient condition of quality assessment for eligibility for federal funds.

Today, to be recognized, an accrediting agency must demonstrate that it is capable of evaluating the educational quality of an institution by virtue of meeting ten criteria. The National Advisory Committee on Accreditation and Institutional Eligibility, a group established by statute and appointed by the Secretary (of Education), is responsible for advising me as to whether an accrediting agency meets those criteria, and also for advising me as to the content of the criteria. There are now eighty-three accrediting organizations recognized by the Department, and they confer their approval on nearly 9,000 institutions.

Accreditation standards, following the standards most commonly used by institutions themselves, have traditionally measured quality in terms of institutional resources—such as endowment per student, percentage of faculty with doctorates, or the number of books in the library—with little or no attention paid as to what effects they have on what results they yield. A 1978 survey of 208 colleges and universities that had engaged in institutional self-studies in preparation for accreditation visits found that only one in three had either generated or examined data on student learning and growth; only 23 percent had examined students' knowledge in their major fields.

I believe that accrediting agencies, and postsecondary institutions themselves, should place as much emphasis on student learning as on the resources and procedures of the institution. Unless they examine student learning, they cannot really gauge educational quality.

Accrediting agencies and our colleges and universities must also reexamine the narrow vocationalism of some current professional requirements in order to restore scope and depth to liberal education. A clear distinction must be made between technical training and the broader goals of higher education so that a sound professional curriculum does not preclude rigorous standards in the general curriculum. In many cases, we have neither.

Thus the guidelines of one professional accrediting association confine one half to two thirds of one student's baccalaureate program to courses in two areas. Another association prescribes approximately 70 percent of the student's four–year program and confines that percentage wholly to two subject areas. And according to the standards of yet another association, the bachelor's degree programs must involve as much as 80 percent of the student's work in the professional field. As a result, some employers are confronting job applicants with a bachelor's degree who are unable to write competently, speak lucidly, or perform more than the most elementary mathematical procedures.

I am concerned that the criteria for determining whether an accrediting agency should be recognized by the Department—last revised in 1974—and the Department's procedures for determining eligibility for recognition may no longer be adequate to their important task. Consequently, I will ask the National Advisory Committee on Accreditation and Institutional Eligibility to conduct a review of the current "Criteria for Recognizing National Accrediting Agencies and Associations" and also to examine the federal process of recognition to determine whether and how these can be strengthened. I will also ask the committee to examine the statutory definition of institutional eligibility and report to me their recommendations for improvements within the limits of our statutory authority. I welcome additional discussion on this subject—by the post-secondary education community, by the public, and by legislators at all levels.

At least one regional accrediting body has begun to assess the quality of higher education through the measurement of student outcomes, not just institutional resources. The Commission on Colleges of the Southern Association of Colleges and Schools, which is the regional association for postsecondary institutions in most southern states, has taken the lead in developing new quality criteria for its member institutions. The Southern Association requires institutions to evaluate the effectiveness of their resources and processes in achieving educational outcomes. In addition, institutions are encouraged to follow changes in the academic achievement of their students by tracking student scores on standardized examinations or locally constructed examinations, the performance of graduates in graduate school, and performance of graduates of professional programs on licensing examinations.

While the Southern Association prescribes no uniform set of procedures or minimum standard for use by an institution, it should be commended for encouraging southern colleges and universities to review their thinking about educational results.

# Other Initiatives by the Department of Education

The Department of Education is taking a number of steps to help improve the quality of postsecondary education. Our Office of Educational Research and Improvement (OERI) is working to improve its ability to provide the nation with accurate and timely information about the quality of education at all levels. Two of the ten newly funded OERI Centers will be encouraged to foster better assessment measures. We will ask the new Center on Postsecondary Management and Governance to become a clearinghouse on state and institutional assessment activities and information, and the new Center on Postsecondary Teaching and Learning to develop new quality indicators.

In addition, we will assist institutions and others in their efforts to develop methods of assessment. Earlier this year the Fund for the Improvement of Postsecondary Education adopted the assessment of student learning and institutional effectiveness as one of its major funding priorities.

# Conclusion

Improving the quality of postsecondary education will require the cooperation of the faculties, administrators, and trustees of individual institutions, state governments, the accrediting organizations, and the federal government. In my remarks this morning, I have suggested some steps that each of these groups can take to meet the problems faced by postsecondary education today. First, and foremost, individual institutions—their, faculty, administrators, and trustees—can undertake a serious effort to assess and improve student learning. Second, state governments can examine their criteria and procedures for recognizing educational institutions. Third, accrediting agencies can take a hard look at their standards and practices. The Department of Education is eager to join with each of these groups in appropriate efforts to strengthen postsecondary institutions.

Today, Mr. Chairman, you are sending a message to the postsecondary education community that we in the federal government share their concern for quality. I thank you for this opportunity to appear before this subcommittee, and I look forward to working with you and with others to improve the accreditation process and the overall quality of postsecondary education.

## VI.4

# Speech to the Harvard Alumni Association

*Delivered on Saturday, September 6, 1986*

## DEREK BOK

It is a great privilege to have all of you in Cambridge for these few days to share our intellectual and cultural life and to celebrate the long, remarkable history of this institution. Many of you have worked to strengthen the University, as your forebears have done since the time of John Harvard and Lady Radcliffe. All of you have enriched us by your presence. To each and every one, I extend our warmest welcome and appreciation.

I always look forward to occasions such as this for the chance they give me to delve again into Harvard history. Nothing could be more therapeutic. No matter what mistakes I make, I invariably find some predecessor who has managed to outdo them. To illustrate, we need only look to the very first year of the College under the reign of my earliest predecessor, Nathaniel Eaton, and his redoubtable bride, Mistress Eaton. Mr. Eaton was barely prevented from beating a teacher to death with a walnut tree plant. Mistress Eaton was accused of putting goat's dung in the hasty pudding. For their sins, they were sacked after only a year of service and the College had to close less than twelve months after it began. Faculty colleagues who grumble about the way they are treated and students who turn up their noses at our cooking should all ponder this episode and put their own complaints in proper historical perspective.

After this modest beginning, Harvard has happily inched forward. Through three and one half centuries, fortunes have been made and unmade, companies have flourished and disappeared, political parties have waxed and waned, yet this venerable institution has persevered, a source of pride to its friends, a cause for apoplexy to its critics but always a force to be reckoned with in American higher education and the country as a whole.

Fifty years have come and gone since we last gathered to celebrate a Harvard anniversary. Looking

Reprinted by permission.

back on the proceedings then, one is sobered by how few glimmerings there were of the great upheavals that would alter Harvard, the nation, and the entire globe in the decades to come. Scarcely a hint appears of the coming transformation of America's role in the world, the quest for greater opportunity by minority groups and women, the vast changes in health care, or the surging growth of technology that would engulf the nation. Still more significant was the failure to anticipate the mounting importance to America of knowledge itself.

Above all else, it is the centrality of knowledge that has changed the face of Harvard and other universities. Starting, ironically, with the last world war, and continuing with the advances in electronics and biotechnology, the growing sophistication of the professions, the use of policy analysis, and the revolution in modern medicine, we have all become much more aware that in a modern society, knowledge, expertise and new discoveries are the critical ingredients of progress.

Since universities are a principal source of these ingredients, they have come to assume much greater importance than our predecessors could have imagined fifty years ago. Fortunately, American universities have responded to this challenge with remarkable zeal and creativity. Many favoring circumstances helped them to succeed. They were fortunate to escape the destruction of World War II that ravaged higher education in so many other countries. They were enriched by an influx of exceptional scientists and scholars fleeing persecution in Europe. They benefited greatly from the support of the world's most prosperous economy. But most of all, they profited from our distinctive way of organizing higher education.

Throughout our history, universities have enjoyed unusual freedom. Public officials have interfered remarkably little with our state institutions, private groups have found it possible to found their own colleges, and all have engaged in a keen but

friendly rivalry for better students, faculty, and facilities. This system is so familiar now that we tend to
take it for granted. In fact, it is virtually unique. In
almost all other countries, universities are heavily
dependent on the government and operate according to the dictates of central planning.

Our free and decentralized system has great
strengths. By permitting many independent centers
of initiative, it encourages innovation and adaptabil-
ity. By avoiding state control, it puts the power to
make decisions in the hands of those most knowledgeable about education and research. By fostering competition, it generates powerful incentives to
excel and improve. The result is a network of universities widely recognized as the finest in the
world in the fruits of their research, the quality of
their professional training, their accessibility to a
wide spectrum of the population, and the variety of
programs they offer to meet the needs of a huge and
diverse student population.

There is good reason, then, to regard this as a
triumphant moment to celebrate the birth of America's oldest university and of American higher education itself. But ours is an institution with Puritan
roots. If there is one characteristic that has marked
Harvard through three and a half centuries, it is an
abiding sense of unease that causes us to worry even
when outward circumstances offer the least excuse
for doing so. By instinct, we feel a pang of guilt
whenever we catch ourselves enjoying our achievements. We struggle not to mention them out
loud . . . with less than total success. We know
how often institutions at their zenith bear within
them the seeds of eventual decline. For us, therefore, it is second nature to shrink from self-congratu-
lation and to ask ourselves instead what hostile
forces, what changes in fortune, what inner contradictions and excesses may come to weaken the
modern university and keep it from making the contributions that modern society demands and hu-
mankind deserves.

In casting about for sources of concern, we can
appropriately begin by looking outside the academy
itself. For success and prosperity attract attention,
not always of a welcome kind. As universities wax in
influence and importance, as their visibility increases and their assets grow, various groups are
naturally tempted to use them for purposes of their
own choosing.

We have seen much evidence of this in recent
years. Military and intelligence agencies have tried
to engage professors in secret research and to impose restrictions to keep our scientific findings out
of enemy hands. Businesses search for relationships
with our scientists that will help them develop new
products. Social activists press the university to use
its stock, its purchasing power, its reputation and
prestige to fight against apartheid and other evils
and injustices. Communities look to our campuses
as sources of wealth and leverage to help solve local
problems.

In responding to such requests, universities must
be keenly aware of their obligation to support the
society that sustains them. The question is how they
can best contribute and what conditions they must
preserve to keep on doing so. All too often, outside
groups mistakenly conclude that since the university is successful in teaching and research, it can
sway political institutions or solve society's problems as well. Frequently, they press the university to
risk its independence by entering into political battles or ask it to act in ways that compromise the
openness and freedom that characterize a healthy
research environment. In all such cases, the problem is not that people seek the university's help to
solve a social problem but that they urge it to act in
ways that contradict its proper nature and threaten
its most essential functions.

Another concern arising in the outside world is
the prospect of excessive government regulation.
As knowledge and advanced education become
more vital to the society, the state will naturally wish
to make sure that institutions supplying these services act according to the public interest. Already,
universities are subject to regulations that prohibit
discrimination, promote affirmative action, insure
accountability for research funds, provide suitable
access for the handicapped, and control access to
student records, among others.

All these regulations are inspired by the best of
motives, and most are perfectly reasonable. The
question is how far the process will continue. The
Reagan years have given us a temporary respite from
further regulation. But plenty of possibilities remain to tempt future administrations: manpower
planning to bring the numbers of graduates into line
with national needs; reviews of new programs and
facilities to avoid duplication and waste; detailed
rules to check the abuses of intercollegiate athletics; and safeguards to protect students from unfair
grades and arbitrary rejections from the admissions
office.

In pondering such regulations, we should clearly
acknowledge that universities must be accountable
to the public. The dilemma that arises is that adding
rules threatens the very qualities that make our universities so successful in serving the public's needs.
Higher education in America has thrived on diversity, local autonomy, and competition. Regulation
implies uniformity, central planning, and bureau-

cratic control. The more rules we impose, the more their cumulative weight threatens to transform the environment that has served so well into the kind of system that has seriously hampered our sister institutions abroad.

The prospects for further regulation are connected to a larger problem of worrisome proportions: the ambivalence many people feel toward major research universities as they grow in visibility, influence, and prestige. You have doubtless seen some of the stories about your *alma mater* that have appeared recently in newspapers and magazines. Their photographs are flattering and their tone, by and large, has been friendly and constructive. In reading them, however, you will have noticed a heavy emphasis on the Harvard mystique — our influence in the society, the size of our endowment, the number of our graduates in high places. However much we protest, I suspect that most of us are secretly pleased to be associated with an institution reputed to have such clout. But we should not forget that such accounts give a distorted picture of what Harvard and other universities actually do or where their true contribution lies.

We can all understand this fixation on the Harvard mystique. Aside from the occasional scientific breakthrough, there is not much drama for the reader in the patient labor of scholars surrounded by their books or the quiet growth of mind and feeling that countless students experience. Yet the images that replace these realities are not entirely harmless. As people read of the monetary value of a Harvard diploma, the swelling size of the Harvard endowment, the fabled influence of the old–boy network, fascination and respect easily turn to envy and resentment.

Although these attitudes are not new, the stakes are infinitely greater now that the state plays such a prominent role in financing scientific discovery and student aid. Federal and state officials give generously to universities, recognizing the importance of education and research. But the effect has been to make our campuses highly dependent on forces beyond their control. As a result, Harvard and institutions like it live a much more precarious existence than our predecessors could imagine fifty years ago, and our continued prosperity is much more dependent on the attitudes of the society at large. As we have learned on several occasions in recent years, resentment over the elitism and arrogance of research universities can easily result in hostile treatment at the hands of legislative bodies and executive agencies.

Although the dangers beyond our gates are real enough, it is quite possible that greater hazards will emerge from tensions within our own community. As President Lowell remarked on this occasion in 1936: "If I read history aright institutions have rarely been killed while they were alive. They commit suicide or die from lack of vigor, and then the adversary closes in and buries them." With this warning in mind, we should take careful note of the inner contradictions and pressures that could limit us in carrying out our responsibilities.

In listing the weaknesses of successful institutions it is fashionable to begin by stressing the danger of complacency. And yet, of all our worries, complacency strikes me as the least significant. In my years at Harvard, I have never seen an institution so conscious of the danger of running downhill or so filled with people determined to do creative work. If we are looking for problems, surely there are other concerns that warrant a greater claim on our attention.

One such problem is the difficulty universities experience in setting priorities and limiting growth. This is an understandable failing. As knowledge and expertise grow more important, their uses multiply, and intriguing opportunities constantly appear. Since universities are anarchic by nature and flourish by giving professors free reign, new initiatives continue to blossom, old programs remain, and the institution grows inexorably.

As this process continues, universities become progressively harder to administer. There are so many programs to keep track of, so many appointments to make, so many places where problems can arise, so many activities clamoring for funds that the demands would tax the capacity of even the most experienced manager. Yet experienced management is precisely what universities must do without. By their nature and function, they need to choose their principal officers from the ranks of the faculty. Untrained in the arts of management, these academic leaders are easily overwhelmed by their administrative responsibilities, leaving them little time for the exciting work of conceiving fresh thoughts about the improvement of education and the emerging opportunities for creative research. We may end, therefore, with the worst of both worlds; appointing leaders for their academic experience who have no chance to think about academic questions. This problem has afflicted presidents for some time. Increasingly, it is affecting provosts, deans, and directors of important programs as well.

The constant growth of universities also requires a relentless quest for funds, as many in this audience will be quick to acknowledge. In the increasingly competitive world of higher education, campus representatives must be more and more resourceful in seeking out money from public and private resources. At best, this pressure results in much good-natured pestering. But in big-time athletics, it often leads to a shameless exploitation of athletes. In science, it generates pressures to enter into arrangements with industry or government which contain elements of secrecy or restrictiveness that compromise a free and open environment for investigation. To those of us who labor in the academic vineyard, such methods often seem purified by the noble purposes we seek to achieve. As Bishop Lawrence once said, on setting out to raise money for Harvard: "When you are serving a truly great cause, you cannot afford to be too scrupulous." To skeptics outside the academy, however, who do not share the Bishop's zeal, the scramble for funds often confirms their belief that universities are just another privileged group trying to further its special interests.

Faculty members too are increasingly caught up in the toils of fundraising and administration as they struggle to develop their departments and maintain their research centers. But many professors are encumbered even more by all the opportunities that come to them in a society hungry for expert knowledge. In professional schools and, increasingly, in Arts and Sciences faculties as well, possibilities abound for consulting, government service, going to conferences, and explaining one's field of knowledge to an interested public. Gradually, quietly, these extramural ventures come to represent for many professors a mounting source of excitement, variety, status, and income.

Such activities are not necessarily harmful. They often serve a valuable purpose by bringing professors into contact with interesting people and events that they might otherwise know only vicariously. Still, the activities do take time away from other pursuits more central to the institution's purpose.

These pressures and distractions are unlikely to recede in the next fifty years. On the contrary. Scholars will find it harder to keep up with their field as the volume of knowledge grows constantly greater. Extramural opportunities will increase as society continues to find new needs for expertise. Faculty members will receive more and more requests to help administer the university as it struggles to maintain a larger portfolio of programs and activities.

As the demands increase, how well will we respond? I scarcely know, yet there are surely grounds for concern. In a world where scholars have to specialize so heavily and rely so much on external sources for recognition and support, loyalties are already divided between the university, the profes-

sion, and the agencies that supply them funds. As these conflicting pressures grow, and faculties are ever more involved with the society that sustains them, can we expect professors to be immune from the prevailing values of our time? A generation of scholars is coming of age that grew up with Watergate and Vietnam and inherited a pervasive distrust of established institutions. We should not assume that they will feel the same institutional loyalties that their predecessors shared any more than we can count on the same loyalties elsewhere in the society. Instead, in a world that honors success and opulent lifestyles, we could easily find ourselves harboring more and more professors who try to combine the freedom and security of a tenure academic post with the income and visibility traditionally reserved for people who take much greater risks and work at much less elevating tasks.

Whether or not these visions materialize, one thing seems certain. In the future, the key ingredient on campus will not be money, important as it is, but time.

Time does not always work in obvious ways. For example, we know from watching our students carefully that those who try to devote every moment to their studies often lower rather than raise, their academic performance. The same may be true of scholars as well. People who are engaged in many absorbing tasks bring an intensity to their work that frequently improves its quality. But we also know that there comes a point when extracurricular burdens become so great that academic work begins to suffer. The possibility we confront in future years is that more and more faculty members will go beyond that point.

If they do, what consequences can we expect? Quite possibly, the effects will not be immediately obvious. Scholarly output may not suffer. Lectures may still be competent and informed. But as time for uninterrupted reflection ebbs away, scholarship may increasingly lack depth and breadth and rely too much on the work of assistants. There will be less opportunity for the casual contacts with students that may seem unnecessary but often provide the most memorable and critical moments in a young person's life at the university. More likely still, there will be no time to make a serious effort to comprehend how students learn and how they can be helped to learn more. Already, we do not understand enough of what our educational programs accomplish nor do we work systematically enough at finding ways to make them better. We talk a lot about how smart our students are when they enroll, but know too little about how much they learn after they arrive. Small wonder that outsiders often ignore the true meaning of a university education and describe it in such crass, material terms.

By now, you have heard enough of our concerns to understand what a harvest of problems our successes have brought us. These problems are very different from the challenges that universities surmounted so effectively in the last fifty years. To address today's agenda, we cannot rely on the forces generated by our system of higher education to move us in the right direction, for the hazards I have described are the products of that very system. To prosper in the future, we will have to make a determined effort to resist the pressures that would deflect us from our appointed mission.

In preparing for this task, we will need to keep one thing firmly in mind. All of the dangers I have described share a single characteristic. Each of them results from a failure to appreciate the proper aims of a university and the conditions essential for achieving them. It is easy to ignore these fundamentals. Many of us take them for granted now that we have grown so accustomed to research universities. Some are tempted to push them aside in order to accomplish other ends that seem particularly urgent. At times, we fail to perceive how unfamiliar circumstances threaten our essential values. Whatever the reason, we will need to be much clearer about the functions that universities perform uniquely well and the conditions required to carry them out.

In particular, we will need to persuade the public and to remind ourselves that we are not corporations, not instruments of national security, not militant bodies anxious to force our vision of social justice on the world. Many organizations can offer advice, or help solve society's problems, or develop new products, or further our military aims. But only universities, or institutions like them, can discover the knowledge on which creative solutions rest and only they can educate the men and women who will eventually make the critical decisions. Many individuals can be entrepreneurs, or advocates, or influential advisors. But only scholars blessed with security and freedom can master the largest subjects and pursue the truth wherever the quest may lead them. Many experiences may temper our judgment and help us grow. But only education can work simultaneously to develop intellectual capacities, awaken new interests, lift aspirations, provoke important questions, deepen understanding—and these, not the reflected lustre of the institution or the influence of its alumni, must be the university's true contribution to its students.

To give these values the eloquence they deserve, let me close with another quotation from President Lowell. For if Lowell could not perceive the great events and transformations that lay ahead for Harvard and the future, any more than we can know them today, he surely understood where Harvard's true salvation lay. In his words,

> As wave after wave rolls landward from the ocean, breaks and fades away . . . , so the generations of [students] follow one another, sometimes quietly, sometimes, after a storm, with noisy turbulence. But whether we think upon the monotony or the violence in human history, two things are always new—youth and the quest for knowledge, and with these a university is concerned. So long as its interest in them is keen, it can never grow old, though it counts its age by centuries. The means it uses may vary with the times, but forever the end remains the same.

VI.5

# To Secure the Blessings of Liberty
*Text of Report on State Colleges' Role*

**A Word to the
American People**

Ignorance is the enemy of democracy. Undeveloped intelligence that falls short of potential is a tragedy for the nation as well as a catastrophic denial of personal opportunity for the individual.

America has far too many people whose abilities are never awakened. This staggering waste and dissipation of our most precious resource means unemployment, unenlightened citizen participation or nonparticipation in elections and other processes of democracy, reduced productivity, and personal stagnation leading to frustration, crime, and abuse of freedom.

This wanton loss occurs because the nation is only partially committed to educating all of its people at a time when our international standing is being threatened and our economic future eroded by highly educated, highly motivated competitors abroad. For the sake of our future and in the interest of our humanity and civility, we must reorder our priorities to make a full and unequivocal commitment to learning.

Is it enlightened reason to take away access to higher education by making massive reductions in federal and state support of education? Under what rationale of priorities do we reduce student aid in the federal budget while increasing spending for the military? Ironically, the enormous cost of sophisticated and complex weapons that require skilled intelligence for utilization as well as advanced technological competence for production and maintenance dictates the very necessity for higher learning and more opportunity for education.

Our nation's economic future, our national security, and the education of our people are all tied together. This structure requires each of the elements of the triad as solid support. Weakening of one threatens the basic strength of the other two. That is why we must have an unprecedented commitment to education. Ignorance is not only costly—it is the passageway to a disastrous fall from which America may never recover. With a high school dropout rate ranging from 25 to 50 percent, and with almost 10 percent of our total population functionally illiterate, who can deny that we have a massive population of undereducated people? The United States is using up its intellectual capital but not replacing it. We must stop acting as though this state of affairs does not exist.

Public officials who propose budget reductions in education at a time when the republic is handicapped by the burden of an undereducated populace are unthinkingly abetting an act of national suicide. Their priorities are wrong. Their lack of insight and their misguided perceptions of the nation's needs contravene fundamental democratic values. They mock their countrymen who so desperately hope for a new era and the dawn of a learning society in America.

The report in its entirety is available from the American Association of State Colleges and Universities, 1 DuPont Circle, Suite 700, Washington D.C. 20036. It is reprinted here by permission of the American Association of State Colleges and Universities.

316

# A Gathering Storm

The National Commission on the Role and Future of State Colleges and Universities sees a storm brewing in U.S. public higher education. Its turbulence will stir up questions about the role and future of state colleges and universities, presenting them with an unprecedented opportunity for answers that can place them in a position of national leadership.

This Report identifies some of the social, political, economic, and educational conditions that forecast the storm, and proposes a series of policy recommendations for governmental and educational leaders to help all Americans secure the blessings of liberty.

The storm warnings are unmistakable: our society is troubled, our economy endangered, our democratic values jeopardized, our international leadership threatened, our educational system embattled.

■ The nation's educational pipeline is contracting as the high school dropout rate mounts to over 25 percent, reaching levels as high as 45-50 percent for minorities in disadvantaged urban areas.

■ Black college students as a percentage of black high school graduates and Hispanic college students as a percentage of Hispanic high school graduates have declined annually since 1975.

■ By 1990, racial and ethnic minorities will account for 30 percent of all 18-22-year olds in the United States.

■ Despite gains in the early 1970s, at the end of the decade blacks still lagged behind whites in both attainment and achievement at each stage of education from high school through graduate and professional studies.

■ The education reform movements, while riveting public attention on the need to improve quality at both the elementary-secondary and the collegiate levels, have failed dismally to address the needs of minority youth, in many cases resulting in the uses of ''excellence'' and ''quality'' as code words for denial of access and opportunity to blacks, Hispanics, and other racial minorities.

■ In today's America, there are at least 23 million adults who have been identified as functional illiterates. In addition, some 13 percent of U.S. teen-agers, and up to 40 percent of minority adolescents, have been found to be functionally illiterate.

■ There are 50 million households in the United States where no family member holds a bachelor's degree—and the figure increases annually.

■ An American underclass is growing at an alarming rate; as many as one-fifth of the nation's children are living in poverty, and nearly half of poverty households are headed by single women.

■ There is an appalling increase in the frequency of adolescent pregnancies, perpetuating a poverty status for females with the greatest need for education but the greatest difficulty in obtaining it.

■ In an era of tight budgets, funds for postsecondary remedial education programs, including special counseling services needed for disadvantaged students, are being sharply curtailed.

■ As college costs have skyrocketed over the past ten years, including the cost of attending public institutions, federal student aid programs have failed to keep up, and have lost considerable ground in real dollars.

■ Across the land, the pendulum of reform in higher education is bringing new laws, policies, and regulations affecting the teaching profession, academic standards, admission and graduation requirements, testing practices, curricula, finance, student services, degree programs, administration procedures, governance, and institutional organization. This has meant that in many states, faculty members, administrators, and trustees at public colleges and universities have permitted their responsibilities for establishing admissions policies and academic standards to erode to the point where such policies are now being shaped in the political arena.

■ A nationwide shortage of elementary and secondary school teachers impends and will soon reach crisis proportions in some cities and states, with the profession needing over one million new teachers by the mid-1990s.

■ A dangerous imbalance in federal student aid programs exists between the percentage of federal support being channeled into grant or work-study programs and the percentage devoted to loans. Whereas in 1980 some 65 percent of federal student aid was in the form of grants or work-study programs, with 35 percent in loans, today that ratio has been reversed, with 65 percent of federal support in loan programs. This means that thousands of college and university graduates are entering the world of work already saddled with huge debts in the America of the late 1980s.

■ An Education Commission of the States (ECS) report found that in 1985 the number of 14-24-year olds who compose America's entry-level labor pool is shrinking, while at the same time "the number of young people who are disconnecting from school, work and the benefits they confer is on the rise." Consequently, poorly motivated teen-agers, lacking fundamental literacy skills and unacquainted with the responsibilities and demands of the work world, are "at risk of never living up to their potential, never leading productive adult lives."

■ Recent studies reveal that American college students, compared with their peers overseas, are poorly informed on global issues and lack an understanding of their country's role in international affairs.

## A "Marshall Plan" for the States

■        These storm signals bode ill for the quality of American life. Nothing short of a creative state-by-state effort to strengthen education at all levels comparable to the Marshall Plan in scope, cost, and dedication, can ensure the preservation of our democratic legacy for the twenty-first century.

■ indicates a Commission recommendation

In the judgment of the Commission, the dimensions of such an effort require that:

- At least 35 percent of American adults should have a college degree by the year 2001.
- State colleges and universities must assume the leadership role in producing the one million additional public school teachers required to meet the needs of elementary and secondary education during the next decade.
- State colleges and universities should direct their academic resources and institutional priorities toward working cooperatively with public schools and community colleges to reduce the high school dropout rate by 50 percent over a ten-year period.

In this Report, the Commission seeks to delineate the role state colleges and universities—a U.S. resource of immeasurable value—must play in that nationwide effort and what public leaders must do to help those institutions fulfill their role as stewards of higher learning.

The Commission has prepared its Report, therefore, as an essentially *political* document—political, in the broad sense that it is addressed to the body politic, both outside and within the higher education community.

The Report is intended for anyone concerned with public policies affecting state colleges and universities. And in contemporary America, that ought to mean everyone, for these are our nation's mainstream campuses—the institutions that should be equipped to offer everyone who wants to earn a bachelor's degree the opportunity to do so.

State colleges and universities today form the centerpiece of the U.S. public higher education system. Chartered to serve the regions and the states in which they are located, positioned between the community colleges and the land-grant/research universities, the state colleges and universities have a pivotal, continuing role as primarily teaching institutions and an emerging mission as centers for basic and applied research and community service. Their continued growth and vitality depend on enlightened academic, fiscal, governance, and management policies developed cooperatively by political and educational leaders committed to the concept that education represents a state's wisest investment in its future.

A major test of the viability of those policies and the effectiveness of that leadership lies just ahead as public higher education faces the complex of social, economic, technological, and demographic changes that are dramatically reshaping American society and profoundly affecting the U.S. role in world affairs.

The Commission perceives these structural changes in our national life as an unprecedented opportunity for state colleges and universities—a test of their resilience and their ability to respond in new and daring ways to challenges to fundamental democratic values, to the imperatives of broadening access to higher education while sustaining program quality, to the urgent needs of business and industry in the realm of economic development, and to the stark facts of international life as an interdependent world prepares to enter yet another dangerous century. All of these challenges will require educational and political leadership of the highest order, with public policies fashioned for the years 2001 and beyond, to build a republic of learners.

# Regarding Public Higher Education and Democratic Values

*Religion, morality, and knowledge, being necessary to good government and the happiness of mankind, schools and the means of education shall forever be encouraged.*
Article Three. The Northwest Ordinance. July 1787

Democracy depends on the informed consent of the governed. Because experience has taught us that being informed cannot be left to chance, schooling and education have been a focus of attention in the United States from the inception of the republic 200 years ago.

Historically, under the Tenth Amendment to the Constitution, public responsibility for the support and control of education is vested in the states, which have been the basic source of laws and charters granted to postsecondary institutions during the past two centuries. In the nation's earliest times, to be a college graduate was to be a part of an elite group. It meant that person was either rich or bright. As the decades went by, the United States came to realize that a small, educated elite was not consistent with its democratic goals, so public policies were developed to break down the barriers to educational opportunity.

After establishment of the public normal schools in Massachusetts in the late 1830s, as America's frontier pushed westward, the early territorial legislatures provided for free public colleges that would be equally open to all—a concept that received great impetus from the passage of the Land-Grant Act of 1862.

With its emphasis on equity and opportunity at all levels, America's public system of education has enriched our society in every conceivable way.

Educated people bring social and economic benefits to the communities and states in which they live. They have learned how to become productive citizens and active, responsible participants in their country's affairs.

Over and over, public schools and colleges have proved to be the wellspring of democracy. In modern times, the GI Bill, the National Defense Education Act of 1958, the Supreme Court's *Brown v. Board of Education* decision, the Higher Education Act of 1965, and its subsequent amendments all attest to that fact. Since 1960, an expanded system of comprehensive state colleges and universities and community colleges has extended educational access to millions who were previously barred from postsecondary education either because of stringent restrictions or because they could not afford it. Recently, these institutions have designed nontraditional programs addressing the learning needs of people where they are—in the work place, including active military service—in terms of their own educational development.

Most Americans view education as a national investment in the preservation and strengthening of social values. Since the time of Thomas Jefferson, our political and governmental system has been predicated on an informed citizenry. "I know of no safe depository of the ultimate powers of the society but the people themselves," Jefferson wrote in 1821, "and if we think them not enlightened enough to exercise their control with a wholesome discretion, the remedy is not to take it from them, but to inform their discretion by education." Between now and the century ahead, our citizens will have to make sophisticated and enlightened judgments about complex scientific, technical, and moral issues, ranging from the international implications of acid rain to the development of nuclear arms.

## Access, Equity, Opportunity

Comprehensive state colleges and universities were developed to make higher education *accessible* to all who seek to continue their education; *affordable*, to put a chance to go to college within everyone's reach; and *accountable* to the states and communities that support them.

But state colleges and universities today face a serious dilemma. Just as the concepts of *equity* and *opportunity* were reinforced by public laws and policies, the current efforts to improve the nation's educational system are guided by an emphasis on the need for *quality* and *excellence*. Therefore, policy makers must face the question of how to reconcile the divergent forces that may be perceived to exist between the goals of excellence and quality, on the one hand, and the goals of equity and opportunity, on the other.

Without quality in education, the nation loses its strength. Without equity in education, democracy ceases to function. The Commission believes that ways must be found to manage the excellence/equity equation so that the boundaries of our public higher education system are extended, not limited.

It is not necessary to give up the goal of educational opportunity in order to achieve excellence. It is not a case of either-or, but both: "True educational excellence in our democracy," the Trustees of the Educational Testing Service have declared, "is not possible without true educational equity."

## The "Low Tuition Principle"

One means of safeguarding and expanding access to postsecondary education in the public sector is to keep tuition at state colleges and universities as low as possible, a principle that has undergirded the development of public higher education from earliest times. According to the low-tuition principle, although costs vary from state to state, tuition levels in the public sector should encourage, rather than deny, access to postsecondary education. The principle is based on the concept that society recognizes the fundamental values inherent in education and that national survival depends on the nourishment of those values. Accordingly, society should bear a significant part of the financial cost of a student's college education.

The parental generation pays, primarily through state and federal taxes, for the education of the younger generation who attend public postsecondary institutions. Then, members of the younger generation, as college graduates, enter the work force, earn income, quickly become taxpayers, and in their productive years pay, in turn, for the public higher education of members of the next generation.

Society's investment in education is thus constantly renewed: by paying taxes, each generation accepts the responsibility to increase educational

■ opportunity for successive generations. The Commission views the low-tuition principle in higher education as an extension of the free public elementary and secondary school system, an extension that becomes all the more necessary as America's technological and social complexity increases, confronting society and education with new problems.

Several of these problems are highlighted by current demographic data showing that the highest birth rate, the lowest high school graduation rate, the lowest rate of participation in higher education, and the highest incarceration rate all describe a single subset of the U.S. population—the growing underclass. Furthermore, the data on the nation's more advantaged populations indicate that the traditional family structure of just two decades ago is changing drastically, including vastly increased numbers of women in the work force, posing dislocations of traditional values and adding to the nation's dilemma.

■ The Commission recommends that, in formulating long-range plans for public higher education, state policy makers strive to keep tuition levels at state colleges and universities as low as possible, and that faculty members, administrators, and trustees at those institutions incorporate a commitment to ''the low-tuition principle'' in policies relating to institutional accessibility.

Low tuition levels require appropriation of state tax funds sufficient to attract and retain highly qualified faculty members, purchase up-to-date equipment, utilize modern instructional technology, and otherwise ensure that requirements for maintaining academic quality are met.

## Higher Education and Public Service

U.S. higher education has a long history of preparing young adults for responsible civic leadership. However, in recent years, with the nation's problems becoming more complex, social scientists and other educators have observed that the interest of college students in their obligations as citizens appears to have diminished. More and more of them, studies show, are preoccupied with personal goals and career aspirations, with such preoccupations being reinforced by curricula that overstress vocationalism and understress the responsibilities of citizenship in a democracy.

To counter this trend, a number of public and private colleges and universities have begun to provide students with the opportunities to participate in public and community service activities as part of their undergraduate experience. Institutional encouragement of students to take advantage of such opportunities benefits society as a whole by extending education, by inducing individual participation in the political process, and by enhancing student understanding of the general welfare.

"Public and community service," the Education Commission of the States (ECS) has reported, "can do more than any academic seminar to counter provincialism and imbue [in students] a sense of responsibility to others."

The social and educational value of public and community service, in the Commission's judgment, is clear. It is a concept that should form the nucleus of the general education component of a student's learning experience, a value basic to enlightened citizenship. The Commission recommends, therefore, that state colleges and universities recognize the value of student participation in public and community service activities and make every effort to integrate public and community service into the undergraduate curriculum.

## Regarding Educational Opportunity in the United States

*In these days. it is doubtful that any child may reasonably be expected to succeed in life if he is denied the opportunity of an education. Such an opportunity. where the state has undertaken to provide it. is a right which must be made available on equal terms.*
The Supreme Court of the United States. in *Brown v. Board of Education*. 1954

In a society in which knowledge is a source of wealth, deprivation of access to higher education is a form of bondage. The social, economic, political, and cultural complexity of contemporary America requires a much higher level of education for everyone than ever before envisioned. Entry level jobs in the increasingly technical service economy require advanced levels of knowledge and skills. Yet only 19 percent of adults over twenty-five in this country have a bachelor's degree.

Only 8.8 percent of black Americans, 7.8 percent of Hispanic Americans, and less than 1.5 percent of Native Americans have a bachelor's degree. Nearly 50 million American families have never had a college graduate in their households. While minority communities are the most rapidly growing segment of our population, their rates of participation in higher education, except for Asian Americans, are actually declining.

To arrest this dangerous trend, we must ensure that all individuals who aspire to earn a bachelor's degree have the opportunity to attempt to fulfill that aspiration. Indeed, in order for the United States to maintain a leadership position in the world, and for its faltering economy to regain its strength in the face of international competition, at least 35 percent of American adults should have a college degree by the year 2001.

To accept this challenge, state colleges and universities will have to embark on an educational venture without precedent. Over the next ten years, these institutions will have major responsibility to produce one million public school teachers capable of working with the most diverse group of students ever to enter America's schools. The state colleges and universities will have to direct their academic resources and efforts toward working with the public schools and the community colleges to cut the high school dropout rate in half by 1996. Only by deliberately reaching out into the elementary and secondary schools and helping to salvage those students who might otherwise drop out will the nation be able to produce the numbers of college-educated people needed for the next century.

Responding to this challenge requires acknowledgment and acceptance: (a) by faculty members, of the necessity to become more skilled and adept in the assessment of student learning and progress; (b) by legislators and institutional leaders, of the imperative to respond effectively to the diverse educational needs of the nation's rapidly growing populations—minorities and new immigrants; (c) by public policy makers and college administrators, of the need to maintain educational support programs, often called remedial education, to overcome handicaps of earlier academic preparation that may have been weak or inadequate; (d) by the nation as a whole, of the need to produce multilingual citizens for a multilingual society and interdependent world; (e) by public officials, of the great national asset represented by the number and diversity of state colleges and universities.

## One Million Teachers

Nowhere is there a greater need for leadership in higher education than in the preparation of teachers for the nation's public schools. The rapidly changing demographic structure of our society is creating serious shortages of teachers at all levels from early childhood education through the high school disciplines. Bilingual and multilingual teachers have been recruited in Europe, for example, to fill this year's positions in American schools.

Just to keep the doors of the public schools open, this country will need one million new elementary and secondary teachers, educational specialists, and school administrators to be trained and placed over the next ten years. With their historic roots as teacher education institutions, America's state colleges and universities are the sector of higher education with the primary responsibility and capacity for meeting this need.

Working in close cooperation with the public schools and teacher organizations, state colleges and universities must:

■ ensure that the academic preparation of teachers meets the highest standards expected by the schools and by the public;

■ attract more talented students, including greater numbers of minority students, into the teaching profession;

■ work in collaboration with teachers in the classrooms at all levels to solve practical problems of improving their teaching skills, developing better methods of student assessment, developing more effective curricula, and enhancing student motivation for learning.

This commitment cannot be made or fulfilled by schools or colleges of education alone. It must be made by all departments and disciplines and reinforced at the top levels of institutional leadership. Every faculty member should be held responsible for making a contribution to raising the level and quality of public education to meet the needs of the next century.

Because the crisis in teacher education is national in scope, the Commission recommends that Congress reinstitute the student loan forgiveness program for college graduates entering the teaching profession.

## Frontiers in Facilitating and Assessing Student Learning

Recent criticisms of higher education have centered on the weaknesses in generic skills that many college graduates reveal. Some state colleges and universities have raised their entrance standards to ensure that all students will perform at a predetermined level, and most rely on traditional course tests and nationally standardized examinations to chart student progress. These approaches to assessment mask the need to search continuously for pedagogical techniques that facilitate learning. Such approaches also exclude many capable students from the opportunity to achieve an education.

State colleges and universities should be in the forefront of the movement to develop more effective methods of assessing the educational progress of students.

Assessment should be seen primarily as a means of enhancing the effectiveness of educational programs, not just as a means of demonstrating academic quality.

Because the Commission is convinced that much of vital importance has yet to be learned and understood about the instructional value of assessment and its use, it recommends that state college and university faculties assign high priority to research on pedagogy at all levels; develop coherent plans for determining when, where, and to what extent each student should demonstrate progress toward an agreed-upon set of bachelor's degree-level skills; and, paralleling such measures, design instructional strategies to correct deficiencies and to assist students to achieve at higher levels.

## Institutional Diversity

Responding to the challenges inherent in meeting different needs and developing diverse talents cannot be accomplished by a monolithic design of higher education. Similarly, no single institution can be expected to offer the complete variety of courses that would permit it to respond to every challenge. It should not be surprising, therefore, that American higher education is by any yardstick the most diversified in the world. Its institutions are large and small, urban and rural, public and private, two-year, four-year, graduate, and professional. They may emphasize graduate and research programs, undergraduate teaching, or cooperative programs with industry. Their students may be historically or predominantly from minority groups. The foregoing characteristics combine in various ways at institutions having two-year or four-year degree programs that range from primarily technical to broad and comprehensive curricula.

State colleges and universities are characterized by diversity. Even when two such institutions may at first glance appear similar, significant differences emerge—between their special curricula (for example, Canadian Studies versus Afghan Studies, or pure mathematics versus mathematics education); their student body (residential versus commuting); purely undergraduate versus graduate; or the socioeconomic compositions of their campuses. In this fashion each state strives within its own higher education governance framework to provide and ensure maximum educational opportunity for its citizens. It is essential, therefore, that every effort be made to maintain such distinctions among institutions and their curricular and instructional programs. Maintaining diversity results in the

cultural and economic enrichment of the communities and regions the institutions are chartered to serve.

Within the context of institutional diversity, special attention is due the significant role the thirty-four public historically black institutions have played and are
expected to play. Established at a time when no other higher educational opportunities were available to the vast majority of black students, they have helped
this country benefit from the development of talents among black Americans.
They have done so under the most adverse conditions and in ways bordering
on the miraculous. They have had to function in a manner that embodies the
essential merits of access and opportunity.

Because our society still needs much progress before black young people
of traditional college age can find at any campus of their choice an environment
conducive to their educational and personal development, the historically black
institutions will continue to occupy an important niche among higher education
institutions in serving their historical clientele.

Enrolling approximately 27 percent of all black students in public four-year
institutions, the historically black public institutions today must be regarded as
playing an expanded role in public postsecondary education. They must be
recognized as having the same kind of regional significance in regard to applied
research and community service that pertains to any other state college or university. Their experiences have made them reservoirs of skills and understanding
for teaching and nurturing underprepared students. They have at the same time
moved into the mainstream of higher education, as evidenced by the proportions of their graduates who have proceeded to earn doctoral degrees. They
possess a rich heritage which, through proper recognition and support, will continue to strengthen and increase access to higher education.

## Remedial Education

Remedial education is not new to American higher education and has existed since 1636. Colleges have provided it for every wave of immigration and
for every new group of students for 350 years. Freshman composition programs,
for example, have always included, at least in part, remedial spelling, grammar,
and rhetorical instruction. Compensatory efforts have long been made to overcome the lack of certain mathematical skills. Such efforts have been accepted
without indictments, given the large differences in the levels of development of
school districts around the country, and have greatly helped to ensure graduation by those admitted to college.

Now, as society becomes ever more diverse, the number and type of educational disparities have increased, and with them, the increasing need for appropriate remedial programs. Recently immigrated students, for example, while
they may be fully qualified for higher education, must continue to become

proficient in the English language while pursuing their studies. Students from inadequate rural or inner-city high schools may be deficient in oral communications skills. Students talented in the arts may need help in mastering the sciences. Almost all students need specific assistance in written expression. But these deficiencies ought not to be permitted to destroy a student's opportunity to pursue a higher education.

For the foreseeable future, state colleges and universities must plan to provide remedial instruction. Recognizing that the foundation of college persistence and achievement is solid academic preparation in high school, state colleges and universities should make a concentrated effort to reduce the incidence of postsecondary remedial education by becoming more actively and directly involved in the preparation of high school students for college study.

More school/college cooperative programs should be developed that not only stimulate the talented, but also guide, enrich, and raise the performance levels of underperforming students. This process ought to include joint meetings of college and high school faculty members and administrators and a sharing of data on student performance.

## Financing Opportunity for All

Basic to our country's approach to education is the pivotal idea that the blessings of liberty should not be dependent on social class. It is, indeed, a moral tenet in America that a class-based society is wrong. One of the goals of the concept of universal education that has guided the development of public elementary, secondary, and higher education systems is to equip each individual to "break out" of underclass status—to "be all that you can be." If educational opportunity is stifled, if the chance to go to college is placed beyond the reach of large numbers of high school graduates, we will produce an elitist system of higher education—the very danger the state colleges and universities were created to guard against.

The GI Bill affirmed the tremendous dividend the American people could earn on their investment in expanding educational opportunities. Then, beginning with the Eisenhower Administration, the nation achieved political consensus on establishment of a federal student financial aid program to enable more students to go to college, so that qualified men and women who wanted to continue their education beyond high school, but who could not afford to do so, would not be denied that opportunity.

Over the years, spanning the presidencies of Kennedy, Johnson, Nixon, Ford, and Carter, such federal aid took the form of Pell Grants, loans, and work-study programs, and the resultant investment in America's economic future has grown. Our economy has been strengthened, our security safeguarded, and our society nourished. Students from families in all walks of life have benefited from that financial aid program. *Seventy-five percent* of all student aid available in U.S. colleges and universities today, in both the public and private sectors, is *federal aid.*

Tragically for the American people, the federal student financial aid program today is on the chopping block in Washington. In 1981, the value of the federal student assistance program was challenged by the new Administration, which began to recommend deep cutbacks in the annual congressional appropriations supporting it. So effective has been that challenge that in the last five years federal student financial assistance purchasing power was cut by 25 percent.

The current Administration, in other words, seeks to cut student financial aid in order to help reduce the deficit. But increases in student aid have *not* added to the deficit. In fact, from 1980 to 1986 the federal deficit *doubled* in constant dollars while federal expenditures for education at all levels *declined* by 16 percent.

In addition, because of increases in college tuition, the percentage of federal student aid awarded as grants has declined, while reliance on student loans has grown, to the point where college graduates today are burdened with debts in excess of $10,000 before they enter the work place. The nation has embarked on an indentured student policy to finance higher education.

Congress should take steps to provide sufficient funds for student financial assistance to rectify the existing imbalance in the federal financial aid program so that the amount of assistance channeled into grants and work-study would be at least equal to that appropriated for student loans.

Our national investment in higher education is not part of the deficit problem. Instead, it is part of the *solution.* An educated populace is a productive populace, earning and returning a portion of that earning power to society in the form of taxes. Education is not a luxury; we cannot be strong either militarily or economically unless we are also strong educationally.

Public policy makers will know that all individuals who aspire to earn a bachelor's degree shall have gained the opportunity to do so, when: (1) cost is not a barrier; (2) minorities are participating in and completing higher education at rates that match their proportions in the population; (3) substantial attention is given to eliminating limitations of access for those having physical disabilities; and (4) adult learners, and particularly single parents, find no roadblocks based on age or gender hindering their access to higher education.

## Regarding Higher Education and Economic Development

Our nation's universities and schools have a vital role to play in revitalizing America's competitiveness. . . . Without strong educational institutions, the United States will not be able to capitalize on our key potential strengths in technology and human resources.
The President's Commission on Industrial Competitiveness, January 1985

**H**istorically, America's economic growth—and thus its national security—has been inextricably linked to the development of human resources and the applications of advances in research and technology to every sector of the nation's business and industry. The greatest threat to the future security and well-being of our nation is the waste of human beings through their inadequate education. Our country must chart a path toward excellence, with policies that encourage all individuals to perform at the peak of their abilities, or risk becoming economically subordinate to those countries willing to do so.

The map of every state is dotted with economic backwaters where educational levels are low, unemployment is high, and prospects for growth are dim. State and local leaders know that such communities, whether rural or urban, will never attract new economic activity unless these conditions are turned around. Recent studies show that in a business' decision to relocate, such factors as the quality of the public schools, local higher education and cultural centers, and communications facilities, are often as important as access to raw materials, markets, or cheap labor.

State colleges and universities have a vital role to play, both in improving the quality of public education in their respective states and regions, and in stimulating the business climate through the application of knowledge resources to business problems.

## Investment in Human Capital

Experience and common sense tell us that educated people:
- bring economic benefits to their communities and states,
- get better jobs,
- earn higher wages,
- pay more taxes,
- stimulate America's cultural, intellectual, and scientific progress,
- and become more productive and responsible citizens.

Today's state colleges and universities are the generators of the service economy, training professionals in business, computer science, engineering, health, teaching, and other service sectors with growing needs for well-educated personnel. By providing access to professional careers for the broadest cross-section of Americans, including women and members of minority and immigrant groups, public colleges and universities represent a pathway into the American mainstream for individuals and families who would otherwise not have the opportunity to make this step, thus helping to ensure the stability of our free economy and our democratic government.

Policy makers should do all in their power to keep the college doors open, both literally and figuratively. Closing the doors of a college or university devalues the state's human capital portfolio and removes its resources from those available for investment in future economic growth—a shortsighted solution to a long-term problem.

When a decision is reached to close a state college or university, such action should be taken only as a last resort—only if the state is certain that its educational investment is being reinvested elsewhere, and only if access to higher education opportunities is not being foreclosed.

## Partners in Regional Economic Development

State colleges and universities link the country in a network of knowledge available for application to problems of regional economic development. They help governments and industries find new uses for old resources to make a region's economy more secure.

A recent study by SRI International provides myriad examples of the positive impact colleges and universities have on the economy of their regions, expanding human capital through education and training, generating new technologies, new products, and new services through basic and applied research, and helping businesses maintain their competitive edge by sharing knowledge resources and transferring innovations from sector to sector throughout our economy.

State governments should examine the role that public higher education can play in regional economic development, including the possible expansion of institutional responsibilities in the areas of research and public service.

Higher education institutions, both public and private, can and should help governments and businesses achieve economic development goals through:

- Economic Research and Analysis, including gathering and housing regional economic data, and assisting governments and business with data analysis,
- Technical Assistance, through faculty consulting or centers organized to assist businesses to increase their competitiveness,
- Research and Development, including cooperative research with business and industry,
- Technology Transfer, applying knowledge, expertise, and technological developments to new sectors of the economy,
- New Business Development, including business incubators, and university entrepreneurship that stimulates local business.

But efforts by individual institutions and the states alone will not ensure that our country's economy will be internationally competitive. Congress should create a national program to enhance the role of colleges and universities in community service and economic development. Such a program should encourage the involvement of higher education institutions with government, labor, business, and industry in planning, research, and development activities that promote expansion and retention of jobs and foster linkages that contribute to regional, state, and national economic growth.

## Adult and Continuing Education

There is little need to search beyond the fact of the increasing average age of those who enroll in college to be convinced that state colleges and universities must address the educational requirements of individuals older than twenty-five. New careers, more effective participation by citizens, continued intellectual vitality, single parenthood, women reentering the work force, expansion of leisure activities—all have been noted as sources of the increase in college participation by adults.

Economic shifts, plant closings, and depressions in the local economy create a particularly poignant need to which public colleges and universities can respond through retraining adult workers for new occupations or upgrading their skills to improve productivity.

In order to respond to these needs, state colleges and universities should restructure their modes of delivery of instruction and services to give adult and part-time students full access to undergraduate and graduate programs. Specifically, institutions committed to serving adult learners should build on tested cooperative models: work-study programs, instructional television, instruction at the work place, and faculty-designed computer-aided instruction.

Access to continuing education programs should be provided in all regions of the states, to give working people the chance to pursue job advancement while fulfilling their civic and family responsibilities.

To ensure that working adults have meaningful access to such programs, the federal government should extend financial aid on a full-parity basis to all part-time and adult students.

## Research

Research as a process of rational and creative inquiry leads to new ideas, concepts, understandings, and products. Because successful, high-quality research depends at its core on the developed skills of critical thinking and reasoning through analysis and synthesis, it is both an integral part and an outcome of higher education.

There has long been an underestimation of the place of both basic and applied research at state colleges and universities. People are often surprised to learn that research at state colleges and universities has resulted in breakthroughs in such areas as robotics, artificial intelligence, and biotechnology, in addition to the excellent social science and historical research and creative scholarly activity focused on the states and communities they serve. The talents among the faculty and students at these institutions have been underestimated and, therefore, underutilized. Over time, however, state colleges and universities have expanded the array of people who have the ability not only to do research themselves but also to teach research skills.

The contributions that can be made by state colleges and universities to the economic development of their regions, as well as the state and the nation at large, depend on the extent to which business and government can capitalize on the knowledge and achievements of their faculties through research, as well as teaching and service.

In the future, comprehensive state colleges and universities can be expected to continue to be involved in innovative research without becoming replicas of the research universities.

Research programs at state colleges and universities should continue to be developed, not only to meet the increasing needs of business and industry, but also to enhance state and regional information resources and to improve the quality of life. Such programs promote private-sector employment by developing a region's natural resources in an environmentally sound manner, while at the same time adapting new technologies to a region's specific economic needs.

# Regarding American Higher Education in an Interdependent World

*No child should grow to adulthood in America without realizing the promise and the peril of the world beyond our borders. Progress made in teaching about world affairs must not lag behind progress made in other areas of American education.*

President Lyndon Johnson's Message to Congress accompanying the International Education Act. 1966

In 1984-85, U.S. higher education was the object of three major critiques examining the state of affairs on the nation's campuses, ranging from the quality of instruction through the performance of students to the scope of the curriculum. Although the reports from the National Endowment for the Humanities, the Association of American Colleges, and the National Institute of Education varied in emphasis, their principal message was essentially the same:

America's colleges and universities have become too utilitarian, too vocational in their orientation, too parochial in their world outlook, with their curricula incoherent and in a state of disarray. Campuses have become "supermarkets," the critics charged, with narrow specialties the order of the day and the humanities on the decline.

Perhaps most alarming were the warnings in all three studies that American college students in the closing years of the twentieth century are seriously deficient in their knowledge of world affairs and their country's role in the international scene. Many colleges and universities in both the public and private sectors were found to be woefully inadequate in giving students an opportunity to study the languages and cultures of other nations; tests revealed Americans from all walks of life to be shockingly ignorant of the political, economic, and social forces that shape our interdependent world.

In examinations administered by the Educational Testing Service, for example, college students were shown to be lacking in understanding such realities of international life as: the relationship of the U.S. economy to the Organization of Petroleum Exporting Countries (OPEC); the causes of inadequate nutrition as a global problem; the comparative world membership of Islam and Christianity; the current patterns of world birth rates and death rates; the reasons for the lack of substantial progress toward world peace during the twentieth century; the significance of nationalism as a political force; or the meaning of sovereignty.

The realities of today's world make it essential that there be a strong international dimension to our educational system from grade school through graduate school. Jet travel has put us only a few hours from any point on the globe. Television satellite transmissions bring acts of terrorism instantaneously into our living rooms. Indeed, the international perspective of many of our citizens is distorted by the constant flow of news about international violence. The economic, cultural, and political events that constitute international relations are submerged by more sensational news. Yet our long-term survival depends on ability to live in the absence of war, not in its presence.

While the United States and other advanced industrialized countries reap the benefits of modern technology, some 800 million people in the Third World, according to the World Bank, currently live at levels that can only be described as abject poverty. Conversely, technology transfer is creating new economic competition in the developing countries. We only need look at our stores and homes to see evidence of the development of Korea, Hong Kong, Taiwan, Singapore, and other Pacific Rim nations. World problems such as strained trade relations, dwindling resources, overpopulation, hunger, pollution, energy, poverty, lack of adequate communication, inflation, and war all require international solutions.

Our lack of knowledge about other cultures can seriously undermine the nation's foreign policy. Americans are prone to assume—quite erroneously—that our economy and our technology are the envy of the rest of the world and that if underdeveloped countries would only follow the U.S. example, they would discover the secrets of economic progress. Yet only a short time ago in Iran, that assumption was perceived to be directly counter to the basic tenets of the Moslem religion and Iranian culture, and it ripped American policy to shreds.

How many U.S. college graduates since World War II were ever exposed to courses dealing with Islamic cultures? How many Americans today understand the religious roots of the war between Iran and Iraq? How many of us had even a casual knowledge about Southeast Asia before the early 1960s? Or about Korea before 1950? Or, for that matter, about Japan before 1941? Yet in our time Americans have fought three wars in the Pacific basin with little or no grasp of the enemy's history, language, religious beliefs, or culture.

## Strengthening International Education

The Commission believes that today's international environment confronts U.S. educators with a threefold challenge:

First, to provide students with an international perspective that reflects the world as it is today in realistic social, political, cultural, and economic terms;

Second, to provide students with international communications skills which will enable them to think, behave, and work effectively in a world of rapid change;

Third, to assist, through research, technical assistance, study, and international service programs, in the resolution of international problems with the same commitment that educational institutions now address domestic issues.

In the Commission's judgment, a critical leadership responsibility for sensitizing Americans and their elected state and national officials to the urgent tasks ahead in the area of international education rests with faculty members and administrators in state colleges and universities. These institutions are regionally based, with roots in every corner of the land. Many of them have already demonstrated extraordinary capabilities in developing outstanding international programs; virtually every state has at least one such institution with a history of overseas ties and commitments, experiences that should be shared across states or regions.

These prototype international programs gauge the extent to which a campus has developed a global perspective, not only in the humanities and social sciences, but also in the total institutional curriculum. They offer an opportunity to encourage the expansion of foreign language and undergraduate area studies programs, not just for social science majors, but also for students in business, engineering, the health professions, and other preprofessional fields. Their guiding premise should be that all students in the university should have a chance to develop an understanding of other cultures, non-Western as well as Western.

Most important for state colleges and universities, which graduate over 50 percent of the teachers annually certified in the United States, is the need to concentrate on improving international education programs for future teachers in the nation's public schools. Some studies brought to the Commission's attention disclose that many social studies teachers today are ill-informed regarding world affairs. In overcoming this "teacher parochialism" in the international area, state colleges and universities must not overlook the imperative to provide opportunities for international experiences for low-income students.

Every scholar who has studied the international education field emphasizes the importance of the institutional mission statement in framing a campus "world outlook." The four Commission-sponsored regional seminars in March and April 1986 urged that the development of such a statement should involve trustees, administrators, faculty members, and professional advisors from other colleges, as well as from abroad. A well-conceived mission statement, in the Commission's opinion, provides a particularly strong incentive to implement international programs in various professional fields, as well as in the liberal arts.

## International Education and U.S. Foreign Policy

At the federal level, the Commission believes that the support of education for international understanding should be a fundamental, ongoing component of U.S. foreign policy, and that initiatives in support of international education should be undertaken on four fronts:

First, that state colleges and universities lead the academic community in renewing and strengthening higher education's ties with the Peace Corps, which were so strong in the 1960s and early 1970s, but which have languished in recent years. One possibility might be a compact in which public postsecondary institutions would agree over a long period of time to link Peace Corps service with academic programs for credit and to support Peace Corps recruiting in fields such as teaching and community development. State colleges and universities would also continue to serve as training sites for Peace Corps Volunteers recruited for service overseas.

Second, that state colleges and universities develop internationally oriented courses of study adapted to the special educational needs of business, industrial, professional, and military personnel scheduled for work abroad, particularly emphasizing language and area studies and courses in intercultural understanding.

Third, that Congress establish a national foundation or trust for international education, both undergraduate and graduate, along the lines of the National Science Foundation and the National Endowments for the Arts and Humanities—a partnership effort involving the academic, industrial, and governmental communities.

Fourth, that Congress authorize a long-term student exchange program designed to bring vastly increased numbers of Third World students to study in the United States and to provide American students with the opportunity to study abroad.

This concept is rooted in the conviction that faculty and student exchange programs constitute vital elements in America's continuing role as an international leader. It also recognizes that, given the financial strictures under which the states will be operating for the foreseeable future, international education must be pursued as a direct, continuing responsibility of the federal government. The proposal is predicated on the assumption that our country would be far wiser and more prudent to export education today than run the risk of importing revolution tomorrow.

## A Word to State Colleges and Universities

Tacit acceptance of old assumptions about higher education leads to hardening of institutional arteries. The world of this century has changed profoundly and rapidly. It is to that changed world that higher education must respond. Hardened arteries can only inhibit an institution's capacity to respond.

Preventive measures must be taken. For this reason, the Commission calls for bold steps—steps sufficiently bold and large that our imaginations and resolve will be stretched to limits heretofore, perhaps, unthinkable. We call for a state-by-state effort comparable to that of the Marshall Plan of the 1940s and 1950s. Such an achievement will entail a combined and concerted undertaking by higher education leaders and the makers of public policy.

The Commission's thinking has led it time and time again to repeat the proposition that all education is an investment in people. Evidence grows that the return on that investment is real and substantial. We believe that the call must now be for a dramatically increased investment at the level of higher education. Educational practices and public policies must work together toward increasing the investment and making its dividends widely available.

Old assumptions that impede this effort must be either rejected or modified. Assuming that higher education will focus principally on "traditional" students; assuming that modern technology will have little impact on modes of teaching and learning; assuming that state colleges and universities will and should return to a condition of "laissez-faire" autonomy; or assuming that it will be impossible to find the resources to respond to these new challenges could halt the effort even before it is attempted.

## Academic Quality

Perhaps no concern about higher education has attracted more attention than the quality of undergraduate education. Most frequently the concern is expressed in terms of deficiencies exhibited by many college graduates in their communication skills, their ability to solve quantitative problems, their knowledge about the world around them, and their competence as critical thinkers.

For example, the three recent national studies by the National Endowment for the Humanities (NEH), the National Institute of Education (NIE), and the Association of American Colleges (AAC) collectively constitute a most serious indictment of U.S. higher education and, indeed, of the entire academic profession. Thus:

"Evidence of devaluation in college curriculums is everywhere. The business community complains of difficulty in recruiting literate college graduates. Remedial programs, designed to compensate for lack of skill in using the English language, abound in the colleges and in the corporate world. Writing as an undergraduate experience, as an exploration of both communication and style, is widely neglected." (AAC)

"The bachelor's degree has lost its potential to foster the shared values and knowledge that bind us together as a society." (NIE)

"A student can now obtain a bachelor's degree from 75 percent of all U.S. campuses without studying European history [and] from 72 percent without studying American literature or history." (NEH)

More recently, three other agencies—the Carnegie Task Force on Teaching as a Profession, the Education Commission of the States (ECS), and the National Governors' Association (NGA)—issued major reports on quality in undergraduate education and the need for dramatic structural changes in policies and practices in the field of teacher education—a professional area of particular concern to state colleges and universities. ECS, in its report, found that "too many students are entering college without the knowledge, skills and attitudes necessary for success in college, a gap [that] will inevitably widen as the nation changes its expectations about what people should know."

Public colleges and universities should respond to these concerns by agreeing on and adopting a set of minimum academic skills and levels of proficiency that all students should attain, preferably by the end of the sophomore year. This should be done on the basis of faculty recommendations and administered in a way that will assure the public that the necessary skills expected from a college education are, indeed, being achieved. Students should be required to match or exceed these threshold requirements, which would provide a basic accountability and a standard upon which individual institutions can build. Each college and university should further specify clearly not only the skills but also the means by which it will facilitate their acquisition by every student before a bachelor's degree is awarded.

Recipients of baccalaureate degrees should have obtained knowledge and experiences that equip them a with sense of competence, relevance, and pertinence for the future. Not only must they function well in a multilingual, technological, global society, but they must also contribute to its advancement and quality. It would be tragic if America's colleges allowed baccalaureate graduates to be monolingual in that global society; to be technologically naive in an age demanding technical skills and sophisticated understandings; or to be uninitiated to the "real-life" worlds of work and of social responsibility.

The dimensions of this undertaking are only gradually being realized:

Study of foreign language and culture should become standard, and over the next fifteen years, state colleges and universities should ensure that all degree recipients master a language other than their native tongue.

Graduates should understand how to use science and technology sufficiently to contribute knowledgeably to public decisions.

Hands-on experiences and internships should expand students' knowledge about the work place and instill a commitment to the public good. At the same time, higher education must continue to increase students' competence and skills; to develop their talent and a love of learning; and to transmit an understanding and appreciation of their own and other cultures.

## Faculty Vitality and Excellence in College Teaching

Faculty vitality and excellence in college teaching go hand in hand. Both are characterized by enthusiasm for the subject taught and delight in seeing evidence of student learning. Both are characterized by persistent curiosity about one's discipline and those of others. Both are characterized by an eagerness in encountering new ideas and new patterns of thought. Both are evidenced by energetic response to the challenge of instructing students who are diverse in their educational, ethnic, and cultural backgrounds.

Dynamism of an institution and the quality of its functioning are determined foremost by the interaction between its faculty and students and among students themselves. Searching for strategies to strengthen that interaction should continue to be a matter of highest priority. There will be, as a consequence, matters of both institutional and public policy that will require special attention of educational and public leaders.

Among these are: a faculty reward system that gives full recognition to outstanding teaching; opportunities to be engaged in and to involve students in research, and scholarly or other creative activity; and support for sabbatical leaves, faculty exchanges, and special provisions for gaining new knowledge and developing new academic skills.

The Commission recommends that state fiscal and institutional policies be adopted or modified to ensure that faculty vitality and excellence in teaching are maintained and enhanced.

## Leadership and Its Newer Dimensions

In recent years higher education institutions have been subjected to increasing pressures stemming from developments such as the decline in high school populations and subsequent college enrollments, changing student interests, and reduced state and federal resources. These pressures have prodded institutions to focus more of their attention on fiscal matters. In response they have turned to corporate models of strategic planning and management. A number of helpful insights have been gained from this perspective, but there is mounting evidence that the corporate perspective has limited applicability to education.

Because business has *profit* as its bottom-line, a business's effectiveness is largely controlled by its competitive edge. The bottom-line outcome of education is improving students' competencies, knowledge and skills. Strengthening an institution's educational effectiveness, then, is to be found in its *cooperative* dimension. When an educational institution sees itself as competing for students and resources, it is hindered in developing productive consortia, sharing instructional strategies, and mounting joint research ventures. By virtue of drawing support from the same ''pie'' of state resources, state colleges and universities have a special mandate to be assertive and responsive in exploring the benefits of cooperation within and among their campuses.

Qualities of creative leadership in the past have been, to a large degree, geared to a frontier spirit. Not all, but much of the educational frontier has been explored and structured. America has become a highly interactive community. Thus the new dimensions of leadership will be measured in terms of cooperative endeavors.

The Commission emphasizes the compelling need for such endeavors because the educational task facing the nation looms large. Support for the effort will be encouraged by discovery of cooperative uses of existing resources, as well as the search for new resources. Cooperation—not competition: this is the new challenge for leadership in higher education.

# Afterword

**O**n September 17, 1987, the United States will observe the 200th anniversary of its Constitution. As we did on July 4, 1976, in celebration of the nation's bicentennial, and again on July 4, 1986, in saluting the Statue of Liberty on her 100th birthday, we the American people will once again count our blessings.

The Commission believes that all Americans will be able to share those blessings fully and fairly only when our society begins to reach the outer limits of its national potential—a dramatic potential that augurs well for our country's stature as a leader in the community of nations.

While we have taken giant steps toward fulfillment of that goal since World War II, much remains to be achieved, with storm clouds threatening to diminish or forestall our accomplishments. We need only to be aware of the growing American underclass and the vast numbers of disconnected and disaffected youth who daily turn their backs on school, to sense what these clouds portend.

The key element in reaching our national potential, in the Commission's judgment, is a public higher education system that offers everyone a chance to go to college. It is the Commission's conviction that the state colleges and universities are the gateways that make broader access to educational opportunity possible. Dedicated principally, as they are, to undergraduate instruction that rests on a solid foundation of general and professional education, and awarding, as they do, more than 30 percent of all bachelor's degrees, their current and future role is indispensable to the accomplishment of broad national educational objectives. Indeed, without the full support and cooperation of the state colleges and universities, it would be impossible for the public schools to effect the basic reforms called for by the National Commission on Excellence in Education in its Report, A *Nation at Risk*, issued in the spring of 1983. As the American Association of State Colleges and Universities said in its policy statement, AASCU *and the Nation's Schools*, adopted in November 1983, the "alumni of 'the colleges of the forgotten Americans' have [as teachers] touched the lives of children in virtually every school district in the land."

Education is basic to every facet of our national life. This Report emphasizes that many, many more Americans need the benefit of the knowledge and skills that a college education can provide. The Commission is persuaded that, unless educational leaders and public policy makers join in a major, new, state-by-state effort to expand educational opportunity, the vitality of our nation will suffer, and our ability to aid in bringing greater stability to the world will disintegrate.

For the United States to shrink from this challenge would be unforgivable.

Those who could not forgive would be those whom we chose, tragically, in the closing years of the twentieth century, not to educate to their fullest potential.

As we prepare to celebrate the beginning of our Constitution's third century, state colleges and universities must squarely face the imperatives of their renewed trusteeship. For they are stewards of the American dream.

## VI.6

# Congressional Economic Panel's Report on Student-Loan Burden

WASHINGTON

*Following is the text of a report—"Student Loans: Are They Overburdening a Generation?"—prepared for the Joint Economic Committee of Congress by Janet S. Hansen, director of policy analysis for the Washington office of the College Board. Opinions are those of the author and do not necessarily reflect the views of the committee or the board. References have been omitted.*

## I. Introduction

■ *Mortgaging a Generation*—a report on student loans by the California Postsecondary Education Commission.
■ *Mortgaged Futures*—a book on how to pay for college by Marguerite J. Dennis.
■ "We've said to young people, if you want an education, here's a loan, pay for it yourself."—Theodore J. Marchese, *Change* magazine, May/June 1986.
■ "The rapidly increasing dependence on loans as a means of financing students is alarming and must end."—Frank Newman, *Higher Education and the American Resurgence.*

As these titles and quotes and the commissioning of a paper by the Joint Economic Committee indicate, concern is mounting about the rapidly growing indebtedness of students pursuing postsecondary education. Attention to this issue is long overdue.

Until recently, research and analysis on student loan programs (most of which involve repayment guarantees and/or subsidies from the federal government) largely focused on their costs to the government or on the level of borrower defaults and how to

reduce them. Because of the need to cut federal deficits and spend federal dollars as wisely as possible, these issues will and should continue to be debated.

Equally important, however, are questions about what large amounts of student debt mean for the economy, for individual borrowers, and for education and society.

Student loans are not new. President Lyndon Johnson, who presided over the creation of the Higher Education Act of 1965 which included student grant, loan, and work programs in its pathbreaking Title IV, was said to have been most interested personally in the Guaranteed Student Loan (G.S.L.) program. He had borrowed to attend college in the 1930's and reportedly felt that loans should be more widely available to students in higher education. In fact, [Robert A.] Caro reports that Johnson borrowed from the bank, from his college, from friends, and even from the local newspaper publisher, and dropped out of school to teach for a while when he couldn't keep up the payments on these debts (and the loan he took out to purchase a used Model A!).

The G.S.L. proposal was designed to facilitate student borrowing by overcoming the reluctance of private lenders to make uncollateralized loans to young persons with no credit history through the provision of repayment guarantees. It also gained support from those wishing to derail college tuition tax credits, which almost passed the Senate in 1964. It was viewed largely as a minimally-subsidized loan of convenience for the middle class; it had an eligibility ceiling of $15,000 in annual income at a time when median family income was $6,957. Needier students already

had access to another federally-sponsored loan program, National Defense (now Direct) Students Loans (N.D.S.L.), which had been enacted as a last-minute substitute for politically-unpopular grants in the National Defense Education Act of 1958. Before the establishment of these federal programs, both colleges and states had created opportunities for students to borrow to help pay the costs of college.

Why are student debt levels the subject of rising concern? Mainly the now huge size of G.S.L. and the large number of students who use it to take out ever larger loans. In 1985-86, 3.6 million students borrowed $8.3-billion in G.S.L.'s. Over 800,000 students took out about $750-million in new N.D.S.L.'s in that year, and other smaller federal loan programs accounted for about $800-million more. Loans are now not just a convenience for the middle class but an important part of the way they and lower-income families finance higher education. This transformation, however, has occurred with relatively little attention paid, either at the beginning or along the way, to what the impact of borrowing for education would be on students who would have to repay the loans.

This paper is an introduction to the complex issue of whether heavy dependence on student loans is creating serious problems for individuals or the society in which they live. While more and more people are looking at this question, it is nevertheless the case that research and analysis are as yet skimpy and fragmentary. Much of the current concern about student indebtedness is based on impressionistic and anecdotal evidence, but data about student loans in general and the G.S.L. program in particular are woefully inadequate for addressing most policy concerns.

This paper, then, is suggestive rather than definitive. It examines the available evidence about student loan rates and levels and how these have changed over time. It identifies some of the major questions that underlie the feeling that reliance on student loans to finance higher education has gone too far, provides some preliminary indications about the extent of the problems, and addresses what can and needs to be done. It establishes a foundation for the task of further marshalling evidence, analysis, and discussion to help determine how great the danger is that we are undesirably mortgaging the futures of college students or jeopardizing national economic growth.

Though existing statistics on loans frequently make it impossible to distinguish borrowing for graduate and professional education from pre-baccalaureate borrowing, this analysis focuses whenever possible on the latter. Graduate students represent only about one and a half million of the approximately 14 million students enrolled in postsecondary education (defined here as including the proprietary sector as well as government and independent nonprofit colleges and universities). Though their borrowing is often large—the average medical student graduates $30,000 in debt—their circumstances are different than undergraduates: they know with some certainty, for example, what careers they will enter and what salaries they can earn. Special programs, moreover, can be and have been created to deal with the pockets of extremely high borrowing found in some graduate and professional fields. Assessing the effects of graduate student borrowing requires an analysis different from the one in this paper; an important contribution on this subject is the study recently published by the Association of American Universities.

Section II of the paper traces the growth of student borrowing over the last two decades. Then, sections III through VI discuss student loans and how they may affect the economy, the well-being of young adults, the achievement of equal educational opportunity, and the educational process. Section VII looks at the risks students face in borrowing to pay for education and at how the United States compares to other countries in protecting students from these risks. A final section indicates what preliminary conclusions can be drawn from this analysis.

## II. Trends in Student Borrowing

Despite the fact that students borrow almost $10-billion annually for postsecondary education, statistics on student loans are poor to nonexistent. Researchers and governing bodies alike have expressed, in various fashion, their frustration over the lack of basic data to answer obvious questions about who is borrowing, how much they are borrowing, and what has happened to borrowing over time.

■ "Currently available data do not permit accurate determination of the actual cumulative debt burdens for Guaranteed Student Loan borrowers in California."

■ "There exists no coherent central data base for the Guaranteed Student Loan Program, no central integrated data base which links the various Title IV programs, and no systematic cross-year data on student aid recipients across programs."

■ "The data suffer from a number of serious limitations precluding, for the most part, any *definitive* assessment of the incidence and level of borrowing among postsecondary students."

■ "The best we can do is read tea leaves and make inferences."

There are almost no data except overall program totals available at the national level for G.S.L., which is far and away the biggest student loan program. Most G.S.L. data comes from state guarantee agencies and varies in amount and quality; one major shortcoming is that state agencies have no way of combining information on students who take out loans guaranteed by more than one agency.

## Table 1: Student Borrowing by Program for Selected Years

| | 1970-71 | 1975-76 | 1980-81 | 1985-86 |
|---|---|---|---|---|
| **Guaranteed Student Loan** | | | | |
| Number of loans (in thousands) | 1,017 | 922 | 2,899 | 3,640 |
| Dollars loaned (in millions) | | | | |
|   Current dollars | $1,015 | $1,267 | $6,187 | $8,288 |
|   Constant 1986 dollars | $2,872 | $2,567 | $8,031 | $8,493 |
| Average loan | | | | |
|   Current dollars | $998 | $1,374 | $2,134 | $2,277 |
|   Constant dollars | $2,824 | $2,784 | $2,770 | $2,333 |
| **National Direct Student Loan** | | | | |
| Number of loans (in thousands) | 452 | 690 | 813 | 854 |
| Dollars loaned (in millions) | | | | |
|   Current dollars | $ 240 | $ 460 | $ 695 | $ 751 |
|   Constant 1986 dollars | $ 680 | $ 932 | $ 902 | $ 770 |
| Average loan | | | | |
|   Current dollars | $532 | $ 667 | $ 853 | $ 880 |
|   Constant dollars | $1,505 | $1,351 | $1,107 | $ 902 |
| **PLUS** | | | | |
| Number of loans (in thousands) | — | — | 6 | 212 |
| Dollars loaned (in millions) | | | | |
|   Current dollars | — | — | $ 14 | $ 548 |
|   Constant 1986 dollars | — | — | $ 18 | $ 562 |
| Average loan | | | | |
|   Current dollars | — | — | $2,333 | $2,585 |
|   Constant dollars | — | — | $3,029 | $2,649 |

— Program not begun.

## Table 2: Average Indebtedness from All Sources for Undergraduates Who Borrow, 1985-86

| Institutional type | After 2 years | After 4 years |
|---|---|---|
| Public 2-year | $3,303 | — |
| Private 2-year | $4,461 | — |
| Public 4-year | $3,217 | $6,685 |
| Private 4-year | $4,340 | $8,950 |

Note: Data are from 485 public 2-year, 107 private 2-year, 335 public 4-year, and 736 private 4-year institutions.

With the exception of a few direct surveys of students or institutions, there are no data on combined borrowing from different programs: G.S.L., N.D.S.L., health professions loans, college and university loan funds, etc.

Thus, it is impossible to assemble precise and comparable nationwide statistics on student borrowing over the past two decades. Nevertheless, a judicious choosing of tea leaves makes it possible to give an impressionistic description of such borrowing and how it has changed in recent years.

Most student borrowing occurs in the three main federal loan programs: G.S.L., N.D.S.L., and Parent Loans to Undergraduate Students (PLUS), a G.S.L. offshoot established in 1980 to provide less-subsidized loans to parents, graduate students, and independent undergraduates. Table 1 gives basic statistics on these three programs for selected academic years since 1970-71, in both current and constant (adjusted for inflation) dollars.

The raw numbers in Table 1 suggest why concern over student loans has been on the rise, showing as they do a startling increase in the amount of borrowing especially under the G.S.L. program. After going along during the early 1970's at slightly over a billion dollars a year, G.S.L. borrowing took off after passage of the Middle Income Student Assistance Act (M.I.S.A.A.) in November 1978 removed all income limits on eligibility. By 1980-81 G.S.L. borrowing had reached over $6-billion and was slowed only temporarily by the reimposition of income restrictions in 1981. By 1985-86 borrowing climbed to over $8-billion in G.S.L.; in addition, students or their families were taking out more than a billion dollars more in N.D.S.L. and PLUS loans. (The exact amount of PLUS loans being taken by students rather than by parents in unknown; some early data indicated it might be about half.)

Table 1 suggests several important qualifiers to the impression that student indebtedness had run wild, however. The size of average annual G.S.L. loans more than doubled over the 15 years shown, but more important to the overall size of the program was the nearly four-fold increase in the number of borrowers. This is especially significant in light of the fact

## Table 3: GSL Indebtedness of Currently Enrolled Borrowers and Repayers in California as of June 30, 1984

| Total borrowed | Currently enrolled borrowers | Repayers |
|---|---|---|
| $0-$2,500 | 56.4% | 63.4% |
| $2,501-$5,000 | 23.7% | 26.2% |
| $5,001-$7,500 | 8.3% | 5.2% |
| $7,501-$10,000 | 6.4% | 3.6% |
| $10,001-$15,000 | 3.6% | 1.4% |
| Over $15,000 | 1.5% | 0.2% |

that postsecondary enrollments have been relatively steady since the mid-1970's, indicating that borrowing is a much more widespread occurrence among postsecondary students in the mid-1980's than it was in the early 1970's. Moreover, Table 1 illustrates that the *value* of the average annual G.S.L. and N.D.S.L. has actually declined over this period when inflation is taken into account. Thus, though many more students are borrowing each year than 15 years ago, on average their loans are smaller in terms of real purchasing power.

The piecemeal available data indicate that cumulative indebtedness of students is rising along with nominal increases in annual borrowing. A 1986 survey of financial aid directors nationwide by the College Scholarship Service (C.S.S.) and the National Association of Student Financial Aid Administrators (NASFAA) provides the best up-to-date indication of the debt levels of undergraduate students completing programs of study in 1985-86. Table 2 shows average debt levels for students who borrow

## Table 5: Cumulative Debt from All Sources of 1984 Seniors at 22 Private Colleges

| | |
|---|---|
| No debt | 27% |
| $1-$2,499 | 4% |
| $2,500-$4,999 | 10% |
| $5,000-$7,499 | 16% |
| $7,500-$9,999 | 20% |
| $10,000-$12,499 | 17% |
| $12,500-$14,999 | 3% |
| $15,000 and over | 3% |

Note: Percentages are not weighted by institutional enrollments or to adjust for differences in response rates. Results are based on 6,668 respondents from 22 institutions.

after two years in public and private two-year colleges and after four years in four-year colleges and universities. The statistics of most interest are those suggesting that student borrowers at public colleges are graduating with an average debt of $6,685, while their private college counterparts have debts averaging $8,950.

Though the data are again spotty, clearly today's students are accumulating more total indebtedness than did their counterparts in earlier years. [Jerry S.] Davis, using data on loans guaranteed by the Pennsylvania Higher Education Assistance Authority, reports that seniors leaving school in 1974-75 had cumulative G.S.L. loans averaging $3,698, a number which grew modestly to $4,474 in 1980-81 and then bounded upward to $7,110 in 1983-84. Elsewhere he reports that in 1980-81 slightly over 600 Pennsylvania undergraduates left school owing more than $7,500 in G.S.L.'s; in 1983-84 about 12,400 undergraduates left school owing this much.

The California Postsecondary Education Commission found evidence of increasing dependence on G.S.L.'s by comparing the accumulated indebtedness of students enrolled in school in 1984 (who are likely to borrow still more before leaving) and borrowers already in repayment (see Table 3) and noting the larger proportions of currently-enrolled borrowers at the higher loan levels. Nearly 20 per cent of those who were currently enrolled already had borrowed over $5,000, as compared to 10 per cent of those who had left school and were repaying their loans.

The cumulative indebtedness of graduating seniors in the University of Wisconsin system rose 19 per cent (from $5,884 to $6,995) between 1982-83 and 1984-85.

Cumulative loan amounts, however, vary widely around the average. Table 4 shows cumulative G.S.L. indebtedness for Pennsylvania seniors leaving school in selected academic years; it indicates both the range of debt and also how cumulative loan levels and the number of borrowers have been rising. It also shows cumulative indebtedness of seniors in New York in 1985-86. The large percentage of students with high debt levels in New York reflects both more recent data and the fact that a high proportion of New York students attend

## Table 4: Cumulative GSL Debt of Seniors in Pennsylvania and New York, Selected Years

| Amount | Pennsylvania | | | | New York |
|---|---|---|---|---|---|
| | 1974-75 | 1977-78 | 1980-81 | 1983-84 | 1985-86 |
| Less than $2,500 ....... | 29.3% | 33.7% | 31.7% | 9.4% | 10.5% |
| $2,501-$5,000 .......... | 45.2% | 34.8% | 35.0% | 17.6% | 18.3% |
| $5,001-$7,500 .......... | 25.5% | 31.3% | 30.4% | 27.2% | 21.6% |
| $7,501-$10,000 ......... | n/a | 0.2% | 2.9% | 43.8% | 38.8% |
| $10,001-$12,500 ........ | n/a | n/a | n/a | 2.5% | 10.8% |
| Number of students .... | 8,065 | 9,185 | 18,672 | 23,023 | 43,080 |

n/a = Not applicable.

private colleges. Table 5 shows the distribution of debt among students graduating in 1984 from 22 schools belonging to the Consortium on Financing Higher Education (COFHE), which represents 30 of the most selective and expensive private colleges in the country. These data, unlike most that are available, indicate how many students graduate without debt as well as the range of debt for those who borrow. At the 22 COFHE schools, only a quarter of 1984 graduates were debt-free, while 43 per cent left school owing $7,500 or more. Table 6 shows the distribution of average debt levels reported by financial aid directors nationwide for 1986 students completing four years of school. It indicates that relatively high levels of borrowing (average cumulative debts exceeding $10,000 for undergraduates) can be found at more than a quarter of private colleges and at a tenth of public ones.

Translating from current to constant dollars modifies the impression of growing indebtedness given by current dollar figures. The C.S.S./ NASFAA survey found current indebtedness among private college graduates who borrowed to be $8,950 in today's (1986) dollars. This would be the same after accounting for inflation as a cumulative indebtedness of $4,285 in 1975. An undergraduate today borrowing $12,500, which was the G.S.L. statutory maximum until legislative changes in October 1986, would be indebted at the same real level as an undergraduate who completed a bachelor's degree in 1975 with $5,985 in debt.

Thus while borrowing is increasing in amount and is certainly more widespread, inflation is an important part of the growth in cumulative debt levels.

Perhaps more important than total debt levels for undergraduates is the fact that borrowing is now so much more common. In the early years of G.S.L. most undergraduate borrowing occurred in colleges and universities, where students were the most likely to complete degree programs and to have higher earnings after graduation. Indeed, an early concern in G.S.L. was bankers' unwillingness to lend to poor students and to those in community colleges and proprietary schools. Illustrative data from two states demonstrated that these restrictions have been overcome. Community colleges led the way in the growth in use of loans in Illinois between [fiscal] 1975 and [fiscal] 1985 (Table 7). In Pennsylvania community college and proprietary school participation in student loans has grown significantly faster than the four-year colleges (Table 8).

Scattered additional evidence from around the country supports the view that there has been a large increase in borrowing among students at schools offering two years of study or less.

This change has been part of a larger transformation in G.S.L. from a program intended mainly to ease the cash-flow problems of non-needy families to a major source of funds for low-income students attempting to pay for college.

In Fiscal Year 1983, 40 per cent of all G.S.L. borrowers came from families with annual incomes under $15,000 (Table 9). Median family income in 1983 was $24,580.

The foregoing data suggest that while student loans are growing, individual indebtedness may not be as alarming as overall program statistics suggest.

But what about the future? Not only does the existing data suggest

## Table 6: Average Debt from All Sources at the End of Four Years, as Reported by Financial-Aid Officers*

| Debt after 4 years | Public 4-year institutions | Private 4-year institutions |
|---|---|---|
| Under $1,000 .. | 0% | 0.4% |
| $1,000-$1,999 .. | 1.5% | 0.5% |
| $2,000-$2,999 .. | 5.1% | 1.5% |
| $3,000-$3,999 .. | 7.8% | 2.2% |
| $4,000-$4,999 .. | 20.4% | 6.8% |
| $5,000-$7,499 .. | 31.8% | 19.3% |
| $7,500-$9,999 .. | 22.8% | 38.7% |
| $10,000-$14,999 | 9.0% | 27.3% |
| Over $15,000 .. | 1.2% | 2.6% |
| n/a ............ | 0.3% | 0.7% |
| Total number of schools ..... | 333 | 736 |
| Approximate mean ....... | $6,685 | $8,950 |

* Percentage distribution represents the distribution of survey respondents (one per school), not the number of students in each category.
n/a = Not applicable.

## Table 7: Undergraduate Borrowing from All Sources by Institutional Type in Illinois, Selected Years

| | Fiscal year 1975 | Fiscal year 1985 | Per cent change |
|---|---|---|---|
| **All schools*** | | | |
| Number of loans ................. | 30,289 | 106,902 | +253% |
| Amount lent ...................... | $ 41,677,113 | $245,682,273 | +489% |
| Average loan ..................... | $ 1,376 | $ 2,298 | + 67% |
| **Public 4-year** | | | |
| Number of loans ................. | 17,299 | 46,937 | +171% |
| Amount lent ...................... | $ 19,418,400 | $ 99,086,187 | +410% |
| Average loan ..................... | $ 1,123 | $ 2,111 | + 88% |
| **Community colleges** | | | |
| Number of loans ................. | 3,659 | 20,666 | +465% |
| Amount lent ...................... | $ 3,813,141 | $ 41,374,398 | +985% |
| Average loan ..................... | $ 1,042 | $ 2,002 | + 92% |
| **Private institutions** | | | |
| Number of loans ................. | 9,331 | 39,299 | +321% |
| Amount lent ...................... | $ 18,445,572 | $105,221,688 | +470% |
| Average loan ..................... | $ 1,977 | $ 2,677 | + 35% |

* Except proprietaries.

## Table 8: Number of Borrowers Leaving School by Sector in Pennsylvania, Selected Years

| Institutional type | 1974-75 | 1983-84 | Per cent change |
|---|---|---|---|
| **In-state** | | | |
| 4-year private | 5,083 | 16,717 | + 229% |
| State universities | 4,890 | 11,426 | + 134% |
| State-related | 4,297 | 13,769 | + 220% |
| Junior colleges | 262 | 1,373 | + 424% |
| Community colleges | 1,117 | 6,975 | + 524% |
| Nursing schools | 569 | 1,665 | + 193% |
| Proprietary schools | 4,443 | 30,829 | + 594% |
| **All out-of-state** | 4,754 | 12,445 | + 162% |

that the rate of increase has picked up in the 1980's, but there are clear signs that indebtedness is likely to continue on its upward course.

The statutory maximum annual loan limit for undergraduate G.S.L.'s was set at $2,500 in 1972, but actual average borrowing has only recently approached this level.

Future increases are unlikely to be constrained, however, since the reauthorization of the Higher Education Act (P.L. 99-498) signed into law on October 17, 1986 raises the undergraduate loan ceiling in G.S.L. to $17,250 and increases borrowing limits under N.D.S.L. as well.

The eligibility of middle-income students for G.S.L. was also curtailed; but states, schools, and private lenders seem likely to develop new borrowing options for this group.

Data from the C.S.S./NASFAA survey of financial aid directors also indicates that borrowing is likely to keep going up.

Table 10 shows that only a minority of respondents favored keeping loan limits where they are, though the range of opinion about what the maximum annual and cumulative loan limits for undergraduates from all sources should be was wide.

Having examined these diverse tea leaves, what inferences can be drawn? The following points sketch what is probably an accurate picture of student borrowing in the United States, the implications of which will be discussed below.

► Of the roughly 14 million students enrolled annually in public, private, and proprietary postsecondary institutions, the evidence suggests that about a third borrow. Since some students may borrow in one year but not another, the proportion of students leaving school with debt is higher. While we lack data to make

ready comparisons with earlier years, it is clear that the proportion of students borrowing to finance higher education has grown greatly in the last decade.

► Data on overall borrowing mask significant differences in the proportion of borrowers of different types. Graduate students probably borrow more frequently and at higher levels than undergraduates, full time students more frequently and at higher levels than part-timers, and students at private institutions more frequently and at higher levels than those enrolled at public, lower-cost schools.

► Among undergraduates, the range in borrowing is wide. Relatively few students leave school having borrowed the maximum for which they are eligible.

► Annual and cumulative borrowing by individuals has grown significantly, but adjusting borrowing levels for inflation modifies the magnitude of the increase. Real indebtedness levels are higher than they were 10 or 15 years ago, but not nearly so much as unadjusted statistics would suggest.

► While student loans used to be viewed as largely for the middle class, they are now used by many

students from lower-income families as well.

► Student borrowing is now common at community colleges and proprietary schools as well as among students in traditional baccalaureate programs, but the heaviest dependence on loans and the highest debt levels are found among students enrolled in private colleges and universities.

## III. Student Loans and the Economy

In 1985 the California Postsecondary Education Commission concluded from a review of the "problems and prospects" of the G.S.L. program in that state that "students with large loan indebtedness will typically have to postpone major purchases for at least a time after entering the work force.... The impact of this increasingly common set of circumstances has major implications for the overall health of the economy."

Concern over these issues has arisen among observers of rising student debt levels at the national level as well. The next section of this paper looks at whether the economic well-being of individuals is likely to be affected by the amounts borrowed for college. Here, we look at whether student borrowing poses a threat to the economy at large.

The question is a complex one and has been the subject of virtually no formal analysis. Therefore, the comments made here (even more so than the rest of this study) must be viewed as tentative and suggestive. At a minimum, we may be able to conclude whether the evidence currently available suggests that a major problem already exists or whether much

## Table 9: Income Distribution of GSL Recipients, Fiscal Year 1983

| Income | Financially dependent students | Financially independent students | All borrowers |
|---|---|---|---|
| Below $15,000 | 34.5% | 48.9% | 39.5% |
| $15,000-$29,999 | 28.6% | 24.4% | 27.1% |
| $30,000-$44,999 | 22.0% | 8.0% | 17.1% |
| $45,000-$59,999 | 7.8% | 2.0% | 5.8% |
| $60,000-$74,999 | 2.1% | 0.4% | 1.5% |
| $75,000 and up | 0.3% | 0.1% | 0.2% |
| Unknown | 4.7% | 16.4% | 8.8% |
| | 100% | 100% | 100% |
| **Percent of total** | 65.1% | 34.9% | 100% |

more detailed analyses would be necessary to draw this conclusion.

The danger to the economy posed by the increasing reliance on student loans is presumably the same danger that economists ascribe to high levels of debt in general. [Charles A.] Luckett and [James D.] August claim that the chief economic problem arising from high debt levels is the constraint imposed on spending when income must be directed to debt service rather than current consumption, though they also recognize the fear that creditors will curtail the availability of credit if high debt levels threaten losses on loans. In either event, spending increases could be constrained and economic growth thereby threatened.

National economic activity is spurred by government and business as well as consumer purchases, so economic growth depends on spending patterns in all three sectors. Therefore, one useful way to put student loans in context is to see what proportion they represent of all borrowing. Table 11 shows that the G.S.L. and PLUS programs (which reflect much but not all student borrowing, with N.D.S.L. the most significant omission) are currently a tiny fraction of the nation's debt. Economic demand seems much more likely to be affected by changes in other areas, such as government spending in this Gramm-Rudman era of budget cuts designed to trim the size of the annual federal deficit, than by what happens in the education loan arena.

Focusing on just household, as opposed to business and government, indebtedness, gives student loans a more visible, though still comparatively small, role. Table 12 shows how G.S.L. and PLUS have changed since 1978 in comparison to consumer installment and mortgage debt. In the Federal Reserve Board's economic reports, student loans that have entered repayment are counted as part of the former. Table 12 indicates that G.S.L./PLUS loans in repayment have grown almost 4½ times faster than installment debt as a whole since 1978, though still a small fraction of such debt. This statistic may overstate the significance of student loans as a constraint on household budgets, however, since these loans typically involve ten-year repayment periods and therefore are counted in the stock of debt longer than other consumer loans that are

| Table 10: Opinions of Financial-Aid Officers About Maximum Debt Levels, by Type of Institution | | | | |
|---|---|---|---|---|
| Issue | Public 2-year | Public 4-year | Private 2-year | Private 4-year |
| Per cent favoring no change in the current statutory annual maximum GSL for undergraduates ($2,500) | 67.0% | 44.8% | 40.7% | 31.1% |
| Per cent favoring increase | 33.0% | 55.2% | 59.3% | 68.9% |
| Per cent favoring no change in the current statutory maximum GSL for all undergraduate years ($12,500) | 53.8% | 41.4% | 40.6% | 25.0% |
| Per cent favoring increase | 46.2% | 58.6% | 59.4% | 75.0% |

usually paid off in one to five years. The extended repayment period means that monthly repayments on student loans are also lower than repayments on similar amounts of other consumer debt.

Whether or not today's historically high consumer debt levels are a problem for the overall economy is the subject of debate. Some analysts conclude after examining the various factors contributing to recent rapid increases that households do not appear in a weakened financial position and that household debt does not seem to be an impediment to future consumer spending, barring a general economic downturn. Others argue that both lenders and borrowers are threatened by recent borrowing patterns that mark a sharp step upward from the trends that have prevailed during most of the past 40 years. The outcome of this debate is unlikely to hinge on the comparatively small portion of household indebtedness that represents student borrowing, though any future consensus that debt levels overall have grown too large would certainly have implications for student loans.

Finally, it is important to note that any detailed assessment of the ef-

### Table 11: Outstanding Indebtedness of Government, Corporations, and Individuals, 1985 (in billions of dollars)

| | |
|---|---|
| Federal government | $1,600.4 |
| State and local government | $ 553.1 |
| Corporations | $1,505.1 |
| Individuals | $3,224.6 |
| GSL and PLUS loans* | $ 36.8 |

*Includes loans to students still in school and those that have entered repayment—fiscal year data.

fects of student loans on the economy would have to take account of the possible spurs to economic growth that these loans represent. This is yet another area where adequate research is lacking, in part because the analytical issues are tremendously complicated and difficult to disentangle. The question of how student aid in general, to say nothing of loans in particular, has affected the economy, among other things, is the subject of much debate and little consensus. But there is clearly a widespread belief that some positive benefits have accrued, despite the problems in measuring and attributing them.

At the most obvious level, loans probably contribute to economic growth by freeing resources that would otherwise have to be spent on education. Delving more deeply, analysts who believe that student assistance programs (grants, loans, and work) have had some positive effects on enrollment rates and educational attainments go on to argue that these effects "unquestionably translate into increases in the national income, the national tax base, employment, and overall productivity." [James C.] Hearn and [Sharon L.] Wilford also cite "a rigorous set of analyses" performed by Susan R. Griffith "examining the question of what the absence of the federal Title IV student aid programs since 1965 might have meant to the nation's economy. Her conclusions were blunt: without the massive federal student aid investment, the nation's unemployment levels and tax base would have suffered appreciably over the past twenty years."

Though Hearn and Wilford acknowledge difficulties with Griffith's study, they are right in looking to these kinds of question in order to get a balanced view of the impact of student aid.

## Table 12: Installment, Student Loan, and Mortgage Debt Outstanding (in billions of dollars)

| | Total GSL/PLUS loans outstanding | (1) Consumer installment credit outstanding | (2) GSL/PLUS loans in repayment | (3) (2) as a per cent of (1) | (4) Mortgage debt outstanding (1-4 family homes) |
|---|---|---|---|---|---|
| 1978 | $ 7.5 | $262.0 | $ 2.9 | 1.1% | $ 753.5 |
| 1979 | $ 9.1 | $296.5 | $ 3.2 | 1.1% | $ 870.5 |
| 1980 | $12.3 | $297.7 | $ 3.8 | 1.3% | $ 963.9 |
| 1981 | $18.5 | $314.3 | $ 4.7 | 1.5% | $1,038.5 |
| 1982 | $22.7 | $327.2 | $ 6.9 | 2.1% | $1,074.7 |
| 1983 | $27.0 | $376.2 | $ 9.5 | 2.5% | $1,192.8 |
| 1984 | $31.9 | $453.6 | $13.0 | 2.9% | $1,329.6 |
| 1985 | $36.8 | $535.1 | $16.1 | 3.0% | $1,469.1 |
| **Percentage Increase 1978-1985** | 390% | 104% | 450% | — | 95% |

Note: Total GSL loans outstanding include loans of students still in school as well as loans that have entered repayment. Only loans that have entered repayment are counted by the Federal Reserve as part of consumer installment credit outstanding.
GSL and PLUS data are for the end of the fiscal year. Consumer credit and mortgage-debt data are for the end of the calendar year.

What conclusions, then, can we draw about student loans and the economy?

► There is virtually no systematic analysis that addresses directly the question of how student loans do or will affect the economy.

► Whether today's historically high levels of government, corporate, and household indebtedness pose a threat to national economic growth is the subject of debate. The outcome of this debate is unlikely to hinge on the comparatively small portion of household indebtedness that represents student borrowing, though any future consensus that debt levels overall have grown too large would certainly have implications for student loans.

## IV. Student Loans and Individual Well-Being

The fact that it has not yet been demonstrated that student loans are negatively affecting the national economy does not mean that individual borrowers might not find their economic well-being threatened by the burden of debt repayment. This section examines the burden imposed on young adults by educational debt.

There has been more research which speaks to this issue than on many questions in the student loan area. As noted at the beginning of this paper, loan defaults have been the object of much attention, mostly because of concern over the costs (both political and monetary) they impose on government programs.

But since the act of defaulting might be considered at least a rough indication that the loan burden had proven unmanageable for the borrower involved, information on who defaults on student loans is also relevant to the issue of loan burden. Addressing the question more directly have been a number of studies attempting to define manageable levels of borrowing for students. Yet another research tack with implications here is analysis of how student loans might affect a borrower's subsequent ability to obtain credit for such things as a house and a car. Finally, there has been some effort to look at whether educational debt affects other life decisions such as career choice, marriage, and having children.

A number of studies have discovered that high cumulative debt levels do not appear to be the culprit in G.S.L. loan default. Rather, high default rates occur among borrowers of smaller amounts, those who take out only one or two loans, those who stay in school for only a year or two, and those who do not obtain their degrees or certificates. Community college and proprietary school students represent a disproportionately high share of defaulters. The total amount of indebtedness incurred appears to be much less a factor in default than does the relationship of this indebtedness to later income, the prospects for which are poorer for dropouts than for graduates and for students who attain lower levels of schooling.

Researchers have periodically attempted to define manageable levels

of indebtedness for college students, usually expressed in terms of the proportion of pre-tax or post-tax income that can reasonably be made available for student loan repayment. [James B.] Stedman reviewed major studies by [Andre] Daniere, [Robert W.] Hartman, [Joseph] Froomkin, and [Dwight H.] Horch and determined that there was "no consensus on where the threshold separating manageable from unmanageable levels of debt should be set." Manageability thresholds derived by these analysts ranged from 3 to 15 per cent of pre-tax income, for example. Nor is the diversity of findings the only problem with this approach. Stedman notes a number of other factors that limit its usefulness.

► Applying manageability thresholds to decisions about how much students can borrow requires information about future incomes and about the exact repayment terms of loans, information which can be difficult to get for a homogeneous group of borrowers (medical students, for example) and almost impossible for a diverse one (all baccalaureate recipients).

► In Stedman's view, many of the calculations used in defining manageable indebtedness are arbitrary.

► Debt manageability thresholds focus mostly on short-term debt burdens, whereas there are also long-range implications that should be considered.

► Relating debt service costs to income is a crude measure of a borrower's capacity to make repayments, a capacity which also depends on such factors as family size, the number of workers per household, and earnings prospects.

► Focusing on the manageability of educational debt alone may shift attention away from how much total indebtedness borrowers can manage and how student debt may cause young adults to be turned down later for additional credit to finance houses, cars, and other goods.

[Robert W.] Johnson and [A. Charlene] Sullivan have addressed this last point. They analyzed eligibility requirements imposed by lenders both for mortgage and consumer credit and assessed the extent to which these requirements were likely to limit individuals with educational debts from obtaining additional credit. Within both sectors the requirements are diverse, but they are less variable and more restrictive in the mortgage lending area. Johnson and Sullivan concluded that student indebtedness as it existed in 1981 (the last year for which they had data) was unlikely to affect the future consumption behavior of young adults. They found that credit markets did not impose particularly effective controls on consumer indebtedness, despite the existence of restrictions on the part of some lenders. In fact, borrowers appeared to be able to obtain "huge" amounts of consumer credit; their own self-imposed limits were responsible for keeping debt levels generally below maximum levels established by the marketplace. Johnson and Sullivan did express concern, based on their projections of future student borrowing and income patterns, that students graduating in the mid-to-late 1980's might find it more difficult to obtain credit for the purchase of residential property. Their projections of future student loan levels appear to be higher than we have actually seen, however, and the analysis would also presumably be affected by the recent and sizeable decline in mortgage interest rates relative to those obtaining when the study was written.

Nevertheless, there are two important points that relate to this issue of how student borrowers will subsequently fare in the credit market. The first is that, contrary perhaps to common expectations, credit markets will *not* keep young adults from getting into financial trouble by restricting the total amount they can borrow for various purposes. In fact, this absence of market discipline appears more evident now than it did three years ago. Sullivan argues that recent developments in the credit market—deregulation, innovations in credit delivery systems and contracts, and increased competition—"have removed some of the forces that have historically operated to limit the amount of credit available, especially to high-risk consumers." This suggests that educational and financial institutions providing student loans to often young, financially-inexperienced individuals have a responsibility to educate them about shopping for and managing credit so that they do not get themselves in over their heads when they leave school and face a host of new credit decisions and few restrictions.

The second point has to do with the future access of student borrowers to *attractive* forms of credit for

their later purchases. Mortgage and consumer credit used to be treated equally under the tax laws, but the tax reform legislation of 1986 gradually removes the deductibility of interest payments, except for interest on home mortgages. For the minority of taxpayers who itemize deductions, this will not only make student loans more expensive because interest will have to be paid with after-tax dollars, but will make second mortgages and other debt instruments based on home equity more attractive ways of borrowing money for whatever purpose than installment loans. If young adults who have borrowed as students find themselves less able than their debt-free peers to buy homes, they may find themselves comparatively disadvantaged in access to the most attractive loans for consumer purchases as well. Since young people have lower in-

comes and are probably less apt to itemize than the general population, however, this problem may turn out to be more hypothetical than real.

A final aspect of the economic well-being issue has to do with whether individuals who borrow for education will be able to repay only at the cost of choosing high-paying careers or delaying marriage or child-bearing. Three researchers who look at this question directly concluded that such was not the case. Davis reported that "Our 1982 follow-up study of 1981 alumni of Pennsylvania institutions found that: (1) only a few borrowers were experiencing loan repayment burdens; (2) there was no relationship between marital statuses and borrowing rates or levels; (3) alumni who had gone to graduate school or were planning on advanced degrees had *higher*, not *lower*, debt levels than others who had complet-

## Table 13: Comparison of Loan Burden Under Various Economic Assumptions

| Assumptions | Aaron | Betty | Colin | Dana |
|---|---|---|---|---|
| Total GSL borrowed | $10,000 | $10,000 | $10,000 | $10,000 |
| Starting salary | $18,800 | $18,800 | $18,800 | $18,800 |
| Expected annual real income growth | 7% | 2% | 2% | 5% |
| Expected annual increase in CPI | 4% | 8% | 3% | 3% |

| Year of repayment | GSL repayments as percentage of pre-tax income | | | |
|---|---|---|---|---|
| 1 | 7.7% | 7.7% | 7.7% | 7.7% |
| 2 | 7.0% | 7.2% | 7.4% | 7.2% |
| 3 | 6.2% | 6.8% | 7.0% | 6.6% |
| 4 | 5.6% | 6.3% | 6.7% | 6.1% |
| 5 | 5.1% | 5.9% | 6.4% | 5.7% |
| 6 | 4.5% | 5.5% | 6.1% | 5.2% |
| 7 | 4.1% | 5.1% | 5.8% | 4.8% |
| 8 | 3.7% | 4.8% | 5.5% | 4.5% |
| 9 | 3.3% | 4.5% | 5.2% | 4.1% |
| 10 | 3.0% | 4.2% | 5.0% | 3.8% |

## Table 14: Comparison of Loan Burden Under Various Economic Assumptions

| Assumptions | Erin | Frank | Grace |
|---|---|---|---|
| Total GSL borrowed | $10,000 | $10,000 | $10,000 |
| Starting salary | $13,500 | $18,800 | $26,100 |
| Expected annual real income growth | 3% | 3% | 3% |
| Expected annual increase in CPI | 4% | 4% | 4% |

| Year of repayment | GSL repayments as percentage of pre-tax income | | |
|---|---|---|---|
| 1 | 10.8% | 7.7% | 5.6% |
| 2 | 10.1% | 7.2% | 5.2% |
| 3 | 9.4% | 6.7% | 4.9% |
| 4 | 8.8% | 6.3% | 4.5% |
| 5 | 8.2% | 5.9% | 4.2% |
| 6 | 7.7% | 5.5% | 4.0% |
| 7 | 7.1% | 5.1% | 3.7% |
| 8 | 6.7% | 4.8% | 3.4% |
| 9 | 6.2% | 4.5% | 3.2% |
| 10 | 5.8% | 4.2% | 3.0% |

352    SPEECHES AND DOCUMENTS

ed baccalaureate degrees; (4) there were no significant differences in first year earnings of borrowers and non-borrowers employed in similar occupations, suggesting that borrowers probably did not obtain higher-paying jobs to repay their loans; and (5) G.S.L.P. debt levels did vary by occupations, with engineers having higher debt levels and marketing and sales personnel having lower debt levels—but engineers earned more and marketing/sales personnel earned less, so their relative situations were similar."

[Dennis J.] Martin reported similar findings from a national sample of borrowers in repayment.

"In general terms, student loans do not appear to have as much adverse impact on borrowers in repayment as many of us, perhaps somewhat viscerally, would have thought. With the exception of the degrees to which loan payments affect their ability to save, the average responses expressed by these borrowers in repayment fall well short of the midpoint in the response range for such value judgments as: the degree to which loan debt affects the decision to marry, to start a family, to take a higher paying job rather than one in a preferred field, to postpone health care, to rent instead of purchase a home, or to drive a used car rather than a new one."

[Kathleen W.] Little reported no significant differences among borrowers and non-borrowers in the classes of 1979 and 1984 at the University of California at Santa Cruz in their patterns of marrying, having children, attending graduate school, buying a house, or owning a car.

All of these studies have problems. Those reported by Davis and Martin are old; they report on students who completed school before the large borrowing years of the 1980's. Martin's results are based on a survey that suffered from a very low response rate and that omitted defaulters from its sample, though borrowers who fail to make their payments might be considered the ones where student loans would have had the greatest impact on later economic decisions. Both Davis and Little (at least for the Class of 1984) surveyed students within a year or so of graduation; perhaps negative economic effects take longer to appear.

Evidence that has been cited in arguing that student loans do affect later decisions unfortunately suffers

from shortcomings of its own. Neither the Carnegie Foundation nor American Council on Education surveys, for example, that imply that comparatively high borrowing levels influence career choice adequately distinguishes between cause and effect: do students borrow more when they expect to enter high-paying fields or do they enter high-paying fields because they have large debts to repay?

These are important questions, especially as debt levels of undergraduates rise. Much more and methodologically more sound research is needed to draw meaningful conclusions, however.

Even though it is virtually impossible as yet to disentangle the knotty question of how much debt students can afford to take on without adverse consequences, however, it is possible to demonstrate that, at the point of borrowing under loan programs as presently constituted, students cannot know what the real burden of the debt they are assuming will be.

How burdensome loans will be during the repayment period is a function of not only how much is borrowed, but also how much the borrower earns and what is happening in the economy at large during repayment, especially to the general level of prices. Inflation, scourge though it may be in many ways, is the friend of debtors with fixed interest obligations, who can repay what they owe in devalued dollars. Students, especially undergraduates, deciding on whether or how much to borrow, however, are not in any position to know how all these factors will interact to determine the real burden of their indebtedness. As they start

school, they cannot be sure of completing their program of study; many will drop out along the way. Most of them will not know with any certitude what careers they will end up pursuing. With borrowing becoming more commonplace, more borrowers will end up having at best just average, rather than above average, income prospects, at least as compared to others with similar educational backgrounds. And future economic conditions, including levels of real wage increases and inflation, are not only beyond their knowing, but beyond the knowing of our most sophisticated economic forecasters as well.

Using a simulation model called the Student Loan Counselor, developed by Dwight Horch of the Educational Testing Service, it is possible to illustrate how variations in the unpredictable circumstances facing student borrowers can affect the burden of student loan repayment. In considering the examples, it is useful to keep in mind as rough benchmarks the following: (1) the debt manageability studies showing the "acceptable" debt repayments ranged from 3 to 15 per cent of pre-tax income; and (2) Johnson and Sullivan's findings that, while consumer credit is easy to find, many banks report the use of guidelines that limit the ratio of mortgage debt service/pre-tax income to 25-28 per cent of income and total mortgage and consumer debt/pre-tax income to 40 per cent, with the latter figure sometimes ranging up to 60 per cent.

The results of the simulations appear in Tables 13, 14, and 15. Seven illustrative borrowers are described there, each of whom borrowed $10,000 in G.S.L.'s with an 8 per cent

## Table 15: Comparison of Loan Burden Under Various Economic Assumptions

| Assumptions | Borrower | | |
|---|---|---|---|
| | Erin 2 | Frank 2 | Grace 2 |
| Total GSL borrowed | $ 7,000 | $ 8,500 | $10,000 |
| Starting salary | $13,500 | $18,800 | $26,100 |
| Expected annual real income growth | 2% | 3% | 4% |
| Expected annual increase in CPI | 4% | 4% | 4% |
| Year of repayment | GSL repayments as percentage of pre-tax income | | |
| 1 | 7.5% | 6.6% | 5.6% |
| 2 | 7.1% | 6.1% | 5.2% |
| 3 | 6.7% | 5.7% | 4.7% |
| 4 | 6.3% | 5.4% | 4.4% |
| 5 | 6.0% | 5.0% | 4.1% |
| 6 | 5.6% | 4.7% | 3.8% |
| 7 | 5.3% | 4.4% | 3.5% |
| 8 | 5.0% | 4.1% | 3.2% |
| 9 | 4.7% | 3.8% | 3.0% |
| 10 | 4.4% | 3.5% | 2.8% |

interest rate in the course of obtaining a bachelor's degree, putting them among the most heavily indebted of today's undergraduates. Each student graduated in 1985 and got a job within a few months. Starting salaries are based on data in Horch's model for 1985, with $18,800 the average for liberal arts and business administration graduates. The loans must be paid back in equal monthly installments over a ten-year period, beginning 6 months after graduation.

Table 13 indicates the influence of income and inflation growth rates on loan burden. [Frank S.] Levy and [Richard C.] Michel have shown how real earnings prospects for men aging from 25 to 35 changed over two recent decades, growing roughly 7 per cent annually in the period 1963-1973 but only about one and a half per cent in the period 1973-1983. The first two students in Table 13, Aaron and Betty, generally illustrate these two real income growth rates. Inflation, however, was low in the first period and high in the second, circumstances that are also reflected in the simulations for Aaron and Betty respectively. The net result is that their loan burden is about the same, demonstrating the fact that, as far as loan repayment is concerned, inflation and real income increases are equally beneficial.

The third case in Table 13, Colin's, shows how debt burdens are higher if both inflation and real income increases are low, as is currently true in the United States. Dana's case is reflective of what might happen if the nation is able to improve earnings somewhat while keeping inflation under control. While none of these repayments would restrict the borrowers' ability to qualify for a mortgage, they affect in different degrees the capacity of a prudent individual to take on additional consumer debt. In no case is additional consumer borrowing ruled out altogether, however.

Table 14 holds student borrowing and economic conditions constant while varying starting salaries. Erin has the typical starting salary of a new teacher in some jurisdictions, Frank the salary of the average liberal arts graduate, and Grace the salary of a new engineer. The teacher clearly has the heaviest burden and, if she should want to buy a house in the years soon after graduation, might feel it unwise to borrow for other purposes. In these first few years, she

will have to use twice the percentage of her salary to repay her student loans as will the engineer.

Table 15 shows the same three students as Table 14, but now assuming that they do not all borrow equal amounts but vary their borrowing to reflect their expected choice of career. In addition, the three careers are assumed to have different earnings prospects from year to year. This table shows that students can equalize their debt burden more than in Table 14 by borrowing less if they expect to enter less lucrative careers; this means, however, that they do not have in fact equal access to loans to help pay for higher education. How, then, can we summarize these diverse findings on student loans and individual well-being?

► Growing student indebtedness has raised fears that repayment obligations are threatening the economic well-being of those who borrow to pay for college. While a number of studies speak to aspects of this issue, they are often old or flawed and come to contradictory conclusions.

► High levels of debt do not appear to be the culprit in loan default. Rather, high default rates occur disproportionately among students who borrow only once or twice, whose cumulative indebtedness is relatively low, who stay in school for only a year or two, and who fail to obtain their degrees or certificates, characteristics that also correlate with lower incomes than those earned by individuals who receive bachelor's degrees.

► Attempts to define "manageable debt limits" for students have resulted in diverse findings and have numerous shortcomings that hamper their usefulness.

► Highly-indebted borrowers with below-average earnings might find their later ability to obtain home mortgages hindered because of restrictions often used by mortgage lenders, but the credit market does not appear to place meaningful limits on borrowers' ability to obtain consumer credit in large amounts.

► This absence of meaningful limits in the credit market suggests that educational and financial institutions that provide student loans have a responsibility to educate their often young and financially-inexperienced clients about managing credit so that they do not get themselves in over their heads financially when they leave school.

► There is little evidence that past borrowers are choosing high-paying careers or delaying marriage and childbearing as a result borrowing to pay for education, though this issue needs much more research that reflects the experience of student borrowers of the mid-1980's, who have borrowed more than earlier graduates.

► Under loan programs as presently structured, students cannot know what the real burden of the debt they are assuming will be. The proportion of later income that individuals will have to devote to student loan repayment rather than to other consumption or saving depends on a variety of factors (ultimate career choice, the prospects for real income increases, and the outlook for inflation) that cannot be reliably predicted by an undergraduate at the time of borrowing.

► Poor productivity growth and lagging incomes in the economy at large will increase the burden of student borrowing. Inflation, on the other hand, while signaling an economy in trouble, lessens the burden of debts with fixed interest rates, which can be paid back in devalued dollars. Relative to student borrowers in the 1960's and 1970's, today's student loan repayers would be most disadvantaged by a combination of low inflation and low real income increases, a situation characteristic of a stagnant economy.

# V. Student Loans and Educational Opportunity

The federal government launched its major student aid programs (embodied in Title IV of the Higher Education Act of 1965) at the height of the War on Poverty. The primary rationale for federal action (and for much of state and institutional aid as well) was and continues to be the need to equalize educational opportunity for traditionally underrepresented groups in higher education: lower-income individuals, minorities, and women.

Concern is mounting that this educational opportunity goal is being threatened by an increasing imbalance in the student aid system between loans and grants; that is, between aid that has to be repaid and that which doesn't. Hard evidence to support or refute this concern is unfortunately difficult to find. Nevertheless, it is clear that whether or not traditionally-disadvantaged students are discouraged from participating in higher education because of the swing toward loans as the major form of available assistance, they will find the burden of loan repayment heavier than their white male counterparts because of continuing disparities in income. Thus loans are not as fair, in the sense of being neutral among different types of students, as are outright grants. Moreover, G.S.L. as currently structured has become increasingly costly to the federal government, which makes this largest of student aid programs a vulnerable target in times of high federal deficits.

To develop these points further first requires some information about available student aid and about how the sources and forms of this aid have shifted over time. As Table 16 shows, in academic 1985-86, $20 billion in various kinds of assistance was available to students at all levels in postsecondary education. The federal government was by far the dominant provider, supplying three-quarters of the total. Thus changes in federal policy, and particularly shifts in emphasis between grants and loans, colored the entire student aid picture.

In 1985-86 almost all federal aid came through the Title IV (or "generally available" aid) programs, but this was not always the case. In the early 1970's, two "specially-directed aid" programs, Social Security student benefits and veterans' educational benefits, accounted for more student assistance than all the Title IV programs. While not intentionally focused on lower-income or disadvantaged students, Social Security and Vietnam-era veterans' benefits probably disproportionately benefited these groups. Both provide outright grant aid.

Two major changes have occurred in federal student aid and thus aid as a whole, both with implications for educational opportunity. First, in the early 1980's inflation-adjusted student aid dropped. Table 17, a constant-dollar version of Table 16, shows a 14-per-cent drop in aid from federally-supported programs between 1980-81 and 1985-86, due entirely to the disappearance of Social Security student benefits and a large decline in aid for veterans. Generally-available federal aid, after suffering a decline in inflation-adjusted dollars in the early 1980's, bounced back somewhat by 1985-86. Thanks more to large real increases in state and institutional grant aid, however, the drop in overall aid available was held to 7 per cent. At the same time that

## Table 16: Aid Awarded to Postsecondary Students in Current Dollars (in millions)

|  | Academic year | | | |
| --- | --- | --- | --- | --- |
|  | 1970-71 | 1975-76 | 1980-81 | Estimated 1985-86 |
| **Federally supported programs** | | | | |
| Generally available aid | | | | |
| Pell grants | $    0 | $   936 | $ 2,387 | $ 3,652 |
| SEOG | $  134 | $   201 | $   366 | $   396 |
| SSIG | $    0 | $    20 | $    76 | $    76 |
| CWS | $  227 | $   295 | $   658 | $   693 |
| NDSL | $  240 | $   460 | $   695 | $   751 |
| GSL and PLUS | $ 1,015 | $ 1,267 | $ 6,201 | $ 8,836 |
| (GSL) | ($ 1,015) | ($ 1,267) | ($ 6,187) | ($ 8,288) |
| (PLUS) | (n/a) | (n/a) | ($    14) | ($   548) |
| Subtotal | $ 1,616 | $ 3,179 | $10,384 | $14,404 |
| Specially directed aid | | | | |
| Social Security | $  499 | $ 1,093 | $ 1,883 | $     0 |
| Veterans | $ 1,121 | $ 4,180 | $ 1,714 | $   667 |
| Other grants | $   16 | $    63 | $   119 | $    48 |
| Other loans | $   42 | $    45 | $    61 | $   248 |
| Subtotal | $ 1,678 | $ 5,381 | $ 3,777 | $   963 |
| Total federal aid | $ 3,295 | $ 8,560 | $14,161 | $15,367 |
| **State grant programs** | $  236 | $   490 | $   801 | $ 1,374 |
| **Institutionally-awarded aid** | $  965 | $ 1,435 | $ 2,138 | $ 3,426 |
| **Total federal, state, and institutional aid** | $ 4,496 | $10,485 | $17,101 | $20,167 |

Note: n/a = Not applicable.

## Table 17: Aid Awarded to Postsecondary Students in Constant 1986 Dollars (in millions)

|  | Academic year | | | |
| --- | --- | --- | --- | --- |
|  | 1970-71 | 1975-76 | 1980-81 | Estimated 1985-86 |
| **Federally supported programs** | | | | |
| Generally available aid | | | | |
| Pell grants | $    0 | $ 1,897 | $ 3,098 | $ 3,742 |
| SEOG | $  378 | $   407 | $   475 | $   406 |
| SSIG | $    0 | $    40 | $    99 | $    78 |
| CWS | $  643 | $   598 | $   855 | $   710 |
| NDSL | $  680 | $   932 | $   902 | $   770 |
| GSL and PLUS | $ 2,872 | $ 2,567 | $ 8,049 | $ 9,054 |
| (GSL) | ($ 2,872) | ($ 2,567) | ($ 8,031) | ($ 8,493) |
| (PLUS) | (n/a) | (n/a) | ($    18) | ($   562) |
| Subtotal | $ 4,574 | $ 6,441 | $13,478 | $14,760 |
| Specially directed aid | | | | |
| Social Security | $ 1,412 | $ 2,214 | $ 2,444 | $     0 |
| Veterans | $ 3,173 | $ 8,468 | $ 2,225 | $   683 |
| Other grants | $   45 | $   128 | $   154 | $    49 |
| Other loans | $  119 | $    91 | $    79 | $   254 |
| Subtotal | $ 4,748 | $10,901 | $ 4,902 | $   987 |
| Total federal aid | $ 9,322 | $17,342 | $18,381 | $15,747 |
| **State grant programs** | $  668 | $   993 | $ 1,040 | $ 1,408 |
| **Institutionally-awarded aid** | $ 2,730 | $ 2,907 | $ 2,775 | $ 3,510 |
| **Total federal, state and institutional aid** | $12,720 | $21,241 | $22,195 | $20,665 |

n/a = Not applicable.

overall aid was declining, however, college costs were rising faster than inflation and real family incomes (Table 18).

The second change is in the balance between types of assistance. Table 19 shows how the proportions of total aid being made available as grants, loans, and work-study have changed. From a high of 80 per cent of all aid in 1975-76, grants declined to 48 per cent 10 years later. Loans now represent almost half of all available aid, up from 17 per cent 10 years earlier.

This shifting balance raises concern over effects on educational opportunity. It is often argued that students from low-income families, minorities, and women are more reluctant to borrow than are white males, though the evidence here is ambiguous. It is clear, however, that these groups earn less than their white male counterparts once they enter the full-time work force, so that the burden of loan repayment will be heavier. Thus, loans, unlike grants, are not neutral among different types of students.

Campus based financial aid officers often report that students from disadvantaged backgrounds, particularly minorities, are reluctant to borrow. [Frank] Newman reiterates this theme, arguing that, "Disadvantaged students find large loans onerous. Minority students, in particular, are less likely to use loans and therefore less likely to enter or stay in college."

A Consortium on Financing Higher Education (COFHE) survey of families in four cities found that women, low-income students, and students with high degree aspirations showed the most concern about undertaking educational debt. Some data suggest that women borrow less often and in lower amounts than men.

Female enrollments have reached all-time highs (women now are the majority of postsecondary students), but black enrollment has been declining, fueling speculation that rising dependence on student aid in the form of loans discourages blacks from participating in higher education. At the same time, there is some evidence that those minority and women students who do enroll are in fact willing to borrow. An unpublished COFHE survey of students graduating from member schools (COFHE represents 30 prestigious private colleges—admittedly not a representative group)

in 1984 found that gender had no relationship to loan indebtedness and that blacks were more likely to report that loans were a major source of funds and a source of funds than were other students.

Women reported more often than men that they expected their parents to help with loan repayments; minorities' expectations of such assistance were noticeably lower.

A study of students enrolled in all sectors of California postsecondary education in 1982-83 had similar results. Virtually identical percentages of men and women applied for guaranteed student loans and blacks applied almost twice as often as whites, undoubtedly reflecting their lower family incomes and greater financial need.

## Table 18: College Costs and Family Incomes in Current and Constant Dollars, Selected Years

| | Academic year | | | |
|---|---|---|---|---|
| | 1970-71 | 1975-76 | 1980-81 | 1985-86 |
| **Current dollars** | | | | |
| Cost of attendance[1] | | | | |
| Private university | $ 3,163 | $ 4,467 | $ 6,566 | $11,100 |
| Private 4-year college | $ 2,598 | $ 3,385 | $ 5,249 | $ 8,480 |
| Public university | $ 1,478 | $ 1,935 | $ 2,711 | $ 4,160 |
| Public 4-year college | $ 1,209 | $ 1,657 | $ 2,420 | $ 3,750 |
| Public 2-year college | $ 1,017 | $ 1,386 | $ 2,020 | $ 3,000 |
| Income[2] | | | | |
| Disposable personal income per capita | $ 3,489 | $ 5,291 | $ 8,422 | $11,817 |
| Median family income | $ 9,867 | $13,719 | $21,023 | $27,735 |
| **Constant 1986 dollars** | | | | |
| Cost of attendance[1] | | | | |
| Private university | $ 8,949 | $ 9,050 | $ 8,523 | $11,374 |
| Private 4-year college | $ 7,351 | $ 6,858 | $ 6,813 | $ 8,689 |
| Public university | $ 4,182 | $ 3,920 | $ 3,519 | $ 4,263 |
| Public 4-year college | $ 3,421 | $ 3,357 | $ 3,141 | $ 3,843 |
| Public 2-year college | $ 2,877 | $ 2,808 | $ 2,622 | $ 3,074 |
| Income[2] | | | | |
| Disposable personal income per capita | $10,101 | $11,051 | $11,490 | $12,349 |
| Median family income | $28,566 | $28,655 | $28,681 | $28,983 |

[1] Cost of attendance includes tuition, fees, room, and board.
[2] Income data are for the calendar year in which the academic year begins.

## Table 19: Grants, Loans, and Work as a Percentage of Total Aid

| | Academic year | | | |
|---|---|---|---|---|
| | 1970-71 | 1975-76 | 1980-81 | Estimated 1985-86 |
| Grants | 66.1% | 80.3% | 55.5% | 47.8% |
| Loans | 28.9% | 16.9% | 40.7% | 48.8% |
| Work | 5.0% | 2.8% | 3.9% | 3.4% |
| Total aid | 100.0% | 100.0% | 100.0% | 100.0% |

## Table 20: Median Incomes of Full-Time, Year-Round Workers by Educational Attainment, 1984

| | 1-3 years of college | 4 years of college |
|---|---|---|
| Males, all races, age 25-34 | $22,260 | $25,754 |
| Females, all races, age 25-34 | $16,152 | $19,068 |
| White males, age 25 and over | $26,302 | $32,022 |
| Black males, age 25 and over | $21,105 | $25,110 |
| White females, age 25 and over | $17,114 | $20,291 |
| Black females, age 25 and over | $15,795 | $20,626 |

If further analysis should show that minorities and/or women react differently to the possibility of borrowing to pay for college than white men, this would be an understandable response to a continuing fact of economic life in America: that significant wage disparities still exist between these groups and white men. Even when such differences as educational attainment, full-time versus part-time work, years of experience, and occupational choice are controlled for, earnings disparities show up. This is not the place for an exhaustive enumeration of comparative statistics, but the few basic numbers in Table 20 give a rough sense of the differences that also show up in more detailed and sophisticated comparisons.

Table 21 shows the difference such disparities can make to workers repaying student loans. The three examples represent (1) a white male (Harry) whose starting salary is the average for liberal arts baccalaureate holders; (2) an individual (Irene) whose starting salary is 70 per cent of the liberal arts average; and (3) another individual (Jesse) whose starting salary is 85 per cent of the liberal arts average. The figures of 70 and 85 per cent were chosen for illustration because they reflect the disparities frequently found in the statistics when comparing earnings of women and minorities who work full time to male counterparts of similar educational and occupational experience. The cases of Irene and Jesse illustrate how much more of their incomes workers with less-than-average income prospects will have to devote to loan repayment rather than to other spending over the 10 years after they leave school.

Loans, then, unlike grants, are not neutral in their effects on different groups of students. Also unlike grants, the G.S.L. program depends on interest rate subsidies to encourage banks and other private lenders to participate and operates as an "entitlement" for eligible students. As a result of liberalized eligibility rules in the 1970's and rising interest rates in the general economy, G.S.L. became an increasingly expensive but unpredictable commitment for the federal government. Changes in 1981 and 1986 imposed new eligibility restrictions and reduced somewhat the government subsidies involved in G.S.L., but the program's basic structure still

results in costs that are highly sensitive to outside economic forces. [Arthur M.] Hauptman and [Michael S.] McPherson describe how this structure evolved and argue that G.S.L.'s high and volatile costs make the program vulnerable in an era when federal expenditures must be reduced to bring budget deficits under control. Another spurt of inflation such as occurred in the early 1980's would drive federal obligations up dramatically: by roughly half a billion dollars annually for each 1-per-cent increase in the Treasury bill rate to which G.S.L. subsidies are tied. One has to wonder just how long the federal government will or should tolerate this kind of financial uncertainty without seeking cost-cutting changes in the program. Such changes could have serious implications for educational access, given the critical role G.S.L. now plays in educational finance for those whose resources are otherwise inadequate to pay for college.

The Higher Education Act reauthorization in 1986 restricted eligibility for G.S.L.'s to students who can demonstrate financial need, a reasonable step in light of the subsidies now involved, But it is a step fraught with irony as well, given the view twenty years ago that the federal government should provide a balanced array of grants, loans, and work opportunities for the disadvantaged and minimally-subsidized loans of convenience for the middle class. The evolution of G.S.L. into the dominant student aid program, combined with increasing levels of subsidy, have gradually and in a largely unexamined way transformed the federal

strategy for using financial assistance to foster equality of opportunity in higher education. This effort is now highly dependent on loans, with uncertain implications for those disadvantaged students who were the original focus of federal concern.

How can we summarize the relationship between student loans and educational opportunity?

► Heavy emphasis on borrowing may discourage traditionally-under-enrolled groups from participating in higher education and hinder the nation's progress toward equal opportunity, though here, as in so many other areas of student aid, the evidence is mixed.

► Women, minority, and low-income students have traditionally been seen as reluctant to borrow. Though female enrollments have increased steadily, black enrollment is dropping. There is much speculation, but little hard data yet to prove, that the shift in student aid policy from heavy reliance on grants to a roughly 50/50 balance between grants and loans, coupled with real declines in student aid available from federal sources, has contributed to this decline.

► Individuals from traditionally-disadvantaged groups who actually enroll in college (as opposed to those who may be discouraged from doing so) may be as willing to borrow as other students, and in fact may be more dependent on loans because they have fewer other resources.

► Because of continuing disparities in income between white males, on the one hand, and women and minorities on the other, even after adjusting for differences in education

## Table 21: Comparison of Loan Burden Under Various Economic Assumptions

| Assumptions | Borrower | | |
|---|---|---|---|
| | Harry | Irene | Jesse |
| Total GSL borrowed | $10,000 | $10,000 | $10,000 |
| Starting salary | $18,800 | $13,160 | $15,980 |
| Expected annual real income growth | 3% | 3% | 3% |
| Expected annual increase in CPI | 4% | 4% | 4% |

| Year of repayment | GSL repayments as percentage of pre-tax income | | |
|---|---|---|---|
| 1 | 7.7% | 11.1% | 9.1% |
| 2 | 7.2% | 10.3% | 8.5% |
| 3 | 6.7% | 9.6% | 7.9% |
| 4 | 6.3% | 9.0% | 7.4% |
| 5 | 5.9% | 8.4% | 6.9% |
| 6 | 5.5% | 7.8% | 6.5% |
| 7 | 5.1% | 7.3% | 6.0% |
| 8 | 4.8% | 6.8% | 5.6% |
| 9 | 4.5% | 6.4% | 5.3% |
| 10 | 4.2% | 6.0% | 4.9% |

and work experience, the latter will find loans more burdensome to repay. In this sense, loans, unlike grants, are not neutral in their effects on different groups.

► As G.S.L. has evolved over 20 years, it has changed from a minimally-subsidized loan of convenience for middle-income families to a highly-subsidized loan for students who can demonstrate financial need. It has also become the dominant student aid program. Thus the federal strategy for fostering equality of opportunity in higher education, which initially focused on a balanced array of grants, loans, and work opportunities for the disadvantaged, has been transformed, with uncertain and largely unexamined implications for the groups who were the original focus of federal concern.

# VI. Student Loans and Education

Before any final conclusions can be reached about the effects of the nation's growing reliance on student loans, yet another issue needs to be addressed: whether loans have implications for the educational process itself. Two kinds of effects seem to be of concern here, tangible ones like whether borrowing affects the choice of major or graduate school plans, and intangible ones relating to educational "values." The tangible effects are easily understood. Marchese gives a good summary of the concerns about values:

"What educational values are prompted by loans? Instrumental values, I believe, values inimical to liberal education, and personalist values, likewise inimical.

"Instrumental values are fostered by loans because loans force a responsible student to think ahead to the necessity for repayment; the incentive of loans is to position yourself through your coursework, major, and degree for a higher-paying job that more readily permits repayment of the loan. In effect, college becomes less and less something done for its own sake and more and more something done for what comes afterwards. Now that is not entirely an unhealthy impulse; but the greater the instrumental purpose the less likely will the student be to 'dally' with the contemplations of liberal and civic learning or 'sacrifice' to develop general intellectual capacity.

"I say 'personalist' because the message to students of loans (as opposed to scholarships, grants, work, and parental contribution, each of which I think carries a more positive set of values with it) is that, 'you go forward on your own nickel.' The response too often evoked becomes, 'I am going to get what is coming to me.' This is what Frank Newman meant in his report last September when he charged that 'excessive loans inadvertently undercut traditional values.' "

Like many other loan issues, this one is complicated. Even more so than on some, the jury is still out. The best this paper can do is to give a sense of the debate and of the evidence on both sides.

First of all, it is worth pointing out that the debate over whether different ways of paying for college affect the educational experience itself is not new. Concern seems to focus on whatever financing mechanism is currently in the spotlight. In 1952 [Richard G.] Axt noted that the boast, " 'I worked my way through college' has been a part of the traditional success story of the self-made man," a tradition boosted by the tough Depression years. Axt also reported, however, that many educators had reservations about the effects of work—especially if it required more than 15 hours per week—on a student's academic and personal life. During the 1950's when Congress was considering proposals to enact the first federal scholarships, critics worried that outright gift aid would negatively affect students' commitment to their studies, in contrast to requirements that they help themselves. Today, with lending at an all-time high, we worry about loans.

Conducting research on the effects of different kinds of financial aid is not easy. As Newman observes, such research is hindered by "the widespread use of aid packages, which introduces the problem of multi-collinearity into statistical analysis." One summary of the "limited" research on financial aid and educational outcomes tentatively concludes that "grants and scholarships have small positive effects on retention and loans generally have negative impacts." A study of new students at a large commuter university by [Richard A.] Voorhees however, found "no support . . . for the claim that loans are detrimental to the persistence of high need freshmen." In addition to such contradictory results, few studies have as yet been done that would capture the effects of the high borrowing of recent years.

One that does is the COFHE survey of the class of 1984 at member schools. While students at these schools (30 of the most expensive and selective undergraduate institutions in the country) are not representative of postsecondary students as a whole in their academic accomplishments, career and income prospects, and so on, they also borrow more frequently and more heavily than most students, as Table 5 in section II showed. Nevertheless, the survey found no evidence of any relationship between undergraduate indebtedness and post-graduation plans, such as attending graduate school or going directly to work. Both this study and a 1984 Carnegie survey show that student borrowing varies by field of study, but neither report shows a formal link between indebtedness and choice of major.

If it is hard to disentangle the tangible effects of different kinds of student aid, it is almost impossible to do so in the area of effects on values. To give but one example: are today's students more preoccupied with economic issues than students of an earlier era because they have to borrow more heavily, or because they are aware that the national economy has been relatively stagnant for over a decade, with some parts of the country suffering from depression-like conditions? Given all the public concern over the state of the economy in recent years, what would be surprising would be to find no tendency for students to be more concerned about their financial futures.

Furthermore, it isn't true that students who receive loans are being told to "go forward on your own nickel." If anything, the message is "you put in two and a half cents and the government will match it;" the subsidy on G.S.L.'s has been 40 to 50 cents for each dollar lent. While students may not be completely aware of the "gift" aspect of loan subsidies, they cannot help but know that some kind of government subvention has been allowing them to borrow at 7 or 8 or 9 per cent during years when general interest rates have been much higher.

Finally, some students apparently prefer loans to work as a form of aid. [James C.] Hearn and [Sharon L.]

Wilford quote Robert Fenske's finding that "aid officers report that certain students for whom grants are not available tend to prefer loans to work-study awards because they believe low-paying jobs interfere with obtaining good grades and completing their programs in timely fashion."

In sum, then,

► Concern is mounting that rising debt levels may affect students' choice of major and graduate school plans and the values they bring to and take from their college educations.

► Much more evidence is needed to draw firm conclusions in this area, including efforts to disentangle the effects of loans from other changes in society at large.

# VII. The Risks of Borrowing: An International Comparison

Section IV concluded by noting the uncertainties about future loan burdens that students face when they borrow because of the unpredictability of both income after graduation and the state of the economy. For the borrower, loans are an investment that carries with it some risk. [Gareth] Williams has articulated this point more fully.

"Higher education as an investment has several characteristics that distinguish it from most other forms of investment: the investment takes a long time to complete, the returns are long-term, and, for any individual, they are very uncertain. So individual investors cannot afford to make mistakes; but at the same time they are not well informed about the implications of different decisions, and most of them are not in a position to make this investment decision more than once. Most successful loan schemes skirt these difficulties by having some form of income-contingent repayment arrangement: the amount a graduate repays in any year depends on his current income. Thus students need not be deterred from borrowing to finance their studies by the fear that their personal investment will be one of the unsuccessful ones. Put another way, an element of insurance is built into the loan schemes."

While Williams overstates the prevalence of such insurance—the

United States and Canada both have successful student loan programs with no formal protections except for death and disability—[D. Bruce] Johnstone provides examples of two countries that do protect students against some of the risks of borrowing: Sweden and West Germany.

In Sweden, as in most of Europe, postsecondary students are not charged tuition or fees but do have to pay living expenses while enrolled in school. Parents are not formally expected to contribute to their children's education, though many do; students are eligible based on their own resources for "Study Means" from the government. Study Means consists mostly of a highly-subsidized loan and a small direct grant. In 1983-84, a little over half of Swedish undergraduates took advantage of the loan portion of Study Means.

Swedish students do not begin repaying their loans until two and a half years after graduation, in contrast to six months in the United States.

In addition to the fact that they are better established in careers when they begin repayment, Swedes also have until their 51st birthdays to repay, in contrast to our 10 years.

The exact period of repayment thus varies with the age of the borrower when he or she enters repayment.

At this point, interest at the rate of 4.2 per cent, which has been accruing during the in-school and post-graduation "grace period" is added to the loan principal to determine the total to be repaid.

This total is divided by the number of years remaining until age 51 to determine the first year's repayment. Each year thereafter, the repayment amount is increased by 4.2 per cent, thus giving Swedish borrowers a graduated repayment plan rather than the level repayments characteristic of U.S. student loans.

In addition to a longer repayment period and graduated payments, a Swedish borrower gets an explicit guarantee against the risk of being overburdened by low income. Debt payments are deferred if the borrower falls below a specified level of financial resources, which include among other things 40 per cent of a spouse's earnings above a certain point. This 40 per cent increases as the spouse's earnings increase. The level of financial resources that triggers the right to defer payment is variable, being higher if the borrower

has children under the age of ten. If as a result of deferrals, the borrower still owes money on a student loan at age 65, the debt is forgiven.

West Germany also has a highly-subsidized loan program called the BAföG to help students pay living expenses. This all-loan program was converted from a largely-grant program in 1984. Probably to make the switch palatable, repayments do not begin until five years after graduation and there is no interest charged at any point. About 30 per cent of German students qualify on the basis of their or their parents' income for this assistance.

Under BAföG a borrower has 20 years to repay and makes equal monthly payments. If his or her income (not considering the income of a spouse) falls below a specified level, payments are deferred. Any remaining debt is canceled after 20 years.

It is worth noting that BAföG in its current form is new and that no students have yet entered repayment. Therefore the German example is not helpful in terms of experience with how its various loan provisions will work out in practice.

Sweden and West Germany do illustrate how various loan features to reduce the risks of unmanageable debt can be designed. These two countries have chosen to subsidize their loan programs more heavily than the United States, but features like graduated repayment, long repayment periods, longer grace periods, and protection against low incomes in theory could be built into less-subsidized programs as well.

In fact, the first two did exist in this country for a short period in the early 1980's under a provision allowing students to consolidate high or multiple loans through the Student Loan Marketing Association.

That loan consolidation authority lapsed in 1983 but was restored in modified form (and with a variety of financial institutions and state agencies authorized to participate) when the Higher Education Act was reauthorized in October 1986.

That act also authorized a small income-contingent loan demonstration project within the N.D.S.L. program to assess the feasibility of a program in which students repay on a variable schedule geared to their adjusted gross incomes.

The issue of whether students could and should be better protected against the risks of borrowing deserves attention.

Loan consolidation may take care of many of our concerns about high indebtedness levels, but will not protect students who borrow at lower levels from the risk that low incomes may force them to commit comparatively high proportions of their resources to loan repayment.

It would be easier to assure groups that are often considered reluctant to borrow, such as minorities and women, that their fears were unfounded if loan programs in fact had protections built into them, which they now do not.

To address head-on the question of cost that would immediately arise should income protection be added to G.S.L., perhaps we should consider whether the current G.S.L. structure of below-market interest rates, subsidies, and fees is optimal. Instead of subsidizing all borrowers based on their or their parents' income at the time the loan is made, may be we should allow all students to borrow at market rates and then use subsidies to offer protection against repayments that are out of proportion to income. As this proposal demonstrates, there are innovative ideas that could be explored, short of starting whole new programs such as the National Student Loan Bank income-contingent loan plan and its variants that have surfaced at various times over the past two decades to insure that student loans will not become the huge burdens so often talked about today.

Furthermore, we need to know more about what kinds of protections student borrowers really want. [Rena] Cheskis-Gold's 1984 survey of alumni of Yale University's Tuition Postponement Option program of the 1970's, one of the few true income-contingent long-term loan programs ever implemented in this country, offers some suggestive findings. While students like low repayments in the early years of work and the income contingency and graduated repayment features of T.P.O., they disliked very long repayment periods (in T.P.O., up to 35 years). Cheskis-Gold's work indicates that the optimal loan program might have moderate payments over a somewhat longer period than currently allowed under G.S.L. and N.D.S.L., rather than small payments over a lifetime, and would offer some protection

when incomes are low relative to debt payments.

To summarize, then, how does the United States stack up in protecting students against the risks of investing in themselves through loans?

► Unlike some European countries, the United States does not build into its loan programs insurance protecting a student borrower from the danger that his investment in himself through education will not result in a level of income sufficient to permit comfortable repayment of the loan.

► Loan consolidation, a feature of U.S. loans which was initiated in the early 1980's but allowed to lapse, was resurrected in the 1986 Higher Education Act reauthorization. It will allow borrowers with large or multiple student loans to pay them over an extended period of time and may offer graduated repayment, but is not a protection for all borrowers against the risk that loan repayment will require an unduly high proportion of income.

► The issue of whether students could and should be better protected against the risks of borrowing deserves attention: innovative ideas exist and need to be investigated, and better information is required about what kinds of protection borrowers and potential borrowers would like to have.

## VIII. Conclusions

In December 1985 the College Scholarship Service of the College Board assembled approximately 50 loan experts (representing educators, students, bankers, and state loan-guarantee agencies) to discuss the problem of student debt burdens and its implications for loan counseling and debt management. Somewhat to the organizers' surprise, however, there was no consensus among those in attendance about what the "problem" was, or even if there *was* a problem. Perhaps this should have been expected, given the paucity of data about student loans and the diversity of American higher education, which makes it hard to give any answer except "it depends" to questions of how much students should borrow.

This paper both reflects those difficulties and gives an illustration of the gaps in knowledge and the conflicting findings that make consensus hard to reach. Better research, even if we

had it, might not tell us what we need to know when we need to know it. Sometimes analysis is a conservative force, since it may be hard to document a problem until the problem becomes so serious that it is overwhelming.

Therefore, while we simply must find ways of obtaining better information than we currently have about our large and growing reliance on student loans to finance higher education, we must also pay attention to the perceptions and impressions of those who are making loans and counseling students and repayers and to the feelings of those who have borrowed. We must take these things seriously, but we must find ways to determine their validity.

Making good policy choices about the future of student loans in financing higher education depends on separating valid from invalid concerns about high borrowing levels. Despite the concerns, many people view student loans not as a problem but as a positive force (along with other student aid programs) in broadening access to college and in spurring the nation's economic and civic growth.

In consumer surveys going back as far as the late 1950's, respondents have listed "financing educational expenses" as either the second or (in the 1983 survey by a narrow margin) third most appropriate reason for borrowing.

Educational borrowing along with borrowing to cover the costs of illness and to purchase a car are the only reasons for borrowing that are approved by a majority of consumers, about 80 per cent of whom support these kinds of loans.

Structuring effective and efficient student loan programs requires attention to many issues in addition to the burden of indebtedness, though we must not neglect the latter. We also need to consider the implications of our growing reliance on loans as the central feature of federal efforts to promote educational opportunity and the appropriateness of loans for different kinds of students in different kinds of institutions. We should also look at whether the evolution of G.S.L. from a minimally-subsidized loan of convenience to a highly-subsidized loan for the financially needy is a backward step to the extent that it limits access to loans for students whose primary need is not subsidies but a means through which to invest in their own futures.

# College Quality from "Time for Results: The Governors' 1991 Report on Education"

*Text of the Report by
the Task Force on Teaching*

## DEFINING THE ISSUES

### A Foundation to Build Upon

For four years, and much longer in many cases, the nation's Governors have championed an agenda to improve teaching. They focused public attention on the importance of good teaching. They created a sense of urgency about the need for action and a political climate that made action possible. Almost every state has taken significant steps to attract and retain able teachers, and many put comprehensive plans in place.

Governors led successful efforts to raise teacher salaries. They insisted on higher standards for teacher training and licensing. Many have programs to recognize outstanding teachers and to draw public attention to the profession's importance and rising standards. They led efforts to create scholarship and loan programs and to widen the pool of teacher candidates.

So why is reform of the teaching profession still on the Governors' agenda? It remains because the nation still faces both a quality and a quantity problem in the teacher workforce. These problems are massive, pervasive, and intertwined with the quality of our economic, civic, and personal lives. It also remains on the agenda because follow-through is everything. Governors achieved some of the reforms in the face of determined opposition; the opposition hasn't gone away. And some innovations need adjustment in the light of experience. No teacher recruitment and retention program will succeed without sustained support from a state's Governor.

How many teachers will we need? The estimates aren't precise (Feistritzer). Projected need is based on federal estimates that assume a constant 6 percent attrition rate, which has not been verified since 1973 (Feistritzer, Mandel). Those figures show that by 1991, the supply of new teachers will be only 68 percent of demand. Some observers think these estimates are conservative because the rising age of teachers will mean a higher attrition rate. They predict that roughly half of the current teaching force will have to be replaced in the next seven years (Mandel). The Carnegie Forum on Education and the Economy concluded that between 1986 and 1992, 1.3 million new teachers will have to be hired. The Forum pointed out that it is unlikely the labor market can meet this need (Carnegie Forum). These are national figures; the state situation may vary. Some states will be in dire need while others will have, or appear to have, all the teachers they need.

Quality in the profession is also uncertain. Teachers score below other college graduates on most standardized tests (Mandel). Those who score high on these tests tend to leave the classroom earlier than others, while those who score the lowest tend to remain (Schlechty and Vance). The highest scorers are less likely to be hired in the first place, but whether this is because they

Reprinted by permission of the National Governors' Association Task Force on Teaching decide not to teach or boards decline to hire them is unknown (Weaver). But some observers see a turnaround in the quality of new teachers. The SAT scores of students who say they plan to teach are rising faster than the average (Feistritzer).

The wrong kind of policy conceals shortages. If certification, hiring, or training standards decline, we won't notice shortages (Spillane). The disturbing fact is that parents and citizens may not be able to readily detect important differences between professional levels of teaching and below-par performance (Palaich). Governors can, however, help force standards in the right direction. We know why teachers leave: the primary reasons are low pay and the absence of a professional work environment (Metropolitan 1986). If Governors help make teaching more attractive, we may both slow the turnover and raise the quality of those who enter the profession. Donna Kerr presented the argument concisely:

> A society's political and economic forces determine in what pursuits intellectual virtuosity will be rewarded. Neither with status nor with prestige nor with money do we reward teaching . . . For those bright and able persons who, against the social and economic grain, would choose to teach, we have failed to structure the work of teaching in a minimally acceptable way.

Governors have a special opportunity now to strengthen teaching. They are experienced in dealing with the problem and can draw on one another's experience. The states have become laboratories for education, and in laboratories, some experiments work, while others don't. It is time to draw lessons from both kinds of experiences and press on.

The national studies of teacher policy this year are a major part of the opportunity; they outline an agenda that builds on what has happened, but is fundamentally different in scope and tone (Carnegie Forum, Holmes, National Commission for Excellence in Teacher Education, California Commission, Committee for Economic Development ECS, reports). The scope is deliberately radical rather than incremental, and the tone is urgent.

The leaders in business, labor, education, the scholarly community, and politics who produced these studies assert a basic argument: modern times are forcing Americans to become much better educated, for economic, civic, and personal reasons.

These studies depict education as the nation's most critical investment program. Achieving new levels of competence will require effective teaching. Now is a particularly difficult time to recruit the teachers we want. To get them, to keep the ones we have, and to make effective use of their talent will require major organizational changes in schools and teaching. The first round of reforms did not attempt those changes (Carnegie Forum).

Policy leaders have started to listen to teachers themselves (Metropolitan, Koppich, Education Commission of the States). While the sad picture that is painted of teacher qualifications is all too accurate in many respects, there is also a multitude of qualified, committed teachers who support change (ECS). Their view of what motivates teachers and what effective teaching requires is sometimes congruent and sometimes at odds with what policy leaders say. Governors, and for that matter, principals, boards, and communities, who tap and focus the energy and commitment of such teachers have powerful allies in support of better education for children.

## What Have the States Done So Far?

Put simply, states have done a lot. The guiding theme has been raising standards at all stages of the teaching career, but especially at training and initial certification. We drew the composite state program that follows from an Education Commission of the States survey of the fifty states (Palaich).

The states' approach to teacher quality has yielded nearly a dozen major programs. The Governors on this task force view these programs not as the resolution of the problem of teacher quality, but as the foundation on which future efforts must build. The issue, after all, is not the ability to pass the reform program; it is the ability and effectiveness of the people we attract to teaching and keep there.

*Financial Aid to Prospective Teachers.* States offer loans for undergraduate teacher education and often forgive repayment in return for a specified number of years of teaching. Some are aimed at math and science shortages or urban teaching; others focus on minority candidates or candidates with very high academic ability. Connecticut's ELEET program is reserved for high school seniors with SAT scores above 1200.

*Teacher Education.* States have raised test scores for admission to teacher training, eliminated education majors and required a liberal arts background. They increased the time and quality of practice teaching under experienced teachers, and reduced the number of specific course requirements for certification.

*Teacher Testing.* Standardized tests of subject matter for new teachers are rapidly becoming the norm in the states. Mississippi has formally committed itself to raising the cutoff scores on those exams in 1986, 1988, and 1990. Also, two states have tested currently certified teachers for basic literacy.

*Alternate Routes to Teaching.* Alternate routes open teaching to those who have not taken collegiate teacher education courses. The New Jersey model requires that candidates have a bachelor's degree and a passing score on a standardized test of subject matter, and that they complete an internship in a local district. The internship involves close supervision and support from a team of administrators and teachers and requires completion of professional training before and during the program. The alternate route replaces emergency programs that admit candidates into areas of shortage, often with few or no requirements. It also creates competition with traditional training programs.

*Increased Salaries.* Higher starting salaries set floors under local salary guides. Some states also have raised salaries across the board. Arkansas increased salaries 10 percent for all teachers and raised the sales tax to pay for it. Other states have created career ladders to make salaries more attractive.

*Career Structures.* Examples of career structures include career ladders of three to five steps, with increasing levels of compensation, selection criteria, and work responsibility. Some states have tried to strengthen the performance of new teachers by assigning experienced teachers to work with them. Some career ladders, such as Tennessee's, are statewide, while others involve searches for alternatives in pilot districts. Arizona, for example, began a five-year experiment in sixteen school districts to design career ladders. Teachers are involved in the design, and improved student achievement is one design criterion.

*Performance Evaluations.* Some states have provided for annual evaluation of all teachers, while others evaluate only the provisional or new teachers at specified intervals. Some specify minimum evaluation criteria and procedures and provide for training of teacher evaluators. Virginia's Beginning Teacher Program provides for a two-year provisional certificate and classroom observation by three professionals to assess the candidates' competence on fourteen specific topics. Candidates who fall short on any of the fourteen receive assistance.

*Teacher Development.* Teacher development efforts include continuing education requirements, teacher academies, and summer institutes. Some require a minimum number of hours of continuing education for credential renewal. Also available are teacher centers and computer demonstration centers. Some states link training to career ladder requirements, and some provide additional state funds to support inservice training. Others require approved training plans; several even spell out the topics: decisionmaking, curriculum development, and community involvement. Maryland has Teacher Assistance Teams in seventeen counties to support teachers who coach their peers. The state provides summer training and three-year grants to the participating schools. The New Jersey Academy for the Advancement of Teaching and Management trains groups of teachers and principals from the same school in effective instruction methods, and then follows up the application of what they learned in their classrooms. The emphasis is on translating theory into practice.

*Teacher Recognition.* Teacher recognition programs include cash awards that sometimes involve teacher development of special projects. They also include individual teacher grants, sometimes of small amounts, but in other cases $15,000 or more. Some of these awards go to groups of teachers, others go to individuals. New Jersey awards $1,000 to one teacher chosen locally in each school in recognition of outstanding teaching. The teacher directs the expenditure of these funds for some educational purpose after participating in a meeting with the Governor.

## What Are the Results?

It is too early to tell in a comprehensive way what the results of these efforts are. There have been successes, but when designing recruitment programs, we ought to give more attention to what motivates which people to teach—or to leave.

It's a complex problem, but our programs don't always reflect that complexity. America gets its teachers from several sources, and they are different enough to require distinct recruiting strategies. Moreover, states and regions within states will depend on these sources in different proportions. Strategies that work in one place may not work elsewhere.

Teachers come from undergraduate teacher training programs for the most part in many states, but undergraduates with other majors might be candidates for graduate or alternate route programs. And a forthcoming Rand study reveals that fewer than half come straight from undergraduate training to the classroom (Darling-Hammond and Haggstrom). Some teachers might be induced to move from other districts. Finally, there is the so-called "reserve pool" of those who once taught but left. We have no reliable estimates for any of these groups, except those in collegiate teacher training, and not all of those people actually enter teaching (Feistritzer).

It is not difficult to illustrate differences in groups of potential candidates, but it is harder to say how these differences affect recruiting. One study of alternate route candidates shows that they are quite unlike their traditional counterparts in test scores, grade point averages, undergraduate majors, and experience (Klagholz).

There are also important differences among reserve pool teachers. The former teacher most likely to be attracted back is female, was very satisfied with teaching, taught elementary school, and left less than two years ago. The one least likely to return is male, taught at the secondary level, was dissatisfied with teaching, and left four or five years ago (Metropolitan 1986). In general, however, the reserve pool is unlikely to be a sufficiently large source of new teachers. The attractions of their new careers simply outweigh those of teaching (Metropolitan 1986).

The motivating factors in teaching are well known. People are attracted to teaching because they want to stay with an academic subject they like and because they simply want to work with children (Lortie, Fuhrman). They become teachers because they want to do something important, to make a difference. Many, of course, have entered because it was easy to do—states that raise certification standards are changing that—or because there were no alternatives elsewhere—and massive social change ended that (Schlechty and Vance).

But again, there are differences among teachers. Secondary school teachers are likely to report that they went into the field because they expected the work to be "interesting or fulfilling." Elementary teachers, younger teachers, and those who majored in education are more likely to cite the preference for working with children (Fuhrman). People who teach are less motivated by salary issues up to a point, but see low salary and low social status as discouraging factors (Rosenholtz and Smylie). We really don't know how sensitive teacher candidates are to increase in starting salaries: how much of an increase is enough? (Hawley and Smylie).

*When* people decide to teach is as important as *why* when it comes to devising recruitment schemes. The person who decides late in college, or perhaps long after college, can face big obstacles in the form of state certification requirements that would send them back to formal training.

Why do teachers leave? Teachers who are more academically gifted than their colleagues are more likely to leave (Rosenholtz and Smylie). The most academically able leave at twice the rate of the least able (Darling-Hammond 1984). Teachers leave because the salaries and status are higher elsewhere, and because of general discontent with the work place (Metropolitan 1986). Teachers with less experience also are more likely to leave. In one state, a quarter of those who entered teaching in the last five years expect to leave (Fuhrman). In the nation, about 40 percent leave in the first two years. This pattern has been consistent over time (Darling-Hammond and Haggstrom).

The rewards that really matter come from the students themselves, and things that get in the way of those rewards create discontent (Fuhrman). Teachers want to be successful with their students, and they want appropriate recognition for that success. They want opportunities for professional growth, variety in their work, and affiliation with colleagues (Hawley, Smylie, and Evertson). These goals are important considerations when designing recruitment and retention strategies.

State policy efforts are just beginning to tap the classroom teacher's perspective through a recent series of interviews, surveys, and discussions. This is an important development for at least two reasons. First, it recognizes the great benefits of teachers' commitment and energy to school improvement. But the second reason bears directly on recruitment and retention efforts. Teachers could be better recruiters than anyone: if they would communicate the value and excitement of teaching to students, recruitment would take care of itself. But too many advise even their own children to avoid the field. Better understanding of what teachers think about their work could lead to policy changes that not only could keep good people from leaving, but could make the work place itself part of the recruiting package.

Teachers say they support many reforms but feel left out of the discussion. They think they could improve their performances if they spent more time with colleagues, but few have the opportunity to do so. They have generally critical views of principals and other school authorities. They feel burdened by nonteaching tasks. They say they love to teach and are generally satisfied with their work, but they feel it isn't respected (Mills and Stout, Fuhrman, Koppich, Metropolitan).

Teachers know schools have changed dramatically in the last two decades because of the changing student body and the intense and distracting social pressures outside of school (ECS National Teacher Forum). Teachers face a tough set of issues: school leadership and the need to create distinct school missions, the decision-making structure of schools and the place of teachers in it, the noninstructional intrusions into professional time, and how and for what to hold schools accountable (ECS National Teacher Forum, Palaich).

How do the state recruiting strategies fit what we know of teacher motivation and opinion? There are two main sets of strategies available to states: those that involve changes in incentives or requirements aimed at the individual, and changes that affect the school as an organization (Palaich). There are many examples of the first type, but few of the second.

The salary improvements, and to a lesser extent, the teacher recognition programs, seem consistent with teachers' opinions. Other programs appear less related to motivation factors to enter and stay in teaching. For example, some teacher testing policies may aggravate the shortage. One study found that states concentrate on screening out the underqualified rather than developing people who might *become* qualified (Goertz, Coley, and Ekstrom). No one disputes the need to allow only the qualified to teach. But according to that study, the policies reduce the likelihood of recruiting minorities. The tests assess few skills that are related to classroom performance. Testing fixes responsibility with teacher education departments in higher education but provides no incentive to other academics who indirectly control teacher preparation. Finally, state teacher policies are put in place without regard for teacher supply and demand. As a result, more than one state has had to reduce teacher test score cutoffs when they didn't recruit enough teachers.

Student loans are another example of the first strategy. A review of state loan programs concluded that most forgiveness loans would have little effect. The people who are attracted would have taught anyway. Exceptions that do attract people who wouldn't have entered otherwise are loan programs that combine significant tuition awards with high academic standards (Spero).

The states approach teacher education from different perspectives. Do we want to eliminate teacher education in its current form by building strong alternative programs? Or deregulate it by removing course requirements? Or regulate it more vigorously by more precisely defining course and certification requirements? Or improve it from within by demanding more imaginative programs? Many, if not all, of these themes appear in the state discussions, and the nationwide trend is not clear.

The very high attrition rate for new teachers (40 percent over the first two years) suggests that states and districts *must* spend more time on retention. It makes no sense to focus on recruiting people if we don't have strategies to keep them. The training costs alone are disturbing with such attrition rates.

States have not tapped the potential of the second strategy, changing the environment of the school itself. Schools are bureaucracies, and many state reforms have made them more so (Darling-Hammond and Wise). Some reforms, by specifying local action in ever greater detail, dampen local commitment (Sykes, interview). Strategies that make the work environment of teaching more attractive are likely to be much more powerful inducements to the people we want in the classroom (Spero, Palaich, Carnegie Forum).

Many other criticisms can be leveled at career ladders, salary programs, alternate routes, and other state initiatives, but one important point must be made in defense of the state efforts. For the most part, the educators have held back and allowed the states' political leadership, with strong backing from the business community, to conceive and guide the reform (Boyer, interview). Although there are many exceptions, teacher unions at the state and local levels generally have not been known as partners in reform, nor have the teacher educators, and the same can be said of other professional groups. This is changing. One of the most important elements of the opportunity that we face now is the strong leadership that is appearing in parts of the educational community itself.

## The Emerging National Agenda to Support Teaching

Several national policy studies in the last twelve months have greatly enhanced the opportunity to strengthen teaching. Together they have not only kept the issue alive, but they also have built a consensus on what ought to be done next. They include *A Nation Prepared*, from the Carnegie Forum; *Investing in Our Children*, by the Committee for Economic Development; *Who Will Teach Our Children*, from the California Commission on the Teaching Profession; *Tomorrow's Teachers*, from the Holmes Group; and *A Call for Change in Teacher Education*, by the American Association of Colleges for Teacher Education. The composite agenda that emerges from these reports is not the agenda of any particular state. The reports themselves disagree on some points. Nevertheless, the areas of agreement are broad. What follows is not a list of unrelated good ideas. The elements comprise a new view of what must be done now to attract and keep able teachers.

## What Do We Do to Attract and Keep Able Teachers?

*Define the Body of Professional Knowledge and Practice that Teachers Must Have.* This is the starting point for everything. Teacher certification and licensing, teacher education, evaluation and the whole effort to improve the attractiveness of teaching must stem from a clear statement of what teachers need to know and be able to do. Certification reform in some states and several teacher education studies developed important approximations of this statement of knowledge and practice (Boyer, Shulman and Sykes, and Holmes). Much more is needed. There is a large body of research that describes productive practice, but teachers also have a perspective, which differs from that of the theoreticians (Mills and Stout). Teachers' knowledge and experience is not systematically tapped (Shulman and Sykes).

*Create a National Board to Define Teacher Standards.* The board would define what teachers need to know and be able to do. It would create and administer a voluntary system to assess that professional capacity. Finally, it would award nationally recognized certificates to teachers who meet the standards (Carnegie, Committee for Economic Development, California Commission). States would, of course, issue teaching licenses. Teachers presently have no influence over standards of professional practice or assessment of that practice (Hawley, Smylie, and Evertson). This board would fill that void because a majority of its members would be teachers, elected by their peers.

*Rebuild the System of Teacher Education.* Teacher education must reflect upon, and contribute to, the emerging consensus on what teachers need to know and be able to do. Teacher educators have announced plans to "make the education of teachers intellectually more solid" (Holmes). These plans involve new reliance on graduate programs, "clinical" schools that would train teachers while educating young people, the elimination of undergraduate education majors, and a closer integration of schools and teacher training institutions. They endorse a liberal arts foundation for all teachers. They also would eliminate many course requirements and concentrate instead on assessment of the knowledge and performance of graduates prior to gaining a state license.

*Redesign the Organization of Schools to Create More Productive Working and Learning Environments.* Schools must focus on student performance. This requires sustained consideration of the conditions that promote teaching and learning in each school. It requires state and especially local monitoring systems that attend to what matters. It also requires more than one education leader. Teachers will have to be involved in decisions about discipline, school goals, their own continuing education, curriculum, and schoolwide problem solving. It also requires a new definition of the principal's job, to emphasize his or her responsibility to develop and use the leadership, professionalism, and participation of teachers (California Commission).

Schools need to build better relationships between union and management, and collaboration in matters outside the scope of collective bargaining. In collective bargaining, conflict is normal and rewarded. But it has costs. On both sides of the bargaining table, the "tough guys" rise to positions of influence. In some districts, work rules specify virtually all areas of contact between teachers and administrators, and collective bargaining continues year round. When conflict ridden relationships are the only ones that link teachers and administration, the improvements in the working and learning place that teachers, administrators, and the public can reasonably expect remain out of reach.

*Redesign the Structure of the Teaching Career.* The teaching career is flat. Advancement means moving out of the classroom. Alternative career structures should provide increasing levels of responsibility and compensation for teachers, with selection criteria based on certified professional competence. These changes would eliminate a major reason for leaving teaching and serve to make better use of teachers' talents. How to develop new career structures is still an open question. Experience reveals several guides: the criteria should be clear and the rewards should be of value to teachers. There should be no arbitrary quotas, training should be available, and teachers should be among the designers of that training (Hawley and Smylie, Carnegie Forum).

*Recruit Able Teacher Candidates.* States need a mix of strategies to recruit minorities, people seeking a second or third career, and those preparing for their first. All have to meet the same standards, but the obstacles, training needs, and inducements may differ, and an effective strategy must recognize that.

*Improve Teacher Compensation, at Entry and Throughout the Career.* Recruiting programs depend on reasonable starting and career salaries. Starting salaries for teaching are low compared to fields that require a similar level of preparation. They also are compressed: there is less than $10,000 difference between the bottom and the top salary levels in most states (Mandel). While average salaries have improved greatly in recent years, teacher salaries have not yet regained the levels of 1970 in real dollars (Kelly, Carnegie Forum).

*Align Teacher Incentives with Schoolwide Student Performance.* Teacher incentives today have little to do with increasing student performance. Salaries increase with seniority and the additional course work chosen without regard for classroom performance. Improving student performance has no effect on individual or group compensation. The most favored teachers get to work with the students who already are the most advanced. In state and federal compensatory education programs, the district allotment actually goes down if performance goes up.

*Improve Teacher Mobility.* There are and will continue to be shortages in one place and surpluses elsewhere. Teachers cannot easily transfer licenses from one state to another. Pension systems often do not permit full transfer of benefits. Local boards often do not give full credit for years of experience out of the district. All of these conditions tend to block market forces that might resolve shortages and surpluses. They also block the force of state recruiting incentives.

*Establish a "Loose/Tight" Approach to State and Local Regulation of Schools.* State and local authorities can deliberate with the educators and then be explicit about expected levels of academic performance. Then they should allow teachers, administrators, and parents to devise ways to meet these levels. Solutions are not obvious here. It is not a matter of defining the courses students must take, but a painstaking and continuing inquiry into what skills students should have, and to what degree.

***Establish the Concept of Educational Bankruptcy.*** Part of the recruitment strategy is to give teachers and principals more responsibility, which able people need to perform at their best. The other side of that is accountability. In rare cases, local systems cannot or will not meet acceptable levels of program or student performance. States should establish a fair, measured process of review against standards, remedial planning, and additional assistance, but with a final recourse to direct state intervention in the school district. This must be a last resort, but an inevitable one in cases of intractable school failure. This procedure is not aimed at teachers but at the organizational conditions under which they work. It makes little sense to abandon able people to a bankrupt organization.

# GOVERNORS' ACTION AGENDA

Without the support of Governors, there will be no progress on the emerging agenda. The agenda is far more difficult than what has been attempted so far. The opportunity is very great, but it will not be realized easily. Perhaps the greatest obstacle is the feeling that "we have already done that." States *should* feel pride in what they have achieved in this area over the last few years. But the quality of education is a major determinant of state and national economic competitiveness. That competition will deal roughly with those who are satisfied with yesterday's accomplishments.

## *Recommendations*

Here are the actions that governors can take now to move that agenda and increase the likelihood of its success:

### *1. Convene a statewide panel to review the national teacher policy reports.*

Among   questions that should be asked of each report are: Is this the right agenda for our state? If it isn't right, what facts show that it isn't? If it is right, what are the obstacles? What will it take to succeed? How will this agenda build upon the work that has already been done? Questions such as these should be posed to a panel that includes education, business, and political leaders of the state. The panel should consider the unusual array of state and national policy studies on teaching that have appeared this year. A year-long commission isn't needed. Finding the appropriate agenda and acting on it is.

### *2. Support the creation of a national board of professional teacher standards.*

The Carnegie Forum on Education and the Economy will convene a planning group to establish the board. Use your state of the state and budget messages to show your support. Speak out on the board's task, and make it clear that the board's standards will have to be rigorous to gain your state's recognition. Direct appropriate state authorities to review policies in relation to the purposes of the board. Ask the teachers in your state to watch the progress of the national board and encourage them to seize this opportunity to strengthen the quality of their profession.

### 3. Develop state initiatives to encourage professional school environments.

This will be an especially difficult item. Many support the value of this approach, but there are few practical guides. Build the case with the public for changing the way schools work. You also might suggest what parents and other citizens could do to support a more productive school environment.

Make it clear to teacher organizations, administrators, and school boards that they must consider a new way of doing business. Governors alone are in a position to set the stage for a new compact between the public and the teachers. The public must offer teachers a professional work environment and all this includes. Teachers must offer a professional commitment to the highest levels of performance. This compact cannot be imposed by government or won at the bargaining table. It can be achieved only over time through discussion, experimentation, and considerable forebearance on all sides. We can fix this item on the public agenda and encourage those willing to work on it.

Direct your commissioner of education to convene superintendents, principals, teachers, boards, unions, and citizens and ask them to identify the opportunities and obstacles. Pledge to remove the obstacles that may exist in regulation. What would a more collaborative school environment look like? What would it take to get it? Propose incentives to test what is known about effective school organizations. A Governor can publicly recognize the schools and districts willing to do this. Say, in essence, "I am looking for a few visionary school principals and teachers, with the superintendents, boards and communities willing to back them up." Put some money behind that challenge. And let teachers and the wider community know about the opportunity.

Provide for the organizational design assistance to administrators and boards that want to redesign the cultures of their schools for greater performance. Support training programs for administrators and others.

Ask questions. What decisions are teachers involved in now? What other decisions should they be involved in? How would their students benefit if they were? What are the obstacles to such involvement? Make it clear that you are willing to relax bureaucratic controls but only for professional controls that guarantee better performance.

The question of how to align teacher incentives to student performance is much debated but not yet answered in a way policymakers can use. Keep asking the question and demand practical answers from the research community and the educators.

### 4. Challenge the higher education community on teacher education.

Enlist the aid of higher education in resolving teacher recruitment and retention problems. Convene the higher education leadership in your state, including presidents, trustees, deans of education, and members of the state board of higher education. Ask these leaders what they should be doing but are not yet doing and what you can do to help.

Should we move toward graduate-level training of teachers? Several recent studies present a strong case for doing so. Others point to the high cost, the impracticality of doing so until teacher salaries justify it, and the time that it will take to overcome the historic antipathy of graduate schools for teacher education. A Governor can encourage competition among various teacher education approaches. If nationally accepted professional standards are in place and tested, the marketplace will decide which training program is superior. Press for an open debate on this subject.

The task is to build alliances with the teacher educators who are willing to assert leadership and set ambitious goals. Hold them publicly accountable, but do what you can to support promising ideas, financially and otherwise.

Again, asking the right questions matters. For example, does the state university endorse the principles asserted by the Holmes Group of education deans? It is for the university community to decide, but a Governor can encourage the faculty to debate this question.

## 5. *Build the case for sustained real dollar increases in education spending.*

Ask the commissioner of education for an accounting of recent education expenditures. How much of the increase goes to instruction and how much has gone for support activities? Are we buying what we really want? Are we saying one thing in our teacher recruitment program and something else in the budget? The budget message is a good time to discuss the implications of these figures. Build a case before the public for sustained growth in instructional support.

## 6. *Define and put in place a comprehensive teacher recruitment strategy.*

Ask for the numbers. What is the projected supply and demand for teachers? What are the assumptions behind those numbers? How do these estimates match state action? Or state reality? Every state has some kind of teacher recruitment program. It is time to assess them. Does anyone conduct entry and exit interviews for teachers? Who enters and who leaves teaching in the state, and why?

Insist that the proper authorities define for new teachers an appropriate mix of strategies that include information to prospective teachers, teacher education, alternate routes, loan programs, placement assistance, and attractive starting salaries.

Support another mix of strategies to recruit the teachers you already have and to keep them from leaving. These strategies might include professional growth opportunities, sabbaticals, teacher recognition programs, and efforts to design more professional work environments.

Governors should lead the state's teacher recruitment efforts personally through public endorsements of the importance and benefits of teaching in the state.

## 7. *Announce the end of emergency teaching licenses.*

Nothing will do more to underscore the seriousness of the standards than for a Governor to declare an end to emergency teacher licenses. Accept temporary shortages and the more aggressive recruiting measures that will be needed. Don't accept unqualified people.

## 8. *Listen to teachers, principals, board members, and others.*

Governors who want to strengthen the teaching profession have many allies that they never see. Create opportunities to listen to small groups of teachers, principals, board members, superintendents, and citizens. What do they think about the emerging teacher policy agenda? In part, these discussions are a search for new ideas. But they are just as important as a way to tap and focus energy and commitment. Talk to the wider public about what you hear from these groups. In so doing, you not only reinforce the agenda, but also demonstrate that it is important for the general public to discuss education and the quality of teaching in a supportive way. And it is most important to find ways to act on and follow through on some of the ideas that come from these meetings.

### 9. Recognize outstanding teaching.

It is impossible to do too much of this. Appoint teachers to boards and panels, and not just to those that have to do with education. Create annual award programs to recognize teachers selected locally. Establish small state grants for distribution to schools through those teachers. Let teachers see that the public believes that teachers have good ideas about education and can wisely apply such funds to education programs.

Create summer symposia for outstanding teachers. Encourage attendance at teacher academies. Hold an annual convocation on excellence in teaching and meet with these teachers to discuss educational matters.

### 10. Establish a state intervention procedure for cases of education bankruptcy.

Initiate legislation to provide for the education of children in districts that cannot or will not respond to repeated evidence of systemwide failure, and repeated efforts to help local authorities correct the situation. The program should include careful monitoring, due process, opportunity for local response, sufficient time, additional resources, firm and effective state intervention if needed, and careful disengagement when the problems are resolved. Such a process would guarantee the safety of the system under the relaxation of specific controls and regulations that we propose elsewhere in this report.

# OVERCOMING OBSTACLES

The conviction that "we have already done that" is a potential obstacle. The facts are that while some states have been enormously creative, no one has done it all. Governors need to convince people that the foundation that has been established in the past is to be built upon, not just celebrated.

The style of confrontation that is normal in collective bargaining is out of place in most other areas of teacher and board relations. When that style of interaction goes beyond the bargaining process, this agenda faces a major obstacle. Governors should point this out and press all parties to find other ways to deal with problems.

The absence of data on supply and demand for teachers is also an obstacle. The numbers can be frustrating when they are incomplete, based on faulty assumptions, or are not used to inform the policy process.

The absence of practical machinery to deal with teachers who respond to recruitment efforts is also an obstacle. When Governors call for teachers, and people want to respond, is there a telephone number to call to find out where current vacancies are?

Also, the misplaced confidence in piecemeal solutions is an obstacle. Whether states adopt this agenda or another one, the solution to teacher recruitment and retention must be comprehensive. The policy process resolves one problem at a time, of course, but it can be guided by an overall sense of direction. When this doesn't happen, a state can end up with strategies that are incomplete or at cross purposes.

Finally, the policy process itself can be an obstacle if it excludes teachers, local boards, and administrators. The agenda we present is really a set of actions Governors can take to create opportunity for others. Thousands of people in classrooms, school board rooms, and administrative offices have to make decisions and take risks for the opportunities to be realized. Governors have to dramatize the importance and benefits of their doing so.

# HOW WILL WE KNOW WE ARE SUCCEEDING?

The agenda of each state will be unique, so a checklist of items that have been attended to will not necessarily demonstrate success. What counts is the kind of teachers the state is able to recruit and keep. Insist that state authorities set recruitment targets and report on the results. What are the average standardized test scores of new teachers? Who leaves?

Set targets for the percentage of real dollar increase in educational expenditure that goes to instruction as opposed to support areas.

Recruiting strategies have to be flexible, and someone has to watch the results and be ready to adjust to changing times. Teacher recruiting strategies are anything but flexible, because most of them are written into law or regulation. Governors will inspire flexibility if they emphasize that it isn't the program they are interested in, but the people—the people who teach children.

**CHAIRMAN**

**Thomas H. Kean**
Governor of New Jersey

**TASK FORCE MEMBERS**

**Bruce Babbitt**
Governor of Arizona
Vice Chairman

**John V. Evans**
Governor of Idaho

**Terry Branstad**
Governor of Iowa

**Joseph E. Brennan**
Governor of Maine

**William A. Allain**
Governor of Mississippi

**James G. Martin**
Governor of North Carolina

**Charles S. Robb**
Former Governor of Virginia

# WORKS CITED

Boyer, Ernest. "A Panel on the Preparation of Beginning Teachers." New Jersey Department of Education, 1984.

Boyer, Ernest. Interview, December 16, 1985.

California Commission on the Teaching Profession. "Who Will Teach Our Children? A Strategy for Improving California Schools." November 1985.

Carnegie Forum on Education and the Economy. "A Nation Prepared: Teachers for the 21st Century." The report of the Task Force on Teaching as a Profession, May 1986.

Committee for Economic Development. "Investing in Our Children." A statement by the research and policy committee of the Committee for Economic Development. New York and Washington 1985.

Darling-Hammond, Linda, and Wise, Arthur. "A Conceptual Framework for Examining Teachers Views of Teaching and Educational Policies." The Rand Corporation, February 1981.

Darling-Hammond, Linda, and Haggstrom, Gus. "Assessing Teacher Supply and Demand." The Rand Corporation (forthcoming, 1986).

Darling-Hammond, Linda. "Beyond the Commission Reports: The Coming Crisis in Teaching." The Rand Corporation, R-3177-RC, July 1984.

Education Commission of the States. "Messages to State Policy Makers." ECS National Teacher Forum (forthcoming).

Evertson, Carolyn M.; Hawley, Willis D.; and Smylie, Marc A. "Improving Teacher Quality and Effectiveness: Issues for the '80s." Vanderbilt University, September 20, 1983.

Feistritzer, C. Emily. "The Conditions of Teaching; A State by State Analysis." The Carnegie Foundation for the Advancement of Teaching, Princeton, New Jersey 1983.

Fuhrman, Susan. "The New Jersey Public School Teacher: A View of the Profession." The Center for Public Interest Polling, Rutgers University, June 1986.

Goertz, Margaret E.; Coley, Richard J.; and Ekstrom, Ruth B. "The Impact of State Policy on Entrance into the Teaching Profession." A final report, NIE Grant #G83-0073, Educational Testing Service, Princeton, New Jersey, October 1984.

Hawley, Willis D.; Smylie, Mark A.; and Evertson, Carolyn. "Improving Teacher Quality and Effectiveness: Issues or the '80's." Vanderbilt University, unpublished paper. September 30, 1985.

The Holmes Group. "Tomorrow's Teachers." East Lansing, Michigan, 1986.

Kelly, James A. "Financing Education Reform." A paper prepared for the Carnegie Forum on Education and the Economy. January 27, 1986.

Kerr, Donna H. "Teaching Competence and Teacher Education in the United States." Teachers College Record, Volume 84, No. 3, Spring 1983.

Klagholz, L. "A Profile of Applicants to New Jersey's Alternate Route to Certification." New Jersey's Department of Education, October 1985.

Koppich, Julia; Gerritz, William; and Guthrie, James. "The View from the Classroom." The California Commission on the Teaching Profession, August 12, 1985.

Lortie, Dan C. "Schoolteacher: A Sociological Study." Chicago: University of Chicago Press, 1975.

Louis Harris Associates. "The American Teacher 1985; Strengthening the Profession." The Metropolitan Life Survey, 1985.

Louis Harris Associates. "Former Teachers in America." The Metropolitan Life Survey, 1986.

Mandel, David. "Teaching Policy: The Data Behind the Debate." Unpublished working paper of the Carnegie Forum on Education and the Economy.

Mills, Richard P., and Stout, Dennis L. "Listening to Teachers." Education Commission of the States, December 1985.

National Commission for Excellence in Teacher Education. "A Call for Change in Teacher Education." American Association of Colleges for Teacher Education, 1985.

Palaich, Robert. "Building State Strategies to Attract and Retain Talented Teachers." Unpublished paper prepared for the National Governors' Association Task Force on Teaching.

Palaich, Robert; Bray, Judith; Flakus-Mosqueda, Patricia; and Wilkens, Joanne. "New Directions for State Teacher Policies." Education Commission of the States. Denver, December 1985.

Rosenholtz, Susan J., and Smylie, Mark A. "Teacher Compensation and Career Ladders." *The Elementary School Journal*, Volume 85, Number 2, 1984.

Schlechty, Phillip C., and Vance, Victor S. "The Distribution of Academic Ability in the Teaching Force: The Policy Implications." Phi Delta Kappan. September 1982, pp. 22–27.

Schulman, Lee, and Sykes, Gary. "A National Board for Teaching?" A paper commissioned for the Task Force on Teaching as a Profession, Carnegie Forum on Education and the Economy, unpublished, January 26, 1986.

Spero, Irene K. "The Use of Student Financial Aid to Attract Prospective Teachers: A Survey of State Efforts.: The College Board—Washington Office, College Entrance Examination Board, New York, February 1986.

Spillane, Robert R. "Agenda for 1986: The Profession of Teaching." Unpublished paper prepared for the National Governors' Association Task Force on Teaching.

Sykes, Gary. Interview, November 20, 1985.

Weaver, W. T. "In Search of Quality: The Need for Talent in Teaching." *Phi Delta Kappan* 61, No. 1, pp. 29–32, 46.

# College Quality from "Time for Results: The Governors' 1991 Report on Education"

*Text of the Report by*
*the Task Force on College Quality*

## DEFINING THE ISSUES

The American system of higher education is an essential component of this nation's continuing economic development, cultural vitality, and general prosperity. By combining the finest research programs with the greatest variety of educational courses and degrees available anywhere, postsecondary institutions provide graduates, and therefore communities, with unparalleled opportunities for personal and professional advancement. Today the percentage of Americans taking advantage of these opportunities for learning is unmatched by any other country in the world. More than 60 percent of this country's high school graduates continue their studies beyond high school.

While student enrollment has tripled since 1965, postsecondary institutions have virtually doubled expenditures to a total of $90 billion in 1984. Both the public and private sectors recognize the critical role of colleges and universities. Funding from local, state, and federal governments account for nearly half of all postsecondary expenditures (Carnes). The private sector provides substantial and steadily increasing support. In 1985 corporations and foundations contributed more than $5 billion to colleges and universities.

But despite obvious successes and generous funding, recent reports have criticized the effectiveness of higher education (Association of American Colleges; National Commission on Excellence in Education; National Commission on Higher Education Issues; National Endowment for the Humanities; National Institute of Education). Both objective data and subjective assessments of higher education indicate disturbing trends. Today's graduates are not as well educated as students of past decades. Gaps between ideal academic standards and actual student learning are widening. Evidence of program decline and devaluation, particularly in the humanities, is becoming increasingly prevalent.

Not enough is known about the skills and knowledge of the average college graduate. However, there is a disturbing trend in the test scores of students graduating from colleges and entering graduate schools. Student performance declined in eleven of fifteen major subject area tests of the Graduate Record Examinations between 1964 and 1982 (Adelman).

College students' attitudes toward their education indicate room for improvement. A 1984 national survey of 5,000 students found that 40 percent of students said no professor took a special interest in their personal academic life and 42 percent felt that most students are treated like numbers in a book (Jacobson).

Other indicators of the deficiencies of higher education come from the employers of graduates. Preliminary screening of ROTC cadets indicates that many cannot pass a basic academic skills test (Tice). These college students are listed as "provisional cadets" until they meet basic quality standards.

Reprinted by permission of the National Governors' Association Task Force on Teaching

Other businesses and professions voice similar frustrations about higher education graduates' readiness for employment. The ever-growing trend of testing elementary and high school teachers has shown that the baccalaureate degree is not a guarantee of even basic literacy, let alone competence in the teacher's subject matter areas. Surveys also indicate substantial levels of dissatisfaction among business employers with the work preparation role of colleges and universities. More than 10 percent of companies surveyed in 1977 provided remedial education, even for college graduates, who tended to be weak in communication and interpersonal skills (Lusterman).

The problems in higher education have been documented by national reports and by key leaders from business, the military, and education itself. Despite this documentation, higher education accrediting agencies apparently are unable to address the decline in academic standards and to hold member institutions accountable for their students' performance. This is especially surprising in light of existing accreditation standards that require a component that considers "outcomes." In practice, however, accrediting associations have focused on campus resources, such as the number of volumes in the library, student/faculty ratio, and structural facilities and physical resources, rather than student learning and abilities. However, even accreditation programs are beginning to note that student progress needs to be substantiated. For example, the Commission on Colleges of the Southern Association of Colleges and Schools has adopted standards for accreditation that include an assessment component.

Improving undergraduate education in the United States will require a coordinated effort by state policymakers, institutional governing boards, administrators, and faculty across all the components of a college education—teaching, academic resources, support services, and curriculum. For schools that offer undergraduate instruction, discussions about the kinds of students the institutions want to develop will naturally lead to decisions to refocus attention and redirect resources to improve undergraduate teaching and learning. Discussions about various approaches to assessment, and specific techniques of assessment, will be a natural follow-up to decisions to improve undergraduate teaching and learning.

As the primary source of funds for public higher education, the states have a major stake in the quality of postsecondary institutions that goes beyond measures of input and processes. State attention must be directed to the outcomes of the higher education system—namely, measuring how much students learn in college.

Assessment is a way that faculty, institutions, and institutional sponsors can focus on outcomes of students, programs, and institutions. Quality can be better determined when information about students, programs, and an institution is regularly collected, analyzed, and used to improve teaching and learning.

Assessment of undergraduate learning and college quality needs, at minimum, to include data about student skills, abilities, and cognitive learning; substantive knowledge of individual students and groups of students at various points in their undergraduate careers; instructional approaches used by faculty; and educational curricula. Because the nature of undergraduate education requires many important skills and cognitive abilities be acquired and developed, colleges and universities should use a number of assessment approaches and techniques.

In 1985, the Southern Regional Education Board stated in its critical report "Access to Quality Undergraduate Education" that quality and access are intertwined. Access is meaningless without considering the quality of the undergraduate program. Yet, there is a fear that assessment procedures will adversely affect students who are underprepared. It is well documented that many of these students perform less well on standardized achievement tests.

An assessment program that uses multiple measures of student learning will more accurately and fairly depict a student's knowledge and abilities, regardless of background or status. Instead of limiting education access, assessment may actually provide incentives to ensure that underprepared students receive the proper counseling, placement, and academic assistance needed to perform in college and to graduate in a reasonable amount of time.

## What have the States Done So Far?

Assessment practices are now in place in a number of states and institutions of higher education. Some of the programs were begun by institutions at their own initiative, while others have been launched as a result of state incentives or mandates. Although our emphasis is on public institutions, we realize there is much to learn from private colleges and universities.

## A Private Innovator

Alverno College, a small, private, liberal arts school in Milwaukee, Wisconsin, offers a model of student assessment. The Alverno faculty conducted a review of curriculum in 1971 and sought a performance-based assessment process. The faculty, lacking higher education models, turned to the corporate community for model programs.

In the Alverno model, the fundamental principles of assessment are specifying criteria; relying on multiple judgments; choosing from alternate performance modes to elicit the full range of the developing ability; and using expert judgment to infer student abilities from this performance. Students also participate in self-assessment. Alverno relies heavily on volunteer assessors from the Milwaukee business and professional community to evaluate student performance. These outside assessors are trained by the Alverno faculty. Their work supplements assessments conducted by the faculty and by the Alverno Assessment Center. The Alverno Office of Research and Evaluation conducts ongoing studies of curriculum in light of assessment data. The major areas of research are what enhances learning, what makes it last, how it is best assessed, how it relates to personal growth, and how it contributes to professional effectiveness.

## A Public Innovator

Northeast Missouri State University (NMSU) adopted a program to assess student learning, often referred to as value-added assessment, in the early 1970s. Scores on tests administered to entering college freshmen are compared with identical tests given to the same students as second semester sophomores to measure gains from the college experience. In addition to the value-added testing, all seniors are required to take a comprehensive exam in their major field of study. Many seniors take standardized exams, and faculty develop examinations for majors that do not have nationally normed tests. Demographic data, and surveys that evaluate the attitudes of students, faculty, alumni, and employers round out information gathered to show the value of an NMSU education.

Northeast Missouri State University's approach to assessment is being adopted by other colleges and universities and is being considered by state legislatures and higher education coordinating boards. The South Dakota Board of Regents has adopted a similar approach for all state colleges and universities in the system. Kean College of New Jersey and the State University of New York, Plattsburgh, are among postsecondary institutions that are developing variations of the value-added program.

## *Statewide Models Of Assessment Programs*

**S** tates are beginning to address the issues of college quality and assessment either singly or in combination with comprehensive reform efforts. The Arkansas Board of Higher Education has asked individual institutions to review, modify, and implement campus assessment plans and report to the board on the specific assessment program initiated on campus. The Louisiana Board of Regents recently examined the core curricula of state institutions in a general education review. The regents have asked state public colleges and universities to assess the outcomes of the newly revamped general education curriculum. However, the decision on the type and form of testing is left to the individual institution. In Illinois, the Committee on the Study of Undergraduate Education of the Board of Higher Education is recommending student assessment programs be instituted to provide information on student performance, but will not mandate the details of the assessment package.

New Jersey has a comprehensive system of entry-level testing in place for incoming college students. An advisory commission has been established to design and implement a long-range College Outcomes Evaluation Project, including student development, research, scholarship, and contributions to community and society. An instrument to test for these student outcomes is planned for development by 1988. A working group appointed by the Maryland State Board for Higher Education has recommended that a general education proficiency test be developed and administered to a sample of students in all statewide public postsecondary institutions at the end of the sophomore year. The Virginia State Council of Higher Education has reviewed existing assessment practices at Virginia postsecondary institutions. While recommending against statewide minimum competency testing for Virginia postsecondary students, all state institutions of higher education have been asked to establish campus-designed procedures for measuring student achievement.

The Colorado higher education reorganization plan requires each state university and college to measure student achievement. Each institution may adopt its own assessment system, depending on its mission. Schools that do not comply by 1990 will lose 20 percent of their state funding appropriation. The Utah Board of Regents is now revising and updating the Master Plan for Higher Education in Utah. Assessment of student outcomes is being considered as part of the revision. Currently, postsecondary institutions are strongly encouraged by the regents to be more active in assessing student learning.

Florida and Tennessee have implemented comprehensive statewide assessment efforts. Florida uses a state-mandated examination to assess basic skills. Students are tested at college entry for placement and remediation, and a standardized exit examination is given to all students before graduation from a Florida community college or entry into upper division courses at state four-year colleges and universities. Students who receive state aid and attend private colleges and universities in Florida must also participate in this testing.

Tennessee's assessment program uses an incentive funding approach. Five percent of each public institution's budget is allocated on the basis of how well the college or university meets five performance criteria, including the assessment of student learning.

Other states have initiated variations of performance funding programs. Missouri rewards individual institutional improvement based on areas of critical state need. New York has an institutional incentive grant program based on the number of degrees conferred. Massachusetts provides funds for Centers of Excellence. Ohio has adopted five specific grant programs to improve higher education, including funding Centers for Excellence and chaired professorships. While these programs are not based specifically on student outcomes, they provide incentives for institutitional improvement. New Jersey also provides special funding to institutions; the Governor's Challenge Funds target state institutions that demonstrate dramatic improvement. South Dakota has begun a performance funding program, and Florida has adopted an initiative to fund Indicators of Progress toward Excellence in Education. The Virginia Fund for Excellence provides grants for institutionally generated, goal-oriented projects.

# WHERE DO WE WANT TO BE IN 1991?

America's institutions of higher education stand as a gateway to opportunity, enterprise, and individual growth. Substantial public and private funds support these institutions. Public policymakers, taxpayers, students, and parents should expect colleges and universities to fulfill their promises. To assure accountability, postsecondary institutions must assess student learning and ability, program effectiveness, and institutional accomplishment of mission.

Although assessment is an area in which only a few institutions of higher education have had long experience, it is an area in which colleges and universities should invest significant time and resources. And colleges and universities are beginning to realize the value of this investment. A 1986 survey by the American Council on Education showed that 91 percent of college and university administrators supported assessment that is linked to improvement of education. Each campus should assess whether the receipt of a baccalaureate degree signifies the acquisition of a core of knowledge, along with the development of abilities to use that knowledge effectively.

Assessment of students' skill levels can and should occur as early as possible in the college program. Results should be used for placement and remediation. The acquisition of knowledge, and the development of abilities, such as thinking critically, solving problems, and synthesizing and drawing inferences from data, are important parts of undergraduate student learning. As students progress in their studies, they should be gaining knowledge and developing higher levels of these fundamental abilities.

Assessment and college quality are not incompatible with the research and graduate functions of postsecondary institutions. In fact, a renewed emphasis on quality at the undergraduate level can revitalize the research and graduate missions of colleges and universities. Quality institutions will aid the cause of research and the creation and application of new knowledge. And better undergraduate students will be better graduate students and professionals.

The benefits of assessment will extend beyond the campus. Graduates of quality institutions will be better prepared to enter the workforce. Assuring the integrity of the college product will enhance the contributions of colleges and universities to the social and cultural development of their communities. And it will promote the link between postsecondary institutions and elementary and secondary schools. A more rigorous undergraduate program will require high schools, middle schools, and elementary schools to do a better job of preparing students to perform college level work.

# GOVERNORS' ACTION AGENDA

## *Recommendations*

### *1. Governors, state legislatures, state coordinating boards, and institutional governing boards should clearly define the role and mission of each public higher education institution in their states. Governors also should encourage the governing boards of each independent college to clearly define their missions.*

By setting goals and objectives, colleges and universities define their particular institutional purposes and develop standards by which to evaluate their progress in achieving those missions. Most colleges and universities will have more than a single function within their mission. Undergraduate instruction may join graduate instruction, research, and public service—or some combination—as a basic function of institutional mission. Institutions should be rewarded fiscally and otherwise as they that take the time to refocus attention on their missions and take steps to evaluate how well goals and objectives central to clearly focused missions are being met. Similarly, independent institutions will be more effective in the competitive arena of higher education as they too refocus attention on roles and missions.

To support these efforts, there are a number of state policy alternatives that can be considered.

● Governors, state legislatures, and coordinating boards should examine the legal and historical basis for the mission of each public college and university in light of current and future state needs.

● Governors, state legislatures, and coordinating boards should determine if state needs are being met by the current configuration of missions among public higher education institutions.

● Governors, state legislatures, and coordinating boards should define, redefine, or refocus the missions of each institution in order to provide a high quality education through a cost-effective delivery system.

● Governors should encourage coordinating boards to review the full range of academic programs in public colleges and universities in light of both institutional mission and program quality.

### *2. Governors, state legislatures, coordinating boards, governing boards, administrators, and faculties should re-emphasize—especially in universities that give high priority to research and graduate instruction—the fundamental importance of undergraduate instruction.*

The predominant model to which most colleges and universities currently aspire is that of the research university. Current reward structures for promotion and tenure in American higher education often encourage faculty to concentrate their efforts on research-oriented tasks. This can lead to a loss of institutional enthusiasm for undergraduate instruction.

Institutions, and the faculty who teach in them, must have the strong encouragement of Governors, legislatures, and coordinating boards to hold undergraduate instruction in special trust and give it special attention.

The task force of Governors fully recognize the synergism that exists among the functions of teaching, research, and public service. Further, the Governors understand that undergraduate students benefit from the enrichment and example of faculty engaged in research and service activities.

There are several ways in which this can be furthered. Governors, state legislatures, and coordinating boards should encourage public discussions of the nature of undergraduate education on each college and university campus, public and private, two-year, and four-year.

Governors, state legislatures, and coordinating boards also are encouraged to develop funding incentives for institutions that reward quality undergraduate teaching and student learning.

**3. *Each college and university should implement systematic programs that use multiple measures to assess undergraduate student learning. The information gained from assessment should be used to evaluate institutional and program quality. Information about institutional and program quality also should be made available to the public.***

Colleges and universities can no longer take for granted the learning that should be occurring on their campuses. In most instances, systematic student assessment, including tough-minded grading, will document the learning that has been taking place. In other instances, a student assessment program will indicate areas in which curriculum and instruction need to be improved. In all instances, regular assessment will provide public institutions with the information they need to document to Governors, coordinating boards, parents, students, and legislatures that tax dollars and other resources are being invested wisely. In a similar vein, independent institutions will be able to demonstrate to their constituencies that the support provided is making a vital difference in the lives of students.

To achieve these goals, Governors should call on colleges and universities to implement programs of undergraduate student assessment that are appropriate to the particular missions of those institutions.

In addition, state coordinating boards, governing boards, and college and university faculties should use the results of assessment programs to improve teaching and learning at each institution.

**4. *Governors, state legislatures, and statewide coordinating boards should adjust funding formulas for public colleges and universities to provide incentives for improving undergraduate student learning, based upon the results of comprehensive assessment programs. Independent colleges and universities should be encouraged to do likewise.***

Although there is justification for allocating resources to public colleges and universities based on enrollment, mission, and other factors, there is also a clear need to reward institutions that can demonstrate that they are doing a good job of educating students. Institutions should be encouraged and rewarded in their efforts to increase the learning of those in their charge. Incentive funding will send a clear signal that policymakers expect and demand proven quality in higher education.

Governors should work with legislatures and coordinating boards to implement a reasonable and substantial incentive funding component in the regular funding formulas for higher education. These same state bodies should recommend special financial incentives—apart from and in addition to the regular funding formula—for public colleges and universities to implement programs of undergraduate student assessment.

Governors should also work with legislatures and coordinating boards to develop funding mechanisms to address deficiencies in student preparation to perform college work, which are identified through assessment programs.

## 5. Governors, state legislatures, coordinating boards, and governing boards should reaffirm their strong commitment to access to public higher education for students from all socio-economic backgrounds.

It is incorrectly assumed that quality and access are competing, antagonistic values in higher education. Although declines in the quality of higher education in the last two decades have occurred during a period when access has been expanded, it is not true that access causes a decline in the quality of higher education.

However, access without quality is a cruel deception, while quality without access is a betrayal of the cherished American ideal of equal opportunity and the belief that it is important to educate all children. In the next decade, an increasing proportion of the nation's youth in the traditional college attendance age categories will have backgrounds that have provided fewer economic and educational advantages. From moral, economic, and national security perspectives the nation simply cannot afford to sacrifice the next generation of emerging Americans in the name of quality enhancement.

College faculties and presidents, governing boards, and state coordinating boards are encouraged to define the prerequisites for success in higher education, including model college preparatory curricula, and to ensure that all parents, students, and school officials are well informed of them.

Institutions, governing boards, and state coordinating boards are encouraged to undertake studies of the patterns of success of the students at each public institution to determine if systematic variations occur among the graduates of particular school districts. The results of these studies should be shared with local school boards so corrective action can be taken as necessary.

## 6. The higher education accrediting community should require colleges and universities to collect and utilize information about undergraduate student outcomes. Demonstrated levels of student learning and performance should be a consideration in granting institutional accreditation.

Although regional accrediting agencies claim to require an outcomes component in their standards, traditionally they have emphasized the availability of institutional resources and processes (education inputs) when deciding to grant accreditation. These resources certainly are fundamental to accomplishing institutional missions; however, they do not by themselves guarantee a high quality, competitive education. Ultimately, institutions must be judged on whether they have, in fact, produced graduates who are intellectually prepared for life and work. For public or private institutions that have undergraduate instruction as one of their functions, programs of student assessment will help demonstrate that students are learning and that the resources and processes are serving the needs of states and the nation.

Governors, state legislatures, and coordinating boards should inform accrediting associations of their expectations that student outcomes be a component in the accreditation of every college and university.

Governors, state legislatures, and coordinating boards should encourage accrediting agencies and public institutions to release detailed assessments of institutional strengths and weaknesses—including reviews of student performance. For purposes of consumer information, Governors, state legislatures, and coordinating boards should request this disclosure from accrediting agencies, and should require it of public institutions.

# HOW WILL WE KNOW WE ARE SUCCEEDING?

**T**o determine and monitor a state's progress in the area of undergraduate student outcomes, Governors can ask the following broad questions:

1. Does each higher education institution in the state have a clear statement of institutional mission?

2. At each institution of higher education in the state with a function of undergraduate instruction, what assessment practices are in place to evaluate student, program, and institutional performance?

3. What state incentives exist to encourage the assessment of undergraduate students, undergraduate programs, and institutions?

4. What information is reported regularly to the public concerning undergraduate student learning, undergraduate program quality, and undergraduate institutional quality?

# OVERCOMING OBSTACLES

**T**he members of the task force realize that a great deal of work must be done in the area of assessing undergraduate education. In some cases, appropriate assessment instruments do not currently exist. Institutions may have to develop their own approaches and instruments—the experience of Alverno College is an example.

Assessment will vary at different institutions, because the mix of programs, missions, and types of students will differ. Each institution will have to determine what it wants to measure before deciding which assessment approaches and techniques are appropriate. The large vendors of standardized and customized tests will need time to design new instruments and approaches to assess higher order abilities.

The Governors on the task force are aware that assessment is currently undertaken by most colleges and universities. From the most basic assessments of student learning, such as grading course examinations and term papers, to sophisticated norm-referenced examinations, colleges and universities already collect information about undergraduate student learning. However, this information is seldom collected systematically or analyzed comprehensively. Such information could be regularly collected and interpreted, supplemented with additional student outcomes information, and used to improve undergraduate teaching and learning.

Implementing a comprehensive undergraduate assessment program will involve certain costs. These costs will vary according to the size of the institution, the nature of the assessment program selected, and the outcomes desired. Peter T. Ewell and Dennis P. Jones in "The Costs of Assessment" state that the question of the cost of assessment is one of how much additional money must be spent to begin a program appropriate to the needs of the institution. Given that dollars currently spent for assessment often can be spent more effectively, and that assessment programs can become more efficiently operated over time, many estimates of new dollars required for implemented comprehensive programs can be substantially reduced.

State leaders can expect opposition from faculty and administrators who fear unintended side effects from the assessment process, such as teaching to the test, limiting the access of the educationally disadvantaged to a college education, narrowing curriculum, and adversely affecting research activities. A 1986 survey by the American Council on Education found the following stumbling blocks to assessment: no funds to develop procedures (71 percent); not clear what to evaluate (64 percent); fears about misuse of results (60 percent); lack of faculty support (58 percent); and no good evaluation instruments (57 percent) (El-Khawas). Faculty and admnistrators must be an integral part of assessment efforts and be seated at the table at the beginning of the discussion. When faculty see the demonstrated benefits of assessment programs, as they have at such diverse schools as the University of Tennessee, Alverno College, and Northeast Missouri State University, they, too, will become standard bearers for achieving more effective college quality through assessment.

This report emphasizes that Governors can take a positive approach in encouraging assessment. The obstacles to assessment are more mythical than real. Peter Ewell states that "statewide approaches should as far as possible be designed to challenge excellence rather than to mandate adequacy. Experience has shown that higher-education institutions are at their best when pursuing the best."

## WORKS CITED

Adelman, Clifford. "The Standardized Test Scores of College Graduates 1964–1982," prepared for the Study Group on the Condition of Excellence in American Higher Education. Washington, D.C.: U.S. Department of Education, National Institute of Education, 1984.

Association of American Colleges. *Integrity in the College Curriculum: A Report to the Academic Community: The Findings and Recommendations of the Project on Redefining the Meaning and Purpose of Baccalaureate Degrees.* Washington, D.C.: Association of American Colleges, 1985.

Carnes, Bruce. Testimony presented to the National Governors' Association Task Force on College Quality. Washington, D.C., 1986.

Ewell, Peter T. "The State Role in Assessing College Outcomes: Policy Choices and Probable Impacts." In *Supporting Works: Task Force on College Quality, Governors' 1991 Report.* Washington, D.C.: National Governors' Association, 1986.

El-Khawas, Elaine. "Campus Trends, 1984." Higher Education Panel Report No. 65. Washington, D.C.: American Council on Education, 1985.

Jacobson, Robert. "Most Students are Satisfied With Their Education, Survey Indicates, But Frustrations are Widespread." *The Chronicle of Higher Education,* February 5, 1986, p. 1.

Lusterman, Seymour. "Education in Industry." Report No. 719. New York: The Conference Board, 1977.

National Commission on Excellence in Education. *A Nation at Risk: The Imperative for Educational Reform.* Washington, D.C.: U.S. Government Printing Office, 1983.

National Commission on Higher Education Issues. *To Strengthen Quality in Higher Education: Summary Recommendations of the National Commission on Higher Education Issues.* Washington, D.C.: National Commission on Higher Education Issues, 1982.

National Endowment for the Humanities (NEH). *To Reclaim a Legacy.* A report written by William J. Bennett, chairman, NEH. Based on findings of the Study Group on the State of Learning in the Humanities in Higher Education. Washington, D.C.: National Endowment for the Humanities, 1984.

National Institute of Education. *Involvement in Learning: Realizing the Potential of American Higher Education.* Study Group on the Conditions of Excellence in American Higher Education. Washington, D.C.: National Institute of Education, 1984.

Tice, Jim. "ROTC Cadet to be Tested on Basic Academic Skills." *Army Times,* March 12, 1984, p. 2.

**CHAIRMAN**

**John Ashcroft**
Governor of Missouri

**TASK FORCE MEMBERS**

**Bob Graham**
Governor of Florida
Vice Chairman

**George Deukmejian**
Governor of California

**John Carlin**
Governor of Kansas

**Harry Hughes**
Governor of Maryland

**Michael S. Dukakis**
Governor of Massachusetts

**George Nigh**
Governor of Oklahoma

**Arch A. Moore Jr.**
Governor of West Virginia

# Carnegie Foundation's Report on Colleges

WASHINGTON

*Following are the prologue and the major recommendations of "College: The Undergraduate Experience in America," a report being issued here this week by the Carnegie Foundation for the Advancement of Teaching.*

Our system of higher education, with its openness, diversity, and scholarly achievement, is the envy of the world. Unencumbered by suffocating ideology, the integrity of the American college and university is unmatched.

And yet, while preparing this report we found that the undergraduate college, the very heart of higher learning, is a troubled institution. Driven by careerism and overshadowed by graduate and professional education, many of the nation's colleges and universities are more successful in credentialing than in providing a quality education for their students. It is not that the failure of the undergraduate college is so large but that the expectations are so small.

During our study we found deep divisions on the campus, conflicting priorities and competing interests that diminish the intellectual and social quality of the undergraduate experience and dramatically restrict the capacity of the college effectively to serve its students. At the colleges and universities we visited, these special points of tension appeared with such regularity and seemed so consistently to sap the vitality of the undergraduate experience that we have made them the focus of this report.

The first problem we encountered is the discontinuity between schools and higher education. Today, educators from the separate levels, with few exceptions, carry on their work in isolation. The curriculum is disjointed and guidance is inadequate. Students find the transition from school to college haphazard and confusing. They are, we found, dissatisfied with recruitment procedures, unclear about requirements for admission, and troubled by the costs. Part-time and older students, a rapidly growing sector part of American higher education, also face disturbing problems of transition.

The separation we found between school and college has led to a mismatch, a disturbing one, between faculty expectations and the academic preparation of entering students. Many young people who go to college lack basic skills in reading, writing, and computation—essential prerequisites for success. Faculty are not prepared, nor do they desire, to teach remediation courses.

We begin this report with the conviction that the nation's education structure should be a seamless web. And we ask: Is it possible for educators from the separate levels to work together to define a basic education and strengthen the proficiency of students in language and computation? How can the procedures for college recruitment, selection, and orientation be improved? And can the nation's colleges expand educational opportunities for the growing number of adults and historically-bypassed students?

The second issue is confusion over goals. Scrambling for students and driven by marketplace demands,

> ## "The undergraduate college, the very heart of higher learning, is a troubled institution."

many undergraduate colleges have lost their sense of mission. They are confused about how to impart shared values on which the vitality of both higher education and society depend. The disciplines have fragmented themselves into smaller and smaller pieces, and undergraduates find it difficult to see patterns in their courses and to relate what they learn to life. Archibald MacLeish observed in 1920, "there can be no educational postulates so long as there are no generally accepted postulates of life itself." And colleges appear to be searching for meaning in a world where diversity, not commonality, is the guiding vision.

Closely related is the conflict between careerism and the liberal arts. Today's students worry about jobs. Narrow vocationalism, with its emphasis on skills training, dominates the campus. Several institutions we visited are virtually torn apart as new majors battle old. A department chairman at a midwest college told us, "They're trying to turn this college into a supermarket where we're willing to put anything in the catalog so long as it will sell." But the president observed, "It's all right to talk about liberal arts goals but we have to face up to what students want today."

These conflicts prompt fundamental questions: Is it possible for administrators, faculty, and students with their separate interests to agree on a vital mission for undergraduate education? Can the curriculum serve individual interests while providing a coherent view of the human condition? Is the academic major simply a means to prepare specialists with narrow technical skills? Above all, can the liberal and useful arts be blended during college, as they must inevitably be blended during life?

The third problem we encountered is divided loyalties within the faculty. Professors are expected to function as scholars, conduct research, and communicate results to colleagues. Promotion and tenure hang on research and publication. But undergraduate education also calls for a commitment to students and effective teaching. Faculty members are torn between these competing obligations.

There is the related matter of faculty renewal. In recent years, career prospects for young professionals have diminished. Opportunities for mobility are slim and options for professional growth restricted. At the same time the number of part-time faculty is increasing. These developments threaten the unity and vitality of the professoriate.

The challenge faced by the faculty is suggested by these questions: What is the balance that should be struck between teaching and research? Is it appropriate for different types of higher learning institutions to have different criteria for faculty evaluation? How can faculty members be professionally renewed?

Fourth, we discovered tensions between conformity and creativity in the classroom. Time and again we heard faculty complain about the passivity of students *whose interests*, they said, *are stirred only when* reminded that *the material being pre-sented will be covered on a test.* In all too many classrooms, we found an absence of vigorous intellectual exchange, a condition for which faculty as often as students bear responsibility.

Still, there remains a vision of the undergraduate college as a place where teachers care about their students, where, in the classroom, traditions can be challenged and new ideas tested. We consider, therefore, the following questions: Is it possible for students, during this era of mass education, to become independent, self-directed learners? How can faculty improve their teaching so as to encourage creativity and critique? And how can all resources for learning, on and off the campus, be connected?

Fifth, we found a great separation, sometimes to the point of isolation, between academic and social life on campus. Colleges like to speak of the campus as *community,* and yet what is being learned in most residence halls today has little connection to the classrooms; indeed, it may undermine the educational purposes of the college. The idea that a college stands in for parents, *in loco parentis,* is today a faded memory. But on many campuses there is great uncertainty about what should replace it. Further, we found that residential and commuter students live in two separate worlds.

We were especially impressed that many faculty and academic administrators distance themselves from student life and appear to be confused about their obligations in nonacademic matters.

How can life outside the classroom support the educational mission of the college?

How should tension between student freedom and institutional authority be resolved?

And how can the college leave space for privacy while also providing activities that sustain community and encourage service?

The sixth problem is the disagreement we found over how the college should be governed. As the complexity of higher education has increased, confidence in the decision-making process appears to have declined. Presidents are caught in the crossfire of conflicting pressures. Faculty feel more loyalty to their discipline than to the institutions where they teach. And when students are asked to participate in campus governance their involvement is sporadic. Can students, faculty, and administrators build community through improved communication?

The next issue is how the outcome of a college education should be measured. Today, the academic progress of students is assessed by each professor, course by course. Class grades are dutifully recorded. The final mark of achievement is the diploma, which presumably signifies an educated person. But good teachers are not necessarily good testers and the college has few ways to evaluate the quality of education overall.

During our study we heard calls for a new approach to evaluation. Increasingly, state and national education officials, lawmakers, parents, and students are wondering just how much is being learned. How can college goals and the evaluation of student achievement be more closely linked? Should there be assessment beyond course grades? Are the testing procedures now used adequate to the task?

This brings us to the final concern. Though listed last, it touches all the rest. We found on most campuses a disturbing gap between the college and the larger world. There is, we sensed, a parochialism that seems to dominate higher education, an intellectual and social isolation that reduces the effectiveness of faculty and limits the vision of the student. We feel compelled to ask: How can the undergraduate college help students gain perspective and prepare them to meet their civic and social obligations in the neighborhood, the nation, and the world?

Here, then, are the eight points of tension: the transition from school to college, the goals and curriculum of education, the priorities of the faculty, the condition of teaching and learning, the quality of campus life, the governing of the college, measuring the outcome, and the connection between the campus and the world.

These problems are not new. They have, in one way or another, troubled higher education for generations. But the points of tension are, we believe, also points of unusual opportunity. On campuses all across the country we found renewed interest in general education, in the quality of teaching, and in the evaluation of the undergraduate experience. Above all, we found a wellspring of tradition and talent waiting to be tapped.

What we urgently need today is a constructive debate about the meaning of the undergraduate college and a willingness to make this part of the educational enterprise a more vital, more enriching institution. At the same time, the diversity of our system must be acknowledged and protected. The responses to the challenge of enriching the baccalaureate experience will surely differ from one institution to another and, in the end, the quality of the effort must be measured not by the certainty of the outcome, but by the quality of the quest.

The American college is ready for renewal, and there is, we believe, an urgency to the task. The nation's colleges have been successful in responding to diversity and in meeting the needs of individual students. They have been much less attentive to the larger, more transcendent issues that give meaning to existence and help students put their own lives in perspective.

This nation and the world need well-informed, inquisitive, open-minded young people who are both

---

> ## "The American college is ready for renewal, and there is an urgency for the task."

---

productive and reflective, seeking answers to life's most important questions. Above all, we need educated men and women who not only pursue their own personal interests but are also prepared to fulfill their social and civic obligations. And it is during the undergraduate experience, perhaps more than at any other time, that these essential qualities of mind and character are refined.

A ringing call for the renewal of the American college may, at first blush, seem quixotic. Not only has cultural coherence faded, but the very notion of commonalities seems strikingly inapplicable to the vigorous diversity of contemporary life. Within the academy itself, the fragmentation of knowledge, narrow departmentalism, and an intense vocationalism are, as we have acknowledged, the

strongest characteristics of collegiate education.

Still, we believe the undergraduate experience can bring together the separate parts, create something greater than the sum, and offer the prospect that the channels of our common life will be deepened and renewed. The college—set apart from graduate and professional education—remains, as Sheldon Rothblatt of the University of California, Berkeley, put it, "the primary form of [higher education] where the well-being of the self and the problem of self and society are central."

To accomplish this essential mission, connections must be made. All parts of campus life—recruitment, orientation, curriculum, teaching, residence hall living, and the rest—must relate to one another and contribute to a sense of wholeness. We emphasize this commitment to community not out of a sentimental attachment to tradition, but because our democratic way of life and perhaps our survival as a people rest on whether we can move beyond self-interest and begin better to understand the realities of our dependence on each other.

We proceed, then, with the conviction that if a balance can be struck between individual interests and shared concerns, a strong learning community will result. And perhaps it is not too much to hope that the college, as a vital community of learning, can be a model for society at large—a society where private and public purposes also must be joined.

## Major Recommendations to Improve the Undergraduate Experience

### I

**Transition: School to College**

The quality of the undergraduate college is measured first by its alliance with the schools, by its willingness to smooth the transition between school and higher education. The way students are recruited shapes their college expectations, and a good college conducts its recruitment and selection to serve the best interests of students.

We found during our study that the path from school to college is poorly marked. Students and their parents urgently need to be better informed about the full range of colleges in America and they should be given better advice about the alternatives they have. Such information is essential if the undergraduate experience is to be strengthened.

► The Educational Testing Service, the College Board, and the American College Testing Program should establish regional advisement centers throughout the country. Such centers would be places where high school counselors could learn about colleges in their own area and nationwide.

► We suggest, too, that these national testing organizations give grants to high schools, especially to those with low college-going rates, to strengthen counseling services. And they should make travel grants available to high school counselors so that they can visit college campuses—and the proposed regional advisement centers—to become better informed about higher education.

► We recommend that the Commission on Self-Regulation of the American Council on Education draw up a strict code of conduct for college recruitment based on the work already done in the nation's registrars and admissions offices. To assure compliance, we urge the nation's six regional accrediting associations to review carefully recruitment procedures at every college and university they accredit.

► We strongly urge that every institution reaffirm, as an essential objective, its commitment to educational opportunity, especially for historically bypassed students. We urge that colleges give priority to need-based student assistance awards. At the federal level, we strongly recommend that Pell grant programs be expanded.

•

► To smooth the transition, we also recommend that every state establish a blue-ribbon panel of school and college educators to consider what students need to know and be able to do in order to prepare effectively for college.

► Meanwhile all colleges and universities should demystify the selection process. Each institution should describe in its literature the various criteria used for selection and give prospective students a profile of the student characteristics that seem most closely linked to the culture of the institution.

► National tests—the S.A.T. and A.C.T.—should be put in appropriate perspective. The vast majority of the nation's colleges and universities are not selective and we strongly urge that if a college does not use the S.A.T. or A.C.T. scores as a significant yardstick for selection of students the tests should not be required.

► When scores are required, the use colleges make of them should be described fully to prospective students. And colleges should report not only the *average* S.A.T. scores, but also the scores of admitted students by quartile.

► Every college and university should ask prospective students to submit an essay as part of their application for admission not only to underline the importance of writing but also as a means of learning more about the needs as well as the strengths of students.

► Throughout the entire selection process, the primary concern of every college should be not just to fill the slots, but to serve the interests of students. Colleges should explain to parents and students the characteristics of those who do *not* succeed at the institutions as well as the characteristics of those who do.

► Colleges should report back to secondary schools on the academic progress of their former students. And we also recommend that every higher learning institution monitor the relationship between selection procedures and the performance of students.

► We conclude that there is an urgent need for new and better ways to assess students as they move from school to higher education. The goal of the new assessment program would be to evaluate not only the *academic* achievement of students—linking it to the curriculum that the students studied—but also to provide *advisement*, to help students make decisions more intelligently about their futures.

► Finally, we recommend the formation of a national panel to study all aspects of the high school–college transition, looking especially for ways to achieve more appropriate matching of the interests of individual students with the purposes of higher learning institutions.

Above all, prospective students and their parents should not be intimidated by the process. It is wrong to believe that there is one type of college that is right for all. A handful of colleges are highly selective, and if attending one of these institutions is a student's goal, some degree of competition must be accepted as a fact of life.

But many lesser-known colleges also offer a solid, challenging undergraduate experience.

## II
### Goals

A quality college is guided by a clear and vital mission. The institution cannot be all things to all people. Choices must be made and priorities assigned. And there is, we believe, in the tradition of the undergraduate college, sufficient common ground on which shared goals can be established and a vital academic program built.

► If the college experience is to be worthwhile, there must be intellectual and social values that its members hold in common, even as there must be room for private preference. A balance must be struck between two powerful traditions—*individuality* and *community*.

► While responding to students' diverse goals, the college has an obligation to give students a sense of passage toward a more integrated, more coherent view of knowledge and of life.

All aspects of college—orientation, curriculum, counseling, instruction, and social life—must contribute to both personal empowerment and social perspective.

The undergraduate experience recognizes both our independence and our interdependence.

It acknowledges the priorities of both individual preferences and community needs.

## III
### Orientation

Most students come to college with high hopes. The transition is a major rite of passage, but undergraduates are often largely uninformed about the values and traditions of higher education. The first days on campus will probably have a significant influence on the entire undergraduate experience.

► All undergraduate colleges should consider an orientation convocation at the beginning of the academic year that would be as significant for matriculating freshmen as the commencement ceremony is for departing seniors.

► We also recommend a preterm orientation session for all new undergraduates, one that may extend into the first semester.

► A short-term credit course—perhaps entitled *The College: Its Values and Traditions*—should be offered to introduce new students to the history of higher education and the unique characteristics and academic procedures of the campus.

► We especially urge the college president to be a leader in introducing new students to the campus. At a college of quality, the president is as involved in welcoming new students to the campus as he or she is in meeting the alumni.

► Special priority should be given to the difficult but essential task of orienting part-time students. Unless these students are taken seriously by the college and integrated into campus life, undergraduate education in America increasingly will become simply a process in which part-time students drift on and off campus and credits are earned and appropriately recorded. In this process, the most essential values of a liberal education will be lost.

► The successful colleges offer a well-planned program of advising for all students, one that provides support throughout the freshman year. Graduate students and upper division students may be effective as aides, especially in advising freshmen.

A successful freshman year program will convince students that they are part of an intellectually vital, caring community.

## IV
### The First Requirement

Proficiency in the written and the spoken word is the first prerequisite for a college-level education. Students need language to grasp and express feelings and ideas effectively. To succeed in college, undergraduates should be able to write and speak with clarity, and to read and listen with comprehension.

► We urge that the reading and writing capability of all students be carefully assessed when they enroll. Those not well prepared in written and spoken English should be placed in an intensive, noncredit, remedial course that meets daily during the academic term. And good English usage must be reinforced by every professor in every class.

► While the need for remedial programs is a fact of life, we are convinced that the long-term answer is better precollegiate education. Every college and university should work closely with surrounding districts to improve the teaching of English in the nation's schools.

► We also recommend that all college freshmen, not just those with special problems, begin their undergraduate experience with a year-long course in English, with emphasis on writing.

► While stressing writing, we also urge that oral communication become an important part of the freshman language course.

Language and thought are inextricably connected, and as undergraduates develop their language skills, they hone the quality of their thinking and become intellectually and socially empowered. The goal must be to extend, through language study, the common knowledge of its students and, in so doing, sustain the heritage of our culture.

## V
### General Education

The weak and ineffective approach to general education—through distribution requirements—should be strengthened. To achieve this essential goal, we propose an approach called an *integrated core*. By the *integrated core* we mean a program of study that introduces a student to essential knowledge, to connections across the disciplines, and, in the end, to the application of knowledge to life beyond the campus.

► To translate the purpose of the *integrated core* into practice, we sug-

gest seven areas of inquiry that touch the disciplines and relate knowledge to experiences common to all people. The following academic framework for general education is suggested:
- *Language: The Crucial Connection*
- *Art: The Esthetic Experience*
- *Heritage: The Living Past*
- *The Social Web*
- *Nature: Ecology of the Planet*
- *Work: The Value of Vocation*
- *Identity: The Search for Meaning*

It seems clear to us that an exploration of these universal experiences—through courses, seminars, all-college convocations, and the like—is indispensable if students are better to understand themselves, their society, and the world of which they are a part. Ideally, general education, the *integrated core*, is not something to "get out of the way," but should extend vertically from freshman to senior year. And in a properly designed baccalaureate program, general education and specialized education will be joined.

## VI
### The Enriched Major

The baccalaureate degree is now divided into two separate parts, general education and the major. We believe these two essential segments of the baccalaureate experience should be blended in the curriculum just as, inevitably, they must be blended during life. Therefore, in tandem with the integrated core, we propose an *enriched major*. By an *enriched major*, we mean encouraging students not only to explore a field in depth, but also to put the specialized field of study in perspective.

► The major, as it is enriched, would respond to three essential questions: What is the history and tradition of the field to be examined? What are the social and economic implications to be understood? and, What are the ethical and moral issues to be confronted and resolved?

► Every student, as an essential part of the undergraduate experience, should complete an *enriched major*. Beyond the separate courses, the field of study should include a written thesis that relates some aspect of the major to historical, social, or ethical concerns. Every student should write a senior thesis and we further suggest that each student par-

ticipate in a senior seminar in which he or she presents the report orally to colleagues and also critiques the papers of fellow students.

As the major begins to intersect with the themes of common learning students return, once again, to the considerations of language, heritage and social institutions, and the rest. At a college of quality when a major is so enriched it leads the student from depth to breadth and focuses, not on mere training, but on liberal education at its best.

## VII
### Faculty Priorities

A coherent curriculum is only the beginning. Good faculty are essential to a good college. Members of the faculty determine the quality of the undergraduate experience. And the investment in teaching is the key ingredient in the building of a successful institution.

► At every research university, teaching should be valued as highly as research and good teaching should be an equally important criterion for tenure and promotion.

► At many research universities, the title Distinguished Research Professor is in place. We recommend that these institutions also establish the rank of *Distinguished Teaching Professor*, extending special status and salary incentives to those professors who are outstandingly effective in the classroom.

► For most of the nation's colleges and universities, where large numbers of undergraduates are enrolled, priority should be given to teaching, not research.

► While not all professors should be publishing researchers, they nonetheless should be first rate *scholars*. Therefore, we urge as the ideal the *scholar-teacher*. We understand this to mean staying on the cutting edge of the profession, knowing the literature in one's field, and skillfully communicating such information to students. To weaken faculty commitment to scholarship, as we define it here, is to undermine the undergraduate experience, regardless of the academic setting.

► Faculty renewal is a crucial component of a good college. A comprehensive plan for the professional development of faculty is important during a period when mobility is restricted. The sabbatical leave is the most common form of faculty renewal, but it is far from universal. We urge that it be available at every institution.

► We recommend that funds be available to help teachers develop new ideas and improve their pedagogical procedures. These grants—to be administered by a campus-wide faculty committee—should be restricted at first to those who engage in undergraduate instruction. We also urge that all colleges have a grant program for faculty research.

► Faculty development programs might also include exchange arrangements and guest lectureships that would move faculty from one campus to another. We recommend that clusters of colleges all across the country organize Regional Faculty Exchange Networks.

► Because department chairs are so important to faculty development, we recommend regional seminars specifically for department chairs to prepare them for leadership.

► A balance must be struck between full- and part-time faculty. Specifically, we propose that no more than 20 per cent of the undergraduate faculty be part-time and that when part-time faculty are used, their employment be educationally justified.

The joy of teaching, engaging the intellect of students, and the satisfaction of participating in the building of an institution of higher learning—these, too, can and should be a source of fulfillment as great as seeing one's name in print in the pages of a professional journal or hearing the applause of one's fellow scholars at a professional meeting.

# VIII

## Creativity in the Classroom

What we found in many classrooms was a mismatch between faculty and student expectations, a gap that left both parties unfulfilled. Faculty, concerned with scholarship, wanted to share ideas with students who are expected to appreciate what professors do, but often this is not the case in lower division courses. Students, remarkably conscious of grades, are willing to conform to the

formula of taking notes and taking tests.

► We urge that top priority be given to classes for freshman and sophomore students. Special efforts should be made, through small seminar units within large lecture sections, to create conditions in the undergraduate classrooms that increase the intellectual exchange between faculty and students.

► The undergraduate experience, at its best, involves active learning and disciplined inquiry that leads to the intellectual empowerment of students.

► The methods used by teachers to measure the progress of their students should be improved. Specifically we recommend that faculty seminars be held on student evaluation to help teachers learn how to give students careful and concise criticisms, how to help them understand the strengths and weaknesses of their performance.

► The evaluation of teachers is also the mark of a good college. We recommend that the performance of each teacher in each classroom be formally assessed by students.

► All members of the faculty should work continuously to improve the content of their courses and their methods of instruction and teacher preparation should begin in graduate school as graduate assistants work with mentors who carefully critique their work.

The undergraduate college, at its best, is an institution committed to knowledge backed by wisdom. This means encouraging students, through creative teaching, to become intellectually engaged.

# IX

## Resources for Learning

The quality of a college is measured by the resources for learning on the campus and the extent to which students become independent, self-directed learners. And yet we found that today, about one out of every four undergraduates spends *no* time in the library during a normal week, and 65 per cent use the library four hours *or less* each week.

The gap between the classroom and the library, reported on almost a

half-century ago, still exists today.

► The college library must be viewed as a vital part of the undergraduate experience. Every college should establish a basic books library to serve the specific needs of the undergraduate program.

► All undergraduates should be introduced carefully to the full range of resources for learning on a campus. They should be given bibliographic instruction and be encouraged to spend at least as much time in the library—using its wide range of resources—as they spend in classes.

► Support for the purchase of books should be increased. A minimum of 5 per cent of the total operating budget of the college should be available for library support.

► The undergraduate college should work closely with surrounding schools and with community libraries to help strengthen library holdings, and provide continued training for school and community librarians.

► The undergraduate college also has a special obligation not only to support adequately the library, but in a larger sense to sustain the culture of the book. Colleges should celebrate the book and schedule activities each year that feature books and reading—bringing authors to the campus, for example—or they can have seminars in which faculty talk about works that were influential in their lives.

•

In the past, technological revolutions bypassed education because teachers were bypassed in the process.

This time it may be different. Today, on many campuses we found teachers more actively involved in the use of computers, and with their help, programming has improved.

► To improve the undergraduate experience—and strengthen the community of learning—the challenge is to build connections between learning resources on and off the campus. The strategy we have in mind is to link technology to the library, to the classroom, and, in the end, to college goals.

► To achieve such integration, we propose three specific recommendations.

First, computer hardware should not be purchased before a comprehensive plan has been developed, one that covers personal computers, information services, and the use of technology by the institution.

► Second, we urge that every college have a high level faculty committee to plan for the integration of learning resources on the campus.

► Third, to broaden their services, we recommend that every college and university also link its library to one or more computer-based networks.

While using technology, students also need to understand how society today is being reshaped by our inventions, just as tools of earlier eras changed the course of history. There is a danger that greater credibility will be given to data than to ideas and that scholars will mistake information for knowledge. The challenge is not only to teach students how to use new technology but also to encourage them to ask when and why it should be used.

# X

## The Quality of Campus Life

The undergraduate college should be held together by something more than plumbing, a common grievance over parking, or football rallies in the fall. What students do in dining halls, on the playing fields and in the rathskeller later at night, all combine to influence the outcome of the college education, and the challenge, in the building of community, is to see academic and nonacademic life as interlocked.

► In a college of quality, faculty will understand the importance of encouraging student participation in campus cultural events. They, too, should be active participants, and attempt to tie their teaching to such activities whenever possible.

► All-college convocations, with careful planning, can be a vital force, stirring discussion and controversy, reflection and commitment. Commencement and alumni weekends can have an equal influence on the campus. And occasionally a college can be brought together to support a worthy cause.

► Even at large complex institutions with their autonomous units, the goals should be to build alliance between the classroom and campus life, to find group activities, traditions, and common values to be shared.

► Further, we strongly urge that intercollegiate sports be organized and operated to serve the students, not the institution. When serious athletic violations are discovered, the accreditation status of the institution should be revoked—along with eligibility for the National Collegiate Athletic Association. We also ask presidents of universities and colleges to say publicly what they acknowledge privately: that big-time sports are out of control.

► All students should be helped to understand that "wellness" is a prerequisite to all else.

They should be taught about good food and exercise, and begin to understand that caring for one's body is a special trust.

Further, a professional nutritionist should advise the campus food service and also be available for students as part of the campus health service.

► We urge that all colleges educate a core of senior students who, in turn, would educate through informal seminars, their fellow students about health, nutrition, and first aid. We also urge that every campus have appropriate health and psychological support services available to which students can be referred.

► Finally, we suggest that leaders of student health centers work directly with their counterparts in food service, intramural athletics, residence hall supervision, student government, and even the academic administration to assure that the "wellness" program has the resources and endorsement of the whole campus. The college of quality remains a place where the curricular and cocurricular are viewed as having a relationship to each other. At a time when social bonds are tenuous, college students should discover the reality of their dependence on each other. They must understand what it means to share and sustain traditions. Community must be built.

# XI

## Residential Living

Administrators, we found, are confused about their obligations to students in nonacademic matters and in the context of student living, the challenge of creating an enthusiastic community of learning must be carefully considered. Are living arrangements simply a convenience or do they contribute to collegiate goals? We find it troubling that students who serve as resident assistants in the dorms are given weighty assignments, when key college administrators, and especially members of the faculty, are far removed from the day to day lives of students.

► We urge that college presidents become directly involved in the planning and oversight of residence hall living and the quality of campus life. The president should receive regular reports on both problems and creative programs in the residence halls.

► We strongly urge that colleges and universities provide intensive workshops for students who agree to serve as resident assistants. We recommend further than R.A.'s have mentors who meet with them regularly and supervise their work and that the R.A.'s be reimbursed adequately.

► It is our position, too, that all colleges need standards—a code of conduct—not just in academic matters, but in nonacademic matters, too. Such standards clarify the expectations of the institution and make rules understandable.

► In a community of learning, as in any community, we need a sense of order to protect the requirements of all, while still respecting the dignity and rights of individuals.

► Specifically we urge that private space should be respected and honored by peers. Loud noise should not be allowed. Sexism, racism, and religious bigotry are offenses to the dignity of other human beings.

► We also recommend that if state laws say alcohol use is illegal for those under 21, colleges should make this fact clearly known to students and affirm the law rather than ignore it.

► Educational programs should be developed in the residence halls to foster a sense of community, and provide an enriching influence.

► Bringing commuter students into the life of the college is an important and growing obligation.

There should be a special office where commuters can go to get help, file complaints, and learn about special programs and services available to them.

A college concerned about community cannot be unmindful of deep divisions on campus. And it is in residence hall arrangements, in private clubs, and the way commuters and part-time students are treated, that some of the most fundamental values of the college are confronted—or avoided.

## XII
### Governing the College

Formal decision-making mechanisms on most campuses are not working very well.

While faculty feel a deep sense of loyalty to their professions, they are less committed to the institutions where they work. We found that, almost without exception, the role of students in campus decision-making is not taken seriously in higher education.

► If the college is to be an effective community, effective governance is essential. At every college and university, forums are needed to address common educational questions and to consider campus-wide matters that cannot be handled in any other way.

► Undergraduates should be encouraged not only to understand how decisions are made at the college where they are enrolled, but also should be asked, indeed expected, to participate as campus citizens as well.

► We urge that the faculty support vigorously a representative campus-wide senate capable of handling all matters relating to the institution's academic goals.

► We further recommend that administrators and board members work with faculty senates to create more inclusive forums to discuss concerns identified in this report—recruitment, orientation and advising, the quality of campus life, student assessment and the rest.

► We especially urge that undergraduates be more fully consulted in the full range of campus life. They should be represented on all standing campus committees that affect the education and social life of the institution.

► In addition to the traditional functions of setting policy, selecting presidents, and approving budgets and key personnel appointments, trustees must participate in shaping institutional priorities. They should involve themselves especially in the reviewing of the quality of the undergraduate experience.

In the end, good governance is to be measured not by the formality of the structure, but by the integrity of the participants, by the quality of communication and above all, by the willingness of individuals to bond together in support of larger purposes.

## XIII
### Measuring the Outcomes

In the measuring of college outcomes we reject paper and pencil tests that focus on simple recall and measure that which matters least. Rather, a quality undergraduate college is concerned about outcomes that transcend what students derive from separate courses.

Students need to think clearly, be well informed, be able to integrate their knowledge, and know how to apply what they have learned.

► Specifically, we recommend that, beyond the evaluation they receive in their separate courses, all students should complete a senior thesis before they graduate.

► This thesis should draw on the historical, social, and ethical perspectives of the major.

► We suggest that students participate in a senior seminar to present orally their theses and participate in the critique of the work of others.

► We also recommend that every college sponsor each year a senior colloquium series in which selected students present their senior papers and respond to questions in a public forum. Such a series would demonstrate to all students the true meaning of a college education.

► Colleges might also ask students to prepare a portfolio that records the activities in which they have engaged as *campus* citizens—student government, clubs, cultural events, and most importantly, voluntary service.

► To gain perspective on how the college experience is perceived retrospectively, colleges also may wish to survey alumni. College officials may interview graduates to determine not only the pattern of former students' further careers education and careers but also how well alumni fulfill their civic and social obligations.

► In measuring outcomes, the task is to strike a balance between the progress of each student—as measured by the courses completed, the grades assigned, and the credits earned—and the overall impact of the undergraduate experience, not just in academic matters but in commitment to community as well.

## XIV
### Values—From Competence to Commitment

Today's students have been labeled the "me generation" concerned only about private ends. We found, however, that undergraduates in this generation have hopes and aspirations that reach beyond themselves.

Undergraduates often are torn by idealism on one hand, and the temptation to pursue narrow career interests on the other. They find themselves politically and socially disengaged.

► We recommend that all students complete a service project—volunteer work in the community or at the college—as an integral part of their undergraduate experience.

► We further urge colleges to offer deferred admission to high school graduates who devote a year to voluntary service before coming to college.

► We also recommend that colleges consider completion of a new "Carnegie Unit"—a term (100 hours) of voluntary service as recommended in our report on high schools—an important criterion in their admissions process.

► Finally, campus life would be enriched if faculty service became more than a catchword.

If service is to become a vital part of the educational experience of every student, faculty must lead the way.

The aim of the undergraduate experience is not only to prepare the young to be productive, but also to enable them to live with dignity and purpose; not only to generate new knowledge, but to channel that knowledge to humane ends; not merely to study government, but to shape a citizenry that can promote the public good.

# Lists and Rankings

VII.1

# Most Effective College Presidents

## Liz McMillan

The most effective college presidents believe less in close collegial relationships than do "typical" presidents, and they rely on respect rather than popularity. according to the preliminary results of a new study.

Effective presidents also work longer hours, make decisions more easily, and confide less frequently in other presidents than do their counterparts at other institutions.

Those are some of the leadership qualities cited by college presidents named as the most effective chief executives. They were nominated as strong leaders in a survey of 485 chief executives, higher-education officials, and scholars who study the college presidency.

### 5 at Top of List

At the top of the list are the Rev. Theodore M. Hesburgh of the University of Notre Dame; Derek Bok of Harvard University; the Rev. Timothy S. Healy of Georgetown University; William C. Friday, president emeritus of the University of North Carolina; and Hanna Gray of the University of Chicago.

The effective college president is a "strong, risk-taking loner with a dream," said James L. Fisher, president emeritus of

the Council for Advancement and Support of Education and co-director of the study.

That image may actually be "antithetical" to traditional notions of the college presidency, Mr. Fisher said.

The study identifies the 100 presidents who received the most nominations as effective leaders in the survey. The list is arranged by type of institution, using the Carnegie classification system (see Page 13).

From the list of 100 presidents, 18 chief executives with the highest number of nominations were selected to participate in personal interviews on the role of the college president. Final results of the survey and interviews will be published in a forthcoming book.

Several presidents on the list, in interviews with *The Chronicle*, indicated that they were pleased to be honored by their colleagues.

"It's always nice to be honored, although I'm not sure what it means," said David Alexander of Pomona College.

Mr. Alexander said the list of the most effective presidents should not be regarded as "definitive."

"To the extent that it purports to be scientific, I think it's misleading," he said. "But to the extent that it represents the opinion of one's peers, it's useful."

Paul A. Elsner, chancellor of the Maricopa County Community College District, said a survey of attitudes might not adequately convey the complexities and "nuances" of the president's job.

"I wouldn't want to reduce the office to the thesis that you have to be a risk-taker," he said. "It takes a lifetime to capture these complexities."

### 315 Respond

In the survey, college leaders were asked about their personal and professional backgrounds. They also completed a questionnaire that examined their attitudes toward leadership and management. Some 315 presidents filled out the questionnaire.

The results were compared with those provided by a group of randomly selected presidents from the *Higher Education Directory*.

Martha W. Tack, co-director of the study and professor of educational administration and supervision at Bowling Green State University, said she had not wanted to define "effectiveness" beforehand but hoped that the presidents themselves would indicate what made them effective.

The two groups showed several differences in attitudes toward the job, Ms. Tack said, although some of the differences were a matter of degree.

Effective leaders take more risks and encourage others to be creative, she said. They care about "little people" at the institution and demonstrate a strong element of "humanity." They also realize they are not "running a popularity contest," and work instead for people's respect, Ms. Tack said.

"They're caught up in a vision of their institution, and they personalize their dream so they can't really separate themselves from the office," she said.

Mr. Fisher is former president of Towson State University and author of *Power of the Presidency*, a guidebook that is widely read by college executives.

He said the survey indicated that "collegial leadership" is a contradiction in terms.

"A president who wants to remain in the classroom should stay there," he said. "That kind of leader cannot represent the collective community as well as a leader who establishes some social distance."

## Grant from Exxon Fund

Mr. Fisher noted that the image of a strong presidential leadership style was contrary to what faculty members and others expect of chief executives. However, it should not threaten the idea of shared governance, he said.

"A close analysis shows that the effective president does believe in shared governance, but he also knows that he is the final authority," he said.

The study, entitled "The Effective College President," is financed by a grant from the Exxon Education Foundation. It will be included in a book to be published next year.

### BOWLING GREEN, OHIO

Following is a list of 100 college and university leaders named as most effective in a survey of 485 presidents, scholars, directors of higher-education associations, and other officials.

The list is organized by institutional categories established by the Carnegie Commission. Included are the presidents who received the most nominations within each category. In the "Doctoral-Granting II" category, only one president received multiple nominations.

Asterisks denote nominees who no longer hold a presidency.

### 4-YEAR COLLEGES AND UNIVERSITIES

#### RESEARCH I
Derek Bok, Harvard U.
John DiBiaggio, Michigan State U.
* William Friday, U. of North Carolina
* Peter Flawn, U. of Texas at Austin
* A. Bartlett Giamatti, Yale U.
Hanna H. Gray, U. of Chicago
Stanley O. Ikenberry, U. of Illinois
C. Peter Magrath, U. of Missouri
Steven Muller, Johns Hopkins U.
Harold T. Shapiro, U. of Michigan
John R. Silber, Boston U.

#### RESEARCH II
Edward J. Bloustein, Rutgers U.
The Rev. William J. Byron, Catholic U. of America
Richard M. Cyert, Carnegie Mellon U.
Lloyd H. Elliott, George Washington U.
The Rev. Timothy S. Healy, Georgetown U.
Robert M. O'Neil, U. of Virginia
* John W. Ryan, Indiana U.
Howard R. Swearer, Brown U.

#### DOCTORAL-GRANTING I
Daniel Berg, Rensselaer Polytechnic Institute
Neil S. Bucklew, West Virginia U.
Thomas J. Clifford, U. of North Dakota
* Norman Hackerman, Rice U.
The Rev. Theodore M. Hesburgh, U. of Notre Dame
James B. Holderman, U. of South Carolina
The Rev. J. Donald Monan, Boston College
Vincent O'Leary, State U. of New York at Albany
Joab L. Thomas, U. of Alabama

#### DOCTORAL-GRANTING II
Herbert H. Reynolds, Baylor U.

#### COMPREHENSIVE I
Ralph W. Adams, Troy State U.
James T. Amsler, Salem State College
Ronald Calgaard, Trinity U. (Tex.)
Ronald E. Carrier, James Madison U. (on leave of absence)
James W. Cleary, California State U. at Northridge
Roland Dille, Moorhead State U.
Paul J. Dovre, Concordia College (Minn.)
Sister Mary Francilene, Madonna College
E. K. Fretwell, Jr., U. of North Carolina at Charlotte
* E. Bruce Heilman, U. of Richmond
Stephen Horn, California State U. at Long Beach
John E. Johns, Furman U.
George W. Johnson, George Mason U.
Msgr. Terrence J. Murphy, College of St. Thomas
* Richard F. Rosser, DePauw U.
Charles E. Smith, U. of Tennessee at Martin
William J. Sullivan, Seattle U.
James F. Vickrey, Jr., U. of Montevallo
James J. Whalen, Ithaca College

#### COMPREHENSIVE II
Merle F. Allshouse, Bloomfield College
Fred B. Bentley, Mars Hill College
J. Richard Chase, Wheaton College (Ill.)
Martha E. Church, Hood College
Norman C. Francis, Xavier U. of Louisiana
Charles E. Glassick, Gettysburg College
Norbert J. Hruby, Aquinas College

#### LIBERAL ARTS I ·
David Alexander, Pomona College
Neal R. Berte, Birmingham Southern College
Paul E. Bragdon, Reed College
Paula P. Brownlee, Hollins College
Colin G. Campbell, Wesleyan U.
* John Chandler, Williams College
* Jill Conway, Smith College
Rhoda M. Dorsey, Goucher College
George A. Drake, Grinnell College
* Robert H. Edwards, Carleton College
Alice F. Emerson, Wheaton College (Mass.)
Richard F. Gross, Gordon College
Paul Hardin, Drew U.
Alice S. Ilchman, Sarah Lawrence College
Philip H. Jordan, Jr., Kenyon College
Nannerl O. Keohane, Wellesley College
Mary S. Metz, Mills College
Gordon J. Van Wylen, Hope College
Richard Warch, Lawrence U.
Kenneth J. Weller, Central U. of Iowa
David K. Winter, Westmont College

#### LIBERAL ARTS II
Hugh M. Gloster, Morehouse College
* Elmer Jagow, Hiram College
* Virginia Lester, Mary Baldwin College
Henry Ponder, Fisk U.
Sister Joel Read, Alverno College
Roy B. Shilling, Jr., Southwestern U.

### 2-YEAR COLLEGES AND INSTITUTES
Nolen M. Ellison, Cuyahoga Community College District
Paul A. Elsner, Maricopa County Community College District
* Carl Gerber, Lakewood Community College
Richard K. Greenfield, St. Louis Community College District
* Richard H. Hagemeyer, Central Piedmont Community College
Joseph N. Hankin, Westchester Community College
Leslie Koltai, Los Angeles Community College District
R. Jan LeCroy, Dallas County Community College
Harold D. McAninch, College of DuPage
Robert H. McCabe, Miami-Dade Community College
Byron McClenney, Alamo Community College District
Lewis Nobles, Clarke College (Miss.)
David H. Ponitz, Sinclair Community College
Joe B. Rushing, Tarrant County Junior College
Bill F. Stewart, State Center Community College District (Cal.)
Lawrence W. Tyree, Gulf Coast Community College District
Bruce E. Whitaker, Chowan College
Jeanette T. Wright, Bay Path Junior College

Copyright: 1986. *The Chronicle of Higher Education.*
Reprinted with Permission.

# Barron's Most Prestigious, Most Popular and Most Exciting Colleges

### MOST COMPETITIVE COLLEGES

| | | | |
|---|---|---|---|
| Adelphi College | NY | Northwestern University | IL |
| Bowdoin College | ME | Princeton University | NJ |
| Brown University | RI | Rice University | TX |
| Bryn Mawr College | PA | Stanford University | CA |
| California Institute of Technology | CA | Swarthmore College | PA |
| Claremont Colleges/Harvey Mudd College | CA | Tufts University | MA |
| | | US Air Force Academy | CO |
| Claremont Colleges/Pomona College | CA | US Coast Guard Academy | CT |
| Columbia University | NY | US Military Academy | NY |
| Cooper Union | NY | US Naval Academy | MD |
| Cornell University | NY | University of Chicago | IL |
| Dartmouth College | NH | University of Notre Dame | IN |
| Duke University | NC | University of Pennsylvania | PA |
| Georgetown University | WDC | Webb Institute of Naval Architecture | NY |
| Harvard University/Radcliffe College | MA | | |
| Haverford College | PA | Wellesley College | MA |
| Johns Hopkins University | MD | Williams College | MA |
| MIT | MA | Yale University | CT |

# HIGHLY COMPETITIVE COLLEGES

| | | | |
|---|---|---|---|
| Bates College | ME | Lafayette College | PA |
| Boston College | MA | Lehigh University | PA |
| Boston University | MA | Macalester College | MN |
| Brandeis University | MA | Miami University | OH |
| Bucknell University | PA | Middlebury College | VT |
| California State University–Dominguez Hills | CA | Mount Holyoke College | MA |
| Carleton College | MN | Oberlin College | OH |
| Carnegie-Mellon University | PA | Randolph Macon Woman's College | VA |
| Centre College | KY | Reed College | OR |
| Claremont Colleges–/McKenna College | CA | Rensselaer Polytechnic Institute | NY |
| Clark University | MA | Rose-Hulman Institute of Technology | IN |
| Colby College | ME | Rutgers University/College of Engineering | NJ |
| Colgate University | NY | Rutgers University/College of Pharmacy | NJ |
| College of the Holy Cross | MA | Rutgers Universty/Rutgers College | NJ |
| College of William & Mary | VA | Smith College | MA |
| Colorado School of Mines | CO | SUNY-Binghamton | NY |
| Columbia University/Barnard College | NY | Stevens Institute of Technology | NJ |
| Connecticut College | CT | Thomas Aquinas College | CA |
| Davidson College | NC | Trinity College | CT |
| Dickinson College | PA | Tulane University | LA |
| Emory University | GA | Union College | NY |
| Franklin and Marshall College | PA | USMerchant Marine Academy | NY |
| Furman University | SC | University of California-Berkeley | CA |
| Georgia Institute of Technology | GA | University of Illinois-Urbana-Champaign | IL |
| GMI Engineering and Management Institute | MI | University of Michigan/Ann Arbor | MI |
| Grinnell College | IA | University of the South | TN |
| Hamilton College | NY | University of Virginia | VA |
| Illinois Institute of Technology | IL | Vanderbilt University | TN |
| Kalamazoo College | MI | Vassar College | NY |
| Kenyon College | OH | Wake Forest University | NC |
| | | Washington & Lee University | VA |
| | | Washington University | MO |
| | | Worcester Polytechnic Institute | MA |

## VERY COMPETITIVE COLLEGES

| | | | |
|---|---|---|---|
| Adelphi University | NY | College of Insurance | NY |
| Agnes Scott College | GA | College of St. Benedict | MN |
| Albany College of Pharmacy | NY | College of the Atlantic | ME |
| Albion College | MI | College of Wooster | OH |
| Albright College | PA | Colorado College | CO |
| Alfred University | NY | Creighton University | NE |
| Allegheny College | PA | DePaul University | IL |
| Alma College | MI | DePauw University | IN |
| American University | DC | Drew University | NJ |
| Augustus College | IL | Drexel University | PA |
| Augustana College | SD | Evergreen State College | WA |
| Austin College | TX | Fairfield University | CT |
| Babson College | MA | Florida Atlantic University | FL |
| Bard College | NY | Florida Institute of Technology | FL |
| Bayamon Technological University | PR | Flordia International University | FL |
| Baylor University | TX | Fordham University/College of Business Administration | NY |
| Beloit College | WI | Fordham University | NY |
| Bentley College | MA | George Washington University | DC |
| Brigham Young University | UT | Gettysburg College | PA |
| California Polytechnic State University | CA | Golden Gate University | CA |
| Canisius College | NY | Grove City College | PA |
| Case Western Reserve University | OH | Gustavus Adolphus College | MN |
| Catholic University of America | DC | Hampshire College | MA |
| Central University | IA | Hanover College | IN |
| Christian Brothers College | TN | Hendrix College | AR |
| City University of New York/ Baruch College | NY | Hobart & William Smith College | NY |
| City University of New York/City College | NY | Hoftsra University | NY |
| | | Houghton College | NY |
| Claremont Colleges/Pitzer College | CA | Huntingdon College | AL |
| Clarkson College | NY | Illinois Wesleyan University | IL |
| Clemson University | SC | Indiana University at Bloomington | IN |
| | | Indiana University of Pennsylvania | PA |

| | | | |
|---|---|---|---|
| James Madison University | VA | Rollins College | FL |
| Knox College | IL | Rutgers University/Cook College | NJ |
| Lake Forest College | IL | Rutgers University/Douglass College | NJ |
| Lawrence University | WI | St. Francis College | PA |
| Le Moyne College | NY | St. John's College | MD |
| Loyola College | MD | St. John's College | NM |
| Loyola University of New Orleans | LA | St. John's University | MN |
| Manhattan College | NY | St. Lawrence University | NY |
| Manhattanville College | NY | St. Mary's College | IN |
| Marquette University | WI | St. Mary's College of California | CA |
| Marygrove College | MI | St. Norbert College | WI |
| Messiah College | PA | St. Olaf College | MN |
| Michigan State University | MI | Santa Clara University | CA |
| Michigan Technological University | MI | Sarah Lawrence College | NY |
| Mills College | CA | Siena College | NY |
| Millsaps College | MS | Simon's Rock of Bard College | MA |
| Milwaukee School of Engineering | WI | Simpson College | IA |
| Mississippi State University | MS | Skidmore College | NY |
| Muhlenburg College | PA | South Dakota School of Mines and Technology | SD |
| New Jersey Institute of Technology | NJ | Southern Methodist University | TX |
| New Mexico Institute of Mining and Technology | NM | Southwestern University | TX |
| New York University | NY | SUNY at Albany | NY |
| North Carolina State University | NC | SUNY at Buffalo | NY |
| Northeast Missouri State University | MO | SUNY at Stony Brook | NY |
| Occidental College | CA | SUNY College at Geneseo | NY |
| Oglethorpe University | GA | SUNY College at Oswego | NY |
| Oral Roberts University | OK | SUNY College of Arts & Sciences | NY |
| Pacific Lutheran University | WA | SUNY Maritime College | NY |
| Pennsylvania State University | PA | Stetson University | FL |
| Pepperdine University | CA | Syracuse University | NY |
| Polytechnic Institute | NY | Texas A&M University | TX |
| Providence College | RI | Texas Christian University | TX |
| Purdue University | IN | Touro College | NY |
| Rhodes College | TN | Trenton State College | NJ |

| | | | |
|---|---|---|---|
| Trinity University | TX | University of Richmond | VA |
| United States International University | CA | University of Rochester | NY |
| | | University of St. Thomas | TX |
| University of California/Irvine | CA | University of Scranton | PA |
| University of California/Los Angeles | CA | University of South Florida | FL |
| University of California/Riverside | CA | University of Southern California | CA |
| University of California/San Diego | CA | University of Texas/Austin | TX |
| University of California/Santa Barbara | CA | University of Vermont | VT |
| University of California/Santa Cruz | CA | University of Washington | WA |
| University of Colorado/Boulder | CA | University of West Florida | FL |
| University of Connecticut | CT | University of Wisconsin/Madison | WI |
| University of Dallas | TX | Ursinus College | PA |
| University of Delaware | DE | Valparaiso University | IN |
| University of Denver | CO | Villanova University | PA |
| University of Detroit | MI | Virginia Polytechnic Institute and State University | VA |
| University of Florida | FL | Washington & Jefferson College | PA |
| University of Iowa | IA | Wheaton College | IL |
| University of Lowell | MA | Whitman College | WA |
| University of Miami | FL | Whittier College | CA |
| University of Michigan at Dearborn | MI | Widener University | PA |
| University of Michigan at Flint | MI | Williamette University | OR |
| University of Minnesota/Morris | MN | Wofford College | SC |
| University of Missouri/Kansas City | MO | Woodbury University | CA |
| University of Missouri/Rolla | MO | Yeshiva University | NY |
| University of New Hampshire | NH | | |
| University of North Carolina/Chapel Hill | NC | | |
| University of Pittsburgh/Johnstown | PA | | |
| University of Puget Sound | WA | | |
| University of Redlands | CA | | |

# COMPETITIVE COLLEGES

| | | | |
|---|---|---|---|
| Alaska Pacific University | AK | Memphis State University | TN |
| Antioch University | OH | Mount Union College | OH |
| Arizona State University | AZ | National College of Education | IL |
| Auburn University | AL | North Texas State University | TX |
| Bennington College | VT | Northern Illinois University | IL |
| Bowling Green State University | OH | Old Dominion University | VA |
| California State Polytechnic University at Pomona | CA | Oregon State University | OR |
| California State University/Fresno | CA | Queens College/CUNY | NY |
| California State University/Fullerton | CA | Roberts Wesleyan College | NY |
| California State University at Long Beach | CA | Rochester Institute of Technology | NY |
| | | St. John's University | NY |
| California State University/ Northbridge | CA | St. Mary of the Woods College | IN |
| California State University/ Sacramento | CA | San Diego State University | CA |
| | | San Francisco State University | CA |
| Central Michigan University | MI | San Jose State University | CA |
| City University of New York/ Hunter College | NY | Sonoma State University | CA |
| | | Southern Illinois University/Carbondale | IL |
| College of New Rochelle | NY | Southwest Texas State University | TX |
| Colorado State University | CO | SUNY at Purchase | NY |
| Eastern Michigan University | MI | Temple University | PA |
| Eckerd College | FL | University of Alabama | AL |
| Eugene Lang College/New School for Social Research | NY | University of Arizona | AZ |
| | | University of California/Davis | CA |
| Friends' World College | NY | University of Centra; Florida | FL |
| Gannon University | PA | University of Cincinnati | OH |
| George Mason University | VA | University of Georgia | GA |
| Georgia State University | GA | University of Hawaii/Mano | HI |
| Grand Valley State College | MI! | University of Illinois at Chicago | IL |
| Illinois State University | IL | University of Kansas | KS |
| Iowa State University | IA | University of Kentucky | KY |
| Lake Erie College | OH | University of Louisville | KY |

| | | | |
|---|---|---|---|
| University of Maryland/College Park | MD | University of Texas/Arlington | TX |
| University of Massachusetts/Amherst | MA | University of Utah | UT |
| University of Minnesota/Twin Cities | MN | University of Wisconsin/Green Bay | WI |
| University of Missouri/Columbia | MO | University of Wisconsin/Milwaukee | WI |
| University of Nebraska/Lincoln | NE | Vermont College/Norwich University | VT |
| University of New Mexico | NM | Washington State University | WA |
| University of Oklahoma | OK | Wayne State University | MI |
| University of Oregon | OR | Wesley College | DE |
| University of Pittsburgh | PA | West Virginia University | WV |
| University of Puerto Rico/Rio Piedras | PR | Western Washington University | WA |
| | | Wichita State University | KS |
| University of South Carolina | SC | World College West | CA |
| University of Tennessee/Knoxville | TN | | |

Source: *Barron's Guide to the Most Prestigious Colleges* and *Barron's Guide to the Best, Most Popular and Most Exciting Colleges*

# Great Teachers of Our Time

**"The unheralded heroes of academe"** was the way Thomas B. McCabe, distinguished alumnus of Swarthmore College, described great teachers and professors he yearned to see recognized nationally for their dedication to students and their careers. Seven years ago, the Council for Advancement and Support of Education organized the first national *Professor of the Year* competition, and in 1981 presented the first grand award to Mary Eleanor Clark, professor of biology at San Diego State University. Since that time almost 800 professors have been nominated by colleges and universities, and awards given to six annual national winners, 20 state winners, and a recipient in Canada.

**The National Award of $5000** is sponsored by the Carnegie Foundation for the Advancement of Teaching, and Dr. Ernest L. Boyer, its distinguished president, chairs the jury for the final selection. During National Higher Education Week in October, the national winner is recognized and the cash award and citation are presented at The Smithsonian Institution, where the professor delivers a public lecture in his/her discipline, demonstrating the abilities and talents which the students have so eloquently extolled in their nominations.

Both the broadcast and print media give extensive coverage to the professor on such programs as the *Today Show,* the Voice of America, and National Public Radio, and in such major newspapers as *The New York Times, The Times of London,* and *The Chronicle of Higher Education.* Many regional media also cover the "top ten national winners" and the *Professor of the Year* recipients in 20 states and Canada. In addition, the national award recipient is requested to tour major cities throughout America to lecture on the college campuses.

**Your Undergraduate Professors** can win these prestigious awards. Each institution may submit up to three nominations made by the dean, president, academic colleagues, and CASE advancement professionals. The nomination letter is supported by a professional resume, schedule of classes, and up to six testimonial letters from present students, former students, and colleagues. The emphasis in selecting recipients is placed on demonstrated evidence of the impact of the professor on the lives and careers of the students. Twenty-five distinguished judges from government, business, education, the media, and the national associations select the final candidates from more than 400 nominated professors from throughout the United States and Canada. Two grand juries select the 20 winning state professors, the Canadian recipient, and national top ten and the *Professor of the Year.*

**State Professors from These Twenty States:** California, Florida, Georgia, Illinois, Indiana, Kansas, Maryland, Massachusetts, Michigan, Minnesota, Missouri, New Jersey, New York, North Carolina, Ohio, Pennsylvania, Tennessee, Texas, Virginia, Washington, and Canada. Professors from all 50 states may compete for the national awards.

*For More Information* and entry forms write: Professor Awards, Council for Advancement and Support of Education, Suite 400, Eleven Dupont Circle NW, Washington DC 20036. Telephone (202) 328-5915. The deadline for submission of official forms is June 1, 1987.

### NATIONAL PROFESSOR OF THE YEAR 1986

Rosemary Tong, Associate Professor of Philosophy, Williams College <u>Massachusetts</u>

### STATE PROFESSORS OF THE YEAR 1986

Robert Brentano, University of California, Berkeley , <u>California</u>

Kalman Goldberg, Bradley University  <u>Illinois</u>

Julius Lester, University of Massachusetts, Amherst, <u>Massachusetts</u>

Sidney Fine, University of Michigan, <u>Michigan</u>

Sharon Browning, Northwest Missouri State University, <u>Missouri</u>

Raybourn Wright, University of Rochester, <u>New York</u>

Florence Wolff, University of Dayton, <u>Ohio</u>

John Wheatcroft, Bucknell University, <u>Pennsylvania</u>

Juanita V. Rodriguez, Tarrant County Junior College, <u>Texas</u>

Eileen Mavis Heatherington, University of Virginia, <u>Virginia</u>

John F. Firkins, Gonzaga University, <u>Washington</u>

## Alabama

**Birmingham-Southern College:** Paul Clinton Bailey, Diane Seymour Brown, Nancy Campbell-Goymer, Henry C. Randa
**University of Alabama:** Barry Mason and Morris L. Mayer

## Arizona

**Pima Community College:** Stanley P. Witt

## Arkansas

**Arkansas State University:** Emma Sue Davidson, Daniel R. Hoyt
**University of Arkansas at Little Rock:** Harper W. Boyd, Bettye Caldwell, and Ralph D. Eberly
**University of Arkansas at Pine Bluff:** Viralene J. Coleman and Rosemarie Holmes Word

## California

**Art Center College of Design:** Gene Fleury and Bernyce Polifka
**California Institute of Technology:** David L. Goodstein
**California Lutheran College:** Michael A. Kolitsky
**California Polytechnic State University:** Adelaide Harmon-Elliott Donald J. Koberg, Philip K. Ruggles, and John E. Trei
**California State University at Dominguez Hills:** Jack Adams, Lloyd Ferguson and Laura J. Robles
**California State University at Fresno:** H. Roger Tatarian
**California State University at Long Beach:** Nicholas Perkins Hardeman, Roberta Hoffman Markman, and Kenneth L. Marsi
**California State University at Los Angeles:** Butrus Abd al-Malik and Lloyd Ferguson
**California State University at Sacramento:** Joseph S. Wu
**California State University at San Bernardino:** Frances F. Berdan and Diane F. Halpern
**Claremont McKenna College:** Stephen T. Davis
**Harvey Mudd College:** J. Arthur Campbell, Thomas M. Helliwell
**Loma Linda University:** V. Bailey Gillespie

Loyola Marymount University: Michael A. Genovese and
    Marie Anne Mayeski
Pepperdine University: Stephen D. Davis
Pomona College: Donald B. McIntyre
San Diego State University: Mary E. Clark, Alvin D. Coox, and
    Thomas M. Davies, Jr.
San Jose State University: Charles Burdick, James M. Freeman,
    and Alan C. Ling
Santa Clara University: Theodore J. Mackin, SJ
Stanford University: David J. Danelski and Robert H. Eustis
University of California, Berkeley: Robert Brentano, Eugene D.
    Commins, Marian Cleeves Diamond, David Littlejohn,
    George C. Pimentel, and Arnold M. Schultz
University of California, Irvine: Eloy Rodriguez and
    William Rost Schonfeld
University of California, Los Angeles: Patricia A. Keating
University of California, San Diego: Thomas Bond and
    Paul D. Saltman
University of California, Riverside: Edwin S. Gaustad
University of California, Santa Barbara: David Cannell
University of California, Santa Cruz: Elliot Aronson and
    Kenneth S. Norris
University of Redlands: Richard I. Kushner
University of San Diego: Iris Wilson Engstrand, Dennis A.
    Rohatyn, and DeForest L. Strunk
University of the Pacific: Paul H. Gross
Westmont College: Robert H. Gundry

## Canada

Brock University (Ontario): William A. Matheson and
    Donald J. Ursino
Carleton University (Ontario): Aviva Kravetz Freedman and
    Brian R. Little
Concordia University (Quebec): Martin Kusy
Dalhousie University (Nova Scotia): James Pincock
McMaster University (Ontario): Herbert M. Jenkins
Selkirk College (British Columbia): Lesley Anderton

Simon Fraser University (British Columbia): Peter E. Kennedy
Technical University of Nova Scotia: Ojars Biskaps and
    Orest Cochkanoff
Trent University (Ontario): John Henry Wadland
University of Manitoba: John Alexander Magill Shaw
University of Ottawa (Ontario): Raymond C. St-Jacques
University of Saskatchewan: Ronald Ernest Verrall
University of Toronto (Ontario): J. Stefan Dupre
University of Toronto at Erindale (Ontario): Desmond Morton
Wilfrid Laurier University (Ontario): Donald F. Morgenson

## Colorado

Colorado Collge: Richard Beidleman and William H. Hochman
Colorado School of Mines: Robert J. Weimer
Colorado State University: Robert M. Lawrence
Regis College: Alice Highman Reich
United States Air Force Academy: William J. Cairney, Lt. Col.
    Daniel G.M. Hannaway, and Lt. Col. Kenneth H. Wenker
University of Northern Colorado: Lynn A. Sandstedt
University of South Colorado: Budge Threlkeld, Sallie A. Watkins

## Connecticut

Central Connecticut State University: Lothar Kahn
University of Bridgeport: Roger S. Pressman
University of Connecticut: Evan Hill, Edwin W. Tucker, and
    Michael T. Turvey
Wesleyan University: Robert A. Rosenbaum

## Delaware

University of Delaware: Roberta F. Colman, E. Wayne Craven,
    Selcuk Guceri, and William I. Homer

## District of Columbia

Georgetown University: Dorothy M. Brown, Leona M. Fisher,
    E. Michael Gerli, Jan Karski and James Slevin

The American University: Allan J. Lichtman, Martha C. Sager,
    Arnold S. Trebach and James H. Weaver
The Catholic University of America: William A. Wallace

## *Florida*

Bethune-Cookman College: Ruel L. Godbey, Jake C. Miller,
    Russell Mootry, Jr., and Roberta G. Weissman
Eckerd College: Julienne H. Empric and William B. Roess
Florida Junior College: Mary Sue Koeppel
Miami-Dade Community College: William R. Alheim,
    George M. Brown, Joseph H. Gibson, and William T. Primus
Rollins College: Barbara H. Carson, Maurice J. O'Sullivan,
    and Karl E. Peters
St. Petersburg Junior College: Helen Weaver Gilbart, Barbara Hull
University of Miami: Howard Pospesel and Harry P. Schultz
University of South Florida: Sara Munson Deats and John Griffith
University of West Florida: Ann T. Agnew
Valencia Community College: Ruth Senterfitt

## *Georgia*

Agnes Scott College: Margaret W. Pepperdene
Clark College: Gloria P. Walker
Emory University: James H. Young
Georgia Institute of Technology: Arthur Beckum, Sherman
    Dallas, William Eberhardt, William Erven Sayle, II, and
    Anderson D. Smith
Georgia State University: Kenneth England, Marion Leathers
    Kuntz, and Michael H. Mescon
University of Georgia: John T. Granrose and Dean Rusk

## *Idaho*

Boise State University: A. Thomas Trusky

## *Illinois*

Aurora University: Peter Adragna
Blackburn College: William E. Werner, Jr.

Bradley University: Alan Galsky and Kalman Goldberg
Chicago State University: Bobbie M. Anthony, Mati Maldre,
    Marilyn W. Sadow, Victor A. Sorell, and Sandra M. Webb
College of Lake County: Douglas Sherman
Concordia College: Merle L. Radke
Eastern Illinois University: Ruth Dow
Illinois Benedictine College: Rose A. Carney
Illinois Insitute of Technology: Earl Frederick Zwicker
Illinois State University: John Dossey and Franzie L. Loepp
Kennedy-King College: Irving Abrahamson
Lake Forest College: Michael Croydon
Lewis University: Paul J. Kaiser
Millikin University: Arvid W. Adell
Moraine Valley Community College: Randy DeVillez,
    Anne B. Donnersberger, Mary Rita Freudenthal, Agita Huns,
    Phyllis Kozlowski, Ray Lehner, Patricia McKeague, and
    Kay Schneegas
Northern Illinois University: Jan Morris Bach
Northwestern University: Richard Kieckhefer
Oakton Community College: Sue Marie Anderson
Quincy College: Leonard Biallas, STD, William Gasser, and
    John J. Natalini
Southern Illinois University at Carbondale: Dale F. Ritter
Triton College: Carole Bauer
University of Chicago: David W. Oxtoby and Herman L. Sinaiko
University of Illinois at Chicago: Edward Minieka,
    W.J. Minkowycz
University of Illinois at Urbana/Champaign: Richard T. Scanlan
Wheaton College: Arthur F. Holmes and Clifford D. Schimmels

## Indiana

Ball State University: Whitney H. Gordon
Butler University: Jack L. Eaton, George Geib, Janos Horvath,
    and Emma Lou Thornbrough
Indiana State University at Evansville: Melvin W. Denner
    and Howard E. Dunn
Indiana University: Kathleen Koval

Manchester College: Edward George Miller
Purdue University: Larry Axel and William H. Hayt
Rose-Hulman Institute of Technology: Herman A. Moench
St. Joseph's College: John D. Groppe
St. Mary's College: Dorothy M. Feigl
University of Notre Dame: Emil T. Hofman
University of Southern Indiana: Wanda B. Hibbitts
Vincennes University: Jay Albert Bardole

## Iowa

Clarke College: Carol Blitgen
Graceland College: Velma N. Ruch

## Kansas

Baker University: Donald L. Hatcher
Emporia State University: Hsien-Tung Liu, Joseph H. Ott,
     Loren Pennington and Melvin G. Storm, Jr.
Kansas Newman College: Charlotte Rohrbach, Surendra P. Singh
Kansas State University: Richard A. Consigli and Don Good
University of Kansas: Clark E. Bricker, Allen J. Cigler, Eldon J.
     Fields, and Lawrence Sherr
Wichita State University: Glen W. Zumwalt

## Kentucky

Kentucky State University: Henry E. Cheaney
Lees College: Donna Snell Smith
Morehead State University: Ruth Barnes and Jules R. Dubar
Transylvania University: Paul E. Fuller and Monroe Moosnick
University of Louisville: Richard Barber, Joseph C. Deck,
     E. Thomas Marsh, and Charles Andrew Plank
Western Kentucky University: Donald R. Tuck

## Louisiana

Centenary College of Louisiana: Earle Labor
Louisiana State University: Lewis P. Simpson
Louisiana Tech University: Sam V. Dauzat

Loyola University: John J. Biguenet
Xavier University: J.W. Carmichael

## Maine

Colby College: Henry A. Gemery
Unity College: David Purdy

## Maryland

College of Notre Dame of Maryland: Sister Maura Eichner
Dundalk Community College: Donald Shaffer
Goucher College: Eli Velder
Loyola College in Maryland: John Gray and George B. Mackiw
Mount St. Mary's College: John L. Morrison
Towson State University: Geneva Ely-Flickinger and
     James M. Furukawa
University of Maryland at Baltimore: Elizabeth Anne Rankin
Western Maryland College: Richard H. Smith, Jr., Ira G. Zepp, Jr.

## Massachusetts

Anna Maria College: Ann Marie L. McMorrow
Babson College: Earl K. Bowen and Laurence S. Moss
Berkshire Community College: Robert Boland, Edwin Clark,
     and Arthur B. Phinney
Boston College: John L. Mahoney and Thomas H. O'Connor
Boston University: Dennis D. Berkey, John G. Gagliardo, Howard
     Clarke Kee, Helen Vendler, and Elizabeth Wiig
Brandeis University: Malcolm W. Watson
Bristol Community College: Raymond J. Lavertue, Sr.
     and Alan Powers
Emmanuel College: Bette F. Weiss
Fitchburg State College: Rita Driscoll
Framingham State College: Joan N. Broadcorens
Gordon College: Marvin Wilson
Harvard University: Robert Coles and Emily Dickinson
     Townsend Vermeule
Massachusetts Institute of Technology: Robert A. Alberty
     and Robert W. Mann

Massasoit Community College: John Chase, Clara Galvin, and Marilyn Maxwell
Mount Holyoke College: Harriet Pollatsek
Northeastern University: Robert W. Case, Robert L. Cord, and Edith E. Flynn
Regis College: Vera Laska
Stonehill College: Chester A. Raymo
Tufts University: Elizabeth Ammons, Sol Gittleman, Martin Jay Sherwin, and Walter C. Swap
University of Massachsuetts at Amherst: Julius Lester, Earl J. McWhorter, and Stephen B. Oates
Wheaton College: Bojan H. Jennings
Williams College: Rosemarie Tong

## *Michigan*

Albion College: Richard Blatti
Alma College: Michael J.J. Smith
Andrews University: Bill Chobotar and Oystein Sakala LaBianca
Aquinas College: Andrew T. Jefchak and Betty Taylor
Central Michigan University: Roy F. Burlington and Lynda King
Eastern Michigan University: Stephen W. Brewer, John W. Moore, and Brigitte D. Muller
Ferris State College: J. Edwards Nicks
Hope College: David G. Myers
Kalamazoo College: David Barclay and Conrad Hilberry
Kalamazoo Valley Community College: Robert G. Badra
Lawrence Institute of Technology: Jerry L. Crist
Marygrove College: Sister Edith Kenny
Michigan State University: Walter Adams and Mordechai E. Kreinin
Michigan Technological University: William W. Predebon
Monroe County Community College: James E. DeVries
Mott Community College: Thom R. Bohnert
Northern Michigan University: Roger D. Barry, Lon L. Emerick
Spring Arbor College: David A. Johnson
University of Michigan: Sidney Fine
Western Michigan University: Stuart Dybek, Oscar H. Horst, Paul L. Maier, and Lawrence Ziring

## Minnesota

College of St. Benedict: Stanley J. Idzerda
College of St. Catherine: Alan N. Graebner and
        Sister Mary E. Thompson
College of St. Scholastica: Sister Mary Richard Boo,
        Chandra M.N. Mehrotra, and Agatha Riehl
Gustavus Adolphus College: Robert Esbjornson and
        Richard M. Fuller
St. Mary's College: Richard V. Kowles
St. Olaf College: Harold H. Ditmanson and Miles H. Johnson
St. Peter's College: Alessandro C. Calianese
University of Minnesota: James C. Cloyd

## Mississippi

Mississippi College: Ronald W. Howard
University of Southern Mississippi: Nettie E. Dubard

## Missouri

Central Missouri State University: Paul H. Engelmann, Donald
        Tibbits, and Lin Welch
Culver-Stockton College: Edward H. Sawyer
Drury College: Victro Agruso
Maryville College: Mary Ellen Finch
Missouri Western State College: Frank Kessler
Northeast Missouri State University: Leon Karel,
        Tom V. Ritchie
Northwest Missouri State University: Sharon Browning
        and George L. Gille
Rockhurst College: Sister Rosemary Flanigan
School of the Ozarks: Marvin DeJong, Stephen John Kneeshaw
Southeast Missouri State University: Robert W. Hamblin
Southwest Baptist University: Bob Derryberry, Twila Miller Smith
Southwest Missouri State University: James Carroll Moyer
St. Louis Community College at Florissant Valley:
        Carol Abe Edwards
St. Louis Community College at Forest Park: T. David Daniel
St. Louis Community College at Meramec: Alice Bante

St. Mary's College of O'Fallon: Anne Marie Carty
University of Missouri-Rolla: William A. Andrews and
        Leonard F. Koederitz
University of Missouri-St. Louis: Charles R. Granger
University of Missouri-Kansas City: Malcolm E. Linville
Westminster College: Frank Brooke Sloss
William Jewell College: Wesley Lee Forbis, Ann Marie Shannon

## Montana

Montana College of Mineral Science Technology:
        Larry G. Tidwell
University of Montana: Ralph J. Fessenden

## Nebraska

Union College: James D. McClelland and Virginia Simmons
University of Nebraska, Lincoln: David W. Brooks, Paul A. Olson,
        and Jerry L. Petr
University of Nebraska, Omaha: John R. Anstey

## New Hampshire

University of New Hampshire: Filson H. Glanz, Manley R. Irwin,
        Allen B. Linden, Donald M. Murray, and Samuel C. Smith

## New Jersey

Fairleigh Dickinson University: Sister Margherita Marchione
Felician College: Marie Callahan and Geri Hennessey
Georgian Court College: Mary Lee Batesko
Montclair State College: Max A. Sobel
Ocean County College: William J. Rickert
Ramapo College: Flavia Alaya and Anthony T. Padovano
Rutgers, The State University of New Jersey: William C.
        McWilliams and Charles Pine
Seton Hall University: Mary A. Boutilier
Upsala College: Starr Roxanne Hiltz

## New Mexico

New Mexico State University: Allan H. Savage

University of Albuquerque: James Morley
University of New Mexico: William F. Coleman

## New York

Adelphi University: Ivory Holmes, Patrick R. Mulene, and
    Dorothy Ramsey
Albany Medical College of Union University: Ray C. Henrikson
    and Michael Donald McGoldrick
Alfred University: Wesley E. Bentz, Ellen Janosik, John L. Stull
Baruch College and Graduate Center: Edward Pessen
Brooklyn College: Vojtech Fried
Canisius College: Larry E. Jones and Marguerite D. Kermis
Cazenovia College: Frederic M. Williams
Clarkson College: Egon Matijevec
Colgate University: Anthony Aveni and James M. McLelland
College of Insurance: Helen Woolsey Steele
College of St. Rose: S.R. Swaminathan
Cornell University: Barbara C. Lust and Daniel G. Sisler
Elizabeth Seton College: Robin Landa
Empire State College: Robert N. Seidel
Fordham University: Irma B. Jaffe
Hobart and William Smith Colleges: Eugen Baer
Hofstra University: Dorothy Cohen
Iona College: George B. Pepper
Ithaca College: Stephen R. Hilbert and Glenn C. Vogel
Le Moyne College: Mary Ann Donnelly and George J. Durr
Long Island University, C.W. Post Campus: Stanley Jarolem
Manhattanville College: Nicole Schupf
Marist College: Joseph R. LaPietra, George J. Sommer,
    and Milton Teichman
Marymount Manhattan College: Denis Miranda
Mercy College: Adma Jeha d'Heurle
Molloy College: John J. Clancy and Catherine M. Dullea
Nazareth College of Rochester: Alexander C. Sutherland
New York City Technical College: Fedele J. Panzarino
New York Institute of Technology: Molly Kyung Sook Chang Lee
    and Luis E. Navia

Queens College: Sheldon C. Seller and Jerry Waxman
Queensborough Community College: Herbert S. Parmet
Rensselaer Polytechnic Institute: Michael M. Abbott, Charles M.
    Close, Robert Doremus, and Robert Resnick
Roberts Wesleyan College: David W. Basinger
Rochester Institute of Technology: Fred L. Wilson
St. Bonaventure University: Boyd Litzinger
St. John's University: Thomas D. Houchin, Richard A. Lockshin
St. Lawrence University: Parker Grimes Marden, Robert N. Wells
State University of New York A and T College at Delhi: Rosalie
    Higgins, Lavonne H. Humphries, and James A. Richards
State University of New York at Albany: Shirley A. Crawford
State University of New York at Geneseo: James H. Willey
State University of New York at Plattsburgh: Lawrence Shaffer
State University of New York at Stony Brook: Robert C. Kerber
State University of New York College at Brockport: Raymond W.
    Duncan, Richard V. Mancuso, and Kazumi Nakano
State University of New York College at Cortland: Judith A. Best
    and Arden P. Zipp
State University of New York College at Oswego:
    Joseph A. Wiecha
State University of New York College at Potsdam: Lynne Sechrist
    Broderick, John T. Omohundro, and Robert Washburn
University of Rochester: Russell A. Peck and Rayburn Wright
Utica College of Syracuse University: William H. Gotwald, Jr.
    and Raymond Simon

## North Carolina

Catawba College: Sanford R. Silverburg
Davidson College: John N. Burnett and Charles E. Ratliff
Elon College: James E. Danieley and John G. Sullivan
Gardner-Webb College: Launita Eye Proctor
Mars Hill College: Harley E. Jolley
North Carolina A and T State University: Myrtle B. Sampson
North Carolina Wesleyan College: David A. Jones
University of North Carolina at Wilmington: Gerald H. Shinn
Wake Forest University: Germaine Bree

Western Carolina University: Joel S. Milner
Winston-Salem State University: Clarence E. Gaines
Winthrop College: Michael Kennedy

## Ohio

Bowling Green State University: Steven O. Ludd, Robert Romans
Capital University: Carl F. Sievert
Case Western Reserve University: Harry W. Mergler
Cuyahoga Community College: Margaret W. Taylor
Cuyahoga Community College, Metro: Joseph F. Clovesko and
      John S. Coleman
Defiance College: Jan J. Younger
Findlay College: Jerry Mallett
John Carroll University: Cyrilla H. Wideman
Kent State University: Lawrence S. Kaplan
Miami University: John P. Maggard and Bruce H. Olson
Muskingum Area Technical College: Timothy L. Berger and
      Terry L. Meyer
Ohio State University: Roger L. Blackwell, Simon Dinitz,
      and Bernard L. Erven
Ohio University: Samuel R. Crowl, Fredrick C. Hagerman, and
      Edgar Whan
Ohio Wesleyan University: Verne E. Edwards
Rio Grande College/Community College: T. Michael Rhodes
Stark Technical College: David Wileman
University of Akron: David L. Jamison and George W. Knepper
University of Cincinnati: Boyd C. Ringo
University of Dayton: Sanford S. Singer, Lawrence P. Ulrich,
      and Florence I. Wolff

## Oklahoma

Oscar Rose Junior College: James H. Lazalier
University of Oklahoma: Thomas J. Hill, Larry K. Michaelsen

## Oregon

Northwest Christian College: Song Nai Rhee

Portland Community College: Alma Sue George
Portland State University: Susan Karant-Nunn
University of Oregon: Richard Koch and Joe H. Mize

## Pennsylvania

Albright College: William R. Marlow
Allegheny College: Bruce L. Clayton, Irwin Gertzog, Samuel S.
     Harrison, and Richard E. Kleeman
Beaver College: William J. Carr
Bloomsburg University: Harold J. Bailey, Peter H. Bohling,
     Andrew J. Karpinski, William S. O'Bruda, and
     Francis J. Radice
Bryn Mawr College: Brunilde Sismondo Ridgway
Bucknell University: John S. Wheatcroft
Cabrini College: Jerome R. Zurek, Jr.
Carlow College: William A. Uricchio
Cedar Crest College: Marion Kayhart
College Misericordia: Lee J. Williames
Community College of Allegheny County: Pearley Cunningham,
     Anne Louise Dailey, and John R. Starmack
Community College of Philadelphia: Dennis R. McGrath
Delaware County Community College: Jane C. Rothrock
Drexel University: Mercia M.T. Grassi, Mark L. Greenberg, Alan
     Lawley, and Joseph L. Rose
Duquesne University: Albert C. Labriola
Elizabethtown College: Donald B. Kraybill
Franklin and Marshall College: Claude Yoder
Gettysburg College: Robert Drane Barnes and Richard T. Mara
Gratz College: Rela Geffen Monson
Indiana University of Pennsylvania: Ronald G. Shafer and
     Howard E. Tompkins
Juniata College: Earl C. Kaylor, Jr. and J. Peter Trexler
King's College: John S. Davis
Lehigh University: Jay Richard Aronson and Peter Beidler
Lincoln University: Judith A. Thomas and Willie Williams, Jr.
Lycoming College: Robert F. Falk
Mansfield University: Arnold George

Messiah College: E. Morris Sider
Montgomery County Community College: Roger P. Willig
Neumann College: Rosalie M. Mirenda
Peirce Junior College: Barbara JoAnn Riebling
Pennsylvania State University: Paul R. Cornwell, Arthur Gold-
   schmidt, Claire Hirshfield, Bruce A. Murphy, and
   Roger Pennock, Jr.
Seton Hill College: JoAnne Woodyard Boyle
St. Francis College: Kirk R. Weixel and Albert A. Zanzuccki
St. Joseph's University: George J. Beichl and James E. Dougherty
St. Vincent College: Michael Wayne Bosko
Temple University: Eudice Glassberg, Charles P. Hall, Jr., Richard
   S. Kennedy, and Russell F. Weigley
Thomas Jefferson University: Mary D. Naylor
University of Pennsylvania: E. Digby Baltzell, Elaine Scarry, and
   Frank W. Warner
University of Pittsburgh: Iain M. Campbell, William J. Chase,
   Vernell A. Lillie, John M. Roberts, and
   Theodore O. Windt, Jr.
University of Scranton: Michael D. DeMichele and Edward Gannor
Ursinus College: Peter F. Perreten
Villanova University: John Immerwahr
Washington and Jefferson College: James Donnelly
Westmoreland County Community College: Barbara A. Stephens
Widener University: Bernard J. Reilly
Wilkes College: Lester J. Turoczi
Wilson College: Harry M. Buck

## Rhode Island

Barrington College: Carlton Gregory
Brown University: Thomas Mutch
Providence College: Mark N. Rerick, Ellen Salvatore, James
   Tattersall, and Paul Van K. Thomson
Rhode Island College: S. Scott Mueller
University of Rhode Island: Frank M. White

## South Carolina

Clemson University: Benjamin C. Dysart, III, Louis L. Henry, and
   Thomas Bruce Yandle, Jr.

Piedmont Technical College: Jane Trammell Rauton
Spartanburg Methodist College: Shannon Wilkerson
University of South Carolina at Spartanburg: William C. Bruce,
    Cecilia Haggerty Cogdell, Eleanor Ladd Kress, and
    Gillian Newberry

## South Dakota

Mount Marty College: Sister Laetcia Kilzer
Northern State University: William E. Haigh, Mavis S. Hamre, A.
    Thomas Hansen, Walter J. King, and Terry Richardson
University of South Dakota: Ray T. Devilbiss and
    Frank A. Einhellig

## Tennessee

East Tennessee State University: Robert J. Higgs
LeMoyne-Owen College: Juanita Williamson
Maryville College: Carolyn L. Blair
Southern College of Seventh-day Adventists: Ray A. Hefferlin
Southern Missionary College: Ray Alden Hefferlin
Southwestern at Memphis: William Larry Lacy
State Technical Institute at Memphis: Cheryl S. Cleaves
Tennessee Technological University: Richard C. Lukas
University of Tennessee at Chattanooga: George C. Conner
    and Benjamin H. Gross
University of Tennessee at Knoxville: William Marvin Bass, III

## Texas

Abilene Christian University: Carl Brecheen and Paul B. Faulkner
Baylor University: Emerson O. Henke
Del Mar College: Ronald John Williams
East Texas State University: Karl Umlauf
Frank Phillips College: Thomas T. Brooks
Howard County Junior College: Paul D. Ausmus
Incarnate Word College: Sister Teresa Grabber and Sister Mary
    Daniel Healy
Lamar University: Ann Die

Odessa College: Don Nichols
Rice University: Katherine Tsanoff Brown
Southwest Texas State University: Clarence C. Schultz, Robert
    W. Walts, and B.L. Williamson
Southwestern Adventist College: Robert Mendenhall and
    Erwin Sicher
Tarrant County Junior College: Juanita V. Rodriguez
Texas A and I University: John C. Perez
Texas A and M University: George F. Bass, James R. Boone,
    Gerald Keim, Ronald D. Macfarlane, and Murray H. Milford
Texas Christian University: R. David Edmunds, Michael D.
    McCracken, and Emmet G. Smith
Texas Lutheran College: Richard L. Torgerson
Texas Tech University: Idris Rhea Traylor, Jr.
Texas Woman's University: Lavon B. Fulwiler
Trinity University: R. Douglas Brackenridge, George B. Cooper,
    Earl M. Lewis, John H. Moore, and Gail E. Myers
University of Dallas: Cherie A. Clodfelter and Richard P. Olenick
University of Houston: Richard I. Evans
University of Texas at Arlington: Thomas W. Hall, Lorrie Norton
    Hegstad, and Allan Saxe
University of Texas at Austin: Robert A. Divine, Austin M.
    Gleeson, Jane N. Lippman, and James W. Vick
University of Texas at Dallas: Rogene A. Buchholz and
    John H. Hoffman
University of Texas at El Paso: Stephen W. Stafford
University of Texas at San Antonio: Marian L. Martinello
University of Texas at Tyler: Olga Howard Fischer
University of Texas Health Science Center at San Antonio:
    John W. Preece
Wayland Baptist University: J. Hoyt Bowers
West Texas State University: Barry L. Duman and Gary T. Garner

## Utah

Brigham Young University: Larry T. Wimmer
University of Utah: Kenneth L. DeVries and Kenneth Eble
Westminster College: Jay Lees and Barry G. Quinn

## Vermont

Lyndon State College: Ferguson McKay
St. Michael's College: John C. Hartnett
University of Vermont: Samuel N. Bogorad and James S. Pacy

## Virginia

College of William and Mary: Ludwell H. Johnson, James C.
    Livingston, and David W. Thompson
Dabney S. Lancaster Community College: Stephen A. Adams
Eastern Mennonite College: Daniel B. Suter
Emory and Henry College: Daniel Leidig and George J. Stevenson
Ferrum College: Douglas W. Foard and Joseph D. Stogner
George Mason University: Evelyn Cohelan, Robert Gilstrap, and
    Bruce B. Manchester
Hampden-Sydney College: Robert G. Rogers
Hollins College: Lawrence Carlyle Becker
James Madison University: Ralph Alan Cohen, Roger Allen Hall,
    Phillip James, Andrew I. Kohen, Virginia Andreoli Mathie,
    and Philip E. Riley
Longwood College: Eleanor Weddle Bobbitt
Marymount College: Sister Marie DeSales Boran and
    Phillipa B. Stevens
Old Dominion University: Raymond H. Kirby
Radford University: Michael W. Cronin and Linda Killen
Randolph-Macon College: Bruce M. Unger
St. Paul's College: Sunday A. Adesuyi
University of Richmond: John R. Rilling
University of Virginia: Eileen Mavis Hetherington and
    Bernard Arthur Morin
Virginia Commonwealth University: A. Bryant Mangum
Virginia Military Institute: Thomas Young Greet
Virginia Polytechnic Institute and State University: McIntyre R.
    Louthan, Jr. and Raymond H. Myers
Virginia Wesleyan College: Betty Jefferson-Harris

## Washington

Clark College: Randall Wulff

Community Colleges of Spokane: Lois J. Roach
Eastern Washington University: S.M. Jameel Hasan and
    John D. Massengale
Gonzaga University: John F. Firkins, David Leigh, Joseph Monks
Pacific Lutheran University: Clifford G. Rowe
Seattle Pacific University: Annalee R. Clemons Oakes
Spokane Falls Community College: Mary Ellen McFadden
St. Martin's College: Norma Shelan
University of Puget Sound: Robert G. Albertson, Michael T.
    Curley, and Kenneth Rousslang
University of Washington: Lee Roy Beach, Don R. Pember, and
    Bonnie S. Worthington-Roberts
Washington State University: Donald Wayne Bushaw and
    Glenn A. Crosby

## West Virginia

Wheeling College: James Goodwin

## Wisconsin

Carroll College: Benjamin Franklin Richason, Jr.
Edgewood College: William B. Duddleston, Jeanette Feldballe
Marquette University: Peter Abramoff
Milwaukee School of Engineering: Marvin Heifetz
St. Norbert College: Robert H. Boyer
Viterbo College: James H. Larson and Laurian Pieterek

## Wyoming

University of Wyoming: George C. Frison, Michael J. Horan,
    and Richard Pasewark

# Sources of University Research Funds

### Ranking of institutions that spent more than $30-million in fiscal 1985

| | Total | Federal government | State, local government | Industry | Institutional funds | Other |
|---|---|---|---|---|---|---|
| 1. Johns Hopkins University | $388,553,000 | $367,063,000† | $ 1,323,000 | $ 0 | $ 4,819,000 | $ 15,548,000 |
| 2. Massachusetts Institute of Technology | 242,908,000 | 189,935,000‡ | 263,000 | 32,007,000 | 1,763,000 | 18,978,000 |
| 3. University of Wisconsin at Madison | 206,425,000 | 123,989,000 | 36,961,000 | 7,217,000 | 27,682,000 | 12,576,000 |
| 4. Cornell University | 203,226,000 | 119,319,000‡ | 26,963,000 | 12,526,000 | 23,274,000 | 19,244,000 |
| 5. Stanford University | 199,165,000 | 172,423,000‡ | 374,000 | 8,044,000 | 7,347,000 | 10,997,000 |
| 6. University of Minnesota | 173,322,000 | 87,776,000 | 19,439,000 | 8,135,000 | 38,231,000 | 19,741,000 |
| 7. University of Washington | 163,962,000 | 135,830,000 | 1,523,000 | 8,887,000 | 5,265,000 | 12,457,000 |
| 8. University of Michigan | 163,713,000 | 106,147,000 | 2,272,000 | 11,677,000 | 35,434,000 | 8,183,000 |
| 9. University of California at Berkeley | 149,900,000 | 96,779,000† | 2,294,000 | 0 | 39,361,000 | 11,466,000 |
| 10. University of California at Los Angeles | 149,744,000 | 109,689,000 | 836,000 | 0 | 19,219,000 | 20,000,000 |
| 11. Texas A&M University | 146,361,000 | 71,346,000 | 52,240,000 | 11,731,000 | 3,636,000 | 7,426,000 |
| 12. University of California at San Diego | 145,650,000 | 115,632,000 | 642,000 | 0 | 14,082,000 | 15,184,000* |
| 13. University of Illinois at Urbana-Champaign | 139,563,000 | 60,536,000 | 18,008,000 | 7,506,000 | 29,257,000 | 4,256,000 |
| 14. Harvard University | 137,853,000* | 103,556,000 | 380,000* | 5,410,000* | 8,651,000* | 19,656,000* |
| 15. Columbia University, main division | 136,577,000 | 120,120,000 | 1,193,000 | 4,027,000 | 2,034,000 | 9,203,000 |
| 16. University of California at San Francisco | 131,348,000 | 95,615,000 | 2,059,000 | 0 | 16,398,000 | 17,276,000* |
| 17. University of Pennsylvania | 130,397,000 | 92,893,000 | 572,000 | 3,685,000 | 14,062,000 | 19,185,000 |
| 18. University of Texas at Austin | 123,337,000 | 62,462,000 | 5,302,000 | 2,136,000 | 40,743,000 | 12,694,000 |
| 19. University of California at Davis | 114,862,000 | 47,652,000 | 3,671,000 | 0 | 52,476,000 | 11,063,000 |
| 20. Pennsylvania State University | 113,196,000 | 70,099,000 | 4,258,000 | 15,715,000 | 22,620,000 | 504,000 |
| 21. Yale University | 107,245,000 | 88,922,000 | 2,765,000 | 1,728,000 | 12,152,000 | 1,657,000 |
| 22. University of Arizona | 105,785,000 | 51,694,000 | 1,336,000 | 9,402,000 | 38,538,000 | 4,798,000 |
| 23. Ohio State University | 103,350,000 | 53,240,000 | 12,207,000 | 7,140,000 | 17,126,000 | 13,637,000 |
| 24. University of Southern California | 97,282,000 | 76,425,000 | 739,000 | 5,361,000 | 14,024,000 | 733,000 |
| 25. University of Maryland at College Park | 96,484,000 | 39,450,000 | 27,194,000* | 8,532,000* | 21,308,000* | 0 |
| 26. University of Colorado | 93,416,000 | 69,359,000 | 251,000 | 2,234,000 | 12,961,000 | 8,611,000 |
| 27. Michigan State University | 92,515,000 | 46,605,000 | 18,794,000 | 2,686,000 | 21,040,000 | 3,390,000 |
| 28. University of Florida | 91,298,000 | 42,031,000 | 4,996,000 | 8,254,000 | 30,748,000 | 5,269,000 |
| 29. Georgia Institute of Technology | 90,445,000 | 50,349,000 | 1,194,000 | 18,730,000 | 20,172,000 | 0 |
| 30. Louisiana State University | 88,953,000 | 25,492,000 | 29,292,000 | 746,000 | 26,209,000 | 7,214,000 |
| 31. Purdue University | 88,866,000 | 58,542,000 | 11,282,000 | 9,583,000 | 17,617,000 | 1,862,000 |
| 32. University of Rochester | 85,850,000 | 64,054,000‡ | 4,456,000 | 6,866,000 | 5,135,000 | 6,100,000 |
| 33. New York University | 83,896,000 | 66,587,000 | 609,000 | 3,742,000 | 11,618,000 | 7,360,000 |
| 34. University of Georgia | 83,548,000 | 28,403,000 | 1,590,000 | 3,729,000 | 49,337,000 | 489,000 |
| 35. Washington University | 80,233,000 | 61,050,000 | 369,000 | 9,617,000 | 4,203,000 | 4,994,000 |
| 36. University of Chicago | 79,929,000 | 66,950,000‡ | 1,193,000 | 1,044,000 | 5,896,000 | 4,846,000 |
| 37. University of Connecticut | 75,155,000 | 38,944,000 | 813,000 | 4,572,000 | 15,532,000 | 15,294,000 |
| 38. Oregon State University | 74,768,000 | 41,117,000 | 16,477,000 | 4,245,000 | 3,199,000 | 9,730,000 |
| 39. North Carolina State University | 74,471,000 | 22,253,000 | 2,074,000 | 8,249,000 | 38,876,000 | 3,019,000 |
| 40. Northwestern University | 72,337,000 | 42,317,000 | 311,000 | 1,690,000 | 23,110,000 | 4,909,000 |
| 41. University of North Carolina at Chapel Hill | 71,644,000 | 56,766,000 | 12,530,000* | 1,177,000 | 0 | 2,501,000 |
| 42. Duke University | 68,899,000 | 56,457,000 | 571,000 | 5,193,000 | 2,943,000 | 3,735,000 |
| 43. Iowa State University | 67,276,000 | 16,030,000‡ | 13,226,000 | 3,131,000 | 32,450,000 | 2,439,000 |
| 44. Yeshiva University | 66,665,000 | 55,764,000 | 0 | 0 | 5,902,000 | 4,990,000 |
| 45. California Institute of Technology | 66,810,000 | 58,855,000‡ | 453,000 | 2,578,000 | 3,891,000 | 1,913,000 |
| 46. University of Iowa | 64,923,000 | 48,059,000 | 160,000 | 1,556,000 | 10,273,000 | 4,875,000 |
| 47. University of Pittsburgh | 63,796,000 | 48,714,000 | 768,000 | 4,069,000 | 4,365,000 | 5,880,000 |
| 48. Baylor College of Medicine | 63,197,000 | 41,749,000 | 0 | 4,241,000 | 8,034,000 | 9,173,000 |
| 49. Virginia Polytechnic Institute & State University | 60,558,000 | 25,650,000 | 19,382,000 | 6,772,000 | 8,754,000 | 0 |
| 50. Carnegie Mellon University | 60,292,000 | 37,666,000 | 3,473,000 | 11,780,000 | 1,626,000 | 5,747,000* |
| 51. Rutgers University | 59,392,000 | 20,561,000 | 10,506,000 | 2,108,000 | 19,914,000* | 2,817,000 |
| 52. Rockefeller University | 59,158,000 | 28,047,000 | 499,000 | 2,961,000 | 16,444,000 | 9,308,000 |
| 53. University of Miami | 58,035,000 | 32,517,000 | 559,000 | 7,892,000 | 13,204,000 | 3,583,000 |
| 54. State University of New York at Buffalo | 57,045,000 | 42,665,000 | 646,000 | 243,000 | 10,554,000 | 2,746,000 |
| 55. University of Texas System Cancer Center | 56,197,000 | 19,408,000 | 0 | 0 | 25,835,000 | 10,894,000 |
| 56. Indiana University | 54,796,000 | 37,527,000 | 523,000 | 2,718,000 | 9,631,000 | 4,397,000 |
| 57. University of Utah | 54,354,000 | 45,564,000 | 1,145,000 | 1,706,000 | 3,380,000 | 2,559,000 |
| 58. University of Hawaii at Manoa | 54,025,000 | 34,886,000 | 16,296,000 | 250,000 | 1,695,000 | 898,000 |
| 59. University of Virginia | 51,653,000 | 35,152,000 | 2,777,000 | 761,000 | 6,897,000 | 6,066,000 |
| 60. Case Western Reserve University | 51,598,000 | 42,182,000 | 370,000 | 2,408,000 | 3,422,000 | 3,216,000 |
| 61. University of Missouri at Columbia | 50,765,000 | 18,577,000 | 9,661,000 | 3,400,000 | 15,624,000 | 3,501,000 |
| 62. Oklahoma State University | 49,084,000 | 11,533,000 | 2,070,000 | 2,972,000 | 28,025,000 | 4,194,000 |
| 63. University of Illinois at Chicago | 48,734,000 | 29,357,000 | 902,000 | 908,000 | 16,311,000 | 4,255,000 |
| 64. University of Nebraska at Lincoln | 47,809,000 | 17,156,000 | 1,293,000 | 2,083,000 | 26,328,000 | 968,000 |
| 65. State University of New York at Stony Brook | 47,495,000 | 31,946,000 | 1,327,000 | 1,412,000 | 7,026,000 | 5,784,000 |
| 66. University of Kentucky | 47,387,000 | 16,497,000 | 11,074,000 | 4,768,000 | 15,048,000 | 0 |
| 67. University of Alabama at Birmingham | 47,167,000 | 39,030,000 | 840,000 | 3,705,000 | 0 | 3,592,000 |
| 68. U. of Texas Health Science Center at Dallas | 46,671,000 | 34,087,000 | 30,000 | 3,967,000 | 64,000 | 8,523,000 |
| 69. New Mexico State University | 46,198,000 | 29,235,000 | 9,049,000 | 1,730,000 | 822,000 | 5,362,000 |
| 70. Princeton University | 46,027,000 | 30,892,000 | 250,000 | 1,184,000 | 9,409,000 | 4,292,000* |
| 71. Washington State University | 45,878,000 | 20,567,000 | 884,000 | 1,465,000 | 14,802,000 | 8,080,000 |
| 72. University of New Mexico | 45,591,000 | 33,640,000 | 4,190,000 | 3,875,000 | 2,738,000 | 1,737,000 |
| 73. University of California at Irvine | 44,458,000 | 34,772,000 | 868,000 | 0 | 2,910,000 | 5,907,000 |
| 74. University of California at Riverside | 44,225,000 | 13,884,000 | 1,970,000 | 0 | 25,187,000 | 3,212,000 |
| 75. Colorado State University | 44,171,000 | 28,702,000 | 5,537,000 | 6,467,000 | 3,201,000 | 264,000 |
| 76. Boston University | 44,135,000 | 38,257,000 | 1,015,000 | 1,994,000 | 2,000 | 2,867,000* |
| 77. Woods Hole Oceanographic Institute | 43,132,000 | 38,560,000 | 3,000 | 646,000 | 679,000 | 3,244,000* |
| 78. University of Cincinnati | 42,709,000 | 24,924,000 | 201,000 | 1,880,000 | 10,654,000 | 5,050,000 |
| 79. University of Oklahoma | 42,290,000 | 17,229,000 | 668,000 | 2,328,000 | 21,254,000 | 811,000 |
| 80. Mississippi State University | 41,376,000 | 11,151,000 | 16,151,000 | 1,606,000 | 11,164,000 | 1,304,000 |
| 81. City U. of New York M. Sinai School of Medicine | 37,750,000 | 29,907,000 | 323,000 | 1,425,000 | 3,742,000 | 2,352,000 |
| 82. University of Massachusetts at Amherst | 37,715,000 | 21,290,000 | 1,863,000 | 1,603,000 | 10,315,000 | 1,274,000 |
| 83. Utah State University | 37,608,000 | 21,718,000 | 8,440,000 | 1,395,000 | 5,680,000 | 375,000 |
| 84. Kansas State University | 37,303,000 | 16,481,000 | 16,501,000 | 721,000 | 6,915,000 | 2,375,000 |
| 85. Auburn University | 36,279,000 | 10,257,000 | 13,670,000 | 2,668,000 | 6,622,000 | 3,061,000* |
| 86. Virginia Commonwealth University | 35,221,000 | 26,816,000 | 1,018,000 | 2,019,000 | 2,568,000 | 2,780,000 |
| 87. Florida State University | 34,969,000 | 16,910,000 | 463,000 | 191,000 | 16,676,000 | 729,000 |
| 88. Vanderbilt University | 34,180,000 | 24,709,000 | 601,000 | 3,376,000 | 2,250,000 | 3,244,000 |
| 89. Clemson University | 32,326,000 | 9,965,000 | 10,216,000 | 1,800,000 | 9,491,000 | 854,000 |
| 90. Emory University | 30,706,000 | 26,136,000 | 408,000 | 2,395,000 | 317,000 | 1,450,000* |
| 91. University of California at Santa Barbara | 30,055,000 | 23,131,000 | 534,000 | 0 | 3,152,000 | 3,238,000 |
| Total, top 91 institutions | $7,637,185,000 | $4,905,717,000 | $526,332,000 | $383,889,000 | $1,263,219,000 | $558,028,000 |
| Total, all institutions* | $9,503,725,000 | $6,002,558,000 | $665,677,000 | $538,203,000 | $1,592,799,000 | $704,489,000 |

† Includes Applied Physics Laboratory with $257-million in federally financed research-and-development expenditures.
‡ Excludes expenditures at university-associated federally funded research-and-development centers.
* Indicates estimated numbers.

SOURCE: NATIONAL SCIENCE FOUNDATION

# Largest Institutions By
# Revenues and Expenditures

| Institution | Financial statistics, 1983-84 4/ (in thousands) | | | Full-time equivalent enrollment, fall 1983 | Full-time equivalent enrollment, fall 1985 |
|---|---|---|---|---|---|
| | Current-fund revenues | Current-fund expenditures | Educational and general expenditures | | |
| 1 | 18 | 19 | 20 | 21 | 22 |
| United States, all institutions ..... | 84,417,287 | 81,993,360 | 63,741,276 | 9,166,399 | 8,943,433 |
| Largest 100 institutions ............... | 24,163,073 | 23,370,949 | 18,089,535 | 2,152,479 | 2,133,835 |
| University of Minnesota, Minneapolis-Saint Paul ......................... | 811,793 | 751,191 | 552,205 | 47,387 | 45,664 |
| Ohio State University, Main Campus ........ | 708,227 | 680,408 | 458,288 | 47,313 | 47,081 |
| University of Texas at Austin ............. | 476,694 | 461,874 | 397,672 | 44,512 | 44,457 |
| University of Wisconsin, Madison ......... | 637,753 | 628,641 | 479,641 | 38,717 | 40,506 |
| Michigan State University ................ | 446,178 | 429,723 | 349,924 | 37,122 | 38,051 |
| Arizona State University ................. | 228,528 | 219,299 | 187,697 | 31,934 | 31,497 |
| University of Maryland, College Park Campus ................................ | 319,541 | 292,943 | 251,026 | 31,521 | 32,558 |
| Miami-Dade Community College .............. | 96,180 | 96,978 | 91,373 | 23,776 | 23,205 |
| University of Illinois, Urbana Campus .... | (5/) | (5/) | (5/) | 32,942 | 34,410 |
| Pennsylvania State University, Main Campus ............................:... | 420,281 | 404,784 | 312,967 | 32,792 | 33,120 |
| Texas A&M University, Main Campus ......... | 527,224 | 453,213 | 380,226 | 34,135 | 33,229 |
| University of Florida ..................... | 423,962 | 414,801 | 377,868 | 32,305 | 32,367 |
| Northeastern University (Mass.) .......... | 178,949 | 178,888 | 159,674 | 27,433 | 25,694 |
| Community College of the Air Force (Ala.) ................................ | (5/) | (5/) | (5/) | 33,055 | 35,212 |
| University of California, Los Angeles .... | 912,662 | 870,916 | 613,628 | 33,388 | 33,064 |
| University of Michigan, Ann Arbor ........ | 844,182 | 806,911 | 488,284 | 32,371 | 32,172 |
| University of Washington .................. | 559,805 | 534,689 | 425,404 | 29,888 | 30,072 |
| San Diego State University (Calif.) ....... | 178,325 | 176,052 | 140,940 | 26,329 | 27,424 |
| Rutgers University, New Brunswick (N.J.) . | 258,427 | 245,398 | 214,562 | 26,538 | 27,239 |
| Purdue University, Main Campus (Ind.) .... | 346,888 | 339,774 | 285,829 | 29,389 | 29,636 |
| Indiana University, Bloomington .......... | 350,059 | 329,277 | 218,237 | 29,429 | 29,419 |
| Northern Virginia Community College ....... | 44,277 | 44,280 | 44,280 | 16,839 | 15,042 |
| New York University ....................... | 646,328 | 620,687 | 392,329 | 23,267 | 23,278 |
| California State University, Long Beach .. | 134,319 | 130,704 | 111,858 | 23,985 | 23,798 |
| University of California, Berkeley ........ | 481,571 | 470,268 | 446,421 | 28,631 | 29,745 |
| University of Arizona ..................... | 400,518 | 398,462 | 272,495 | 25,797 | 25,478 |
| University of Iowa ........................ | (5/) | (5/) | (5/) | 26,036 | 25,929 |
| University of Southern California ......... | 422,768 | 422,505 | 371,216 | 23,171 | 23,694 |
| Temple University (Pa.) ................... | 367,108 | 361,820 | 226,286 | 21,553 | 22,878 |
| University of Cincinnati, Main Campus (Ohio) ............................... | 402,609 | 376,682 | 212,091 | 22,685 | 21,732 |
| University of Houston, University Park (Tex.) ................................ | 178,985 | 176,857 | 148,539 | 20,843 | 22,957 |

| Institution | Financial statistics, 1983-84 4/ (in thousands) | | | Full-time equivalent enrollment, fall 1983 | Full-time equivalent enrollment, fall 1985 |
| | Current-fund revenues | Current-fund expenditures | Educational and general expenditures | | |
| 1 | 18 | 19 | 20 | 21 | 22 |
| Brigham Young University, Main Campus (Utah) ................... | (5/) | (5/) | (5/) | 26,019 | 25,824 |
| Louisiana State University and A&M College ...................... | 274,380 | 265,704 | 214,902 | 27,025 | 26,180 |
| Macomb Community College (Mich.) ......... | 44,159 | 44,366 | 41,785 | 14,614 | 12,729 |
| University of Pittsburgh, Main Campus (Pa.) ............................. | 344,746 | 341,345 | 269,233 | 22,242 | 22,166 |
| Wayne State University (Mich.) ........... | 216,810 | 208,584 | 198,136 | 21,556 | 19,784 |
| California State University, Northridge .. | 116,021 | 112,847 | 96,284 | 21,361 | 21,501 |
| University of South Florida .............. | 164,428 | 161,826 | 143,786 | 18,785 | 19,528 |
| University of Massachusetts at Amherst ... | (5/) | (5/) | (5/) | 23,969 | 24,098 |
| Iowa State University of Science and Technology .......................... | 285,444 | 279,379 | 198,950 | 24,404 | 24,935 |
| Boston University (Mass.) ................. | 336,927 | 320,307 | 273,232 | 21,727 | 21,949 |
| University of New Mexico, Main Campus .... | 143,444 | 138,100 | 118,060 | 17,903 | 18,653 |
| Oakland Community College (Mich.) ........ | 43,960 | 43,492 | 40,451 | 16,244 | 15,586 |
| Central Piedmont Community College (N.C.) | 26,464 | 26,361 | 24,333 | 10,244 | 12,986 |
| University of Wisconsin, Milwaukee ........ | 125,097 | 123,354 | 105,740 | 19,403 | 19,209 |
| University of Akron, Main Campus (Ohio) .. | 104,004 | 97,768 | 86,189 | 19,463 | 18,951 |
| Houston Community College (Tex.) ......... | 48,827 | 46,407 | 46,362 | 10,747 | 11,095 |
| University of Georgia ..................... | 308,564 | 304,278 | 277,575 | 22,847 | 23,260 |
| University of Tennessee, Knoxville ........ | 202,845 | 199,623 | 157,317 | 22,878 | 21,843 |
| San Jose State University (Calif.) ........ | 128,546 | 111,367 | 104,931 | 19,412 | 19,104 |
| University of Kansas, Main Campus ......... | 172,542 | 168,269 | 137,360 | 20,421 | 21,119 |
| University of Utah ........................ | 317,672 | 305,911 | 216,291 | 19,645 | 19,760 |
| Northern Illinois University .............. | 128,014 | 129,253 | 97,409 | 19,841 | 19,961 |
| North Carolina State University, Raleigh . | 260,101 | 255,605 | 222,921 | 18,910 | 20,057 |
| Virginia Polytechnic Institute and State University ............................. | 237,180 | 238,710 | 210,195 | 21,074 | 21,764 |
| El Camino College (Calif.) ............... | 37,105 | 39,271 | 34,699 | 14,645 | 12,088 |
| San Francisco State University (Calif.) .. | 121,790 | 106,630 | 98,715 | 18,506 | 18,548 |
| Cuyahoga Community College District (Ohio) ............................... | 68,797 | 62,503 | 57,898 | 14,727 | 13,088 |
| University of Illinois at Chicago ......... | (5/) | (5/) | (5/) | 20,915 | 20,730 |
| Tarrant County Junior College (Tex.) ..... | 47,856 | 45,797 | 41,539 | 14,973 | 12,920 |
| University of Nebraska, Lincoln .......... | 202,716 | 201,425 | 162,924 | 21,675 | 20,904 |
| University of Kentucky Community College System ............................... | 45,113 | 43,853 | 41,021 | 15,536 | 14,731 |
| De Anza College (Calif.) ................. | (5/) | (5/) | (5/) | 10,728 | 7,108 |
| Texas Tech University ..................... | 170,631 | 156,704 | 128,478 | 21,282 | 21,085 |
| Indiana University-Purdue University, Indianapolis .......................... | 325,702 | 308,292 | 155,552 | 14,683 | 14,786 |
| Cleveland Institute of Electronics (Ohio) ............................... | 14,773 | 12,900 | 5,750 | 12,470 | 8,031 |
| University of South Carolina at Columbia . | 156,617 | 156,200 | 132,780 | 19,077 | 19,126 |
| Milwaukee Area Technical College (Wis.) .. | 76,064 | 75,897 | 71,288 | 11,575 | 10,677 |
| University of Texas at Arlington ......... | 94,226 | 92,218 | 77,719 | 18,803 | 18,541 |
| | 195,386 | 188,970 | 167,703 | 18,665 | 18,570 |

| Institution | Financial statistics, 1983-84 4/ (in thousands) | | | Full-time equivalent enrollment, fall 1983 | Full-time equivalent enrollment, fall 1985 |
| | Current-fund revenues | Current-fund expenditures | Educational and general expenditures | | |
|---|---|---|---|---|---|
| 1 | 18 | 19 | 20 | 21 | 22 |
| University of Missouri, Columbia ......... | 338,718 | 323,583 | 210,206 | 21,674 | 20,627 |
| California State University, Fullerton ... | 86,334 | 84,743 | 78,008 | 17,213 | 17,204 |
| State University of New York at Buffalo, Main Campus ........................ | (5/) | (5/) | (5/) | 18,490 | 18,505 |
| University of Colorado at Boulder ........ | 199,078 | 197,346 | 158,798 | 20,705 | 21,216 |
| Southern Illinois University, Carbondale . | 189,809 | 185,388 | 160,839 | 20,950 | 20,169 |
| College of DuPage (Ill.) ................. | 41,323 | 40,805 | 36,507 | 11,230 | 11,549 |
| California State University, Sacramento .. | 105,261 | 94,419 | 86,804 | 17,794 | 18,472 |
| San Francisco Community College District (Calif.) ............................. | 60,337 | 63,955 | 63,278 | 12,621 | 12,195 |
| Long Beach City College (Calif.) ......... | 38,063 | 37,209 | 34,747 | 10,627 | 10,627 |
| University of North Carolina at Chapel Hill ................................. | 418,153 | 392,812 | 332,258 | 20,038 | 20,243 |
| San Antonio College (Tex.) .............. | 43,558 | 43,176 | 41,161 | 15,125 | 13,183 |
| Orange Coast College (Calif.) ........... | (5/) | (5/) | (5/) | 13,262 | 12,712 |
| University of Pennsylvania .............. | 717,481 | 699,022 | 381,771 | 18,941 | 18,957 |
| University of Oklahoma, Norman Campus .... | 203,551 | 198,228 | 111,797 | 19,527 | 18,483 |
| Oklahoma State University, Main Campus ... | 184,137 | 171,055 | 128,032 | 21,074 | 19,462 |
| Georgia State University ................ | 94,167 | 92,972 | 89,723 | 14,689 | 14,748 |
| Florida State University ................ | 155,210 | 155,090 | 134,326 | 17,959 | 18,634 |
| Saddleback Community College (Calif.) .... | 34,450 | 33,895 | 33,895 | 10,110 | 9,067 |
| University of Toledo (Ohio) ............. | 89,959 | 87,512 | 74,488 | 16,271 | 16,117 |
| Illinois State University ............... | (5/) | (5/) | (5/) | 18,195 | 18,693 |
| North Texas State University ............ | 100,326 | 97,660 | 78,378 | 16,243 | 17,214 |
| Syracuse University, Main Campus (N.Y.) .. | 213,916 | 213,405 | 166,123 | 16,928 | 16,876 |
| Western Michigan University ............. | 115,078 | 114,578 | 88,198 | 16,062 | 16,265 |
| Santa Ana College (Calif.) ............. | 37,076 | 35,524 | 33,995 | 9,600 | 8,775 |
| Pima Community College (Ariz.) .......... | 33,190 | 33,710 | 31,776 | 10,661 | 10,042 |
| Memphis State University (Tenn.) ......... | 83,453 | 81,483 | 70,371 | 16,510 | 15,447 |
| Harvard University (Mass.) .............. | 586,338 | 586,078 | 509,139 | 15,353 | 17,386 |
| University of Kentucky .................. | 352,353 | 328,346 | 230,253 | 18,302 | 17,259 |
| Kent State University, Main Campus (Ohio) | 118,962 | 112,960 | 86,736 | 16,555 | 16,539 |
| Nassau Community College (N.Y.) .......... | 60,912 | 61,124 | 60,672 | 14,693 | 13,586 |

# One Hundred Largest
# Colleges and Universities

Selected statistics for the 100 college and university campuses enrolling the largest number of students in 1985: United States, 1983 to 1985

| Institution | Rank order 1/ | Control 2/ | Type 3/ | Total enrollment, fall 1984 | Total enrollment, fall 1985 | Enrollment by sex, fall 1985 Men | Women | Enrollment by attendance status, fall 1985 Full-time | Part-time | Enrollment by level, fall 1985 Under-graduate | Postbacca-laureate | Earned degrees conferred, 1983-84 Associate | Bachelor's | First-professional | Master's | Doctor's |
|---|---|---|---|---|---|---|---|---|---|---|---|---|---|---|---|---|
| | 2 | 3 | 4 | 5 | 6 | 7 | 8 | 9 | 10 | 11 | 12 | 13 | 14 | 15 | 16 | 17 |
| United States, all institutions ..... | --- | --- | --- | 112,241,940 | 112,247,055 | 5,818,450 | 6,428,605 | 17,075,221 | 15,171,834 | 110,596,674 | 11,650,381 | 452,240 | 974,309 | 74,407 | 284,263 | 33,209 |
| Largest 100 institutions ............. | --- | --- | --- | 2,763,397 | 2,771,063 | 1,425,466 | 1,345,597 | 11,749,393 | 11,021,672 | 2,227,540 | 543,525 | 46,577 | 277,189 | 19,592 | 92,576 | 17,571 |
| University of Minnesota, Minneapolis–Saint Paul ................. | 1 | 1 | 1 | 62,266 | 63,067 | 31,942 | 31,125 | 35,326 | 27,741 | 49,904 | 13,163 | 298 | 5,886 | 700 | 1,840 | 495 |
| Ohio State University, Main Campus ....... | 2 | 1 | 1 | 53,446 | 53,199 | 28,898 | 24,301 | 43,555 | 9,644 | 40,828 | 12,371 | 141 | 6,967 | 727 | 2,046 | 521 |
| University of Texas at Austin ......... | 3 | 1 | 1 | 47,973 | 47,838 | 25,718 | 22,120 | 41,169 | 6,669 | 36,633 | 11,205 | 0 | 7,127 | 545 | 1,716 | 427 |
| University of Wisconsin, Madison ........ | 4 | 1 | 1 | 44,218 | 45,050 | 23,865 | 21,185 | 37,707 | 7,343 | 31,617 | 13,433 | 0 | 5,466 | 436 | 2,062 | 630 |
| Michigan State University .......... | 5 | 1 | 1 | 42,193 | 42,746 | 21,175 | 21,571 | 34,504 | 8,242 | 33,365 | 9,381 | 1 | 7,050 | 298 | 1,790 | 355 |
| Arizona State University .......... | 6 | 1 | 1 | 40,538 | 40,529 | 20,688 | 19,841 | 25,722 | 14,807 | 30,319 | 10,210 | 0 | 4,873 | 141 | 1,151 | 130 |
| University of Maryland, College Park Campus ............ | 7 | 2 | 1 | 38,307 | 38,679 | 20,392 | 18,287 | 28,837 | 9,842 | 30,556 | 8,123 | 0 | 5,131 | 0 | 1,040 | 307 |
| Miami-Dade Community College ........... | 8 | 1 | 3 | 37,675 | 37,082 | 16,010 | 21,072 | 13,069 | 24,013 | 37,082 | 0 | 5,024 | 0 | 0 | 0 | 0 |
| University of Illinois, Urbana Campus ..... | 9 | 1 | 1 | 34,670 | 35,997 | 20,249 | 15,748 | 32,859 | 3,138 | 27,232 | 8,765 | 0 | 6,060 | 307 | 2,041 | 538 |
| Pennsylvania State University, Main Campus ............ | 10 | 1 | 1 | 34,401 | 35,699 | 20,096 | 15,603 | 31,370 | 4,329 | 29,637 | 6,062 | 55 | 7,255 | 0 | 1,108 | 364 |
| Texas A&M University, Main Campus ....... | 11 | 1 | 1 | 36,827 | 35,675 | 21,484 | 14,191 | 31,393 | 4,282 | 29,089 | 6,586 | 0 | 5,874 | 173 | 1,014 | 298 |
| University of Florida ......... | 12 | 1 | 1 | 35,496 | 35,334 | 19,756 | 15,578 | 29,832 | 5,502 | 27,438 | 7,896 | 1,168 | 4,774 | 524 | 1,075 | 294 |
| Northeastern University (Mass.) ......... | 13 | 2 | 1 | 35,219 | 35,271 | 20,003 | 15,268 | 18,205 | 17,066 | 30,167 | 5,104 | 361 | 3,498 | 162 | 927 | 30 |
| Community College of the Air Force (Ala.) ............. | 14 | 1 | 3 | 33,055 | 35,212 | 31,339 | 3,873 | 35,212 | 0 | 35,212 | 0 | 5,020 | 0 | 0 | 0 | 0 |
| University of California, Los Angeles ..... | 15 | 1 | 1 | 34,501 | 34,501 | 17,939 | 16,562 | 31,717 | 2,784 | 22,893 | 11,608 | 0 | 4,699 | 598 | 2,151 | 465 |
| University of Michigan, Ann Arbor .......... | 16 | 1 | 1 | 34,467 | 34,456 | 19,253 | 15,203 | 30,458 | 3,998 | 22,093 | 12,363 | 0 | 5,352 | 745 | 3,087 | 738 |
| University of Washington .......... | 17 | 1 | 1 | 34,450 | 34,086 | 17,913 | 16,173 | 27,033 | 7,033 | 23,696 | 10,390 | 0 | 5,063 | 417 | 1,590 | 358 |
| San Diego State University (Calif.) ......... | 18 | 1 | 2 | 33,698 | 33,898 | 16,366 | 17,532 | 21,708 | 12,190 | 27,787 | 6,111 | 0 | 4,424 | 0 | 1,154 | 0 |
| Rutgers University, New Brunswick (N.J.) . | 19 | 1 | 1 | 33,724 | 33,524 | 15,912 | 17,612 | 24,144 | 9,380 | 25,821 | 7,703 | 0 | 4,471 | 0 | 1,271 | 362 |
| Purdue University, Main Campus (Ind.) ..... | 20 | 1 | 1 | 31,852 | 32,822 | 19,611 | 13,211 | 28,214 | 4,608 | 27,197 | 5,625 | 610 | 5,329 | 86 | 1,175 | 383 |
| Indiana University, Bloomington .......... | 21 | 1 | 1 | 32,715 | 32,816 | 15,962 | 16,854 | 27,585 | 5,231 | 25,493 | 7,323 | 45 | 4,269 | 270 | 1,824 | 417 |
| Northern Virginia Community College ....... | 22 | 1 | 3 | 32,053 | 32,282 | 13,977 | 18,305 | 6,656 | 25,626 | 32,282 | 0 | 1,784 | 0 | 0 | 0 | 0 |
| New York University .......... | 23 | 2 | 1 | 33,014 | 32,266 | 14,676 | 17,590 | 18,192 | 14,074 | 14,782 | 17,484 | 231 | 2,541 | 698 | 3,694 | 418 |
| California State University, Long Beach .. | 24 | 1 | 2 | 31,124 | 31,124 | 15,038 | 16,086 | 18,261 | 12,863 | 25,625 | 5,499 | 0 | 4,054 | 0 | 717 | 0 |
| University of California, Berkeley ....... | 25 | 1 | 1 | 31,007 | 31,007 | 17,470 | 13,537 | 28,265 | 2,742 | 21,765 | 9,242 | 0 | 4,810 | 373 | 1,901 | 698 |
| University of Arizona ........... | 26 | 1 | 1 | 30,307 | 30,864 | 16,250 | 14,614 | 22,695 | 8,169 | 22,959 | 7,905 | 0 | 3,757 | 231 | 1,287 | 259 |
| University of Iowa ........... | 27 | 1 | 1 | 30,798 | 30,611 | 15,574 | 15,037 | 23,150 | 7,461 | 21,738 | 8,873 | 0 | 3,041 | 464 | 1,275 | 273 |

| Institution | Rank order [1] | Control [2] | Type [3] | Total enrollment, fall 1984 | Total enrollment, fall 1985 | Enrollment by sex, fall 1985 | | Enrollment by attendance status, fall 1985 | | Enrollment by level, fall 1985 | | Earned degrees conferred, 1983-84 | | | | |
|---|---|---|---|---|---|---|---|---|---|---|---|---|---|---|---|---|
| | | | | | | Men | Women | Full-time | Part-time | Under-graduate | Postbacca-laureate | Associate | Bachelor's | First-professional | Master's | Doctor's |
| 1 | 2 | 3 | 4 | 5 | 6 | 7 | 8 | 9 | 10 | 11 | 12 | 13 | 14 | 15 | 16 | 17 |
| University of Southern California | 28 | 2 | 1 | 30,373 | 30,373 | 18,634 | 11,739 | 19,151 | 11,222 | 16,221 | 14,152 | 0 | 2,797 | 664 | 2,909 | 424 |
| Temple University (Pa.) | 29 | 1 | 1 | 28,772 | 30,277 | 15,519 | 14,758 | 19,178 | 11,099 | 20,938 | 9,339 | 145 | 2,999 | 637 | 1,151 | 243 |
| University of Cincinnati, Main Campus (Ohio) | 30 | 1 | 1 | 30,830 | 30,205 | 16,211 | 13,994 | 18,674 | 11,531 | 24,133 | 6,072 | 549 | 2,842 | 300 | 937 | 202 |
| University of Houston, University Park (Tex.) | 31 | 1 | 1 | 31,095 | 29,944 | 15,864 | 14,080 | 15,823 | 14,121 | 19,495 | 10,449 | 0 | 2,549 | 378 | 1,092 | 145 |
| Brigham Young University, Main Campus (Utah) | 32 | 2 | 2 | 29,571 | 29,800 | 16,361 | 13,439 | 22,156 | 7,644 | 26,626 | 3,174 | 419 | 4,769 | 159 | 1,012 | 129 |
| Louisiana State University and A&M College | 33 | 1 | 1 | 30,186 | 29,727 | 15,587 | 14,140 | 24,208 | 5,519 | 24,100 | 5,627 | 0 | 3,234 | 266 | 819 | 108 |
| Macomb Community College (Mich.) | 34 | 1 | 3 | 30,892 | 29,491 | 14,470 | 15,021 | 5,176 | 24,315 | 29,491 | 0 | 2,560 | 0 | 0 | 0 | 0 |
| University of Pittsburgh, Main Campus (Pa.) | 35 | 1 | 1 | 29,197 | 28,710 | 14,879 | 13,831 | 17,805 | 10,905 | 19,003 | 9,707 | 0 | 2,968 | 443 | 2,005 | 389 |
| Wayne State University (Mich.) | 36 | 1 | 1 | 29,070 | 28,424 | 13,917 | 14,507 | 14,297 | 14,127 | 19,217 | 9,207 | 0 | 2,541 | 498 | 1,328 | 147 |
| California State University, Northridge | 37 | 1 | 2 | 28,144 | 28,144 | 12,786 | 15,358 | 16,478 | 11,666 | 23,164 | 4,980 | 0 | 3,726 | 0 | 630 | 0 |
| University of South Florida | 38 | 1 | 2 | 27,690 | 28,032 | 12,879 | 15,153 | 14,183 | 13,849 | 21,581 | 6,451 | 378 | 3,648 | 92 | 821 | 39 |
| University of Massachusetts at Amherst | 39 | 1 | 2 | 27,162 | 27,852 | 14,273 | 13,579 | 22,095 | 5,757 | 21,341 | 6,511 | 105 | 3,517 | 0 | 920 | 268 |
| Iowa State University of Science and Technology | 40 | 1 | 1 | 26,994 | 27,182 | 16,698 | 10,404 | 23,263 | 3,919 | 22,591 | 4,591 | 0 | 3,876 | 116 | 597 | 228 |
| Boston University (Mass.) | 41 | 2 | 1 | 27,630 | 27,181 | 13,296 | 13,885 | 19,334 | 7,847 | 17,143 | 10,038 | 31 | 3,144 | 678 | 1,657 | 333 |
| University of New Mexico, Main Campus | 42 | 1 | 1 | 26,079 | 26,628 | 12,445 | 14,183 | 14,458 | 12,170 | 22,112 | 4,516 | 229 | 1,745 | 186 | 787 | 114 |
| Oakland Community College (Mich.) | 43 | 1 | 3 | 26,605 | 26,553 | 11,208 | 15,345 | 8,460 | 18,093 | 26,553 | 0 | 1,679 | 2 | 0 | 0 | 0 |
| Central Piedmont Community College (N.C.) | 44 | 1 | 3 | 26,235 | 26,550 | 11,818 | 14,732 | 6,313 | 20,237 | 26,550 | 0 | 777 | 0 | 0 | 0 | 0 |
| University of Wisconsin, Milwaukee | 45 | 1 | 2 | 26,464 | 26,213 | 12,535 | 13,678 | 14,975 | 11,238 | 21,721 | 4,492 | 0 | 2,279 | 0 | 1,003 | 42 |
| University of Akron, Main Campus (Ohio) | 46 | 1 | 2 | 26,644 | 26,025 | 12,964 | 13,061 | 15,007 | 11,018 | 21,511 | 4,514 | 922 | 2,005 | 189 | 592 | 67 |
| Houston Community College (Tex.) | 47 | 1 | 3 | 25,118 | 25,415 | 11,703 | 13,712 | 2,935 | 22,480 | 25,415 | 0 | 485 | 0 | 0 | 0 | 0 |
| University of Georgia | 48 | 1 | 1 | 25,230 | 25,408 | 12,325 | 13,083 | 21,373 | 4,035 | 19,958 | 5,450 | 0 | 3,513 | 306 | 1,244 | 270 |
| University of Tennessee, Knoxville | 49 | 1 | 1 | 26,158 | 25,397 | 13,275 | 12,122 | 18,948 | 6,449 | 19,263 | 6,134 | 0 | 3,571 | 247 | 1,047 | 250 |
| San Jose State University (Calif.) | 50 | 1 | 2 | 24,843 | 24,843 | 12,272 | 12,571 | 14,661 | 10,182 | 19,504 | 5,259 | 0 | 3,614 | 0 | 853 | 0 |
| University of Kansas, Main Campus | 51 | 1 | 1 | 23,901 | 24,774 | 12,768 | 12,006 | 19,001 | 5,773 | 18,155 | 6,619 | 0 | 2,985 | 198 | 1,083 | 241 |
| University of Utah | 52 | 1 | 1 | 24,566 | 24,770 | 14,250 | 14,520 | 15,154 | 9,616 | 20,617 | 4,153 | 5 | 2,547 | 230 | 720 | 162 |
| Northern Illinois University | 53 | 1 | 1 | 23,689 | 24,311 | 10,831 | 13,480 | 17,132 | 7,179 | 18,217 | 6,094 | 0 | 3,653 | 73 | 1,222 | 71 |
| North Carolina State University, Raleigh | 54 | 1 | 1 | 23,733 | 24,294 | 15,297 | 8,997 | 16,863 | 7,431 | 20,673 | 3,621 | 115 | 2,912 | 0 | 679 | 210 |
| Virginia Polytechnic Institute and State University | 55 | 1 | 1 | 23,303 | 24,193 | 14,241 | 9,952 | 20,735 | 3,458 | 18,368 | 5,825 | 0 | 3,849 | 62 | 1,003 | 271 |

| Institution | Rank order[1] | Control[2] | Type[3] | Total enrollment, fall 1984 | Total enrollment, fall 1985 | Enrollment by sex, fall 1985 Men | Women | Enrollment by attendance status, fall 1985 Full-time | Part-time | Enrollment by level, fall 1985 Undergraduate | Postbaccalaureate | Earned degrees conferred, 1983-84 Associate | Bachelor's | First-professional | Master's | Doctor's |
|---|---|---|---|---|---|---|---|---|---|---|---|---|---|---|---|---|
| | 2 | 3 | 4 | 5 | 6 | 7 | 8 | 9 | 10 | 11 | 12 | 13 | 14 | 15 | 16 | 17 |
| El Camino College (Calif.) | 56 | 1 | 3 | 24,476 | 24,179 | 11,123 | 13,056 | 6,044 | 18,135 | 24,179 | 0 | 1,147 | 0 | 0 | 0 | 0 |
| San Francisco State University (Calif.) | 57 | 1 | 2 | 24,170 | 24,170 | 10,416 | 13,754 | 13,956 | 10,214 | 18,339 | 5,831 | 0 | 3,279 | 0 | 994 | 5 |
| Coyahoga Community College District (Ohio) | 58 | 1 | 3 | 24,972 | 24,159 | 8,939 | 15,220 | 7,069 | 17,090 | 24,159 | 0 | 1,906 | 0 | 0 | 0 | 0 |
| University of Illinois at Chicago | 59 | 1 | 2 | 24,067 | 24,158 | 13,079 | 11,079 | 17,792 | 6,366 | 17,081 | 7,077 | 0 | 2,791 | 461 | 1,052 | 112 |
| Tarrant County Junior College (Tex.) | 60 | 1 | 3 | 25,990 | 24,135 | 11,351 | 12,784 | 5,449 | 18,686 | 24,135 | 0 | 1,179 | 0 | 0 | 0 | 0 |
| University of Nebraska, Lincoln | 61 | 1 | 1 | 24,228 | 24,020 | 13,344 | 10,676 | 18,590 | 5,430 | 19,911 | 4,109 | 179 | 2,883 | 147 | 706 | 215 |
| University of Kentucky Community College System | 62 | 1 | 3 | 23,742 | 23,767 | 8,376 | 15,391 | 10,337 | 13,430 | 23,767 | 0 | 2,617 | 0 | 0 | 0 | 0 |
| De Anza College (Calif.) | 63 | 1 | 3 | 26,256 | 23,743 | 9,586 | 14,157 | 5,596 | 18,147 | 23,743 | 0 | 869 | 0 | 0 | 0 | 0 |
| Texas Tech University | 64 | 1 | 2 | 23,406 | 23,457 | 13,227 | 10,230 | 18,789 | 4,668 | 19,632 | 3,825 | 0 | 2,935 | 210 | 548 | 102 |
| Indiana University-Purdue University, Indianapolis | 65 | 1 | 2 | 23,366 | 23,430 | 10,441 | 12,989 | 9,569 | 13,861 | 16,910 | 6,520 | 599 | 1,545 | 658 | 594 | 11 |
| Cleveland Institute of Electronics (U....) | 66 | 2 | 3 | 23,373 | 23,373 | 22,205 | 1,168 | 0 | 23,373 | 23,373 | 0 | 16 | 0 | 0 | 0 | 0 |
| University of South Carolina at Columbia | 67 | 1 | 1 | 23,301 | 23,263 | 10,856 | 12,407 | 15,878 | 7,385 | 15,089 | 8,174 | 330 | 3,124 | 275 | 1,303 | 138 |
| Milwaukee Area Technical College (Wis.) | 68 | 1 | 3 | 20,783 | 23,173 | 10,556 | 12,617 | 6,518 | 16,655 | 23,173 | 0 | 1,366 | 0 | 0 | 0 | 0 |
| University of Texas at Arlington | 69 | 1 | 2 | 23,397 | 23,109 | 13,132 | 9,977 | 13,336 | 9,773 | 18,618 | 4,491 | 0 | 2,222 | 0 | 558 | 27 |
| University of Connecticut | 70 | 1 | 1 | 22,976 | 23,063 | 10,864 | 12,199 | 16,319 | 6,744 | 16,096 | 6,967 | 0 | 2,825 | 182 | 1,066 | 195 |
| University of Missouri, Columbia | 71 | 1 | 1 | 23,585 | 23,047 | 12,015 | 11,032 | 19,305 | 3,742 | 17,271 | 5,776 | 0 | 3,678 | 220 | 1,069 | 245 |
| California State University, Fullerton | 72 | 1 | 2 | 23,034 | 23,034 | 10,743 | 12,291 | 12,937 | 10,097 | 19,138 | 3,896 | 0 | 3,140 | 0 | 781 | 0 |
| State University of New York at Buffalo, Main Campus | 73 | 1 | 2 | 22,953 | 22,896 | 13,175 | 9,721 | 16,341 | 6,555 | 16,628 | 6,268 | 68 | 2,590 | 248 | 1,011 | 208 |
| University of Colorado at Boulder | 74 | 1 | 1 | 22,299 | 22,767 | 12,445 | 10,322 | 20,112 | 2,655 | 18,568 | 4,199 | 0 | 3,123 | 142 | 731 | 258 |
| Southern Illinois University, Carbondale | 75 | 1 | 1 | 22,776 | 22,553 | 14,214 | 8,339 | 18,014 | 4,539 | 18,530 | 4,023 | 717 | 4,427 | 150 | 698 | 152 |
| College of DuPage (Ill.) | 76 | 1 | 3 | 18,648 | 22,537 | 9,725 | 12,812 | 5,965 | 16,572 | 22,537 | 0 | 1,005 | 0 | 0 | 0 | 0 |
| California State University, Sacramento | 77 | 1 | 2 | 22,483 | 22,483 | 10,441 | 12,042 | 15,237 | 7,246 | 18,197 | 4,286 | 0 | 3,281 | 0 | 728 | 0 |
| San Francisco Community College District (Calif.) | 78 | 1 | 3 | 21,344 | 22,416 | 10,638 | 11,778 | 6,850 | 15,566 | 22,416 | 0 | 1,456 | 0 | 0 | 0 | 0 |
| Long Beach City College (Calif.) | 79 | 1 | 3 | 22,245 | 22,245 | 10,119 | 12,126 | 5,225 | 17,020 | 22,245 | 0 | 1,169 | 0 | 0 | 0 | 0 |
| University of North Carolina at Chapel Hill | 80 | 1 | 1 | 21,652 | 22,066 | 9,552 | 12,504 | 18,567 | 3,499 | 14,943 | 7,123 | 0 | 3,338 | 463 | 1,103 | 283 |
| San Antonio College (Tex.) | 81 | 1 | 3 | 22,274 | 22,041 | 9,888 | 12,153 | 7,311 | 14,730 | 22,041 | 0 | 968 | 0 | 0 | 0 | 0 |

| Institution | Rank order 1/ | Control 2/ | Type 3/ | Total enrollment, fall 1984 | Total enrollment, fall 1985 | Enrollment by sex, fall 1985 Men | Women | Enrollment by attendance status, fall 1985 Full-time | Part-time | Enrollment by level, fall 1985 Under-graduate | Postbacca-laureate | Earned degrees conferred, 1983-84 Associate | Bachelor's | First-professional | Master's | Doctor's |
|---|---|---|---|---|---|---|---|---|---|---|---|---|---|---|---|---|
| 1 | 2 | 3 | 4 | 5 | 6 | 7 | 8 | 9 | 10 | 11 | 12 | 13 | 14 | 15 | 16 | 17 |
| Orange Coast College (Calif.) ............. | 82 | 1 | 3 | 21,581 | 21,925 | 10,838 | 11,087 | 6,157 | 15,768 | 21,925 | 0 | 1,131 | 0 | 0 | 0 | 0 |
| University of Pennsylvania ............... | 83 | 2 | 1 | 22,065 | 21,870 | 11,944 | 9,926 | 17,501 | 4,369 | 11,747 | 10,123 | 60 | 2,372 | 639 | 1,737 | 406 |
| University of Oklahoma, Norman Campus .... | 84 | 1 | 1 | 21,365 | 21,748 | 12,328 | 9,420 | 15,364 | 6,384 | 15,825 | 5,923 | 0 | 2,357 | 229 | 702 | 154 |
| Oklahoma State University, Main Campus ... | 85 | 1 | 1 | 22,237 | 21,639 | 12,331 | 9,308 | 17,574 | 4,065 | 17,180 | 4,459 | 56 | 2,920 | 71 | 648 | 197 |
| Georgia State University ................. | 86 | 1 | 2 | 21,366 | 21,612 | 9,260 | 12,352 | 9,081 | 12,531 | 15,038 | 6,574 | 51 | 2,012 | 0 | 1,520 | 98 |
| Florida State University ................. | 87 | 1 | 1 | 20,984 | 21,537 | 10,184 | 11,253 | 16,684 | 4,853 | 16,652 | 4,885 | 454 | 3,625 | 196 | 816 | 273 |
| Saddleback Community College (Calif.) .... | 88 | 1 | 3 | 21,493 | 21,493 | 8,381 | 13,112 | 4,504 | 16,989 | 21,493 | 0 | 839 | 0 | 0 | 0 | 0 |
| University of Toledo (Ohio) .............. | 89 | 1 | 1 | 21,039 | 21,238 | 10,652 | 10,586 | 12,725 | 8,513 | 18,171 | 3,067 | 812 | 1,804 | 221 | 543 | 50 |
| Illinois State University ................ | 90 | 1 | 2 | 20,903 | 21,178 | 9,827 | 11,351 | 17,051 | 4,127 | 18,490 | 2,688 | 0 | 3,419 | 0 | 524 | 29 |
| North Texas State University ............. | 91 | 1 | 2 | 21,414 | 20,996 | 10,075 | 10,921 | 13,704 | 7,292 | 15,155 | 5,841 | 0 | 1,977 | 0 | 987 | 176 |
| Syracuse University, Main Campus (N.Y.) .. | 92 | 2 | 1 | 21,044 | 20,980 | 10,964 | 10,016 | 14,824 | 6,156 | 13,940 | 7,040 | 23 | 2,665 | 212 | 1,286 | 157 |
| Western Michigan University .............. | 93 | 1 | 1 | 20,233 | 20,963 | 10,266 | 10,697 | 13,629 | 7,334 | 15,958 | 5,005 | 0 | 3,145 | 0 | 1,025 | 45 |
| Santa Ana College (Calif.) .............. | 94 | 1 | 3 | 20,253 | 20,843 | 10,270 | 10,573 | 3,512 | 17,331 | 20,643 | 0 | 339 | 0 | 0 | 0 | 0 |
| Pima Community College (Ariz.) ........... | 95 | 1 | 3 | 20,862 | 20,801 | 9,894 | 10,907 | 4,662 | 16,139 | 20,801 | 0 | 1,010 | 0 | 0 | 0 | 0 |
| Memphis State University (Tenn.) ......... | 96 | 1 | 2 | 21,296 | 20,749 | 9,785 | 10,964 | 11,819 | 8,930 | 16,005 | 4,744 | 0 | 1,609 | 151 | 710 | 59 |
| Harvard University (Mass.) ............... | 97 | 2 | 1 | 19,977 | 20,711 | 12,964 | 7,747 | 14,174 | 6,537 | 7,965 | 12,746 | 20 | 1,679 | 774 | 2,236 | 457 |
| University of Kentucky ................... | 98 | 1 | 1 | 20,637 | 20,421 | 10,338 | 10,083 | 15,755 | 4,666 | 15,911 | 4,510 | 0 | 2,807 | 326 | 775 | 153 |
| Kent State University, Main Campus (Ohio) | 99 | 1 | 1 | 20,324 | 20,406 | 8,985 | 11,421 | 14,604 | 5,802 | 16,451 | 3,955 | 0 | 2,320 | 0 | 822 | 124 |
| Nassau Community College (N.Y.) .......... | 100 | 1 | 3 | 21,132 | 20,320 | 8,860 | 11,460 | 10,269 | 10,051 | 20,320 | 0 | 3,054 | 0 | 0 | 0 | 0 |

1/ Institutions ranked by size of total enrollment in fall 1985.
2/ Publicly controlled institutions are identified by a "1"; privately controlled, by a "2."
3/ The types of institutions are identified as follows: "1", universities; "2", other 4-year institutions; "3", 2-year institutions.
4/ Totals for the United States and the 100 largest colleges include estimates for nonrespondents.
5/ Data not reported.

SOURCE: U.S. Department of Education, Center for Statistics, "Fall Enrollment in Colleges and Universities", "Earned Degrees Conferred", and "Financial Statistics of Institutions of Higher Education" surveys (September 1986).

# The top 100 institutions in total federal obligations for fiscal 1985

| Institution | Research and development[1] Amount | Rank | Total federal obligations[1] Amount | Rank |
|---|---|---|---|---|
| Johns Hopkins U.[2] | $429,180,000 | 1 | $448,068,000 | 1 |
| Massachusetts Institute of Technology | 187,649,000[3] | 2 | 211,480,000 | 2 |
| Stanford U. | 174,961,000[3] | 3 | 203,707,000 | 3 |
| U. of Washington | 146,179,000 | 4 | 183,352,000 | 4 |
| Howard U[4] | 13,769,000 | 110 | 163,879,000 | 5 |
| Columbia U., Main Division | 127,331,000 | 6 | 155,971,000 | 6 |
| Cornell U. | 119,966,000[3] | 8 | 155,831,000 | 7 |
| U. of California, Los Angeles | 128,211,000 | 5 | 151,180,000 | 8 |
| U. of Wisconsin, Madison | 124,604,000 | 7 | 148,703,000 | 9 |
| U. of Minnesota | 103,272,000 | 14 | 142,497,000 | 10 |
| Yale U. | 109,227,000 | 10 | 133,756,000 | 11 |
| U. of Michigan | 108,035,000 | 11 | 133,679,000 | 12 |
| Harvard U. | 109,414,000 | 9 | 131,790,000 | 13 |
| U. of California, Berkeley | 106,710,000[3] | 12 | 129,841,000 | 14 |
| U. of Pennsylvania | 103,119,000 | 15 | 126,523,000 | 15 |
| U. of California, San Diego | 103,603,000 | 13 | 117,937,000 | 16 |
| U. of California, San Francisco | 98,536,000 | 16 | 114,634,000 | 17 |
| Pennsylvania State U.[5] | 76,723,000 | 19 | 111,279,000 | 18 |
| U. of Southern California | 89,646,000 | 17 | 102,542,000 | 19 |
| U. of Illinois, Urbana-Champaign | 83,122,000 | 18 | 99,423,000 | 20 |
| U. of Colorado | 71,424,000 | 23 | 90,793,000 | 21 |
| New York U. | 74,577,000 | 20 | 89,244,000 | 22 |
| Ohio State U. | 56,065,000 | 30 | 87,154,000 | 23 |
| U. of Chicago | 71,194,000[3] | 24 | 83,957,000 | 24 |
| Washington U. | 71,978,000 | 22 | 82,607,000 | 25 |
| Duke U. | 69,169,000 | 26 | 81,712,000 | 26 |
| U. of Rochester | 70,379,000 | 25 | 81,073,000 | 27 |
| U. of Texas, Austin | 72,379,000 | 21 | 78,729,000 | 28 |
| U. of Pittsburgh | 58,620,000 | 28 | 76,163,000 | 29 |
| Purdue U. | 51,475,000 | 34 | 75,298,000 | 30 |
| Northwestern U. | 48,747,000 | 39 | 75,285,000 | 31 |
| U. of North Carolina, Chapel Hill | 63,105,000 | 27 | 73,431,000 | 32 |
| Michigan State U. | 46,945,000 | 42 | 72,795,000 | 33 |
| U. of Florida | 47,656,000 | 41 | 72,675,000 | 34 |
| U. of Iowa | 55,117,000 | 31 | 70,326,000 | 35 |
| U. of Arizona | 49,740,000 | 37 | 67,080,000 | 36 |
| Indiana U. | 39,660,000 | 48 | 65,013,000 | 37 |
| U. of Maryland, College Park | 51,013,000 | 35 | 64,646,000 | 38 |
| Yeshiva U. | 56,968,000 | 29 | 64,623,000 | 39 |
| U. of Utah | 50,938,000 | 36 | 63,837,000 | 40 |
| Texas A&M U. | 39,041,000 | 49 | 62,003,000 | 41 |
| Gallaudet U.[4] | 2,173,000 | 207 | 61,173,000 | 42 |
| Georgia Institute of Technology | 51,585,000 | 33 | 59,606,000 | 43 |
| Boston U. | 46,152,000 | 43 | 59,387,000 | 44 |
| U. of Alabama, Birmingham | 44,093,000 | 45 | 59,373,000 | 45 |
| California Institute of Technology | 55,083,000[3] | 32 | 58,499,000 | 46 |
| Inter American U. of Puerto Rico, San German | $ 0 | — | $57,591,000 | 47 |
| Case Western Reserve U. | 47,994,000 | 40 | 56,465,000 | 48 |
| Carnegie Mellon U. | 48,872,000[3] | 38 | 54,052,000 | 49 |
| U. of California, Davis | 43,156,000 | 46 | 52,247,000 | 50 |
| Louisiana State U. | 34,764,000 | 54 | 51,155,000 | 51 |
| Baylor C. of Medicine | 45,837,000 | 44 | 49,670,000 | 52 |
| U. of Miami | 33,709,000 | 58 | 47,726,000 | 53 |
| U. of Kentucky | 21,931,000 | 83 | 47,300,000 | 54 |
| Vanderbilt U. | 39,909,000 | 47 | 47,096,000 | 55 |
| U. of Virginia | 37,416,000 | 51 | 46,858,000 | 56 |
| Oregon State U. | 33,746,000 | 57 | 46,154,000 | 57 |
| North Carolina State U. | 27,357,000 | 68 | 45,515,000 | 58 |
| Rutgers U. | 26,889,000 | 70 | 45,442,000 | 59 |
| U. of New Mexico | 31,362,000 | 62 | 44,189,000 | 60 |
| U. of Georgia | 23,800,000 | 76 | 44,092,000 | 61 |
| U. of Texas Health Science Center, Dallas | 37,432,000 | 50 | 43,495,000 | 62 |
| U. of Puerto Rico, Regional Colleges Administration | 0 | — | 43,014,000 | 63 |
| U. of Connecticut | 32,775,000 | 59 | 42,941,000 | 64 |
| U. of Illinois, Chicago | 28,172,000 | 65 | 42,395,000 | 65 |
| U. of Massachusetts, Amherst | 25,780,000 | 72 | 41,249,000 | 66 |
| U. of Cincinnati | 27,886,000 | 67 | 41,117,000 | 67 |
| Princeton U. | 34,720,000[3] | 55 | 41,091,000 | 68 |
| New Mexico State U. | 24,861,000 | 73 | 40,883,000 | 69 |
| U. of Tennessee, Knoxville | 23,226,000 | 79 | 39,665,000 | 70 |
| U. of Kansas | 20,676,000 | 86 | 39,505,000 | 71 |
| U. of Hawaii, Manoa | 29,090,000 | 63 | 39,084,000 | 72 |
| State U. of New York, Stony Brook | 35,059,000 | 53 | 39,068,000 | 73 |
| U. of California, Irvine | 31,515,000 | 60 | 38,927,000 | 74 |
| Tufts U. | 34,495,000 | 56 | 38,036,000 | 75 |
| Virginia Polytechnic Institute & State U. | 24,565,000 | 75 | 37,878,000 | 76 |
| Rockefeller U. | 35,285,000 | 52 | 37,745,000 | 77 |
| Virginia Commonwealth U. | 28,896,000 | 64 | 37,706,000 | 78 |
| Colorado State U. | 24,767,000 | 74 | 37,331,000 | 79 |
| Rochester Inst. of Technology | 1,356,000 | 230 | 36,582,000 | 80 |
| U. of Missouri, Columbia | 22,343,000 | 81 | 36,552,000 | 81 |
| State U. of New York, Albany | 11,530,000 | 117 | 34,448,000 | 82 |
| Iowa State U. | 14,555,000[3] | 106 | 34,276,000 | 83 |
| Woods Hole Oceanographic Institute | 31,392,000 | 61 | 33,814,000 | 84 |
| Temple U. | 18,954,000 | 92 | 33,564,000 | 85 |
| Emory U. | 27,005,000 | 69 | 33,161,000 | 86 |
| Utah State U. | 22,067,000 | 82 | 32,415,000 | 87 |
| Brown U. | 26,029,000 | 71 | 31,178,000 | 88 |
| City U. of New York, Mount Sinai School of Medicine | 28,059,000 | 66 | 31,054,000 | 89 |
| Oklahoma State U. | 10,666,000 | 124 | 30,629,000 | 90 |
| U. of California, Santa Barbara | 23,602,000 | 78 | 30,145,000 | 91 |
| U. of Oregon, Main Campus | 17,445,000 | 94 | 29,843,000 | 92 |
| Washington State U. | 17,381,000 | 95 | 29,614,000 | 93 |
| Puerto Rico Jr. C. | 0 | — | 29,341,000 | 94 |
| Mississippi State U. | 14,459,000 | 107 | 29,186,000 | 95 |
| Georgetown U. | 18,194,000 | 93 | 27,929,000 | 96 |
| State U. of New York, Buffalo | 23,051,000 | 80 | 27,842,000 | 97 |
| Wayne State U. | 16,598,000 | 100 | 27,282,000 | 98 |
| Syracuse U. | 17,035,000 | 97 | 26,803,000 | 99 |
| Kansas State U. | 9,871,000 | 129 | 26,539,000 | 100 |
| Total, 100 institutions | $5,326,087,000 | | $7,151,433,000 | |
| Total, all institutions | $6,379,151,000 | | $10,984,597,000 | |

Note: Federal obligations are funds set aside for payment. Institutions do not always receive them during the year in which they were obligated.

[1] Amounts shown represent total obligations from 15 federal agencies that accounted for about 95 per cent of all federal obligations to universities and colleges in the United States and for virtually all federal obligations to such institutions for research and development. Amounts shown represent awards to individual institutions. Awards to the administrative offices of university systems are excluded from institutional totals because final allocation of funds is unknown, but are included in "Total, all institutions."

[2] Includes $299-million obligated to the Applied Physics Laboratory, considered a federally financed research-and-development center until fiscal 1978.

[3] Excludes research and development obligations to university-administered federally financed research-and-development centers.

[4] Howard U. and Gallaudet U. receive substantial appropriations from Congress each year for general operating expenses.

[5] Includes $8-million obligated to the Applied Research Laboratory, considered a federally funded research-and-development center until fiscal 1978.

SOURCE: NATIONAL SCIENCE FOUNDATION

# *Freshman Merit Scholars*
## Institutions enrolling the most in 1986

This table shows the top 41 colleges and universities attended by freshman Merit Scholars named in 1986. The rankings were determined by *The Chronicle* from an alphabetical listing supplied by the National Merit Scholarship Corporation.

The first column lists the total number of Merit Scholarship winners, while the second column shows the number whose scholarships were paid for by the institution, not by the National Merit Scholarship Corporation or other corporate sponsors.

Over all, 6,026 freshman Merit Scholars were enrolled—3,648 at 232 private institutions and 2,378 at 152 public institutions.

| | Number of scholars | Number sponsored by institution |
|---|---|---|
| 1. Harvard and Radcliffe Colleges | 297 | — |
| 2. University of Texas at Austin | 270 | 210 |
| 3. Yale University | 183 | — |
| 4. Rice University | 176 | 125 |
| 5. Stanford University | 172 | — |
| 6. Princeton University | 140 | — |
| 7. Georgia Institute of Technology | 130 | 98 |
| 8. Northwestern University | 117 | 75 |
| 9. University of Chicago | 115 | 73 |
| 10. Texas A&M University at College Station | 112 | 77 |
| 11. Massachusetts Institute of Technology | 106 | — |
| 12. Carleton College | 104 | 81 |
| 13. Michigan State University | 102 | 83 |
| 14. Duke University | 90 | 7 |
| 15. University of California at Los Angeles | 83 | 60 |
| 16. University of Michigan | 78 | — |
| 17. Trinity University | 73 | 65 |
| 18. Washington University | 72 | 48 |
| 19. University of Minnesota–Twin Cities | 71 | 58 |
| 19. Oberlin College | 71 | 57 |
| 21. University of Florida | 70 | 61 |
| 22. Cornell University | 68 | — |
| 23. University of California at Berkeley | 66 | 4 |
| 24. University of Virginia | 62 | — |
| 25. Brown University | 61 | — |
| 26. University of Houston | 59 | 48 |
| 27. University of Pennsylvania | 57 | — |
| 28. Baylor University | 56 | 42 |
| 29. Ohio State University at Columbus | 55 | 42 |
| 30. Miami University | 49 | 28 |
| 31. Harvey Mudd College | 47 | 33 |
| 32. Auburn University | 46 | 31 |
| 33. Brigham Young University | 45 | 30 |
| 33. Dartmouth College | 45 | — |
| 35. Emory University | 43 | 34 |
| 35. University of Illinois at Urbana–Champaign | 43 | — |
| 37. University of California at Santa Barbara | 41 | 34 |
| 38. Williams College | 39 | — |
| 39. Rose-Hulman Institute of Technology | 38 | 32 |
| 40. University of Notre Dame | 37 | — |
| 41. Case Western Reserve University | 35 | 24 |
| 41. University of Miami | 35 | 27 |

SOURCE: NATIONAL MERIT SCHOLARSHIP CORPORATION

# Edward B. Fiske's Best and Most Interesting Colleges

## ALABAMA

Alabama, University of—Tuscaloosa
Auburn University
Birmingham–Southern College
Tuskegee Institute

## ARIZONA

Arizona State University
Arizona, University of

## ARKANSAS

Arkansas, University of

## CALIFORNIA

California Institute of Technology
California State University and Colleges
California, University of—Berkeley
California, University of—Davis
California, University of—Irvine
California, University of—Los Angeles
California, University of—Riverside
California, University of—San Diego
California, University of—Santa Barbara
California, University of—Santa Cruz
Claremont-McKenna College (Claremont
    Colleges)
Harvey Mudd College (Claremont Colleges)
Mills College
Occidental College
Pacific, University of the
Pepperdine University
Pitzer College (Claremont Colleges)
Pomona College (Claremont Colleges)
Redlands, University of
San Francisco, University of
Santa Clara University
Scripps College (Claremont Colleges)
Southern California, University of
Stanford University
Whittier College

## COLORADO

Colorado College
Colorado School of Mines
Colorado, University of—Boulder
Denver, University of

## CONNECTICUT

Connecticut College
Connecticut, University of
Fairfield University
Trinity College
Wesleyan University
Yale University

## DELAWARE

Delaware, University of

## DISTRICT OF COLUMBIA

American University
Catholic University of America
George Washington University
Georgetown University
Howard University

## FLORIDA

Eckerd College
Florida Institute of Technology
Florida State University—Tallahassee
Florida, University of—Gainesville
Miami, University of
Rollins College
South Florida, University of (including New
    College)
Stetson University

## GEORGIA

Agnes Scott College
Clark College (Atlanta University Center)

Emory University
Georgia Institute of Technology
Georgia, University of
Mercer University
Morehouse College (Atlanta University Center)
Morris Brown College (Atlanta University Center)
Spelman College (Atlanta University Center)

### IDAHO

Idaho State University

### ILLINOIS

Chicago, University of
DePaul University
Illinois Institute of Technology
Illinois, University of, at Urbana–Champaign
Knox College
Lake Forest College
Northwestern University
Principia College
Wheaton College

### INDIANA

DePauw University
Earlham College
Indiana University
Notre Dame, University of
Purdue University
Rose–Hulman Institute of Technology
Wabash College

### IOWA

Cornell College
Grinnell College
Iowa State University
Iowa, University of

### KANSAS

Kansas, University of

### KENTUCKY

Centre College
Louisville, University of

### LOUISIANA

Louisiana State University
Loyola University

Tulane University/Sophia Newcomb College
Xavier University

### MAINE

Atlantic, College of the
Bates College
Bowdoin College
Colby College
Maine, University of—Orono

### MARYLAND

Goucher College
Hood College
Johns Hopkins University
Maryland, University of—College Park
St. John's College
St. Mary's College of Maryland

### MASSACHUSETTS

Amherst College
Babson College
Boston College
Boston University
Brandeis University
Clark University
Gordon College
Hampshire College
Harvard University
Holy Cross, College of the
Massachusetts Institute of Technology
Massachusetts, University of—Amherst
Mount Holyoke College
Northeastern University
Smith College
Tufts University
Wellesley College
Wheaton College
Williams College
Worcester Polytechnic Institute

### MICHIGAN

Albion College
Alma College
Calvin College
Hope College
Kalamazoo College
Michigan State University
Michigan, University of

## MINNESOTA

Carleton College
Macalester College
Minnesota, University of—Minneapolis
St. John's University
St. Olaf College

## MISSISSIPPI

Millsaps College

## MISSOURI

Missouri, University of—Columbia
St. Louis University
Washington University

## MONTANA

Montana College of Mineral Science and
  Technology

## NEBRASKA

Nebraska, University of

## NEW HAMPSHIRE

Dartmouth College
New Hampshire, University of

## NEW JERSEY

Drew University
Fairleigh Dickinson University
New Jersey Institute of Technology
Princeton University
Rutgers University
Seton Hall University
Stevens Institute of Technology

## NEW MEXICO

New Mexico Institute of Mining and Technology
New Mexico, University of
St. John's College

## NEW YORK

Adelphi University
Alfred University
Bard College
Barnard College (Columbia University)

CUNY—Baruch College
CUNY—Brooklyn College
CUNY—City College of New York
CUNY—Community Colleges
CUNY—Hunter College
CUNY—John Jay College of Criminal Justice
CUNY—Lehman College
CUNY—New York City Technical College
CUNY—Queens College
Colgate University
Columbia College (Columbia University)
Cooper Union
Cornell University
Fordham University
Hamilton College
Hartwick College
Hobart and William Smith Colleges
Hofstra University
Houghton College
Ithaca College
Long Island University—Southampton College
The New School for Social Research
New York University
Pratt Institute
Rensselaer Polytechnic Institute
Rochester Institute of Technology
Rochester, University of
St. Lawrence University
Sarah Lawrence College
Skidmore College
SUNY—Albany
SUNY—Binghamton
SUNY—Buffalo
SUNY—Purchase
SUNY—Stony Brook
Syracuse University
Union College
Vassar College
Wells College
Yeshiva University

## NORTH CAROLINA

Davidson College
Duke University
North Carolina State University
North Carolina, University of, at Chapel Hill
North Carolina, University of, at Greensboro
Wake Forest University

## OHIO

Antioch College
Case Western Reserve University
Cincinnati, University of
Dayton, University of

Denison University
Kent State University
Kenyon College
Miami University
Oberlin College
Ohio State University
Ohio Wesleyan University
Wittenberg University
Wooster, College of

## OKLAHOMA

Oklahoma, University of—Norman
Oral Roberts University
Tulsa, University of

## OREGON

Lewis and Clark College
Oregon State University
Oregon, University of
Reed College
Willamette College

## PENNSYLVANIA

Allegheny College
Bryn Mawr College
Bucknell University
Carnegie–Mellon University
Chatham College
Dickinson College
Drexel University
Duquesne University
Franklin and Marshall College
Gettysburg College
Haverford College
Lafayette College
Lehigh University
Muhlenberg College
Pennsylvania State University
Pennsylvania, University of
Pittsburgh, University of
Swarthmore College
Temple University
Ursinus College
Washington and Jefferson College

## RHODE ISLAND

Brown University
Rhode Island, University of

## SOUTH CAROLINA

Charleston, College of
Clemson University
Furman University
South Carolina, University of

## TENNESSEE

Fisk University
Rhodes College
South, University of the—Sewanee
Vanderbilt University

## TEXAS

Austin College
Baylor University
Dallas, University of
Houston, University of—University Park
Rice University
Southern Methodist University
Southwestern University
Texas A&M University
Texas Christian University
Texas, University of—Austin
Trinity University

## UTAH

Brigham Young University
Utah, University of

## VERMONT

Bennington College
Marlboro College
Middlebury College
Vermont, University of

## VIRGINIA

Hollins College
Randolph–Macon Woman's College
Richmond, University of
Sweet Briar College
Virginia Polytechnic Institute and State
   University
Virginia, University of
Washington and Lee University
William and Mary, College of

## WASHINGTON

Evergreen State College
Puget Sound, University of
Washington, University of
Whitman College

## WEST VIRGINIA

West Virginia University

## WISCONSIN

Alverno College
Beloit College
Lawrence University
Marquette University
Ripon College
Wisconsin, University of—Madison

Source: Edward B. Fiske: Selective
Guide to Colleges (TimesBooks)

# Collective Bargaining

# Unionization Among College Faculty
## *January 1–December 31, 1986*

Joel M. Douglas
Professor of Public Administration
Baruch College, City University of New York

## Introduction

The number of unionized institutions, campuses and faculty in higher education continued to increase during 1986, albeit at a slower rate than previous years, and has now reached its highest level to date. Over 208,000 faculty are now covered by collective bargaining agreements, more than at any other time in the history of academic unionism. The steady growth of faculty unionism indicates a continued approval of collective bargaining as a means of governance. The acceptance of academic unionism as measured by the number of certified agents grew at a rate of 2.7% during 1986 and was not restricted to any one geographic area as faculty agents were elected in nine different states. There are now 458 reported faculty bargaining agents, an increase of 12 from 1986. Over one thousand campuses are involved in faculty collective bargaining with certified academic unions. For the first time in seven years, no faculty union was reported decertified either as the result of court action, litigation, or a challenge to agent status. The record indicates that once faculty unionize, they rarely elect decertification.

## Public vs. Private Dichotomy

As in previous years, public sector institutions continued to dominate academic collective bargaining. Only one of the seventeen elections held during 1986, was conducted at a private institution, the College of Insurance. The largest number of elections was held in Illinois, one of the states with the most recent legislation. Public sector collective bargain-

ing is directly related to the passage of enabling legislation, and since none was enacted during 1986, the effect in forthcoming years may be damaging for faculty unionists. Of the 458 recognized faculty agents, 381 (83.2%) are at public institutions. Of the 381 public institutions now unionized, 88 are four-year colleges, while the remaining 293 are two-year institutions. Unionized public sector campuses now total 921 and account for 61% of the 1501 campuses in that category. In the private sector, approximately 5% of the 1830 campuses are unionized.

It is evident that the ruling by the United States Supreme Court in *NLRB v. Yeshiva University*, 444 U.S. 672 (1980), which prohibited faculty members who were adjudicated as possessing the "indicia of managerial status" from bargaining under the protection of the National Labor Relations Act, has virtually eliminated private sector higher education union organizing. While there were no *Yeshiva* decertifications this year, faculty unions trying to organize at private institutions continue to experience great difficulty in overcoming its impact.

## Agents Elected

Seventeen bargaining agent elections were held in 1986; 14 of which resulted in a decision by the professoriate to engage in or to continue to participate in the collective bargaining process. Of the 17, 13 were considered "new" elections, while the other four were challenges to an existing agent by a competing one. In eight of the thirteen "new" elections, faculty selected bargaining agents, while in two, the results are still pending, although at this writing, the pro-collective bargaining vote is greater than that of

"No-Agent." In three elections, "No-Agent" was the faculty choice. An analysis of faculty union organizing and agent elections follows:

# AFT

The American Federation of Teachers and their local affiliates were involved in 12 elections; winning six and losing five, with the results in one still pending. New AFT locals include units at Kishwaukee Community College, Lassen Community College, the University of Maine (Systemwide), and Washington Community College, District XII. The AFT also retained bargaining rights at Portland Community College in Oregon, and their affiliation with APSCUF at the Pennsylvania State College and University System.

At Kishwaukee Community College, the AFT won bargaining rights for a unit of 80 faculty by defeating an independent local, 38-4. At Lassen Community College, the AFT defeated the NEA for the right to represent a unit of 50 faculty by a vote of 31-7. One unit of part-time faculty, 288 members at the University of Maine (Systemwide), joined the ranks of the AFT when they defeated the NEA and "No-Agent" by a vote of 153-28-26.

In elections involving a "change in agent" status, the AFT won bargaining rights from the NEA for a unit of 288 faculty at Washington Community College, District XII in the State of Washington by a vote of 122-90 over the NEA. In another "change in agent" status election in the Pennsylvania State College and University System, the 3,700 member faculty unit voted to retain their affiliation with APSCUF/AFT over that of APSCUF/AFT/AAUP by a vote of 827-299. The former agent had been a three-member consortium consisting of APSCUF, AFT and AAUP and now is a dual affiliation between APSCUF and AFT. The representation rights for one AFT local, Portland Community College was unsuccessfully challenged by the NEA and "No-Agent." In that election the AFT retained bargaining rights by a vote of 207-92-15.

The AFT was involved in three "No-Agent" elections last year. At the University of California System, they were defeated by "No-Agent," of 1734-470 in a representation election for a unit of 3,600 academic researchers. In Illinois, the AFT was defeated by "No-Agent" for a faculty unit of 762 at Illinois State University at Normal by a vote of 383-223. The AAUP, also involved in the same election, received 64 votes. At Northern Illinois University, the UPI-AFT coalition, while victorious in the initial election over AAUP and "No-Agent," was defeated in a run-off by "No-Agent," 398-371.

The AFT was the most active among faculty unions in terms of new organizing in 1986. They were involved in 12 faculty elections; winning six, losing five, with the results of one still pending. Their affiliates, including joint affiliations with other agents, currently represent over 88,000 faculty at 140 colleges and universities for the purpose of collective bargaining.

# NEA

The National Education Association and their affiliates were involved in eight organizing elections this year; winning three, losing four, with the results in one still pending. New NEA locals include the faculty units Oakton Community College in Illinois, Antelope Valley Community College in California, and the Division of Continuing Education of the Massachusetts Community College System. At Oakton, the NEA defeated the AFT by a vote of 78-60 to win bargaining rights for a unit of 149 faculty members. At Antelope Valley, an NEA/CTA consortium defeated the AFT/CFT local by a vote of 100-82 to represent a unit of 250 faculty members. In the largest of the new units to elect an agent this year, the NEA and its affiliate, the MCCC, defeated "No-Agent" by a vote of 631-516 for bargaining rights for a new unit of 1,800 faculty of the Division of Continuing Education, Systemwide, of the Massachusetts Community College System. At Hocking Technical College in Ohio, the NEA and its Ohio affiliate, the OEA, continued to lead in a challenged election to represent 109 faculty members at this institution. The OEA/NEA received 52 votes, "No-Agent" 46 votes, with 25 votes still challenged.

In terms of elections involving established bargaining relationships, the NEA was unsuccessful in its attempt to unseat the AFT for the bargaining rights for 350 faculty at Portland Community College. The NEA received 92 votes and "No-Agent" 15 votes, while AFT continued its certification with 207 votes. The NEA lost the bargaining rights for a unit of 288 faculty members at Washington Community College, District XII to the AFT by a vote of 122-AFT to 90 for NEA. The NEA was not involved in any "No-Agent" votes during 1986.

The NEA and its affiliates continue to represent the largest number of unionized institutions, 207. The number of faculty covered contracts negotiated by NEA affiliates, including joint affiliations, exceeds 77,000.

# AAUP

The American Association of University Professors was involved in six elections this year; winning two and losing four. They are the only faculty agent to have organized a private college, winning bargaining rights for a unit of 20 faculty at the College of Insurance in New York State. In that election the AAUP received 16 votes, while "No-Agent" received one. The AAUP was also successful in retaining bargaining rights at Portland State University for a unit of 548 faculty. The AAUP received 260 votes against 211 for a "No-Agent" challenge.

The AAUP lost representation rights as a member of the APSCUF bargaining agent coalition at the Pennsylvania State College and University System. In a "change of agent status" election concerning affiliation and bargaining rights, APSCUF and either AFT or AAUP, a unit of 3,700 faculty members selected the APSCUF/AFT affiliation over the AAUP by a vote of 827-299.

The AAUP was involved in two elections within the Illinois State University System. At Illinois State University at Normal, the AAUP and AFT were defeated by "No-Agent" for representation rights for a unit of 762 faculty by a vote of 383-"No-Agent," 223-AFT and 64-AAUP. At Northern Illinois University, the AAUP and AFT, competed with "No-Agent" for a unit of 908 faculty. The first election resulted in none of the three receiving a majority of votes cast; UPI-AFT 318, "No-Agent" 273, AAUP 186. In a run-off election between the UPI-AFT and "No-Agent," "No-Agent" received 398, while UPI-AFT received 371.

The AAUP, its locals and joint affiliations represent over 59,000 faculty at 51 colleges and universities.

# Independent

Independent faculty unions were involved in two elections last year, winning one and losing the other. The faculty at Santa Barbara Community College, a unit of 740, elected an "Independent" over "No-Agent" by a vote of 250-37. The other election involving an "Independent" was at Kishwaukee College where they were defeated by the AFT by a vote of 38-4 for the bargaining rights of a unit of 80 faculty.

# "No-Agent"

Three "No-Agent" elections were reported in 1986, each of which involved relatively large bargaining units. In the University of California System, a unit of 3,600 academic researchers rejected unionization and chose "No-Agent" over AFT by a vote of 1734-470. In two institutions in the Illinois State University System, "No-Agent" was the faculty choice instead of unionization. At Illinois State the faculty elected "No-Agent" over the AFT and AAUP by a vote of 383-223-64. In a run-off election at Northern Illinois University, a unit of 908 faculty also rejected collective bargaining. In the first election, the UPI-AFT received 318 votes, "No-Agent" 273 and AAUP 186, necessitating a second election. It is interesting to note that the combined faculty pro-collective bargaining vote in the initial election was 504 in favor of one or the other agents, while 233 selected "No-Agent." However, since none of the parties received a majority, a run-off was required. In that election, "No-Agent" defeated the UPI-AFT by 26 votes out of nearly 800 votes cast by a vote of 398-371.

# Strikes

There were 12 reported faculty work stoppages during 1986, nine of which were considered "fall back-to-school" strikes. Of the 12 strikes, half involved faculty at two-year institutions, while the other six were at four-year institutions. Three private colleges, Fairleigh Dickinson, Roger Williams and the Berklee College of Music were involved in stoppages.

The nine "fall back-to-school" strikes at the outset of the 1986-1987 fall semester was the highest reported total during the last seven years. Of these strikes, four occurred at two-year institutions, while five were at four-year colleges. The average length of these strikes was 9.1 days. Set forth below are the institutions, size of faculty unit, faculty agent and length of strike data. "Fall back-to-school" strikes occurred at:

1) Bellevue Community College: 250 full/part-time faculty, NEA, 7-days;
2) Fairleigh Dickinson University: 495 full/part-time faculty, AAUP, 7 days;
3) Lake Land College: 104 faculty, AFT, 20 days;
4) Mercer Community College: 127 faculty, NEA, 3 days;

5) Mott Community College: 196 faculty, NEA, 7 days;

6) Roger Williams College: 108 full-time and 44 part-time faculty, NEA, 2 days;

7) Temple University: 1,052 faculty, AAUP, 15 days;

8) Thornton Community College: 138 faculty, AFT, 35 days;

9) Wayne State University: 1,378 faculty, AAUP, one day.

Strikes reported during the 1986 spring semester included two simultaneous 14-day stoppages at Berklee College of Music, one each by full-time and part-time faculty. Both units are represented by the AFT. The other spring strike occurred at Jefferson Technical College where the NEA local engaged in a 96-day strike over the terms and conditions of their initial contract. The unit at Jefferson consists of 46 faculty members. For a complete analysis of work stoppages during 1986, the reader is referred to NCSCBHP *Newsletter*, Vol. 14, No. 5.

# Legislation

No faculty collective bargaining enabling legislation was passed during 1986. While several bills were discussed, most notably in Wisconsin, the State of Washington and Maryland, none were enacted. The number of states with enabling legislation for collective bargaining now stands at 26. Additionally, four states allow collective bargaining pursuant to the regulatory framework established by university governing boards. Faculty organizations continue to be active in lobbying efforts to secure collective bargaining legislation in those states without bills. For a complete listing of collective bargaining legislation, see *Directory of Contracts and Bargaining Agents, Table No. Eleven.*

# Demographic Analysis

Accounting for an exact number of college faculty is a troublesome assignment since the total is relatively fluid. Furthermore, using any one date as a reference point subjects the researcher to certain statistical biases inherent in that selection. Nevertheless, we have developed our own procedure which is set forth below:

1) The number of institutions and campuses is obtained from the National Center for Education Statistics (NCES), the Higher Education Directory and the NCSCBHEP data bank. The last NCES reports are for the 1982-1983 academic year, the HED data is as of 1985, while NCSCBHEP Reports reflect the period through January 1, 1987.

2) The total number of faculty is derived from NCES statistics and is not divided into full- and part-time. Unit size is tabulated from reporting institutions, faculty organizations and our own data bank. Faculty are recorded as being represented by collective bargaining agents and agreements, and do not reflect union membership.

The number of faculty covered by collective bargaining increased from 195,570 to 208,147, a rise of 6.4%. Part of this growth is due to improved reporting procedures by the national faculty organizations and individual institutions and to better research methods being employed at NCSCBHEP, and does not necessarily reflect increased organizing.

The number of public sector faculty represented by faculty unions increased by 6.7% from 186,326 in 1986 to 198,647 in 1987, while a 2.7% rise, 9,244 to 9,500 was reported in private college faculties represented by unions during this time period. Adjunct faculty are included in the total count as efforts to isolate this category have not yet proved workable. As long as faculty units continue to contain both full- and part-time faculty, difficulties will be experienced in this calculation. Although the *Directory* includes data pertaining to faculty collective bargaining agreements in Canada, the demographic analysis reflects only colleges in the United States.

# First Contract Signed

Collective bargining involves a time lag between unit certification and the negotiation of the initial contract. Six "first faculty bargaining contracts" were signed in 1986, all of which involved units which achieved their initial certifications in previous years.

The University of California System signed two "first contracts," one with nurses and the other with lecturers. The California Nurses Association was originally certified as agent for this 5,000 member unit in 1983. The lecturers, a unit of 1877 represented by the AFT since 1984, also signed their first agreement. A faculty unit of 402 at Cabrillo College certified and represented as an AFT affiliate in 1984, signed their initial contract. Two Ohio community colleges, Jefferson Technical and Terra Technical, both represented by the NEA, signed initial contracts in 1986. The NEA obtained bargaining rights for these units in 1985. In Illinois, the AFT, representing the 97 faculty at Rend Lake College since 1985, also signed their initial agreement.

# Summary and Conclusions

Nineteen hundred and eighty-six may be viewed as a year in which the proponents of faculty collective bargaining achieved mixed results. While the number of collective bargaining units and contracts, as well as the number of faculty represented is higher than it has ever been, two major setbacks for academic unionists were noted.

The "No-Agent" elections at Illinois State University and Northern Illinois University, as well as the contested election at Sangamon State, represent long and devisive struggles over the issue of faculty collective bargaining. The failure of the AFT-UPI and the AAUP to present a united front at Sangamon, where the results are still pending, and at Northern, where "No-Agent" won in a run-off election, probably accounted for the defeat of faculty unionization at these institutions. At Sangamon, 73 votes were needed to elect a faculty agent, the combined pro-collective bargaining vote yielded 83, however, that was split between 69 for the AFT and 14 for the AAUP. At Northern, the combined vote of AFT-UPI and AAUP generated a vote of 504 for collective bargaining against 273 for "No-Agent." This margin of almost 2-1 favor of an agent, without any one party receiving a majority, resulted in a run-off election in which "No-Agent" narrowly defeated the AFT by 27 votes out of 768 cast. For reasons that are unique to the academic community, certain faculty who voted for a bargaining agent in the initial election chose "No-Agent" in the run-off as opposed to an agent from another organization. This phenomenon remains peculiar to academic collective bargaining where the failure of the three national organizations to present a united front continues to result in "No-Agent" wins.

While the number of agents and contracts have increased, the absence of any new enabling legislation is expected to produce a leveling off in public sector organizing. In those states where faculty unions lobbied for new legislation, efforts are expected to continue; however, in the absence of any new bills, faculty organizing in those states will become more difficult. The new area of union growth appears to be in organizing the unorganized in those states where legislation has already been enacted. Further attempts to organize adjunct faculty, as was done this year in the University of Maine and the Massachusetts Community College Systems are also expected. Other potential areas of new unionization drives are in selected groups of academic researchers, support staff, and nontenure-track faculty members.

While challenges and raids by one agent against another for the rights to represent existing faculty units will probably continue, most of those involve local issues and do not appear to constitute a trend or a predictable pattern. No evidence is available to indicate any change in the cooperative postures of the three national organizations vis-a-vis each other. The failure of faculty unionization at Northern and Sangamon (thus far) are illustrative of this point.

The number of *Yeshiva*-related decertifications is expected to diminish since most of the cases in the litigation pipeline have already been adjudicated. There are no new lead cases currently before the U.S. Supreme Court concerning the application of the doctrine at this time. Observers have noted, however, that the *Yeshiva* question may now shift to challenges to public sector institutions where collective bargaining legislation is already in place.

The gap between the private sector and public sector is expected to continue to grow. With no statutory or judicial relief predicted for private sector faculty who wish to bargain in spite of the legal environment, faculty unions are devoting their energies, almost exclusively, to public sector organizing. As a result, the number of faculty at private sector colleges who are unionized will either diminish or stabilize. Faculty collective bargaining continues to remain a viable form of governing one's employment relationship and is solidly entrenched in our nation's colleges and universities.

Table One

Faculty Bargaining Agents and Collective Bargaining Agreements
Public and Private Institutions, 1974 – 1986

Table Two

# Faculty Bargaining Agents and Collective Bargaining Agreements in Two- and Four-year Institutions, 1974 – 1986

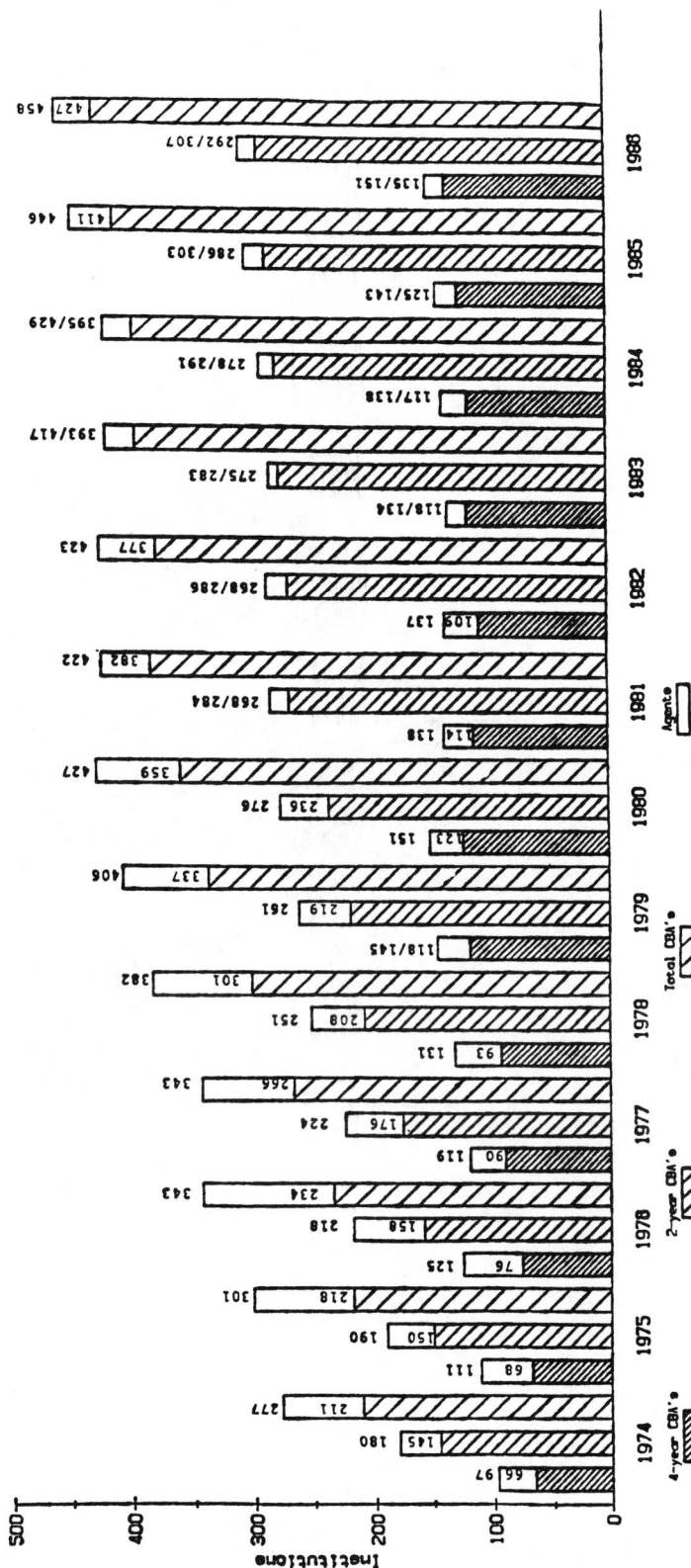

Institutions

Legend: Agents | Total CBA's | 2-year CBA's | 4-year CBA's

1974: 66/97; 145/180; 211/277

1975: 68/111; 150/190; 218/301

1976: 76/125; 158/218; 234/343

1977: 90/119; 176/224; 266/343

1978: 93/131; 208/251; 301/382

1979: 118/145; 219/261; 337/406

1980: 123/151; 236/276; 359/427

1981: 114/138; 268/284; 382/422

1982: 101/137; 268/286; 377/423

1983: 118/134; 275/283; 393/417

1984: 117/138; 278/291; 395/429

1985: 125/143; 286/303; 411/446

1986: 135/151; 292/307; 427/458

**Table Three**

**Recognized Faculty Bargaining Agents in Two and Four-Year Institutions, 1987**

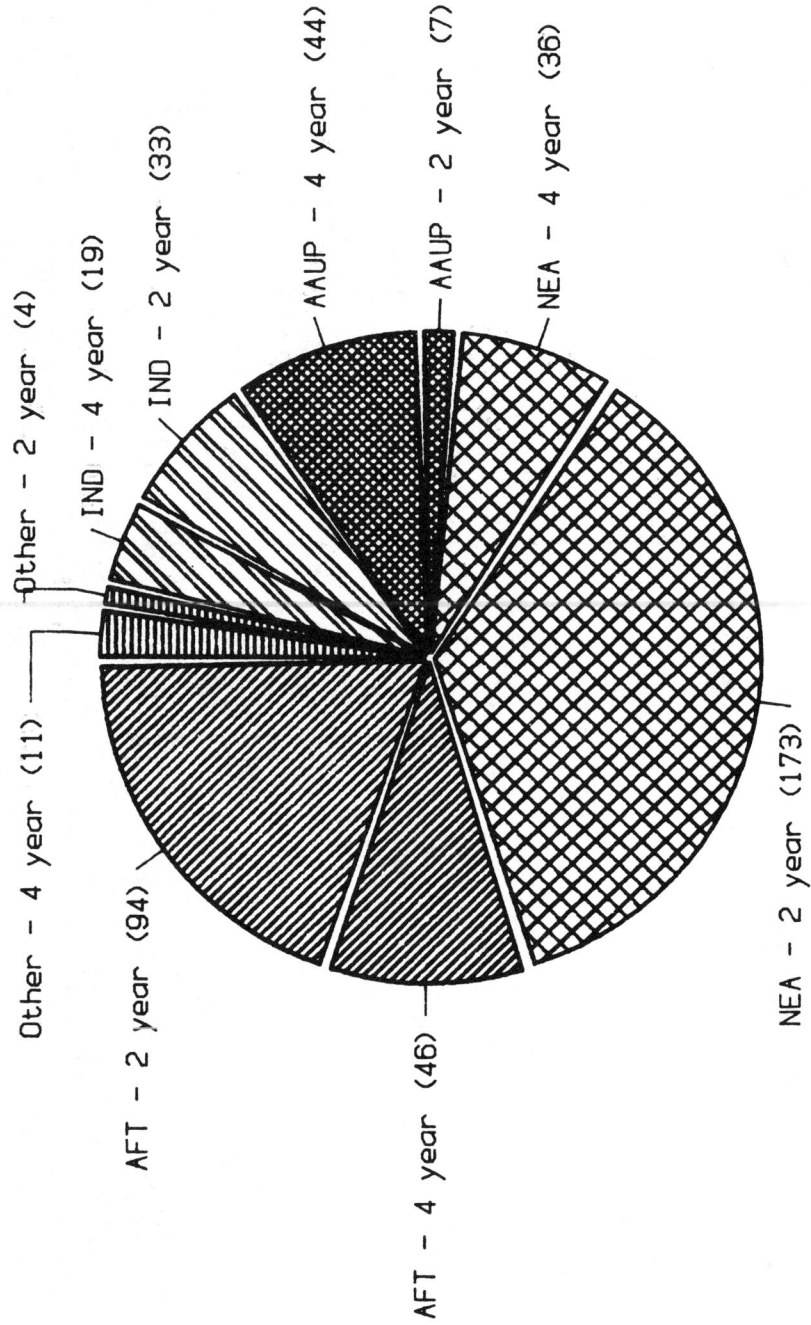

Other – 2 year  (4)

IND – 4 year  (19)

IND – 2 year  (33)

AAUP – 4 year  (44)

AAUP – 2 year  (7)

NEA – 4 year  (36)

Other – 4 year  (11)

AFT – 2 year  (94)

AFT – 4 year  (46)

NEA – 2 year  (173)

Dual agent affiliation membership status credited to both organizations.

TABLE FOUR

RECOGNIZED FACULTY BARGAINING AGENTS -- PUBLIC AND PRIVATE
1987

| | YEAR | AAUP | AFT | NEA | IND | AAUP/AFT | AFT/NEA | AAUP/NEA | AFT/IND | AAUP/IND | AFGE | AFSCME | OTHER | TOTAL |
|---|---|---|---|---|---|---|---|---|---|---|---|---|---|---|
| PUBLIC INSTITUTIONS | 4 | 23 | 25 | 20 | 10 | 1 | 0 | 2 | 0 | 0 | 2 | 1 | 4 | 88 |
| | 2 | 3 | 87 | 166 | 29 | 1 | 1 | 1 | 0 | 1 | 0 | 2 | 2 | 293 |
| TOTAL | | 26 | 112 | 186 | 39 | 2 | 1 | 3 | 0 | 1 | 2 | 3 | 6 | N=381 |
| PRIVATE INSTITUTIONS | 4 | 17 | 19 | 14 | 7 | 0 | 0 | 0 | 1 | 1 | 0 | 0 | 4 | 63 |
| | 2 | 1 | 5 | 5 | 3 | 0 | 0 | 0 | 0 | 0 | 0 | 0 | 0 | 14 |
| TOTAL | | 18 | 24 | 19 | 10 | 0 | 0 | 0 | 1 | 1 | 0 | 0 | 4 | N=77 |
| SUMMARY OF RECOGNIZED AGENTS | 4 | 40 | 44 | 34 | 17 | 1 | 0 | 2 | 1 | 1 | 2 | 1 | 8 | 151 |
| | 2 | 4 | 92 | 171 | 32 | 1 | 1 | 1 | 0 | 1 | 0 | 2 | 2 | 307 |
| TOTAL | | 44 | 136 | 205 | 49 | 2 | 1 | 3 | 1 | 2 | 2 | 3 | 10 | N=458 |

TABLE FIVE

FACULTY COLLECTIVE BARGAINING AGREEMENTS
1987

| | YEAR | AAUP | AFT | NEA | IND | AAUP/ AFT | AFT/ NEA | AAUP/ NEA | AFT/ IND | AAUP/ IND | AFGE | AFSCME | OTHER | TOTAL |
|---|---|---|---|---|---|---|---|---|---|---|---|---|---|---|
| PUBLIC INSTITUTIONS | 4 | 23 | 21 | 20 | 6 | 1 | 0 | 2 | 0 | 0 | 2 | 1 | 3 | 79 |
| | 2 | 3 | 81 | 163 | 24 | 1 | 1 | 1 | 0 | 1 | 0 | 2 | 2 | 279 |
| TOTAL | | 26 | 102 | 183 | 30 | 2 | 1 | 3 | 0 | 1 | 2 | 3 | 5 | N=358 |
| PRIVATE INSTITUTIONS | 4 | 16 | 18 | 12 | 6 | 0 | 0 | 0 | 1 | 1 | 0 | 0 | 2 | 56 |
| | 2 | 1 | 5 | 5 | 2 | 0 | 0 | 0 | 0 | 0 | 0 | 0 | 0 | 13 |
| TOTAL | | 17 | 23 | 17 | 8 | 0 | 0 | 0 | 1 | 1 | 0 | 0 | 2 | N=69 |
| SUMMARY OF BARGAINING AGREEMENTS | 4 | 39 | 39 | 32 | 12 | 1 | 0 | 2 | 1 | 1 | 2 | 1 | 5 | 135 |
| | 2 | 4 | 86 | 168 | 26 | 1 | 1 | 1 | 0 | 1 | 0 | 2 | 2 | 292 |
| TOTAL | | 43 | 125 | 200 | 38 | 2 | 1 | 3 | 1 | 2 | 2 | 3 | 7 | N=427 |

## TABLE SIX

### ANALYSIS OF BARGAINING AGENTS & COLLECTIVE BARGAINING AGREEMENTS

| | YEAR | AAUP | AFT | NEA | IND | AAUP/AFT | AFT/NEA | AAUP/NEA | AFT/IND | AAUP/IND | AFGE | AFSCME | OTHER | TOTAL |
|---|---|---|---|---|---|---|---|---|---|---|---|---|---|---|
| RECOGNIZED AGENTS | 4 | 40 | 44 | 34 | 17 | 1 | 0 | 2 | 1 | 1 | 2 | 1 | 8 | 151 |
| | 2 | 4 | 92 | 171 | 32 | 1 | 1 | 1 | 0 | 1 | 0 | 2 | 2 | 307 |
| TOTAL | | 44 | 136 | 205 | 49 | 2 | 1 | 3 | 1 | 2 | 2 | 3 | 10 | N=458 |
| COLLECTIVE BARGAINING AGREEMENTS | 4 | 39 | 39 | 32 | 12 | 1 | 0 | 2 | 1 | 1 | 2 | 1 | 5 | 135 |
| | 2 | 4 | 86 | 168 | 26 | 1 | 1 | 1 | 0 | 1 | 0 | 2 | 2 | 292 |
| TOTAL | | 43 | 125 | 200 | 38 | 2 | 1 | 3 | 1 | 2 | 2 | 3 | 7 | N=427 |
| BARGAINING UNITS WITHOUT AGREEMENTS | | 1 | 11 | 5 | 11 | 0 | 0 | 0 | 0 | 0 | 0 | 0 | 3 | N=31 |

**Table Seven**

# Faculty Represented by Certified Bargaining Agents, 1987

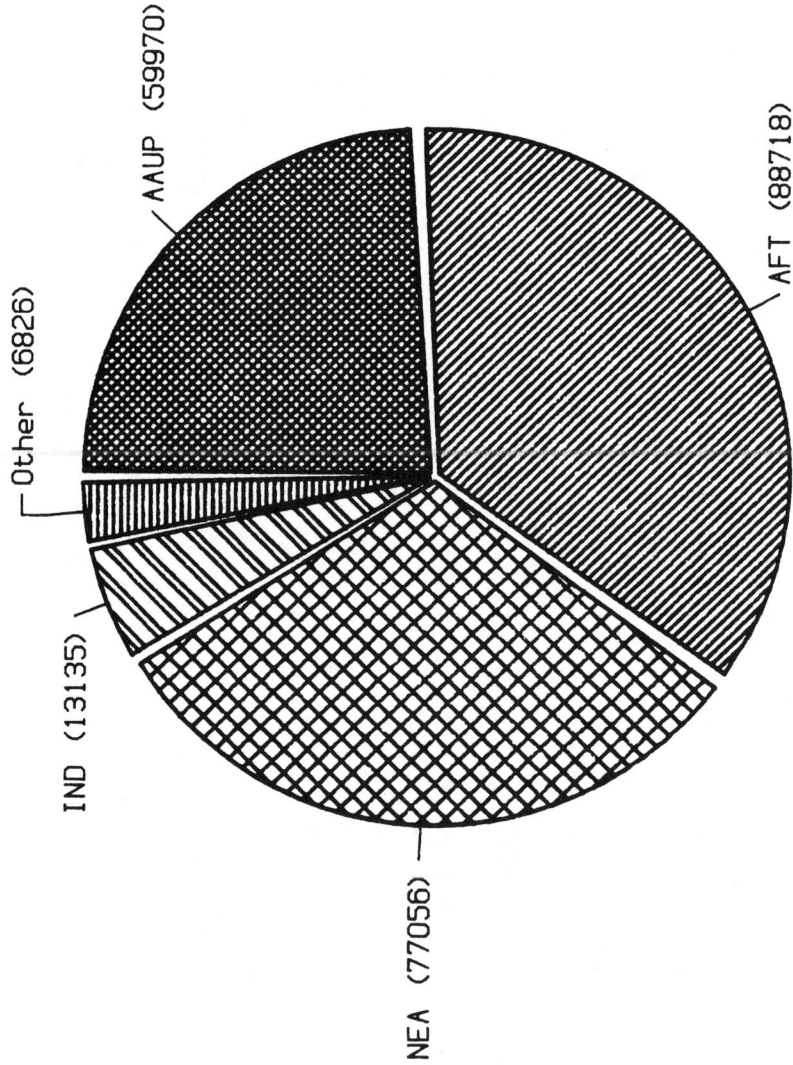

AAUP (59970)

AFT (88718)

Other (6826)

IND (13135)

NEA (77056)

Dual agent affiliation membership status credited to both organizations.

TABLE EIGHT[1]

FACULTY REPRESENTED BY CERTIFIED BARGAINING AGENTS
IN PUBLIC AND PRIVATE, TWO- AND FOUR-YEAR INSTITUTIONS
1987

| | YEAR | AAUP | AFT | NEA | IND | AAUP/ AFT | AFT/ NEA | AAUP/ NEA | AFT/ IND | AAUP/ IND | AFGE | AFSCME | OTHER | TOTAL |
|---|---|---|---|---|---|---|---|---|---|---|---|---|---|---|
| PUBLIC | 4 | 18,964 | 37,509 | 18,785 | 2,849 | 14,521 | 0 | 20,700 | 0 | 0 | 126 | 279 | 5,450 | 119,183 |
| | 2 | 813 | 33,546 | 35,055 | 7,970 | 120 | 189 | 285 | 0 | 850 | 0 | 125 | 511 | 79,464 |
| TOTAL | | 19,777 | 71,055 | 53,840 | 10,819 | 14,641 | 189 | 20,985 | 0 | 850 | 126 | 404 | 5,961 | N=198,647 |
| PRIVATE | 4 | 2,679 | 2,376 | 1,919 | 407 | 0 | 0 | 0 | 35 | 858 | 0 | 0 | 335 | 8,609 |
| | 2 | 180 | 422 | 123 | 166 | 0 | 0 | 0 | 0 | 0 | 0 | 0 | 0 | 891 |
| TOTAL | | 2,859 | 2,798 | 2,042 | 573 | 0 | 0 | 0 | 35 | 858 | 0 | 0 | 335 | N=9,500 |
| SUMMARY OF UNIT SIZE | 4 | 21,643 | 39,885 | 20,704 | 3,256 | 14,521 | 0 | 20,700 | 35 | 858 | 126 | 279 | 5,785 | 127,792 |
| | 2 | 993 | 33,968 | 35,178 | 8,136 | 120 | 189 | 285 | 0 | 850 | 0 | 125 | 511 | 80,355 |
| TOTAL | | 22,636 | 73,853 | 55,882 | 11,392 | 14,641 | 189 | 20,985 | 35 | 1,708 | 126 | 404 | 6,296 | N=208,147 |

[1]Represents both full-time and part-time faculty members included in certified bargaining units. No distinction is made with respect to union membership.

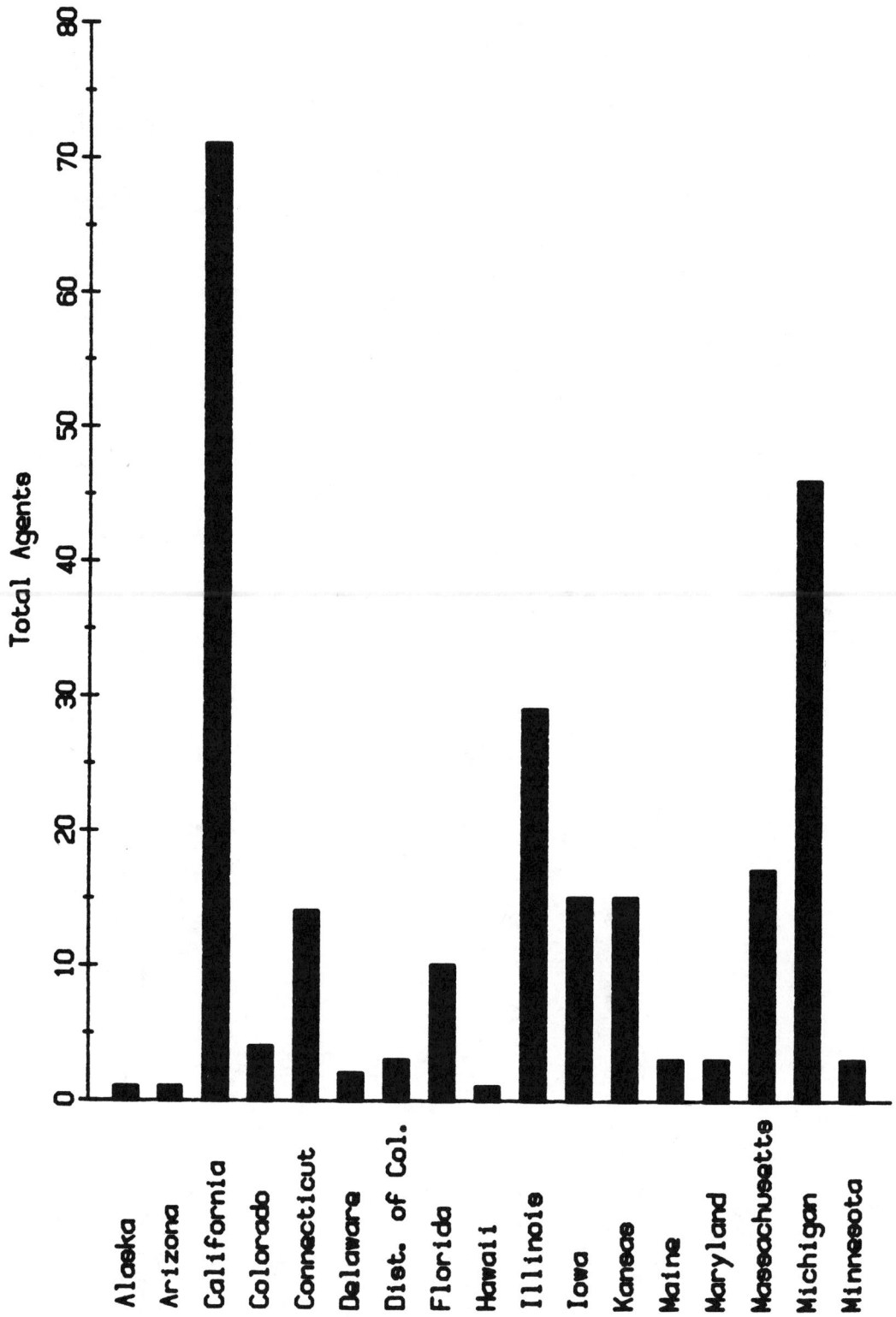

Table Nine
Geographic Distribution of Faculty Bargaining Agents, 1987

Total Agents

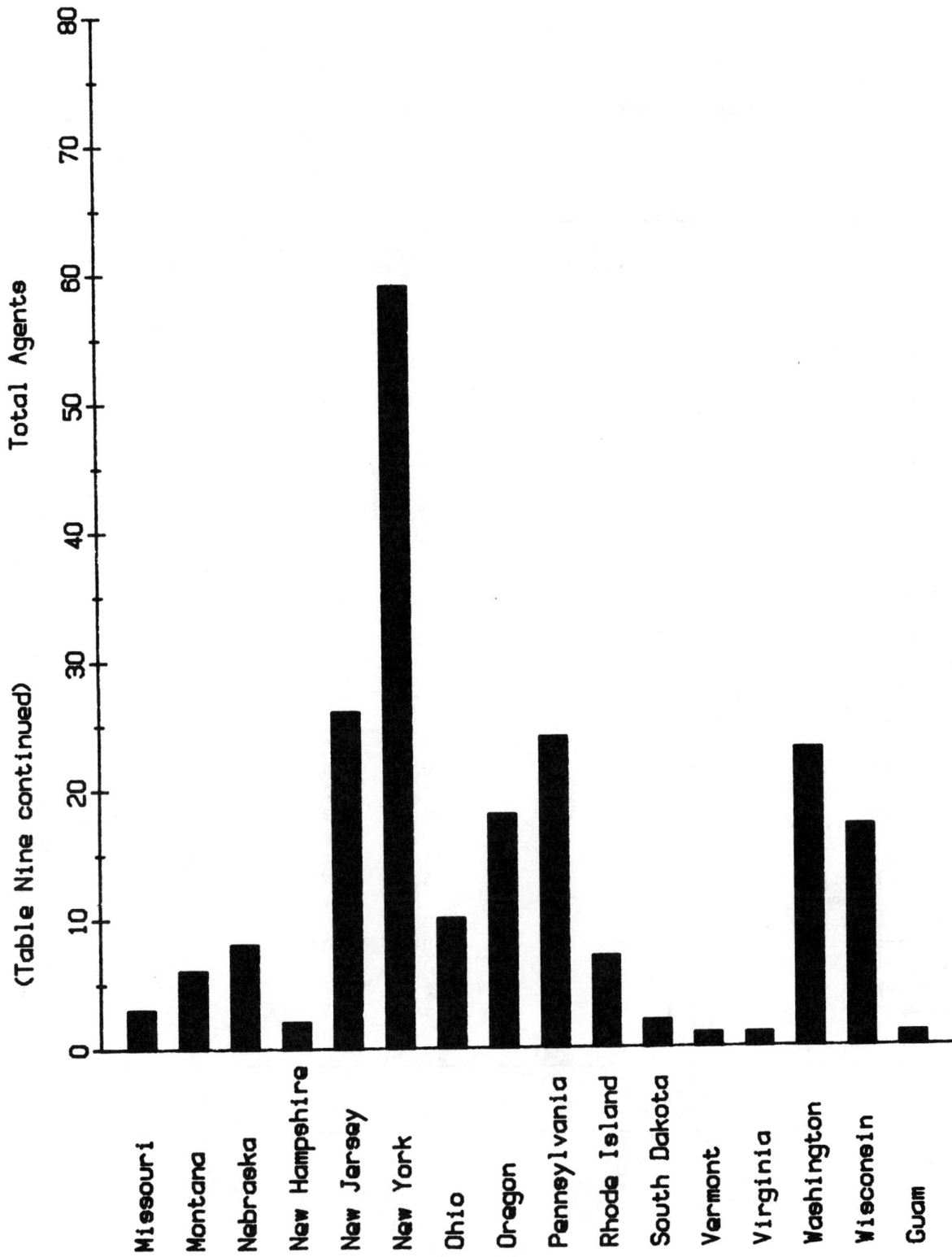

(Table Nine continued)

TABLE TEN

GEOGRAPHIC DISTRIBUTION OF BARGAINING AGENTS AND COLLECTIVE
BARGAINING AGREEMENTS IN TWO- AND FOUR-YEAR INSTITUTIONS
1987

| State | 4-Year Agents/Contracts | | 2-Year Agents/Contracts | | Total Agents/Contracts | |
|-------|---|---|---|---|---|---|
| Alaska | 0 | 0 | 1 | 1 | 1 | 1 |
| Arizona | 0 | 0 | 1 | 1 | 1 | 1 |
| California | 12 | 11 | 59 | 56 | 71 | 67 |
| Colorado | 3 | 2 | 1 | 0 | 4 | 2 |
| Connecticut | 9 | 9 | 5 | 4 | 14 | 13 |
| Delaware | 2 | 2 | 0 | 0 | 2 | 2 |
| District of Columbia | 3 | 3 | 0 | 0 | 3 | 3 |
| Florida | 3 | 2 | 8 | 7 | 11 | 9 |
| Hawaii | 1 | 1 | 0 | 0 | 1 | 1 |
| Illinois | 1 | 1 | 28 | 26 | 29 | 27 |
| Iowa | 2 | 2 | 13 | 13 | 15 | 15 |
| Kansas | 1 | 1 | 14 | 13 | 15 | 14 |
| Maine | 2 | 1 | 1 | 1 | 3 | 2 |
| Maryland | 1 | 0 | 2 | 2 | 3 | 2 |
| Massachusetts | 12 | 10 | 5 | 4 | 17 | 14 |
| Michigan | 17 | 16 | 29 | 29 | 46 | 45 |
| Minnesota | 2 | 2 | 1 | 1 | 3 | 3 |
| Missouri | 1 | 1 | 1 | 1 | 2 | 2 |
| Montana | 4 | 4 | 2 | 2 | 6 | 6 |
| Nebraska | 3 | 2 | 5 | 5 | 8 | 7 |
| New Hampshire | 2 | 2 | 0 | 0 | 2 | 2 |
| New Jersey | 9 | 8 | 17 | 17 | 26 | 25 |
| New York | 24 | 19 | 40 | 39 | 64 | 58 |
| Ohio | 7 | 7 | 8 | 8 | 15 | 15 |
| Oregon | 6 | 6 | 13 | 11 | 19 | 17 |
| Pennsylvania | 10 | 9 | 14 | 14 | 24 | 23 |
| Rhode Island | 6 | 6 | 1 | 1 | 7 | 7 |
| South Dakota | 2 | 2 | 0 | 0 | 2 | 2 |
| Vermont | 1 | 1 | 0 | 0 | 1 | 1 |
| Virginia | 1 | 1 | 0 | 0 | 1 | 1 |
| Washington | 1 | 1 | 23 | 21 | 24 | 22 |
| Wisconsin | 2 | 2 | 15 | 15 | 17 | 17 |
| Guam | 1 | 1 | 0 | 0 | 1 | 1 |
| TOTAL | 151 | 135 | 307 | 292 | 458 | 427 |

## TABLE ELEVEN

### COLLEGE CLOSINGS[1]

| Institution | State | Agent | Unit Size | 2/4 Year | Closing Date |
|---|---|---|---|---|---|
| *Central YMCA Community College | IL | AFT | 80 | 2 | 1983 |
| *Colorado Women's College | CO | AAUP | 42 | 4 | 1982 |
| *Detroit Institute of Technology | MI | NEA | 34 | 4 | 1981 |
| *Milton College | WI | AFT | 35 | 4 | 1982 |
| *Nasson College | ME | AFT | 30 | 4 | 1983 |
| *Shaw College at Detroit[2] | MI | NEA | 37 | 4 | 1983 |
| Springfield Campus - University of South Dakota | SD | NEA | -- | 4 | 1984 |

[1]Institution previously cited in the _Directory_ as having negotiated collective bargaining agreements.

[2]U. S. Bankruptcy Court judge orders permanent closing of institution. (March, 1984)

# TABLE TWELVE

BARGAINING AGENTS

| | |
|---|---|
| AAUP | American Association of University Professors |
| ACCF | Associated Community College Faculties |
| ACPU | Association Canadien des Professeur's d'Universite |
| AFGE | American Federation of Government Employees |
| AFSCME | American Federation of State, County and Municipal Employees |
| AFT | American Federation of Teachers |
| APSCUF | Association of Pennsylvania State College and University Faculties |
| CAUT | Canadian Association of University Teachers |
| CEQ | Centrale de l'Enseignement du Quebec |
| CFA | California Faculty Association |
| CNA | California Nurses Association |
| CSEA | California State Employees Association |
| CSN | Confederation des Syndicats Nationaux |
| CTA | California Teachers Association |
| CWA | Communication Workers of America |
| ELIFA | English Language Institute Faculty Association |
| FAC | Florida Academic Congress |
| FAPUQ | Federations des Associations de Professeurs des Universites du Quebec |
| FUSA | Faculty United Service Association |
| GFT | Guam Federation of Teachers |
| IFT | Illinois Federation of Teachers |
| IND | Independent |
| MCCC | Massachusetts Community College Council |
| MSP | Massachusetts Society of Professors |
| MTA | Massachusetts Teachers Association |
| NEA | National Education Association |
| NYEA | New York Educator's Association |
| NYS Fed. Phy. Dent. | New York State Federation of Physicians and Dentists |
| NYSUT | New York State United Teachers |
| OEA | Ohio Education Association |
| OEA | Oregon Education Association |
| OPEIU | Office of Professional Employees International Union |
| OPSEU | Ontario Public Service Employees Union |
| PaFT | Pennsylvania Federation of Teachers |
| PCFA | Post College Faculty Association |
| PSC | Professional Staff Congress |
| SCEA | State Colleges Education Association (Nebraska) |
| SCFA | Santa Cruz Faculty Association |
| SEIU | Service Employees' International Union |
| SPSE | Society of Professional Scientists and Engineers |
| SRFBC | Simon's Rock Faculty Bargaining Council |
| TAA | Teaching Assistants Association |
| UAPD | Union of American Physicians and Dentists |
| UCCFF | United Community College Faculty of Florida |
| UEA | University Education Association |
| UFF | United Faculty of Florida |
| UFL | University Federation of Librarians |
| UHPA | United Hawaii Professional Assembly |
| UPC | United Professors of California |
| UPI | United Professionals of Illinois |
| UPU | Union De Profesores Universitaros |
| UUP | United University Professions |
| WEA | Wisconsin Education Association |

TABLE THIRTEEN

CAMPUSES REPRESENTED BY RECOGNIZED FACULTY
BARGAINING AGENTS - PUBLIC AND PRIVATE
1987

| | YEAR | AAUP | AFT | NEA | IND | AAUP/ AFT | AFT/ NEA | AAUP/ NEA | AFT/ IND | AAUP/ IND | AFGE | AFSCME | OTHER | TOTAL |
|---|---|---|---|---|---|---|---|---|---|---|---|---|---|---|
| PUBLIC INSTITUTIONS | 4 | 42 | 110 | 75 | 14 | 12 | 0 | 22 | 0 | 0 | 0 | 4 | 66 | 347 |
| | 2 | 13 | 182 | 286 | 49 | 9 | 1 | 10 | 0 | 12 | 2 | 8 | 4 | 574 |
| TOTAL | | 55 | 292 | 361 | 63 | 21 | 1 | 32 | 0 | 12 | 2 | 12 | 70 | N=921 |
| PRIVATE INSTITUTIONS | 4 | 21 | 19 | 15 | 8 | 0 | 0 | 0 | 1 | 2 | 0 | 0 | 9 | 75 |
| | 2 | 2 | 7 | 5 | 2 | 0 | 0 | 0 | 0 | 0 | 0 | 0 | 0 | 16 |
| TOTAL | | 23 | 26 | 20 | 10 | 0 | 0 | 0 | 1 | 2 | 0 | 0 | 9 | N=91 |
| SUMMARY | 4 | 63 | 129 | 90 | 22 | 12 | 0 | 22 | 1 | 2 | 2 | 4 | 75 | 422 |
| | 2 | 15 | 189 | 291 | 51 | 9 | 1 | 10 | 0 | 12 | 0 | 8 | 4 | 590 |
| TOTAL | | 78 | 318 | 381 | 73 | 21 | 1 | 32 | 1 | 14 | 2 | 12 | 79 | N=1,012 |

TABLE FOURTEEN

## The Extent of Faculty Unionization
## by Two- and Four-year Campuses, 1987

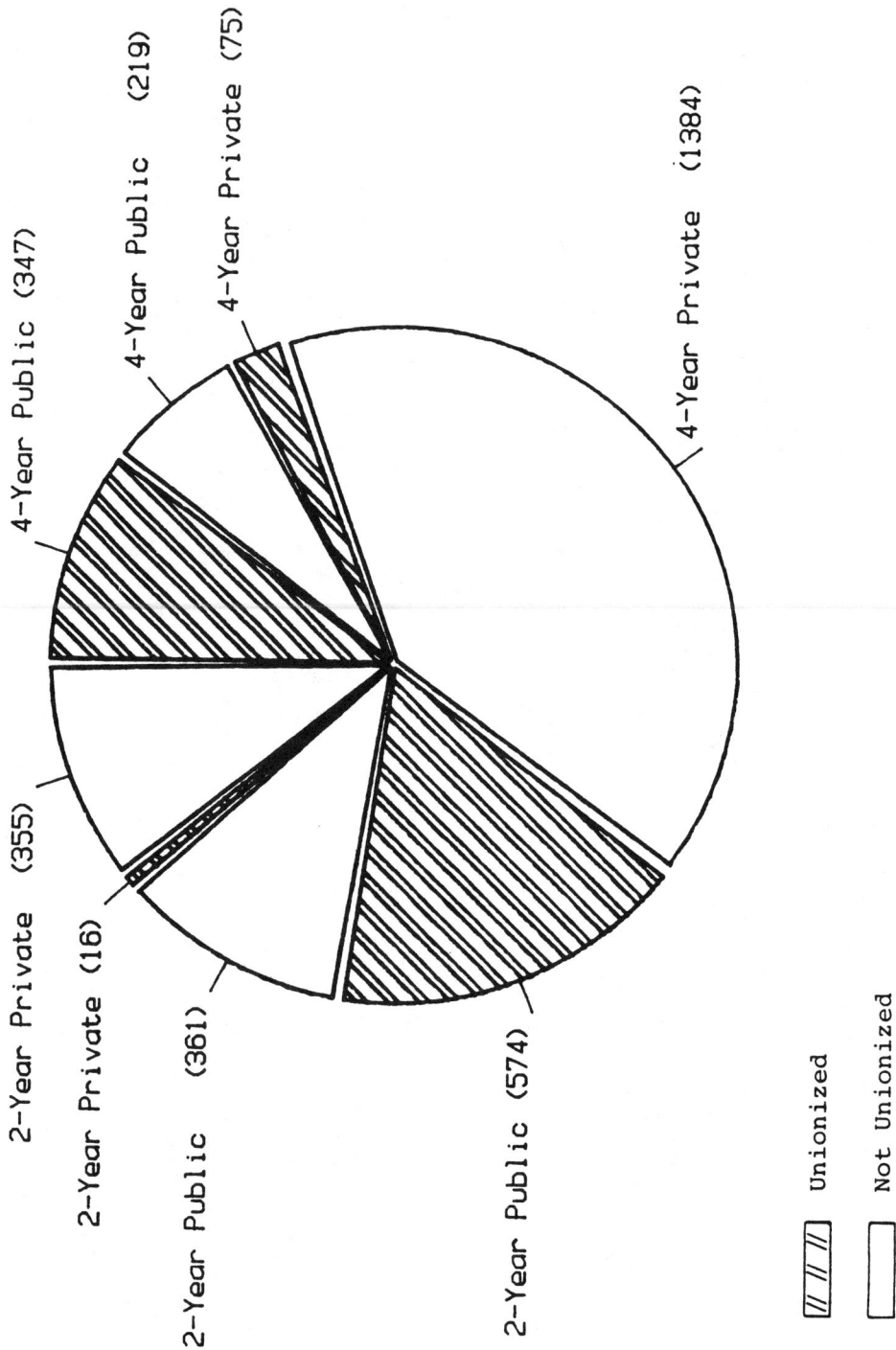

- 4-Year Public (347)
- 4-Year Public (219)
- 4-Year Private (75)
- 4-Year Private (1384)
- 2-Year Private (355)
- 2-Year Private (16)
- 2-Year Public (361)
- 2-Year Public (574)

Unionized

Not Unionized

for Tables 1-14

Source: Directory of Faculty Contracts and Bargaining Agents in
Institutions of Higher Education, Volume 13, January 1987
(The National Center for the Study of Collective Bargaining
in Higher Education and the Professions, Baruch College,
City University of New York)

# Corporate Aid to Education

# Part I.
# National Trends in Corporate Support of Education

Corporate support of education rose to an estimated $1.875 billion in 1985, an increase of 10.3 percent over the revised estimate of $1.700 billion for 1984. This increase of $175 million occurred despite a 5.3 percent decline in pretax net income (PTNI) to the second-lowest level since profits peaked in 1979. The share of corporate pretax net income given in support of education, 0.84 percent, is the highest since 1950, the first year for which there is an estimate.

Total corporate contributions exhibit a similar pattern. They rose by $400 million, 10 percent above 1984, to reach an estimated $4.4 billion. Again, because of the decline in profits, the 1.97 percent of PTNI represented by corporate gifts is the highest level on record.

During the 15-year span covered in **Table I**, there have been three periods when pretax net income declined—1974-75, 1979-82, and 1984-85. In 1975, gifts to all causes and to education both remained at about the same level as in the previous year despite the profit decline. For the other two periods the situation is dramatically different. Both total contributions and support of education have grown in the face of diminishing or stagnant profits. Profits in 1985 were 13.2 percent below their 1979 peak of $257.2 billion, yet both total and education contributions were approximately twice their 1979 levels.

In constant dollars, profits have fallen by 42 percent since 1978, while over the same period contributions to all causes and to education have increased by 28 percent and 46 percent respectively, again in constant dollars. This suggests that the corporate commitment to charitable contributions generally, and to education in particular, remains very strong despite the profit setbacks.

The ability of corporate contributions programs to expand during periods of profit decline has been due in large part to the existence of corporate foundations. They are the buffer against changes in corporate fortunes. When parent companies reduce their contributions during periods of stagnant profits, the foundations maintain and even increase their grants by using earnings on their assets, by drawing down assets or by a combination of the two. In periods of high profits, on the other hand, corporations pay into their foundations more than the foundations pay out and thus rebuild foundation assets.

## Table I
## National Trends in Corporate Pretax Net Income and Contributions

| Year | Corporate Pretax Net Income* (billions of dollars) | Corporate Contributions** (millions of dollars) | | Contributions as a Percentage of Corporate Pretax Net Income | | Educational Support as a Percentage of Total Contributions |
|---|---|---|---|---|---|---|
| | | Total** | Education*** | Total | Education | |
| 1970 | 75.4 | 797 | 320 | 1.06 | 0.42 | 40.2 |
| 1971 | 86.6 | 865 | 345 | 1.00 | 0.40 | 39.9 |
| 1972 | 100.6 | 1,009 | 365 | 1.00 | 0.36 | 36.2 |
| 1973 | 125.6 | 1,174 | 410 | 0.93 | 0.33 | 34.9 |
| 1974 | 136.7 | 1,200 | 445 | 0.88 | 0.33 | 37.1 |
| 1975 | 132.1 | 1,202 | 450 | 0.91 | 0.34 | 37.4 |
| 1976 | 166.3 | 1,487 | 560 | 0.89 | 0.34 | 37.7 |
| 1977 | 200.4r | 1,791 | 665 | 0.89r | 0.33r | 37.1 |
| 1978 | 233.5r | 2,084 | 780 | 0.89r | 0.33r | 37.4 |
| 1979 | 257.2r | 2,288 | 880 | 0.89r | 0.34r | 38.5 |
| 1980 | 237.1r | 2,359 | 980 | .99r | 0.41r | 41.5 |
| 1981 | 226.5r | 2,514 | 1,090 | 1.11r | 0.48r | 43.4 |
| 1982 | 169.6r | 2,906 | 1,250r | 1.71r | 0.74r | 43.0r |
| 1983 | 207.6r | 3,627r | 1,525r | 1.74r | 0.73r | 42.0r |
| 1984 | 235.7 | 4,000***r | 1,700r | 1.70r | 0.72r | 42.5r |
| 1985 | 223.2 | 4,400*** | 1,875 | 1.97 | 0.84 | 42.6 |

*U.S. Department of Commerce.
**Internal Revenue Service.
***CFAE estimate.
r Revised.

*Note:* The figures for total corporate contributions and corporate contributions to education are not completely comparable. The former is an IRS figure that *includes* company grants to their own sponsored foundations and *excludes* the gifts and grants made by these foundations. As a consequence, they understate the consolidated total of corporate and corporate-foundation contributions for the period after 1979 and other years in which foundation giving is larger than company grants to their foundations (see Table VI). The figures for corporate contributions to education, on the other hand, are CFAE estimates that include the grants made by both corporations and corporate foundations. As a result the large changes in educational support as a percentage of total contributions are heavily influenced by this lack of comparability.

Another factor enabling corporations to maintain their levels of giving in years of soft earnings stems from the growing significance of gifts of company products and property to corporate support programs. For the third year in a row, following the Economic Recovery Tax Act of 1981, there have been relatively large increases in donations of company products to educational institutions for research or training in research. Gifts of inventory are especially attractive to corporations in recession periods. They lower the value of inventory, provide a tax deduction and do not act as a drain on cash.

The total contributions reported in Table I are those reported to the Internal Revenue Service (IRS) on corporate income tax returns. The figures include transfer payments from the corporations to their foundations but do not include contributions made by the foundations. Since 1980, payments into the largest foundations have been less than the grants made by these foundations, a common occurrence when profits decline (see Table VI, p. 8 for the figures reported in 1980–85). The figures reported to the IRS thus understate the actual flow of corporate dollars to philanthropic causes between 1980 and 1985.

CFAE's estimates of education support, on the other hand, include the gifts and grants made *by the* foundations but exclude company payments *to them*. This provides a more accurate estimate of corporate monies actually received by the donees than do the government figures.

## Effect of Inflation

During the last 15 years inflation has accounted for much of the growth in both total corporate contributions and in education's share of these grants. The average annual growth rates for the Consumer Price Index (CPI), as well as for pretax net income and corporate contributions—both total and to education—between 1970 and 1985 are shown below.

### Average Annual Growth Rates

| | CPI | PTNI | Corporate Contributions | |
| --- | --- | --- | --- | --- |
| | | | Total | Education |
| 1970-75 | 6.7% | 11.9% | 8.6% | 7.1% |
| 1975-80 | 8.9 | 12.4 | 14.4 | 16.8 |
| 1980-85 | 5.5 | -1.2 | 13.3 | 13.9 |
| 1970-85 | 7.0 | 7.5 | 12.1 | 12.5 |

Although the average annual increase in the CPI, the most commonly used measure of inflation, was

7.0 percent from 1970 to 1985, individual yearly figures ranged from 3.2 to 13.5 percent. The effect of inflation on corporate contributions is shown graphically in **Chart I.** When adjusted for changes in the CPI, the 12.5 percent annual rate of increase in current dollars for corporate support of education since 1970 translates into 5.1 percent in constant dollars, still a most respectable gain.

## The Importance of Corporate Support to Higher Education

The $1.875 billion estimate for corporate support of education in 1985 is a measure of all corporate charitable contributions to education. Approximately 70 to 75 percent of this total is support of colleges and universities, with the remaining 25 to 30 percent accounted for by support of individual students, precollege education, economic education and other education-related organizations.

**Chart 1**
**Estimated Corporate Contributions to Education, 1970-1985** (millions of dollars)

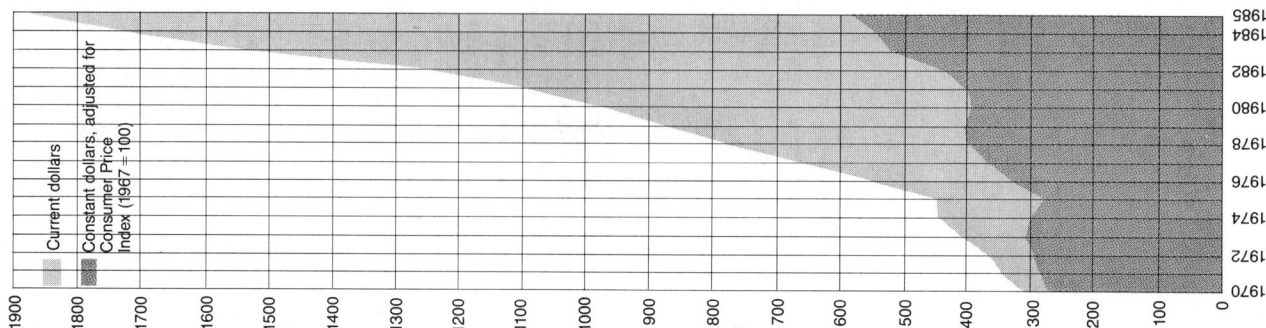

**Table II**
**Corporate Support of Colleges and Universities in Relation to Total Voluntary Support and Institutional Expenditures**

| Year | Total Expenditures of Institutions of Higher Education* (billions of dollars) | Voluntary Support of Institutions of Higher Education** (millions of dollars) | | Voluntary Support as a Percentage of Institutional Expenditures | | Corporate Support as a Percentage of Total Voluntary Support |
|---|---|---|---|---|---|---|
| | | Total | Corporate | Total | Corporate | |
| 1970-71 | 26.9 | 1,860 | 259 | 6.9 | 1.0 | 13.9 |
| 1971-72 | 29.1 | 2,020 | 275 | 6.9 | 0.9 | 13.6 |
| 1972-73 | 31.3 | 2,240 | 318 | 7.1 | 1.0 | 14.2 |
| 1973-74 | 34.2 | 2,240 | 354 | 6.5 | 1.0 | 15.8 |
| 1974-75 | 38.9 | 2,160 | 357 | 5.6 | 0.9 | 16.5 |
| 1975-76 | 42.6 | 2,410 | 379 | 5.6 | 0.9 | 15.7 |
| 1976-77 | 46.1 | 2,670 | 446 | 5.8 | 1.0 | 16.7 |
| 1977-78 | 49.4 | 3,040 | 508 | 6.1 | 1.0 | 16.7 |
| 1978-79 | 54.1 | 3,230 | 556 | 6.0 | 1.0 | 17.2 |
| 1979-80 | 62.5 | 3,800 | 696 | 6.1 | 1.1 | 18.3 |
| 1980-81 | 70.5 | 4,230 | 778 | 6.0 | 1.1 | 18.4 |
| 1981-82 | 77.3 | 4,860 | 976 | 6.3 | 1.3 | 20.1 |
| 1982-83 | 83.3 | 5,160 | 1,112 | 6.2 | 1.3 | 21.5 |
| 1983-84 | 90.1 | 5,600 | 1,271 | 6.2 | 1.4 | 22.7 |
| 1984-85 | 95.5 | 6,320 | 1,574 | 6.6 | 1.6 | 24.9 |
| 1985-86p. | 102.6 | 7,000 | 1,650 | 6.8 | 1.6 | 23.6 |

*U.S. Department of Education.
**Estimates by CFAE from Surveys of Voluntary Support of Education.
p.Preliminary.

Table II focuses on corporate giving to colleges and universities in relation to total voluntary support of higher education and to institutional expenditures.

For the past 15 years, corporate support of higher education has risen steadily. Since 1970, corporate gifts to higher education have grown by an average 13.1 percent a year, well above the average annual increase in the Consumer Price Index of 7.0 percent over the same period. Since total private gifts did not expand as fast as corporate contributions, corporate support has provided an increasing share of the pie.

At the present time, corporate gifts account for approximately 24 percent of all voluntary support received by the colleges and universities. Indeed, during the academic year 1984-85, the business community provided more support than any of the traditional donor categories—alumni, other individuals, foundations, religious and other organizations.

The estimates shown in Table II derive from reports from the colleges to the Council's annual survey of all voluntary support of education.★ The survey of voluntary support of education differs from the corporate survey in several significant ways. For example, the data are generated by the *donee* institutions rather than by the *donor* corporations; and the study covers the July 1 through June 30 period rather than the calendar year because the academic and fiscal years of most institutions coincide.

Respondents to the two surveys give different values to certain in-kind gifts which provided a significant portion of the big rise in corporate support in 1984-85. The donee colleges report such gifts—primarily company products—at fair market value, while the corporations report them at close to production cost, a much lower figure. The difference between the two valuations—perhaps some $200 million—tends to inflate the college statistics.

Whatever the differences between campus-based and company-based surveys, there are suggestions from

★ *Voluntary Support of Education* is published annually by the Council and is an essential reference for the education community. An increasing number of corporate and foundation donors also look to it for guidance in making decisions with respect to education support. The 1984-85 survey is available from the Council for $25 prepaid; the 1985-86 survey will be off the press in late spring 1987.

both that the rapid growth of corporate support is slowing. Preliminary data from the colleges for 1985–86 suggest another increase in company gifts, but it appears smaller than in the past. As for calendar year 1986, a representative group of corporate donors checked by the Council at midyear predicted no change in 1986 over 1985. The corporations reporting in this survey, however, estimated their total giving for all of 1986 would be down an average 2.5 percent compared to 1985.

This is not good news for the higher education institutions. For the past ten years, gifts to education —total and corporate—have risen faster than institutional spending, and thus have provided an increased share of support for college budgets. For the past five years, education costs have grown at 3 percent above inflation and are expected to increase faster than the consumer price index for the remainder of the decade. If voluntary support slows, the financial pressures on the institutions will increase.

These pressures are already considerable, a legacy in part from the 1970s. Inflation—especially surging energy costs—hit the colleges hard. As a result, maintenance of the education plant and upgrading of research facilities were deferred, and faculty and staff salaries did not keep pace with the cost of living.

Education is highly labor-intensive, and faculty compensation constitutes by far the largest share of institutional expense. (The fact that a large part of the faculty consists of older persons, tenured with average salaries at the upper end of their ranges, adds to the problem.) The need to restore to the teaching profession some of the real income lost since the mid-1970s will require faculty salary increases at least 1 percent above the rate of inflation for several more years.

It is estimated that one half of higher education's physical plant is more than 25 years old; one quarter of it was built before World War II. On average, university research equipment is twice as old as comparable equipment in industry. Renewing and replacing the higher education infrastructure could cost between $30 billion and $40 billion.

Demographic change also is creating new financial problems for education. The decline in the size of the traditional college-going age group, and the fact that a larger proportion of the group comes from low-income households, make it harder for institutions to generate additional revenue from tuition. Federal student aid programs have lagged rising costs, and as a consequence institutions are forced to divert more of their own resources to provide a greater share of the financial aid packages.

Finally, the nation's colleges and universities are under increasing pressure to upgrade the quality of undergraduate education and to adapt to the needs of a changing work force. The type of work performed in the U.S. has changed dramatically; new kinds of education programs are needed to keep pace with new job requirements and to assist adult workers with retraining. All this means additional investment in equipment, curriculum development and faculty.

Corporate contributions are important now, and will become even more so, in helping the colleges and universities deal with these challenges.

## Table III
### Percentage Distribution of Corporate Contributions

| | 1984 (415) | 1985 (436) |
|---|---|---|
| Education | 38.9% | 38.3% |
| Health and Human Services | 27.7 | 29.2 |
| Culture and Art | 10.7 | 11.1 |
| Civic Activities | 18.8 | 16.5 |
| Other | 3.9 | 4.9 |
| | 100.0% | 100.0% |

(Numbers in parentheses show the number of companies reporting.)

# Part II.
# The Survey Results

The 1985 Annual Survey of Corporate Contributions, conducted jointly by the Council for Financial Aid to Education and the Conference Board, reports on the charitable giving of the largest U.S. corporations with contributions programs.

The 439 companies participating in this survey reported contributions of $1.71 billion in 1985, a 17.5 percent increase over the amount reported in 1984 by 422 companies. Support of education in this period rose 15.7 percent, from $561.7 million in 1984 to $650 million in 1985.

## Profile of Survey Respondents

Survey participants were almost evenly split between the manufacturing and nonmanufacturing sectors —225 manufacturing companies and 214 nonmanufacturing. A questionnaire was mailed to the *Fortune* 1,000 manufacturing companies, the *Fortune* 50 or 100 companies of each of the nonmanufacturing industry groups, and other companies with contributions budgets of $100,000 or more.

While these companies represent a very small part of the corporate universe, their contributions constitute a very large share of total corporate giving nationwide. Research by CFAE has found that the largest corporations with substantial contributions budgets provide well over half of all corporate support. The most recent study of federal corporate income tax filings found that corporations reporting gifts of $100,000 or more, although less than 1 percent of all corporations, account for 65 percent of corporate giving. Among this year's respondents, only 9 companies, or 2 percent of the sample, had contributions budgets less than $100,000, while 56 percent made contributions in excess of $1 million. In addition, 75 percent of the companies reported worldwide assets of more than $1 billion.

Analysis of survey responses takes two forms: a look at contributions patterns and relationships over time; and comparisons of the participants by various groupings such as industry, company size and metropolitan area.

## Where the Corporate Contributions Dollar Goes

Table III shows that the largest share of corporate contributions goes to education. Between 35 to 41 percent of total corporate contributions has flowed to education since this joint survey was begun in 1974. Approximately 70 percent of every

education dollar goes to colleges and universities.★

In 1985, the steady decline in the proportion of corporate gifts flowing to health and human-service organizations stopped and these gifts increased for the first time in ten years to 29.2 percent. In 1975, these causes received 42.1 percent of every contributions dollar; over the next nine years, their proportion of total corporate giving decreased by 1 to 2 percent each year.

## Company-Product Gifts Continue Growing

Survey results confirm the growing importance of noncash contributions to corporate philanthropy. Over one fifth of total contributions in 1985 took the form of company products and surplus property (**Table IV**).

---

★Education support includes donations to institutions of higher education, elementary and secondary schools, state and local educational fund-raising groups, individual scholarships, economic education groups and other education-related organizations. Program support for research projects funded from the contributions budget is included, while support of contractual research is excluded. Educational programs such as employee tuition-refund programs are excluded when funded out of the personnel, public relations or other expense budgets.

**Table IV**
**Company Gifts by Type**
**(millions of dollars)**

| | 1984 | | 1985 | |
|---|---|---|---|---|
| | Amount | % of Total | Amount | % of Total |
| Cash | $1,119.07 (405) | 77.8 | $1,330.50 (427) | 79.5 |
| Securities | 14.09 (12) | 1.0 | 7.43 (11) | 0.4 |
| Company Products | 147.37 (74) | 10.2 | 190.30 (80) | 11.4 |
| Other Property | 157.41 (79) | 11.0 | 144.84 (80) | 8.7 |
| Total | $1,437.94 (405) | 100.0 | $1,673.07 (427) | 100.0 |

(Numbers in parentheses show the number of companies reporting.)

**Table V**
**Gifts of Company Products, by Industry**
**(thousands of dollars)**

| | 1984 | | | | 1985 | | | |
|---|---|---|---|---|---|---|---|---|
| | Total | % of Total | Education | Ed. as % of Total | Total | % of Total | Education | Ed. as % of Total |
| Electrical Machinery | $43,201 | 29.3 | $37,261 (12) | 86.3 | $94,666 | 49.8 | $74,411 (12) | 78.6 |
| Pharmaceuticals and Chemicals | 35,232 | 23.9 | 5,058 (1) | 14.4 | 54,137 | 28.4 | 7,459 (7) | 13.8 |
| Telecommunications | 33,346 | 22.6 | 33,346 (1) | 100.0 | 8,471 | 4.4 | 7,471 (1) | 88.2 |
| Transportation Equipment | 13,934 | 9.5 | 13,816 (2) | 99.2 | 11,753 | 6.2 | 11,484 (3) | 97.7 |
| All Others | 21,664 | 14.7 | 1,548 (14) | 7.1 | 21,272 | 11.2 | 309 (11) | 1.4 |
| Total | $147,377 | 100.0 | $91,029 (30) | 61.8 | $190,299 | 100.0 | $101,134 (34) | 53.1 |

(Numbers in parentheses show the number of companies reporting.)

Gifts of company products alone showed an increase of 29 percent. This growth did not come at the expense of cash contributions, which increased by 18.8 percent. The survey has collected information on product and property gifts since 1982, following the Economic Recovery Tax Act of 1981 which provided enhanced deductions for inventory items given for research training and research in science/engineering at institutions of higher education. The $190.3 million in product donations in 1985 was almost twice the amount reported in 1982.

Product and property gifts are an especially important component of education-support programs. Company products account for 16 percent of all giving to education; property 3 percent. Education causes received 53 percent of total product gifts and 13 percent of all property gifts reported by survey respondents. **Table V** shows that manufacturers of electrical machinery, a category that includes computers, made by far the largest product donations.

The size of company-product gifts varied widely among respondents. The largest amount given in products to education by a single company was $21.1 million, the smallest was $3.1 million. The mean amount was $3.1 million, but the median was $115,341, indicating that many companies made relatively small product donations. These amounts were those reported for income tax purposes as charitable deductions and may differ significantly from the values shown by recipients, which usually report list price, a higher figure.

Many companies also donate excess company products and other used property without taking the charitable deduction. In 1985, 90 companies gave $55.6 million worth of products and property over and above the amounts reported as charitable deductions.

Most property and product gifts were made directly from corporations. Gifts from company-sponsored foundations were almost exclusively cash.

## The Role of Foundations

Tables VI through IX detail the importance of company-sponsored foundations to corporate contributions programs. When corporate philanthropy is disbursed solely from corporate funds it tends to rise and fall with corporate profits over the course of a business cycle. By funding their foundations in years of high profits, corporations set aside reserves of money to be used in years of poor profits. In effect, they insulate recipients from the ups and downs of the business cycle.

In 1985, 269 companies, or 61 percent of the survey respondents, reported having company-sponsored foundations. Close to two fifths of total contributions came in the form of foundation gifts. Ten years ago, only 42 percent of the survey participants reported having company-sponsored foundations.

Table VI presents the consolidated

**Table VI**
**Structure of Corporate Contributions (millions of dollars)**

| | 1980 | 1981 | 1982 | 1983 | 1984 | 1985 |
|---|---|---|---|---|---|---|
| Total Company Gifts | $ 944.7 (709) | $1,039.1 (768) | $1,116.8 (519) | $1,250.7 (484) | $1,448.9 (404) | $1,666.5 (423) |
| Less: Gifts to Company Foundations | 381.4 (249) | 361.6 (239) | 367.1 (186) | 435.7 (159) | 562.2 (157) | 614.0 (182) |
| Direct Company Gifts to Others | 563.3 (661) | 677.5 (735) | 749.7 (494) | 815.0 (461) | 886.7 (388) | 1,052.5 (395) |
| Plus: Company Foundation Gifts | 431.3 (353) | 493.3 (359) | 531.9 (286) | 553.0 (270) | 569.2 (230) | 658.4 (256) |
| Total Corporate Contributions | $994.6 (732) | $1,170.8 (789) | $1,281.6 (534) | $1,368.0 (503) | $1,455.9 (422) | $1,710.9 (439) |
| Difference Between Foundation Receipts and Foundation Gifts | –$49.9 | –$131.7 | –$164.8 | –$117.3 | –$ 7.0 | –$44.4 |
| Cumulative Change from 1974 | +112.4 | – 19.3 | – 184.1 | – 301.4 | –308.4 | – 352.8 |
| Number of Companies with Foundations | 376 | 389 | 297 | 283 | 243 | 269 |

(Numbers in parentheses show the number of companies reporting.)

**Table VII**
**Percentage of Reporting Companies with Corporate Foundations, by Industry, 1985**

| Industry | Percentage | Industry | Percentage |
|---|---|---|---|
| **MANUFACTURING** | | **NONMANUFACTURING** | |
| Transportation Equipment (14) | 93.3 | Engineering & Construction (2) | 66.7 |
| Primary Metals (13) | 86.7 | Insurance (28) | 65.1 |
| Stone, Clay & Glass (6) | 85.7 | Banks (39) | 63.9 |
| Fabricated Metals (8) | 80.0 | Telecommunications (7) | 63.6 |
| Machinery (15) | 78.9 | Finance (3) | 60.0 |
| Paper & Allied Products (11) | 78.6 | Business Services (4) | 50.0 |
| Pharmaceuticals (10) | 76.9 | Merchandising (8) | 44.4 |
| Food, Beverage & Tobacco (18) | 75.0 | Utilities (13) | 25.5 |
| Rubber (3) | 75.0 | Transportation (1) | 14.3 |
| Electrical Machinery (24) | 72.7 | All Nonmanufacturing (105) | 50.7 |
| Chemicals (19) | 70.4 | ALL COMPANIES (269) | 63.1 |
| Textiles & Apparel (2) | 66.7 | | |
| Petroleum & Gas (14) | 63.6 | | |
| Printing & Publishing (6) | 60.0 | | |
| Mining (1) | 33.3 | | |
| All Manufacturing (164) | 74.9 | | |

(Numbers in parentheses show the number of foundations.)

**Table VIII**
**Foundation Cash Flow, by Industry, 1985**

| Industry | Payments into Foundations | Earnings | Grants Made by Foundations | Net Change |
|---|---|---|---|---|
| **MANUFACTURING** | | | | |
| Chemicals(14) | $ 30,029,554 | $ 6,146,752 | $ 33,087,280 | + $ 3,089,026 |
| Electrical Machinery(14) | 42,915,500 | 17,591,956 | 52,007,178 | + 8,500,278 |
| Fabricated Metals(5) | 6,100,000 | 1,008,454 | 6,036,985 | + 1,071,469 |
| Food, Beverage & Tobacco(10) | 19,626,818 | 26,314,709 | 24,685,040 | + 21,256,487 |
| Machinery(11) | 10,709,530 | 1,314,790 | 10,642,226 | + 1,382,094 |
| Paper & Allied Products(4) | 3,528,475 | 1,176,078 | 3,598,272 | + 1,106,281 |
| Petroleum & Gas(7) | 93,847,535 | 36,449,959 | 126,977,917 | + 3,319,577 |
| Pharmaceuticals(7) | 23,475,000 | 1,962,214 | 20,984,240 | + 4,452,974 |
| Primary Metals(6) | 2,554,971 | 540,272 | 2,657,774 | + 437,469 |
| Printing & Publishing(4) | 4,936,081 | 243,656 | 5,066,785 | + 112,952 |
| Rubber(2) | 520,000 | 1,389,692 | 1,412,153 | + 497,539 |
| Stone, Clay & Glass(2) | 2,203,772 | 699,491 | 2,058,878 | + 844,385 |
| Textiles & Apparel(1) | 400,000 | 25,105 | 622,604 | – 197,499 |
| Transportation Equipment(8) | 100,171,023 | 43,051,116 | 47,265,858 | + 95,956,281 |
| .Total(95) | $341,018,259 | $137,914,244 | $337,103,190 | + $141,829,313 |
| **NONMANUFACTURING** | | | | |
| Banks(17) | $ 20,488,327 | $ 4,237,895 | $ 26,597,092 | – $ 1,870,870 |
| Business Services(2) | 28,017,500 | 409,822 | 1,895,436 | + 26,531,886 |
| Finance(3) | 1,543,216 | 1,026,969 | 1,770,438 | + 799,747 |
| Insurance(12) | 55,473,181 | 13,203,408 | 30,926,684 | + 37,749,905 |
| Merchandising(3) | 15,743,000 | 1,676,692 | 19,635,638 | – 2,215,946 |
| Telecommunications(5) | 64,428,873 | 8,469,412 | 25,608,242 | + 47,290,043 |
| Utilities(9) | 15,354,794 | 2,962,510 | 12,350,409 | + 5,966,895 |
| Total(51) | $201,048,891 | $ 31,986,708 | $118,783,939 | + $114,251,660 |
| GRAND TOTAL(146) | $542,067,150 | $169,900,952 | $455,887,129 | + $256,080,973 |

(Numbers in parentheses show the number of companies reporting.)

contributions of corporations and their foundations over the last six years, deducting the funds turned over by parent companies to their foundations. In each of these years, foundation contributions exceeded receipts from parent companies, a common occurrence in years of lackluster profits. In 1985, the gap between gifts made by corporate foundations and the funds they received from their sponsoring companies was $44 million. Note that about one third of the companies with foundations (87 cases) made no payments into their foundations in 1985.

Grants to foundations from their parent companies are only one index of the foundations' grant-making capability. Also important are the earnings on the foundations' accumulated assets. Table VIII summarizes, by industry, the degree to which investment income serves as a source of funds in situations in which the sponsoring companies pay in less than their foundations pay out as charitable gifts. Note that three industry groups drew on foundation assets to cover grants.

Not all of the respondents were able to give complete data about foundation earnings and assets; the number in each industry therefore varies from table to table. The important conclusion from this sample is that foundation earnings make it possible to increase contributions above the corporations' payments and can add to foundation assets for use in future years.

Another measure of the value of foundations is the size of their assets. Table IX shows the changes in assets for foundations in 1985, by industry. This table reflects changes in market value of foundation assets as well as changes affected by cash flow. The 221 companies providing information reported an increase in assets of $363.2 million in 1985. The $2.2 billion in assets provides a large cushion for the giving programs of these companies.

## Contributions, PTNI and Assets

The relationships between contributions and two financial measures—pretax net income and assets—are shown in **Table X** for companies reporting financial data on a worldwide basis and for those reporting on United States operations only.

Between 1984 and 1985, the ratios of total giving and education giving to pretax net income increased for both worldwide and U.S.-only operations. Contributions increased more than profits. On the other hand, there was a decline in the ratio of contributions and education support to assets, owing to the fact that assets increased more than either measure of contributions. As a share of total contributions in both groups, education support continued to account for approximately 38 percent in 1985.

Since the number of companies responding to the survey varies from year to year, the significance of changes is best judged by examining the 344 "core" companies that reported in both years (see **Table XI**).

**Table IX**
**Changes in Market Value of Corporate Foundation Assets, by Industry, 1985**

| | Assets as of 12/31/84 | Assets* as of 12/31/85 | Net Change in Assets* | % Change |
|---|---|---|---|---|
| **MANUFACTURING** | | | | |
| Chemicals(18) | $ 72,391,069 | $ 75,513,733 | +$ 3,122,664 | + 4.3 |
| Electrical Machinery(22) | 195,340,023 | 207,358,608 | + 12,018,585 | + 6.2 |
| Fabricated Metals(7) | 20,819,436 | 23,064,409 | + 2,244,973 | + 10.8 |
| Food, Beverage & Tobacco(11) | 53,479,937 | 58,087,420 | + 4,607,483 | + 8.6 |
| Machinery(15) | 41,734,470 | 44,163,106 | + 2,428,636 | + 5.8 |
| Mining(1) | 10,887,949 | 12,346,482 | + 1,458,533 | + 13.4 |
| Paper & Allied Products(9) | 57,521,579 | 65,970,454 | + 8,448,875 | + 14.7 |
| Petroleum & Gas(11) | 284,518,904 | 283,359,607 | − 1,159,297 | − 0.4 |
| Pharmaceuticals(9) | 44,412,774 | 49,967,961 | + 5,555,187 | + 12.5 |
| Primary Metals(12) | 195,363,611 | 215,859,363 | + 20,495,752 | + 10.4 |
| Printing & Publishing(4) | 3,572,624 | 4,415,433 | + 842,809 | + 23.6 |
| Rubber(3) | 18,065,629 | 23,698,434 | + 5,632,805 | + 31.2 |
| Stone, Clay & Glass(3) | 5,227,981 | 6,012,176 | + 784,195 | + 15.0 |
| Textiles & Apparel(2) | 11,151,172 | 11,542,284 | + 391,112 | + 3.5 |
| Transportation Equipment(13) | 274,079,306 | 406,740,224 | + 132,660,918 | + 48.4 |
| Total(140) | $1,288,566,464 | $1,488,099,694 | +$ 199,533,230 | + 15.4 |
| **NONMANUFACTURING** | | | | |
| Banks(33) | $ 81,115,415 | $ 80,957,929 | −$ 157,486 | − 0.2 |
| Business Services(3) | 4,777,466 | 31,559,139 | + 26,781,673 | +560.6 |
| Engineering & Construction(1) | 862,544 | 652,159 | − 210,385 | − 24.4 |
| Finance(3) | 8,029,191 | 11,464,332 | + 3,435,141 | + 42.8 |
| Insurance(22) | 220,255,441 | 267,818,802 | + 47,563,361 | + 21.6 |
| Merchandising(6) | 23,493,391 | 25,616,467 | + 2,123,076 | + 9.0 |
| Telecommunications(5) | 137,528,604 | 220,211,174 | + 82,682,570 | + 60.1 |
| Utilities(8) | 31,026,801 | 32,509,507 | + 1,482,706 | + 4.8 |
| Total(81) | $ 507,088,853 | $ 670,789,509 | +$ 163,700,656 | + 32.3 |
| GRAND TOTAL(221) | $1,795,655,317 | $2,158,889,203 | +$ 363,233,886 | + 20.2 |

(Numbers in parentheses show the number of companies reporting.)

*Some of the companies reported face value of bonds, which did not change during the year. Since some foundations were not established until 1985, changes in their asset values are not reported in this table, and the net change in these values will therefore differ from those reported in Table VIII.

**Table X**
**Total Contributions and Support of Education in Relation to Worldwide and U.S.-Only Pretax Net Income and Assets (000 omitted)**

| Worldwide | 1980 659 companies | 1981 712 companies | 1982 513 companies | 1983 471 companies | 1984 392 companies | 1985 409 companies |
|---|---|---|---|---|---|---|
| Total Contributions | $ 959,249 | $ 1,116,261 | $ 1,255,464 | $ 1,329,633 | $ 1,423,855 | $ 1,636,412 |
| Support of Education | 362,494 | 407,270 | 511,725 | 518,713 | 553,517 | 626,794 |
| Pretax Net Income | 164,735,000 | 165,277,000 | 134,746,000 | 152,832,000 | 147,716,000 | 159,974,004 |
| Assets | 2,642,819,000 | 2,959,364,000 | 2,921,421,000 | 2,852,949,000 | 2,593,032,000 | 3,260,887,200 |
| Total Contributions as % of: | | | | | | |
| Pretax Net Income | 0.582 | 0.675 | 0.932 | 0.870 | 0.964 | 1.023 |
| Assets | 0.036 | 0.038 | 0.043 | 0.047 | 0.055 | 0.050 |
| Support of Education as % of: | | | | | | |
| Pretax Net Income | 0.220 | 0.246 | 0.380 | 0.339 | 0.375 | 0.392 |
| Assets | 0.014 | 0.014 | 0.018 | 0.018 | 0.021 | 0.019 |
| Support of Education as % of Total Contributions | 37.8 | 36.4 | 40.8 | 39.0 | 38.9 | 38.3 |

| U.S. Only | 1980 477 companies | 1981 525 companies | 1982 383 companies | 1983 368 companies | 1984 340 companies | 1985 364 companies |
|---|---|---|---|---|---|---|
| Total Contributions | $ 532,260 | $ 681,494 | $ 918,595 | $ 1,011,374 | $ 1,168,161 | $ 1,361,629 |
| Support of Education | 192,482 | 235,115 | 358,383 | 405,969 | 438,060 | 511,583 |
| Pretax Net Income | 65,963,000 | 81,833,000 | 79,334,000 | 89,035,000 | 89,013,000 | 98,461,592 |
| Assets | 1,190,370,000 | 1,552,140,000 | 1,637,241,000 | 1,600,112,000 | 1,540,271,000 | 2,256,935,806 |
| Total Contributions as % of: | | | | | | |
| Pretax Net Income | 0.807 | 0.833 | 1.158 | 1.136 | 1.312 | 1.383 |
| Assets | 0.045 | 0.044 | 0.056 | 0.063 | 0.076 | 0.060 |
| Support of Education as % of: | | | | | | |
| Pretax Net Income | 0.292 | 0.287 | 0.452 | 0.456 | 0.492 | 0.520 |
| Assets | 0.016 | 0.015 | 0.022 | 0.025 | 0.028 | 0.023 |
| Support of Education as % of Total Contributions | 36.2 | 34.5 | 39.0 | 40.1 | 37.5 | 37.6 |

**Table XI**
**Support of Education, Two Survey Years (344 Companies Participating in Both Surveys)**

| Industry | 1984 Worldwide Pretax Net Income (millions) | 1984 Support of Education Amount (000) | 1984 % of PTNI | 1984 % of Total Contributions | 1985 Worldwide Pretax Net Income (millions) | 1985 Support of Education Amount (000) | 1985 % of PTNI | 1985 % of Total Contributions | % Change 1984-1985 Education | % Change 1984-1985 PTNI | % Change 1984-1985 Total Contributions |
|---|---|---|---|---|---|---|---|---|---|---|---|
| **MANUFACTURING** | | | | | | | | | | | |
| Chemicals(26) | $ 12,949 | $ 56,336 | .435 | 42.2 | $ 8,471 | $ 65,680 | .775 | 45.4 | + 16.6 | − 34.6 | − 8.4 |
| Electrical Machinery(22) | 20,922 | 105,966 | .506 | 54.5 | 19,484 | 114,489 | .588 | 51.3 | + 8.0 | − 6.9 | + 14.9 |
| Fabricated Metals(8) | 495 | 2,639 | .533 | 39.3 | 383 | 2,447 | .639 | 33.0 | − 7.3 | − 22.6 | − 10.4 |
| Food, Beverage & Tobacco(17) | 5,458 | 13,778 | .252 | 24.6 | 7,381 | 26,446 | .358 | 28.7 | + 91.9 | + 35.2 | + 64.1 |
| Machinery(14) | 452 | 9,493 | 2.100 | 43.6 | 941 | 9,136 | .971 | 35.8 | − 3.8 | +108.1 | + 17.2 |
| Mining(2) | 163 | 1,360 | .837 | 64.4 | 136 | 1,057 | .777 | 56.7 | − 22.3 | − 16.4 | − 11.7 |
| Paper & Allied Products(11) | 1,458 | 7,619 | .522 | 43.9 | 1,466 | 5,796 | .395 | 35.3 | − 23.9 | + 0.5 | − 5.3 |
| Petroleum & Gas(20) | 38,324 | 125,779 | .328 | 45.6 | 32,709 | 128,116 | .392 | 47.0 | + 1.9 | − 14.7 | − 1.2 |
| Pharmaceuticals(9) | 4,364 | 19,995 | .458 | 32.4 | 4,834 | 17,991 | .372 | 26.6 | − 10.0 | + 10.8 | + 9.6 |
| Primary Metals(10) | 756 | 8,053 | 1.065 | 47.4 | 886 | 8,392 | .947 | 43.0 | + 4.2 | + 17.2 | + 14.9 |
| Printing & Publishing(8) | 1,287 | 4,401 | .342 | 36.2 | 1,294 | 5,618 | .434 | 33.3 | + 27.7 | + 0.6 | + 38.6 |
| Rubber(4) | 954 | 2,888 | .303 | 41.4 | 264 | 2,240 | .850 | 28.3 | − 22.4 | − 72.4 | + 13.6 |
| Stone, Clay & Glass(3) | 375 | 1,297 | .346 | 21.8 | 387 | 1,304 | .337 | 21.1 | + 0.6 | + 3.3 | + 3.8 |
| Textiles & Apparel(3) | 189 | 1,625 | .858 | 18.2 | 56 | 1,856 | 3.340 | 51.9 | + 14.2 | − 70.7 | + 60.0 |
| Transportation Equipment(10) | 13,392 | 49,609 | .370 | 42.9 | 11,886 | 46,993 | .395 | 34.3 | − 5.3 | − 11.2 | + 18.3 |
| Total(167) | $101,537 | $410,840 | .405 | 43.9 | $ 90,577 | $437,562 | .483 | 42.0 | + 6.5 | − 10.8 | + 11.4 |
| **NONMANUFACTURING** | | | | | | | | | | | |
| Banks(49) | $ 4,580 | $ 17,554 | .383 | 24.9 | $ 6,461 | $ 19,405 | .300 | 24.6 | + 10.5 | + 41.1 | + 11.8 |
| Business Services(5) | 764 | 1,820 | .238 | 30.8 | 790 | 4,393 | .556 | 50.9 | +141.4 | + 3.4 | + 46.2 |
| Engineering & Construction(1) | − 9 | 106 | — | 31.7 | 5 | 106 | 1.958 | 35.4 | + 0.2 | — | + 10.2 |
| Finance(5) | 925 | 2,841 | .307 | 41.4 | 1,443 | 2,935 | .203 | 35.9 | + 3.3 | + 56.0 | + 19.3 |
| Insurance(39) | 2,784* | 20,988 | .754 | 16.6 | 4,187* | 21,963 | .525 | 19.2 | + 4.6 | + 50.4 | − 9.8 |
| Merchandising(15) | 4,214 | 6,838 | .162 | 12.6 | 4,366 | 9,191 | .211 | 14.2 | + 34.4 | + 3.6 | + 18.5 |
| Telecommunications(6) | 5,433 | 49,843 | .917 | 67.5 | 3,681 | 29,248 | .794 | 47.2 | − 41.3 | − 32.2 | − 16.0 |
| Transportation(6) | 433 | 682 | .157 | 10.0 | 342 | 1,549 | .453 | 20.9 | +127.1 | − 21.0 | + 9.2 |
| Utilities(51) | 16,298 | 12,292 | .075 | 26.0 | 15,905 | 13,961 | .088 | 26.8 | + 13.6 | − 2.4 | + 10.4 |
| Total(177) | $ 35,422 | $112,964 | .319 | 28.8 | $ 37,181 | $102,752 | .276 | 25.9 | − 9.0 | + 5.0 | + 1.0 |
| GRAND TOTAL(344) | $136,960 | $523,804 | .382 | 39.4 | $127,759 | $540,314 | .423 | 37.6 | + 3.2 | + 6.7 | + 8.3 |

(Numbers in parentheses show the number of companies reporting in both surveys.)
*Insurance company figures are based on "net gain from operations after dividends to policyholders and before federal income tax, excluding capital gains and losses"—the closest measure to pretax net income of corporations generally.

Their giving patterns differ from those in the national estimates in degree but not in direction. They confirm the national trends seen earlier in Table I. Overall, pretax net income fell by 6.7 percent while total contributions and education support increased by 8.3 percent and 3.2 percent respectively. These increases were considerably smaller than the 24 percent increases in both total contributions and education gifts reported by the 304 "core" companies in both the 1983 and 1984 surveys.

Segmenting these core companies into manufacturing and non-manufacturing sectors uncovers some interesting facts. For the manufacturing group, profits fell, yet total contributions and education support rose. In contrast, the 177 nonmanufacturing companies experienced a 5 percent increase in pretax net income, while their total contributions increased by only 1 percent and education support actually declined by 9 percent between 1984 and 1985.

## Comparisons by Groupings

Contributions patterns differ by metropolitan area, by size of company and by industry. These patterns are detailed in Tables XII through XIV.

### By Metropolitan Area

Companies can be compared geographically as is done in **Table XII.** This table shows education support

## Table XII
## Support of Education by Major Metropolitan Areas, 1985

| Metropolitan Area | Worldwide Pretax Net Income (millions) | Support of Education (000) | Support of Education as % of PTNI | | Total Contributions (000) | Support of Education as % of Total Contributions | |
|---|---|---|---|---|---|---|---|
| | | | % | Rank | | % | Rank |
| Baltimore(5) | $ −266 | $ 1,774 | — | — | $ 4,836 | 36.7 | 11 |
| Boston(11) | 1,783 | 9,587 | .538 | 4 | 22,557 | 42.5 | 5 |
| Chicago(32) | 13,123 | 39,146 | .298 | 12 | 106,400 | 36.8 | 10 |
| Cincinnati-Dayton(8) | 1,882 | 8,318 | .442 | 5 | 22,197 | 37.4 | 9 |
| Cleveland(6) | 1,692 | 13,416 | .793 | 1 | 28,358 | 47.3 | 3 |
| Dallas-Ft. Worth(9) | 1,605 | 3,904 | .243 | 14 | 11,434 | 34.1 | 12 |
| Detroit(9) | 11,834 | 35,212 | .298 | 12 | 110,849 | 31.8 | 14 |
| Hartford(9) | 2,746 | 9,887 | .360 | 10 | 25,284 | 39.1 | 7 |
| Houston(10) | 4,806 | 20,116 | .419 | 6 | 40,146 | 50.1 | 2 |
| Los Angeles(16) | 4,889 | 19,844 | .406 | 8 | 65,344 | 30.4 | 15 |
| Milwaukee(5) | 600 | 1,150 | .192 | 15 | 5,115 | 22.4 | 17 |
| Minneapolis-St. Paul(18) | 3,506 | 25,223 | .719 | 2 | 87,071 | 29.0 | 16 |
| New York, Westchester, Southern CT/NJ(72) | 58,372 | 226,876 | .389 | 9 | 588,045 | 38.6 | 8 |
| Philadelphia(18) | 8,760 | 31,430 | .359 | 11 | 68,736 | 45.7 | 4 |
| Pittsburgh(14) | 4,488 | 24,368 | .543 | 3 | 58,377 | 41.7 | 6 |
| St. Louis(8) | 4,390 | 11,210 | .255 | 13 | 34,319 | 32.7 | 13 |
| San Francisco(13) | 10,733 | 44,280 | .413 | 7 | 87,849 | 50.4 | 1 |
| Total(263) | $134,943 | $525,741 | .390 | | $1,366,917 | 38.4 | |

(Numbers in parentheses show the number of companies reporting.)
Metropolitan areas with fewer than five respondents are not listed.

## Table XIII
## Contributions by Manufacturing Companies, by Size of Worldwide Pretax Net Income and Assets, 1985

| Pretax Net Income | % of PTNI | | Support of Education as % of Total Contributions |
|---|---|---|---|
| | Total | Education | |
| Net Loss(10) | | | 42.8 |
| Net Income less than $5 million(2) | 15.979 | 6.290 | 39.3 |
| $ 5 million under $ 10 million(3) | 13.151 | 6.216 | 47.3 |
| $ 10 million under $ 25 million(16) | 2.047 | .537 | 26.2 |
| $ 25 million under $ 50 million(24) | 5.117 | 2.569 | 50.2 |
| $ 50 million under $100 million(27) | 2.077 | 1.149 | 55.3 |
| $100 million under $250 million(56) | 1.290 | .441 | 34.2 |
| $250 million under $500 million(25) | 1.527 | .540 | 35.4 |
| $500 million under $ 1 billion(27) | 1.283 | .496 | 38.6 |
| $ 1 billion and over(20) | .791 | .378 | 47.8 |
| All Manufacturing Companies(210) | 1.092 | .472 | 43.2 |

| Assets | % of Assets | | Support of Education as % of Total Contributions |
|---|---|---|---|
| | Total | Education | |
| $100 million under $250 million(12) | .213 | .059 | 27.5 |
| $250 million under $500 million(24) | .124 | .042 | 34.1 |
| $500 million under $ 1 billion(30) | .140 | .041 | 29.6 |
| $ 1 billion under $ 2.5 billion(56) | .142 | .067 | 47.0 |
| $2.5 billion under $ 5 billion(36) | .119 | .040 | 33.3 |
| $ 5 billion under $ 10 billion(25) | .138 | .058 | 41.7 |
| $ 10 billion and over(27) | .096 | .044 | 46.0 |
| All Manufacturing Companies(210) | .110 | .048 | 43.2 |

(Numbers in parentheses show the number of companies reporting.)

## Chart 2
## Comparative Rankings Of Education Support, by Industry, 1985

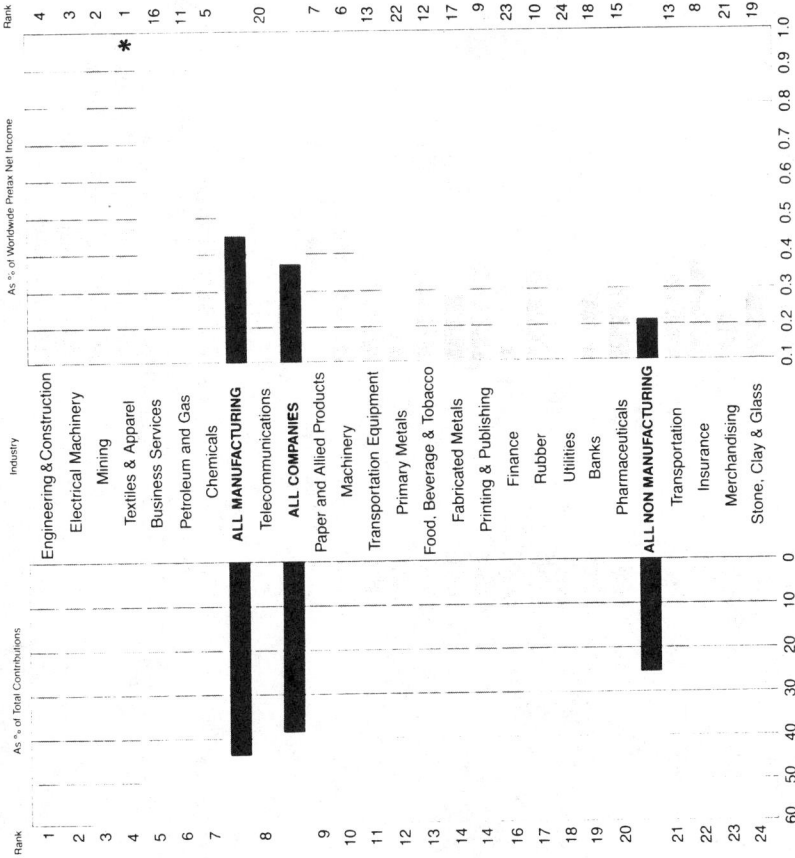

| Rank (As % of Total Contributions) | Industry | Rank (As % of Worldwide Pretax Net Income) |
|---|---|---|
| 1 | Engineering & Construction | 4 |
| 2 | Electrical Machinery | 3 |
| 3 | Mining | 2 |
| 4 | Textiles & Apparel | 1 * |
| 5 | Business Services | 16 |
| 6 | Petroleum and Gas | 11 |
| 7 | Chemicals | 5 |
| | ALL MANUFACTURING | |
| 8 | Telecommunications | 20 |
| | ALL COMPANIES | |
| 9 | Paper and Allied Products | 7 |
| 10 | Machinery | 6 |
| 11 | Transportation Equipment | 13 |
| 12 | Primary Metals | 22 |
| 13 | Food, Beverage & Tobacco | 12 |
| 14 | Fabricated Metals | 17 |
| 14 | Printing & Publishing | 9 |
| 16 | Finance | 23 |
| 17 | Rubber | 10 |
| 18 | Utilities | 24 |
| 19 | Banks | 18 |
| 20 | Pharmaceuticals | 15 |
| | ALL NON MANUFACTURING | |
| 21 | Transportation | 13 |
| 22 | Insurance | 8 |
| 23 | Merchandising | 21 |
| 24 | Stone, Clay & Glass | 19 |

As % of Total Contributions: 0 10 20 30 40 50 60

As % of Worldwide Pretax Net Income: 0.1 0.2 0.3 0.4 0.5 0.6 0.7 0.8 0.9 1.0

* For 1985 support of education by textile companies as a percent of worldwide PTNI jumped to 3.243 In 1984 the figure was 5.32. Much of the increase was due to decreased earnings

---

their contributions programs than did the smaller companies.

### By Industry

For industry comparisons, the most common measures are the proportion of total contributions devoted to education and the ratio of contributions to pretax net income. **Chart 2** ranks the industries first according to education's share of their total contributions and then according to the ratio of education support to the industry's worldwide PTNI.

**Table XIV** presents these comparisons and also indicates the ratio of education support and total contributions to worldwide assets. The pretax net income of the manufacturing companies is slightly over twice that of the nonmanufacturers, while the assets of the nonmanufacturing companies are twice as large as those of the manufacturers. In 1985, total contributions of manufacturing companies were 2.6 times greater than those of their nonmanufacturing counterparts, while support of education by manufacturers was 4.4 times greater than that of the nonmanufacturers. The manufacturing sector accounted for 81.7 percent of all education support.

### Individual Company Data

Tables **XV** and **XVI** present profiles of the top 25 contributors to education in both the manufacturing and nonmanufacturing sectors.

These 50 companies together provided $418.6 million in education support, which was 64.4 percent of the total $650 million reported by all.

---

as a percentage of PTNI and of total contributions for 263 companies headquartered in 17 major cities.

The ranges both of dollar figures and of percentages are large, partially because of the wide variation in the number of companies reporting from each of the locations. Comparisons and rankings among cities, particularly those represented by a very small number of companies, should therefore be approached cautiously. Relationships by geographic location vary from year to year because of changes both in the sample and in business conditions. Thus the relative positions of the various metropolitan areas with respect to PTNI and contributions vary over time.

### By Company Size

**Table XIII** compares the manufacturing companies by size of worldwide pretax net income and assets. More than half of the reporting companies have PTNI greater than $100 million and assets over $1 billion.

In general, there is an inverse relationship between contributions and corporate size. The larger the PTNI or assets of the 210 manufacturing companies reporting these data, the smaller the percentages given for all philanthropic purposes and for support of education.

On the other hand, the importance of education support to total contributions is directly related to the size of the manufacturing companies. The largest companies gave more generously to education as part of

**Table XIV**
**Total Contributions and Support of Education in Relation to**
**Worldwide Pretax Net Income and Assets, 1985**

| Industry | Pretax Net Income (millions) | Assets (millions) | Total Contributions (000) | Support of Education (000) | Total Contributions as % of: | | Support of Education as % of: | | Education Support as % of Total Contributions |
|---|---|---|---|---|---|---|---|---|---|
| | | | | | PTNI | Assets | PTNI | Assets | |
| **MANUFACTURING** | | | | | | | | | |
| Chemicals(26) | $ 9,632 | $ 93,021 | $ 126,497 | $ 57,643 | 1.313 | .136 | .598 | .062 | 45.6 |
| Electrical Machinery(30) | 21,557 | 163,078 | 279,751 | 161,318 | 1.298 | .172 | .748 | .099 | 57.7 |
| Fabricated Metals(9) | 602 | 5,598 | 5,670 | 1,765 | .942 | .101 | .293 | .032 | 31.1 |
| Food, Beverage & Tobacco(21) | 11,419 | 85,060 | 125,454 | 39,837 | 1.099 | .147 | .349 | .047 | 31.8 |
| Machinery(18) | 1,742 | 25,722 | 24,282 | 8,557 | 1.394 | .094 | .491 | .033 | 35.2 |
| Mining(3) | 168 | 3,179 | 2,832 | 1,555 | 1.688 | .089 | .927 | .049 | 54.9 |
| Paper & Allied Products(14) | 1,816 | 34,457 | 22,335 | 8,176 | 1.230 | .065 | .450 | .024 | 36.6 |
| Petroleum & Gas(19) | 37,042 | 378,049 | 282,005 | 131,792 | .761 | .075 | .356 | .035 | 46.7 |
| Pharmaceuticals(11) | 6,110 | 32,735 | 74,989 | 19,182 | 1.227 | .229 | .314 | .059 | 25.6 |
| Primary Metals(13) | 2,105 | 27,885 | 11,742 | 3,930 | .558 | .042 | .187 | .014 | 33.4 |
| Printing & Publishing(10) | 1,789 | 10,465 | 21,819 | 6,779 | 1.220 | .208 | .379 | .065 | 31.1 |
| Rubber(3) | 556 | 9,604 | 6,923 | 1,991 | 1.246 | .072 | .358 | .021 | 28.8 |
| Stone, Clay & Glass(6) | 750 | 9,533 | 14,204 | 2,062 | 1.895 | .149 | .275 | .022 | 14.5 |
| Textiles & Apparel(2) | 56 | 2,922 | 3,424 | 1,802 | 6.162 | .117 | 3.243 | .062 | 52.6 |
| Transportation Equipment(15) | 15,432 | 154,642 | 153,068 | 52,594 | .992 | .099 | .341 | .034 | 34.4 |
| Total(200) | $110,774 | $1,035,951 | $1,154,996 | $498,982 | 1.043 | .111 | .450 | .048 | 43.2 |
| **NONMANUFACTURING** | | | | | | | | | |
| Banks(58) | $ 8,804 | $1,041,072 | $ 97,822 | $ 25,234 | 1.111 | .009 | .287 | .002 | 25.8 |
| Business Services(6) | 1,188 | 13,653 | 7,709 | 3,644 | .649 | .056 | .307 | .027 | 47.3 |
| Engineering & Construction(3) | 201 | 6,140 | 2,414 | 1,406 | 1.203 | .039 | .701 | .023 | 58.2 |
| Finance(4) | 1,443 | 122,942 | 6,630 | 2,026 | .459 | .005 | .140 | .002 | 30.6 |
| Insurance(39) | 5,471* | 499,990 | 115,240 | 21,455 | 2.106 | .023 | .392 | .004 | 18.6 |
| Merchandising(19) | 5,232 | 119,740 | 74,480 | 11,834 | 1.423 | .062 | .226 | .010 | 15.9 |
| Telecommunications(8) | 10,902 | 128,844 | 75,357 | 29,757 | .691 | .058 | .273 | .023 | 39.4 |
| Transportation(8) | 495 | 11,031 | 8,190 | 1,689 | 1.653 | .074 | .341 | .015 | 20.6 |
| Utilities(51) | 17,591 | 226,168 | 55,154 | 14,350 | .314 | .024 | .082 | .006 | 26.0 |
| Total(196) | $ 51,328 | $2,169,581 | $ 442,997 | $111,394 | .863 | .020 | .217 | .005 | 25.1 |
| GRAND TOTAL(396) | $162,102 | $3,205,532 | $1,597,993 | $610,376 | .986 | .049 | .377 | .019 | 38.2 |
| 1984 Grand Total(369) | $149,493 | $2,489,922 | $1,389,387 | $540,212 | .929 | .056 | .361 | .022 | 38.9 |

(Numbers in parentheses show the number of companies reporting.)
*Insurance company figures are based on "net gain from operations after dividends to policyholders and before federal income tax, excluding capital gains and losses"—the closest measure to pretax net income of corporations generally.

**Table XV**
**Top 25 Manufacturing Companies Ranked by Education Support**

| Company Rank | Corporate Contributions (thousands of dollars) | | Educational Support as a Percentage of Total Contributions | Corporate Pretax Net Income (millions of dollars) | Contributions as a Percentage of Corporate Pretax Net Income | |
|---|---|---|---|---|---|---|
| | Education | Total | | | Education | Total |
| 1 | 60,000 | 104,900 | 57.2 | 11,619 | .516 | .903 |
| 2 | 32,105 | 60,063 | 53.4 | 9,529 | .337 | .630 |
| 3 | 28,620 | 87,694 | 32.6 | 4,621 | .619 | 1.898 |
| 4 | 20,739 | 25,394 | 81.7 | 758 | 2.736 | 3.350 |
| 5 | 18,500 | 27,200 | 68.0 | 3,621 | .511 | .751 |
| 6 | 16,589 | 34,771 | 47.7 | 3,562 | .466 | .976 |
| 7 | 14,905 | 31,102 | 47.9 | 4,808 | .310 | .647 |
| 8 | 13,186 | 20,026 | 65.8 | 2,732 | .483 | .733 |
| 9 | 12,510 | 40,802 | 30.7 | 445 | 2.811 | 9.169 |
| 10 | 12,073 | 23,678 | 51.0 | 3,811 | .317 | .621 |
| 11 | 11,657 | 12,183 | 95.7 | 36 | 32.381 | 33.842 |
| 12 | 11,362 | 29,423 | 38.6 | 1,854 | .613 | 1.587 |
| 13 | 11,058 | 25,207 | 43.9 | 1,097 | 1.008 | 2.298 |
| 14 | 8,933 | 16,750 | 53.3 | 876 | 1.020 | 1.912 |
| 15 | 8,359 | 19,925 | 42.0 | 4,309 | .194 | .462 |
| 16 | 8,197 | 9,033 | 90.7 | 80 | 10.246 | 11.291 |
| 17 | 7,695 | 16,139 | 47.7 | 1,004 | .766 | 1.607 |
| 18 | 7,677 | 15,545 | 49.4 | 530 | 1.448 | 2.933 |
| 19 | 5,942 | 8,574 | 69.3 | 1,773 | .335 | .484 |
| 20 | 5,608 | 10,492 | 53.4 | 797 | .704 | 1.316 |
| 21 | 5,416 | 11,809 | 45.9 | 1,083 | .500 | 1.090 |
| 22 | 5,408 | 9,515 | 56.8 | 431 | 1.255 | 2.208 |
| 23 | 5,341 | 5,999 | 89.0 | 79 | 6.761 | 7.594 |
| 24 | 5,108 | 10,444 | 48.9 | (20) | * | * |
| 25 | 4,845 | 12,818 | 37.8 | (201) | * | * |
| Total | 341,833 | 669,486 | 51.1 | 59,234 | .577 | 1.130 |

*Company showed loss

**Table XVI**
**Top 25 Nonmanufacturing Companies Ranked by Education Support**

| Company Rank | Corporate Contributions (thousands of dollars) | | Educational Support as a Percentage of Total Contributions | Corporate Pretax Net Income (millions of dollars) | Contributions as a Percentage of Corporate Pretax Net Income | |
|---|---|---|---|---|---|---|
| | Education | Total | | | Education | Total |
| 1 | 21,111 | 38,215 | 55.2 | 2,546 | .829 | 1.501 |
| 2 | 6,836 | 18,375 | 37.2 | N.A. | — | — |
| 3 | 5,667 | 23,228 | 24.4 | 1,654 | .343 | 1.404 |
| 4 | 3,123 | 51,776 | 6.0 | 438 | .714 | 11.821 |
| 5 | 2,843 | 8,031 | 35.4 | 442 | .644 | 1.818 |
| 6 | 2,828 | 6,603 | 42.8 | 526 | .538 | 1.255 |
| 7 | 2,686 | 9,700 | 27.7 | 1,651 | .163 | .588 |
| 8 | 2,582 | 7,500 | 34.4 | 855 | .302 | .877 |
| 9 | 2,398 | 7,583 | 31.6 | 427 | .562 | 1.777 |
| 10 | 2,382 | 9,075 | 26.2 | 1,716 | .139 | .529 |
| 11 | 2,366 | 3,977 | 59.4 | 468 | .506 | .851 |
| 12 | 2,262 | 7,795 | 29.0 | 898 | .252 | .868 |
| 13 | 2,200 | 10,551 | 20.9 | 1,891 | .116 | .558 |
| 14 | 2,137 | 9,863 | 21.7 | 329 | .649 | 2.997 |
| 15 | 1,874 | 6,742 | 27.8 | 1,739 | .108 | .388 |
| 16 | 1,752 | 5,032 | 34.8 | 24 | 7.330 | 20.967 |
| 17 | 1,665 | 3,807 | 43.7 | 307 | .543 | 1.240 |
| 18 | 1,509 | 4,918 | 30.7 | 495 | .305 | .994 |
| 19 | 1,450 | 9,723 | 14.9 | 683 | .212 | 1.424 |
| 20 | 1,327 | 4,293 | 30.9 | 104 | 1.276 | 4.128 |
| 21 | 1,237 | 3,251 | 38.1 | 943 | .131 | .345 |
| 22 | 1,157 | 5,015 | 23.1 | 1,683 | .069 | .298 |
| 23 | 1,145 | 4,495 | 25.4 | 434 | .264 | 1.036 |
| 24 | 1,136 | 1,566 | 72.5 | 115 | .988 | 1.362 |
| 25 | 1,129 | 6,332 | 17.8 | 195 | .579 | 3.248 |
| Total | 76,802 | 267,446 | 28.7 | 20,563 | .374 | 1.301 |

N.A. Not available

Source: Corporate Support of Education
(Council for Financial Aid to Education, Inc.
680 Fifth Avenue New York, NY 10019)

# Selected State Reports on Higher Education

# X.1

# Arkansas

## Board of Higher Education
### Membership

The members of the State Board of Higher Education (SBHE) during 1986 were Mr. Nicky Hargrove, Chairman, Mrs. Corliss Howard, Vice Chairperson, Mrs. Mary Faye Black, Secretary, Mr. David Dubbell, Mr. Woody Freeman, Dr. Kemal Kutait, Dr. Dave Luck, Mr. Dan Pierce, and Dr. Clifton Roat. Mr. Perrin Jones was appointed to fill the vacancy on the SBHE created by the resignation of Mr. Sheffield Nelson.

### Meetings

Regular quarterly meetings of the SBHE were held at the University of Arkansas for Medical Sciences, Southern Arkansas University – Tech, the University of Arkansas at Little Rock, and the Holiday Inn West in Little Rock. In addition, policy discussion sessions were conducted about the budget process, the enrollment projection process, the role of the SBHE, and the unique history and mission of the two – year institutions.

### 25th Anniversary

A special evening meeting and social activity, including present and former members of the SBHE, was held in honor of the 25th anniversary of the SBHE.

## Finance
### 1987 – 89 Higher Education Budget Recommendations

The SBHE recommended to the General Assembly and the Governor that the state budget for the 1987 – 89 biennium include approximately $311 million in 1987 – 88 and approximately $347 million in 1988 – 89 for operating funds for the 20 state institutions of higher education. The amount recommended for 1987 – 88 is approximately the same as the amount appropriated by the General Assembly two years ago for 1986 – 87. Full funding of the SBHE recommendation would restore the budget cuts that have been absorbed during the past two years.

The SBHE also made recommendations for capital improvements and maximum salary levels for faculty and administrative positions at the institutions. The presidents and chancellors of all state institutions supported the SBHE budget recommendations.

### Economic Feasibility of Bond Issues and Loans

The SBHE verified the economic feasibility of proposed bond issues or bank loans at Garland County Community College, Phillips County Community College, the University of Arkansas for Medical Sciences, the University of Arkansas at Monticello, and the University of Central Arkansas.

## Academic Affairs
### New Degree Programs

The SBHE approved the following new degree programs:

| | |
|---|---|
| Arkansas State University | B.S. – International Business Studies |
| University of Arkansas at Little Rock | B.S. – Computer Engineering Technology |
| University of Central Arkansas | M.S. – Health Education |

## Discontinued Degree Programs

The SBHE received letters of notification that the following degree programs were discontinued:

| | |
|---|---|
| Southern Arkansas University-El Dorado | A.A.S.–Chemical Technology |
| University of Arkansas at Little Rock | A.S.–Engineering Master of Library Science and Information |
| University of Arkansas at Pine Bluff | B.S.–Library/Media B.S.–Industrial Arts Education |
| University of Central Arkansas | B.B.A. & A.A.–Executive Secretarial Administration |

## Changes in Organizational Structures

The SBHE approved proposals to restructure or rename existing organizational units to create the following:

| | |
|---|---|
| Arkansas Tech University | School of Business |
| University of Arkansas at Pine Bluff | School of Agriculture, Home Economics, and Technology |
| | School of Business and Management |
| | School of Education |
| | School of Arts and Sciences |
| | Center for Multi-Disciplinary Research and Sponsored Programs |
| Westark Community College | Division of Computer and Information Management Systems |

## Certification of Out-of-State and Non-Public Institutions

Based on recommendations by the Institutional Certification Advisory Committee, the SBHE certified Webster University, Southern Illinois University, and the Southern Technical College campuses at Little Rock and Texarkana, and recertified Pikes Peak Community College, Stephens College, Arkansas College of Technology, Cleveland Institute of Technology, and the International Correspondence Schools Center for Degree Studies to offer college credit in Arkansas.

## Quality Higher Education Study Committee Recommendations

The Arkansas Department of Higher Education (ADHE) produced a report on the progress made by institutions of higher education in implementing the recommendations of the Quality Higher Education Study Committee. Significant progress was noted in the areas of admissions, student assessment and advising, partnerships with public schools and businesses, teacher education, and the general education core curriculum. Copies of the report were sent to the Governor, members of the General Assembly, members of the SBHE, and campus administrators.

## Arkansas Transfer Advisory Committee

The Arkansas Transfer Advisory Committee was created as an on-going mechanism to facilitate transfer of academic credits between the thirty-two state and independent institutions of higher education in Arkansas. The Committee recommends policies to make the transfer process smoother, coordinates transfer agreements between institutions, and produces several publications concerning institutional transfer policies and course equivalencies. The ADHE provides staff assistance for the Committee.

In addition, each of the 32 institutions has designated a transfer officer to provide information about the institution's transfer policies. A roster of all of the transfer officers was distributed to the academic administrators and department heads for use in advising students.

## Review of Mathematics Programs

A review was conducted by the ADHE of the mathematics programs at all ten state two-year institutions and all state universities, except for the University of Arkansas for Medical Sciences. The team of out-of-state consultants was generally very positive about mathematics education at Arkansas state institutions of higher education. The main concern expressed in the report was that many entering freshmen are not properly prepared to handle college-level mathematics. The consultants recommended that successful completion of algebra I and II and geometry in high school should be required for unconditional admission to any of the state universities.

## Teacher Education Standards

A committee of chief academic officers was formed by the ADHE to recommend ways to strengthen teacher education programs. The chief academic officers recommended and the presidents and chancellors agreed to implement the new standards that were to be considered by the State Board of Education for approval of teacher education programs. The State Board of Education subsequently adopted the strengthened standards, which include the following:

- All teacher education majors will take, as a minimum, the same general education requirements as other baccalaureate degree programs.
- Secondary education majors will major in an academic discipline in addition to taking teaching methods courses.
- Teacher education students will be introduced to teacher education at the freshman or sophomore year through observation and experience.
- All professional education content/methods courses will be taught at the upper division.
- A minimum of twelve weeks of practice teaching (practicum) will be required.
- Admission requirements to teacher education will require passage of basic communications skills and core general knowledge test (NTE Pre-Professional Test); demonstrated proficiency in written and oral communication; and a 2.5 grade-point average.

## Student Assessment and Retention Standards

A committee of chief academic officers was formed by the ADHE to recommend minimum activities to be conducted by institutions to evaluate students' academic abilities and to provide academic support services. The chief academic officers recommended and the presidents and chancellors agreed to work with their faculties to implement the following standards:

- Students at all institutions will be assigned to an academic advisor throughout their enrollment.
- Some institutions offer developmental activities to help students bring their competencies to a level at which they can pass college-level work. Those institutions which offer developmental activities will adopt the following plan:
  - Students will be evaluated to determine their proficiency in English grammar, reading and

mathematics, and developmental activities will be provided for those students with deficiencies;
  - Developmental work will continue until a minimum competency is achieved;
  - Developmental work will not apply to a baccalaureate degree program or associate degrees which transfer to baccalaureate programs; and
  - Developmental activities will be evaluated to determine their effectiveness.

## Guidelines for Telecourses

Changes in telecommunications technology make telecourses offered through video cassettes or broadcasting an attractive and convenient form of learning. In order to assure quality in the offering of telecourses by institutions in Arkansas, the chief academic officers were asked by the ADHE to consider the guidelines for telecourses recommended by a Telecommunications Task Force. The guidelines received a favorable response from the group of chief academic officers for implementation by institutions which offer telecourses.

## Grants to Improve Public School Teaching

The ADHE, in cooperation with the State Department of Education, selected projects at 15 state and independent institutions of higher education in Arkansas for funding through the federal Education for Economic Security Act to improve the teaching of math and science in the public schools.

## Statewide Basic Skills Tests

Committees of English and mathematics department heads and faculty members were formed by the ADHE to make recommendations regarding basic skills tests for students at all state institutions of higher education. Two types of tests are being considered. The first would be used to identify freshmen who might be unprepared for college-level math and English courses so that those students can be assigned to non-credit remedial courses. The second type of test would assess whether students had mastered the expected level of learning in reading, math, and writing by the end of the sophomore year in order to be eligible to continue into the junior year.

The staff of the Southern Regional Education Board (SREB) will assist Arkansas with this project.

The ADHE director and several institutional officials attended a meeting at the SREB offices in Atlanta concerning statewide testing programs for college students.

## Transfer of Credits to Nursing Programs

The ADHE worked with the heads of nursing education programs at Arkansas institutions of higher education to facilitate transfer of credits between nursing programs at different institutions, as mandated by Act 88 of 1979.

## Academic Common Market

The ADHE administered the participation of Arkansas in the Academic Common Market of the Southern Regional Education Board. During 1986, 69 additional Arkansas residents enrolled in university programs in other southern states which are not available in Arkansas and the students paid in-state tuition through the Common Market program. These programs inclued library science, commercial music, aerospace engineering, petroleum engineering, fire service administration technology, nursing (doctorate), and counseling and personnel services (doctorate).

## Criteria for New Program Proposals

The ADHE revised the publication entitled, *Criteria and Procedures for Preparing Proposals for New Academic Programs,* and provided copies to campus officials.

# Student Financial Aid Programs

## State Student Assistance Grant Program

The ADHE awarded $4,128,372 for 1985–86 and $4,702,064 for 1986–87 to 12,938 needy students at state and independent institutions of higher education, vocational–technical schools, and proprietary schools in Arkansas. Administration of the program included determining the financial need of all 19,399 applicants.

## Governor's Scholars Program

The ADHE coordinated the selection of the 100 high school seniors to receive $2,000 Governor's Scholarships for attendance as freshmen at Arkansas state and independent institutions of higher education in the fall 1987 semester. The ADHE also transferred the funds to the institutions for scholarships for the three classes (almost 300 students) of Governor's Scholars enrolled in the fall of 1987. Finally, the ADHE assisted with the coordination of a conference and banquet honoring the Governor's Scholars.

## Math/Science Teacher Loan Program

The ADHE coordinated, with the assistance of the Department of Education, the selection of undergraduate students for participation in the Math/Science Teacher Loan Program during the 1986–87 year. The loans are forgiven if the recipients teach math or science in the public schools after graduation. A total of $130,766 was loaned to 68 students for 1986–87.

## Teacher/Administrator Loan Program

The ADHE administered the Teacher/Administrator Loan Program for public school teachers and administrators in Arkansas who either did not pass the teacher competency test or need additional university courses in order to be recertified. The loans are forgiven for the teachers and administrators who continue to work in the public schools of Arkansas. A total of $458,220 was loaned during 1985–86.

## Congressional Teacher Scholarship Program

The ADHE, with the assistance of the Department of Education, established the procedures for administering the Congressional Teacher Scholarship Program. This new federal program will provide $5,000 annual scholarships to encourage some of the brightest students to pursue teacher education degrees as undergraduates.

## Scholarships for Survivors and Dependents

The ADHE administered programs of scholarships to children of Arkansas law enforcement officers and firemen and dependents of Arkansas military personnel killed or missing in action. In 1985–86, scholarships totaling $23,390 were provided to sixteen students.

# Planning and Research

The ADHE Planning and Research Division collected, analyzed, and reported information about a variety of areas related to higher education in Arkansas. Publications included the following:

- *Geographic and Institutional Origin of Arkansas College Students. Fall 1985.*
- *Arkansas High School Graduates: Projections to 1999–2000.*
- *Student Retention — An Issue of the 80's.*
- *Spring On–Campus Full–Time Equivalent Enrollment, 1986.*
- *Annual Full–Time Equivalent Enrollment and Student Semester Credit Hour Production in Arkansas State Institutions of Higher Education, 1984–85.*
- *Degrees Granted by Arkansas Institutions of Higher Education, 1984–85.*
- *Fall On–Campus Enrollment, 1985.*
- *Degrees by Classification of Instructional Program Code.*
- *On–Campus Enrollment in Arkansas Institutions of Higher Education.*
- *Annual Full–Time Equivalent Enrollment and Student Semester Credit Hour Production in Arkansas State Institutions of Higher Education, 1985–86.*

# Arkansas Desegregation Plan
## Annual Report to Office of Civil Rights

The ADHE monitored compliance by state institutions of higher education with the commitments made in the Arkansas Desegregation Plan, and submitted an annual report to the U.S. Office of Civil Rights.

## Public Forum on Desegregation

Presentations were made by representatives of the ADHE, SBHE, and state institutions of higher education at the Public Forum on the Status of Desegregation in Public Institutions of Higher Education in Arkansas sponsored by the Advisory Committee to the U.S. Commission on Civil Rights.

# Liaison with Branches of State Government
## Governor's Office

The ADHE provided information and assistance to the Governor's Office on a variety of issues and projects. In addition, the ADHE director attended meetings of the Governor's Cabinet and represented Governor Clinton at a meeting of a national task force on improving higher education.

## Legislature

The ADHE provided information and assistance to legislative committees, to individual legislators, and to legislative staff members on a variety of issues. Also, the ADHE director met individually with 69 members of the General Assembly to learn of their views about higher education in Arkansas and the role of the SBHE and the ADHE.

## State Agencies

The ADHE provided information and assistance to a number of state agencies on a variety of issues and activities.

# Other Activities
## Data Processing Purchases

The ADHE reviewed and made decisions on requests from state colleges and universities to purchase computer hardware and software. Decisions were made on requests by campuses to spend more than $4.5 million.

## Energy Conservation

Assistance with energy conservation was provided by ADHE to state and independent colleges and universities through a special grant to the ADHE from the Department of Energy. An engineer, with expertise in energy conservation, served on the ADHE staff and coordinated this effort.

## Economic Development Projects

The ADHE approved proposals and distributed over $3 million to the state institutions of higher education for special activities designed to enhance the economic development of Arkansas. The ADHE also coordinated a meeting for institutional officials involved in these projects, and collected and analyzed information from the institutions regarding the impact of the economic development activities.

## College Attendance

The ADHE coordinated the annual statewide effort to increase the number and percentage of high school graduates who enroll in college. A booklet entitled, *Your Future Starts Now,* was distributed by institutional representatives to eighth graders during special visits to junior high schools. A slide-tape presentation entitled "Go For It" was also shown to eighth graders during these visits. The booklet and slide show stress the lifelong benefits of college attendance, the availability of financial aid, and the importance of taking rigorous academic courses in high school in order to be able to enter and succeed in college.

The percentage of high school graduates attending a college or university in Arkansas increased from 39.4 percent in the fall of 1984 to 42 percent in the fall of 1985.

The 1985 fall headcount enrollment of 74,594 at Arkansas state and independent institutions of higher education was the highest ever.

## Higher Education Conference

The ADHE helped coordinate a statewide higher education conference, which was attended by more than 200 administrators and faculty members from state and independent colleges and universities in Arkansas.

## Representation on Committees and Boards

The ADHE director served on the following committees and boards:

- Arkansas Science and Techology Authority Board
- Committee on Jobs for Arkansas' Future
- Arkansas State Technical Institute Advisory Committee
- Arkansas State Job Training Coordinating Council
- Governor's Economic Development Board
- Economic Expansion Study Commission

## Newsletters

The ADHE published and distributed four issues of the *Arkansas Higher Education Review,* a newsletter about higher education in Arkansas.

## Speeches

The ADHE director made speeches to the following groups:

- Commencements
  - Arkansas State University—Jonesboro
  - East Arkansas Community College
  - Garland County Community College
  - Southern Arkansas University—El Dorado
- Civic Clubs
  - Arkadelphia Rotary Club
  - Benton Lions Club
  - Conway Rotary Club
  - Little Rock Optimist Club
  - Little Rock Toastmasters Club
  - North Little Rock Lions Club
  - North Little Rock Rotary Club
  - Pine Bluff Kiwanis Club
  - Stuttgart Lions Club
- Other
  - American College Personnel Association
  - Arkansas Association of Community Service/Continuing Education Administrators
  - Arkansas College Personnel Association
  - Arkansas Tech University Freshmen Leadership Program
  - Asssociation of Community and Junior Colleges of Arkansas
  - Intergovernmental Relations Committee
  - Phi Delta Kappa—Little Rock Chapter
  - Rural Leadership Training Program
  - "The Global Revolution in Technology"—Symposium held at the University of Arkansas at Pine Bluff
  - University of Arkansas at Little Rock Faculty Assembly
  - University of Central Arkansas College of Education Faculty
  - University of Central Arkansas Division of Student Affairs

ADHE staff members and SBHE members made speeches to the following groups:

- Association of Arkansas College and University Registrars
- Arkansas Deans Association
- East Arkansas Economic Conference
- Science Information Liaison Office—Conference on Small Business Development in Arkansas
- "Winning the Race with Change"—Conference

sponsored by the Arkansas Science and Technology Authority
- American Association of Affirmative Action Officers
- Arkansas Association of Student Assistance Programs
- Arkansas Association for Developmental Education

## Campus Visits

The ADHE director visited all 20 state and 10 of the 12 independent colleges and universities in Arkansas for campus tours and meetings with the presidents and chancellors and other administrators. In addition, the director, other ADHE staff members, and SBHE members visited campuses for a variety of meetings and events.

# ADHE Staff
## New Staff Members

The following individuals joined the ADHE staff:

- Dr. Diane Gilleland, Associate Director for Finance

- Margaret Lincourt, Coordinator of Student Financial Aid
- John McGrath, Financial Officer
- Marh Lingo, Administrative Assistant
- Charlene Williams, Receptionist
- Joyce Davis, Secretary
- Joe Schrameyer, Word Processing Operator

## Staff Development Workshops

Staff development workshops were conducted on the following topics:

- History and role of the SBHE and the ADHE
- Public speaking
- Time management
- The performance evaluation process and the grievance procedure for state employees
- Use of the telephone system
- Use of the word processing system
- The Arkansas Science and Technology Authority — Dr. John Ahlen
- The Vocational–Technical Division — Dr. Barry Ballard

# Connecticut:
## *Board of Governors for Higher Education*

The year 1985–86 was one of accomplishment and anticipation for the Board of Governors for Higher Education. With many of its initiatives in place, the Board's attention turned to the future. In its first statewide plan, the Board offers a bold vision of the future and an ambitious agenda for making Connecticut's colleges and universities among the nation's best by the year 2001.

Established in 1983, the Board of Governors is the state coordinating and policy-making agency for Connecticut colleges and universities. While the Board coordinates policy with the private sector, it has primary responsibility over the public system consisting of the University of Connecticut, its health center and regional campuses; four state universities; twelve regional community colleges; five state technical colleges; and the Board of State Academic Awards' Charter Oak College.

Chief among the Board's duties are the development of consolidated operating and capital budget requests, licensure and accreditation of academic programs and institutions (both public and independent), administration of state student financial assistance programs, campus facilities development and research and information services. Its goals are to promote academic excellence, student access, responsiveness and the effective use of resources.

The Board has eleven public members. Seven are appointed by the Governor and four by the legislative leaders of the Governor's opposite political party. As of July 1986 members were: Jeremiah J. Lowney, Jr., Lebanon, Chairman; Anne Boyd Kraig, New Canaan, Vice Chairman; Thomas A. Aquila, Weston; Russell D'Oench, Jr., Middletown; Sal J. Giudice, Colchester; Sidney P. Marland, Jr., Hampton; William J. McCue, New Britain; Edmund B. Piccolino, Darien; and Betty L. Tianti, Newington. Two vacancies exist. The Board has an advisory committee of 22 academic representatives.

The Department of Higher Education, the Board's administrative arm, has three Divisions for Academic Affairs, Financial Affairs and Research and Information Services, an Office of Educational Opportunity and the Office of the Commissioner. Working with colleges, the Board and its staff sought to assure the system meets today's needs as well as tomorrow's challenges.

# Investing in Connecticut's Future

Capping nine months of study with college and industry advisors, the Board in June completed *Investing in Connecticut's Future: A Strategic Plan for Higher Education.* Stressing that the state's future prosperity rests on the quality of education, the five-year plan urges a major commitment to colleges and universities. Among its forty strategies, the plan calls for strengthening funding, attracting more minority students and faculty, improving services for part-time students, enhancing quality in the liberal arts and in teacher preparation, and expanding industry-related programs. Its recommendations will form the basis of many of the Board's 1986–87 legislative and budget proposals.

# Striving for Excellence

Highlighting efforts to strengthen quality was the Board's award of $1.4 million to eight Centers of Excellence in fields ranging from biotechnology to international relations. The Board won legislative approval for a complementary program, an Endowed Chair Investment Fund, through which state monies will be matched with private sector support for eminent faculty scholars.

As the nation's attention focused on the quality of teachers, so did the Board's. It obtained legislative support to create an Institute for Effective Teaching which will explore ways to enhance education curricula and expand professional development opportunities for college faculty.

To improve teaching skills in science, mathematics and computers, five public and independent colleges received $307,000 in grants under the federal Education for Economic Security Act. Some 315 students were awarded incentive loans which are later "forgiven" in return for teaching service. The need for attracting more students to the profession was underscored by a Department of Higher Education study showing that colleges are awarding fewer bachelor's degrees in education than ever before, presaging a serious shortage of teachers by 1990.

In light of national calls for strengthening the liberal arts, the Board now requires that one-third of baccalaureate work be completed in general education as part of its new regulations for licensure and accreditation. The procedures also specify the number of credits students can earn in non-collegiate sponsored instruction and experiential learning.

In all, the Board authorized or re-authorized thirteen programs at public institutions and fourteen at independent institutions. New offerings include the state's first doctoral program in business administration at the University of Connecticut, a sixth-year certificate program for science and mathematics teachers at Southern Connecticut State University and an optical engineering program at Norwalk State Technical College.

# Responding to State Needs

Assuring that Connecticut institutions of higher learning serve the needs of citizens and employers remained a key Board priority.

At the two-year level, a Board task force called on the regional community and state technical colleges to develop more cooperative offerings, especially in "low technology" fields, remedial education and short-term training. To help students take courses in both systems at once, the technical colleges will, in fall 1987, adopt the semester-based calendar used systemwide.

Responding to temporary labor needs, the Board contracted for thirty spaces for transfer students in electrical and mechanical engineering and dental hygiene at the University of Bridgeport, and for an additional twenty in hotel and restaurant management at the University of New Haven. The spaces will be available for two years starting in fall 1986. The Board also recommended expanding entering

classes in engineering at the University of Connecticut and in dental hygiene at Tunxis Community College.

Twenty outstanding students received High Technology Graduate Scholarships, double the number awarded previously. The Scholarships encourage new research and add to faculty resources.

Expanding its service to the public, the Department of Higher Education assumed responsibility for the Education and Employment Information Center, a statewide source of free information on learning and career opportunities. Public inquiries to the Center's toll-free hotline (1-800-842-0229) doubled since its move to the Department.

# Securing Adequate Finances

To sustain adequate and equitable funding for public higher education, the Board developed its 1986–87 operating budget using formulas for instruction, libraries and campus maintenance. The formulas distribute funds according to factors such as numbers of students, levels of programs, and size and role of institutions.

For 1986–87, the Board succeeded in obtaining an overall 10.9 percent increase in operating funds. The total net FY 1987 general fund operating budget for higher education is $316.3 million, representing a $31.6 million or 11.1 percent increase over FY 1986 expenditures. This includes approximately $4.6 million in the form of a supplemental appropriation from the state's FY 1986 surplus. The budget also includes funding for an additional 150 general fund positions. The combined increase in both general fund and tuition fund support is $36.2 million or a 10.9 percent increase.

For the University of Connecticut, the budget provides additional support for physical plant operations, long–range data processing, engineering spaces and equipment, and instructional and support positions. At the UConn Health Center, funds will enhance programs in imaging science, arthritis, neuroscience, bone and connective tissue, oncology, poison control and adolescent medicine. Funds are also provided to expand oncology services and establish a hospice program at Uncas–on–Thames Hospital.

For Connecticut State University, additional support is provided for instruction, libraries, physical plant operations, long–range data processing, equipment, and administrative and support positions. Funds for the regional community colleges will support new positions and physical plant improvements while the state technical colleges will use their additional resources for libraries, equipment, a pilot technology transfer program and moving Greater New Haven State Technical College to its new Orchard Hill site.

The Board obtained funds for its Institute for Effective Teaching, Minority Advancement Initiative, Endowed Chair Investment Fund, Centers of Excellence, student financial aid, and contracting arrangements for student spaces with independent colleges.

# Restoring Campus Facilities

The Board's emphasis on renovating campus facilities was strongly endorsed by the Governor and General Assembly. Forty percent of all capital funds for 1986–87 were authorized for renovation and only 31.9 percent for new construction.

The FY 1987 capital budget totals $44.2 million of which $38.3 million is in general obligation bonds and $5.9 million is in self-liquidating bonds. Highlights include $4.5 million to complete Phase II of the Central Naugatuck Valley Region Higher Education Center, $5 million for building renovations at the University of Connecticut, $3.1 million to complete UConn's student recreation and athletic facility, and $2.7 million for a permanent home for Greater New Haven State Technical College. Equipment funds increased to 4.2 percent of the capital budget as institutions sought to upgrade equipment that has been in use since World War II.

The Board's annual financing plan for campus facilities is a part of a five–year plan to eliminate health, fire, or safety hazards and architectural barriers; increase energy conservation; maintain and renovate existing facilities; replace existing leased or deteriorated facilities; and create facilities for new or consolidated programs only when space is not available.

During the year, the Board authorized bonding for equipment for Waterbury State Technical College's "Factory of the Future," making the college the first in New England with an automated model factory. Construction began at Central Connecticut State University to renovate the Stanley Street School into a fine arts center. The Board also issued a ranking of building conditions of the state technical colleges, citing $10.8 million worth of needed repairs.

# Assuring Student Equity and Access

Assuring equity in state support for all students is the goal of another Board initiative. Part–time students, whose numbers are rapidly growing, pay considerably more than full–time students for the same instruction. To correct this inequity, the Board proposes to transfer costs for credit instruction to the state's general and tuition funds over five years at a cost of $14.5 million. Part–time students will pay a prorated share of tuition and fees charged to full–time students.

In March the Department of Higher Education forecast a loss to the state of $700,000 in federal student aid money if provisions of the Gramm-Rudman-Hollings deficit reduction measure were enacted. The report led Governor O'Neill to name a task force of lawmakers and education officials to study ways to compensate for shortfalls in student aid.

During 1985–86, student assistance programs administered by the Department of Higher Education provided $11.3 million in aid, including $989,000 in federal funds, to approximately 14,000 Connecticut residents. A total of $6 million was distributed to students at independent colleges and approximately $5.3 million was made available through seven other programs including the State Scholastic Achievement Grant Program. In addition, state–supported colleges provided approximately $7.1 million in tuition waivers to needy students.

The Board continued to promote access and equity by implementing recommendations contained in its 1985 *Strategic Plan to Ensure Racial and Ethnic Diversity in Connecticut Public Higher Education.* In accordance with Board requirements, public colleges developed plans to diminish by half, within five years, disparities between the enrollment and graduation rates of minorities and non–minorities. The plans were evaluated by a special peer review committee. Based on its recommendations, the Board granted six institutions one-year approvals and six three–year approvals and the remaining 11 received five-year approvals.

In a new effort, the Board developed the Minority Advancement Program (MAP), a three-pronged approach designed to increase minority enrollment, professional recruitment and developmental opportunities. This initiative, also tied to the *Strategic Plan,* includes three programs: (1) the Minority Enrollment Incentive Program; (2) the Minority Staff Development/Recruitment Program; and (3) the

Connecticut Collegiate Awareness and Preparation (CONNCAP) Program.

To promote early awareness initiatives, the Department's Office of Educational Opportunity provided technical assistance to the Stamford Higher Education Project (SHEP) and the Hartford Consortium for Higher Education's Career Beginnings grant effort. SHEP replicates the Department's earlier program, the Minorities in Higher Education Project, by matching minority middle- and high-school youngsters with successful professionals or mentors who counsel them on academic and career plans.

Career Beginnings is a two-year program operated by the Hartford Consortium for Higher Education in partnership with the Private Industry Council, Greater Hartford Community College, UConn—Hartford Campus, and Hartford State Technical College. The program will help Hartford high school juniors learn about college and career options, and was developed in part by the Department's Office of Educational Opportunity.

As part of the Department's internal affirmative action efforts, the agency developed a new staff recruitment procedure and career counseling system. Seven staff participated in workshops conducted by the Commission on Human Rights and Opportunities. The Department's affirmative action plan was approved by the Commission.

In March the Department met its set-aside goal for small business contracts and minority businesses. The Department continued to maintain data on all small and minority business contracts awarded through June. Final goal attainment for small business contracts was 37 percent, some 8 percent above the agency's goal and for minority business enterprises, 29 percent, some 14 percent above the agency's goal.

# Student and Degree Profiles

Connecticut public and independent institutions of higher education enrolled 160,148 students in 1985–86, less than one percent below last year's headcount total. In the public sector, losses occurred primarily at the two-year institutions. Declines in the independent sector were modest.

A total of 27,016 degrees were awarded in spring 1985 by Connecticut institutions, continuing a ten-year trend despite changes across disciplines. The most marked change was the drop in the number of bachelor's degrees awarded in education, down to 5.4 percent of all degrees, compared to 19.1 percent ten years ago. Bachelor's degrees in business and management are now the most popular.

Public colleges are awarding fewer bachelor's and master's degrees while the state's independent institutions are granting more. This new trend reflects the growing numbers of part-time students attending public colleges. These shifts have important implications for the state's future workforce and for colleges in terms of budget allocations, faculty assignments and program growth and standards. The Board of Governors will continue to monitor these changes as it carries out the goals of its *Strategic Plan for Higher Education.*

## X.3

# Kentucky

## Higher Education in Kentucky 1986

Higher education in Kentucky was highlighted by several advances in 1986, including the first steps in implementing the state's first Strategic Plan for Higher Education, approved by the Kentucky Council on Higher Education in November 1985, the founding of a citizens' advocacy group for higher education, enhanced financial and quality programs support from the Kentucky legislature, a new capital program, increased enrollments, and a new community college and expanded independent college.

The year began with a concerted effort by the supporters of the state's eight public universities, thirteen community colleges and twenty-one private colleges and universities to gain greater support for higher education in Kentucky. The Kentucky Advocates for Higher Education, Inc., a group of business and civic leaders, had been formed in October 1985 to develop statewide support for higher education. The Kentucky Advocates sponsored eight rallies throughout the state on January 6, the day before the 1986 biennial General Assembly convened, and held another rally on February 5 in the capital city of Frankfort, which was attended by over 5,000 citizens from all parts of the state.

Kentucky Governor Martha Layne Collins made higher education one of the top priorities in her 1986–1988 biennial budget recommendations to the state legislature. In the final budget the 1986 General Assembly appropriated more to higher education than was in the recommendations of the Governor and the house and senate Appropriations and Revenue Committees and approved for perhaps the first time higher education programs that were aimed specifically at increasing the quality of higher education throughout the public system. Among the legislative actions were the following:

• Appropriations for the public higher education

system of $481,282,500 for FY 1986/87 (an 8.33 percent increase over the previous year) and $535,349,400 for FY 1987/88 (an 11.23 percent increase). This amounted to more than a 20 percent increase of state support for higher education over the biennium. (Because of a revenue shortfall, the budget was reduced by 2 percent in November 1986.)

• Appropriations for the Kentucky Higher Education Assistance Authority of $8,574,900 for FY 1986/87 and $8,817,100 for FY 1987/88. Students at both the public and private institutions receive financial assistance through KHEAA.

• New bonding authority totaling approximately $147.3 million for new facilities, deferred maintenance, major renovation, and equipment.

• A Commonwealth Centers program, to establish centers of excellence, which will offer a set of disciplines representing related areas of intellectual or artistic enterprise. Centers will be awarded to the public universities and community colleges on a competitive basis.

• An Endowed Chairs program, to establish endowed chairs — again, on a competitive basis — to support and attract outstanding scholars to the Kentucky public higher education system.

• A Salary Incentive Fund, to reward and recognize superior performance of faculty and staff members at the universities and community colleges. The biennial budget appropriated some $5 million for this fund in FY 1986/87, and some $9.5 million in FY 1987/88.

• Participation in the National Science Foundation's Experimental Program to Stimulate Competitive Research (EPSCoR) to assist young scientific and technical researchers in Kentucky develop in their profession and to increase the level of sponsored research in the state.

• The Governor's Minority Student College Preparation Program, to develop methods of better preparing minority students to persist in college to graduation. This program, funded at $250,000 for each year of the biennium, is aimed at intervention activities with students at the middle–school/junior–high–school level.

• Major additions to the higher education system, including a new community college, a Robotics Center, and a supercomputer. A total of $228 million, from all sources, was authorized for capital projects for higher education.

## Enrollment

Increasing educational attainment levels for Kentucky's citizens is one of the principal goals of Kentucky's Strategic Plan for Higher Education. In the fall of 1986 enrollment rose at both the public and private colleges and universities, even though the number of spring 1986 high school graduates declined by 3.2 percent. The public universities and community colleges, which account for approximately 85 percent of the higher education enrollment in Kentucky, had a headcount enrollment of 115,346, up 3.9 percent over fall 1985. The increase was even more dramatic for first-time freshmen, with a fall 1986 increase of over 6 percent. There were 19,858 students enrolled at the independent institutions, a 2.5 percent increase over fall 1985; the first-time freshmen increased by 2.3 percent. The total headcount enrollment for higher education in Kentucky in fall 1986 was 136,204.

## Degrees Conferred

During the 1985/86 fiscal year, Kentucky's institutions of higher education conferred 20,618 degrees. The eight public universities conferred 1,418 associate degrees, 9,444 bachelor's degrees, 2,908 master's or specialist's degrees, 151 doctorate degrees, and 691 first-professional (medicine, law, dentistry, pharmacy) degrees. The thirteen University of Kentucky community colleges conferred 2,613 associate degrees. The sixteen independent senior institutions conferred 385 associate degrees, 2,320 bachelor's degrees, 349 master's or specialist's degrees, and four doctorate degrees. The five independent junior colleges conferred 335 associate degrees.

The total degrees awarded by type of institution were: state-supported senior institutions, 14,612; UK community college system, 2,613; all state–supported institutions, 17,225; independent senior institutions, 3,058; independent junior institutions, 335; all independent institutions 3,393.

## New, Enhanced Institutions

In July 1986 Owensboro Community College was founded, the first new community college in Kentucky in almost twenty years. In fall 1986 Lindsey Wilson (Columbia, Ky.), formerly a two–year college, became a four–year institution.

## Higher Education Systems in Kentucky

The Kentucky Council on Higher Education serves as the coordinating agency for public community colleges and universities in the state. The independent colleges are organized into a twenty-one–member group, the Council of Independent Kentucky Colleges and Universities. The two councils work closely together in setting higher education policy. Postsecondary vocational schools and adult programs are operated by the Kentucky Department of Education and the Kentucky Superintendent of Public Instruction. Certificate programs are offered at this level; the associate degree and certificate level programs are coordinated through cooperative arrangements between the Council on Higher Education and the Department of Education. A number of for-profit schools are organized by statute under the Kentucky Board for Proprietary Education.

## Governance and Coordination of Public Higher Education

Kentucky Statutes mandate a shared responsibility for the governance and coordination of public higher education between the individual institutional governing boards and the Council on Higher Education. Among the various forms in the fifty states, Kentucky's system is generally classified as a coordinated—as opposed to a governance—system. In Kentucky, management and operational responsibilities and authority are vested in the governing board of each institution. The Council on Higher Education is a policy–making body for the system of higher education. In the fulfillment of its statutory charges, the Council on Higher Education's decisions and policies may affect institutional management and operations, but the Council does not manage or operate any college or university. Thus the responsibilities to define and deliver a co-ordinated system of higher education in the state are shared among the individual governing boards of the public institutions and the Council on Higher Education.

# Higher Education Institutions

The institutions that compose the Kentucky system of higher education are:

*Public Universities:*
Eastern Kentucky University, Richmond
Kentucky State University, Frankfort
Morehead State University, Morehead
Murray State University, Murray
Northern Kentucky University, Highland Heights
University of Kentucky, Lexington
University of Louisville, Louisville
Western Kentucky University, Bowling Green.
*University of Kentucky Community College System:*
Ashland Community College, Ashland
Elizabethtown Community College, Elizabethtown
Hazard Community College, Hazard
Henderson Community College, Henderson
Hopkinsville Community College, Hopkinsville
Jefferson Community College, Louisville

Lexington Community College, Lexington
Madisonville Community College, Madisonville
Maysville Community College, Maysville
Owensboro Community College, Owensboro
Paducah Community College, Paducah
Prestonsburg Community College, Prestonsburg
Somerset Community College, Somerset
Southeast Community College, Cumberland.
*Independent Senior Colleges and Universities:*
Alice Lloyd College, Pippa Passes
Asbury College, Wilmore
Bellarmine College, Louisville
Berea College, Berea
Brescia College, Owensboro
Campbellsville College, Campbellsville
Centre College, Danville
Cumberland College, Williamstown
Georgetown College, Georgetown
Kentucky Christian College, Grayson
Kentucky Wesleyan College, Owensboro
Lindsey Wilson College, Columbia
Pikeville College, Pikeville
Spalding University, Louisville
Thomas More College, Crestview Hills
Transylvania University, Lexington
Union College, Barbourville.
*Independent Junior Colleges:*
Lees College, Jackson
Midway College, Midway
St. Catharine College, St. Catharine
Sue Bennett College, London.

# Mississippi:

## A Summary of Activities in Institutions of Higher Learning, State of Mississippi, July 1, 1985–June 30, 1986

Fiscal year 1985–86 held financial challenges for the Board of Trustees of State Institutions of Higher Learning as it experienced two mid-year budget cuts and a reduction in appropriations for FY 1986–1987 by the 1986 legislature. Faced with lack of adequate financial support for the institutions, the Board made an agonizing decision and sent recommendations to the 1986 legislature to restructure higher education. Such a decision indicated the depth of Board's concern for maintaining quality. Despite financial difficulties, the Board continued its commitment to maintain quality education and to streamline programs and operations.

## Legislative Appropriations

Appropriations made to the institutions of higher learning by the 1986 legislature totaled $239,379,656 compared to appropriations of $297,110,532 made during the 1985 legislature. Current appropriations are below FY 1985–86 by $57,730,876 or 19.43 percent.

Of this appropriation, general support of the eight universities totals $142,688,479 for FY 1986–87. This represents a reduction of $24,000,682 or 14.4 percent below the level appropriated by the 1985 legislature. This reduction represents the total appropriation for FY 1985–86 received by Alcorn State University, Mississippi University for Women, and Mississippi Valley State University. In response to these funding cuts, tuition at the eight universities increased by approximately $200 at the comprehensive universities and $400 at the regional universities. Total tuition charges replaced approximately $11 million of the $24 million cut in state appropriations. Of the remaining reduction of $13 million, approximately $6 million was reduced mid year in FY 1985–86.

With over 250 employees taking advantage of the early retirement option and with the elimination of positions as they became vacant, budget reductions in July 1986 resulted in the termination of 235 employees. For 1986–87 there are no direct funds for support of library catch-up and no funds for salary adjustments. Only by eliminating items not considered critical were the universities able to budget for inflation in utilities and supplies.

All budgetary units under the governance of the Board received budget reductions for FY 1986–87. The University of Mississippi Medical Center received reductions of $10,010,815 or 16.17 percent; Agriculture, Forestry, and Veterinary Medicine received cuts of $5,522,570 or 21.79 percent; and the Cooperative Extension Service received reductions of 19.61 percent. Student Financial Aid received the largest percentage reduction when their budget was reduced 55.78 percent, more than half of the previous year's appropriation.

Appropriations to higher education for FY 1986–87 are below the appropriated levels of FY 1984–85. The Universities will begin to reverse the progress they have made in previous years if funding levels continue to decline in this manner. Higher education since FY 1981–82 has received budget cuts in all but one year, or five out of the past six years.

## Board's Recommendation to Restructure Higher Education

After experiencing two budget cuts in 1985–86, with inadequate funding likely for 1986–87, in January 1986 the Board decided that restructuring higher education was necessary. The Board determined that only through closing some schools and reallocating funds could the quality of the remaining schools be retained.

At the January 16, 1986, meeting the Board passed

a resolution recommending closure of the University of Mississippi School of Dentistry, Mississippi State University College of Veterinary Medicine, Mississippi University for Women, and Mississippi Valley State University. The resolution also recommended that off–campus degree–granting programs be eliminated, that the Gulf Coast Research Laboratory be placed under the administrative control of the University of Southern Mississippi, and that regional universities be designated as colleges. The legislature did not pass the resolution, and all of the universities were forced to seek ways to compensate for reduced funding.

# Programs Reviewed

The review of university programs, which continued in 1985–86, is part of the Board's general plan to attain the highest quality possible within the resources available without needless duplication.

During 1985–86 the Board evaluated 61 doctoral programs remaining from previous review. In the current review, each of the five doctoral–granting universities prepared a self-study for each of its doctoral programs. These self–studies were evaluated by Dr. Paul Sharp, the Board's external consultant for doctoral programs, prior to site visits of the respective doctoral campuses during his visit to Mississippi from April 30 through May 3, 1986. Following the completion of Dr. Sharp's report, the Board is expected to take action on doctoral programs in July 1986.

Also during the fiscal year, the Board conducted a rereview of programs that received a less–than–approval rating in the April 1984 review of academic programs below the doctoral level. Of the original 133 programs in rereview, 100 were either eliminated or upgraded by June 30, 1986. The Board is expected to take final action on the remaining 33 programs between July and November 1986.

# Upgrading Programs

The Board continually seeks ways to provide citizens with quality education. During 1985–86 the Board's action concerned certain requirements improving students' preparedness for college and their education while in college.

## *Requirements for Entering Students*

In July 1982 the Board had adopted a policy requiring 13½ specific high school units in English, math, science, and social science as part of admission requirements for entering freshmen, effective fall 1986. In preparation for this change, the Board conducted surveys to determine if the courses were available to students and if students would complete the requirements by fall 1986.

The survey in July 1985 determined that public and private high schools were offering courses required for college admission. The September 1985 survey determined that 44 percent of the graduating seniors surveyed would complete the 13½ units. This survey also indicated that the new requirements were not likely to cause a great decline in freshman enrollment. The survey indicated that graduating seniors planning to attend a state university numbered 6,538, or 14 percent more than graduating seniors attending the state universities in fall 1984.

Since Mississippi is the first state in the South to put into effect its requirement of high school courses for university admission, the Board determined that the admission policy needed some flexibility in its first year. In November 1985 the Board adopted a transition-year policy allowing deferrals and exemptions of coursework. Under the policy, students may defer no more than two courses until the first semester of enrollment when the work must be made up. In addition, the policy allows a limited number of freshmen to be exempt from no more than two of the required courses.

## *Requirements for Teacher Candidates*

The Board believes that one way to improve education is to improve teacher education standards. Therefore, the Board raised admission standards to teacher education programs in November 1981 by approving the College Outcome Measures Program (COMP), a competency test to be used as a condition of admittance to teacher education programs. The program, begun in February 1983, requires that all students desiring to enter professional teacher education programs score at least 170 on the Composite Examination of the COMP, 17 on the speaking portion, and 17 on the writing portion. In addition, students must have a 2.25 GPA on a 4.0 scale through the end of the sophomore year. Students with an 18 on the ACT or a 3.2 GPA through the first semester of their sophomore year have to take only the speaking and writing portions and may bypass the Composite Examination. This standard became effective with the fall semester of 1983.

By October 1985 after three years of testing, some 79 percent of the students who had taken the COMP since spring 1983 had passed all required parts. Of those who were required to take only the Speaking and Writing Areas of the COMP, some 85 percent passed both parts on the first attempt.

## Requirements for University Graduates

The Board continued its policy requiring that students entering the universities take a prescribed core curriculum of 24 hours. This policy ensures that all students graduating from the state universities in Mississippi will have had the opportunity for diverse knowledge from their college courses. The minimum core curriculum requires 6 hours of English composition, 3 hours of algebra, 6 hours of a laboratory science, and 9 hours of humanities and fine arts courses. The policy was approved March 1984 and began fall 1984.

# Board's Participation Benefits All Areas of Education

The Board along with the State Department of Education was awarded a federal grant for improving instruction in mathematics, science, and computer learning in elementary and secondary schools. The grant funds programs which support the Education Reform Act of 1982. As part of the grant, university faculty train teachers to teach their colleagues in staff development courses which provide additional teacher training. The higher education portion of the grant was divided into three subgrants administered by the Mississippi Association of Colleges of Teacher Education (MACTE) and began in 1985.

In September 1985 the Board of Trustees of State Institutions of Higher Learning and the State Board of Education met for the first time. Members of the boards discussed what they were doing to improve education in the state.

During the fiscal year, the Board of Trustees and the Board of Education worked together to collect information about students' preparation for the new admission standards which require 13½ high school units in English, mathematics, science, and social science. In July 1985 a survey was sent to private and public school principals to determine if high schools were offering curricula that met the new entrance requirements. The survey sent September 1985 assessed how many seniors would actually complete the 13½ units.

The Board again sponsored the MINDPOWER essay competition for high school seniors in public and private schools in the state. The first, second, and third place winners received $1000, $500, and $250 scholarships respectively to the state universities of their choosing.

The Board continued the Math–Science Teacher Education Scholarship and Summer Math–Science Teacher Retraining Program which provide certified teachers of mathematics and the sciences to help meet the critical needs for teachers in these fields. In 1985–86, the Math–Science Teacher Education Scholarship was awarded to 232 students, and the Summer Math–Science Teacher Retraining Program made awards to 29 teachers. Seventy-three more math and science teachers have resulted from the program.

The program was begun April 1983 when legislative funding allowed the Board to establish scholarships for educating teachers in mathematics and in sciences such as physics, biology, earth science, general science, and chemistry. Those eligible for the scholarships must be (1) a teacher holding a current or expired teaching certificate and desiring to be licensed in math or science; or (2) a full-time student admitted to a teacher education program leading to a Class A certification in math and science. The scholarship may be used at any of the state colleges or universities which have teacher education programs.

# Student Financial Aid

The Mississippi Guarantee Student Loan Agency, operated by the Board of Trustees of State Institutions of Higher Learning, guaranteed approximately $50 million in loans from July 1, 1985, through June 30, 1986. During this time, 24,667 loans were guaranteed at 941 schools and originated by 128 lenders in Mississippi banks, savings and loans, credit unions, insurance companies, and education institutions. This cooperative effort among statewide lenders has allowed most students to secure loans in their hometowns. However, should they not be able to secure the loan with a hometown lender, statewide lenders and a lender of last resort will provide for their needs. From its first loan in April 1982 until June 30, 1986, the Agency guaranteed $172 million in 80,871 loans.

When the Agency began, its major goal was to provide qualified students with complete access to these student loans in Mississippi. With 117 active lenders throughout Mississippi participating in this loan program, the Board believes it has realized this goal. The loans available through the Mississippi Guarantee Student Loan Agency are in addition to other loan programs funded by the state and administered through the office of the Board of Trustees of State Institutions of Higher Learning.

# Donation for Medical and Nursing Financial Assistance

For the fourth year, a gift of $100,000 funded the Special Medical and Nursing Assistance Program. The gift to the Board of Trustees established financial assistance for students in their junior and senior years at the University of Mississippi Medical School and for students enrolled in nursing education programs leading to a baccalaureate degree in nursing. The donor intends to make an annual grant of $100,000 through the 1987–88 academic year.

# Library

The need for new library acquisitions has been a major point of emphasis for all universities. In 1985–86, the legislature made a special appropriation of $3,061,500 for support of the libraries at the eight public universities and the Gulf Coast Research Laboratory. This special appropriation for libraries began in 1970–71 to bring university libraries up to the standards of the Association of College and Research Libraries.

The 1986 legislature, however, made no appropriation for libraries. During 1986–87 despite the lack of special library appropriations, the universities have continued their commitment to libraries by budgeting $3.8 million of general support funds for book purchases.

# Buildings

During 1985–86 the following construction projects were completed on university campuses: at Mississippi Valley State University, the Laundry Facility, $518,423.89; at Mississippi State University a total of $5,432,767.35 of which $4,514, 438.08 was for the Creative Arts Complex; and at Mississippi Agriculture and Forestry Experiment Station (MAFES) a total of $384,405.40. Major repair and renovation projects on the campuses totaled $6,903,192.83 as allocated by the Bureau of Building, Grounds and Real Property Management.

# Other Board Actions

In August 1985 Dr. Donald W. Zacharias was named President of Mississippi State University.

Board members attended a leadership seminar at Mississippi State University on October 4–5, 1985. They considered the Board's role and responsibilities and issues in higher education.

In May 1986 the Board agreed to sponsor a joint project with the Research and Development Center and the Institute for Technology Development (ITD). The project links science and technology research in the universities with application in government, business, and industry. The Board began asking university faculty to submit information about their abilities so that a databank could be created. The databank resource will match business and industry's needs with university expertise.

# Enrollment and Degrees
## Enrollment

Enrollment figures for the fall term of 1985 show an on-campus headcount enrollment of 48,153 and an off-campus headcount enrollment of 2,953. On-campus full–time equivalent (FTE) enrollment totaled 43,464 while off–campus degree–granting centers enrolled 929 FTE students. The off–campus FTE enrollment includes students attending classes at eight degree–granting off–campus centers and four resident centers. Extension classes offered by six of the universities had a total enrollment of 732.

## Degrees

During the academic year 1985–86, the institutions awarded 7,674 bachelor's degrees; 1,883 master's degrees; 131 specialist or sixth-year degrees; 262 doctoral degrees (other than in Medicine); 139 Doctor of Medicine degrees; 41 Doctor of Dentistry degrees; 144 Law degrees, and 25 Doctor of Veterinary Medicine degrees. The universities presented awards to 141 students completing less than four–year programs. A total of 10,440 degrees and awards were granted in 1985–86.

# Conclusion

Despite financially troubled times, the Board maintained a wise management of resources and continued progress in upgrading educational requirements and programs so that the citizens of Mississippi could best be served.

# New York:

## *Higher Education in New York State 1986*

All colleges and universities in New York State—public, independent non–profit, and proprietary—are members of The University of the State of New York, an entity established in the State Constitution that embraces all education in New York, public and private, at all levels from prekindergarten to postdoctoral. The University is governed by the Board of Regents, a lay board composed of sixteen persons elected by the Legislature to seven–year terms.

The higher education portion of The University of the State of New York, at the end of 1986, is composed of 247 public, independent, and proprietary degree-granting institutions. The degree-granting institutions comprise 137 independent colleges and universities, 27 proprietary colleges, and 2 public university systems. Of these last, one, the State University of New York (SUNY), has sixty-four campuses; the other, The City University of New York (CUNY), has nineteen campuses.

The State University of New York has campuses across the State. Thirty–four of them are fully State–operated; of that number, thirteen offer study through the doctoral level (including four comprehensive university centers), fourteen offer undergraduate and master's degree study, three offer programs to the baccalaureate level, and four are two–year colleges. The other thirty campuses are community colleges that are sponsored by local government units (usually counties), under State University's supervision. One community college offers baccalaureate and master's degree programs; the other twenty-nine are two–year colleges. The City University of New York is located in New York City. It has twelve senior colleges (one offering study through the doctoral level, eight offering undergraduate and master's degree programs, two offering programs to the baccalaureate level, and a school of law) and seven community colleges (one of which is a four–year college). There are 137 independent colleges and universities in New York State; most of them have been chartered (incorpo-

rated) by the Regents or by special acts of the Legislature. Of them, 33 offer study through the doctoral level (including 12 comprehensive universities); 79 offer study through the baccalaureate and/or master's degree level; and 25 are two–year colleges. Most of the 27 proprietary colleges specialize in the fields of business and commerce. All but 2 are two–year institutions; one offers baccalaureate programs; one offers baccalaureate and master's degree programs.

# Enrollments

Between the fall of 1985 and the fall of 1986, statewide, total headcount enrollments declined by an estimated 0.4 percent, from 977,399 in the fall of 1985 to an estimated 973,932 in the fall of 1986. This decline continues a trend that began with the fall of 1984. Enrollment declines in the 80's and 90's have been projected by the Regents for several years. The present rate of decline is very close to the projection made in The Regents Statewide Plan for the Development of Postsecondary Education in New York State, 1984. Since the peak of higher education enrollments (999,175) in 1983, total headcount enrollment has declined by an estimated 2.5 percent by the fall of 1986. Headcount enrollments in the State University of New York grew by about 0.4 percent between fall 1985 and fall 1986, but declined by 3.6 percent from the fall of 1983. In The City University of New York, fall 1986 enrollments were 0.9 percent more than fall 1985, and 0.7 percent more than 1983 levels. Both independent and proprietary institutions experienced a 1.5 percent decline in enrollments between the fall of 1985 and the fall of 1986. Since 1983, independent sector enrollments have declined 2.9 percent; those in the proprietary sector have declined 3.9 percent.

In their 1984 Statewide Plan, the Regents projected a decline of about 111,000 students, overall, between 1983 and 1992, resulting in total enrollments in New York slightly below the number in 1973. This projection is based on current demographic data, elementary and secondary enrollments, participation rates, and similar factors, and assumes no policy changes that could lead to either increases or decreases in overall enrollments.

By sector, in the fall of 1986 almost 41 percent of total enrollment was at independent colleges and universities, almost 38 percent was at the State University of New York, almost 19 percent at The City University of New York, and almost 3 percent was at proprietary colleges. These proportions are approximately the same as they were in the fall of 1985.

# State Funds for Higher Education

For the 1986–87 State fiscal year, New York State appropriated $2,984.9 million in support of higher education, a $131.4 million increase over the 1985–86 appropriation ($2,853.5 million). In both years, the largest proportion of State appropriations was to support the operating budget of the State-operated campuses of the State University of New York. These funds were $1,300.3 million in 1985–86 and $1,323.7 million in 1986–87 (almost 46 percent in each year). The second largest category was State aid for The City University of New York's senior colleges, about 21 percent in 1985–86 ($588.1 million) and in 1986–87 ($623.5 million). This was followed by appropriations for New York's State–funded student aid programs ($425.8 million in 1985–86, and $429.4 million in 1986–87, about 15 percent of the total each year). State aid for the community colleges of the State University of New York and The City University of New York comprised almost 11 percent of appropriations for higher education in 1985–86 ($302.2 million) and in 1986–87 ($306.5 million). Direct State aid to eligible independent colleges and universities was $125.7 million in 1985–86 and $131.0 million in 1986–87 (between 4 and 5 percent of the total each year). Support for special opportunity programs for educationally and economically disadvantaged students at public and independent institutions totaled $59.1 million in 1985–86 and $60.2 million in 1986–87, about 2 percent of the total higher education appropriation in each year. Other categorical programs comprise the balance of funds appropriated in each year. New York State appropriations in support of higher education for the 1986–87 State fiscal year equaled about 12.2 percent of the State's estimated revenues for the year.

# Student Financial Aid

New York State maintains one of the most broad and comprehensive programs of student financial aid in the nation, comprised of both noncompetitive tuition grants for undergraduate and graduate study in New York and competitive scholarship and fellowship programs. In addition, the State administers Federal Guaranteed Student Loans.

In 1985–86, under the Tuition Assistance Program (TAP), New York's principal entitlement program for need–based aid, the State paid $369.2 million to 289,608 low– and middle–income New Yorkers studying full–time as undergraduate or graduate students at eligible public, independent, and proprietary institutions in the State. In 1985–86, the TAP program provided grants equal to tuition, up to a maximum of $2,700, for undergraduates at the lowest income levels, with awards scaled back as income rose. For graduate study, the maximum award was $600. In 1986, the Legislature enriched the TAP schedule, effective for the 1986–87 academic year, to increase the maximum award to equal tuition up to a ceiling of $2,850, and the minimum award from $300 to $350, for undergraduates; to increase the ceiling on New York net taxable income for a maximum award from $5,000 to $6,500, and for a minimum award from $29,000 to $32,000; to increase the maximum award for graduate study from tuition up to $600 to tuition up to $1,200; and to make other beneficial changes in the Tuition Assistance Program.

In 1986, the Legislature created a new program of 1,000 Empire State Scholarships of Excellence, which will provide $2,000 awards to the recent high school graduates in each county in New York who receive the highest score on the examination used to determine the recipients of Regents College Scholarships. (The Regents College Scholarships, established in 1913, are the oldest State–supported competitive undergraduate scholarship program in the nation.)

# Access for Minorities

Several new scholarship programs were established in 1985 to increase the participation of economically disadvantaged and minority students in scientific, technical, and professional careers. The Regents Health Care Scholarship Program provides aid of up to $10,000 per year to minority or economically disadvantaged students in medical or dental schools. The Regents Professional Opportunity Scholarship Program provides awards of up to $5,000 per year for such students in programs leading to licensure in a variety of other professions, including social work, engineering, accountancy, law, architecture, and psychology. For 1986–87, one hundred awards are available under each program.

In 1985, the Legislature created the Science and Technology Entry Program (STEP) to assist colleges and universities to work in collaboration with secondary schools that have a significant proportion of minority pupils. STEP's purpose is to assist and encourage high school students who are economically disadvantaged or members of historically underrepresented minority groups to undertake studies that will assist them to enter postsecondary programs leading to careers in scientific, technical, health, and health-related professions. Specific activities include diagnostic testing, special instruction, tutoring, enrichment activities, counseling, and program evaluation. Grants may be made up to $100,000. For the 1986–87 State fiscal year, $1.6 million was appropriated for the STEP program.

In 1986, the Legislature established a Collegiate Science and Technology Program (CSTEP) as a complement to STEP. CSTEP authorizes grants to colleges and universities to provide aid and supportive services to undergraduate and graduate students from economically disadvantaged or historically underrepresented minority groups who seek to study in fields leading to careers in scientific, technical, health, or health-related professions.

# Other Highlights

The principal responsibilities of the Regents in the area of higher education are to coordinate, to evaluate quality, and to plan. On behalf of the Regents, the State Education Department promulgates quality standards for the registration (accreditation) of credit-bearing programs of study; every curriculum creditable towards a degree at any public, independent, or proprietary degree-granting institution in New York State must be registered (accredited) as meeting those standards before the institution may offer that program. This evaluation process applies not only to new curricula but to the periodic review of existing curricula for adherence to quality standards. At the end of 1986, there were some 16,150 programs registered at New York's 247 degree-granting institutions. During 1986, recognition of the Regents as a Nationally-Recognized Accrediting Agency was renewed by the U.S. Secretary of Education. The New York State Board of Regents is the only state higher education agency in the nation to hold such recognition.

In 1984, the Regents adopted the Regents Statewide Plan for the Development of Postsecondary Education in New York State, 1984, the sixth quadrennial Statewide Plan for higher education since 1964. During 1986, the Regents issued The 1986 Progress Report on their 1984 Statewide Plan.

Based largely on responses by 229 colleges and universities to a structured questionnaire, the 1986 Progress Report offers substantive evidence of progress being made by New York's colleges and universities in advancing the five goals set by the Regents in their 1984 Statewide Plan: Access, Excellence, Employment and Economic Development, Diversity, and the Effective Use of Resources. It reveals progress in extension of access to higher education, strengthening of curricula, collaboration by higher education institutions with elementary and secondary education, and interaction with business and industry. It also reveals several areas in which continued attention is needed during the remaining two years of the 1984 Statewide Plan.

During 1986, the Regents authorized three institutions to confer degrees for the first time (one seminary and two hospital-based nursing schools) and approved amendments of institutional master plans to authorize one institution to operate new branch campuses. One institution was authorized to award doctoral degrees for the first time, and two two-year colleges were granted authority to offer baccalaureate degrees. One proprietary college closed during 1986.

This year marks the fifteenth anniversary of the creation of the Regents College Degrees and Examinations, the nation's first "examining university." Established in 1971 as the Regents External Degree Program, today the Regents College Degrees offers courses of study leading to associate and baccalaureate degrees in the liberal arts and sciences, business, nursing, and technology. It is accredited by the Commission on Higher Education of the Middle States Association of Colleges and Schools, and its nursing programs are accredited by the National League for Nursing. Offering no classroom instruction of its own, Regents College Degrees grants credit and confers degrees on the basis of the learning demonstrated by its students, without regard to the ways in which that learning was acquired. In its first fifteen years, Regents College Degrees has awarded 31,735 associate and baccalaureate degrees. Currently it has an active enrollment of some 16,000 students worldwide.

On July 7, 1986, Gordon M. Ambach, President of The University of the State of New York and Commissioner of Education since 1977, announced his intention to resign that office not later than June 30, 1987.

# Oklahoma:
## *General Progress of the State System*

1985–86 had an auspicious beginning when the State Regents at a special July 31 meeting allocated $524.5 million for State System operating budgets. Included in the allocation was $425.8 million in state-appropriated funds, the largest higher education appropriation in state history. The balance was made up of $98.6 million in estimated revolving fund income. The State Regents had requested a total of $575.5 million in their recommendation to the legislature and the amount allocated represented an increase of $58.1 million in state funds over the amount allocated for 1984–85 and over 92 percent of the Regents' recommendation for 1985–86.

In addition, the Regents allocated $17 million for capital improvements in the State System at their September meeting, including a total of $10 million to complete the state's commitment for the funding of the Energy Center at the University of Oklahoma and the 21st Century Center for Agriculture and Renewable Natural Resources at Oklahoma State University, the two largest capital projects in the history of the State System. At the same meeting the Regents adopted an operating budget recommendation for 1986–87 of $603.5 million, including $507.8 million in state–appropriated funds.

The increased funding came about as a result of a tax program passed by the 1985 legislature in the face of the declining oil and gas revenues but by mid–year it had become apparent that the state's revenue collections were continuing to decline and the Regents in December reduced State System budgets by $12.8 million, holding that amount over to apply to 1986–87 budgets. The Regents' reductions were equal to an annualized rate of three percent of the state-appropriated funds in the 1985–86 State System budget.

The State Board of Equalization had certified that 1986–87 revenue available for appropriation by the legislature from the general revenue fund would be some $197 million less than the comparable 1985–86 amount. When the 1986–87 higher education appropriation was finalized, it amounted to a reduction of 9.5 percent from the $425 million appropriated for 1985–86.

The 1985 legislature did not raise limits on general enrollment fees and tuition for 1985–86, but did give the State Regents authority to raise general fees and tuition between June 1, 1986 and January 1, 1987. The 1985 fee law also recognized the State Regents' long-standing position that resident students should pay, on the average, 25 percent of their instructional costs and that nonresident students should pay, on the average, 75 percent of their instructional costs at state colleges and universities.

The law further provides that the State Regents submit a plan to the legislature by January 1, 1987, detailing how this policy might be implemented gradually, provided that yearly increases amount to no more than 10 percent in general enrollment fees or 15 percent in nonresident tuition.

Following a public hearing on the matter, the Regents acted to increase fees at all three types of institutions by 10, 12, and 15 percent effective with the 1986 fall semester. The differing rates of increase were intended to help alleviate some inequities in the fee structure that developed from across-the-board 10 percent increases in general enrollment fees and 15 percent in nonresident tuition in past years. As a result, students at some academic levels were paying a significantly higher percentage of their instructional costs than others in the same institution.

While increasing fees on the one hand, the State Regents also increased their fee waiver scholarship program. Under the policy change, State System institutions are authorized to waive students' fees in an amount not to exceed two percent of the previous year's operating budget. The old rate was 1.5 percent. The change in fee waivers will allow scholarships for 1986–87 to increase from $6.9 million to $9.3 million. Nearly 14,000 students received State

Regents' fee waiver scholarships in the previous year.

The 1985 legislature, through the passage of Senate Bill No. 304, changed the structure of the three higher education center boards. Under provisions of the new law, the centers now have boards of trustees instead of advisory boards, with more direct responsibility for the services and facilities of the centers. Governor George Nigh subsequently announced the appointments to the Boards of Trustees for the University Center at Tulsa, the Ardmore Higher Education Program and the McCurtain County Higher Education Program. The University Center board accepted a gift of land from the City of Tulsa for construction of the permanent UCT campus on the near north side of Tulsa. Construction will be financed by a special city sales tax approved by the voters of Tulsa earlier in the year. Educational programs at the three centers continue to be provided through consortia of State System institutions and the State Regents continue to allocate budget funds for the operation of the centers.

The State Regents ratified an agreement with the Gansu Province Bureau of Education of the People's Republic of China for a cooperative exchange of educational materials, students, faculty and visiting scholars. This agreement came about as a result of the trade and educational mission to China in September of 1985 led by Governor Nigh. The agreement was signed in Gansu Province on behalf of the State Regents by Dr. Dan S. Hobbs, Senior Vice Chancellor for Planning and Policy Research, who accompanied the mission. The agreement provided for an observation team of Gansu higher education officials to visit Oklahoma colleges and universities in 1986 with a similar visit to China by Oklahoma representatives later.

In October the Regents approved three new academic policies — on awarding associate degrees, on advanced standing and credit by examination, and on academic program review. The new policy on associate degrees was recommended by the National Association of Community and Junior Colleges and simplifies the number and type of associate degrees. After July 1, 1986, State System institutions authorized to offer associate degrees will confer the Associate in Arts and Associate of Science on students completing programs for transfer to upper–division baccalaureate degree programs. Students completing programs designed to lead them directly to employment in a specific career will receive the Associate in Applied Science degree. After the effective date on the new policy, no other associate degrees than the three enumerated may be conferred.

The revised policy on advanced standing credit provides a procedure by which institutions may recognize educational experiences students have received outside an accredited institution of higher education, such as training in the armed services and the like. Students are to be evaluated using standardized tests such as CLEP or tests developed at the institution. Institutions offering advanced standing credit may do so only for courses taught at the awarding institutions.

The policy on program review is designed to give institutions a tool by which to evaluate their own programs and to provide the State Regents with comparable information on similar programs in like–type institutions in the State System. In essence the policy provides criteria for institutions to use in evaluating their own academic programs, measuring their vitality, uniqueness and applicability to the institutions' mission. Under a provision of the policy 20 percent of State System programs would be systematically reviewed every year beginning with the 1985–86 academic year, so that all programs are reviewed over a 5-year period. Program recommendations made by institutions after implementation of the policy are to be made on the basis of data gathered in the program review process. Institutional program reviews will be further reviewed at the State Regents' office in keeping with the Regents' constitutional responsibility for academic program approval.

The State Regents gave approval to a plan for the State of Kansas to reserve a minimum of two positions in the Northeastern State University's College of Optometry for Kansas students. According to the agreement approved by the Regents, Kansas would pay the projected per–student program cost for the contract year less the annual fee paid by the student. The agreement between NSU and Kansas came about as a result of a request by the State Regents in 1984 that State System professional schools— medicine, dentistry, veterinary medicine, osteopathic medicine, and optometry—investigate the possibility of contracting with other states if enrollment by resident students is declining. The NSU– Kansas Board of Regents agreement is the first to be proposed since the 1984 request. The contract period begins July 1, 1986, and extends through June 30, 1987, with a provision for annual renewal.

In another matter related to higher education in other states, the State Regents took under consideration in January the possible participation by Oklahoma in the Academic Common Market program operated by the Southern Regional Education Board which Oklahoma joined by act of the 1985 Oklahoma Legislature. The idea behind the program is to provide students in member states with access to expensive academic programs, especially at the graduate and professional levels, without each state having to shoulder the cost of maintaining every program available. Under provisions of the Academic Common Market program which has been in operation since 1974, Oklahoma students would pay resident tuition to attend other states' programs not available in Oklahoma on a space–available basis. At their June meeting the State Regents approved the state's participation in the Academic Common Market.

Oklahoma filed a "final" report with the U.S. Office for Civil Rights on the state's desegregation of higher education. Oklahoma's most recent state plan for civil rights compliance expired at the end of 1985 and the narrative report summarized the progress made by the state. However, the report went beyond the twelve years under which Oklahoma operated under federally approved civil rights plans, going back to 1955 when segregation was ended in the State System. The State Regents and State System institutions continue their concerns regarding the employment of minority faculty and enrollment of minority students through the State Regents' policy on Social Justice even though the federally mandated desegregation plan has expired.

The Regents' annual report on research in the State System released in February revealed that Oklahoma higher education attracts two dollars in external funds for every state dollar invested in the function of research. 1985 research expenditures in the State System topped $100 million for the first time, surpassing the $93.7 million spent the previous year. Research expenditures rose 6.8 percent in the State System while over-all E & G expenditures went up only 3.4 percent. In 1975 the total expenditure for organized research in the State System was $9.5 million compared with the 1985 total of $32.1 million, an increase of 237.4 percent. Organized research increased at more than twice the rate of sponsored research during the same ten–year period reflecting the State Regents' increased commitment to funding research at State System institutions. The University of Oklahoma Health Sciences Center attracted more than $16 in sponsored research for every state dollar invested in organized research there in 1985.

Following some eighteen months of work, the State Regents' Physician Manpower Advisory Committee made its report to the Regents in May. Nine recommendations were made in the report by the advisory committee which has been studying Oklahoma's health needs projected to the year 2000. Included among the recommendations, which were taken under study by the Regents, were proposals to reduce gradually the maximum number of medical students authorized by 8 percent, to make the Physician Manpower Committee permanent and to revise Oklahoma's physician goals when an anticipated national goal revision takes place. The committee also recommended uniform standards of education for public allopathic and osteopathic medical colleges in Oklahoma and encouraged the State Regents to develop expanded programs of graduate education for internship and residency training at the osteopathic college. Other recommendations dealt with physician shortages in fields such as psychiatry and child psychiatry, a concern over the qualifications of foreign medical graduates practicing in Oklahoma, and funding for medical education.

In March Governor George Nigh announced the appointment of Tulsa businessman Julian J. Rothbaum to the State Regents for a nine–year term. He succeeded State Regent Eugene Swearingen also of Tulsa whose term expired in May 1985 but who, under provision of law, continued to serve until his replacement was appointed. In May Govenor Nigh announced the reappointment of Enid banker Bert H. Mackie to a second nine–year term on the State Regents. Mr. Mackie was first appointed to the board in June of 1977, succeeding John J. Vater, Jr, also of Enid, and served as Chairman of the Regents in 1984–85.

Dr. Larry Nutter, Vice Chancellor for Student Affairs, resigned from the State Regents' staff to accept the presidency of Rose State College, effective January 1, 1986. Dr. Le Z. Walter was named by the State Regents as Dr. Nutter's replacement. Dr. Walter was formerly Associate Director of the Oklahoma Network for Continuing Higher Education and was previously associated with the State Regents' Guaranteed Student Loan Program. Dr. Walter will supervise the work of the Student Affairs Division in which a variety of federal and state financial assistance programs are administered.

The largest of these financial aids programs is the Guaranteed Student Loan Program which has been in operation since 1966 with nearly 200,000 student loans having been made since that time, amounting to more than $308 million. Collections of past–due student loans surpassed $2 million during the years as the State Regents continued their efforts to collect defaulted loans. Although Oklahoma's default rate is well below the national rate, greatly increased loan volume, stricter enforcement of the Regents' lender reporting policy and active collection efforts have pushed collections up dramatically. As a result of new legislation, federal and state tax refunds of those who have defaulted on student loans may be intercepted. Some 13,000 loans have been defaulted in the twenty years of operation of the Guaranteed Student Loan Program, of which over 5,000 have been repaid or are currently being collected.

New student assistance programs implemented or created during the year include the federal Carl D. Perkins Scholarship program to assist students in teacher education. This federal assistance program complements two state programs, the Future Teacher Scholarships and the Oklahoma Teacher Education Loan Program. In addition the 1986 legislature created the William P. Willis Scholarship Fund in honor of the long–time Tahlequah representative who announced his retirement from the Oklahoma Legislature. The legislature established a $250,000 trust fund to support the scholarships which are to be awarded to low–income, full–time undergraduate Oklahoma residents enrolled at State System colleges and universities.

In December the Regents approved the selection of five university graduate students as the first State Regents' minority doctoral scholars under a new program designed to encourage outstanding minority graduate students to pursue faculty careers. Nominees for the awards which carry a $1,000 scholarship each are made by the graduate deans at the doctoral degree granting institutions participating in the program, with the final selections made by the State Regents. Each of the five students selected is a current recipient of the Regent's Minority Doctoral Study Grant Program from which the nominations are made.

Ninety-one percent of the students attending State system colleges and universities are Oklahoma residents according to a study on institution selection by students from 1981 to 1985. The report, prepared by the State Regents' Planning and Policy staff, shows five percent of the students enrolled in institutions of higher education are residents of other states while another four percent come from foreign countries. Stated another way, students come to state colleges and universities from all 77 Oklahoma counties, from 49 other states and from 126 foreign countries.

It has been just over a year since the W. K. Kellogg Foundation of Battle Creek, Michigan, announced its gift of $5.8 million to the Oklahoma State System of Higher Education to develop a state–wide network of continuing higher education. The Kellogg grant to the State System is the second largest the foundation has ever made. Two Oklahoma foundations, The Noble Foundation of Ardmore and Sarkeys Foundation of Norman, later announced grants

supporting the Leadership Development portion of the network project and the 1986 Oklahoma Legislature appropriated $2 million in matching funds for the development of a state–wide telecommunications system, also a part of the network project. During the first twelve months a great deal of progress was made toward implementation of the seven programs within the projected three–year network project which has already drawn national attention and promises to be exemplary for the State System of higher education.

## Technical–Occupational Programs

During the academic year 1985–86, technical programs were evaluated at OSU Technical Branch, Oklahoma City, El Reno Junior College, Oklahoma City College, and Rose State College.

An inventory of technical educational programs conducted in 1986 reveals that there are currently 598 technical-occupational programs being offered at 24 state institution campuses with a projected full–time–equivalent enrollment of 19,685 and 29,165 head–count students expected for the 1986–87 academic year.

## New Educational Programs

During the past fiscal year, 1985–1986, no new doctoral programs were approved. One master's degree, three bachelor's degrees, nine associate degrees, and six certificate programs were approved for implementation in 1986–87 at colleges and universities in the State System.

| Institution | Master's Degree |
| --- | --- |
| Central State University | Psychology — Master of Arts |
| | **Bachelor's Degree** |
| East Central University | Engineering Technology — Bachelor of Science |
| University of Oklahoma | Musical Arts — Bachelor of Musical Arts |
| University of Science and Arts of Oklahoma | Early Childhood Education — Bachelor on Science in Education |
| | **Associate Degree and Certificates** |

| | |
|---|---|
| Oklahoma State University OSU Technical Branch, OKC | Industrial Loss Prevention — Associate in Technology Management — Associate in Management Technology and Certificate Systems Maintenance Administration — Certificate |
| Eastern Oklahoma State College | Computerized Machine Technology and Robotics — Associate in Technology Welding Technology — Certificate |
| Northern Oklahoma College | Banking and Finance — Associate in Business |
| Oklahoma City Community College | Biomedical Equipment Technology — Associate in Technology |
| Tulsa Junior College | Avionics — Associate in Engineering Technology Retail Management — Associate in Business and Certificate Telecommunications — Associate in Engineering Technology Computer Maintenance Technology — Certificate |
| Western Oklahoma State College | Real Estate — Associate in Applied Science |
| Sayre Junior College | Medical Technology — Certificate |

## Teacher Education

In 1980 the Oklahoma Legislature passed House Bill No. 1706, a comprehensive measure designed to upgrade the quality of teacher preparation in Oklahoma higher education and to improve the caliber of elementary and secondary school teachers certified to teach in public school systems and other accredited Oklahoma schools. Among the many provisions of that legislation is a program designed to help induct first-year elementary and secondary teachers into the teaching profession — the Entry-

Year Assistance Program. Under this program, a three-member Entry-Year Assistance Committee is created for each first-year teacher licensed by the State Board of Education. An Entry-Year Committee is comprised of (1) a teacher consultant, (2) a principal or assistant principal designated by the local board, and (3) a teacher educator from a college or university in Oklahoma.

The 1986 Oklahoma Legislature in House Bill No. 1611 appropriated the sum of $2,147,189 and $71,573 in carryover funds for a total of $2,218,762 to implement higher education's responsibilities for the Entry-Year Assistance Program.

The following calculations anticipate the division of funds available in 1986-87 by category:

| | |
|---|---|
| Planning and Development (public colleges) | $ 558,917 |
| Entry-Year Committees and Travel (public and private) | 1,616,600 |
| State-Level Administration and Planning | 43,245 |
| TOTAL FOR 1986-87 | $2,218,762 |

## Ardmore Higher Education Program

The Ardmore Higher Education Program had its beginning as a three-year pilot program in the summer of 1974 with classes on the Ardmore High School campus. In August, 1974, the program was moved to renovated facilities at the Mount Washington School north of Ardmore, which served the Ardmore Higher Education Center for six years. A new building, consisting of a library, student lounge, two talkback television receiving classrooms, and administrative offices, was constructed and occupied in November, 1980. The 7,200 square-foot facility was provided at a cost of approximately $400,000 funded from private contributions to match an equal amount of challenge grant from the Noble Foundation.

The construction of a Noble Foundation financed 5,000 square-foot library, computer lab, and faculty office addition was completed in January, 1986. A science lab and classroom, financed by state funds, is scheduled for completion in January, 1987. Additional classrooms are leased from the adjacent high school.

The enrollment of the Ardmore Higher Education Center has grown from a fall 1974 headcount of 283 in 24 classes to a fall 1986 headcount enrollment of almost 1,100 in 78 classes.

Institutions offering instruction at the Ardmore Higher Education Center are Southeastern Oklahoma State University, Murray State College, and East Central University.

*McCurtain County Higher Education Program.* The McCurtain County Higher Education Program in Idabel had its beginning in the fall of 1976. In 1978, the people of McCurtain County voted to build a new facility for the Center through a bond issue to be paid by a county–wide tax levy. The new facility was completed in the late summer of 1980 and was first used for classes that fall. The building was dedicated on October 3, 1980 as the E. T. Dunlap Center for Higher Education.

Since that time, classes have been taught in this modern 27,000 square-foot structure, which consists of two talkback television receiving classrooms, a library, student and faculty lounges, a science center, an art center, a business/accounting center, several large classrooms, and administrative offices.

The headcount enrollment has grown from 279 students in 20 classes in the fall of 1976 to 809 students in 115 classes in the fall of 1986.

Institutions offering instruction through the McCurtain County Higher Education Program are Carl Albert Junior College, Eastern Oklahoma State College, and Southeastern Oklahoma State University.

## University Center at Tulsa

The University Center at Tulsa was authorized by Senate Bill No. 480 of the 1982 Oklahoma Legislature and was signed into law on April 16. The law directed the State Regents to establish and operate the University Center, giving upper division and master's level courses and programs, drawing on the resources of existing universities. The law also stipulated that UCT would not duplicate the offerings of Tulsa Junior College or the Langston University Urban Center programs. Senate-Bill No. 304 of the 1985 Oklahoma Legislature created a nine–member Board of Trustees with administrative responsibility for the University Center at Tulsa but left the mission of UCT unchanged.

The University Center opened in the fall of 1982 with degree programs offered by The University of Oklahoma, Oklahoma State University, Northeastern State University, and Langston University. The administrative offices and most classes are housed in the Tulsa State Office Building, but additional facilities used by UCT are located in The University of Oklahoma Tulsa Medical College, the Oklahoma College of Osteopathic Medicine and Surgery, the Tulsa Public Schools and the Tulsa City-County libraries.

The City of Tulsa has donated 200 acres near downtown for the construction of a campus for the University Center at Tulsa. $15 million have been committed from city sales tax revenue for construction of the first phase of the physical facilities scheduled for completion in late summer 1988.

The headcount enrollment in the fall 1982 semester was 1,862 in 192 classes. In the fall 1986 semester, headcount enrollment had grown to 2,849 in 512 classes.

*Robert S. Kerr Conference Center.* In February 1978, the Kerr Foundation, Inc. donated to the State of Oklahoma for educational purposes the Robert S. Kerr home and approximately forty acres of land on which the house is located. The site is in LeFlore County, near the city of Poteau.

The State Regents, with the aid and cooperation of other state and federal agencies, converted the Kerr home into a conference center which was dedicated Thursday, October 29, 1983.

The conference center has the capacity for housing approximately twenty and provides dining for approximately fifty people. The three conference/seminar rooms available for carrying out the functions of the center are connected with the Oklahoma Higher Education Televised Instruction System (Talkback TV). Space has been made available at the center for the Eastern Oklahoma Historical Society Museum.

Some 204 conferences and seminars were held there during the 1985–86 fiscal year.

## Off–Campus Classes

Each semester certain institutions offer classes at locations other than the home campus. The basic purpose of off–campus and extension classes as noted in the comprehensive policy statement adopted by the Oklahoma State Regents on September 22, 1981, and revised on October 2, 1983, is to provide continuing higher education for adult part–time students where educational needs are not being met through the on–campus efforts of any higher education institution in the immediate locale. The staff is continuing to work with advisory groups in developing a new comprehensive policy on educational outreach which will include standards, coordination and planning, out–of–state offerings, and non-credit courses.

From the 1985 summer term through the 1986 spring semester there were 12,500 enrollments creating 31,146 credit hours at various locations throughout the state and around the world. Within Oklahoma, public colleges and universities have offered classes at nearly 150 locations leaving no region unserved.

## Televised Instruction System

A contract was awarded to Fanning Engineers to provide consultative services to the Oklahoma State Regents on the enhancement of the Televised Instruction System to provide duplex capability statewide while providing additional capacity in data and voice transmission. A final report from Fanning will be made to the Chancellor and staff by June 30, 1986.

Thus far, the Oklahoma Educational Television Authority building and the Televised Instruction System headquarters have been connected via a duplex microwave linkage. The Oklahoma State University Educational Television Services location and TIS have been connected by duplex fiber optics linkage and the University of Oklahoma Health Sciences Center and TIS have been connected by a duplex fiberoptics linkage. These linkages, made possible through an appropriation by the legislature and a substantial grant by the W. K. Kellogg Foundation, will broaden the potential service capabilities of the enhanced system.

The Oklahoma College of Osteopathic Medicine and Surgery, located in Tulsa, is offering continuing medical education via the system to practitioners in the field. Good responses have been received from doctors. The three major osteopathic hospitals, located at Enid, Oklahoma City, and Tulsa are now fully operational TIS receiving sites.

Sequential course offerings leading to the completion of a program or degree plan are still emphasized in the programming priorities. The Master's in Environmental Science (OU) is available to students throughout the state via Talkback Television. In addition, more time is continuing to be scheduled for staff meetings and for use by entities of government. Each transmitting institution has time and channel allocations to facilitate long-range programming.

There were 102 enrollments at 8 locations in the fall of 1971 when the system became operational as compared with 989 enrollments at 53 locations in the fall of 1985.

## Electronic Media

At the July 27, 1983, meeting the State Regents approved the first institutional requests to offer classes by way of satellite transmission via the Oklahoma Educational Television Authority. Offering of courses by other electronic media such as cable and

the Oklahoma Higher Education Televised Instruction System dates from the early 1970's.

Fourteen institutions submitted annual reports as directed by the State Regents. Four of those institutions reported offering 92 courses by cable with 2,916 enrollments and 8,925 credit hours and the fourteen institutions reported offering 119 courses by satellite via the Oklahoma Educational Television Authority with 2,593 enrollments and 7,688 credit hours.

The institutions provided demographic data on telecourse students. The typical telecourse student is described as being married, caucasian, female, older than regular on–campus students, employed full–time or has small children at home, has been to college before, and has definite educational goals. The reasons most often cited for taking telecourses were that the on–campus sections conflicted with work schedules, family responsibilities, and transportation problems. The flexible schedule observed with telecourses allows older adults with responsibilities of maturity to fulfill their educational goals. Completion rates and grade point averages tend to be on par with those of on-campus students. These students tend to go to college part–time.

## Oklahoma Network of Continuing Higher Education

The Oklahoma Network of Continuing Higher Education is funded by grants from the W. K. Kellogg Foundation of Battle Creek, Michigan, and The Noble and Sarkeys Foundations of Oklahoma. The project has completed its first year of developing services for a statewide network of continuing higher education.

Over 1,200 participants, including regent, presidents, administrators, and faculty, attended leadership development seminars. Needs assessment surveys were sent to 9,000 persons in various roles from community leaders to higher education, business, and citizens. Plans for a research center enhancement were developed with the University of Oklahoma. Fifty–four educational information centers were given computerized guidance and counseling software, including fourteen public libraries. Interprofessional development strategies were outlined for the health sciences field to round out the continuing professional educations segment of the project.

Phase I of the statewide telecommunications network enhancement was completed linking broadcast, satellite, and production capabilities to the existing microwave network. Consultant reports laid the ground work for the buinding of nearly 2,000 voice and data channels to expand communications among colleges, universities, public libraries, county extension offices and other locations. Implementation of the network will be phased, with an expected completion date of fall 1987.

## Faculty Salaries

The average salary paid all regular full-time teachers in the State System institutions in 1985–86 was $30,285 for the 9–10 month academic year. The figure represents a 9.1 percent increase over the $27,748 average salary paid in 1984–85. The average salary at the universities was $32,660, which is an increase of 9.1 percent over the $29,926 of 1984–85. The average salary at the four-year colleges was $30,435, a 9.4 percent increase over the 1984–85 average of $27,823. At the two–year colleges the 1985–86 average salary was $26,245, a 9.1 percent increase over the $24,056 average of 1984–85.

## Current Operating Expenditures

There was a total of $812,227,807 expended for current operations in The Oklahoma State System of Higher Education in the fiscal year 1985–86. Of this amount, $506,142,267 was expended for the Educational and General — Part I Operating Budget; $72,050,726 was expended for the Education and General — Part II Operating Budget (Sponsored Research and Programs); $39,830,442 was expended for Student Aid; and $194,204,372 was expended for Auxiliary Enterprises (housing, food services, student unions, etc.). Of the total current budget, 62.3 percent was expended for the regular educational and general operating budget, and 37.7 percent was expended for Sponsored Research and Programs, Student Aid and Auxiliary Enterprises.

## Capital Improvements

Colleges and universities in the State System have been engaged in a capital improvements program planned for accomplishment during the period 1965–75. Part I, 1965 to 1970, was accomplished at a cost of $63,508,695 with $38,500,000 of the funding coming from state funds, and $29,008,695 from federal and private funds.

In 1968, the people authorized a bond issue to provide the state's part of the funding for Phase II of the Capital Improvements Program. The bond issue contained $34,250,000 for regular campus improvements and $26,870,000 for improvements at the University of Oklahoma Health Sciences Center.

This Phase II Program was delayed by the federal government's curtailing federal funding to match state monies to underwrite projects. Although funds for health-related projects were delayed, federal funds were finally made available for construction at the Health Sciences Center. Only a small portion of federal funds was made available for regular campus projects.

In the spring of 1973, the Oklahoma Legislature in its adoption of Senate Concurrent Resolution No. 8 authorized the State Regents to proceed with allocation of state funds to accomplish as much of the capital improvements which had been planned for colleges and universities as could be done with state funds. Federal funds had not been made available and it became necessary that the Regents and institutions move forward with making certain improvements at the campuses.

The resolution also expressed intent of the legislature that the State Regents in revising Campus Master Plans of projects to be accomplished give priority to the modernization and repair and provide modernized equipment for good, old buildings on the campus.

The State Regents adopted a set of guidelines and procedures for carrying out legislative intent expressed in SCR No. 8 and requested that each institution file a revised Campus Master Plan of projects to be accomplished with the limited amount of state funds available to underwrite the costs. These campus plans subsequently were revised and priorities established and were submitted for the approval of the State Regents. Upon approval, the Regents authorized allocation of funds for accomplishing projects in priority order to the extent funds were available.

In 1979, a revised campus Master Plan of projects was approved for all institutions in the State System. This plan was modified through December 1984 to show an estimated cost for all approved projects of $288,501,740. Of this total, it was proposed that state funds would be needed in the amount of $131,352,270 with the balance to come from other sources. Through December 1984, a total of $51,962,953 in state funds had been appropriated for these projects.

## Social Justice

In 1982 the State Regents adopted a policy on Social Justice that seeks to propel the State System beyond its civil rights compliance activities toward a broader concern for equity not only for Blacks, but also for Native Americans, Hispanics, Asian-Americans, women and the handicapped.

The Regents' long–standing advisory committee on civil rights compliance was subsequently reconstituted as an advisory committee on social justice with membership expanded to include representation of the various minorities toward which the Regents' social justice policy is aimed.

In March, 1986, the State Regents co-sponsored with the advisory committee a two-day Conference on Social Justice in Oklahoma Higher Education in Tulsa which was attended by some eighty participants. Out of that conference is planned a series of reports intended to assist the State Regents in planning social justice programs and initiatives, building upon those civil rights programs and activities already in place, in an effort to assure equity to all in Oklahoma higher education.

# Tennessee:
## *Tennessee Higher Education*

## Background

Tennessee recognizes the importance and value of higher education. Public colleges and universities are located throughout the state, offering comprehensive programs and ensuring services ranging from occupational training to the arts and sciences to law and health sciences. Institutional policies have been developed with the belief that all qualified individuals should have equal access to higher education opportunities. The institutions operate with the support of state tax dollars, federal funds, private and corporate contributions, and student tuition and fees.

Public higher education in Tennessee is coordinated by the Tennessee Higher Education Commission and consists of two systems — the University of Tennessee campuses governed by the University of Tennessee Board of Trustees and the state universities, community colleges, technical institutes and area vocational – technical schools governed by the Board of Regents of the State University and Community College System of Tennessee.

The Higher Education Commission, the University of Tennessee Board, and the Board of Regents are composed of lay citizens appointed by the governor to ensure public direction and policy guidance in higher education. All three bodies employ chief executive officers and are legislative entities with defined purposes and responsibilities.

A movement was begun in the early eighties in Tennessee to ensure excellence and accountability in higher education through several initiatives: Performance Funding Program, Centers of Excellence, Campus Centers of Excellence, Chairs of Excellence, Undergraduate Excellence, and Academic Scholars Program.

A Performance Funding Program was begun in Tennessee in 1980, making it the first statewide program in the country to provide incentives to colleges and universities for improving the quality of academic performance. Institutions are evaluated by standards of performance and may earn up to 5 percent additional funding beyond the institution's regular state funding. The purpose of these funds is to recognize and reward efforts on the part of institutions to evaluate and improve instructional quality. The Tennessee program continues to be viewed nationally as the most outstanding program of its kind. The standards of performance are: achievement of accreditation in accreditable fields, performance of graduating students on tests in their major fields, performance of graduating students in universities on a test of general education, performance of graduating students in community colleges on a test of general education and on finding employment, performance of graduating students in technical institutes on finding employment, surveys of employers, alumni, and students, and plans for improving instruction.

The Centers of Excellence concept was introduced in 1982 and first funded in 1984–85. Tennessee leaders chose this program to emphasize and capitalize on the best programs the state has to offer. The program focuses extensive resources on outstanding academic programs at Tennessee universities. There are thirty–two Centers of Excellence on the university campuses, fourteen of which were begun in 1984–85, twelve more added in 1985–86, and six more in 1986–87. For every two dollars of state funding for Centers of Excellence, the institution is required to match one dollar with institutional funds. The state has invested approximately $45 million in Centers during the first three years of the program.

Guidelines for the Centers are developed each year by the staffs of the Higher Education Commission, the University of Tennessee, and the State Board of Regents. Benchmarks or measures of accountability for evaluating progress are developed by the institutions, working in cooperation with these staffs, and are reported annually to the Governor and the General Assembly. Basically, centers are evaluated on faculty publications, faculty presentations, credentials of new faculty, special recognition of faculty, and the ability to generate external funding.

In 1986, five Centers of Excellence at Tennessee universities were selected by the Tennessee Higher Education Commission to receive Performance Par Excellence awards and a total of $266,000 in extra funding for their outstanding work and achievements over the first three years of the Centers' program.

The Chairs of Excellence program originated in 1984. As of April 1987, sixty-five chairs have been funded, of which forty chairs have been matched on a one for one basis with private and institutional funds. Each matched Chair of Excellence is filled by a distinguished scholar who is nationally recognized. This program is an integral part of Tennessee's successful efforts in bringing nationally-known scholars to its universities.

A new program establishing fifteen Campus Centers of Excellence at two-year colleges and technical institutes was recommended and begun in FY 1986-87. These centers enhance distinctively superior programs of instruction and public service.

The Undergraduate Excellence Programs are corollary to the Chairs of Excellence Program. Central to each of the Undergraduate Excellence Program is a visiting professor who focuses on improving instruction in writing, math, and other fields.

The Tennessee Academic Scholars Program is an endowment program which provides $4,000 scholarships to outstanding Tennessee high school students for enrollment in one of the state's public or private colleges or universities. This program was begun to encourage Tennessee's top high school graduates to attend college in Tennessee. Since those who attend colleges out-of-state are less likely to return home and put their considerable talents to use in Tennessee, higher education officials and legislators believe it is a good investment in the state's economy to try to retain these top students. This program began in 1986.

# Highlights of 1986-87
## Funding

Full funding of the higher education formula was achieved for FY 1986-87. The $628.7 million state appropriation represented a fourteen percent increase over FY 1985-86. This funding level placed Tennessee third in the nation among states showing an increase in funding for higher education.

## Approaches to Excellence

| | |
|---|---|
| Centers of Excellence | $20,266,000 |
| Campus Centers of Excellence | 1,400,000 |
| Chairs of Excellence | 15,000,000 (endowments) |
| Undergraduate Excellence | 900,000 |
| Academic Scholars | 900,000 (endowments) |

## Growth Patterns

With the headcount enrollment for Fall, 1986 at 147,064 students, Tennessee's public colleges and universities experienced a 1 percent increase in enrollment between Fall, 1985 and Fall, 1986. In a period of enrollment decline, nationally, this increase is attributed to more aggressive recruiting, enticements for better students, attractive programs for part-time students, and a renewed dedication to the basics of a college curriculum.

## Financial and Administrative Innovations

The Performance Funding Program, which has operated in Tennessee since 1980, provides incentive funding to colleges and universities which document that they are doing a good job. The purpose of these funds is to recognize and reward efforts on the part of institutions to evaluate and improve instructional quality.

The Tennessee Foreign Language Institute was authorized by the General Assembly in 1986 to serve the needs of prospective and existing businesses in the state, as well as the needs of students learning a new language at all grade levels and in colleges and universities. The venture, funded by a $500,000 endowment which required matching from private gifts and grants was a cooperative effort among a number of state agencies and private industries.

## Plans for the Future

- To increase compatibility between high school graduation requirements and admission requirements of postsecondary institutions
- To improve articulation between secondary and postsecondary education
- To strengthen teacher education programs

# Texas:
## *Highlights of 1986*

## Planning for the Future Top Priority

Strengthening standards in higher education, as well as planning for the future, were top priorities for the Coordinating Board, Texas University and College System in 1986. Higher admission standards, along with a ban on credit for remedial courses, will help strengthen the quality of higher education in Texas in addition to other measures. An advisory committee made recommendations to test freshmen for basic skills, while the Select Committee on Higher Education looked at the overall condition of higher education in Texas. These actions and the two special legislative sessions made 1986 a year which fundamental questions were raised concerning higher education. The answers are still pending.

### *Budget Crisis*

As the Texas Legislature met in two special sessions during August and September 1986, budget cuts were of special concern to higher education. The special sessions were called by Gov. Mark White to respond to a state budget deficit estimated at $2.8 billion. Following a report on the anticipated deficit by State Comptroller Bob Bullock in February, Gov. White issued Executive Order MW – 36 requesting 13 percent across – the – board cuts in state agency and higher education spending.

Bullock's estimate was based on the dramatic drop in spot market oil prices which hit a seven – year low in February. Taxes on oil and gas production would constitute almost one – third of Texas' anticipated tax revenue during the two – year budget period ending August 1987. The budget, required by the constitution to be balanced, was based on predictions that oil would sell for an average of $25 a barrel during the year ending in August 1986 and just over $24 during the twelve months ending in August 1987. Oil prices dropped to about $10 a barrel in August 1986.

During the two special sessions, cuts to colleges and universities originally feared to be as high as 34 percent brought an outcry from regents, faculty, staff, alumni, students and higher education advocates. That figure was later dropped to 13 percent and in the second special session the House and Senate agreed to 10.5 percent cuts for senior colleges and 9 percent cuts for junior colleges for the 1986 – 87 biennium.

### *Decline in Enrollment*

Four-year universities in Texas experienced their first enrollment drop in more than thirty years, according to fall 1985 enrollment figures. Twenty-eight of the thirty-seven campuses had lower enrollments, as did fifteen of the thirty-eight independent four-year institutions. Community colleges also reported shrinking enrollment in thirty-seven of the forty-nine districts. Overall, state colleges and universities reported a decrease of nearly 2 percent from the previous year.

Declines also were seen in the public and independent medical schools, while dental enrollments continued a planned enrollment reduction. Total enrollment at the four public technical institutions was up slightly.

The U.S. Department of Education projected smaller numbers of students nationwide for the next few years, citing census data showing that the 18 – 24 age group will shrink through 1995. The Coordinating Board forecast similar trends for Texas even though the state's population is growing faster than the national average.

Enrollment growth in Texas higher education is expected to hover around 1 percent annually through the year 2000, according to forecasts adopted by the Board in January. The Board's projections are updated every two years and are used in planning and estimating future funding needs of public colleges and universities.

## Slowdown on Construction

The state's 1986 fiscal crisis, coupled with an enrollment decline, resulted in a Board resolution restricting consideration of new construction on university campuses. The resolution passed in April calls for a halt on most new construction until the Legislature and governor address the financial conditions of the state and higher education.

Proposed by Board member Ray Clymer of Wichita Falls, the resolution did not call for a construction moratorium, although university officials withdrew or requested deferral of most new building plans throughout fiscal year 1986. Buildings approved this year would add to the state's future costs for utilities and maintenance under the formula funding system, the resolution notes.

Board members agreed they would prefer to encourage repair or rehabilitation of existing buildings rather than authorize new construction during the fiscal crisis.

## Faculty Salaries Up

Although state agencies and institutions of higher education saw budget cuts, one area managed to show gains. Faculty salaries at Texas' public universities showed improvement as salaries averaged 5.1 percent higher over the previous year. According to a survey by the Coordinating Board, the gain is outpacing the annual inflation rate of 3.2 percent recorded by the Consumer Price Index.

However, the increase may not be enough to keep Texas from losing ground to the competition, Commissioner Kenneth Ashworth said. With funding cuts in higher education, Ashworth says Texas may dip below the national average again.

Average salaries at Texas public universities for 1985–86 stand at $42,436 for full professors; $32,159 for associate professors; $26,928 for assistant professors; and $20,513 for instructors. At the state's public community colleges, faculty salaries in general academic programs are 3.8 percent higher than last year, averaging $29,916.

## 1985 Fall Headcounts: Enrollment in Texas Higher Education

| | Fall 1985 Enrollment | Change from 1984 |
|---|---|---|
| **Public Institutions** | | |
| Universities | 361,052 | −2.64% |
| Community Junior Colleges | 289,532 | −3.70 |
| Total | 650,584 | −3.12 |
| **Independent Institutions** | | |
| Senior Colleges and Universities | 77,900 | 0.81 |
| Junior Colleges | 1,151 | −7.03 |
| Total | 79,051 | 0.68 |
| **Texas State Technical Institute** | 8,667 | 1.39 |
| **Medical, Dental and Allied Health Schools** | | |
| Public Institutions | 9,216 | −2.57 |
| Independent Institutions | 1,484 | −1.00 |
| Veterinary Medicine* | 1,436 | −3.56 |
| Total | 12,136 | −2.50 |
| **TOTAL — All Institutions** | **750,438** | **−2.67** |

* Includes Texas A&M University College of Veterinary Medicine for the first time.

## Investing in the Future

"An important investment in the future of Texas," is what Chairman Temple called $35 million in research grants awarded to state universities under the Texas Advanced Technology Research Program. In October, the Board made awards to eighty-seven projects at eleven universities.

A committee was formed at the direction of the Legislature to select university research which would stimulate growth of new industry. The Board distributed the money based on recommendations by a team of fourteen nationally eminent scientists. Frederick Seitz, former president of the National Academy of Sciences and retired president of Rockefeller University, chaired the panel, which evaluated more than 500 proposals by university researchers.

The largest number of awards were made in biotechnology, with funding given to twenty-nine projects. Nineteen grants were awarded for research in microelectronics and telecommunications.

The University of Texas at Austin received funding for twenty-nine projects. Eleven projects were funded at Texas A&M University and thirteen more at A&M's Agricultural and Engineering Experiment Stations. Eighteen projects at the University of Houston received funding.

Projects in The University of Texas and Texas A&M University Systems obtained a total of $23.3 million. Projects for other universities totaled $11.7 million. The Legislature specified that the UT and A&M Systems could receive no more than two-thirds of the $35 million.

## Committees at Work

Concern for the future of higher education in the state was evident with the formation of the Select Committee on Higher Education. In accordance with HCR 105 passed by the 1985 Legislature, the committee met throughout the year examining teacher education, remedial courses, facility use, governance, and the quality of academic and research programs. A report is expected in January 1987 when the 70th Legislature convenes.

Coordinating Board Chairman Larry Temple of Austin was named by the governor to head the committee. Members were appointed by Gov. White, Lt. Gov. Bill Hobby and House Speaker Gib Lewis, who also serve on the committee.

## Basic Skills Test

The advisory committee on testing was appointed by Chairman Temple to assist the Board in recommendations to the 1987 Legislature on a standardized skills test for Texas public university students.

"At least 30,000 freshmen who enter Texas public colleges and universities each year cannot read, write or compute at levels needed to perform effectively in higher education," said Robert Hardesty, chairman of the advisory committee on testing and president of Southwest Texas State University.

Beginning in 1988, all freshmen in public colleges and universities should be tested in reading, writing and mathematics, the committee recommended. The group suggested that test scores would not affect admission but rather assist in the process of locating students needing remedial training.

Following a ten-month study, the panel recommended that the Legislature fund $500,000 to develop the test and $3 million to administer it each year. Another $2 million would be needed for remedial courses.

## Ban on Remedial Credit

Rules prohibiting state universities and community colleges from offering degree credit for remedial course work were approved by the Coordinating Board in an effort to maintain the integrity of the college degrees. Board members set fall 1986 as a cutoff date to stop awarding degree credit for remedial courses.

A survey in fall 1985 showed that at least six state universities and twenty-nine community colleges were awarding degree credit for courses below college level.

State funding will not be affected by the Board's action. Community colleges have had statutory responsibility since 1973 for meeting the needs of students who are deficient in reading, writing, and mathematics. Universities, however, may obtain formula funding for three hours of remedial English and three hours of remedial mathematics.

## New Responsibilities

The Division of Community Colleges and Technical Institutes was created at the beginning of fiscal year 1986. The new division reflected the Board's increased role in coordinating those sectors as it implemented the new legislation which transferred responsibility for administration of postsecondary technical and vocational education programs from the Texas Education Agency to the Coordinating Board. Previously TEA had authority in technical-vocational programs while the Coordinating Board had authority in academic areas. With that transfer also came $215.5 million in state support for technical-vocational education. In conjunction with the transfer, the Board assumed the oversight of the four campuses of the Texas State Technical Institute, which continues to be governed by its own board of regents.

Because of the magnitude of the responsibility, the Commissioner of Higher Education appointed an advisory committee to assist in developing policies and procedures for technical-vocational education. In April, the advisory committee submitted its report on planning, operating procedures and recommended guidelines.

## Desegregation Progress Report

The five-year Texas Equal Educational Opportunity Plan for Higher Education, developed under an agreement with the federal Office for Civil Rights, entered its third year of implementation in 1986. Although some major problem areas remain, such as enrollment of minority students, the plan has been successful in improving physical plants, programs and faculty salaries at Prairie View A&M University and Texas Southern University.

Renovation and repair projects are nearing completion at the state's two traditionally black institutions, Prairie View A&M and TSU. The two universities also are meeting the requirements for new programs as proposed in the plan. Since the plan was implemented in 1983, TSU has added five new programs, while Prairie View A&M has added seven. The plan requires six new programs during the five-year period.

Texas public universities are finding it difficult to meet the goals for recruiting minority students under the federally ordered desegregation plan. Despite an overall increase in black and Hispanic enrollment, the numbers declined during 1985–86 at fifteen of twenty-six institutions compared to the 1978–79 base year. In addition, the Texas plan commits the state to reduce by at least 50 percent the disparities between the proportion of white first–time–in–college, full–time and undergraduate transfers and black and Hispanic first–time–in–college freshmen and undergraduate transfers who attend traditionally white institutions. Currently, 39% of white high school graduates enter traditionally white colleges, while blacks enroll at a 12 percent rate and Hispanics at 16 percent in the same colleges.

An advisory committee asked the Board to consider additional steps to boost the statewide effort. Some of the steps include encouraging secondary and community college students to prepare for a college education, seeking more state support for tutoring and counseling at universities, and increasing financial aid for minority students.

In other areas of the Texas plan, faculty salaries at TSU and Prairie View A&M moved closer to the comparable traditionally white institutions. Compared to six traditionally white universities, TSU and Prairie View A&M made gains at all levels except that of professor in closing the gap between average salaries.

The Coordinating Board submitted its second annual narrative report for the 1984–85 academic year in August 1985 and awaits an evaluation from the U.S. Department of Education Office for Civil Rights. The third annual narrative report for academic year 1985–86 was submitted in August 1986 and an evaluation is expected in the spring of 1987.

## Campuses Sharing Facilities

The Board in October approved procedures for establishing partnerships between public community colleges and upper-level university centers that share facilities. Legislation passed in 1985 allows upper–level and community colleges to split costs of salaries, supplies, library operations, food service and building maintenance. Five upper–level centers share facilities with public community colleges.

# Financial Planning: Budget Crisis Hampers Higher Education

As fiscal year 1986 came to a close, the Texas Legislature was heading into a second back-to-back special session to deal with a projected deficit of $2.8 billion for 1987. The House and Senate stood divided on budget cuts in higher education, finally agreeing to a 4.5 percent cut in 1986 and a 6 percent cut in 1987.

Budget cuts coupled with a hiring freeze caused immediate problems on many campuses including the elimination of class sections due to a lack of professors and reduced services, such as shorter library hours.

University officials across the state expressed concern with the long–term effects of budget cuts especially in the areas of faculty recruitment and retention. Other concerns were voiced about university research in the state, since many legislators and university officials believe that research is the key to economic diversification.

## Formula Funding

During 1986 the Board recommended a significant increase in funding faculty salaries in the next biennium and advocated stronger support for organized research. The Board approved funding formulas for fourteen areas of operation at state universities which, if fully funded by the 70th Legislature, would provide $2.3 billion for the next biennium.

Separate formulas were approved which would generate $1.1 billion in support for public community college programs. For the first time, the Board's recommendations for community college funding apply not only to academic programs but also to technical and vocational training. Formulas for postsecondary technical–vocational programs were proposed in the past by the Texas Education Agency, but in 1985 legislators transferred responsibility for such programs to the Coordinating Board.

For the current biennium, formula–generated funds account for approximately three–fourths of total appropriations to Texas public universities. An annual inflation rate of 4 percent was figured into the Coordinating Board recommendations.

## Faculty Salaries Competitive

Average faculty pay at Texas public universities should reach the level of the ten most populous states under formula funding recommendations adopted by the Board in January. In an effort to keep

Texas competitive, the Board agreed that salaries should be measured against the ten-state average instead of the national average.

The gap in the average salaries between Texas and its competitors threatens to make it difficult to recruit and retain outstanding faculty. Data from 1985–86 shows an average salary of $31,640 for Texas, compared to $32,180 for the nation as a whole, and $34,490 for the ten most populous states.

With Texas threatening to fall further behind while states undergoing economic recovery invest heavily in higher education, the Board voted to ask the 1987 Legislature to increase formula funding for faculty salaries by 8.7 percent the first year of the coming biennium and 10.9 percent the following year.

## Community Colleges

Community college formula recommendations were based on an analysis of administrative and instructional costs per contact hour for 1985. The formulas would generate $553 million for technical and vocational programs and $548 million for academic programs over the next biennium, about 25.5 percent above current biennial levels. Formula funding is recommended for the Texas State Technical Institute and the lower–level Lamar University centers in Orange and Port Arthur for the first time.

## Tuition Raised

The first major tuition increase since 1957 went into effect during 1986. The new rates were expected to generate $263.7 million in additional state revenues for the current biennium. Minimum rates at community colleges were unchanged.

Resident tuition rates were raised from $4 per semester hour to $12, effective for the fall 1985 semester. Rates will rise to $16 per hour in fall 1986, gradually increasing to $24 per hour by 1995. Minimum tuition levels were raised from $50 to $100 per semester.

The non–resident undergraduate rate increased from $40 per semester hour to $120 in fall 1985; following that hike, the rate will be indexed to cover 100 percent of costs. Average costs will be calculated biennially by the Coordinating Board.

In resetting tuition rates for medical and dental school programs, the Legislature sought to make tuition offset 10 percent of costs. Tuition for Texas residents will rise from $400 per year to $1,219 in fall 1986. Further increases are scheduled annually, bringing the rate to $5,463 in 1989.

## Appropriations Request

The Board in July adopted a $225 million appropriations request for fiscal years 1988 and 1989. The request is approximately $19.4 million more than the 1986–87 appropriation.

The 1988–89 request includes 17 trusteed funds. One of the largest jumps in trusteed funds is in the Minority Scholarship Program, up $1.2 million from 1987 to $1.5 million in 1988 and $2.5 million in 1989. The increase in funding is due to the state's commitment to the Texas Equal Opportunity Plan for Higher Education.

Trusteed funds requested for the 1988–89 biennium include $178.8 million plus $27.3 for eight new programs to help increase student access and performance, for a total of $206.2 million. That compares to $191.9 million for the 1986–87 trusteed funds request.

State funding for the private Baylor medical and dental schools was reduced in the special session from 1984–85 levels of $87.3 million to $74.4 million.

## Average Budgeted Salaries: Public College and University Faculty, 1980–81 to 1985–86

**Public Universities**

| Year | National Average[1] | Texas Average[1] | Percent Increase | Inflation Rate[2] |
|---|---|---|---|---|
| 1985–86 | $34,479 | $33,117 | 4.7% | 3.5% (1985) |
| 1984–85 | 32,180 | 31,640 | 3.1 | 3.4 (1984) |
| 1983–84 | 30,100 | 30,700 | 5.1 | 3.0 (1983) |
| 1982–83 | 29,100 | 29,200 | 8.6 | 6.0 (1982) |
| 1981–82 | 26,900 | 26,900 | 17.5 | 10.2 (1981) |
| 1980–81 | 24,800 | 22,900 | 8.2 | 13.5 (1980) |

**Public Community Colleges**

| Year | Texas Average[3] | Percent Increase | Inflation Rate[2] |
|---|---|---|---|
| 1985–86 | $29,916 | 3.8% | 3.5% (1985) |
| 1984–85 | 28,832 | 7.3 | 3.4 (1984) |
| 1983–84 | 26,870 | 6.4 | 3.0 (1983) |
| 1982–83 | 25,247 | 10.5 | 6.0 (1982) |
| 1981–82 | 22,849 | 13.4 | 10.2 (1981) |
| 1980–81 | 20,151 | 10.8 | 13.5 (1980) |

[1] American Association of University Professors annual reports for public categories I and IIA combined (full-time faculty for the first four ranks)
[2] Bureau of Labor Statistics — Consumer Price Index
[3] Coordinating Board salary survey, average budgeted salaries to full-time faculty in general academic courses only

## Research Up

Support for state university research programs from all sources grew by 16.3 percent in fiscal year 1986. Of the approximately $302.7 million available for the programs, more than one-half came from the federal government and just above 23 percent from the state.

A 13.6 percent jump occurred in research funds for public health science centers from $147.2 million in 1984 to $167.3 million in 1985. Slightly more than 52 percent came from federal sources and about one-fourth from the state.

# Facilities Development: Board Policy Restricts New Construction

New construction on Texas college and university campuses was sharply curtailed during 1986 because of a resolution passed by the Board in April. The resolution did not call for a construction moratorium, although university officials withdrew or requested deferral of all new building proposals throughout fiscal year 1986.

The resolution stated that the Coordinating Board will limit consideration of adding new educational and general space through construction to projects clearly justified as critical to the role and scope of the university. The policy will be in effect at least until the Select Committee on Higher Education makes its report to the Legislature in January 1987.

Board members agreed they would rather repair or rehabilitate existing buildings than authorize new construction. A recent study by the Coordinating Board shows that $300 million is needed to remodel and repair buildings on the senior university campuses in Texas to put them in satisfactory condition. The Board also pointed out that buildings approved this year would add to the state's future costs for utilities and maintenance under the formula funding system.

## Construction Down

Institutions gained Board approval during fiscal year 1986 for 42 campus construction and renovation proposals compared with 29 the previous year; cost estimates totaled more than $93 million and were substantially lower than the $128 million spent in 1985. Thirteen property acquisitions were authorized at an expected cost of $15 million, while 18 property acquisitions totaled $3.7 million in 1985.

The Coordinating Board approved $46 million in projects funded by the Higher Education Assistance Funds. It deferred some $73.5 million and disapproved $4 million in such projects. Additional funding from the HEAF included $8 million in land acquisitions. Other projects the Coordinating Board approved includes those financed by $43.8 million in Permanent University Fund bonds.

Fiscal year 1986 marked the first use of the Higher Education Assistance Fund approved in 1984 by state voters for institutions other than the University of Texas and Texas A&M Systems.

## Campus Planning Activities

The Division of Campus Planning requested that all public universities and medical institutions file updated campus master plans with the Board. The long-range projects of campus and student needs are used in the Board's review of proposals for new construction, renovation projects and land acquisitions.

The 12th annual Facilities Inventory Workshop focused on reporting procedures, methods used for space planning, ways for institutions to utilize inventory data, and analysis of facilities inventory profiles. Seventy-eight representatives from sixty-two public, private and medical institutions attended the workshop. Some 154 institutional records are in the facilities inventory file.

The annual survey of campus student housing for fall 1985 found 88 percent occupancy for public senior universities, the same as the fall 1984 survey indicated. Public community colleges reported an occupancy rate of 89 percent, down 9.9 percent from 1984. Of the fifty-eight community colleges responding to the fall 1985 survey, thirty offer housing to students. Independent senior and junior colleges student housing occupancy was 89 percent, up 6 percent from the previous year.

# Financial Aid: Gramm–Rudman Causes Cuts in Student Aid

The Gramm–Rudman–Hollings Act, officially known as the Balanced Budget and Emergency Control Act, will cause an approximate 4.3 percent decrease in federal student financial aid programs in the 1986–87 academic year. An additional 11 percent cut is predicted the following year.

For 1986, the 4.3 percent decrease is predicted to cost $14.3 million in aid for 16,500 Texas students. This figure includes a one-time only 6.6 percent decrease in Pell grants due to a funding shortfall.

The additional 11 percent cut expected next year will cost the state's students about $24.6 million in the 1987–88 academic year.

## Legislative Changes

Changes in state legislation affecting Texas students include the tuition bill, HB 1147, adopted by the 69th Legislature in 1985. The bill includes a provision to open the Texas Public Educational Grant Program to foreign students, a group which has been excluded in the past. Further, non–residents are no longer restricted to 10 percent of the total fund. Instead, funds going to foreign and non–resident students must come from money set aside from foreign and non–resident students' tuition. That figure is set at 5 percent of the tuition for 1986 and 1987.

Under the tuition bill, college officials will be required to accurately monitor the non–resident set–asides. The bill also raises the question of how to assess foreign student need.

TSTI students also were brought into the TPEG program as were professional medical and dental students. Schools are obligated to maintain set–asides for all students, and to establish grant programs which include all student categories.

Also included in HB 1147 are limitations on several waiver programs which in the past allowed certain non-resident students to pay resident tuition rates.

## Hinson–Hazlewood Loans Down

The Board loaned $11.8 million to students through the Hinson–Hazlewood program in 1986, down $6 million from 1985. The 33 percent decline from last year is partially due to commercial lenders becoming more active in student loans. However, Student Services officials anticipate a turnaround in that trend since the Hinson–Hazlewood loan now offers a lower interest rate and application procedures have been streamlined. An average $2,672 was loaned to 4,413 student borrowers in the program during 1986. Compared to 1985, a smaller number of students are taking out larger loans. Last year an average of $2,250 went to 6,761 students.

Collections totalled $18.2, as compared to $17.2 million in 1985. The Hinson–Hazlewood program continues to show a low default rate, with suits filed within the year against approximately 4.8 percent of borrowers in the repayment process.

Guaranteed Student Loans were made by the Board to some 3,711 students and account for $8.5 million of Hinson–Hazlewood funds loaned in 1985. Health Education Assistance Loans made up a smaller portion of Hinson–Hazlewood lending with 585 students receiving $3 million.

Auxiliary Loans to Assist Students were awarded to 117 students and totalled $322,944. The number of recipients remained about the same as in 1985, but the total was down from $345,000 last year.

Interest rates for the Hinson–Hazlewood loans guaranteed through the Health Education Assistance Loan program were dropped in 1986 from 9.5 percent to 8.75 percent. The HEAL program is operated by the U.S. Department of Health and Human Resources. Interest rates also were lowered for Guaranteed Student Loans from 9 percent to 8 percent. Rates for the Auxiliary Loans to Assist Students were lowered from 12 percent to 10 percent.

In other changes, the Hinson–Hazlewood College Student Loan Program was altered to allow proprietary school students who were unable to obtain loans from commercial lenders to apply directly for loans through the Hinson–Hazlewood program. At public and private schools in the state, Hinson–Hazlewood applications are processed at the institution and forwarded to the Coordinating Board for further processing. Proprietary school students will apply directly to the Coordinating Board, by–passing the institutional steps.

## Equalization Grants Decrease

The Board distributed some $17.3 million to students in independent colleges and universities in 1986 for tuition equalization grants. The state provides the grants to help needy students meet higher tuition costs at private institutions. Some 14,318 students received funds, with the total amount down from $20.8 million awarded the previous year. Funding is expected to continue to decrease due to the state budget crisis. The Legislature had already cut appropriations to $35.9 million for the 1986–87 biennium, compared to $41 million for the 1984–85 biennium, prior to the special sessions, when additional cuts were made.

The Commissioner appointed a Tuition Equalization Grant Advisory Committee to review the TEG allocation process. Allocations have been based on full-time headcount enrollments at participating institutions.

The committee will make recommendations on equitably allocating funds under a formula which considers student need for full– and part–time students. The committee, chaired by Dr. Robert Sasseen of the University of Dallas, will present its findings and recommendations at the January 1987 meeting.

Some 3,604 students in independent colleges received $2.7 million through the State Student Incentive Grant Program, with the state's 50 percent matching share provided through the Tuition Equalization Grant Program.

In addition, $1.4 million was awarded to 4,790 students in public colleges, with the state's 50 percent matching share provided through institutional contributions from the Texas Public Educational Grant Program.

## Teacher Loans, Grants Underway

During 1986, the Teacher Education Loan Program loaned $1.2 million to 1,368 students, while the Future Teacher Loan Program distributed $379,563 to 234 students.

The Future Teacher Loan Program and the Teacher Education Loan Program were authorized by the Legislature in 1984 to allow student borrowers the opportunity to have their loan debts canceled by teaching in Texas public schools. The Board gave final approval to rules governing the program in October 1984 and in January 1985 placed the interest rate at 12 percent. A higher interest rate was set than for other state-administered student loans, since cancellation is expected in nine out of ten cases. The higher rate will encourage students to honor their commitment to a career in teaching.

The Board in October awarded the bulk of $1.8 million in federal grant funds earmarked for higher education projects to strengthen teaching in mathematics, science, foreign languages and computer science. Funding was awarded to thirty-three projects at public and independent universities and public community colleges.

## State Scholarships Awarded

Scholarships totalling $425,840 were awarded to 514 students in the State Scholarship Program for Ethnic Recruitment. Those figures are about the same as 1985 when $472,108 was given to 646 students. The scholarships are targeted for minorities who make up less than 40 percent of the student population. Such scholarships encourage desegregation as required by a federally ordered equal opportunity plan.

During fiscal year 1986, the Coordinating Board changed the procedures for disbursing the scholarship funds, in an effort to increase the state's ability to monitor the use of funds and ease the transfer of funds from schools not active in the program to

schools needing additional funds. Student applications are now processed by the Coordinating Board, with checks issued by the State Treasury. Checks are sent directly to the schools for disbursement. In previous years the program worked as an on-campus operation.

Administration of the Good Neighbor Scholarship was transferred to the Coordinating Board from the Texas Education Agency in 1985. Through the program, qualified students from eligible countries in the Western Hemisphere are awarded tuition exemptions while attending a public college in Texas.

The program provides 235 exemptions each semester and each summer term. For a student enrolled in 15 semester hours, the scholarship is worth $1,800 per semester or $3,600 for the academic year.

The Board considered increasing the academic standards required for the Good Neighbor Scholarship; however, international student advisors from a number of institutions successfully argued against the requirements in light of social and other adjustments faced by new foreign students attending Texas schools. The decision was made to require students to meet institutional academic requirements for the student's particular field of study.

# Programs: Board Action Assures Continued Quality

The Coordinating Board initiated several new actions in 1986 to insure continued quality in Texas public colleges and universities. Several of these initiatives concerned courses. A study comparing televised instruction with on-campus courses was completed as was a survey of the characteristics of shortened-format courses. Untaught courses have been removed from course inventories and pre-college level courses will no longer count toward academic degrees.

Also in 1986, mission statements describing the fundamental purposes of each institution were adopted for approximately half of the state's senior colleges.

## Board Action

The Board adopted rules prohibiting state universities and community colleges from applying remedial course credit toward degrees. Guidelines adopted previously for English and mathematics limit formula funding to three credit hours of remedial work in each area.

More than 10,000 course offerings that went untaught for three consecutive years at Texas public universities have been struck from course inventories since the beginning of 1985. Some 6,500 courses were deleted last year, and an additional 3,665 deletions were reported in January. The Board sought the elimination of dormant course offerings to discourage unauthorized program growth and to avoid "false advertising" through catalogs. A survey will be conducted annually to seek out dormant courses; however, Coordinating Board officials do not anticipate many more.

In other matters concerning courses, the Board in July heard an analysis of campus policies on shortened format classes. Most of the institutions submitted guidelines which stipulated the same number of class hours in a short course as in a regular semester course—which is 45 hours of class contact for 3 semester credit hours. However, others submitted less contact time, stating that class material could be covered within a shorter time.

In a continuing effort, the Board in July approved an updated transfer curriculum for the agricultural sciences, joining fifteen others established in recent years to help students transfer among public institutions without losing course credits. The Board in 1979 began a study of all the transfer of credit policies and since then has adopted fifteen new or revised transfer curricula and other transfer policies.

In April 1985, the Coordinating Board adopted new rules permitting Texas public universities to apply for approval to offer degree programs on military bases.

## Telecourses Effective

A review of research on the effectiveness of televised instruction was presented at the July Board meeting. Research suggests that the achievement of students taking courses via television is equivalent to that of students taking instruction via traditional methods.

Data obtained from eleven community colleges or systems and four universities comprised the basis of a first-year status report which also was presented at the July meeting.

Community colleges reported offering 131 telecourses to 18,996 students in the 1985–86 academic year. Three universities offered 82 courses to 889 students via live, interactive delivery systems. Student achievement in televised courses at Texas institutions was found to be comparable to that of students in equivalent on-campus courses.

During 1986, eight additional community colleges received Board authority to offer televised instruction, bringing the total number of institutions so authorized to twenty–three.

## Academic Degrees Approved

In 1986, Board approval was given for twelve new degree offerings proposed by universities including two doctoral, five master's, three bachelor's and two associate–level programs. Two master's level requests and one bachelor's level request were withdrawn by universities, and the Board denied one baccalaureate level and one master's level request.

In addition, the Board discontinued unauthorized master's and doctoral programs at Texas Woman's University in marriage and family therapy. One of the new doctoral programs approved for Texas A&M University is in archaeology with a concentration in nautical archaeology. This program is unique to the state and is expected to attract worldwide attention.

The Board endorsed 18 graduate degree programs by ten Texas public universities through the SREB common market in the 1985–86 academic year. Texas is one of fourteen states participating in the exchange, which allows students to enroll in university programs in other states at resident tuition rates. Texas has participated since 1977. In 1985 it sent nine students to other states and hosted forty–eight students.

## Certificate of Authority Awarded

Regulations for private degree-granting institutions were amended by the Board in October. The rules revise procedures and criteria for evaluating non-exempt private institutions of higher education offering academic degrees or seeking to use the term "college" or "university."

At the Coordinating Board's request, the prosecuting attorney of Travis County successfully sought a permanent injunction against the American College of Health Science and the College of Life Science for offering degrees and using the term "college" without a certificate of authority from the Board as required by state law. On Aug. 15, 1986, Judge Bob Jones of the 167th Judicial District Court of Travis County ordered that the institutions cited "desist and refrain" from the prohibited activities without a certificate of authority issued by the Coordinating Board.

In April, the Board issued a certificate of authority to the Texas Chiropractic College to award the bachelor of science in human biology degree. The certificate is valid for two years.

## Standards Increased

Admission standards were increased during the year as eight of the twenty-four state-supported four-year campuses either raised their SAT and ACT score requirements or set minimum scores for the first time. Also four universities have added specific requirements for high school preparation, bringing the total to fifteen institutions with high school course prerequisites.

## Campus Missions Defined

Formal establishment of the missions of state universities and health science centers is an on-going Board project. By mid–1986 mission statements from seventeen institutions had been approved by the Board. Fourteen more have had their initial statements endorsed by the Board while four are in active negotiations regarding their statements. Work continues on eight institutions.

This on–going effort of establishing mission statements for each institution will aid the Board in evaluating program proposals from a statewide perspective and will assist schools in concentrating their resources to maintain quality programs.

# Utah

It was exactly one year ago that Governor Norman H. Sangerter declared a state of educational ALERT in Utah. The Governor, in his ALERT proclamation, called upon all citizens to join with him in marshaling the economic and human resources of this state to meet our educational needs. The 1986 year has been a year of marshaling the troops to face the educational challenges in Utah. Every major event in higher education has been within the ALERT framework.

## Budget Matters

The most dramatic evidence of the educational ALERT was the 94 percent budget reallocation ordered by the Governor in June in response to worsening economic forecasts. The Governor ordered all agencies, including higher education, to identify 6 percent of their budgets that could be reallocated to other higher priority areas in 1987–88.

The 94 percent budget reallocation was a wrenching experience on Utah's nine colleges and university campuses. Presidents set out to define their highest priority programs under an extremely short time frame and under great pressure from their campuses and local communities.

Nevertheless, the System of Higher Education identified $15.4 million from the $257,248,500 state funded appropriation to be reallocated. This included the elimination of 159 full-time equivalent faculty positions, 13 full-time equivalent executive positions and 272 full-time equivalent staff positions. Some 102 programs were eliminated, 130 were reduced and 20 were consolidated.

The State Board of Regents recommended in its 1987–88 budget request that reallocated funds be spent to close part of the compensation equity gap between Utah and peer institutions and for other highest priority institutional needs, including such items as library books and vocational equipment. Beyond the reallocation, the Board of Regents also identified other urgent institutional needs, such as cost of living increases, enrollment increases and state insurance needs. A 6 percent budget increase would be required to fund these needs. Other identified needs, including further salary increases and implementation of a state statute on reimbursed overhead, required a 10.2 percent budget request under the Board of Regents proposal.

The Governor, in his budget recommendations to the Legislature, reflected virtually the same priorities as the Board of Regents. His budget reflected a 5.7 percent increase, including implementation of the reimbursed overhead statute.

The above budget matters all relate to the 1987–88 budget, but they impacted directly on higher education matters in 1986, because budget considerations for next year signal to faculty members whether the state of Utah is willing to make the necessary investment in higher education.

Regarding the 1986–87 budget, two critical budget cuts have been absorbed by the System of Higher Education. The first cut—3 percent—came just after the budget year began in July because of revenue shortfalls. The Board of Regents imposed a one–time tuition surcharge on students at all nine institutions for winter and spring quarters to absorb part of the 3 percent cut. The remainder of the cut will be absorbed through reduced library and equipment expenditures and reduced hiring of part-time faculty and staff. Some class sections will also be cut. The second cut of 1 percent came in late November during a special session of the Legislature. Institution presidents are still determining how that cut can be absorbed.

## Master Plan

A new Master Plan for the Utah System of Higher Education was endorsed by the Board of Regents in December. The Master Plan provides a guide for higher education in Utah through the year 2000. It reflects the same priorities as the Governor's educational ALERT, including preserving open access to the System of Higher Education while redirecting enrollment toward community colleges.

The Master Plan calls for enrollment targets to be set at each of the nine institutions, with at least one third of all students directed to community colleges by the year 2000. The technical colleges will be renamed community colleges and will offer associate degrees and certificates that respond to community needs as authorized by the board if necessary legislation is approved. Legislation will also be sought to eliminate the requirement that 75 percent of all courses at the technical colleges be vocational.

Tuition policies will be altered to reflect higher tuition at the higher cost research universities, medium tuition at the state colleges and relatively modest tuition at the community colleges. Admission standards will be differentiated similarly.

A moratorium is declared on any expansion of institutional missions construed as academic drift until quality deficits such as competitive salaries, libraries, computer and laboratory equipment and academic support have been corrected and the issues of quality and access reconciled.

A strong commitment to vocational-technical education is reflected in the Master Plan through the recommended adoption of a funding formula to address the fact that many vocational programs are more costly than general education/transfer programs. The Master Plan also calls for short–term non–credit vocational training to be funded through the State Board of Vocational Education and flow to higher education, area vocational centers, or school districts in a coordinated manner to conserve state resources.

The Master Plan calls for experimentation with different scheduling and calendaring plans to promote greater use of telecommunications instruction and other proven but less expensive teaching techniques.

# Revision of the Education Article

The Governor, Legislature and general public all endorsed a revision of the Education Article this year. The revision includes the Utah System of Higher Education in the Constitution, thus ending years of debate about the constitutionality of Utah's system of educational governance.

The constitutional revision clearly establishes a public education system and a higher education system. The Legislature has given authority to the Board of Regents to govern higher education.

The Education Article Revision reflects the governor's ALERT declaration because it enhances the partnership between public and higher education. The governor's ALERT proclamation states that a continuing cooperative partnership between public and higher education is of fundamental importance in dealing with the challenges of managing growth and improving quality.

# X.10

# West Virginia

## Highlights of the Annual Report 1985 – 86

The 1985 – 86 fiscal year was the first year of implementation of the *Agenda for Action 1985 – 1990: A Master Plan of Goals and Services for Public Higher Education in West Virginia.* This Master Plan emphasized institutional cooperation, improved access and enhanced resources for higher education. Increased coordination among the colleges and universities was a major theme to ensure access to quality higher education for West Virginians in the most cost effective manner. Other strategic goals in this plan include bringing West Virginia's college-going rate to the SREB average and increasing salaries for higher education personnel to at least the SREB averages by 1990.

Relative to previous years, fiscal 1985 – 86 represented the second successive good year with respect to public higher education in West Virginia. Legislative support was demonstrated by the passage of a number of important bills which impacted favorably on higher education, and the absence of mid-year budget cuts (totalling $32 million over the previous three years) allowed institutions to fulfill their budgeted commitments during the year. Faculty and staff salaries increased by approximately 8.2 percent and overall state support for higher education improved by 10 percent over the previous year. A capital construction and renovation program was funded by a $73 million revenue bond issue as part of the largest capital improvement project in history for West Virginia public higher education.

Among other highlights of the 1985 – 86 Report are the following:

### Statistical Information

- The total enrollment in Fall 1985 was 66,744, a decrease from 68,533 the preceding year. The average in-state resident student enrollment for all institutions was 80 percent.

- The number of full-time enrolled (41,528) comprised 62.2 percent of the total headcount; 54.9 percent female.

- A total of 708 certificate and degree programs was offered consisting of 46 one-year certificate programs, 219 associate degree programs, 272 baccalaureate programs, and 171 graduate and professional degree and certificate programs.

- A total of 10,854 degrees was conferred; 2,056 associate, 6,580 baccalaureate, and 2,228 graduate and professional degrees (a 2.3 percent decrease from 1984 – 85).

### Basic Academic Programs and Student Services

- The five-year cycle of academic program reviews and evaluations continued. A total of 162 programs was reviewed at thirteen of the sixteen institutions. Of these, two programs at West Virginia University and one at West Virginia Northern Community College were identified as programs of excellence, an additional 137 were recommended for continuation, 8 were discontinued, and 16 were deferred for further consideration.

- The ten baccalaureate-granting institutions continued to preserve a basic complement of degree programs in the traditional liberal arts and sciences, with a total of 131 baccalaureate degree programs available at all West Virginia public institutions. The number of such degree programs per institution ranges from six to fourteen at the four-year institutions. West Virginia University and Marshall University each offers 23 undergraduate majors in the liberal arts and sciences.

- Graduate and professional school opportunities for West Virginia residents were augmented through a continuation of contractual arrangements with other states and through the SREB Academic Common Market program; 142 West Virginia residents enrolled in out-of-state programs not available in West Virginia.

## Career and Professional Programs

- Approximately 89 percent of all associate degrees and 75 percent of all degrees were in career fields.
- A total of 9,268 students was enrolled at the three community colleges and an additional 9,907 in the community college components, constituting 28.7 percent of the total enrollment.
- Funds were allocated involving the Education and Economic Security Act (EESA) and the West Virginia Council on Economic Education (WVCEE) toward programs designed to improve teacher effectiveness in West Virginia public schools.

## Programs for Adults and Non-Traditional Learners

- Demographic projections for West Virginia from 1980 to 1990 indicate a 47.2 percent increase in the 35–44 age group, a 13.5 percent increase in the 25–34 age group, and a 10 percent decline in the population of the traditional college age cohort.
- Adult and non–traditional students are principally part–time and constituted 37.8 percent of the total enrollment.
- Off–campus classes comprised 9.4 percent of all classes offered; enrollment in television courses totalled 3,004.

## Other Activities

- The appropriation of $100,000 by the 1985 Legislature for the Eminent Scholar Endowment Trust Fund Program was matched by contributions from Marshall University and West Virginia University to establish chairs at these institutions.
- A number of cooperative programs was developed including consortia in Charleston, Wheeling, and Parkersburg.
- The Center for Economic Research and the Institute for Public Affairs at West Virginia University and the Center for International Trade at Marshall University were established during the 1986 legislative session. The Economic Development Act of 1986 established the Higher Education–Industry Partnerships (HEIP), and the Board of Regents' Center for Education and Research with Industry was relocated at Marshall University.

A special aspect of the performance of the West Virginia system of higher education as it relates to budget is the quality, performance and salary level of its faculty. Salary level is one of the most important factors in ensuring the State's ability to attract and retain good faculty. West Virginia's public institutions still compare rather poorly with national averages and with the averages of the fifteen SREB states. However, in 1985–86, the West Virginia Legislature continued steps begun the previous year in addressing the faculty salary problem. Passage of a salary schedule for classified staff during the 1986 legislative session forms a basis for similar improvements in staff salaries.

On another positive note, in terms of tax effort and legislative effort toward the support of higher education in West Virginia, the state compares better with national averages. While it is indeed a fact that faculty and staff salaries are low, and that dollars spent per full time equivalent student are also well below the national average, West Virginia moved up in national rank from 37th for 1985–86 appropriations to 35th for 1986–87. Passage of key legislation in 1986 authorizing transfer of up to five percent among the four line items of state general revenue appropriation and the Higher Education Student Assistance Program will also have a positive impact on higher education, effective with the 1986–87 fiscal year.

Section II of the Report provides a detailed analysis of total operating and capital budgets, as well as educational and general revenues and expenditures for 1985–86. The total operating budget for all institutions combined was $412.6 million. Also included in this section are excerpts from individual institutional reports identifying financial issues that have resulted in limitations on institutional performance imposed by fiscal stringency.

Unique and significant institutional activities and accomplishments are included in Section III of the Report for each college and university.

## X.11

# U.S. Department of Education Office of Postsecondary Education

The Office of Postsecondary Education (OPE) administers the largest share of the Department's funding. During FY 1986, more than $14 billion was awarded under the various postsecondary education programs, including:

- more than $3.5 billion in Pell Grant assistance to needy students;
- more than $8 billion loaned to students under the Guaranteed Student Loan program;
- almost $2 billion awarded to students through the various Federal financial aid programs administered by eligible colleges and universities;
- more than $135 million awarded to colleges and universities to assist in their institutional development;
- almost $169 million to colleges and nonprofit organizations for recruitment and support of disadvantaged students;
- more than $30 million for a variety of international programs, including fellowships, language center support, and international studies support; and
- more than $50 million for support of facilities on college campuses.

In addition to making awards under these programs, OPE is responsible for monitoring expenditures of program funds, validating information submitted by millions of student applicants, training administrators in the operation of Federal programs, reviewing over 5,000 institutional audits per year, supporting projects which promote innovation and excellence, and a variety of other program-related activities.

OPE has also become quite active in the collection of debts owed as a result of defaults under the various loan programs it administers. These defaults range from more than $5 billion under the student loan programs to $84.4 million defaulted by higher education institutions under the college housing loan program. Through stepped-up collection efforts, the amount collected has increased significantly over the past four years, totaling about $200 million during FY 1986.

Highlights of other OPE accomplishments during FY 1986 are:

## Student Financial Assistance

The Office of Student Financial Assistance implemented a new program of scholarship assistance for outstanding high school graduates who plan to pursue careers as teachers. Regulations were developed and procedures implemented for the Congressional Teachers Fellowship Program, formerly the Carl Perkins Scholarship Program. It will provide $9.57 million to the States, administrators of the program.

## Improved Verification Process

For several years, the Office of Student Financial Assistance has verified information provided by applicants for Pell Grants. Applicants must submit documentation of information provided in their applications. The verification system was expanded to cover all the student aid programs, including the Guaranteed Student Loan program and the Federal student assistance programs administered by recipient institutions (the Supplemental Educational Opportunity Grant, National Direct Student Loan and College Work Study programs). Significant savings of taxpayer dollars are expected as a result of identifying misreporting through this improved verification process.

Full implementation of this new procedure required a series of verification training workshops for the financial aid community, conducted shortly after publication of the regulations announcing the new verification procedures. More than 10,000 financial aid administrators attended the sixty–six workshops conducted by OSFA.

## Need Analysis for Guaranteed Student Loan Applicants

A major legislative accomplishment was the requirement that all loans granted under the Guaranteed Student Loan program be based upon financial need. This requirement will result in savings through elimination of unnecessary loan amounts borrowed by applicants without financial need. This loan volume reduction reduces the interest and special allowance subsidies paid to lenders and reduces costs associated with defaulted loans.

## Income Contingent Loan Program

Another major legislative achievement was the authorization of a pilot program to award unsubsidized, income contingent loans. Under this program, student loan recipients will repay their loans at a rate pegged to actual income after graduation. Interest will accrue at a market-indexed rate. Such a program will reduce default and interest subsidy costs significantly and also ease the debt burden on students who require major loan assistance to achieve their academic objectives.

## "Gateway" Electronic Reporting

Each year, more than 3,000 institutions of postsecondary education participating in the Perkins Loan (formerly National Direct Student Loan), Supplemental Educational Opportunity Grant, and Work Study programs must submit a complex and lengthy document in order to report expenditures and request new funding. Many of these reports contain errors that are resolved only through a detailed and time-consuming editing process. This year OPE made it possible for participating institutions to submit their reports electronically through the "Gateway" project. This system utilizes specially developed computer disks which can be used on many types of personal computers. The 796 participants in this project have been overwhelmingly enthusiastic, and it is expected that many more institutions will participate next year. As a result of the

"Gateway" project and other improvements, the Department will be able to issue final allocations to institutions five weeks earlier than last year.

## Collections on Defaulted Student Loans

Perhaps the greatest accomplishment in the area of collections was the implementation of the Internal Revenue offset program. This effort involved working with the Internal Revenue Service to identify defaulters who had filed tax returns claiming income tax refunds. Thousands of defaulters were advised that their refunds had been applied to their debt to the Federal government. Last year, more than $120 million was collected through this offset method.

A number of major steps have resulted in significant increases in the amount of collections received from borrowers who defaulted on student loans. These steps include:

- A full implementation of the authority which enabled reporting of debtors to national consumer credit bureaus in order to prevent them from easily obtaining other credit financing. Collections offices are now reporting an average of 75 to 100 calls a week from delinquent borrowers as a result of this measure.

- A coordinated effort between the Departments of Justice and Education to pursue litigation on default cases. Effective publicity of the success of this effort (such as some cases in which luxury automobiles have been impounded) has also spurred defaulted borrowers to contact collections for repayment.

- Implementation of a private sector initiative that assigned defaulted loans to experienced private sector loan collection agencies. This initiative allowed the Department to reduce its collections work force in the regions.

- Implementation of procedures to identify, locate and offset the salaries of Federal employees who have failed to repay student loans has succeeded in recovering more than $10 million.

## Institutional Quality Control Pilot Project

Since the inception of Federal student financial aid programs, the Department and education institutions have been concerned about the quality of delivery in these programs. In spite of audits, program reviews, and data verification to reduce errors, program–wide payment errors still remain unacceptably high. To achieve a breakthrough in reducing these errors, OPE implemented a pilot project to install quality control systems at the points where services are actually delivered to students: the institutions.

## Teacher Education — Institutional Aid Programs

In response to the Secretary's Objective on Teacher Improvement, historically Black colleges and universities were given the opportunity to amend their Institutional Aid grants and obtain supplemental funding to improve the quality of teacher education preparation. Twenty-four institutions chose to accept the supplemental funding to conduct a systematic re-examination of their teacher training programs. The funding also provided for an internal competency assessment, including but not limited to competencies identified by the faculty and other standard competency measures.

## Title VII — Academic Facilities

New funding by the Congress for Academic Facilities Construction Grants (Title VII, Part B) required development of regulations and procedures to make new awards under the program. This process was successfully completed, and the first competition was conducted for the nearly $38 million in grant assistance.

# Major Court Decisions Affecting Colleges and Universities 1986

Reprinted by permission of the *College Administrator and the Courts, Annual Review.*

## XI.1

# Academic Affairs

## —Grade Appeal
## —Unfavorable Letter Placed in Student's File by Professor

HARRIS V. BLAKE, 798 F. 2D 419. United States Court of Appeals, Tenth Circuit, 1986.

FACTS: A graduate student in the University of Northern Colorado's Center for Special and Advanced Programs was enrolled in a counseling course but was allowed to withdraw administratively after the normal drop date. The professor for the course wrote the following letter which was placed in his file:

> This letter concerns when Henry Harris was registered for and his withdrawal from my Introductory Practicum Counseling, PCG 612, during Spring Quarter of 1979. Mr. Harris was allowed to withdraw by the Dean of Students, long after the drop date and after he had exhibited specific behaviors of being incompetent and unethical in his supervised practicum.
>
> It is my belief that Henry should not be allowed to register for a practicum and that if he does, the practicum should be aware of his past performance.

After the letter was written, the Advisory Committee determined that no action should be taken to remove the student from the program but that future instructors should be informed of his performance in the counseling practicum course which he dropped. The student continued to take courses.

After attempts to obtain a copy of the letter by mail, he was eventually given a copy of the letter when he went to the office of the academic coordinator of the program. Later the Dean of the College of Education determined that the placement of the letter in the file was "most inappropriate" and had it removed from the file.

The student received two grades which lowered his average below the required minimum and he was thus required to withdraw from the program. He logged an official grievance with the academic appeal board. He alleged that the two professors who had given him low grades had seen the letter in his file and were prejudiced against him by the letter. The academic appeal board upheld the grades which he received.

The student brought suit alleging that he was deprived of a property interest in continued enrollment and a liberty interest in his ability to pursue a career in psychology. He claimed that he was deprived of both procedural and substantive due process in that he had been treated arbitrarily and capriciously.

ISSUE: According to the facts of this case, was the student denied either procedural or substantive due process by virtue of the placement of the unfavorable letter in his file and/or the receipt of low grades following that placement.

ANSWER: No.

REASONING OF THE COURT: The court first declared that the student did have a property interest in his enrollment in the program and was thus entitled to procedural due process. However, it pointed out that the United States Supreme Court has emphasized that less stringent procedural requirements attach when a school makes an academic judgment about a student than when it takes a disciplinary action. (**Board of Curators v. Horowitz** reported in *The College Student and the Courts*).

The Court concluded that the decisions regarding the student were academic rather than disciplinary and that the procedural due process afforded the student was more than adequate to protect his property interest in continued enrollment. The Court also noted that the student had a right to place his own explanatory letter in his file.

As to whether the student had been deprived of substantive due process by arbitrary or capricious treatment, the court reasoned that the decisions regarding the student were made "conscientiously and with careful deliberation" and that there was no evidence of a "substantial departure from accepted academic norms as to demonstrate that the person or committee responsible did not actually exercise professional judgment." The court based its conclusion on the United States Supreme Court decision in **Regents of the University of Michigan v. Ewing.** (Reported in *The College Student and the Courts*)

The court noted that the student was given the opportunity to challenge the letter placed in his file and the subsequent grades he received before the academic appeal board. It further noted that there was no evidence that any of the professors or administrators who were involved harbored nonacademic or unconstitutional motives for affecting his withdrawal. The court concluded that the decision of the board was made with conscientious deliberation through the exercise of professional judgment. The court concluded by declaring that it was undisputed that unbiased faculty members considered the student's case and exercised their own judgment concerning the propriety of the grades that compelled the student's withdrawal.

# — Professor's Alleged Promise Does Not Create Property Interest in Academic Credit

Easley v. University of Michigan Board of Regents, 627 F. Supp. 580. United States District Court, E.D. Michigan, S.D., 1986.

Facts: A student at the University of Michigan Law School was not allowed to graduate because he had accumulated only eighty (80) credit hours when the minimum number of credits required for graduation was eighty-one (81). The student claimed that he had earned six credit hours in the course, Civil Procedure, instead of the normal five hours granted for successful completion of that course.

The student had received permission to take the course examination at a later date because of claimed family troubles. He further claimed that the professor promised him that upon successful completion of the course he would receive six credit hours. The professor denied making any such promise and, in fact, did not have the authority to grant six hours credit for a five credit hour course.

The student brought suit alleging that the withholding of his degree violated his due process rights. He claimed that the alleged promise by the professor created a property interest in the sixth hour which granted him due process rights.

Issue: According to the facts of this case, does an alleged promise by a professor of an additional credit hour, beyond the established number given for a course, create a property interest for the student which would trigger due process protection?

Answer: No.

Reasoning of the Court: The court first pointed out that a professor in the University of Michigan Law School did not have any discretion regarding the number of credit hours for an established course such as Civil Procedure. It did note that individual professors do have discretion to determine the number of credit hours a student may receive for an independent study course. There was no evidence that the professor had actually promised the student six credit hours for successful completion of the course.

In ruling against the student, the court reasoned that even if the professor had in fact promised the student six credit hours for the course, he would still lack a protected property interest in the sixth hour. The court pointed out that not every subjective belief creates a protected interest which would trigger due process protection. It further declared that the course, civil procedure, is a five hour course and that no promise by a professor could change that.

Additional Comments: The student also alleged that although the eighty-one (81) hours required for graduation did apply to his class, that requirement did not bind him since he claimed that he did not receive at the beginning of the term a copy of the new regulations which increased from eighty (80) to eighty-one (81) the hours required for graduation. The court declared that the student's claim was groundless and frivolous since the new regulations were distributed with other orientation material at the beginning of each term. Also, the regulations were readily accessible throughout the year in the administrative offices of the law school.

## XI.2

# Administrative Employment

## — President's Offer of Multi – Year Contract to Coach

UNIVERSITY OF ARIZONA V. COUNTY OF PIMA, 722 P. 2D 352.   Court of Appeals of Arizona, Division 2, 1986.

FACTS:   In 1982, Ben Lindsey was offered the position of head basketball coach at the University of Arizona. Although Lindsey's contract covered one year, the president of the university orally assured Lindsey that he would have four years to rebuild the program, and that his contract would be resubmitted to the board each of those four years.

Lindsey brought this suit when he was terminated after one year of employment. The board argued that any multi – year contract with Lindsey was void under Arizona statutes which provide that the state may not incur an obligation against the state for any expenditure not authorized by appropriation and allotment. This statute, the board argued, prohibits any offer of multi – year employment to Lindsey. The question of the interpretation of the statute was accepted by the appellate court.

ISSUE:   Does a state appropriations statute, prohibiting the state or any of its agencies from obligating the state beyond current appropriations, prevent a university from offering a person a *de facto* multi – year contract?

ANSWER:   No.

REASONING OF THE COURT:   The court held that the statute does not prevent an agreement to resubmit a one – year contract to the board for a multiple of years, but rather subjects that contract to the discretion of the legislature to avoid obligation for any term beyond the current fiscal year, and current appropriations. Here, the legislature's power to

avoid any expenditure for the second year or beyond does not relieve the university of its agreement to resubmit the contract each year to the board, for four years. Rather, the statute subjects the additional years' agreements to state funding.

Here, the university continued the operation of its basketball program, demonstrating the appropriation and allotment of funds. Therefore, Lindsey's entitlement to employment may be judged by contract principles, with no invasion of the statute's prohibitions.

ADDITIONAL COMMENTS:   The court likened the promise to Lindsey to the university's tenure policy, which provided that the contract of a tenured faculty member would be submitted each year to the board for reappointment, subject to appropriation of funds by the state.

Many jurisdictions have statutes prohibiting the incurring of multi – year fiscal obligations, which may, in certain jurisdictions, also violate the state constitution. This case is important in that it prevents the university from offering multi – year employment contracts (common for coaches), or promises for renewal of one-year contracts, and then attempting to avoid such a contract under an appropriations statute. Equally important, however, is the court's recognition of the state's power to avoid such obligations. This power is significant but not absolute, as demonstrated here, where the university enjoyed funding for the continuing of its basketball program.

It is common practice to offer head coaches multi – year contracts, and such practice will continue at many universities; however, it should be recognized that the holding in this case places the university in the position of having to consider a settlement of a multi – year offer where it seeks to terminate a coach before the end of his promised "tenure." Such "buy – outs" have a double impact upon athletic department budgets, and represent a kind of "de facto tenure" not enjoyed by other administrative employees of the university.

539

## XI.3

# Administrator Employment

## — Race Discrimination

CRAIG V. ALABAMA STATE UNIVERSITY, 804 F. 2D 682. United States Court of Appeals, Eleventh Circuit, 1986.

FACTS: In 1978, the United States District Court for the Middle District of Alabama found that Alabama State University had engaged in a pattern or practice of discrimination against whites in the hiring of administrative staff, and faculty. The court entered a judgment ordering the university to refrain from further discrimination in hiring.

In 1983, Moore, a white female, applied for the position of Federal Relations Director at ASU. She was employed, on an interim basis, at acting assistant director, under a contract covering the period July 1–September 30, 1983. At the time, she was also given a contract for the period October 1, 1983 to September 28, 1984, with the understanding that the position would eventually have to be advertised. Subsequently, in August, 1983, the board of trustees of the university, having not been informed of the second contract, concluded that the position was open as of October 1, 1983. On being informed by the president of ASU that her first contract was "terminal," Moore agreed to the advertisement of the position, and applied for it.

During this time, Williams, a black female employee of the university, was on a two–year study leave, providing for her return in 1983, to a "faculty, or other mutually acceptable position" at her previous salary of $31,420.00 per year. When Williams notified the university of her availability for work, the search for the federal relations position was discontinued, and she was hired at her previous salary, more than $6,000.00 above the advertised salary for the position. Moore and others brought this suit, alleging a violation of the district court's injunction in the prior lawsuit. The district court held that Williams was hired as federal relations director because of the contractual obligation to her upon her return

from study leave, and that the federal relations position was the only available job meeting the university's commitment. Moore appeals.

ISSUE: Did ASU discriminate against Moore in its hiring of Williams, in violation of the federal court order?

ANSWER: Yes.

REASONING OF THE COURT: Citing **Griggs v. Duke Power Company** (*The College Administrator and the Courts,* Casebook), the court held that a policy of hiring from within, albeit facially neutral, becomes discriminatory when applied in a context of a past pattern or practice of discrimination in hiring of a racial group. In this context, the failure to consider outside applicants necessarily operates more harshly upon the affected class (here whites) because the policy causes their total exclusion from consideration, thus benefiting the employer's racially distorted workforce.

The court rejected the university's reliance upon the agreement with Williams as business necessity (see **Griggs**), holding that it was not obligated to enter into it in the first instance, and that it had an obligation not to use selection criteria which maintained the status quo of its racially imbalanced workforce. The business necessity justification for an otherwise discriminatory hiring pattern must involve a business purpose sufficiently compelling to override any negative racial impact, and there must be no acceptable alternative which would better accomplish the business purpose or accomplish it equally well with a lesser negative racial impact. In short a practice with discriminatory racial impact must "(foster safety and efficiency, and must be essential to that goal)."

ASU offered no evidence that its study leave policy was essential to insure a necessary quality in staff, particularly where, as here, the favored employee was an administrator, not a member of the

540

faculty. Moreover, it is arguable that the university might better achieve its goal of improving its workforce by opening all vacant positions to the widest applicant pool, rather than limiting its hiring to promotions from within a racially imbalanced workforce.

ADDITIONAL COMMENTS: The court observed that the federal relations position required only a masters degree, which Williams possessed before taking her study leave, and that her study was unrelated to the duties of the federal relations position. Thus, a proper search could have produced a more qualified candidate for the position, at a lower salary.

The court held that it was not invalidating, the university's study leave policy generally, but rather only as applied in this case, where the university's administrative and professional workforce was more than 90% black.

## XI.4

# Affirmative Action

## —Denial of Tenure
## —Failure to Consider AA Plan

SOLA V. LAFAYETTE COLLEGE, 804 F. 2D 40. United States Court of Appeals, Third Circuit, 1986.

FACTS: Lafayette College operated pursuant to a tenure policy which provided, *inter alia,* that not more than two-thirds of the faculty of any department could be tenured members of the faculty, absent "an exceptional guideline-breaking candidate." In 1982, Sola, a female, applied for tenure. The chairman of her department gave her a qualified recommendation, noting that the department was only one position short of its "tenure quota," and that a male professor, whom he viewed to be "stronger" than Sola, would be eligible for tenure in the future.

The college's published tenure criteria included consideration of enrollment trends, the need for a desirable mix of specialties, tenure guidelines, "principles of Affirmative Action (sic)," economic priorities, and other relevant needs of the college.

Ultimately, the president of the college approved a recommendation of the college's faculty tenure committee that Sola not be awarded tenured status. The Pennsylvania Human Relations Commission denied Sola's formal charge of sex discrimination, and she filed this lawsuit in federal court, claiming wrongful discharge, breach of contract, and intentional infliction of emotional distress. The district court dismissed her claims, and she appeals.

ISSUE: Did the trial court err in refusing to consider Sola's claim that the college breached its employment agreement with her by refusing to consider its stated affirmative action criteria when determining her application for tenure?

ANSWER: Yes.

REASONING OF THE COURT: The court of appeals held that Sola properly raised, in her complaint, the issue whether the college breached its employment contract with Sola by refusing to consider her gender as a positive factor in the tenure decision process. Noting that her claim was based upon the provisions of the faculty handbook, as incorporated by reference into her employment contract, and was not a civil rights claim, the court of appeals directed the federal trial court to determine whether Pennsylvania state law recognizes a claim for breach of contract based upon a college's voluntary affirmative action plan or criteria.

The court rejected Sola's claim of wrongful discharge (a tort claim), holding that she failed to prove that she was denied tenure because of her sex.

ADDITIONAL COMMENTS: The issue raised by this case is important in light of recent United States Supreme Court opinions upholding voluntary affirmative action plans. The breach of contract claim is, of course, distinct from a claim of violation of court ordered affirmative action, including numerical hiring goals, or the enforcement of a consent decree containing a race-conscious promotion plan, as approved by the Supreme Court in **Local 28, Sheet Metal Workers' International Association v. E.E.O.C.** and **Local No. 98, International Association of Firefighters v. City of Cleveland** (See *The College Administrator and the Courts*).

The Sola case contains a noteworthy discussion of the issue whether a tort claim of wrongful discharge is precluded in federal court where that claim has been determined adversely to the claimant in a state administrative agency proceeding.

# — Preference for Female Applications
# — Fair Practices Code (Maine)

DORAN V. UNIVERSITY OF MAINE AT FARMINGTON, 505 A. 2D 483. Supreme Judicial Court of Maine, 1986.

FACTS: Pursuant to a plan for consolidation of academic departments, the University created a new position of director of a center for human, health and family studies. Under a written faculty senate procedure, full-time faculty nominated candidates for such a position. Doran was nominated and was selected by a vote of ten to eight over a female nominee. The university's provost rejected Doran, citing his concern about the failure of any of the university's centers to nominate a female for the position of director.

At the time of this action, the university had in place a written affirmative action plan, encouraging women and minorities to apply for positions, and offering assurance of equal and fair consideration to all qualified candidates.

Doran brought this action, alleging that the rejection of his nomination, in favor of the female nominee, violated the state's Human Rights Act, prohibiting employment discrimination based upon sex. The university admitted this violation, but alleged the state's Fair Practices Code required or permitted affirmative action such as that engaged in with regard to the selection of center directors. The trial court held in favor of the university and Doran appeals.

ISSUE: Does the state's Fair Practices Code permit the rejection of Doran's nomination in favor of the preference of a female applicant solely because of the sex of the applicants?

ANSWER: No.

REASONING OF THE COURT: The code does require each state agency or department to prepare and follow an affirmative action plan. However, nothing in the code requires that a plan include requirements for the preference of women to other possible candidates. The university's plan encourages women to apply for positions and seeks to expand the applicant pool in this regard. However, the plan does not provide for the promotion of a minimum number of female applicants, for denying a male promotion in favor of a female, or for any preference of females solely because of sex, unless sex is a bona fide occupational qualification.

ADDITIONAL COMMENTS: Since the case was based upon alleged violations of state law, the court rejected the invitation of the university to look to federal cases, including U.S. Supreme Court cases interpreting the provisions of Title VII of the Civil Rights Act, insofar as it applies to the validity of voluntary affirmative action plans, or plans approved by a federal court pursuant to a consent decree. See **United Steelworkers of America** v. **Weber,** and **Firefighters Local Union No. 1784** v. **Stotts,** *The College Administrator and the Courts,* Revised Edition, and **Local 93 etc,** v. **City of Cleveland.**

## XI.5

# Defamation

## —Letter of Recommendation

GOLDMAN V. WAYNE STATE UNIVERSITY
BOARD OF GOVERNORS, 390 N.W. 2D 672.
Court of Appeals of Michigan, 1986.

FACTS: A student at Wayne State University brought this action alleging that a letter of recommendation, sent by a university committee concerning his suitability to pursue a medical career, constituted defamation in the form of libel. The committee is designed to assist students in their application process to health related professional schools. The committee collects relevant data (transcripts, letters of recommendation, and MCAT scores) and submits this information along with their own recommendation and ranking based on all interviews. When the student submitted a letter of recommendation from his mother, an English professor at Wayne, without stating her relationship to him, it was suggested by the committee that the letter be withdrawn. The student did so. Later the committee determined that the student had enrolled in two classes which met at the same time. He made an A in both classes but never attended one of them. The class in which he made an A but never attended was his mother's English course.

The committee decided not to recommend the student for admission to medical school and included in his materials a letter stating "doubts about his suitability for a profession that values personal integrity." The student was rejected at every medical school where he had applied.

The lower court granted a summary judgment favoring the university and the student appealed.

ISSUE: Was there sufficient evidence of defamation to preclude a summary judgment favoring the university?

ANSWER: No.

REASONING OF THE COURT: Where a summary judgment is issued there must be no issue of material fact that can be cited. If there are such issues then the case must be submitted to a jury rather than being decided only on the basis of law. In this instance the student was unable to show actual malice which is a necessary requisite in proving defamation. In other words, the student had to at least provide sufficient evidence to raise the issue that the committee acted with knowledge that their letter was false or with reckless disregard for its truth or falsity. The student did not provide any evidence but simply alleged that there was malice. "It is a well established rule of law that general allegations of malice will not suffice to establish a genuine issue of material fact." The court also noted that far from establishing any evidence beyond mere allegations ". . . all indications are that the committee's opinion, as set forth in the letter, is based on true and undisputed facts."

544

# XI.6

# Faculty Contracts

## — Letters Promising Tenure

LEWIS V. LOYOLA UNIVERSITY OF CHICAGO, 500 N.E. 2D 47. Appellate Court of Illinois, First District, 1986.

FACTS: In 1979, Lewis was approached by a search committee of Loyola University for the position of Chairman of the Department of Pathology of Loyola's medical college. During several months of negotiation, the dean of the college sent Lewis two letters, the first addressing Lewis' administrative salary and practice stipend for clinical work, staffing, departmental space allocation, and tenure. In the second letter, the dean stated that, assuming that both Lewis and the college administration would be satisfied with the employment relationship, the dean would propose early approval of tenure for Lewis, in September, 1981.

Subsequently, Lewis received a formal letter of appointment listing his salary, and appointing him as professor of pathology. A transmittal letter detailed his salary. Although Lewis' appointment was renewed for 1981–82 and 1982–83, the dean failed to submit his name for tenure consideration. Recognizing that he could have submitted his own name, Lewis deferred to his dean's promise to correct the "oversight."

In 1982, the dean resigned his administrative post without acting as promised, and Lewis was relieved of his chairmanship and advised that his appointment was terminal. He brought this action alleging breach of contract. The university argued that the letters from the dean were superceded by the formal contract, and could not be considered in construing its obligation to Lewis. Judgment was entered for Lewis and the university appealed.

ISSUE: Were the letters referred to above properly considered by the court in determining the terms of Lewis' employment with the university?

ANSWER: Yes.

REASONING OF THE COURT: The court held that, where a formal contract is not expressive of the complete agreement and understanding of the parties, consideration of antecedent proceedings does not vary the agreement, but serves to exemplify its terms. In this regard, any relevant evidence may be considered to determine whether the final contract does contain the complete agreement of the parties. Finally, whether a written document containing the essential terms of a contract contemplates the execution of a later formal document, the determination whether the former is a contract, or merely negotiation, is dependent upon the intent of the parties.

The final letter of appointment, although containing Lewis' name, and a statement of compensation, contained no reference to the position he accepted, nor references to staffing, departmental space, etc. These matters were covered in the two additional letters, which contained the statement that, if Lewis accepted the position offered, a formal letter of appointment would follow. The earlier communications thus constitute a part of Lewis' contract, and not merely negotiation.

As to tenure there was a promise to consider Lewis in 1981. Evidence was introduced to show that, although a dean's submission was not binding, it was followed in virtually all cases. It was therefore within the trial court's discretion to find that, if the dean had complied with his written representation, Lewis would have been tenured, pursuant to the terms of his contract.

ADDITIONAL COMMENTS: The court upheld the trial court's award of damages sustained by Lewis in 1984, but reversed and remanded the lower court's award of future damages of $100,000.00 per year, as speculative.

This case demonstrates that courts will generally not require the formation of a contract for reappointment, where the plaintiff has an adequate remedy in damages for breach of contract. The question in this case, on remand, is the amount of future damages to be awarded to Lewis.

# — Replacing Full – Time Faculty with Part – Time Faculty

VANDEVER V. JUNIOR COLLEGE DISTRICT OF KANSAS CITY, 708 S.W. 2D 711.  Missouri Court of Appeals, Western District, 1986.

FACTS:  In 1975, the district adopted a master plan establishing a 55–45 ratio between full time and part-time faculty employed by the district. Pursuant to this plan, many full–time, non–probationary faculty members, including Vandever, received notice that they would be placed on unpaid leave. Vandever was placed on leave at the close of the fall semester, 1979.

Thereafter, the district substantially increased its employment of part–time faculty to teach courses previously taught by full–time faculty. The pattern of course assignments for part–time faculty was such that, in many instances, the fifteen hour courseload of a former full–time faculty member would be divided among three to five part–time faculty, at a substantial savings in payroll.

Vandever brought this suit alleging that the action of the district amounted to a breach of contract in that it violated the district's own written policy that "A non-probationary faculty member's *place* will not be filled by a replacement within a period of two years unless he/she has been offered reappointment and has declined." (emphasis added) The district contended that the term "place" means a full–time appointment, including office hours, curriculum development, and other non–teaching duties. Part-time faculty, the district argued were responsible only to prepare lessons and teach assigned classes.

The trial court directed a verdict in favor of the district, and Vandever appeals.

ISSUE:  Is Vandever entitled to a jury determination whether she has been replaced by part–time employees, in violation of the above quoted terms of her employment contract?

ANSWER:  Yes.

REASONING OF THE COURT:  Vandever presented evidence that the district's intent in using the word "place" was to mean a fifteen–hour teaching load, and not a "full–time" as opposed to "part–time" position. Vandever's witness, who had arguably drafted or participated in the drafting of the policy, indicated that the term was understood to mean such by teachers. Further, Vandever offered evidence that forty–two part–time faculty were hired to teach courses previously taught by fifteen full–time faculty, and that she herself was offered a total of twenty–one hours, part–time at two different colleges within the district.

Within this context, the court held the contract susceptible to two meanings, which should be submitted to the jury. If a "place" means fifteen credit hours, and Vandever can establish that a "place" became available within two years, she is entitled to an offer of reappointment under the district's policy.

ADDITIONAL COMMENTS:  The majority of the court indicated that the district's argument as to the meaning of the term "place" would subject Vandever's entitlement to reinstatement to the district's absolute discretion whether to recreate full–time positions, as defined by the district. Vandever's argument on the other hand is that when part–time faculty have been employed to teach fifteen hours of courses previously taught by her, and which she remains qualified to teach, she has been "replaced."

# Faculty Employment

## —Age Discrimination

DiBENEDETTO V. COMMONWEALTH, 497 N.E. 2D 266. Supreme Judicial Court of Massachusetts, 1986.

FACTS: DiBenedetto applied for and was hired into the position of lecturer in Italian at the University of Massachusetts, after his former college closed in 1975. In 1979, he applied for an advertised, tenure-track position in the Spanish Department at the university. During a telephone conversation with the chairman of the Spanish Department (which DiBenedetto recorded without the knowledge of the chairman). DiBenedetto was told that the department "was looking for younger people." Nonetheless, the chairman encouraged DiBenedetto to submit his vitae, and DiBenedetto was ultimately interviewed as a finalist candidate for the position by a faculty selection committee. The chairman was a nonvoting member of that committee. The position was offered to an applicant who was thirty-three years old.

DiBenedetto, who was fifty-one years old, brought this suit in state court, alleging employment discrimination under the federal Age Discrimination in Employment Act. The jury, in its answers to special interrogatories, stated that the university's department chairman did discriminate against DiBenedetto, but that the university did not fail to hire DiBenedetto because of his age. On the basis of these answers, the trial judge dismissed DiBenedetto's claim of age discrimination, and he appeals.

ISSUE: Did the trial judge act within his discretion in dismissing plaintiff's claim where the jury found discrimination by the chairman, but not ultimately in the hiring decision?

ANSWER: Yes.

REASONING OF THE COURT: The court first reaffirmed that in an age discrimination action, the

plaintiff has the same burden of proof as in a Title VII action alleging employment discrimination. Specifically, plaintiff must prove, by the greater weight of the evidence, that (1) he applied for an advertised position; (2) that he was within the protected age range of 40–70 years; (3) that he was qualified for the position; (4) that, despite his qualifications, he was not hired; (5) that a younger person with equal or inferior qualifications was hired; and (6) that the reasons given for rejecting plaintiff's application were "a pretext or cover-up for not hiring him."

Emphasizing the necessity of proof on the sixth factor, the court held that, although plaintiff need not prove his age was the sole factor in the decision not to hire him, he must prove that his age was "a determining factor" in that decision. On this issue, although the chairman may have had some bias for a younger applicant, the jury found that his bias did not influence the hiring decision.

ADDITIONAL COMMENTS: Citing **McDonnell Douglas Corporation** v. **Green**, and **Kumar** v. **Board of Trustees** (reported in *The College Administrator and the Courts*), the court emphasized that the plaintiff must prove more than discrimination; he must prove that the discrimination had a "causative impact" on the decision not to hire. In other words, that but for the discriminatory consideration of age, plaintiff would have been hired. It was due to plaintiff's failure to prove causation that his claim was dismissed.

The court did not cite the U.S. Supreme Court's decision in **Texas Department of Community Affairs** v. **Burdine** (*The College Administrator and the Courts*, Second edition); however, its rationale is in accord with the **Burdine** court's holding that a plaintiff in a Title VII action must prove that a stated reason for an employment decision is a pretext for illegal discrimination.

Although not affecting this case, the Age Discrimination in Employment Act amendments of 1986 (see Appendix, *The College Administrator and the*

*Courts,* Second edition), grant additional employment protections to those outside the upper age range of seventy years.

# — Handbook Terms as Part of Employment Contract

PUNDT V. MILLIKIN UNIVERSITY, 496 N.E. 2D 291. Appellate Court of Illinois, Fourth District, 1986.

FACTS: After being hired as a probationary employee of Millikin University, Pundt received a copy of the university's staff handbook. The handbook stated, in part, that it was promulgated to provide information to the employee regarding the employment practices of Millikin, and the benefits and responsibilities of employment. Regarding retention, the handbook stated that the faculty "may only be terminated (sic) for just cause outlined in the handbook, or as otherwise determined in the good judgment and fair treatment of Millikin." Although the term "just cause" was defined as not limited to the certain offenses listed in the handbook, the handbook repeated, in its grievance procedure, that a regular, full-time employee "may be discharged for cause only."

Pundt was promoted to permanent status, but was thereafter terminated. He brought this action, in state court, alleging that his termination was without cause as outlined in the staff handbook, and was therefore in breach of his employment contract with Millikin. The university argued that, since the handbook was not specifically incorporated into Pundt's employment contract, the university was not contractually bound by its provisions. The trial court agreed, and dismissed Pundt's claim. He appeals.

ISSUE: Was the university's staff handbook a part of its employment contract with Pundt?

ANSWER: Yes.

REASONING OF THE COURT: The court held that the question whether a university's handbook is a part of its employment contract with an employee is to be determined by the court, not a jury. In deciding the question, the court held that the university was not required to publish a handbook; however, once it did, stating its purpose, and providing that a permanent employee may be dismissed only for cause, the employee had a right to

expect the handbook to be followed in termination actions.

Thus, the court held, the handbook is properly a part of the employee's contract.

ADDITIONAL COMMENTS: The court did not determine the merits of Pundt's allegations that he was discharged without just cause. It held only that, in determining cause for dismissal, the university was bound to follow its employee manual.

The court recognized that some state courts have held that an employee handbook may not be considered a part of the employment contract where the employee has not given independent consideration for the promises in the handbook, or where the employer has retained the right to unilaterally amend or withdraw the handbook, citing **Reynolds Manufacturing Co.** v. **Mendoza,** 644 **S.W.** 2d 536, and **Johnson** v. **National Beef Packing Co.,** 551 **P.** 2d 779. However, the **Pundt** court reasoned that, where there is a mutuality of obligation existing for the contract, the employee furnishes adequate consideration for the handbook's statements when he or she continues to work under the handbook's provisions.

The cases cited by the court include those in which the employee worked under a written contract which specifically incorporated by reference a staff handbook. However, the **Pundt** court clearly did not view this specific incorporation by reference as a condition precedent to the finding that the handbook is a part of the employment contract. *Cf.* **Piper** v. **Board of Trustees,** 426 **N.E.** 2d 262 (1981).

In this regard, the editors note that the incorporation of the staff handbook, as well as other university regulations in the employee's contract of employment may benefit the university as much as the employee. This question is certainly appropriate for counsel, who should be involved in the review of the staff handbook prior to its promulgation.

# — Reclassification of Position as Sex Discrimination

GRIFFIN V. BOARD OF REGENTS OF REGENCY UNIVERSITY, 795 F. 2D 1281. United States Court of Appeals, Seventh Circuit, 1986.

FACTS: Griffin was hired in 1974 as a temporary faculty member in the Department of Sociology at

Illinois State University. At the time of her being hired, she did not have her doctorate. In 1977, Griffin applied for a regular faculty position, but was rejected in favor of a male applicant with a Ph.D., prior teaching experience at Yale and Princeton, and experience in applied research. Griffin's resume indicated no expertise in these areas. In 1978, a tenured faculty member resigned, and Griffin apparently sought the vacant position. The position was reclassified as temporary, pursuant to university regulations.

Regular faculty positions are tenure track positions, subject to national search, and usually require a doctorate. Temporary positions do not require the doctorate, and are one-year appointments, renewable for up to three years.

Griffin filed a charge of sex discrimination with the federal Equal Employment Opportunity Commission (EEOC). Griffin who, had now received her doctorate, was not offered a position for 1980–81 because of a university rule placing a three-year upper limit upon temporary status faculty appointments. Subsequently, the board rejected a settlement offer by the EEOC. She brought this action in federal court, which entered a preliminary injunction, reinstating her to a part-time position. The court then certified a class action on behalf of similarly situated females, on the basis of Griffin's claim of a pattern or practice of sex discrimination in employment by ISU. The trial court found in favor of the university and Griffin appeals.

ISSUE: (1) Did the university discriminate against Griffin on the basis of her sex in rejecting her original bid for regular status, or her application for the vacant position?

(2) Did the university engage in a pattern or practice of sex discrimination in the establishment or filling of regular faculty positions?

ANSWER: No, to both questions.

REASONING OF THE COURT: As to her individual claim of sex discrimination, plaintiff failed to prove either that she was qualified for the one open regular position for which she applied, or that the selection of a male with a Ph.D. and direct experience, which Griffin lacked, was a pretext for sex discrimination. Similarly, there was no evidence that the university's policy to reclassify a vacant regular position as temporary is motivated by considerations of sex of its faculty.

As to the class action claims, the court found no persuasive evidence of a pattern or practice of sex discrimination. The dual classification of positions,

the court found, is typical in higher education. Such a dual system is not illegal, unless women are treated differently than men within the same faculty class, regular or temporary.

The court rejected plaintiff's claim that women, who occupy a greater percentage of temporary positions than regular positions compared to males, perform the same work in temporary positions as males do in regular positions. The court found a difference in qualifications and responsibilities between regular and temporary faculty; moreover, any concentration of women in temporary positions is related to demand, not gender motivated selection or classification.

In sum, there is no persuasive statistical evidence that women are classified on the basis of their sex, or any showing of criteria for classification which is sex-based. Even assuming a disproportionate classification, the dual classification system serves a valid business purpose, in that ISU used temporary faculty (who, like Griffin, may be pursuing a doctorate) much the same way as a university with a graduate program would use graduate assistants. In this way the university is adequately staffed, without having a particular department becoming too heavily tenured.

ADDITIONAL COMMENTS: The court suggested that a disproportionate impact analysis might, in any event, be inappropriate in cases of faculty hiring, since hiring decisions at the professional level are inherently subjective. The court seemed to be persuaded that a showing of disparate treatment of individuals, rather than merely a statistical showing of disparate impact of classification upon women as a class, is more appropriate in a faculty hiring case. The court noted a split of opinion among the federal circuit courts on this issue.

# — Sex Discrimination
# — Damages

SELLERS V. DELGADO COLLEGE, 781 F. 2D 503. United States Court of Appeals, Fifth Circuit, 1986.

FACTS: Sellers, a candidate for a master's degree in journalism, was hired by the college in 1975 at a salary of $9,000 for the academic year, and $3,000 for the summer term. She was classified as an instructor, but was generally assigned administrative duties in public relations, including preparation of press releases, brochures, and other materials regarding events at the college. She requested, but was not offered, a formal job description.

In 1976, the college hired a male assistant professor, with a master's degree and experience in journalism, at a salary of $10,500 for the academic year. His assignments soon encroached upon Sellers' areas of responsibility, and, ultimately, he was presented to staff as "Co-ordinator of Information Services." Sellers was given additional teaching duties with no extra pay.

After unsuccessful requests to speak with her superiors about her job, Sellers resigned and filed a charge of employment discrimination with the Equal Employment Opportunity Commission. That charge led to this lawsuit, which alleged discrimination on the basis of sex, and constructive discharge.

The trial court (magistrate) found sex discrimination and awarded Sellers back pay of $2044.50 for a nine-month period immediately preceding her resignation. The court also awarded Sellers $18,200, an amount equal to that which the male counterpart earned the year following Sellers' resignation. The damage award is appealed.

ISSUE:   Were the above damage awards proper?

ANSWER:   No.

REASONING OF THE COURT:   Citing the United States Supreme Court's decision in **County of Washington v. Gunther** (452 **U.S.** 161), the Court held that a Title VII plaintiff arguing disparate pay based upon sex, must show: (1) that she and the subsequently hired male performed essentially the same jobs, but received different pay; (2) the degree to which the relevant jobs overlapped; (3) the time at which the overlap occurred (for purposes of a back pay award).

Back pay may be awarded for a period not to exceed two years prior to timely filing of the EEOC charge and extending to the date of judgment. In this case the period for which back pay was awarded should be explained in that it did not recognize Sellers' period of unemployment subsequent to her resignation. It should be stated whether the award was predicated upon the provisions of Title VII, or Equal Pay Act. As to the $18,200, "front pay" is "calculated to terminate on the date a victim of discrimination attains an opportunity to move to her rightful place, rather than upon the date the order granting of relief is entered." (Citing **Patterson v. American Tobacco Co.,** 535 **F.** 2d 257.) Without proper explanation, there is doubt as to the validity of any "front pay" award. This matter should be considered upon remand.

ADDITIONAL COMMENTS:   Although the amount of a damage award is not normally instructive for general application, this case is helpful to the administrator in discussing with legal counsel the monetary consequences of liability in an employment discrimination case.

## XI.8

# Faculty Evaluation

## —Denial of Promotion
## —Alleged Discrimination

ANDERSON V. UNIVERSITY OF NORTHERN IOWA, 779 F. 2D 441. United States Court of Appeals, Eighth Circuit 1985.

FACTS: Anderson, a sixty–three–year–old black female, was originally hired by the university as an assistant professor in the college of social and behavioral sciences. In 1973, she was promoted to the rank of associate professor. In 1977, 1979 and 1982, she applied for, but was denied promotion to the rank of professor, the stated reason being her lack of scholarly productivity.

In 1983, Anderson filed suit, claiming violations by her employer of Title VII of the Civil Rights Act, and the Equal Pay Act. She alleged that the university has promoted only one of seven eligible black faculty, and that her personal salary was $2,000 less than that of a comparable white male faculty member.

The district court found that Anderson's ability as a teacher was undoubted and that her student and peer evaluations were consistently favorable. However, the court held, these factors do not, standing alone, establish a case of discrimination as alleged. The court dismissed Anderson's claims, and she appealed.

ISSUE: Did the university deny Anderson promotion because of her race, or discrimination against her on the basis of her sex, in the payment of salary?

ANSWER: No.

REASONING OF THE COURT: It is appropriate for the university to establish performance criteria, including scholarship, as a basis for the competitive evaluation of faculty for promotion in rank.

Judged by such criteria, Anderson had a lower output of scholarship than anyone else on the social and behavioral sciences faculty.

Statistics such as those cited by Anderson are not controlling. They establish only a prima facie case, which may be rebutted by a showing of justifiable reasons for refusal to rehire, promote, or the like. Anderson failed to carry the ultimate burden of proof that the decision in her case was motivated by considerations of her race.

Anderson's claims of salary discrimination are barred under a settlement agreement in an earlier class action suit against the university.

ADDITIONAL COMMENTS: The court's decision as to Anderson's burden of proof is consistent with the United States Supreme Court's decision in **Texas Department of Community Affairs v. Burdine.** The decision is also in accord with federal common law that a public university is free to adopt promotion criteria which require the peer evaluation of one's teaching, scholarship and service. Such criteria, although requiring the subjective judgment of peers involved in the promotion or tenure process, are constitutionally valid, so long as they are applied without regard to race or sex, or other protected characteristics. See *e.g.,* **Green v. Texas Tech University,** *The College Administrator and the Courts,* Casebook, Revised Edition.

## —"Early" Evaluation

SMITH V. STATE, 389 N.W. 2D 808. Supreme Court of North Dakota, 1986.

FACTS: Smith was employed as a probationary, nontenured professor at the University of North Dakota, beginning with the fall semester, 1982. She was evaluated by her department (sociology) at the end of that semester, and again in February, 1983. In February, she was informed of deficiencies in her

551

teaching, including method of instruction, student retention, and materials selection. Her contract was renewed for 1983–1984. In November, 1983, she was again evaluated, and informed that these deficiencies were still evident. Ultimately, in December, 1983, she received notice of nonrenewal, effective at the end of the 1983–84 academic year.

She brought this action, alleging that her department's recommendation of nonrenewal was invalid for failure to comply with published university procedures. Specifically, she alleged that those procedures required that she be evaluated at the end of the first semester, and at the end of the first year, not in February, as was the case. Further, she alleged that the evaluation of her teaching was not based upon a fair cross section of student opinion. Finally she alleges procedural errors in the university proceedings. The trial court dismissed her action on the merits and she appeals.

ISSUE:   Did the university's actions, in evaluating Smith "early" in 1983, amount to a breach of her employment contract?

ANSWER:   No.

REASONING OF THE COURT:   The court held that, although the university did depart from the strict requirements of its published evaluation schedule, its evaluations of Smith, which included an additional evaluation in the fall semester of 1983,

represented substantial compliance, and served to give Smith fair notice of her deficiencies and an opportunity to improve her performance. The court held that while strict compliance with published policy is preferable, failure to conform to every technical detail of university procedures is not dispositive, where no prejudice is shown. The determination whether there has been substantial compliance is a question of fact.

On the question of student evaluations, the court held that the university had considered student evaluations in all classes except one, and had considered opinions of eleven of the twelve graduate students in the department. In the class not considered, Smith failed to conduct the evaluation as scheduled, and had altered procedures for the evaluation.

ADDITIONAL COMMENTS:   In approving the "substantial compliance" rationale, the court cited with approval **Stensrud v. Mayville State College,** and **Piacitelli v. Southern Utah State College,** both reported in *The College Administrator and the Courts,* Revised Edition.

The court emphasized that, although Smith may have offered substantial evidence of her teaching abilities, and although the decision not to retain her might have been bad judgment, a court should not substitute its judgment for that of the university, where substantive and procedural fairness are evident.

## XI.9

# Faculty Separation

## —Constructive Discharge

KLINE V. NORTH TEXAS STATE UNIVERSITY, 782 F. 2D 1229. United States Court of Appeals, Fifth Circuit, 1986.

FACTS: Kline was hired in 1976 as Associate Dean and acting chairman of the Department of Pediatrics at the medical branch of North Texas State University. He also held the rank of tenured professor of pediatrics. In 1978, the dean of the medical college notified Kline by letter of the termination of his assistant deanship, noting several days later that the termination was "for the good of the institution." Approximately one month later, Kline requested of the president of the university reasons for the termination of his appointment as assistant dean. He received no response and was not offered a hearing on the matter.

During this same general period of time, Kline, became involved in a dispute between two members of his departmental faculty. He allegedly sought, but was unsuccessful in obtaining, the support of his dean in resolving this dispute. Subsequently, Kline alleges, one of the faculty members involved in the dispute engaged in harassment of Kline by spreading rumors about Kline and a colleague, reading Kline's patient charts without permission, and consistently complaining about Kline. The most serious aspect of this dispute involved alleged fiscal mismanagement of Kline's department, including an allegation that Kline's faculty "adversary" was diverting clinic funds. The chief fiscal officer of the university ordered an audit which disclosed fiscal mismanagement of the department.

Apparently in response to these disputes, Kline took a leave of absence for one year. His departmental "adversary" was appointed acting chairman of the department. At the end of the year's leave, Kline sought to return, stating a willingness to serve only as tenured professor, and relinquishing his chairmanship. The acting chairman allegedly refused Kline permission to return except as a research professor, with no privileges to practice medicine at the medical center. Kline refused this offer and accepted employment at another institution.

He subsequently filed this lawsuit in federal court, alleging that the termination of his deanship and the related disputes amounted to a constructive discharge without cause, and in violation of his rights under the first amendment to the U.S. Constitution. A jury awarded Kline damages and the university appealed.

ISSUE: Was Kline constructively discharged without cause, and in retaliation for his exercise of protected speech?

ANSWER: No.

REASONING OF THE COURT: To find constructive discharge, it must be evident from the record that the employer has deliberately created a condition so intolerable that the employee is forced to involuntarily resign his position. Kline failed to show how the university, or its president and dean, forced his resignation. The dean sought to insure that the audit report of Kline's department absolved Kline of blame for fiscal mismanagement; further, in granting Kline's leave of absence, he did not demand a resignation. More important, he accepted Kline's early request to return to the faculty, a request he could have denied. Kline himself refused to respond to a letter from the dean offering him his teaching position on terms outlined in the letter.

Neither did Kline show that the university chief fiscal officer or the associate chairman of the department of pediatrics deliberately created conditions mandating Kline's resignation. It is questionable whether these individuals even had a duty to act on Kline's behalf in the matters at issue.

The person most actively challenged by Kline — his departmental "adversary" and successor as department chairman — was not named in the lawsuit.

ADDITIONAL COMMENTS: The court refused to consider the matter of the termination of Kline's tenure as associate dean, holding that the applicable statute of limitations had run, thus barring a suit based upon that action.

In support of its definition of "constructive termination," the court cited **Young v. Southwestern Savings & Loan Association,** 509 F. 2d 140 (5th Cir. 1975).

## XI.10
# Faculty Termination

## —Dismissal of Tenured Faculty for Cause
## —Due Process

AGARWAL V. REGENTS OF THE UNIVER-SITY OF MINNESOTA.  United States Court of Appeals, Eighth Circuit, 1986.

FACTS:  Agarwal, a tenured professor at the university, was dismissed for plagiarism in the preparation of three science laboratory manuals, and on the basis of student complaints from eight physics majors, alleging incompetency in teaching and harassment of students, as well as unprofessional behavior toward colleagues. The charges supporting dismissal were communicated to Agarwal, and heard by a university faculty committee and the board of regents.

Agarwal filed this action in federal court, alleging that the university's action was motivated by consideration of his East Indian origin, in violation of Title VII of the Civil Rights Act. He also claimed that the dismissal denied him due process. He appeals the Trial Court's decision in favor of the university.

ISSUE:  Was the university's action in dismissing Agarwal for cause for plagiarism proper and non-discriminatory?

ANSWER:  Yes.

REASONING OF THE COURT:  Citing the procedural requirements for termination, as outlined in the Riggins case, this supplement, the court held that Agarwal had been properly notified of the grounds for his dismissal, and enjoyed an opportunity to respond to their validity, including formal post–termination hearings at which he was represented by counsel. The requirements of procedural due process in such cases do not necessitate that he

be afforded prior notice and an opportunity to correct deficiencies in a case such as this, nor is he entitled to prior notice that student evaluations will be considered in determining his employment status.

There is no evidence that the decisions were motivated by consideration of his national origin. Although there was some testimony of possible plagiarism by other professors, there was no evidence that the university condoned such acts, or would discriminate on the basis of national origin in enforcement of its employment policies in this regard.

ADDITIONAL COMMENTS:  Agarwal unsuccessfully argued that his dismissal was unjustified by university rules regarding tenure, which define cause for dismissal as "such as seriously interfere with the person's capacity competently to perform his duties, or with his usefulness to the university." The court held that Agarwal's actions, as described above, would support dismissal on the latter ground. This finding is noteworthy as allowing the university discretion in interpreting these terms, but may also caution against a too narrow specification of cause in university policy statements.

## —Due Process Procedures in Terminating Tenured Faculty

JOHNSON V. ALABAMA AGRICULTURAL & MECHANICAL UNIVERSITY, 481 SO. 2D 336. Supreme Court of Alabama, 1985.

FACTS:  Johnson, a tenured member of the university's faculty, was notified in a letter from the vice–president for academic affairs that the university proposed to terminate Johnson's employment. The letter specified the charges against her, and named five individuals, three of whom would be selected by the president, to hear the case for termination. The letter also disclosed a list of witnesses for the university and the charges to which their testimony would relate. This information was provided pursuant to procedures outlined in the faculty handbook.

Johnson was notified, in the letter, that she was to notify the vice–president of any objection to the five proposed members of the hearing panel. She filed no objection. She was also notified to her right to present witnesses on her behalf and her right to cross-examine university witnesses, but was advised that she could not be represented by legal counsel at the hearing.

The hearing panel found the charges valid, but recommended against termination, in recognition of Johnson's fourteen years of service to the university. The recommendation was forwarded to the university's president, who sought the counsel of an "executive planning" group, an advisory committee to the president. That group recommended strict probation.

Johnson was notified of the probation. Subsequently, on request of an associate dean, the matter was reconsidered, with Johnson's agreement, by the executive advisory committee to the president. Both Johnson and the associate dean appeared before the committee. After the reconsideration, the president notified Johnson that it had been decided that she would be terminated from her employment. She filed this action, alleging the invalidity of her removal. Specifically, she asserted that the university's policy of denying legal representation at faculty termination hearings violated procedural due process mandates. The trial court dismissed her claims and she appeals.

ISSUE: Did the university's procedures utilized in this case violate Johnson's due process rights?

ANSWER: No.

REASONING OF THE COURT: The court actually avoided a direct holding on the issue of the right of a tenured faculty member to legal representation at a collegial termination hearing, on the ground that Johnson had not raised this objection prior to or at the hearing. (Normally, a nonjurisdictional issue may not be raised for the first time on appeal.) Furthermore, the court held, Johnson

demonstrated no special need for legal counsel at the hearing.

The court rejected Johnson's claim that the president was not entitled to examine her personnel file in reaching his decision in this case. It held that, since the president could have dismissed Johnson on the charges presented, in any event, she was not prejudiced by his examination of her general personnel file. Moreover, although generally held to the record, the president may look at other evidence upon which a reasonable person would rely in making a decision as to personnel action to be taken.

As to the reconsideration itself, the court noted Johnson's consent and appearance, and her constructive awareness that a different recommendation was possible as a result of the second hearing of her case.

# — Failure to Perform Duties After Reassignment

JOSBERGER V. UNIVERSITY OF TENNESSEE, 706 S.W. 2D 300. Court of Appeals of Tennessee, 1985.

FACTS: Josberger held positions as dean of the college of nursing, and as a member of the university's faculty. She resigned those positions, and accepted another assignment. She later repudiated the subsequent assignment, which repudiation was not accepted by the university.

After taking approximately one month's sick leave, Josberger was terminated on the basis of her failure to complete the duties of her reassignment. The termination was accompanied by notice of reasons, and a hearing. Both the president of the university and its board of trustees approved the termination. Josberger sought judicial review of the action, and the court affirmed the university's decision. She appealed.

ISSUE: Were the grounds for termination and the manner of its implementation valid?

ANSWER: Yes.

REASONING OF THE COURT: The termination was based upon sound evidence presented at the hearing, and was justified. A faculty member cannot be heard to complain of procedures which are in accord with fundamental due process, where they are followed as outlined in the faculty handbook.

# — Financial Exigency
# — Burden of Proof

PACE V. HYMAS, 726 P.2D 693. Supreme Court of Idaho, 1986.

FACTS: In 1981, the Idaho legislature increased its appropriation to the Agricultural Research and Co-operative Extension Service of the University (hereafter ARCES) to $12.1 million. This appropriation was approximately $500,000 less than the university had requested/budgeted. In additional action, a house concurrent resolution called for an across-the-board salary increase, which was funded by an appropriation of $667,800.00. These appropriations were enhanced by a net surplus from the ARCES's previous year's budget.

In reaction to this financial picture, the university determined that its budget was inadequate, and laid off Pace, a senior member of the tenured faculty of ARCES. Pace filed this suit claiming that the university's decision violated due process guarantees, and the university's tenure policies, which provided, among other things, that:

> After tenure has been awarded, the faculty member's service can be terminated only for adequate cause, . . . or under conditions of financial exigency as declared by the Board. . . .

University policies defined financial exigency as:

> a demonstrably *bona fide* imminent financial crisis which threatens the viability of an agency, institution, office, or department as a whole, or one or more of its programs, or other distinct units, and which cannot be adequately alleviated by means other than a reduction in the employment force. . . .

The trial court placed the burden of proof of financial exigency upon the university, and it filed this interlocutory appeal.

ISSUE: Where a university initiates a lay-off of tenured faculty on grounds of financial exigency, does it carry the burden of proof on that issue, if the lay-off is challenged on due process grounds by the affected faculty?

ANSWER: Yes.

REASONING OF THE COURT: Where a faculty member subjected to lay-off on grounds of financial exigency sues on a theory of denial of due process of law, in violation of Section 1983 of the Civil Rights Act, he or she must prove a violation of the underlying constitutional right. However, the burden of proof does not extend to all issues. The burden is on the defendant employer to prove affirmative defenses, such as good faith, or immunity. Defendants also shoulder the burden of proof of other exceptional circumstances justifying their actions, in selected cases, where plaintiff establishes a prima facie case of discrimination, *e.g.,* in cases alleging race or sex discrimination in employment.

Although these cases are not directly on point with the instant case, they support the conclusion that an employer claiming financial exigency as grounds for dismissal of a member of the university's tenured faculty must prove that such exigency was demonstrably *bona fide.* A tenured faculty member is guaranteed continued employment, absent cause, or bona fide financial crisis. To require him/her to prove the "nonexistence" of such crisis would be contrary to the implication of his entitlement to continued employment and inconsistent with common sense.

Moreover, where evidence necessary to establish a fact lies peculiarly within the knowledge of defendant, then defendant generally has the burden of coming forward with the evidence on that issue.

Substantial evidence exists to support the conclusion that the university did not sustain its burden on this issue. The ARCES 1982 budget was more than $750,000 greater than its 1981 appropriation; the 1982 appropriation included a substantial amount for salary increases, which the university did not implement across-the-board; a 1981 budget surplus of more than $100,000 was uncommitted for 1982. The board was uninformed of this surplus before declaring the exigency, and did not examine alternatives other than reduction in work force, including reductions in salaries, travel, supplies, equipment, or capital outlay.

ADDITIONAL COMMENTS: The court cited several cases reported in *The College Administrator and the Courts,* in support of its decision, including **Browzin v. Catholic University of America, Bignall v. North Idaho College, Brenna v. Southern**

**Colorado College,** and **AAUP v. Bloomfield College.**

Citing **Levitt v. Board of Trustees,** and **Johnson v. Board of Regents** (reported in *The College Administrator and the Courts*), the court remanded for Pace to show that the absence of bona fide financial exigency demonstrated that her dismissal — in breach of her contract of employment — was without rational basis, and therefore in violation of Section 1983 of the Civil Rights Act.

# — Financial Exigency
# — Elimination of
# Language Program

MILBOUER V. KEPPLER, 644 F. SUPP. 2021. United States District Court, District of Idaho, 1986.

FACTS: In June, 1982, the Governor of Idaho issued an executive order requiring an across-the-board budget reduction of 9 percent among all state agencies for fiscal year 1983. In response to a directive from the state board of education to respond to the mandate, the President of Boise State University (hereafter BSU) testified before the board that a financial exigency existed at BSU.

Policies of the state board of education define financial exigency as a demonstrably *bona fide* imminent financial crisis which threatens the viability of an agency, institution, office or department, as a whole, or one or more of its programs or units, and which cannot be alleviated by means other than a reduction in employees.

The university submitted a plan for cutbacks, including the elimination of its German language program. The plan was approved, and pursuant to the recommendation of the Dean of Arts and Sciences, the foreign language program was eliminated. This action resulted in the layoff of the department's faculty, including Milbouer.

Milbouer brought this action, alleging breach of contract, wrongful discharge, and violation of due process rights embodied in Section 1983 of the Federal Civil Rights Act. Milbouer alleged that BSU enjoyed a surplus from fiscal year 1982 in the amount of $300,000.00, and that, after the layoffs, BSU hired more than fifteen new faculty in other programs. She also alleged that she received inadequate notice of layoff, and that proper procedures were not followed in dealing with affected faculty.

ISSUE: Was Milbouer's termination invalid on substantive or procedural grounds?

ANSWER: No.

REASONING OF THE COURT: The court held that the university met its burden of proof that it was confronting a situation of *bona fide* financial exigency. In support of this holding, the court noted that the university actually enjoyed only a $27,000.00 surplus from fiscal 1982, an amount inadequate to respond to the fiscal needs of BSU's academic programs as they existed.

Speaking to the viability of plaintiff's academic program, the court noted that student enrollment in German languages was extremely low, and that only four students had graduated from the program from 1980 to 1982. In light of this low student enrollment, the plaintiff's program was, in the opinion of the court, subordinate to the needs of programs which were a viable part of the university's curriculum. In this regard, the court noted that plaintiff was not selected from among German language colleagues for layoff, but was a part of the disestablishment of the entire department. Further, none of the new hirings were in areas previously staffed by faculty subject to the layoff.

Recognizing the university's obligation to attempt to relocate affected faculty within the university, the court found that Milbouer had been offered, and rejected, a part-time position in the English department, and had abandoned her program of retraining (study) which would have qualified her for a position as a linguistic specialist in the business field.

Finally, the court held that plaintiff had received adequate notice, by cable to her temporary address in Germany, and letter to her permanent address, of the termination, including copies of relevant policies on financial exigency and a copy of the budget reduction plan. In addition, she was offered, and received a hearing on the matter of her challenge to the plan, during which she was allowed to voice her response and to question the dean, executive vice-president, and president of the university.

ADDITIONAL COMMENTS: The court distinguished the decision of the Supreme Court of Idaho in **Pace v. Hymas** (this supplement) as involving a different fiscal year, and a different surplus situation.

The decisions should be compared, as to interpretation of the definition of financial exigency. The **Milbouer** Court interpreted language virtually identical to that at issue in **Pace** to permit the university to consider, as its primary criteria in responding to staff reductions, the viability of essential university programs. This discretion included the appropriateness of hiring new faculty in viable programs, while terminating tenured faculty in "low priority" programs. **Cf. AAUP v. Bloomfield College,** and other cases cited in the Additional Comments to **Pace v. Hymas.**

# —Hearings for Nontenured Faculty

MOORE V. UTAH TECHNICAL COLLEGE, 727 P. 2D 634. Supreme Court of Utah, 1986.

FACTS: Moore was employed by Utah Technical College in 1977, as an instructor, without tenure. At the time of his initial appointment, college policies regarding nonrenewal of faculty appointments provided, *inter alia,* for three months notice of nonretention, and stated that the affected faculty member "shall be afforded due process." In 1978, Moore was notified of his reappointment for the 1978–79 academic year.

During the 1978–79 academic year, the college amended its policy on nonrenewal of faculty appointments to authorize the president of the college to extend probationary appointments beyond the third year of appointment, not to exceed two additional years. The amended policy continued three months notice of nonreappointment, but deleted the "due process" provision.

In 1979 and 1980, Moore received additional one–year reappointments, without tenure. The 1980 appointment, for 1980–81, was Moore's fourth one year appointment.

During the 1980–81 academic year, pursuant to direction of its board of regents, the college again amended its policy on termination of faculty appointments to provide for six month advance notice of nonreappointment to faculty with two or more years of service. The amended policy further reinstated a requirement for "procedural due process" in those cases involving a faculty member's charge of employment discrimination or violation of constitutional rights in the nonrenewal of his/her contract.

On March 5, 1981, Moore was given three months advance notice that his contract would not be renewed for 1981–82. Subsequent to this notice, the amended policy on nonrenewal of appointments was forwarded to, and approved by the board of

regents. Moore requested a hearing on the matter of the nonrenewal of his appointment, alleging that he was protected by the notice and/or due process requirements of the 1977, or the 1981 policy. When his request was denied, he brought this suit, which was dismissed. He appeals.

ISSUE: Did Moore have a right to a hearing on the matter of the nonrenewal of his employment?

ANSWER: No.

REASONING OF THE COURT: Noting at the outset of its opinion that Moore was not tenured, the supreme court held that he had no constitutional entitlement to a hearing on the matter of his nonreappointment. His claim was based entirely upon an alleged contract entitlement.

The court rejected the claim of breach of contract, holding that, when the board of regents assumed control of the state's technical colleges in 1978, state law provided that the president of such colleges could approve policies governing nonretention of faculty. The 1979 policy, providing for three months notice, and eliminating the general "due process" requirement was valid, as approved by Utah Tech's president, and governed Moore's appointment, until modified by the 1981 policy. That policy, the court held, was by its terms, not in place until January, 1981. Thus, it was not intended to apply to require six months advance notice of nonreappointment for those, such as Moore, appointed in 1980–81. To apply it to Moore's contract would be to require his automatic reappointment for 1981–82. Such retroactive impact would be unreasonable.

The 1979 policy, which governed Moore's appointment, was followed by the college in terminating Moore's appointment. He was given the requisite notice, and was not entitled to a hearing.

ADDITIONAL COMMENTS: The court's decision that Moore had no constitutional entitlement to a hearing challenging the nonrenewal of his appointment is generally in accord with the U.S. Supreme Court's holding **Perry v. Sindermann,** that a nontenured public employee enjoys no property interest in his continuing appointment, absent a contract commitment to reappointment (usually stated in the form of an appointment, with tenure). However, the companion case of **Board of Regents v. Roth,** not relied upon in the **Moore** case, continues to provide for a qualified right to a hearing, in cases involving the implication, by the state (the public college), of an employee's personal reputation in the community. See *e.g., The College Administrator and the Courts.*

# —Nonrenewal of Nontenured Faculty Without Cause —Statements Made By Dean

LOVELACE V. SOUTHEASTERN MASSACHUSETTS UNIVERSITY, 793 F. 2D 419. United States Court of Appeals, First Circuit, 1986.

FACTS: Lovelace was employed as a teacher, without formal tenure, under a contract for "the period September 1, 1982 to June 30, 1983." On February 28, 1983, the university sent him a letter, notifying him that his contract would not be renewed. Lovelace brought this action alleging, among other things that he could not be terminated except for cause related to his teaching, or other duties, and that his termination was in retaliation for his exercise of rights protected by the First Amendment.

Specifically, Lovelace claimed that he had a property interest in continued employment, absent just cause, under a clause in the collective bargaining agreement between the university and its organized faculty. That clause provided that "in the development of all recommendations for reappointment or nonrenewal, justification of all recommendations *(sic)* must be included." He also claimed that he was given oral assurances by his dean that his contract would be renewed. In the alternative, Lovelace claimed that he was entitled to be rehired because his notice of nonrenewal was received too late under university rules. Finally, he claimed that his termination was in retaliation for his refusal to change his course and grading standards.

The trial court found in favor of the university on all claims, and Lovelace appeals.

ISSUE: (1) Did Lovelace have a property interest in continued employment, entitling him to a hearing on the grounds for his nonreappointment?

(2) Were oral representations by Lovelace's dean that he would be rehired, if his student evaluations improved, a binding offer to rehire?

(3) Did the university fail to give timely notification to Lovelace of the nonrenewal of his contract?

(4) Did the university violate Lovelace's right to free speech where it considered his refusal to mod-

ify course or grading standards in its decision not to renew his employment?

ANSWER: No, to all questions.

REASONING OF THE COURT: (1) Lovelace's contract clearly specified the duration, and terminal date of his employment. The collective bargaining agreement did nothing to extend that appointment, or to compromise the university's discretion to exercise its judgment in deciding to whom it will grant reappointment or tenure. The provision simply "proceduralized the information gathering process and served to facilitate the president in exercising his judgment . . . by ensuring that he would have the written opinions of relevant persons in the university hierarchy before him when he was ready to act."

(2) University policy specified that notice of nonrenewal must "be given by March 1." He did not receive the notice until approximately March 7. This "trivial tardiness" does not require reappointment. First, there is no provision that lateness of notice results in automatic rehire, as is the case under the statutes of some jurisdictions. The policy merely calls for notice, one way or the other, on the decision to reappoint. Thus, when he had not received the notice, Lovelace had no cause to believe anything other than that the notice was late—not that he had been reappointed.

(3) The dean's representations, even if true, could not contradict the requirements of the university's formal tenure procedures. Where Lovelace was aware of these procedures, he could not justifiably rely upon oral assurances of employment outside the formalized system. In any event, the president had the discretion to view Lovelace's student evaluations and to determine if he should be reappointed.

(4) The university has the right to determine general policy as to course content, homework load, and grading policy. The First Amendment does not require that the university allow Lovelace, or any other nontenured professor, to unilaterally determine the total parameters of his coursework, or his standards for evaluating student performance. A university may consider the pedagogical style and philosophy of a nontenured teacher in light of the university's educational mission.

ADDITIONAL COMMENTS: In affirming the university's general freedom to determine who may teach, what may be taught, how it may be taught, and who may be admitted to study, the university cited the U.S. Supreme Court's decision in **Regents of the University of California v. Bakke** (*The Col-*

*lege Administrator and the Courts,* Revised Edition). Compare **Hillis v. Stephen F. Austin State University** (*The College Administrator and the Courts,* Revised Edition), discussing whether a professor's direct refusal to change a grade may be considered insubordination.

# — Relationship of Bargaining Agreement and Tenure Act to Termination

WILLIAMS V. WEAVER, 495 N.E. 2D 1147. Appellate Court of Illinois, First District, 1986.

FACTS: Williams was employed as a probationary faculty member by the board of trustees of the community college district, and taught business education at Malcolm X College. His contract provided, in part, that he was employed for a stated one–year period, and that he would be notified, by October 1, 1978, whether he would be employed for the following year.

A collective bargaining agreement between the board and its teachers stated that recommendations regarding renewal of employment contracts were to be made by eligible faculty within the appropriate academic department, according to published criteria and procedures. These procedures included an evaluation by all eligible faculty, of the candidate for retention.

On September 28, 1978, the department chairman notified Williams that his employment would not be renewed for the 1979 academic year. Although eligible faculty had not completed evaluations of Williams' performance, they concurred in the chairman's recommendation on the basis of Williams' poor performance. Thereafter, in November, 1978, the board notified Williams that he would not be retained.

Subsequent to this action, the state legislature passed the 1981 "Tenure Act," providing, in part, that the board "shall provide for a procedure to evaluate the performance and qualifications of nontenure (sic) faculty members. . . ."

Williams sued in state court, alleging breach of contract, and tortious interference by the board and the above–referenced individuals with his prospective business and economic advantage. His complaint was dismissed and he appeals.

ISSUE: (1) Was the board bound by the collective bargaining agreement insofar as it required

prior evaluation by faculty of a candidate for retention?

(2) Did the Tenure Act require the board to provide for formal collegial evaluation of Williams' performance prior to his termination?

ANSWER: No, to both questions.

REASONING OF THE COURT: The court refused to retroactively apply the 1981 Tenure Act to employment action taken in 1978. It therefore left open the question whether the act required faculty evaluation of probationary teachers prior to the board's decision to terminate their employment, and to what extent the board was bound by faculty recommendations.

The court held that, in the absence of statutory provision to the contrary, the board's authority to hire and terminate is discretionary, and may not be superceded, modified, or conditioned upon the terms of a collective bargaining agreement.

Plaintiff's claim of tortious interference with his business advantage was rejected on the ground that he had no "reasonable" expectation of continued employment, beyond the expired year, and thus had no business or economic advantage subject to tortious interference. Even assuming such an expectation, the court held, plaintiff's argument of tortious interference depends upon the illogical conclusion that the board should be held liable for interfering with its own business relationship with him. As to the individual chairman and faculty members, the court held a claim of tortious interference with contract could not be maintained, where the board was in no way bound to seek or follow their evaluations, had they been completed.

# — Tenure Rights of "Visiting Professor"

TETLOW V. LOYOLA UNIVERSITY OF NEW ORLEANS, 403 SO. 2D 1242. Court of Appeals of Louisiana, 1986.

FACTS: In January, 1979, Dr. Tetlow executed a contract with the university, specifying his employment as a full-time "visiting associate professor." In 1981, he applied for, but was not awarded tenure. He was informed at that time that his 1982–83 contract would be terminal.

He brought this action alleging that his years of continuous employment entitled him to tenure under the provisions of the faculty handbook. The trial court upheld his claim, and the university appealed.

ISSUE: Is a faculty member appointed by written agreement as a "visiting" professor entitled to tenure on the basis of years of service as specified for "tenure track" faculty?

ANSWER: No.

REASONING OF THE COURT: Tetlow agreed to an appointment on "visiting" status when he signed the contract of appointment. Under applicable university policy, time in that status does not count toward tenure.

Even assuming the appointment was on a "tenure track," the court stated in *dicta* that Tetlow was not entitled to "automatic" tenure until he was offered and had accepted a fifth year appointment, following four years of residence. In this case, his fourth year contract was specifically stated to be terminal. He thus had no right or entitlement to tenure.

ADDITIONAL COMMENTS: This decision reaffirms the U.S. Supreme Court's landmark holding in **Perry v. Sindermann** (*The College Administrator and the Courts,* Casebook) that a public university faculty member has no unilateral expectation of tenure which is enforceable. Rather, any interest in continued employment must be supported by a bilateral understanding reduced to contract, or evident in clear policies or practices of the institution.

The decision obviously advises that the institution should have an established tenure policy, and clear definitions of faculty positions, specifying those "special" appointments which are not "tenure track" positions. Tenure status of a position, its duration, and its eligibility for tenure should be defined, if not in the contract, then in policy statements incorporated by reference in the contract and available to faculty (as in a faculty handbook).

# —Work Load Basis for Alleged Sex Discrimination

O'CONNER V. PERU STATE COLLEGE, 781 F. 2D 632. United States Court of Appeals, Eighth Circuit, 1986.

FACTS: O'Conner was hired by Peru State College as a physical education teacher and women's basketball coach for the 1981–82 academic year. She was assigned an average teaching load in terms of credit hours, but was given a large number of "activity" classes that required two or three hours of classroom supervision for each credit hour earned. She had to teach several dance classes, and since she had no training in this area, she had to spend abnormally large amounts of time for preparation. Her other duties included coaching the women's junior varsity basketball team, recruiting high school athletes, organizing a girls' high school invitational basketball tournament, assisting with the women's track team, and chaperoning and transporting the cheerleaders to men's events.

Despite low evaluations, she was rehired for the 1982–83 year. However, on December 9, 1982, she was notified that she would not be rehired for the 1983–84 year because PSC wanted to "establish confidence" in the women's basketball program. At a hearing in February 1983, PSC alleged that O'Conner: (1) missed a national athletic association meeting; (2) failed on one occasion to send a team roster to tournament officials; (3) arrived late to basketball games; (4) scheduled a varsity and a junior varsity game for the same day in different cities; (5) used an unauthorized assistant; (6) left basketball practice unsupervised when she had to be absent; (7) engaged in poor recruiting; (8) had poor staff relations; (9) generated organizational problems regarding the high school invitational tournament; and (10) was inattentive to detail in keeping track of basketball expenses.

After PSC reaffirmed its employment decision, O'Conner first sought a temporary restraining order or preliminary injunction. Both were denied. In April of 1983, she filed this suit and a complaint with the Office of Civil Rights of the U.S. Department of Education. OCR investigators concluded that PSC had been in violation of Title IX when O'Conner was employed because of inequities in certain portions of its men's and women's athletic programs. OCR also found that the college would be found in compliance because PSC was already implementing a plan that would correct the disparities within a reasonable time. The trial court dismissed all of O'Conner's claims and she appealed challenging the trial court's findings of fact.

ISSUE: Were the reasons given by the college for terminating O'Conner's employment merely a pretext for sex discrimination?

ANSWER: No.

REASONING OF THE COURT: The trial court found that new instructors were routinely assigned the schedules of their predecessors, without regard to sex. Further, the fact that females traditionally taught dance classes was found to be insufficient, standing alone, to demonstrate that O'Conner's class assignments were based upon her sex.

O'Conner asserted that males in the physical education department were never assigned to do general admission work for the college when a class failed to fill, as she was. Although one male coach testified in support of this general allegation, even he noted the substitution, on occasion, of additional coaching duties. Moreover, male faculty from other departments of the college were assigned administrative duties when classes failed to fill. Thus, it was not clearly erroneous that the trial court failed to characterize one possible isolated incident as a sexually discriminatory employment condition. The record was clear as to O'Conner's outside duties, but it failed to show that male faculty had fewer outside duties.

O'Conner also contended that there was a disparity in recruiting and that she was required to report her absences while male coaches did not have to report their absences. The only disparity in recruiting related to private (booster) support for men's athletics. This singular disparity does not support a finding of sex discrimination as to O'Conner.

O'Conner failed to show disparate treatment of male and female coaches regarding tardiness or absence from practices. O'Conner was not penalized for absence or tardiness, *per se,* but rather for her failure to notify the team, and to appoint an authorized assistant with assigned directions.

Citing **Texas Department of Community Affairs v. Burdine,** the court held that O'Conner was required to ultimately demonstrate a pretextual (discriminatory) *motive* on the part of PSC, refuting the college's stated reasons for its personnel action. On this question, there was evidence to support the trial court's conclusion that the college's stated reasons (noted above) were not pretextual.

In rejecting O'Conner's claim that the college violated Title IX of the education amendments, the court held that the college's athletic coaching program was not a direct beneficiary of federal financial assistance.

ADDITIONAL COMMENTS: In deciding O'Conner's claims, the appellate court applied the **Burdine** test, which requires that: (1) the plaintiff must establish a *prima facie case,* facts sufficient to give rise to an inference that the termination was motivated by discrimination; (2) the employer must then articulate an alternative, legitimate reason for the discharge sufficient to dispel the unfavorable inference; and (3) the plaintiff must show that the reason given by the employer was pretextual and the employer was actually improperly motivated.

## XI.11

# Governance

## —Trustees Authority to Issue Rules for Financial Aid Program

BOARD OF TRUSTEES OF STATE INSTITU-
TIONS V. WOOD, 779 F. 2D 1106. U.S. Court
of Appeals, Fifth Circuit, 1986.

FACTS: The Board of Trustees of State Institutions of Higher Learning in Mississippi adopted rules and regulations governing loans to medical students designed to encourage needed medical practices in Mississippi communities of 10,000 and under. A medical student applied for and was granted a loan at a time when the rules and regulations provided for residency training only in the specialties of Family Practice, Internal Medicine, and Pediatrics. The rules and regulations were a part of every loan contract and provided that any breach of contract matured the loan and, upon demand, made liquidated damages of $5,000 for each unfulfilled year of the required five years of practice then due and payable.

The student graduated and requested that the Board of Trustees waive the residency restrictions and allow him to pursue a residency in obstetrics and gynecology. The board refused his request whereupon he ignored the loan contract and did pursue a residency in obstetrics and gynecology.

The board then brought action to recover the loan with interest and liquidated damages. The student, now a medical doctor, claimed that the rules of the board were not authorized by the Mississippi statutory scheme governing medical loans and converts the liquidated damage provision incorporated in the statutes into an impermissible penalty.

ISSUE: Does the board of trustees have the power to promulgate the rules and regulations nec-

essary to carry out the purposes of the loan programs?

ANSWER: Yes.

REASONING OF THE COURT: In ruling that the board had the statutory authority to promulgate appropriate rules and regulations necessary to carry out the purposes of the loan program, the court reasoned that the statutory authority was broad enough to encompass the limitation on residency training. It declared "The choice to permit only certain specialization by those returning to community practice serves a central aim of the loan program, i.e. to secure the most needed types of practice."

The court pointed out that the rules and regulations were incorporated into the contract prior to its execution by the student. It declared that he ". . . has chosen to pursue his post-graduate residency training in a specialty not permitted by his contract and has consequently breached its terms."

The court ruled that the statutory scheme imposing liquidated damages with interest did not constitute an impermissible penalty. It noted that an estimation of the degree of damages flowing to the state as a result of a loan recipient's failure to return to practice medicine only in one of the designated specialties would be difficult to measure or establish. It declared "In Mississippi, where such damages for breach are both 'uncertain and difficult of estimation,' such a provision has regularly been construed as one for liquidated damages."

ADDITIONAL COMMENTS: This case illustrates that students should be made aware when they execute loan contracts that the provisions contained therein are indeed binding. Students should be on notice that governments are not always prone to forgive loans or ignore provisions contained in loan contracts which may be distasteful to students.

# Jurisdiction

## —Employment Discrimination Case Hearing in State Court

CLIFTON V. MIDWAY COLLEGE, 702 S.W. 2D 835. Supreme Court of Kentucky, 1986.

FACTS: Clifton was first employed by the Midway College in 1955. She served as registrar, but was demoted in October, 1978 to the position of assistant registrar. On June 16, 1981, she was discharged.

She filed a charge of employment discrimination with the Equal Employment Opportunity Commission, alleging that she was terminated because of her age, or sex, or both. The EEOC referred her claim to the state commission for human rights. Subsequently, the state agency relinquished the case to the EEOC, which issued a "right to sue" notice to Clifton. She filed this action in state court against the college.

The state trial court dismissed her complaint on the ground that it lacked jurisdiction. An intermediate appeals court affirmed and the state supreme court agreed to hear the jurisdictional dispute.

ISSUE: Did the State trial court have jurisdiction to hear this case in the posture above noted?

ANSWER: Yes.

REASONING OF THE COURT: A claimant is not precluded from bringing an action in state court under state statutes regarding employment discrimination, where the appropriate state agency has failed to consider the claim or issue an order in the matter. Clifton received no hearing on the merits of her claim, and no determination was made by any agency which would prevent that claim from being considered by an appropriate state court.

ADDITIONAL COMMENTS: The administrator should be aware of the separate jurisdiction of state and federal trial courts in employment discrimination cases, and that state statutes establish separate claims from those asserted under Title VII of the federal Civil Rights Act, which is judicially enforced by suit in the appropriate federal district court. State statutes regarding employment discrimination also differ from state to state, and may provide for administrative, as well as judicial enforcement.

## XI.13
# Open Meetings Laws

## —Meetings of Committee Appointed to Investigate Student Athletes' Academic Achievements

ABELL PUBLISHING COMPANY V. BOARD OF REGENTS, 514 A. 2D 25. Court of Special Appeals of Maryland, 1986.

FACTS: Following the cocaine–related death of Lenard Bias, a student athlete at the University of Maryland, news reports highlighted his alleged substandard academic achievements, and made more visible the question of the scholarship of student athletes. In response to this issue, the chancellor of the university appointed two task forces, one of which was charged to examine the academic achievement of student athletes. The academic task force was divided into subcommittees, each of which indicated their intent to meet in closed session.

Abell, as publisher of the Baltimore *Sun* newspaper, brought this action, alleging that closed meetings of the subcommittee violated the state's open meetings statute. That statute, as read by Abell, governs a committee created by rule, resolution, or bylaw of the board of regents.

The trial court denied Abell's petition for an injunction, prohibiting closed meetings and the newspaper appeals.

ISSUE: Are the task force and its subcommittees public bodies within the Maryland open meetings statute?

ANSWER: No.

REASONING OF THE COURT: The decision to appoint the task force was within the discretion of the university chancellor. His appearance before the board of regents was essentially for the purpose of informing the board of his decision to appoint the task force, rather than seeking the board's approval, as a condition precedent to his action. In fact, the board passed no resolution concerning the chancellor's recommendation, but rather expressed concurrence with his decision in its minutes.

The task force was to report to the chancellor, who in turn would report to the university's president. The president would report to the board. Thus, the task force was a committee of the chancellor, and not the board. The open meetings statute does not apply to such committees.

ADDITIONAL COMMENTS: The court held that the subcommittee's meetings were not investigations involving sworn testimony and were thus not open to media under the Maryland Declaration of Rights.

Obviously, open meetings statutes differ from jurisdiction to jurisdiction, including in their definition of public bodies subject to the requirement of public sessions. It is noteworthy, in cases of this type, to consider that even if a committee of this type is generally subsumed by the open meetings statute, discussions of the academic or disciplinary record of particular students may be protected under federal or state privacy statutes, *i.e.,* the Family Education and Privacy Rights Act, and the "little FEPRA's" passed by many states.

An appellate court in Florida has recently ruled that the state's open meetings law is subordinate to the state's statute respecting the privacy of student records, thus preventing a newspaper from attending a student disciplinary hearing without the consent of the student.

## XI.14
# Religion

## —State Institution's Cosponsorship of Lectures with Church

BILL OF RIGHTS LEGAL FOUNDATION V. EVERGREEN STATE COLLEGE, 723 P. 2D 483. Court of Appeals of Washington, Division 2, 1986.

FACTS: Evergreen State College and First United Methodist Church, of Olympia, Washington, cosponsored a lecture series comprised of nine lectures between January and May, 1983. The university provided $250 for the series. The church provided a room at the church, refreshments, and parking. The two entities cooperated in the selection and scheduling of speakers.

The foundation brought suit, alleging that the university's expenditure of state funds for this program violated the establishment clause of the first amendment to the United States Constitution, representing an impermissible entanglement between the state and a religious institution. From a dismissal of its action, the foundation appeals.

ISSUE: Did ESU's cosponsorship and expenditure of state funds for a limited lecture series, held in a room at the church, violate the United States Constitution?

ANSWER: No.

REASONING OF THE COURT: Citing **Lemon v. Kurtzman** (see *The College Administrator and the Courts,* Basic Casebook), the court held that a finding of excessive entanglement between church and state requires an examination of benefit received by a church institution, as a result of state action. Here, there is no showing of any "tangible" benefit to the church as a result of the lecture series. Any aid from the state was incidental, and therefore not of constitutional magnitude under **Lemon.**

Under current Supreme Court cases, impermissible aid is that which is direct, such as payment by the state for its teachers who provide remedial instruction to parochial students, or similar payment for auxiliary services, books, and the like. Such aid is not involved in this case.

More dispositive of the case is the fact that this lecture series involves no relationship between the state and the church. Precedent cases are concerned with state oversight of joint programs which are ongoing in nature. This program involved and required no state oversight to guard against the fostering of religion. The setting was far different than that of a sectarian school, with a captive audience. Here, the program was open to the public, and was directed to a voluntary downtown "lunch hour" audience of workers and other townspeople. The lectures were arguably secular in nature, and the program was temporary.

ADDITIONAL COMMENTS: The series included lectures by a state supreme court justice, a lobbyist, a university faculty member, a physician, and a radio news director, and covered subjects such as legal rights and morality; the ethics of the legislative process; a defense of secular humanism; the growth of private schools; changes in education; and media and government.

# XI.15
# Salary

## — Change in Job Classification Related to Salary

WALCH V. UNIVERSITY OF MONTANA, 716 P. 2D 640.  Supreme Court of Montana, 1986.

FACTS:  In 1982, the University of Montana reorganized its division of physical plant maintenance. As a result of the reorganizaton, Walch's position was split into two separate positions, and he was reclassified from maintenance superintendent, grade 16, to maintenance superintendent, grade 15. Pursuant to a pay plan exception, allowing the university to use a formula "to maintain a differential between craft salaries and [management salaries] in the physical plant." Walch's salary remained the same. Walch challenged the action under the state's administrative procedures act.

A state hearing officer held that Walch's responsibilities justified his reclassification to maintenance services manager I, grade 16. She held that the university should "continue to pay Mr. Walch in accordance with the formula designed for the management staff" in the physical plant, but to make appropriate changes in his "pay grade level." The university made no change in Walch's pay and he sought judicial interpretation of the order of the hearing officer as to his pay.

ISSUE:  Did the ordered change in Walch's job classification require a change in his current salary?

ANSWER:  No.

REASONING OF THE COURT:  The order of the hearing officer indicated that the university should "continue" to pay Walch according to the formula. Had the hearing officer meant for the uni-

versity to pay Walch under the state's regular pay matrix, she would have so stated. Her use of the word "continue" is indicative of her intent.

Walch's contention that, without change in pay, the order is meaningless, is rejected. Walch's reclassification title and pay grade level will be of importance in future determination of his salary.

ADDITIONAL COMMENTS:  This case represents an interpretation of the ruling of the state hearing officer as to an employee's pay. It suggests that the hearing officer could have required a pay adjustment, although it does not so hold. In any event, provisions of state pay plans and state administrative procedures statutes differ from jurisdiction to jurisdiction. Thus, decisions such as this are no more than persuasive in a proceeding in another state.

## — Reduction of Salary After Resigning Administrative Position

FRANKEN V. ARIZONA BOARD OF REGENTS, 714 P. 2D 1308.  Court of Appeals of Arizona, 1985.

FACTS:  In 1973 Dr. Franken was recruited to the University of Arizona to chair the department of optical sciences. He has been a tenured professor since his arrival at the university. He was a full–time administrator from 1975 until the 1984–85 school year when he voluntarily resigned his administrative position to engage in full–time teaching and research. His resignation resulted in a decrease in salary.

Franken sued for breach of contract, declaratory

568

judgment, wage discrimination and denial of a property right to his salary. The trial court granted the university motion for summary judgment. Franken appealed.

ISSUE: Can the university decrease the salary of a tenured professor who voluntarily resigns an administrative position to return to teaching and research?

ANSWER: Yes.

REASONING OF THE COURT: Since Franken was tenured only as a teacher and not as an administrator, his administrative appointment was "at-will." Franken was not entitled to the higher rate of pay simply because he had always received it, especially considering the fact that he resigned the higher paying position.

# Staff Dismissal

## —Due Process in Dismissal Procedures

RIGGINS V. BOARD OF REGENTS OF THE UNIVERSITY OF NEBRASKA, 790 F. 2D 707. United States Court of Appeals, Eighth Circuit, 1986.

FACTS: Riggins, a Hispanic female, was employed by the University of Nebraska, in its division of custodial services. University records indicated an employment history of difficulty between Riggins and co-workers. In 1983, Riggins had an encounter with a co-worker, which resulted in Riggins's filing a complaint with police authorities. She reported sick the day following this incident. On the same day, one of her supervisors wrote her a letter, notifying her of her assignment to a different building and a different shift. The supervisor telephoned Riggins, requesting that she report to a designated work area, where he intended to give her the letter. She was apparently met at this location by both of her supervisors, and, according to their version of the incident, refused to meet with them together. They allege that she "walked away down the hall."

Riggins subsequently met with her two supervisors and the university's affirmative action officer, and was told that she was being suspended for insubordination. She was informed that the basis of the decision was the "walking away" incident, especially in light of her previous work history. Following this meeting, Riggins had a lengthy meeting with an appropriate university superior, during which she stated her account of the incident in question, including her reasons for not wanting to meet with her supervisors. The university officer discussed with Riggins' supervisors her version of the incident, and subsequently decided that Riggins should be terminated.

Riggins knew that the university had a written grievance procedure, published in its employee handbook, but chose not to use the procedure. Instead, she filed a complaint with the State Equal Opportunity Commission, which claim was settled for $4,000.00. In the settlement, she reserved the right to pursue a federal action alleging a civil rights violation. She filed this action in federal court, and appeals the court's decision in favor of the university.

ISSUE: Did the university's handling of the charges against Riggins afford her sufficient procedural due process under the Constitution?

ANSWER: Yes.

REASONING OF THE COURT: Citing the decision of the U.S. Supreme Court in **Cleveland Board of Education v. Loudermill** (*The College Administrator and the Courts,* Revised Edition), the court of appeals held that the hearing in this case by the University was not required to be formal. It need only be an initial check against mistaken decision — "especially a determination of *(sic)* whether there are reasonable grounds to believe that the charges against the employee are true and support the proposed action."

In this case, the university provided fundamental procedural due process requirement: notice and an explanation of the evidence, including a detailed formal report of the incident; an opportunity to respond (in this case twice); and a check by the university into the validity of the employee's version of the matter.

Assuming that a more thorough post-termination process were required, the university had a formal grievance procedure, which Riggins chose not to use.

ADDITIONAL COMMENTS: The court held that the key factor in overturning the termination in **Loudermill,** was that the employees were not given an opportunity to respond to the charges against them before they were fired. See **Arnett v. Kennedy,** *(The College Administrator and the Courts).*

In what may be instructive dictum, the court outlined what it believed to be the necessary components of due process in the termination of a tenured university employee for cause:

1. clear and actual notice of the charges, in sufficient detail to enable the employee to rebut them;
2. notice of the names of those making the charges, and the nature of their factual evidence;
3. a reasonable time and opportunity for the employee to present testimony in her defense;
4. a hearing before an impartial board or tribunal.

The court held that the hearing need not include the opportunity to confront and cross-examine opposing parties.

# —Unprofessional Behavior of Staff —Exercise of Free Speech

LEIPHART V. NORTH CAROLINA SCHOOL OF THE ARTS, 342 S.E. 2D 914. Court of Appeals of North Carolina, 1986.

FACTS: Leiphart was director of student activities at NCSA, reporting to the dean of student services. The dean held regular staff meetings, at which she encouraged discussion of complaints or problems relating to her department. On October 21, 1983, knowing that the dean would be out of town, Leiphart called a staff meeting for the purpose of presenting complaints which he had collected concerning the dean. These complaints were apparently collected during a several week period, but not presented by Leiphart during regular staff meetings. When several staff members protested the nature of the called meeting, he "closed his folder" and terminated the meeting. When the dean returned from her trip, she met with Leiphart on October 24, and challenged his conduct in calling the meeting during her absence. Leiphart had the opportunity to respond to the dean's charge that his actions were inappropriate.

On November 18, the dean informed Leiphart in writing that he was being dismissed from his employment for cause. The letter specifically detailed the incident of the October 21 meeting, and concluded that Leiphart's actions in compiling complaints, and purposefully presenting them in the dean's absence, constituted unprofessional behavior which was disruptive of the productive working relationships within the department. The letter informed Leiphart of his right to appeal the decision to the state personnel commission.

Leiphart appealed, and the commission, after hearing, affirmed the decision. Leiphart brought this appeal, alleging that the decision denied him due process and violated his rights under the First Amendment.

ISSUE: Was the school's dismissal of Leiphart procedurally adequate and in accord with the protections afforded him under the First Amendment's free speech provisions?

ANSWER: Yes.

REASONING OF THE COURT: The court held that Leiphart received notice of the nature of the charges against him at the pretermination meeting with the dean on October 24, and then had the opportunity to respond to those charges. Following his discharge, he was afforded a full hearing by the appropriate state commission. The charges themselves are supported by the evidence, which included statements of co–directors that they could not trust Leiphart and that their working relationship with him had been strained by his actions.

The court further held that state statutes requiring a written statement of charges prior to dismissal are satisfied where the charges are known, and formalized in the actual letter of dismissal. The statute's purpose, the court held, is to prevent the employer from firing an employee and then searching for a reason to justify the dismissal.

The court rejected Leiphart's claim that the school's failure to afford an internal grievance hearing, prior to appeal to the state commission, denied due process. Although it would have been better practice to have had such a hearing, the court held, in this case there is no evidence to show that the result would have been affected, since the chancellor had already approved the dismissal.

# Staff Employment

## —Accommodating Religious Beliefs of Staff

PENNSYLVANIA STATE UNIVERSITY V. PENNSYLVANIA HUMAN RELATIONS COMMISSION, 505 A. 2D 1053. Commonwealth Court of Pennsylvania, 1986.

FACTS: Wallace Swinehart was employed by the Pennsylvania State University Hershey Medical Center (hereafter the medical center) as a security guard. In the fall term, 1980, the medical center determined the need to increase weekend security patrol during the daylight shift to three officers. Swinehart declined to work on Saturday on the ground that it was his Sabbath, as observed by the Worldwide Church of God. The medical center attempted to locate volunteers to cover the weekend time Swinehart was scheduled to work, or to transfer him to a position where he would not be required to work during the daytime on Saturday. Neither alternative could be implemented.

Declining to incur additional expense, the Medical Center terminated Swinehart. He filed a charge of discrimination in employment on the basis of religion, which charge was determined in his favor by the commission. The university appeals.

ISSUE: Was the university required to grant Swinehart twenty-six Saturday leave days per year, and to replace him with university or outside employees at premium pay, or additional pay?

ANSWER: No.

REASONING OF THE COURT: The court held, initially, that the test to be applied in this case should be analogous to that applied by the federal courts in cases alleging discrimination on the basis of religion in violation of Title VII of the Civil Rights Act, 42 U.S.C., Sec. 2000e(j) (See Appendix I). Citing the U.S. Supreme Court's decision in **Trans World Airlines v. Hardison** (*The College Administrator and the Courts,* Revised Edition), the court considered this test to include consideration whether the employer is unable to reasonably accommodate an employee's religious belief, without undue hardship on the conduct of the employer's business.

Implicit in this analysis is consideration of the nature of the employer's business, the frequency and permanent nature of the accommodation, and the nature of the employee's work. Here, both Swinehart's supervisory status and the need for continuous security operations must be addressed. To use volunteers, or to use temporary help from an outside security agency has not been shown to constitute an equivalent replacement for Swinehart's role as a supervisor of the patrol force.

Finally, to burden other employees by compelling them to replace Swinehart on twenty-six Saturdays, even with premium pay, would constitute an unreasonable burden on those employees, and would excessively involve the state in the implementation of a religious belief, by interfering with individual choices of third persons in order to accommodate one employee.

ADDITIONAL COMMENTS: The court analogized the need in **TWA v. Hardison,** for twenty-four hour per day aircraft maintenance, and the employer's efforts at reasonable accommodation. The court interpreted **Hardison** to reject requiring an employer to incur substantial increases in cost, to accommodate an employee's religious beliefs, stating that such could amount to a preference on the basis of religion.

## —Alleged Discrimination on Basis of National Origin
## —Statute of Limitations

KELLER V. ASSOCIATION OF AMERICAN MEDICAL COLLEGES, 644 F. SUPP. 459. United States District Court, District of Columbia, 1986.

FACTS: Keller, a nontenured employee of defendant association, of Hispanic origin, was placed on probation for thirty days in February, 1982. Subsequently, in 1983, the association determined the need to reorganize its membership and publications section, on account of a decline in workload brought on by a reduced demand for AAMC publications. This fact, and the management decision to computerize a portion of AAMC membership and publications orders functions resulted in the termination of one of the organization's two book order clerk positions.

At this time, the supervisor of the publications orders area stepped down from her supervisory role, retaining her clerical duties. Of the two remaining book order clerks, AAMC chose to terminate plaintiff, and to retain a Ms. Thomas, a co-employee of plaintiff. This decision was justified by Ms. Thomas' higher performance evaluations. The association hired a new employee to replace the supervisor, justifying the new hire on the ground that none of its current book order employees had computer skills or knowledge.

Keller filed a complaint against AAMC with the District of Columbia Office of Human Rights on November 30, 1983. The complaint, which alleged national origin discrimination, was cross filed with the Equal Employment Opportunity Commission. She then brought this action, alleging a violation of Section 1981 of the Federal Civil Rights Act and the Title VII of that act, prohibiting employment discrimination based upon national origin. AAMC argued that Keller's claims were barred by applicable periods of limitation, and that, in any event, she was not the victim of employment discrimination.

ISSUE: (1) Were Keller's claims barred by applicable statutes of limitations?
(2) Was Keller's termination motivated by considerations of her national origin?

ANSWER: (1) Yes, (2) No.

REASONING OF THE COURT: The court held that Keller's claim under Section 1981 of the Civil Rights Act was governed by the District of Columbia's one year statute of limitations for civil rights claims. Since Keller did not file her claim until December, 1984, more than one year after her termination in November, 1983, the issue is not viable.

Keller's Title VII claim is similarly subject to dismissal for not having been filed within 300 days from the date of the accrual of her cause of action, under 42 U.S.C., Sec. 2000e-5(e). She was placed on probation in February, 1982, but did not file her

complaint with the D.C. Office of Human Rights and EEOC until November 30, 1983. Her charge was not deemed filed with the EEOC until January, 1984, more than 300 days after the alleged discriminatory act.

In any event, plaintiff was not the victim of employment discrimination. She was not replaced by any applicant, unless one considers hiring of a new supervisor a replacement of Keller. This hire was justified on the basis of the need for computer skills, not possessed by current staff, an allegation established by affidavit of defendant, and not disputed by plaintiff. The retention of Thomas was justified by her superior performance evaluation, which showed an accuracy in her work substantially above that of plaintiff. Thomas' performance evaluations were consistently above average, while Keller's declined from above average to average from 1980 to 1983.

As to the decision to cut back one position, AAMC adequately demonstrated a significant decline in book sales, including a 32% drop in sales of major publications from 1978-79 to 1982-83, and a 13% decline from 1983 to 1984.

ADDITIONAL COMMENTS: In deciding plaintiff's substantive claim of national origin discrimination, the court followed the test outlined in **Texas Department of Community Affairs v. Burdine,** frequently cited in *The College Administrator and the Courts,* and its supplements.

# —Discipline of Campus Police Officer for Possession of Controlled Substance

FLORIDA STATE UNIVERSITY V. MOORE, 492 SO. 2D 703. District Court of Appeal, First District, 1986.

FACTS: Moore was dismissed from her position as a university security officer for conduct unbecoming a public employee, based upon her possession of controlled substances. She sought, and was granted a de novo hearing by the state's career service commission, a quasi-judicial body empowered to hear cases involving final employment action by state agencies against permanent status—career service—employees.

The commission agreed with the university's finding of cause for personnel action, but reduced the penalty from dismissal to thirty-day suspension based upon the possession being minimal and indirect. The university appeals the commission's order.

ISSUE:  Does the state career service commission have the authority to reduce the severity of personnel action taken by a university?

ANSWER:  Yes.

REASONING OF THE COURT:  In an extremely brief opinion, citing **Department of Business Regulation v. Jones,** 474 So. 2d 359 (Fla. App. 1985), the court held that Florida Statutes, Section 110.309(4) authorizes the commission to amend personnel action taken by a university, where the commission's findings in support of its order are supported by the record in the case.

ADDITIONAL COMMENTS:  In Florida, the career service commission considers appeals of dismissals or suspensions of career service employees (nonfaculty) of most state agencies, including, but not limited to the state universities.

# — Reclassification of Position

DUKE V. ARIZONA BOARD OF REGENTS, 721 P. 2D 1159.  Court of Appeals of Arizona, Division 2, 1986.

FACTS:  Duke was employed by the university as a Maintenance Mechanic II. His principal job was the inspection of university fire extinguishers; he was not otherwise involved in university fire safety programs. In 1979, the university established geographic divisions for its maintenance operations and designated the position of plan maintenance team leader for the various maintenance groups. Plaintiff was not so designated because his responsibilities included little if any supervision of others.

In 1980, pursuant to statutory mandate that the board of regents establish uniform job and position classifications, wage scales, and uniform position descriptions among the three state universities, the University of Arizona adopted a plan for compensation equity. This plan provided for pay ranges related to classification of positions and specific compensation within those ranges as determined by the director of personnel or his designee. In 1984, a personnel systems audit resulted in Duke's position being reclassified as fire systems technician, pay

grade 16. He brought this action, claiming that he was contractually entitled to reclassification as a supervisor, or team leader, pay grade 19. The board here appeals a jury verdict in his favor.

ISSUE:  Did the above audits, and reevaluations by the university of its job classifications entitle Duke to reclassification as a supervisor?

ANSWER:  No.

REASONING OF THE COURT:  At no time did Duke's duties as a fire extinguisher inspector require the type of foreman or supervisory duties included within the team leader position. Nor did the audits require his reclassification as a supervisor. The statutory audit and reclassification of positions was required to establish uniformity among the state's three universities in the classification of positions, job descriptions and the like.

As to individual classifications, and pay equity, authority was vested in the director of personnel or his designee. Moreover, job classifications were exempted from staff grievance procedures. These factors indicate that those establishing the above plans did not intend to create any contractual right to reclassification. The comparable pay for comparable duties provision of the universities' pay equity policies, as stated in employee manuals, does not amount to a contract right to reclassification as a supervisor, where work performed has been consistently determined to be nonsupervisory in nature.

# — Research Grant as Employment Contract

TIDWELL V. EMORY UNIVERSITY, 349 S.E. 2D 245.  Court of Appeals of Georgia, 1986.

FACTS:  Tidwell was hired by the university as an "at will" research technician. Being overqualified for that position, he was told by his supervisor that, "if things worked out, (the university) would think about trying to keep him on, maybe getting him a non-tenured faculty position." Subsequent to this interchange, Tidwell assisted his supervisor in applying to the American Cancer Society for a two-year research grant. The grant application listed Tidwell as participating in the proposed research as co-investigator, at a salary higher than he enjoyed as a technician.

When the grant was awarded, Tidwell was informed that he would not participate in the project, principally because of his problems in relating to other employees. Several months later, Tidwell was terminated from his employment as a technician because of alleged poor relations with co-workers.

He brought this suit, alleging breach of a contractual obligation to employ him as co-investigator of the ACS project. He appeals a summary judgment in favor of the university.

ISSUE: Did the university's grant application constitute a contract of employment, or binding offer of employment?

ANSWER: No.

REASONING OF THE COURT: The court of appeals held that, in soliciting and accepting the grant, the university did not obligate itself to hire Tidwell. The mere fact that he would benefit from the acceptance of the grant does not, *per se,* establish a contractual entitlement to employment. Moreover, Tidwell was not promised employment, orally, or in writing; nor did the grant application require that he, or any other specific individual be employed on the project.

ADDITIONAL COMMENTS: The portion of the grant quoted by the court indicated that the conduct of the investigation would be under the direction of the "grantee institution," without apparent qualification.

The case, on appeal, did not raise an issue as to the cause for Tidwell's ultimate discharge.

# — University Staff Doing Business with the University

IN RE BEYCHOK, 484 SO. 2D 912. Court of Appeal of Louisiana, First Circuit, 1986.

FACTS: Beychok was a member of the board of supervisors of Louisiana State University (hereafter LSU or the university). He was also president, chief executive officer, director and majority stockholder of WBC, Inc., a bakery products company. From 1981 through 1984, the university solicited sealed competitive bids for bakery products. WBC submit-

ted sealed bids, and was awarded contracts in the approximate amount of $200,000.

During this same time period, Beychok, as CEO of WBC, Inc., negotiated with the university's athletic director, and was granted a lease for advertising space on the university's football scoreboard/clocks. WBC paid approximately $6500 for leased space. The university's board of supervisors took no part in this decision, which was made without solicitation of competitive bids.

In August, 1984 Beychok and others sought a ruling from the state's ethics commission regarding the propriety of board members entering into contracts with the university. The commission concluded that state statutes prohibited board members from entering into such business transactions with the university. Following a nonfinal judicial proceeding, the commission issued an order cancelling the contracts and ordering that the university should refrain from entering into future contracts with members of the governing board. Beychok appeals.

ISSUE: (1) Was WBC's receipt of bakery sales contracts in violation of the state's ethics code?
(2) Was Beychok's negotiation of the lease in violation of the code?

ANSWER: (1) No; (2) Yes.

REASONING OF THE COURT: The Appellate Court held that members of the board may not enter into bid contracts with the university, unless such contracts are awarded as a result of sealed, competitive bids; the recipient is the low competitive bidder; and the board member does not participate in the acceptance of the bid. Thus Beychok's negotiation of the lease agreement is in violation of the code. However, the award of the bakery sales contracts is not invalid under the code.

The commission's order prohibiting all future contracts is invalid. Whether contracts are in accord with the code depends upon compliance with the procedures above described.

ADDITIONAL COMMENTS: Administrators should consult counsel concerning the requirements of their state's ethics codes for public employees. Statutes in some jurisdictions may place greater or lesser limitations upon business dealings between the public officer in his private capacity, and a state agency.

## XI.18

# Staff Termination

## —Alleged Age Discrimination
## —Prior Administrative Rulings Do Not Preclude Defenses

JOHNSON V. UNIVERSITY OF WISCONSIN-MILWAUKEE, 738 F. 2D 59. United States Court of Appeals, Seventh Circuit, 1986.

FACTS: Johnson was hired in 1965 as a secretary. Thereafter, during the period from 1973–1981, she worked in the fringe benefits office, and the payroll office, in employment counseling positions. She was discharged in 1981, and contested the discharge through arbitration proceedings. It was the university's position that Johnson was unable to complete routine assignments, attempted to avoid work, and performed work incorrectly, Johnson alleged that she was terminated in retaliation for her son's legal action against the university.

The arbitrator found that, although Johnson was not discharged for proper cause, she was not the subject of illegal discrimination on the basis of age, handicap, or in retaliation for her son's actions. The arbitrator found just cause for a ten–week suspension without pay, and ordered reinstatement with pay, less that ten–week salary, and less earnings received from alternative employment during the period of her separation.

During an unemployment compensation hearing following her termination, the hearing officer determined that, although Johnson had made some errors in her job, the university's disciplinary proceedings were, in part, contrived.

She brought this action alleging age discrimination. In the suit, she argued that the university should be precluded, by the arbitrator's findings

and the decision of the unemployment compensation appeals board, from raising the defense of legitimate cause for termination. The trial court permitted the introduction of the arbitrator's decision, but ruled against the admissibility of the unemployment compensation board's findings. The jury found that Johnson was not the victim of age discrimination under federal law and she appeals, after denial of her post-trial motions.

ISSUE: (1) Do the administrative agency findings have a preclusive effect in the federal suit alleging age discrimination?
(2) Was the federal court's exclusion of evidence of defendant's alleged retaliatory motive improperly excluded by the court?

ANSWER: No, to both questions.

REASONING OF THE COURT: The general rule is that a prior arbitration is not preclusive on the issue of impermissible discrimination under Title VII. This is so because the arbitrator is generally bound by the contract before him.

State administrative decisions have been given preclusive effect, if the state agency acted in a judicial capacity, with opportunity for full hearing by the parties, and where the issues are identical in the two proceedings. In this case, the issue before the unemployment tribunal was Johnson's alleged misconduct, not whether there were general, legitimate business reasons for her termination, sufficient to contradict an allegation of age discrimination.

The evidence of alleged retaliation (for her son's actions) was properly excluded from the federal action. Although a retaliatory discharge would be improper, it has no bearing on the issue of age discrimination—the basis for Johnson's federal lawsuit.

ADDITIONAL COMMENTS: As the case implies, Johnson could have alleged a count of retaliatory discharge, under Title VII and in a court sounding in constitutional rights violation. However, as a litigant, she is bound by the parameters of the statutes upon which she bases her federal cause of action in this case.

# — Violation of Procedures — Discrimination and Retaliation

LOYOLA UNIVERSITY V. HUMAN RIGHTS COMMISSION, 500 N.E. 2D 639. Appellate Court of Illinois, First District, 1986.

FACTS: Loyola University has a personnel policy providing for classifications of employee misconduct into four levels, and providing for disciplinary action of varying degree from warning to termination, depending upon the level of the offense, and prior offenses. Irvin, a black male security officer, with two formal employee evaluations rating him as "excellent" and "promotable," filed a charge against Loyola with the state department of human rights, alleging that he was denied promotion because of his race.

Three weeks later, Irvin was charged with sexual harassment of a female co-worker, a level 3 offense, calling for a five-day suspension for the first offense. Specifically, Irvin was alleged to have suggested, in response to her statement that she was tired during a shift in the medical college, that she rest on a table in the gynecology and obstetrics department because the stirrups on the table were good to "hold the legs apart." Irvin was also alleged to have made other suggestive or insulting remarks to the co-worker, including that she should leave him a "wake-up call." Prior to this charge, Irvin had been disciplined for three separate and unrelated level 1 offenses.

Irvin denied the sexual harassment charge, and filed a retaliation charge with the department. Two weeks later he was fired for sexual harassment and for being generally disruptive. The department filed a complaint with the state human rights commission, which held, after a hearing, that Irvin was discriminated against on account of his race. In support of its holding, the commission cited three comparable cases involving white employees of the university. In those cases, the employees, who had a prior history of level 2 offenses, were warned, or suspended, but not terminated, for admitted sexual harassment which, in each instance involved the indecent touching of a female co-worker, and, in two of the three cases, solicitous or lewd remarks.

The university appealed a trial court affirmance of this holding.

ISSUE: Did the termination of Irvin for a first-time level 3 offense constitute racial discrimination, where white employees received lesser punishments in similar or more serious cases?

ANSWER: Yes.

REASONING OF THE COURT: The court limited its review by holding, at the outset, that a commission's finding should not be overturned unless contrary to the manifest weight of the evidence.

Citing **McDonnell Douglas Corp. v. Green** and **Texas Department of Community Affairs v. Burdine** *(The College Administrator and the Courts),* the court held that Irvin established a prima facie case by showing the short period between his original charge of employment discrimination and his termination, and the disparate treatment of other employees charged with sexual harassment. At this point, the burden shifted to the university to state a nondiscriminatory reason for its actions. When the university met this burden by alleging that Irvin's conduct was premeditated, and that his history of misconduct justified termination, the ultimate burden was upon Irvin to show that these reasons were pretextual for discrimination on the basis of race.

The court held that Irvin met this burden by showing that the white co-workers were similarly situated as to the nature of the sexual offense, as well as prior conduct record. The type of conduct involved in the three cases of white workers was more serious than Irvin's yet he received a harsher penalty. Moreover, the white workers in the other three cases had a history of level 2 infractions, compared to Irvin's level 1 infractions.

The fact that, unlike Irvin, the white employees admitted their offenses does not justify the university's termination of Irvin for a first offense.

Irvin's alleged general disruptive influence is rebutted by the university's own formal evaluations of him as an excellent employee, immediately qualified for promotion.

ADDITIONAL COMMENTS: The court held that its inquiry did not challenge the harshness of the university's penalty, per se, but only whether the punishment was consistent with that imposed upon similarly situated persons of another race.

## XI.19
# Tort Liability

## —Suit Against College for Improper Instruction

MOORE V. VANDERLOO, 386 N.W. 2D 108. Supreme Court of Iowa, 1986.

FACTS: In November, 1978, Linda Moore began chiropractic treatments with Dr. Vanderloo. After undergoing a cervical manipulation by Vanderloo, Moore suffered a sudden onset of symptoms and was taken to a hospital. At the hospital her condition was diagnosed as a cerebral stroke. Moore ultimately suffered permanent bodily and emotional impairment.

Prior to the treatment, Moore had used a birth control aid, manufactured by Ortho Company.

Moore brought suit against Vanderloo, Ortho, and Palmer College of Chiropractic, the institution from which Vanderloo received his degree. The claim against Vanderloo was based upon medical negligence (malpractice), and lack of informed consent (to the procedure employed by Vanderloo). The claim against Ortho was based upon strict products liability, for manufacture of a defective product. Palmer College was sued for breach of warranty and for negligence in failing to properly research and teach Vanderloo the risk of stroke from manipulation of the neck.

The claim against Vanderloo was settled prior to trial, and the claim against Palmer College dismissed. Judgment was entered after trial in favor of Ortho. Moore appeals.

ISSUE: Did Moore state a cause of action against Palmer College for breach of warranty or improperly instructing a student?

ANSWER: No.

REASONING OF THE COURT: The Uniform Commercial Code, governing a claim of breach of warranty, covers goods, not services. Moreover, Moore is not in privity with Palmer, and there is no consideration for an alleged warranty between her and the college. If a court were to hold that a diploma created an express warranty between the college and a third party dealing with the graduate, absent privity, or reliance, there would be an open door to unlimited liability of educational institutions. Furthermore, the state issues a license to a chiropractor, based upon his/her completion of a competency test. Thus, if there were an implied warranty regarding the training of a chiropractor, it would be from the state, not an educational institution.

The court rejected a claim of educational malpractice on public policy grounds. *First,* the court held that a standard of care for instruction would be difficult to formulate. *Second,* there are inherent problems in such cases in determining the nature and cause of damages. *Third,* to allow such a cause of action would create a flood of litigation against colleges, where graduates fail to measure up to professional standards. *Finally,* the court should not interfere with legislatively created standards for professional competency.

ADDITIONAL COMMENTS: Although it is doubtful that the decision would have been different in a degree privilege state, it is interesting to raise the question whether a claim of negligence against the college would have survived a motion to dismiss where a state competence exam was not required. In this regard, the court's opinion begs the question whether a cause of action may be advanced against the state. The "floodgate of litigation" rationale, as well as the court's concern for the formulation of a standard of care, could be debated. The better rationale, aside from the minimum competency argument, is that most states have formulated by statute a professional standard of care in medical malpractice cases which references prevailing medical practice in the same or similar community, or the medical skills of the average member of the profession, in good standing. Finally, it may be argued that the educational institution cannot insure the continuing education or training of the physician, or his implementation of acquired skills in accord with professional standards in the medical community.

# — Trampoline Accident
# — Comparative Negligence

WHITLOCK V. UNIVERSITY OF DENVER, 712 P.2D 1072. Colorado Court of Appeals, 1985.

FACTS: Whitlock, a student at the University of Denver, injured his neck on a trampoline owned by a fraternity recognized by the university and located on its campus. The injury rendered Whitlock a quadriplegic.

The trampoline had been located, for a significant period of time, on the lawn of the fraternity house, which was leased from the university. The university was aware of the presence and use of the trampoline by the fraternity, and previous injuries of students using them. The university's director of athletics testified as to the danger of trampolines and stated that he had placed a school owned trampoline in a locked room, allowing its use only with supervision by a coach.

The lease between the university and the fraternity established university control over the property and fraternity affairs, and revealed university maintenance responsibilities.

A jury assessed Whitlock's damages at $7.3 million, but reduced them to $5.2 million, on the basis of its finding of a degree of comparative negligence on the part of Whitlock in using the trampoline. The trial court set aside the jury's verdict, holding that Whitlock's negligence was greater than the university's negligence. It further ordered a reduction of the verdict to $4 million, in the event its judgment

was overturned and the jury verdict reinstated on appeal. Finally it granted the university's alternative motion for new trial. Both parties appealed.

ISSUE: Did the trial court have adequate grounds for setting aside the jury's verdict, or ordering the alternative reduction in that verdict?

ANSWER: No.

REASONING OF THE COURT: The above evidence of the formal agreement between the university and the fraternity, the university's right of control, and its knowledge of the risks inherent in use of trampolines, the use of this trampoline, and prior injuries, are sufficient to establish a duty on the part of the university to exercise reasonable care in matters involving students' use of such equipment. The evidence presented was sufficient to support a jury finding of negligence on the part of the university. The degree of that negligence, as compared to alleged negligence of the student, is, in most cases, a question for the jury. Here the evidence was conflicting as to the degree that either party contributed to Whitlock's injury. Reasonable minds could draw different conclusions regarding respective degrees of fault of the parties; thus the matter was properly decided by the jury.

There was no prejudice shown as to the jury, or that it was improperly influenced by the mere presence of plaintiff in the courtroom.

Finally, the amount of damages awarded by the jury was affirmed by the appellate court. The record established that Whitlock's economic losses alone were $4 million. Thus, considering pain and suffering, loss of time and enjoyment of life, and other noneconomic losses, the trial court's reduction of damages was in error.

ADDITIONAL COMMENTS: Since the early 1970s, most jurisdictions have abrogated the doctrine of contributory negligence, which denied an injured any recovery from a negligent defendant, if the injured party's own negligence substantially contributed to his injury. The more favored doctrine applied in cases such as the instant case is that of "comparative negligence." This doctrine does not bar recovery by a plaintiff who was himself negligent, if the defendant's negligence was a legal cause of the plaintiff's injuries. The "pure" form of this doctrine, adopted first in Florida in the case of **Hoffman v. Jones** (followed in California in **Li v. Yellow Cab Co.**), apportions recovery in direct relation to the relative degree of fault of the parties. Thus, in the instant case, where the university is 75 percent negligent (its relative degree of fault, as a legal cause of plaintiff's injuries, on the scale of 100 percent, is 75 percent), plaintiff (Whitlock) will recover 75 percent of his damages. His damages are reduced by 25 percent or the jury's assessment of the degree of his own lack of reasonable care, as a legal cause of his injuries.

Variations of the doctrine allow recovery by the plaintiffs, unless their negligence is equal to or greater than that of the defendant, in which case, recovery may be denied. Administrators should consult counsel to determine the rule applied in a particular jurisdiction, and how it affects the evaluation of a negligence case filed against the university.

# Campus and Community: Boston University

Reprinted by permission of John H. Silber, President, Boston University.

# Boston's University:
# Campus and Community

BOSTON UNIVERSITY has always enjoyed a symbiotic relationship with Greater Boston. The University benefits from the vitality and resources of the city, and in turn provides the community with a wide range of educational, cultural, legal, and medical services. The University also has a decisive impact on its region as an economic partner, employer, and property owner.

## Boston University and the Economy of Boston

The growing financial strength of Boston University has immensely improved the economy of the Greater Boston area. From a financial perspective, the University is correctly described as a vast interregional transfer mechanism for bringing funds into metropolitan Boston from other parts of the state and nation. Since the work of the University is highly labor-intensive, the direct economic effect of its $400 million budget is far greater than that of a manufacturing plant of comparable budget. If all its employees are counted—full-time, part-time, student, and temporary—Boston University is the second largest private employer in Boston and the eighth largest in Massachusetts, with a payroll of more than $180 million. Although a non-profit institution, the University has always paid real estate taxes to the City on commercial properties, and in addition has paid real estate taxes to the City on *all* properties acquired since June 1980. Together with in-lieu-of-tax payments, these payments amounted to $1.9 million in 1985. Moreover, the $81 million in research and training grants that flowed to Boston University in 1985 also contributed to local economic and industrial development.

The University also contributes to the economic health of the region through its educational programs and scholarships. In addition to scholarships provided under the Boston Scholars Program, described later in this chapter, graduate management scholarships valued at $80,000 annually are provided for qualified City employees to help upgrade their management skills. The University has recently offered Executive Education Programs for John Hancock, General Electric, Raytheon, and a number of other firms. Extensive programs at off-campus sites educate the personnel of firms such as GTE Sylvania and General Electric, improving skills and productivity in such fields as robotics, computer-aided design, manufacturing engineering, and basic computer science.

Boston University's College of Communication conducts programs for employees in firms throughout metropolitan Boston in writing, marketing, public relations, speaking, and video, and conducts executive training directed toward the needs of public utilities, agencies, and professional associations. In the College of Engineering, the University's Late Entry Accelerated Program (LEAP) allows qualified adults with some technical background to become engineers; faculty and administrators of the College of Engineering are actively recruiting women and members of minorities. Consequently, the proportion of women and minority students in the College has consistently ranked among the highest in the nation.

Boston University also seeks to stimulate and to improve the local economy through numerous centers, institutes, and programs. The Medical Center, which itself employs over 2,300 residents of the South End and Greater Boston, has fostered the development of a new South End Technology Square Association, a non-profit corporation designed to stimulate commercial development and increased employment opportunities in the South End. The School of Medicine's Technology Transfer Program allows participating firms to collaborate with medical faculty in biomedical research of mutual interest. The University's Small Business Development Program, undertaken in conjunction with Dr. James M. Howell, Senior Vice President of the Bank of Boston, Chairman of the Council for Economic Action, and Trustee of Boston University, brings together business leaders and academicians to offer training and encouragement for entrepreneurs hoping to start small businesses. The program actively seeks out potential entrepreneurs, identifies local markets and growth industries, and seeks to provide access to capital for graduates of the program who have developed a business plan based on their training. In its first year, the program enrolled 180 students, 80 percent of them from minority groups. The program's initial cycle has launched twenty-two new businesses employing ninety people. These businesses were established by the provision, through the program, of $600,000 in capital investment.

A number of Boston University's programs bring together local, national, and international businessmen. The Manufacturing Roundtable is an international working partnership between fifteen manufacturing executives and faculty of the School of Management and the College of Engineering. The Human Resources Policy Institute, consisting of forty member companies under the direction of Professor Fred K. Foulkes, identifies research projects relevant to industry needs, which are then funded with donations from the Institute's membership.

Other Boston University programs develop forward-looking working relationships between business, the academic world, and government. The Center for Technology and Policy, directed by Professor Gerald Gordon, investigates the social implications of emerging technology and assists in the formation of a national policy in this area. The Center is in the process of forming a Technical Strategy Council which will include representatives from industry, government, and the University working in cooperation to identify major areas of research to be addressed. The Institute for Employment Policy, under the direction of Professor Peter Doeringer, studies the economies of local industries and the efficiency of governmental programs; faculty provide *pro bono* assistance to Private Industry Councils functioning under the federal Job Training Partnerships Act, and to many other non-profit and public agencies.

The development and extension of the University's relationships with business and industry, especially in the areas of science, engineering, and technology, is a primary responsibility of Dr. Russel C. Jones, who in 1985 was named Vice President for Academic Affairs and Academic Development. A civil engineer, Dr. Jones came to Boston University in 1981 after having been a faculty member at Massachusetts Institute of Technology, a department chairman at Ohio State University, and Dean of Engineering at the University of Massachusetts. Dr. Jones is assisted in his efforts by Dr. Aviva Brecher, Director of Academic/Corporate Relations, who is studying the feasibility of a formal University/industry collaborative program.

Like its relationship to industry, Boston University's relationship to the City of Boston is one of partnership. When, in 1984, the City asked the State Legislature for assistance in increasing its revenue, Boston University was among the City's strongest supporters. President Silber published a widely read article endorsing the City's request, joined other college presidents in testifying before the State Legislature, and encouraged the University's alumni to write in support of the City's proposals. Nearly 40,000 alumni responded.

## Boston University and Its Neighborhood

Fourteen of the University's sixteen schools are located on the Charles River Campus. In this urban setting, cut through by major thoroughfares, the campus in 1971 required extensive efforts of beautification, repair, and development. By 1985, following policies of adaptive re-use and the creation of green spaces within its urban environment, Boston University had made major progress in enhancing the attractiveness of its campus. Along Commonwealth Avenue, the ground floor of a large dormitory was remodeled, and small stores and restaurants set into street frontage formerly occupied by a garage. A block away, along the tree-lined quiet of Bay State Road, elegant Victorian townhouses, apartment buildings, and mansions were restored and preserved by the University. Containing offices for departments and institutes as well as residences, Bay State Road, following the riverbank, leads toward a complex of modern buildings which includes the University's main library, law library, and student union.

The University's diverse campus now reflects a commitment to urban civility, with open spaces interspersed among refurbished buildings whose attractiveness and character have been consciously preserved. The University's contributions to the neighborhoods of Brookline, Allston-Brighton, and Kenmore Square are also apparent. University buildings in these areas have been attractively remodeled with improved flow of local traffic. Through its property acquisitions and renovations, the University has contributed to the rehabilitation of entire neighborhoods. Its Office of Buildings and Grounds maintains and cleans streets, sidewalks, and trees all along Commonwealth Avenue from Kenmore Square to Allston. The skillful and dedicated work of Boston University's Buildings and Grounds employees is an outstanding example not only of service to the University but of service to the public. The University's 41-member police department offers protection to residents of Kenmore Square, Allston, Audubon Circle, and Cottage Farm in Brookline. In off-campus areas patrolled by the Boston University police, serious crime has dropped by 19 percent since 1980.

The development of the Boston University Campus has anchored the revitalization of Kenmore Square and the area to its west, an area which had suffered urban blight since the middle 1960s. Boston University, represented by then Vice President Daniel J. Finn, was one of the founders of the Kenmore Business Association. It was the University's initiative which led the Association, in 1978, to form the Kenmore Study Group. Made up of organizations with a direct interest in the revitalization of Kenmore Square—among them the Boston Red

Sox, the Charlestown Savings Bank (now the Neworld Bank), and the First National Bank of Boston (now the Bank of Boston)—as well as Boston University and the Office of the Mayor, the Group assessed the mutual interests of the University, the City, and the neighborhoods and laid out a plan for the future.

Again, it was Boston University that was responsible for the most significant steps taken in recent years to realize this plan. The most dramatic development to date came to completion in September of 1983 with the transformation of a Kenmore Square building into the Boston University Bookstore. The largest in New England, and one of the best and most diverse bookstores in the world, it reflects the creativity and energy the University has marshaled to transform its campus and enrich its environment. (See Chapter 4 for further information on the Boston University Bookstore.)

Three formerly vacant or underutilized buildings adjacent to Kenmore Square now house part of the Arthur G. B. Metcalf Center for Science and Engineering, an educational resource serving regional and national high-technology needs. In 1979 the University purchased the former Kenmore Hotel, which had been for years a dormitory of Grahm Junior College. Responding to the request of the City, the University forewent its plan to use the facility as a dormitory and instead put it back on the tax rolls and sold the building to a private developer to be converted into low-cost housing for the elderly.

In 1970, Audubon Circle, a once-thriving neighborhood in close proximity to the Boston University campus, was in decline. Predominantly a student neighborhood since the 1960s, its residents attended a number of institutions close by. Beginning in 1966 with the purchase of the building at 38 Buswell Street for student housing, Boston University started a gradual renewal in the neighborhood. This process continued through the late 1960s and accelerated through the 1970s as the University acquired additional property in the area. Buildings were refurbished for the safety and comfort of the students and other tenants who inhabited them, and yards and parkways were landscaped. The property at 22-24 Buswell Street may serve as an example: When purchased by the University in 1978, it had exposed wiring, staircases in danger of falling through to the basement, an inactive sprinkler system, and inadequate entry and egress. The cost to the University of rehabilitating this property in 1978 was nearly $1 million.

From 1977 to 1980, the University spent nearly twice as much renovating the 379 units it acquired as it had spent to acquire them: total major renovation costs of $4.7 million represent 180 percent of the acquisition cost. This is a fair measure of the extent to which Boston University has rehabilitated what had been a derelict neighborhood.

By 1983, Boston University had spent $11.2 million to rehabilitate and landscape properties in Audubon Circle. It had also paid the City over $420,000 in taxes owed by previous owners of buildings it had acquired. The University continues to spend $1.3 million annually on property management and maintenance.

As it renovated and upgraded its properties in Audubon Circle, the University also augmented its police patrols in the area. Boston University's security forces were enlarged by 40 percent, from 29 to 41 persons, between 1980 and 1982.

Gradually, as many of the buildings in Audubon Circle were rehabilitated rather than demolished and replaced, the neighborhood began to recover something of its traditional character. Businesses began to move back. Audubon Circle has recently seen the establishment of a food market, a home cleaner, a laundry, a dry cleaner, and a sandwich shop in storefronts which were previously boarded up. The number of vacant apartments, nearly 25 percent of the total available in 1970, has declined to less than ten percent today.

This extensive program of refurbishing, upgrading, and maintaining the area, something which only a major institution with a commitment to the neighborhood was in a position to do, transformed Audubon Circle. The area began to attract, alongside the students of Boston University and other schools, an increasingly stable and prosperous population. Home ownership in the neighborhood has increased five times since 1977. This development could never have taken place apart from the improvements Boston University had made in the neighborhood prior to 1977.

Audubon Circle would not be the attractive neighborhood it is today without Boston University. The continued strong presence of the University is a guarantee of the neighborhood's future stability. Boston University will continue to cooperate with other residents of a revitalized Audubon Circle, and to provide high-quality living space for its students there.

In Brookline, the University meets on a regular basis with the Board of Selectmen to discuss neighborhood issues. After consultation with the Historical Commission of Brookline, Boston University took on itself the restoration of the historic house at 25 Lenox Street. At a total cost of more than $430,000, the house has now been restored to a condition that preserves its mid-nineteenth century character. The University has joined with Brookline in having the Fuller Building, designed by Albert Kahn, the foremost industrial architect of the twentieth century, placed on the National Registry of Historic Places.

Since 1960, the University has been involved in the process of purchasing the Commonwealth Armory. While the desirability of the University's acquisition of the Armory has been recognized by Governors Volpe, Sargent, King, and Dukakis, and while the Legislature passed, in 1982, a bill authorizing and directing the Commonwealth of Massachusetts to sell the property to the University, negotiations are still in progress to complete the purchase. Meanwhile, the University has built an indoor track in the Armory, which it makes available to more than thirty public and parochial schools in the Boston area.

Through the Boston University Task Force, the University seeks cooperation and communication with more than twenty neighborhood groups. The University plans to continue its regular meetings with these groups, and to share with them its plans for future development.

## The University's Contributions to Local Education

Boston University considers it imperative that it contribute not only to the higher education of its students, but to education at all levels throughout the city where it resides. Each year, under the Boston Scholars Program, the University offers three four-year scholarships to graduates from each of the high schools of Boston and Brookline. The value of these 232 scholarships exceeds $2.3 million annually.

In the spring of 1986, the University announced its establishment of fourteen full-tuition Medeiros Scholarships for outstanding students of Boston's parochial schools. Named in honor of Humberto Cardinal Medeiros, this scholarship program was established to recognize the contribution of the parochial schools of the Boston area, and to extend the University's longtime efforts on behalf of the students of the Boston area to outstanding graduates of the parochial system. The first

generation of Medeiros Scholars will enter Boston University in the fall
of 1987.

Recognizing the service and sacrifice made by firefighters to the
City and to Boston University, the University has established four-year
scholarships for the children of Boston and Brookline firefighters who
have died in the line of duty. (In recognition of the hazards faced by
these brave public servants, the University has purchased 400 personal
distress locators for the Fire Departments of Boston and Brookline.
These devices, also known as PDL-5s, have been specially tested and
modified in accordance with the specifications of the Boston/Brookline
Firefighters. They emit an audible signal should the firefighter fail to
move for a specified length of time. The PDL-5s, presented to the Fire
Departments by the University in March of 1986, can make the difference between life and death for firefighters who have been trapped or
rendered unconscious.)

Other Boston University scholarship programs have been established
for graduates of Roxbury Community College, employees of the City of
Boston, and local high school teachers. In response to the need for more
qualified science teachers, the University offers training in computer
science to teachers at the Boston Latin School. A Science Seminar Program provides local science teachers with updated teaching materials
and methods.

Many other educational programs, with virtually every School and
College of Boston University contributing, demonstrate the University's commitment to Boston and to her students. The following are
some of the University's most notable educational contributions to
the community:

• Since 1981, the School of Education's Literacy and Language Institute
has provided assessment and has developed programs for more than 100
learning-impaired or disabled students. The Institute has also held
more than 150 seminars attended by thousands of teachers and administrators throughout the Greater Boston area.

• The Adult Literacy Program, a pathbreaking and nationally recognized initiative, addresses an area of increasing national concern. More
than 175 adults have benefited from this program.

• University programs at Norfolk Prison, founded and directed by Professor Elizabeth Barker, have given convicts the opportunity to study
toward bachelor's degrees awarded by Boston University's Metropolitan
College. Initiated in 1972 with the encouragement of President Silber,
the program enrolls between 60 and 80 prisoners each year; since 1977
it has awarded 45 degrees. No former prisoner who has received a
degree from the program has ever gone back to prison.

• The Evergreen Program offers people over sixty a program which
combines physical education and courses on, among other topics, current events, international relations, philosophy, and foreign languages.
Since it began in 1980, the program has enrolled more than two thousand citizens of the Boston area at a nominal fee of $10. The University
also opens all its regular courses to participants in the Evergreen Program and all other senior citizens, on a space-available basis, at a fee of
$10 per course.

• The Elementary School Physical Education Program each week
serves 360 children from Cambridge, Brighton, and Boston.

In addition to its direct contributions to education, the University
has played a prominent role in seeking to improve secondary education

throughout the Boston area. It took the lead in drafting an agreement under which twenty-five Boston-area colleges and universities agreed to assist local schools and actively recruit their graduates. In 1982, President Silber appointed as his Special Assistant Dr. Robert Sperber, former Superintendent of the Brookline Public Schools. In this capacity, Dr. Sperber oversees the University's Collaborative Office, the Urban Schools Task Force, and the Educational Consortium in their efforts to foster educational excellence at the secondary level, without which excellence in higher education cannot be achieved.

In recent years, the University has shown increasing concern over public school education in Boston. Responding to widespread criticism of the Boston Public Schools, President Silber suggested a remedy, proposing that the Boston Public School Committee contract with the University for it to manage the school system for five years. Under this plan, the resources of Boston University in personnel, in budgeting, in curriculum planning, and in various other management areas would be used to set up the information systems and the management procedures necessary to operate a large school system.

Although the Boston Public School System did not respond to President Silber's initiative in 1985, three other communities have approached Boston University about obtaining its services for their school systems.

## Contributions to Cultural Life

As a major center of culture in Boston and New England, the University is committed to making its musical, artistic, dramatic, scholarly, and literary resources available to the public. It also provides a forum from which major political figures may address significant public issues. The following are a few examples of the University's many contributions to the cultural life of the area.

• Each year the University offers the Greater Boston community over 350 concerts and recitals by superb artists, including members of the faculty and guest artists. All concerts sponsored by the School of Music are open to the public, and most are free.

• To encourage the development of musical talent in the Boston area, Boston University's music students conduct a workshop for high school composers each year.

• Outstanding music students from twelve to eighteen years of age are invited into the Greater Boston Youth Symphony Orchestra (GBYSO), founded by the University in 1958 and run in cooperation with a community board of directors. Members of the orchestra receive training from faculty and students of Boston University's School of Music, which also provides rehearsal space. The services of GBYSO's Music Director, Eiji Oue, a faculty member of the School of Music, are contributed by the University. Students in the Greater Boston Youth Symphony Orchestra have come from over 100 communities in the area. GBYSO has appeared at Symphony Hall in Boston, Carnegie Hall in New York, the United Nations, the White House, and in a number of foreign countries, including Israel.

• The Boston University Art Gallery carries at least one exhibition of a Boston-area artist annually.

• Each year the Huntington Theatre offers a series of five plays, including classics and the works of contemporary playwrights. For each production, the Huntington provides special matinee performances for high school students and discounts for senior citizens. Three performances of each production, including one student matinee, conclude with an open-audience discussion at which time cast, crew, and director discuss the play and its performance with the audience.

• In 1986, funded by a grant from the National Endowment for the Humanities, the University is sponsoring the Young Critics Institute. This program offers selected high school students an opportunity to observe each Huntington Theatre production as it progresses through rehearsal to opening, to attend lectures on the play by a Boston University faculty member and by a journalist or theatre critic, and to write an independent review of the final production.

• Hundreds of lectures, free and open to the public, are given under the auspices of Boston University each year. The University Lectures provide an annual forum for a distinguished Boston University scholar to address the campus, scholars from neighboring institutions, and the public at large. The Center for International Relations, the Institute for Philosophy and Religion, and the Boston Colloquium for the Philosophy of Science also provide outstanding lecture series.

• Throughout the year, the Marsh Chapel provides lectures for the public as well as broadcasts on WBUR of Sunday morning worship services.

• Boston University's Center for Archaeological Studies offers public participation in the excavation of local archaeological sites such as the Paul Revere House.

• The Astronomy Department opens its observatory to the public every week, and has sponsored special programs on Halley's Comet for high school and junior high school students.

Other cultural activities of Boston University are described in the section on the School for the Arts and elsewhere in Chapter 3, and in the section on the University's Centers and Institutes in Chapter 6.

## The University's Contributions to the Health of Greater Boston

When, in 1972, the Boston University School of Medicine assumed full responsibility for all medical services at Boston City Hospital, it continued a tradition of service to the South End that stretches back to 1873. City Hospital had become, and continues to be, a major provider of medical care for a great portion of Boston's indigent citizens. The Boston University School of Medicine now budgets well in excess of $1 million annually to help support the salaries of City Hospital's department staffs. A training program in primary care developed at City Hospital has been emulated in other large city hospitals around the nation.

Boston's underprivileged residents have benefited from many innovative programs developed by the School of Medicine in areas ranging from mother and infant care to problems such as drug abuse and teenage pregnancy. Boston University medical students collaborate with the Boston Area Health Education Center to provide health care in medically underserviced neighborhoods. The Health Education Center identifies and recruits minority and disadvantaged Boston high school students interested in careers in the health professions; approximately thirty participate in a tuition-free program each year. Faculty and students of the Boston University Medical School also work at University Hospital, the Boston Veterans Administration Medical Center, and at twenty other affiliated health care institutions. University Hospital's Home Medical Service, the oldest continuously operating home-care service in the United States, works in conjunction with the School of Medicine to care for 850 homebound men and women in Boston's Back Bay, Dorchester, Fenway, Roxbury, South Boston, and South End neighborhoods.

Sargent College's Occupational Therapy Department operates a free clinic for Boston area children with sensory-motor problems and provides free services to dozens of schools, hospitals, and community health programs; the Physical Therapy Department also operates a free clinic. The Speech, Language and Hearing Clinic offers reasonably priced diagnostic and treatment services for the hearing-impaired, as well as testing and evaluation of hearing. Many faculty of Sargent College are consultants to hospitals, clinics, and school systems.

Baccalaureate and graduate students in the School of Nursing intern in about 130 health agencies, many in the underserviced areas of Roxbury, Dorchester, and South Boston. The Goldman School of Graduate Dentistry provides, at greatly reduced fees, complete dental care for more than 650 inner-city Boston children; a team of faculty and dental students work in the South End, and in Chinese and Hispanic communities, providing free oral screenings and working to improve awareness of dental health needs. The Center for Industry and Health Care assists retirees, health maintenance organizations, employees, and employers in developing affordable health plans.

Boston University also engages in or sponsors many programs which contribute to the skills of health-care professionals, or which advance the frontiers of research. The School of Public Health offers practicing health professionals the opportunity to upgrade their skills in the only part-time evening public health program in Massachusetts. Researchers at the School conduct studies on many health issues of vital importance to the community, for example, the effects of alcohol consumption on prenatal development, and the safety of backyard pesticides. The School's Drug Epidemiology Unit, located in Brookline, conducts major health studies on drug use and its effects on the health of adults, children, and the unborn.

The Boston University Medical Center, one of the nation's leading centers of health-related research, includes facilities devoted to Parkinson's disease, muscular dystrophy, Alzheimer's disease, sports medicine, high blood pressure, amyloid disease, aphasia, and stroke and heart attack. The Hubert H. Humphrey Cancer Research Center is a leading research operation assisting in the treatment of between three and four hundred cancer patients per year at University Hospital. The staff of the Medical Center are also actively involved in supporting the first state alliance for the mentally ill in Massachusetts. The Center for Law and Health Sciences conducts research on risk to health among consumers, in the workplace, and from the environment.

## Programs, Faculty, and Students Contributing to the Region

In addition to its massive contributions to the health of metropolitan Boston, the University offers numerous other programs that serve the region. A few examples follow.

• The Legal Aid Program in the Boston University School of Law, with one of the largest and most experienced groups of full-time clinical instructors of any law school in the country, represents about 300 indigent clients from the Greater Boston area in civil cases each year. Under the auspices of the Student Defender and Prosecutor Programs, law students each year also represent about 350 indigent clients charged with misdemeanors and less serious felonies.

• The Law School's Graduate Tax Program sponsors an Institute on Federal Taxation that is widely attended.

• The Center for Applied Social Science provides *pro bono* consulting services to schools and other non-profit organizations.

• The Danielsen Institute is establishing a pastoral counseling center as part of the St. Paul African Methodist Episcopal Church's community project for the needy in Cambridge.

• The Boston University Chapel offers organizational assistance to charitable and social-service agencies and direct assistance to the needy.

• In the College of Liberal Arts, members of the Geology Department conduct ongoing research with direct application to the management of the New England coastal zone; community groups and state agencies frequently consult with the Department on these issues. Research on surface and subsurface waters and water pollution contributes to conservation efforts throughout New England.

• The Office of Public Archaeology, a part of the Center for Archaeological Studies, conducts resource impact studies required on projects supported or licensed by the federal or state governments.

• In the College of Communication, a joint venture with the Boston Cable Community Access Foundation presents five nightly half-hour newscasts each week, covering major local news stories.

• Non-profit organizations seeking advertising and public relations services can find them in the College of Communication's Ad Lab, which recently promoted a Students Against Drunk Driving presentation.

• Public Radio station WBUR, the recipient of numerous awards for excellence in FM programming, is owned and operated by the Board of Trustees of Boston University, which provides the station's facilities and a major portion of its operating budget.

In addition to its many programs serving the Greater Boston area, the University encourages its students to contribute individually to the welfare and vitality of their city. The Martin Luther King, Jr., Center, Marsh Chapel and the University Chaplains, the Student Activities Office, the Office of Residence Life, and the Office of Orientation and Off-Campus Services coordinate the activities of more than three thousand Boston University students who serve the community through some 250 public service agencies and organizations. Their principal activities include:

Counseling and reading internships in the Boston Public Schools

Blood pressure screening in the Boston Head Start Programs

Crisis Intervention Counseling

The United Way Blood Drive Program

The Special Olympics

Work for the *Globe* Santa

Shopping trips for the elderly (a student government project)

The Friendship Network – Conversation Partners

Art Education Projects in Children's Hospital, Perkins School for the Blind, and other agencies for children's welfare

The Boston University Community Experience Program, providing supportive and structured social gatherings for mentally retarded citizens

Internships for art history students in the Museum of Fine Arts, The Boston Society, and the Massachusetts Art Commission

Participation in OXFAM America: In 1984 and 1985, in cooperation with University Dining Services, more than three thousand Boston University students donated the food costs of one day's meals to OXFAM.

College Work-Study: Over the past fifteen years, fifteen thousand Boston University Work-Study students have been employed in support roles with non-profit organizations; over two thousand community agencies have benefited through payroll savings in excess of $10 million.

Volunteer social work: Each year the School of Social Work places nearly three hundred students in social welfare agencies.

Boston University's faculty serve in leadership positions in the Massachusetts Public Health Association, the Boston Center for Blind Children, the Newbury and Triton Regional School Committee, the American Heart Association, the Roxbury Comprehensive Community Health Center, the Massachusetts Advocacy Center, the Massachusetts Food and Agriculture Coalition, and literally hundreds of other civic, educational, and charitable organizations. Faculty of the College of Communication have served on the Boston Cable Community Access Foundation and many other public-service groups and boards. In 1985, University employees contributed more than $123,000 to the annual United Way Campaign.

Since 1971, a long tradition has been greatly expanded and intensified: no institution of higher education now matches Boston University in service to the people, the neighborhoods, and the charitable and governmental institutions of Boston and its surrounding communities.

# Centenaries and Anniversaries

## 25th Anniversary                    1987

| | |
|---|---|
| Allentown College of St. Francis de Sales | PA |
| California State University, San Bernardino | CA |
| College of Insurance | NY |
| College of the Virgin Islands | VI |
| Detroit College of Business | MI |
| Franklin Pierce College | NH |
| Inter-American University | PR |
| Mount Senario College | WI |
| Troy State University, Dothan | AL |
| University of Puerto Rico (Humcao) | PR |

### Two-Year Colleges

| | |
|---|---|
| Anson Technical College | NC |
| Arizona Western College | AZ |
| Barstow College | CA |
| Big Bend Community College | WA |
| Nlue Mountain Community College | OR |
| Central Carolina Technical College | NC |
| City Colleges of Chicago-Loop College | IL |
| Clark Technical College | OH |

| | |
|---|---|
| Cochise College | AZ |
| Edison Community College | FL |
| Greenfield Community College | MA |
| Greenville Technical College | SC |
| Highland Community College | IL |
| Kent State University-New Philadelphia | OH |
| Lake City Community College | FL |
| Merced College | CA |
| Newbury College | MA |
| Niagara County Community College | NY |
| Onondaga Community College | NY |
| Patrick Henry Community College | VA |
| Randolph Technical College | NC |
| St. Louis Community College-Forest Park | MO |
| San Diego Mesa College | CA |
| Suffolk County Community College Ammerman Campus | NY |
| Sullivan County Community College | NY |
| Treasure Valley Community College | OR |
| Tri-County Technical College | SC |
| Ulster County Community College | NY |
| University of Alaska Community College –Sitka | AK |

50th Anniversary        1987

| | |
|---|---|
| Cardinal Stritch College | WI |
| Missouri Southern State College | MO |

Pepperdine University –
    Malibu
      Los Angeles                                              CA

Queen's College, Flushing                                      NY

Two-Year Colleges

College of Eastern Utah                                        UT

Meridian Junior College                                        MS

Stenotype Institute                                            NY

University of Netucky, Ashland Community College  KY


60th Anniversary                1987

Austin Peay State University                                   TN

Bob Jones University                                           SC

Eastern Montana College                                        MT

Edgewood College                                               WI

Jersey City State College                                      NJ

Menlo College                                                  CA

Pan American University                                        TX

Parks College of St. Louis                                     IL

Regis College                                                  MA

Rutgers University College of Pharmacy                         NJ

Southwestern Assemblies of God College                         TX

University of Arkansas at Little Rock                          AR

University of Bridgeport                                        CT

University of Houston (University Park)                         TX

University of North Carolina, Asheville                        NC

University of Pittsburgh, Johnstown                            PA

| | |
|---|---|
| University of Tennessee at Martin | TN |

Two-Year Colleges

| | |
|---|---|
| Arkansas State University, Beebe Branch | AR |
| Butler County Community College | KS |
| East Mississippi Junior College | MS |
| Glendale Community College | CA |
| Long Beach City College | CA |
| Marshalltown Community College | IA |
| Moberly Area Junior College | MO |
| Northwest Mississippi Junior College | MS |
| Porterville College | CA |
| Southern Ohio College, Cincinnati | OH |
| Texarkana Community College | TX |
| Thornton Community College | IL |
| Yuba College | CA |

Centenary                              1987

| | |
|---|---|
| Alverno College | WI |
| Bethel College | KS |
| California State University | CA |
| Campbell University | NC |
| Catholic University of America | WDC |
| Cedarville College | OH |

| | |
|---|---|
| Central State University | OH |
| Clark University | MA |
| Florida A&M University | FL |
| Gonzaga University | WA |
| Illinois Benedictine College | IL |
| Moorhead State University | MN |
| Nebraska Wesleyan University | NE |
| Occidental College | CA |
| Pembroke State University | NC |
| Pomona College | CA |
| Pratt Institute | NY |
| Troy State University | AL |
| Whittier College | CA |

Two-Year Colleges

| | |
|---|---|
| Sinclair Community College | OH |

150th Anniversary        1987

| | |
|---|---|
| Cheyney University | PA |
| Davidson College | NC |
| DePauw University | IN |
| Guilford College | NC |
| Knox College | IL |
| Marshall University | WV |
| Mount Holyoke College | MA |

| | |
|---|---|
| Muskingum College | OH |
| West Liberty State College | WV |

Bicentennial          1987

| | |
|---|---|
| Castleton State College | VT |
| Franklin and Marshall College | PA |
| University of Pittsburgh | PA |
| York College | PA |
| Louisburg College | NC |

## 25th Anniversary    1988

| | |
|---|---|
| American College of Puerto Rico, Bayamon | PR |
| Coleman College | CA |
| College of Boca Raton | FL |
| La Roche College | PA |
| Long Island University, Southampton | NY |
| Oral Roberts University | OK |
| Pace University, Briarcliff/Pleasantville | NY |
| Pitzer College | CA |
| Sacred Heart University | CT |
| Saginaw University State College | MI |
| Southwest State University | MN |
| University of Central Florida | FL |
| University of Maryland, Catonsville Campus | MD |
| University of Missouri – St. Louis | MO |
| University of Pittsburgh, Bradford | PA |
| University of Pittsburgh, Greensburgh | PA |
| University of West Florida | FL |

## Two-Year Colleges

| | |
|---|---|
| Bay de Noc Community College | MI |
| Borough of Manhattan Community College | NY |
| Carteret Technical College | NC |
| Central Piedmont Community College | NC |

| | |
|---|---|
| Columbus Technical Institute | OH |
| Crowder College | MO |
| Cumberland Community College | NJ |
| Dalton Junior College | GA |
| Florence Darlington Technical College | SC |
| Gaston College | NC |
| ICM School of Business | PA |
| Indiana Vocational Technical College. Indianapolis | IN |
| Indiana Vocational Technical College Columbus | IN |
| Indiana Vocational Technical College Gary | IN |
| Indiana Vocational Technical College Madison | IN |
| Indiana Vocational Technical College Evansville | IN |
| Indiana Vocational Technical College Richmond | IN |
| Jefferson College | MO |
| Kingsborough Community College, Brooklyn | NY |
| Lorain County Community College | OH |
| Mount San Jacinto College | CA |
| Mount Wachusett College | MA |
| Northeast Alabama State Junior College | AL |
| Quinsigamond Community College | MA |
| St. Louis Community College, Florissant Valley, St. Louis | MO |
| St. Louis Community College, Meramec, Kirkwood | MO |

| | |
|---|---|
| Spokane Community College | WA |
| Sandhills Community College | NC |
| Sumter Area Technical College | SC |
| Thames Valley State Technical College | CT |
| University of Kentucky Hendersom Community College | KY |
| West Valley College | CA |

### 50th Anniversary   1988

| | |
|---|---|
| California State Polytechnic | CA |
| King's College, Briarcliff | NY |
| Siena College | NY |
| Valley Forge Christian College | PA |

### Two-Year Colleges

| | |
|---|---|
| Brainerd Community College | MN |
| El Reno Junior College | OK |
| Henry Ford Community College | MI |

### 60th Anniversary   1988

| | |
|---|---|
| Angelo State University | TX |
| Hartwick College | NY |
| Kendall School of Design | MI |
| Mount Mercy College | IA |

### Two-Year Colleges

| | |
|---|---|
| Copiah-Lincoln Junior College | MS |

| | |
|---|---|
| East Central Junior College, Union | MS |
| East Central Union College, Decatur | MS |
| Hutchinson Community College | KS |
| Jones County Junior College | MS |
| Jackson Community College | MS |
| National Education Center – Spartan School of Aeronautics | OK |
| Westark Community College | AR |
| Yakima Valley Community College | WA |

## CENTENARY  1988

| | |
|---|---|
| Central New England College | MA |
| New Mexico State University | NM |
| St. Paul's College | VA |
| Salem College | WV |
| University of Charleston | WV |
| University of Puget Sound | WA |
| University of Scranton | PA |
| Utah State University | UT |
| Wheelock College | MA |

### Two-Year Colleges

| | |
|---|---|
| Eastern Arizona College | AZ |
| Interboro Institute | NY |
| Muskegon Business College | MI |

Ricks College                                          ID

Snow College                                           UT

<u>150th Anniversary</u>          1988

Duke University                                        NC

Virginia Commonwealth University                       VA

Westfield State College                                MA

# Institution Changes

# Institution Changes

## New Institutions

| Alabama | FICE No.: |
|---|---|
| International Bible College | 021997 |

| California | |
|---|---|
| American Technical College for Career Training | 010314 |
| Brooks Institute | 001123 |
| California College for Health Sciences | 022061 |
| Edison Technical Institute | 022885 |
| Queen of The Holy Rosary College | 029377 |

| Florida | |
|---|---|
| Florida Bible College | 023022 |
| National School of Technology | 021218 |

| Iowa | |
|---|---|
| Emmaus Bible College | 023289 |

| Kansas | |
|---|---|
| The Brown Mackie College | 006755 |

| Maine | |
|---|---|
| YDI Schools | 022772 |

| Michigan | |
|---|---|
| Great Lakes Junior College of Business | 006770 |

| Minnesota | |
|---|---|
| Saint Paul Technical Vocational Institute | 005533 |

| Missouri | |
|---|---|
| Dickinson Junior College | 022032 |

| New Mexico | |
|---|---|
| Albuquerque Vocational-Technical Institute | 004742 |

| New York | |
|---|---|
| Catholic Medical Center of Brooklyn and Queens School of Nursing | 012364 |
| Long Island Seminary of Jewish Studies | 011993 |
| New York Institute of Technology Central Office | 007968 |
| Ohr Somayach Institutions | 023201 |
| Rabbinical College Kamenitz Yeshiva of America | 004810 |
| Sara Schenirer Teachers Seminary | 011995 |
| Shaarei Zion Academy | 023037 |
| United Talmudical Academy of Monsey | 023039 |

| Ohio | |
|---|---|
| RETS Institute of Technology | 020990 |

| Pennsylvania | |
|---|---|
| Biblical Theological Seminary | 023230 |
| CHI Institute | 022898 |
| ICS Center for Degree Studies | 004049 |
| Pinebrook Junior College | 009908 |
| Reconstructionist Rabbinical College | 022734 |
| RETS Electronics Schools | 007781 |

| Texas | |
|---|---|
| Houston Graduate School of Theology | 023202 |
| Northeast Texas Community College | 023154 |

| Vermont | |
|---|---|
| New England Culinary Institute | 022540 |

| Virginia | |
|---|---|
| Institute of Textile Technology | 003717 |

| Wisconsin | |
|---|---|
| Wisconsin Conservatory of Music | 003913 |

## Institutions that Closed During 1986

| Arizona | FICE No. |
|---|---|
| The College of Granado (closed) | 010878 |

| Arkansas | |
|---|---|
| American College (No longer accredited as a junior college of business by the Association of Independent Colleges and Schools) | 010821 |

| California | |
|---|---|
| Holy Family College (Closed) | 012313 |
| Sysorex Institute (No longer a candidate for accreditation as a junior college by the Western Association of Schools and Colleges) | 029330 |

| Florida | |
|---|---|
| Spurgeon Baptist Bible College (No longer a candidate for accreditation by the American Association of Bible Colleges) | 029309 |

| Illinois | |
|---|---|
| George Williams College (Closed) | 001683 |
| Sherwood Conservatory of Music (No longer offers degrees) | 001755 |

| Indiana | |
|---|---|
| Holy Cross Junior College (No longer 3IC certified) | 007263 |

| Kansas | |
|---|---|
| Saint John's College (Closed) | 001942 |

| Missouri | |
|---|---|
| Saint Paul's College (Closed) | 002510 |

| New Hampshire | |
|---|---|
| Magdalen College (No longer a candidate for accreditation by the New England Association of Schools and Colleges, Commission on Vocational, Technical, Career Institutions) | 029299 |

| New Mexico | |
|---|---|
| University of Albuquerque (Closed) | 002662 |

| New York | |
|---|---|
| Bais Fruma (No longer 3IC certified) | 029358 |
| Beth Rochel Seminary (No longer 3IC certified) | 022644 |
| Hadar Hatorah Rabbinical Seminary (No longer 3IC certified) | 004791 |

Rabbinical Seminary Beth Yitzchok D'spinka                    029110
  (No longer a candidate for accreditation by the Association
  of Advanced Rabbinical and Talmudic Schools)
Stenotype Institute                                          011996
  (Closed)
Yeshiva Chofetz Cham Radun                                   010944
  **(No longer 3IC certified)**

### Oklahoma
Oklahoma Missionary Baptist College                          029348
  **(No longer 3IC certified)**

### Pennsylvania
Faith Theological Seminary                                   003264
  **(No longer 3IC certified)**
FPM Data School, Inc.                                        021330
  (Closed)
Median School of Allied Health Careers                       008568
  (Degree-granting program to be discontinued June 1987)

### South Dakota
Freeman Junior College                                       003462
  (Closed)

### Washington
Cogswell College North                                       022917
  (No longer a candidate for accreditation by the Northwest
  Association of Schools and Colleges)

## Name Changes

The first line is the institution's former name. The indented
line is its new name.

### Alabama       *FICE No.*
Gadston State Community College
  Gadston State Junior College                          001017
Troy State University at Dothan-Fort Rucker
  Troy State University at Dothan                       001048

### Arizona
Miller Institute
  ITT Technical Institute                               020652

### California
California Lutheran College
  California Luthern University                         001133
Condie Junior College of Business and Technology
  Condie Junior College                                 029250
Heald College, Santa Rosa
  Heald College, Rohnert Park                           022623
Marymount Palos Verdes College
  Marymount College                                     010470
Riverside City College
  Riverside Community College                           001270
Samuel Merritt Hospital College of Nursing
  Samuel Merritt College of Nursing                     007012
San Jose Community College District System Office
  San Jose/Evergreen Community College
    District Systems Office                    029042
University of Santa Clara
  Santa Clara University                                001326

### Colorado
Rocky Mountain School of Art
  Rocky Mountain College of Art and Design              007649

### Florida
Florida Junior College at Jacksonville
  Florida Community College at Jacksonville             001484
Morris Junior College of Business
  Phillips Junior College of Business                   029123

### Georgia
Clayton Junior College
  Clayton State College                                 008976
Draughon's Junior College
  South College                                         013039
Mercer University Main Campus
  Mercer University, Macon                              001580
Tift College
  Tift College of Mercer University                     001595

### Illinois
Sauk Valley College
  Sauk Valley Community College                         001752

### Indiana
Indiana Central University
  The University of Indianapolis                        001804

### Iowa
Faith Baptist Bible College                                  007121
  Faith Baptist Bible College and Seminary

### Kentucky
Draughon's Junior College of Business
  Career Com Junior College of Business                 005202
Lexington Technical Institute
  Lexington Community College                           029210

### Massachusetts
Central New England College of Technology
  Central New England College                           010306
Marian Court Junior College of Business
  Marian Court Junior College                           006873

### Michigan
Baker Junior College of Business
  Baker College                                         004673
College of Art and Design
  College of Art and Design—Center for Creative Studies  006771

### Mississippi
Phillips College
  Phillips Junior College of the Mississippi Gulf Coast  009221

### New York
City University of New York, York College
  The York College of the City University of New York    004759
Polytechnic Institute of New York
  Polytechnic University                                002796
Seminary of the Immaculate Conception
  Seminary of the Immaculate Conception of the
    Diocese of Rockville Center                002683
State University of New York Downstate Medical Center, Brooklyn
  State University of New York Health Science Center
    at Brooklyn                                002839
State University of New York Upstate Medical Center, Syracuse
  State University of New York Health Science Center
    at Syracuse                                002840
Torah Temimah Talmudical Seminary
  Yeshiva and Mesivta Torah Temimah Talmudical Seminary  029304
Wendell Castle Workshop                                      022370
  Wendell Castle School

### North Dakota

Mary College
  University of Mary                               002992
Standing Rock Community College
  Standing Rock College                       029129

### Ohio

Shawnee State Community College
  Shawnee State University                 012748
University of Steubenville
  Franciscan University of Steubenville   003036
Wright State University Western Ohio Branch
  Wright State University Lake Campus   009169

### Oklahoma

Bethany Nazarene College
  Southern Nazarene University        003149
Northeastern Oklahoma State University
  Northeastern State University         003161
Oklahoma State University—School of Technical Training
  Oklahoma State University Technical Branch, Okmulgee   003172
Oklahoma State University Technical Institute
  Oklahoma State University Technical Branch,
    Oklahoma City                          003171

### Pennsylvania

American Institute of Drafting
  American Institute of Design         011006
Community College of Allegheny County North Campus
  Community College of Allegheny County College
    Center—North                       029101
Pennsylvania State University Capitol Campus
  Pennsylvania State University Capitol College   006814
Philadelphia College of Art
  Philadelphia College of the Arts       003350

### Puerto Rico

Colegio Universitario Metropolitana
  Universidad Metropolitana         029278
Instituto Commercial De Puerto Rico Junior College
  ICPR Junior College               011940

### South Dakota

University of South Dakota Main Campus
  University of South Dakota         003474

### Tennessee

Martin College
  Martin Methodist College         003504

### Texas

Criswell Center For Biblical Studies
  Criswell College                 029351
Henderson County Junior College
  Trinity Valley Community College     003572
Hill Junior College
  Hill College of the Hill Junior College District   003573
Texarkana Community College
  Texarkana College               003628

### Vermont

College of Saint Joseph The Provider
  College of Saint Joseph          003685

### Virginia

Marymount College of Virginia
  Marymount University           003724

### Washington

Cornish Institute
  Cornish College of the Arts       012315
Fort Steilacoom Community College
  Pierce College                005000

## Merged Institutions

### Iowa

Open Bible College *into*         004601
Eugene Bible College (in Oregon)     029251

### Michigan

Muskegon Business College *into*     002296
Baker College                  004673

### Minnesota

Saint Mary's Junior College *into*    002381
College of Saint Catherine       002342

### Pennsylvania

New School of Music *into*        011146
Temple University (Esther Boyer College of Music)   003371

Source: HEP HIgher Education Directory

# Bibliography

# Books

## Academic Programs

Clifton, Conrad F. *Academic Program Reviews: Institutional Approaches, Expectations, and Controversies* (Association for the Study of Higher Education, 1986).

## Academic Excellence

Gilley, J. Wade. *Searching for Academic Excellence: Twenty Colleges and Universities on the Move and their Leaders* (American Council on Education, Macmillan Publishing Company, 1986).

## Admissions

American Association of Collegiate Registrars and Admissions Officers. *Transfer Credit Practices of Designated Educational Institutions* (AACRO, 1986).

College Board. *Measures in the College Board Admissions Process* (College Board Publications, 1986).

*College Admissions Data Handbook 1986–87* (27th Edition, Orchard House, 1986).

## Architecture

Grant, Christin. *New Ideas for a New Building: The Roll Building Project at Kellogg Community College* (Facility Management Institute, 1986).

## Associations

Bloand, Harland G. *Associations in Action: The Washington D.C. Higher Education Community* (Association for the Study of Higher Education, 1985).

## Athletics

Richard E. Lapchick and Robert Malekoff. *On the Mark: Putting the Student Back in the Student Athlete* (Lexington Books, 1986).

## Business – Higher Education Linkage

American Association of State Colleges and Universities. *The Higher Education – Economic Development Connection* (AASCU, 1986).

Fenwick, Dorothy C. *Guide to Campus – Business Linkage Programs: Education and Business Prospering Together* (American Council on Education, 1986).

Stankiewicz, Richard. *Academics and Entrepreneurs: Developing University – Industry Relations* (St. Martin's Press, 1986).

## Career Guide

Rose, Suzanne. *Career Guide for Women Scholars* (Springer Publishing Company, 1986).

## Communications

*Campus Telephone Systems: Managing Change* (National Association of College and University Business Officers, 1986).

## Community Colleges

Diener, Thomas. *Growth of an American Invention: A Documentary History of the Junior and Community College Movement* (Greenwood Press, 1986).

Mahoney, James R. *Community, Technical and Junior Colleges: A Statistical Analysis* (American Association of Community and Junior Colleges, 1986).

Puyear, Donald E. *Maintaining Institutional Integrity* (Jossey–Bass, 1986).

Roueche, John E. and George A. Baker. *Access and Excellence: The Open Door College* (American Association of Community and Junior Colleges, 1986).

Dziech, Billie Wright. *Controversies and Decision Making in Difficult Economic Times* (Jossey–Bass, 1986).

## Computers

Hollander, Patricia A. *Computers in Education: Legal Liabilities and Ethical Issues Concerning their Use and Misuse* (College Administration Publications, 1986).

Rohrbaugh, John, and Anne Taylor. *Applying Decision Support Systems in Higher Education* (Jossey–Bass, 1986).

*Directory of Computing Facilities in Higher Education.* Warlick (University of Texas, 1985).

## Conferences

Ilsley, Paul J. *Improving Conference Design and Outcomes* (Jossey–Bass, 1985).

## Consortia

Baus, Frederick, and Teresa LaRocco. *1986 Consortium Directory* (Council for Interinstitutional Leadership, 1986).

## Continuing Education

Beder, Hal. *Marketing Continuing Education* (Jossey–Bass, 1986).

Charner, Ivan, and Catherine A. Rolzinski. *Responding to the Educational Needs of Today's Workplace* (Jossey–Bass, 1986).

Gessner, Quentin H. *Handbook on Continuing Higher Education* (American Council on Education/Macmillan Publishing Co, 1986).

National University Continuing Education Association. *Handbook and Directory 1985–86* (NUCEA, 1986).

## Crisis Management

Hoverland, Hal. *Crisis Management in Higher Education* (Jossey–Bass, 1986).

Steeples, Douglas W. *Institutional Revival: Case Histories* (Jossey–Bass, 1986).

## Cross–National Orientation

Clark, Burton R. *Higher Education System: Academic Organization in Cross–National Perspective* (University of California, 1986).

Paige, Michael. *Cross–Cultural Orientation: New Conceptualizations and Applications* (University Press of America, 1986).

## Directories

*Accredited Institutions of Postsecondary Education, Programs, Candidates 1985–86* (American Council on Education/Macmillan Publishing Company, 1986).

Carol M. Thomas, *Directory of College Facilities and Services for the Disabled* (Oryx Press, 1986).

*World of Learning* (Europa, 1986).

## Endowments

Vigeland, Carl. *Great Good Fortune: How Harvard Makes Its Money* (Houghton Mifflin, 1986).

## Enrollment

*Getting Students Ready for College: Why and How We Must Change What We Are Doing* (Southern Regional Education Board, 1986).

Hossler, Don. *Managing College Enrollments* (Jossey–Bass, 1986).

## Essays

Smart, John C. *Higher Education: Handbook of Theory and Research* (Agathon Press, 1986).

## Ethics

Cahn, Steven M. *Saints and Scamps: Ethics in Academia* (Rowman and Littlefield, 1986).

## Evaluation

*Defining and Assessing Baccalaureate Skills: Ten Case Studies* (American Association of State Colleges and Universities, 1986).

Andrews, Hans A. *Evaluating for Excellence* (New Forums Press, 1985).

## Faculty

Baldwin, Roger G. *Incentives for Faculty Vitality.* (Jossey–Bass, 1986).

Beckham, Joseph C. *Faculty/Staff Nonrenewal and Dismissal for Cause in Institutions of Higher Education* (College Administration Publications, 1986).

Biles, George E. *Part–time Faculty Personnel Management Policies* (American Council on Education/Macmillan Publishing Company, 1986).

Bowen, Howard Rothmann. *American Professors; A National Resource Imperiled* (Oxford University Press, 1986).

Bowker, Lee H. *Role of the Department Chair* (American Sociological Association, 1985).

Boyer, Carol M. *And On the Seventh Day: Faculty Consulting and Supplemental Income* (Association for the Study of Higher Education, 1985).

Creswell, John W. *Faculty Research Performance: Lessons from the Sciences and Social Sciences* (Association for the Study of Higher Education, 1985).

Elman, Sandra E. *Professional Service and Faculty Rewards: Towards an Integrated Structure* (National Association of State Universities and Land Colleges, 1985).

Floyd, Carol E. *Faculty Participation in Decision Making: Necessity or Luxury?* (Association for the Study of Higher Education, 1986).

Licata, Christine M. *Post–Tenure Faculty Evaluation: Threat or Opportunity?* (Association for the Study of Higher Education, 1986).

Mortimer, Kenneth P. *Flexibility in Academic Staffing: Effective Policies and Practices* (Association for the Study of Higher Education, 1986).

*National Faculty Directory, 1987* (17th Edition, Gale Research, 1986).

UNESCO. *Academic Staff Development in Higher Education* (Unipub, 1986).

Yuker, Harold E. *Faculty Workload: Research, Theory and Interpretation* (Association for the Study of Higher Education, 1985).

## Finance

Berg, David J. *Making the Budget Process Work* (Jossey–Bass, 1986).

Dresner, Bruce M. *Results of the 1984 NABUCO Comparative Performance Study and Investment* (National Association of College and University Business Officers, 1985).

Foose, Robert A. and Joel W. Meyerson. *Alternative Approaches to Tuition Financing; Making Tuition More Affordable* (National Association of College and University Business Officers, 1986).

Hyatt, James A. and Aurora A. Santiago. *Financial Management of Colleges and Universities* (National Association of College and University Business Officers, 1986).

Johnstone, Bruce. *Sharing the Costs of Higher Education* (College Board Publications, 1986).

Marsee, Jeff. *Cash Management for Colleges and Universities* (National Association of College and University Business Officers, 1986).

Matkin, Gary W. *Effective Budgeting in Continuing Education: A Comprehensive Guide to Improving Program Planning and Organizational Performance* (Jossey–Bass, 1985).

## Foreign Students

Institute of International Education. *Open Doors 1985/86: Report on International Educational Exchange* (IIE, 1987).

## Fund Raising

Dannelley, Paul. *Fund Raising and Public Relations: A Critical Guide to Literature and Resources* (University of Oklahoma Press, 1986).

Dunn, John A. *Enhancing the Management of Fund Raising* (Jossey–Bass, 1986).

## General

Bok, Derek. *Higher Learning* (Harvard University Press, 1986).

Levine, David O. *American College and the Culture of Aspiration. 1915–1940* (Cornell University Press, 1986).

Lynton, Ernest A., and Sandra E. Elman. *New Priorities for the University: Meeting Society's Needs for Applied Knowledge and Competent Individuals* (Jossey–Bass, 1986).

Nelson, William A. W. *Universities in Crisis: A Medieval Institution in the 21st Century* (Institute for Research on Public Policy, 1986).

Schrecker, Ellen. *No Ivory Tower: McCarthyism and the Universities* (Oxford University Press, 1986).

Smart, John E. *Higher Education: Handbook of Theory and Research* (Agathon Press, 1986).

## Government Relations

Bernstein, Melvin H. *Higher Education and the State: New Linkages for Economic Development* (National Institute for Work and Learning, 1986).

*Transforming the State Role in Undergraduate Education: Time for A Different View* (Education Commission of the States, 1986).

Feller, Irwin. *Universities and the State Governments: A Study in Policy Analysis* (Praeger Publishers, 1986).

Johnson, Janet R., and Laurence R. Marcus. *Blue Ribbon Commissions and Higher Education: Changing Academia from the Outside* (Association for the Study of Higher Education, 1986).

Levy, Daniel C. *Higher Education and the State in Latin America: Private Challenges to Public Dominance.* (University of Chicago Press, 1986).

Sabatier, Paul. *Academics and the Legislature: Case Studies in Scientific Advice* (University of California Press, 1986).

## History

Alberts, Robert C. *Pitt: The Story of the University of Pittsburgh, 1787–1987* (University of Pittsburgh Press, 1986).

Aloian, David. *College in a Yard II* (Harvard University Press, 1986).

Bailyn, Bernard. *Glimpses of Harvard Past* (Harvard University Press, 1986).

Bratton, Mary Jo Jackson. *The East Carolina University: The Formative Years, 1907–82* (East Carolina University, 1986).

Brooke, Christopher. *History of Gonville and Caius College* (Cambridge University Press, 1986).

Caine, L. Vernon. *To Heights Beyond: The Story of the Illinois College, 1866–1973* (Southern Illinois University Press, 1986).

Harrington, Michael F. *Ouachita Baptist University: The First 100 Years* (August House, 1985).

McCurdy, Michael. *Words* (Globe Pequot Press, 1986).

Morrison, Jr., James L. *The Best School in the World: West Point; The Pre–Civil War Years, 1833–1866* (Kent State University Press, 1986).

Munroe, John A. *The University of Delaware: A History* (University of Delaware Press, 1986).

Niederer, Francis J. *Hollins College: An Illustrated History* (University Press of Virginia, 1986).

Oren, Dan. *Joining the Club: A History of Jews and Yale* (Yale University Press, 1986).

Rutkoff, Peter M. and William B. Scott. *New School: A History of the New School for Social Research* (Free Press, 1986).

Schmuhl, Robert. *University of Notre Dame: A Contemporary Portrait* (University of Notre Dame Press, 1986).

Smith, Richard Norton. *The Harvard Century: The Making of a University to a Nation* (Simon & Schuster, 1986).

*United Negro College Fund Archives: A Guide and Index* (University Microfilms International, 1986).

## Instructional Technology

Voegel, George. *Advances in Instructional Technology* (Jossey–Bass, 1986).

## Interdisciplinary Programs

Newell, William H. *Interdisciplinary Undergraduate Programs: A Directory* (Association for Integrative Studies, 1986).

## Law

Pavela, Gary. *Dismissal of Students with Mental Disorders: Legal Issues, Policy Considerations, and Alternative Responses* (College Administration Publications, 1985).

Rosenthal, William. *Use of Data in Discrimination Issue Cases* (Jossey–Bass, 1986).

## Leadership

Bogue, E. Grady. *Enemies of Leadership: Lessons for Leaders in Education* (Phi Delta Kappa Publications, 1986).

Callan, Patricia M. *Environmental Scanning for Strategic Leadership* (Jossey–Bass, 1987).

Kerr, Clark. *Presidents Make a Difference: Strengthening Leadership in Colleges and Universities* (Association of Governing Boards of Colleges and Universities, 1985).

## Management

White, Gregory P. *Management Science: Applications to Academic Administration: An Annotated and Indexed Bibliography* (Council of Planning Librarians, 1985).

## Marketing

Constantine, Karen Krall. *Annotated and Extended Bibliography of Higher Education Marketing* (American Marketing Association, 1986).

## Minorities

Schlachter, Gail Ann. *Directory of Financial Aids for Minorities* (Reference Service Press, 1986).

Taylor, Charles A. *Handbook of Minority Student Services* (NMOC Inc., 1986).

Western Interstate Commission for Higher Education. *Minorities in Higher Education: The Changing Southwest* (WICHE, 1986).

## Office Procedure

*Administrative Procedures for Small Institutions* (National Association of College and University Business Officers, 1985).

## Presidency

Cohen, Michael D. *Leadership and Ambiguity: American College President* (Harper & Row, 1986).

Kerr, Clark. *Many Lives of Academic Presidents: Time, Place and Character* (Association of Governing Boards of Universities and Colleges Press, 1986).

Vaughan, George B. *Community College Presidency* (American Council on Education, 1986).

## Private & Public Institutions

Gardner, John W. *Cooperation and Conflict: The Private and Public Sectors in Higher Education* (Association of Governing Boards of Universities and Colleges, 1986).

Geiger, Roger L. *Private Sectors in Higher Education: Structure, Function and Change in Eight Countries* (University of Michigan Press, 1986).

Locke, Elizabeth H. *Perspectives for Change: American Private Higher Education* (Duke Endowment, 1986).

## Professional Education

Stark, Joan S., Malcolm Lowther, and Bonnie M. K. Hagerty, *Responsive Professional Education; Balancing Outcomes and Opportunities* (Association for the Study of Higher Education, 1986).

## Public Relations

Rowland, Westley. *Key Resources on Institutional Advancement: A Guide to the Field and Its Literature* (Jossey–Bass, 1986).

Ryans, Cynthia C., and William L. Shanklin. *Strategic Planning, Marketing and Public Relations and Fund–Raising in Higher Education: Perspectives, Reading and Annotated Bibliography* (Scarecrow Press, 1986).

## Public Colleges

Ohles, John F. *Public Colleges and Universities* (Greenwood Press, 1986).

## Public Services

Crosson, Patricia. *Public Service at Public Colleges: Mission and Management* (American Association of State Colleges and Universities, 1985).

## Rankings

Webster, David S. *Academic Quality Rankings of American Colleges and Universities* (Schenkman Publications, 1986).

## Reading

Baker, David. *Student Reading Needs and Higher Education* (American Library Association, 1986).

## Reforms

*The Next Wave: Synopsis of Recent Education Reform Reports* (Education Commission of the States, 1986).

## Religious Education

Solberg, Richard. *Lutheran Higher Education in North America* (Augsburg Publishing House, 1986).

## Research

Cresswell, John W. *Measuring Faculty Research Performance* (Jossey–Bass, 1986).

Quay, Richard H. *Research in Higher Education: A Guide to Source Bibliographies* (Oryx Press, 1986).

Von Blum, Paul. *Still–Born Education: A Critique of the American Research University* (University Press of America, 1986).

## Research Parks

Levitt, Rachelle L. *Research Parks and Other Ventures: The University/Real Estate Connection* (Urban Land Institute, 1985).

## Scholarships

Bailey, Robert Leslie *How and Where to Get Scholarships and Financial Aid for College.* (Arco, 1986).

*College Cost Book, 1986–87* (Macmillan, 1986).

*College Facts Chart, 1986–87* (National Beta Club, 1986).

Hegener, Karen C. *College Money Handbook: The Complete Guide to Expenses, Scholarships, Loans, Jobs, and Special–Aid Programs at Four–Year Colleges* (Peterson's Guides, 1986).

Leider, Robert. *Don't Miss Out: The Ambitious Student's Guide to Financial Aid* (Octameron Associates, 1986).

## Special Interests

Wallenweldt, E. C. *Roots of Special Interest in American Higher Education: A Social, Psychological and Historical Perspective* (University Press of America, 1985).

## State Universities

Koepplin, Leslie W. *Future of State Universities: Issues in Teaching, Research and Public Service* (Rutgers University Press, 1985).

## Statistics

*Factbook on Higher Education, 1986–87.* Compiled by Cecilia A. Ottinger (American Council on Education, 1986).

*Compendium of University Statistics.* Text in English and French (Association of Universities and Colleges of Canada, 1986).

*Financial Statistics of Universities and Colleges, 1983–84* (Association of Universities and Colleges of Canada, 1985).

## Student Development

Amprey, Joseph L. *Student Development on the Small Campus* (National Association of Personnel Workers, 1986).

Barrow, John C. *Fostering Cognitive Development of Students* (Jossey–Bass, 1986).

Cornett, Lynn M. *Improving Student Preparation: Higher Education and the Schools Working Together* (Southern Regional Education Board, 1986).

Creamer, Don C. *Opportunities for Student Development in Two–Year Colleges* (National Association of Student Personnel Administrators, 1986).

Dalton, Jon C. *Promoting Value Development in College Students* (National Association of Student Personnel, 1985).

Giddans, Norman S. *Journey of Youth: Psychological Development During College* (Character Research Press, 1985.)

Noel, Lee. *Increasing Student Retention: Effective Programs and Practices for Reducing the Dropout Rate* (Jossey–Bass, 1986).

Olivas, Michael. *Latino College Students* (Teachers College Press, 1986).

Richardson, Richard C. *Students in Urban Settings: Achieving the Baccalaureate Degree* (American Association for Higher Education, 1986).

Schuh, John C. *Handbook for Student Group Advisers* (American College Personnel Association, 1985).

Talley, Joseph E. *Counselling and Psychotherapy with College Students: A Guide to Treatment* (Praeger, 1986).

Ware, Mark E. *Handbook on Student Development: Advising, Career Development and Field Placement* (Lawrence Erlbaum Associates, 1986).

Whitman, Neal A. *Increasing Students' Learning: A Faculty Guide to Reducing Stress Among Students* (Association for the Study of Higher Education, 1986).

Zikopoulos, Marianthi. *Choosing Schools from Afar. The Selection of Colleges and Universities in the United States by Foreign Students* (Institute of International Education, 1986).

## Student Guides

*Barron's Profiles of American Colleges* (15th Edition, 2 vols, Barron's 1986).

*Barron's Guide to the Best, Most Popular and Most Exciting Colleges* (4th Edition, Baron's 1986).

*Barron's Guide to the Most Prestigious Colleges* (4th Edition, Barron's 1986).

*Chronicle's Four–Year College Databook, 1986–87* (Chronicle Guidance Publications, 1986).

*Index of Majors, 1986–87* (College Entrance Examination Board, 1986).

*College Handbook,* 1986–87 (24th Edition, College Entrance Examination Board, 1986).

Doughty, Harold R. *Guide to American Graduate Schools* (5th Edition, Penguin, 1986).

Edelstein, Scott. *A User's Manual: All the Important Things No One Else Will Tell You About Colleges and College Life* (Bantam, 1985).

Fiske, Edward B. *Selective Guide to Colleges, 1986–87* (Times Books, 1986).

Hawes, Gene R. *College Board Guide to Going to College While Working: Strategies for Success* (College Board, 1985).

Kesslar, Oreon Pierre. *Financial Aids for Higher Education: A Catalog for Undergraduates* (12th Edition, William C. Brown, 1986).

Lehman, Andrea E., and Eric A. Suber. *The 1987 College Money Handbook* (Peterson's Guides, 1986).

Liscio, Mary Ann. *Guide to Colleges for Hearing Impaired Students* (Academic Press, 1986).

*Guide to Colleges for Mobility Impaired Students* (Academic Press, 1986).

*Guide to Colleges for Visually Impaired Students* (Academic Press, 1986).

*Peterson's Annual Guides to Graduate Study* (21st Edition, Peterson's Guides, 1987).

*Randax Education Guide to Colleges Seeking Students* (Education Guides, 1985).

Rugg, Frederick E. *Rugg's Recommendations of the Colleges* (4th Edition, Whitebrook Books, 1986).

Sjogren, Cliff. *Diversity, Accessibility and Quality: A Brief Introduction to American Education for Non-Americans* (College Board Publications, 1986).

*Yale Daily News. Insider's Guide to the Colleges* (12th Edition, St. Martin's Press, 1986).

## Student Press

Schuh, John H. *Enhancing Relationships with the Student Press* (Jossey-Bass, 1986).

## Student Services

Cohen, Robert D. *Working with the Parents of College Students* (Jossey-Bass, 1986).

Garland, Peter H. *Serving More than Students: A Critical Need for College Student Personnel Services* (American Association for Higher Education, 1986).

Kuh, George D. *Private Dreams, Shared Visions: Student Affairs Work in Small Colleges* (National Association of Student Personnel Administrators, 1986).

Leafgren, Fred. *Developing Campus Recreation and Wellness Programs* (Jossey-Bass, 1986).

Scovitch, Linda. *Standards and Guidelines for Student Services* (Council for the Advancement of Standards, University of Maryland, 1986).

## Teacher Education

Galambos, Eva. *Improving Teacher Education* (Jossey-Bass, 1986).

## Teaching and Learning

Beidler, Peter G. *Distinguished Teachers on Effective Teaching* (Jossey-Bass, 1986).

Breivik, Patricia S. *Managing Programs for Learning Outside the Classroom* (Jossey-Bass, 1986).

Carnegie Forum. *A Nation Prepared: Teachers for the 21st Century. The Report of the Task Force on Teaching as a Profession* (Carnegie Forum on Education and the Economy, 1986).

Civikly, Jean M. *Communicating in the College Classrooms* (Jossey-Bass, 1986).

Daloz, Laurent A. *Effective Teaching and Mentoring: Realizing the Transformational Power of Adult Learning Experiences* (Jossey-Bass, 1986).

Daly, William. *College-School Collaboration: Appraising the Major Approaches* (Jossey-Bass, 1986).

Elbow, Walter. *Embracing Contraries: Explorations in Learning and Teaching* (Oxford University Press, 1986).

Friedman, Paul. *Fostering Academic Excellence through Honors Programs* (Jossey-Bass, 1986).

Knowles, Malcom S. *Using Learning Contracts: Practical Approaches to Individualizing and Structuring Learning* (Jossey-Bass, 1986).

Meyer, Chet. *Teaching Students to Think Critically: A Guide for Faculty in all Disciplines* (Jossey-Bass, 1986).

Nelson, Cary. *Theory in the Classroom* (University of Illinois Press, 1986).

Milton, Ohmer. *Making Sense of College Grades: Why the Grading System Does not Work and What Can Be Done About It* (Jossey-Bass, 1986).

Ross, Elinor, and Betty Roe. *The Case for Basic Skills Programs in Higher Education* (Phi Delta Kappa, 1986).

Tchudi, Stephen N. *Teaching Writing in the Content Areas: College Level* (National Education Association, 1986).

Wood, Nancy V. *College Reading and Study Skills: A Guide to Improving Academic Communication* (Holt, Rinehart & Winston, 1985).

Wright, Richard A. *Teaching in the Small College: Issues and Applications* (Greenwood Press, 1986).

## Technology Transfer

*Trends in Technology Transfer in Universities: Report of the Clearinghouse on University–Industry Relations* (Association of American Universities, 1986).

## Tests

*College Planning/Search Book,* 1986–87 (American College Testing Program, 1986).

## Texas

Haigh, Berte R. *Land, Oil and Education* (Texas Western Press, 1986).

Whisenhunt, Donald W. *Encyclopedia of Texas Colleges and Universities: An Historic Profile* (Eakin Publications, 1986).

## Trustees

Wood, Miriam Mason. *Trusteeship in the Private College* (Johns Hopkins Press, 1985).

## Unions

Frank Geltner. *Acuition, or the Act of Sharpening Acuteness or Perceptiveness of Mind: Computer Applications: Current Developments in College Union Activities.* (Association of College Unions, 1986).

Girard, Kathryn. *Peaceful Persuasion: A Guide to Creating Mediation Resolution Programs on College Campuses* (Mediation Project, University of Massachusetts, 1986).

Hall, Laura. *Lectures Programming* (Association of College Unions International, 1985).

Temte, Anne. *Union Recreation Area* (Association of College Unions International, 1985).

## Who's Who

*Who's Who Among Students in American Universities and Colleges* (Randall Publishing Company, 1986).

## Women

Fritsche, Joanne M. *Toward Excellence and Equity: The Scholarship on Women as a Catalyst for Change in the University* (University of Maine at Orono, 1986).

Hoferek, Mary J. *Going Forth: Women's Leadership Issues in Higher Education and Physical Education* (Princeton Books, 1986).

Simeone, Angela. *Academic Women: Working Towards Equality* (Bergin & Garvey, 1986).

Theodore, Athena. *Campus Troublemakers: Academic Women in Protest* (Cap & Gown Press, 1986).

## Work Programs

Gold, Gerard G., and Ivan Charner. *Higher Education Partnerships: Practices, Policies and Problems* (National Institute for Work and Learning, 1986).

# Articles

## Academic Freedom

Academic Freedom and Tenure: Pennsylvania State University Academe 72:15a–19a May–June 1986.

Academic Freedom and Tenure: Talladega College. *Academe* 72:6a–14a, May–June 1986.

Institutional Openness and Individual Faculty Academic Freedom. M. Glicksman, *Academe* 72:16–18 September–October 1986.

## Academic Reform

Reflections of Academic Reform. A. W. Ostar. *Academe,* 72–41, September–October 1986.

## Accreditation

Accreditation of Schools: Why it Must be Improved. G. Dumke *Educational Digest* 52:18–20 December 1986.

## Administration

Administrators vs Faculty: How to Change the Good Guys–Bad Guys Scenario. E. E. Walker *Change* 18:9 March/April 1986.

The Triadic Format of Administrative Accountability. B. Gunn. *Journal of College & University Personnel Association* 37:10–17 Winter 1986.

## Admissions

The Emergence of the Admissions Profession in the 1960s. N. K. Howard. *Journal of College Admissions.* 114:21–7 Winter 1987.

## Affirmative Action

Mainstreaming Affirmative Action—A Practitioner Speaks. P. J. Coughlin *Journal of College & University Personnel Association* 37:27–8 Winter 1986.

## Age

Age Differences in College Values and Perceived Quality of College Life M. A. Okun et al. *Educational Gerontology* 12 5:409–16 1986.

## Assessment

The Push to Assess: Why It's Feared and How to Respond. S. D. Spangehl. *Change* 10:35–9 January–February 1987.

## Blacks

The Five Most Important Problems Confronting Black Students Today. J. H. Smith et al. *Negro Educational Review* 37:52–61 April 1986.

## Campus Autonomy

Campus Autonomy and its Relationship to Measures of University Quality. J. F. Volkwein. *Journal of Higher Education* 57:510–28 September–October 1986.

## Chairperson

Managerial Behavior of College Chairpersons and Administrators. A. C. Bare. *Research in Higher Education* 24 2:128–38 1986.

## Classroom

Proximity and Student Density as Ecological Variables in a College Classroom. W. B. Hoffman and H. N. Anderson. *Teaching of Psychology* 13:200–3 December 1986.

## College Presidents

Educational Leadership: College Presidents in the Decade Ahead. M. Brown and W. R. Walworth *College Board Review* 138:22–3+ Winter 1985–86.

Successful Colleges Found Headed by Presidents Who Are People–Oriented, Doggedly Persistent. B. T. Watkins, *Chronicle of Higher Education* 32:20 + June 4 1986.

## Costs

College Costs: Have They Gone too High too Fast? M. O'Keefe. *Change* 18:6–8 May–June 1986.

The Marginal Costs of Instruction. S. A. Hoenack et al. *Research in Higher Education* 24 4:335–417 1986.

Over a Barrel: The High Costs of Rising Tuitions. R. A. Yanikoski *Educational Record* 67:12–25 Summer 1986.

Under the Gun: Why College Is So Expensive. S. Hackney. *Educational Record* 67:8–10 Spring–Summer 1986.

Who Should Pay for College and When? M. McPherson. *Change* 18:9 May–June 1986.

## Counseling

The Relationship of Career Exploration, College Jobs and Grade Point Average. C. C. Healy and D. L. Mourton. *Journal of College Student Personnel*. 28:28–34 January 1987.

Student Characteristics as Predictors of Perceived Academic Advising Needs. *Journal of College Student Personnel* 28:60–5 January 1987.

## Crisis Management

Crisis Management in Higher Education. H. Hoverland et al. *New Directions in Higher Education* 55:1–116 1986.

## Curriculum

On Defining Coherence and Integrity in the Curriculum. J. S. Stark. *Research in Higher Education* 24 4:433–6 1986.

## Discipline

Dealing with the Disruptive College Student: Some Theoretical and Practical Considerations. G. Amada. *Journal of American College Health* 34:221–5 April 1986.

## Enrollment

Coping with Competition for Students in a Period of Decline. F. Wing and G. I. Rowse. *Planning for Higher Education* 14 1:6–15 1985–86.

Managing College Enrollments. D. Hossler. *New Directions in Higher Education*. 53:5–108 1986.

## Ethics

Ethics for Survival: Constructing Commission Rates for University Development Officers. W. S. Brown. *Journal of College and University Personnel Association* 37:20–3 Summer 1986.

The University and Morality: A Revised Approach to University Autonomy and its Limits. J. C. Alexander. *Journal of Higher Education* 57:463–76 September–October 1986.

## Evaluation

Assessment of Institutional Effectiveness. K. M. Moore. *New Directions in Community Colleges* 56:49–60 1986.

Developing Policies and Procedures for Evaluating Instruction. M. Y. Janners and P. M. Tampas. *Engineering Education* 76:675–9 1986.

Evaluation and Accreditation of Institutions of Postsecondary Education. T. E. Manning. *North Central Association Quarterly* 61:261–7 Fall 1986.

Faculty Role in Presidential Evaluations. J. J. Dennis and K. Bullerdieck. *Journal of College & University Personnel Association* 37:1–4 Fall 1986.

Performance Evaluation for Tenured Faculty: Issues and Research. B. Reisman. *Liberal Education* 72:73–87 September 1986.

Predictors of Faculty Dissatisfaction with an Annual Performance Evaluation. J. E. Ormrod. *Journal of College & University Personnel Association* 37:13–18 Fall 1986.

Research Fundamentals and the Interrelation of Emotions, Grades and Evaluations. R. Pasnak. *Teaching of Psychology* 13:30–2 February 1986.

Student Opinion of the Value of Student Evaluations. M. Mirion and E. Segal. *Higher Education* 15:259–65 1986.

## Excellence

Planning for Excellence. D. W. Farmer. *College Board Review* 139:8–9 Spring 1986.

## Faculty

Aging and the Quality of Faculty Job Performance. R. T. Blackburn and J. H. Lawrence. *Review of Educational Research* 56:265–90 Fall 1986.

B–I–T–E: A Back–in–Touch Experience for Faculty Development. C. Licata and D. Pike. *Business Education Forum* 40:31–3 March 1986.

The Case for an Institutional Perspective on Faculty Development. S. M. Clark et al. *Journal of Higher Education* 57:176–95 March–April 1986.

Conceptions of Faculty Development. R. P. Riegle. *Educational Theory* 37:53–9 Winter 1987.

Faculty Development for Teacher Educators. R. I. Arends et al. *Journal of Teacher Education* 37:17–22 September–October 1986.

Faculty Development in Teacher Education: An Agenda. R. Brittingham *Journal of Teacher Education* 37:2–5 September–October 1986.

Faculty Development via Field Programs for Middle-aged, Disillusioned Faculty. R. Boice. *Research in Higher Education* 25 1:115–35 1986.

The Faculty Dilemma: A Short Course. J. H. Schuster. *Phi Delta Kappan* 68:275–82 December 1986.

Faculty Evaluation: Selected Views. *Engineering Education* 76:680–4 April 1986.

Faculty Roles and Role Preferences in Ten Fields of Professional Study. J. S. Stark et al. *Research in Higher Education* 25 1:3–30 1986.

The Faculty's Future: A Quest for Grace Under Pressure. M. McPherson. *Change* 18–48 July–August 1986.

Faculty Work Harder in a No–Growth Era. E. H. El–Khawas. *Educational Record* 67:48–51 Fall 1986.

Grievance Procedures. *Academe* 72:6–24 May–June 1986.

The Myth that's Responsible for Faculty Malaise. F. W. Fletcher. *Chronicle of Higher Education* 32:92 April 23, 1986.

A Nobel Laureate on the Faculty: What it Really Means to a University. M. Freedman. *Chronicle of Higher Education* 33:48–9 November 5, 1986.

On Future Demands for Older Professors. M. W. Riley. *Academe* 72:14–16 July–August 1986.

The Outlook for the American Professoriate. H. R. Bowen and J. H. Schuster. *Education Digest* 51:36–9 March 1986.

Peer Evaluations for Salary Increases and Promotions Among College and University Faculty Members. E. Spaights and E. Bridges. *North Central Association Quarterly* 6:403–10 Winter 1986.

Practical Ways to Build Student–Faculty Rapport. R. J. Menges and others. *Liberal Education* 72:145–55 Summer 1986.

Promotion of Academic Staff: Reward and Incentive. I. Moses. *Higher Education* 15 1–2:135–49 1986.

Scholarship for the Teaching Faculty. F. S. Weaver. *College Teaching* 34:51–8 Spring 1986.

Six–Year Case Study of Faculty Power Reviews, Merit Ratings and Pay Awards in a Multidisciplinary Department. T. H. McIntosh and T. E. Van Koevering. *Journal of College & University Personnel Association* 37:50–14 Spring 1986.

## Finance

Financing Higher Education: A Proposal for Reform. C. H. Karelis and O. Sabot. *Liberal Education* 73:40–2 January–February 1987.

Funding Over Time: Measuring Institutional Finance. W. H. Pickens. *New Directions in Institutional Research* 52:57–67 1986.

## Financial Aid

Toward Integrity in Financial Aid Counseling. P. O. Cleary. *Journal of College Admissions* 110:29–35 Winter 1986.

## Future

Higher Education: Circa 2000. F. D. Fisher. *Change* 19:40–5 January–February 1987.

Leading Higher Education into the 21st Century. H. D. McAninch. *Community, Technical and Junior College Journal* 56:14–17 June/July 1986.

The 21st Century: Will Higher Education Prepare America? C. E. Rickard and S. Hankins. *College Board Review* 139:20–1 Spring 1986.

Who Will Offer the Degrees of the Future? D. M. Arlton and T. J. Kalikow. *North Central Association Quarterly* 60:379–85 Winter 1986.

## General

Academe Must be Wary of Hazards Within and Without. Derek Bok. *Chronicle of Higher Education* 33:88 September 17, 1986.

Changling Higher Education: Unraveling the Gordian Knot. F. W. Lutz and I. K. Arney. *Journal of Research and Development in Education* 20:32–9 Winter 1986.

Higher Education in the 1980s: Examining the Conventional Wisdom. L. L. Leslie and C. E. Conrad. *College Board Review* 138:12–17 Winter 1986.

The Incredible Shrinking College: Downsizing as Positive Planning. H. L. Smith. *Educational Record* 67:38–41 Spring/Summer 1986.

In Loco Parentis Reinventis: Is There Still a Parenting Function in Higher Education? D. E. Gregory and R. A. Ballou. *NASPA Journal* 24:28–31 Fall 1986.

Judging a Good College: Importance of the 'Voice' of the Institution. B. DeMott. *Change* 19:5 January–February 1987.

A Musing Look at American Higher Education. P. I. Dressel. *Research in Higher Education* 24 3:318–24 1986.

The Unintended Revolution in America's Colleges Since 1940. T. N. Bonner. *Change* 18:44–51 September–October 1986.

When Will Universities Become Their Own Model? C. Fincher. *Research in Higher Education* 25 3:299–303 1986.

## Humanities

Present Rhetoric and Future Opportunities in the Humanities. S. Jeffords. *Liberal Education* 72:101–8 Summer 1986.

## Language

On Higher Educationspeak. M. Green. *Liberal Education* 72:51–5 September 1986.

## Learning

The University as a Place of Learning. D. O'Brien. *Liberal Education* 72:139–44 Summer 1986.

## Mentally Inferior Students

Autonomy and Theoretical Orientation of Remedial Non-remedial College Students. J. Koutrelakos. *Journal of Negro Education* 55:29–37 Winter 1986.

## Mission

Mission, Organization and Leadership. P. L. Dressel. *Journal of Higher Education* 58:101–9 January–February 1987.

The University's Statement Goals: An Idea Whose Time Has Arrived. R. D. McKelvie. *Higher Education* 15 1–2:151–163 1986.

The University Mission Statement: A Tool for the University Curriculum, Institutional Effectiveness and Change. M. E. Mouritsen. *New Directions in Higher Education* 55:45–52 1986.

## Morality

The University and Morality: A Revised Approach to University Autonomy and its Limits. J. C. Alexander. *Journal of Higher Education* 57:463–76 September–October 1986.

## Neo–Conservatism

Neo–Conservatism and Social Darwinism: Implications for Higher Education. P. Sola et al. *Journal of Negro Education* 55:3–20 Winter 1986.

## Organization

Organizing the Resources That Can Be Effective. A. S. Graff. *New Directions in Higher Education* 53:89–101 1986.

## Personnel Practices

Career Alternatives: A Model for Calculating Financial Costs and for Making Policy Decisions. K. E. Renner. *Research in Higher Education* 25 1:42–54 1986.

## Planning

An Integrated Decision Support System for Academic Effort Planning and Review. C. H. Chung and J. D. F. Chen. *Journal of Educational Technology Systems* 15 2:159–70 1986–87.

Planning and Resource Allocation Management. J. W. Coleman *New Directions in Higher Education* 55:53–61 1986.

## Private Colleges

Private Liberal Arts Colleges and Teacher Preparation. N. F. Daly. *New Directions for Teaching and Learning* 27:83–90 1986.

Stewardship of Resources for Private Higher Education. D. R. Moore. *New Directions in Higher Education* 55:17–23 1986.

## Productivity

The Elusive Nature of Institutional Productivity Ratings. D. R. Dillon. *Reading Research and Instruction* 26:50–7 Fall 1986.

Productivity of Faculty in Higher Education Institutions. J. J. Denton et al. *Journal of Teacher Education* 37:12–16 September/October 1986.

## Publishing

Academic Affiliations of Social Work Authors: A Citation Analysis of Six Major Journals. B. A. Thyer and K. J. Bentley. *Journal of Social Work Education* 22:67–73 Winter 1986.

Institutional Productivity Ratings Based on Publications in Reading Journals, 1973–1983. J. L. Johns et al. *Reading Research and Instruction* 25:102–7 Winter 1986.

Publications of Reading Educators: The Authors and their Articles. M. Abram et al. *Reading Improvement* 23:162–7 Fall 1986.

Writing Method and Productivity of Science and Engineering Faculty. R. T. Kellogg. *Research in Higher Education* 25 2:145–63 1986.

## Quality

Assessment of Quality in Higher Education: A Critical Review of the Literature and Research. D. L. Tan. *Research in Higher Education* 24 3:223–65 1986.

## Research

Academic Research vs the Liberal Arts. R. W. Merriam. *Journal of College Science Teaching* 16:105–9 November 1986.

Measuring Faculty Research Performance. J. W. Creswell. *New Directions in Institutional Research* 50:1–102 1986.

Trees without Fruit: The Problem with Research about Higher Education. G. Keller. *Change* 18:7–10 July–August 1986.

What Characterizes a Productive Research Department? L. Baird. *Research in Higher Education* 25 3:211–23 1986.

## Retention

The Coming Revolution in College Retention Strategies. T. B. Smith. *NASPA Journal* 24:10–13 Fall 1986.

## Salary

The Annual Report on the Economic Status of the Profession. 1985–86. *Academe* 72:3–71 March–April 1986.

Faculty Salary Analyses by Region, Rank and Discipline from 1977–78 to 1983–84. D. Q. Mohanty et al. *Research in Higher Education* 24 3:304–17 1986.

From Evaluations to an Equitable Selection of Merit–Pay Recipients and Increments. W. F. Koehler. *Research in Higher Education* 25 3:253–63 1986.

## Scholarship

The Pursuit of Scholarship. G. B. Vaughan. *Community, Technical Technical College Journal* 56:12–16 February–March 1986.

## Sexual Harassment

Graduate Women, Sexual Harassment, and University Policy. B. E. Schneider. *Journal of Higher Education* 58:46–65 January–February 1986.

## State Agencies

State Coordinating Agencies and Academic Innovation: A Policy Sector Perspective. S. L. Schachter. *Higher Education* 15 3–4:333–42 1986.

## State Universities

The Dilemma of the State University in the 1980s: Quality vs Comprehensiveness. M. F. Hammond and L. D. Tompkins. *College Board Review* 139:12–19 September 1986.

Educational Quality, Access, and Tuition Policies at State Universities. J. J. Seneca and M. K. Taussig. *Journal of Higher Education* 58:25–37 January–February 1987.

Recognizing Problems in State Universities. C. J. Ping. *New Directions in Higher Education* 55:9–16 1986.

## Stress

The Hectic Life of Faculty Members: Three Professors Describe How Stress Affects their Jobs, Families. *Chronicle of Higher Education* 33:11 February 4, 1987.

Job–related Tension and Anxiety Taking a Toll Among Employees in Academe's Stress Factories. L. McMillen. *Chronicle of Higher Education* 33:1+ February 4, 1987.

Studying Stress among Student Services and Professionals: An Interactional Approach. R. D. Brown et al. *NASPA Journal* 23:2–10 Spring 1986.

## Student Quality

The Crisis of Student Quality in Higher Education. L. C. Solmon and M. A. La Porte. *Journal of Higher Education* 57:370–92 July–August 1986.

## Students

Greek Affiliation and Attitude Change in College Students. D. H. Wilder et al. *Journal of College Student Personnel* 27:510–30 November 1986.

The Impact of Living Group Social Climate on Student Academic Performance. R. H. Schrager. *Research in Higher Education* 25 3:265–76 1986.

An Investigation into the Relationship Between University Faculty Attitude Toward Student Rating and Organizational and Background Factors. T Avi–Itzhak and L. Kremer. *Educational Research Quarterly* 10 2:31–8 1985–86.

Irrational Beliefs, Depression and Anger among College Students. J. A. Hogg and J. L. Deffenbacher. *Journal of College Student Personnel.* 27:349–53 July 1986.

Loneliness among Adolescent College Students at a Mid-western University. N. Medora and J. C. Woodward. *Adolescence* 21 391–402 Summer 1986.

Students' Contribution to their College Costs and Intellectual Development. T. D. Erwin. *Research in Higher Education* 25:195–203 1986.

Student Coping Mechanisms in Sexist and Non–sexist Professors' Classes. L. B. Rosenfeld and M. W. Jarrard. *Communication Education* 35:157–62 April 1986.

Student–Faculty Relationships and Intellectual Growth among Transfer Students. J. F. Volkwein et al. *Journal of Higher Education* 57:413–30 July–August 1986.

## Student Press

Student Affairs Professionals and the Student Press. D. A. DeCoster and L. Krager. *New Directions in Student Services* 33:45–56 1986.

## Teaching

Assigned Reading Activity: An Alternative to Lecture/Discussion. N. K. Buchanan. *College Teaching* 34:111–13 Summer 1986.

Confessions of a Reformed Textbook Junkie: Kicking the Habit Improved my Teaching. M. F. Rogers. *Chronicle of Higher Education* 33:36–7 February 4, 1987.

Excuse Me, but I Actually Like Being a College Professor. S. Pinsker. *Chronicle of Higher Education* 32:128 March 19, 1986.

Experiencing the Dual Role of College Teacher and College Student. A. Chavez. *College Student Journal* 20:21–2 Spring 1986.

Hours of Contact and their Relationship to Student Evaluations of Teaching Effectiveness. N. Dawson. *Journal of Nursing Education* 25:26–9 June 1986.

The Ideal Professor of Education. R. Wisniewski. *Phi Delta Kappan* 68:288–92 December 1986.

Improving Faculty Teaching: Effective Use of Student Evaluations and Consultants. R. C. Wilson. *Journal of Higher Education* 57:196–211 March–April 1986.

Improving the Lecture through Active Participation. J. Nelson. *College Student Journal* 20:315–20 Fall 1986.

Interfaculty Differences in Classroom Teaching Behaviors and their Relationship to Student Instructional Ratings. S. Erdle and H. G. Murray. *Research in Higher Education* 24 2:115–27 1986.

Matching College Instruction to Student Learning Style. K. V. Lundstrom and R. E. Martin. *College Student Journal* 20:270–4 Fall 1986.

A New Look at the Effect of Course Characteristics on Student Ratings of Instruction. P. A. Cranston and R. A. Smith. *American Educational Research Journal* 23:117–28 Spring 1986.

Peer Perspectives on the Teaching of Science. S. Tobias. *Change* 18:36–41 March–April 1986.

Planning Lectures that Start, Go, and End Somewhere. R. M. Schlenker and C. M. Perry. *Journal of College Science Teaching* 15:440–2 March/April 1986.

The Quest for Excellence in University Teaching. T. M. Sherman et al. *Journal of Higher Education* 58:66–84 January–February 1987.

Selecting Instructional Strategies. C. Weston and P. A. Cranton. *Journal of Higher Education* 57:259–88 May–June 1986.

A Synthesis of Research on the Characteristics of Teacher Educators. M. B. Troyer. *Journal of Teacher Education* 37:6–11 September–October 1986.

Twenty Ways to Raise Student Ratings–No Teaching Required. R. E. Ciscell. *Contemporary Education* 57:144–5 Spring 1986.

Using Interactive Images in the Lecture Hall. R. L. Weaver and H. W. Cotrell. *Educational Horizons* 64:180–5 Summer 1986.

## Tenure

Academic Promotion and Tenure. R. I. Miller. *Journal of College and University Personnel Association* 37:19–25 Winter 1986.

The Tenure System, not Flexible Staffing Preserves Excellence. E. Benjamin. *Academe* 72:61 January–February 1986.

## Urban University

The Enigma of the Urban University. E. Spaights and W. C. Farrell. *Education* 106:356–61 Summer 1986.

## Values

Postsecondary Educational Attainment and Humanitarian and Civic Values. E. T. Pascarella et al. *Journal of College Student Personnel.* 27:418–25 September 1986.

## Women

Academic Woman: Twenty-Four Years of Progress? J. E. Stecklein and G. E. Lorenz. *Liberal Education* 72:63–71 Spring 1986.

Annie Mae in Academe: Professionalization as Sabo-tage. S. Radford Hill. *Women's Studies Quarterly* 14:21–2 Spring–Summer 1986.

The Gender Gap in Library Education and Publication. C. Beghtol. *Journal of Education for Library and Information Science* 27:12–30 Summer 1986.

Increasing the Productivity of Women in Higher Education. R. R. Daniels et al. *College Studies Journal* 20:236–41 Fall 1986.

Networking–Mentoring: Career Strategy of Women in Academic Administration. M. J. Swoboda and S. B. Millar. *Journal of National Association of Women Deans, Administrators and Counselors* 50:8–13 Fall 1986.

Organizations and Inequality: Sources of earnings differentials between male and female faculty. P. S. Tolbert. *Sociological Education* 59:227–36 October 1986.

Women in the Adult Education Professoriat. *H. Y. Williams Journal of National Association of Women Deans, Administrators & Counsellors* 50:20–5 Fall 1986.

Women Who Write: Prolific Female Scholars in Higher Education and Student Affairs Administration. D. E. Hunter. *Journal of National Association of Women Deans, Administrators and Counsellors* 50:33–9 Fall 1986.

## Writing

The Professor as a Writer. R. T. Oliver. *Communication Education* 35:186–92 April 1986.

# Index